PSYCHOLOGY
The Science of Mind and Behaviour

PSYCHOLOGY
The Science of Mind and Behaviour
Richard D. Gross

SECOND EDITION

Hodder & Stoughton

LONDON SYDNEY AUCKLAND

A companion Study Guide is now available to accompany this coursebook. Written by Richard Gross and Paul Humphreys (Chief Examiner, AEB Psychology A-level), it is available through your usual supplier.

034 0 58736 9   Psychology: The Science of Mind & Behaviour Study Guide

The National Extension College has developed a modular open-learning course for the AEB A level in psychology using *Psychology: The Science of Mind and Behaviour* as the core text. The course is available from the National Extension College with or without tutorial support. For further details, write or phone: National Extension College, 18 Brooklands Avenue, Cambridge, CB2 2HN. Tel: 0223 316644

British Library Cataloguing in Publication Data

Gross, Richard D.
  Psychology: Science of Mind and
  Behaviour. – 2Rev.ed
  I. Title
  150

  ISBN 0–340–56136–x

First published 1992
Fifth impression 1993

Typeset by Wearset, Boldon, Tyne and Wear
Printed in Great Britain for the educational publishing division of Hodder & Stoughton Ltd, Mill Road, Dunton Green, Sevenoaks, Kent by Butler & Tanner Ltd, Frome, Somerset

CONTENTS

Preface   xiv

Acknowledgements   xvii

**PART ONE: THE NATURE AND SCOPE OF
PSYCHOLOGY**   1

1. *What is Psychology?*   3
   Definitions; The Process Approach (the biological bases of
   behaviour; learning; cognitive processes; comparative
   psychology); The Person Approach (social psychology;
   developmental psychology; individual differences): Educational Psychology; Clinical Psychology; Industrial or
   Occupational Psychology; Chartered Psychologists;
   Schools of Thought or Theoretical Approaches; The Language of Psychology; Psychology and Common Sense.

2. *Is Psychology a Science?*   21
   Philosophy and Psychology (empiricism; positivism);
   What is Science? (induction and scientific method); The
   Subject-matter of Psychology (what makes a good
   theory?); The Methodology of Psychology (replicability;
   cause and effect; control and objectivity; the psychology
   experiment as a social situation); Reductionism; The
   Mind–Body Problem (interactionism; epiphenomenalism;
   psychophysical parallelism; idealism, materialism; identity
   theory; alternatives to dualism and monism); Free Will
   Versus Determinism (Skinner's rejection of free will).

3. *Psychology and Ethics*   51
   The Psychologist as Scientist/Investigator (human sub-
   jects/participants; animal subjects); The Psychologist as
   Practitioner (psychology as value-free science; therapists as
   value-neutral and non-directive).

**PART TWO: THE BIOLOGICAL BASIS OF
BEHAVIOUR AND EXPERIENCE**   71

4. *The Nervous System*   73
   An Overview of the Human Nervous System—Structure
   and Function; The Central Nervous System (methods of
   studying the brain); Development of the Brain; The Major
   Structures and Functions of the Brain (the forebrain; the
   midbrain; the hindbrain); The Spinal Cord; The Localization of Brain Function (split-brain patients); The Autonomic Nervous System; The Endocrine System.

5. *States of Consciousness*   103
Consciousness and Self-consciousness; Meanings of 'Consciousness'; Consciousness, Arousal and Alertness (tonic alertness; phasic alertness); Consciousness and Attention (focal attention); The Functions of Consciousness; Two Kinds of Consciousness; Consciousness and the Electroencephalogram; Sleep (sleep and the circadian rhythm; the physiology of sleep; the varieties of sleep and the ultradian rhythm; sleeping and dreaming; the effects of sleep deprivation; theories of sleep; theories of dreaming); Hypnosis (the hypnotic procedure; trance or role-playing? hypnosis and pain); Meditation; Biofeedback.

6. *Motivation, Emotion and Stress*   127
Motivation: The 'Why' of Behaviour (philosophy and psychology in the study of motivation; homeostatic drive theory; drive-reduction theory; competence motives; play and motivation; motivation and adaptation) Arousal and Personality (the need for control; cognitive motives); Emotion: Adding Flavour to Behaviour (theories of emotion); Stress: When Emotions Become Harmful (what causes stress? how do we react to stress? stress, disease and personality; how do we cope with stress?).

7. *Learning*   164
(Learning as 'what is learned' and as 'how it is learned' How can learning be defined? learning versus performance; learning and other abilities; some basic questions about learning); Behaviourist Approaches (classical conditioning; operant or instrumental conditioning; the antecedents of behaviour; does conditioning work in the same way for all species? is conditioning more complex than it seems?); Tolman's Cognitive Behaviourism; Applications of Conditioning; (linear versus branching programmes; how effective is programmed instruction?); Social Learning Theory and Observational Learning (reinforcement as information about the future; the role of cognitive factors in observational learning); Insight Learning; Do we Have to Choose Between Trial-and-Error and Insight? (Gagné's hierarchy of learning; Harlow's concept of learning sets; learning set and transfer of learning).

PART THREE: SENSORY AND COGNITIVE PROCESSES   **199**
8. *Sensory Processes*   201
How are Sensation and Perception Related? The Senses—Providing the Raw Material of Perception; Classification of Sensory Systems; Characteristics of Sensory Systems; The Visual System (the sense organ; is the eye a camera? the receptors; visual pathways; colour vision and colour blindness; retinex theory and colour constancy); The Auditory System (the sense organ; the receptors; the auditory

pathways; auditory sensory processing and hearing defects).

9. *Perception* 223
Gregory's Theory (perceptual constancy; illusions; evaluation of Gregory's theory); Gibson's Theory of Direct Perception (evaluation of Gibson's theory); Gestalt Psychology (the principles of perceptual organization); Marr's computational theory of vision (working out the computational theory; 3-D model representation of object recognition; evaluation of Marr's theory; the influence of set on perception; what determines set? context, instructions and other situational variables; effects of emotional connotation; effect of the value of objects); Depth Perception (monocular pictorial cues; monocular non-pictorial cues; binocular non-pictorial cues); Pattern Recognition; Theories of Pattern Recognition (template-matching hypothesis; prototype theories; feature detection theories; the importance of context).

10. *Perception: the Nature–Nurture Debate* 262
The Study of Perceptual Development (an overview of the evidence); Studies of Human Cataract Patients; Animal Experiments; Perceptual Adaptation/Readjustment Studies; Cross-cultural Studies; Studies of Human Infants (asking the right questions; methods of studying infant perception; studying what the baby possesses; perception of colour; perception of brightness; perception of movement; visual acuity); Studying What the Baby Does (perception of pattern or form; facedness; perception of depth and 3-D objects; the visual constancies; conclusions).

11. *Attention* 296
(Definitions of attention; methods of studying attention); Theories of Selective Attention (Broadbent's 'filter model'; Treisman's attenuator model; the pertinence model; an evaluation of single channel models); Studies of Divided Attention (automatic versus controlled processing; automaticity and practice; conclusions).

12. *Memory* 309
The Concept of Memory; The Study of Memory; Storage (sensory memory; short-term memory; long-term memory); Retrieval; The Multi-store Model; What is the Evidence for the Multi-store Model? (two-component tasks; coding; brain-damaged patients); Alternatives to the Multi-store Model (episodic and procedural memory; levels of processing; working memory); Theories of Forgetting (trace decay; displacement; interference; the Gestalt theory of forgetting; prevention of consolidation; cue-dependent forgetting; motivated forgetting); Special Issues (semantic memory and knowledge; organization; imagery; recon-

structive memory and eye-witness testimony); Conclusions.

13. *Language and Thought*   360
Does Language Determine Thought? (the linguistic relativity hypothesis; peripheralism; restricted and elaborated codes; Labov and black English); Are Language and Thought Separate and Independent? (Vygotsky's theory of the language–thought relationship); Conclusions.

14. *Thinking, Problem-solving and Artificial Intelligence*   375
Early Studies of Problem-Solving; Classifying Problems; Early AI Research into Problem-Solving; Solving Non-adversary Problems (means end analysis; state-space theory); Solving Adversary Problems; Expert Versus Novices (Expert Systems); What Computers Can and Cannot Do; What is AI? What is a Computer? What Can Computers Do? And How Do They Do It? Strong and Weak AI and the Computational Theory of Mind; The Chinese Room and the Turing Test; Connectionism or Parallel Distributed Processing (what is a connectionist machine? so what's new about connectionist machines?); Conclusions.

PART FOUR: SOCIAL BEHAVIOUR   401

15. *The Ethological and Sociobiological Approach to the Study of Behaviour*   403
Experimental and Naturalistic Approaches; Ethological Questions and Methods; The Evolution of Ethology; Ethology and Psychology; Evolutionary Theory; The Concept of Instinct (fixed action patterns; sign stimuli, releasers and supernormal stimuli; the role of environmental factors; the role of hormonal factors and their interaction with the environment; innate releasing mechanisms; criticisms of the ethological approach; the social nature of FAPs; conflict and displacement activity; displacement activity, FAPs and evolution); Courtship and Mating; How do Animals Fall in Love? Social Structure; Territoriality; Parental Care and Imprinting (critical and sensitive periods; reversibility); Sociobiology (biological altruism; the paradox of altruism; the sociobiological solution; sociobiology and human nature).

16. *Pro- and Anti-social Behaviour*   431
Biological and Psychological Altruism (biological altruism in humans; psychological altruism; bystander intervention; defining the situation; diffusion of responsibility; the cost of intervention; the cost of time; the costs of helping different kinds of victim); Aggression; The Nature and Nurture of Aggression (the ethological approach; the neurophysiological approach; the psychoanalytic approach; the learning theory approach; social learning theory: the influence of observing aggression; television

violence and catharsis; television and pro-social behaviour); Aggression and De-individuation.

17. *Interpersonal Perception*   463
Definitions and Models of Interpersonal Perception; Forming Global Impressions of People (central versus peripheral traits; the primacy-recency effect; social roles; role conflict); Judging the Causes of Behaviour (Jones and Davis's correspondent inference theory; Kelley's co-variation model; sources of error and bias in the attribution process); Inferring what People Are Like (individual stereotypes; group stereotypes; the nature of stereotypes; stereotypes and behaviour); Influencing How Others See Us (impression management; self-disclosure; self-monitoring).

18. *Interpersonal Attraction*   492
Relationships Must be Rewarding (exchange and equity; the matching hypothesis); Compatibility; Specific Factors Influencing Attraction (proximity, exposure and familiarity; personal space; similarity; complementarity; reciprocal liking; competence; physical attractiveness; culture; gender; context); Liking and Loving; The Break-down of Relationships (why do relationships go wrong? how do relationships break down?).

19. *Attitudes, Attitude Change and Prejudice*   514
What are Attitudes? Attitudes, Beliefs and Values; Attitudes and Behaviour; Measurement of Attitudes; Persuasive Communication (the source; the message; the recipient; situation or context); Theories of Attitude Change (cognitive dissonance; evaluation of dissonance theory); Prejudice (some demonstrations of prejudice; origins of prejudice; personality theories; social psychological theories; the reduction of prejudice); Conclusions.

20. *Social Influence*   554
Social Facilitation; Leaders and Leadership (the trait approach; the situational approach; Fiedler's contingency model of leader effectiveness; leadership and communication networks); Leadership and Power; Conformity (empirical studies of conformity; individual differences in conformity; conformity and non-conformity); Theories of Conformity (criticisms of conformity experiments); Obedience (Milgram; so why do people obey in the Milgram experiment? criticisms of Milgram); Conclusions.

PART FIVE: DEVELOPMENTAL PROCESSES   587
21. *Childhood and Adolescence—Development of Personality and the Self-concept*   589
Freud's Psychoanalytic Theory (biographical sketch; influences on Freud's thought; the structure of personality); Conflict and the Ego; Freud's Instinct Theory (psychosex-

ual development; oral stage; anal stage; phallic stage; latency; evidence for the Oedipus complex; seduction theory and child abuse; psychosexual development and personality types; is there any evidence to support Freud?); Development of the Self-concept (consciousness and self-consciousness; what is the self? components of the self-concept; self-image; self-esteem; ideal self); Theories of Self (factors influencing the development of the self-concept; reaction of others; comparison with others; social roles; identification; developmental changes in the self-concept; self-recognition; self-recognition in non-human species; self-recognition in human infants; self-definition; the psychological self; the categorical self; adolescence and the self-concept; anorexia nervosa); Erikson's Psychosocial Theory of development (similarities between Erikson and Freud; differences between Erikson and Freud; Erikson's psychosocial stages; basic trust versus basic mistrust; autonomy versus shame and doubt; initiative versus guilt; industry versus inferiority; identity versus role confusion; work as a source of identity; evaluation of Erikson's Theory; other theories of adolescence).

22. *Attachment and Separation: The Effects of Early Experience*   645
The Nature of Attachment (concept of attachment; the gradual development of attachments; the other side of attachment; attachment, attachment behaviour and bonds; different kinds of attachment; the study of attachments; the stability of attachments; attachment and social competence); Theories of Attachment (cupboard love theories; Bowlby's monotropy theory; factors influencing attachment; intensity of interaction; sensitivity and the mother's personality; consistency; social responsiveness and the child's personality); The Effects of Separation: Bowlby's Maternal Deprivation Hypothesis; Effects of Deprivation (short-term; long-term); Effects of Privation (affectionless psychopathy; developmental retardation; critical or sensitive periods; reversibility of long-term effects; studies of adoption; studies of children suffering extreme privation; studies of isolated rhesus monkeys); Conclusions.

23. *Sex and Gender*   674
Terms Relating to Sex and Gender; Biological Categories; Hermaphroditism (testosterone insensitivity; adrenogenital syndrome); Gender Role Differences (gender role identity; the biological approach; biosocial theory; Freud's psychoanalytic theory; social learning theory; cultural relativism; cognitive–developmental theory; stages of gender identity); Androgyny.

24. *Adulthood and Old Age—Development of Personality and the Self-concept*   700
Stage Theories of Adulthood; Levinson et al's (1978) 'Seasons of a Man's Life' (early adult transition; entering

the adult world; age thirty transition; settling down; mid-life transition; entering middle adulthood; age fifty transition; culmination of middle adulthood; late adult transition); Gould's Theory of the Evolution of Adult Consciousness; An Evaluation of Stage Theories of Adulthood; Is the 'Mid-life Crisis' a Developmental Stage?; The Effects of Unemployment (what specific factors related to unemployment cause distress?); Retirement (differences between retirement and unemployment) Ageing (ageism; the ages of me); Life-span and Life-expectancy; Physical Aspects of Ageing (smaller; slower; weaker; lesser; fewer); Intelligence, IQ and Ageing (the definition of intelligence; intelligence tests; cross-sectional versus longitudinal studies; cognitive changes in adulthood and old age); Ageing and Memory; Social Change in Old Age (social disengagement theory); Activity (or Re-engagement) Theory; Social Exchange Theory; An Evaluation of Theories of Ageing; Erikson's Psychosocial Theory; Bereavement; Grief and Mourning (normal and abnormal grieving; the causes of pathological grief; death of the self).

25. *Cognitive Development*   738
Piaget's Theory (intelligence: trait or process; the nature of intellectual development); Stages of Cognitive Development (the sensorimotor stage; the pre-operational stage; the concrete operational stage; the formal operational stage; Piaget on play; evaluation of Piaget's theory); Bruner's Developmental Theory (enactive; iconic; symbolic; language and cognitive development); Vygotsky's Developmental Theory.

26. *Language Development*   768
What is Language? (phonology; semantics; syntax; linguistics and psychology—psycholinguistics); Describing Language Development (pre-linguistic stage; one-word stage; two-word stage); Theories Explaining Language Development (selective reinforcement and imitation; language acquisition and the biological aspects of language; an evaluation of Chomsky's theory); Teaching Language to Non-humans (evaluation; is the language of children and chimps qualitatively different? helping chimps be more like children); Conclusions.

27. *Moral Development*   802
Freud's Psychoanalytic Theory (psychosexual and moral development; are males morally superior to females? is a guilty conscience the sign of a moral or an immoral person? an evaluation of Freud's concept of conscience; generality versus specificity in moral conduct); Learning Theory Approach (the contribution of classical conditioning; the contribution of operant conditioning); Social Learning Theory (what characteristics of models are important for imitation? learning versus performance and the role of reinforcement; evaluation of experimental studies of imita-

tion; imitation and identification; role of cognitive variables); The Cognitive–Developmental Approach (Piaget's theory; Kohlberg's theory).

PART SIX: INDIVIDUAL DIFFERENCES   **837**

28. *Intelligence*   839

Definitions of Intelligence; Factor Analytic Theories of Intelligence (Spearman's two-factor theory; Burt and Vernon's hierarchical model; Thurstone's primary mental abilities; Guilford's 'structure of intellect' model; criticisms of factor analysis); Alternative Models of Intelligence; Intelligence Tests (a brief history of intelligence tests; individual and group tests; mental age and IQ; the relationship between intelligence and IQ; the criteria of an intelligence test; the cultural nature of intelligence and intelligence tests; psychophysiological approaches to measuring intelligence); The Heredity–Environment Issue (proposition 1, proposition 2, proposition 3, proposition 4); Conclusions (race and IQ, conclusions).

29. *Personality*   879

Introduction (the place of personality in psychology as a whole; how do theories of personality differ? the nomothetic versus idiographic approach; Allport's trait theory; behaviour); The Type and Trait Approach— Eysenck and Cattell (factor analysis; Eysenck's type theory; introversion–extroversion neuroticism and psychoticism; personality questionnaires; the biological basis of personality; the relationship between personality and conditionability; personality and criminality; psychiatric diagnosis; an evaluation of Eysenck's theory as a whole; Cattell's Trait Theory; first- and second-order factors: Cattell and Eysenck compared; evaluation of the 16PF; personality and behaviour); Kelly's Personal Construct Theory (the repertory grid technique; an evaluation of PCT); Humanistic Theories (Maslow's hierarchy of needs; who achieves self-actualization? empirical studies of self-actualization; Rogers's self theory); Psychoanalytic Theories; Freud's Psychoanalytic Theory (dreams; neurotic symptoms; defence mechanisms; Freud's theory of the mind; 'our reasons' versus 'the reasons'; the psychopathology of everyday life); Evaluation of Freud's Theory (empirical studies of Freud's theories; is the theory scientific? how valid is the case study method? how representative were the subjects studied by Freud? biological factors; reification); Jung's Analytical Psychology (structure of the personality and levels of consciousness; other similarities and differences between Jung and Freud); Adler's Individual Psychology (the origins of inferiority; factors contributing to inferiority; neurosis and therapy; evaluation).

30. *Psychopathology* 929
The Concept of Abnormality (the statistical criterion; deviation-from-the-norm criterion; the adequacy or mental health criterion; abnormality as personal distress; abnormality as maladaptiveness; the mental illness criterion); The Concept of Mental Illness (comparison between DSM-III-R and ICD-10); Neurotic Disorders (anxiety neurosis; phobias; obsessive–compulsive neurosis; somatoform disorders; dissociative disorders; psychosomatic disorders); Organic Mental Disorders; Schizophrenia and Related Disorders (schizophrenia; theories of schizophrenia); Mood Disorders (manic disorder; depressive disorder; bi-polar disorder; seasonal affective disorder); Personality Disorders (anti-social personality; obsessive–compulsive personality; paranoid personality; schizoid personality); Retardation; Problems with the Classification of Mental Disorder (reliability; validity) Conclusions.

31. *Treatments and Therapies* 961
A Classification of Treatments and Therapies; Physical or Organic Approaches (drug therapy; electro-convulsive therapy; side-effects of ECT; is ECT effective? how does ECT work? psychosurgery); Psychodynamic Approaches (Freud's theory of psychological disorder; the aims of psychoanalysis; therapeutic techniques; the concept of cure; psychoanalytically-oriented psychotherapy); Behavioural Approaches (models of psychological disorder; behaviour therapy; behaviour modification); Cognitive Approaches (cognitive-behaviour therapy; personal construct therapy; the aims of therapy; therapeutic techniques); Humanistic–Phenomenological Approaches (client-centred therapy; the aims of therapy; the therapeutic process; CCT and counselling; encounter groups); Action Therapies (Gestalt therapy; transactional analysis; primal therapy; Erhard seminars training; psychodrama; existential approaches); Treatment Effectiveness; Conclusions.

References and Further Reading 995

Index 1023

PREFACE

This book aims to provide a self-contained introduction to all major aspects of psychology. The content is based on the revised [1987] Associated Examining Board (AEB) A-level psychology syllabus, but it should also be useful if you are studying for the Joint Matriculation Board (JMB) A-level or an International Baccalaureate examination in psychology, or if you are starting a psychology degree or studying psychology as a subsidiary subject in some other area of higher education.

In writing the book I have made use of many years' teaching of A-level to attempt to give an up-to-date coverage of all aspects of the AEB syllabus in a way that avoids either superficiality or excessive detail.

I have tried to raise all the important questions about each topic discussed, to help you get a firm grasp of the topic as a whole. (You will sometimes find that a date quoted in the text for a specific reference differs from the date given in the list of references. Often the same work will be published by different publishers or in different editions – the date in the text normally refers to the original date of publication, while that in the list of references indicates the particular editions which I consulted. Such discrepancies do not, of course, arise in the case of journal/magazine articles.)

The book is not intended to be read in sequence from cover to cover, like a novel. Instead, each chapter can be regarded as a self-contained 'unit', to suit different sequences of tackling the overall subject-matter. Extensive cross-referencing between chapters had been included both to facilitate this and show how different topics and parts of the syllabus are interrelated – I am sure that your class discussions will soon show that to divide human behaviour and experience into separate 'bits' is quite artificial but not to divide them up in some way seems to make things impossibly difficult for students, teachers and textbook writers alike. (The details given in the Contents list are only a very general guide to what each chapter discusses – a full index has been included to help locate specific points and details.)

I have tried to make the tone as light-hearted as I could without detracting from the basic seriousness of the topics under discussion. I have also tried not to 'preach' or talk *at* you, the reader, but to address you as directly as possible, asking you questions from time to time, and to present the subject-matter in a way that will both help you write your essays and/or seminar papers and also stimulate discussion with fellow students and teachers.

Compare this work with others. Write to the publishers about it, if you wish. In short, *use* it.

PREFACE TO THE SECOND EDITION

Much has changed in psychology since 1987 when this book was originally published. This has made it necessary to update material in all chapters and in the case of Ethics and Artificial Intelligence to write two new chapters. However, much remains from the first edition, often in its original form.

At the same time, there have been no syllabus changes (except for the introduction of AS level), and basic issues in teaching psychology and writing textbooks remain the same: (1) how to achieve an integrated, coherent coverage of a vast subject while having to divide it up into sections, and (2) how to achieve a balance between breadth and depth, trying to provide an overview of the essential features of a topic while covering it in sufficient detail to prevent the reader from having to do enormous amounts of extra reading. As if this wasn't a tall enough order, the style must also be readable!

I hope (and believe) that all the positive features of the first edition have been retained. In addition, I have tried to respond to the inevitable criticisms made by students and teachers alike, the single most common being the lack of photographs, diagrams and other pictorial material. Overall, I think the page design is far more attractive and much easier to read. I have also tried to correct factual errors and errors of interpretation. Thanks to those who have pointed these out to me. The order of chapters has been changed quite extensively and they are now grouped into sections; this should make the book as a whole much easier to use.

No single book, of course, can meet all the needs of every student/reader but I believe that this one will meet most of the needs of most of its readers. If that sounds immodest, please let me know what you think after you have used it for a while.

DEDICATION

To all those who, in their various ways, have made this book possible, including readers – past, present and future – and, of course, Jan, Tanya, and especially Jo, who is so much better now. With love and thanks.

ACKNOWLEDGEMENTS

I would like to thank the following: Tina Roszcyzk for word-processing and printing, often at very short notice; Jan Gross, for word-processing and printing, for which she received no payment but much aggravation; Tanya Gross, for her creative suggestions for the cover design; Paul Humphreys, for reading the manuscript and making many helpful and interesting comments; Tim Gregson-Williams, for his continuing editorial support.

The author and publishers would like to thank the National Extension College and their A level psychology course team for their constructive criticism and input to the second edition.

The publishers would like to thank the following for permission to reproduce photos and diagrams.

Page 3, Wide World Photos, Inc.; pp. 4t, 4b, Bettmann Archive, Inc.; p. 5, Freud Museum Publications Ltd; p. 9, The Hulton Picture Company/Bettmann Archive, Inc.; pp. 85–8, Science Photo Library; p. 143, 'Unmasking the Face' by P. Ekman and W. V. Friesen, Consulting Psychologists Press, 1984; p. 166, Science Photo Library; p. 171, The Hulton Picture Company/Bettmann Archive, Inc.; p. 190, Albert Bandura, Stanford University; p. 238, Weidenfeld and Nicholson Ltd; pp. 420tl, 420m, 420b, Bruce Coleman Ltd; p. 420tr, Eric and David Hosking; p. 422, Radio Times Picture Library; p. 524, by permission of the Health Education Authority; p. 565, William Vandivert, Dennis, MA, USA/Scientific American; p. 576, by permission of Harper Collins Publishers, New York; p. 577, Stanley Milgram, 1965. From the film 'Obedience', distributed by the Pennsylvania State University, Audio-Visual Services; p. 601, UPI/Bettmann Archive, Inc.; p. 624, Olive Picrle/Black Star; p. 651, Harlow Primate Laboratory, University of Wisconsin; pp. 678–9, by permission of the Johns Hopkins Press, Maryland, Baltimore; p. 738, Yves de Braine/Black Star; p. 743, by permission of Paul Hamlyn Publishing/Reed International Books; p. 766, by permission of Harvard University Press; p. 798, by permission of Georgia State University/Enrico Ferrorelli/Colorific!; p. 817, Albert Bandura, Stanford University; p. 820, Walter Mischel, Columbia University; p. 817, Albert Bandura, Stanford University; p. 820, Walter Mischel, Columbia University; p. 882, UPI/Bettmann Archive, Inc.; p. 887, Times Newspapers Ltd, London; p. 894, Lawrence Erlbaum Associates, Inc.; p. 898, Ohio State University Archives; p. 902, Special Collections Department, Brandeis University, Waltham, MA, USA; p. 905, Bettmann Archive, Inc.; p. 921, The Hulton Picture Company/Bettmann Archive, Inc.; p. 926, Bettmann Archive, Inc.; p. 969, Freud Museum Publications Ltd.

PART 1

The Nature and Scope of Psychology

1 WHAT IS PSYCHOLOGY?

DEFINITIONS

When a psychologist meets someone for the first time at, say, a party, and replies to the standard 'opening line', 'What do you do for a living?', the reaction of the newly made acquaintance is likely to fall into one of the following categories:

(i) 'Oh, I'd better be careful what I say from now on,' (partly defensive, partly amused);
(ii) 'I bet you meet some right nutters in your work,' (partly intrigued, partly sympathetic);
(iii) 'What exactly is psychology?' (partly inquisitive, partly puzzled).

What these betray (especially the first two) is an inaccurate and incomplete understanding of the subject. The first reaction seems to imply that psychologists are mind-readers and have access to other people's thoughts. *They do not.* The second reaction seems to imply that psychologists work only or largely with people who could variously be described as 'mentally ill', 'emotionally disturbed' or 'mad'. *They do not.* The third reaction perhaps implies that the borderline between psychology and other subject disciplines is not clearly drawn. *It is not*, and what this chapter attempts to do is provide a general answer to (c) by doing three things:

(i) looking at some changing definitions of psychology and some of the major schools of thought within psychology as a whole;
(ii) outlining the major subdivisions of the subject-matter of psychology, and seeing what different psychologists actually do;
(iii) looking at the relationship between psychology and common sense.

1. *Do Psychologists Agree Among Themselves as to What Psychology Is?*

The word *psychology* is derived from two Greek words, *psyche* (mind, soul or spirit) and *logos* (discourse or study) which, put together, produce 'Study of the mind'.

The appearance of psychology as a subject discipline in its own right is generally dated at 1879, when Wilhelm Wundt (Fig. 1.1) opened the first psychology laboratory, at the University of Leipzig in Germany. Wundt and his co-workers were attempting to investigate 'the mind' through *introspection*, that is, observing and analysing the structure of their own conscious mental processes (thoughts, images, feelings) as they occurred. Their aim was to analyse conscious thought into its basic elements, perception into its constituent sensations, etc., much as chemists analyse compounds into elements (hence *structuralism*). They recorded and measured the results of their introspections under *controlled* conditions,

Figure 1.1 Wilhelm Wundt (1832–1920). Wide World Photo, Inc.

Figure 1.2 *William James (1842–1910). The Bettmann Archive*

Figure 1.3 *John Broadus Watson (1878–1958). The Bettmann Archive*

ie under the same physical surroundings, using the same 'stimulus' (eg a clicking metronome), giving the same verbal instructions to each person (subject) who participated, and so on. It was this emphasis on measurement and control that marked the separation of the 'new psychology' from its parent discipline of philosophy.

For many hundreds of years philosophers had been reflecting on and speculating about 'the mind'. Now, for the first time, scientists (Wundt was actually a physiologist by training) were applying some of the basic methods of scientific investigation to the study of mental processes:

> Psychology is the Science of Mental Life, both of its phenomena and of their conditions ... The Phenomena are such things as we call feelings, desires, cognition, reasoning, decisions and the like. (William James, 1890) (Fig. 1.2)

However, by the second decade of the twentieth century, the validity and usefulness of this method were being seriously questioned, in particular by an American psychologist, John B. Watson (Fig. 1.3). Watson believed that introspection produced results which could never be proved or disproved, eg if my introspection produces different results from *yours*, how can we ever decide whose is correct? Of course, we cannot, because there is no objective way of doing so: we cannot 'get behind' the introspective report to check its accuracy. Introspection is subjective and only the individual can observe his/her own mental processes—it cannot be done by another person. Consequently, Watson proposed that psychologists should confine themselves to what is measurable and observable by more than one person, namely *behaviour*:

> For the behaviourist, psychology is that division of Natural Science which takes human behaviour—the doings and sayings, both learned and un-learned—as its subject matter. (John B. Watson, 1919)

So a new brand of psychology had emerged, known as *behaviour-ism*. It largely replaced Wundt's Introspectionism, advocating that human beings should be regarded as complex animals and studied using the same scientific methods as used by chemistry and physics. This was the only way, Watson believed, that psychology could make any claims to being a science itself: to emulate the natural sciences, psychology must adopt its objective methods. The study of inaccessible, private, mental processes was to have no place in a truly scientific psychology.

Behaviourism (in one form or another) was to remain the dominant force within psychology for the next thirty years or so, especially in the USA and, to a lesser extent, in Britain. The emphasis on the role of learning (in the form of *conditioning*) was to make that topic one of the central areas of research in psychology as a whole. Behaviourist theories of learning are often referred to as Stimulus–Response (S–R) theories, because of their attempt to analyse all behaviour into stimulus–response units, no matter how complex the behaviour. (Strictly, only *classical* conditioning fits the S–R model. The other major form of conditioning, *operant conditioning*, is significantly different but is often included under the S–R rubric—see Chapter 7.) A reaction against Behaviourism came in the form of the *Gestalt* school of psychology, which emerged in the 1920s and 1930s in Austria and Germany. The Gestalt psychologists were mainly interested in perception and believed that perceptions could not be broken down in the way that behaviourists advocated for behaviour; one of their central beliefs was that 'the whole is greater than the sum of its parts'. Equally, they rejected the Structuralism of Wundt and others like Titchener in America.

Starting in 1900, in Austria, Sigmund Freud (Fig. 1.4) was beginning to publish his theory of personality in which the *unconscious mind* was to play such a crucial role. Freud's *psychoanalytic theory* also represented a challenge, and a major alternative, to behaviourism.

During the 1950s and 1960s, many psychologists began to look to the work of computer scientists in trying to understand the more complex behaviour which, they felt, Learning (Conditioning) Theory had either neglected altogether or greatly oversimplified. The behaviour in question was what Wundt and the early scientific psychologists had called '*Mind*' or mental processes, but which were now referred to as *cognition* or Cognitive Processes (see James's 1890 definition above). This involves all the ways in which we come to *know* the world around us, how we *attain*, *retain* and *regain* information, through the processes of attention, perception, memory, problem-solving, language and thinking in general.

Figure 1.4 *Sigmund Freud (1856–1939). Marcel Sternberger, Freud Museum Publications Ltd*

The cognitive psychologist sees the person as an *information-processor* and cognitive psychology has been heavily influenced by computer science, with human cognitive processes being compared with the operation of computer programs (the *computer analogy*). Cognitive psychology now forms part of *cognitive science*, which emerged in the late 1970s, along with Artificial Intelligence, Linguistics, Philosophy, Anthropology and Neuroscience (see Fig. 1.7).

As we noted earlier, what makes mental (or cognitive) processes different from behaviour is that they are essentially 'private' in that, at best, you can only *infer* from, say, a person's furrowed brow or head-scratching that they are trying to puzzle out a problem or make up their mind about something. You can also ask them what they are doing, but ultimately you cannot prove or disprove their account of what is going on inside their head, because nobody else can get inside their head to find out.

Thus we have come full circle—back to the behaviourists' original criticisms of introspection. However, mental processes are now accepted as being valid subject-matter for psychology, provided we can objectify or externalize them (make them 'public'), as in memory tests or problem-solving tasks. Consequently, what a person says and does are perfectly acceptable sources of data (information) *about* their cognitive processes, although the processes themselves remain inaccessible to the observer, who can study them only indirectly:

> Psychology is usually defined as the scientific study of behaviour. Its subject matter includes behavioural processes that are observable, such as gestures, speech and physiological changes, and processes that can only be inferred, such as thoughts and dreams. (K. Clark & G. Miller, 1970)

And more recently (and more concisely):

> The scientific study of behaviour and mental processes . . . (Atkinson et al, 1990)

2. How can we Divide up the Work that Psychologists Do?

As we have seen, behaviourist and cognitive psychology have been very influential in determining the general direction that psychology has taken in the last sixty or seventy years, and this is reflected in the definitions of their subject which psychologists have given. However, much more goes on under the general heading of 'psychology' than we have outlined so far: there are other schools of thought, other aspects of human (and animal) activity that constitute the special focus of study, and finally different kinds of work that different psychologists do.

A distinction which may prove helpful is that between the *academic* and the *applied* branches of the subject (Fig. 1.5). The academic psychologist carries out research (scientific investigation) in a particular area (eg perception) and is attached to a university, polytechnic or research establishment where they will also teach first degree students (undergraduates) and may supervise the research of postgraduates.

Research is of two major kinds: *pure*, ie done for its own sake and intended, primarily, to increase our knowledge and understanding; and *applied*, ie aimed at solving a particular problem, usually a social problem such as alcoholism or juvenile delinquency. Applied psychology is usually funded by a government institution, like the Home Office or the Department of Education and Science, or by some commercial or industrial institution.

However, neither of these distinctions is hard and fast: many psychologists work in both academic and applied/practical settings, clinical psychologists especially are engaged in research as an integral part of the evaluation of their work (see below), and pure research may be used for practical ends just as applied research is part of the general 'store of knowledge' which comprises psychology. It may be more useful to distinguish between the psychologist as *investigator* (scientist) and as *practitioner*.

The range of topics that may be investigated is as wide as psychology itself, but a way of classifying them has been suggested by Legge (1975), namely, those which focus on the *processes* or *mechanisms* underlying various aspects of behaviour, and those which focus more directly on the *person*.

THE PROCESS APPROACH

This category itself divides into four main areas—the biological bases of behaviour, learning, cognitive processes and comparative—and is collectively known as *experimental psychology*. (This is something of a misnomer, as the experimental method is used in almost all areas of psychology, including the person-oriented approach; it was originally used to distinguish scientific psychology from the philosophy from which it emerged. Sometimes the term 'general' is used instead of 'experimental.')

1. *THE BIOLOGICAL BASES OF BEHAVIOUR (CHAPTERS 4–6)*

(Neuro)physiological psychologists are interested in the physical basis of behaviour, how the functions of the nervous system (in particular the brain) and the endocrine (hormonal) system are related to and influence behaviour and mental processes. For example, are there parts of the brain specifically concerned with particular behaviours and abilities (*localization of brain function*)? What role do hormones play in the experience of

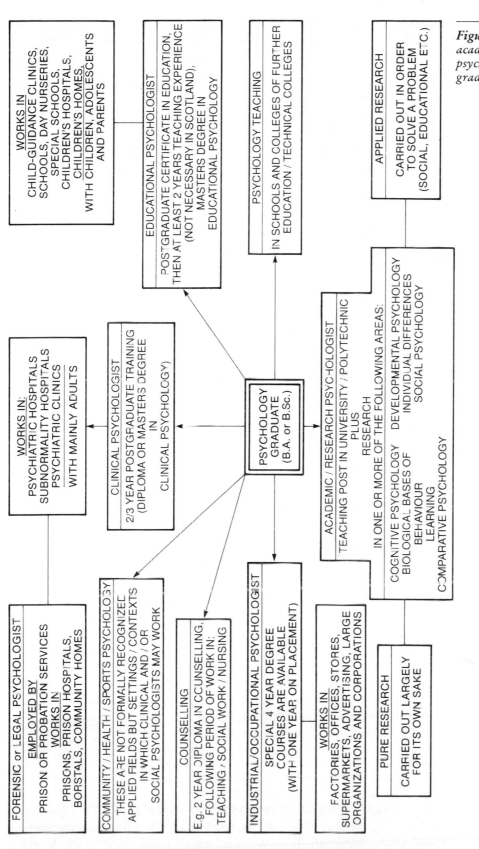

Figure 1.5 *The major areas of academic and applied psychology open to psychology graduates*

emotion and how are these linked to brain processes? What is the relationship between brain activity and different *states of consciousness* (including *sleep*)? What changes occur in the brain when we say that learning has taken place or that a memory has been established? These are just some of the questions that (neuro)physiological psychologists try to answer.

However, we must be aware of the philosophical issue of *reductionism* which, although it does not apply just to neurophysiological psychology, has become focused on the 'Mind–Body' issue (see Chapter 2). Briefly, some physiologists believe that the 'mind' can be 'reduced' to or explained (in principle) totally in terms of brain processes, etc. The implication is that once we know enough about how the brain works, psychology will no longer have a role to play.

Related to interest in (neuro)physiological processes is that in the biological process of genetic transmission (the science of *genetics* existing in its own right.) The *Heredity–Environment* (or *Nature–Nurture*) issue, which runs right through psychology, makes use of what geneticists have discovered about what kinds of characteristics can be passed from parents to offspring, how this takes place and how genetic factors interact with environmental ones (see Chapters 10, 15, 24, 26, 28 and 30).

Other topics which fall within this area are *motivation* and *stress*. (*Sensory Processes* are also biological processes but because of their close connection with perception are dealt with in Chapter 8).

2. *LEARNING (CHAPTER 7)*

The learning process permeates most other subdivisions of psychology. This is partly a reflection of the impact of behaviourism on psychology as a whole (at least up to the 1950s), since learning plays such a central part in behaviourist theory where it is studied in the form of *Conditioning*. But there is much more to learning than conditioning. We shall be discussing the work of Social Learning theorists who, while sharing many of the basic principles of Conditioning theory, also believe that conditioning alone cannot account for much human behaviour. They have focused on *Observational Learning* (Modelling) as an important additional learning process—especially in children. (See also Chapter 27.)

Learning which is closely related to cognitive processes, such as language and perception, is also considered to be different from conditioning; thus Gestalt psychology's *Insight* learning and the learning by rats of 'mental maps' (Tolman, 1948) are examples of *cognitive* learning. All three kinds of learning (plus others) will feature prominently in the discussion of development (especially Chapters 25 and 27) and the applications of theories of learning are important in the treatment of behaviour disorders (see Chapter 31).

(We should perhaps make a distinction between: (i) '*theories of learning*', which include all three types mentioned above; and (ii) '*learning theory*', which usually refers to the behaviourist theories of conditioning, eg Pavlov, Watson and Skinner.)

3. *COGNITIVE PROCESSES (CHAPTERS 9–14)*

As we noted earlier, *cognition* means knowing, so cognitive (or mental) processes refer to all those ways in which knowledge of the world is attained, retained and used, including *attention*, *memory*, *perception*, *language*, *thinking*, *problem-solving*, *reasoning* and *concept-formation* ('higher-order' mental activities). As we have seen, these are processes which can only be inferred and which cannot be seen directly. Although these are often studied for their own sake, they may have very important practical implications too, for example, understanding the memory processes involved in eye-witness testimony. Much social psychology (listed here as belonging in the Person category) is cognitive in flavour, that is, concerned with the mental processes involved in interpersonal perception (eg stereotyping) and attitude change (eg cognitive dissonance) and is known as *social cognition*. Also, Piaget's theory of development (again, belonging to the Person category) is concerned with *cognitive development*.

Because of the major influence of computer science on cognitive psychology, and the fact that cognitive psychology now forms part of *cognitive science*, the relationship between human problem-solving and *Artificial Intelligence* is discussed in this section of the book (Chapter 14). According to cognitive science, both computers and human problem-solvers are *information-processing machines*.

Figure 1.6 Charles Darwin (1809–1882)

4. *COMPARATIVE PSYCHOLOGY (CHAPTER 15)*

This is often used synonymously with *animal* psychology, but the word 'comparative' implies the original purpose of studying animals, namely to increase our understanding of human behaviour. The study of animal behaviour was inspired by Darwin (Fig. 1.6), whose 1859 theory of evolution made it seem quite reasonable to believe that, by studying the more simple species from which we have evolved, we should learn more about ourselves.

However, there is a great temptation to extrapolate directly from non-human species to ourselves (see Chapter 2). Moreover, much study of animal behaviour takes place for its own sake and is perhaps more appropriately called 'animal' psychology. At the same time, animals continue to be used as experimental subjects, in many areas of psychology, when for moral and practical reasons humans cannot be used (see Chapter 3).

Ironically, the study of animals was first taken up by psychologists (as opposed to biologists, which Darwin was) and much of their research took place in the laboratory (including Watson's work and that of the behaviourists who followed him). More recently (especially since the 1950s) *zoologists* have been advocating the 'naturalist' approach to the study of animal behaviour, observing animals in their natural habitats. This *ethological* approach is associated particularly with Niko Tinbergen and Konrad Lorenz. A development of ethology since the late 1970s is *sociobiology* (Wilson: see pages 427–30), which attempts to explain all social behaviour (animal and human) in terms of evolutionary forces.

Naturalistic methods of studying people (especially children) have been inspired by the ethologists and Bowlby's theory of attachment in human infants (Chapter 22) was greatly influenced by Lorenz's study of *Imprinting* in goslings.

THE PERSON APPROACH

1. SOCIAL PSYCHOLOGY (CHAPTERS 16–20)

Some psychologists would claim that 'all psychology is social psychology' because all behaviour takes place within a social context and, even when we are alone, our behaviour continues to be influenced by others (eg their potential response to what we are doing). Our self-concept is in large measure a reflection of how others have treated us and responded to us in the past, (this is actually discussed in Chapter 21) but others may have a more immediate and direct influence upon us when we are actually in their presence (social facilitation, leadership, conformity and obedience).

Social psychology is also concerned with interpersonal perception (forming impressions of others), interpersonal attraction (why we like some people more than others), attitudes and attitude change, prejudice and pro- and anti-social behaviour (including aggression). Social psychologists tend to draw on the work of general psychology in order to see how this can help them understand the behaviour that goes on between people.

2. DEVELOPMENTAL PSYCHOLOGY (CHAPTERS 21–27)

Developmental psychology studies the physical, intellectual, social and emotional changes that occur in the individual over time. One very significant change that has occurred within developmental psychology during the past twenty years or so is the recognition that development is not confined to childhood and adolescence, but is a lifelong process (referred to as the *Lifespan Approach*). While the ageing process has been studied for many years, the emphasis has tended to be on physical aspects and the associated psychopathology (or mental illness, especially senile dementia); it has not had the 'flavour' of a stage of development, unlike pregnancy, infancy, toddlerhood and so on. Also, 'growing old' has, traditionally, had very negative connotations, compared with 'growing up', which is normally taken to be something desirable and almost an end in itself. It is now generally accepted, however, that adulthood is a developmental stage, quite distinct from adolescence and old age.

The first major theorist to acknowledge the lifelong nature of development ('cradle-to-grave') was Erik Erikson, who described the 'Eight Ages of Man', each of which presents the individual with a new developmental task to be worked on.

Developmental psychology is not an isolated or independent field and advances in it depend on progress in the entire realm of psychology, for example, behavioural genetics, (neuro)physiological psychology, learning, perception and motivation. This is reflected in the wide-ranging methods and techniques of study that are used. But developmental psychology also contributes to other areas of psychology; for example, although Piaget's theory of cognitive development was meant to map the changes that take place up to about fifteen years of age, he is considered to have made a massive contribution to psychology as a whole.

Developmental psychology also provides an important 'testing ground' for general psychological principles, many of which have derived from laboratory studies on animals: the study of developmental changes can indicate just how valid these principles are when applied to human beings in the real world. It was Darwin's *Origin of Species* (1859) which inspired the view that the child is a rich source of potential information about the nature of the human species as a whole. By careful observation of the developing infant and child, the evolution and development of the human species (*Phylogeny*) can be traced. (*Ontogeny* is the evolution and development of the individual.) The developing organism can be regarded as a microcosm of the species as it developed. (A microcosm is a smaller-scale example of some larger process or situation, eg the family is a microcosm of society.)

3. *INDIVIDUAL DIFFERENCES (CHAPTERS 28–31)*

As the name suggests, this is concerned with the ways in which people can differ from one another, in particular personality and intelligence.

Personality can be thought of as those relatively stable and enduring aspects of individuals which distinguish them from others, making them unique, but which at the same time allow people to be compared with each other. Within that general definition, there are several different theoretical approaches, including the trait and type approach (Eysenck and Cattell), the psychodynamic (Freud, Jung, Adler), the humanistic (Maslow, Rogers), the social learning approach (Mischell) and the cognitive (Kelly). The first of these, the trait and type approach, is closely related to *psychometrics* ('mental measurement'), since this approach makes great use of standardized tests of personality on which to compare large numbers of individuals and groups or classes of individuals.

Similarly, the study of *intelligence* is very much concerned with differences between individuals and groups (eg racial and age-groups) and a great deal of time and money has been invested since 1905 (when Binet and Simon devised the first intelligence test) in constructing new tests and refining old ones. One of the most hotly debated issues in psychology is how to account for differences in measured intelligence between different racial groups in terms of genetic factors (nature or heredity) or environmental factors (nurture or environment). The status of the tests used is problematic, as is the attempt to define the term 'intelligence' itself.

Also included is *psychopathology* (or *abnormal psychology*). This studies the underlying causes of what is variously called mental illness, behaviour disorder, emotional disturbance and various forms of deviancy (which may include criminality, sexual perversions, drug abuse and alcoholism); it is closely linked with one of the applied areas of psychology, namely, clinical psychology (see below). Clearly, there is also overlap between abnormal psychology and the study of (normal) personality: we have to know what the range of individual differences is before we can begin to classify people (or their behaviour) as abnormal or deviant. We shall also be discussing different kinds of treatment and therapies.

Two other major sources of individual differences are *age* and *gender*. These are both dealt with as part of *developmental* psychology.

Is there a real difference between the Process and the Person approaches after all? I have tried to show how different research areas overlap with others and how, in practice, it is very difficult to separate them, even if it can be done theoretically.

However, there are differences (mainly of degree) which are worth mentioning:

The *Process approach* is much more confined to the laboratory, makes far greater use of animals as subjects, and makes the general and basic assumption that psychological processes (particularly learning) are essentially the same in *all* species: any differences that are found between members of different species are only *quantitative* (differences of degree). In contrast, the *Person approach* makes much greater use of field studies (eg observing subjects in their natural environments) and of non-experimental methods (eg correlational studies). In the main, human subjects are used and it is assumed that *qualitative* differences (differences in kind) exist between humans and other animals.

Our discussion of the Person/Process approaches has been concerned with the *academic* branch of psychology. Fortunately, the situation is a little more straightforward as far as applied psychology is concerned, partly because of the special training required (over and above the minimum requirement that all psychologists must possess a psychology degree) and partly because of the place and type of work involved. The three major areas of applied psychology are Educational, Clinical and Industrial (or Occupational). (As these are all concerned with people, they may be considered the applied aspects of the Person approach.)

EDUCATIONAL PSYCHOLOGY

The educational psychologist has had at least two years teaching experience and has gained a postgraduate qualification in educational or child psychology. The main areas of responsibility include:

(i) administering psychological tests, particularly intelligence or IQ tests, as part of the assessment of learning difficulties;
(ii) the planning and supervision of remedial teaching;
(iii) research into teaching methods, the curriculum (subjects taught), interviewing and counselling methods and techniques;
(iv) the planning of educational programmes designed to meet the needs of mentally and physically handicapped (including the visually handicapped and autistic) and other groups of children and adolescents who are not attending ordinary schools (ie *special education*).

Educational psychologists are usually employed by the Local Education Authority (LEA) and work in one or more of the following: child guidance clinics (usually staffed by a psychiatrist, one or more educational psychologists, several psychiatric social workers, one or more child psychotherapists, and, sometimes, a speech therapist); the Schools Psychological Service; hospitals, day nurseries, nursery schools, special schools (day and residential) and residential children's homes. The age of clients is up to 18 years, but most will fall into the 5 to 16 age-group.

Working very closely with parents and teachers, educational psychologists advise both groups how to deal with children and adolescents who have mental and/or physical handicaps, behaviour problems or learning difficulties. They are also involved in teacher training.

CLINICAL PSYCHOLOGY

Clinical psychologists are by far the most numerous single group of psychologists: more than one-third of all psychologists classify themselves as clinical and a further 10 per cent or so call themselves 'counselling psychologists' (they tend to work with younger clients in colleges and universities rather than in hospitals).

The clinical psychologist has trained for two or three years as a post-graduate and is qualified to:

(a) Assess the mentally handicapped, administer psychological tests to brain-damaged patients, devise rehabilitation programmes for long-term psychiatric patients and assess the elderly for their fitness to live independently in their own homes.

(b) Plan and carry out programmes of therapy, usually *behaviour therapy/modification* (both derived from Learning theory principles), but occasionally they may choose *psychotherapy* (group or individual) in preference to, or in addition to, behavioural techniques (see Chapter 31).

Psychotherapy is usually carried out by *psychiatrists* (who are doctors who specialize in psychological medicine) or *psychotherapists* (who are often social workers who undergo a special training, which includes their own psychotherapy) and is based on the psychoanalytic (psychodynamic) theories of personality associated with Freud (see Chapters 29 and 30). Patients may be of any age but are usually adults, of whom many will be elderly; the clinical psychologist works in psychiatric and subnormality hospitals, psychiatric wards in general hospitals and psychiatric clinics. Many are engaged in conducting research into abnormal psychology, including the effectiveness of different treatment methods.

Working with the families of patients, clinical psychologists are increasingly involved in community care as psychiatric care in general moves out of the large psychiatric hospitals. They are also engaged in teaching other groups of professionals, such as nurses, psychiatrists and social workers.

A special sub-group of clinical psychologists is the *forensic* or *legal psychologist*, who is employed by the prison or probation service. The forensic psychologist may be called as an expert witness in court trials to testify regarding: (i) the credibility of witnesses and defendants; (ii) the fitness of individuals to stand trial; (iii) any other matter seen as requiring the expert opinion of a psychologist (eg handwriting). They may work in community homes (once called approved schools), detention centres, youth custody centres and prisons or prison hospitals (for the criminally insane) such as Broadmoor and Rampton.

INDUSTRIAL OR OCCUPATIONAL PSYCHOLOGY

The responsibilities of the industrial or occupational psychologist include:

(a) The selection and training of individuals for jobs and vocational guidance, which often involves giving aptitude tests and tests of interest and is sometimes the responsibility of individuals trained in personnel management, which has a large psychology component.

(b) Industrial rehabilitation, ie helping people who, for reasons of illness, accident or redundancy, need to choose and re-train for a new career.

(c) Designing training schemes, as part of *'fitting the person to the job'*; this is particularly important at a time when new technology is replacing old methods and sometimes taking over totally the jobs done by particular workers. Teaching machines and simulators (eg of an aeroplane cockpit) often feature prominently in such training schemes.

(d) 'Fitting the job to the person' (*human engineering* or *ergonomics*) whereby applications from experimental psychology are made to the design of equipment and machinery, in order to make the best use of human resources and to minimize accidents and fatigue. Examples of how engineering psychologists have been consulted include telephone dialling codes (memory and attention) and the design of decimal coinage (tactile and visual discrimination); these illustrate very well the interplay between applied and pure research where the former very often depends on the latter and any complete separation between them is not possible.

(e) Advising on working conditions so as to maximize productivity as another facet of ergonomics (the study of efficiency of people in their working environments). Occupational groups involved include computer/VDU operators, those working on production lines and air traffic controllers.

(f) Helping the flow of communication between departments or sections in government institutions or 'industrial relations' in commerce and industry (often called *organizational psychology*). Here the emphasis is on the social, rather than the physical or practical, aspects of the working environment.

(g) Helping to sell products and services through advertising and promotions. Many psychologists are employed in the advertising industry, where they draw on what experimental psychologists say about human motivation, attitudes, cognition and so on.

CHARTERED PSYCHOLOGISTS

Since 1987, the British Psychological Society (the only scientific and professional body for British psychologists incorporated by Royal Charter) has been authorized under its Charter to keep a Register of Chartered Psychologists. Entry to the Register is restricted to members of the Society who have applied for registration and who have the necessary postgraduate qualifications or experience to have reached a standard sufficient for professional practice in psychology without supervision (Gale, 1990).

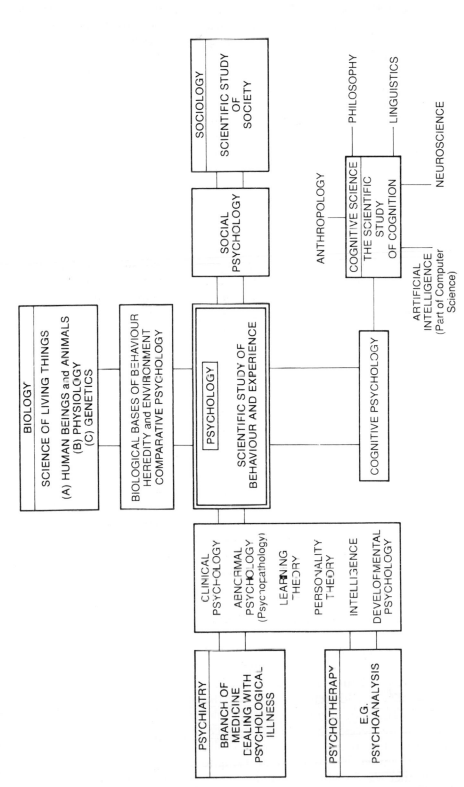

Figure 1.7 The relationship between psychology and other scientific disciplines

SCHOOLS OF THOUGHT OR THEORETICAL APPROACHES

Throughout our discussion so far, we have had cause to refer to behaviourist, or psychoanalytic, or cognitive theories or perspectives (Fig. 1.7); it should be apparent by now that we cannot talk about psychologists as if they all shared some basic theory about 'what makes people tick', nor indeed do they agree about what sort of terminology or methodology to use when carrying out their research or formulating their theories.

Different psychologists make different assumptions about what particular aspects of a person are worthy of study, sometimes to the exclusion of others, and this helps to determine an underlying *model* or *image* of what human beings are like. In turn, this model or image determines a view of psychological normality, the nature of development, preferred methods of study, the major cause(s) of abnormality and the preferred methods and goals of treatment. These issues and the position of five major theoretical approaches (psychoanalytic, behaviourist, humanistic-existential, neurobiological and cognitive) regarding them are summarized in Table 1.1.

These (together with different versions of each) are the major theoretical approaches that will make their appearance throughout the book (particularly in relation to development). It should be evident from even a cursory glance at the table how different and distinctive is the *language* used by each approach. So let us now take a closer look at some of the language used in psychology as a whole.

THE LANGUAGE OF PSYCHOLOGY

As in all sciences, there is a special set of technical terms (jargon) to get used to and this is generally accepted as an unavoidable feature of studying the subject. But over and above these technical words, which scientists speak to fellow scientists, psychologists use words that are familiar to us from everyday speech and it is here that 'doing psychology' can become a little confusing.

Some examples of this are 'behaviour' and 'personality'. For parents to tell their child to 'behave yourself' is meaningless to a psychologist's ears because behaving is something we are all doing all the time (even when asleep) and to say someone 'has no personality' is equally meaningless, because as personality refers to what makes a person unique and different from others you cannot help but have one! Other terms, which denote large portions of the research of experimental psychology, such as memory, learning and intelligence are called *hypothetical constructs*, that is, they do not refer to anything that can be directly observed but can only be inferred from observable behaviour. Equally important, they seem to be necessary in order to account for the behaviour that is observed; but there is a danger of thinking of them as 'things' or 'entities', rather than as a way of trying to make sense of behaviour.

Another way in which psychologists try to make sense of something is by comparing it with something else (often something complex is compared with something more simple), that is, they use an *analogy*. Since the 1950s and the development of computer science, the *computer*

Table 1.1 Five major approaches in psychology

	(1) PSYCHO-ANALYTIC OR PSYCHO-DYNAMIC (EG FREUD)	(2) BEHAV-IOURIST OR STIMULUS–RESPONSE (EG SKINNER)	(3) HUMAN-ISTIC-EXISTENTIAL (EG MASLOW)	(4) NEURO-BIOLOGICAL OR BIOGENIC	(5) COGNITIVE
Nature of human beings	Individual is in conflict due to opposing demands made by different parts of the personality— ID, EGO, SUPEREGO. Behaviour is largely determined by unconscious forces.	Human behaviour is shaped by environmental forces (REINFORCE-MENT) and is a collection of learned responses to external stimuli. The key learning process is conditioning (classical and operant).	The individual is unique, free, rational and self-determining. Free-will and self-actualization make human beings distinct from animals. Present experience is as important as past experience.	Behaviour is determined by genetic, physiological and neurobiological factors and processes. The influence of the central nervous system (especially the brain) is crucial.	The human mind is compared to a computer. People are INFORMA-TION-PROCESSORS, selecting information, coding it, storing it and retrieving it when needed. Memory, perception and language are central.
Nature of psychological normality	Adequate balance between id, ego, superego. But conflict is always present to some degree.	Possession of an adequately large repertoire of adaptive responses.	Ability to accept oneself, to realize one's potential, to achieve intimacy with others, to find meaning in life.	Properly functioning nervous system.	Proper functioning of cognitive processes and the ability to use them to monitor and control behaviour.
Nature of psychological development	PSYCHO-SEXUAL stages: oral (0–1); anal (1–3); phallic (3–5/6); latency (5/6–puberty) genital (puberty–maturity). Sequence determined by maturation. The individual is shaped by early childhood experiences.	None as such. No stages of development. Different behaviour is selectively reinforced at different ages but the differences between a child and an adult are merely QUANTITAT-IVE.	Development of self-concept, in particular self-regard (self-esteem). Satisfaction of lower-level needs as prerequisite for higher-level (growth) needs.	Stages of behavioural/psychological development based on changes in brain growth which are genetically determined (ie maturation).	● Stages of Cognitive Development (eg Piaget): sensorimotor (0–2), pre-operational (2–7); concrete operational (7–11); formal operational (11–15). ● Information-Processing approach— development of memory, perception, language, attention, etc.

Table 1.1 Continued

	(1) PSYCHO-ANALYTIC OR PSYCHO-DYNAMIC (EG FREUD)	(2) BEHAV-IOURIST OR STIMULUS–RESPONSE (EG SKINNER)	(3) HUMAN-ISTIC-EXISTENTIAL (EG MASLOW)	(4) NEURO-BIOLOGICAL OR BIOGENIC	(5) COGNITIVE
Preferred method(s) of study	Case-study (Clinical method)	Experiment (Animals and humans)	Case-study	Experiment (Animals and humans)	Experiment (Mainly humans) *Artificial intelligence*
Major cause(s) of abnormal behaviour	Emotional disturbance or neurosis caused by unresolved conflicts stemming from childhood. Abnormal behaviour is symptomatic of such conflicts. Main feature is anxiety.	The learning of maladaptive responses or the failure to learn adaptive ones in the first place. No distinction between symptoms and the behaviour disorder.	Inability to accept and express one's true nature, to take responsibility for one's own actions and to make authentic choices. Anxiety stems from denying part of self. Referred to as identity crisis or ontological insecurity.	Genetic disorders, organic (bodily) disorders (e.g. brain disease or injury), chemical imbalance, food allergies. MENTAL ILLNESS gives rise to behavioural and psychological symptoms.	Unrealistic or irrational ideas and beliefs about self and others. Inability to monitor or control behaviour through appropriate cognitive processes.
Preferred method(s) of treatment	Insight-oriented psychotherapy (eg psychoanalysis). The unconscious is revealed through dream interpretation, free-association, transference.	Behaviour therapy or modification. Eg systematic desensitization, aversion therapy, flooding, behaviour shaping, token economy.	Client-centred therapy; insights come from the client as present experiences are explored with the therapist.	Physical treatments. Eg chemotherapy (drugs), electro-convulsive therapy (E.C.T.), psychosurgery.	Eg cognitive–behaviour therapy, rational–emotive therapy, Zen meditation and behavioural self-control.
Goal(s) of treatment	To uncover and work through unconscious conflicts to make them conscious. To achieve reasonable balance between id, ego and superego.	To eliminate maladaptive responses and to acquire adaptive ones.	To rediscover the *Whole self*, which can then proceed towards self-actualization.	To alleviate symptoms and/or to actually reverse the underlying cause(s) of the illness.	To correct these unrealistic/irrational ideas and beliefs so that thinking becomes an effective means of controlling behaviour.

analogy has become very popular as a way of trying to understand how the brain works; as we have seen, the language of computer science has permeated the cognitive view of human beings as information processors. A *model* is a kind of metaphor: it is not meant to be taken too literally but is more of a suggestion as to how we might think of peoples' behaviour, again in order to understand it better. A model entails a single, fundamental idea or image and is not as complex as a theory (although sometimes the terms are used interchangeably).

In Chapter 2, a *theory* is defined as a complex set of interrelated statements which attempt to explain certain observed phenomena. (But this is only one of many definitions that you might come across in your reading!) Although, strictly speaking, the role of theory is to explain, in practice, when we refer to a particular theory (eg that of Freud or Piaget), we often include description as well.

Thomas (1985) defines a theory as, 'an explanation of how the facts fit together' and he likens a theory to a lens through which to view the subject matter, filtering out certain facts and giving a particular pattern to those it lets in.

A *hypothesis* is defined in Chapter 2 as a testable statement about the relationship between two or more variables. The term is sometimes used to mean something very similar to 'theory' but these two meanings should be kept separate.

Psychology and Common Sense

A common reaction among psychology students, when discussing the findings of some piece of research, is to say 'But we knew that already' implying that 'It's only common sense'. Alternatively, they might say 'But that's not what we normally understand by such-and-such', implying that the research is in some way wrong. So it seems that psychology is often in a 'Catch-22' position—either it merely *confirms* common sense or it *contradicts* it, in which case psychology seems to be the less credible.

Whereas only a few of us would think of ourselves as physicists or doctors, engineers or novelists, unless we had received a special education, or training, or had special talent, we all consider that we know something about people and why they behave as they do. So there is a sense in which we are all psychologists!

This is a theme explored at length by Joynson in *Psychology and Common Sense* (1974). He begins by stating that human beings are not like the objects of natural science—we understand ourselves and can already predict and control our behaviour to a remarkable extent. This creates for the psychologist a paradoxical task: what kind of understanding can you seek of a creature which already understands itself?

For Joynson, the fundamental question is, 'If the psychologist did not exist, would it be necessary to invent him?' For Skinner, 'it is science or nothing' and Broadbent, another leading behaviourist, also rejects the validity of our everyday understanding of ourselves and others (Joynson calls it 'the behaviourists' prejudice'). Yet it seems inevitable that we try to make sense of our own and other people's behaviour (by virtue of our cognitive abilities and the nature of social interaction) and to this extent we are all psychologists. (This is discussed further in relation to Interpersonal Perception—see Chapter 17.)

Heather (1976) points to ordinary language as embodying our 'natural' understanding of human behaviour; in his view, as long as human beings have lived they have been psychologists, and language gives us an 'elaborate and highly refined conceptual tool, developed over thousands of years of talking to each other'. So how can we resolve the dilemma? Legge (1975) and others resolve it by distinguishing between *formal* and *informal* psychology (or professional versus amateur, scientific versus non-scientific). Our common sense, intuitive or 'natural' understanding is unsystematic and does not constitute a body of knowledge; this makes it very difficult to 'check' an individual's 'theory' about human nature, as does the fact that each individual has to learn from his/her own experience. So part of the aim of formal psychology is precisely to provide such a systematic body of knowledge, which represents the unobservable bases of our 'gut-reactions'.

But it could be argued that informal psychology does provide a 'body of knowledge' in the form of proverbs or sayings or folk wisdom, handed down from generation to generation, for example, 'birds of a feather flock together', 'too many cooks spoil the broth' and 'don't cross your bridges before you come to them'. Perhaps these contain at least a grain of truth. But the problem is that for each of them we can find yet another proverb which states the opposite—'opposites attract', 'many hands make light work' and 'time and tide wait for no man' (or 'nothing ventured, nothing gained'). Common sense does not help us to reconcile these contradictory statements—but formal psychology can! Indeed, there does seem to be some evidence to support both proverbs in the first pair (see Chapter 18 on Interpersonal Attraction); formal psychology tries to identify the *conditions* under which each statement holds true—they only appear contradictory if we assume that only one or the other can be true! In this way, we can see scientific psychology as throwing light on our everyday, informal understanding, not necessarily as negating or invalidating it.

Legge believes that most psychological research should indeed be aimed at demonstrations of 'what we know already' but that it should aim to go one step further; only the methods of science, he believes, can provide us with the public, communicable body of knowledge that we are seeking. According to Allport (1947), the aim of science is 'Understanding, prediction and control above the levels achieved by unaided common sense' and this is meant to apply to psychology as much as it does to the natural sciences. Just what science involves, and how appropriately we can study people scientifically, is the subject of the next chapter.

2 Is Psychology a Science?

Philosophy and Psychology

In trying to answer the important and complex question of whether psychology is a science, it is instructive to take a brief look at some of the major philosophical influences that helped to create psychology as a separate discipline and which help to explain what psychology is today. 'Is psychology a science?' is essentially a philosophical question; it cannot be answered without taking the meaning of certain concepts into account, in particular, the concept of a science. The two major philosophical influences I will describe here are *Empiricism* and *Positivism*.

EMPIRICISM

The *Empiricists* were seventeenth-century British philosophers (notably Locke, Hume and Berkeley) who believed that the only source of true knowledge about the world is *sensory experience*, that is, what comes to us through our senses or what can be inferred about the relationships between such sensory facts. This fundamental belief proved to be one of the major influences on the development of physics and chemistry. Indeed, the word '*empirical*' ('through the senses') is often used synonymously with 'scientific', implying that what is at the heart of scientific activity is the observation and measurement of the world and the collection of data. Empiricist philosophers were usually contrasted with *Rationalists or Nativists* who believed that knowledge of the world is largely innate or inborn.

Although Wundt had been influenced by empiricism through its impact on science as a whole (including physiology) it was behaviourism which was to embody empiricist philosophy within psychology. Locke maintained that the mind at birth was a *tabula rasa*, a blank slate on which experience made its imprint, and this extreme environmentalism is built into the behaviourist view of learning, whereby the child is totally malleable and can be made into anything the environment wants it to become. According to George Miller (1962), the implications of empiricism for psychology, in addition to the emphasis on the senses as the 'doors to the mind', include: (i) the analysis into *elements* (eg conscious mind into simple ideas or overt behaviour into Stimulus–Response units); and (ii) a theory of *association* necessary for explaining how simple elements can be combined to form more complex elements or compounds.

Thus empiricism provided for psychology both a *theory* (tabula rasa view of the mind) and a *methodology* (central role of observation and measurement), and this corresponds to a very important distinction between two kinds of behaviourism—philosophical and methodological. *Philosophical behaviourism*, in its most extreme form, is Watson's rejection of mind, the view that, for example, thinking is nothing but a series of vocal or sub-vocal verbal responses; less extreme is Skinner's belief that mental concepts are irrelevant in trying to predict and control human behaviour. *Methodological behaviourism* refers to the emphasis on observation, the collection and measurement of data, the importance of the experiment and so on. Despite the decline of philosophical behaviourism, methodological behaviourism has continued to exert its influence—most psychologists today are behaviourists in this second sense and it underlies the way psychology is taught.

POSITIVISM

The philosophy of Auguste Comte (1842), positivism was directly influenced by the achievements of the natural sciences during the seventeenth, eighteenth and nineteenth centuries. In essence, Comte advocated the application of the methods and principles of natural science to human behaviour, institutions and political organizations (which is why he is regarded as the father of sociology).

According to Heather (1976), there are two significant events that marked the impact of positivism on psychology; first, the publication in 1859 of Darwin's *Origin of Species*, outlining his theory of evolution, which enabled psychology to be placed firmly within the biological sciences ('man as organism'); and, secondly, the opening of the first psychology laboratory by Wundt in 1879, which created the precedent for the experimental basis on which academic psychology has rested ever since.

The work that Comte began in 1842 culminated in the 1920s in the formation of the Vienna Circle, a group of philosophers (including A. J. Ayer), mathematicians and scientists who attempted to rid philosophy of any statements which could not be publicly verified or empirically tested (ie metaphysical statements). They believed that the scientific path was the only one that could lead to 'the truth' and advance human progress. These *Logical Positivists* were strong supporters of early behaviourism which, in rejecting introspectionism and the study of private, subjective, experience, was trying to put psychology on a public footing, whereby any number of observers could agree about 'the facts'. (We shall discuss later some of the consequences of the behaviourist attempt to confine 'the data' to purely 'objective' facts.) Related to logical positivism is *Materialism* (or *Physicalism*), the belief that all valid propositions (including those to do with consciousness) must be capable of being translated into the language of physics. From this it follows that, eventually, psychology will be 'swallowed up' in the universal science of physics (having first been replaced by physiology and biochemistry etc). This represents an extreme form of *Reductionism* which we shall discuss in detail later in the chapter.

WHAT IS SCIENCE?

A science may be defined in various ways, but there are certain criteria that must be met:

(a) There must be a definable *subject-matter*, that is, what the science is *about*, the range of objects or phenomena it studies.
(b) There must be some kind of *theory* construction and *hypothesis*

testing. A theory is a complex set of interrelated statements which attempts to explain certain observed phenomena; from a theory, particular statements can be inferred which constitute testable statements about the relationship between two or more variables. These testable statements usually take the form of predictions about what will happen under certain specified conditions and are known as *hypotheses*; it is hypotheses, rather than whole theories, which are empirically tested in scientific research.

(c) Facts cannot be established through rational argument (despite the attempts of philosophers or 'armchair' psychologists) but through the use of *empirical* methods of investigation, that is, observation, measurement and other *objective* ways of gathering information (data-collection). The major methods used in psychology are summarized in Figure 2.1.

(d) Science should attempt to discover general *laws* or principles that govern, in the case of psychology, human behaviour and mental processes and which are intended to be applicable to every member of the human species (ie *universal*).

INDUCTION AND SCIENTIFIC METHOD

What we have said so far about what constitutes a science would probably be agreed by most psychologists and philosophers of science. But this does not necessarily tell us how scientific activity proceeds, the sequence of 'events' or the precise relationship between theory, hypothesis-testing and the collection of data.

The classic picture of how scientific method goes on is called *induction* (the Inductive Method). Briefly, as a form of reasoning, it involves moving from the particular to the general, that is, drawing general conclusions from a number of separate observations. Medawar (1963) describes the inductive method as a process of scientific discovery that begins with simple, unbiased, unprejudiced observation and out of this sensory evidence, embodied in the form of simple propositions or declarations of fact, generalizations will grow up and take shape, 'Out of the disorderly array of facts an orderly theory, an orderly general statement will somehow emerge'. But three main problems arise from this picture:

(a) There is no such thing as 'unbiased' or 'unprejudiced' observation— our perception is always selective and we always interpret what we see (see Chapter 9). As Popper (1972) says, observation is always pre-structured and directed and this is as true of physics as it is of psychology.

(b) Induction does not enable us to *prove* general statements, although it may enable us to discover relationships among sense-data, ie, what is observed. (We shall discuss this further when we take a closer look at the psychological experiment.)

(c) The sum of inductive statements (separate observations) is unable, logically, to lead to generalizations which are more than the sum of those statements. (This too is discussed later.)

The first problem in particular has led Popper to revise the stages of the scientific process as presented by the inductive method and it may be useful to compare Popper's revised version with the original (Table 2.1).

Figure 2.1 *The major criteria of a science and the empirical methods used in psychology*

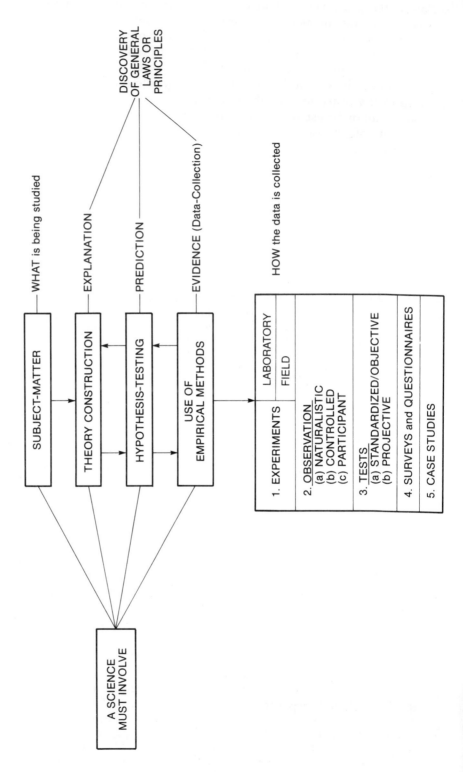

INDUCTIVE METHOD (CLASSICAL VIEW OF SCIENCE)	POPPER'S VERSION
1. Observation and method 2. Inductive generalization 3. Hypothesis 4. Attempted verification of hypothesis 5. Proof or disproof 6. Knowledge	1. Problem (usually a refutation of an existing theory or prediction) 2. Proposed solution or new theory 3. Deduction of testable statements from the new theory (ie hypotheses) 4. Tests or attempts to refute by methods including observation and experiment 5. Establishing a preference between competing theories

Table 2.1 Comparison of the classical, inductive view of science and Popper's revised version

Popper's version shows quite clearly that observation does not go on in a 'theoretical vacuum' but is related, more or less directly, to some theory:

> Sense-data, untheoretical items of observation, simply do not exist. A scientific theory is an organ we develop outside our skin, while an organ is a theory we develop inside our skin. (Popper, 1968)

This point is discussed at length by Deese (1972), who argues that, despite the essential reliance (like all science) on observation, empirical information (data) plays a more modest role than is normally supposed. The function of empirical observation is *not* to find out what causes what or how things work in some ultimate sense but simply to provide justification for some particular way of looking at the world. In other words, observation justifies (or not) a theory that we (or someone else) already hold and it is theories which determine what kinds of data are collected.

The interdependence between theory and data is shown in Deese's belief that: (i) theory in the absence of data is *not* science; and (ii) data alone do not make a science. So both theory and data are necessary for science. But 'data' are not 'facts' in the ordinary sense—they are part of the information needed to establish psychological facts, which depend on the interpretation of data in the light of a theory. 'Data' in Deese's sense correspond to the 'unbiased' observation of the classic, inductive, view of science; 'facts' in Deese's sense correspond to Popper's alternative view. So for Deese, a *Fact* equals *Data* plus *Theory*. When we talk about 'evidence' we normally mean measurement, numbers, recordings etc, which are interpretable in terms of a particular theory, *not* 'pure observations'. (This relates to the issue of objectivity which we shall discuss below.)

THE SUBJECT-MATTER OF PSYCHOLOGY—WHAT IS IT ABOUT?

As we saw in Chapter 1, definitions of psychology have changed during the past hundred years or so. However, even if there were a single definition that all or most psychologists could agree about, the fact would remain that different schools of thought define the subject-matter rather differently. In particular, each school rests upon a different image of what human beings are like, which in turn determines *what* is important to study as well as *how* to study it. Consequently, not only do different schools represent different facets of the same discipline but they seem to comprise self-contained disciplines. In the words of Kuhn (1962), this state of affairs amounts to the lack of a *paradigm*. According to Kuhn, a philosopher of science, the role of theory is absolutely central to the definition and state of a science and a field of study can only be properly considered a science if a majority of its workers subscribe to a common global theory or perspective, that is, a paradigm. Specifically, a paradigm provides answers to the following questions:

(i)   What are the fundamental entities which constitute the subject-matter?
(ii) How do these (fundamental entities) interact with one another and with the human senses?
(iii) What questions may be legitimately asked about such entities and what techniques used in seeking solutions to them?

In the case of biologists, it is Darwin's Theory of Evolution which unites them and helps to give them an identify which distinguishes them from say, physicists, whose unifying theory is Einstein's relativity theory. This shared set of assumptions, methods and 'language' is clearly lacking in psychology.

Kuhn identifies three historical stages in the development of a science (Table 2.2). According to Kuhn, science is *not* the steady, cumulative

Table 2.2 Kuhn's three stages in the development of a science		
Pre-science	No paradigm has been developed and there are several schools of thought.	
Normal science	A paradigm has emerged and this dictates the kind of research carried out; the results are interpreted so as to be consistent with it. The details of the theory are filled in and workers explore how far the theory can go; disagreements may arise but these can be resolved within the limits allowed by the paradigm.	
Revolution	A point is reached, in almost all established sciences, where the conflicting evidence becomes so overwhelming that the old paradigm has to be abandoned, and a new one takes its place (*paradigm-shift*); for example, Copernican physics was replaced by Newtonian, which itself was displaced by Einstein's theory. When this paradigm-shift occurs, there is a return to normal science.	

acquisition of knowledge that used to be the picture painted, but an endless succession of long peaceful periods (normal science) and scientific revolutions.

In terms of Kuhn's three stages of scientific development, psychology is still a pre-science. However, Palermo (1971) believes that psychology has already gone through several paradigm shifts. The original paradigm was *Structuralism*, represented most clearly in Wundt's introspectionism, with its emphasis on identifying the elements of the conscious thoughts and feelings of normal human adults. This was replaced by *Behaviourism*, with its emphasis on the objective observation of the behaviour of adults, children and animals. More recently, the rise of

Cognitive Psychology has once again put 'mind' back on the psychological map; while recognizing that cognitive processes can only be inferred from observable behaviour, it is understood that they can none the less be studied using experimental techniques.

Finally, Valentine (1982) claims that behaviourism comes as close to a paradigm as anything could. It provides:

(a) A clear definition of the subject-matter, namely behaviour as opposed to mental/cognitive processes or experience.
(b) Fundamental assumptions in the shape of the central role of learning (in particular, conditioning) and the analysis of behaviour in stimulus–response terms, the emphasis on the *functional analysis* of behaviour, allowing prediction and control (as opposed to explanation or understanding).
(c) A methodology, with the controlled experiment at its core.

However, a number of points need to be made about Valentine's position. In terms of the distinction made earlier between philosophical and methodological behaviourism, the strongest claim that could be made is that what unites psychologists is *methodological behaviourism*. However:

(i) clearly not all psychologists are methodological behaviourists, eg psychoanalytic and humanistic psychologists;
(ii) methodological behaviourism, as already explained, refers to a *way of conducting research* and is *not* a theory about the subject-matter of psychology!

It seems difficult not to agree with Kuhn that psychology is still in a pre-scientific stage of its development.

There is also a rather ironic twist to Valentine's claim about behaviourism being a paradigm, and that is that the most famous and influential behaviourist, Skinner, is an 'enemy' of theories in psychology! He maintains (Skinner, 1950) that psychology should aim to predict and control behaviour, not to explain it by use of theory. Theories, he claims, whether they deal with mental processes, physiological processes, or anything else, are not only unnecessary but can create new problems of explanation, which can then become 'covered up' and may generate wasteful research. Instead he advocates a much more direct approach, which stresses the pursuit of functional laws based directly on empirical research.

Skinner's empirical approach rests on the assumption that 'facts' can exist without theory ('pure' facts) and that observation can be non-selective or 'unprejudiced'. But we saw earlier that this is a mistaken view. Also, it seems that prediction of behaviour pre-supposes some theory as to what 'underlies' the behaviour but this is precisely what Skinner's *atheoretical* approach denies.

According to Kline:

> ... Now in psychology most of the work is of the detailed kind, as if there were an accepted paradigm. Yet ... this is by no means the case. In fact, there are various models of psychology, all of which involve different paradigms. Furthermore ... it is the uncritical acceptance of what are manifestly absurd paradigms and the refusal to examine them or consider a paradigm that is adequate for the nature of man that is at the root of the failure of experimental psychology. (Kline, 1988)

WHAT MAKES A GOOD THEORY?

Popper believes that:

> Theories are nets cast to catch what we call 'the world', to rationalize, to explain and to master it. (Popper, 1959)

Valentine (1982) believes that theories are both logically and psychologically necessary. But they also serve a very important practical (*heuristic*) function, that is, they guide research; as Allport (1955) puts it, 'theory is the stage upon which experiments are conducted' and it allows us to select from an infinite number of possible experiments.

Given the crucial role of theory in scientific activity, we now want to ask how we decide whether a particular theory is 'good' or not. Thomas (1985) lists nine criteria for evaluating a theory. Taken as a whole, these are not limited to *scientific* criteria, that is, a 'good' theory is not simply one that is 'scientific' and there are other important dimensions of a theory that are taken into account.

1) Perhaps the most important of the scientific criteria is to do with *falsifiability* or *refutability*. The logical positivists advanced the principle of *verification*, which maintains that for a statement to be factually 'true', it must be possible to know how to demonstrate its truth, that is, what observations would lead us, under certain conditions, to accept the statement as being true or reject it as being false. So they believed that science should only concern itself with that which can be completely 'nailed down' or tested—anything else is a pseudo-problem or pseudo-statement (and included in this latter category was Freud's psychoanalytic theory) (see Chapter 29).

However, Popper (1959) argued that the principle of verification was invalid as a way of distinguishing between science and non-science. He maintained that it was too easy to obtain evidence to support a theory; this is precisely the appeal of Freudian theory, according to Popper, because it can explain anything! Since, as we have already seen, observational statements and statements of experimental results are always *interpretations* of the data in the light of theories, it is deceptively easy to verify a theory. A more stringent and meaningful requirement, according to Popper, is to attempt to *falsify* the theory. But whereas for the logical positivists a non-scientific statement was a meaningless statement, Popper never dismissed non-scientific theory as having no value (as the logical positivists had misinterpreted him as saying). On the contrary, he thought that non-scientific observations might be of considerable importance and he realized that science in the past had emerged from metaphysical or mythical-religious conceptions of the world.

According to Kline (1988), many working scientists follow Popper's scientific logic and accept the view that science is concerned with the refutation of hypotheses, that:

> ...All scientific knowledge is thus provisional. At any point it may be refuted. (Kline, 1988)

In psychology, a large number of experiments are conducted on this principle—but the *practice* may be different from the principle:

> ...an important distinction is drawn by philosophers of science. If a theory yields new and surprising hypotheses, especially when contra-

intuitive, then confirmation is considered good support for theory. This is confirmation of bold conjectures. On the other hand, cautious conjectures that follow easily from the theory are only interesting if falsified ... in psychology this approach has been grossly abused. Psychologists rarely go in for bold conjectures. Rather they use cautious conjectures and regard the theory as confirmed if they are supported. This is particularly true of the users of cognitive models ... (Kline, 1988)

2)   A second major criterion is that a good theory should accurately reflect the reality it is trying to explain—this is to do with its *truth value*. The danger with this is that, if used alone or as the major criterion, it forces us to choose between competing theories; for if, for instance, Freudian theory is 'correct' or 'true', then how can Skinner's also be correct or true? Perhaps the solution to this dilemma is to say that these theories are sufficiently different for us to regard both as being 'partially true', they each 'tell the truth' but only about part of the total 'jigsaw' (see Table 1.1.) Alternatively, we might say that a statement (about some aspect of behaviour or experience) is only true (if at all) *relative* to a particular theoretical perspective—'truth' does not exist independently, in some absolute way. In relation to what we said in Chapter 1 about informal psychology, a further requirement of a good theory connected to its truth value is that it should be *reflexive*. This means that any theory of human behaviour must be able to explain how the theory itself came about, because formulating theories is part of the human behaviour the theory is attempting to explain in the first place. Everything that goes under the name of 'scientific activity' is part of the totality of human activity, so psychologists are in the unique position of having to account not only for the behaviour of those they are studying but at the same time having to account for their *own* behaviour in so doing! The psychologist as scientist is engaging in the very same (or at least very similar) activity as the objects of study are engaged in—they are part of their own subject-matter! As Heather (1976) puts it, the psychologist is making observations about observers, experimenting with experimenters and theorizing about theorizers.

This conundrum was solved very neatly by Kelly in his *Personal Construct Theory*, in which he proposes the model of 'man the scientist' (see Chapter 29). Heather (1976) believes that the acid test of any psychological theory is whether or not it is capable of explaining its own creation and no behaviourist theory, he maintains, can pass the test! (Much of Chapter 17 is concerned with how we can all be considered psychologists.)

3)   A good theory should be stated in such a way that it can be clearly understood by anyone who is reasonably competent in English, maths and logical reasoning. Many students complain that psychology textbooks are too wordy and use unnecessarily complex language, and many psychologists criticize certain theories (eg those of Piaget and Freud) for being too vague or imprecise or complex.

4)   A good theory should be able to explain not only past events but also accurately *predict future events*. In addition, it should enable us to make accurate predictions about the behaviour of a particular individual rather than dealing with general statements about groups of people. This relates to the distinction between *idiographic* and *nomothetic* approaches. Idiographic (from the Greek *idio* meaning 'own', 'personal'

or 'private') refers to the study of individuals, while 'nomothetic' ('law-giving' or law-like) refers to the study of groups.

The case study, clearly, is the idiographic method par excellence; Freud used it exclusively (although this did not prevent him formulating a theory meant to apply to *all*). But the case study method makes the use of statistical analysis impossible and mainstream experimental psychology is rooted in the nomothetic approach of natural science, which is concerned with trying to discover general laws. The idiographic approach is concerned with people as unique individuals, as 'singular events' rather than instances of universal laws and, as such, it does not enable generalization beyond the single case, although it may suggest hypotheses that can be tested with other subjects. The nomothetic approach, as it involves several subjects, does enable us to make generalizations about people; it also requires verification through experimental replication and statistical analysis of the results. Perhaps the most crucial difference is that the nomothetic approach enables us to *predict* with some accuracy future *group* results but it *cannot* help predict the behaviour of an *individual*—the uniqueness of each response is to a large degree 'swallowed up' in the group score. By contrast, the idiographic approach deals with events which never recur in the same form—they can neither be replicated nor predicted!

Allport (1961) believes that psychology should be concerned with the study of the *individual*, not the group, with uniqueness and not commonalities. He used a biographical-type case study which some critics would say is more suitable for history and literature than science. To the extent that scientific psychology must be (predominantly) nomothetic, Allport would conclude that psychology cannot (or should not) be a science (see Chapter 29).

5)   A good theory should be *internally consistent*, that is, the different parts of the theory should all fit together to form a coherent structure; there should not be any contradictions between one part of the theory and another, and the terms and concepts used should be logically connected.

6)   A good theory should also be *economical*, in the sense that it is based on as few unproven assumptions as possible. Also, the mechanisms it suggests to explain the phenomena in question should be as simple as possible. These requirements are sometimes summed up in '*the law of parsimony*' or 'Occam's razor', that is, if we have to choose between two theories which are equally 'good' in all other respects, we should choose the simpler, more economical, theory.

7)   A good theory generates a great deal of new research and stimulates general interest and discussion. This is known as the '*fertility criterion*' and can take several forms, eg direct replication studies, testing certain assumptions or principles not previously tested, verification studies (to test whether some theoretical assumption is born out in real life), 'population applicability' (for example, cross-cultural research), and 'extended theorizing' (developing and modifying the original theory, for example, the Neo-Freudians, such as Jung, Adler and Erikson, and Neo-Behaviourists, such as the Social Learning Theorists).

8)   A good theory is one we find self-satisfying; this has to do with its intuitive or even aesthetic appeal, which can in no way be measured. It has to do with a feeling that the theory has captured the essence of what

it is trying to explain, it 'feels right'. Clearly this is the least scientific of all the nine criteria.

9) A good theory should offer practical guidance in solving every-day problems (eg child-rearing, crime, mental illness). According to Garnham:

> '... Scientific explanations differ from other types of explanation in the potential they provide for prediction and control. This potential is reflected in the way science has changed our lives ... (Garnham, 1991)

How appropriate are prediction and control as aims of *psychological* theories?

In 1969, the American Psychological Association took at its annual conference the theme of 'Psychology and the Problems of Society'. George Miller, who was then president, took as the title of his address 'Psychology as a Means of Promoting Human Welfare'. In it, he made the distinction between psychology as a natural science and as a means of changing our image of ourselves.

Psychology as a natural science aims, theoretically, at providing the 'true' view of man's psychological nature and, practically, at applying the theoretical principles discovered to provide behavioural technologies, that is, ways of manipulating our circumstances and behaviour to make them fit our desires and goals. (Examples can be found in behaviour therapy and modification and intelligence testing.) In this context, psychologists become 'the experts', the professionals, who present their findings to the rest (the public at large) and apply these findings in the form of behavioural control. But Miller is unhappy with the idea of psychologists as experts; he believes that of the three aims of psychology as a science, understanding and prediction are more appropriate than control, with understanding being the primary goal. Included in this aim is *self-understanding* (see Chapter 3).

In its other role, often implicit and unconscious, psychology seems to work to change our beliefs about what we are like as human beings. Rather than discovering means to ends, it may have the effect of influencing the very nature of those ends themselves, helping to create a:

> ... new and different public conception of what is humanly possible and what is humanly desirable. (Miller, 1969)

This suggests a tenth criterion of a theory to add to the nine already discussed: a good theory is one which has had a distinct impact upon our image of ourselves, what we think we are like and are capable of, and—in this indirect way—a good theory is one which has an impact upon the way we behave. Indeed, Miller cites Freud's theory in exactly this context and sums up by saying:

> ... the impact of Freud's thought has been due far less to the instrumentalities he provided than the changed conception of ourselves that he implied. (Miller, 1969)

Freud could be seen as having changed the nature of the problems human beings face and it is in this way, rather than through providing practical solutions to those problems we already have, that psychology in general, and theories in particular, might exert their most powerful and significant influence.

THE METHODOLOGY OF PSYCHOLOGY

In this section, I shall focus on the *experiment*, as this is usually taken to be the most scientific of all methods, the 'method of choice'. This is for three main reasons: (i) it is *replicable*; (ii) it allows us to make statements about *cause* and *effect*; and (iii) it permits a considerable degree of *control* which helps to make it the most *objective* method.

How applicable is the experimental method to the study of people?

REPLICABILITY (REPEATABILITY)

A fundamental requirement of all scientific research is that workers in the field should be able to check each others' findings; the purpose of publishing a detailed report of a piece of research is precisely so that others can see for themselves exactly what was done. This is not because of a lack of trust, but because we cannot *generalize* from the results of a single experiment; this may be due to the fact that the sample used in a particular study was unusual or atypical in some way and hence was *unrepresentative*. (This often happens in A-level experiments because of the difficulty of finding a wide range of subjects.) As most scientific theories are intended to apply to *all* cases of a similar kind (eg all situations in which two chemicals are combined or where human subjects have to recall a list of words in any order), we must try to ensure that the results reflect the theory rather than the particular sample of subjects used. The more often an experiment is repeated (which necessarily entails different samples being used each time), with the same results obtained, the more confident one can be that the theory being tested is valid.

> Whatever the *logical* aspects of scientific method may be (deriving hypotheses from theories, the importance of refutability etc.), it is a very *social* business. Yet this exposure of scientific activities to national and international comment and criticism is what distinguishes it from the 'folklore' of informal theories. This is achieved in several ways. The procedures have to be qualified and quantified for the benefits of others, so that they may be replicated by others.
>
> In this way the procedures, instruments and measures become standardized so that scientists anywhere in the world can check the veracity of observations and findings reported. This also implies, then, the use of universally agreed conventions about the reporting of these observations and findings. (Richardson, 1991)

So science does not take place in a social vacuum but is a human activity which is part of an international community. To the extent that there are agreed conventions and criteria as to what counts as 'good' or acceptable science, science cannot be regarded as a totally objective means of discovering the 'truth'—it is a human activity like any other. And yet it is those very conventions and socially agreed criteria which make scientific knowledge so much *more* objective and reliable than 'common sense' or informal knowledge ('folklore').

Perhaps a more fundamental reason for repeating a study is that no one test of a theory can ever completely *prove* it. The concept of proof in science (as opposed to, say, maths) is very complex and to ask 'Is theory X true?' or 'Has theory Y been proved?' is really to ask the wrong kinds of questions. More usefully, we should ask 'How much, or what kind of, evidence is there to support the theory?' In practice, what often happens is that part of a theory finds fairly consistent support while another part does not. (Remember, only *parts* of a theory are tested at one time, not the whole theory.) The important point here is that there is no such thing as absolute proof in psychology or any other science; there can only be a series of tests of a particular hypothesis (sometimes with variations), an accumulated series of results which, on balance, tend to support (or otherwise) the theory from which the hypothesis has been derived.

Use of Statistics

Once we have collected our data it has to be interpreted: what do our facts and figures mean, what do they tell us, how do they relate to our hypothesis? Usually, this interpretation involves the use of statistical procedures which both *describe* the data, thus making it easier to understand, and, through the use of tests of significance, tell us the *probability* of our results having occurred by chance alone. It is important to note here that probability is the best we can hope for—there is no certainty in science; in any particular study, the most we can conclude is that the hypothesis has been supported *on this occasion*. The more times that different researchers produce evidence to support the hypothesis, the more 'faith' we can put in it; belief in the validity of a theory is very much a matter of faith, but it is faith based on 'public' evidence.

Returning to our original theme of replicability, another fundamental reason for repeating experiments is to do with the continued influence of induction, the basis of which is reasoning from the *particular* to the *general*, from particular observations to general conclusions. (This influence remains, despite the criticisms of the inductive method which we discussed earlier. The major alternative model of the scientific process is the *hypothetico-deductive* method which, as the name implies, refers to the testing of theories by deducing specific hypotheses and collecting evidence for these. However, these need not be seen as mutually exclusive but as representing different stages of the scientific process, both necessary and neither sufficient without the other; Coolican, 1990.) However many observations of the 'same' phenomenon are made, each observation (which can include an experiment to test a hypothesis) is only a *specific* observation and there can be no logical certainty that the observation will be made again, even under 'identical' conditions. A classic philosophical example is that although the sun has always risen in the past, there is no certainty that it will rise tomorrow! (although there's a very good chance that it will). Therefore we need as many demonstrations of a particular hypothesis as possible, as there is no logical guarantee that the same results will be obtained next time.

But in what sense is a replication a test of the same hypothesis? Clearly, there is a sense in which any experiment can only be carried out *once* (just as a teacher can only give the 'same' lesson once or a cook make the 'same' meal once): it is a unique event. What is being repeated is a test of the *essential characteristics* of the experiment, but just what these are can be a matter of interpretation. This can be seen by asking the following three questions:

(i) How typical of people in general are the human *subjects* used by psychologists?

(ii) How typical of real-life situations are the *situations* in which psychologists study people?

(iii) How typical of human behaviour is the behaviour of *non-human subjects* used by psychologists?

1)   We said earlier that one reason for replication is that we cannot generalize from the results of a single experiment, often because the subject sample is unrepresentative. It is certainly much more difficult to generalize about people than it is about, say, chemicals; in other words, particular human subjects are much *less representative* of people in general than a particular sample of a certain chemical is of that chemical. This raises the question of *biased* or unrepresentative sampling.

   George Miller (1962) estimated that 90 per cent of American experiments have used college students (who are accessible and 'cheap') and yet the results still tend to be generalized to the American population as a whole, and often beyond that to Britain, Western Europe, etc. But there is no reason to believe that American college students are typical of any other group in terms of gender, intelligence, age, personality, social class background or any other *subject variables* which can influence how subjects will perform in any experimental situation. What's more, these student subjects are often Psychology students who are *required* to participate in research as a course requirement!

2)   Most experiments are conducted in laboratories—strange and contrived environments in which people are asked to perform unusual or even bizarre tasks. How can we be sure that the way people behave in the laboratory is an accurate indication of how they behave outside, in 'real life'? Heather (1976) believes that we cannot. In his view:

> Psychologists have attempted to squeeze the study of human life into a laboratory situation where it becomes unrecognizably different from its naturally occurring form. (Heather, 1976)

The artificiality of the lab, together with the 'unnatural' things that the subjects may be asked to do, jointly produce a distortion of behaviour. The very term 'subject' implies that the participant is being treated as something less than a person, a dehumanized and depersonalized 'object' that fits the mechanistic view of man which is at the root of empirical (methodological) behaviourism. The most recent set of guidelines for conducting research with human beings, published by the British Psychological Society, is entitled *Ethical Principles for Conducting Research with Human Participants* (1990). These are discussed in Chapter 3. However, 'subject' is the term which will be used for the most part throughout this book, as that is how most psychologists still refer to those they study. Experiments *can* be conducted in natural settings, in which case they are called *field experiments*. An experiment is defined not by where it is conducted but by *how* it is conducted—it is the experimenter's manipulation of the independent variable, plus the control of all the other relevant variables, that makes an investigation experimental. But for practical reasons, experiments are usually carried out in a laboratory setting.

3)   The question of *animal experiments* is important because of the extent to which they are used in many areas of psychology. Clearly, although a great deal of animal research is conducted for its own sake,

much is also undertaken to help us understand human behaviour. How can it do this?

(a) There is an underlying evolutionary continuity between humans and other species which gives rise to the assumption that differences between humans and other species are merely *quantitative* (as opposed to qualitative), ie other species may display more simple behaviour and have more primitive nervous systems than humans but they are not of a different order from humans. So, it is believed, it is valuable to study these more simple cases in order to understand the more complex ones.

(b) Animals are smaller and therefore easier to study in the laboratory. They also have much shorter life-spans and periods of gestation and maturation, so it is much easier to study their development—many generations can be studied in a relatively short time.

(c) Animal studies can provide useful hypotheses for subsequent testing on human subjects and, equally important, animals can be used to test cause-and-effect relationships where the existing human evidence is only correlational (eg the relationship between smoking and lung cancer).

(d) It is legally permitted to use much more rigorous experimental controls with animals than with humans, for example, inter-breeding (to study genetic influences), subjecting young animals to all kinds of deprivation (sensory, perceptual, maternal, social, etc), surgically, and in other ways, eg interfering with their brains.

The ethical status of these experiments is often very dubious (see Chapter 3). However, we can never be *certain* that the mechanisms involved in the behaviour of one species are the same as those involved in others; ultimately, we have to test the particular species whose behaviour we are trying to explain and this is true even when the species being compared are very closely related on the evolutionary scale. Humans are *not* chimpanzees, rats or pigeons, and even if human behaviour *appears* to be very similar to that of some simple species, we cannot be sure that it 'works' in exactly the same way (see Chapter 15). When we try to explain human behaviour in terms of how rats perform in Skinner boxes, for example, we are committing the sin of *ratomorphism* (Koestler, 1970a). The opposite, but equally sinful, error is that of *anthropomorphism*, that is, attributing human-like qualities or motives to non-human organisms or objects.

CAUSE AND EFFECT

This represents another aspect of induction, as well as another 'symptom' of the positivistic/mechanistic nature of academic psychology. According to Heather (1976), to say that psychology is mechanistic in nature implies a view of people as some complex piece of machinery, inert and passive, propelled into motion only by the action of some force (either external or internal) upon them; their behaviour is fully explicable, in principle, in terms of 'causes' over which they have no control.

The notion of cause is a complex one and there are different opinions regarding exactly what constitute the logical grounds for inferring a cause-and-effect relationship for some empirical observation. But it is generally agreed that a 'cause' cannot be *directly* observed; strictly speaking, all that can be observed are two events appearing close together in space and/or time (the principle of *contiguity*). 'Cause', and 'effect' are *constructs*.

One view is that the cause must be both a *necessary* and *sufficient* condition for the appearance of the effect and (usually) the cause must *precede* the effect. To take the biological example of the knee-jerk reflex, the reflex will *only* occur when the knee is struck in a particular spot (corresponding to the tap on the knee as a *necessary* condition) and it occurs *every time* the knee is tapped (corresponding to the tap on the knee as a *sufficient* condition). The tap on the knee, of course, also precedes the leg shooting up in the air.

To put it more formally:

(i)   A (the tap on the knee) *must* occur for B (the reflex) to occur and, in the absence of A, B never happens;

(ii) B always occurs when A occurs—A never happens without B following.

This relationship must, of course, be demonstrated on several occasions, and the more often this happens, the more confident we can be that a cause-and-effect relationship does exist.

According to Watson's early brand of behaviourism, the cause (or antecedent events) was presumed to be limited to events in the outside world, the 'stimuli', which elicited responses (effect) from the passive organism (see Chapter 7). Although this philosophical behaviourism has now largely been replaced by methodological behaviourism, the basic mechanistic notion of cause still tends to dominate. Sometimes the Independent Variable (IV) is thought of as a cause and the Dependent Variable (DV) as the effect. But the IV and DV are much more general than cause and effect: the IV is what the experimenter manipulates (systematically varies), for example, the amount of sleep subjects have, and the DV is some aspect of the subject's behaviour (which varies as a function of differences in the IV), for example, the ability to recall a poem.

Using the necessary and sufficient condition criteria, we could not say (assuming that subjects with no sleep do significantly worse than the others) that lack of sleep is a *necessary* condition of poor recall (since other factors could also account for the poor recall, eg alcohol), but it could be a *sufficient* condition (the lack of sleep alone produced poor recall). The lack of sleep also preceded the poor recall. However, as alcohol could produce similar results as well, lack of sleep can hardly be thought of as a sufficient condition of poor recall in the way that a tap on the knee is a sufficient condition of the knee-jerk reflex. Most human behaviour has multiple causes.

Because of the complexity of the notion of cause, as well as the complexity of most behaviour, psychologists tend to avoid the terms cause and effect altogether. More commonly they talk about, 'variable X systematically varying as variable Y is varied' or, 'changes in variable X producing changes in variable Y' or, 'the conditions under which such-and-such behaviour occurs'.

Deese (1972) makes the important point that, ultimately, what is taken as a cause-and-effect is an inference arising *not* from direct observation but from the theory which states what is necessary and sufficient for the production of certain events—it is the theory which states what is supposed to influence what.

An alternative view altogether is put forward by Heather (1976), namely, that human beings are the causes of their own behaviour. This view regards people as *agents*, in sharp contrast to the mechanistic view described at the beginning of this section (and see Chapter 3). This is a characteristic of *humanistic* theories, such as those of Maslow and Rogers (see Chapter 28).

Another alternative view is the *Psychology of Action*, according to which:

> ... Psychology cannot be a science based on the discovery of causes and their effects, nor can its best work have any special claim to universality. The task of psychology, as a science, must then, be the attempt to find out the systems of tacit rules and conventions that are followed in the creation of everyday life ... (Harré et al, 1985)

CONTROL AND OBJECTIVITY

The purpose of control is to enable the experimenter to isolate the one key variable which has been selected (the IV), in order to observe its effect on some other variable (the DV); control is intended to allow us to conclude that it is the IV, and nothing else, which is influencing the DV.

But how do we know when we have controlled *all* the relevant variables? It is fairly easy to control the more obvious ones (eg *situational* variables, such as room temperature, noise levels and instructions, and *subject* variables, such as gender, age and intelligence), but for every variable that is controlled there is probably at least one which is not! It is the purpose of different kinds of *experimental design* to control subject variables. But it is never possible to control these completely; it is the *variability* of human beings that makes them so much more difficult to study scientifically than, say, chemicals. The important point here is that what is controlled and what is not is based on the judgement and intuition of the experimenter—what he/she thinks is important (and possible) to control. This is hardly the kind of degree of objectivity normally associated with the scientific experiment!

Clearly, control and objectivity are matters of *degree* only and it is unreasonable and unrealistic to expect total objectivity in any science, even physics. Popper (1972) has pointed out that it is unrealistic— because impossible—to regard any observation as being totally objective, value-free or uninfluenced by the experimenter's interests, preferences or expectations.

In addition to the impossibility of complete control, there is a problem involved in assuming that the IV (or 'stimulus' or 'input') is identical for *all* subjects and that the DV (or 'response' or 'output') is dependent on what the former is, in some objectively definable sense. Many psychologists are very critical of this assumption (eg Joynson, 1974; Heather, 1976). The notion of a stimulus (as defined by behaviourists, anyway) implies that it can be defined independently of the particular subject presented with it and that it has a standard effect on all subjects; but it seems, in practice, very difficult to attempt to give a completely objective definition.

One such attempt was made by Broadbent (1961), who defined a stimulus in terms of the physical stimulation impinging on the subject's sense organs; but this completely ignores the distinction between sensation—what 'the eye' sees—and perception—what 'the seer' sees (see Chapter 9). Perception involves an *interpretation* of the sense-data provided by the stimulus; the subject's past experience, motivational state, expectations and so on help to determine the *meaning* of the stimulus for the subject and, in turn, the meaning helps determine the subject's response. There is a sense in which, in a purely objective way, the stimulus does not exist: what the stimulus really is, is how it is interpreted by the subject and this will differ from subject to subject.

If the stimulus has meaning for the subject, then it follows that the response is not a passive reaction produced by the stimulus but is itself meaningful; and it acquires its meaning through what the subject is trying to do. Heather (1976) argues that a 'science of persons' would stress that human action is always directed to the *future*, rather than being reactions to past events (ie the stimulus). Broadbent gives an objective definition of a response as, 'events at those parts of the body which act on the outer world' or, 'muscular contractions'. But 'muscular contractions' or movements have no meaning in themselves—they only acquire their meaning when they form part of a series of movements intended to achieve some goal (in which case we call them *actions*). It is no easy matter trying to describe what we do except in terms of what we are trying to achieve by doing it, whether it is scratching your back, writing an essay or eating. The further we go in trying to break these actions down into their component parts (ie the muscle movements involved), the further removed we become from the categories we normally use to think about human behaviour. And the further we go, the less meaningful the descriptions become, for example we could analyse 'eating' by describing the individual action of picking up the fork, moving it down towards the plate, piercing a piece of food, etc., but could we analyse each of these further and still be describing actions (as opposed to movements)? What Broadbent is advocating is a form of *Reductionism*, an attempt to 'reduce' actions to muscle movements in the name of objectivity.

Another famous advocate of objectivity, but this time from the perspective of personality theory, is Cattell, who argues that:

> ... The scientific study of personality seeks to understand personality as one would the mechanism of a watch, the chemistry of the life processes in a mammal or the spectrum of a remote star. That is to say it aims at objective insights; at the capacity to predict and control what will happen next; and at the establishment of scientific laws of a perfectly general nature. (Cattell, 1981; quoted in Kline, 1988)

According to Kline, Cattell's analogy is not a good one because:

(a) While there is no disagreement as to what a watch is or isn't, this cannot be said of personality. Personality is a *hypothetical construct* and has no independent existence beyond the mind which conceived it:

> ... Thus, whatever studying objectively the processes of personality may mean, it certainly is quite unlike studying the finite mechanisms of a watch ... (Kline, 1988)

(b) A mammal is a definite organism, its life processes are finite, chemical and electrical events. Of course, objective study of these is perfectly possible and infinitely superior to endless speculation about say, the nature of blood, but:

> . . . There can be no descent into a physiological universe of discourse. Of course, it is possible to study the human physiology by the scientific method, but this is not studying personality or psychology. Even if physiology is studied alongside behaviour it adds nothing to our understanding of psychology. Suppose that cortical cells A and B always fired when I saw red and at no other time.
> What does this tell us about my experience of red? Indeed it is banal because it goes without saying that there must be neural, biochemical or electrical changes underlying experience, for there can be no others. (Kline, 1988)

Kline is advocating a *rejection* of Reductionism; we shall return to this issue later.

THE PSYCHOLOGY EXPERIMENT AS A SOCIAL SITUATION

Another way of exploring the issue of objectivity is to look more closely at what is involved in an experiment where a human experimenter tests a human subject. Clearly, the situation is not equivalent to that in which a human experimenter investigates some part of the physical world—people are *not* inanimate objects but animate, conscious, thinking beings.

A more accurate way of thinking about the psychological experiment is as a *social situation*, which entails mutual expectations by participants. How are the expectations of the subject and the experimenter related?

The Subject's Expectations

On the subject's side are what Orne (1962) has called the *demand characteristics* of experiments. Whereas in the mechanistic model the emphasis is usually on what is *done to* the (passive) subject, Orne is interested in what the human subject *does* (which implies *participant* as a more appropriate term). Subjects' performance in an experiment could almost be conceptualized as *problem-solving behaviour* since, at some level, they see it as their task to ascertain the true purpose of the experiment and to respond in a manner which will support the hypothesis being tested. In this context, the totality of *cues* which convey an experimental hypothesis to the subject become significant determinants of the subject's behaviour and it is the sum total of those cues that Orne labels the '*demand characteristics of the experimental situation*'.

So the subject is on a constant 'look-out' for cues about how to behave—what do these cues include? As well as the actual communication during the experiment itself (both explicitly in the form of instructions and implicitly in the form of non-verbal communication), cues include whatever the subject might already have heard about the experiment (eg from other subjects), the way the subject is approached initially and asked to volunteer, the person of the experimenter and the setting of the experiment. It is very difficult in practice to find truly naïve subjects who do not believe they have at least some familiarity with psychology, or who cannot infer the purpose of the experiment from the procedure. The central point is that subjects are not passive responders but are actively engaged in trying to work out what is going on and how they should perform.

This tendency to identify the demand characteristics is related to the tendency to play the role of 'a good experimental subject', wanting to please and co-operate with the experimenter and not to 'upset the experiment'. It is mainly in this sense that Orne sees the experiment as a 'social situation'. The demand characteristics of the situation help define the role of 'good experimental subject' and the subject's responses are a function of the role that is created.

The Experimenter's Expectations

On the other hand, the experimenter unconsciously conveys to the subject how the subject should behave: this is referred to as *experimenter bias*. The point is that the experimenter is unaware of the influence he or she may be exerting (often in the form of non-verbal messages) on the subject. This was demonstrated by Rosenthal (1966) who put hundreds of his psychology students in the role of experimenter with rats as subjects. He told half the experimenters that they would be studying a strain of 'maze-bright' rats (bred from intelligent stock) and the other half that they would be studying 'maze-dull' rats. In fact, the rats were all 'average' and were randomly allocated to the two groups, yet the first group of experimenters reported significantly better performance on maze-learning for their rats than the second group.

With human subjects, the experimenter's expectations are likely to be all the more important since, as we have seen, they are looking for all the available cues to help them successfully play their 'role'; and so, unwittingly, the experimenter may be influencing the subject's actual behaviour!

Removing Bias

Can anything be done to prevent these sources of bias?

The answer is, 'Yes', first by making sure that the subjects do not know under what conditions they are being tested. This, in fact, is standard practice but will never elimininate the impact of demand characteristics altogether. Perhaps the clearest example of where this can be effective is in tests of drug-effects, where control subjects are given a sugar pill or other 'placebo' while the experimental subjects receive the real drug (*single-blind technique*).

The second, and better way of reducing experimenter bias is to ensure that the experimenter also does not know which subjects have been given the drug and which the placebo; for example, the experimenter who administers the drug or placebo is not the one who measures the effects (*double-blind technique*).

However, by using these two methods of control, we have not changed the nature of the experimental situation from a social to a non-social one: we have merely altered certain aspects of the situation in which subjects try to make sense of an often bewildering and apparently senseless experience. Perhaps by removing some of the potential sources of bias, the experience is made all the more bewildering and their need to search for demand characteristics is made all the more necessary.

REDUCTIONISM

Earlier we criticized the attempt (by extreme behaviourists) to 'reduce' actions to 'muscular contractions' by pointing out that, whereas actions are meaningful (and purposeful), muscle movements are not. What Broadbent advocates stems from his attempt to make psychology objective, to rid it of all 'mentalistic' language, as 'muscle movements' are publicly observable while 'thoughts' and 'intentions', etc. are private and inaccessible to others. So we can say that philosophical behaviourists are trying to reduce 'the mind' to a series of muscle movements (often they make do with talking about Stimulus–Response or S–R connections). The logical conclusion of this is to explain mental processes and behaviour in terms of physiology (especially neurophysiology), biochemistry, chemistry and ultimately, physics (the primary science). It we want to get to the 'ultimate truth' of something, we must seek more minute units of analysis; even to talk about 'S–R connections' represents a much 'larger' unit of analysis than, for instance, a description of the neurons (brain cells) involved in those connections, with 'muscular contractions' representing an intermediate unit. Similarly, an account of the neurons represents a 'larger' unit of analysis than an account of the atoms and molecules of which they are composed.

According to this view, behaviourism could be regarded as an intermediate or transitional stage in the ultimate rejection of traditional, mentalistic, psychological concepts: that is, psychology (in any form) will ultimately be reduced to (and replaced by) microphysics:

> For a very long time reductionism remained the generally accepted philosophical aim of the natural sciences as well of psychology. It was supposed that the basic goal of science is to reduce complex phenomena. (Luria, 1987)

Luria traces the origins of reductionism to the mid-nineteenth century view in biology that the organism is a complex of organs and the organs are a complex of cells. So, in order to explain the basic laws of the living organism we have to study as carefully as possible the features of separate cells. From its biological origins, reductionism was extended to science in general, as reflected by Rose et al (1984) who define it as:

> ...the name given to a set of general methods and modes of explanation both of the world of physical objects and of human societies. Broadly, reductionists try to explain the properties of complex wholes—molecules, say, or societies—in terms of the units of which those molecules or societies are composed.

For example, the properties of a protein molecule could be uniquely determined or predicted in terms of properties of the electrons or protons of which its atoms are composed. Similarly:

> ...The properties of human society are no more than the sums of the individual behaviours or tendencies of the individual humans who compose it. For example, societies are 'aggressive' because the individuals who compose them are 'aggressive' (Rose et al, 1984)

As related specifically to psychology, one definition of reductionism is that it refers to:

> ...the idea that psychological explanations can be replaced by explanations in terms of brain functioning or even in terms of physics and chemistry...(Garnham, 1991)

Although, ultimately, the aim (according to reductionism) is to account for *all* phenomena in terms of microphysics, *any* attempt to explain something in terms of its component parts may be thought of as reductionist. Figure 2.2 gives some examples of reductionism drawn from various areas of psychology (with the appropriate chapters in the book indicated alongside the examples).

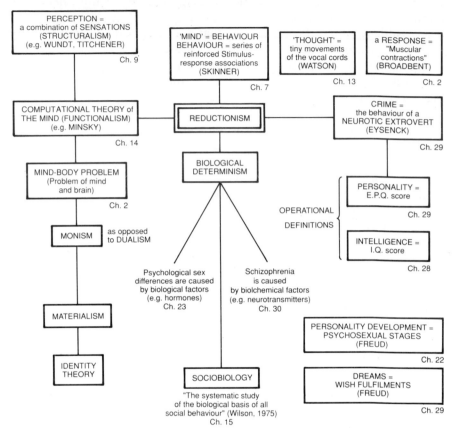

Figure 2.2 Examples of Reductionism relating to various topic-areas within psychology as a whole

But is this reductionist approach acceptable or even meaningful? Can a thorough knowledge of the primary sciences (even if this is attained) ever replace the need for psychological explanations? There are several objections, which have been raised by psychologists and others.

First, Legge (1975) considers the example of signing our name. Although this could (in principle) be explained in terms of nerve activity and muscle movement, the real importance of a signature is its *social* (psychological) meaning. As we saw above, only *actions* are meaningful and the vast majority of our actions derive their meaning from their relevance to our interactions with others.

Secondly, even if we could reduce signing our name in this way, we would only be specifying what nerve activity and muscle movements are involved in a *particular instance* of name-signing, and not every possible instance. The point is that we can sign our name in many different ways, for example, by holding the pen in our mouth, or using a stick in the sand or using chalk on a wall, and each involves a different combination of brain and muscle activity; the 'act' of signing our name is largely *independent* of any particular physiological activity that may be involved. Clearly, even with a complete knowledge of physiology, a psychological explanation is more appropriate and useful, which raises the issue of *levels* of *explanation*.

Rose (1976) argues that the controversy surrounding the reductionist issue stems from a semantic confusion (a confusion over word-meanings), namely, an equation of 'explaining' and 'explaining away'. If we are trying to get rid of psychological explanations altogether, replacing them with neurophysiological ones, then this is the 'unacceptable face' of reductionism. But if an explanation of brain function is used to enhance or complement our psychological explanation, then this is no threat to psychology.

Rose believes that the confusion between 'explaining' and 'explaining away' can be removed by introducing the concept of a *hierarchy of levels of explanation* (Fig. 2.3).

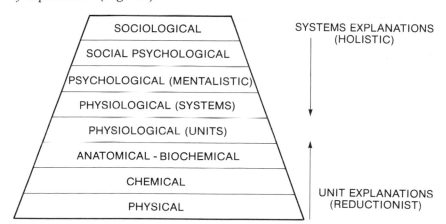

Figure 2.3 Hierarchical levels of explanation. (From Rose, 1976)

These different hierarchical levels correspond to different scientific disciplines; as you move up the hierarchy, the size of the unit of description increases (*holistic*) but there is an inverse relationship between size and complexity, so that as you move up the units also become less complex. By the same token, as you move down the hierarchy, the units become smaller and more complex (*reductionist*). Also, the fundamental explanations in a particular discipline can be found at some lower or more basic level. For example, what physics can tell us about atoms can provide explanations relevant to chemistry (eg how atoms are joined to form molecules), and psychology can be seen as providing 'basic' explanations for sociology (eg how memory and perception work).

Rose's major point is that each level involves a different '*universe of discourse*', that is, a different set of concepts and terminology, a different way of conceptualizing the 'same' phenomena and, because they are different, one cannot be substituted for another. Levels lower down in the hierarchy cannot replace levels higher up because they are doing essentially different jobs; each is valid in its own right and what makes one level of explanation the 'right' one is the *purpose* of the explanation at any particular time, what sort of answer we want and why we want it. For example, as the larger, higher-level explanations are more 'economical' than the smaller, lower-level ones (ie it is easier and faster to talk about 'signing our name' than to describe all the brain and muscle activity involved), the former will generally be more effective for the purposes of communication, either between individuals or within one's own head.

We saw earlier that Kline (1988) also talks about different universes of discourse when rejecting Cattell's analogy between understanding personality and understanding the chemistry of the life processes in a mammal. He goes on to say:

> ... It is true that scientific method has worked well in engineering, biology and astronomy but the human psyche is not an essentially mechanical object. The human brain is susceptible to much study but the mind belongs to a different universe of discourse where methods such as these do not seem to apply ... It is clear that the scientific method is unsuited to psychology because the subject matter of psychology is conceptually different from that of the classical sciences for which the method was developed. This is a fundamental problem of the scientific method in psychology. (Kline, 1988)

To give a specific example from auditory perception to match Kline's earlier example of seeing red:

> ... If we ascertain that a sound applied at the ear of an observer produces a regular pattern of electrical response in the brain, then we can feel certain that some internal connections between the peripheral sensory system (the ear) and the central nervous system (the brain) are present. However, regularity of brain response tells us nothing, unfortunately, about how or even whether the observer actually *perceives* the sound; hence, information about perception based on electrophysiological data is weak. (Even if two different stimuli give rise to two distinctly different patterns of electrical activity in the brain, we would still not know whether the two stimuli were perceived, or whether they were perceived as different.) If, however, we were able to instruct or train the observer to respond behaviourally to a sound, or in one way to one sound and in another way to another sound, our information would be so strong that ... we would possess incontrovertible evidence of perception ... (Bornstein, 1988)

Perception, as a *psychological* experience, cannot be reduced to the *neurophysiological* events which (usually) accompany it.

Finally, Garnham (1991) gives the example of evolutionary biology and biochemistry. Breakthroughs in biochemistry in the 1950s and beyond have uncovered in increasing detail the mechanisms by which offspring inherit their parents' characteristics. We can now see how, in principle, a theory of evolution fits together with a biochemical account of inheritance. But:

> ... a scientific theory of evolution still needs concepts such as gene pool and evolutionary stable strategy, which cannot be defined in biological terms.
>
> Similarly, although a scientific approach to cognition assumes that perceiving and thinking depend on brain functioning, there will always be a need for a level of explanation in which cognitive concepts play a role. Cognitive science will no more be replaced by physiology than the theory of evolution has been replaced by biochemistry'. (Garnham, 1991)

The Reductionist controversy has probably generated more heat over the *mind–body* problem than any other, and to this we now turn.

THE MIND–BODY PROBLEM (OR THE PROBLEM OF MIND AND BRAIN)

This is concerned with the relationship between mind (or consciousness) and neurophysiological processes, in particular, brain activity. Much of the controversy within psychology regarding the place of 'mind' in a scientific psychology, culminating in the rise of behaviourism in America, stems from the *dualism* of the seventeenth-century French philosopher, Déscartes, who distinguished between 'mind' and 'body', the latter being 'reduced' to a machine driven by a hydraulic system of vital liquids running through the nerves. According to Déscartes, the mind (or soul) was located in the brain's pineal gland, and was seen as driving the body through the brain and nerves, but it is qualitatively different from the body, non-physical and non-material. His famous *'cogito ergo sum'* ('I think, therefore I am') implied that what makes human beings different from animals is the possession of a mind or soul, and this is the essence of man. While everything else can, in principle, be doubted, it is impossible for any person to doubt his or her existence as a thinking being. Dualism remained the dominant view of the mind–body issue until Watson's behaviourist manifesto in 1913.

If we accept that mind and body are fundamentally different, the problem remains as to how we are to understand their relationship. The major proposed solutions are summarized in Figure 2.4.

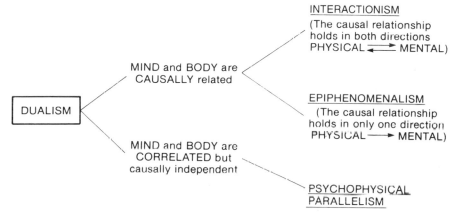

Figure 2.4 *The dualism between mind and body*

INTERACTIONISM

Both common sense and ordinary language seem to attribute both mental and physical events with causal power. For instance, we talk about 'mind over matter' and there seems to be some medical support for this view—as in the case of cancer patients who beat their disease through their determination to get better. Psychosomatic illness is usually defined as caused by stress or other psychological factors, although the physical symptoms are very real, eg stomach ulcers, and the whole concept of voluntary actions and movements depends upon the belief that willing or deciding to move our arm, for example, will result in our arm moving. Similarly, we often attribute changes in our perceptions to 'mind-changing' drugs (eg the hallucinogens) through their effect on brain chemicals, or changes in intelligence or personality to brain damage or surgery.

But despite these examples, it is difficult to understand how something physical and spatial can influence something that is non-physical and non-spatial (and vice versa). Where, for instance, does the interaction occur?

Valentine (1982) believes that in the case of apparent interaction (as in the examples above), we simply choose to focus attention on one aspect of the cause and the other aspect of the effect, and this does not preclude the existence of the other correlated aspect. For example, we may choose to say that some psychological stress has caused a stomach ulcer, but this does not preclude some unmentioned physiological state that is correlated with the stress.

Boden (1972) prefers to think of 'the mind' as guiding, rather than causing, physical movements.

EPIPHENOMENALISM

While granting that mental and physical events are different, epiphenomenalists argue that mental experiences or processes are non-causal by-products of physical processes; only physical processes have causal power. A consequence of this view is that mental processes have no part to play in the explanation of behaviour and so can be disregarded for that purpose; this is a view adopted by Skinner, although he is often taken to reject the concept of mind altogether (as did Watson).

PSYCHOPHYSICAL PARALLELISM

It was the philosopher Leibniz (in 1714) who first argued that mental and physical events occur simultaneously (like two synchronized clocks or orchestras) but do not causally influence each other. In psychology, Wundt was one early advocate of this view, as were the Gestalt psychologists (see Chapter 9) who maintained that there is a one-to-one correspondence between how a stimulus is perceived and how it is represented in the brain, a correspondence they called *isomorphism*. A good deal of physiological psychology also assumes this view.

But clearly, any kind of simple correlation is often missing; for example, depression could be associated with a variety of physical states and, conversely, the same physical state (eg arousal) could be associated with a number of psychological states. (Correlation may also be missing due to a difference in the *levels* at which the two exist—eg the example of name-signing given when discussing Reductionism). If we reject Dualism, the main alternative is Monism, which can take two major forms, as seen in Figure 2.5.

Figure 2.5 Monism

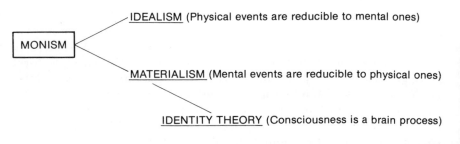

IDEALISM

According to this view, only mental phenomena are real. Berkeley (1710) argued that *'esse'* is *'percipi'* (to be is to be perceived); the universe is occupied only by minds, physical objects being entirely dependent on these and existing solely as ideas in someone's mind.

Most psychologists and philosophers would not accept this view and it also seems to be anti-common-sense. But humanistic psychologists, strongly influenced by *phenomenology*, do stress the fundamental nature of *experience* and the dependence of our knowledge of the external world on how we interpret and define it. It is, of course, a view which is rejected out of hand by philosophical behaviourists.

MATERIALISM (OR PHYSICALISM)

This maintains the opposite of idealism, namely, that only physical phenomena are real, and lies at the heart of the Reductionist approach; Watson favoured this view. But how would it explain, for instance, non-organic psychological disorders (eg neurosis)? Psychiatrists tend to be materialists and assume that, eventually, organic causes will be found for all kinds of disorder (see Chapter 30).

Freud was a materialist who set out to provide a materialist account of human behaviour. His intention was to:

> ... furnish a psychology that shall be a natural science: that is to *represent* psychical processes as quantitatively determinate states of specifiable material particles ... (Freud, 1895; quoted in Flanagan, 1984)

However, while remaining a materialist, he came to the view that no single scientific vocabulary (eg anatomy) could adequately describe—let alone explain—all facets of the material world. He upheld the *thesis of the autonomy of psychological explanation*, which meant he completely rejected his original reductionist project:

> ... psychoanalysis must keep itself free from any hypothesis that is alien to it, whether of an anatomical, chemical or physiological kind and must operate with purely auxiliary ideas. (Freud, 1919)

While materialism and reductionism usually go hand-in-hand, they do not *necessarily* do so (Flanagan, 1984).

IDENTITY THEORY

This is a recently popular form of materialism which claims that consciousness *is* a brain process, in the same way that 'heat is mean kinetic energy' or a 'gene is a section of the DNA molecule'. This form of identity is *contingent* (true as a matter of fact) as opposed to logical (true by definition), the latter being stronger; but contingent identity is stronger than correlation. When we say that consciousness is a brain process, what is implied is that both consciousness and the brain process refer to the same thing (contingent identity), but they do not have the same meaning (as do 'brother' and 'male sibling', for example).

An important difference between Materialism and Identity Theory is that, if mental processes are contingently identical with brain processes (as the latter maintains), then mental processes, as much as brain processes, are capable of causally influencing behaviour.

Joynson believes that Identity Theory represents a:

> . . . purely verbal solution which dissolves into what is effectively dualism, at any attempt to put it into practice. (Joynson, 1971)

Identity Theory would also seem to face many of the problems faced by the signing-one's-name example, which we discussed in relation to Reductionism.

ALTERNATIVES TO DUALISM AND MONISM

1)   More radical solutions have been proposed by those who reject both Dualism and Monism. For example, Ryle (1949) believes that the distinction between mind and body is purely grammatical, whereby matter is usually described using nouns and pronouns, and mind using verbs, adverbs and adjectives. So all language describing states of mind can be shown, on analysis, to be about behaviour and possible behaviour (Ryle's position is known as *logical behaviourism*).

2)   Valentine (1982) believes that the best solution may be the *double-aspect theory*, a sophisticated variant of parallelism, which gives credence to the reality of mental and physical processes but claims that these are merely two aspects of the same fundamental underlying reality. The main philosophical objection to this view is that the 'underlying reality' remains essentially unknowable. In terms of the hierarchical levels of explanation that we discussed above, Rose (1976) believes that the concept of mind resides at a higher hierarchical level than the concept of brain processes.

3)   *Naturalistic Functionalism* was a view put forward by William James, which sees consciousness or *Conscious Mental Life* (CML) as a feature which has emerged via natural selection in creatures with our particular kind of biological organization. Instead of thinking of CML as a *thing*, James (1904) views it as a *function*. Using an analogy with walking and breathing, mental states are functional states/properties of the complex interaction between ourselves and the outside world, a functional outcome of brain–world interaction.

Similarly, Dewey (1922) claimed that:

> Breathing is an affair of the air as truly as of the lungs, digesting an affair of the food as truly as of the tissues of the stomach. Seeing involves light just as certainly as it does the eye and optic nerve . . .'

So CML ('the mind') is an 'emergent property' of the physical brain but is distinct from it, since mental events refer to *interactions between* brains and environment, which cannot be separated.

4)   Figure 2.2 gives as an example of reductionism the Computational Theory of the Mind which represents a brand of functionalism. Essentially, what the CTM claims is that the key to understanding the 'mind' (intelligence) is to understand the logical operations performed by it (ie the function it performs). In computer terms, the *software* is what is crucial: the 'mind' does *not* depend on any particular *physical (hardware)* realization, so that the kind of brain we have is largely irrelevant.

So CMT proposes a solution to the mind–brain controversy in terms of the software/hardware distinction: the mind is to the brain what software is to hardware. The objections to this view (eg Flanagan, 1984; Searle, 1980, 1987) are discussed in detail in Chapter 14.

FREE WILL VERSUS DETERMINISM

Like the mind–body issue, free will versus determinism is one of the most intractable philosophical problems that still 'haunts' psychology. It also seems to capture the basic conflict between the common sense view of ourselves and the view that is offered by scientific psychology.

Our everyday, intuitive, common sense understanding is that people have the ability to choose their own course of action, to determine their lives and, to this extent, have free will. At the same time, this freedom is exercised only within certain limits set by physical, political, sociological and other environmental factors.

The concept of free will is also inextricably linked to the concept of *responsibility*; we normally think of people as being *morally responsible* for what they do since they are the 'cause' of what they do—they are not driven by powerful outside forces. This view is embodied in the law, of course, which allows for exceptional cases, such as 'diminished responsibility' or 'unfit to plead because of insanity' (see Chapter 30).

Yet the positivistic/mechanistic nature of scientific psychology implies a very different view, namely that behaviour is determined by external events or stimuli and that people are passive responders and, to this extent, are not free. Determinism also implies that behaviour occurs in a regular, orderly manner which is totally predictable (at least in principle) and that every human action has a cause.

Several points need to be made here:

1) First, from our discussion above of the inductive nature of science, it should be clear that total predictability is impossible (Popper, 1950). The past does not logically guarantee the future; and if this is true of classical physics, how much more true is it of human behaviour? So if determinism's main requirement is that behaviour should be completely predictable, it does not seem to pose the same 'threat' to the free-will view after all.

2) We have already argued that the free will view regards people as the cause of their own behaviour, so the two views are not opposed on the grounds of whether or not behaviour is *caused*, but rather in relation to the source and nature of the cause. (The opposite of 'caused', strictly speaking, is 'random' and no one would seriously argue that human nature is random; indeed, it would be difficult to reconcile moral responsibility with the idea of randomness.)

3) An important distinction can be made between coercion or compulsion on the one hand and determinism on the other. Free acts are free from coercion or compulsion, but this is consistent with them being determined, a view which James called *soft determinism*. He argued that the question of free action depends on the *type*(s) of cause(s) our behaviour has. In particular, if our actions have as their proximate cause something like *conscious mental life*, we can regard them as free, rational, voluntary, purposive actions.

Freud, as we have seen, was a materialist and not a reductionist, but he was also a determinist, rejecting the possibility of free will. For him the 'coercion' or 'compulsion' comes from within the individual's own unconscious mind; for Skinner, they *are* external.

So '*soft determinism*' represents one attempt to reconcile the free will and determinism arguments. Another is provided by Heather (1976), who points out that we can describe human behaviour in lawful terms and still 'give man his freedom'. How? By thinking of the person *as a rule-following animal*. Much of our social behaviour is highly predictable and there is a great deal of regularity about it; for instance, 'Would you pass the salt, please?', followed by, 'Yes certainly'. Although the response is very predictable it is far from being inevitable, nor is it 'caused' by the initial request; in principle, at least, we are free to ignore the request or we may give an unexpected reply, such as 'Why, what's wrong with my cooking?'.

The 'rules' of social interaction are, of course, often *implicit* and should not be equated with the formal or explicit rules of a game of football. None the less, to see human behaviour as governed by rules allows us to: (i) predict it, within certain limits; and (ii) continue to think of humans as fundamentally free.

SKINNER'S REJECTION OF FREE WILL

Probably the most outspoken advocate of the view that the person is *not* free is Skinner (see Chapters 7 and 31). In *Beyond Freedom and Dignity* (1971) he argues that *behavioural freedom is an illusion*.

When negative reinforcers (ie consequences that an organism will work to escape from or avoid) are considered along with positive ones ('rewards'), then almost *all* behaviour is controlled by the contingencies of reinforcement which occur constantly in the environment. When we believe we are behaving 'freely' we are merely free of negative reinforcement or its threat; our behaviour is still *determined* by the pursuit of things that have been positively reinforcing in the past, and consists of responses that have previously been positively reinforced. When we perceive others as behaving 'freely' we are merely unaware of their reinforcement histories and the contingencies that govern their behaviour. So, for Skinner, the doctrine of 'autonomous man', upon which so many social institutions are based, is illusory.

Based on his work with rats and pigeons, which shows that behaviour is more efficiently controlled through the use of positive reinforcement (rather than negative reinforcement or punishment), Skinner advocates that we should abandon our illusory beliefs in behavioural freedom, accept the inevitability of control, and design an environment in which behaviour will be directed towards socially desirable ends exclusively through the use of positive reinforcement. This is the key to Skinner's imaginary utopia described in his 1948 novel *Walden Two*.

If Skinner is advocating positive reinforcement as a *means* to achieving a socially desirable goal, the question still remains as to who is to say what those goals should be. Skinner urges psychologists themselves not to be shy about participating in the shaping of policies of control; but in so doing, would they not be exercising their free will? For Skinner, there seems to be no contradiction in the idea of a few, more powerful, individuals deciding to create a totalitarian society in which the majority is controlled, externally, through conditioning techniques, which is what he describes in *Walden Two* and subsequently advocated for the 'real' world.

3 PSYCHOLOGY AND ETHICS

In discussing the issue of psychology as a science in Chapter 2, we noted that one of the unique features of psychology is that the subject-matter (what is being studied) is essentially the same kind of thing as those carrying out the study—people in both cases.

Compared with physics or chemistry, this means that the subjects in a psychological investigation are capable of thoughts and feelings, whereby they try to understand what is going on and respond emotionally to what is going on—either positively or negatively. Biologists and scientists working in medical research share with psychologists the problem of subjecting living, sentient, things to what are often painful, stressful or simply unpleasant experiences and it is because their subjects have feelings, etc. that they face questions of *ethics* about what they do.

Just as Orne (1962) regards every psychology experiment as primarily a *social* situation (which, as we saw in Chapter 2, raises questions of objectivity), we could also regard every psychological investigation as an *ethical* situation (raising questions of propriety and responsibility). Just as *methodological* issues permeate every area of psychology, so do *ethical* issues, and they each recur throughout the chapters that follow. But psychologists are not just scientists or investigators, they are also *practitioners*, that is, they work in practical and clinical settings in which people with psychological problems require help (see Chapter 1). Whenever the possibility of *changing* people in some way arises, ethical issues also arise, just as they do in medicine and psychiatry (and, to some degree, in teaching).

In this chapter, we shall look at the psychologist as a scientist/investigator, both of humans and animals, and as practitioner. It might be useful at this point to list some of the published *Codes of Ethics*, etc. which psychologists are meant to follow (see Fig. 3.1). (Unless otherwise stated, quotes will be from the British Psychological Society's (BPS) ethical principles.)

THE PSYCHOLOGIST AS SCIENTIST/INVESTIGATOR

HUMAN SUBJECTS/PARTICIPANTS

The introduction to the *Ethical Principles for Conducting Research with Human Participants* (BPS, 1990) states that:

> Participants in psychological research should have confidence in the investigators. Good psychological research is possible only if there is mutual respect and confidence between investigators and participants. Psychological investigators are potentially interested in all aspects of human behaviour and conscious experience. However, for ethical reasons,

Figure 3.1 Major Codes of Conduct/ Ethical Guidelines published by the British Psychological Society (BPS) and American Psychological Association (APA)

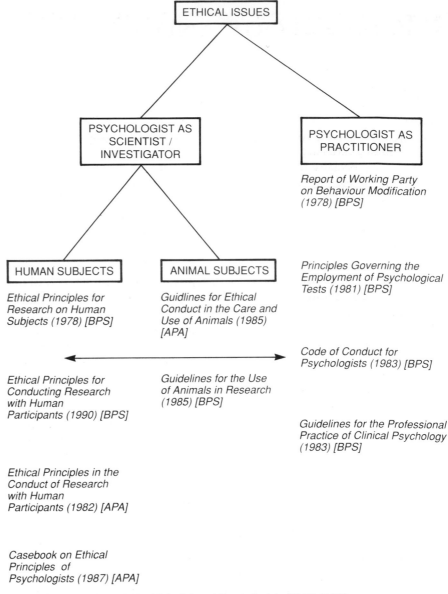

some areas of human experience and behaviour may be beyond the reach of experiment, observation or other form of psychological investigation. Ethical guidelines are necessary to clarify the conditions under which psychological research is acceptable. (paragraph 1.2)

Psychologists are urged to encourage their colleagues to adopt the Principles and to ensure that they are followed by all researchers whom they supervise (including *all* students—GCSE, 'A' and 'AS' level and above):

In all circumstances, investigators must consider the ethical implications and psychological consequences for the participants in their research. The essential principle is that the investigation should be considered from the standpoint of all participants; foreseeable threats to their psychological well-being, health, values or dignity should be eliminated . . . (paragraph 2.1)

This may require consulting with members of various ethnic, racial, sex, age or social class populations.

Consent and the Right to Withdraw

Participants should be informed of the objectives of the investigation and all other aspects of the research which might reasonably be expected to influence their willingness to participate—only such information allows *informed consent* to be given (paragraph 3.1). If this is not possible, additional safeguards are needed to protect the welfare and dignity of the participants, especially in the case of children and those with psychological impairments (eg mental retardation) which limit understanding and/or communication (paragraph 3.2) But even here, real (informed) consent should be obtained and, in addition, all below-16-year-olds should have parental consent (or consent from those in *loco parentis*) (paragraph 3.3).

Special care needs to be taken when research is conducted with detained persons (those in prison, psychiatric hospital, etc.), whose ability to give free informed consent may be affected by their special circumstances (paragraph 3.5).

Investigators must realize that they often have influence over participants, who may be their students, employees or clients: this relationship must not be allowed to pressurize the participants to take part or remain in the investigation (paragraph 3.6). Nor must payment be used to induce participants to risk harm beyond that which they risk without payment in their normal lifestyle (paragraph 3.7) We should note in relation to paragraph 3.6 that it is standard practice in American Universities for psychology students to participate as subjects in research as part of their course requirements. (They receive payment and credits, which go towards their final grade, and are free to choose which research to participate in—but they are *not* free to participate or not.)

> If harm, unusual discomfort or other negative consequences for the individual's future life might occur the investigator must obtain the disinterested approval of independent advisors, inform the participants and obtain informed, real consent, from each of them. (paragraph 3.8)

A study which is invariably (almost inevitably) cited in relation to ethical issues is Milgram's Obedience Experiment, which is discussed in detail in Chapter 20. Very briefly, subjects initially volunteered for a study of memory, which then turned out to be a study of the effects of punishment on learning. The subject was paired with a confederate who always 'chose' the role of learner, which left the subject as the teacher who had to punish the learner with increasingly strong electric shocks each time he made a mistake on the learning task. Milgram wanted to see how obedient subjects were as measured by the shock level they were prepared to go to.

One of Milgram's critics, Baumrind (1964), expressed concern for the welfare of the subjects—were adequate measures taken to protect them from the undoubted stress and emotional conflict which they experienced? Milgram replied that this presupposes that the outcome of the experiment was expected—Baumrind is confusing the (unanticipated) outcome with the basic experimental procedure. The production of stress was *not* an intended and deliberate effect of the manipulation—it was discussed with colleagues beforehand and none anticipated the reactions which occurred. He asked some of his students and a group of psychiatrists to predict when, on average, subjects would stop obeying the experimenter: they estimated that most would stop at the point when the learner began to protest, thus implying that there would be very little conflict experienced by subjects:

> Understanding grows because we examine situations in which the end is unknown. An investigator unwilling to accept this degree of risk must give up the idea of scientific inquiry. (Milgram, 1974)

You cannot know your results in advance!

However, while this might meet Baumrind's original criticism, it does not get rid of the charge of *deception* (which is a feature of most psychological research and is certainly not peculiar to Milgram). To the extent that subjects are deceived as to the true purpose of the study, they cannot give informed consent (deception is discussed separately on p. 55).

Another famous and controversial study (also discussed in detail in Chapter 20), is the Prison Simulation experiment (Zimbardo et al, 1973), in which subjects volunteered for a study of the psychological effects of imprisonment and were randomly allocated to the role of prisoner or prison guard. Once again, some subjects (the prisoners) experienced (largely) unanticipated distress but there was little in the way of deception and informed consent was obtained for a study which took place in a specially converted basement at Stanford University:

> The legal counsel of Stanford University was consulted, drew up a formal 'informed consent' statement and told us of work, fire, safety and insurance requirements we had to satisfy (which we did). The 'informed consent' statement signed by every participant, specified that there would be an invasion of privacy, loss of some civil rights and harassment. Neither they, nor we, however, could have predicted in advance the intensity and extent of these aspects of the prison experience. We did not, however, inform them of the police arrests, in part, because we did not secure final approval from the police until minutes before they decided to participate and, in part, because we did want the mock arrests to come as a surprise. This was a breach, by omission, of the ethics of our informed consent contract. The staff of the university's Student Health Department was alerted to our study and prior arrangements made for any medical care which might be required.
>
> Approval was officially sought and received in writing from the sponsoring agency ONR, the Psychology Department and the University Committee of Human Experimentation . . . (Zimbardo, 1973)

The study was planned to last for two weeks but was abandoned after six days because of the distress the prisoners were suffering. By contrast, once Milgram saw the degree of distress his subjects were experiencing, why didn't he call a halt to the experiments there and then? This relates to the question of *withdrawal from the investigation*.

Along with the provision of information, which forms the basis of informed consent, investigators should make plain to the participants their right to withdraw from the study at any time, regardless of any payment or other inducement offered. This may be difficult in certain observational or organizational settings but must be an aim and applies to children as much as to adults (paragraph 6.1). In the light of experience of the investigation, or as a result of debriefing (see below), participants have the right to withdraw their consent retrospectively and to require their own data (including any recordings) to be destroyed (paragraph 6.2). (In longitudinal research, consent may need to be obtained on more than one occasion and so retrospective withdrawal of consent could involve a considerable amount of data collected over a substantial period of time.)

Coolican (1990) believes that Milgram flagrantly contravened all principles regarding the right to withdraw at any point and to terminate proceedings when distress levels are substantially higher than anticipated or than is acceptable. Each time a subject expressed the wish to stop giving shocks, he was ordered to continue, with the prods and prompts becoming increasingly harsh. Coolican points out that the APA (1987) stresses special vigilance when the investigator is in a position of power over the participant, a position that was, of course, very forcefully exploited by Milgram.

So why did Milgram allow the experiments to continue?

He acknowledges that he *could* have stopped them but felt that 'momentary excitement is not the same as harm' and he did not feel that the stress was sufficiently intense to warrant abandoning the research. (He was largely vindicated by the results of his debriefing—see below).

At a more abstract level, Milgram started out with the belief that every person who came to the laboratory was free to accept or reject the dictates of authority: far from being a passive creature, subjects are active, choosing adults. If *some* subjects could defy the experimenter, this surely demonstrates that others were free to do likewise. Indeed, the final prod 'You have no other choice, you *must* go on!' was often the occasion for subjects to break off, and say something like 'That's where you're wrong, I do have a choice!'

Colman (1987) points out that an ethical committee of the APA investigated Milgram's research not long after its first publication (during which time Milgram's APA membership was suspended) and eventually found it ethically acceptable. In 1965 he was awarded the prize for outstanding contribution to social psychological research by the American Association for the Advancement of Science.

Deception

> Intentional deception of the participants over the purpose and general nature of the investigation should be avoided whenever possible. Participants should never be deliberately misled without extremely strong scientific or medical justification. Even then there should be strict controls and the disinterested approval of independent advisors. (paragraph 4.2)

The decision that deception is necessary should only be taken after determining that alternative procedures avoiding concealment or deception are not available, ensuring that the participants will be *debriefed* at the earliest opportunity and consulting on how the withholding of information and deliberate deception will be received.

Coolican (1990) cites a study by Menges (1973) who reviewed about 1000 American studies and found that 80 per cent involved giving participants less than complete information. In only 3 per cent were they given complete information about the independent variable, and only in 25 per cent of cases was complete information given about the dependent variable.

In terms of the likely harm to the participant, clearly some cases of deception are less serious than others; perhaps most serious are those likely to affect the participants' self-image, particularly self-esteem. This is why studies like Milgram's and that of Zimbardo et al have proved so controversial. It could be argued that it is in *social psychology* generally that the most potentially damaging deception goes on, since it is in this kind of research that people are most likely to learn things about themselves *as a person*, things which will be of much greater emotional significance than, say, one's ability to perceive, remember or solve problems (the concern of *cognitive psychology*).

A form of deception used almost exclusively in social psychology is the confederate (or stooge) who (usually) pretends to be another subject (as in Milgram's experiments). This involves an elaborate 'staging' of events into which the naïve subject has to fit unwittingly—but at least debriefing (see below) allows the confederate to be revealed for what he/she really is.

However, in *field* experiments of bystander intervention (see Chapter 16), emergencies are staged in real-life situations which do not permit any debriefing to occur (eg actors pretending to collapse in the New York subway—Piliavin et al, 1969). This means that such unsuspecting participants never find out that they were participating in an experiment at all and so never find out that they have been deceived—a double deception!

Can deception ever be justified?

Aronson defends Milgram on the grounds that unless he had used deception, he would have found results:

> ... which simply do not reflect how people behave when led to believe they are in real situations. (Aronson, 1988)

It may be the best and (perhaps) the only way to get useful information about how people behave in most complex and important situations. Each year Aronson asks his psychology students how they would have behaved if they had been one of Milgram's subjects? About 1 per cent each year say they'd go all the way. Does this mean they are nicer people than Milgram's subjects? Aronson doesn't think so. It means that if given half a chance, most people will try to 'look good'.

This in theory raises the fundamental question as to the value of finding out about obedience, eg only if we believe it is of general social significance to understand the processes involved (the *end*) can we begin to justify deception as a *means* of studying it and even then it may only be a *partial* justification.

Indeed, Aronson believes that, 'It is simply unethical to tell lies to people'—lying is *in and of itself*, objectionable.

Protection of Participants

Investigators have a primary responsibility to protect participants from physical and mental harm during the investigation. Normally, the risk of harm must be no greater than in ordinary life, ie participants should not be exposed to risks greater than or additional to those encountered in their normal life styles ...

Participants must be asked about any factors in the procedure that might create a risk, such as pre-existing medical conditions and must be advised of any special action they should take to avoid risk. (paragraph 8.1)

Fortunately, there are relatively few cases in which actual physical harm (eg pain) comes to subjects, although Little Albert (who was made to fear a white rat through the association of the rat with a hammer smashing down on a steel bar right behind his head) is a notable exception (see Chapter 7) and many have involved electric shock, extreme noise levels, food and sleep deprivation, anxiety or nausea, etc. (Coolican, 1990). But in many of these cases the adult subjects give informed consent, especially in sleep and food deprivation, where there is often no need for deception, and the right to withdraw at any time acts as an additional safeguard (at least in theory).

However, Little Albert was too young to give consent (informed/otherwise) although his mother presumably did. (It's actually not clear what she knew in advance.) But there is no doubt that she exercised her right to withdraw her son from the experiment to save him any more 'punishment'. There is also no doubt that having a hammer crash down on a 4 foot steel bar right behind your ear is very painful (Albert may have suffered permanent hearing loss as a result) but equally worrying is the distress—the 'mental harm'. The point of the experiment was to induce a phobia of rats (and other 'furry' things) and this was undoubtedly achieved.

According to Aronson:

> ... The experimenter must take steps to ensure that subjects leave the experimental situation in a frame of mind that is at least as sound as it was when they entered. This frequently requires post-experimental 'debriefing' procedures that require more time and effort than the main body of the experiment. (Aronson, 1988)

So debriefing (along with *confidentiality* and the right to withdraw) can be regarded as a major means of protecting participants where mental suffering has occurred—with or without deception—and participants must also be protected from the stress that might be produced by disclosing highly personal and private information. They must be reassured that they are *not* obliged to answer such questions.

Debriefing

As mentioned above, debriefing may be necessary to ensure that participants leave the experimental situation in a frame of mind at least as good as that when they arrived.

Where no undue suffering is experienced but subjects are deceived regarding the real purpose of the experiment:

> ... the investigator should provide the participant with any necessary information to complete their understanding of the nature of the research. The investigator should discuss with the participants their experience of the research in order to monitor any unforseen negative effects or misconceptions. (paragraph 5.1)

However:

> ... some effects which may be produced by an experiment will not be negated by a verbal description following the research. Investigators have a responsibility to ensure that participants receive any necessary de-briefing in the form of active intervention before they leave the research setting. (paragraph 5.3)

This is more like a 'therapeutic' measure than it is a matter of 'good manners'. Examples of this second kind of debriefing (which also incorporates the first) can be found in both the Zimbardo et al and Milgram experiments:

> Following the study, we held a group and individual de-briefing session, had all the subjects return post-experimental questionnaires several weeks later, several months later, and at yearly intervals. Many submitted retrospective diaries and personal analyses of the effects of their participation. We have met with most of the subjects since the termination of the study singly or in small groups, or where that was not possible, have discussed their reactions in telephone conversations. We are sufficiently convinced that the suffering we observed and were responsible for, was stimulus-bound and did not extend beyond the confines of the basement prison. (Zimbardo, 1973)

In Milgram's experiments, a very thorough debriefing ('dehoax') was carefully carried out with all subjects during which: (i) they were reunited with the unharmed actor-victim; (ii) were assured that no shock had been delivered; and (iii) Milgram and the subject had an extended discussion. Obedient subjects were assured that their behaviour was entirely normal and their feelings of conflict and tension were shared by other subjects, while defiant subjects were supported in their decision to disobey the experimenter. All subjects were told they would receive (and did) a comprehensive report when all the experiments were over, detailing the procedure and the results. They were also sent a follow-up questionnaire regarding their participation. There was a 92 per cent response rate to this and the only difference between those who responded and those who did not was that more younger people did not respond. Nearly 84 per cent said they were glad or very glad to have participated while less than 2 per cent said they were sorry or very sorry. 80 per cent felt that more experiments of this kind should be carried out and 74 per cent had learned something of personal importance.

Milgram points out that the debriefing and assessment were carried out as a matter of course and *not* stimulated by the distress the subjects (unexpectedly) experienced.

One year after the completion of the experiments, an impartial psychiatrist interviewed 40 subjects, several of whom had experienced extreme stress; none showed any signs of having been psychologically harmed or having suffered any traumatic reactions:

> The central moral justification for allowing a procedure of the sort used in my experiment is that it is judged acceptable by those who have taken part in it. Moreover, it was the salience of this fact throughout that constituted the chief moral warrant for the continuation of the experiments. (Milgram, 1974)

He goes on to say that any criticism of the experiment which does not take into account the tolerant reactions of the participants is hollow:

> Again, the participant, rather than the external critic must be the ultimate source of judgement. (Milgram, 1974)

According to Aronson (1988), not only is debriefing valuable as a means of undoing any discomfort or deception which might have occurred during the experimental session, but it also provides the experimenter with an opportunity to provide additional information about the topic under investigation, so the experiment can become an educational experience for subjects. In addition, the experimenter can determine to what extent the procedure worked:

> ... and find out from the one person who knows best (the subject) how the procedure might be improved. In short, the prudent experimenter regards subjects as colleagues—not as objects ... (Aronson, 1988)

(This touches on the more general issue of the mechanistic nature of psychology—see Chapter 2. 'Subject' has rather different connotations from 'participant', a term much more compatible with the concept of 'person'.)

One final point:

> Debriefing does not provide a justification for unethical aspects of an investigation. (paragraph 5.2)

Confidentiality

> Subject to the requirements of legislation, including the Data Protection Act, information obtained about a participant during an investigation is confidential unless otherwise agreed in advance ... Participants in psychological research have a right to expect that information they provide will be treated confidentially, and, if published, will not be identifiable as theirs. In the event that confidentiality and/or anonymity cannot be guaranteed, the participant must be warned of this in advance of agreeing to participate. (paragraph 7.1)

> Apart from the ethical considerations, a purely pragmatic argument for guaranteeing anonymity is that members of the public would soon stop volunteering if their identity was disclosed without their permission. (Coolican, 1990)

If subjects have been seriously deceived they have the right to witness destruction of any such records they don't wish to be kept. Results are usually made anonymous as early as possible by use of a letter/number instead of name.

Are there special circumstances in which the investigator might contravene the confidentiality rule?
Yes, namely where there are clear/direct dangers to human life. Eg participant observation of gang life where a serious crime is planned/or a psychiatrist's patient plans to kill himself, etc.:

> The ethical principles involved here are broader than those involved in conducting scientific research. (Coolican, 1990)

Involuntary Participation and Observational Research

> Studies based upon observation must respect the privacy and psychological well-being of the individuals studied. Unless those observed give their consent to being observed, observational research is only acceptable in situations where those observed would expect to be observed by strangers. Additionally, particular account should be taken of local cultural values and of the possibility of intruding upon the privacy of individuals who, even while in a normally public space, may believe they are unobserved. (paragraph 9.1)

In the case of *naturalistic observation* the essential ethical issue is one of *consent*—not only can informed consent not be given, *no consent at all can be given*. At the same time, the possibility of any kind of debriefing is virtually nil, from a practical point of view. Even more serious is participant observation, where peoples' private lives may be invaded. Coolican (1990) cites a study by Humphreys (1971) of the behaviour of consenting homosexuals. He acted as public washroom 'lookout'. Those being studied were completely unaware of being studied and of the fact that their car registration numbers were recorded in order to obtain more background information later on. We mentioned earlier the case of *field experiments*, where people are unwitting, unsolicited subjects in an experiment, and where, implicitly, demands are made on them in the form of an actor pretending to collapse in a public place. This puts them under some degree of obligation and, depending on their participation or otherwise, they may experience a range of feelings, including guilt/ embarrassment/disgust/helplessness, etc. There may be twice the amount of deception involved, but instead of receiving twice the amount of debriefing, they don't receive any!

Colleagues

> Investigators share the responsibility for the ethical treatment of the research participants with their collaborators, assistants, students or employers. A psychologist who believes that another psychologist or investigator may be conducting research that is not in accordance with the principles above should encourage that investigator to re-evaluate the research. (paragraph 11.1)

Publication and Access to Data

This is made explicit by the APA (1981)—psychologists as scientists must accept primary responsibility for the selection of research topics, research methods, analysis and reporting. Data must not be suppressed, alternative hypotheses and explanations must be acknowledged. Researchers must only take credit for what they have done—so those who have made equal or unequal contributions must be named—either as a co-author or in footnotes or elsewhere (including research assistants, who often do much of the 'donkey-work', clerical assistants, etc.). A basic requirement of research papers, etc. is to provide a sufficiently detailed account to enable other researchers to test the hypothesis for themselves (*replication*). In the light of this, perhaps the greatest sin that can be committed by a scientist is what it is generally agreed was done by Burt, who was accused of making up data for his Twin Studies to support his genetic theory of intelligence (see Chapter 28).

Conclusions

> Psychologists respect the dignity and worth of the individual and strive for the preservation of fundamental human rights. They are committed to increasing knowledge of human behaviour and of peoples' understanding of themselves and others and to the utilization of such knowledge for the promotion of human welfare. (APA, 1981)

This general statement is echoed by Aronson who argues that, in a real sense, social psychologists are:

> ...obligated to use their research skills to advance our knowledge and understanding of human behaviour for the ultimate aim of human

betterment. In short, social psychologists have an ethical responsibility to the society as a whole . . . (Aronson, 1988)

Aronson goes on to say that there may sometimes be a conflict between this general responsibility to society and the more specific responsibility to each individual subject, and that this is most likely to arise when studying such important issues as conformity, obedience and helping behaviour. In general, the more important the issue: (i) the greater the potential benefit for society as a whole; and (ii) the more likely an individual subject will experience discomfort, anxiety and upset. Can this conflict be resolved?

> . . . No code of ethics can anticipate all problems, especially those created when subjects discover something unpleasant about themselves or others in the course of their participation [eg in the Milgram or Zimbardo et al experiments]. (Aronson, 1988)

The basic dilemma facing experimental Social Psychologists is the belief in the value of free scientific enquiry and that in the dignity of humans and their right to privacy. This dilemma must be squarely faced every time an experiment is designed and conducted, as:

> . . . there is no concrete and universal set of rules or guidelines capable of governing *every* situation. (Aronson, 1988)

ANIMAL SUBJECTS

The Scientific Affairs Board of the BPS published their *Guidelines for the Use of Animals in Research* (1985), in conjuction with the Committee of the Experimental Psychological Society. They offered a checklist of points, which investigators should carefully consider when planning experiments with living animals.

Researchers have a general obligation to:

> . . . avoid, or at least to minimize, discomfort to living animals . . . discuss any future research with their local Home Office Inspector and colleagues who are experts in the topic . . . seek . . . Widespread advice as to whether the likely scientific contribution of the work . . . justifies the use of living animals, and whether the scientific point they wish to make may not be made without the use of living animals . . . (BPS, 1985)

This raises two fundamental questions:

(i) how do we know animals suffer?
(ii) what (goal) can ever justify the subjection of animals to pain?

How do we Know Animals Suffer?

According to Dawkins, the question of how much we know regarding the suffering of an animal of another species is:

> . . . fundamental to many of the current debates about animal welfare . . . (Dawkins, 1980)

What criteria should be used to judge animal suffering?

1) Are the animals physically healthy? Disease and injury are generally acknowledged to be major causes of suffering. For this reason, experiments like the Executive Monkey experiments (in which pairs of monkeys were attached to apparatus which gave electric shocks, such

that the 'executive' could prevent the shock by pressing a lever but the other could not, with the effect that the former developed ulcers and eventually died) would be unlikely even to be debated in the current climate (Mapstone, 1991) (see Chapter 6). It is self-evident that these monkeys were suffering and the experiments were quite rightly condemned by the scientific community. But even if we are sure that they are not suffering, we would still have to decide:

> ... Whether their confinement imposed mental suffering which did not affect their external condition ... (Dawkins, 1980)

Apparently healthy zoo and farm animals often show bizarre abnormal behaviour (bobbing up and down, eating faeces, etc.). An animal may also suffer intensely but too transiently for any overt signs of injury to make themselves obvious (transporting food animals may produce subtle physiological effects, eg changes in the ammonia content of the muscles, or hormone levels).

2) The biggest difficulty is not being able to *ask* animals what they are feeling. But with greater knowledge of the animals themselves, the lack of words may not turn out to be such a formidable barrier. The animals' behaviour may provide evidence enough, eg a fairly direct way of getting animals to express what they feel by their behaviour is to give them access to switches which control their environment in some way. For example, what happens when pigs are given the opportunity to adjust their own levels of illumination? Work at the Agricultural Research Council has shown that pigs quickly learn what light switches are for and can be effectively asked what sort of lighting they like and when they like the lights to go on and off.

3) We must *find out* about animal suffering by careful observation and experimentation:

> ... Because different species have different requirements, different life-styles, and, for all we know, different kinds of emotions, we cannot assume that we know about their suffering or well being without taking the trouble to study them species by species ... (Dawkins, 1980)

To build up a picture of what an animal might be feeling, we need a great deal of factual information about its biology. More specifically, before we can claim to be able to recognize its signs of suffering in a particular species we need to:

(a) Document its signs of illness and health, including physiological disturbances which may be hidden from the unaided observer.
(b) Try to find out how each species expresses its various emotional states. (We might begin by studying animals in the wild or in a relatively unrestricted state and compare it with the behaviour of captive animals.)
(c) Find out whether these behaviour restrictions lead to suffering, eg frustration or merely to the innocuous signs of captivity.
(d) Discover the animals' own preference for different environments/ conditions, as this might well alter our picture of how much they were suffering in a given instance.

> Science ... has ... a major and positive contribution to make [to animal welfare]. By studying animals, we can learn how they express themselves and the conditions under which they suffer physically and mentally.

Through this knowledge we have a much better chance of being able to ensure that they do not suffer while they are in our care. (Dawkins, 1980)

Why do Animal Experiments?

The question of suffering wouldn't arise if animals were not being used in experiments in the first place.

According to Gray (1987), the main justifications for animal experimentation are: (i) the pursuit of scientific knowledge; and (ii) the advancement of medicine. In either case, for the argument to be valid, we must be able to rule out the fact that the experimenter is deriving pleasure from the animals' suffering (ie that this is the major reason the experiment is done!)

The guidelines state that if the animals are confined, constrained, harmed or stressed in any way, the experimenter must consider whether the knowledge to be gained justifies the procedure. Some knowledge is trivial and experiments must not be done simply because it is possible to do them.

To take the example of the Executive Monkeys again, the medical justification (to discover why business executives develop ulcers) was insufficient to justify the continuation of these experiments. The monkeys' obvious suffering superseded even the combination of scientific and medical justification. But there are other cases where, while the scientific justification may be apparent, the medical justification is much less so, eg experiments where animals' brains are stimulated through implantation of permanent electrodes (electrical brain stimulation—EBS) (eg Olds and Milner, 1954; see Chapter 6).

Whatever practical application such experiments may have subsequently had (eg pain/anxiety relief in psychotics, epileptics and cancer patients), they don't seem to have been conducted with such human applications in mind. Can the scientific knowledge gained about ESB as a very powerful positive reinforcer justify, *on its own*, the fact that the rats were eventually 'sacrificed' (ie killed)?

The very least that can be required of researchers is that every step is taken to ensure the minimum of suffering is caused, both during and following any surgical procedure and by any electric shock or food deprivation, which are such common features of laboratory experiments.

Gray (1987) claims that rats are the most commonly used experimental subjects in psychology, with food deprivation and electric shock being the most objected-to treatments. He claims that food deprivation is *not* a source of suffering and that the rats are either fed once a day when the day's experimentation is over or are maintained at 85 per cent of their free-feeding (*ad lib.*) body weight, and that both are actually *healthier* than allowing them to eat *ad lib*. Regarding shock, Gray claims this may cause *some* pain but not *extreme* pain (based on observations of the animals' behaviour). The level permitted is controlled by the Home Office (HO) inspectors—the average level used in the UK is 0.68 milliamperes, for an average of 0.57 seconds. This usually produces an unpleasant tickling sensation in humans.

The Guidelines point out that procedures causing pain or distress are illegal unless the experimenter holds an HO licence and relevant certificates. Even then, there should be no alternative ways of conducting the experiment without the use of aversive stimulation.

Similarly, it is illegal to perform any surgical or pharmacological procedure on vertebrates in the UK without an HO licence and relevant certification. Such procedures must be performed by experienced staff and it is a particular responsibility of senior staff to train and supervise others. Experimenters must be familiar with the technical aspects of anaesthesia and appropriate steps should be taken to prevent post-operative infection in chronic experiments.

Throughout the Guidelines, the importance of understanding species differences is emphasized in relation to: (i) caging and social environment; (ii) the stress involved in marking wild animals for identification or attaching them with radio transmitters; and (iii) the duration of food/drink deprivation.

Paragraph 8 also states that field workers should disturb animals as little as possible:

> ... Even simple observation on wild animals can have marked effects on their breeding and survival ... (paragraph 8)

A case in point is Cayo Santiago (the oldest continuously maintained primate colony in the world—established in 1939) a Caribbean island that is almost literally a laboratory in the field ('open-air laboratory'). The rhesus monkeys which inhabit the island are given provisions, so that some aspects of their feeding ecology cannot be studied. But it is possible to follow the behaviour, development and population dynamics of a species over many generations. Each year the monkeys are trapped and the youngsters born that year are tattooed and blood samples are taken—the colony is still used partly for medical research, but these are the only interventions. Without this, the age, sex and maternal geneology of every individual (plus a detailed biography) would not be known (Rawlins, 1979).

Prior to 1970, Cayo's primary purpose was to supply monkeys for medical research (having already deprived them of their natural habitats) and behavioural studies were not allowed to interfere with this. Since 1970, no animal has been captured and the developmental study of the free-ranging monkeys is at least as important as the medical research. But what if there were an outbreak of some infectious disease which threatened the colony; this would pose a dilemma between practical and moral considerations. Interference to save the monkeys could be defended and attacked on moral grounds: the scientists' moral duty is to save them if they have the power to do so. However, the scientists are also bound to retain and preserve the naturalness of Cayo, so should the monkeys be free to die? This dilemma seems to underline and reflect the dual nature of Cayo both as natural and man-made, 'field' and laboratory (Gross, 1990).

Gray (1991) extends the 'medical justification' argument by claiming that, while most people (both experimenters and animal rights activists) would accept the ethical principle that inflicting pain is wrong, we are sometimes faced with having to choose between different ethical principles (ie we have to make moral choices), which may mean having to choose between human and animal suffering. He believes that *speciesism* (discriminating against and exploiting animals because they belong to a particular (non-human) species; Ryder, 1990) *is* justified, and argues that:

... not only is it not wrong to give preference to the interests of one's own species, one has a duty to do so ... (Gray, 1991)

Such a moral choice involves establishing a calculus (Dawkins, 1990) which pits the suffering of the animals against the human suffering which the use of animals will alleviate:

> In many cases the decision not to carry out certain experiments with animals (even if they would inflict pain or suffering) is likely to have the consequence that more people will undergo pain or suffering that might otherwise be avoided ... (Gray, 1991)

One of the problems associated with the pro-speciesism argument, according to Gray, is that medical advance may only become possible after extensive development of knowledge and scientific understanding in a particular field; in the interim:

> ... scientific understanding may be the only specific objective that the experiment can readily attain ... (Gray, 1991)

It is at this interim stage that the suffering imposed on the animals in experiments will far outweigh any (lesser) suffering eventually avoided by people—this is at the core of the decisions that must be made by scientists and ethical committees.

Gray has been criticized by Ryder (1991) for being inconsistent between declared ethical principles and action. If Gray believes his own principle that, 'if it is wrong to inflict pain unnecessarily, it is equally wrong whether the pain is inflicted upon a human being, a rat or a spider', then he should abandon painful research upon animals—ie *there can be no exceptions*. But this seems to assume that Gray's distinction between ethical principles and moral choices is false and this seems to hinge upon the interpretation of 'unnecessarily'. Surely Gray's argument is about what are *justifiable exceptions* to the general ethical rule that inflicting suffering is wrong—if the animal's suffering is a means to an end (ie the prevention of human suffering) then it is *not* unnecessary. Ryder's reply would be that 'unnecessary' does *not* imply 'necessary' (ie the experimenter has a moral duty to perform the research) but Gray believes that it does!

THE PSYCHOLOGIST AS PRACTITIONER

According to Fairbairn and Fairbairn (1987), the *Guidelines for the Professional Practice of Clinical Psychology* (1983) attempt to spell out in detail sound practice as well as ethical advice: (i) the need to maintain professional competence; (ii) not allowing the false impression of competence to be entertained by others; (iii) safeguards for the work of trainees; (iv) the need to obtain valid consent for treatment; and (v) the problems of privacy and confidentiality.

Paragraph 1 states that psychologists, '... shall hold the interests and welfare of those in receipt of their services to be paramount at all times ...' But psychologists may face split loyalties—as part of an interdisciplinary team they may have obligations to both the client and, say, the psychiatrist in charge. The Guidelines make it clear that, in cases of conflict, it is the psychologist's responsibility to ensure that, '... the client receives the care that he or she is considered to require ...', ie loyalty to the client predominates over any loyalty to colleagues.

The Guidelines also state that the psychologist must not unreasonably impose his or her values (nor those of the institution) on the client, nor should they:

> ... condone, use or participate in the application of psychological knowledge or technology in any way that infringes human rights. (paragraph 13.1)

Unlike the psychologist as researcher, the clinical psychologist (like educational psychologists, psychotherapists, psychiatrists, social workers, nurses, counsellors and special needs teachers) is involved with bringing about *psychological change* (although the physical benefits to the client may often be the primary aim, as in the treatment of severely self-mutilating clients). It is in their capacity as *agents of change* that clinical psychologists, etc. face their greatest ethical challenges:

> Practitioners in the caring professions face moral decisions every day. They must decide how to allocate their time and the other resources at their disposal, who to help and who not to help. They must decide how they will interact with those who seek their help; for example, whether in general they will regard them as autonomous beings with rights and responsibilities, or rather as helpless individuals, incapable of rational choice ... All ... face the problems of confidentiality that being in possession of privileged information causes. And all face the problem of deciding how much of themselves to give to their professional work and how much to keep for themselves, their families and friends ... (Fairbairn and Fairbairn, 1987)

Fairbairn and Fairbairn (1987) believe that ethics has received relatively little attention in psychology as compared with other caring professions, such as medicine, nursing and social work, yet, '... a consideration of the ethical dimensions of psychological change is fundamental to the development of practice ...'. They argue that two not uncommon beliefs which are likely to lead away from an explicit consideration of professional ethics and values in psychological practice are: (i) that psychology is a value-free science; and (ii) that therapists should be value-neutral or 'non-directive'.

PSYCHOLOGY AS VALUE-FREE SCIENCE

Fairbairn and Fairbairn cite Sutton (1981), who claims that:

> ... in one respect psychological practice faces unique problems, because psychology stands at the intersection of the helping professions with 'science' ...
>
> ... Psychological science has traditionally been thought of as developing through careful, value-free investigations. The notion of an objective (and hence, so it is thought, value-free) clinical psychology, favoured by many psychologists, rests on the possibility of a foundation in a positivist science ... (Fairbairn and Fairbairn, 1987)

This raises the debate about the nature of psychology as a whole. According to Shotter (1975), psychology as a discipline should be thought of as a 'moral science of action' as opposed to a 'natural science of behaviour' (see Chapter 2).

But to what extent are the ideas and techniques of clinical psychology actually founded on systematic scientific research? Quoting Sutton again:

If the practising psychologist is to retain his status as a scientist rather than to be simply a purveyor of ideas and techniques developed by other psychologists, then (s)he has an obligation to undertake scientific work. (Sutton, 1981)

Similarly, Dallos and Cullen (1990) argue that the model which has become central for clinical psychology is the *scientist-practitioner model*, which sees clinical psychology as being guided by, and operating within, the framework of general scientific method.

However, according to Fairbairn and Fairbairn (1987), the greater the emphasis on the scientific credibility of research, the less likely interpersonal or professional values or ethics are to be widely and seriously debated. If clinical psychologists view clinical psychology as having firm foundations in positivist science, they may disregard ethics because these are not amenable to objective consideration. However:

> ... Even if the psychological knowledge utilised in clinical practice was always the result of the application of an objective scientific method, at the point at which it is applied, moral questions of an interpersonal kind are bound to arise ... Similarly, applications of findings in ... behaviour modification and intelligence testing bring along with them questions of ethics. (Fairbairn and Fairbairn, 1987)

This distinction between possession of knowledge and application of that knowledge ('science' versus 'technology') is fundamental to any discussion of ethics because it is related to the notion of *responsibility*. Presumably, the clinical psychologist chooses which techniques to use with clients and how these are to be used: the mere existence (and even the demonstrated effectiveness) of certain techniques does not *in itself* mean that they must be used.

Similarly, the kind of research which clinical psychologists consider worth doing (and which, then, provides the scientific basis for the use of particular techniques) is a matter of choice and reflects views as to the nature of human beings and how people can be changed. In this respect, perhaps, the clinical psychologist is different from the atomic physicist or geneticist, whose discoveries may be abused (in the form of atomic bombs or genetic engineering) *by others* (governments, dictators, etc.) with greater power and authority: the clinical psychologist is both researcher and practitioner, scientist and technocrat.

So what is the view of the person underlying the practice of a scientifically-based clinical psychology?

According to Trower (1987), the two major criticisms of scientific behaviour therapy or modification are that:

(a) Because of (rather than despite) its espoused status as a value-free, applied science it tends to devalue and thereby dehumanize its clients and it does this by treating people for 'scientific' purposes as if they were 'organisms' as opposed to 'agents' who are helpless victims of forces outside their control. This criticism also applies to medical psychiatry and classical psychoanalysis, except that both see the controlling forces as being internal (organic abnormalities or intrapsychic forces, respectively) as opposed to environmental contingencies.

(b) Clients (soon come to) believe (given the overwhelming 'scientific' ethos) that they are abnormal organisms (deficient, ill, etc.) and that they are not only helpless but also worthless, because this is part of the culture-wide stereotype of 'mental illness' and allied terms (see Chapter 30).

Negative self-evaluation and passivity characterize many, if not the majority of, mental health clients, ie clients think and behave like passive organisms and this is precisely the problem. Trower believes that the solution lies in helping people recover or discover their agency:

> ... The criticism of scientific behaviour therapy is that along with medical psychiatry, it tends to work against this objective by encouraging clients, relatives, friends, and the helping professionals alike to think of clients in terms of passive, deficient, helpless organisms. (Trower, 1987)

THERAPISTS AS VALUE-NEUTRAL AND NON-DIRECTIVE

If psychology as a value-free science is about not regarding or treating clients fully as human beings, this second major issue is about the therapist or psychologist functioning as something less than a complete person in the context of the therapeutic situation.

According to Fairbairn and Fairbairn (1987), providing help and support in a non-directive, value-free way is a tradition for psychotherapists and counsellors. But this may seem to require remaining aloof and distant from the client, not being 'personally present', not 'standing alongside' the client. Doesn't this, in turn, entail not treating the client with respect as a person, which can never be in the client's best interests?

> ... if the therapeutic relationship is to be based on respect for clients as people, as it must be if the client is to be treated as a person, then it also has to be acknowledged that it takes place between two people. We cannot respect another as a person unless we recognize that he is a person like us; and we cannot do this in a therapeutic situation unless we are present, as a person, with the other. (Fairbairn and Fairbairn, 1987)

Adopting what is thought to be a value-free position in therapy may lead the therapist to deny the importance or influence of his or her own moral values, which are often hidden in therapy:

> ... But the purpose of the psychologist is commonly to promote change which frequently involves movement towards the therapist's best, ie valued, solution: that is, in some sense, by some means, the therapist's values are imposed upon the client, albeit implicitly rather than explicitly. (Fairbairn and Fairbairn, 1987)

> ... even for the most ardent adherent ... of a value-free science in therapy, there may be limitations to the extent to which they can, in conscience, remain morally neutral. For example, even such therapists may feel direct influence is necessary where moral positions involving violence or serious crime are concerned. (Fairbairn and Fairbairn, 1987)

Fairbairn (1987) believes that the principle of respect for individuals as persons is central to the positive ethical evaluation of any changes brought about by psychologists. Respecting others as people involves helping them to make responsible decisions about their lives, 'because taking responsibility for one's own life is at least part of what it is to function fully as a person ...'.

Lindley (1987; cited by Fairbairn, 1987) argues that many psychotherapies, because they aim at increasing autonomy, are based on the assumption that, '. . . taking control of one's own life is itself an essential part of human flourishing', ie they would seem to be based on respect for persons.

Fairbairn (1987) argues that respecting a person's wishes is essentially about respecting the person as autonomous, ie a self-governing being and regards this as the most important aspect of the attitude of respect for persons.

Psychologists who have responsibility for clients over whom they can exert power and influence must give them opportunities to be, or encouragement in being, responsible for themselves. For some clients it would involve providing opportunities for exercising choice and directing the course of their lives. This is perhaps especially true in the case of patients in long-stay psychiatric and mental handicap wards, where opportunities for responsible choice and decision-making may be systematically removed in the interests of safe, secure and easily maintained wards (Fairbairn, 1987). (Compulsory treatment under Mental Health Legislation is largely about removing responsibility from individuals who are thought, at least temporarily, to be incapable of responsible action and who constitute a risk to themselves and/or others. The difficulty is deciding just how much responsibility it is appropriate to remove and to give back.)

To conclude, Hawks (1981) (cited by Fairbairn and Fairbairn, 1987) believes that prevention rather than cure should be a primary aim of psychology, enabling people to cope by themselves, without professional help, thus 'giving psychology away' to the people/client. (This was the theme of George Miller's 1969 Presidential Address to the American Psychological Association—see Chapter 2 and Gross, 1990.):

> The value of understanding human functioning does not inhere in its application in the usual sense but in its possession . . . In order to help a person who is in psychological difficulties we work to enhance his understanding of himself and of his relationships to others. If we think in terms of traditional roles, then the significant place in society of the psychologist will be more that of the teacher than expert or technician. (Bakan, 1967; quoted in Fairbairn and Fairbairn, 1987)

PART 2

The Biological Basis of Behaviour and Experience

4 The Nervous System

The biological basis of behaviour is an integral part of the study of psychology. The important point to remember is that psychologists are interested in biology *not* for its own sake but for what it can tell them about behaviour and mental processes.

A few other important points should be made about the relationship between psychology and biology:

(a) The kind of behaviour of which an animal species is capable depends very much on the kind of *body* it possesses; humans can flap their arms as much as they like but they will never fly (unaided) because arms are simply not suited to flight, they are not designed for it, while wings are. However, we are very skilled at manipulating objects (particularly small ones) because that is how our hands and fingers have developed during the course of evolution.

(b) The possession of a specialized body is of very little use unless the nervous system is able to control it; of course, evolution of the one usually mirrors evolution of the other. The kind of behaviour of which a species is capable is determined by the kind of *nervous system* it possesses.

(c) The kind of nervous system also determines the extent and the nature of the *learning* of which a species is capable. As you move along the phylogenetic–evolutionary scale, from simple, one-celled amoebae, through insects, birds and mammals, to primates, including *Homo sapiens*, the nervous system becomes gradually more complex and behaviour becomes increasingly the product of learning and environmental influence, as distinct from instinct and other innate, genetically-determined factors.

An Overview of the Human Nervous System (NS)—Structure and Function

As you can see from Figure 4.1, the NS involves a number of sub-divisions. Before looking at these in detail, we need to look at some of the general characteristics of the NS:

1) The NS as a whole comprises between 10 and 12 billion (ie 10 to 12 thousand million) nerve cells or *neurons*; these are the basic structural units or building blocks of the NS.

2) Other kinds of cell in the NS include *glial* ('glue') cells, which are mostly smaller than neurons and ten times more numerous; they supply nutrients and structural support to the neurons and provide a barrier to certain substances from the bloodstream.

Figure 4.1 Major sub-divisions of the human nervous system (including the main sub-divisions of the brain)

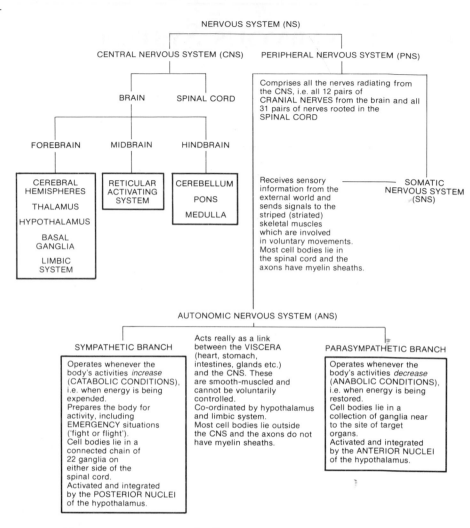

3) About 80 per cent of all neurons are found in the brain, in particular, in the cerebral cortex, the topmost outer layer.

4) Information is passed from neuron to neuron in the form of *electrochemical impulses*; these constitute the 'language' of the NS.

5) Neurons are of three main kinds: (i) *sensory* (or afferent), which carry information from the sense organs to the CNS; (ii) *motor* (or efferent) which carry information from the CNS to the muscles and glands; and (iii) *interneurons* (or connector), which connect neurons to other neurons and integrate the activities of sensory and motor neurons. Interneurons are the most numerous and constitute about 97 per cent of the total number of neurons in the CNS, which is the only part of the NS in which they are found.

6) Although no two neurons are identical, most share the same basic structure and they work in essentially the same way. Figure 4.2 shows a typical motor neuron.

The *cell body* (or soma) houses the nucleus (which contains the genetic code), the cytoplasm (which feeds the nucleus) and the other structures common to all living cells. The *dendrites* branch out from the cell body; it is through the dendrites that the neuron makes electrochemical contact with other neurons, by *receiving* incoming signals from neighbouring

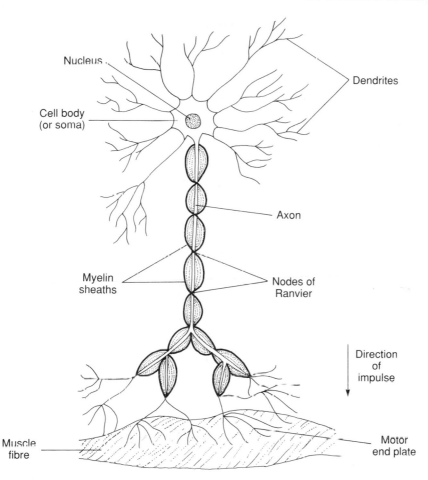

Figure 4.2 A typical motor neuron

Nucleus

Cell body (or soma)

Dendrites

Axon

Myelin sheaths

Nodes of Ranvier

Direction of impulse

Muscle fibre

Motor end plate

neurons. The *axon* is a thin cylinder of protoplasm, which projects away from the cell body and carries the signals received by the dendrites to other neurons. The *myelin sheath* is a white, fatty substance, which insulates the axon and speeds up the rate of conduction of signals down the axon and towards the *terminal buttons* (or boutons, or synaptic knobs). The myelin sheath is not continuous but is interrupted by the *Nodes of Ranvier* (see p. 76).

As Figure 4.3 shows, the terminal buttons house a number of tiny sacs or *synaptic vesicles*, which contain between 10 and 100,000 molecules of a chemical messenger, called a *neurotransmitter*. When an electrochemical impulse has passed down the axon it arrives at a terminal button and stimulates the vesicles to discharge their contents into the minute gap between the end of the terminal button (the *presynaptic membrane*) and the dendrite of the receiving neuron (the *postsynaptic membrane*) called the *synaptic cleft* (or gap).

The neurotransmitter molecules cross the synaptic gap and combine with special receptor sites in the post-synaptic membrane of the dendrite of the receiving neuron. The term '*synapse*', therefore, refers to the junction between neurons (there is no actual physical contact between them) at which signals are passed from a sending to a recipient neuron through the release of neurotransmitters.

However, some neurons use a form of direct electrical influence (these

Figure 4.3 *The synapse*

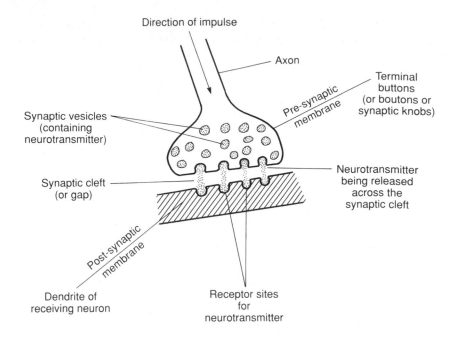

'electrotonic' synapses are not well understood) and synapses are sometimes found between dendrite and dendrite, axon and cell body and between axon and axon. However, the most common arrangement is for neurons to interconnect at synapses where a form of chemical communication is used (Iversen, 1979).

7)   The electrochemical signal which passes down the axon is called an *action potential*. Before the action potential occurs, an inactive neuron contains positively charged *potassium* (K^+) ions (electrically charged potassium atoms) and large, negatively charged protein molecules. Outside the neuron, in the surrounding fluid, there are concentrations of positively charged *sodium* ions (Na^+) and negatively charged *chloride* ions (Cl^-). The large, negatively charged, protein ions are trapped inside the neuron, while the positively charged sodium ions are kept out by the action of the sodium–potassium pumps in the cell membrane, which allow potassium (and chloride) ions to move in and out fairly freely.

The overall effect of this uneven distribution of ions is that the *inside* of the cell is electrically *negative* relative to the outside (by about 70 millivolts). The neuron is said to be *impermeable* to the positively charged sodium ions; this situation describes its resting state or *resting potential*.

When an action potential occurs, the inside of the neuron momentarily changes from negative to positive (+ 40 millivolts), the sodium channels are opened (for 1 millisecond) and sodium ions flood into the neuron (it is now permeable to sodium ions). This sets off a chain reaction, whereby the sodium channels open at adjacent membrane sites all the way down the axon. But almost as soon as the sodium channels are opened, they close again and potassium channels are opened instead, allowing potassium ions *out* through the membrane and restoring the negative resting potential.

Because the myelin sheath is not continuous but segmented (so that at the *Nodes of Ranvier* the axon is actually exposed), the action potential jumps from one node to another down the axon; this is called *saltatory conduction* and is actually faster than if the sheaths were continuous (see Fig. 4.2.)

8) Some synapses are *excitatory* (they 'instruct' the receiving neuron to 'fire', ie to conduct an action potential) while others are *inhibitory* (they 'instruct' the receiving neuron *not* to 'fire'). Because each neuron may have between 1000 and 10,000 synapses, some of which will be excitatory and some inhibitory, the 'decision' to fire or not to fire will depend on the *combined* effect of all its receiving synapses; if enough excitatory synapses are active, their combined effect may add up to exceed the threshold for firing of the receiving neuron (this is called *summation*).

9) Inhibitory synapses are important because they help control the spread of excitation through the highly interconnected NS and so keep activity channelled in appropriate networks or 'circuits'; epileptic seizures or fits, for example, may be caused by excitation of many different brain circuits at the same time and, if it were not for inhibition, we might all be having seizures much of the time.

10) The stimulus to the neuron must be intense enough to produce an action potential, that is, it must exceed the *threshold of response*, but once this has been passed, it travels, at the same speed, to the end of the axon. So an impulse is either present or absent (the *all-or-none rule*).

11) Action potentials are all of the same strength (amplitude), so the intensity of the stimulus is measured by:

(a) The *frequency* of firing, whereby the stronger the stimulus, the more often the neuron will fire (a *very* strong stimulus producing a volley of impulses).
(b) The *number* of neurons stimulated, whereby the stronger the stimulus, the greater the number of neurons stimulated.

12) However strong the stimulus, there is always a very short interval after each firing (one or two milliseconds) during which no further impulse can pass; this is the *absolute refractory period*. This is followed by a *relative refractory period*; the stronger the stimulus, the shorter the interval between the absolute refractory period and the next impulse.

13) Neurons vary considerably in size; for example, a neuron in the spinal cord may have an axon two or three feet long, running from the tip of the spine down to the big toe, while in the brain, neurons are only a few one-thousandths of an inch long.

14) Axons of motor neurons which terminate in muscles end in a series of branches, tipped by motor end plates, each of which is attached to a single muscle fibre; impulses at the motor end plate cause the muscle to contract (eg the arm is raised).

15) A *nerve* is a bundle of elongated axons belonging to hundreds or thousands of neurons. Nerves spread out to every part of the body and connect with sense receptors, skin, muscles and internal organs. Twelve pairs of *cranial nerves* leave the brain through holes in the skull and 31 pairs of *spinal nerves* leave the spinal cord through the vertebrae; together, they constitute the nerves of the peripheral nervous system (PNS) (see Fig. 4.9).

Nerves are usually large enough to be seen with the naked eye, while neurons can only be seen with the help of a powerful microscope.

16) What makes a synapse either excitatory or inhibitory is the particular *neurotransmitter(s)* contained within the vesicles of the synaptic button. As we have seen, neurotransmitter molecules cross the synaptic cleft and then attach themselves to specific receptor sites in the post-synaptic membrane; these sites actually consist of large protein molecules. A region on the surface of the receptor site is precisely tailored to match the shape of the transmitter molecule (in a lock-and-key fashion). The effect of the transmitter is brought to an end either by *deactivation* (where it is destroyed by special enzymes) or by *re-uptake* (where it is pumped back into the pre-synaptic axon, either for destruction or recycling).

According to Iversen (1979) and others there are at least thirty different neurotransmitters in the brain, each with its specific excitatory or inhibitory effect on certain neurons; the various chemicals are localized in specific groups of neurons and pathways and are not randomly distributed throughout the brain. Some of the major transmitters and their effects are shown in Table 4.1.

There is some evidence that more than one kind of transmitter may be released from the same synaptic button depending on the pattern of action potentials reaching it (Lloyd et al, 1984).

A distinction is sometimes made between: (i) *neurotransmitters* which have a fairly direct influence on receiving neurons; and (ii) *neuromodulators*, which 'tune' or 'prime' neurons so that they will respond in a particular way to later stimulation by a neurotransmitter.

Included among this group of neuromodulators are certain neuropeptides (which are included in Table 4.1), notably the *encephalins* ('in the head') and the *endorphins* ('morphine-within'), which are also known as *optoids* because functionally they resemble the opium drugs morphine, heroin and opium itself.

Morphine is commonly used for the relief of severe, intractable pain and the discovery of 'opiate receptors' in the neurons strongly suggested that the brain creates its own powerful pain-killer; encephalins and endorphins seemed to fit the bill and they may work by interfering with the release of transmitters from the pre-synaptic membrane of neurons which transmit information about pain.

It is thought that they are released during acupuncture and hypnosis, producing a reduction in perceived pain, although pain-information probably still reaches the brain (as it is not the pain receptors which are directly influenced; see Chapter 5).

It is also believed that placebos ('dummy drugs') work by influencing the release of endorphins which may be important in the way in which animals deal with pain and stress.

Other neuromodulators are the *prostoglandins*, which cause long-term shifts in neuronal sensitivity (Lloyd et al, 1984); it is believed that a deficiency in prostoglandins may cause schizophrenia.

Other neuropeptides are found as *hormones*, including: (i) *vasopressin*, which is thought to play a role in memory; (ii) *corticosteroids* ('stress hormones') and *adrenocorticotrophic hormone* (ACTH), which are involved in stress reactions and emotional arousal (see Chapter 6); and (iii) *androgens* (male sex hormones), which regulate sex drive in both sexes (see the later section on the Endocrine System).

Table 4.1 *Major neurotransmitters and their effects*

NEUROTRANSMITTER	EFFECT ON RECEIVING NEURON	RELATED BEHAVIOUR
1. Acetylcholine (ACh)	Generally *excitatory* but can be *inhibitory*, depending on the type of receptor molecule involved	Voluntary movement of muscles, behavioural inhibition, drinking, memory
2. Noradrenaline (norepinephrine)	*Inhibitory* (in CNS) and *excitatory* (in ANS)	Wakefulness and arousal—behavioural and emotional, eating. Some forms of recurrent *depression* associated with low levels and *mania* with high levels
3. Dopamine	*Inhibitory* and *excitatory*	Voluntary movement, emotional arousal. *Parkinson's disease* caused by atrophy of dopamine-releasing neurons (which link the midbrain to the corpus striatum). *Schizophrenia* may be caused by over-activity of dopamine in the hypothalamus, limbic system and medial forebrain bundle which mediate emotion and thought. Abnormally high concentrations of dopamine and dopamine receptors in brains of deceased schizophrenics (Snyder, 1980) (see Chapter 30)
4. Serotonin	*Inhibitory* and *excitatory*	Sleep, temperature regulation
5. GABA (gamma-amino butyric acid)	*Inhibitory* It is the most common inhibitor in the CNS (up to one-third of all the brain's synaptic buttons) and is found in all parts of the CNS	Motor behaviour. The inherited disease *Huntington's chorea* may result from degeneration of GABA cells in the corpus striatum which is involved in motor control
6. Glycine	*Inhibitory* Found in the spinal cord	Spinal reflexes and other motor behaviour
7. Glutamate	*Excitatory*	Unknown
8. Aspartate	*Excitatory*	Unknown
9. Peptides	*Inhibitory* and *excitatory*	Sensory transmission, especially pain

(Items 2–4, Noradrenaline, Dopamine and Serotonin, are bracketed together as Monoamine transmitters.)

17)   The *effect* of *drugs* on *behaviour* is mediated by their effect on neurotransmitters. The drugs which psychologists are particularly interested in are *psychoactive* drugs, those which produce mental effects ('active' in the 'psyche') and directly alter the level of activity in one or more brain systems (either increasing or decreasing it). Table 4.2

Table 4.2 The effect of major psychoactive drugs on neurotransmitters, physiology, mood and behaviour

DRUG	NEUROTRANS-MITTERS AFFECTED	EFFECTS ON PHYSIOLOGY, MOOD AND BEHAVIOUR
1. Curare (used by South American Indians to poison their arrows)	Acetylcholine (ACh) prevented from acting because the curare molecules cover up the post-synaptic receptor sites of the muscle neurons	Fatal muscular paralysis. The brain is not affected—but all other muscles, including respiratory muscles, are paralysed
2. Botulinum toxin (present in improperly-prepared food)	Acetylcholine (ACh)	Paralysis which is often fatal (=botulism)
3. Nerve gases and insecticides	Acetylcholine (ACh)	Fatal muscular paralysis
4. *Amphetamines* ('speed or uppers') eg Benzedrine Dexedrine Methedrine Drinamyl ('Purple Hearts')	Dopamine and noradrenaline— their re-uptake is blocked, making them effective for longer	Seem to act more as psychomotor *stimulants* than anti-depressants (which is how they are often prescribed). Increase alertness, counteract fatigue and lethargy and produce feelings of confidence and decisiveness. Suppress appetite (through stimulation of Reticular Activating System which controls overall level of arousal and 'mimicking' the sympathetic branch of the ANS). But high doses can induce symptoms identical with paranoid schizophrenia
5. *Antidepressants* *A. Tricyclics* imipramine (Tofranil) amitriptyline (Tryptizol)	Work by blocking the breakdown of *noradrenaline* and *serotonin*	Feeling of euphoria. They block rapid eye movement (REM) sleep (see Chapter 5)
B. Monoamine oxidase (MAO) Inhibitors phenelzine (Nardil) tranylcypromine (Parnate)	These inhibit the enzyme *Monoamine oxidase* (MAO) which breaks down the *monoamine transmitters* subsequent to their release	
6. L-dopa	Dopamine The body converts the drug into dopamine	Prescribed for patients with Parkinson's disease. Can sometimes produce symptoms of schizophrenia

Table 4.2 Continued

DRUG	NEUROTRANS-MITTERS AFFECTED	EFFECTS ON PHYSIOLOGY, MOOD AND BEHAVIOUR
7. *Major tranquillizers* phenothiazines ('anti-schizophrenic drugs') chlorpromazine (Largactil or Thorazine) trifluoperazine (Stelazine)	Dopamine They bind to dopamine receptor sites (they are dopamine-antagonists) and so prevent dopamine from reaching those receptor sites	Reduce schizophrenic—and other psychotic—symptoms. The Reticular Activating System is *not* affected, nor the Electroencephalogram (EEG). But electrical activity in hypothalamus and limbic system is suppressed
8. *Minor tranquillizers* benzodiazepines ('anti-anxiety drugs' or anxiolytic sedatives) diazepam (Valium) chlordiazepoxide (Librium) meprobamate (Miltown)	Inosine (which might be a neurotransmitter modulator) binds with the same receptor sites as these drugs. It could be the body's own anxiety reliever. GABA	A calming effect, reducing anxiety and tension without depressing the level of alertness. Valium prescribed to patients with Huntington's Chorea may help by stimulating GABA receptors
9. *Hallucinogenic drugs* LSD (lysergic acid diethylamide) psilocybin ('magic mushroom')	Structurally similar to serotonin	Produce feelings of calm, contentment, inner peace, increased appetite and possible disorientation (cannabis); illusions, hallucinations, distortions of time perception and contact with 'reality' (LSD)
Mescaline	Structurally similar to noradrenaline and dopamine	
Cannabis (marijuana, hashish, pot, weed, grass, etc.)	They seem to work by blocking the effects of *serotonin*, which usually inhibits thought processes and emotions	Overdoses of LSD can cause psychotic reactions and could kill
Phencyclidine (PCP or 'Angel Dust')	May attach themselves to serotonin receptor sites, preventing the sites from receiving it. The result is that consciousness	LSD, *psilocybin* and *mescaline* are also referred to a 'psychedelics'. All hallucinogenic drugs are also called 'psychotomimetic', which means 'imitation of psychosis', because some produce effects very similar to schizophrenia

Table 4.2 Continued	DRUG	NEUROTRANS-MITTERS AFFECTED	EFFECTS ON PHYSIOLOGY, MOOD AND BEHAVIOUR
		becomes flooded with remote associations and feelings	
	10. *Sedatives (or depressants)* barbiturates (Luminal—phenobarbitone Amytal—amylobarbitone Nembutal, Seconal, Pentothal) alcohol	In large quantities these are sleep-inducers (*hypnotics*) and may act in a similar way to certain anaesthetics. In smaller doses, they act more like (minor) tranquillizers. Combined with alcohol, they can be fatal	In small amounts, barbiturates and alcohol can act as stimulants by reducing anxiety and reducing inhibitions. Larger quantities induce sedation, stupor (sleep), anaesthesia, loss of consciousness and death (Ornstein, 1977). Larger amounts may cause people to become belligerent and abusive, disorientated and confused and may experience hallucinations. Addicts who are withdrawn from alcohol often suffer 'delirium tremens' (the D.T.s) which can be fatal
	Opiates (narcotics) (codeine, morphine, heroin)	Opium comes from the juice of certain types of poppy, its active ingredients are *codeine* and *morphine*. Morphine is stronger than codeine and *heroin* (derived from morphine) is the strongest narcotic of all. Neural tissue is eventually destroyed after prolonged use of heroin and the *endorphins* are under-produced	At first heroin produces intense pleasure but repeated use produces *tolerance*—ie ever-increasing amounts must be taken to achieve the same effect. Tolerance soon gives way to physical and psychological *dependence*, otherwise known as *addiction*
	11. *Stimulants* caffeine nicotine cocaine	Caffeine is found in tea and coffee and many carbonated drinks, particularly colas	*Nicotine* may have a relaxing or stimulating effect, depending on circumstances. It is addictive. Effects of *cocaine* similar to those of amphetamines but former is addictive

summarizes the effects on mood and behaviour of some major drugs, together with effects on neurotransmitters.

THE CENTRAL NERVOUS SYSTEM (CNS)

METHODS OF STUDYING THE BRAIN

How do we Know What we Know?

1) One of the earliest methods used to study the CNS was the study of patients who had suffered brain damage, either as the result of an accident or a stroke or tumour. A famous and early use of this method led to the discovery of a specialized area of the brain for speech.

In 1869, a French physician, Paul Broca, reviewed evidence from a number of cases of brain damage and concluded that injury to a certain part of the left cerebral hemisphere caused the patient's speech to become slow and laboured but that the ability to understand speech was almost completely unaffected. What is now called *Broca's Area* seems to control the ability to *produce* speech and damage to it causes *motor* (or expressive) *aphasia*.

In 1874, Carl Wernicke reported that injury to a different part of the left hemisphere caused *receptive aphasia*, that is, the inability to *understand* speech (one's own or someone else's).

These *clinical* studies of the brain have normally been conducted in parallel with *anatomical* studies, usually during the course of postmortems where human beings are involved. Studying *structure* and *function* in a complementary way is essential for an adequate understanding of such a complex organ as the brain.

2) Where *animal experiments* are concerned (as in other areas of psychology), parts of the brain may be *surgically removed* (either through cutting or burning out with electrodes—a method called *ablation*) or an area of the brain may be damaged (rather than removed), in which case a *lesion* is produced. An early user of the first method was Karl Lashley, working with rats in the 1920s, and it has been used extensively to study the role of the brain in eating (see Chapter 6).

One major exception to the rule that the subjects in these surgical experiments are always animals is *split-brain* patients, who have undergone surgery for epilepsy when all other treatments have failed. The surgery involves cutting the tissue which connects the two halves of the brain (the corpus callosum) and Roger Sperry and his colleagues in the 1960s and 1970s made full use of the unique opportunity to study these 'split brains'. Their work will be discussed in detail later in the chapter (see p. 96).

3) Instead of surgically removing or damaging the brain, it can be *stimulated*, either chemically (using micro-pipettes to drop transmitter substances onto specific areas of the brain) or, more commonly, electrically, using *micro-electrodes*, whereby precise locations can be stimulated. Again, where humans are the subjects, they are usually already undergoing surgery for a brain tumour or some other abnormality (such as epilepsy) and the neurosurgeon takes advantage of the fact that the patient is conscious, alert and able to report memories, sensations and so on produced by the stimulation. Penfield pioneered this kind of research in the 1950s.

4) *Microelectrodes* are also used to *record* the electrical activity in individual neurons when the subject (usually a cat or monkey) is

presented with various kinds of stimuli. This method was used by Hubel and Wiesel in the 1960s to study visual feature detectors (see Chapters 8 and 9).

5) The electrical activity of the brain can also be recorded from the outside by fitting electrodes to the scalp. The activity can be traced on paper and typical brainwave patterns associated with various states of arousal have been found. This is the *electroencephalogram* (EEG), which records action potentials for large groups of neurons and has been used extensively in the study of states of consciousness, including sleep (see Chapter 5).

A brief change in the EEG may be produced by the presentation of a single stimulus but the effect may well be lost (or obscured) in the overall pattern of waves. However, if the stimulus is presented repeatedly, and the results averaged by a computer, other waves cancel out and the evoked response can be detected. This technique is known as the *Average Evoked Potential* and has shown, for example, that an identical visual stimulus yields different AEPs according to the meaning the subject attaches to it.

6) A relatively recent method of studying the CNS involves *radio-active labelling*, which takes advantage of the brain's flexible use of blood-carried oxygen. A radioactive isotope is added to the blood, causing low levels of radioactivity, which increase as greater blood flow occurs to more active areas of the brain. A scanner next to the head feeds radiation readings to a computer, which produces a coloured map of the most and least active brain regions; different regions change colour as the person attempts a variety of tasks or is presented with a variety of stimuli.

7) Another use of computers is the CAT scan (Computerized Axial Tomography). A moving X-ray beam takes pictures from different positions around the head and these are converted by the computer into 'brain slices'—apparent cross-sections of the brain. CAT scanning is used primarily for the detection and diagnosis of brain injury and disease but is not as effecient as the more recent PET (Positron Emission Tomography), which uses the same computer-calculation approach as CAT but uses radiation for the information from which the brain slices are computed. A radioactive tracer is added to a substance used by the body (eg oxygen or glucose); as the marked substance is metabolized, PET shows the pattern of its use, for example, more or less use of glucose could indicate a tumour, and changes are revealed when the eyes are opened or closed.

More recently still, Nuclear Magnetic Resonance imaging (NMR; or magnetic resonance imaging, MRI; Schulman, 1983) applies a magnetic field and measures its effects on the rotation of atomic nuclei of some element in the body; again, a computerized cross-sectional image is produced (Fig. 4.4). So far only hydrogen nuclei have been used.

What can These Methods Tell Us?

As psychologists, of course, we must not lose sight of the significance of these methods—we are not interested in the brain for its own sake (as fascinating as this may be) but for what it can tell us about the control of psychological functions and abilities, both subjective and behavioural. It

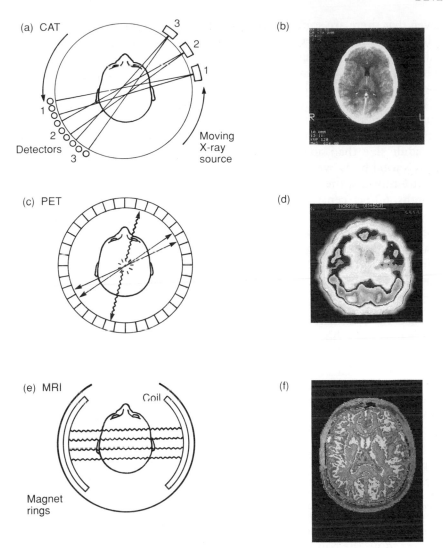

Figure 4.4 Non-invasive techniques (a), (c) and (e) used to study detailed sections of the living human brain (b), (d) and (f)

is tempting to infer that if damage to (or loss of) a particular brain area is associated with the loss of (or reduction in) a particular ability, that part of the brain normally controls that ability; unfortunately, there are other possibilities. For example, the damaged area might itself be controlled by a different (undamaged) area or the damage may have disrupted the normal functioning of nearby, or related, intact areas. We shall return to some of these issues later when we discuss split-brain patients.

DEVELOPMENT OF THE BRAIN

One of the most remarkable things about the human brain is not its size or even the number of neurons of which it is composed, but rather the staggering complexity of the *interconnections* between the neurons;

given that there are somewhere between 8 to 10 billion neurons, each of which may have between 1000 and 10,000 synaptic connections with other neurons, it has been estimated that there are more possible ways in which the neurons of a single human brain can be interconnected than there are atoms in the known universe!

It is the development of synaptic connections which accounts for much of the increase in brain weight after birth. At birth, the baby has almost its full complement of neurons and the brain is closer at birth to its adult size than any other organ. (It represents 10 per cent of the baby's total body weight compared with 2 per cent of the adult's.)

At 6 months, the brain is already half its eventual adult weight; at 12 months, 60 per cent; at 5 years, 90 per cent and at 10 years 95 per cent. The increase in weight is almost 200 per cent in the first three years and the brain reaches its maximum weight by about 20 years. The average male adult brain weighs 1375 grammes (about 3 pounds) and the average female brain weighs 1250 grammes. While the major development before birth is the growth of neurons, brain growth after birth is the result of four major changes:

(a) We have already mentioned the growth of *synaptic* connections between neighbouring neurons. The continued growth or survival of any given neuron in fact depends on the establishment of synaptic connections with other neurons, and the death of individual neurons is extremely common during brain development. Indeed, the period of *peak* development in any one brain area is marked by the *greatest* rate of cell death in that area that will occur during the lifetime of the organism, a much higher rate than is associated with ageing, for example (see Chapter 24).
(b) The neurons do actually increase in *size* (but not in number).
(c) *Glial* cells develop (and are ten times more numerous than neurons); they 'pad out' the space in between neurons and supply them with vital nutrients.
(d) *Myelin sheaths* grow around the axons to insulate the neuron and speed up the conduction of action potentials.

Once fully grown, the brain loses weight by about 1 gramme each year.

If it were the absolute size of brains which determined level of intelligence, then humans would certainly be surpassed by many species, and even if we take *brain size:body size* ratio, we would still find that house mice, porpoises, tree shrews and squirrel monkeys come higher in the intelligence league than ourselves.

Clearly, it is the *kind* of brain which is important, and what seems to be unique about the human brain is the proportion of it which is *not* devoted to particular physical and psychological functions and which is, therefore, 'free' to facilitate our intelligence, our general ability to think, reason, use language and learn.

THE MAJOR STRUCTURES AND FUNCTIONS OF THE BRAIN

The brain is normally subdivided into three: (i) the forebrain; (ii) the midbrain; and (iii) the hindbrain. We shall discuss them in this order.

1. *THE FOREBRAIN*

The Cerebral Hemispheres (or Cerebrum)

The cerebral hemispheres are the two largest structures at the top of the brain which enfold (and, therefore, conceal from view) most other brain structures—if you were to remove an intact brain, its appearance would be dominated by the massive hemispheres, with just the cerebellum showing at the back (as in Fig. 4.5).

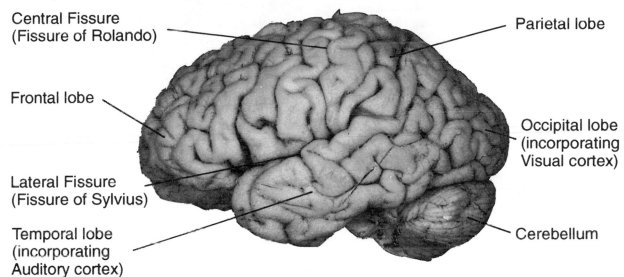

Central Fissure (Fissure of Rolando)

Parietal lobe

Frontal lobe

Occipital lobe (incorporating Visual cortex)

Lateral Fissure (Fissure of Sylvius)

Temporal lobe (incorporating Auditory cortex)

Cerebellum

Figure 4.5 Lateral (side-on) view of the human brain (left cerebral hemisphere)

The top layer of the cerebrum (about 1 cm at its deepest) is the *cerebral cortex* (usually just called 'cortex', which means 'bark'); it is highly convoluted (wrinkled; see Fig. 4.5), which is necessary in order to pack its $2\frac{1}{2}$ square-foot surface area into the relatively small space inside the cranium.

The cortex is pinkish-grey in colour (hence 'grey matter') but below it the cerebrum consists of much thicker white matter, which consists of myelinated axons (the cortex consists of cell bodies).

There is a large crevice running along the cerebrum from front to back (the *longitudinal fissure* or *sulcus*), which divides the two hemispheres, although they are connected further down by a dense mass of commissural ('joining') fibres called the *corpus callosum* (or 'hard body').

There are two other natural dividing lines in each hemisphere: (i) the *lateral fissure* (or fissure of Sylvius); and (ii) the *central fissure* (or fissure of Rolando). The lateral fissure separates the *temporal lobe* from the *frontal lobe* (anteriorly) and from the *parietal lobe* (posteriorly), while the central fissure separates the frontal and parietal lobes. The *occipital lobe* is situated behind the parietal lobe and is at the back of the head (see Fig. 4.5). (Remember, this division of the cortex into four lobes—named after the bones beneath which they lie—is a feature of *both* hemispheres, which are mirror-images of each other.)

The *visual cortex* is found in the occipital lobe (Fig. 4.6), the *auditory cortex* in the temporal lobe, the *somatosensory* (or body-sense) *cortex* in the parietal lobe and the *motor cortex* in the frontal lobe (see Chapter 8).

The somatosensory cortex and motor cortex are perhaps the most well-defined areas and both show *contralateral control*, that is, areas in

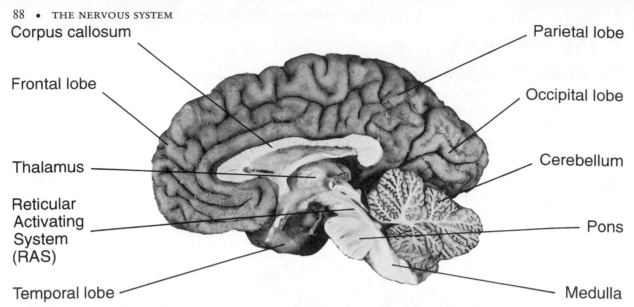

Corpus callosum

Frontal lobe

Thalamus

Reticular
Activating
System
(RAS)

Temporal lobe

Parietal lobe

Occipital lobe

Cerebellum

Pons

Medulla

Figure 4.6 Front-to-back cross-section of the right cerebral hemisphere

the *right* hemisphere receive information from and are concerned with the activities of the *left* side of the body—and vice versa. The crossing over takes place in the medulla (part of the brain stem) and is called *corticospinal decussation*. These areas represent the body in an upside-down fashion, so information from the feet, for example, is received by neurons at the top of the area.

Figure 4.7 Basal (from underneath) view of the human brain

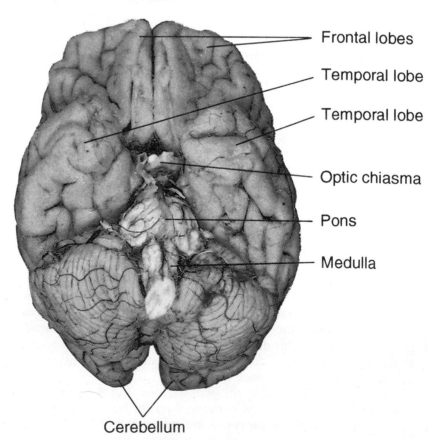

Frontal lobes

Temporal lobe

Temporal lobe

Optic chiasma

Pons

Medulla

Cerebellum

Furthermore, the *amount* of cortex taken up with the motor activities of, or sensory information from, different parts of the body is associated *not* with the size of that body part but with the degree of precise motor control or the sensitivity of that part of the body. So fingers, for example, have much more cortex devoted to them than the trunk in the motor cortex and the lips have a very large representation in the somatosensory cortex (Fig. 4.8).

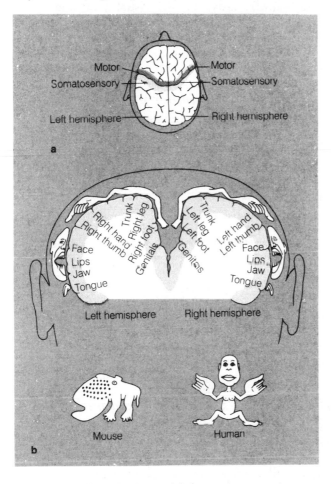

Figure 4.8 Animunculi and homunculi showing how much cortical tissue is devoted to each body area. The mouse explores with its nose and each whisker has its own cortical area. We can use our hands for sensing, although we normally rely more on vision. The large face of the homunculus reflects the large cortical areas necessary for the control of speech

Broca's area is found in the frontal lobe and Wernicke's area borders the temporal and parietal lobes but in the *left* hemisphere only. (We shall say more about this under *localization* of brain function, see p. 93.)

About three quarters of the cortex does not have an obvious sensory or motor function and is known as the *association cortex*; this is where the 'higher mental functions' (cognition)—thinking, reasoning, learning, etc.—probably 'occur' but, except for certain aspects of memory and perception, these aspects of human intelligence have resisted attempts to localize them. However, there is no doubt that the cortex is not necessary for biological survival (this is controlled by various *sub-cortical* structures), as some species do not have one to begin with (eg birds) and in those that do, surgical removal does not prevent the animal from displaying a wide range of behaviour—although it becomes much more automatic and stereotyped. The human brain has a greater proportion of association cortex than any other species.

According to Suomi (1982), what makes the cortex of special interest to the developmental psychobiologist is: (i) that it is the last part of the brain to stop growing and differentiating; (ii) it undergoes greater structural change and transformation *after* birth than any other part of the brain; and (iii) a greater number of neural interconnections are made *after* birth than during the pre-natal period.

The sequence of cortical development seems to be: (i) the motor area; (ii) the somatosensory area; (iii) the visual area; and (iv) the auditory area. It is interesting to try to relate this sequence to the nature–nurture debate on perception (see Chapter 10) and Piaget's theory of cognitive development, in which sensory-motor activity plays such a vital part (see Chapter 25).

The Thalamus ('Deep Chamber')

There are actually two thalami, situated deep in the forebrain (between the brain-stem and the cerebral hemispheres). Each is an egg-shaped mass of grey matter and represents a crucial link between the cerebrum and the sense organs. *All* sensory signals pass through the thalamus, which serves as a relay station or major integrator of information flowing in from the sense organs to the cortex; each contains nuclei which are specialized to handle particular types of signal:

(i)   the *ventrobasal complex*, which takes information fed in from the body via the spinal cord;
(ii) the *lateral geniculate* ('bent') *body* (LGB), which processes visual information (see Chapter 8);
(iii) the *medial geniculate body*, which processes auditory information (see Chapter 8).

The thalamus also receives information from the cortex, mainly dealing with complex limb movements, and these are directed to the cerebellum. Another part of the thalamus plays a part in sleep and waking.

The Hypothalamus ('Under the Thalamus')

For its size (about the size of the tip of your index finger) the hypothalamus is a remarkable and extremely important part of the brain. It plays a major part in *homeostasis* (control of the body's internal environment) and *motivation*, including eating and drinking, sexual behaviour and emotional arousal.

Seven areas can be identified, each with its own special function: (i) *posterior*, sex drive; (ii) *anterior*, water balance; (iii) *supraoptic*, also water balance; (iv) *presupraoptic*, heat control; (v) *ventromedial*, hunger; (vi) *dorsomedial*, aggression; and (vii) *dorsal*, pleasure. (The role of the hypothalamus, particularly in relation to hunger and eating, is discussed in detail in Chapter 6.)

The hypothalamus works basically in two ways:

(i)   by sending electrochemical signals to the entire autonomic nervous system (ANS: Fig. 4.1), so that it represents a major link between the CNS and the ANS;
(ii) by influencing the *pituitary gland*, to which it is connected by a network of blood vessels and neurons.

The pituitary gland is situated in the brain, just below and to one side of the hypothalamus, but it is not part of the CNS; it is in fact part of the *endocrine* (hormonal) *system*, which we shall discuss later in the chapter (and see Chapter 6).

Basal Ganglia ('Nerve Knots')

These are embedded in the mass of white matter of each cerebral hemisphere and are themselves small areas of grey matter, in fact comprising a number of smaller structures: (i) the *corpus striatum* ('striped body'), composed of the lentiform nucleus and caudate nucleus; (ii) the *amygdala* ('almond'); and (iii) the *substantia nigra*. These structures are closely linked to the thalamus and they seem to play a part in muscle tone and posture by integrating and co-ordinating the main voluntary muscle movements, which are the concern of the great descending motor pathway (the *pyramidal system*). Information from the cortex is relayed to the brain stem and cerebellum.

The Limbic System ('Bordering')

This is not a separate structure but comprises a number of highly interrelated structures which, when seen from the side, seem to nest inside each other, encircling the brain-stem in a 'wishbone'.

The major structures are: (i) the thalamus; (ii) hypothalamus; (iii) mamillary body; (iv) anterior commissure; (v) septum pellucidum; (vi) cingulate gyrus; (vii) hippocampus; (viii) amygdala; (ix) fornix; and (x) olfactory bulb.

The human limbic system is very similar to that of primitive mammals and so is often called 'the old mammalian brain'. It is also sometimes called the 'nose brain' because much of its development seems to have been related to the olfactory sense (and, of course, the olfactory bulb is one of its components).

It is closely involved with behaviours which satisfy certain motivational and emotional needs, including feeding, fighting, escape and mating, and its role in relation to aggression is discussed in Chapter 16.

The hippocampus is involved in memory; someone whose hippocampus is damaged is very easily distracted and they will be unable to carry out an intended sequence of actions (eg making a cup of tea) because they have forgotten what they had planned to do (see Chapter 12).

The limbic system as a whole serves as a meeting place between the cortex (or 'neocortex', in evolutionary terms the most recent part of the brain to have developed) and older parts of the brain, such as the hypothalamus. From the cortex it receives interpreted information about the world and from the hypothalamus information about the body's internal state; these are integrated and the 'conclusions' are fed back to the cortex and to the older, sub-cortical areas.

2. THE MIDBRAIN

This is really an extension of the brain stem and connects the forebrain to the spinal cord. The main structure is the *Reticular Activating System* (RAS), which ascends from the spinal cord to the forebrain carrying mainly sensory information (the ARAS) and descends from the forebrain to the spinal cord carrying mainly motor information.

The ARAS is vitally important in maintaining our general level of arousal or alertness (and is often called the 'consciousness switch') and plays an important part (but by no means the only one) in the sleep–waking cycle (see Chapter 5). It also plays a part in selective attention and, although it responds unselectively to all kinds of stimulation, it helps to screen extraneous sensory information by, for example, controlling *habituation* to constant sources of stimulation and making us alert and responsive mainly to *changes* in stimulation (see Chapter 11).

Sleeping parents who keep 'one ear open' for the baby who might start to cry are relying on their ARAS to let only very important sensory signals through, so it acts as a kind of sentry for the cortex. Damage can induce a coma-like state of sleep.

The midbrain also contains important centres for visual and auditory reflexes, including the *orienting reflex*, a general response to a novel stimulus. Birds which sight, track and capture prey in flight have very prominent and bulging areas in their midbrain and bats have a very prominent auditory area in the midbrain.

3. *THE HINDBRAIN*

Cerebellum ('Little Brain')

Like the cerebrum, the cerebellum consists of two halves, or hemispheres, and is even more convoluted than the cortex. It synthesizes all sensory information from vision, the inner ear (which controls balance), the muscles and the joints and can calculate the movements required in a particular sequence of behaviour. So the cerebellum plays a vital role in the co-ordination of voluntary (skeletal) muscle activity, balance and fine movements (such as reaching for things). Motor commands which originate in higher brain centres are processed here before transmission to the muscles.

Damage to the cerebellum can cause hand tremors, drunken movements and loss of balance. The inability to reach for objects normally (*ataxia*) and hand tremors are quite common amongst the elderly.

The cerebellum also controls the intricate movements involved in the swimming of a fish, the flying of a bird, playing a musical instrument or driving a car. Once learned, complex movements such as are involved in signing our name, picking up a glass, walking, and even talking, seem to be 'programmed' into the cerebellum, so that we can do them 'automatically', without having to think consciously about what we are doing; the cerebellum acts like an 'automatic pilot' inside the brain.

The cerebellum accounts for about 11 per cent of the entire brain weight and only the cerebrum is larger. Its grey matter in fact consists of three layers of cells, the middle layer of which—the *purkinje* cells—can link each synapse with up to 100,000 other neurons, more than any other kind of brain cell.

The Pons ('Bridge')

This is a bulge of white matter which connects the two halves of the cerebellum. It is an important connection between the midbrain and the medulla and is vital in integrating the movements of the two sides of the body. Four of the twelve cranial nerves (which originate in the brain) have their nuclei ('relay stations') here, including the large trigeminal nerve. It is the middle portion of the brain stem.

The Medulla Oblongata ('Rather Long Marrow')

This is a fibrous section of the lower brain stem (about 2 cm long) and is really a thick extension of the spinal cord. In evolutionary terms, it is the oldest part of the brain and it is the site of the crossing-over of the major nerve tracts coming up from the spinal cord and coming down from the brain. It contains vital reflex centres, which control breathing, cardiac function, swallowing, vomiting, coughing, chewing, salivation and facial movements.

The midbrain, pons and medulla together make up the *brain-stem*.

THE SPINAL CORD

About the thickness of a little finger, the spinal cord passes from the brain-stem down the whole length of the back and is encased in the vertebrae of the spine. The spinal cord is the main communication 'cable' between the brain (CNS) and the peripheral nervous system (PNS), providing the pathway between body and brain.

Messages enter and leave the spinal cord by means of 31 pairs of spinal nerves; each pair innervates a different and fairly specific part of the body and are 'mixed nerves', ie they contain both motor (carrying information from the nervous system to the muscles) and sensory (carrying information from the sensory receptors to the nervous system) neurons for most of their length. However, at the junction with the cord itself, the nerves divide into two roots—the *dorsal root* (towards the back of the body), which contains sensory neurons, and the *ventral root* (towards the front of the body), which contains motor neurons (Fig. 4.9).

The spinal cord constitutes a simplified model (compared with the brain) of a neurological system which receives sensory information, processes it and then delivers impulses to the muscles for the initiation and co-ordination of motor activity. The basic *functional* unit of the NS is the spinal reflex arc, for instance, the *knee-jerk reflex* involves just two kinds of neurons: a sensory neuron conveys information about stimulation of the patella tendon to the spinal cord and this information crosses a single synapse within the grey 'butterfly' (which runs inside the centre of the cord). This causes a motor neuron to stimulate the appropriate muscle groups in the leg, which causes the leg to shoot up in the air.

However, most spinal reflexes are more complex than this. For example, withdrawing your hand from a hot plate will involve an interneuron (as well as a sensory and motor neuron) and two synapses. Commonly, the experience of pain follows one or two seconds after you have withdrawn your hand—this is how long it takes for sensory information to reach the cortex.

THE LOCALIZATION OF BRAIN FUNCTION

So far we have said that the cerebral hemispheres: (i) are mirror-images of each other; (ii) both divide into four lobes; and (iii) that Broca's area and Wernicke's area (which deal with speech production and comprehension, respectively) appear only in the *left* hemisphere.

Figure 4.9 *The spinal cord and spinal nerves. (From Rosenzweig and Leiman, 1989)*

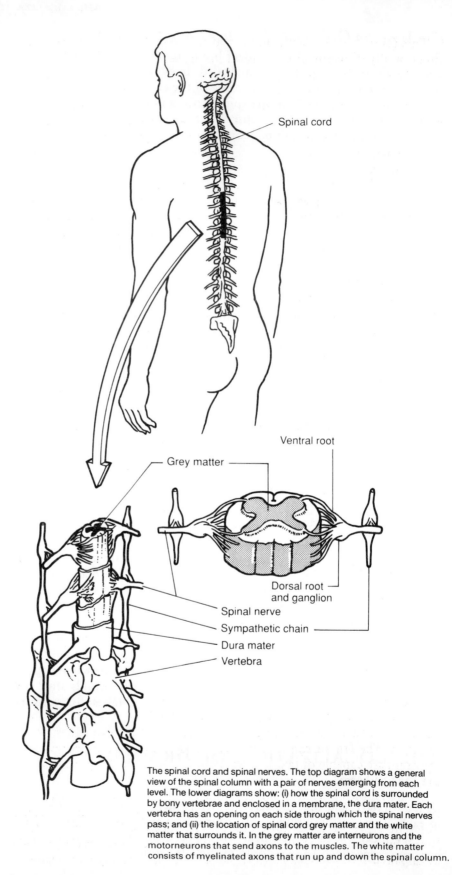

Spinal cord

Ventral root

Grey matter

Dorsal root and ganglion

Spinal nerve

Sympathetic chain

Dura mater

Vertebra

The spinal cord and spinal nerves. The top diagram shows a general view of the spinal column with a pair of nerves emerging from each level. The lower diagrams show: (i) how the spinal cord is surrounded by bony vertebrae and enclosed in a membrane, the dura mater. Each vertebra has an opening on each side through which the spinal nerves pass; and (ii) the location of spinal cord grey matter and the white matter that surrounds it. In the grey matter are interneurons and the motorneurons that send axons to the muscles. The white matter consists of myelinated axons that run up and down the spinal column.

This (and other evidence) has led to the view that the hemispheres are functionally different (*functional lateralization*) and much of the discussion has focused on language. From studies of stroke victims in particular it is generally agreed that for the majority of *right*-handed people their *left* hemisphere is *dominant* for speech (and language ability in general); someone who is paralysed down their *right* side must have suffered damage to the *left* hemisphere and, if they have also suffered *aphasia*, then we can infer that language is normally controlled by the *left* hemisphere.

One of the difficulties associated with generalizations in psychology (even with something as 'biological' as cerebral function) is the existence of individual differences. Some people seem to have much more lateralized brains than others; others have language more or less equally represented on both sides (*bilateral representation*) (Beaumont, 1988). As far as the left hemisphere being dominant for language, this seems to be true for 95 per cent of right-handed patients, while only 5 per cent had their right hemisphere dominant. But with left-handers, things are much less clear-cut: 75 per cent had their left hemisphere dominant, none had the right dominant but 25 per cent showed bilateral representation (based on a review by Satz (1979) of all studies between 1935–75; cited in Beaumont, 1988). Over and above this left–right handed difference, is the finding that women show less lateralization than men; for example, damage to one side will, on average, affect a woman's brain less than a male's. Similarly, damage to the right hemisphere will interfere with a man's spatial abilities more than a woman's. So, the left–right specialization is most prevalent in right-handed men (and not 'all people'! (Ornstein, 1986)) (see Chapter 23).

In the majority of right-handed people, is the dominance of the left hemisphere a built-in characteristic or is it modifiable?

According to Zaidel (1978), the two hemispheres are fairly equal up until about five years of age. In general, a child's brain is much more *plastic* (flexible) than an adult's (Rose, 1976); for example, in children up to three years, brain trauma produces similar effects regardless of which site is damaged. Provided the lesion is not too severe, or if it occurs on one side only, considerable recovery is possible—the corresponding area on the other side takes over the function of the damaged area and this seems to be especially true of speech.

This seems to support the conclusions of Lashley who (in the 1920s) studied the effects of brain destruction on rats' learning ability. His (1929) *law of mass action* states that the learning of difficult problems depends upon the *amount* of damage to the cortex and *not* on the position or site of the damage. So, the *greater* the cortical damage, the *greater* the learning difficulty, but Lashley could not find *specific* neural circuits related to the learning of, or memory for, particular types of problem. The *law* of *equipotentiality* states that corresponding parts of the brain are capable of taking over the function normally performed by the damaged area.

Similarly, the *principle* of *multiple control* maintains that any particular part of the brain is likely to be involved in the performance of many different types of behaviour. For example, rats with lesions in their lateral hypothalamus show deficits in certain learning situations, as well as impaired feeding. Conversely, the same behaviour (eg aggression or emotion) normally involves a number of brain sites and the logical conclusion of this seems to be that the brain functions as a complete unit, an integrated whole. (We shall return to this issue below.)

SPLIT-BRAIN PATIENTS: ONE BRAIN OR TWO? ONE MIND OR TWO?

Remember that split-brain patients have undergone surgery (normally in the treatment of epilepsy) to cut their corpus callosum, which normally joins the two hemispheres and allows an exchange of information from one to another. While the surgery may relieve the suffering, it has a major side-effect, namely, the two hemispheres become functionally separate, ie they act as two separate, independent brains.

Sperry (based on a number of studies in the 1960s and 1970s, for which he was awarded the Nobel Prize for Medicine in 1981) and Ornstein (1975) believe that split-brain studies reveal the 'true' nature of the two hemispheres, and that each embodies a different kind of consciousness (see Chapter 5).

In a typical experiment (Sperry, 1968), subjects sit in front of a screen with their hands free to handle objects that are behind the screen but which are obscured from sight by the screen. While fixating on a spot in the middle of the screen, a word (eg 'key') is flashed onto the *left* side of the screen for one-tenth of a second to ensure that the word is only 'seen' by the *right* hemisphere (see Fig. 4.10).

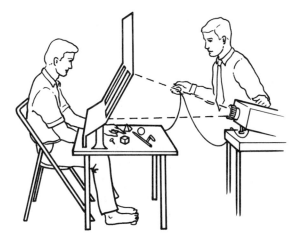

Figure 4.10 Apparatus for studying lateralization of visual, tactual, lingual and associated functions in the surgically separated hemispheres. (From Sperry, 1968)

If asked to pick out the key from a pile of objects with the *left* hand (still controlled by the *right* hemisphere), this can be done quite easily; however, the subject is unable to *say* what word appeared on the screen (because the *left* hemisphere did not receive the information from the right as it would in a normal subject). The subject literally does not know why they choose that object.

Again, a word (eg 'heart') is flashed on a screen, with 'he' to the left and 'art' to the right of the fixation point. If asked to *name* the word, subjects will say 'art' (because this is the portion of the word projected to the *left* hemisphere) but when asked to point with the left hand to one of two cards on which 'he' and 'art' are written, the left hand will point to 'he' (because this was the portion projected to the *right* hemisphere).

These examples show that the right hemisphere is not completely without language ability—otherwise subjects could not successfully point or select—but it clearly lacks the left hemisphere's ability to name and articulate what has been experienced. In the second example, both hemispheres are handicapped if information is not conveyed from one to the other—the whole word ('heart') is not perceived by either!

A similar but perhaps more dramatic example involved sets of photographs of different faces—a beautiful young female model, a podgy-cheeked boy, an old man and so on. Each photo was cut down the middle and the halves of two different faces were pasted together. They were then presented to subjects in such a way that the left side of the photo would only be visible to the right hemisphere and vice versa. So, for example, with a picture of an old man to the right and a young boy to the left, subjects were asked to *describe* what they had seen (the *left* hemisphere responding). They said 'an old man'. But if asked to *point* with their left hand to the complete photo of the person they had seen (the *right* hemisphere responding) they would point to the 'young boy'. It seems that two completely separate visual worlds can exist within the same head!

These and many more, equally dramatic, experiments led Sperry, Ornstein and others to conclude that each of the separated hemispheres has its own private sensations, perceptions, thoughts, feelings and memories—in short, that they constitute two separate minds, two separate spheres of consciousness (Sperry, 1964; see Fig. 4.11).

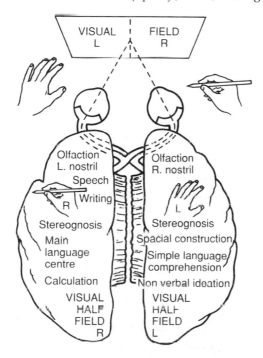

Figure 4.11 Schematic outline of the functional lateralization evident in behavioural tests of patients with forebrain commissurotomy. (From Sperry, 1968)

Levy-Agresti and Sperry concluded that the:

...mute, minor hemisphere is specialized for Gestalt perception, being primarily a synthesist in dealing with information input. The speaking, major hemisphere, in contrast, seems to operate in a more logical, analytic, computer-like fashion... (Levy-Agresti and Sperry, 1968)

Ornstein (1986) summarizes the differences like this:

(a) The left is specialized for analytic and logical thinking (ie breaking things down into their component parts), especially in verbal and mathematical functions, processes information sequentially (one item at a time) and its mode of operation is primarily linear (straight-line).

(b) The right is specialized for synthetic thinking, (bringing different things together to form a whole), particularly in the area of spatial tasks, artistic activities, crafts, body image and face recognition, processes information more diffusely (several items at once) and its mode of operation is much less linear (more holistic).

Cohen (1975) argues that long-standing pre-surgical pathology might have caused an abnormal reorganization of the brains of these split-brain patients, so that generalizing to normal people might not be valid. She cites a study by Kinsbourne in which the left hemisphere of aphasic patients was anaesthetized but that they continued to speak fluently but unintelligibly, suggesting that the abnormal speech is produced by the non-specialist *right* hemisphere. This seems to contradict the conclusions of split-brain studies that the right hemisphere has some understanding of language but is *mute*!

A number of attempts have been made to move beyond the simplistic left hemisphere/right hemisphere, verbal/non-verbal distinction, both in normal subjects and in split-brain patients. In a review of recent research, Annett (1991) says that, '. . . it is evident that each hemisphere has some role in the functions assigned to the other'. For example, the right hemisphere has a considerable understanding of language and it has been suggested that it might be responsible for semantic errors made by deep dyslexics. Similarly, the left hemisphere is almost certainly responsible for the production of imagery, 'which is likely to be required in much spatial thinking'.

But are there any distinctive left hemisphere skills?

Annett believes the best candidate is sensitivity to differences in rapidly changing acoustic cues, crucial to speech recognition. Another possibility is the production of movement sequence over time, involved in both speech and skilled hand movement.

She cites an interesting study by Poizner et al (1987) of six cases of deaf users of American Sign Language (ASL), all right handers, who had used ASL since early childhood; three suffered a left hemisphere stroke, three suffered a right hemisphere stroke. The former suffered loss of ASL, often remarkably similar to the kinds of disorder seen in normal speakers who suffer strokes at similar locations. The three right hemisphere stroke patients showed no significant loss of ASL:

> . . . It is clear that left hemisphere specialization for language can occur for a language that is not based on speech . . . (Annett, 1991)

It seems that there might be a physiological basis for left hemisphere specialization, namely the *planum temporale* (PT), a region adjacent to the auditory receiving area and so well placed to analyse speech sounds. In about 66 per cent of brains, the PT is larger on the left, in about 11 per cent it is larger on the right and in the rest it is about equal. This has been found in fetal brains from about three weeks of pregnancy.

While arguing that right hemisphere processing of language is extremely rare and is found in normal people only as a result of early left hemisphere damage, Gazzaniga (1985) also claims that it is not at all clear that the traditional interpretation of split-brain studies is correct. He argues that the brain is organized in a *modular* fashion, ie organized into relatively independent functioning units, which work in *parallel*. (This is consistent with current connectionist models in artificial intelligence; see Chapter 14.) Many of the modules operate at a non-conscious level, in parallel to our conscious thought; the left hemisphere tries to assign interpretations to the processing of these modules. So brains are organized such that many mental systems coexist in a 'confederation' (similar to Fodor's (1983) idea of mental modules):

> ... Although Gazziniga's view is not the common one among neuropsychologists, not all neuropsychologists accept the degree of separation between the hemispheres suggested by Sperry and his co-workers ...
> (Sternberg, 1990)

An alternative view is one of *integration*, ie the two hemispheres should be seen as playing different parts in an integrated performance (Broadbent, 1985; cited by Sternberg, 1990).

Similarly, Cohen is also critical of studies of hemispheric lateralization using normal subjects. She concludes by arguing that the two sides of the brain do not function in isolation but form a highly integrated system. Most everyday tasks involve a mixture of 'left' and 'right' skills—in listening to speech, for instance, we analyse both the words *and* the intonation pattern, while an integrated perception of linguistic and musical elements occurs in the appreciation of opera and analysis of visual shapes and linguistic knowledge are both required in reading; these may be accompanied by imagery and sub-vocal speech. Far from doing their own thing, the two hemispheres work very much together (Cohen, 1975).

THE AUTONOMIC NERVOUS SYSTEM (ANS)

As Figure 4.1 shows, the ANS is the part of the PNS, which controls the internal organs and glands of the body over which we have little (or any) voluntary control.

It comprises two branches, the *sympathetic*, which takes over whenever the body needs to use its energy, as in an emergency situation (the 'fight of flight' syndrome) and the *parasympathetic*, which is dominant when the body is at 'rest' and energy is being built up.

Essentially, therefore, the two branches work in *opposite* ways but they are both equally necessary for the maintenance of the delicately balanced internal state of homeostasis (see Chapter 6).

Sometimes a sequence of sympathetic and parasympathetic activity is required: in sexual arousal in men, erection is primarily parasympathetic while ejaculation is primarily sympathetic.

The ANS produces its effects in two ways: (i) by direct neural stimulation of body organs; and (ii) by stimulating the release of hormones from the endocrine glands; in both cases, the *hypothalamus* is the orchestrator. Table 4.3 summarizes the major sympathetic and parasympathetic effects on the organs and glands and the ANS will be discussed further in Chapter 6 in relation to emotional stress.

Table 4.3 Major sympathetic and parasympathetic reactions

ORGAN OR FUNCTION AFFECTED	SYMPATHETIC REACTION	PARASYMPATHETIC REACTION
1. Heart-rate	Increase	Decrease
2. Blood-pressure	Increase	Decrease
3. Secretion of saliva	Suppressed (mouth feels dry)	Stimulated
4. Pupils	Dilate (to aid vision)	Contract
5. Limbs (and trunk)	Dilation of blood vessels of the voluntary muscles (to help us run faster, for example)	Contraction of these blood vessels
6. Peristalsis (Contraction of stomach and intestines)	Slows down (You don't feel hungry in an emergency)	Speeds up
7. Galvanic Skin Response (GSR) (Measure of the electrical resistance of the skin)	Decreases (due to increased sweating, associated with increased axiety)	Increases
8. Bladder muscles	Relaxed (there may be temporary loss of bladder control)	Contracted
9. Adrenal glands	Stimulated to secrete more adrenaline and noradrenaline	Reduced secretion
10. Breathing rate	Increased (through dilation of bronchi)	Decreased
11. Liver	Glucose (stored as glycogen) is released into the blood to increase energy	Sugar is stored
12. Emotion	Experience of strong emotion	Less extreme emotions

THE ENDOCRINE SYSTEM

As we have said, many of the bodily reactions which result from the ANS are produced by its effect on the *endocrine* glands, which secrete *hormones* (chemical messengers which, unlike neurotransmitters, are released directly into the bloodstream and are carried throughout the body).

The effect of hormones is much slower than that of neurotransmitters: an electrochemical impulse can convey a message in a matter of milliseconds while several seconds may be required for the stimulation, release and arrival of a needed hormone at its destination. Consequently, where an immediate behavioural reaction is required (eg a reflex action),

Table 4.4 Major pituitary hormones and their effects

HORMONE	ENDOCRINE GLAND OR ORGAN STIMULATED	EFFECTS
Growth hormone (somatotropin)	Body tissues	Increases growth of bones and muscles, particularly in childhood and adolescence. Too little produces *pituitary dwarfism* and too much *gigantism*
Gonadotrophic hormones 1. Luteinizing hormone (LH)	Gonads (Testes—Male, Ovaries—Female)	Development of sex (germ) cells —⟨ Ova (Female) / Sperm (Male); Production of sex hormones —⟨ Oestrogen and Progesterone (Female) / Testosterone (Male)
2. Follicle-stimulating hormone (FSH)	Ovaries	Production of follicles in ovary during ovulation
Thyrotrophic hormone (TTH)	Thyroid gland	Secretion of *thyroxin* which controls metabolic rate—too little causes lethargy and depression, too much causes hyperactivity and anxiety
Lactogenic hormone (Prolactin)	Breasts	Milk production during pregnancy
Adrenocorticotrophic hormone (ACTH)	Adrenal glands 1. Adrenal medulla 2. Adrenal cortex	Secretion of adrenaline and noradrenaline. Secretion of adrenocorticoid hormones (or corticosteroids), eg cortisol and hydrocortisone (important in coping with stress) (see Chapter 6)
Oxytocin	Uterus (Womb)	Causes contractions during labour and milk release during breast-feeding
Vasopressin (Also a neurotransmitter)	Blood vessels	Causes contraction of the muscle in the walls of blood vessels and so raises blood pressure
Antidiuretic hormone (ADH)	Kidneys	Regulates the amount of water passed in the urine

Anterior pituitary (rows: Growth hormone through Adrenocorticotrophic hormone)

Posterior pituitary (rows: Oxytocin through Antidiuretic hormone)

Other endocrine glands include:
(A) *Thymus*—situated in the chest; functions are unknown but thought to involve production of antibodies (see Chapter 6).
(B) *Pancreas*—secretes *insulin* (Anti-diabetic hormone), given in the treatment of diabetes. Controls the body's ability to absorb and use glucose and fats.
(C) *Pineal body/gland*—situated near corpus callosum, functions unknown but may play a role in sleep–waking cycle (see Chapter 5).

the NS plays a major role: hormones are better suited to communicating steady, relatively unchanging, messages over prolonged periods of time (eg the body changes associated with puberty).

Endocrine glands are ductless and are contrasted with *exocrine* glands (such as salivary, sweat and tear glands) which do have ducts and secrete fluids directly onto the body surface or into body cavities; their influence is, consequently, much less widespread than that of endocrine glands.

The major endocrine gland is the *pituitary gland* which, as we have seen, is physically (but not functionally or structurally) part of the brain (situated just below the hypothalamus). It is often called the 'master gland' because it produces the largest number of different hormones and also because it controls the secretion of several other endocrine glands.

The pituitary comprises two independently functioning parts: (i) the *posterior*; and (ii) the *anterior*. The former transmits hormones which are thought to be manufactured in the hypothalamus, while the latter is stimulated by the hypothalamus to produce its own hormones. The major hormones of the posterior and anterior lobes of the pituitary are shown, with their effects, in Table 4.4.

Other important endocrine glands are the *adrenals* (situated just above the kidneys), each of which comprises the adrenal *medulla* (inner core) and the adrenal *cortex* (outer layer). As Table 4.4 shows, the medulla secretes adrenaline and noradrenaline which are the transmitter substances for the sympathetic branch of the ANS; consequently, the 'fight or flight' syndrome is often kept going by a 'closed circuit', whereby the sympathetic NS stimulates the adrenals to produce adrenaline and noradrenaline (initiated by the hypothalamus, which stimulates the pituitary gland to secrete ACTH which, in turn, stimulates the adrenals) which then stimulate the sympathetic nerves, and so on. This closed circuit explains why your heart continues to pound for several seconds after a dangerous or stressful situation has passed (see Chapter 6).

5 STATES OF CONSCIOUSNESS

CONSCIOUSNESS AND SELF-CONSCIOUSNESS

Whereas animals may be said to have consciousness, only human beings have self-consciousness, a special relationship we have with ourselves whereby we are able to treat ourselves as if we were objects or things through thought and reflection.

Consciousness is usually discussed in relation to humans and nothing more will be said in this chapter about the consciousness of other species, but because of the diverse ways in which psychologists have studied the topic (including animal experiments), some of what we say will have direct bearing on animal consciousness.

MEANINGS OF 'CONSCIOUSNESS'

We use the term 'consciousness' in a variety of ways in everyday language, for example:

(a) When we are awake we are conscious but when we are asleep, in a coma or we have been 'knocked out' by a punch to the head, we are unconscious (the term 'unconscious' is often reserved for the last two examples but, as we shall see, when we fall asleep, we do 'lose consciousness').

(b) When we do something consciously we do it deliberately or knowingly, but to do something automatically or without having to think about it (eg an experienced driver or typist) is to do it unconsciously.

(c) Advertising campaigns (eg anti-drug) are aimed at increasing public consciousness or awareness of the risks and dangers associated with taking drugs.

Similarly, psychologists and other scientists interested in trying to understand consciousness define it in different ways. Freud, for example, saw consciousness as a whole comprising three levels: (i) the conscious, which refers to what we are fully aware of at any one time; (ii) the pre-conscious, which refers to what we could become aware of quite easily if we switched our attention to it; and (iii) the unconscious, which refers to what we have pushed out of our conscious minds, through repression, making it extremely inaccessible, although it continues to exert an influence on our thoughts, feelings and behaviour (see Chapter 29).

Although most psychologists would agree that thoughts, feelings, memories, etc. differ in their degree of accessibility (that is, they could all be placed on a *continuum* of consciousness, with 'completely conscious' at one end and 'completely unconscious' at the other), most would not accept Freud's formulation of the unconscious (based on repression). Indeed, other psychodynamic theorists, in particular Jung, disagreed fundamentally with Freud's view of the unconscious. Although he admitted the existence of repression, Jung distinguished between the personal and the collective unconscious, the former being based on the individual's personal experiences, the latter being inherited and common to all human beings (or at least to all members of a particular cultural or racial group; see Chapter 29).

Rubin and McNeil (1983) define consciousness as, 'our subjective awareness of our actions and of the world around us'. Ruch gives it a much more cognitive emphasis by defining it as:

> . . . a process of experiencing the external and internal environment in ways that separate immediate stimuli from immediate responses, that is, stimuli are processed and 'understood' in some sense as against leading directly to mechanical responses. (Ruch, 1984)

Both definitions share a view of consciousness as pointing inwards, towards our thoughts, feelings, actions, etc. and outwards, towards external, environmental, events (including other people). Emphasis on the internal world is, of course, where psychology began as a separate discipline, with Wundt's study of conscious thought through introspection, but this was soon replaced by a dramatic shift in the opposite direction, when Watson rejected consciousness as a valid object of scientific investigation as part of his 'behaviourist manifesto' (see Chapters 1 and 2).

Since the late 1960s, the pendulum has begun to swing back towards an interest in consciousness, particularly in exploring different states of awareness and how changes from one state to another take place. While humanistic psychologists, such as Maslow, may be primarily concerned with a person's subjective experience, physiological psychologists are more interested in trying to correlate subjective states of awareness with objective, physiological measures of consciousness, such as electroencephalograms (EEGs—'brain waves'), breathing and heart rates, blood pressure, and so on.

CONSCIOUSNESS, AROUSAL AND ALERTNESS

The physiological measures described above (and other correlates of consciousness) are often described as measures of level of *arousal* or *alertness*. Both subjectively, and in terms of overt behaviour, there is an obvious difference between being sleepy and being wide-awake in terms of degree of arousal or alertness; less obvious are the smaller changes which occur during normal wakefulness and which are of two kinds— tonic and phasic—mediated by different brain systems (Lloyd et al, 1984).

TONIC ALERTNESS

Changes in *tonic alertness* reflect intrinsic (and usually quite slow) changes of the basic level of arousal throughout a 24-hour period (or even across a lifetime) and so are closely related to various biological rhythms, in particular the circadian rhythm (see below). It was originally thought that the Reticular Formation or Reticular Activating System (RAS) was solely responsible for arousing and maintaining consciousness (in Chapter 4 the RAS was described as a 'consciousness switch'); for instance, if the brain-stem is severed below the RAS, the animal will be paralysed but will remain fully alert when awake and will show normal sleep–wake EEG patterns, but if it is sectioned above the RAS the animal will fall into a state of continuous slow-wave sleep.

Again, Moruzzi and Magoun (1949) found that electrical stimulation of the RAS of anaesthetized cats produced long-lasting signs of arousal in their EEGs; in cats that were not anaesthetized, the effect of RAS stimulation was to produce behavioural signs of arousal, alertness and attention. According to Moruzzi and Magoun, sleep occurs when the level of activity of the RAS falls below a certain critical level.

However, it is now known that other brain structures (both in the thalamus and hypothalamus) are involved in the sleep–wake cycle and the co-ordination of all these systems is necessary for the initiation and maintenance of conscious awareness.

Both during wakefulness and during sleep, there are periodic, fairly predictable, changes in the degree of alertness; the day-time changes are governed by a *diurnal rhythm* and the sleep (night-time) changes by an *ultradian rhythm*.

PHASIC ALERTNESS

Changes in *phasic alertness* involve short-term, temporary, variations in arousal, over a period of seconds, initiated by novel and important environmental events. An important component of these changes is the *orienting response* to arousing stimuli (which involves a *decrease* in heart-rate and breathing rate, pupil dilation, a tensing of the muscles and characteristic changes in the EEG, which becomes desynchronized). If the stimuli are continuously presented, the orienting response is replaced by *habituation*, whereby the person or animal stops responding to them.

Habituation

Habituation is, in fact, a form of adaptation; it is more important from a survival point of view to respond to novel stimuli rather than constant ones and since most stimuli are relatively constant, we need to be able to attend selectively to those which are different and/or unexpected. So it is the *changing* aspects of the environment which demand, and usually receive, our attention and the nervous systems of animals and humans have evolved in such a way as to make them especially responsive to change.

CONSCIOUSNESS AND ATTENTION

Another way in which experimental psychologists have studied consciousness is through the concept of attention. Although consciousness is difficult to describe because it is fundamental to everything we do (Rubin and McNeil, 1983), one way of trying to 'pin it down' is to study what we are *paying attention* to, that is, what is in the forefront of our consciousness and, according to Allport (1980a), 'attention is the experimental psychologist's code name for consciousness'.

FOCAL ATTENTION

Focal attention (or focal awareness) is what we are currently paying deliberate attention to and what is in the centre of our awareness (this corresponds to Freud's 'conscious'); all those other aspects of our environment, or our own thoughts and feelings which are on the fringes of our awareness but which could easily become the object of our focal attention, are within our *peripheral attention* or awareness (which corresponds to Freud's 'pre-conscious'; see Chapter 11).

How Important is Focal Attention?

We do seem capable of doing many things quite unconsciously (ie automatically, without having to think about what we are doing) and this perhaps is best illustrated by our perceptual abilities. It is difficult to imagine what it would be like if we were aware of how we perceive. For example, to select consciously one version of the ambiguous lady cartoon (see Fig. 9.11) we must either know that there is a young and an old lady 'in' the picture or we must have already *perceived* both versions (in which case, how did the original perception come about?). You may have had difficulty yourself perceiving the old lady if your immediate perception was of the young lady, even though you consciously 'searched' for and tried to see the alternative version. (This underlines the very important difference between *conception* and *perception*.)

Using a rather different (but popular) example, something which we normally do quite automatically (such as walking down stairs) might well be disrupted if we try to bring it into focal awareness. Again, this makes sense in terms of freeing us to attend to those environmental events which are unfamiliar or threatening in some way; if we had to think about our bodily movements when walking, this would add to the long list of sources of stimulation competing for our attention! (see Chapter 11).

Perhaps only when first negotiating stairs as a toddler did we ever have to attend focally to ascending and descending them; but even with skills which do require focal attention when they are first acquired (eg driving, playing the piano), once they have been mastered, they become automatic and, as Lloyd et al (1984) put it, unconscious processes seem to be 'precipitates' of earlier conscious processes.

Nisbett and Wilson (1972) go so far as to claim that all psychological activities (including social behaviour) are governed by processes of which we are unaware. If people are asked about what they think governed their behaviour after participating in a social psychology experiment, the answers they give do not usually correspond very well with the explanations which psychologists offer for the same behaviour (and which they believe are the *real* reasons). Nisbett and Wilson argue that our belief that we can account for our own behaviour ('common-sense' or intuitive explanations) is illusory because what really guides our behaviour is not available to consciousness (compare this with Freud's distinction between 'our' reasons and 'the reasons'; see Chapter 29).

However, as we saw in Chapter 1, many psychologists take the view that people are psychologists and that commonsense explanations may be as valid as theoretical, scientific ones (Joynson, 1974; Heather, 1976), which seems to be in direct conflict with Nisbett and Wilson.

THE FUNCTIONS OF CONSCIOUSNESS

Like perception, many cases of problem-solving seem to involve processes which are 'out of consciousness'; for example, answers often seem to 'pop into our head' and we do not know how we reached them. If what is important is the solution (as opposed to the process involved in reaching it), then consciousness may be seen as incidental to information-processing.

The complexity of our nervous system which makes our consciousness possible provided our ancestors with the flexibility of behaviour which helped them survive. However, it is less obvious whether consciousness was *itself* adaptive or simply a side-effect or by-product of a complex nervous system.

Some psychologists and biologists believe that consciousness is a powerful agent for controlling behaviour which has evolved in its own right. Accordingly, non-conscious problem-solving systems are seen as the *servants* of consciousness; they are guided and integrated by consciousness but carry out automated routines (Ruch, 1984).

According to Hilgard's (1977) 'neo-dissociation' theory, the consciousness which *solves* a problem may be different from that which *reports* the solution; neither is 'higher' or 'lower' than the other, they are simply different. This theory is based on Hilgard's work with hypnosis and consistent with the work on split-brain patients (discussed in Chapter 4).

TWO KINDS OF CONSCIOUSNESS

As we saw in Chapter 4, the two cerebral hemispheres are specialized (although they share the potential for many functions and both participate in most psychological activities), so that each is dominant with respect to particular functions.

Ornstein (1986) believes that these two modes of operation represent two distinct modes of consciousness; in daily life we normally just alternate between the two and, although they might complement each other, they do not readily substitute for one another (as when you try to describe a spiral staircase or how you tie a shoe-lace).

Galin and Ornstein (1972; cited in Ornstein, 1986) recorded changes in subjects' EEGs when presented with either verbal or spatial tasks. On *verbal* tasks, alpha rhythms (associated with a waking adult with their eyes closed) in the right hemisphere *increased* relative to the left, while on *spatial* tasks, the reverse was true. The appearance of alpha rhythms indicates a 'turning off' of information processing in the area of the brain involved so, on verbal tasks, information processing is being turned off in the right hemisphere, which is the side of the brain *not* being used (as if to reduce the interference between the two conflicting modes of operation of the two hemispheres).

Similarly, people with damage to the left hemisphere have greater problems with consciously-executed writing, while those with right-hemisphere damage have greater problems with more automatic writing, such as signing their name. This suggests that the left hemisphere may be more involved in highly conscious processes which require intentional behaviour and the focusing of attention, while the right may be more involved with automatic or unconscious actions and more sensitive to material outside the conscious focus of attention.

CONSCIOUSNESS AND THE ELECTROENCEPHALOGRAM (EEG)

As we saw in Chapter 4, a major method (since the 1930s) of studying the working of the brain is to monitor the electrical activity of the brain; exactly the same information can be used to throw light on consciousness, because particular patterns of electrical activity are correlated with other indices of arousal and alertness.

Electroencephalography (literally, 'electric-in-head writing') detects the output of minute electrical 'ripples', caused by changes in the electrical charges in different parts of the brain (usually the synchronized activity of large groups of neurons); although there are characteristic patterns which are common to all individuals of a particular age or developmental stage, each individual's brain activity is as unique and distinctive as their fingerprints.

The electroencephalogram (EEG) has wires, an amplifier, electromagnetic pens and paper revolving on a drum. One end of each wire is attached to the scalp (with the help of special jelly) and the other to the amplifier, which can register impulses of 100 microvolts (1/10,000 of a volt) or less and magnifies them 1 million times; the impulses are traced on paper by pens and appear as rows of oscillating waves (see Fig. 5.1). The waves vary in frequency and amplitude:

(a) *Frequency* is measured as the number of oscillations per second—the more oscillations, the higher the frequency. One complete oscillation is a *cycle* and the frequency is expressed as cycles per second (cps) or Hertz (Hz).
(b) *Amplitude* is measured as half the height from the peak to the trough of a single oscillation. Frequency is the more important of the two measures.

The four major types of wave (measured in frequency) are:

(a) *Delta* (1–3 Hz)—these are found mainly in infants, sleeping adults or adults with brain tumours.
(b) *Theta* (4–7 Hz)—these are found mainly in children aged 2 to 5 years and in psychopaths; they may be evoked by frustration.
(c) *Alpha* (8–13 Hz)—these are found mainly in adults who are awake, relaxed and whose eyes are closed. They are most reliably recorded from the back of the scalp.
(d) *Beta* (13 Hz and over)—these are found mainly in adults who are awake, alert, whose eyes are open and who may be concentrating on some task or other. They are most reliably recorded from the front and middle of the scalp and are related to activity in the sensory and motor cortex.

Computerized electroencephalography has recently been used to detect *evoked potentials*, minute voltage changes induced in the brain by fairly specific visual and auditory stimuli; often the average of a number of responses to similar kinds of stimuli is used (the Average Evoked

Potential or AEP) in order to amplify the signal-to-noise ratio. AEPs are used to study newborns, some children with learning problems, patients in a coma, stroke victims, tumour patients and patients with multiple sclerosis, but for certain brain conditions, brain-scanning has largely replaced the EEG in the past few years. (The Diagram Group, 1982).

SLEEP

1. *SLEEP AND THE CIRCADIAN RHYTHM*

Blakemore (1988) asks what would happen if we removed all the *external* cues to the nature of time—both natural and manufactured (clocks, meal-times, day and night). Could our bodies still have their own rhythmic existence?

In 1972, Michel Siffre, a young French cave explorer, spent 7 months underground with no cues as to the time of day. He had adequate food, water, books and exercise equipment and his only contact with the outside world was via a telephone which was permanently staffed. He was linked-up to a computer and video-camera by which scientists on the surface could monitor his physiological functions and state of mind.

He organized his life into a fairly normal pattern of alternating periods of activity and sleep—his 'day' was broken up by a normal meal pattern. The remarkable finding was that he chose to live a 25-hour day (not 24). For every real day that passed, he rose an hour later—the clock in his brain was running a little slow:

> For all the advances of modern society, we cannot afford to ignore the rhythms of the animal brain within us, any more than we can neglect our need to breathe or eat. Without the biological clocks in our brains, our lives would be chaotic, our actions disorganized. The brain has internalized the rhythms of Nature, but can tick on for months without sight of the sun . . . (Blakemore, 1988)

Most animals display a *circadian rhythm* ('circadian' from the Latin 'circa dies' = 'about one day'), a periodicity or rhythmical alternation of various physiological and behavioural functions, synchronized to the 24-hour cycle of light and dark. So, during a 24-hour period, there is a cycle of several physiological functions (eg heart-rate, metabolic rate, breathing rate, body temperature) which all tend to reach maximum values during the late afternoon and early evening and minimum values in the early hours of the morning.

Rats, like humans, have an *inherent* rhythm of about 25 hours which dictates their cycle of sleep and waking if they are put in the dark. This internal clock is as reliable and regular as most manufactured ones—the rhythm deviates by no more than a few minutes over several months.

So how is the internal clock re-set each day to the cycle of the real world and where is the clock to be found?

It is thought to be a tiny cluster of neurons, the *suprachiasmatic nucleus* (SN), situated in the hypothalamus. Damage to the SN in rats produces complete disappearance of the circadian rhythm—periods of sleep, eating and drinking, etc. beome completely random during the course of the 24-hour period.

The SN is situated directly above the optic chiasma (the junction of the two optic nerves *en route* to the brain; see Chapter 8). A tuft of thin nerve fibres branches off from the main nerve and penetrates the hypothalamus above, forming synaptic connections with cells in the SN. This anatomically insignificant pathway is the link between the outside world and the brain's own clock (Blakemore, 1988). So the retina projects directly onto the SN, which ensures that the sleep–wake cycle is tuned to the rhythm of night and day—if this connection with the retina is severed, the cycle goes 'haywire'.

Therefore, in human adults, at least, it appears that the circadian rhythm does not depend primarily on external cues (although, presumably, it can be adjusted if necessary, using these external cues). But could not the rhythm have been learnt as a result of years of environmental experience?

Animal experiments, in which the length of 'day' can be manipulated, show that this is true, but only up to a point. Animals can be adjusted to cycles which vary by up to four or five hours above or below 24 but there are limits beyond which the cycle cannot be environmentally manipulated, just as hibernation cycles cannot be adjusted to fit experimentally manipulated 'seasons'. (The stress-producing effects of disrupting the circadian rhythm—as in shiftworkers and jet-lag—are discussed in Chapter 6.)

The circadian rhythm (or 'biological clock'), therefore, seems to be predominantly an *internal* property of the system, and sleep is part of that rhythm. So if external cues are largely irrelevant, what are the internal events which cause sleep?

2. *THE PHYSIOLOGY OF SLEEP*

First, we must qualify what we have said about the role of environmental cues. When darkness falls, the eyes indirectly inform the *pineal gland* (the 'third eye')—a tiny structure at the top of the brain-stem, which keeps track of the body's natural cycles and registers external factors such as light and darkness. This secretes *melatonin* in response to darkness, making us drowsy; Downing (1988) calls melatonin 'nature's sleeping draught'. Melatonin is a hormone that affects brain cells which produce *serotonin*, a sleep-related transmitter substance. In turn, serotonin is concentrated in the *raphe nuclei* (situated near the pons), which secrete a substance that acts on the RAS to induce light sleep. Jouvet (1967) found that lesions of the raphe nucleus in cats produce severe insomnia and naturally-occurring lesions in humans seem to have a very similar effect.

Another important sleep centre is the *locus coeruleus*, a tiny structure (on each side of the brain-stem) whose cells are rich in noradrenaline, which it is thought might be involved in inducing active (or rapid eye movement, REM) sleep (see below). We have already discussed the role of the reticular activating system (RAS) in maintaining a general level of arousal (see p. 105): if the level of activity in the RAS falls below a certain critical level, sleep will occur (Moruzzi and Magoun, 1949) and it is quite clear that, in sleep, sensory input to the RAS is reduced and that the electrical activity sweeping from the RAS up through the cortex drops below the level required to keep us awake (The Diagram Group, 1982).

Finally, there is evidence that a substance called *factor S* accumulates gradually in the brains of animals while they are awake and that, if this is removed from the fluid surrounding the brain and transferred into another animal, sleep will be induced. It is likely that factor S contributes to our feelings of sleepiness (The Diagram Group, 1982).

3. THE VARIETIES OF SLEEP AND THE ULTRADIAN RHYTHM

In the typical sleep laboratory, a subject settles down for the night with not only EEG wires attached but also wires from an electrooculogram or EOG ('oculo' meaning 'eye') and from an electromyogram or EMG ('myo' meaning 'muscle'; Fig. 5.1).

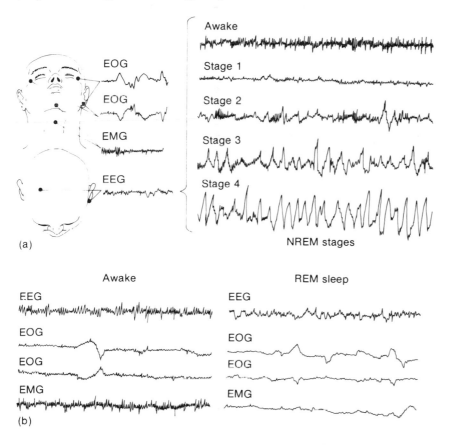

Figure 5.1 Comparison of physiological measures for different types of sleep
(a) The non-rapid-eye-movement (NREM) stages are represented in typical order of appearance; in reality each one gradually blends into the next.
(b) Rapid eye movement (REM) sleep is in some ways similar to waking but in others quite different; the EEG is more similar to waking than to that of any NREM stage and REMs are present, but the body muscles are deeply inhibited

A typical night's sleep comprises a number of *ultradian* cycles (approximately 90 minutes duration) and each cycle comprises a number of stages:

Stage 1: When we first fall asleep, we enter stage 1 sleep; the EEG is irregular and lacks the pattern of alpha waves which characterizes the relaxed waking state. There is at first a reduction in frequency of the alpha waves, which are then replaced by a low voltage, slow wave (2–7 Hz), accompanied by slow rolling eye movements. The heart-rate begins to slow down, the muscles relax and it is easy to be woken-up (The transitory stage from being awake to entering stage 1 sleep is called the *hypnogogic period* and is sometimes used to include stage 1.)

Stage 2: This is a deeper state of sleep than stage 1 but it is still fairly easy to wake someone. The EEGs show bursts of activity called 'spindles' (13–15 Hz) which last for about 25 seconds. There are also occasional sharp rises and falls in amplitude of the whole EEG (*K complexes*), which last up to about 2 seconds.

Stage 3: Sleep is becoming deeper, the spindles disappear and are replaced by long slow delta waves for up to 50 per cent of the record. The sleeper is now quite unresponsive to external stimuli and so is difficult to wake; heart-rate, blood pressure and body temperature all continue to drop.

Stage 4: The sleeper now enters 'delta sleep' (deep or 'quiet sleep') (50 per cent and more of the record consists of delta waves) and will spend up to 30 minutes in stage 4; about an hour has elapsed since stage 1 began. It is difficult to wake the sleeper—as in stage 3—but something highly personally relevant (eg a baby crying) can rouse even a deep sleeper.

The cycle then goes into reverse, so the sleeper re-enters stage 3, then stage 2, but instead of re-entering stage 1, a different kind of sleep (*Active sleep*) appears: pulse and respiration rates increase, as does blood pressure, and all three processes become less regular, EEGs begin to resemble those of the waking state (showing that the brain is active) and yet it is even more difficult to wake someone from this kind of sleep than the deep stage 4 sleep, and for this reason it is referred to as 'paradoxical' sleep (Aserinsky and Kleitman, 1953). Another characteristic of active sleep are the rapid eye movements (the eye-balls moving back and forth, up and down, together) under the closed lids (hence *'rapid eye movement'* or *REM* sleep). Finally, while the brain may be very active, the body is not; REM sleep is characterized by muscular paralysis (especially the muscles of the arms and legs) so that all the tossing and turning and other typical movements associated with sleep in fact occur during stages 1 to 4, which, collectively, are called *NREM* sleep, ie *non-rapid-eye-movement* sleep. (The distinction between REM and NREM sleep was originally made by Dement and Kleitman, 1957.)

After 15 or so minutes in REM sleep, we re-enter NREM sleep (stages 2 to 4) and so another ultradian cycle begins. However, with each 90 minute cycle, (of which there are four or five on average per night) the duration of the REM sleep increases and that of NREM sleep decreases; the first cycle normally provides the deepest sleep and the shortest REM period and, as the night goes on, we spend relatively more time in REM and less in NREM sleep. In later cycles, it is quite common to go from REM to stage 2 and then straight back into REM sleep (by-passing stages 3 and 4) and natural waking usually occurs during a period of REM sleep (see Fig. 5.2).

This sleep pattern is not only typical but seems to be universal. However much peoples' lifestyles may vary during the day, sleep proceeds in the same regular pattern, obeying the same rules. There are no apparent differences between men and women, introverts and extroverts, the more and less intelligent (Empson, 1989), although there are important developmental changes:

> ... The most striking thing about sleep patterns within a broad age group, however, is how remarkably uniform they are' (Empson, 1989)

> ... While most all-night recording experiments are over brief periods (of up to a week), some very extended studies have been done and there is no

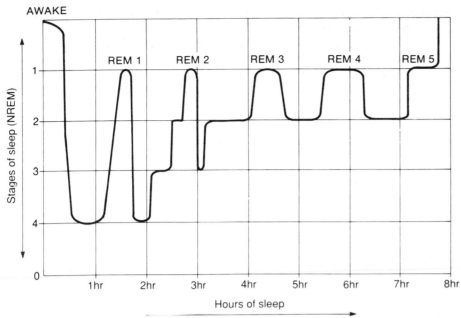

AWAKE

Stages of sleep (NREM)

Hours of sleep

Figure 5.2 A typical night's sleep (note the disappearance of stages 3 and 4 and the relative increase in the length of REM periods)

evidence that the patterns of sleep we observe over short periods (after the first night) are in any way peculiar to the unfamiliarity of the laboratory environment. (Empson, 1989)

4. *SLEEPING AND DREAMING*

Sleeping subjects, if woken during REM sleep, will report that they have been dreaming about 80 per cent of the time, while being woken from NREM sleep only produces a 15 per cent 'dreaming rate'.

REMs seem to be a very reliable indicator that someone is dreaming (especially in combination with the fairly high frequency and low amplitude brain waves). To some extent, the nature of the REMs reflects the content of the dream (for instance, dreaming about a tennis match and a back-and-forth movement of the eyes—as would happen in waking life), but it is now generally agreed that there is no one-to-one correspondence between dream action and eye movement, although cues about the general nature of the dream can often be gleaned from the REM record. For example, if the eye movements are small and sparse, we are probably having a peaceful, fairly passive dream, whereas larger and more continuous REMs suggest a more active and emotional dream (Faraday, 1972). (Faraday also notes that research has shown that movements of the inner ear also occur during sleep and may be correlated with the auditory content of dreams.)

Not only is there a difference in the number of times that dreams are reported when subjects are woken from REM and NREM ('orthodox') sleep, but the *kind* of mental activity associated with each is very different. Subjects woken from NREM sleep tend to report dreams which are shorter, less vivid and less visual than REM dreams and, in fact, subjects often describe themselves as having been 'thinking' rather than dreaming; NREM sleep is also associated with sleep-walking (somnambulism), sleep talking and some types of nightmare.

REM sleep has been called 'dream sleep' or the 'D-state' and some have gone as far as to call it the 'third state of existence', because it is in many ways as different from NREM sleep (the 'S-state') as it is from waking. This leads us to ask why we need to dream.

But is it possible that the difference between REM and NREM sleep regarding the dreaming which goes on is actually an artifact of the ability to *recall* dreams following the 'rude awakening'? Beaumont (1988) argues that being awoken from NREM may lead to the dream being forgotten before the subject is sufficiently awake to report it (since this is a deeper kind of sleep in which the brain is much less active), while being woken from REM may allow the ongoing dream to be remembered and then reported (here the brain is much more active).

Clearly, if this is so, then we have stumbled upon a major confounding variable which challenges the very basis of much of the sleep/dream research. There is evidence that an appreciable amount of mental activity does occur during NREM sleep and there are no completely consistent differences between dream reports obtained when subjects are woken from either kind of sleep.

However, evidence from studies of *sleep deprivation* does seem to support the view of REM sleep as a dream-state sleep quite independently of the sleeper's report of having dreamed (or not).

5. *THE EFFECTS OF SLEEP DEPRIVATION—THE REM REBOUND*

Webb and Bonnet (1979) (cited in Lahey, 1983) limited subjects to two hours sleep on one particular night. They suffered no ill effects the following day but that night they fell asleep more quickly and slept longer than usual. Longer periods of sleep deprivation may result in some unpleasant psychological effects but people are remarkably able to do without sleep. Webb and Bonnet gradually reduced the length of sleep in a group of volunteers from 8–4 hours per night over a 2-month period with no detectable effect.

However, when sleep is *abruptly* reduced (as, say, in the case of hospital doctors, who may be on duty for 72 hours at a stretch), the effects are rather more serious—irritability, intellectual inefficiency and an intense fatigue and need for sleep. And interestingly, these are more or less the same effects as are produced by depriving subjects of approximately 2 hours of *REM sleep* (but otherwise allowing them to sleep normally)—the following night, there is an increase in REM sleep (so as to compensate for the previous night's loss—this is the *REM rebound*).

When volunteers are able to get by on greatly (but *gradually*) reduced amounts of sleep it is apparently because they pack their 2 hours of REM tightly into the sleeping time they do have (thus reducing the amount of NREM sleep in between their dreams). When sleep is *abruptly* reduced, there is no time to adopt this additional dreaming-sleep pattern.

There has been a good deal of support for the REM-rebound phenomenon.

Dement (1960) woke subjects from their REM sleep on five successive nights (while a control group were only woken during NREM sleep periods). When they were allowed to sleep uninterruptedly, they did 60 per cent more dreaming until they had made up their lost REM time. For as many as five nights following their REM deprivation, they spent more time in REM than usual and on some nights they doubled their REM time.

These results were consistent with the idea that REM sleep and the dreaming associated with it are especially important, perhaps representing the most important function of sleeping (Empson, 1989).

Dement also reported that his subjects tended to become paranoid while deprived of REM sleep, ascribing sinister motives to the researcher, developing all kinds of unreasonable suspicions and even hallucinating, as well as becoming nervous, irritable and unable to concentrate.

However, he later maintained that these symptoms were *not* reliably caused by lack of REM sleep and that they were more likely to have been caused by the researcher's expectations, communicated (ironically) through concern for their welfare—Dement had told his subjects what he thought the probable results would be, and that a psychiatrist would be on duty all the time. After the third day, little sleep at all was being had (since they had more frequent REM periods and so were woken more frequently) and the symptoms were the combined effects of total sleep deprivation and suggestion. (This is a good example of *demand characteristics*—see Chapter 2).

Dement replicated his earlier study in 1965 and found no evidence of psychiatric symptoms with REM sleep deprivation (Empson, 1989).

6. *THEORIES OF SLEEP*

> Our planet is a dangerous place; there is ruthless competition for limited resources and only the fittest survive. And yet all the most advanced animals, normally alert, shrewd, watchful, drop their defences to sleep. Even human beings, the most spectacularly successful species, spend one-third of their lives more or less paralysed and senseless.
>
> If sleep is so risky, it must bestow a huge benefit on animals that indulge in it, or it would have been eliminated by the powerful forces of natural selection. Animals that did not need sleep would surely have evolved and prevailed over their sleepy competitors ... sleep must surely be valuable ... (Blakemore, 1988)

According to Empson (1989), even though psychologists have made great strides in understanding sleep mechanisms, this hasn't greatly helped in understanding what sleep is *for*; only a larger understanding of the role of sleep in human functioning (including its psychology) can answer that question.

In cats too, it seems that NREM alone is inadequate. Jouvet (1967) placed cats on a small island surrounded by water and allowed them either to remain awake or to go into NREM sleep. However, whenever they entered REM sleep, they tended to slip into the water and woke up; prolonged deprivation of REM produced abnormal behaviour, including hypersexuality and, eventually, death.

Many drugs, including alcohol and various sleeping pills, suppress REM sleep without affecting NREM sleep (which is ironic, because the body seems to need REM more). If people or cats are deprived of *all* sleep for a period of days, they will eventually go to sleep standing up, but the body seems to have a specific need for REM and, after REM deprivation, subjects go straight into REM sleep.

While sleep has the features of a *primary drive* (such as hunger and sex), what makes it unique as a primary biological drive is that the need for sleep is reflected in *decreased* levels of arousal and its satisfaction is associated with further decreases. Sleep, therefore, represents a serious exception to the view that organisms seek a single optimal level of (non-specific) arousal (Lloyd et al, 1984) (see Chapter 6).

The Restoration Theory

The *Restoration theory* (Oswald, 1966) maintains that both REM and NREM sleep serve a restorative, replenishing, function. NREM restores bodily processes which have deteriorated during the day, while REM sleep is a time for replenishing and renewing brain processes through the stimulation of protein synthesis.

The theory also accounts for the large proportion of babies' sleeping-time spent in REM sleep; only gradually do we acquire sleep–wake patterns which we associate with the circadian rhythm. During much of their first year, babies are sleeping for about 18 hours per 24, by about 12 months they have two periods of sleep every 24 hours (one day-time and one night-time) and not until about 5 years has an 'adult' pattern become established (probably as a result of both environmental and maturational factors).

Within these changing patterns, the relative proportions of REM and NREM sleep change quite dramatically: whereas the newborn spends half of its 18 hours in REM sleep, adults usually spend only one-quarter of their 8 hours in REM sleep. The developing brain needs a great deal of protein synthesis for cell manufacture and growth and REM sleep helps to achieve this (see below).

What evidence is there to support Oswald? In patients who survive drug overdoses and withdrawal and other brain 'insults', such as intensive electro-convulsive therapy (see Chapter 31), there are prolonged increases in REM sleep, which are consistent with the estimated time for the half-life of proteins in the brain, ie in a 6-week period, about half the brain's total protein is replaced, and this is the approximate length of the increased REM period (somewhere between 6 and 8 weeks).

Nocturnal secretion of growth hormone (which produces *bodily* protein synthesis) depends on uninterrupted stage 4 sleep and in adults a chronic lack of normal stage 4 is found in fibrositis sufferers, whose EEG during sleep is characterized by 'alpha–delta' patterns, a mixture of sleeping and waking EEG. This is typically experienced as fitful, 'unrestorative sleep'. The disturbance of stage 4 in healthy volunteers produces the symptoms of fibrositis:

> ...All this evidence is consistent with a general anabolic function for sleep: REM sleep subserving brain growth, repair and memory functions, and slow wave (stage 4) sleep promoting bodily growth and repair. (Empson, 1989)

However, cell repair goes on 24 hours a day (even though it reaches a peak at night) but a more serious objection to the theory is that, far from being a restful state, REM sleep, as we have seen, is an active state (at least as far as the brain is concerned) and probably burns up a substantial amount of energy. Indeed, blood flow to the brain increases during REM sleep and this would actually *prevent* high levels of protein synthesis. In view of this kind of evidence, Oswald (1974) maintains that *both* types of sleep are involved in the process of restoring *bodily* tissue.

Evolutionary Theory (Meddis, 1975, 1977)

Different species characteristically sleep for different periods; those at risk from predators, which cannot find a safe place to sleep or which spend large parts of each day searching for and consuming food and water (such as herd animals), sleep very little, while predators that sleep in safe places and can satisfy their food and water needs fairly quickly (such as lions), sleep for much of the day (Lloyd et al, 1984).

The *Evolutionary theory* of sleep maintains that sleep is an advantage because it keeps the animal *immobilized* for long periods, being immobile it will be less conspicuous to would-be predators and, therefore, safer. The safer the animal from predators, the longer it is likely to sleep, as we noted above.

Meddis also argues that the long sleep periods of babies have evolved to prevent exhaustion in their mothers and, in this sense, sleep is still functional—at least for mothers of babies and small children! As for the need for immobilization, this no longer seems viable as an explanation of sleep in humans and so may be regarded as a remnant of our evolutionary past.

A variant of the evolutionary theory is *Hibernation theory*, which argues that elaborate mechanisms of sleep have evolved solely to keep us quiet in the dark; animals hibernate to conserve energy and to stay out of possible danger during the winter months.

Any *evolutionary theory* (like Meddis's) must be able to explain the variety of lifestyles across modern species, involving very great differences in total sleep time. Why has this particular instinct become a universal, while others are as diverse as the habitats of the creatures exhibiting them? Why does almost every known animal show the same patterning of sleep (although there is a great variation in total quantity)?

Despite enormous differences in lifestyle, all mammals seem to have to find time for a minimum amount of sleep. If there was no other evidence for the absolute necessity of sleep, the finding that the porpoise has evolved a system of sleeping with the two sides of its brain alternately would be eloquent enough on its own:

> ...This clearly suggests that sleep has acquired an essential role in physiology, whatever the evolutionary pressures which led to its appearance in primeval reptiles. (Empson, 1989)

Empson (1989) characterizes Meddis's theory as a 'waste of time' theory and claims that it is contradicted by the fact that it is universal among animals, as well as by the finding that sleep deprivation can be fatal (Kleitman, 1927).

A weaker version of the 'waste of time' theory was proposed by Horne (1988), who distinguishes between *core sleep* (which is necessary) and *optional sleep* (which isn't). Evidence from sleep deprivation experiments (both partial and total) shows that accumulated sleep 'debts' are made up to some extent on recovery nights, but never entirely. Thus, REM rebound accounts for approximately 50 per cent of the REM lost during selective awakenings; so only the first three hours of sleep are truly necessary (core sleep) and the rest is optional (having no physiological function). In animals which sleep longer than three hours, it seems to reduce energy expenditure and keep them immobile.

Empson (1989) criticizes the distinction as being not very useful—

most of us eat more than we absolutely need to in order to keep body and soul together, both in variety and quantity, but no biologist would say that, because a proportion of feeding was optional that feeding was only partly functional:

> ... sleep appears to be ubiquitous and necessary; it is a complex function of the brain involving far-reaching changes in body physiology as well as brain physiology. It is difficult to believe that it does not have an important function and the restorative theories provide a coherent account of what this might be. (Empson, 1989)

7. THEORIES OF DREAMING

While a great deal has been discovered about the physiology of sleep, and psychologists have developed reliable techniques for establishing when people are likely to be dreaming, there has not been an equivalent amount of progress in understanding the nature of dreams. A starting point for any analysis of this nature must be to establish clearly how dreaming differs from waking consciousness. (Empson, 1989)

Empson goes on to identify four such differences:

(a) Dreams happen to us as opposed to being a product of our conscious control:

> ... When dreaming we are the spectators of an unfolding drama, and only rarely does one have the impression of being in control ... (Empson, 1989)

'Lucid dreaming', in which the dreamer 'knows' he or she is dreaming and decides how the dream plot should develop, is very rare.

(b) The logic of waking consciousness is suspended (as indeed Freud believed—see Chapter 29).

(c) Dreams reported in the laboratory tend to be mundane and lack the bizarre quality of 'normal' dreams. This is probably because only the strangest experiences are remembered when we wake normally after a night's sleep. Also, Faraday (1972) points out that the last dreams of the night tend to be more vivid than earlier ones.

(d) Dreams are certainly odd. Empson refers to what has been called the *single mindedness* of dreams: the imagery of the dream totally dominates the dreamer's consciousness while, when awake, we normally reflect on the stream of consciousness as it goes on and can be aware of one thing but simultaneously imagine something else.

Reorganization of Mental Structures

According to Ornstein (1986) REM sleep and dreaming may be involved in the re-organization of our *schemas* (mental structures) so as to accommodate new information. People placed in a 'disturbing and perplexing' atmosphere for four hours just prior to sleep (asked to perform difficult tasks with no explanation) spend longer in REM sleep than normal. REM time also increases after people have had to learn complex tasks.

This may explain why REM decreases with age; as we have seen, newborns spend 50 per cent of their (approximately) 18 hours of sleep in

REM (active) sleep compared with 25 per cent spent by adults in their (approximately) 8 hours.

Oswald suggested that babies' brains need to process and assimilate the flood of new stimuli pouring in from the outside world and that this is (partly) achieved through REM sleep.

Activation–Synthesis Model (Hobson and McCarley, 1977; McCarley, 1983)

The cortex is highly active during REM sleep, although it receives little external stimulation. Although the motor cortex is highly active (generating activity which would normally produce bodily movement) these commands don't reach the muscles of the limbs but are 'switched off' at a relay station at the top of the spinal column, so we are effectively paralysed. (This explains the loss of tone in the neck muscles under the chin—one defining feature of REM sleep.)

Not only is the cortex isolated (unable to control muscles) but there is also inhibition of incoming signals produced by the sensory systems (so perceptions of the 'real' world are selectively attenuated). Hindbrain and midbrain structures, normally associated with relaying sensory information to the cortex, spontaneously generate signals responsible for cortical activation and are also indistinguishable from signals which would normally have been relayed from the eyes/ears. This activity is under the control of a periodic triggering mechanism in the *pontine brainstem* (top of the spinal column, at the base of the brain). *Giant cell* activity precedes REMs in animals and there is no evidence that cortical activity can influence these cells (Empson, 1989).

So the brain is very active during REM (*activation*) and dreams are a consious interpretation (*synthesis*) of all this activity. While awake, the mental operating system organizes sensory information into the simplest meaningful interpretation. Supposing the same system is at work during dreams, mental processes attempt to organize diverse material, eg the sensation of falling (from *vestibular* activity), the experience of paralysis (from blocking of *motor output*) and specific events of the day all need to be made sense of.

A dream, therefore, is the simplest way of interpreting these diverse experiences by combining them into some meaningful whole. It is the unusual intensity and rapidity of brain stimulation (often involving simultaneous activation of areas not usually activated together when we are awake) which accounts for the highly changeable and sometimes bizarre content of dreams.

Many dream experiences do seem to reflect the brain's and body's state (and so can be thought of as *interpretations* of these physical states), eg being chased, locked up or frozen with fear may well reflect the blocked motor commands to the muscles, floating, flying and falling experiences may reflect vestibular activation and the sexual content of dreams may reflect vaginal engorgement and penile erection (Ornstein, 1986).

Evaluation of Theories of Dreaming

(a) A similar *neural* theory (Rose, 1976) explains dreaming in terms of the relatively random inputs which trigger memory sequences at a time when 'waking' control mechanisms (which normally keep a fairly close watch over these sequences) are either reduced or absent.

(b) Perhaps there is a sense in which we dream *instead* of *acting* (maybe suggesting the need for rest/restoration for the body)—cats with brain-stem injury act out their dreams, by, for example, chasing the mouse of their dreams while ignoring the real mouse in their cage, ie they are not paralysed in the normal way during REM sleep.

(c) Dreams are often incoherent and bizarre. Abrupt shifts in imagery may simply be the brain's, 'making the best of a bad job in producing partially coherent dream imagery from the relatively noisy signals sent up . . . from the brain stem' (Ornstein, 1986).

(d) Does the truth of the activation–synthesis model *exclude* other theories of dreams? Not necessarily. It may account for 'where dreams come from' but not 'what dreams are for'. *Psychological* theories focus on the *synthesis* component (much more than on the activation component) and try to explain its significance for the dreamer. Freud's is probably the best known (and most controversial)—dreams are wish-fulfilments and, like Jung, he saw *symbolism* as of central importance. Both saw dreams as putting the dreamer in touch with parts of the self usually inaccessible during waking life (see Chapter 29).

Hall (1966) saw dreams as, 'a personal document, a letter to oneself', and, like Jung, advocated the study of dream *series* rather than single, isolated, dreams.

(e) The activation–synthesis model has been elaborated by Crick and Mitchison (1983). According to them, we dream in order to forget!

The cortex (unlike other parts of the brain) is composed of richly inter-connected *neuronal networks* in which each cell (neuron) has the capacity to excite its neighbours. Memories are encoded in these networks, with neurons and their many synapses representing different features of memory. These networks are like spider's webs—when one point is excited, a pulse travels throughout the network.

The problem with such a network system is that it malfunctions when there is overload of incoming information (eg fantasies, obsessions, hallucinations). To deal with such overload, the brain needs a mechanism to 'debug' or tune the network; this would work best when the system is isolated from external inputs and would have to be able to randomly activate the network in order to eliminate spurious (or 'parasitic') connections (Atkinson et al, 1990).

Learning requires constant modification of the brain circuits. Whatever rule is used by the brain to guide the strengthening/weakening of synaptic connections, it surely makes mistakes, in the form of:

> odd backwaters of neural circuitry . . . little unwanted pieces of modified circuitry that would disturb the progress of normal learning, if left unpruned . . . (Blakemore, 1988).

The random pontine brainstem activity which stimulates the cortex during REM sleep has the function of erasing memories which have become 'parasitic'—interpretations which, whatever their origin, have no place in our latest view of the world and are redundant—but persistent:

... This accumulation of nonsense is expressed in dreams created only in order to be forgotten ... (Empson, 1989)

... Dreams are, quite literally, a kind of shock therapy, in which the cortex is bombarded by barrages of impulses from the brainstem below, while a different mode of synaptic modification ensures that the unwanted elements of each circuit are unlearned. The perceptual content of dreams would, then, correspond to the internally generated patterns of activity set up in the cerebral cortex as a result of the barrage from below. The fact that the narrative of a dream, though sometimes bizarre, is at least coherent (the dream tells some sort of story) must surely reflect interpretive processes, at higher levels of the brain, probably in the frontal lobes, trying to impose order or plausability on the chaos of activity in the sensory area of the cortex ... (Blakemore, 1988)

REM sleep is, then, the mechanism for 'cleaning up' the network; we awake with a cleaned-up network and the brain is ready for new input. Trying to remember our dreams, according to Crick and Mitchison, may *not* be a good idea—they are the very patterns of thought the system is trying to tune out.

What Would Happen to an Animal that Couldn't Dream?

Its cortex would fill up rapidly with the unwanted junk of unrepresentative experience.

In order to survive *without* dreams, an animal would need a much larger cortex. Two higher mammals which seem to have no REM sleep are the spiny ant-eater (an Australian marsupial) and the dolphin. Both have an abnormally large cortex for their size and evolutionary development. Their oversized brains are needed to accommodate all their useless memories since they have little or no ability to unlearn them (Blakemore, 1988).

'What is a Dream?' (Seligman and Yellen, 1987)

Seligman and Yellen (1987) have tried to map the psychological reality of dreaming onto contemporary neurophysiological evidence of brain function during sleep, accounting for both the emotional quality and visual content of dreaming.

They base their ideas on three sources of evidence, which are:

(a) Neurophysiological evidence suggesting the hindbrain is in control of the generation and maintenance of REM sleep (as stated by the *activation* synthesis model).

(b) REMs are *not* continuous during REM sleep but appear in periodic bursts, typically lasting 2–10 seconds and separated by periods of sleep of up to 3 minutes. Subjects woken during REM bursts reported highly vivid experiences (*primary visual experiences/PVEs*) much more frequently than those woken from periods of REM 'quiescence' (*secondary cognitive elaboration/SCEs*). Eighty-two per cent of mental activity when woken from REM bursts were of PVEs, compared with 80 per cent SCEs when woken from periods of quiescence.

So REM bursts seem to be characterized by visual (and auditory) hallucinatory sensations.

(c) How can the cortex construct sense out of the chaos produced by the random discharges from the pontine brainstem (a part of the brain we share with the humblest reptiles)? Seligman and Yellen surveyed students about their dreams and concluded that:

> ... the same process by which individuals make coherent the externally generated visual episodes of daily life is at work during dreaming; when an individual encounters the internally generated visual episodes in REM sleep, he develops this ability (in whatever measure he possesses it) to make this encounter coherent. (Seligman and Yellen, 1987, quoted in Empson, 1989)

Hypnosis

Rubin and McNeil define hypnosis as:

> an altered state of consciousness, in which the hypnotized subject can be influenced to behave and to experience things differently than she would in the ordinary waking state. (Rubin and McNeil, 1983)

Elsewhere, they define it as:

> a state of increased suggestibility (or willingness to comply with another person's directions) that is brought about through the use of certain procedures by another person, the hypnotist. (Rubin and McNeil, 1983)

This notion of *suggestibility* is often thought to be at the core of hypnosis and a great deal of research has attempted to identify personality types which are high and low in 'hypnotizability'. Hilgard (1970) believes that people can be classified in this way; for example, among student subjects, 'highs' are often humanities majors and are able to lose themselves in individual pursuits (such as reading) while 'lows' are often science majors and are more likely to participate in group activities. (Compare this with Eysenck's description of introverts and extroverts; see Chapter 29.)

About 5 per cent of the population can be induced to a deep hypnotic trance and about 10 per cent do not respond at all, with the majority falling somewhere in between these two extremes.

THE HYPNOTIC PROCEDURE

According to Hilgard hypnosis is:

> the state of consciousness caused in a subject by a systematic procedure for altering consciousness, usually carried out by one person (the hypnotist) to alter the consciousness of another (the subject). (Hilgard, 1975)

The typical procedure begins with a 10–15 minute induction of verbal suggestions designed to induce a passive, sleeplike (but waking) state. For the next 45 minutes or so, the subject is asked to perform a number of tasks, which may be based on the Stanford Hypnotic Susceptibility Scales (Weitzenhoffer and Hilgard, 1965). These scales are heavily weighted with: (i) ideomotor ('thought–movement') tasks, such as 'posture sway' (falling without forcing), 'arm immobilization' (the arm rises less than one inch in 10 seconds) and 'verbal inhibition' (not being able to give their name within 10 seconds); but also include (ii) sensory hallucinations (eg imagining a fly is in the room and behaving in some appropriate way); (iii) temporary amnesia (only being able to recall three or fewer items from a longer series); (iv) age regression (eg the subject is taken back in time and asked to describe events and people in their childhood); and (v) post-hypnotic suggestion (eg after being 'awakened' the subject opens the window when the hypnotist gets out his handkerchief, a signal given to the subject while in the hypnotic state).

The more items the subject 'passes', the higher his/her susceptibility score; using these scales, men and women have been found to be equally hypnotizable and people with vivid imaginations and who feel comfortable taking orders from others also tend to be hypnotized more easily. Susceptibility seems to reach a peak up to the age of ten years and declines steadily after that.

TRANCE OR ROLE-PLAYING?

What is the evidence that the hypnotic state constitutes a *qualitatively different state of consciousness*, as Hilgard claims?

There is no doubt that the hypnotic state is *not* a state of sleep (using EEGs and other criteria), although subjects often report dream-like imagery and may show REMs while 'dreaming'. Some report feeling bored but relaxed, others seem to attain a kind of controlled hypnogogic state (neither fully awake nor asleep) and almost all remain aware of who and where they are; some of the more responsive subjects, however, may not remember what they did and may think only a few minutes have passed (Ruch, 1984).

Some of the evidence seems quite convincing; for example, touching the skin with a pencil may cause blisters if the subject has been told it is red hot and touching the skin with a Japanese wax-plant may fail to cause a skin reaction if the subject believes it is a harmless chestnut leaf.

Again, telling subjects that they have just eaten a large, fatty, meal causes the body to secrete lipase (a fat-digesting enzyme); when they think the meal was rich in protein, pepsin and trypsin are secreted (protein-digesting enzymes). Hypnosis can also affect breathing rate, heart-rate and various kinds of glandular activity (The Diagram Group, 1982).

However, Barber (1969) believes that all hypnotic phenomena are due to motivational and social-psychological factors. The 'hypnotic trance' does not constitute a unique state (there is no distinctive EEG, for instance) and the 'hypnotized' person is simply highly motivated to co-operate with the hypnotist's suggestions and is good at 'role-playing'; anything that can be done in the hypnotized state can be done while 'awake'.

A similar argument is made by Orne (1970), who paid a group of subjects (and trained them) to pretend they were hypnotized; an experienced hypnotist could not tell them apart from a group who had actually been hypnotized, despite sticking them with pins and asking them to engage in all sorts of unusual behaviour.

HYPNOSIS AND PAIN

It has been claimed by many critics of hypnosis that the only distinctive psychological change which it produces is *relaxation* (which can just as easily be produced by other techniques, such as meditation, relaxation exercises, etc.).

However, Hilgard, one of the leading researchers in the field, believes that hypnosis has been successfully used with dental patients, burn victims, women in childbirth and terminal cancer patients to reduce their pain. One experimental technique for studying pain is the *cold pressor response*, where subjects immerse their arm in freezing water and are asked to report how painful it is over a 30-second period.

Hypnotized subjects are told that the experience will not be painful and usually report very little pain (a 'slight tingle', for example). However, physiological measures of pain (such as heart-rate and blood pressure) are usually extremely high and this led Hilgard to propose his Neo-Dissociation Theory (1974, 1977). Dissociation refers to a separation between different aspects of consciousness: in the case of pain, there are at least two components: (i) a sensory component; and (ii) an emotional component, and hypnosis only influences the latter. Unlike drugs, hypnosis does not prevent pain information from reaching the brain—so the pain information is available and, if pressed, the hypnotized subject may be able to report the pain.

Hypnotized subjects who reported no pain were asked if some other part of themselves (*a hidden observer*) might know more; if such a hidden observer was contacted, it often reported knowledge of some degree of pain (although this was usually less than for the same subject when not hypnotized; Hilgard, 1978).

Hypnosis has been successfully used in psychotherapy and has also been used as a memory enhancer for witnesses to accidents and criminal cases. However, because of the possibility of accidentally creating pseudo-memories (Hilgard, 1981), testimony given under hypnosis is usually inadmissible in court. (For an excellent review, see Wagstaff, 1987; summarized in Gross, 1990.)

MEDITATION

Meditation has been defined as a clearing or emptying of the mind through a narrowly focused thought process; the special word or phrase (the *mantra*) used in Transcendental Meditation is an example of this.

According to Burns and Dobson (1984), the different forms and varieties of mediation are all ways of achieving an inner quiet and a heightened awareness and can be thought of as the art of being in the 'here and now'.

Meditation, originally practised in India and other Eastern countries, became popular in the West in the late 1960s, as part of the 'flower power' phenomenon which was, among other things, a rejection by the youth of traditional materialistic values which were seen as severely limiting people's individual freedom.

Since then, meditation has been studied by psychologists as a state of consciousness (and a technique for bringing that about) using fairly traditional, scientific techniques (which is ironic when you consider that Western science was one of the institutions rejected by 'flower power').

There are many reported cases of yogis who manage to control their autonomic functions quite voluntarily through meditation, enabling them to endure all kinds of injury and deprivation, without suffering any apparent physical harm. A famous example is Ramanand Yogi, a 46-year-old Hindu who, through the practice of yoga ('union'), managed to survive for over five hours in a sealed metal box in 1970. He was filmed and various physiological measurements were taken while he was inside: he used just over one-half of the calculated minimum amount of oxygen needed to keep him alive (and during one hour, he was averaging just one-quarter).

The secret of yogis' science-defying feats seem to be the *trance*-like state which is induced by meditation techniques, whereby the body's metabolism is slowed down considerably. However, others believe that meditation (like hypnosis) is simply an elaborate way of inducing quite normal *relaxation responses* and that there is nothing unique or magical about meditation.

Over and above any religious beliefs surrounding it, meditation requires: (i) a quiet environment where the meditator will not be interrupted; (ii) a mental device on which to concentrate (such as the mantra, which is repeated continuously); (iii) a passive attitude as opposed to an active, striving one; and (iv) a comfortable position. Regular use of this simplified form of meditation encourages a relaxation response, which triggers the parasympathetic branch of the ANS. Ornstein (1986) has suggested that meditation is primarily a right hemisphere 'intuitive' activity and practising meditation for long periods may induce a relative shift in hemisphere dominance. Some research has shown that meditators do better than non-meditators on certain right-hemisphere tasks, such as remembering musical tones, but they do worse on verbal problem-solving tasks. However, we cannot be sure that these differences arose *because* of meditation as the evidence is correlational and there may be other important differences between meditators and non-meditators apart from meditation.

BIOFEEDBACK

What yogis seem to be able to do through meditation can apparently be achieved in a much more scientifically-orientated way through biofeedback. Simply, individuals are provided with information (feedback) about specific aspects of their biological functioning (eg heart-rate, breathing rate, blood pressure, EEG and galvanic skin response (GSR)) and, on the strength of this information, are trained to control these biological functions (of which we are normally completely unaware) at will.

In a typical training session, a subject is connected to various recording machines and when, say, blood pressure falls within a certain pre-determined range, a signal is given (a buzzer sounds or a flashing light is switched on): this signal, of course, is the feedback.

Biofeedback techniques grew out of experiments with rats (Miller and Dicara, 1967; Dicara and Miller, 1968), in which, it was claimed, involuntary, autonomic, responses were brought under control using operant conditioning. (Briefly, paralysed rats were rewarded by hypothalamic electrical stimulation whenever their breathing rate—and other autonomic functions—changed in the desired direction.) This was quite a startling finding because until then it had been believed that autonomic behaviour could only be conditioned using classical methods and that operant conditioning could only be applied to voluntary behaviour (see Chapter 7).

However, these results have always been considered highly controversial and have never been replicated (Walker, 1984). Indeed, Miller himself (1978) has spoken out against accepting the results from any experiments using curarized (paralysed) animals.

Nevertheless, research into biofeedback has continued, with mixed fortunes. Many studies have claimed that a wide range of autonomic functions can be brought under voluntary control. Early biofeedback experiments seemed to show that subjects could control their EEGs without any specific training and many have attempted to get subjects to produce alpha waves, with apparent success.

High blood pressure, migraine headaches, some types of vomiting and secretion of stomach acids which can cause ulcers can all be modified by biofeedback, as can skin temperature and salivation.

However, these results have not always been replicated and may turn out to be artificial. For instance, eye movements can produce changes in the electrical field which block input to an ordinary alpha recorder, that is, the apparent control of alpha waves may be the result of changes in eye movements as opposed to actual changes in brain activity.

Similarly, electrocardiograms (ECGs) revealed that yogis who claimed to be able to stop their hearts had in fact learnt to control pressure in the thoracic cavity and could shut off the return of blood to the heart, thereby eliminating the characteristic heartbeat noise—their hearts were beating *faster* than normal.

Other studies have shown that blood pressure and heart-rate can be controlled through subtle muscular movements or sometimes through breathing changes. So the learning of blood pressure and heart-rate control, etc. might, in fact, be a *consequence* of control over muscular responses.

Biofeedback has been applied to an enormous variety of clinical problems but there is serious doubt about its effectiveness, especially compared with other procedures. Many believe that simple training in voluntary muscle relaxation is often at least as effective—and sometimes more so—as biofeedback in the control of tension.

LeFrançois (1983) argues that the application of biofeedback in medicine has tremendous, but largely unproven, potential, and Miller (1978), whose studies of rats provided the stimulus, believes that most biofeedback research has been conducted at the first stage of scientific research, namely, pilot studies which have shown promise. What is needed now, he says, are controlled comparisons, where new treatments, such as biofeedback, are compared with other treatments and with placebos.

6 MOTIVATION, EMOTION AND STRESS

MOTIVATION: THE 'WHY' OF BEHAVIOUR

Trying to define *motivation* is a little like trying to define psychology itself; each major theoretical approach tries to account for what causes human behaviour and the underlying image of human beings implicit in each theory is, in essence, a theory of the causes of behaviour (see Table 1.1). Motives are a special kind of cause which:

> ...energize, direct and sustain a person's behaviour (including hunger, thirst, sex and curiosity). (Rubin and McNeil, 1983)

The word 'motive' comes from the Latin for 'move' and this is captured in George Miller's definition:

> The study of motivation is the study of all those pushes and prods— biological, social and psychological—that defeat our laziness and move us, either eagerly or reluctantly, to action. (Miller, 1962)

Motivated behaviour is goal-directed, purposeful, behaviour and it is difficult to think of any behaviour (animal or human) which is not motivated in this sense. However, exactly how the underlying motives are conceptualized and how they are investigated depends very much on the persuasion of the psychologist; for instance, a *psychoanalytic* psychologist will try to discover *unconscious* motives and wishes, a *behaviourist* will search for *reinforcement schedules, a humanistic* psychologist will relate behaviour to *self-actualization,* a *neurobiological* psychologist will look for processes taking place in the *nervous system* and a *cognitive* psychologist will try to relate behaviour to the person's *thinking.*

Even these superficial examples will indicate that motives may differ with regard to a number of features or dimensions, including: (i) internal or external; (ii) innate or learned; (iii) mechanistic or cognitive; and (iv) conscious or unconscious. A number of attempts have been made to classify different kinds of motives, and these loosely correspond to the major psychological theories outlined above.

Murray (1938) identified twenty different human motives (which he called needs), including dominance, achievement and autonomy. Rubin and McNeil (1983) classify motives into two major categories: (i) survival or physiological motives; and (ii) competence or cognitive motives, with social motives representing a third category. Clearly, humans share survival motives with all other animals and, as we shall see below, we also share certain competence motives. But other motives are peculiarly and uniquely human, notably self-actualization, which lies at the peak of a 'hierarchy of needs' in Maslow's (1954) humanistic theory. (This is discussed in detail in Chapter 29).

In Chapter 29 we shall also discuss Freud's psychoanalytic theory (together with other related theories) as a theory of personality but, as the emphasis is upon dynamic forces which operate within each one of us (rather than how people differ), it can just as well be regarded as an account of human motivation.

In Chapter 7, we shall discuss laboratory studies of learning, in particular, of conditioning. For Skinner, 'motivation' is too mentalistic a term to be acceptable and, besides, behaviour can be analysed in terms of reinforcement schedules which leave nothing 'behind' the behaviour to be explained. However, not all learning theorists agree with Skinner, notably the social learning theorists, and in this chapter we shall discuss the Drive-Reduction theory of Clarke L. Hull, which differs from Skinner's theory in several important ways.

We will also take a close look at physiological theories of motivation (on which Hull's Drive-Reduction theory is partly based) as well as competency motives, including what Murray called achievement motivation or need for achievement (nAch). Another of the needs identified by Murray was affiliation, that is, the need for the company of, and interaction with, other people; social needs are discussed, in various ways, in Chapters 15 to 20.

PHILOSOPHY AND PSYCHOLOGY IN THE STUDY OF MOTIVATION

As with many other aspects of psychology, the study of motivation has its roots in philosophy. *Rationalists* saw human beings as free to choose between different courses of action and so, in a sense, the concept of motivation becomes unnecessary—we behave as we do because we have chosen to do so and it is our reason which determines our behaviour. This idea of freedom and responsibility is a basic premise of both humanistic and cognitive approaches.

The seventeenth-century British philosopher, Hobbes, proposed the theory of *hedonism*, which maintains that all behaviour is determined by the seeking of pleasure and the avoidance of pain—these are the 'real' motives (whatever we believe our motives to be) and this basic idea is an important one in Freud's psychoanalytic theory. Similarly, the basic principles of positive and negative reinforcement can be seen as corresponding to the seeking of pleasure and avoidance of pain, respectively, and these are central to Skinner's operant conditioning.

Freud's theory is often referred to as an instinct theory and the concept played a major role in early psychological approaches to motivation. Largely inspired by Darwin's (1859) Theory of Evolution, which argued that humans and animals differ only quantitatively and not qualitatively, a number of psychologists (including William James and William McDougall) identified human instincts meant to explain human behaviour. McDougall (1908), for example, originally proposed twelve, and by 1924 over 800 separate instincts had been identified. But to explain behaviour by labelling it is to *explain* nothing (eg 'We behave aggressively because of our aggressive instinct' is a circular statement) and this, combined with the sheer proliferation of instincts, seriously undermined the whole approach. (However, the concept of instinct—with certain important modifications—remains a central feature of the *ethological* approach to behaviour, in particular, animal behaviour, which is discussed in Chapter 15.)

During the 1920s the concept of instinct was largely replaced by the concept of *drive*, a term first used by Woodworth (1918), who compared human behaviour with the operation of a machine: the mechanism of a machine is relatively passive and drive is the power applied to make it 'go'.

The Concept of Drive

The concept of drive has taken two major forms: (i) the *homeostatic drive* theory (Cannon, 1929), which is a physiological theory; and (ii) the *drive-reduction* theory (Hull, 1943) which is primarily a theory of learning.

i) HOMEOSTATIC DRIVE THEORY

The term *homeostasis* was coined by Cannon in 1929 to refer to the process by which an organism maintains a fairly constant internal (bodily) environment, that is, how body temperature, blood-sugar level, salt concentration in the blood, etc. are kept in a state of relative balance or equilibrium. The basic idea is that when a state of imbalance arises (eg through a substantial rise in body temperature) something must happen to correct the imbalance and restore equilibrium (eg sweating). In this case, the animal does not have to 'do' anything because sweating is completely automatic and purely physiological. However, in the case of the imbalance which is caused by the body's need for food or drink (tissue-need), the hungry or thirsty animal has to behave in a way which will procure food or water and it is here that the concept of a homeostatic *drive* becomes important: tissue-need leads to internal imbalance, which leads to homeostatic drive, which leads to appropriate behaviour, which leads to restoration of internal balance, which leads to drive reduction.

As Green (1980) points out, the internal environment requires a regular supply of raw materials from the external world but while oxygen intake, for example, is involuntary and continuous, eating and drinking are voluntary and discontinuous (or spaced) and while we talk about a hunger and thirst drive, we do not talk about an 'oxygen drive'. Because of the voluntary nature of eating and drinking, hunger and thirst have been the homeostatic drives most researched by physiological psychologists.

Hunger

Hunger arises from the body's need for the nutrients used in growth, bodily repair, the maintenance of health and the production of energy. Cannon originally believed that the hunger drive was caused by stomach contractions ('hunger pangs') and that food reduces the drive by stopping the contractions.

In an experiment by Cannon and Washburn (1912), Washburn swallowed a balloon so that his stomach contractions could be measured; as predicted, there was a high correlation between contractions and hunger. However, this hardly proves that the contractions actually *caused* the hunger and, indeed, the balloon itself may have been the cause of the contractions.

There are several other important objections to Cannon's theory of hunger: (i) people whose stomachs have been surgically removed still feel hungry, and hunger persists even when neural pathways from the stomach to the brain have been cut; (ii) even a full stomach can 'feel' hungry if the passage to the small intestine is blocked (LeFrançois, 1983); (iii) the duodenum is probably more involved in hunger feelings than the stomach (Schachter, 1971); and (iv) people in affluent societies like our own very rarely experience hunger pangs (even though we may express our hunger by saying 'I'm starving').

Green (1980) refers to studies with rats in which the oesophagus is cut (producing an 'oesophagael fistula') so that food may be taken in through the mouth (so by-passing the stomach) or placed directly into the stomach (so by-passing the mouth). The results suggest that short-term regulation of food intake (as measured by how much food is eaten and over what length of time) could be controlled by either oral or gastric (stomach) factors; although neither is actually necessary, the presence of food in the stomach and small intestine is more important, although being able to taste and chew our food seems to be essential for a feeling of being full and sated.

Compared with these *'peripheral'* influences on the hunger drive, most recent research has focused on *'central'* influences, that is, the role of brain centres which respond to change in blood-sugar level and fat content in the bloodstream, in particular, the hypothalamus.

Research with rats in the 1940s identified the hypothalamus as playing a crucial role in eating behaviour. For example, lesions in the lower, central, portion of the hypothalamus (the *ventro-medial* nucleus, VMH) cause *hyperphagia*, that is, the rat will carry on eating until it becomes grotesquely fat—doubling or even trebling its normal body weight. This suggests that the normal function of the VMH is to *inhibit* feeding when the animal is 'full'; hence the VMH became known as the 'satiety centre'; it has been found in rats, cats, dogs, chickens and monkeys (Teitelbaum, 1967).

Just as there is a centre which stops feeding, so there seems to be a part of the hypothalamus which normally *stimulates* feeding in the first place: the lateral hypothalamus (LH), if damaged, would cause the animal to starve (even in the presence of food) to the point of death; this failure to feed is called *aphagia*.

An interesting finding is that the *taste* of food seems to be especially important in hyperphagic rats; whereas most animals will eat even bad-tasting food ('you'll eat anything if you're hungry enough'), hyper-phagic rats are very fussy and will refuse their regular food if quinine is added to it, even if this means that they become underweight (Teitelbaum, 1955). Similar results have been found with obese humans.

Why?

Internal and External Cues for Eating

One possible explanation is that the VMH lesion reduces the rat's sensitivity to *internal* cues of satiation (eg blood-sugar level and body fat content) and instead it becomes more responsive to *external* cues (eg taste). Schachter (1971) reports that overweight people also seem to pay little attention to internal cues (eg hunger pangs) and base their eating habits more on external cues (eg the availability and taste of food). However, although there is some evidence that hypothalamic tumours are associated with obesity in obese humans, there is no evidence that the hypothalamus does not function properly in overweight people generally, although it is still possible that it works *differently* in 'fat' and 'thin' eaters.

Schachter et al (1968) found that while normal-weight subjects responded to the internal cue of stomach distention ('feeling bloated') by refusing any more food, obese subjects tended to go on eating. Similarly, when a group of normal subjects and a group of obese subjects were deprived of one meal and then half of each group was given a roast-beef sandwich and the other half left hungry, only the normal weight subjects who had eaten the sandwich ate fewer crackers when allowed to eat their fill—the fact that some of the obese subjects had eaten a sandwich made no difference to the number of crackers they ate.

Schachter (1971) suggests that it is the *availability* of food to which the obese subjects were responding. However, he also found that obese subjects are less prepared than normal-weight subjects to make an effort to find food (eg go into the next room to get sandwiches) or to prepare the food in some way (eg shell peanuts); so the former tend to keep on eating as long as food is in sight or is ready-to-eat, regardless of whether their physiological needs have been met, while the latter are more willing to search for food but only if they are genuinely hungry.

Overweight people also tend to report that they feel hungry at prescribed eating times even if they have eaten a short while before; normal-weight individuals tend to eat only when they feel hungry, and this is relatively independent of clock-time.

Needs Without Specific Drives—Learning What to Eat

Clearly, with persistent deprivation, the resulting drive can come to dominate all aspects of a person's behaviour. Keys et al (1950) studied a group of volunteer subjects who spent six months in a state of semi-starvation (less than half their normal caloric intake). Their thoughts, dreams and conversations soon became dominated by food; their gum-chewing, coffee-drinking and smoking all increased markedly and, as time went on, they spent more and more time collecting 'pin-ups' of recipes and cooking utensils and devising elaborate menus.

These subjects' drive for food and their psychological need for food were clearly highly correlated, but this connection is not always so evident; a good example of this is how we (and animals) know what to eat for a nutritionally-balanced diet. While we all need vitamin C, for example, we do not actively seek it out if we are deprived of it, nor, if we did, would we have any easy way of detecting it with any of our senses in the food we eat.

Many Arctic explorers used to die of scurvy (a severe vitamin C deficiency) while the Eskimos were thriving (by eating animal fat, for example, which is rich in vitamin C); the explorers tended to retain their practice of eating lean meat even in a situation which necessitated a change.

If specific glands in rats are removed (eg the pancreas), they compensate by eating increased or decreased amounts of appropriate food (eg decreased amounts of sugar). If their diet is made deficient in certain essential vitamins and minerals, they soon develop an aversion to this diet and come to prefer new food; the aversion persists even after the deficiency is corrected. So rats, at least, seem to learn (presumably through taste and odour cues) which diets best meet their biological needs.

Presumably, we can do the same and cultural evolution helps the selection of balanced diets. Mexicans increased the calcium in their diet by mixing small amounts of mineral lime into their tortillas. In Britain and the USA, by contrast, we seem to prefer diets which are fundamentally deterimental to our health, although in recent years there has been a strong campaign in favour of healthy eating.

Needs Without Specific Drives—Learning How Much to Eat

It seems that even people who do not continuously monitor their weight manage to keep it within a range of a few pounds, despite great variations in physical activity and the nutritional value of various foods they eat.

Similarly, laboratory animals with access to unlimited amounts of food will regulate their body weights very precisely within a certain range, and the hypothalamus seems to play a vital role in this process of weight regulation. While hunger seems to be initiated by low blood-sugar levels, it usually stops before any increase could register in the hypothalamus; the hypothalamus also monitors fat content and when this rises above a certain point eating is inhibited, thus enabling humans and other animals to maintain a remarkably stable weight.

Despite the importance of the hypothalamus, it is now generally accepted that to think of the VMH as a satiety centre and the LH as a feeding centre is not the most useful or accurate way of characterizing the hypothalamic role. Hyperphagia is probably the result of interruption of nerve fibres passing through the hypothalamus, and obesity may be produced by cutting these fibres behind the hypothalamus. Similarly, LH aphagia may be 'mimicked' by damage to a bundle of fibres running from the brain-stem to the corpus striatum in the forebrain (Green, 1980).

The hypothalamus is probably a neural transmitting station to other parts of the brain and so it is the severing of neural pathways which seems to cause aphagia and hyperphagia rather than the destruction of a specific brain structure.

There is also some evidence that neurotransmitters are centrally involved in the control of appetite. Appetite in obese rats can be reduced by one of a number of hormones belonging to the *peptide* group and injections of *beta-endorphins* (opiate-like chemicals produced by the brain that reduce the perception of pain) have been found to increase appetite (see Chapter 4).

Thirst

We can go without food substantially longer than water; while pangs of hunger may fade after a few days, sensations of thirst soon become maddening and thirsty rats will learn to find a reward of water faster than an equally hungry rat will learn to find a food-reward.

A dry mouth and throat are obvious cues to thirst but there are, like hunger, delicate biochemical processes within the body. A lesion in the LH causes *adipsia* (a prolonged refusal to drink) and, conversely, simulation of parts of the hypothalamus by angiotensin (a neurotransmitter) causes a previously water-sated rat to start drinking within seconds (Green, 1980).

The hypothalamus contains specialized cells (*osmoreceptors*) which are sensitive to osmotic pressure and others which detect changes in salt concentration; if a small amount of salt soloution is injected into the hypothalamus of a goat, it proceeds to drink several gallons of water.

Exercise or increase in body temperature causes us to sweat which, as well as cooling the body, takes water from the blood. With less water, the concentration of salt in the blood increases (because the same amount of salt is dissolved in less water) and this high salt concentration stimulates the specialized cells in the hypothalamus—which causes drinking.

The hypothalamus also stimulates the posterior lobe of the pituitary gland to release the antidiuretic hormone (ADH), which in turn stimulates the kidneys to reduce the excretion of water (ie more concentrated urine). (It is thought that ADH is actually manufactured in the hypothalamus itself.)

Like hunger, thirst and drinking seem to stop long before enough time has elapsed for the body to have absorbed the water from the stomach and for the water–salt balance in the blood to have been restored. So what makes us stop drinking?

Stomach distention is one important factor; cold water is more thirst-quenching because it moves out of the stomach much more slowly and so provides a clearer stomach-distention signal to the brain. Another is the mouth-metering mechanism, which gauges the amount of water being ingested and compares the amount needed to restore the water balance.

ii) DRIVE-REDUCTION THEORY

As indicated earlier, Hull's motivational theory must be considered in the context of his theory of learning. Drive-reduction was intended to explain the fundamental principle of *reinforcement*, both *positive* (the reduction of a drive by the *presentation* of a stimulus) and *negative* (the reduction of a drive by the *removal* or *avoidance* of a stimulus).

As we have seen in discussing homeostasis, a physiological or tissue need gives rise to a corresponding drive and behaviour which removes the need and consequently reduces the drive. The needs and drives in which Hull was interested were the *primary* (physiological), homeostatic, needs and drives of hunger, thirst, air, avoiding injury, maintaining an optimum temperature, defecation and urination, rest, sleep, activity and propagation (reproduction) and Hull believed that *all* behaviour (human and animal) originates in the satisfaction of these drives. The essence of drive-reduction theory is represented in Figure 6.1.

While the terms need and drive are often used interchangeably, there is a fundamental difference between them—needs are physiological and can

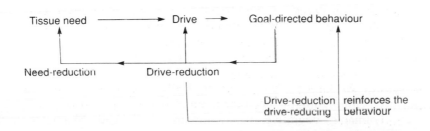

Figure 6.1 Summary of drive-reduction theory

be defined objectively (eg in terms of hours without food or blood-sugar level) and drives are psychological (behavioural) and constitute *hypothetical constructs* (although drives are operationalized as hours of deprivation in Hull's equations—see below). Hull proposed a number of equations which were meant to be testable in laboratory experiments. Perhaps the most important of these was:

$$sEr = D \times V \times K \times sHr$$

where sEr stands for the intensity or likelihood of any learned behaviour which can be calculated if four other factors are known, namely D (the drive or motivation, measured by some indicator of physical need, such as hours of deprivation), V (the intensity of the signal for the behaviour), K (the degree of incentive, measured by the size of the reward or some other measure of its desirability) and sHr (habit strength, measured as the amount of practice given, usually in terms of the number of reinforcements; Walker, 1984).

Criticisms of Homeostatic Drive-reduction Theory

Hull's basic premise that animals (and, by implication, people) *always* learn through primary drive-reduction and *never* learn if drive-reduction does not occur can be criticized from several directions:

1) Even in the case of primary drives, their relationship to *needs* is very unclear, as we saw when discussing the eating behaviour of obese people; at its simplest, drives *can* occur in the absence of any obvious physiological need.

One example of a non-homeostatic drive in animals is electrical self-stimulation of the brain (ESB). Olds and Milner (1954) found that rats stimulated by an electrode implanted near the septum (part of the limbic system) would make between 3000 and 7500 lever-pressing responses (the response producing shock) in a 12-hour period. Olds (1956) reported that one rat stimulated itself more than 2000 times per hour for 24 consecutive hours and in 1958 reported that rats which normally press a lever 25 times per hour for a food reward will press 100 times per *minute* for a reward of ESB.

So powerful a reinforcer is brain stimulation that a male rat with an electrode in its LH will self-stimulate in preference to eating if hungry, drinking when thirsty or having access to a sexually receptive female. This effect has been found in rats, cats, monkeys and pigeons (and humans, occasionally). According to Green (1980) and Beaumont (1988), the main reward site for ESB is the median forebrain bundle or MFB, a fibre tract which runs from the brain stem up to the forebrain through the LH and the effect seems to depend on the presence of the synaptic transmitters dopamine and noradrenaline (the catecholamines). There are also brain sites which, when stimulated, motivate the animal to *terminate* stimulation.

These reward centres are generally thought of as the neural substrate of 'pleasure', so that any behaviour defined as pleasurable involves their activation. As Green (1980) puts it, ESB is seen as a 'short-cut' to pleasure, 'eliminating the need for natural drives and reinforcers'.

2) Tolman's cognitive behaviourism challenged Skinner's S–R

psychology because it showed that learning could take place in the absence of reinforcement (latent learning). As Hull was defining reinforcement in terms of drive-reduction, and was claiming that learning could not occur without drive-reduction, it follows that Tolman was also showing that learning *could* take place in the absence of drive-reduction (see Chapter 7).

3) Hull's theory was also inadequate in that it emphasized primary (homeostatic) drives to the exclusion of secondary (non-homeostatic) drives: primary drives are based on primary (innate) needs while much human (and, to a lesser extent, animal) behaviour can only be understood in terms of secondary (acquired) drives. A number of researchers, notably Miller (1948), Mowrer (1950) and Dollard and Miller (1950) modified Hull's theory to include acquired drives (in particular, anxiety) which led in the 1950s to a great deal of research on avoidance learning (see Chapter 7).

The attachment of babies to their mothers has been explained in terms of a secondary drive (acquired through classical conditioning by associating her with the reduction of the primary hunger drive; see Chapter 22). Phobias can be understood in terms of avoidance learning (whereby avoiding the feared object or situation reduces the fear and so, through negative reinforcement, makes avoidance more likely; see Chapters 7, 30 and 31).

For Mowrer (1950), the secondary drive of anxiety is one of the main instigators of behaviour; striving for social approval, success, power and money can all be seen as being motivated by the wish to *avoid* the unpleasant consequences which, early in life, became associated with loss of parental love, failure or weakness.

4) Although not everyone would agree with this interpretation, it does underline the inadequacy of drive-reduction theory which, in Maslow's terms, deals only with *survival* needs and ignores completely the *self-actualization* (or 'growth') needs, which make human motivation distinctively different from that of animals. However, just as ESB cannot be accommodated by drive-reduction when considering only animal motivation, so animals seem to have other non-homeostatic drives which they share, to some degree, with humans. The rest of this part of the chapter will be devoted to these important, and pervasive, non-homeostatic needs and drives.

COMPETENCE MOTIVES—MOTIVES WITHOUT SPECIFIC PRIMARY NEEDS

According to White (1959), the 'master reinforcer' which keeps most of us motivated over long periods of time is the need to confirm our sense of personal *competence*; competence is defined as our capacity to deal effectively with the environment. It is *intrinsically* rewarding and satisfying to feel that we are capable human beings, to be able to understand, predict and control our world (which, as you may have spotted, also happen to be the major aims of science—see Chapter 2).

Unlike hunger, which comes and goes, competence seems to be a continuous, on-going, motive. We cannot satisfy it and then do without it until it next appears because it is not rooted in any specific physiological need and for this reason it is not very helpful to think of the competence motive as a drive which pushes us into seeking its reduction.

Another important difference between competence motives and homeostatic drives is that the former often involve the *search for stimulation* rather than an attempt to reduce it, as in the latter.

One way of seeking stimulation is through *curiosity* and *exploration*, which has been demonstrated in a number of species. If rats are allowed to become thoroughly familiar with a maze and then the maze is changed in some way, they will spend more time exploring the altered maze, even in the absence of any obvious *extrinsic* reward, such as food: they are displaying a *curiosity drive* (Butler, 1954).

Butler (1954), Harlow (1953) and Harlow et al (1950, 1956) gave monkeys mechanical puzzles to solve, eg undoing a chain, lifting a hook and opening a clasp. The monkey did these puzzles over and over again, for hours at a time, with no other reward: they were displaying their *manipulative drive* (Harlow et al, 1950).

PLAY AND MOTIVATION

Much of the behaviour normally described as play can be thought of in terms of the drives for curiosity, exploration and manipulation, indeed, play and exploration are often equated. But is this valid?

Hutt (1966) distinguished between *specific* and *diverse* exploration and believes that play may be similar to the latter, but not the former. However, as Fisher (1980) points out, these are difficult to distinguish in practice in babies and young children, partly because both are facilitated by novelty and complexity. It seems that, almost from birth, babies show a preference for novel and more complex stimuli, although the level of complexity preferred is a function of the baby's age (which, of course, is correlated with perceptual and other aspects of development—see Chapter 10).

The purpose of play from the child's point of view is simple enjoyment; it does not consciously engage in play to find out how things work, to try out adult roles or to exercise its imagination but because it is fun and intrinsically satisfying. Any learning which does result is quite incidental, although for the young child there is no real distinction between 'work' and 'play' in an adult sense. Piaget (1951) distinguishes between play, which is performed for its own sake (and which allows the child to practise its skills and abilities in a relaxed and carefree way) and 'intellectual activity' or learning, in which there is an external aim or purpose; this distinction is meant to apply to the three major types of play he identifies (mastery, symbolic or make-believe and play with rules) but is more blurred in the first. (Piaget's theory is discussed in more detail in Chapter 25, and two other major theories, those of Freud and Erikson, are both discussed in Chapter 21.)

It is not just humans who play—the young of many species engage in activities which seem to have little to do with the homeostatic or survival needs; however, the higher up the evolutionary scale the species is, the more apparent and purposeful the play becomes and the more the nature of play changes as the young animal develops. As Fontana (1983) points out, even in monkeys, play is mainly confined to physical movement of some kind, such as chasing and romping, and it usually involves other young monkeys; but in humans, play goes through a series of stages (Piaget, 1951) and there is a great variety of types of play, including manipulation of physical objects, physical play with other people, symbolic or imaginative play and so on.

MOTIVATION AND ADAPTATION

Piaget saw play as essentially an adaptive activity and, throughout development, play helps to consolidate recently acquired abilities as well as aiding the development of additional cognitive and social skills (Rubin et al, 1983).

In the same way, the competence motives of curiosity, exploration and manipulation undoubtedly have adaptive significance for an individual and, ultimately, for the species. Although the internal conditions which give rise to competence motives are not apparent (in contrast with physiological drives) and although they do not have any obvious, immediate, consequences for the fulfilment of biological needs, investigating and exploring the environment equips an animal with 'knowledge' which can be used in times of stress or danger (Bolles, 1967).

According to *optimal-level* (or *arousal*) theories (Berlyne, 1969; Arkes and Garske, 1977), these kinds of behaviours are based on an in-built tendency to seek a certain 'optimum' level of stimulation or activity (not unlike a homeostatic model of drive-reduction).

According to Berlyne (1969), exploring the unfamiliar increases arousal. However, if the unfamiliar is too different from what we are used to, arousal will be too high (we feel anxious and tense) while if it is not different enough, arousal is too low (we soon become bored). Our optimum level of arousal is partly determined by how relaxed we are feeling initially: when we are relaxed we are more likely to welcome novel and challenging experiences (to increase arousal) whereas when we are already tense, we prefer to deal with what is already familiar and relatively undemanding. (This applies to animals too.)

A number of *sensory deprivation* experiments, involving mature animal and human subjects, lend support to optimum-level theories. Butler (1954) kept monkeys in small, barren cages and pressing a button brought a reward of opening a small observation window, through which they could see, for example, an electric train. In the classic experiments on sensory deprivation carried out by Hebb and his colleagues at McGill University in the 1950s (Bexton et al, 1954; Heron, 1957), subjects almost completely cut off from their normal sensory stimulation (by wearing blindfolds, ear-muffs, cardboard tubes on their arms and legs, etc.) soon began to experience extreme psychological discomfort, reported hallucinations and could not usually tolerate their confinement for more than three days (see Figs 6.2 and 6.3).

Cohen and Taylor (1972) studied the psychological effects of long-term imprisonment and found that sensory deprivation and monotony are experiences which are shared by prisoners, explorers, space travellers and round-the-world sailors.

Conversely, excessive stimulation ('sensory overload') is also debilitating and may be responsible for some kinds of psychological disorders in our highly urbanized society.

AROUSAL AND PERSONALITY

Clearly, different individuals can tolerate different levels of arousal; one

Figure 6.2 *Sensory deprivation cubicle (Heron, 1957)*

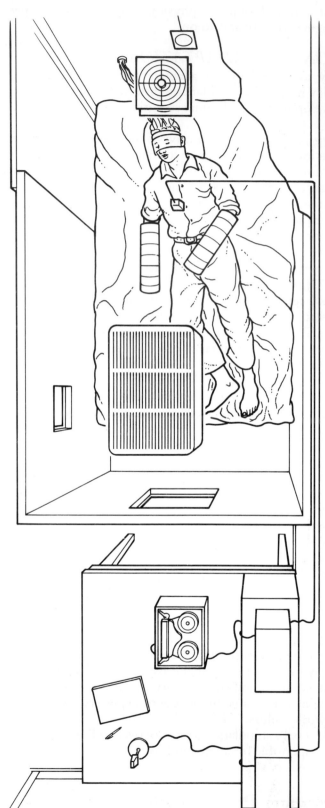

EXPERIMENTAL CUBICLE constructed at Mc Gill University in Montreal to study the effects of perceptual isolation is at the right in this semischematic drawing from above. The subject lies on a bed 24 hours a day, with time out for meals and going to the bathroom. The room is always lighted. The visual perception of the subject is restricted by a translucent plastic visor; his auditory perception, by U-shaped pillow covering his ears and by the noise of an air conditioner and a fan (ceiling of cubicle). In the experiment depicted here a flat pillow is used to leave room for the wires attached to the subject's scalp, which are connected to an electroencephalograph in an adjacent room. The subject's sense of touch is restricted by cotton gloves and long cardboard cuffs. The experimenter and the subject can communicate by means of a system of microphones and loud speakers.

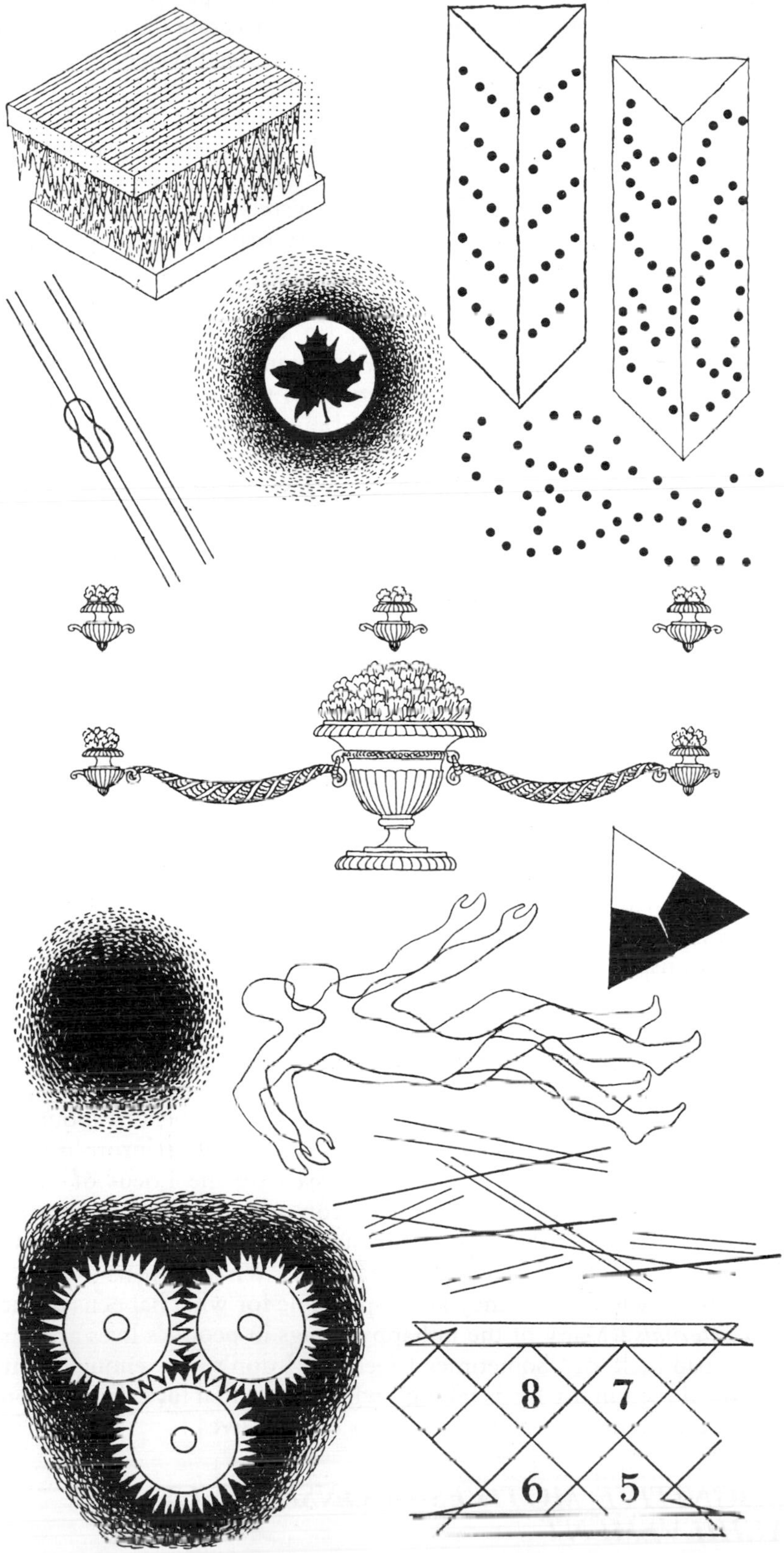

Figure 6.3 Hallucinations of sensory-deprived subjects (Heron 1957)

person's optimum may be 'overload' for another person and 'deprivation' for someone else. Perhaps those who can tolerate (indeed, seek) the highest levels of arousal are those who take life-threatening risks (by climbing mountains, parachuting, performing stunts, etc.).

Ogilvie (1984) interviewed a group of top international athletes and found them to be: (i) strongly in need of success and recognition; (ii) highly autonomous and needing to dominate; (iii) self-assertive and forthright; (iv) loners, preferring transitory relationships to deep emotional ties; and (v) very low in anxiety, very realistic and having a high degree of emotional control. In sum, they are 'stimulus addictive', needing to extend themselves periodically to the limits of their physical, emotional and intellectual capacities, 'in order to escape from the tensionless state associated with everyday living'.

Zuckermann (1978) gave personality tests to over 10,000 people and divided them into *augmenters*, whose brains become more responsive the greater the stimulation, and *reducers*, whose brains exercise some kind of inhibition, whereby they become less responsive with increased stimulation.

Thus some people tend to thrive on stimulation and actively seek to increase it while others seek to reduce it (compare this with Eysenck's theory of Introversion–Extroversion, see Chapter 29).

THE NEED FOR CONTROL

Another major kind of competence motive is the need to be in control of our own destiny and not at the mercy of external forces (Rubin and McNeil, 1983). The need for control is closely linked with the need to be free from the controls and restrictions of others, to dictate our own actions and not be dictated to. According to Brehm (1966), when our freedom is threatened, we tend to react by reasserting our freedom, which he called *psychological reactance*.

When people initially expect to have control over the outcomes of their actions, the first experience of not being in control is likely to produce reactance (Wortman and Brehm, 1975) but further bad experiences are likely to result in *learned helplessness* (Seligman, 1975), to which we shall return in the section on stress.

Again, there are important individual differences. Rotter (1966) proposed the *locus of control* concept to refer to our beliefs about what controls events in our everyday lives and how we are reinforced for our actions. Locus of control was first assessed by the Locus of Control Scale, a self-administered questionnaire comprising twenty-three pairs of opposed statements; the scale contrasts *internals* (eg 'People's misfortunes result from the mistakes they make' or, 'What happens to me is my own doing') who believe they are responsible for what happens to them, with *externals* ('Many of the unhappy things in people's lives are partly due to bad luck' or, 'Sometimes I feel that I don't have enough control over the direction my life is taking') who believe that luck, fate and other people and events control most aspects of their lives.

COGNITIVE MOTIVES—CONSISTENCY AND ACHIEVEMENT

Perhaps one of the most researched cognitive motives is the need for *cognitive consistency*, which is discussed in Chapter 19 in relation to attitudes and attitude change.

Another which has generated an enormous amount of research and theorizing is *achievement motivation* or Need for Achievement (nAch), which was one of the twenty human motives identified by Murray in 1938. He drew a sharp distinction between 'psychogenic' or psychological needs, which are learned, and 'viscerogenic' or physiological needs, which are innate.

Based on his acceptance of Freud's belief that people express their true motives more clearly in free-association than in direct self-reports (or questionnaire-type personality tests), Murray (together with Morgan, 1935) devised the Thematic Apperception Test (TAT), which consists of a series of twenty pictures, presented one at a time, ten in each of two sessions separated by at least one day. Slightly different versions are used for men and women, boys and girls. The subject is told the TAT is a test of imagination and asked to make up a story that describes:

(i)   what is happening and who the people are;
(ii) what has led up to the situation;
(iii) what is being thought and what is wanted and by whom;
(iv) what will happen, what will be done.

The pictures are sufficiently ambiguous with regard to the events depicted and the emotions of the characters (Fig. 6.4), to allow a wide range of interpretations and how a person interprets them reveals their

Figure 6.4 Sample TAT picture

unconscious motives; hence the TAT is a major *projective* test used in motivation and personality research. Its inter-judge reliability is quite high but test–retest reliability is lower. A person who scores high on nAch is concerned with standards of excellence, high levels of performance, recognition of others and the pursuit of long-term goals (ie they are ambitious).

McClelland (McClelland et al, 1953, 1958) is the major figure associated with nAch research and has found that high scorers tend to perform better on a number of tasks, including anagram puzzles, are generally more persistent and prefer an 'expert' to a 'friendly' work partner. They also tend to attribute their performance to *internal* factors (ability, effort, etc.), while low scorers are more likely to attribute theirs to *external* factors (ease of the task, luck, etc.). Two very important variables which interact with nAch are: (i) fear of failure; and (ii) fear of success. Atkinson (1964) argued that achievement-related behaviour is powerfully affected not just by nAch but also by *fear of failure*. He proposed a modified theory of achievement behaviour, incorporating nAch, fear of failure and certain contextual variables (in particular the perceived probability of success or failure and the incentive associated with success or failure).

It has been found consistently that nAch scores do not predict the actual behaviour of females as well as that of males. Why should this be? According to Maccoby (1963), females, traditionally, have not been encouraged to be successful in those areas in which men are expected to excel (and which are reflected in nAch scores), but Horner (1970, 1972), using a story completion task, found that female students showed significantly greater *fear of success* than male students. This fear of success is likely to influence behaviour in competitive situations and situations in which success is seen by women as coming into conflict with their relationships with men and their success as women.

Hoffman (1977) followed-up Horner's subjects and found that the high fear of success scorers married and had children sooner than low scorers; having a baby reaffirms their sense of femininity, removes them from the competitive arena and re-establishes their dependency on their husbands. Significantly, many become pregnant when faced with the possibility of success in an area where they might have been in competition with their husbands.

EMOTION: ADDING FLAVOUR TO BEHAVIOUR

Mr Spock in *Star Trek* is often pointing out to Captain Kirk how much energy human beings waste through reacting emotionally to things when a more logical and rational approach would be more productive. But would we be human at all if we did not react in this way? This is not to advocate 'being emotional' in the sense of losing control of our feelings or being unable to consider things in a calm and detached way; however, it is the richness of our emotions and our capacity to have feelings as well as to think and reason which makes us unique as a species. Emotions set the tone of our experience and give life its vitality and, like motives, they are internal factors which can energize, direct and sustain behaviour (Rubin & McNeil, 1983).

Many attempts have been made by psychologists to *classify* emotions:

(a) Wundt (1896) believed that emotional experience can be described in terms of combinations of three dimensions—pleasantness/unpleasantness, calm/excitement and relaxation/tension (based on introspection).

(b) Schlosberg (1941) also identified pleasantness/unpleasantness, together with acceptance/rejection and sleep/tension (based on photographs of posed facial expressions).

(c) Osgood (1966) also saw pleasantness as one dimension plus activation and control, which correspond to the evaluative, activity and potency factors of the semantic differential—see Chapter 19 (based on live emotional display).

(d) Ekman et al (1972) and Ekman and Friesen (1975) identified six primary emotions (surprise, fear, disgust, anger, happiness and sadness) which they believe are universal, ie they are expressed facially in the same way, and which are recognized as such by members of a diversity of cultures, and so are probably innate (based on photos of posed facial expressions (Fig. 6.5).

     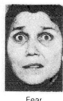

Happiness   Disgust   Surprise   Sadness   Anger   Fear

Figure 6.5 Six universal facial expressions

(e) Plutchik (1980) identifies eight primary emotions (which correspond to Ekman and Friesen's six, except that 'joy' and 'sorrow' are used for 'happiness' and 'sadness', respectively, plus acceptance and expectancy).

For each emotion that we may identify, there are three *components*: (i) the *subjective experience* of happiness, sadness, anger etc; (ii) the *physiological changes* which occur, involving the nervous system and the endocrine system, over which we have little, if any, conscious control although we may become aware of some of their effects (such as 'butterflies in the stomach', gooseflesh, sweating etc, see Chapter 4); and (iii) the *behaviour* associated with a particular emotion, such as smiling, crying, frowning, running away, being frozen to the spot, etc.

How these three components are related, the relative emphasis given to one or more of them and how they are related to our *cognitive appraisal* or interpretation of the emotion-producing stimulus or situation, are what distinguish competing theories of emotion.

THEORIES OF EMOTION

a) The James–Lange Theory

If there is a commonsense theory of emotion, it is that something happens which produces in us a subjective emotional experience and, *as a result* of this, certain bodily and/or behavioural changes occur. James (originally in 1878 and then in 1890) and Lange, (at first independently of James), turned this commonsense view on its head and argued that our emotional experience is the *result*, not the cause, of perceived bodily changes. To give an example used by James, the commonsense view says that we meet a bear, are frightened and run; the James–Lange theory maintains that we are frightened *because* we run! Again, 'We feel sorry because we cry, angry because we strike, afraid because we tremble...'

> ...the bodily changes follow directly the perception of the exciting fact, and ... our feeling of the same changes as they occur *is* the emotion (James, 1890).

The crucial factor in the James–Lange theory is *feedback* from the bodily changes (Fig. 6.6). We label our subjective state by *inferring* how

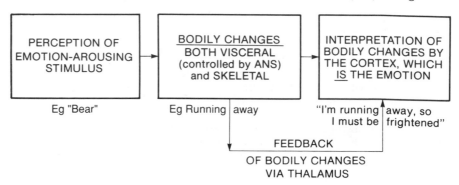

Figure 6.6 *The James–Lange theory of emotion*

we feel based on perception of our own bodily changes ('I'm trembling so I must be afraid') which is rather similar to Bem's self-perception theory (see Chapter 19). How feasible is this theory?

You may be able to think of situations in which you have reacted in a fairly automatic way (eg you've slipped coming down the stairs) and only after you have grabbed the bannisters do you become aware of feeling frightened (and a little shaken)—it is almost as if the sudden change in your behaviour has caused the fear, quite apart from *why* you grabbed the bannisters.

The theory implies that by controlling (deliberately altering) our behaviour we can control our emotional experiences. Try smiling—do you feel any happier? A crucial test (which James admitted would be very difficult to perform) would be to examine the emotional experience of someone who is completely anaesthetized but not intellectually or motor-impaired.

In the examples that James himself gives of inferring emotion from bodily changes (eg running away from the bear), he is clearly attaching much more importance to *skeletal* as opposed to visceral changes. In this respect, the James–Lange theory probably differs from other theories, which usually talk about *physiological changes* meaning visceral changes.

To this extent, there are two important studies which lend support to the James–Lange theory. The first is by Valins (1966), who provided male subjects with feedback of their supposed heart-rate while watching slides of semi-nude *Playboy* females. The heart-rate was pre-recorded and programmed to increase in apparent response to presentation of half the slides, so that subjects believed they were reacting to these pictures.

These slides were rated as more attractive than those supposedly associated with unchanged heart rate.

The second is by Laird (1974), in which thirty-two students were falsely told that they were to participate in an experiment to measure activity in the facial muscles. Bogus electrodes were attached to their faces (as if to measure physiological responses) and the subjects were instructed to raise their eyebrows, contract the muscles in their forehead and make other facial expressions without their realizing the emotional significance of what they were doing. Cartoon slides were then projected onto a screen and, regardless of their content, subjects rated as funnier those they saw while 'smiling'; also, when rating their own emotion, subjects described themselves as happier when they were smiling, angrier when frowning and so on.

So, to some extent, overt behaviour can serve as a *cause* of subjective feelings, and yet in the James–Lange theory, these bodily changes occur *spontaneously*, not consciously and deliberately, so perhaps we cannot draw too many conclusions from studies like Laird's. Besides, there are other, equally serious objections to the theory, in particular, those made by Cannon in 1927.

However, both studies strongly suggest that physiological arousal is not sufficient to account for emotional experience and, the fact that subjects in the Valins study were prepared to *infer* emotion on the basis of information about their reactions to stimuli, suggests it may not even be necessary and that *cognitive* factors may be sufficient (Parkinson, 1987).

b) *The Cannon–Bard Theory*

According to Cannon, there are four major faults with the James–Lange theory:

1) The theory implies that for each subjectively distinct emotion there is a corresponding set of physiological changes enabling us to label the emotion we are experiencing. Cannon argued that:

> ... the same visceral changes occur in very different emotional states and in non-emotional states. (Cannon, 1929)

But is there any evidence that such physiological differences actually exist?

According to Wolf and Wolff (1947), although it is possible to make physiological distinctions between certain emotions (eg anger is generally associated with an increase in gastric activity and fear with an inhibition of gastric activity), efforts to find clear-cut physiological differences between some of the more subtle emotions have not been as successful (eg depression, feeling overwhelmed).

Ax (1953, 1957) reported that fear is associated with increased heart-rate, skin conduction level, muscle action potential frequency and breathing rate (corresponding to the effects of *adrenaline*) while anger is accompanied by increased diastolic blood pressure, frequency of spontaneous skin conduction responses and action potential size (indicating the greater influence of *noradrenaline*).

Ax's findings have been confirmed by others (eg Frankenhaeuser (1975). Schachter (1957) confirmed that fear is influenced largely by adrenaline but found that anger produces a mixed adrenaline–

noradrenaline response and pain produces a noradrenaline-like pattern. However:

> Whether or not there are physiological distinctions among the various emotional states must be considered an open question. Any differences which do exist are at best rather subtle and the variety of emotion, mood and feeling states do not appear to be matched by an equal variety of visceral patterns. (Schachter and Singer, 1962)

According to Lloyd et al (1984), the research does not allow us to distinguish between the effects of general autonomic feedback and differentiated arousal patterns but, to be fair to James (as we noted earlier), he was probably more concerned with *expressive* behaviour (running away, trembling, etc.) than he was with visceral responses (which the research we have just reviewed focused on) and it could be argued that Cannon's first criticism is, therefore, not strictly relevant. (Indeed, since we are almost completely unaware of these visceral changes, it would have been very difficult for James to have claimed that it is 'visceral feedback' which constitutes the emotion.)

2) Even if there were identifiable patterns of physiological response associated with different subjective emotions, Cannon argued that such physiological changes themselves do not necessarily produce emotional states, ie physiological arousal is not sufficient.

He based this on a famous study by Marañon (1924) who injected 210 subjects with adrenaline: 71 per cent said they only experienced physical symptoms, with no emotional overtones at all, and most of the rest reported 'as *if*' emotions; the few who experienced genuine emotion had to imagine (or remember) a highly emotional event. More recently, Hohmann (1966) studied twenty-five adult males with spinal cord injuries who suffered corresponding damage to their autonomic nervous system and who reported significant changes in the nature and intensity of certain emotional experiences, particularly, anger, fear and sexual feelings. Generally, the higher up the spinal cord the lesion, the greater the disruption of visceral responses and the greater the disturbance of normal emotional experiences; like Marañon's subjects, they too reported 'as if' emotions, a 'mental kind of anger', for example.

Therefore it would seem that physiological changes, after all, although not sufficient for the experience of 'full-blooded' emotions, are *necessary*. However, even though Marañon's and Hohmann's subjects did not experience 'real' emotions, it is significant that they experienced *particular* 'as if' emotions rather than a generalized state of arousal; clearly, perception of an eliciting stimulus is needed to give an emotion a full-bodied flavour. According to Schachter, what Marañon's and Hohman's subjects reported:

> . . . is precisely what should be anticipated from a formulation of emotions as a joint function of cognitive and physiological factors. (Schacter,1964)

3) A third criticism is to do with whether or not the physiological changes associated with emotion are even necessary (let alone sufficient). Cannon (1927) removed the sympathetic nervous system of cats and Sherrington (1900) severed the spinal cord and vagus nerves of dogs; in both cases, feedback from the viscera to the brain was prevented but the animals showed apparently normal emotional reactions. However, as Lloyd et al (1984) point out, we do not know about their emotional experience.

Yet Dana's (1921) study of a patient with a spinal cord lesion lends support to Cannon—despite having no sympathetic functioning and extremely limited muscular movement, the patient showed a range of emotions, including grief, joy, displeasure and affection. But we cannot generalize from a single case, although the Valins and Laird studies both support Dana.

4)   Cannon also argued that, as we often feel emotions quite rapidly, and as the viscera are quite slow to react, how could the physiological changes be the source of such sudden emotion (as required by the James–Lange theory)?

So what is different about Cannon's theory (known as the Cannon–Bard theory)?

As Figure 6.7 shows, the subjective emotion is quite *independent* of

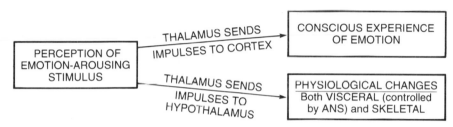

Figure 6.7 The Cannon–Bard theory of emotion

the physiological changes involved: the emotion-producing stimulus is processed by the thalamus, which sends impulses: (i) to the cortex, where the emotion is consciously experienced; and (ii) to the hypothalamus, which sets in motion certain autonomic physiological changes.

c) *Schachter's Cognitive Labelling Theory*

According to Schachter (1964), Cannon was wrong in thinking that bodily changes and the experience of emotion are independent and the James–Lange theory is mistaken in claiming that physiological changes cause the feeling of emotion. However, he shares the James–Lange belief that physiological changes *precede* the experience of emotion because the latter depends *both* on physiological changes *and* on the interpretation of those changes—we have to *decide* which particular emotion we are feeling, and the label we attach to our arousal depends on to what we *attribute* that arousal (see Fig. 6.8.) (Schachter is saying that physiological arousal is *necessary* for the experience of emotion but the nature of arousal is immaterial—it is how we interpret the arousal that matters, and so the theory is also known as the 'Two factor theory of emotion'.)

The classic experiment which demonstrates the cognitive theory of emotion is that of Schachter and Singer (1962) described in Box 6.1.

The experiment was, in fact, testing three interrelated hypotheses regarding the *interaction* between physiological and cognitive factors in the experience of emotion:

(a) If an individual experiences a state of physiological arousal for which he/she has no immediate explanation, he/she will 'label' this state and describe it in terms of the cognitions available. So precisely the same state of arousal could receive different labels (eg 'euphoria'/ 'anger'—Groups B and C). (Physiological arousal *and* cognitive labelling are necessary).

(b) If an individual experiences a state of physiological arousal for which

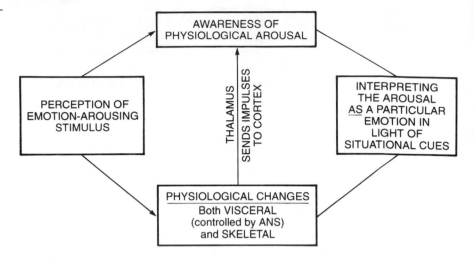

Figure 6.8 Schachter's cognitive labelling theory (or two-factor theory)

Box 6.1: Schachter and Singer's (1962) Adrenaline Experiment

Subjects were given what they were told was a vitamin injection in order to see its effect on vision; in fact, it was adrenaline. Subjects were tested under one of four conditions:

Group A Subjects were told the *real* side-effects of the injection (namely palpitations, tightness in the throat, tremor, sweating, etc).
Group B Subjects were given *false* information about the effects of the injection (eg itching and headache).
Group C Subjects were given *no* information about the effects of the injection (eg true or false).
Group D Control group subjects were given a saline injection (and otherwise treated like group C subjects).

While waiting for a 'vision test', each subject (one at a time) sat in a waiting room with another 'subject' (in fact, a confederate of the experimenters). For half the subjects in each condition, the confederate acted in a happy, frivolous way (making paper aeroplanes, laughing out loud and playing with a hula hoop) (*euphoria*) while for the other half, he acted very angrily (eventually tearing up the questionnaire which he and the subject were both asked to complete) (*anger*). (In fact, the group B condition was only run with a euphoric stooge.)

Subjects' emotional experiences were assessed by: (i) observers' ratings of the degree to which they joined in with the confederate's behaviour; and (ii) self-report scales. What were the results?

As predicted, groups A and D were much less likely to join in with the confederate and to report feeling euphoric or angry, while group B and C subjects assumed the confederate's behaviour and emotion. Why? While group A could attribute their arousal to the injection and so did not need to explain it in emotional terms, groups B and C attributed *their* arousal to 'emotional' factors, using the confederate's behaviour as a *cue* for identifying their own state of arousal as either euphoria or anger.

---

he/she has a completely appropriate explanation (eg 'I've just been given an injection of adrenaline') he/she will 'label' this state accordingly (Group A).

(c) Given the same circumstances, an individual will react emotionally

> *Box 6.2: Falling in Love on a Suspension Bridge (Dutton and Aron, 1974)*
>
> The subjects were unsuspecting males, aged 18–35, who were visiting the Capilano Canyon in British Columbia, Canada. An attractive female experimenter approached the men and asked them questions as part of a survey she was supposedly conducting on reactions to scenic attractions. One of the things they were asked to do was to invent a short story about an ambiguous picture of a woman, which was later scored for the amount of sexual content, taken to reflect their sexual attraction towards the interviewer.
>
> Some men were interviewed on an extremely unstable suspension bridge, 230 feet above the Canyon (high-arousal condition) and others on a solid wooden bridge upstream (low-arousal condition); as predicted, the stories of the former group contained significantly more sexual imagery.

or describe his/her feelings as emotions only to the extent that he/she experiences a state of physiological arousal (all 3 groups). (Physiological arousal is *necessary*.)

Schachter and Wheeler (1962) confirmed these results by injecting subjects either with adrenaline or chlorpromazine (which inhibits arousal); controls were injected with a placebo. While watching a slapstick comedy, the adrenaline-subjects laughed more, and the chlorpromazine subjects less, than the control subjects.

Another supporting study is that by Dutton and Aron (1974) (Box 6.2). This study confirms Schachter's theory that the autonomic arousal which accompanies all emotions is similar and that it is our *interpretation* of that arousal that is important, even though this sometimes results in our *mis-identifying* our emotions; Dutton and Aron's suspension bridge subjects seemed to be mis-labelling their fear as sexual attraction to the interviewer. (What do you think would have been the outcome if the interviewer had been male?)

Evaluation of the Cognitive-Labelling Theory

1) According to Parkinson (1987), the predominant influence in the study of emotion since Schachter has been a cognitive one. The focus of Schachter's model is an atypical state of affairs where the subject is unsure about the cause of arousal (Groups B and C). But Schachter (1964) admitted that we usually *are* aware of a precipitating situation prior to the onset of arousal (which usually takes 1–2 seconds to reach consciousness) and so it is normally perfectly obvious to the person what aspects of the situation have initiated the emotion. However, even here the meaning of the emotion-inducing circumstances requires some cognitive analysis before the emotion can be labelled. Schachter claims that although the *quantitative* aspect of emotion can arise without cognitive mediation ('am I in a state of emotional arousal?') (eg Valins) the *qualitative* aspect requires prior cognition ('what emotion is it I am experiencing?') (eg Laird). Mandler (1984) has called Schachter and Singers' theory the 'jukebox' theory—arousal is like the coin which gets the machine going and cognition is the button we push to select the emotional tune. According to Parkinson:

> . . . this view that affect is post cognitive is now probably the most popular attitude among emotion theorists. (Parkinson, 1987)

2) Are environmental cues really as easily accepted as the basis for inferences about our own feelings as Schachter claims (Fiske and Taylor, 1984)? Using the original Schachter–Singer paradigm, several studies (Plutchik and Ax, 1967; Marshall and Zimbardo, 1979; Maslach, 1979) have concluded that subjects' efforts to understand an unexplained state of arousal is more extensive than a quick examination of salient cues in the surrounding environment.

3) One of the ways in which Schachter's work has influenced the cognitive approach to emotion is in the form of an *attributional theory* of emotion—ie the nature and/or intensity of an emotion seems to depend largely on the causes to which the individual attributes his/her physiological changes (see Chapter 17). For example, Peterson and Seligman (1980) and Abramson and Martin (1981) grafted attribution principles onto Seligman's (1975) theory of *learned helplessness* in order to try to explain clinical depression. Clearly, the experience of the inability to control the outcome of one particular situation (helplessness) does not inevitably lead to clinical depression in most people. So what other factors are involved? Abramson and Martin (1981) believe that depression only occurs when subjects make certain attributions about their helplessness, specifically, when they believe it is caused by *internal* factors (as opposed to environmental), which are perceived as *stable* (as opposed to variable) and that are believed to reflect a *global deficiency* (as opposed to one related to a particular kind of bad experience). So people become depressed when they conclude that helplessness is likely to pervade all aspects of their future lives. Schachter's theory implies that emotional reactions induced by a threatening experience can be reattributed to a neutral or less threatening source, eg if you blame some external stimulus rather than your own inadequacies, you may calm down sufficiently to break the vicious circle. A number of experiments using this kind of intervention have found support for the re-attribution approach (Fiske and Taylor, 1984).

4) In turn, this is related to stress (see below). Cox (1978) argues that the experience of stress is usually described in ways associated with emotions—anger, anxiety, depression, fear, grief, guilt, jealousy and shame: the experience of stress is indeed an emotional one. Lazarus (1976) refers to these as the 'stress emotions'. Agreeing with Schachter, Kagan (1975) believes that it is how an individual cognitively appraises the situation which shapes basic feelings into a specific emotion. This, of course, raises again the question of just how flexible/labile is emotional experience and implies the crucial question as to how much stress can be reduced (or prevented) by changing people's cognitive appraisal of the situation.

A famous study by Speisman et al (1964) involved showing subjects a film on anthropology (*Subincision in the Arunta*) in which the penises of aboriginal boys are seen being cut with a jagged flint knife as part of a puberty rite. This normally causes high levels of stress. However, the sound track was manipulated, so that: (i) the pain, jaggedness of the knife, etc. were emphasized (*trauma*); (ii) the boys' anticipation of entering manhood was stressed (*denial*); (iii) the emotional elements were ignored and the traditions of the tribe were stressed (*intellectualization*); or (iv) there was no commentary at all (*silent control*). As predicted, arousal (measured by GSR and heart-rate) was highest in (i), next highest in (iv) and lowest in (ii) and (iii). What we tell ourselves about external situations influences the level of arousal we experience. But we should also ask if the converse is true—does the level of arousal influence how we appraise the situation. Those studies that have failed to replicate Schachter and Singer's findings all suggest that emotion is rather less malleable than Schachter believed: (i) if the dosage is high enough, adrenaline seems to produce an unpleasant mood—even in the Group B condition and in the presence of the euphoric 'stooge'; (ii) Group B and Group C were both more likely to interpret the unexplained arousal negatively—regardless of the mood of the stooge.

5) Finally, Hilgard et al (1979) make some important criticisms:

(a) Adrenaline does not affect everyone in the same way and Schachter and Singer in fact eliminated from their analysis five subjects who later reported they experienced no physiological symptoms.

(b) No assessment was made of subject's mood *before* the injections; presumably, a subject in a better mood to begin with might respond more positively to a playful stooge.

(c) How comparable are arousal states created by drugs and manipulated in the laboratory to naturally-occurring, real-life emotions?

d) Cognitive Appraisal or Affective Primacy—Which Comes First, Thought or Feeling?

Perhaps the best example of a *cognitive appraisal* theory is that of Lazarus (1982) which is a development of Schachters' cognitive labelling theory. According to Lazarus, some degree of cognitive processing is an essential prerequisite for an affective reaction to a stimulus to occur:

> Cognitive appraisal (of meaning or significance) underlines and is an integral feature of all emotional states. (Lazarus, 1982)

A good demonstration of cognitive appraisal is the Speisman et al (1964) study. As we saw, denial and intellectualization both led to substantial reductions in stress. So it seems that:

> ... manipulating an individual's cognitive appraisal when confronted by a stressful event can have a significant effect on physiological stress reactions. (Parkinson, 1987)

Lazarus proposes that cognitive appraisal invariably precedes any affective reaction, although it *does not* have to involve any *conscious* processing. Zajonc (1984) argues that there is generally little direct evidence of either the existence or nature of such pre-conscious cognitive processing but the study of *subliminal perception* (see Chapter 9) suggests otherwise. Zajonc (1980) argues that cognition and affect operate as independent systems and an emotional response may *precede* cognitive processes under certain circumstances; we often make affective judgements about people even though we have processed very little information about them. For example, we may meet someone very briefly and form a positive or negative impression, despite not being able to remember any detailed information about them later, eg hair or eye colour (Eysenck and Keane, 1990).

Zajonc seems to over-estimate the amount of cognitive processing which Lazarus and other cognitive appraisal theorists are claiming. For example, Lazarus simply argues that some minimal cognitive analysis at some level always precedes emotional experience, but this does not have to be a thoroughgoing processing of the stimulus:

> ... emotion results from evaluative perception of a relationship (actual, imagined or anticipated) between a person (or animal) and the environment. (Lazarus, 1982)

As such, emotion is necessarily preceded by appraisal of the implications of the stimulus event for the subject's well-being. But is Lazarus claiming, effectively, that an experience cannot be called an 'emotion' *unless* some cognitive appraisal is involved, ie is it part of the *definition* of an emotion? This is a way of evading the *empirical* question of affective primacy (Zajonc, 1984).

Many of the examples Zajonc gives seem *not* to be examples of emotional states at all. For example, startle occurs automatically. It is essentially a *reflex* response and Lazarus would not argue that any cognitive appraisal was involved. Similarly, Ekman et al (1985) claim that startle is produced automatically in all subjects by the same stimulus (eg a sudden loud noise), whereas the whole history of the psychology of emotion attests to the fact that there is no known stimulus which will reliably produce the same emotion in all subjects:

> There is no doubt that Lazarus's studies have far more direct relevance to everyday emotional experiences than do those of Zajonc. This provides grounds for assuming (albeit tentatively) that emotional experience is generally preceded by cognitive processes, even if that is not invariably the case. (Eysenck & Keane, 1990)

STRESS: WHEN EMOTIONS BECOME HARMFUL

While there is no single definition of stress, we have all experienced it at one time or another and, because of its potential harm, physiologically and psychologically, psychologists, psychiatrists and others agree that it is essential that we try to understand it in order to prevent it or at least minimize it.

Cox (1975) identifies three models of stress around which definitions and research have revolved:

1) The *engineering model* sees external stresses giving rise to a stress reaction, or strain, in the individual, so the stress is located in the stimulus characteristics of the environment; stress is what *happens to* a person (not what happens within a person).

The concept is derived from Hooke's Law of Elasticity in physics, which deals with how loads (stress) produce deformation in metals. Up to a point, stress is inevitable and can be tolerated; indeed, moderate levels may even be beneficial and complete absence of stress (as measured, say, by anxiety or physiological arousal) could be positively detrimental (for instance, being so relaxed that you fail to notice the car speeding towards you as you are crossing the road).

There is no doubt that stress helps to keep us alert, providing us with some of the energy required to maintain an interest in our environment, to explore it and adapt to it; in these respects, stress is similar to motivation and emotion (or is a component of both). However, when stress becomes intolerable (when we are stretched beyond our limits of elasticity) it becomes positively harmful.

2) The *physiological model* is primarily concerned with what happens *within* the person, that is, with the 'response' aspects of the engineering model, in particular the physiological (and, to a lesser extent, the psychological) changes which occur as a result of stress.

The impetus for this view of stress was Selye's (1956) definition that, 'stress is the non-specific response of the body to any demand made upon it'. Selye's original observations were made when he was a medical student and noticed a general malaise or syndrome associated with 'being ill', regardless of the nature of the illness. The syndrome was characterized by: (i) a loss of appetite; (ii) an associated loss of weight and strength; (iii) loss of ambition; and (iv) a typical facial expression associated with illness. Further examination of extreme cases revealed major physiological changes, including enlargement of the adrenal cortex, shrinkage of the thymus, spleen and lymphatics (all involved in the body's immune system) and, eventually, deep bleeding ulcers of the stomach and upper gut (confirmed by Cox, 1978). These changes, representing the non-specific response to illness, were supposed to reflect a genuine phenomenon not embraced by specific responses and Selye called them the *General Adaptation Syndrome* (GAS)—we shall discuss this further below.

3) The *transactional model* represents a kind of blend of the first two models and sees stress as arising from an *interaction* between people and their environment, in particular, when there is an imbalance between the person's perception of the demand being made of them by the situation and their ability to meet the demand, and when failure to cope is important. Because it is the person's *perception* of this mis-match between demand and ability which causes stress, the model allows for important individual differences in what are sources of stress and how much stress is experienced; people may also differ in terms of characteristic physiological responses to stress (over and above the GAS). For instance, some will typically have migraine headaches, others break out in a rash, others have stomach pains and so on. There are also wide differences in how people attempt to cope with stress, psychologically and behaviourally, and we shall discuss some of these below.

The Engineering Model may be seen as primarily concerned with the question 'What *causes* stress?', and the Physiological Model with the question, 'How do we *react* (physiologically) to stress?'. The Transactional Model is concerned with both these questions plus the question, 'How do we *cope* with stress?'. We shall now look at these three major issues.

WHAT CAUSES STRESS?

i) Frustration and Conflict

We saw in relation to the transactional model that perceived mis-match between demand and ability causes stress, and so anything which prevents us from achieving our goals is a potential source of stress. Indeed, *frustration* is usually defined as some kind of negative emotional state which occurs when we are prevented from reaching a goal (Coon, 1983) and so is a common source of stress. But what causes frustration?

Our own inadequacies can prevent us from achieving our goals and ambitions (eg we want to be a basketball player but are very short, or we want to be a doctor but cannot stand the sight of blood). Or we can be thwarted by a whole host of external/environmental factors over which we have little or no control (although no less than we have over some personal factors, eg being short), such as the train being cancelled, the telephone being out of order, or the weather changing for the worse! We shall say more about these everyday hassles below.

Conflicts develop when a person experiences two or more competing or contradictory motives or goals:

(a) *Approach–approach* conflicts involve having to choose between *two equally attractive alternatives*, eg two equally delicious-sounding dishes on the same menu or two equally interesting courses at college or university (see Cognitive Dissonance Theory in Chapter 19 for a discussion of how such conflict is resolved once the decision has been made).

(b) *Avoidance–avoidance* conflicts involve having to choose between *two equally unattractive alternatives*, eg going to the dentist or putting up with awful toothache, deciding whether to do your psychology or your sociology essay first. It is a case of having to choose 'between the devil and the deep blue sea'.

(c) *Approach–avoidance* conflicts involve the *same person or situation having both very desirable and undesirable qualities*, eg you are really interested in psychology but you are not so sure about the statistics, or you want to go to university but you would like to be working and earning some money.

ii) *Disruption of Circadian Rhythms*

As we saw in Chapter 5 the word *circadian* comes from the Latin *circa dies* and means 'about one day'. It describes a particular periodicity or rhythm of a number of physiological and behavioural functions which can be seen in almost all living creatures.

It seems that most species synchronize their bodily rhythms to the 24-hour cycle of light and dark, so that during a 24-hour period there is a cycle of many physiological functions (eg heart-rate, metabolic rate, breathing rate, body temperature) which all tend to reach maximum values during the late afternoon and early evening and minimum values in the early hours of the morning (Colquhoun and Edwards, 1970). It might seem fairly obvious that such a rhythm would occur as it is likely that physiological functions would increase during the day when we are active and become depressed at night when we are asleep and inactive. However, many studies have shown that these rhythms persist if we suddenly reverse our activity pattern and sleep during the day and are active during the night (Colquhoun and Edwards, 1970).

There is evidence that these rhythms are internally controlled (endogenous) but that their timing synchronizes and coincides with external (exogenous) environmental cues. So if we persist with our reversal of sleep and activity, after a period of acclimatization the body's circadian rhythms will have reversed and become synchronized to the new set of exogenous cues.

Individuals differ considerably in how quickly they can reverse their rhythms; it can take 5–7 days for some and up to 14 days for others, and some may never achieve a complete reversal. Also, not all physiological functions reverse at the same time—body temperature usually reverses inside a week for most people, while the rhythms of adrenocortical hormone takes much longer. During the changeover period all the body's functions are in a state of *internal desynchronization* (Aschoff, 1964), which is very stressful and accounts for much of the exhaustion, malaise and lassitude associated with changing work shifts.

Psychological functions also seem to follow a well-defined circadian rhythm; for instance, we generally perform most psychological tasks most efficiently when our body temperature is highest and least efficiently when it is lowest. However, one notable exception is short-term memory which is negatively correlated with body temperature (Colquhoun, 1971, 1972).

So what happens to job performance (and, therefore, job efficiency) when body temperature and other physiological functions alter rhythm as a result of change in work shift? Hawkins and Armstrong-Esther (1978) studied eleven nurses during the first seven nights of a period of night duty and found that performance was significantly impaired on the first night but improved progressively on successive nights; body temperature had not fully adjusted to night-working after seven nights. There were significant differences between individual nurses, with some appearing relatively undisturbed by working nights and others never really adjusting at all. (The effects of lack of sleep were discussed in Chapter 5.)

Shift workers often report experiencing insomnia, digestive problems, irritability, fatigue, even depression. Workers who rotate shifts each week also have more accidents on the job and lower productivity. Blakemore (1988) refers to a study of workers at the Great Salt Lake Mineral and Chemical Corporation in Utah, who worked a three-weekly schedule: the first week a day shift, second week a night shift, third week an evening shift and so on:

> ... This is one of the most common shift schedules used in industry, but it seems almost deliberately designed to present the worst possible challenge to the rhythms of the body ... (Blakemore, 1988)

Blakemore says it is like travelling constantly from west to east and never quite overcoming the resulting jet lag (more of that below). Laboratory animals subjected to this kind of rotating schedule of light and dark suffer from increased heart disease and a shorter life-span.

The Utah workers were forced to rotate their biological clock *backwards* by eight hours per week. A psychologist, Czeisler, recommended that: (i) the shifts rotate *forwards* in time (taking advantage of the body's natural preference for a 25-hour cycle; and (ii) each shift should last for three weeks (as most people take more than a week to adjust to a new time zone).

The results of these changes were quite dramatic, rapid and

remarkable—workers liked the new schedules, enjoyed better health and made better use of their leisure time; productivity rose by 22 per cent.

Another occupational group who are very much affected by disruption to their circadian rhythms are airline pilots who experience 'jet-lag' because they cross time-zones during the course of the flight. If you have ever travelled across a time-zone, you will know what it is like to have your biological rhythms 'out of sync' with your surroundings: if you arrive in Washington DC at, say, 9 a.m. (after an eight-hour flight from London) you may be ready intellectually to start the day but as far as your body is concerned, it is still sleeping-time (back in London it is 3 a.m., the middle of the night).

Knowledge of the characteristics of the biological clock help us to understand an apparently curious feature of jet-lag, namely that most people suffer much *less* when travelling in an *east–west* direction than a west–east direction.

When going west ('chasing the sun'), the day is temporarily *lengthened*—because the *natural* cycle of the biological clock is 25 hours (see Chapter 5), an *increase* in day-length is much easier to deal with than a decrease. Indeed, the ideal way to travel would be to always be going east–west, in short hops of *one* time-zone each day, making each day of the journey precisely equal to the body's natural 25-hour rhythm.

Melatonin (a hormone produced by the pineal gland) plays a crucial role in the experience of jet-lag: its secretion reaches a peak during the night (helping to make us sleepy in the first place—see Chapter 5) and, after a long flight, the cyclical release of melatonin stays locked into the day/night pattern of the home country for some days. This could account for the fatigue felt during the day and the insomnia at night. If jet-lagged volunteers are given melatonin during the evening, far fewer report feeling jet-lagged than controls who receive only a placebo (Blakemore, 1988).

iii) *Life Changes*

Holmes and Rahe (1967) examined 5000 patient records and made a list of 43 life events, of varying seriousness, which seemed to cluster in the months preceding the onset of their illness; out of this grew the *Social Readjustment Rating Scale* (SRRS), a self-administered pencil-and-paper measure on which subjects check all those things which have happened to them in some specified time period (usually six to twelve months).

As shown in Table 6.1, the life events are ranked from 1 to 43 and each is assigned a mean value (from 100 for 'death of spouse' to 11 for 'minor violations of the law'); these mean values (or item weightings) were obtained empirically by telling 100 judges that 'marriage' had been assigned an arbitrary value of 500 and asking them to assign a number to each of the other events in terms of how much change in someone's life pattern it would involve *relative* to marriage. The average of the numbers assigned each event was divided by 10 and the resulting values became the weighting of each life event; an individual's SRRS score is the sum of the values for each life event which is ticked.

The assumption underlying the scale is that stress is created by events which require change (whether they are desirable or undesirable). Life changes are a mixed blessing—while we may welcome the variety and novelty they provide they also prevent us from achieving certain (other)

RANK	LIFE EVENT	MEAN VALUE
1	Death of spouse	100
2	Divorce	73
3	Marital separation	65
4	Jail term	63
5	Death of close family member	63
6	Personal injury or illness	53
7	Marriage	50
8	Fired at work	47
9	Marital reconciliation	45
10	Retirement	45
11	Change in health of family member	44
12	Pregnancy	40
13	Sex difficulties	39
14	Gain of new family member	39
15	Business readjustment	39
16	Change in financial state	38
17	Death of close friend	37
18	Change to different line of work	36
19	Change in number of arguments with spouse	35
20	Mortgage over $10,000	31
21	Foreclosure of mortgage or loan	30
22	Change in responsibilities at work	29
23	Son or daughter leaving home	29
24	Trouble with in-laws	29
25	Outstanding personal achievement	28
26	Wife begins or stops work	26
27	Begin or end school	26
28	Change in living conditions	25
29	Revision of personal habits	24
30	Trouble with boss	23
31	Change in work hours or conditions	20
32	Change in residence	20
33	Change in schools	20
34	Change in recreation	19
35	Change in church activities	19
36	Change in social activities	18
37	Mortgage or loan less than $10,000	17
38	Change in sleeping habits	16
39	Change in number of family get-togethers	15
40	Change in eating habits	15
41	Vacation	13
42	Christmas	12
43	Minor violations of the law	11

Table 6.1 Social Readjustment Rating Scale *The amount of life stress a person has experienced in a given period of time, say one year, is measured by the total number of life change units (LCUs). These units result from the addition of the values (shown in the right column) associated with events that the person has experienced during the target time period (see text).*

Source: Holmes,T. H. and Rahe, R. H. (1967) The Social Readjustment Rating Scale. *Journal of Psychosomatic Research, II*, 213–218.

goals and may force us into setting ourselves new goals and objectives which we have not anticipated. The SRRS was intended to predict the onset of illness; how well has it fared?

A number of studies have shown that people who experience many significant life changes (ie a score of 300 life change units or over) are more susceptible to phsyical and mental illness than those with lower scores, eg correlations are usually small but significant and the range of associated symptoms is wide, including sudden cardiac death, heart attacks (non-fatal), TB, diabetes, leukaemia, accidents and even athletics injuries.

However, we should be careful not to draw the wrong conclusions from this data, which is only correlational; for instance, rather than claiming that life events cause illness, it could be that some life events are themselves early manifestations of an illness which is already developing, eg being fired from work, sexual difficulties, trouble with in-laws, change in sleeping habits (Brown, 1986).

The Controllability of Life Events

Life changes may only be stressful if they are unexpected and, in this sense, uncontrollable.

Studies have shown that when subjects are asked to classify the undesirable life events on the SRRS as either 'controllable' or 'uncontrollable', only the latter are significantly correlated with subsequent onset of illness.

As Brown (1986) suggests, perhaps it is *perceived* uncontrollability which makes life-change stressful and, hence, dangerous to health. Using Rotter's (1966) *Locus of Control Scale*, and devising a new scale (the Life Events Scale), Johnson and Sarason (1978) found that life events stress was more closely related to psychiatric symptoms (in particular, depression and anxiety) among people rated as high on *external* Locus of Control than among those rated as high on *internal* Locus of Control.

Related to Locus of Control is Seligman's (1975) concept of *learned helplessness* (see Chapter 7): when dogs, mice, cats and people discover that their behaviour and the delivery of electric shock are independent (ie nothing the subject does will make any difference—the shock will be given anyway), this learned helplessness is generalized to other situations in which shock is *in fact* contingent on the subject's behaviour.

Seligman (1975) believes that human depression can be explained in terms of learned helplessness—the original state of anxiety is replaced by depression when the individual realizes that trauma cannot be controlled and is said to be in a state of inaction (inhibition of coping behaviour) which places him/her in a highly vulnerable biological position. Learned helplessness is also thought to be involved in drug abuse. We saw above how, for example, Peterson and Seligman (1980) have combined the theory of learned helplessness and attribution theory to explain depression (see Chapter 17).

In Brady's (1958) Executive Monkey experiment, pairs of monkeys were yoked by an apparatus which gave electric shocks: whenever one received a shock, so did the other (and this happened at 20-second intervals for six hours at a time over a period of several weeks). One of the pair (the 'executive') could prevent shock by pressing a lever; the other also had a lever but pressing it had no effect. The executive developed severe ulcers and eventually died; the other member of the pair showed no apparent ill effects. This is in contradiction to the belief that control over the situation usually *reduces* stress.

Two important points need to be made: (i) Brady's monkeys were *not* randomly assigned to the executive and non-executive conditions but had been selected on the basis of how quickly they learned to avoid shock (Seligman et al, 1971); and (ii) in a partial replication of Brady's experiment, Weiss (1972) using rats, preceded the shock by a *warning signal* for the executives who had much *less* stomach ulceration than their partners. By contrast, Brady's executives had to be constantly vigilant—without a warning signal, they could never be sure whether they would be successful in avoiding the *next* shock –very stressful! Human executives (many of whom are Type A personalities—see below) are also particularly prone to stress-related diseases and air-traffic controllers (who have to be constantly vigilant) have the highest incidence of stomach ulcers in the USA.

iv) *The Hassles and the Uplifts of Everyday Life*

The SRRS is useful but, by definition, most of the 43 changes are not an everyday occurrence.

Lazarus et al (1981) designed a *hassles scale* (comprising 117 items, including 'concerns about weight', 'misplacing or losing things', 'rising price of common goods') and an *uplift scale* (135 items including 'relating well with spouse/lover', 'feeling healthy', 'meeting your responsibilities').

In a study of 100 men and women, aged 45–64, over a 12-month period, Lazarus et al confirmed the prediction that hassles were positively related to undesirable psychological symptoms and that uplifts were negatively related. They also found that hassles were a more powerful predictor of symptoms than life events (as measured by SRRS) ('divorce', for example, may exert stress by any number of component hassles, such as cooking for oneself, handling money matters and having to tell people about it).

Brown (1986) believes that we need to be able to use the hassles scale to predict *somatic* symptoms, because psychological symptoms occur very close in time to the hassles themselves.

v) *Personality and Stress*

Having already discussed depression in relation to learned helplessness, it seems important to describe the *Type A* personality, which, according to Brown (1986) has become common in twentieth-century, industrialized/urbanized societies.

The Type A personality (Friedman and Rosenman, 1974) is, typically, a middle-class American male who has a chronic sense of time urgency, an excessive competitive drive and is prone to free-floating but extraordinarily well-rationalized hostility. He is always setting himself deadlines, has 'hurry sickness', cannot bear waiting his turn, has to do several things at once, is insecure about his status and needs the admiration of peers to bolster his self-esteem. The Type B person may be equally ambitious but it seems to steady him, give him confidence, rather than goad and irritate him.

How does this relate to stress?

The Type A personality is seen as being at risk, specifically for high blood pressure and coronary heart disease. A longitudinal study (Rosenman et al, 1975) was begun in 1960–1 and involved 3000 men, aged 39–59, all well at the start of the study, which continued for $8\frac{1}{2}$ years. Type A men were almost $2\frac{1}{2}$ times as likely to develop coronary heart disease than their Type B counterparts; when adjustments were made for traditional risk factors (eg age, smoking, blood cholesterol, blood pressure, heart disease in the family), Type A men were still *twice* as likely to suffer heart attacks, etc. These findings have been replicated in

Sweden, Belgium, Honolulu, England, New Zealand and Canada.

However, there are also several studies which have failed to support the concept of a distinct Type A personality. In a review of the research, Evans (1990) concludes that, as a global measure, Type A has yet to show itself as an indisputable risk factor for coronary heart disease.

HOW DO WE REACT TO STRESS?

We have already mentioned the General Adaptation Syndrome or GAS which Selye (1956, 1976) believes represents the body's defence against stress.

Selye argues that the initial symptoms of almost any disease or trauma are virtually identical, that is, the body responds in the same way to *any* stressor (source of stress), whether it is external and environmental or whether it arises from within the body itself. He has defined stress as:

> . . . the individual's psychophysiological response, mediated largely by the autonomic nervous system and the endocrine system, to any demands made on the individual. (Selye, 1956)

The GAS comprises three stages:

1) *Alarm reaction.* This involves physiological changes generally associated with emotion: the sympathetic nervous system is activated and in turn stimulates the adrenal medulla to secrete increased levels of adrenaline and noradrenaline. These are associated with sympathetic changes such as increased blood-sugar level, increased heart-rate and blood pressure, increased blood flow to the muscles, pupil dilation and decreased GSR (see Chapter 4).

The amount of adrenaline and noradrenaline (catecholamines) in the urine reflects the degree of sympathetic-adrenomedullary activity taking place and is correlated with how much stress people report experiencing.

The action of the catecholamines is to mimic sympathetic arousal and, in fact, noradrenaline is the transmitter at the synapses of the sympathetic branch of the ANS. Consequently, noradrenaline from the adrenals prolongs the action of noradrenaline released at synapses in the ANS. This means that, even if the stressor is short-lived and even after it has been removed, sympathetic arousal will continue. (This is a 'closed-loop' process, making a stress reaction self-perpetuating.)

2) *Resistance.* If the stressor is not removed, the body begins to recover from the initial alarm reaction and to cope with the situation. There is a decrease in sympathetic activity, a lower rate of adrenaline and noradrenaline output, but an increase in output from the other part of the adrenal gland, the adrenal cortex.

The adrenal cortex is controlled by the amount of adrenocorticotrophic hormone (ACTH) in the blood. ACTH is released from the anterior pituitary (the 'master' endocrine gland) upon instructions from the hypothalamus. The adrenal cortex is essential for the maintenance of life and its removal results in death.

The glucocorticoid hormones (chiefly cortisol and corticosterone) control and conserve the amount of glucose in the blood, which helps to resist stress of all kinds. Selye believes that increases in blood-sugar levels occur as the person or animal is exposed to stress and, if the stress continues, they return to normal levels and remain so during the resistance stage.

3) *Exhaustion*. The body's resources are now becoming depleted, the adrenals can no longer function properly, blood glucose levels drop and, in extreme cases, hypoglycaemia could result in death. It is at this stage that psychophysiological (or *psychosomatic*) disorders develop, including high blood pressure, heart disease, asthma, ulcers and so on.

STRESS, DISEASE AND PERSONALITY

An important way in which stress may result in disease is through its influence on the body's immune system, a collection of billions of cells which travel through the bloodstream and move in and out of tissues and organs, defending the body against invasion by foreign agents (eg bacteria, viruses, cancerous cells); the study of the effect of psychological factors on the immune system is called *psychoimmunology*. People often catch a cold soon after a period of stress (eg final exams) because stress seems to reduce the immune system's ability to fight off cold viruses. But there are some interesting personality variables involved. For example, students with hard-driving personality styles (similar to Type A) were the most stressed by exams, had the lowest antibody levels and caught more colds than other students (Jermott et al, 1981).

A study by Greer et al (1979) in England of women who had been diagnosed as having breast cancer (and actually had a mastectomy) found that those who reacted either by denying what had happened or by showing a 'fighting spirit' were significantly more likely to be free of cancer five years later than women who stoically accepted it or felt helpless.

A powerful stressor is the death of a close relative (it comes at the top of the SRRS) and there is considerable documentation of surviving relatives dying themselves within weeks or even minutes of the death of a spouse or a child. In the 18 months following such a loss, people have a greater risk of death from a variety of illnesses (including heart attacks and cancer) than others of the same age and gender (see Chapter 24).

While heart attacks and strokes may involve changes in the ANS, infectious diseases and cancer are more directly associated with impairment of immune functions and bereaved people definitely have reduced resistance to disease. It seems that adrenaline can inhibit the ability of certain lymphocytes to release chemicals that kill invading germs or cells (including cancer cells) which the body recognizes as foreign. Corticosteroids also prevent immature lymphocytes from maturing and, therefore, from properly carrying out their disease-fighting functions.

Finally, Locke (1982) found that 'good copers' deal effectively with shocks and challenges while 'poor copers' easily become depressed, anxious and develop a sense of helplessness. At times of major life changes, the latter showed a diminished level of a certain type of white blood cell ('natural killer cells') which normally fight off viruses and cancer cells.

HOW DO WE COPE WITH STRESS?

This final section will deal with coping as a *psychological* process. The GAS describes a physiological attempt to cope with stress but there are other methods of trying to control physiological reactions to stress which are, in themselves, psychological, in particular meditation and biofeedback (which we discussed in Chapter 5) and progressive relaxation (see Chapter 31).

The major psychological methods of coping to be discussed here are: (i) defence mechanisms and (ii) coping mechanisms.

(a) The *ego defence mechanisms* (discussed in detail in Chapter 29) are mainly associated with the anxiety produced by conflict, as described in Freud's Psychoanalytic Theory. All we shall say here is that, by their nature, defence mechanisms involve some degree of distortion of reality and self-deception and, while desirable in the short-term, as long-term solutions to stress they are unhealthy and undesirable.

(b) *Coping mechanisms*, by contrast, are conscious ways of trying to adapt to stress and anxiety in a positive and constructive way, by using thoughts and behaviours oriented towards searching for information, problem-solving, seeking help from others, recognizing our true feelings and establishing goals and objectives. Eight major coping mechanisms described by Grasha (1983) are shown in Table 6.2, together with the equivalent defence mechanisms.

One important coping mechanism not discussed by Grasha is *control*. Brown (1986) cites several studies in which subjects in a simulated dental surgery have had access to a button to signal to the 'dentist' when their pain becomes intolerable; the effect is usually to reduce anxiety over possible pain and actually to *increase* the amount of pain that subjects will put up with before using the button (if they use it at all).

Being warned of possible pain and other discomforts, and having treatment explained to you, is called *information control* and it seems that not to have information control can be very stressful, as found in a study of the residents of Three Mile Island, in the USA, scene of a nuclear energy plant accident (a less well-known disaster than the 1986 Chernobyl disaster). The risks from nuclear radiation that frighten people most are those that are unobservable, unknown to science and which lie in the future (eg leukaemia, which may develop 20 years after exposure).

Another kind of control is *cognitive control*. Langer et al (1975) asked patients awaiting elective surgery (such as hernia repairs, hysterectomies) in hospital to think about a time when they were too busy to attend to a minor cut and to compare it with a time when they had been free to lavish concern on a comparable cut. They were told that pain is extremely subjective and that stress can be controlled by controlling attention to the negative and positive aspects of surgery (eg being in hospital gives you a chance to withdraw from everyday hassles). These *cognitive control* patients were compared with a group of patients who were told what was going to happen to them and warned of post-operative discomforts but reassured about their safety and the quality of care they would receive, etc. (the *information-control* group).

Both methods were found to help patients cope (compared with a control group) but cognitive control proved more beneficial than information control in reducing anxiety, requesting sedatives, etc. Knowing enough so that you do not have to let your imagination run wild, but not knowing too much so that stress is, unwittingly, increased (information control), combined with thinking about the situation in a

COPING MECHANISM	DESCRIPTION	CORRESPONDING DEFENCE MECHANISM	
1. Objectivity	Separating one thought from another, or our feelings from our thoughts, which allows us to obtain a better understanding of how we think and feel and an objective evaluation of our actions	Isolation	*Table 6.2 Some major coping mechanisms and their corresponding defence mechanisms*
2. Logical analysis	Carefully and systematically analysing our problems in order to find explanations and to make plans to solve them, based on the realities of the situation	Rationalization	
3. Concentration	The ability to set aside disturbing thoughts and feelings in order to concentrate on the task in hand	Denial	
4. Empathy	The ability to sense how others are feeling in emotionally-arousing situations so that our interactions take account of their feelings	Projection	
5. Playfulness	The ability to use past feelings, ideas and behaviour appropriately so as to enrich the solution of problems and to otherwise add some enjoyment to life	Regression	
6. Tolerance of ambiguity	The ability to function in situations where we or others cannot make clear choices—because the situation is so complicated	—	
7. Suppression	The ability consciously to forget about or hold back thoughts and feelings until an appropriate time and place to express them arises	Repression	
8. Substitution of thoughts and emotions	The ability consciously to substitute other thoughts or feelings for how we really think or feel in order to meet the demands of the situation	Reaction formation	

Sublimation can be thought of as a Coping Mechanism *and* a Defence Mechanism, because it involves channelling anxiety in socially desirable ways and so is positive and constructive

constructive way which helps you get things in perspective (cognitive control), would seem to be an ideal way of coping with a stressful situation.

7 Learning

We have already seen how the behaviourist approach has exerted a major influence in psychology. In view of the central role of learning in philosophical behaviourism, it is not surprising that the topic of learning should itself be one of the most researched and discussed in the whole of psychology.

However, the concept of learning illustrates very well the discrepancy between the everyday, commonsense use of a term and its technical, scientific, use (see Chapter 1).

LEARNING AS 'WHAT IS LEARNED' AND AS 'HOW IT IS LEARNED'

When the layperson talks about learning the emphasis is usually on *what* has been learned, for example, learning to drive or to use a computer, learning French or learning about the causes of the Vietnam war. But when psychologists use the term, their focus is on the *process* of learning itself, almost irrespective of the end product; they ask 'How does it work?' rather than, 'What does it lead to?'.

Another important difference is that when we focus on the end product we tend to judge the learning to be deliberate; when you learn to drive, for example, you pay to acquire certain specific skills which will get you your driving licence. But, for the psychologist, learning can take place without there being a 'teacher' as such: we can learn by merely observing others, who may not even know they are being watched, let alone trying to teach us anything. We can also learn without other people being involved at all; for example, if two 'events' occur often enough in the environment (eg lightning followed by thunder) then we can learn about how they are related without anyone trying to teach us.

HOW CAN LEARNING BE DEFINED?

As we saw in Chapter 1, learning is a hypothetical construct, that is, it cannot be directly observed but can only be inferred from observable behaviour. So, for example, if a person's performance on a task at Time 1 differs in any particular way or to some degree from performance on the task at Time 2, we may infer that learning has taken place. But if that change is observed on just that one occasion we would be much more hesitant about making such an inference. Learning, therefore, normally implies a fairly permanent change in a person's behavioural performance. Again, temporary fluctuations in behaviour can occur as a result of fatigue, drugs, temperature changes, and so on, and this is another reason for taking *permanence* as a minimum requirement for saying that learning has taken place.

However, permanent changes in behaviour can also result from things that have nothing to do with learning, for example, the effects of brain damage on behaviour, or the changes associated with puberty and other maturational processes. So to call behavioural change a case of learning, the change must be linked in some way to past experience of some kind (regardless of whether there was any attempt to bring about that change).

For these reasons, psychologists usually define learning as:

> . . . a relatively permanent change in behaviour due to past experience. (Coon, 1983)

or:

> . . . a relatively permanent change in behavioural potential which accompanies experience but which is not the result of simple growth factors or of reversible influences such as fatigue or hunger. (Kimble, 1961)

LEARNING VERSUS PERFORMANCE

Kimble's definition has one major advantage over Coon's, namely, it implies a distinction between *learning* (behavioural potential) and *performance* (actual behaviour). Think of all the things you know and can do but which you are not displaying at this present moment—if you can swim you are almost certainly not doing so as you read this chapter but you could readily do so if faced with a pool full of water! So what you could do (potential behaviour based on learning) and what you are actually doing (current performance) are two different things, but ultimately, of course, the only proof of learning is a particular kind of performance (such as exams).

We can relate the learning–performance distinction to what we said earlier about what counts as learning. Performance, but not learning, can fluctuate due to fatigue, drugs, emotional factors, etc. and so is much more variable than the more permanent learning. (Exams come to mind again—many students have left an exam knowing what they could not demonstrate during the exam itself.)

LEARNING AND OTHER ABILITIES

A rather different kind of definition is offered by Howe, for whom learning is:

> . . . a biological device that functions to protect the human individual and to extend his capacities. (Howe, 1980)

In this context, learning is neither independent of nor entirely separate from several other abilities, in particular memory and perception. Indeed, learning and memory may be regarded as two sides of the same coin (see Chapter 12).

According to Howe, learning is also *cumulative*, ie what we learn at any time is influenced by our previous learning, so that developmental and learning processes are closely interlinked. Also, most instances of learning take the form of adaptive changes whereby we increase our effectiveness in dealing with the environment; this has undoubted survival value.

SOME BASIC QUESTIONS ABOUT LEARNING

If it is generally agreed by psychologists that learning is: (i) relatively permanent; and (ii) due to past experience, then there is much less agreement about: (a) exactly what changes when learning takes place;

and (b) what kinds of past experience are involved. Put another way, how do the changes occur and what mechanisms are involved?

A dimension along which psychologists differ regarding (a) and (b) is the extent to which they focus on the overt, behavioural changes as opposed to the covert, cognitive changes. As we have seen in Chapters 1 and 2, behaviourists such as Watson and Skinner emphasize the former to the exclusion of the latter, while cognitive psychologists are more interested in the latter as they are reflected in the former.

We will now take a detailed look at different theories of learning.

BEHAVIOURIST APPROACHES—LEARNING THEORY (CLASSICAL AND OPERANT CONDITIONING)

Figure 7.1 shows the major figures in the behaviourist tradition and how

Figure 7.1 Major figures in the behaviourist (learning theory) tradition

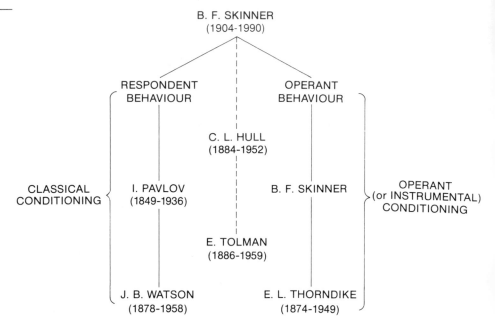

they relate to each other. Historically (or chronologically) Skinner does not belong at the top but at the bottom—he was born several years after the others. But he appears at the top because of the distinction he made (in 1938) between *respondents* (or respondent behaviour), which are triggered automatically by particular environmental stimuli, and *operants* (or operant behaviour) which are not tied to stimuli in that way and which are essentially voluntary.

Related to this distinction is that between Classical (Pavlovian) conditioning and Operant (Instrumental or Skinnerian) conditioning. Although both represent the behaviourist Stimulus–Response (S–R) approach to learning, there are some important differences between them, hence Skinner's distinction. Neither Hull nor Tolman fits easily into either of the two major types of conditioning, which is why they are placed between the others (Hull's theory was discussed in Chapter 6).

Figure 7.2 Ivan Pavlov (1849–1936)

CLASSICAL CONDITIONING (OR, WHY DO DOGS DROOL OVER BELLS?)

Ivan Pavlov (Fig. 7.2) was a physiologist interested in the process of digestion in dogs, for which research he was awarded the Nobel Prize in 1904 (the year Skinner was born). He developed a surgical technique whereby a dog's salivary secretions could be collected in a tube attached to the outside of its cheek so the drops of saliva could be easily measured (Fig. 7.3). In the course of his physiological investigations Pavlov noticed

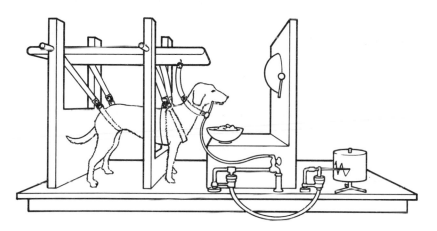

Figure 7.3 The apparatus used by Pavlov in his experiments on conditioned reflexes

that the dogs would often start salivating *before* any food was given to them, for example, when they looked at the food, or saw the feeding bucket or even when they heard the footsteps of the approaching laboratory assistant who was coming to feed them.

These observations led to the study of what is now called Classical (or Pavlovian) Conditioning, whereby a stimulus (a bell) which would not normally produce a particular response (salivation) eventually comes to do so by being paired with another stimulus (food) which *does* normally produce the response. The basic procedure is summarized in Figure 7.4.

Before conditioning, the taste of food will naturally, and automatic-

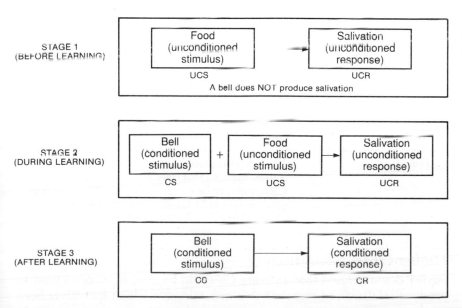

Figure 7.4 The basic procedure involved in classical conditioning

ally, make the dog salivate but the sound of a bell will not; so the food is referred to as an *unconditioned stimulus* (UCS) and the salivation is an *unconditioned response* (UCR)—an automatic, reflex, biologically built-in response. The dog does not have to learn to salivate in response to food, it can do so naturally. During conditioning the bell is paired with the food. Because the bell does not naturally produce salivation it is referred to as a *conditioned stimulus* (CS), ie its coming to produce salivation is *conditional* upon it being paired with the UCS. (It is also *neutral* with regard to salivation prior to conditioning.)

If the bell and food are paired a sufficient number of times the dog starts to salivate as soon as it hears the bell and before the food is presented. When this occurs we say that conditioning has occurred and the salivation is now referred to as a *conditioned response* (CR) because it is produced by a conditioned stimulus (CS)—the bell.

This basic procedure can be used with a variety of conditioned stimuli, eg buzzers, metronomes, lights, geometric figures and so on. The exact relationship between the CS and the UCS can also be varied to give different kinds of conditioning. For example, in the example shown in Figure 7.4, the CS is presented about half a second before the UCS and is called *delayed* or *forward conditioning*. This and three other alternatives are shown in Table 7.1.

Table 7.1 Four types of classical conditioning based on different CS–UCS relationships	1. *Delayed or forward*	The CS is presented before the UCS and remains 'on' while the UCS is presented and until the UCR appears. Conditioning has occurred when the CR appears before the UCS is presented. A half second interval produces the strongest learning—as the interval increases so the poorer the learning becomes. This is the kind of conditioning typically used in the laboratory, especially with animals
	2. *Backward*	The CS is presented after UCS; generally, this produces very little, if any, learning in laboratory animals. However, much advertising uses backward conditioning (eg the idyllic, tropical, scene is set and then the coconut bar is introduced)
	3. *Simultaneous*	The CS and UCS are presented together; conditioning has occurred when the CS on its own produces the CR. This kind of conditioning occurs frequently in real-life situations (eg the sound of the dentist's drill accompanies the contact of the drill with your tooth)
	4. *Trace*	The CS is presented and removed before the UCS is presented, so that only a 'memory trace' of the CS remains to be conditioned. The CR is usually weaker than in Delayed or Simultaneous conditioning

Higher Order Conditioning

Pavlov demonstrated that a strong CS could be used in place of food to produce salivation in response to a new stimulus which had never been paired with food. For example, if the CS is a buzzer, it can be paired with, say, a black square in such a way that after ten pairings (using delayed conditioning) the dog will salivate a small but significant amount at the sight of the black square before the buzzer is sounded.

Remember that the black square had never been associated with food directly but only indirectly, through association with the buzzer which *had* been associated with food; it is as if the CS were functioning as a UCS. The buzzer and food situation is referred to as *first order* conditioning and the black square and buzzer situation as *second order* conditioning. Pavlov found that, with dogs at least, learning could not go beyond third or fourth order conditioning. Even so, conditioning is beginning to look a rather more complex process than it did when we first described it.

Generalization and Discrimination

Other phenomena involved in classical conditioning (as well as in operant) which make it a more complex and versatile process are generalization and discrimination.

In *generalization* the CR transfers spontaneously to stimuli that are similar to, but different from, the original CS. For example, if a dog is trained using a bell of a particular pitch and it is then presented with a bell a little higher or lower in pitch, it will still salivate, although only one bell (the original CS) was actually paired with food. However, if the dog is continually presented with bells that are increasingly different from the original, the CR will gradually weaken and eventually stop altogether; the dog is showing *discrimination* (see Fig. 7.5).

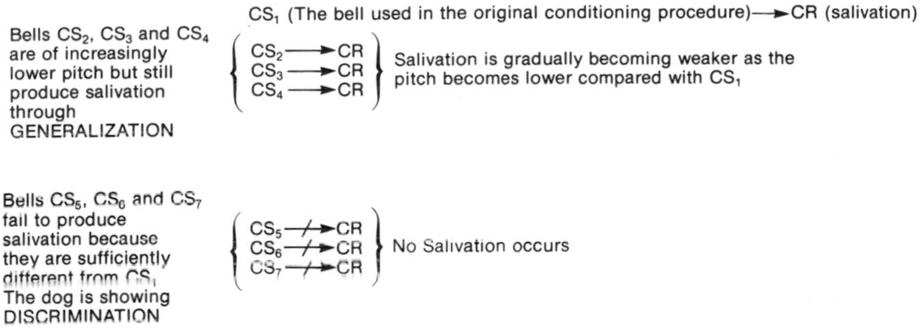

CS_1 (The bell used in the original conditioning procedure) $\longrightarrow$ CR (salivation)

Bells CS_2, CS_3 and CS_4 are of increasingly lower pitch but still produce salivation through GENERALIZATION

$\left. \begin{array}{l} CS_2 \longrightarrow CR \\ CS_3 \longrightarrow CR \\ CS_4 \longrightarrow CR \end{array} \right\}$ Salivation is gradually becoming weaker as the pitch becomes lower compared with CS_1

Bells CS_5, CS_6 and CS_7 fail to produce salivation because they are sufficiently different from CS_1. The dog is showing DISCRIMINATION

$\left. \begin{array}{l} CS_5 \longrightarrow\!\!\!\!/\, \blacktriangleright CR \\ CS_6 \longrightarrow\!\!\!\!/\, \blacktriangleright CR \\ CS_7 \longrightarrow\!\!\!\!/\, \blacktriangleright CR \end{array} \right\}$ No Salivation occurs

Figure 7.5 An example of discrimination occurring spontaneously as a result of generalization stopping

In addition to spontaneous discrimination, as in the above example, Pavlov trained dogs to discriminate in the original conditioning procedure. For example, if a high-pitched bell is paired with food but a low-pitched bell is not, the dog will start salivating in response to the former but not to the latter (discrimination training).

An interesting phenomenon related to discrimination is what Pavlov called *experimental neurosis*. He trained dogs to salivate to a circle but not to an ellipse, and then gradually changed the shape of the ellipse until it became almost circular. As this happened the dogs started behaving in 'neurotic' ways—whining, trembling, urinating and defecating, refusing to eat and so on. It was as if they did not know how to respond—was the stimulus a circle (in which case, through generalization, they 'ought' to salivate) or was it an ellipse (in which case, through disrimination, they 'should not' salivate)?

Extinction and Spontaneous Recovery

After dogs had been conditioned to salivate to a bell, if the bell was repeatedly presented without food, the CR of salivation became gradually weaker and eventually stopped altogether; this is called *extinction*.

When this happens it might seem as if the association between the bell and the food has faded so that the dog has 'unlearnt' the original connection. But this is not the case: when dogs were removed from the experimental situation, following extinction, and then put back a couple of hours or so later, and Pavlov re-presented the bell, the dogs started salivating again. Although there had been no further pairing of the bell and food, the CR of salivation reappeared in response to the bell, a phenomenon called *spontaneous recovery*. It shows that extinction does not involve an 'erasing' of the original learning but rather a learning to inhibit or suppress the CR when the CS is continually presented without a UCS.

Does Classical Conditioning Apply to Human Behaviour?

Certainly, there have been many laboratory demonstrations with human subjects and the basic procedure is useful as a way of thinking about how certain fairly automatic responses may be acquired in real life. Also, as we shall see in Chapter 31, the impact of conditioning principles (both classical and operant) within clinical psychology has been considerable, ie they can be used deliberately to change people's behaviour in a certain direction (see also Table 1.1, p.17, comparing different theoretical approaches).

The first attempt to apply Pavlov's findings with dogs to humans was made by J.B. Watson, the founder of Behaviourism. Working with Rayner (1920), Watson succeeded in inducing fear in a young child through classical conditioning (Box 7.1).

Box 7.1   The Case of Little Albert (Watson and Rayner, 1920)

Albert B's mother was a wet-nurse in a children's hospital. Albert was described as, 'healthy from birth' and, 'on the whole stolid and unemotional'. When he was about nine months old his reactions to various stimuli were tested—a white rat, a rabbit, a dog, a monkey, masks with and without hair, cotton wool, burning newspapers, and a hammer stiking a four-foot steel bar (just behind his head). Only the last of these elicited a fear response and so constituted the UCS (with the fear the UCR); the other stimuli were neutral because they did not produce fear.

When Albert was just over eleven months old the rat and the UCS were presented together; this occurred seven times altogether over the next seven weeks, by which time the rat (CS) on its own came to produce the fear response (now a CR).

The CR transferred spontaneously to the rabbit, the dog, a seal-skin fur coat, cotton wool, Watson's hair and a Santa Claus mask, but it did not generalize to Albert's building blocks or to the hair of two observers (ie Albert showed discrimination).

Five days after conditioning the CR produced by the rat persisted; ten days after conditioning it was 'much less marked' but one month after conditioning it was still evident.

Whether Watson and Rayner had intended to remove the CR is not known—Albert's mother removed him from the hospital.

Watson and Rayner might have attempted to remove little Albert's fear using the method of 'direct unconditioning' employed by Jones (1924) to treat *Little Peter* (Box 7.2).

Box 7.2   The Case of Little Peter (Jones, 1924)

Little Peter was a 2-year-old living in a charitable institution. Jones was mainly interested in those children who cried and trembled when an animal (eg a frog, rat or rabbit) was shown to them and Peter, who in other respects was regarded as well-adjusted, had an extreme fear of rats, rabbits, fur coats, feathers, cotton wool, frogs and fish (it was not known how these fears had arisen).

Jones, supervised by Watson, put a rabbit in a wire cage in front of Peter while he ate his lunch and, forty sessions later, Peter ate his lunch with one hand and stroked the rabbit (now on his lap) with the other. In a series of 17 steps the rabbit (in the cage) had been brought a little closer each day, was then let free in the room and eventually sat on Peter's lunch tray.

This is an early example of a method of removing fears (or phobias) called *systematic desensitization*; it is used a great deal today (see Chapter 31).

If a fear of rats can be deliberately induced (as in Little Albert's case) or removed (as in Little Peter's), does classical conditioning also help to explain how fears are acquired, spontaneously, in everyday life?

We can see how, for example, a fear of the dentist could be learnt in this way, eg:

Drilling hitting a nerve (UCS)→ pain/fear (UCR)
Sound of drill (CS) + drill hitting nerve (UCS)→ pain/fear (UCR)
Sound of the drill (CS)→ fear (CR)

You could become conditioned to more than one CS in the same 'sitting'—it all depends on what you notice at the time. For example, if you are looking at the dentist peering into your mouth, you may become afraid of 'faces seen upside down' or if the dentist is wearing a mask you may acquire a fear of masks too. Also through generalization, you can come to fear all drill-like noises or white coats worn by medical personnel or lab technicians, and so on.

Generalization may be useful up to a point but discrimination may be just as important; carpenters need to use an electric drill and it is necessary for them to do so without trembling with fear. (Of course, not everyone's conditioned fear responses are of equal strength—mine could be extreme compared with yours, although we may both have acquired the fear through classical conditioning.)

As we shall see in Chapter 30, human fears may often be kept going through avoiding the object of our fears, ie we do not give the fear a chance to undergo extinction. (This occurs in conjuction with operant conditioning whereby the avoidance behaviour becomes strengthened through negative reinforcement, which will be discussed later in this chapter.)

OPERANT OR INSTRUMENTAL CONDITIONING (OR WHY DO RATS PRESS LEVERS?)

When Skinner (Fig. 7.6) drew the distinction between respondent and

Figure 7.6 B. F. Skinner (1904–1990) (Bettman Archive Inc.)

operant behaviour, he was not rejecting the discoveries of Pavlov and Watson but arguing that most animal and human behaviour is not elicited by specific stimuli in the way they described. Instead, he was interested in how animals *operate* on their environment and how this operant behaviour is *instrumental* in bringing about certain *consequences* which then determine how probable that behaviour is to be repeated.

Skinner saw the learner as much more *active* than did Pavlov or Watson, for whom behaviour was automatically brought about by stimuli—unconditioned stimuli before learning and conditioned stimuli after learning. In classical conditioning, there is a certain necessity and inevitability about the response—the animal has no choice but to respond in a particular way. But in operant conditioning things are much less certain; behaviour is *emitted* by the organism (not *elicited* by the stimulus) and so is essentially *voluntary* (as opposed to reflex or involuntary) and the likelihood of a particular behaviour being emitted is a function of the past consequences of such behaviour.

Just as Watson's ideas were based on the earlier work of Pavlov, so Skinner's study of operant conditioning grew out of the earlier work of another American, Edward Thorndike.

Thorndike and the Law of Effect

Thorndike built puzzle-boxes for use with cats; their task was to operate a latch which would automatically cause the door to spring open. Each time they managed to escape there was a piece of fish waiting for them, which was visible from inside the puzzle-box (Fig. 7.7). (The cats

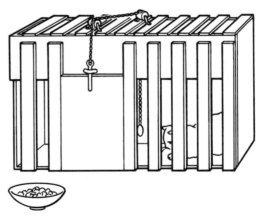

Figure 7.7 Thorndike's puzzle box

were deprived of food for a considerable time before the experiments began and so were highly motivated.) Each time, after eating the fish, they were put straight back in and the whole process was repeated.

At first the cats struggled to get out, behaving in a purely random fashion, and it was only by chance that the first escape was made. But each time they were returned to the puzzle-box it took them less time to operate the latch and make their escape. For instance, with one of the boxes, the average time for the first escape was five minutes but after ten to twenty trials this was reduced to about five seconds. How did Thorndike account for this?

The learning, he said, was essentially random or *trial-and-error*; there was no sudden flash of insight into how the releasing mechanism worked but rather a gradual reduction in the number of errors made and hence escape time. As to exactly what was being learned in this trial-and-error way, Thorndike proposed a 'connection between the situation and a certain impulse to act', or between the stimulus (the manipulative components of the box) and the response (the behaviour which allowed the cat to escape). Further, the stimulus response connection is, 'stamped in when pleasure results from the act, and stamped out when it doesn't'—this is Thorndike's famous *law of effect* (1898).

The Law of Effect is crucially important as a way of distinguishing classical and operant conditioning (as Skinner was to do forty years later):

(a) It points out that what happens *as a result* of behaviour will influence that behaviour in the future, whereas in classical conditioning it is, in a sense, what happens *before* behaviour (pairing of the CS and UCS) that is crucial and which determines the behaviour.

(b) It points out that the animal is not indifferent to the nature of those consequences—responses that bring about 'satisfaction' or pleasure are likely to be repeated, those which bring about 'discomfort' are likely not to be. (In classical conditioning the UCS works essentially in the same way whether it is food (something pleasant) or electric shock (something unpleasant or aversive), since the response is produced *by* it and not vice versa.)

Skinner's 'Analysis of Behaviour'

We saw in Chapter 1 that Skinner's approach was atheoretical, that is, he was attempting to control and predict behaviour, not to explain it. He used a form of puzzle-box known as a Skinner box, which was designed for a rat or pigeon to do things in rather than escape from. This box has a lever (in the case of rats), under which is a food tray, and the experimenter decides exactly what the relationship shall be between pressing the lever and the delivery of a food pellet. In this sense, the experimenter has total control of the animal's environment but it is the rat that has to do the work (Fig. 7.8).

Another modification of Thorndike's work was Skinner's use of the term *strengthen* in place of 'stamping in' and *weaken* in place of 'stamping out' in Thorndike's Law of Effect; for Skinner, Thorndike's terms were too mentalistic and his own more objective and descriptive. The analysis of behaviour, according to Skinner, requires an accurate but neutral representation of the relationship (or *contingencies*) between: (i) *antecedents* (the stimulus conditions, eg the lever, the click of the food dispenser, a light that may go on when the lever is pressed); (ii) *behaviours* (or *operants*, eg pressing the lever); and (iii) *consequences* (what happens as a result of the operant behaviour). We shall look at (i) and (iii) in more detail.

'Behaviour is Shaped and Maintained by its Consequences'

This quote from Skinner represents his version of the Law of Effect; the consequences of operants can be; (i) a *positive reinforcement*; (ii) a *negative reinforcement*; or (iii) a *punishment* and their effects on behaviour can be summarized as in Figure 7.9.

You will see that positive and negative reinforcement have the same effect on behaviour, namely *strengthening* it (making it more probable),

Figure 7.8 A rat in a skinner box

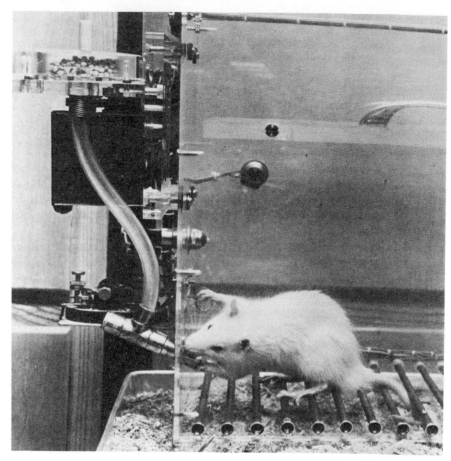

but each works in a different way, from the opposite direction. *Positive reinforcement* involves presenting something the animal likes (eg food) while *negative reinforcement* involves the removal or avoidance of some 'aversive' (literally 'painful') state of affairs (eg electric shock).

Punishment has the opposite effect on behaviour—it *weakens* it (making it less probable)—through the presentation of an aversive stimulus.

Let us take the example of a rat pressing a lever in a Skinner box (Fig. 7.10).

The difference between negative reinforcement and punishment should now be clear: in the former, an aversive stimulus comes to an end or is avoided altogether, while in the latter, the aversive stimulus begins.

Figure 7.9 The consequences of behaviour and their effects

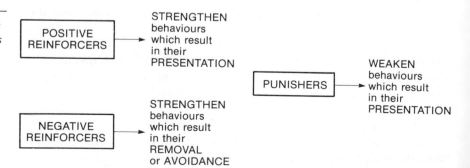

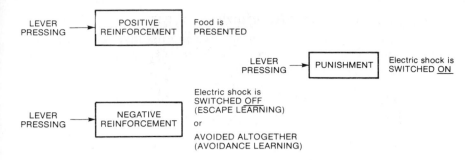

What is the Difference Between a Reinforcer and Reinforcement?

You may have spotted that in Figure 7.9 the term Reinfor*cer* (and Punis*her*) is used while in Figure 7.10 I have referred to Reinforce*ment* (and Punish*ment*); the difference is between a thing and a process. Food itself is a reinforcer, electric shock a punisher; the process whereby food is presented as a result of lever-pressing is (positive) reinforcement and when electric shock is presented instead it is called punishment.

But we should note here just how Skinner defines these terms or, more accurately, how he decides that something is or is not a reinforcer or a punisher. It is, in fact, a decision that must be made retrospectively, that is, after food or shock, etc., has been made contingent on, say, lever-pressing on a number of occasions. So, if the behaviour is strengthened when followed by food, we can call the food a reinforcer, and if the shock weakens it we can call the shock a punisher; therefore, reinforcers and punishers cannot be defined independently of the effects they have on behaviour.

This kind of definition could be accused of circularity ('a reinforcer is whatever strengthens behaviour' and 'whatever strengthens behaviour is a reinforcer') and it seems to make the task of predicting behaviour rather tricky because Skinner is saying that we have to 'wait and observe' just what the effects on behaviour are.

A partial solution (of an empirical if not a logical kind) is to ensure that rats and pigeons are highly motivated to learn the relationship between pressing levers or pecking discs and receiving food by starving them for several hours before the experiments begin!

A partial justification for 'waiting and seeing' is that, according to Skinner, this is a more rather than a less scientific way of going about things, since the intended effect may not always coincide with the actual effect. Take an example from parent–child interaction: if children who feel deprived of their parents' attention find that the parents respond when they are naughty, they are more likely to go on being naughty, even if the parents' response is to shout or smack. Being shouted at, or being smacked, is at least a form of attention and is preferable to being ignored. So, whereas the parents' intention is to stop the child being naughty, the actual effect may be the opposite, ie an intended punishment may turn out to be a positive reinforcement!

Similarly, a positive reinforcement can only loosely be called a reward as 'reward' implies that the rewarder expects to strengthen behaviour, whereas 'positive reinforcement' refers to what has been shown to strengthen the behaviour of the rewarded person or animal.

Primary and Secondary Reinforcers

As well as the distinction between positive and negative reinforcement, an important distinction also exists between two types of reinforcer, primary and secondary. *Primary reinforcers* (eg food, water, sex) are naturally reinforcing, reinforcing in themselves, whereas *secondary reinforcers* acquire their reinforcing properties through association with primary reinforcers, that is, we have to *learn* (through classical conditioning) to find them reinforcing.

Examples of human secondary (or conditioned) reinforcers are money, trading stamps, cheques and tokens (see Chapter 31 for a discussion of token economy programmes used with psychiatric patients and other groups).

In a Skinner box situation, if a click accompanies the presentation of each pellet of food, the rat will eventually come to find the click on its own reinforcing; this is demonstrated by using the click as a reinforcer for getting the rat to learn some new response.

A famous demonstration of the power of response of secondary reinforcers is the study by Wolfe (1936). He used the Chimp-O-Mat machine, which chimpanzees learned to operate to obtain poker chips, as a secondary reinforcement for solving problems.

Secondary reinforcers are often important because they 'bridge the gap' between the response and the primary reinforcer which may not be immediately forthcoming.

Schedules of Reinforcement

Another important aspect of Skinner's work (Ferster and Skinner, 1957) is concerned with the effects on behaviour of how frequently and how regularly (or predictably) reinforcements are presented. He identified five major schedules, each of which is associated with a characteristic pattern of responding and, as Walker (1984) observes, this part of Skinner's research is in large measure counterintuitive, which makes it all the more interesting.

To summarize, first, rats and pigeons (and probably most mammals and birds) typically 'work harder' (eg press the lever at a faster ate) for scant reward: when reinforcements are: (i) relatively few and far between; and (ii) relatively irregular or unpredictable, not only will they go on working but will do so long after the reinforcement has actually been withdrawn altogether!

So each schedule can be analysed in terms of: (i) pattern and rate of response; and (ii) resistance to extinction. This is summarized in Table 7.2.

A convenient way of displaying visually the rate of response is to plot responses cumulatively, as steps along a vertical axis, against the time when they are made along the horizontal axis; Skinner called this a 'cumulative record' and an example is shown in Figure 7.11.

A continuous schedule is usually only used when some new response is being learned; once it is being emitted regularly and reliably it can be maintained by using one of the four *partial* or *intermittent* schedules. But, of course, this change must be gradual: if the animal is used to being reinforced every time it makes a certain response, and it is then switched to a Variable Ratio (VR) 50 (ie on average, every 50th response is reinforced), it will soon stop responding.

Table 7.2 *Common reinforcement schedules and associated patterns of response and resistance to extinction*

REINFORCEMENT SCHEDULE	EXAMPLE	PATTERN AND RATE OF RESPONDING	RESISTANCE TO EXTINCTION	EXAMPLE OF HUMAN BEHAVIOUR
1. Continuous reinforcement (CRF)	Every single desired response is reinforced	Response rate is low but steady	Very low—the quickest way to bring about extinction	1. Receiving a high grade for every assignment. 2. Receiving a tip for every customer served
2. Fixed interval (FI)	A reinforcement is given every 30 seconds (FI 30)—provided the response occurs at least once during that time	Response rate speeds up as the next reinforcement becomes available; a pause after each reinforcement. Overall response rate fairly low	Fairly low—extinction occurs quite quickly	1. Being paid regularly—every week or month. 2. Giving yourself a 15-minute break for every hour's studying done
3. Variable interval (VI)	A reinforcement is given on average every 30 seconds (VI 30)—but the interval varies from trial to trial. So the interval on any one occasion is unpredictable	Response rate is very stable over long periods of time. Still some tendency to increase response rate as time elapses since the last reinforcement	Very high—extinction occurs very slowly and gradually	Many self-employed people receive payment irregularly—depends when the customer pays for the product or service
4. Fixed ratio (FR)	A reinforcement is given for a fixed number of responses—however long this may take. Eg one reinforcement for every 10 responses (FR 10)	There is a pronounced pause after each reinforcement and then a very high rate of responding leading up to the next reinforcement	As Fixed Interval	1. Piecework—the more work done, the more money earned. 2. Commission—extra money for so many goods made or sales completed
5. Variable ratio (VR)	A reinforcement is given on average every 10 responses (VR 10) but the number varies from trial to trial. So the number of responses required on any one occasion is unpredictable	Very high response rate—and very steady	Very high—the most resistant of all the schedules	Gambling

Skinner (1938) originally used an interval schedule because a reinforcer is guaranteed, sooner or later, so long as one response is made in the interval.

Figure 7.11 *Typical cumulative records for a response (such as lever-pressing) reinforced using five schedules of reinforcement*

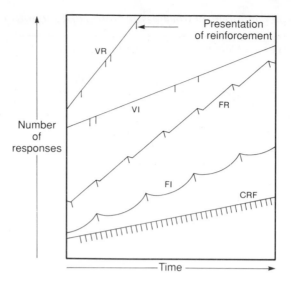

Shaping—the Reinforcement of Successive Approximations

Reinforcement can also be used to build up relatively complex behaviour—behaviour which the animal does not normally display or which is not part of its natural repertoire—by reinforcing closer and closer approximations to the desired behaviour.

First, the behaviour must be broken down into a number of small steps, each of which is reinforced in sequence, so that gradually what the animal can do is much more like what the experimenter is trying to teach it. This is what animal trainers have been doing for hundreds of years and is the method of reinforcement Skinner used to teach pigeons to play ping-pong or turn a full (anti-clockwise) circle. Most skills in humans are learned in this step-by-step manner, whether this happens deliberately and consciously (as in driving) or spontaneously and unconsciously (as in acquiring speech).

Shaping also provides an important foundation for behaviour modification, used to teach mentally handicapped children and adults to use the toilet, feed and dress themselves and other social skills. It has been used also to develop speech in autistic children (see Chapter 31).

Superstitious Behaviour

An interesting example of the role of reinforcement is the situation where a certain behaviour is strengthened, by chance, because it happens to precede a reinforcement; the relationship between the behaviour and the reinforcer is accidental (not contingent), ie the reinforcer would have occurred anyway.

Skinner (1948) first noticed this phenomenon while training pigeons to peck at a disc. Sometimes they would engage in some irrelevant behaviour (eg turning in circles, hopping from side to side) just before pecking the disc and the resulting reinforcer would strengthen both the disc-pecking *and* the irrelevant response. Of course, so long as the required response of pecking was emitted the reinforcer would follow, whether or not the pigeon turned around or hopped from one side to another.

Whenever we 'keep our fingers crossed' or engage in any type of ritual (as is quite common amongst actors and sportsmen and women, while 'warming up' for competition) we, in Skinner's terms, are displaying superstitious behaviour.

Negative Reinforcement—Escape and Avoidance Learning

Figure 7.10 shows that two forms of negative reinforcement are *Escape* and *Avoidance Learning*; these are the two major ways in which negative reinforcement has been studied in the laboratory. Escape learning is relatively simple; for example, rats can learn to press a lever to turn off electric shock. Avoidance learning is more complex and more relevant to certain aspects of human behaviour.

Most laboratory studies have used a 'shuttle box', a box divided into two compartments, sometimes with a barrier or door between the two compartments, and electric shock can be delivered through the floor of either compartment independently of the other. Neither side is permanently safe, but only one is electrified at a time; the problem for the animal is to find which is the safe side on any one occasion. A warning signal is given whenever the electrified side is to be changed, so the animal can always avoid being shocked if it switches sides when it hears (or sees) the warning signal. But why should it? According to Walker (1984) the only theory of avoidance learning worth considering is the Two Factor Theory (Mowrer, 1960) or the Two Process Theory (Gray, 1975)— the two processes or factors being classical and operant conditioning. According to Mowrer, the animal first learns to be afraid (through classical conditioning the light or buzzer warning signal elicits an anticipatory emotional response of fear or anxiety) and then learns a response to reduce the fear (jumping the barrier is negatively reinforced through avoiding the shock before it is switched on).

Miller (1948) attempted to separate out the classical from the operant factors. At first he trained rats to run out of a white room, through a small door, into a black room by giving them shocks in the white room. After pre-training, the door was closed and could only be opened by the rat turning a wheel. Even though no further shocks were given, the residual 'aversiveness' of the white room (acquired through classical conditioning) was sufficient to motivate the rats to learn quickly to turn the wheel so that they could run through into the 'safe' room, thus relieving their anxiety (negative reinforcement).

An interesting and important difference can now be seen between positive and negative reinforcement in relation to extinction. If we try to teach a rat a new response in order to get it into a black box which used to contain food, it will soon stop responding; but if a rat successfully escapes from a white room which used to be dangerous, it may go on escaping indefinitely. In the former case it soon 'discovers' that the food is no longer available but in the latter it does not stay around long enough to 'discover' that the shock is no longer available.

Therefore, responses which are motivated by conditioned fear or anxiety should persist longer (take longer to extinguish) than those motivated by positive incentives. Avoidance learning prevents the learner from 'testing reality' and this has been found in dogs and humans (Solomon and Wynne, 1953; Turner and Solomon, 1962). In humans, phobias may be seen as becoming persistent in this way and one therapeutic attempt to bring about extinction through forced reality testing is called flooding or implosion therapy (see Chapter 31).

Punishment

Skinner has always maintained that positive reinforcement (and, to a lesser extent, negative reinforcement) is a much more potent influence on behaviour than punishment, both with animals and humans, largely because the latter can only make certain responses less likely—you cannot teach an animal or a person anything new by punishment alone.

Other psychologists either disagree with Skinner or emphasize different reasons for the ineffectiveness of punishment.

Campbell and Church (1969) argue that punishments are, if anything, a stronger influence on behaviour than the incentive effects of reinforcements (at least as far as laboratory animals are concerned). The problem, however, is the unpleasant side-effects of stress, anxiety, withdrawal, aggression and so on (see Chapter 27 for discussion of this in relation to children).

Estes (1970) trained two groups of rats to press a lever for food, after which they were given extinction trials. For Group A, the first few extinction trials involved strong electric shock every time they pressed; from then on, the food was simply withheld. For Group B, food was withheld on all the extinction trials (and no shocks).

In the first stage of extinction, Group A rats did make fewer responses but they later resumed their previous rate of responding and, by the end of the experiment, had made as many responses as Group B. Estes concluded that punishment merely *suppressed* the lever pressing in the short term, but did not weaken it.

Other experiments have shown that the strength and duration of the suppression effect depend on the *intensity* of the punishment and the degree of deprivation. However, the response is still suppressed rather than unlearned.

Howe (1980) points out that when alternative ways of obtaining reinforcers are available, punishment has a more powerful suppressive effect on the punished behaviour. For example, Azrin and Holtz (1966) combined punishment and reinforcement so that response A was punished while response B, incompatible with A, was positively reinforced. This is something that Skinner advocates with human beings.

THE ANTECEDENTS OF BEHAVIOUR—STIMULUS CONTROL

A crucial difference between classical and operant conditioning is to do with the role of the stimulus in relation to the response. Whereas in classical conditioning the stimulus *elicits* or *triggers* the response in an automatic way, in operant conditioning the stimulus indicates the likely consequence of *emitting* a particular response, ie the operant behaviour is more likely to occur in the presence of some stimuli than others. If the rat has been reinforced for pressing the lever, it is more likely to go on emitting that response as the lever becomes associated both with reinforcement and the action of pressing (probably through classical conditioning). Technically, lever pressing has now come under the control of the lever stimulus—but there is still no inevitability about pressing it, only an inceased probability. (This is why the term 'S–R psychology' is sometimes used only to refer to *classical* conditioning.)

Similarly, drivers' behaviour is brought under the stimulus control of traffic signals, road signs, other vehicles, pedestrians and so on. Much of our everyday behaviour can be seen in this way; sitting on chairs, answering the telephone, turning on the television, etc., are all operants which are more likely to occur in the presence of those stimuli because of the past consequences of doing so.

A special case of stimulus control is a *discriminative stimulus*. In the Skinner box, for example, if a rat is reinforced for lever pressing *only* when a light is on, the light soon becomes a discriminative stimulus, ie the rat only presses when the light is on. If you learn to ask your teachers questions only when they are sitting at their desk (and not when standing by the board) because this has been the occasion for discussion in previous lessons, then your question-asking behaviour is under the stimulus control of your teachers' behaviour.

DOES CONDITIONING WORK IN THE SAME WAY FOR ALL SPECIES?

According to Walker (1984), the fact that many experiments involving a variety of species can all be described as classical conditioning (since in all cases a response comes to be elicited by a new stimulus) does *not* in itself mean that there is only one mechanism involved or only one explanation which applies, equally, to all species and all cases.

Although conditionability seems to be an almost universal property of nervous systems (including those of sea snails, flatworms and fruit flies) many psychologists have argued that there can be no general laws of learning (Seligman, 1970). But what might such laws be?

One example is the law of *contiguity*: events (or stimuli) which occur close together in time and space are likely to become associated with each other. Most of the examples of conditioning we have considered so far would appear to 'obey' the law of contiguity. But can we find exceptions and, if so, how can we explain them?

A famous and important exception are *taste aversion* studies (Garcia and Koelling, 1966; Garcia et al, 1966). In the Garcia et al study, rats were given a novel-tasting solution, eg saccharine-flavoured water (the CS), prior to a drug, eg apomorphine (the UCS), which has a delayed action, inducing severe intestinal illness (the UCR). In two separate experiments the precise time-lapse between tasting the solution and the onset of the drug-induced nausea was either (A) 5, 6, 7, 8, 9, 10, 11, 12, 15, 16, 17, 18, 19, 20, 21 and 22 minutes, or (B) 30, 45, 75, 120 and 180 minutes. In (A), the rats received just four treatments (one every third day) and in (B) five were given (one every third day) and in all cases a conditioned aversive response to the solution was acquired (ie intestinal illness became a CR—a response to the solution alone). In some replications, just a single treatment has been needed. Illness seems to be naturally attributed to tastes.

Findings such as these show that the use of slow-acting rat poisons are really a waste of time and effort because the interval between food consumption and illness can be several *hours* without abolishing the aversion (ie the *association* between the poison and the illness is still learnt).

However, as Mackintosh (1984) has pointed out, the time interval does have some effect—everything else being equal, 30 minutes will show a more marked aversion than 300 minutes (although there will be some learning in the latter).

Control groups of rats, which either received apomorphine injection with ordinary water or saline injection with saccharine solution, suggest that the aversion to the saccharine solution is a genuine CR as a result of association with the apomorphine (the illness is 'attributed' to the solution) as opposed to neophobia (the tendency to avoid any novel substance, made stronger by the experience of illness).

Rats can also be conditioned to novel smells:

> ... The omnivorous rat displays a bias, probably established by natural selection, to associate gustatory and olfactory cues with internal malaise, even when these stimuli are separated by long time periods ... (Garcia et al, 1966)

However, auditory, visual and tactile stimuli are not so readily associated with internal illness—but are more easily associated with peripheral pain.

Turning to pigeons, it is impossible to deter them from water and, for other species, taste aversions are very difficult to establish, even if the animal is made very ill. In almost all species aversions are learned more easily to new flavours than to familiar ones (saccharine solution is a novel taste for the rat).

Thus there seem to be definite biological limitations on the ability of animals to develop a conditioned aversion. Similarly, the average rat will learn very quickly to avoid shock in a shuttlebox and will also learn very quickly to press a lever for food. However, rats do not learn very readily to press a lever to avoid shock. Again, pigeons can be trained quickly to fly from one perch to another in order to avoid shock but it is almost impossible to train them to peck a disc to avoid shock.

Is there any evidence that contiguity is not necessary to experimental situations other than conditioned taste aversion? Mackintosh (1984) cites a study by Bow Tong Lett in which rats were removed from a maze immediately after choosing on each trial, regardless of whether they were right or wrong and only several minutes later were they returned to receive food in the maze if they had chosen correctly. They learned successfully with delays of at least five minutes:

> The association span of the rat, it appears, is capable of bridging quite long intervals. (Mackintosh, 1984)

But clearly this is not always so. Why not?

Mackintosh (1984) argues that if we assume that the function of conditioning is to enable organisms to find out what signals or produces certain important events, ie to attribute the occurrence of, say, food or danger to their most probable antecedent causes, it makes no sense for an animal to associate the occurrence of food with any or every event that has happened in the preceding hour. The mechanisms of conditioning are nicely designed, he says, to help an animal distinguish between the probable causal relations and occasional chance conjunctions of events. Conditioning, therefore, makes some functional sense.

While it is true that successful conditioning can occur to a stimulus even though there is a substantial interval between it (CS) and the reinforcer (the UCS), such conditioning will be prevented if there is some other event which predicts the occurrence of the reinforcer more accurately. As Mackintosh says:

> Conditioning occurs selectively, to good predictors of reinforcement at the expense of poorer predictors. (Mackintosh, 1984)

He cites a study by Williams in which pigeons learnt to peck at a disc briefly illuminated with a red light despite a 10 second delay between such pecks and the delivery of food. However, this was effectively abolished if some other stimulus (eg a brief green light) occurred in the interval between the peck on the red disc and food. It is as if they attribute food to the more recent event (green light) as opposed to the earlier red light.

These findings suggest that whether or not a particular event is associated with a particular reinforcer does not depend solely on the relation holding between the two (as the traditional learning theories would have it) but also on whether other intervening events are more easily associated with that reinforcer. This explains why even short intervals between stimulus and reinforcer can prevent conditioning. It also explains why conditioning can still occur despite the often long intervals in the taste-aversion experiments—the animal is denied access to food or drink other than the saccharine-solution or whatever the CS happens to be.

Findings like these have led Bolles (1980) and others to conclude that we cannot regard the basic principles of learning as applying equally to all species in all situations; we must take into account the evolutionary history of the species as well as the individual organism's learning history.

An important idea in this context is Seligman's concept of *preparedness* (1970). Animals are biologically prepared to learn actions that are closely related to the survival of their species (eg learned water or food aversions) and these prepared behaviours are learned with very little training. By the same token, there are also 'contra-prepared' behaviours, which are contrary to an animal's natural tendencies and so are learned with great difficulty, if at all. Seligman believes that most of the behaviour studied in the laboratory falls somewhere in between these two extremes.

Oakley (1983) believes that preparedness in conditioning is an inherited characteristic. If, in the history of a species, individuals have often been exposed to certain biologically significant kinds of association, then the ability to learn rapidly about such associations becomes genetically transmitted. These genetic constraints apply to both classical and operant conditioning.

What about preparedness in humans? Much of the relevant data relates to how easily certain conditioned fear responses can be induced in the laboratory or how common certain phobias are compared with others (the 'naturally occurring ones'). For instance, Ohman (1975) and Hygge and Ohman (1978) paired slides of snakes and spiders with a strong electric shock and quickly established conditioned emotional responses to these slides but not to slides of flowers, houses or berries.

Seligman (1972) observed that human phobias tend to fall into certain narrow categories, most of them being of animals or dangerous places. Most common of all were the fear of snakes, spiders, the dark, high places and closed-in places and often there is no previous evidence for the fear actually having been conditioned (this is discussed further in Chapter 31).

Another interesting finding is that classically conditioned responses extinguish faster in humans than animals. According to Weiskrantz (1982) this is because the CRs are modulated by more complex human memories.

These findings in turn raise further questions, including: (i) what exactly is learned during conditioning; and (ii) what is the role of cognitive factors in conditioning? I shall treat these as two parts of the same question.

IS CONDITIONING MORE COMPLEX THAN IT SEEMS? THE ROLE OF COGNITION

1) According to Mackintosh (1978), conditioning is *not* reducible to the strengthening of S–R associations by the automatic action of a process called reinforcement. It is more appropriate to think of it as a matter of detecting and learning about *relations between events*, whereby animals typically discover what signals or causes events that are important to them, such as food, water, danger or safety. Mackintosh goes on to say that instead of treating salivation or lever-pressing as what is learned, we could regard it simply as a convenient *index* that the subject has detected certain relationships in its environment (see the references to Mackintosh in the previous section).

Indeed, Pavlov himself described the CS as a 'signal' for the UCS, the relationship between CS and the UCS as one of 'stimulus substitution' and the CR as an 'anticipatory' response, suggesting that his dogs were *expecting* the food to follow the bell, etc.

To support this interpretation, Rescorla (1968) presented two groups of animals with the same number of CS–UCS pairings, but the second group also received additional presentations of the UCS on its own without the CS. The first group showed much stonger conditioning than the second, indicating that the most important factor (in classical conditioning anyway) is how *predictably* the UCS follows the CS, not *how often* the CS and UCS are paired.

Again, Rescorla (1967) presented the CS at irregular intervals both before and after the UCS (eg five seconds before, then five seconds after, then ten seconds before, etc.) so that the animal 'learnt' that the CS is not related to the UCS in any systematic way; this may make it difficult to condition the animal to the same CS in later experiments since it has already learned that it is not systematically related to past events.

2) Many investigators regard conditioning as involving the formation of central representation of causal relations (or, at least, predictive ones) between events: stimulus event A predicts stimulus event B (the CS predicts the UCS). But the learning may also take the form: stimulus event A predicts that stimulus event B will *not* occur; this is called *conditioned suppression* or *inhibition*.

Pavlov (1927) first trained a dog with three separate stimuli: a flashing light, the tone of C sharp and a rotating disc; all of these were signals for food. Then an 'inhibitory combination' was formed by sounding a metronome along with the rotating disc, this combination never being followed by food: the dog learned not to salivate. Then the metronome was sounded along with the tone and flashing light, which produced a virtual elimination of salivation. Pavlov concluded that the metronome had become a 'conditioned inhibitor'.

3) Another demonstration of the complexity of conditioning is the phenomenon of *blocking* (Kamin, 1969). If, for example, an animal is shown a light, quickly followed by an electric shock, the light soon comes to elicit fear as a CR. If a noise is then added (Noise + Light + Shock), then the noise should also soon become a CS, because it too is being paired with shock.

However, this is not what happens; if the noise is later presented alone, it fails to produce a CR. Why? It seems that the noise has somehow been 'blocked' from becoming a CS because of the previous conditioning to the light; in cognitive terms, since the light already predicts shock, the noise is irrelevant, it provides no additional information—the animal already 'knows' that shock will follow the light.

4) Turning now to operant conditioning, the complexity of learning is well illustrated by *learned helplessness* (Seligman, 1974, 1975). Dogs were strapped into a harness and given a series of shocks from which they could not escape. They were later required to learn avoidance behaviour in a shuttle-box—they had to jump a barrier within 10 seconds of a warning signal or suffer 50 seconds of painful shock. Whereas control dogs, which had not been subjected to the inescapable shocks, learned the avoidance response very quickly, about two-thirds of the experimental dogs seemed unable to do so. They seemed passively resigned to suffering the shock and even if they did successfuly avoid the shock on one trial, they were unlikely to do so on the next. Some dogs had to be pushed over the barrier 200 times or more before this learned helplessness wore off.

So the dogs, according to Seligman, learned that no behaviour on their part had any effect on the occurrence (or non-occurrence) of a particular event (ie the shock). This has been demonstrated using human subjects by Miller and Norman (1979), and Maier and Seligman (1976) have tried to explain depression in humans in terms of learned helplessness (see Chapters 5 and 30).

5) Skinner's claim that reinforcements and punishments automatically strengthen and weaken behaviour has been challenged by many, including Bandura (1977), who maintains that: (i) they provide the learner with *information* about the likely consequences of certain behaviour under certain conditions, that is 'what leads to what', and whether we are 'right' or 'wrong' (*feedback*); and (ii) they motivate us by causing us to *anticipate future outcomes*—our present behaviours are largely governed by the outcomes we expect them to have.

While Bandura is addressing his comments primarily to human behaviour, one of the earliest challenges to Skinner's view came from a fellow student of learning in rats, Edward Tolman.

Tolman's Cognitive Behaviourism— Latent Learning and Cognitive Maps

Tolman, although working within the behaviourist tradition in the 1920s, 1930s and 1940s, would today be regarded as a cognitive psychologist, because he explained the learning of rats in terms of inferred cognitive processes, in particular 'cognitive' or mental maps. He also distinguished between learning and performance (or 'knowing' and 'doing').

Tolman and Honzik (1930) showed that learning *can* take place in the absence of reinforcement (contrary to Skinner's position) in the following way: Group 1 were reinforced every time they found their way through a maze to the food box; Group 2 were never reinforced; and Group 3 received no reinforcement for the first ten days of the experiment but did so from day eleven.

Group 1, as you might expect, learned to run the maze quickly and made fewer and fewer mistakes. Again, not surprisingly, Group 2 never decreased the time it took them to find the food and they wandered the same maze aimlessly much of the time. Group 3, however, having apparently made no progress during the first ten days (of no reinforcement) showed a sudden decrease in the time it took to reach the goal-box on day eleven when they received their first reinforcement and caught up almost immediately with Group 1 (Fig. 7.12).

Clearly the Group 3 rats had been learning their way through the maze during the first ten days but that learning was *latent* (or 'behaviourally silent'), that is, it did not show up in their actual behaviour (performance). With the incentive of the reinforcement on day eleven, that previously 'hidden' learning was demonstrated, allowing Group 3 rats to catch up very quickly with the Group 1 rats, which had been reinforced from the beginning. So Tolman and Honzik had produced

Figure 7.12 The results of Tolman and Honzik's study of latent learning in rats

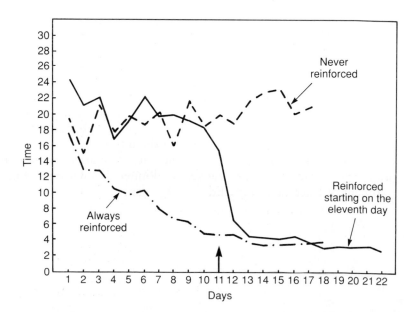

evidence for the view that reinforcement may be important in relation to *performance* of learned behaviour but that it is not necessary for the learning itself.

Having established the role of reinforcement, Tolman wanted to know exactly what it is that is learned (and which does not require reinforcement). Tolman's theory (1948) of *sign-learning* (or place-learning) maintains that rats learn something *about* 'what leads to what' in the maze, that is, they learn *expectations* as to which part of the maze will be followed by which other part of the maze. These expectations Tolman called *'cognitive maps'* and they represent a primitive kind of perceptual map of the maze, an understanding of the spatial relationships that constitute the maze (much like the mental map you or I have of familiar streets, those that lead to your home or to college).

What is the evidence for this?

Of course, like all cognitive processes, a cognitive map cannot be directly observed but only inferred from actual behaviour. However, it is difficult to know how else to explain the findings that rats, which have originally learned to run through a maze, could then swim through it (if it was flooded), roll through it, take short-cuts or how, if the maze were rotated, they could find the usual food location from several different starting points (Fig. 7.13).

These findings suggest that it is *not* the individual movements of walking or swimming, etc. that constitute the learning of the maze (as the Chain Response or Reflex Theory would maintain) but rather something

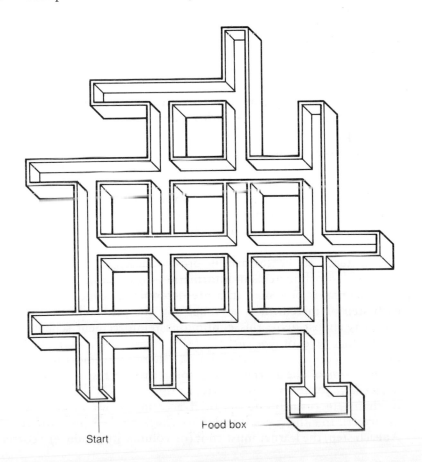

Start

Food box

Figure 7.13 The maze used in Tolman and Honzik's study of latent learning in rats

to do with the geographical characteristics of the maze (Sign Learning Theory). In a direct test between these two opposed theories, Restle (1957) flooded a maze immediately after a group of rats had learnt to run it and they were able to swim to the goal-box with no more errors than when they had walked. This clearly supports Tolman's theory of sign learning.

APPLICATIONS OF CONDITIONING

The three major ways in which conditioning principles have been put to practical use with people are:

(a) *Behaviour therapy* or *modification*, which constitutes a major form of treatment of behaviour disorders (and which is discussed in detail in Chapter 31).
(b) *Biofeedback*, a way of bringing automatic, physiological processes under voluntary control (and which was discussed in detail in Chapter 5.
(c) *Programmed learning* or *instruction*:

> . . . a method of instruction that systematically applies the principles of operant conditioning to the learning situation. (Haber and Runyon, 1983)

The first 'teaching machine' was devised by Pressey, an educational psychologist, in 1926. It consisted of a series of multiple choice questions used for testing what students had already been taught. Skinner (1954, 1958) advocated the extension of this technique for initial *learning*.

Not only did Skinner believe that all learning (human and animal) takes place according to the principles of (operant) conditioning but that the usual classroom situation is not an ideal situation for learning to happen: the teacher typically has little control over crucial variables such as students paying attention, their motivation and the reinforcements they receive, and often it is the aversive consequences of the classroom which dominate (such as trying to avoid failure or the teacher's disapproval).

Skinner also believed that much conventional teaching–learning is slow and inefficient. Programmed instruction can remove these obstacles to learning on the basis of six principles:

(a) The material to be learned is broken down into a number of elements—separate items of information (or frames).
(b) The material is presented in a pre-determined sequence, such that each step or increment is so small that the probability of making errors is almost zero; this continuous reinforcement schedule ensures a high level of *motivation*.
(c) For every correct response, an immediate reinforcement is provided in the form of the learner being told that the response is correct (*immediate feedback*); an incorrect response takes the learner back to that item (usually after a brief account of why the answer is incorrect). In either case, learners are checking their own progress.
(d) At each step, the learner must emit (or voluntarily produce) a correct

answer in order to receive a reinforcement; in this way, reinforcement is *contingent* upon appropriate behaviour and learners are *actively participating* in their learning.

(e) The reinforcement of correct responses to a number of small steps (successive approximations) making up the material to be learned represents a form of *shaping*.

(f) Learners work at their own pace, which allows for any individual differences in speed of learning.

LINEAR VERSUS BRANCHING PROGRAMMES

The kind of programmed learning which Skinner devised and advocated is *linear*; it comprises a predetermined sequence of steps, which is the same for all students and each must be correctly answered before moving on to the next. By contrast, *branching* programmes usually comprise larger frames (chunks of information and explanations rather than very short, simple, questions and bits of information) and they allow alternative routes through the material, depending on the accuracy of the learner's answers. This allows more able students to skip familiar material and move on to more advanced material. Branching also enables a learner who makes an error to find out *why* the answer is wrong by directing them to branch off from the main stem of the programme and work through some special review material.

Both linear and branching programmes can take the form of: (i) *books* (programmed texts); (ii) *teaching machines* (in which, for example, a frame is exposed in the left-hand window and the student writes the answer in the right-hand window or pulling a lever moves the answer under a perspex cover, revealing the correct answer and the next frame); or (iii) *Computer Assisted Instruction* (CAI). CAI usually involves an elaborate, complex, branching programme; the learner either operates a teletype keyboard or uses a special probe to indicate the answer on a monitor

HOW EFFECTIVE IS PROGRAMMED INSTRUCTION?

To compare programmed instruction (often called self-instruction) with traditional teaching methods is no simple matter, partly because each can vary so much and each may interact with a number of other variables.

Schramm (1964) reviewed 165 studies and concluded that students do learn from programmed instruction but, in general, it is neither superior nor inferior to conventional teaching methods. It seems that both the type of material and the type of students will have a major bearing on the relative effectiveness of methods of instruction.

SOCIAL LEARNING THEORY AND OBSERVATIONAL LEARNING

A major alternative to conditioning (as an attempt to understand learning) comes from Social Learning Theory. This originated in the USA in the 1940s and 1950s as an attempt to re-interpret certain aspects of Freud's psychoanalytic theory in terms of conditioning theory (or Orthodox Learning Theory) (Dollard and Miller, 1950). This was carried

Figure 7.14 *Albert Bandura (born 1925)*

on in the 1960s and 1970s, notably by Albert Bandura (Fig. 7.14), who tried to make Freud's concept of identification more objective and scientifically viable by studying it in the laboratory in the form of imitation (see Chapter 23).

1) Along with other behaviourist psychologists, the Social Learning (SL) theorists believe that all behaviour is learned through the same mechanisms, according to the same principles of learning. However, where they differ significantly from Pavlov, Watson, Skinner and so on, is in their interest specifically in human learning, especially the acquisition of social and moral behaviour (we shall be discussing both theories in relation to moral development in Chapter 27). According to McLoughlin (1971), social learning is 'behaviour learned in interpersonal situations and linked to the needs that require for their satisfaction the mediation of other people'.

2) Although SL theorists agree that we should observe what is observable, they also believe that there are important cognitive or mediating variables which intervene between stimulus and response and without which we cannot adequately explain behaviour. These cognitive variables cannot be directly observed but can only be inferred from observing actual behaviour. We shall say more about this later on.

3) SL theorists do not deny the importance of classical and operant conditioning but they do think that these learning processes cannot adequately account for the appearance of *novel* behaviour, that is, behaviour which the individual has not displayed before; classical conditioning can explain how a response shifts from one stimulus to another (stimulus substitution) while operant can explain how spontaneously-produced responses, through selective reinforcement and shaping, become more likely to be repeated. But if these were the *only* two kinds of learning, the child's behavioural repertoire would be very limited indeed.

Consequently, the SL theorists have emphasized a kind of learning that is distinct from conditioning, namely *observational learning*, that is, learning through watching the behaviour of another person. There are several important points to note about the concept of observational learning:

(a) The person whose behaviour is observed is called the *model*; hence 'modelling' is normally used synonymously with 'observational learning'.

(b) The learning takes place spontaneously, with no deliberate effort on the learner's part or any intention to teach on the model's part.

(c) Both fairly specific behaviours (eg nailbiting) and more general, emotional states (eg fear of the dentist) can be modelled (the latter through facial expressions, body posture, etc.).

(d) Observational learning, as such, takes place without any reinforcement (Bandura, 1965); mere exposure to the model is sufficient for learning to occur. However, whether the learning actually reveals itself in the behaviour (ie *imitated*) depends, among other things, on the *consequences* of the behaviour, both for the model and the learner (Bandura et al, 1963). So, whereas for Skinner the role of reinforcement is central to the learning process itself, for the SL theorists it is important only in so far as it determines the likelihood of learned responses actually being demonstrated. This, of course, is the crucial distinction between learning and performance which we came across when discussing Tolman's cognitive behaviourism.

(e) Much of the SL theorists' research has centred on the characteristics of models that make them more or less likely to be imitated and the conditions under which the learning will be performed.

REINFORCEMENT AS INFORMATION ABOUT THE FUTURE

We noted above that Bandura takes a very different view of how reinforcement works to Skinner and this relates directly to the learning–performance distinction which Bandura makes but which Skinner does not.

According to Skinner, reinforcement works *automatically*; the strengthening of a response simply 'happens' and the learner, human or animal, is not required to assess or evaluate the effects of their behaviour. Bandura on the other hand, maintains that:

> Reinforcement serves principally as an informative and motivational operation rather than as a mechanical response strengthener. (Bandura, 1977)

By *informative* he means that the consequences of our behaviour (reinforcement or punishment) tell us under what circumstances it would seem wise to try a particular behaviour in the future, that is, they improve our prediction of whether a given action will lead to pleasant or unpleasant outcomes in the future. While Skinner believes that a consequence exerts its influence in *reverse* (ie strengthening the behaviour that *preceded* the reinforcement or punishment), Bandura argues that the consequence exerts its influence forwards, *into the future*, by giving the learner information about what effects can be expected if they behave that way again in similar circumstances.

For these reasons, we can learn from observing others (as well as from our own behaviour), because watching others can provide the same information as to what kind of behaviour leads to which consequence.

By *motivational*, Bandura means that we are more likely to try to learn the modelled behaviour if we value the consequences related to that behaviour. But as Bandura also makes the distinction between learning and performance, the motivational effect of reinforcement (as we noted above) may be greater in relation to demonstration of learning rather than the learning itself.

THE ROLE OF COGNITIVE FACTORS IN OBSERVATIONAL LEARNING

The learning process is a much more complex one for Bandura than it is for Skinner. In Bandura's view:

> ...contrary to mechanistic metaphors, outcomes change behaviour in humans through the intervening influence of thought. (Bandura, 1974)

Bandura believes that there are five major functions involved in observational learning:

1) *Paying attention*. The learner must attend to the pertinent clues in the stimulus situation and ignore those aspects of the model and the environment that are incidental and do not affect the performance the learner seeks to learn. Especially with complex behaviour, failure to reproduce the behaviour properly later on is often due to misdirected attention at the time of modelling.

2) Recording a *visual image* or *semantic code* for the modelled behaviour in memory. Without an adequate coding system the learner fails to store what has been seen or heard (see Chapter 12). There are obvious developmental trends in the ability to learn from models; whereas an infant's use of modelling is confined mainly to immediate imitation, the older child can defer (postpone) imitation because of its superior use of symbols. The codes must, of course, be suitable for transforming into overt actions (see Chapter 25).

3) *Memory permanence*. This refers to devices such as rehearsal and use of multiple codes to help *retain* the stored information over long periods.

4) *Reproducing the observed motor activities accurately*. This usually requires a number of trials to get the muscular *feel* of the behaviour (through feedback). Again, there are developmental trends involved here, whereby the older child enjoys greater muscular strength and control.

5) *Motivation*. Behaviourists have traditionally equated this with the role of the *consequences of behaviour* and we have already discussed the differences between Bandura's and Skinner's interpretation of the nature of reinforcement and how it works. Some evidence for the role of cognitive factors is provided by a study by Bandura et al (1963) in which children were asked to reproduce the actions of a model seen on a film. Group 1 simply watched the film, Group 2 were asked to describe the model's actions as they saw them on the film and Group 3 were asked to count while watching the film (an interfering task). It was found that Group 2 children were able to reproduce the behaviour of the model most accurately and thoroughly through the aid of verbalization. As expected, Group 3 children did worst of all, with Group 1 children somewhere in between.

We shall have more to say about the role of cognitive factors in modelling in Chapter 27 on moral development.

INSIGHT LEARNING

Insight learning represents a view of learning as 'purely cognitive' and stems from a theoretical approach in psychology which is diametrically opposed to the S–R approach, namely, the *Gestalt* school. The Gestalt psychologists are best known for their work on perception (see Chapter 9) and their view of learning is directly linked to their view of perception; indeed, insight learning can be defined as a perceptual restructuring of the elements that constitute a problem-situation, whereby a previously missing 'ingredient' is supplied and all the parts are seen in relation to each other, forming a meaningful whole (see Chapter 14 for a discussion of Gestalt studies of problem-solving).

For example, imagine a chimpanzee, in its cage, reaching for a banana which lies outside the cage; its arm is not long enough to get the banana, but also outside the cage is a stick which the chimp can reach and which is long enough to reach the banana. After reaching with its arm unsuccessfully, it suddenly reaches for the stick and uses it to rake in the banana.

Köhler (1925), one of the leading Gestalt psychologists, used this and similar problems to demonstrate *insight-learning*, which he saw as opposed to the *trial-and-error* learning involved in S–R approaches. In the latter, stimulus and response become associated when, by chance, the animal produces the correct response (or 'solves the problem') and is reinforced for doing so. However, the correct response does not appear suddenly, it merely takes less and less time to be made on each subsequent trial and there is no 'understanding' involved (eg Thorndike's cats in puzzle boxes).

By contrast, in insight learning a sudden solution is the rule (usually preceded by long pauses, during which there is inspection of the whole visual field) and, once the solution has appeared, it can be repeated immediately the next time the problem is confronted. What is learned is not a specific set of conditioned associations but a cognitive relationship between a means and an end, and this makes *transfer* to other, similar, problem situations easier.

For example, Sultan (Köhler's most intelligent chimp) was able to pull into the cage the longer of two sticks by using the shorter one and then, with the longer one, was able to pull in a piece of fruit. Again, he was able to join two sticks together in order to make a stick long enough to rake in some fruit. In a different kind of problem, he learned to stack boxes, one on top of the other, to reach bananas suspended from the ceiling (see Fig. 7.15).

However, a couple of qualifications need to be made:

(a) Animals do not usually demonstrate insight learning very easily unless all the elements that constitute the problem are in their field of vision at the same time. For example, the chimp has to be able to see the fruit and sticks (or boxes) together before it can grasp their relationship and solve the problem. People, by contrast, could immediately *think* of a stick and go looking for one; language is an important tool for thinking in this kind of problem-solving situation.

(b) Köhler has been criticized for his belief that insight involves a sudden re-structuring of the situation independent of the animal's past experience. There is evidence that insightful solutions can be facilitated by 'hints' or cues, especially if the elements of the problem situation are already familiar to the learner. This is captured especially well in another solution that Sultan found to the banana problem; he succeeded in breaking off a branch from a sawn-off castor-oil bush, located inside the cage, which he used to rake in a banana lying outside the cage. Although Köhler described this as happening in 'one single quick chain of action', and despite its appearance as a 'flash of insight', it did not come 'out of the blue', out of nowhere. Sultan was very familiar with bananas and with castor-oil bushes, as well as with sticks.

According to Arthur Koestler (1970), all acts of 'creation', whether in

Figure 7.15 Köhler's experiments with chimpanzees

painting, humour, poetry or science, share one basic characteristic, namely the juxtaposition of two concepts or ideas or images which were previously separate. When two things, previously unrelated, are seen as belonging together in some way, a joke or a scientific discovery is made. He cites the story of Archimedes, who was asked to judge whether a beautiful crown, allegedly made of pure gold, had in fact been adulterated with silver. Short of melting it down, he was stumped—he knew the specific weight of gold (its weight per volume unit) but how was he to measure the volume of such a complicated and ornate object as the crown?

One day, while getting into his bath, Archimedes noticed the familiar sight of the water-level rising and, in a flash ('Eureka!') he realized that the volume of water displaced was equal to the volume of his immersed body and that here was a way that the volume of the crown could also be measured. So, two already familiar pieces of knowledge, first the specific weight of gold, and secondly, water displacement equalling object immersion, were, for the first time, related to each other and, in that moment, a discovery was made. Only someone with Archimedes' knowledge could have made such a discovery; in Koestler's terms, he was *ripe* for making the discovery.

In the case of chimpanzees, their ripeness includes their manual dexterity, their advanced sensory motor co-ordination (biological) and their familiarity with sticks, bananas, etc. (experiential or environmental); the former are reminiscent of Seligman's concept of preparedness and the latter is demonstrated by a study by Birch (1945). Monkeys which were allowed to play with sticks for three days solved the food-raking problem faster than monkeys without such experience.

Do We Have to Choose Between Trial-and-Error and Insight?

Koestler believes that the debate between the S–R and the cognitive psychologists derives to a large extent from a refusal to take seriously the notion of ripeness. Rats and cats have generally been presented with tasks for which they are biologically ill-fitted and so the resulting learning was bound to appear gradual, piecemeal, and at first quite random.

Köhler and the Gestalt school, by contrast, set chimps problems for which they were (almost) ripe and so gave the impression that all learning is based on insight.

So, is there a middle ground?

GAGNÉ'S HIERARCHY OF LEARNING

Gagné (1974) has attempted to answer the question regarding the relationship between simple and complex forms of learning. Is there a continuity between them and, if so, what form does this take? His solution is to regard eight major varieties of learning as *hierarchically* related, each building on earlier, more simple abilities, which therefore, represent prerequisites for later, more complex abilities. These are summarized in Table 7.3.

1. *Signal learning*	The establishment of a simple connection in which a stimulus takes on the properties of a signal *(classical conditioning)*	*Table 7.3 Gagné's hierarchy of learning*
2. *Stimulus–Response learning*	The establishment of a connection between a stimulus and a response where the response is a voluntary movement and the connection is instrumental in satisfying a need or motive *(operant conditioning)*	

1 and 2 are prerequisites for:

3. *Chaining*	The connecting of a sequence of two or more previously learned stimulus–response connections
4. *Verbal association*	The learning of chains that are specifically verbal, important for the acquisition and use of language. Enables a number of learned connections involving words to be emitted in a single sequence

3 and 4 are prerequisites for:

5. *Discrimination learning*	Making different responses to similar stimuli. Involves more than simply making isolated stimulus–response connections because it is necessary to deal with the problem of interference between similar items

5 is a prerequisite for:

6. *Concept learning*	Learning to make a common response to stimuli that form a class or category but which differ in their physical characteristics. Requires representing information in memory, classifying events and discriminating between them on basis of abstracted properties

6 is a prerequisite for:

7. *Rule-learning*	A rule is a chain of two or more concepts (eg 'if A then B')

7 is a prerequisite for:

8. *Problem-solving*	Involves re-combining old rules into new ones, making it possible to answer questions and solve problems, especially important for real-life human problem-solving situations.

HARLOW'S CONCEPT OF LEARNING SETS

According to Harlow (1949), S–R learning and insight learning are related; essentially, they are two different phases of the same, continuous process, with S–R learning predominant in the early stages and insight developing out of prior S–R connections. Harlow suggests that the concept of a *learning set* (or 'learning to learn') represents an intervening process between S–R and insight learning; the greater the number of sets, the better equipped the learner is to adapt to a changing environment, and a very large number of different sets, 'may supply the raw material for human thinking'.

To study learning sets, Harlow gave monkeys a variety of discrimination tasks. In the simplest, the monkey had to choose between two objects, one of which was designated the 'correct one'. In a more complex task the monkey had to find the 'odd-one-out' of three objects. In both types of task, the pair of objects or set of three was changed each time a correct discrimination was made. So, for example, the monkey might be shown a small red square and a large blue circle and would be given six trials in which to choose the 'correct' one (for which a food reward was given). When this had been achieved a different pair of objects (eg a green triangle and a black circle) was presented and once again the monkey had six trials in which to make the correct discrimination.

In one study, involving 344 of these two-object tasks, the results were dramatic. Learning the first few discriminations was difficult but it gradually became easier as the number of different tasks increased, until after 300 the solution was immediate (solved on the first trial). Remember that the same pair of objects was never used more than once.

There were certain kinds of errors to which different monkeys were prone that made it quite systematic. For example, choosing the object on the right, alternating sides from trial to trial or always choosing the larger object. Such errors gradually dropped out as the monkey realized that none of these was relevant to the solution; once this happened, the monkey could adopt a new strategy that was appropriate to *all* the tasks and which did not depend on the specific stimuli used. According to Harlow, a learning set involves learning a general skill applicable to a whole new class of problems, or again, it consists of learning a simple rule or code, based on a *conceptual* (not a perceptual) relationship (1959). To this extent, Harlow demonstrated that insightful learning itself is (at least partially) learned and grows out of more random, trial-and-error learning.

Bruner (1966) reported similar findings in rats running mazes: after learning to take the route involving a series of left/right/left/right turns, they took substantially less time than before to learn to reverse the sequence (right/left/right/left), that is, they had learned to alternate.

LEARNING SET AND TRANSFER OF LEARNING

Learning set represents a special case of a more general phenonemon known as transfer of learning (or training). Essentially, transfer refers to the influence of earlier learning on later learning which we saw, when defining learning at the beginning of the chapter, to be an inherent feature of the learning process in general (Howe, 1980).

Howe maintains that some kinds of transfer take the form of simple stimulus generalization (equivalent to Gagné's Signal Learning) while in more complex learning situations transfer may depend on the acquisition of rules or principles that apply to a variety of different circumstances (Gagné's Concept, Rule Learning and Problem-solving). Learning sets can be viewed as intermediate between simple generalization and the more complex transfer phenomena involved in hierarchically organized skills.

It used to be thought that certain disciplines (such as Latin or maths) were so general in their transferability that they could 'train the mind' to cope with almost any demand that might subsequently be made of it. (This was the thinking behind the 'classical' education of the public schools.) However, it is now recognized (especially for motor skills) that the effect of training is much more limited and is restrained by the degree of similarity of the components of different tasks; and yet the notion of similarity itself is a complex one.

For instance, in a *mirror-drawing* task, practice under one condition (eg drawing the outline of a star without the mirror) *interferes* with performance under the other conditions (drawing using only the mirror-image of the star) producing *negative transfer*. Yet tracing patterns of very different appearance might seem to constitute dissimilar tasks but in fact there is considerable *positive transfer* from practising one pattern using only the mirror-image to being able to trace another under the same conditions. Positive transfer also occurs when subjects practise with their non-preferred hand. The normal laboratory procedure for studying transfer is as follows:

Experimental group	Learns A	Learns B	Tested on B
Control group	Learns B	Tested on B	

If learning A enhances the learning of B, then we say that positive transfer occurs; if A interferes with B then we speak of negative transfer and if A makes no difference either way then there is no transfer.

Transfer is commonly analysed in S–R terms: (i) where the S–R relationships are the same (eg A and B require the same response) then we expect to find positive transfer; (ii) where the S–R relationships are different (A requires one response and B a different, incompatible response) then we expect negative transfer.

Again, when an *old* response is required by a *new* stimulus there is *positive* transfer; when a *new* response is required by an *old* stimulus there is *negative* transfer. Learning sets, of course, are one form of positive transfer and positive transfer in general illustrates the cumulative nature of learning, whereby new learning builds on prior learning. Not only is learning cumulative but, as we said early in the chapter, it is closely intertwined with other processes, particularly perception and memory which are covered in the next section of the book (Chapters 9 and 11).

Sensory and Cognitive Processes

8 Sensory Processes

When we move our eyes or our heads, the objects we see around us remain stable. Similarly, when we follow an object that is itself moving, we attribute the movement to the object and not to ourselves. When we approach somebody in the street we do not experience them as gradually growing 'before our very eyes', and objects seen from various angles are still recognized as 'the same' object as they are when seen from head-on.

These examples of how we experience the world may seem so common-place as not worth mentioning until we realize what is actually taking place physically. If we compare what we experience (namely, a world of objects that remain stable and constant) with what our sense organs receive in the form of physical stimulation (an almost continuous state of flux) it is almost as if there are two entirely different worlds involved: the one we are consciously aware of is a world of 'things' and people (*perception*) and the one we are not aware of is a world of sense-data (*sensation*).

How are Sensation and Perception Related?

Essentially, perception cannot occur in the absence of sensation, but the sense-data constitute only the 'raw material' from which our conscious awareness of objects is constructed. So, to the extent that we perceive the world as it really is, we do this *indirectly*, through analysing, interpreting and trying to make sense of sensations. It seems that we are in direct and immediate contact with the world as we do not have to work out consciously what objects are (not usually, at least). However, our awareness of things is the end product of a long and complex process, which begins with physical energy stimulating the sense organs (light in the case of vision, sound waves in the case of hearing and so on) and ends with the brain interpreting the information that it has received from the sense organs. (We shall look later at how the visual system processes visual information.) So whereas the visual system as a whole is involved in (visual) perception, in sensation only the sense organs (the eyes) are directly stimulated; but, of course, the sense organs are part of the perceptual system as a whole.

The Senses—Providing the Raw Material of Perception

According to Ornstein (1975) we do not perceive objective reality but, rather, our *construction* of reality—our sense organs gather information which the brain modifies and sorts and this 'heavily filtered input' is compared with memories, expectancies and so on until, finally, our consciousness is constructed as a 'best guess' about reality.

In a similar vein, James maintained that:

> . . . the mind, in short, works on the data it receives much as the sculptor works on his block of stone. (James, 1902)

However, different artists use different materials and, similarly, different sensory systems provide different kinds of sense-data for the perceiver-sculptor to 'model'. Perhaps it is unnecessary to spell out that each of our various sensory systems is only designed to respond to a particular kind of stimulation but a related, and equally important point (often overlooked) is that they also function as *data-reduction systems* (Ornstein, 1975).

To the extent that something cannot be sensed (ie our senses are not responsive or sensitive to it) it does not exist for us; while we normally regard our senses as the 'windows' to the world, a major job they perform is to discard 'irrelevant' information and to register only what is likely to be of practical value (clearly, something which has occurred as a result of evolutionary forces). We would be overwhelmed if we responded to the world as it is; different forms of energy are so diverse that they are still being discovered and all species have developed particular sensitivity to certain of these which have aided their survival.

The frog is a useful example here: in the visual system there are specialized kinds of detectors, one of which responds only to small, dark, objects coming into the field of vision and which move quite close to the eye (a net convexity detector). Clearly, the frog has evolved its own specialized 'bug-perceiving' sub-system (Lettvin et al, 1965).

Bruce and Green (1990) define perception as the ability to detect structures and events in the surroundings. This requires that an animal be sensitive to at least one form of energy which can provide information about the environment, eg chemical substances diffusing through the air or water, mechanical energy (pressure on the body surface, forces on limbs and muscles or waves of sound pressure in the air or water), electric or magnetic fields:

> Sensitivity to diffusing chemicals and to mechanical energy gives an animal considerable perceptual abilities but leaves it unable to obtain information rapidly about either its inanimate world or about silent animals at a distance from itself . . . The form of energy that can provide these kinds of information is light, and consequently most animals have some ability to perceive their surroundings through vision . . . (Bruce and Green, 1990)

Light is one form of *electromagnetic radiation*:

> a mode of propagation of energy through space which includes radio waves, radiant heat, gamma rays and X-rays. (Bruce and Green, 1990)

The human eye responds to radiant electromagnetic energy in the visible spectrum. Although the entire spectrum ranges from less than 1 billionth of a metre to more than 100 metres, we can 'see' only the tiny portion between 380 and 780 billionths of a metre (nanometres) which we call light. Infra-red radiation, ultrasonics, pressure, mechanical vibrations in the air and other forms of energy are all around us and yet, by design, the eye only responds to that very limited part of the visible electromagnetic spectrum. (Although pressure on the eyeball produces sensations of light, it is external sources of light which normally produce the sensation; Fig. 8.1).

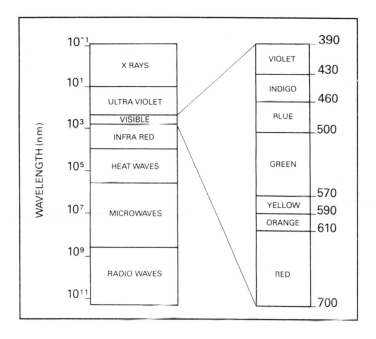

Figure 8.1 The spectrum of electromagnetic radiation. Wavelengths are given in nanometres (1 nm = 10^{-9} m). The visible part of the spectrum is shown on the right, with the colours of different wavelengths of light. (From V. Bruce, & P. R. Green, (1990) Visual Perception. Hillsdale, New Jersey, Lawrence Erlbaum Associates Inc.)

CLASSIFICATION OF SENSORY SYSTEMS

The senses have been classified in several ways. For example, Sherrington (1906) identified three kinds of receptors:

(i)   *exteroceptors* (which tell us about the external environment);
(ii) *interoceptors* (which tell us about the internal environment);
(iii) *proprioceptors* (which deal with the position of our body in space and its movement through space).

Exteroception includes the five 'traditional' senses of *sight* (vision), *hearing* (audition), *smell* (olfaction), *taste* (gustation) and *touch* (cutaneous or skin senses). *Interoception* includes the internal receptors for oxygen, carbon dioxide, blood glucose and so on. *Proprioception* is usually sub-divided into: (i) the *kinaesthetic sense* which monitors movements of the limbs, joints and muscles; and (ii) the *vestibular sense*, which responds to gravity and the movements of the head.

Gibson (1966) rejected proprioception as a distinct sensory system (and saw taste and smell as representing the same system), and Legge (1975) includes proprioception under the general heading of interoception.

CHARACTERISTICS OF SENSORY SYSTEMS

However we classify them, sensory systems (or modalities) have certain characteristics in common:

(a) As we have already seen, they each respond to particular forms of energy or information.

(b) They each have a *sense organ* (or accessory structure), which is the first 'point of entry' for the information that will be processed by the system (the sense organ, as it were, 'catches' the information).

(c) They each have *sense receptors* (or transducers), specialized cells which are sensitive to particular kinds of energy and which then convert it into electrical nerve impulses, the only form in which this physical energy can be dealt with by the brain (see Chapter 4).

(d) They each involve a specialized part of the brain which interprets the messages received from the sense receptors and (usually) results in conscious awareness of an object, a person, a word, a taste, etc. (ie, we perceive).

(e) A certain minimum stimulation of the sense receptors is necessary before any sensory experience will occur; this is known as the *absolute threshold*. In practice, instead of finding a single intensity value below which subjects never detect the stimulus and above which they always detect it, a range of values is found and the absolute threshold is taken to be the value at which the stimulus is detected 50 per cent of the time.

Table 8.1 summarizes the major sense organs, sense receptors and brain areas involved in the six major sensory systems.

Not only does the absolute threshold vary from individual to individual but it varies for the same individual at different times, depending on physical state, motivation, physical conditions of presentation and so on.

The *difference threshold* is the minimum amount of stimulation necessary to discriminate between two stimuli and is also known as the *just noticeable difference* (jnd). Weber's law states that the jnd is a constant value but this, of course, will differ from one sense modality to another; for example, 1/133 is the value needed to tell apart the pitch of two different tones and 1/5 for discriminating between saline solutions.

Fechner (1860) reformulated Weber's law, and the Weber–Fechner law (as it has come to be known) states that large increases in the intensity of a stimulus produce smaller, proportional, increases in the perceived intensity. Fechner's was one of the first attempts to express mathematically a psychological phenomenon and was an important contribution to *psychophysics*, which studies the relationship between physical stimuli and the subjective experience of them and which is of enormous historical importance in the development of psychology as a science.

The Weber–Fechner law holds only approximately through the middle ranges of stimulus intensities and an alternative approach is *signal detection theory*, which rejects the notion of thresholds altogether. Each sensory channel always carries *noise* (any activity which interferes with the detection of a signal); the stronger the stimulus, the higher the signal-to-noise ratio and the easier it is to detect the stimulus. The detection of a stimulus, therefore, then becomes a statistical matter.

SENSE MODALITY	SENSE ORGAN (ACCESSORY STRUCTURE)	SENSE RECEPTOR (TRANSDUCER)	BRAIN AREA (CORTEX UNLESS OTHERWISE INDICATED)
Vision (Sight)	Eye (in particular, the lens)	Rods and cones (in the retina)	Occipital lobe— striate cortex, extrastriate, (prestriate) cortex (via optic nerve)
Audition (Hearing)	Outer ear (pinna) Middle ear (eardrum and ossicles) Inner ear (cochlea)	Specialized hair cells in the organ of corti situated in the cochlea	Temporal lobe (via auditory nerve)
Gustation (Taste)	Tongue (in particular, the taste buds and papillae, the ridges around the side of the tongue)	Special receptors in the taste buds which connect with sensory neurons (nerve-cells)	Temporal lobe (via gustatory nerve)
Olfaction (Smell)	Nose (in particular, the olfactory mucosa of the nasal cavity)	Transducers in the olfactory mucosa	Temporal lobe and limbic system (via olfactory bulb and olfactory tracts)
Skin or cutaneous senses (Touch)	Skin	There are about 5 million sensors of at least 7 types, eg: 1. Meissner's corpuscles (touch); 2. Pacinian corpuscles (stretching and vibration) 3. Krause end bulbs (cold)	Parietal lobe (somatosensory cortex) and cerebellum
Proprioception— kinaesthetic and vestibular senses	Inner ear (semicircular canals) (in particular, the vestibular sacs)	Vestibular sensors or otoliths ('earstones'), tiny crystals attached to hair cells in vestibular sacs which are sensitive to gravity	Cerebellum (via vestibular nerve)

Table 8.1 Sense organs, sense receptors and brain areas for the six major sensory systems/modalities

THE VISUAL SYSTEM

An important initial question is: how does light carry information about the environment? A useful concept here is the *ambient optic array* (Gibson, 1966). Imagine an environment illuminated by sunlight and, therefore, filled with rays of light travelling between surfaces. At any point, light will converge from all directions and we can imagine the point surrounded by a sphere divided into tiny solid angles. The intensity of light and the mixture of wavelengths will vary from one solid angle to another, and this spatial pattern of light is the optic array:

> ... Light carries information because the structure of the optic array is determined by the nature and position of the surfaces from which it is reflected. (Bruce and Green, 1990)

The fundamental job of a single-chambered eye (such as the human eye) is to map the spatial pattern in the optic array onto the retina by forming an image: all light rays striking the eye from one point in space are brought to a focus at one point on the retina (Bruce and Green, 1990). *Visual acuity* is a way of describing the efficiency with which the eye does this ('the ability of a person or animal to detect fine spatial pattern...' (Bruce and Green, 1990)) and acuity is limited by several processes, in particular:

(a) The efficiency with which the optical apparatus of the eye maps the spatial pattern of the optic array on to the retina.
(b) The efficiency with which the receptor cells convert that pattern into a pattern of electrical activity.
(c) The extent to which information available in the pattern of receptor cells activity is detected by the neural apparatus of the retina and the brain.

We shall look at each of these aspects of acuity in turn.

THE SENSE-ORGAN—THE EYE

Ornstein (1975) describes the eye as, 'the most important avenue of personal consciousness' and it is estimated that 90 per cent of the information we receive about the external world reaches us through the eyes. The great majority of research interest has focused on vision, both as a sensory system and a perceptual system.

The sense organ of vision is the eye and its major structures are shown in Figure 8.2.

The *conjunctiva* is a transparent, delicate membrane, covering the inside of the eyelids and the front of the eye. It contains nerves and many tiny blood vessels which dilate (expand) if the eye is irritated or injured (the eye becomes bloodshot). The *cornea* is a transparent membrane which protects the lens and through which light enters the eye.

The *pupil* regulates the amount of light entering the eye via the *iris* (the coloured part of the eye), which has tiny sets of muscles that dilate and contract the pupil. (Pupil size is also regulated by the ciliary muscles.) In bright light, the pupil contracts to shut out some of the light rays; when light is dim or we are looking at distant objects, the pupils dilate to let more light in; here it is sensitivity rather than acuity which is crucial. Ultimately, pupil size is controlled by the Autonomic Nervous System (ANS) and so is outside conscious control; the parasympathetic branch

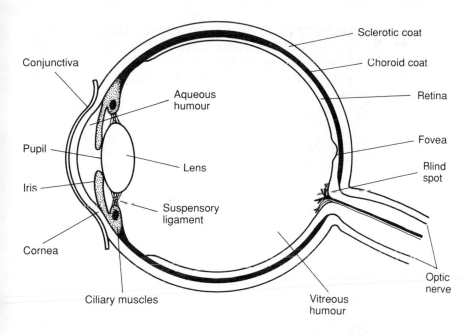

Conjunctiva

Sclerotic coat

Choroid coat

Aqueous humour

Retina

Pupil

Fovea

Lens

Blind spot

Iris

Suspensory ligament

Cornea

Ciliary muscles

Vitreous humour

Optic nerve

Figure 8.2 The major structures of the human eye

of the ANS controls change in pupil size as a function of change in illumination, while the sympathetic branch dilates the pupils under conditions of strong emotional arousal (eg an 'emergency' situation when we need to see 'better'; see Chapter 4). The pupil's function is to reduce the aperture of the lens in bright light and so reduce the blur of the image due to spherical or other optical aberrations.

The *lens*, situated just behind the iris, is enclosed in a capsule held firmly in place by the *suspensory ligaments*. It focuses light on the retina as an inverted (upside-down) image and its shape is regulated by the *ciliary muscles*. Along with certain reptiles, birds and other mammals, the lens of the human eye thickens and increases its curvature (and the ciliary muscles contract) when focusing on nearby objects; when viewing more distant objects, it becomes flatter (and the ciliary muscles are fully relaxed). This process is called *accommodation* and increases the power of the lens (a measure of its performance)—the ability to accommodate over a wide range is clearly useful to primates, which typically examine the detail of objects at close range:

> If the eye is optimally focused, the spatial pattern in the optic array is transformed into a pattern of light intensity on the retina with a minimum degree of blur. (Bruce and Green, 1990)

Between the cornea and the lens is the *anterior chamber* filled with *aqueous humour*, a clear, watery fluid, and behind the lens is the *posterior chamber* (larger than the anterior) and filled with *vitreous humour*, a jelly-like substance. Both fluids give the eyeball its shape and help to keep it firm.

The *sclerotic coat* is the thickest layer of the eyeball and forms the outer, white part of the eye. It consists of a strong, fibrous membrane, except in the front where it bulges to form the cornea. The *choroid coat* is a dark layer containing black-coloured matter which darkens the chamber of the eye and prevents reflection of light inside the eye; in front, it becomes the iris which is seen through the transparent cornea.

Primates' eyes make the largest, most rapid and most precisely controlled eye movements of all animals except the chameleon. The human eye is held in position by a dynamic balance between three pairs of antagonistic muscles and instability in this balance produces a continuous, small-amplitude *tremor*, which means that the retinal image is in constant motion.

Sampling the optic array is achieved by three kinds of movement:

(a) Sudden, intermittent jumps of eye position (*saccades*) occur when trying to fixate an object when looking directly at it (foveal vision). Even when we think we are looking steadily at something and when we read, or look at a picture, our eyes make several saccades each second to scan it.

(b) Once an object has been fixated, *pursuit movements* keep it in foveal vision as the object or the observer moves.

(c) If the distance of the object from the observer changes, *convergence* movements keep it fixated by the foveas of both eyes.

Both (b) and (c) are smooth and continuous.

According to Bruce and Green, the human eye at any instant samples a relatively large portion of the optic array (the *perhipheral* visual field) with low acuity and a much smaller portion (the *central* or foveal visual field) with high acuity.

Beaumont (1988) believes that constant alteration of the retinal image serves three useful purposes:

(a) It gives more time to the pigments to replace themselves after bleaching (see below).

(b) Any nervous tissue becomes less responsive with repeated stimulation and so also needs a chance to recover.

(c) It helps reduce the probability that parts of the retina will become obscured by blood vessels by giving an opportunity for slightly different parts of the stimulus to be viewed by different sets of receptors.

IS THE EYE A CAMERA?

In a camera, light striking each light-sensitive grain in the film comes from a narrow segment of the optic array, and this is also true of the retinal image (Bruce and Green, 1990). Both also have a lens which projects the image onto the film or the retina. So the camera is a useful analogy for understanding the optics of the eye. However, Bruce and Green point out a number of important differences:

(a) Judged by the same standards as a camera, even the most sophisticated eye forms an image of an extremely poor quality. Optical aberrations produce blur, aberrations of the lens and cornea cause distortions in the image, and the curvature of the retina means that images of straight lines are curved and metrical relations in the image do not correspond to those in the world.

(b) As we have seen, the image is constantly moving; a camera which moved in this way would produce blurred pictures.

(c) The retinal image has a yellowish cast, particularly in the macular region, and contains shadows of the blood vessels which lie in front of the receptor cells in the retina. Could the retinal image be 'cleaned up' to the point where it resembles a photograph?

(d) The question implies that the role of the eye is to take a snapshot of the world at each fixation and send a stream of pictures to the brain to be examined there. But while the purpose of a camera is to produce a picture to be viewed by people, the purpose of the eye and brain is to extract the information from the changing optic array needed to guide a person's actions or to specify objects or events of importance. The extraction of information about pattern begins in the retina itself—the optic nerve does not transmit a stream of pictures to the brain (as a TV camera does to a TV set) but instead transmits *information* about the pattern of light reaching the eyes. The brain then has to interpret that information.

The *retina* is the innermost layer of the eyeball, formed by the expansion of the optic nerve which enters at the back and a little to the nasal side of the eye. It is a delicate membrane, comprising three main layers:

(a) *Rods and cones*, photosensitive cells which convert light energy into electrical nerve impulses (and which form the rear layer of the retina).
(b) *Biopolar cells*, connected to the rods, cones and ganglion cells.
(c) *Ganglion cells*, whose fibres (axons) form the beginning of the *optic nerve* leading to the brain.

THE RECEPTORS—RODS AND CONES

Most of the eye's structures are, in fact, accessory structures and Gregory (1966) has estimated that only about 10 per cent of the light entering the eye actually reaches the transducers (rods and cones), the rest being absorbed by the accessory structures.

The *rods* are one thousand times more sensitive than cones and are far more numerous—in each retina there are 120 million rods and 7 million cones. Their distribution around the retina also differs: *cones* are much more numerous towards the centre of the retina, in particular, the *fovea* (a pit-like depression which is in fact part of a cone-rich area called the macula lutea), where there is a concentration of about 50,000 cones, while the rods are distributed fairly evenly around the periphery (but none is to be found in the fovea). The rods are specialized for vision in dim light (including night-time vision) and contain a photosensitive chemical (rhodopsin) which changes structure in response to low levels of illumination; they help us see black, white and intermediate greys (achromatic colour) and this is referred to as *scotopic vision*. The cones are specialized for bright light vision (including daylight) and contain iodopsin; they help us see chromatic colour (red, green, blue, etc.) and provide *photopic vision* (from 'photon', the smallest particle of light which travels in a straight line). (Colour perception and defects in perceiving colour are discussed below.)

Human vision, like that of most species, must be adapted to operate in a range of light intensities and this is reflected in the structure of the retina. Rods have a deeper stack of pigment-filled layers of folded membrane in the outer segment than cones; this means that a photon passing through a rod is less likely to come out the other end, making rods far more sensitive than cones (ie they are more likely to respond to low levels of illumination). According to Bruce and Green (1990), this difference explains the correlation between the rod:cone ratio in an animal's retina and its ecology: diurnal animals (those which are active by day and sleep at night) have a higher proportion of cones than nocturnals, though pure-cone retinas are rare (mostly confined to lizards and snakes), as are pure-rod retinas (confined to deep-sea fish and bats, which never leave their dark habitats).

A further adaptation of the retina in animals active in dim light is in the form of a silvery *tapetum* behind the retina, which reflects light back through it, so giving the rods a second 'bite' at the stream of photons (although at the cost of increasing blur through imperfect reflections). This explains the glow of a cat's eyes when caught in a car's headlights (Bruce and Green, 1990).

When focusing on objects in bright light, the most sharply-defined image is obtained by looking directly at them, thereby projecting the light onto the fovea (which, remember, is packed with cones). In night-light, however, the sharpest image is actually produced by looking slightly to one side of the object (eg, a star in the sky), thereby stimulating the rods which are found in the periphery of the retina.

The dense packing of cones helps explain acuity—the more densely packed the receptors, the finer the details of a pattern of light intensity which can be transformed into differences in electrical activity. The differences between a human's acuity and, for example, a falcon's is the result of a difference in receptor packing, with receptors being three times more densely packed in the falcon.

The chemical difference between the rods and cones also explains the phenomenon of *dark adaptation*. If you go into a dark cinema from bright sunlight, you will experience near blindness for a few seconds because the rods need a little time to take over from the cones, which were responding outside (ie the rhodopsin in the rods is being regenerated or re-synthesized, having been 'bleached' by the bright sunlight). It takes 30 minutes for the rods to reach their maximum level of responding.

The 127 million rods and cones are 'reduced' to one million ganglion cells which make up the optic nerve; this means that information reaching the brain has already been 'refined' to some extent compared with the relatively 'raw' information received from other sensory nerves. However, the degree of 'reduction' or *summation* differs considerably for different areas of the retina: in the periphery, up to 1200 rods may combine to form a single ganglion cell and thus to a single axon in the optic nerve, providing only very general visual information; while at the fovea, perhaps only ten to twelve cones are summed for each ganglion cell and this provides much more detailed information. Two other kinds of cell, *horizontal* and *amacrine*, interconnect with groups of the other cells and connect them together, which increases further the degree of information-processing which takes place in the retina itself. Horizontal cells interconnect receptors and bipolar cells, while amacrine cells interconnect bipolar and ganglion cells.

The first step in analysing the transformation of pattern occurring in the retina is to establish the relationship between input and output (ie the pattern of light falling on the retina and the rate at which ganglion cells fire impulses). Each ganglion cell has a *receptive field*, a region of the retina, usually roughly circular, in which stimulation affects the ganglion cell's firing rate. There are (at least) three kinds of ganglion cell, each with a different kind of receptive field:

(a) *On-centre* cells are more neurally active when light falls in the centre of the receptive field but less active when it falls on the edge.
(b) *Off-centre* cells work in the opposite way.
(c) *Transient* cells have larger receptive fields and seem to respond to movements, especially sudden ones.

The combined activity of on-centre and off-centre cells provides a clear definition of contours ('edges') where there is a sudden change in brightness. These contours are essential in defining the shape of objects to be perceived (Beaumont, 1988). (Further analysis of contours takes place in the striate cortex by simple, complex and hypercomplex cells—see below.) As Beaumont (1988) points out, the retina *appears* to be built back-to-front: the receptors don't point to the source of the light but towards the supporting cells at the back of the eye. Before it arrives at the receptors, light must pass through the layers of retinal cells and blood vessels inside the eye. In view of all this, it is surprising that such high-quality vision can still be achieved (Fig. 8.3). (You may sometimes

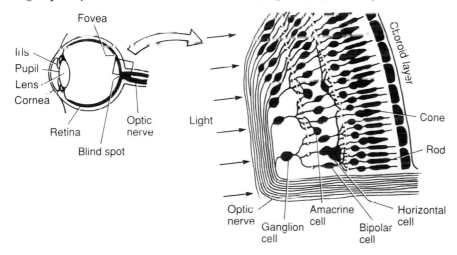

Figure 8.3 A diagrammatic section through the eye and a section through the retina at the edge of the blind spot. (From R. L. Atkinson, R. C. Atkinson & E. R. Hilgard (1983) Introduction to Psychology, 8th edn. New York, Harcourt, Brace Jovanovich Inc.)

become aware of this in the form of a tree-like after-image after a lightning flash, which are the shadows of the blood vessels thrown upon the retina, or when you look up at the sky, especially a cloudless, blue sky, and you see small transparent bubbles floating in front of you, which are red blood cells.)

VISUAL PATHWAYS—FROM EYE TO BRAIN

As we have seen, the 127 million receptors in each eye are combined to form the 1 million optic nerve fibres, which means that there is a massive integration and channelling of information

As you can see from Figure 8.4, the pathways from the half of each retina closest to the nose cross at the *optic chiasma* (or chasm) and travel to the *opposite* hemisphere (crossed pathways), while the pathways from the half of each retina furthest from the nose (uncrossed pathways) travel to the hemisphere on the *same* side as the eye. This means that if

Figure 8.4 *The visual system*

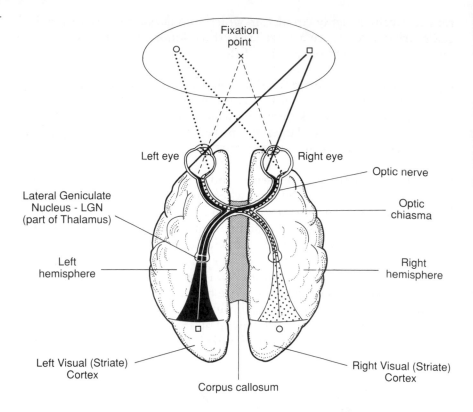

somebody fixates on a point straight ahead of them, so that the eyes converge, the image of an object to the *right* of fixation falls on the left half of each retina and information about it passes along the crossed pathway from the right eye to the left hemisphere and along the uncrossed pathway from the left eye to the *left* hemisphere—no information is passed directly to the right hemisphere. All these relationships are reversed for an object to the *left* of the fixation point, so that information is passed directly only to the *right* hemisphere. Therefore it follows that any damage to the visual area of just one hemisphere will produce blind areas in *both* eyes; however, the crossed pathway ensures that complete blindness in *either* eye will *not* occur. Also, the position of visual information on the cortex approximates the locations of the real world in that adjacent areas of the visual world fall side-by-side on the cortex. However, the *amount* of cortex devoted to different areas of the world differs—that portion of the visual field falling on the fovea is greatly emphasized, with the peripheral areas receiving relatively little cortical representation (Frisby, 1980).

Before reaching the cortex, the optic nerve travels through the *lateral geniculate nucleus* (LGN) which is part of the thalamus; optic nerve fibres terminate at synapses with LGN cells arranged in layers (laminae). Each lamina contains a retino-optic map of half the visual field.

LGN cells have concentric receptive fields similar to those of retinal ganglion cells and each is thought to be driven by one or more of the same receptive field type. Axons of LGN cells form the optic radiations and project to the occipital lobe. In monkeys, all LGN cells project to area 17, which is the *visual or striate cortex* (called the *geniculostriate* path). The existence of a feedback path from the cortex to the LGN suggests strongly that the LGN is not simply a relay station for retinal visual information to the cortex—but this path is not currently understood (Bruce and Green, 1990).

In humans, the geniculostriate path must be intact for conscious experience of vision to be possible—people with damage to their visual cortex will report complete blindness in part or all of the visual field. Even so, they will show some ability to locate or even identify objects which they cannot consciously see (what Weiskrantz, 1986, calls *blindsight*). The most thoroughly investigated patient is D.B., who had an operation meant to reduce the number of severe migraines he suffered. He was left with an area of subjective blindness but was able to detect whether or not a visual stimulus had been presented to the blind area and could also identify its location, although he seemed to possess only a rudimentary ability to discriminate shapes.

This suggests that, while most visual functions rely on the 'primary' geniculostriate path, the 'secondary' *retinotectal path* (some ganglion cells are projected to the paired *superior colliculi* structures in the midbrain) carries enough information to guide some actions in an unconscious way. However, in the intact brain, those two paths do not function independently: the *corticotectal* path provides the superior colliculi with input from the cortex. (The superior colliculi seem to play an important role in the control of several visual reflexes, including eye movements and perception of the location of objects. The receptive fields of cells in this area are larger than those in the cortex and are more evenly spread in the periphery of the retina, an area particularly sensitive to moving stimuli.)

The first recordings from single cells in the striate cortex of cats and monkeys were made by Hubel and Wiesel (1959, 1962, 1968). They found cells with concentric fields in a layer of the cortex where input fibres from the LGN terminate (*simple* fields), but in other layers cells had quite different receptive fields (*complex* fields). They identified three kinds of cortical cells:

1) *Simple* cells respond only to particular features of a stimulus (eg straight lines, edges and slits) in particular *orientations* and in particular *locations* in the animal's visual field. For example, a bar presented vertically may cause a cell to 'fire' but if the bar is moved to one side or out of vertical, the cell will not respond.

2) *Complex* cells also respond to lines of particular orientation—but location is no longer important, eg a vertical line detector will respond wherever in the visual field it is. It seems that complex cells receive inputs from larger numbers of simple cells sharing the same orientation sensitivity.

3) *Hypercomplex* cells, which are 'fed' by large numbers of complex cells and are similar to complex cells except that they take *length* into account too (ie they are most responsive to a bar or edge not extending beyond their receptive field).

However, some researchers have come to doubt the existence of a third distinct class of cell (Bruce and Green, 1990). Despite this, the visual cortex is by no means a homogeneous mass of tissue with cells of different kinds randomly scattered; instead, it shows astonishingly precise and regular arrangement of different cell types (what Hubel and Wiesel (1962) called the 'functional architecture' of the visual cortex).

The six main layers of the striate cortex can be recognized under the microscope. The cortical area devoted to the central part of the visual field is proportionately larger than that devoted to the periphery. Hubel and Wiesel (1977) suggest that the cortex is divided into roughly square blocks of tissue (about 1 mm square), extending from the surface down to the white matter, which they call *hypercolumns*; within these, cells have different receptive fields, with a good deal of overlap, but all falling within some single retinal area (or *aggregate field*).

Two further patterns of organization are:

(a) Cells fall into two groups according to which eye is most effective in eliciting a response. Although cells in some layers have binocular fields (ie they respond to their optimal stimulus whichever eye the stimulus is presented to), they always respond more strongly to a stimulus in one eye than the other (*ocular dominance*). Cells sharing the same ocular dominance are grouped together into bands running across the cortex.

(b) Cells are arranged in columns according to their orientation preference. If an electrode penetrates the cortex perpendicular to the surface, all the cells (both simple and complex) which it encounters will have the same orientation preference. These hypercolumns are about 0.05 mm across (Bruce and Green, 1990).

Are there other regions of the cortex where visual information is processed?

Single-cell recordings have revealed many regions of the *extrastriate* (or *prestriate*) cortex, anterior to the striate, which can be considered 'visual areas'. But it has proved more difficult to map these, compared with the striate cortex.

Maunsell and Newsome (1987) reviewed studies involving macaque monkeys and concluded that there are nineteen visual areas, covering large areas of the occipital, temporal and parietal lobes (Fig. 8.5). The deep folding of the cortex means that some areas, lying within folds (*sulci*) are not visible from the exterior; for this reason, two important areas not shown in Figure 8.5 are V3 (lying in the lunate sulcus between V2 and V4), and the middle temporal area (MT) in the superior temporal sulcus (anterior to V4).

Figure 8.5 Side-view of the right cerebral hemisphere of a macaque monkey. Area V1 is the striate cortex. (From J. H. R. Maunsell & W. T. Newsome (1987) Visual processing in monkey extrastriate cortex, Annual Review of Neuroscience, 10, 363–401)

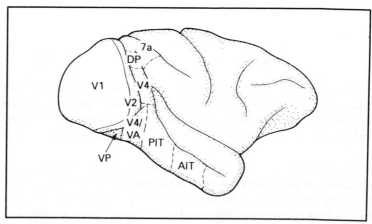

Each area sends output to several others and most, if not all, connections are matched by reciprocal connections running in the opposite direction. Van Essen (1985) lists ninety-two pathways linking the visual areas. Most can be classified as either ascending (leading away from V1) or descending (leading towards V1); when classified in this way, a consistently hierarchical pattern emerges, with areas placed at different levels (Fig. 8.6).

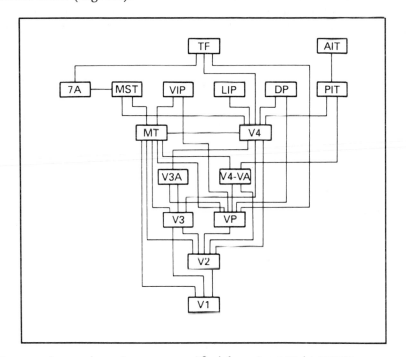

Figure 8.6 The hierarchical organization of extrastriate visual areas in the macaque monkey as proposed by Maunsell and Newsome. (From J. H. R. Maunsell & W. T. Newsome (1987) Visual processing in monkey extrastriate cortex. Annual Review of Neuroscience, 10, 363–401)

Does each area have its own specified function? Zeki (1978) proposed a 'parcelling model', whereby the simple representation of the visual field in V1 and V2 is parcelled out to be analysed by a number of areas working in parallel, one analysing patterns of motion, another colour, etc.

But Maunsell and Newsome (1987) and Van Essen (1985) believe that there might be two main pathways operating in parallel, one concerned with the analysis of motion and spatial layout, the other with colour, form and object recognition. Some of the evidence regarding processing of colour is discussed in the next section.

COLOUR VISION AND COLOUR BLINDNESS

Light can be described *physically* by its energy spectrum (intensities at different wavelength), or *phenomenologically* by three dimensions—(i) *brightness* (perceived intensity); (ii) *hue* (perceived colour); and (iii) *saturation* (the purity of hue, ie how much colour, or how much white). Although both hue and saturation are aspects of 'colour', it is hue which is intended when discussing theories of colour vision and colour vision defects.

As we have already seen, it is the cones which are the photoreceptors responsible for chromatic vision. We have also seen that the rods and cones contain photosensitive pigments (which change their chemical constitution on exposure to light—like photographic film), rhodopsin ('visual purple') in the case of rods and iodopsin in the case of cones.

Rushton and Campbell (1954; cited by Rushton, 1987) were the first to measure the visual pigments in the living human eye, applying the familiar observation that a cat's eye will reflect back light shone in its eye. Using a photomultiplier tube, they measured the very faint light reflected from the human eye (we have a very black surface behind the retina—the choroid coat—instead of the cat's shining *tapetum lucidium*) and identified rhodopsin, plus red and green pigments. However, insufficient blue light is reflected to measure the blue cone pigment (Rushton, 1987).

Later, Marks et al (1964; cited by Rushton, 1987), in the USA, used fresh retinas from monkeys and human eyes removed during surgery, to measure visual pigments in single cones. They found the blue-, green- and red-sensitive cones, thus supporting the Young–Helmholtz Trichromatic Theory; Rushton and Campbell's findings were also confirmed using living colour-blind subjects who possessed only one of the two pigments measured by them (Rushton, 1987).

The Trichromatic Theory

The Trichromatic Theory (Young, 1801), claims that colour is mediated by three different kinds of cone, each responding to light from a different part of the visible spectrum—blue-sensitive, green-sensitive and red-sensitive cones are maximally responsive to short, medium and long wavelengths, respectively. While the sum of the three wavelengths (B + G + R) determines brightness, their *ratio* (B:G:R) determines colour. This is essentially what is believed today (Rushton, 1987). As Atkinson et al put it:

> ... The quality of colour is coded by the *pattern* of activity of three receptors rather than by specific receptors for each colour. (Atkinson et al, 1990)

This explains the painter's experience that mixing a few paints will produce a whole range of colours. It also implies that every colour (including white) should excite B, G, and R cones in a characteristic set of ratios, such that a mixture of red and green and blue lights, adjusted to produce this same set of ratios, should appear white or whatever the initial colour was. This was systematically tested by Maxwell (1854) who found that every colour can be matched by a suitable mixture of blue, green and red 'primaries' (the trichromacy of colour). This was later confirmed by Helmholtz (Rushton, 1987).

The Opponent Colour Theory

The major alternative to the Trichromatic Theory is the Opponent Colour (Tetrachromatic) Theory (Hering, 1878), which claims that colour analysis depends on the action of two types of detector, each having two modes of response—one signals either red or green, the other signals yellow or blue. (Brightness depends on a system that signals white or black—therefore, one can see colour that looks greenish and bluish and dark but *not* one that looks both reddish and greenish *or* both light and dark, etc.; Troscianko, 1987).

What evidence is there to support the Opponent Colour (or Opponent Process) theory?

1)   If you stare at a coloured surface (eg red) and then look at a plain surface, you will perceive an after-image which is coloured in the 'opposite-direction' (ie green). This is called a *complementary* (or *negative*) *after image*.

2)   People with defective colour vision (usually called 'colour-blind') usually fail to distinguish between red and green; this is the most common form of defect, caused by a recessive sex-linked gene, which affects more males (about 8 per cent) than females (about 0.4 per cent). Sufferers have dichromatic vision (whereas those with normal vision have *trichromatic*) such that they possess only red- *or* green-sensitive cone pigments, but they can match every colour of the rainbow exactly with a suitable mix of only two coloured lights (eg red and blue)—most people need the green primary as well if every colour is to be matched.

Next most common is true colour-blindness, whereby there is an absence of any cones at all (these people have *monochromatic* vision), and least common of all is yellow–blue blindness. These findings are clearly consistent with the Opponent Colour theory.

3)   While the retina encodes in terms of three constituent components (a blue, green, red 'component' system) output through the ganglion cells and onto the LGN becomes recoded in terms of *opponent processes* (DeValois et al, 1966). There seem to be four kinds of LGN cells—those which increase activity to red light but decrease with green ($R+G-$), those which increase activity to green light but decrease with red ($G+R-$), and similarly for blue and yellow ($B+Y-$) and yellow and blue ($Y+B-$). Still other LGN cells simply respond to black and white (Beaumont, 1988).

Evidence such as this has led to the generally held view that a complete theory of colour vision must draw on elements from *both* theories; indeed, Helmholtz himself showed that the two theories are not incompatible, as a simple transformation could change the three receptor outputs to two different signals plus one additive signal (Troscianko, 1987).

RETINEX THEORY AND COLOUR CONSTANCY

Any chromatic light hitting the retina is composed of different amounts of the three primary colours (eg turquoise might be 70 per cent blue, 30 per cent green) so blue-sensitive cones would 'fire' quite quickly and green-sensitive ones quite slowly (and red-sensitive would not fire at all).

However, *perceived* colour is not solely determined by the wavelength composition of the light reflected from the object (the spectral reflectance of the object) but by several other factors including:

(a) The relative proportions of different wavelengths in the light falling on the object (the spectral composition of the illumination).
(b) *Prior stimulation* of the retina (as shown by complementary or negative after-images).
(c) The *nature* of the *surroundings*, such as the simultaneous contrast created by adjacent areas of different colour or brightness (eg a grey square will look brighter set against a black background than against a white background).
(d) Our familiarity and knowledge of an object's colour, which is part of

the *psychological* phenomenon of *colour constancy* (see next chapter).

> Our visual system is built to tell us about the permanent colours of objects as opposed to the spectral composition of the light falling on a local area of the retina . . . (McCann, 1987)

and a powerful demonstration of colour constancy is provided by Land (1964, 1977), the inventor of the Polaroid camera. His 'Mondrian' experiment and Retinex Theory are described in Box 8.1.

Box 8.1 Land's (1964, 1977) 'Mondrian' experiment and Retinex Theory of Colour Constancy

Land used a large, complex display ('colour Mondrian')—a patchwork of different coloured matt papers, randomly arranged so that each colour was surrounded by several others. The display is illuminated by mixed light from projectors with red, green and blue filters. Each projector also had an independent brightness control.

Observers selected one of the papers (eg white) and Land measured the amounts of red, green and blue light coming from the white paper. They then selected a second paper (eg red) and once again the amounts of red, green and blue light were measured.

Land then changed the illumination so that the red light from the red paper was exactly equal to the red light from the white paper (this required only a small change, since roughly the same amounts of red light are reflected from a red and white paper). A substantial change was required to adjust the other projectors so that exactly the same amounts of green and blue came from the red paper as had previously come from the white paper (much less green and blue are reflected from a red paper). When all three projectors were turned on together, each observer reported 'red' despite the fact that the physical properties of the light from that paper were the same as the light from the white paper (using previous illumination).

In this way, Land went from paper to paper and showed that nearly the full range of colour sensations could be produced from a single mixture of red, green and blue light (thus supporting the trichromatic theory).

If perceived colour were determined solely by the spectral composition of the reflected light, the initially red paper would be seen as white. But observers displayed *colour constancy* and this led Land to propose his *retinex theory* (1977), whereby the information from each of the sets of receptor mechanisms produces a separate lightness image, a comparison of these images is carried out and it is this comparison which determines the colour which is perceived. Again, the three lightnesses provide the co-ordinates of a 3-D space and, whereas a colour space based on the *absolute* absorptions in the three classes of receptor will predict only whether two physical stimuli will *match*, a space based on the three lightnesses will predict how colours actually *look*, because between them they give the reflectance of the object in different parts of the spectrum (ie a measure of the *relative absorptions*).

'Retinex' ('retina' and 'cortex') implies that the formation of lightnesses could occur in the retina or cortex; the retinal–cortical structure acts as a whole.

THE AUDITORY SYSTEM

THE SENSE ORGAN—THE EAR

When we hear sounds we are detecting changes in air pressure as they occur at the ear. These changes have a cyclical pattern and move in a wave-like fashion. So sounds (ie pure *tones*, a sound which corresponds to a sine wave) can be thought of as having a *frequency* (the number of cycles per second, measured in Hertz) and *intensity* (the height or amplitude of the wave). Real sounds, of course, are complex and comprise many components with different frequencies and intensities (but these can be thought of as composed of a collection of pure tones; Beaumont, 1988).

Sound waves arrive at the *pinna* (Fig. 8.7), where they are 'trapped'

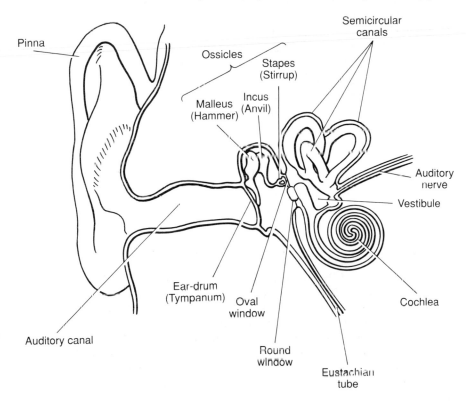

Figure 8.7 The major structures of the human ear

and passed into the *auditory canal* (the two structures comprise the *outer* or *external* ear). From here, the sound waves travel to the ear-drum (*tympanum* or *tympanic membrane*) which is deflected so that it moves with the same frequency as the sound waves. Linked to the ear-drum is the first of three small bones, the *malleus* ('hammer'), which transmits the ear-drum's movements to the *incus* ('anvil') which in turn passes vibrations onto the *stapes* ('stirrup'). This mechanical arrangement not only transmits but amplifies the wave. The three bones are collectively known as the *ossicles* and they, together with the ear-drum, comprise the *middle ear*.

From here sound passes into the *inner ear* via the stapes which rests against the *oval window* which is the 'gateway' to the *inner ear* and the receptors.

THE RECEPTORS

The auditory receptors are contained in the *cochlea*, a fluid-filled structure, consisting of a coiled tube of bone, resembling a snail's shell. It is divided into sections of fluid by various membranes, including the *basilar membrane*. Pressure at the oval window causes pressure changes in the cochlear fluid which in turn causes the basilar membrane to vibrate. This has the effect of bending the *hair cells* of the *organ of corti* (attached to the basilar membrane). These hair cells are the auditory receptors and synapse with neurons with long axons, which form part of the auditory (cochlear) nerve. The hair cells are forced against the fairly rigid *tectoral membrane* and this contact produces nerve impulses in the hair cells, which pass to ganglion cells and then to the cortex via the auditory nerve.

When pressure waves are transmitted to the basilar membrane, one part vibrates much more strongly than the rest, depending on the frequency of the original sound wave—high frequency sounds vibrate the end near to the middle ear, while low frequency sounds vibrate the other end (von Bekesy, 1960). However, the precise mechanism by which hair cells produce neural potentials is still poorly understood (Beaumont, 1988).

(The *inner ear* also contains sensory receptors for balance and positional sense—the vestibular and kinaesthetic senses—in particular, the vestibular sacs contained within the semi-circular canals).

THE AUDITORY PATHWAYS

The auditory nerve (the 8th cranial nerve) comprises about 31,000 neurons (compared with approximately one million in the optic nerve) and travels through the *medial geniculate body* (MGB), part of the thalamus, *en route* to the upper part of the *temporal lobe*. Unlike vision, cortical cells are not arranged topographically (in terms of the spatial location of the stimulus), so that different groups of cells seem to deal with different frequencies.

Impulses from the auditory nerve at one side of the head pass up to the MGB and the cortex on *both* sides of the brain (in vision, remember, the visual field at one side only projects to the opposite hemisphere). But it is still true that the pathway from one ear to the *opposite* hemisphere is larger and more important than that passing to the same-side hemisphere. Damage to the auditory nerve on one side of the head will cause deafness in the ear on that side. However, deafness rarely results from brain damage, due to the projection from each ear to both sides of the brain (bilateral projection). Brain damage is usually on one side only, thus altering hearing thresholds (acuity) but not producing complete deafness (Beaumont, 1988).

AUDITORY SENSORY PROCESSING AND HEARING DEFECTS

The major psychological (phenomenological) aspects of sound are: (i) *pitch*; (ii) *loudness*; (iii) *timbre*; and (iv) *location* (or localization).

1) *Pitch* is the equivalent of hue in relation to light. It corresponds to the frequency of the sound wave, which, as we have seen, is encoded by the vibration of different regions of the basilar membrane. Throughout

the auditory system there are neurons which respond most actively to stimulation of a given frequency; this information can, therefore, be passed fairly directly to the cortex. But most cells do not respond to a highly specific frequency and some respond over quite a broad range. There is also a curious *absence* of cells responsive to *lower* frequencies (although there is good discrimination of pitch at this level; Beaumont, 1988).

Young adults can hear frequencies between 20 and 20,000 hertz. Dogs, bats, and porpoises can detect much higher frequencies. The jnd is less than 1 Hz at 100 Hz and 100 Hz at 10,000 Hz.

2)   *Loudness* or intensity involves more complex coding. It is not coded independently of frequency, so the response of a given cell in the auditory pathway will differ for two tones, even if they are of the same loudness. There seem to be insufficient neurons to separately encode all the levels of loudness we can detect at each frequency, so the coding of loudness must involve the joint activity of several cells (Beaumont, 1988).

Loudness is measured in decibels (dB): a change of 10 dB corresponds to a change in sound power of 10 times, 20 dB: 100 times, 30 dB: 1000 times and so on (Atkinson et al, 1990).

3)   *Timbre* is the quality of sound (for example, the sound of different musical instruments producing the same note). We do not usually hear pure tones but tones composed of a *fundamental* plus a range of harmonics and overtones. In everyday life, complex sounds comprise a bundle of different frequencies. Some cells in the auditory cortex might only respond to complex sounds.

4)   *Location* of sound is identifying where the sound is coming from and, as with visual depth perception (see Chapter 9), there is more than one cue involved: two major cues are *phase differences* and *intensity differences*. Both of these are related to the fact that our ears occupy different positions on our heads, so that sound has to travel less distance to reach one ear than the other, thereby involving an *inter-aural time difference*.

In *phase differences*, pressure waves originating from the sound source are likely to arrive at the two ears at a different phase in their cycles—at a given moment the wave arriving at, say, the left ear maybe going up while that at the right may be going down. As there are cells which respond at particular phases in the cycle, these phase differences can be detected by cells higher up in the auditory system. Unless the stimulus is directly in front or behind, some pattern of phase differences will be generated by any complex sound. This cue is used for *low* frequency sounds.

Intensity differences refers to the fact that intensity will be greater at the nearer ear. The head produces a 'sound shadow', which *decreases* the intensity of the sound reaching the further ear and, as the head blocks high frequencies more than low frequencies, this cue is used for *high* frequency sounds. If you wear stereo headphones and increase the relative loudness in one ear, the sound will appear to shift towards that side of space. The same effect can be produced to some extent by altering the balance control on a stereo system (Beaumont, 1988).

The fact that we tend to confuse sounds coming from in front with those coming from behind is consistent with this two-cue 'theory'—

phase and intensity differences are virtually non-existent for sound sources directly in front of, or behind, the observer.

Finally, the two main kinds of hearing deficits are: (i) *conduction loss*, in which thresholds are raised roughly equally at all frequencies due to poor conduction in the middle ear, and (ii) *sensory–neural loss*, in which threshold increase is unequal, with large increases occurring at higher frequencies. This usually results from inner ear damage, often involving some destruction of the hair cells (which do not regrow). This is quite common in elderly people, rock musicians, airport-runway crews and pneumatic drill operators (Atkinson et al, 1990).

9 PERCEPTION

Chapter 8 began with the claim that sensation and perception, although related, are distinct. Perception requires stimulation of the sense organs (and, more importantly, the sense receptors) but there is more to perception than just this physical stimulation, which merely provides the 'raw material' for perception. But what is the 'extra' ingredient that turns a merely *physical* process (sensation) into a *psychological* one (perception)? And is this a valid way of thinking about the relationship between two such interdependent processes? What assumptions are being made when such a distinction is drawn?

These questions touch on some of the fundamental similarities and differences between major psychological *theories* of perception. Two major issues which different theories attempt to resolve are:

1)   Is our awareness of the world of objects, people, etc., essentially determined by the information presented to the sensory receptors, so that we perceive what things are like in a fairly direct way, based on sensory information ('*bottom-up processing*'), or is perception the end-result of a process which begins with sensory stimulation but which also involves making *inferences* about what things are like, so that we perceive them *indirectly*, drawing on our knowledge and expectations of the world ('*top-down*' processing)?

2)   Is the way we perceive largely the result of learning and experience (*empiricism*) or is it essentially an innate ability, requiring little if any learning (*nativism*)? (This is, of course, an example of the Nature–Nurture issue and is dealt with in Chapter 10.)

Fortunately, it is relatively easy to classify the major theories of perception in terms of these two issues, since researchers who believe that perception is an indirect process, based on top-down processing, also tend to be empiricist (Bruner, 1957; Neisser, 1967; Gregory, 1972, 1980), while the major theorist who believes in direct perception (bottom-up processing) is Gibson (1966, 1979) who is also an empiricist. Bruce and Green (1990) also refer to the indirect/top-down theories as 'traditional' and Gibson's direct theory as 'ecological' (indeed, this was Gibson's own term, implying basically that visual information from the whole physical environment is available for analysis by retinal receptor cells). The Gestalt Psychologists represent the major *nativist* approach (see Table 9.1).

In the first part of this chapter, we shall concentrate on one of each kind of theory, namely Gregory's, Gibson's and the Gestalt theory (the 'three Gs').

Table 9.1 *A classification of theories of perception*

	DIRECT (BOTTOM-UP) (ECOLOGICAL)	INDIRECT (TOP-DOWN) (TRADITIONAL)
EMPIRICIST	Gibson	Gregory, Bruner, Neisser, Marr
NATIVIST	Gestalt	

GREGORY'S THEORY—PERCEPTION AS INFERENCE

Definitions of perception (as given in textbooks of psychology) are usually drawn from theories like Gregory's and these definitions make clear that there *is* a difference between sensation and perception. For example:

> Perception is not determined simply by stimulus patterns; rather it is a dynamic searching for the best interpretation of the available data ... perception involves going beyond the immediately given evidence of the senses. (Gregory, 1966)

> ... the process of assembling sensations into a useable mental representation of the world. (Coon, 1983)

And again:

> Perception creates faces, melodies, works of art, illusions, etc. out of the raw material of sensation. (Coon, 1983)

These definitions also make it clear that perception does involve sensory stimulation which, in turn, makes it necessary to distinguish between perception proper and experiences which are indistinguishable from these but which do not involve sensory stimulation, namely hallucinations (see Chapter 30), eg 'seeing pink elephants' in the absence of any.

Coon's reference to illusions suggests another distinction, namely that between accurate (true or veridical) perception, whereby our interpretation matches the objective nature of the object or stimulus, and mistaken or *false* perception, where we in some way mis-interpret what is presented to the senses. Illusions, of course, are examples of mistaken perception (while hallucinations are generated by the brain and involve no external stimulus).

Illusions have been used a great deal by Gregory (and other empiricists) to demonstrate how accurate or veridical perception works (see below).

But why should it be necessary to '*explain*' perception at all?

> Usually, perception seems so immediate and instantaneous that it is difficult to understand that there is anything to be explained. But there is, and psychologists see this explanation of how we are able to perceive the world around us through our senses ... as a *problem* ... (Greene, 1990)

One special problem, according to Greene (1990), is to explain the process by which *physical* energy received by the sense organs forms the basis of perceptual *experience* (the sensation/perception distinction again). If you think of some of the ways in which the eye is *not* a camera and how the retinal image is distorted (relative to the object which projects it; see Chapter 8), then you will have some idea of the 'problem of perception'. Further, the retinal image is inverted (and yet we see the world the right way up) and it is 2-dimensional (the retina is curved and flat) yet we see a 3-dimensional world, which suggests that our perception of objects, etc. cannot be adequately accounted for by the facts of sensory stimulation alone. *Perceptual constancy* and *illusions* also demonstrate the interpretative, indirect, 'top-down' nature of perception.

1) *PERCEPTUAL CONSTANCY*

Just as it is necessary to *select* from all the available sensory stimulation which surrounds us (otherwise we would become overwhelmed—'sensory overload'), so it is often necessary to *supplement* it, because the total information that we might need could be missing (not directly available to the senses). This is what Gregory means by 'going beyond the immediately given evidence of the senses' (ie inferences).

We often view objects from angles such that their 'true' shape and size is not reflected in the retinal image they project; for example, rectangular doors often project trapezoid-shaped images, round cups often project elliptical-shaped images and people of normal size often project very small images, and yet we usually perceive them as rectangular, round and normal-sized, respectively. These are examples of shape and size *constancy*, the ability to perceive objects as we know them to be despite changes in the sensory stimulation which they produce; whether this ability is learned or inborn is discussed in the next chapter (compare this ability with Piaget's concept of conservation—see Chapter 25).

An impressive demonstration of the mechanisms which produce constancy is *after-images*. If you stare at a bright light for a few seconds, the after-image this causes has a fixed size, shape and position on the retina. But if you quickly look at a nearby object and then at one further away, the after-image seems to shrink and swell, seeming largest when we are looking at the most distant object. Why should this happen? A real object casts a smaller image the further away it is and to maintain perceptual constancy, the image is 'scaled up' by the brain (*constancy scaling*); the same scaling effect is applied to after-images, producing changes in their apparent size. Another easy but quite convincing demonstration is to draw your outline in the mirror in a steamy bathroom, closing one eye as you do so—the image, which appeared life-size as you drew it (guided by constancy), seems half the normal size as you stand back from it.

However much you incline your head, you still perceive trees or telegraph poles as vertical and, similarly, with horizontal lines. But do *size* and *shape constancy* always work?

Clearly, there are times when they do not: your conceptual knowledge that those things moving about down there are cars and people does not convince your perceptual experience when you look down from a very tall building—they do *look* more like ants than people! But this is an exception to the rule.

As we move our heads around, we, in fact, produce a constantly changing pattern of retinal images and yet we do not perceive the world spinning around; kinaesthetic feedback from the muscles and the organs of balance in the ear is integrated with the changing retinal stimulation by the brain so as to *inhibit* perception of movement—this is called *location constancy*. To keep the world from swinging crazily every time we move our eyes, the brain subtracts the eye-movement commands from the resulting changes on the retina and this helps to keep people and objects 'in their place'.

In *colour constancy*, familiar objects retain their colour (strictly, they retain their hue) under a variety of lighting conditions (including night-light), provided there is sufficient contrast and shadow. Again, this is not a fool-proof process and we do sometimes make mistakes, but clearly, there is not a one-to-one correspondence between wavelength of light and colour perception (see Chapter 8).

Related to colour constancy is *brightness constancy*; for example, we perceive coal as black even in bright sunlight and paper as white even in deep shadow, although the coal may actually be reflecting more light than the paper (as measured by a photometer or light meter).

Another example of inference is when we attribute to an object characteristics which we could only know directly if we were to use one or more senses other than the one we are using at the time—for example, we choose an apple because it *looks* sweet, juicy, crisp and so on.

So visual information from the retinal image is often sketchy and incomplete and the visual system has to 'go beyond' the retinal image in order to test hypotheses which fill in the 'gaps' (rather like the Gestalt principle of Closure—see below) (Greene, 1990).

In order to make sense of the various sensory inputs to the retina, the visual system must draw on all kinds of evidence, including distance cues, information from other senses and expectations based on past experience. For all these reasons, perception is an indirect process involving a construction based on physical sources of energy.

2) ILLUSIONS

Illusions represent yet another example of how we go beyond the information given, whereby what we perceive may not be physically present in the stimulus (and hence not present in the retinal image). Gregory (1983) has identified four types of illusion:

1) *Distortions*, such as the Müller–Lyer, Horizontal–Vertical, Ponzo, Poggendorff and Circle illusions (Fig. 9.1(a–e); here we are genuinely misperceiving, that is, making a perceptual *mistake*.

2) *Ambiguous figures*, such as the Rubin Vase (see Fig. 9.9) and the Necker Cube (Fig. 9.1 (f)); here, the *same* input results in *different* perceptions through a switch of attention.

3) *Paradoxical figures*, such as the Penrose impossible objects (Fig. 9.1 (g) and (h)). In the case of the 'impossible' triangle', we make the false assumption that the three corners are all the same distance away from us. A 3-dimensional 'version' of the triangle can be made, but the corners are not actually touching—they may appear to do so, however, when viewed from a particular angle.

4) *Fictions*, such as the Kanizsa triangle (Fig. 9.1 (i)) in which we see what is literally not there, not 'given' in the stimulus (an absence of data).

When perceptual cues conflict, the visual system has to 'bet' as to what the correct interpretation is. For instance, in the Ponzo illusion, it can either accept the equal lengths of the two central lines as drawn on the

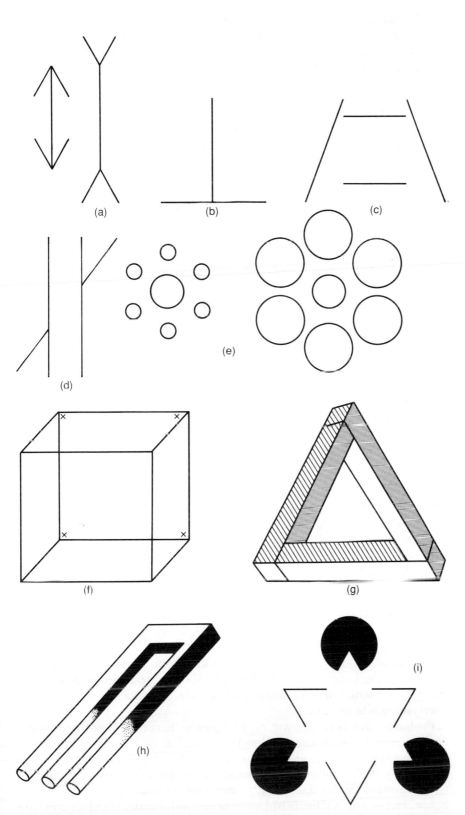

Figure 9.1 *Common illusions (a) Müller–Lyer illusion (1889). The arrow with the outgoing fins is seen as longer, but they are the same length; (b) Horizontal–vertical illusion (Fick, 1851). The vertical line is seen as longer, but they are the same length; (c) Ponzo illusion (1928). The top line of the two central lines is seen as longer, but they are the same length; (d) Poggendorff illusion (Zöllner, 1860). A diagonal line appears bent—but it is not; (e) the Titchener circles (Wundt, 1898). The central circle in the left-hand group is seen as larger than that in the right-hand group, but they are the same size; (f) Necker cube. The crosses can be seen as being drawn either on the back side of the cube or on the top side (looking down); (g) the Penrose impossible triangle; (h) another impossible object; (i) the Kanizsa triangle*

page (a flat, 2-D surface), which would involve the assumption that they are equi-distant from the observer, or it can 'read' the whole figure as *representing* a railway-track converging into the distance, so that the two horizontal lines represent sleepers, the top one of which would be further away from the observer (nearer the horizon) but appears longer since it 'must' be longer in order to produce the same length image on the retina.

Clearly, the second interpretation is inappropriate, since the figure is in fact drawn on a flat piece of paper (ie there are no actual distance differences) and the result is the illusion-experience. But this case of mistaken perception illustrates (as do all illusions) how the perceptual system *normally* operates, namely formulating a *perceptual hypothesis*, a 'best guess' which is then tested against sensory inputs:

> ... perception is an active process of using information to suggest and test hypotheses. (Gregory, 1972)

What we perceive is not the data but the interpetation of it:

> ... a perceived object is a hypothesis, suggested and tested by sensory data ... (Gregory, 1966)

Again:

> ... perceptions are representations of reality and not, so to speak, samples of reality which a passive theory of perception would maintain. They are, rather, brain descriptions in a sort of internal brain language. Brain states represent the world rather as letters on a page represent fiction or truth ... (Gregory, 1983)

In the case of ambiguous figures, we make two alternative hypotheses about what sort of object could be responsible for that sort of pattern on our retina—clearly, the sensory information is not adequate in accounting for the perceptual experience since the figure can be *seen* in more than one way (ie there cannot be a one-to-one correspondence between sensation and perception). With the Necker cube, for example, a spontaneous 'flipping' occurs—but the sensory stimulation has not changed in any way. The same applies to reversible figures like the Rubin vase and Leeper's Ambiguous Lady (see pp. 240 and 242).

But Gregory stresses that the hypothesis is not a separate process from the perception itself:

> ... the experience that one has in perception *is* a hypothesis. I wouldn't separate the hypothesis from the perception ... perceptions are predictive hypotheses. They're suggested by available data ... (Gregory, 1983)

He goes on to point out that the 'data' can be a, 'surprising absence of signals'. Take, for example, the fictional Kanizsa triangle, in which it is the gaps (absence of stimulation) which are the data for the apparent overlying white triangle.

Probably the best known of Gregory's 'perception-as-hypotheses' explanations involves the Müller–Lyer illusion (itself one of the most famous and most discussed illusions amongst psychologists).

Gregory explains illusions in terms of a perceptual hypothesis which is not confirmed by the 'data', that is, our attempt to interpret the stimulus figure turns out to be misplaced or inappropriate, resulting in the experience of an illusion. It is our attempt to construe the stimulus in keeping with how we normally construe the world which misleads us, in particular, reading depth and distance cues into 2-D drawings.

According to Gregory, the arrow with the *ingoing fins* provides linear perspective cues which suggest it could be the *outside corner* of a building; the ingoing fins, accordingly, are seen as walls receding away from us so that the shaft is *closer* to us. For the arrow with the *outgoing fins*, the situation is reversed; perspective cues suggest it could be the *inside corner* of a room so that the outgoing fins are seen as walls approaching us, in which case the shaft is in some sense *further away* from us (Fig. 9.2.)

However, the retinal images produced by the shafts are *equal* and, according to *size constancy*, if equal-sized images are produced by two lines, one of which is further away from us than the other, then the line which is further away *must actually be longer!*

All this interpretation is, of course, taking place quite unconsciously and so quickly that we perceive the illusion immediately.

The role of learning in perception of the illusion also tends to support Gregory's interpretation as evidenced by the study of cataract patients and cross-cultural studies (see Chapter 10).

However, if (as in Fig. 9.3) the perspective cues are removed but the illusion remains then this strongly suggests that Gregory's 'misapplied size constancy theory' is itself misapplied. Also, Robinson (1972) suggests that it is more likely that the apparent distance of the shaft is caused *by* the apparent size of the shafts than vice versa (as claimed by Gregory).

Robinson (1972), also cites a study by Morgan (1968) using a Müller–Lyer figure (Judd, 1899) with a dot placed half-way along the shaft (Fig. 9.4). The dot clearly seems to be nearer the left-hand end and it seems the only way Gregory could explain this is to suppose that the arrowheads make the shaft appear to slope away from the observer, thus offering a rather odd perspective interpretation of the figure. Gregory (1971) in fact claims to have demonstrated such a slope using an

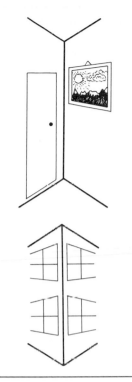

Figure 9.2 A representation of Gregory's explanation of the Müller–Lyer illusion in terms of depth cues and size constancy

Figure 9.3 The Müller–Lyer illusion with the depth cues removed. (a) Delboeuf (1892); (b) Delboeuf (1892), Brentano (1892); (c) Delboeuf (1892)

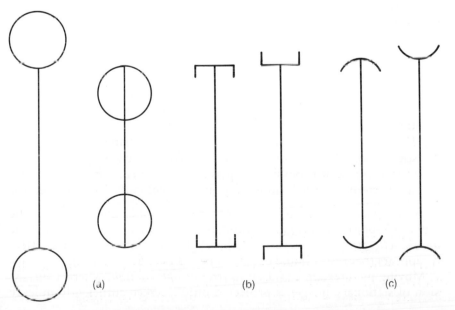

(a)   (b)   (c)

Figure 9.4 Judd's (1899) Müller–Lyer figure used by Morgan (1969)

apparatus designed to measure apparent depth. Using both eyes, the subject, in the dark, sees a small light which can be adjusted in distance.

Using only one eye, the subject sees a luminous display of the Müller–Lyer (or some other) illusion and by means of a sheet of neutral tinted perspex at 450 degrees to the line of sight, the light can be superimposed onto the luminous display. So the light can be put at different points on the display, thus mapping the apparent distance of various parts of the figure. Gregory has shown that the outgoing fins do appear to be closer to the observer than the shaft, (ie they represent inside corners), while the ingoing fins appear to be further away (ie outside corners), thus supporting his applied constancy-scaling explanation.

However, Eysenck and Keane (1990) believe that Gregory was mistaken when he claimed that *everyone* perceives the luminous figure as 3-D, and when the illusion is perceived, it may be due simply to the fact that the apparently longer shaft is part of a longer (overall) object (Eysenck, 1984).

Clearly, not all illusions can be explained in terms of the same (unconscious) processes (eg size-constancy):

> The large number and the variety of illusions give little reason to suppose . . . that they can be explained by a single principle. The most likely outcome is that a fairly small number of principles will be found which, working together can account for the data . . . (Robinson, 1972)

> . . . Our understanding of illusions is still remarkably incomplete in spite of the volume of research that they have inspired . . . (Robinson, 1972)

We have been talking about illusions so far in a very restricted and special sense, namely, visual stimuli which have been deliberately created to be illusions; however, we are surrounded by illusions which we do not normally think of in this way, partly, perhaps, because they are so commonplace:

(a) All drawings, paintings, etc. are 2-D, however, because of perspective cues used by the artist, we *infer* depth and distance (the third dimension); we add something which is not physically present in the stimulus. This also applies to the images projected onto our television and cinema screens, which also employ another kind of illusion—of movement.

(b) *Illusions of movement.* Just as it is possible for changes in patterns of stimulation on the retina not to be accompanied by perception of movement, so it is possible to perceive movement *without* a successive pattern of retinal stimulation (ie *apparent movement* or *motion*).

If you look at a spot of light in an otherwise completely dark room, the light will appear to move (even though it is stationary); this is called the *autokinetic effect.* However, if other lights are introduced, the effect disappears (because a frame of reference has been introduced).

Moving pictures are based upon *stroboscopic motion*, where a succession of stationary images is projected onto a screen sufficiently quickly to produce an illusory impression of continuous movement. A simpler form of this is the *phi phenomenon*, much researched in the lab, whereby a number of separate lights turned on and off in quick succession will create the impression of a *single* light moving from one position to another.

Finally, when the only information we have about movement is visual (that is, there are no proprioceptive cues), we tend to assume that larger objects remain stationary while smaller ones move. A famous demonstration of this was carried out by Duncker (1939) who shone a light onto a screen and then moved the screen to one side; most subjects reported that they saw the light move (in the opposite direction to the actual movement of the screen). This is an example of *induced movement*. Other examples include the moon seen through a thin cover of moving clouds (where it is the moon—the smaller object—which is seen to move) and the common experience of sitting in a train alongside another train and not being sure which one has started to pull out of the station.

Veridical Perception of Movement

What these movement illusions show is that the brain normally uses more than just retinal images when perceiving *real* movement. The assumption that larger objects are less likely to be moving than smaller ones is one extra 'rule' that is used, so that judgements about relative size are important extra bits of information; however, as we have seen, this can mislead us as much as it can inform us.

Clearly, there must be changes in the retinal image; indeed, it seems that the receptors only respond to *changes* in the environment. As we saw in Chapter 8 the eyes are constantly making minute, oscillatory, movements which keep the receptors stimulated. A device for stabilizing the retinal image (Cornsweet, 1970) shows that these movements are necessary for seeing things *at all*. A tiny slide projector, mounted on a contact lens, is attached to the cornea and a slide projected onto a screen; since the lens and the projector move with the eye, the retinal image is stablized (ie eye movements and the movement of the image on the screen 'cancel each other out' and so the retinal image stays in the same place). After initially seeing the picture with normal acuity, within a few seconds it begins to fade and after a minute disappears altogether.

As we have said, if you turn your head slowly around with your eyes open, you will create a succession of different retinal images—but you will *not* perceive movement; clearly, therefore, changes in the retinal image cannot be a sufficient basis for the perception of movement. Conversely, when an unchanging object moves across your visual field and you follow it with your eyes, the retinal image remains the same but you *do* perceive movement.

Another important cue to movement is *configuration change*. Objects moving in the environment usually do so against a background of stationary (or differently moving) objects, and the nose and other anatomical borders to the visual field also provide a stationary reference point against which to judge movement (which causes a configuration change or change in the overall pattern and interrelationship between objects). However, although in practice this is often an important source of information, it may not be a necessary one. Gregory (1973) points out that if a lighted cigarette is moved about in a dark room it will be perceived as moving, even though there are no background cues or frame of reference.

It seems that the brain is capable of distinguishing between eye movements which signal movement of objects (real movement) and eye movements (and movements of the head) which do not (as when you scan a stationary scene and things stay in their proper place). Probably the superior colliculus plays an important role in making this distinction. Gregory (1973) describes two systems: (i) the image–retina system, which responds to changes in the visual field which produce changes in the retinal image; and (ii) the eye–head system, which responds to movements of the head and eyes. He argues that the perception of movement is the product of an interplay between the two systems.

EVALUATION OF GREGORY'S THEORY

Gordon (1989) describes Gregory's theory as representing, '. . . the most explicit and fullest treatment of the central idea of empiricism . . .'. But he also argues that there is a serious problem regarding the relationship between knowledge and hypotheses—for example, illusions persist despite full knowledge of why they occur, so why doesn't this knowledge enable us to modify our hypotheses in an adaptive way? And just what are these hypotheses? How do we modify them? And what's the difference between different kinds of learning which do occur, some very rapid (for example, having the Old Lady pointed out to us in the Ambiguous Lady—see p. 242), some very slow (for example, adapting to wearing distorting goggles—see Chapter 10)?

Gordon (1989) believes that the *computational* approach to vision (such as Marr's (1982) which we shall discuss later in the chapter) shows that it *is* possible to give much more detailed accounts of what the central *constructive* processes ('top-down processing') might be than anything Gregory offers.

Another interesting point made by Gordon (1989) is that, if perception is essentially constructive, how does it ever get started? How is it that there seems to be such communality among the perceptions of different people if we have all had to construct our own idiosyncratic worlds? Brunswick's answer would be in terms of *probabilistic functionalism* (1952, 1956), namely, that the selection of appropriate cues is vital to survival, ie the world is common to all perceivers and this may account for regularities in the perceptions of all creatures sharing a particular ecological niche.

Are our retinal images really as impoverished as Gregory claims? If they are, how does he account for the fact that perception is typically accurate, that our hypotheses are usually correct? Illusions are not 'paradigm' (typical) cases of perceptual experience. Eysenck and Keane (1990) suggest that Gregory is perhaps more successful in explaining visual illusions than perception as a whole, since illusions are artificial, simplified, unrealistic stimuli compared with naturally-occurring objects and scenes.

Support for the constructivist theory comes from studies of the importance of *context* on perception (see below) which usually involve very brief presentations of stimuli, thus maximizing the impact of knowledge, expectations etc ('top-down' processes) and reducing the impact of 'bottom-up' processes.

> ... since these conditions probably obtain only relatively infrequently in everyday life, constructivist theories may have less relevance to normal situations than to artificial laboratory situations' (Eysenck and Keane, 1990).

GIBSON'S THEORY OF DIRECT PERCEPTION (1950, 1966, 1979)

In the real world, retinal images only rarely contain projections of single, isolated objects; usually they are much richer than this, and typically include other objects, background, even the distant horizon.

In addition, movement is a vital part of perceiving, something that is often overlooked in laboratory research.

In summing up Gregory's contribution, Gordon states that:

> ... empiricists may have underestimated the richness of sensory evidence when perceivers operate in the real world ... (Gordon, 1989)

and:

> ... it is possible that we perceive constructively only at certain times and in certain situations. Whenever we move under our own power on the surface of the natural world and in good light, the necessary perceptions of size, texture, distance, continuity, motion, and so on, may all occur directly and reflexively ... (Gordon, 1989)

These are some of the basic ideas of Gibson's theory of direct perception and ecological optics (a 'bottom-up' approach).

1)   While for the empiricists the starting point in trying to explain perception is the retinal image, for Gibson this involves the mistake of describing the input for a perceiver in the same terms as that for a single photoreceptor, namely a stream of photons. But the correct starting point for Gibson is a pattern of light extended over time and space, which can be thought of as an *optical array* containing all the visual information from the environment striking the eye. It provides unambiguous, invariant information about the layout of objects in space and this information takes three main forms: *optic flow patterns*, *texture gradient* and *affordances*.

Perception essentially involves 'picking up' the rich information provided by the optic array in a direct way which involves little or no (unconscious) information processing or computations or internal representation.

2)   In the Second World War Gibson was given the task of preparing training films which would describe the problems pilots experience when taking off and landing. He needed to know exactly what information pilots have available to them. His answer was *optic flow patterns* (OFPs) which can be illustrated by considering a pilot approaching the landing strip (Fig. 9.5)—the point towards which the pilot moves appears motionless, with the rest of the visual environment apparently moving away from that point, ie all around that point there is an apparent radial expansion of textures flowing around one's head. This lack of apparent

Figure 9.5 *Optic flow as a pilot approaches the landing strip. (From Gibson, J. J. (1950).* The Perception of the Visual World. *Boston: Houghton-Mifflin)*

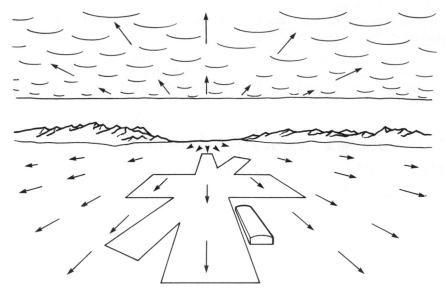

movement of the point towards which we move is an invariant, unchanging, feature of the optic array. Such OFPs can provide pilots with unambigious information about their direction, speed and altitude. Gibson was so impressed by the wealth of sensory information available to pilots in OFPs that he subsequently devoted himself to analyzing the kinds of information available in sensory data under other conditions (Eysenck and Keane, 1990).

3) Gibson called one such set of conditions *texture gradients* (or gradient of texture density). Textures expand as you approach them and contract as they pass beyond your head; this happens *whenever you move towards something*, ie over and above the behaviour of each texture element, there is a 'higher-order' pattern or structure, available as a source of information about the environment; the flow of the texture is *invariant*. This is an example of an important cue to depth, which is perceived directly (ie without the need for any inferences). Other examples of directly perceived, invariant higher-order features of the optic array relevant to depth perception include *linear perspective* and *motion parallax* (see section on Depth cues, p. 257). So for Gibson the third dimension (depth) is available to the senses as directly as the other two dimensions, *automatically* processed by the sense receptors and automatically producing the perceptual experience of depth.

4) The third major feature of the optic array, *affordances*, is closely tied up with Gibson's concept of '*ecological optics*'. To understand an animal's perceptual system we need to consider the environment in which the system has evolved, particularly the patterns of light (optical array) which reach the eye from the environment (ecological optics). When an object moves further away from the eye its image gets smaller (*relative size*), most objects are bounded by texture surfaces and the *grain of texture* gets finer as the objects recede, objects obscure a part of the textured ground against which they are seen (*superimposition*) and the further away an object is, the closer it will be to the horizon (*height in the horizontal plane*). The crucial point here is that objects are not judged in complete isolation—the optical array commonly contains far more information than that associated with a single stimulus object,

something overlooked by the use of classical optics and laboratory experiments (Gordon, 1989).

EVALUATION OF GIBSON'S THEORY

1) According to Marr (1982), Gibson asked the critically important question: 'How does one obtain constant perception in everyday life on the basis of continually changing sensations?' This is exactly the right question, showing that Gibson correctly regarded the problem of perception as that of recovering from sensory information 'valid properties of the external world'.

But he failed to realize two equally critical things, namely, that:

> First, the detection of physical invariants, like image surfaces, is exactly and precisely an information-processing problem, in modern terminology. And second, he vastly underrated the sheer difficulty of such detection. (Marr, 1982)

Workers in Artificial Intelligence (of whom Marr is one) have set themselves explicit goals, including devising a system which will simulate the process of seeing: trying to create some model which will actually extract variants has proved very difficult. But Gordon (1989) wonders whether, equally, Marr has underemphasized the importance of motor activity.

2) An interesting study by Lee and Lishman (1975) at Edinburgh involves the use of a specially built swaying room (suspended above the floor) designed to bring texture flow under experimental control. As the room sways (thus changing the texture flow), adults typically make slight unconscious adjustments and children tend to fall over. Normally, the brain is very skilled at establishing correlations between changes in the optic flow, signals to the muscles and staying upright.

This tends to lend support to Gibson's belief in the importance of movement in perception and the artificiality of separating sensory and motor aspects of behaviour. Arguably, the single most important reason for having a visual system is to be able to anticipate when contact with an approaching object is going to be made. Lee and Lishman (1975), for example, believe that estimating 'time to contact' is crucial for actions such as avoidance of objects and grasping them and thus represents extremely important ecological information. (This can be expressed as a formula, ie

$$\text{Time to contact} = \frac{\text{Size of retinal image}}{\text{Rate of expansion of retinal image}}$$

and is a property shared by *all* objects, hence another invariant and a demonstration of the unambiguity of the retinal image.)

Measures of optical flow have also provided some understanding of how skilled long-jumpers control their approaches to the take-off position (Gordon, 1989).

3) The concept of affordance has perhaps proved the most controversial. These are directly perceivable potential uses of objects (eg a ladder 'affords' ascent/descent, a chair 'affords' sitting) and which are detected will depend on the perceiver's species and current psychological state. The concept of affordances forms part of Gibson's (1979) attempt to show that all the information needed to make sense of the visual environment is directly

available in the visual input (Eysenck and Keane, 1990), ie a pure bottom-up approach.

According to Bruce and Green (1990), the concept is at its most powerful/useful in the context of simple visually-guided behaviour, such as that of insects. It makes sense here to speak of an animal detecting the information available in the light needed to organize its activities and the idea of the animal needing to have a conceptual representation of its enviroment seems redundant.

But what about people? Gibson's concept may apply to the detection of distance and other variables involved in the guidance of locomotion, but humans don't just perceive and act in a physical environment but also in a *cultural* environment. Is Gibson seriously claiming that no *knowledge* of writing or the postal system is needed in order to detect that a pen affords writing or that a letter-box affords posting a letter, that these are directly perceived invariants?

Fodor and Pylyshyn (1981) believe that the terms 'invariant' and 'directly detected' are so vague as to be meaningless. However, they can be made more precise and useful by using a 'sufficiency criterion': the pattern of light reflected from a looming surface is sufficient to produce perception of an impending collision (as shown by experiments with artificial simulation of such a pattern) and so it makes sense to speak of an invariant property of this pattern being detected directly. But can a sample of light from a Leonardo da Vinci painting be sufficient to recognize it as one of his works? Surely further information beyond what is contained in the light is necessary, ie we must already have knowledge (stored in memory) about his paintings! (Bruce and Green, 1990).

Fodor and Pylyshyn distinguish between 'seeing' and 'seeing as':

> What you see when you see a thing depends upon what the thing you see is. But what you see the thing as depends upon what you know about what you are seeing . . . (Fodor and Pylyshyn, 1981)

This view of perception as 'seeing as' is the fundamental principle of the *transactionalists* (eg Ames: see Ittelson, 1952). They argue that, because the sensory input is always ambiguous, the interpretation selected is the most likely one in the light of what has been perceived in the past. A very famous demonstration is the Ames Distorted Room (Fig. 9.6), which is

Figure 9.6 The Ames distorted room

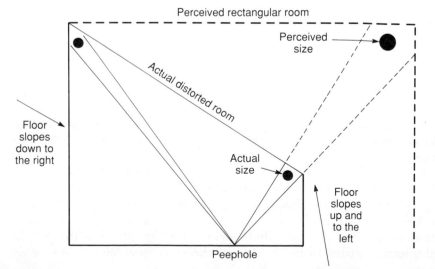

constructed in such a way that when viewed with one eye through a special peephole, a person at one end may look like a dwarf and a person at the other end like a giant and if they cross the room they appear to change size. The perceiver is put into a situation of having to choose between two different beliefs about the world built up through past experience: (i) rooms are rectangular and consist of right angles, etc. (and as seen through the peephole, the Ames room looks perfectly normal and regular); and (ii) people are usually of 'average' height. Most subjects choose the former and so judge the people to be of an odd size—but the case of a wife who saw her husband in the Ames Room, and judged the room to be odd shows that particular past experience can override more generalized beliefs about the world.

Fodor and Pylyshyn (1981) believe that Gibson's ecological approach has little useful to say about seeing as but provides useful insights into seeing. Bruce and Green agree, saying:

> ... Most human activity takes place within a culturally defined environment and ... people see objects and events as what they are in terms of a culturally given conceptual representation of the world. (Bruce and Green, 1990)

4) The Ames Room is, of course, another kind of visual *illusion* and it is the near impossibility of Gibson's theory to account for mistaken (non-veridical) perception which is perhaps its greatest single weakness. He argues that most laboratory demonstrations of 'mistakes' occur in circumstances very different from those prevailing in the natural environment (eg 2-D illusions, presented briefly as opposed to 3-D objects perceived over relatively long periods). But his claim that illusions are merely trick figures dreamt up by psychologists to baffle ordinary people does not apply to all cases; at least some produce effects similar to those found in normal perception (eg the vertical–horizontal illusion; Eysenck and Keane, 1990).

One particularly striking example is the 'hollow face' illusion (Fig. 9.7)—there is sufficient information here to see the mask as hollow but we stubbornly fail to do so. If we move our head from side to side, the face appears to follow us, in blatant disregard of the actual motion perspective present (Bruce and Green, 1990). Gregory's (1971) explanation is simply that the improbability of it being a hollow face and not a normal face is so great that the truth is totally rejected:

> The hollow face is not an example of an illusion which involves static observers or monocular viewing and is a difficult one for the ardent Gibsonian to discuss as a laboratory trick. We must invoke a memory of some sort here to explain why we see what we are used to seeing despite useful information to the contrary. (Bruce and Green, 1990)

For Gibson, there is no distinction between sensation and perception; indeed, his 1966 book is entitled *The Senses Considered as Perceptual Systems*. If all perception were veridical, his case might be stronger. Eysenck (1984) claims that, in a sense, Gibson's theory is *too* good because he is arguing that stimulation of the sense receptors provides so much valuable information that space perception is essentially perfect (which, clearly, it is not).

5) However, since we have also considered limitations of Gregory's theory (the main alternative to Gibson's) and since *both* would agree

Figure 9.7 *Picture of the inside of a hollow mask—but it is impossible not to see it as a normal face. (From Gregory, R. L. (1970).* The Intelligent Eye. *London, Weidenfeld & Nicolson)*

that: (i) visual perception is mediated by light reflected from surfaces and objects; (ii) some kind of physiological system is needed to perceive; and (iii) perceptual experience can be influenced by learning, is there a middle-ground between the two positions, a theoretical synthesis?

According to Eysenck and Keane (1990), the relative importance of bottom-up and top-down processes is affected by a variety of factors: bottom-up may be crucial when viewing conditions are good but top-down may become increasingly important if the stimulus is presented very briefly and/or the stimulus is ambiguous, etc. Gibson seems to have concentrated on *optimal viewing conditions*, while Gregory and other constructivists have tended to use *sub-optimal viewing conditions*.

Clearly, in most circumstances, both bottom-up *and* top-down processes are needed: the most clearly worked out model of such interdependence is Neisser's *analysis-by-synthesis* (1976) (Fig. 9.8). He assumes a *perceptual cycle* involving *schemata*, *perceptual exploration* and *stimulus environment*. Schemata contain collections of knowledge based on past experience (see Chapter 12) which serve the function of directing perceptual exploration towards relevant environmental stimulation. Such

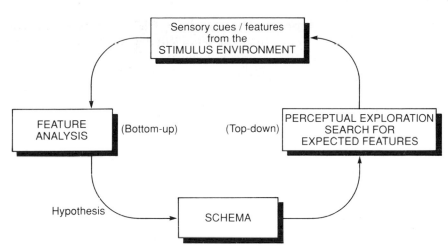

Figure 9.8 Neisser's (1976) Analysis-by-Synthesis model of perception

exploration often involves moving around the environment and leads the perceiver to sample actively the available stimulus information. If the sampled information fails to match that in the relevant schema, then the hypothesis is modified accordingly. An initial *analysis* of the sensory cues/features (bottom-up) might suggest the hypothesis that an object is, say a chair. This will set in motion a search for the expected features (eg four legs and a back), based on our schema of a chair (*synthesis*—a top down process). But if the environmental features start to disconfirm the original hypothesis (eg there are only three legs and no back), then a new hypothesis must be proposed and tested (this is a stool) and the appropriate stool-schema activated.

So perception never occurs in a vacuum, since our sampling of sensory features of the environment is always guided by our knowledge and past experience. In this way, perception is also seen as an *interactive* process, involving both *bottom-up* feature analysis and *top-down* expectations.

GESTALT PSYCHOLOGY—PERCEPTION IS ORGANIZED

If the key process in Gregory's theory is inference and in Gibson's direct perception of invariants, then the key concept in the Gestalt approach is that of *organization*.

As we saw when discussing Reductionism in Chapter 2, the Gestalt psychologists were reacting against the structuralism of Wundt and Titchener, who tried to analyse perceptual experience in terms of its basic elements (sensations).

Ehrenfels (1890) claimed that many groups of stimuli acquire a pattern quality which is over and above the sum of their parts; for example, a square is more than a simple assembly of lines—it has 'squareness'. This 'emergent property' he called *Gestalt qualität* (from quality).

Wertheimer (1880–1943) began work in 1910 on the phi phenomenon, which demonstrates that the perception of (apparent) movement occurs as a result of the temporal and spatial relationships between the (component) stimuli: the whole is greater than the sum of its parts. Wertheimer worked at Frankfurt University with the assistance of two young psychologists, Köhler (1887–1967) and Koffka (1886–1941) and these are the three central figures in Gestalt psychology.

(j)

Figure 9.9 *The Rubin vase*

According to Gordon (1989), the discoveries of Gestalt theory, '. . . are now part of our permanent knowledge of perception . . .' and that includes the distinction between Figure and Ground demonstrated by the famous Rubin's vase (Rubin, 1915; Fig. 9.9).

A major philosophical influence on Gestalt psychology was *phenomenology*, the belief that a perceptual theory should be trying to explain everyday experience. For example, Koffka asked, 'Why do things look as they do?' (which Gordon (1989) claims is, '. . . the most famous question in the history of perception'). A perceptual theory must explain the stability and coherence of our world of everyday experience—we perceive objects, not sensations, and the proper approach to this world is that of the phenomenologist:

> There seems to be a single starting point for psychology, exactly as for all the other sciences: the world as we find it, naïvely and uncritically. (Köhler, 1947)

THE PRINCIPLES OF PERCEPTUAL ORGANIZATION

If it is true that we perceive objects *not* as combinations of isolated sensations (colours, shapes, sizes, etc.) but as *Gestalten* (variously translated as 'organized wholes', 'configurations' or 'patterns'), how is this achieved?

We apply certain principles which can all be summarized under the *Law of Prägnanz*, which was defined by Koffka:

> Psychological organization will always be as 'good' as the prevailing conditions allow. In this definition, the term 'good' is undefined. (Koffka, 1935)

But again:

> Of several geometrically possible organizations, that one will actually occur which possesses the best, simplest and most stable shape. (Koffka, 1935)

Attneave (1954) defined 'good' as possessing a high degree of internal *redundancy*, ie the structure of any unseen part is highly predictable from the visible parts, and Hochberg's 'minimum principle' (1978) maintains that if there is more than one way of organizing a given visual stimulus, the one most likely to be perceived is the one requiring the *least* amount of information to describe it.

In practice, the 'best' way of perceiving is the symmetrical, uniform and stable and this is achieved through *proximity*, *closure*, *continuity* and *symmetry*, *similarity*, *Figure–Ground* and the *part-whole relationship*: these are all manifestations of the more general, inclusive, *Law of Prägnanz* (Fig. 9.10).

a) Proximity

Elements which appear close together—in space or time—tend to be perceived together, so that Figure 9.10(a) is normally seen as three pairs of parallel lines and 9.10(b) as a group of three dots, followed by a pair, followed by a single dot. An auditory example would be the perception of a series of musical notes as a melody because they occur soon after one another in time.

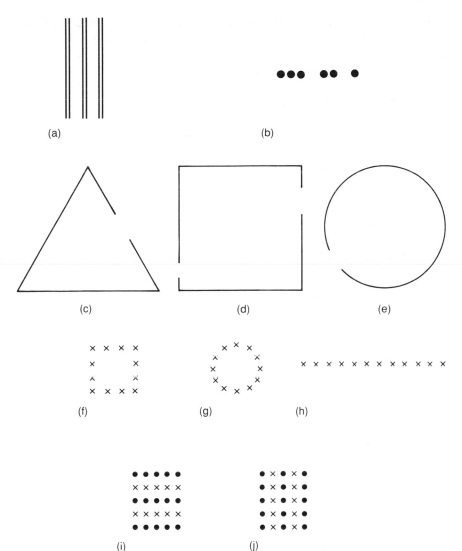

Figure 9.10 The Gestalt principles of organization (a) Proximity; (b) proximity; (c) closure; (d) closure; (e) closure; (f) continuity and symmetry; (g) continuity and symmetry; (h) continuity and symmetry; (i) similarity; (j) similarity

b) Closure

Closed figures are more easily perceived than open or incomplete ones, so that we tend to close incomplete figures, as in Figure 9.10(c), (d) and (e), in order to give their familiar meaning.

c) Continuity and Symmetry

Similar parts of a figure which appear in straight or curved lines tend to stand out; when they make recognizable shapes (such as circles and squares) they become conspicuous. So, for example, the crosses in Figure 9.10(f) are seen as composing a square, those in 9.10(g) a circle and those in 9.10(h) a straight line. Again, music is perceived as continuous rather than a series of distinct, separate sounds and the same applies to speech.

d) Similarity

Like-elements tend to be perceived together, as belonging to the same pattern. In Figure 9.10(i), for example, we tend to see alternating rows of dots and crosses (rather than columns of dots and crosses intermingled); if we turn it on its side (9.10(j)), we now see columns of dots alternating with columns of crosses. When we hear all the separate voices in a choir as one entity, the principle of similarity is operating.

e) *Figure–Ground*

Some part of a stimulus always stands out as being in the foreground (the Figure) and everything else as background (Ground); the Figure is what we attend to at any particular time and the Ground represents the context in which the Figure is presented and from which it derives its meaning.

According to Rubin (1915), the Figure has 'thinglike' qualities, while the Ground is relatively uniform; the Figure also seems to be nearer and the Ground extends unbroken behind it.

Figure 9.9 (p. 240) (the famous Rubin vase) illustrates the Figure-Ground principle and is also *reversible*, ie it can be seen in two ways—when we attend to the vase, the profiles constitute Ground and when we switch attention to the profiles, they become the Figure.

A famous example of a reversible Figure–Ground phenomenon is Leeper's Ambiguous Lady (Fig. 9.11). Can you see an attractive young lady and an old hag? Objectively, they are both present in the picture—but it is impossible to see them both simultaneously. A map is another example—we normally see the land as Figure and the sea as Ground, since we are more familiar with the shape of Africa, for example, than the shape of the Atlantic.

An auditory example is following one conversation out of several going on in a 'cocktail party' situation (usually the one we are involved in); but a reversal can occur if, for example, our name is mentioned by someone on the other side of the room. Try repeating 'over-run' out loud and you will find the two words alternating as Figure and Ground.

f) *Part–whole Relationship*

Figure 9.10(f), (g) and (h) illustrate the principle that, 'the whole is greater than the sum of its parts': each pattern is composed of twelve crosses but the gestalts are different despite the similarity of the parts (and are determined largely through proximity and continuity/ symmetry).

Another example is the case of water (H_2O), which is composed of a mixture of hydrogen (H) and oxygen (O) but the properties of water are very different from those of hydrogen or oxygen taken separately. Again, the notes in a musical scale played up the scale produce a very different sound compared with the same notes played down the scale and the same melody can be recognized when hummed, whistled or played with differert instruments and in different keys.

ASSESSMENT OF GESTALT PRINCIPLES

According to Gordon (1989), most contemporary psychologists would agree that the Gestaltists were correct about many things: geometric illusions continue to fascinate both theorists and experimenters, we do seem to respond to relationships between stimuli rather than to absolute values, wholes are more than the sum of their parts and stimuli are organized into patterns:

The spontaneous groupings in perception are fascinating and reliable

Figure 9.11 *Leeper's ambiguous lady*

phenomena and are still being researched 80 years after Wertheimer's demonstration . . . (Gordon, 1989)

And:

The most comprehensive account of perceptual grouping is still that provided by the Gestalt psychologists in the 1920s . . . (Roth, 1986).

However, many writers agree that the laws (especially Prägnanz) are (as originally expressed) at best only descriptive, and at worst extremely vague, imprecise and difficult to measure. For example, Greene (1990) asks what exactly makes a circle or square a 'good' figure? Again:

. . . some of their 'Laws' of perceptual organization today sound vague and inadequate. What is meant by a 'good' or a 'simple' shape, for example? Recent workers have attempted to formalize at least some of the Gestalt perceptual principles. (Bruce and Green, 1990)

There has been a recent revival of interest in Gestalt principles and many experiments (as opposed to verbal reports or 'demonstrations') have been carried out. According to the principles, some figures should look 'better' than others: will people recognize good figures when they see them? (Greene, 1990).

Experimental Tests of Gestalt Laws

1)   Pomerantz (1981) reviewed a number of experiments which provide objective measures of perceptual grouping. If a set of elements lend themselves to perceptual grouping, then subjects should have difficulty responding to one element of the set while ignoring others. Conversely, if a set of elements *don't* lend themselves to grouping, it should be *easy* to do this.

One objective measure of grouping is how quickly subjects can sort or classify one element presented with others which they must try to ignore. For example, Pomerantz and Garner (1973) gave subjects a pile of cards, each with a pair of brackets printed on. They had to sort the cards into two piles (A and B) according to whether the *left-hand bracket* on each card looked like '(' or ')'. Subjects were told to ignore the right-hand bracket completely. In one condition, the pair of elements were predicted to be *groupable*, in the other condition, *non-groupable*. (There was an Experimental and a Control pack in each condition; see Fig. 9.12.)

The results confirmed the hypotheses, showing that there are objective correlates for the perceptual phenomenon of grouping. Elements seen as grouped are also processed differently—less efficiently (more slowly) because subjects were trying to select out one element from a group. Under conditions where subjects are required to attend to *all* elements of a group, groupable elements are processed more efficiently.

What is it about the groupable elements which make them groupable? Presumably, similarity and proximity are involved.

2)   Pomerantz and Schwaitzberg (1975) systematically manipulated proximity by using cards with brackets drawn further and further apart. Given a suitable separation between the paired elements, grouping effects disappeared (ie there was no longer a difference between sorting times for control/experimental packs of 'groupable' stimuli). But similarity in orientation of 'groupable' elements is also important (Olson and Attneave, 1970).

Figure 9.12 *Experimental test of grouping used by Pomerantz and Garner (1973)*

		SORT INTO PILE			
		A	B	B	A
GROUPABLE STIMULI	CONTROL	((	) (	) (	((
	EXPERIMENTAL	((	) (	))	( )
NON-GROUPABLE STIMULI	CONTROL	⌐	⌐	⌐	⌐
	EXPERIMENTAL	⌐	⌐	⌐	⌐

Figure 9.12 *Experimental test of grouping used by Pomerantz and Garner (1973)*

3)   Garner and Clement (1963) asked subjects to rate on a 'goodness' scale the groups of dots (A/B/C; Fig. 9.13); generally, they rated A as 'better' than B and B 'better' than C. Pomerantz (1981) showed subjects the same groups of dots which they could join up as they wished (as in dot-to-dot). He predicted that nearly all would join up simple or 'good' figures in the same way, while 'non-good' figures would be joined in various ways. The prediction was supported.

4)   Navon (1977) tested the hypothesis that the overall Gestalt should be perceived before the individual (component) parts) He distinguished *local* (more specific and so 'part-like') and *global* (more whole-like) features. Subjects looked briefly at a large (*global*) letter composed of many small (*local*) letters while deciding as quickly as possible whether an H or an S had been presented auditorily. When the *global* letter was the same as the auditory letter, auditory discrimination was faster, but when they were different, there was an interference effect and it was much slower.

More surprisingly, performance on the auditory task was totally unaffected by the nature of the *local* letters—most subjects failed to notice that large letters were constructed from smaller ones. This

Figure 9.13 *Experimental test of grouping used by Garner and Clement (1963) and Pomerantz (1981)*

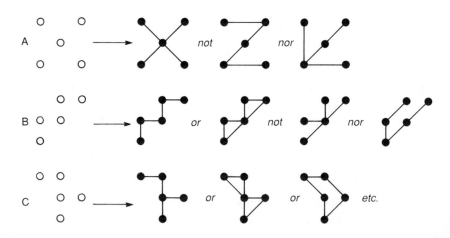

suggests that global features are perceived more readily than local—as predicted by Gestalt principles. Why?

Perhaps when there is only enough time for a partial perceptual analysis, it is usually more valuable to obtain information about the general structure of a perceptual scene than about a few isolated details. The experiment shows that the *whole* can be perceived *before* its parts—but it is not clear how much control people have over their perceptual processes. For example, if someone wanted to perceive the local features while ignoring the global, could they? (Eysenck and Keane, 1990). Navon (1977) tried to answer this in a further experiment, using the same kinds of stimuli. This time subjects had to decide as quickly as possible whether the global letter was an H or an S or, alternatively, whether the local letters were H's or S's. On half the trials, the local and global elements matched (Fig. 9.14(a)), while on the other trials, they didn't (Fig. 9.14(b)).

Decision speed with global letters was unaffected by the nature of the local letters, but decision speed with local letters was greatly slowed when there was a *mismatch* (Table 9.2):

> ...This latter finding suggests that it is difficult or even impossible to avoid perceiving the whole and that global processing necessarily occurs before any more detailed perceptual analysis. (Eysenck and Keane, 1990)

Similarly, Palmer (1977) argues that visual form is analysed *hierarchically*, from overall configuration moving down to basic features or elements, at each level. Gestalt principles were found to help determine how the low-level units are combined to form more organized gestalten at that level. Marr (1976) also found the Gestalt principles useful in achieving accurate *segmentation*, that is, how visual information is used to decide which regions of a visual scene belong together and form coherent structures. He devised a computer program aimed at achieving segmentation (of a teddy bear, for example) using the Gestalt principles and obtained very encouraging results, obtaining appropriate segmentation of the teddy's outline, eyes and nose. However, some scenes are ambiguous and require using knowledge about objects in order to achieve segmentation (eg two leaves overlapping substantially in a bowl of flowers; Marr, 1982):

> ...Navon's (1977) work implies that the notion that perceptual analysis involves building up a representation of a visual scene from its individual elements may be misguided. Instead initial global structuring is often fleshed out by progressively more and more fine-grained analysis. There is obvious sense in having the perceptual system operate in this fashion, because it enables important objects in the visual scene to be identified and perceived with minimal delay... (Eysenck and Keane, 1990)

However, the perceptual system doesn't invariably work like this, and

Figure 9.14 Example of (a) matching and (b) non-matching local and global letters, as used by Navon (1977)

CONDITION	TIME IN M/SECS TO RESPOND TO 'GLOBAL' OR 'LOCAL'	
	MATCH	MISMATCH
Global	471	477
Local	581	664

Table 9.2 Decision time for global and local letters under match or mismatch conditions. (Based on Navon, 1977)

Navon's global letters were quite small (never exceeding 5.5 degrees of the visual angle, ie the angle formed at the eye by light rays from the extremities of an object). Kinchla and Wolf (1979) used similar but large stimuli (up to 22.1 degrees of the visual angle) and found that local letters were easier to respond to than global when the latter exceeded 8 degrees. They concluded that those forms in the visual field having an optimal size are processed first:

> In sum, the Gestalt notion that Pattern Recognition often depends on the overall shape of a visual stimulus rather than on its individual features has received some support. However, there are clearly cases in which it does not apply. Factors such as the sizes of the local and global features, the viewing conditions and the nature of the observer's task are all likely to play a part in determining the role played by individual features in Pattern Recognition... (Eysenck and Keane, 1990)

> ...It seems obvious that in everyday life it is sometimes earier to process 'forests' and sometimes it is easier to process 'trees'. (Roth, 1986)

CONCLUSIONS

> The Gestalt laws are still accepted as descriptions of grouping phenomena. However, they have limited explanatory value... (Roth, 1986)

More recent work has looked for *explanations* within the framework of cognitive psychology and Artificial Intelligence.

The Gestalt laws are difficult to apply to the perception of solid (3-D) objects, (as opposed as 2-D drawings). Our eyes evolved to see 3-D objects and when 3-D arrays have been studied, Gestalt laws don't always stand up so well. Many of the Gestalt displays have very low *ecological validity*, ie the:

> ...naturalness of stimuli, how representative they are of the objects and events which organisms must deal with in order to survive. (Gordon, 1989)

Part of this low ecological validity is the Gestalt emphasis on *single* objects—in the real world we're faced with 'whole' scenes in which the 'parts' are single objects (Humphreys and Riddoch, 1987).

MARR'S COMPUTATIONAL THEORY OF VISION

To the extent that Gibson believes that all the information we need for veridical perception is contained in the retinal image, there is no 'problem' of perception that needs resolving. For Gregory, there is a problem: How do we account for our (usually) accurate perception given the highly ambiguous and often incomplete nature of the retinal image? But he was not concerned with spelling out the precise mechanisms by which useful information about a scene is extracted from an image of that scene. Marr (1982), however, was and his whole theory is an attempt to propose a solution to the '*Vision Problem*'

A way of putting the 'problem' in perspective is to consider what would be necessary if we were to attempt to design a computer to perform certain tasks which people can do relatively easily. It turns out that what comes 'naturally' to us is in fact so complex and so poorly understood, that attempts to give a machine this ability prove astonishingly unsuccessful (see Chapter 14).

Frisby (1986) asks us to imagine that we are trying to design a robot capable of assembling some blocks (as part of an industrial assembly process). How would we go about designing a visual system that could match the visual capabilities of a person for seeing what needs to be done to construct a tower?

First, the robot needs an optical device of some kind (eg a TV camera) that could capture one or more images of the scene. Secondly, the images would have to be analysed and interpreted in some way to provide useful information about the scene (eg information about the distance of the blocks from the robot, their shape, etc.):

> All this information is so readily provided by our own visual system that it is natural to think it must be easy to enable a robot to extract such information from its input images. But it is not! (Frisby, 1986)

So the *vision problem* can be defined as finding out how to extract useful information about a scene from images of that scene; 'useful information' is that which will guide the thoughts or actions of the total system of which the visual system is a part.

So vision is sometimes described as the business of making *explicit* information about a scene which is only *implicit* in the original image—the *computational approach* aims to specify the computations which are necessary to extract useful information from images.

Marr (a mathematician by training) began by studying the computations performed by the cerebellum but soon became dissatisfied with speculating about neural structures as such and decided what was missing was an analysis of the *functions* they perform. Even if you knew the functions of every cell or connection in the brain this still would not be enough—he said it would be like trying to understand flight simply by examining a bird's feathers (Gardner, 1985):

> ...Marr's lasting influence will probably be the way he has brought a deeper realization to those investigating biological visual systems of the need to study, not just the phenomena of biological vision, nor just the neural mechanisms that might underlie them, but, at least as important, the nature of the visual task being solved by those visual systems. (Frisby, 1986)

This reference to the 'task' of the visual system relates to the first of three levels at which, according to Marr, any process must be understood, namely: (i) computational theory (why/what for?); (ii) algorithm (how?); and (iii) hardware implementation (in what form?).

He illustrated the three levels by taking an example of an information-processing task which can definitely be performed by a machine, namely a cash register:

(a) *Computational theory*. The key question here is, 'What is the goal of the computation, why is it appropriate and what is the strategy by which it can be carried out?' (Marr, 1982). The cash register's function is to add sums of money and it is this procedure of addition which brings it within the class of 'information-processing' devices (it carries over subtotals, etc.). The computational theory here is simply the *rules of arithmetic*; these describe what the machine achieves as well as the constraints on it which allow the process within the machine to be defined. At this stage, there may be complete ignorance as to *how* the machine does its arithmetic (Gordon, 1989).

So, in the case of vision, how do we derive properties of the world from images of it? What is being computed and why is this a useful piece of information to compute? In what way is a 2-D image related to the 3-D world? What are the constraints which make it possible to recover the properties of the scene from the related image (how is it interpreted)? For example, how is it possible to recover the shape of a rotating body from fleeting images? How is stereoscopic vision possible? (Gardner, 1985).

Vision must start with an image on the retina but what we experience is the external world. Light stops at the retina and from then on all there is are nervous impulses—there are no pictures in our head (but that's what we experience). It follows that this neural activity is representing the world *symbolically* and these symbolic representations of various aspects of the world, initially obtained from the retinal image, are combined into the description we call seeing (Marr, 1982).

(b) *Algorithm*. The key question here is, 'How can the computational theory be implemented?' (Marr, 1982). In particular, how are the input and output represented and what is the algorithm (precise set of rules or procedures) for the transformation of input into output? For the cash register, input and output are represented in decimal notation, but exactly what does it do in order to convert input and output? Whatever the algorithms turn out to be in vision, Marr wanted them to be consistent with what we know about neuropsychology and psychophysics.

(c) *Hardware implementation*. 'How can the representation and algorithm be realized physically? (Marr, 1982). How does the machine actually work? It might contain interlocking cogs (like old-fashioned mechanical calculators) or (most likely) it uses a series of electronic switches. We want to know how the physical components actually operate.

WORKING OUT THE COMPUTATIONAL THEORY

Marr believed that the theory should see the main job of vision as deriving a representation of *shape*. Vision can do much more than this, of course, but he believed that information about brightness, colour, etc. is of secondary importance. So how is the visual system able to derive reliable information regarding the shapes of objects in the real world from information contained in the retinal image?

His answer was that vision is organized as an information-processing system comprising a series of successive stages which represent independent visual *modules*:

> ... vision is considered to be a sequence of processes that are successively extracting visual information from one representation, organizing it and making it explicit in another representation to be used by other processes. Viewed in this way it is conceptually convenient to treat vision as computationally *modular* and *sequential* ... (Mayhew and Frisby, 1984; quoted in Frisby, 1986)

The four basic stages of visual representation are summarized in Box 9.1

Box 9.1   *The four stages (modules) of Marr's Computational Theory of Vision*

The Image (or Grey-Level Description)

Its function is to represent intensity of light at each point in the retinal image, so as to discover regions in the image and their boundaries. Regions and boundaries are parts of images—*not* part of things in the world, so this represents the starting point of the process of seeing.

Primal Sketch

Its function is to make explicit the properties of the 2-D image, from the kinds of intensity change within a scene (areas of grey/relative brightness as opposed to darkness) to a primitive representation of the local geometry. It describes the scene in terms of a vast collection of features, such as edges, lines and blobs and is the initial symbolic representation of the 'raw information' contained in the image. It is formed by processing mechanisms which are completely independent of any 'high level' knowledge about objects. Changes in intensity occur in a scene at the point where edges and changes in surface contour are likely to occur, so the primal sketch makes possible the detection of boundaries in the image. (It provides a more useful, less cluttered, description of the image—hence 'sketch').

$2\frac{1}{2}$-D Sketch

Its function is to make explicit the orientation and depth of visible surfaces, as if a 'picture' of the world is beginning to emerge. It is no longer an image because it contains information about things in the world which provide the image. But what's emerging is organized only from the viewpoint of the observer—it is not a description of a stable, external environment which is independent of some observer, so it cannot explain perceived constancy of shape despite movement on the observer's part. (Information about absolute distance of surfaces from the observer is incomplete/inaccurate, hence '$2\frac{1}{2}$-D'.)

3-D Model Representation

Its function is to make shapes and their spatial organization explicit as belonging to particular 3-D objects, independently of any particular position or orientation on the retina (ie independent of any particular observer). The observer now has a model of the external world. Knowledge about the nature and construction of the object is now made use of ('top-down' processing). It can be thought of as 'object recognition'.

3-D MODEL REPRESENTATION AND OBJECT RECOGNITION

Having referred to the 3-D model representation as involving top-down processes (drawing on stored knowledge about what objects look like), Marr, in fact, argued that in *many* cases, 3-D structures can be derived from the $2\frac{1}{2}$-D sketch using only general principles of the kind used in the earlier stages. His basic insight rests on the simple observation that *stick-figure representations* (especially of animals and plants) are easy to recognize (Garnham, 1991). The brain automatically transposes the contours derived from the 2½-D sketch onto axes of symmetry which resemble stick figures composed of pipe cleaners (Gardner, 1985). The 3-D model will comprise a unique description of any object one can distinguish—the same object should always produce the same unique description no matter what the angle of viewing.

But how are these stick figures related to the people, animals and plants, etc. we usually see?

Marr argued that peoples' bodies, etc. can be represented as jointed cylinders, or, more realistically, as *generalized cylinders* which change their size along their length (Fig. 9.15). He then showed that the cylinders which compose an object can be computed from the 2½-D sketch: the lines running down the centre of these cylinders (important

Figure 9.15 *Cylinders of various sizes can be combined to represent the shapes of various (parts of) objects). (From Marr, D. and Nishikara, H. K. (1978). Representation and recognition of the spatial organization of three-dimensional shapes.* Proceedings of the Royal Society of London, *200 (Series B), 269–294)*

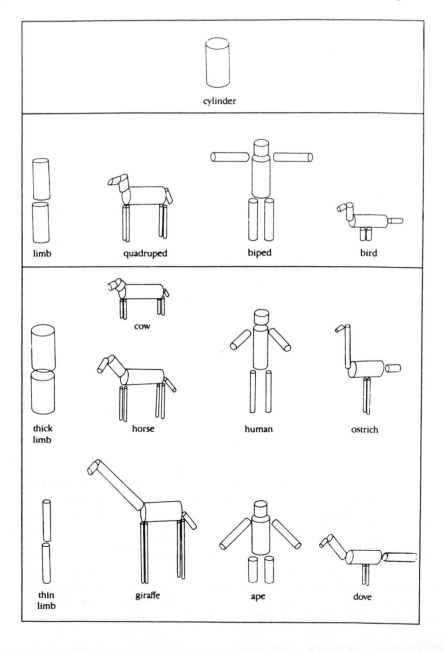

cylinder

limb   quadruped   biped   bird

cow

thick limb   horse   human   ostrich

thin limb   giraffe   ape   dove

in the recognition process) make up the stick figures.

Once a generalized cylinder representation of objects in a scene has been computed, it can be compared with stored representations of objects in a *catalogue of 3-D models*, where objects are represented in 'standard' orientations (Garnham, 1991).

EVALUATION OF MARR'S THEORY

1) Marr attempted to integrate knowledge from neuropsychology and artificial intelligence because this was necessary to understand how (visual) perception works. He argued strongly that studying the hardware (whether it is cortical cells such as the simple, complex and hypercomplex cells discussed in Chapter 8, or computer components) is itself insufficient—it is understanding the nature of the *task* the hardware is performing which is crucial (ie how does the hardware implement the computational theory?

> Emphasis on devising well-founded methods for solving visual process tasks irrespective of the design of any particular hardware for implementing those methods is *the* salient feature of Marr's approach...
> (Frisby, 1986)

Without this topmost level of analysis (the computational theory) we shall never have a deep understanding of the biology of the visual system, because we shall never know *why* the hardware it possesses is designed (evolved) that way. The basic idea that the *goal* of vision should feature large in any explanation of vision is obviously a form of top-down processing.

2) Gordon (1989) says that Marr's work is regarded by many as the most important development in perception theory in recent years. But the account of the 3-D model is clearly much weaker than the earlier stages. Gordon sees this as not surprising since the problems are much more formidable:

> ... whilst his ideas seem quite plausible in terms of machine recognition of objects, the evidence that this is how a living visual system might function is not at all compelling ... to date, the only occasion when machine systems do recognize objects is when they are operating in artificially constrained worlds—worlds typically comprising only blocks or prisms.
> (Gordon, 1989)

3) While clearly guided by many top-down considerations, much of his detailed work concentrated on bottom-up processes (eg those involved in contour extraction and texture discrimination), and these are the most convincing. However, when he speculates about processes involving knowledge of the world and acting in a top-down way, his ideas become much less convincing; for example, do we really carry in our heads those generalized cylinders which he claims are the 'primitives' for 3-D shape perception? How could we test this possibility?

4) Gardner (1985) largely agrees with Gordon's assessment. Most of Marr's account focuses on the steps prior to recognition of real objects in the real world ('... the most central part of perception ...'):

> ... the procedures he outlined for object recognition may prove applicable chiefly to the perception of figures of a certain sort—for example, the mammalian body, which lends itself to decomposition in terms of generalized cylindrical forms. (Gardner, 1985)

5) Despite these misgivings, Gordon (1989) concludes that Marr's *'Vision'* (1982) is a, '... landmark in the history of perceptual theory'.

THE INFLUENCE OF SET ON PERCEPTION

Many very important and famous studies of perception relate, directly or indirectly, to the concept of *set*, one which lies at the heart of the view that perception is an active process involving selection, inference and interpretation (ie the empiricist approach). We shall see that Bruner is referred to several times in this regard—his name appears in Table 9.1, along with Gregory and Neisser—as one of the leading top-down theorists.

Allport defined perceptual set as:

> ... a perceptual bias or predisposition or readiness to perceive particular features of a stimulus. (Allport, 1955)

That is, the tendency to perceive or notice some aspects of the available sense-data and ignore others.

Bartlett defined a schema as:

> ... an active organization of past reactions and of past experiences which must always be supposed to be operating in any well-adapted organic response. (Bartlett, 1932)

and Vernon defined schemas as:

> ... persistent and deep-rooted, well-organized classifications of ways of perceiving, thinking and believing. (Vernon, 1955)

Vernon maintains that set works in two ways: first as a *selector*, whereby the perceiver has certain expectations which help focus attention on particular aspects of the incoming sensory stimulation; and, secondly, as an *interpreter*, whereby the perceiver knows how to deal with the selected data, how to classify, understand and name it and what inferences to draw from it.

WHAT DETERMINES SET?

There are several factors which can influence or induce set, most of which are to do with the perceiver (*perceiver* or *organismic variables*), some of which are to do with the nature of the stimulus or the conditions under which it is being perceived (*stimulus* or *situational variables*). However, whether they arise primarily within the perceiver or from outside, they only indirectly influence perception through directly influencing set which, as such, is of course itself a perceiver variable or characteristic (Fig. 9.16).

CONTEXT, INSTRUCTIONS AND OTHER SITUATIONAL VARIABLES

Chapman (1932) gave a classic demonstration of how instructions can induce set. Subjects saw a series of cards on which were printed several capital letters; the cards varied according to: (i) the number of letters (four to eight); (ii) the identity of the letters; and (iii) their spatial arrangement. They were presented tachistoscopically (ie for very brief measured periods of time) so that ability to recognize them would be less than perfect and set was manipulated by instructing subjects to report on

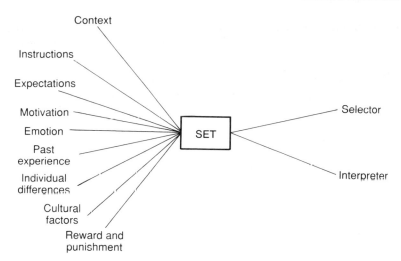

Figure 9.16 The indirect influence of perceiver and stimulus variables on perception through their direct influence on set

one of the three characteristics of a card on each exposure (number of letters, which they were, and spatial arrangement). Compared with subjects given instructions after exposure (which, presumably, had no influence on set), those given instructions before exposure made fewer errors, on all three attributes.

The way that instructions create set is, essentially, through inducing *expectations* on the perceiver's part. There are many examples of selective perception outside the laboratory where set is a key variable: a great deal of occupational and professional training can be seen as equipping the trainee with a system of sets which will enhance performance in various ways, such as a policeman being trained to notice and remember car registration numbers, or the physical characteristics of (potential) law-breakers.

Often, there is an interaction between *expectation* and *context*, as in the letter/number series below:

$$\text{E D C \, 13 \, A} \qquad \text{16 \, 15 \, 14 \, 13 \, 12}$$

The physical stimulus '13' is the same in each case but is perceived differently because of the context in which it appears; we expect it to be a letter B when in a sequence of other letters and the number 13 when in a sequence of other numbers (Minturn and Bruner, 1951).

We may fail to notice printing errors or writing errors for the same reason, for example, 'The cat sat on the map and licked its whiskers'. If you can't spot the deliberate mistake, look at Figure 9.17. What do you read in the triangles? What words are actually written in the triangles? What you perceive and what is physically present should, in each case, be different.

These last three examples demonstrate the interaction between

Figure 9.17 What is actually written in the triangles?

expectation and *past experience*; a classic experimental demonstration of this is the study by Bruner and Postman (1949). Subjects were presented with unusual playing cards, ie with the colour and suit combinations reversed (eg black hearts and red spades). The cards were presented tachistoscopically and, not surprisingly perhaps, at very short exposures the subjects tended to report that the cards were normal (basing their reports on one feature and assuming that the other matched it). But at longer exposures, they sometimes reported 'brown or purple hearts' or 'cards in black with red edges', which suggested a genuine perceptual distortion ('compromise perceptions', an almost literal blending of stimulus information and stored information).

Allport (1955) distinguished six types of motivational–emotional influence on perception: (i) bodily needs (normally studied as the effects of physiological deprivation); (ii) reward and punishment; (iii) emotional connotation; (iv) individual values; (v) personality; and (vi) the value of objects.

Two principles of perception related to the concept of set are *perceptual accentuation/sensitization*, whereby things that are relevant or salient for us are perceived as larger, brighter, more attractive, more valuable, etc. and *perceptual defence*, whereby things that are threatening or anxiety-provoking in some way are more difficult to perceive at a conscious level (McGinnies, 1949).

EFFECTS OF EMOTIONAL CONNOTATION— PERCEPTUAL DEFENCE

McGinnies (1949) coined the term 'perceptual defence' to refer to the findings from laboratory experiments that subliminally-perceived words (below the threshold of consciousness) which evoke unpleasant emotions take longer to perceive at a conscious level than neutral words.

Perceptual defence is, in turn, linked to the more general—and less defence-orientated—concept of subliminal perception, ie:

> . . . perception occurring even though the stimulus input is presented so briefly or at such low intensity as to be below the threshold of conscious awareness. (Eysenck and Keane, 1990)

A number of studies have shown that recognition can occur before perception enters conscious awareness ('autonomic discrimination without awareness'—the 'subception effect'). Somehow, enough information about the stimulus is transmitted to the autonomic nervous system to determine different levels of GSR but not enough reaches the brain centres responsible for correct verbal identification. Another way this phenomenon has been studied is through what cognitive neuropsychologists call 'blindsight' (Weiskrantz, 1986; see Chapter 8). Eysenck and Keane (1990) claim that blindsight seems to provide very strong evidence, '. . . that extensive perceptual processing can occur despite an absence of conscious awareness'.

Dixon (1971) reviewed a number of studies which showed that verbal stimuli which are too quick or too dim to be consciously perceived, will none the less affect the subject's associative processes. It has been found that: (i) associations following the subliminal perception of a word were linked to its meaning (Marcel and Patterson, 1978); (ii) subjects' self-ratings of anxiety increased following the subliminal presentations of unpleasant words, such as 'cancer' (Tyler et al, 1978); (iii) GSRs increase to the subliminal presentation of emotive picture stimuli, such as a breast (O'Grady, 1977).

McGinnies (1949) presented subjects, on a tachistoscope, with eleven emotionally neutral words (such as 'apple', 'broom' and 'glass') and seven emotionally-arousing, taboo words (such as 'whore', 'penis', 'rape', 'bitch'). Each word was presented for increasingly long durations until it was named and there was a significantly higher recognition threshold for the taboo words (ie, it took longer for subjects to name them). The taboo words also produced a greater GSR and more of them were distorted when being named.

A number of studies have challenged McGinnies's conclusion regarding perceptual defence. Howes and Solomon (1950) argued that subjects' higher threshold for taboo words was due to their greater reluctance to say them out loud without more confidence in their guesses. Some support for this criticism comes from a study by Aronfreed et al (1953) in which female subjects were tested by a male experimenter. Higher recognition thresholds and greater GSRs were produced for the taboo words compared with those produced when other combinations of subject and experimenter were used. (Note that McGinnies found no significant sex difference either in perceptual defence or emotionality during the pre-recognition period.) Support also comes from Bitterman and Kniffin (1953) who found that there was no perceptual defence effect if subjects were allowed to write down their answers instead of saying them aloud. The perceptual defence effect could also be eliminated by warning subjects that taboo words would be shown (Lacy et al, 1953; Postman et al, 1953).

However, Beier and Cowen (1953) found that even when subjects were warned about sexual words, most still perceived them more slowly and they also reported that they did *not* consciously stop themselves from uttering them.

Another criticism is to do with the lower frequency of occurrence of the taboo words in written English, ie they are less familiar than the neutral words and this *alone* could explain the differences in recognition threshold (Solomon and Howes, 1951). They obtained a list of the frequency of about 30,000 words in print and chose 60 (all non-taboo) of varying frequencies and determined their recognition thresholds. Using a similar procedure to McGinnies, they found a high negative correlation (−0.79) between frequency of word in print and recognition threshold. In a more direct test of the word-frequency explanation, Postman et al (1952) determined how frequent the taboo words were in print and matched them with neutral words of the same frequency; they found no support for perceptual defence—in fact, the threshold for the taboo words was significantly *lower* (probably due to underestimation of the taboo word frequency).

However, none of these studies measured GSR. Cowen and Beier (1954), on the other hand, demonstrated the emotional effects of sexual words *independently* of their frequency. Again, it is difficult to estimate the actual familiarity of individual subjects with taboo words just from their frequency in written English; several words used in these various experiments are sexual slang ('balls', 'screw') and how familiar subjects are will depend on their particular social experience (Vernon, 1962). To get around these problems, Lazarus and McCleary (1951) created traumatic or neutral stimuli by pairing five nonsense syllables with shock during a training period (while another five were not paired). After a sufficient number of trials, the shock-paired syllables became threatening to the subjects, despite there being no threat involved in their being uttered. (This got round the problem of response-withholding.) Also, all the nonsense-syllables (by definition) were equally unfamiliar. Following training, recognition thresholds were measured in the usual way, plus GSR. On those trials when subjects made incorrect guesses, there was a higher GSR to shock-paired than neutral syllables, strongly supporting the idea of automatic discrimination without awareness (and so, indirectly, of perceptual defence).

But is perceptual defence a truly *perceptual* phenomenon or is the increased recognition threshold for taboo words due to some kind of *response bias*? (Eysenck, 1984). Hardy and Legge (1968) asked subjects to detect the presence of a faint auditory stimulus while watching a screen on which emotive or neutral words were presented subliminally. Though nearly all failed to notice that any words had been presented, the auditory threshold was *higher* when emotive words were being presented. This effect was due to reduction in sensitivity to stimulation as opposed to a shift in response bias—the experimental design effectively precluded any report suppression. Hardy and Legge concluded that perceptual defence is a genuine perceptual phenomenon.

However, there remains a paradox. According to Howie (1952), when we talk about perceptual defence we are speaking of, 'perceptual processing as somehow being both a process of knowing and a process of avoiding knowing', ie how is it that the perceiver can selectively defend him/herself against an emotional stimulus *unless* he/she has already perceived and identified it? (Eysenck, 1984).

The concept of subliminal perception in general, and perceptual defence in particular, becomes more acceptable if perception is thought of *not* as a unitary process but one involving multiple processing stages and mechanisms, with consciousness perhaps representing just the final level of processing (Erdelyi, 1974; Dixon, 1981). Put another way, consciousness may not be essential to cognition (Eysenck, 1984). As Baddeley says:

> . . . there is by now relatively substantial evidence to suggest that a subject's behaviour may be influenced by information that he is not able to report consciously . . . (Baddeley, 1990)

EFFECT OF THE VALUE OF OBJECTS

This relates to the phenomenon of perceptual accentuation/sensitization. In a famous study, Bruner and Goodman (1947) required children to turn a knob which controlled a circular patch of light on a screen, so that the patch of light was the same size as coins of various denominations. All children tended to over-estimate the coins (compared with a control group who estimated the size of cardboard discs) but children from poor families did so to a greater extent than wealthy children. Presumably, money is perceived as more valuable by children who have less of it.

In a replication study, Carter and Schooler (1949) found that over-estimation of coins only occurred when judgements were made from memory, not when direct matching was required; this was in fact the opposite of what Bruner and Goodman had found. Ashley et al (1951) confirmed the original findings when subjects were hypnotized into believing that they were rich or poor.

Finally, Solley and Haigh (1958) asked 4- to 8-year-olds to draw pictures of Santa Claus at intervals during the month before Christmas and the two weeks following. As Christmas approached, so the pictures became larger, as did Santa's sack of toys, but afterwards his toys shrank and so did Santa.

DEPTH PERCEPTION

As we saw when discussing his theory, Gibson believed that many cues to depth are included among the physical invariants which are directly perceived—they are included among the *pictorial* cues below.

Depth cues can be classified in terms of: (i) *monocular–binocular*; and (ii) *pictorial–non-pictorial* (or secondary–primary) and these are summarized in Table 9.3. *Monocular* cues are those that can be detected with

	MONOCULAR	BINOCULAR
Pictorial (secondary)	1. Relative size 2. Relative brightness 3. Superimposition (overlap) 4. Linear perspective 5. Aerial perspective 6. Height in the horizontal plane 7. Light and shadow 8. Texture gradient 9. Motion parallax	
Non-Pictorial (Primary)	Accommodation	1. Retinal disparity 2. Convergence (see Chapter 8)

Table 9.3 A classification of depth cues

one eye only and so are not primarily dependent on biological processes—except in the case of accommodation. The vast majority of monocular cues are *pictorial*, that is, they are features of the visual field itself (and they are also *static*) but *binocular* cues depend upon the structure and function of the *two* eyes.

MONOCULAR—PICTORIAL CUES

(a) *Relative size*. In an array of different-sized objects, smaller ones are usually seen as more distant, (particularly if they are known to have a constant size).
(b) *Relative brightness*. Brighter objects normally appear to be nearer.
(c) *Superimposition* (or overlap). An object which blocks the view of another is seen as being nearer.
(d) *Linear perspective*. Parallel lines (eg railway tracks) appear to converge as they recede into the distance.
(e) *Aerial perspective*. Objects at a great distance appear to have a different colour (eg, the hazy, bluish, tint of distant mountains).

(f) *Height in the horizontal plane*. When looking across a flat expanse (eg across the sea), objects which are more distant seem 'higher' (ie closer to the horizon) than nearer objects, which seem 'lower' and closer to the ground.

(g) *Light and shadow*. Three-dimensional objects produce variations in light and shade (eg we normally assume that light comes from above).

(h) *Texture gradient*. Sand, for instance, is perceived as being more textured close-to but as it stretches away from us it looks more uniform, smooth and fine-grained.

(i) *Motion parallax*. This is the major *dynamic* cue to depth (either monocular or binocular) and refers to the speed of apparent movement of objects nearer or further away from us. Generally, objects further away seem to move more slowly than nearer objects (eg telegraph poles seen out of a train window flash by when they are close to the track).

MONOCULAR—NON-PICTORIAL CUES

Accommodation. Refers to the change in the shape of the lens depending on the distance of the object—it flattens for distant objects and thickens for closer ones (and provides depth cues within about 4 feet).

BINOCULAR—NON-PICTORIAL CUES

(a) *Retinal disparity*. Because our eyes are (approximately) 6 cm apart, they each receive slightly different retinal images; the superimposition of these two images is *stereoscopic vision*. (Close each eye in turn and you'll see the difference!) Related to this is convergence.

(b) *Convergence*. Refers to the simultaneous orienting of both eyes towards the same object—when we look at a distant object (25 feet or more) the line of vision of our two eyes is parallel but the closer the object, the more our eyes turn inwards towards each other. (If the object is too close, we go 'cross-eyed' and cannot focus properly.)

PATTERN RECOGNITION—WHAT MAKES A 'T' A 'T'?

In a sense, pattern recognition is the central problem of perception and is almost synonymous with perception itself—how are we able to recognize, identify and categorize objects? What are the processes by which sensory information is converted into a psychologically meaningful perception?

Eysenck (1984) defines pattern recognition as 'assigning meaning to visual input by identifying the objects in the visual field' and believes that the ease with which we normally succeed in identifying objects in fact conceals the, 'amazing flexibility of the human perceptual system as it copes with a multitude of different stimuli', a remarkable achievement.

A common way of illustrating the problem is to think of all the different ways in which a particular stimulus might be presented; for instance, letters of the alphabet, as in Figure 9.18. What do all these

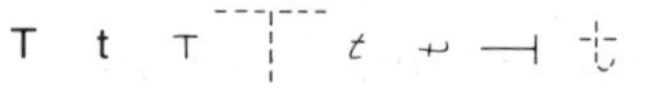

T t τ Ţ *t* ⊣ ⊣ Ṫ

Figure 9.18 *What makes a 'T' a 'T'?*

marks on the page have in common? To say that obviously they are all letter 'T's is too easy and, in a sense, begs the question. How are we able to recognize them as 'T's, what makes them identifiable in this way, what makes a 'T' a 'T'? These are what theories of pattern recognition (PR) attempt to answer.

THEORIES OF PATTERN RECOGNITION

There are three major kinds of theory: (i) *template-matching*; (ii) *prototype*; and (iii) *feature detection*.

TEMPLATE MATCHING HYPOTHESIS

As with all pattern recognition (PR) theories, the template matching hypothesis (TMH) sees PR as the comparison of information which has just stimulated the sense organs (retained in sensory memory) with the relatively permanent information acquired during our lifetime, ie a match is made between the incoming sensory information and something in our long-term stores. But what exactly is this something? According to the TMH, the memory system stores a large number of constructs or internal representations (*templates*) and we compare incoming stimulus information with these miniature copies of previously presented patterns or objects. But if there is an unlimited number of ways of presenting the letter 'T' for example, it follows that there would have to be an unlimited number of templates, one for each *particular* instance of the letter.

The TMH seems unable to explain how we could recognize even slightly unfamiliar patterns, and not only would the number of templates required be neurologically impossible, because it would have to be infinite, but the hypothesis ends up *assuming* what it is trying to explain (Donahoe and Wessels, 1980). (Incidentally, template-matching is the basic technique used by computers to 'read', which is one reason why they are so bad at recognizing any slight deviation from the highly specific configurations in their memories—see Chapter 14. It is also the basis of price-coding in supermarkets—each packet has a special bar code which identifies the item for which the computer supplies the price; this is then entered on the cash-register tape.)

PROTOTYPE THEORIES

Instead of proposing that what we store is a template for each individual pattern, we could suggest a smaller number of *prototypes*, 'abstract forms representing the basic elements of a set of stimuli' (Eysenck, 1984). Whereas template theories treat each stimulus as a separate entity, prototype theories maintain that similarities between related stimuli play an important part in PR, whereby each stimulus is a member of a *category* of stimuli and shares certain basic properties with other members of the category (Posner, 1969; Read, 1972).

While the idea of a prototype is intuitively appealing, the precise nature of prototypes and the matching process is not very explicit and prototype theories fail to explain how PR is affected by the context as well as by the stimulus itself (Eysenck, 1984). Just what those properties are which are shared by a category of stimuli is what we want to know but what prototype theories fail to tell us; this is where the third type of theory comes into its own.

FEATURE DETECTION THEORIES

By far the most researched and influential theories of PR maintain that each stimulus pattern can be thought of as a configuration of elementary features. Letters of the alphabet, for example, are composed of combinations of about twelve basic features (including straight vertical lines, horizontals and closed curves) so an 'A' may be analysed into two diagonals, one horizontal, a pointed head and an open bottom. The evidence for this is of two main kinds: behavioural and neurological.

Behavioural Studies

A common experimental technique is a visual scanning task in which subjects search lists of letters as rapidly as possible in order to find a specified target letter which occurs in unpredictable positions in the lists. Clearly, finding the target letter involves recognizing a particular pattern and rejecting others and if recognition entails the detection of elementary features, then the task should be more difficult the more features the target and non-target letters have in common.

This was confirmed by Neisser (1964) and Rabbitt (1967). Subjects found 'Z' much faster in a list comprising C, G and O than when M, X and E were the non-target letters. Similarly, Gibson et al (1968) found that it took longer to decide that P and R are different than to distinguish between G and W.

Neurological Studies

There is considerable evidence that the visual systems of a wide variety of vertebrates contain both peripheral (retinal) and central (cortical) cells that respond only to particular features of visual stimuli (Hubel and Wiesel, 1959, 1962, 1963, 1968; Barlow et al, 1972).

As we saw in Chapter 8, Hubel and Wiesel, for example, using cats and monkeys, identified three kinds of cortical cells, simple, complex and hypercomplex. But do these different kinds of cell constitute the feature detectors postulated by feature detection theories?

Marr (1982) tried to construct a computerized feature-detection system and found that the activity in any one cell is too variable and ambiguous to be thought of as feature detection as such; however, it might provide the first step in the analysis of features present in the visual input. Perhaps these neurological detectors are a necessary precondition for any higher-level (cognitive) pattern analysis taking place.

However, there are also some more basic criticisms. Eysenck (1984), for example, argues that feature theories typically assume a *serial* form of processing, with feature extraction being followed by feature combination and, finally, by PR. Hubel and Wiesel (1962) saw the sequence of simple, complex and hypercomplex cells representing a serial flow of information, whereby only particular information is processed at any one time before being passed on to the next level upwards and so on.

However, Lennie (1980) reviewed the literature and concluded that a great deal of non-serial processing takes place in the visual cortex and that the relationship between the three kinds of cell is more complex than originally thought.

An interesting and famous example of non-serial processing is Selfridge's (1959) computer program for the recognition of Morse code and a small set of hand-written letters, which he called *Pandemonium* (the capital of Hell in Milton's *Paradise Lost*). The components are four kinds of *demons*:

(a) *Image demons*, who simply copy the pattern—much as the retina records visual patterns.
(b) *Feature demons*, who analyse the information from the image demons in terms of combinations of features.
(c) *Cognitive demons*, who are specialized for particular letters and will 'scream' according to how much the input from the feature demons matches their special letter.
(d) A *decision demon*, who chooses the 'loudest scream' and, hence, the *name* of the letter.

Because it is able to deal with many options simultaneously (eg is this letter an A, B, C or D, etc.?), Pandemonium is an example of *parallel processing* (as opposed to serial processing).

THE IMPORTANCE OF CONTEXT

A number of writers have pointed out that feature detection theories do not take sufficient account of the *context* and certain perceiver variables, such as expectations (Palmer, 1975; Norman, 1976; Massaro et al, 1978; Eysenck, 1984) and we saw some examples of their influence earlier in this chapter. Clearly, the same features can produce different patterns (especially if they are ambiguous) and different features can produce the same pattern depending on context, which can tell us what patterns are *likely* to be present and hence what to expect. Indeed, we may *fail* to notice the absence of something or a distorted form of a stimulus (eg typographical errors) because of its high predictability.

This influence of context and expectation on the analysis of sensory features illustrates 'top-down' or *conceptually-driven processing*; processing which begins with the elementary features and works 'upwards' towards PR is 'bottom-up' or *data driven* and most feature detection theories to date seem to fall into this latter category.

One effect of context on PR may be to allow a partial and selective analysis of the stimuli to be recognized, ie PR involves selectively attending to some aspects of the presented stimuli but not others. PR and selective attention, therefore, can be seen as closely related (Solso, 1979). We will discuss attention in Chapter 11.

10 Perception: the Nature–Nurture Debate

The heredity–environment (or nature–nurture) aspect of perception has been hotly debated in psychology. This chapter will consider the evidence supporting both sides of the argument.

However, we should not expect any simple answers. As we saw in Chapter 9, perception is a complex set of different but interconnected and overlapping abilities (eg perception of depth, colour and movement) and several sense modalities are involved. To ask whether perception is learnt or innate is to oversimplify the issue. Philosophers, who considered this question long before psychologists began to study it scientifically, tended to oversimplify their questions and, consequently, produced oversimplified answers, which were of two distinct types.

1) The *nativists* believed that we are born with certain capacities to perceive the world in particular ways; these capacities are often immature or incomplete at birth but develop gradually thereafter. Psychologists of a nativist persuasion believe that this development after birth proceeds through the genetically-determined process of maturation, with learning playing only a minor role—or none at all. This type of philosophy is best illustrated by the Gestalt school of psychology.

2) The *empiricists* maintained that all our knowledge and abilities are acquired through experience, that is, are learned (the word 'empirical' means 'through the senses'). As we saw (Chapter 9), *transactionalists* are one school of psychology embodying the empiricist philosophy.

Most present-day psychologists would consider themselves neither nativists nor empiricists but rather *interactionists*, believing that we may be born with capacities to perceive the world in certain ways but that stimulation and environmental influences in general are crucial in determining how—and even whether—these capacities actually develop. Different perceptual abilities may be more or less affected by genetic or environmental factors, but it is certain that any perceptual ability is the product of an interaction between both sets of factors; both are always involved, although it is not always obvious exactly what part they play.

The Study of Perceptual Development

What kind of evidence is relevant?

1) The *perceptual abilities* of *newborn babies* represent the most direct way of investigating the nature–nurture issue. In general, the earlier a particular ability appears, the more likely it is to be under the influence

of genetic factors. However, the fact that it develops some time after birth does not necessarily mean it has been learnt, as it could take time to mature. There are other special difficulties involved in studying speechless subjects, as we shall see below.

2) *Animal experiments* often involve depriving animals in some way of normal sensory and perceptual stimulation and recording the long-term effects of this deprivation on their sensory and perceptual abilities. Some studies reverse this and actually provide the animals with 'extra' experience and stimulation. Still others study the animal's brain to see how it controls perceptual abilities. From a research point of view, the main advantage of studying animals is that we can manipulate their environments in ways which are not permissible with human subjects. Deprivation studies can tell us how much and what kinds of early experience are necessary for normal perceptual development in those species being studied, but we must be very cautious about generalizing these findings to humans (and we must be aware of the ethical objections to such research—see Chapter 3).

3) *Studies of human cataract patients* represent the human counterpart to animal deprivation studies. These patients have been deprived of normal visual experience through a physical defect, rather than through experimental manipulation or interference, and constitute a kind of 'natural experiment'. Their vision is restored through surgical removal of the cataract and the abilities that are evident immediately after removal of the bandages are normally taken to be innate and unlearned. However, there are special problems involved here too: generalizing from 'unusual' adults to 'normal' babies can be hazardous and it is not always obvious whether abilities that do not appear have to be learned or are 'present' but not being used.

4) In *studies of perceptual adaptation* or *readjustment*, human subjects wear special goggles which distort the visual world in various ways. If they can adapt to such a distorted-looking world then human 'perceptual habits' cannot be as fixed or rigid as they would be if they were under genetic control—perhaps the way we perceive is itself originally learned. However, we need to ask what kind of adaptation is taking place: is it actually perceptual or is it merely motor, that is, learning to move about successfully in a very different-looking environment? If the latter is the case, then we cannot conclude necessarily that our perceptual 'habits' are habits at all (ie learned in the first place) but only that we are good at changing our body movements to 'match' what we see.

5) *Cross-cultural studies* attempt to test whether or not the way that we, in Western culture, perceive things is universal, that is, perceived in the same way by people who live in cultures very different from our own. The most common method of testing is to present members of different cultural groups with the same stimulus material, usually visual illusions.

A major advantage of cross-cultural studies is that they act as a buffer against generalizing from a comparatively small sample of the earth's population (Price-Williams, 1966), ie unless we study a particular process in different cultures, we cannot be sure what contributory influences are on that process. So, if we find consistent differences between different cultural groups, unless we have good, independent reasons for believing that these differences are biologically caused, then we are forced to attribute them to environmental factors, be they social customs, ecological, linguistic or some combination of these. Such studies, therefore, enable us to discover the extent to which perceiving is structured by the nervous system (and so common to all human beings) and to what extent by experience. However, as we shall see, psychologists cannot agree as to the key features of such cultural experience.

AN OVERVIEW OF THE EVIDENCE

Having said that most psychologists regard perceptual abilities as the product of an interaction between genetic factors (nature) and environmental factors (nurture), some attempts have been made to test directly the merits of the nativist and empiricist positions and we shall discuss some of these when we look at the work of Bower, with infants.

By the same token, most of the evidence which supports the nativist theory derives from infant studies. As we said above, the earlier a particular ability appears, the less opportunity there has been for learning to have occurred and so the more likely it is that the ability is under genetic control.

Although the bulk of the evidence supports the interactionist position, there are grounds for concluding that relatively simple perceptual abilities are more under genetic control and less susceptible to environmental influence, while the situation is reversed in the case of more complex abilities. The most clear-cut demonstration of this comes from human cataract patients and so we shall start with these.

STUDIES OF HUMAN CATARACT PATIENTS

These really represent the 'natural' counterpart in humans of the animal experiments described below. They are based on case-studies of patients who have undergone an operation for the removal of cataracts to 'restore' their sight (a cataract is a film over the lens of the eye and can either be present at birth or develop any time afterwards). Most of the evidence comes from the work of von Senden, a German doctor who, in 1932, reported on 65 cases of people who had undergone cataract-removal surgery; the earliest case was reported in 1700, the latest in 1928.

Von Senden's original data was taken up again by Hebb in 1949, who analysed the findings in terms of: (i) *figural unity*, the ability to detect the presence of a figure or stimulus; and (ii) *figural identity*, being able to name or in some other way identify the object, to 'say' what it is. Hebb concluded that while (i) seemed to be innate, (ii) seemed to require learning.

Initially, cataract patients are typically bewildered by an array of visual stimuli (rather like the 'blooming, buzzing confusion' which William James believed was the perceptual experience of newborn babies). However, they can distinguish figure from ground (ie some object from its background), fixate objects, scan them and follow moving objects with their eyes. But they cannot identify by sight alone those objects which are already familiar through touch (and this includes faces), distinguish between various geometrical shapes without counting the corners or tracing the outline with their fingers, or say which of two sticks is longer without feeling them (although they can tell there is a difference).

They also fail to show perceptual constancy. For example, even after visual identification has occurred (ie things are recognized through sight alone) there may be little generalization to situations other than that in which the object was originally recognized, eg a lump of sugar held in someone's hand may not be identified as such when suspended from a piece of string. Another example would be the failure to recognize a triangle as being the same geometrical shape when its white side is turned over to reveal a red side or when viewed under different lighting conditions. (Interestingly, as we shall see later in the chapter, Bower believes that size and shape constancy are probably innate; Hebb's findings suggest this is not so.)

So the more simple ability of figural unity seems to be available very soon after cataract removal and seems not to be dependent on prior visual experience, while the more complex figural identity seems to require a long period of training. Hebb believes that this is how these two aspects of perception normally develop. Further evidence comes from the case of S. B. (Box 10.1).

Box 10.1   The Case of S. B. (Gregory and Wallace, 1963)

S. B. was 52 when he received his sight after a corneal graft operation. His judgement of size and distance were good, provided that he was familiar with the objects in question. He could recognize objects visually if he was already familiar with them through touch while blind so, unlike most of the 65 cases analysed by Hebb, he displayed good cross-modal transfer, ie recognition through one sense modality (touch) being substituted by another (vision). However, he seemed to have great difficulty in identify-ing objects visually if he was not already familiar with them in this way: a year after his operation he still could not draw the front of a bus although the rest of the drawing was very well executed (Fig. 10.1). S. B. was never able to use his new-found ability to see its fullest extent; for instance, he did not bother to turn on the light at night but would sit in the dark all evening.

As the months passed, it became clear that S. B. was in some ways like a newborn baby when it came to recognizing objects and events by sight alone. For instance, he found it impossible to judge distances by sight alone—he knew what windows were, from touching them both from inside a room and from outside (while standing on the ground). But, of course, he had never been able to look out from a top-floor window and he thought, 'he would be able to touch the ground below the window with his feet if he lowered himself by his hands' (Gregory and Wallace, 1963) The window in question was the one in his hospital room—40 feet above the ground!

He never learnt to interpret facial expressions such as smiles and frowns, although he could infer a person's mood from the sound of their voice.

Figure 10.1 This was drawn after S. B. had had some experience of sighted travel. Basically it shows the parts he knew by touch. But clearly he had also, by this time, noticed the bright advertisement for Typhoo Tea on the side of the bus

---

Although these 65 cases seem to underline the importance of experience as far as all but the most simple perceptual abilities are concerned, there are certain problems involved in interpreting the results:

1)   Adult patients are not the same as babies; while the sensory systems of babies are all relatively undeveloped, adults have other well-developed

sensory modalities which tend to compensate for the lack of vision (touch and hearing in particular). These other channels may actually hinder visual learning because the patient, in order to use vision, may have to actually 'un-learn' previous experience. As people tend to find it easier to use the channel they already know best, or use most often, S. B.'s ability to recognize familiar objects through vision alone but continued preference for touch over vision may reflect this tendency to stick with what is familiar rather than experiment with the unknown. This may be a safer conclusion to draw than Hebb's, which is that figural identity is (normally) largely learned.

2)   It seems that, traditionally, cataract patients have not been very adequately prepared for their 'new world of vision'; their resulting confusion and general emotional distress following the operation may result in a rather inaccurate picture of what they can and cannot actually see. Referring to S. B. again, when blind he would cross the street on his own, but once he could see the traffic it frightened him so much that he refused to cross on his own. In fact, he died three years after his operation, at least partially from depression. (Depression was also common amongst von Senden's cases.)

3)   We do not know what physical deterioration of the visual system may have occurred during the years of blindness and so cannot be sure that the absence of figural identity is due to lack of visual stimulation and learning (which Hebb believes are responsible) rather than to some physical damage.

4)   The reliability of the case histories themselves is open to doubt; presumably the standards for reporting in 1700 were not as strict as they are today, so that there is great variability in the ages of the patients when they underwent surgery, and when their cataracts first appeared, hence in the amount of visual experience prior to the defect.

ANIMAL EXPERIMENTS

Riesen (1947) deprived one group of chimps of light by raising them in darkness, except for several 45-second periods of exposure to light while they were being fed; this continued until they were sixteen months old, when they were compared with a group of normally-reared chimps. The deprived group showed markedly inferior perceptual abilities when tested at sixteen months. While they did show pupil constriction to light and were startled by sudden, intense illumination, they did not blink in response to threatening movements made towards their faces or show any interest in their toys unless they accidentally touched them with some part of their bodies.

As Weiskrantz (1956) pointed out, the visual deficiencies in the deprived group were probably due to failure of the retinas to develop properly; when the retina is not stimulated by light, fewer of the retinal cells develop and the visual cortex too may begin to degenerate. So, Riesen's experiment may show only that a certain amount of light is physically necessary to maintain the visual system and allow it to mature normally. In an effort to overcome these objections to his original study, Riesen later (1965) reared three chimps from birth to seven months of age, under three different conditions:

(i) *Debi* spent the whole time in darkness;
(ii) *Kova* spent $1\frac{1}{2}$ hours per day exposed to diffuse or unpatterned light by wearing translucent goggles; the rest of the time was spent in darkness;
(iii) *Lad* was raised in normal lighting conditions.

As expected, only Debi suffered retinal damage. Lad was no different, perceptually, from any other normally-reared chimp. It was Kova who was of special interest because, while she did not suffer any retinal damage, she was only exposed to unpatterned light, so that she did not see 'objects' as such but only patches of light, different colours and brightnesses—not distinguishable shapes or patterns. She was noticeably retarded. For example, she needed six days of training (receiving two electric shocks per day from a yellow and black striped disc) before she even whimpered when the disc was shown. She was also very slow to follow a moving object with just her eyes.

Riesen also fitted translucent goggles to monkeys, chimps and kittens for the first three months of their lives. Some simple perceptual abilities remained intact, such as differentiating colours, size and brightness, but more complex abilities did not, eg following a moving object, differentiating between geometrical shapes, perceiving depth and distinguishing a moving object from a stationary one. Riesen's studies as a whole suggest that:

(a) Light is necessary for normal physical development of the visual system (at least in chimps, some monkeys and kittens).
(b) Patterned light is also necessary for the normal development of some of the complex visual abilities (in those species).

Therefore, environmental stimulation of certain kinds seems to be essential for normal perceptual development. If perception were wholly innate, environmental factors (over and above those which can actually harm the developing organism or actively prevent maturation from taking place) should not have any effect; Riesen has shown, however, that they do.

Other animal experiments have also shown the impact of early experience on perceptual abilities.

Hubel and Wiesel (1962) used cats reared in full or partial blindfolds (translucent goggles); the receptive fields of the latter failed to develop normally (see Chapter 8). In a later study, Hubel (1979) found evidence that the brain itself can be affected by visual deprivation. He surgically closed either the left or right eyelid of several monkeys when they were two weeks old. This reduced the amount of light striking the retina; the eyelid remained closed until eighteen months of age. He then opened the eye and injected a radioactive substance, which would be transported to the visual cortex, into the non-deprived eye. Pictures were taken of slices of cortex with radiation-sensitive film, allowing a study of the *ocular dominance columns,* which are groups of cells in the cortex that respond to input from either the right or the left eye (see Chapter 8). The columns of the open eye were greatly expanded while those of the closed eye had shrunk dramatically. Also, there seems to be a critical period for the development of these areas of the visual cortex, lasting from three to six weeks after birth.

Blakemore and Cooper (1970) looked at more specific environmental effects. They raised kittens from birth in darkness, except for a five-hour period each day when they were placed in a large drum or round chamber which had either vertical or horizontal stripes on the walls. A collar prevented the kittens from seeing their own bodies, so that the stripes were the only visual stimuli they encountered.

At five months old, the kittens were tested for line recognition by being presented with a moving pointer held either vertically or horizontally. Those reared in the 'vertical world' would only reach out to touch a vertical pointer, while those raised in the 'horizontal world' reached only for a horizontal pointer. Depending on the kind of visual experience they had had for the first five months, the kittens acted as if they were blind in the presence of the other kind of visual stimulus. This 'behavioural blindness' mirrored 'physiological blindness'. By placing microelectrodes into individual cells in the visual cortex, Blakemore and Cooper found that those kittens raised in a vertically-striped environment did not possess cells that fired in response to bars of light moved horizontally, and the reverse was true for the kittens raised in the horizontally-striped environment. The only receptive fields to have developed were those which reflected the early visual experience of the kittens.

However, this does not show conclusively that responding to lines at different angles develops solely through environmental influence: it is possible that receptive fields for all angles are present at birth and that where a kitten sees only vertical lines, those fields which would otherwise have responded to horizontal lines are 'taken over' by vertical fields. Another possibility is offered by Leventhal and Hirsch (1975), who found that exposure to horizontal and vertical lines prevents the appearance of any cells responsive to diagonals, but cells responsive to horizontals and verticals can be found even after exposure to diagonal lines only. This suggests that the horizontal and vertical cells are in some way more basic and robust than diagonal cells.

However, these findings seem to suggest very strongly that the type of environment is important in the development of at least certain kinds of perceptual ability in some species: in kittens, perception does seem to be at least partly learned.

Held and Hein (1963) were concerned with the effects of deprivation on the ability of kittens to guide their movements through vision. Given that a kitten's perceptual abilities are not entirely innate, to what extent is the acquisition of these abilities dependent on exposure to visual stimulation *and* motor activity? They found that only by moving about in a visually rich environment will normal sensory–motor co-ordination develop—passive exposure to such an environment is not sufficient.

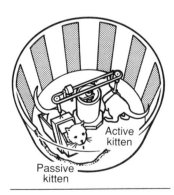

Figure 10.2 *The kitten carousel. (From Held, 1965)*

Held and Hein used an apparatus called the kitten carousel (Fig. 10.2). For the first eight weeks after birth, kittens were kept in darkness and then spent about three hours each day in the carousel (the rest of the time being spent in the dark). The 'active' kitten could move itself around (its legs were free) and its movements were transmitted to the 'passive' kitten via a series of pulleys, ie every time the active kitten moved the passive kitten moved the same distance, at the same speed, etc. The significant thing to note is that both kittens had exactly the same visual experience (both type and amount) but one could move itself about while the other was dependent on the first one's movements.

After several weeks of this arrangement, they were tested for 'paw–eye co-ordination'. The active kittens were markedly superior; for example, after thirty hours exposure they all showed visually-guided paw place-ment (if gently lowered towards the floor, they extended their paws, which is a typical response for normally-reared kittens). None of the passive kittens could do this after thirty hours, nor did they blink in response to an approaching object. They also failed to show the normal reluctance to step onto the deep side of the visual cliff apparatus (see below, p. 289 and Fig. 10.11). But does this mean that they could not actually perceive depth?

It seems that this would be a premature conclusion, as the 'passive' kittens soon learned the normal avoidance responses when allowed to run around in a lighted environment. This suggests that, rather than having failed to learn depth perception as such, they simply had not learned the correct motor responses associated with depth perception.

So we must distinguish between perception on the one hand and sensory–motor co-ordination on the other (see perceptual readjustment studies, below).

A general problem with animal studies (as with studies of human infants) is that we can only infer their perceptual experiences through observing their behaviour or their physiological responses—they cannot tell us more directly what they can or cannot see. We cannot be certain that animals deprived in particular ways do not perceive particular stimuli, *only that they do not behave as if they do*. It is possible that certain perceptual abilities have developed, but if they have not become linked to the animal's behaviour, we may have no way of knowing.

PERCEPTUAL ADAPTATION/ READJUSTMENT STUDIES

The basic hypothesis being tested in these studies is that human beings are capable of perceiving the world in a different way from normal and adjusting to this altered perception, thus demonstrating that perception is largely learned. The greater the degree of adaptation to a new perceptual world, the more significant the role of learning is taken to be. (Compared with other species that have been tested, human beings come out on top as far as this adaptability is concerned.)

It follows that the less adaptation a particular species shows, the greater the control by genetic factors in the perceptual abilities of that species. This has been clearly demonstrated by Sperry's (1943) experi-ment with salamanders and Hess's (1956) experiment with chickens.

Sperry rotated the eyes of salamanders through 180 degrees so that images on the retina were inverted (upside-down) compared with the normal eye. When presented with a stimulus moving upwards, the salamanders moved their heads downwards—they moved according to what they saw. But they showed no tendency to adapt over time and had to be force-fed, or fed in the dark.

Hess's subjects were chickens. They were fitted with prisms which shifted the image seven degrees either to the left or the right. Chickens which wore left shifting prisms always pecked to the left of the grain by seven degrees; similarly, those fitted with right-shifting prisms always pecked to the right by seven degrees. Like the salamanders, the chickens did not show any signs of adapting, however many times they pecked.

One of the earliest recorded human studies was that of Stratton (1896; Box 10.2).

Box 10.2   Stratton (1896)

Stratton fitted himself with a telescope on one eye which 'turned the world upside down'. (The other eye was kept covered—if both eyes had worn telescopes it would have proved too much of a strain, especially to the eye-movement muscles.) He wore the telescope for a total of 87 hours over an eight-day period; he wore blindfolds at night and at other times when not wearing the inverting lens. As far as possible he went about his normal routine. For the first three days he was aware that part of his environment—the part not in his immediate field of vision but on the periphery—was in a different orientation. But by the fourth day he was beginning to imagine unseen parts as also being inverted, and by the fifth day he had to make a conscious effort to remember that he actually had the telescope on. He was able to walk round the house without bumping into furniture and, when he moved, his surroundings looked 'normal'; however, when he concentrated hard and remained still, thigs still appeared upside down. By the eighth day, everything seemed 'harmonious'; he began to 'feel' inverted but this was quite normal and natural to him.

When Stratton removed the telescope, he immediately recognized the visual orientation as the one that existed prior to the start of the experiment. He found it surprisingly bewildering, although definitely *not* upside-down. This absence of an inverted after-image or after-effect is quite a crucial finding: it means that Stratton had not actually learnt to *see* the world in an upside-down fashion, or removal of the telescope would have caused the now normal (right-way up) world to look upside-down again! Instead, it suggests that the adaptation has taken the form of learning the appropriate motor responses in an upside-down-looking world. (Compare this with the question of depth-perception in Held and Hein's kittens that we discussed earlier.)

Having said this, Stratton did experience an after-effect which caused things before him to 'swing and sweep' as he moved his eyes, showing that location constancy (seeing things as stable and remaining in the same place) had been disrupted. In another experiment, Stratton made goggles which visually displaced his body so that he always appeared horizontally in front of himself—wherever he walked he 'followed' his own body image, which was suspended at right angles to his actual body. When he lay down, his body would appear above him, vertically, again at right angles (Fig 10.3). After three days, he was able to go out for a walk on his own—and lived to tell the tale!

Figure 10.3 One of Stratton's experiments in which goggles displaced the wearer's body image at right angles

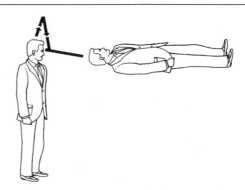

Gilling and Brightwell (1982) report a recent replication of Stratton's inverted goggles experiment (Box 10.3).

Box 10.3   The Case of Susannah Fienues (Gilling and Brightwell, 1982)

Susannah Fienues, a young art student, wore inverted goggles (fitted with a prism as opposed to a lens), for a period of seven days.
    After first putting them on she reported:

> The cars are going upside down. They're going the wrong way. It's all going completely the wrong way to what you'd expect. It's really strange.

After one hour, she reported:

> . . . In fact, looking at people in cars was quite normal, I didn't think they were upside down, and I just got adjusted to it, I think. But the difficult thing is just walking and being very disorientated, because how you feel is completely different to what you're doing . . . As for things being upside down, it just doesn't feel like that at all because I know very well that I'm sitting here and so I think my brain still knows that, so it's all right.

Like Stratton, she at first had great difficulty in pouring milk from a jug into a glass.
    By the fourth day, she could walk without difficulty, even with poise, from the bedroom to the sitting room. And she could now pour the milk! She felt, 'Just fine . . . I don't notice that things are upside down at all.'
    She could write her name normally—but only if she closed her eyes and didn't see her hand as she wrote it. With her eyes open, she could write it so that it appeared normal to her—but inverted to anyone else!
    By seven days her early problems seemed to have vanished—she could ride her bike, walk, run, climb stairs, turn corners, make coffee, and put records on, 'The only thing that's still quite difficult is eating and using a knife and fork.' Again:

> It's become more and more difficult to imagine myself standing upright or sitting down normally. I almost want to sit upside down because I can't quite imagine myself sitting normally.

This account supports the view of vision as an active process, enabling us to deal with the world. When she removed the goggles, she was annoyed that nothing seemed any different! She reverted to normal vision within a few minutes, very relieved that the experiment was over! Like Stratton, she learnt to match her vision with signals reported by the rest of her body:

> . . . She was not just seeing, but sampling the world as a whole with her senses, and organizing them so that they told stories which could be sensibly related to each other. She saw with her whole body, the whole apparatus of her senses, as it were, and not just with her eyes . . .

Snyder and Pronko (1952) made goggles which inverted and reversed the visual world. Their subjects wore them continually for thirty days and were able to adapt to the changes. Two years after the experiment, these subjects coped just as well when refitted with the goggles as first-time subjects at the end of the thirty-day period, showing that motor adaptations are extremely resistant to forgetting.

Kohler (1962) used an optical device which inverted the image without reversing left and right (more like Stratton's than Snyder and Pronko's). His subjects were disoriented and even nauseous at first but after several days adjusted and lived reasonably normally. Köhler concluded that upright vision could be achieved if the subject moved about and touched objects in the environment and the more familiar the object was, the easier this could be achieved. The fact that some of the subjects had an inverted after-effect when they removed the apparatus also suggests that the adaptation may actually be visual in nature and not simply sensory–motor. However, the after-effect lasted only for the first few minutes, which suggests that any purely perceptual learning that did occur was not very substantial. Similarly, when subjects wore goggles, such that the left half of each lens was red and the right half green, the visual world at first looked red when the subject looked to the left and green when the subject looked to the right. But adaptation to this occurred after only a few hours. Upon removal of the goggles, the visual world seemed to be coloured in the opposite direction to that experienced when the goggles were being worn. Yet, as with the inverting goggles, this after-effect lasted only a short time.

The importance of moving about in the physical environment when adapting to a perceptually distorted world was confirmed by Held. Based on his work with the kitten carousel, discussed earlier, he got one human subject to push another around on a trolley inside a large drum, while both wore goggles that shifted everything to one side. They both had identical visual experiences (as did the active and passive kitten) but the one who did the pushing made a faster and more efficient adjustment (as did the active kitten).

So what can we conclude from these studies?

(a) It seems that when subjects adapt to a distorted perceptual world, they are not, for the most part, actually learning to see 'normally' but instead are developing the appropriate motor behaviour which helps them to get around and function efficiently in their environment. What is learnt is not a new way of perceiving the world but a new set of body movements.

(b) The visual system, at least in adults, is extremely flexible and can adjust to distorted conditions. This strongly suggests that learning plays an important role in perceptual development, since a totally or largely innate system would not allow such adaptation to occur.

(c) Because the subjects are adults, who have already undergone a great deal of learning, and in whom maturation has already taken place, it is difficult to generalize from these studies to how babies develop under normal circumstances. Just because an adult is able to learn to perceive the world in a different way, we cannot automatically assume that babies originally have to learn to perceive the world as they do.

CROSS-CULTURAL STUDIES

These have mainly involved testing members of different cultural groups using the same test materials, usually visual illusions. The two most commonly used have been the Müller–Lyer and the horizontal–vertical (see Chapter 9).

The pioneering study was carried out by Rivers et al in 1901. They went to the Murray Islands, a group of islands situated in the Torres Straits (between New Guinea and Australia). Compared with English adults and children, the Murray Islanders were less prone to the Müller–Lyer. This was attributed to the fact that the natives limited their attention strictly to the task they were asked to perform (ie judge the length of the arrow shafts), while European subjects tended to regard the figure as a whole (including the arrowheads). By contrast, the horizontal–vertical illusion was *more* marked among the Murray Island men; this, together with the pronounced character of the illusion in children, led Rivers to conclude that it was due to some physiological condition or, at least, to some simple and primitive psychological condition (Price-Williams, 1966).

Probably the largest study was that of Segall et al (1963) who spent six years studying African children and adults, and inhabitants of the Philippines, and comparing them with each other as well as with South Africans of European descent and Americans from Illinois (in the American mid-west). On the Müller–Lyer illusion, the Africans and Philippinos were much less susceptible than the other two groups, but there were some interesting results for the horizontal–vertical illusion.

Two of the African tribes studied, the Batoro and the Bayankole, were at the top end of the illusion scale, that is, they were most likely to see it. Both tribes live in high, open country where you can see for miles without 'interference'; hence, vertical objects, such as trees or mountains, become important focal points and are used to estimate distances.

A third tribe, the Bete, who live in a jungle environment, were at the bottom end of the scale—they were least likely of all the groups to see the illusion. Europeans and Americans tended to come somewhere in between the three African tribes.

The implication is that ecology, ie the physical environment which a cultural group occupies, is closely tied to the susceptibility of that group to visual illusions; as we shall see below, some psychologists believe that ecology actually determines susceptibility.

Another illusion that has been used in cross-cultural research, but less often than the other two, is the rotating trapezoid. This is attached to a motor and revolves in a circle. It has horizontal and vertical bars fixed to it to give the impression of a window (see Fig. 10.4.)

Most Western observers report seeing a rectangle that oscillates to and

Figure 10.4 The rotating window. (As used by Allport and Pettigrew, 1957)

fro, backwards and forwards, rather than a trapezoid revolving through 360 degrees (which is what it actually is and does). This seems to be based on the assumption that it is a window (or window-type object). (This effect is reduced when it is viewed binocularly, ie with both eyes, rather than monocularly, ie with one eye closed; it is also reduced when the horizontal bars are removed.)

On the assumption that it is normally interpreted as a window by people who are used to seeing windows, and who bring with them expectations of rectangularity, we might expect that people from cultures where windows (as we know them) are not an everyday sight might see the rotating trapezoid for what it is.

One such cultural group are the Zulus, who not only do not have western-style windows but tend to live in a rather circular environment. Allport and Pettigrew (1957) compared urban and rural Zulus with each other and with Europeans.

Under optimal conditions (using one eye and further away) there were no differences between the three groups. But under less-than-optimal conditions (using both eyes and from a shorter distance) the rural Zulus—who live in the traditional circular culture—were less likely to perceive an oscillating rectangle than the other two groups and were more likely to perceive a rotating trapezoid.

Stewart (1973) found that rural Tongan children were less likely to see the Ames distorted room than children living in the city of Lusaka (Zambia) and European children. She found the same differences for other illusions (including the Müller–Lyer) and, interestingly, the greater the exposure to a 'rectangular' environment, the greater the susceptibility to the Müller–Lyer illusion. How can we account for the differences?

One of the first attempts to explain the results of cross-cultural studies was Segall et al's (1963) 'carpentered world hypothesis'; referring to members of Western culture they say:

> We live in a culture in which straight lines abound and in which perhaps ninety per cent of the acute and obtuse angles formed on our retina by the straight lines of our visual field are realistically interpretable as right angles extended in space. (Segall et al, 1963)

What they are saying, in effect, is that we tend to interpret illusion figures, which are usually 2-D drawings, in terms of our past experiences, so that in Western culture (which is a 'carpentered world') we add a third dimension (depth), which is not actually present in the drawing. This misleads us as to the true nature of the stimulus, resulting in what we call an illusion. This explanation is very similar to Gregory's (see Chapter 9). We are more or less likely to experience the illusion depending on what our cultural experience tells us the drawing *could* represent. If we are not used to straight lines and right angles, why should we think there is any difference in the length of the shafts of the arrows in the Müller–Lyer figure? Similarly, if we live in a circular environment, why should we see the rotating trapezoid as an oscillating rectangle? (We shall see later that the very tendency to interpret 2-D diagrams or pictures in 3-D terms may itself be something that is culturally determined.)

However, apart from certain theoretical and methodological criticisms of the carpentered world hypothesis, there is also substantial evidence which does not support it. Mundy-Castle and Nelson (1962) studied the Knysma forest dwellers, a group of isolated, white, illiterate South Africans. Despite the rectangularity of their environment, they were unable to give appropriate 3-D responses to 2-D symbols on a standard test, and on the Müller–Lyer figure their responses were not significantly different from non-Europeans, although they differed significantly from literate, white adults.

Jahoda (1966) compared the Lobi and Dagomba tribes of Ghana, who live in open parkland in round huts, with the Ashanti, who live in dense forest in roughly rectangular huts. The prediction that the Lobi and Dagomba would be significantly more susceptible to the horizontal–vertical while the Ashanti would be significantly more susceptible to the Müller–Lyer was not supported.

Finally, Gregor and McPherson (1965) found no significant differences between two groups of Australian aborigines on the two illusions, despite one group living in a relatively urbanized, carpentered environment and the other living primitively out of doors. However, both groups were significantly *less* prone to the Müller–Lyer than Europeans and *more* prone to the horizontal–vertical.

Consequently, Mundy-Castle and Nelson, Jahoda, and Gregor and McPherson, have suggested that Campbell et al exaggerated the influence of ecology on cultural differences in perception. Jahoda, for example, has stressed the importance of considering the possible effects of exposure to Western education and other cultural variables (which were largely overlooked in the Segall et al study). He believes that many of the findings may reflect the inability of some cultural groups to interpret 2-D drawings or other representations of the 3-D world, something which we take so much for granted because we encounter them from birth onwards. But it may be very difficult for people who are not familiar with them through a lifetime of exposure to interpret them in this way: the tendency to see pictures as depicting objects in the real world may itself be culturally determined.

It seems there are two separate processes involved when we 'read' pictures. First, we must learn to make perceptual inferences about the real world (what is the picture of?), and secondly, we must learn the conventions which the picture-maker is using in order to assess the real world (for instance, all the depth cues, such as linear perspective, relative size and superimposition; see Chapter 9).

Cross-cultural research, mainly in Africa, shows that the interpretation of pictures is far from automatic; rather than an inborn ability, it is a skill of considerable complexity. Three very famous studies seem to lend support to this view—the first indirectly, the second two directly.

Turnbull (1961) studied the Bambuti pygmies, who live in the dense rain forests of the Congo, a closed-in world without open spaces. Turnbull brought a pygmy out to a vast plain where a herd of buffalo was grazing in the distance. The pygmy said he had never seen one of those insects before; when told they were buffalo, he was offended and Turnbull was accused of insulting his intelligence. Turnbull drove the jeep towards the buffalo; the pygmy's eyes widened in amazement as he saw the insects 'grow' into buffalo before him. He concluded that witchcraft was being used to deceive him.

This is a good illustration of lack of size constancy, an important cue we use to 'read' pictures. The sight of the buffalo from such a distance was so far removed from the pygmy's experience that he could only believe that they were small animals (insects) rather than much larger ones (buffalo) which only *looked* smaller (by virtue of the small retinal image produced by large objects viewed from a distance). He could not apply size constancy for such great distances (but presumably he could for shorter ones) and if he could be deceived in this way when looking at real, live buffalo, how much more insulted would he have felt if he had been shown a photograph of the same scene?

Directly relevant to this question is a study by Deregowski (1972) in which he refers to a description given by a Mrs Fraser (who taught health care to Africans in the 1920s) of an African woman slowly discovering that a picture she was looking at portrayed a human head in profile:

> She discovered in turn the nose, the mouth, the eye, but where was the other eye? I tried by turning my profile to explain why she could see only one eye, but she hopped round to my other side to point out that I possessed a second eye which the other lacked.

The woman was treating the picture as an object rather than as a 2-D representation of an object—she had not learnt to 'infer' the depth in the picture, the parts that were not immediately visible (which clearly she could do when looking at a real face). Her 'object' turned out to have only two dimensions and this is what she found bewildering.

Hudson (1960) used a series of pictures depicting hunting scenes (two of which are shown in Fig. 10.5). They have been used in many parts of Africa with subjects drawn from a variety of tribal and linguistic groups. Subjects were shown one picture at a time and asked to name all the objects in the picture in order to determine whether or not the elements were correctly recognized. Then they were asked about the relationship between the objects—'What is the man doing?' 'What is closer to the man?' and so on. If subjects take note of the depth cues and make the 'correct' interpretations, they are classified as having 3-D depth perception; if not, they are judged to have 2-D perception:

> ... The results from African tribal subjects were unequivocal: both children and adults found it difficult to perceive depth in the pictorial material. The difficulty varied in extent but appeared to persist through most educational and social levels. (Deregowski, 1972)

However, it may not be a simple matter of cultural differences in the ability to identify 2-D pictorial representations of the 3-D world but under what conditions subjects from different cultural groups are asked to recognize things depicted in pictures. There seem to be three important questions we should ask about such studies (Gross, 1990):

(a) Do these studies make it difficult for non-Western subjects to give 'correct' responses?
(b) Could it be that the drawings used in some of these studies emphasize certain depth cues while ignoring others, thus putting non-Western perceivers at a double disadvantage?
(c) Is it also possible that what is taken as a difference in perception is really a matter of stylistic preference?

To answer (a), Deregowski et al (1972) studied the Me'en tribe of Ethiopia, who live in a remote area, still largely unaffected by Western

Figure 10.5 Pictorial depth perception is tested by showing subjects a picture such as the top illustration. A correct interpretation is that the hunter is trying to spear the antelope, which is nearer to him than the elephant. An incorrect interpretation is that the elephant is nearer and is about to be speared. The picture contains two depth cues: overlapping objects and known size of objects. The bottom illustration depicts the man, elephant and antelope in true size ratios when all are the same distance from the oberver. (From Hudson, 1960)

culture. When members of the tribe were shown drawings of animals they responsed by feeling, smelling, tasting or rustling the paper, showing no interest in the visual content of the picture itself.

However, when the unfamiliar paper was replaced by pictures painted on (familiar) cloth, they responded to the drawing of the animal. These animals were 30 cm high (compared with only 5 cm on the paper) and, without exception, despite almost certainly not having seen a picture before, seven out of ten correctly identified the first cloth picture as a buck, and ten out of ten identified the second as a leopard. As Serpell says:

> Given a sufficiently salient stimulus, with distracting cues removed such as the novelty of paper or the distinct white band of the border, immediate recognition may be possible simply by stimulus generalization, one of the most basic characteristics of learning. (Serpell, 1976)

At the same time, several subjects misidentified the buck and leopard as other four-legged animals and, in some cases, recognition seems to have been built up gradually, by helping the subject to trace the outline of the animal with a finger. Deregowski et al note the similarity in this respect of their subjects' verbal responses to those of young American children shown successively clearer images for identification, starting with a completely blurred image (Potter, 1966; cited by Deregowski et al, 1972).

Another way of simplifying the task is to ask the subject to recognize an object without having to identify it by name. Deregowski (1968b) gave a recognition task to boys and men in the 'relatively pictureless' Bisa community (a region of Zambia remote from main roads). They had to select from an array of eighteen model animals the one depicted in a black-and-white photo. Six were commonly seen in the area, the rest were very exotic. The boys were better at finding the strange animals than the men (they had received more schooling) but the men (mainly hunters) were better with familiar animals.

Under optimal conditions, pictures do seem to be recognizable without any prior learning; unlike words, most pictures are not entirely arbitrary representations of the real world—their arbitrariness:

> ... lies in what features they choose to stress and what features to leave out and it is these conventions governing this choice which the experienced picture perceiver must learn. (Serpell, 1976)

In answer to (b), one of the things the experienced picture perceiver has learned is the Western artist's use of *relative size* to represent distance. So, in Hudson's pictures a major cue to the relationship between the man, elephant and antelope is their relative size against the background knowledge of their normal sizes. Hudson also uses the cues of overlap (or superimposition) and linear perspective (see Chapter 9), eg in one drawing the elephant and a tree were shown near the apex of a pair of converging straight lines representing a road. Since the laws of perspective were a late discovery in European art (Gombrich, 1960) and the assumption of parallel edges to a road is promoted by a 'carpentered' environment, it is not too surprising that African children seldom understand this cue. Hudson (1960) found overlap (if noticed) to be the most effective of his three cues (confirmed by Kilbride et al, 1968, with a sample of Ugandan schoolchildren).

There is also a contradiction between these depth cues and others in the real world, namely *binocular disparity* and *motion parallax*, both of which are missing from Hudson's pictures (and, indeed, from *all* pictures). Also missing is *gradient of density* (or texture gradient). Gibson (1950) and Wohlwill (1965) found these all to be more important as depth cues in pictures than in 3-D displays for Western subjects over a wide age-range. Serpell (1976) refers to an unpublished report by Kingsley et al in which an artist redrew one of Hudson's pictures adding pebbles to the road and grass in open terrain, each surface showing a gradient of density, while everything else remained unchanged. Twelve-year-old Zambian children gave 64 per cent 3-D answers under these conditions compared with 54 per cent on Hudson's original. When colour and haze around distant hills, etc. were added, the figure rose to 76 per cent.

In answer to (c), much of the research seems to imply a belief that the Western style of pictorial art represents the real world in an objectively correct fashion; by implication, the subject who does not understand it is 'deficient' in some way. But since 'artistic excellence' is not identical with 'photographic accuracy' (Gombrich 1960), Serpell (1976) asks if it may be possible that subjects in different cultures 'reject' Western art forms on *aesthetic* grounds and that all the research has mistakenly described a *stylistic* preference as a difference in perception.

Hudson (1962) and Deregowski (1969b, 1970) found that African subjects with limited Western education slightly preferred unfolded, 'split', 'developed' or 'chain-type' drawings (Fig. 10.6 (left)) to 'ortho-gonal' or perspective drawings (as in Fig. 10.6 (right)). Why? Often it is because the latter fails to show some of the important features (recall the African woman shown the photograph by Mrs Fraser).

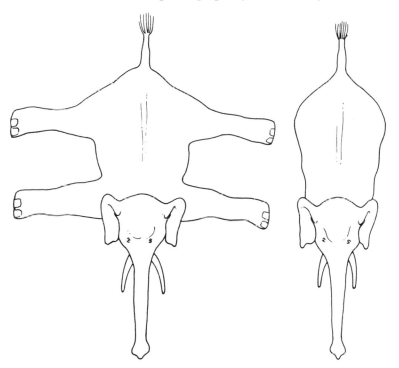

Figure 10.6 The split-elephant drawing (left) was generally preferred by African children and adults to the top-view perspective drawing (right). One person, however, did not like the split drawing because he thought the elephant was jumping around in a dangerous manner. (From Deregowski, 1972)

The importance of artistic convention increases the more symbolic and abstract the art is—the convention is part of the fund of common experience shared by the artist and the audience. Duncan et al (1973) point out that the small lines used by cartoonists to imply motion are the least understood of all the pictorial conventions which have been shown to rural African schoolchildren. And where the artist had drawn a boy's head in three different positions above the same trunk to indicate the head was turning around half the children thought he was deformed.

Likewise, Western observers require guidance from an anthropologist to understand the art forms of American Indians (Boas, 1927) or Nuba personal art in the Sudan (Faris, 1972; Fig. 10.7).

STUDIES OF HUMAN INFANTS

To repeat a point made earlier, studies on human infants represent the most direct way of trying to settle the nature–nurture issue. But, of course, the fact that the baby cannot tell us what it sees and hears, etc. presents problems of its own, the most important being that the investigator has to *infer* what the baby perceives; we can never be sure that the inference is correct.

Figure 10.7 Stylized bear rendered by the Tsimshian Indians on the Pacific coast of British Columbia is an example of split drawing developed to a high artistic level. According to anthropologist Franz Boas, the drawings are ornamental, and not intended to convey what an object looks like. The elements represent specific characteristics of the object. (From Deregowski, 1972)

Again, if newborns do not show a particular ability this does not necessarily mean that such abilities have to be learnt—they may develop sometime after birth through the action of genetic 'time switches' involved in the process of maturation. The general rule is that the earlier an ability appears, the more likely it is to be genetically controlled, and not the result of learning. Clearly, as was pointed out at the beginning, perception is not a single ability but a series of abilities. (Vision has been most widely studied, both in infants, adults and animals, and most of this chapter so far has concentrated on this sense modality. We shall be emphasizing vision in this section too.)

Vision involves perception of colour, shape, size, depth, movement, etc. Some of these may be largely innate, while others may be largely due to the effects of experience. We must be specific about which aspect of perception we are talking about when trying to establish to what extent, and in what ways, genetic and environmental factors have their influence.

ASKING THE RIGHT QUESTIONS

In 1890 William James wrote, 'the baby, assailed by eyes, ears, nose, skin and entrails at once, feels it all as one great blooming, buzzing confusion'.

Until quite recently, many people (including psychologists) agreed with James that the baby's perception of the world is hazy, poorly defined, unstructured, even chaotic. Many have gone so far as to believe that babies are born blind. But studies of newborns in the last twenty years or so have taught us that to ask, 'Can the baby see or not, or hear or not?' is the wrong kind of question. Instead, we should ask; 'What and how well can the baby see and hear?'

METHODS OF STUDYING INFANT PERCEPTION

Psychologists make inferences about infants' perception in two ways: first, by looking at what the baby *possesses* by way of sensory equipment (its structural and physical attributes), and secondly, by observing what the baby *does* (including physiological changes in the presence of various stimuli). In both cases we ask, 'What is the baby likely to be seeing or hearing?' and, 'How soon can particular abilities be expected, or seem to, develop?'

More specifically, what are some of the methods used to study infant perception? (These relate mostly to what the baby does rather than what it possesses.)

(a) A general and widely used method is to present two stimuli simultaneously. If the infant spends more time looking at one than the other, then it is inferred that:

    (i) it can actually tell the difference (discriminate) between them;

    (ii) that it prefers the one it looks at longer. This is called the *spontaneous visual preference technique* (or preferential looking). The same basic technique has been used to study other modalities, including taste and smell.

For example, Steiner (1977, 1979) studied newborns' differential responses to tastes and smells by their facial expressions. The psychophysical evidence is compelling that four basic qualities together make up taste experience, namely: sweet, salt, sour and bitter. Steiner systematically gave the newborns sweet, sour and bitter substances and photographed their 'gustofacial' responses. Sweet produced expressions of 'satisfaction', often accompanied by a slight smile and sucking movements. Sour produced lip-pursing, often accompanied by or followed by nose wrinkling and eye blinking. Bitter produced expressions of dislike and disgust and rejection, often followed by spitting or even pre-vomiting movements. He also observed nasofacial expressions in response to smells placed on cotton swabs held under the babies' nose. Butter and banana produced positive expressions, vanilla produced positive or indifferent ones, fish produced some rejection and rotten eggs led to unanimous rejection.

Cernoch and Porter (1985) compared breast-fed babies with bottle-fed babies, 12–18 days old, for olfactory recognition of their mother, father and a stranger. They were photographed while exposed to pairs of gauze pads worn under the arm by each of the adults the previous night. Only breast-feeding babies showed a clear preference for their own mother's scent, no baby recognized its father's scent and nor did the bottle-fed recognize their mother's. (Mothers can recognize their baby's scents after 1–2 days.)

(b) Another method involves *reflecting light on the cornea* to monitor the baby's vision and then filming the reflection of the cornea. This gives the researcher a more precise reading of what the baby is looking at than is possible from simply noting the orientation of the head or the general direction of the gaze (as in (a)).

(c) Another approach is to *measure the baby's sucking rate*, via a dummy or pacifier, as a response to different stimuli. A baseline rate is recorded before the stimulus is presented (ie the baby's normal or spontaneous sucking rate). When the stimulus is presented, the baby at first tends to suck noticeably slower or faster but after a while *habituation* sets in (that is, the baby stops responding to it as a novel stimulus) and a return to the baseline rate occurs.

The stimulus is then changed in some way and if there is another increase or decrease in sucking rate, it is inferred that the baby can tell the difference—it is responding to the change as a novel stimulus.

(d) *Habituation* is used as a method in its own right and has been used to study perception in every modality. It presumably reflects two components: (i) the baby's developing mental representation of a stimulus and; (ii) the continuing comparison of whatever stimulus is present with that representation. If an external stimulus and a mental representation match, the baby 'knows' the stimulus, so there is little reason for it to continue looking. But mismatches maintain the baby's attention, so that a novel (and discriminable) test stimulus presented after habituation to a familiar one, typically re-excites attention. This method has been used especially to study the perception of form, orientation, location, movement and colour (Bornstein, 1988).

(e) *Conditioned head rotation* involves the baby sitting on its (usually) mother's lap. On one side is a loudspeaker and when a tone or speech syllable is played through the speaker and the baby responds by orienting towards it, it receives a positive reinforcement in the form of a colourful mechanical toy which appears just above the speaker. This method can help measure the development of several abilities basic to sound perception, such as detection of sounds of different frequencies, localization of sound in space and response to complex sounds which specify speech (Bornstein, 1988).

(f) A sixth method is to attach a dummy or nipple to audio-visual equipment so that when the baby sucks, a tape-recording is switched on or an image projected onto a screen can be brought into sharper focus the harder the baby sucks.

(g) Two important physiological measures are the baby's heart rate and breathing rate—a decrease in these is usually taken to indicate that something has caught the baby's attention.

These methods may be combined with each other and also with study of the visual apparatus (or any other) itself to help us infer what the baby actually perceives.

There are important differences between these different methods regarding the ambiguity of the results they produce. For example, Bornstein (1988) points out that while, for example, demonstrable preferences offer good evidence for the existence of absolute and difference thresholds (see Chapter 8), *any failure to demonstrate* a preference is fundamentally ambiguous. For example, a baby in the laboratory may orient towards its mother and a stranger equally, but still be able to smell them apart and show clearly which it prefers under particular circumstances. But conditioned head rotation and habituation are less ambiguous because they, '...draw even more actively on definitive behavioural acts...' (Bornstein, 1988) and for this reason are currently among the most widely used methods.

1) *STUDYING WHAT THE BABY POSSESSES*

What can we tell about the infant's visual perception from studying its visual apparatus?

We know that the nervous system as a whole is still immature (as we might expect). The optic nerve is thinner and shorter than an adult's and is only partially myelinated (insulated by a myelin sheath), so that visual information is transmitted inefficiently to a similarly undeveloped cortex for interpretation. However, myelination is complete by about 4 months after birth. (Without myelination of the optic nerve, we could probably only see diffuse flashes of light.)

The human eye at birth is about half the size and weight of an adult's; the eyeball is shorter and this reduces the distance between the retina and the lens, making vision less efficient. However, the newborn's eyeball is anatomically identical to the adult's—all the parts are there but their relationship to each other is different and they do not all develop at the same rate; for example, the cornea is much closer to its final form than the iris.

PERCEPTION OF COLOUR

According to Bornstein (1988), studying colour presents formidable technical problems, one of them being the fact that colour (hue) and brightness co-vary; clearly each must be controlled in order to study the other. Adults, at least can be *asked* to match brightness.

Bornstein (1976) used a habituation technique with three-month-olds and found they could discriminate blue–green from white and yellow from green (these tests are normally failed by red–green 'colour-blind' people).

These findings have been confirmed in a number of studies; for example, Packer et al (1985) used a choice–preference technique with babies as young as one month old. Bornstein sums up their findings by saying that:

> . . . infants 1 month and certainly 2 months of age and older are known to possess largely normal colour vision, based on their discrimination of colour stimuli in the absence of brightness cues. (Bornstein, 1988)

(See Chapter 13 on Language and Thought for a further discussion on colour perception.)

The retina is fairly well developed at birth; the rods and cones are also fairly well developed, so the basis for colour vision is present in the newborn. (These two kinds of retinal cells become differentiated by the seventh month of pregnancy at the latest.)

PERCEPTION OF BRIGHTNESS

The fovea (which is packed with cones and thus provides the clearest image of an object when viewed in daylight or other bright light) is fairly well developed at birth; by four months after conception it has become structurally differentiated.

We know that babies react to bright light while still in the womb—if a bright light is shone on a pregnant woman's belly, the baby may move towards it. (Perhaps some of the baby's movements in the womb, known as 'quickening', which usually begin around the fourth month, stem from this attraction to light.) Also, the pupillary reflex (a response to bright light whereby the pupil contracts, thus reducing the amount of light that enters the eye) is present even in premature babies. Similarly, the blink reflex to bright light is present at birth.

So, clearly, the neonate is sensitive to differences in the intensity of light. A five-day-old infant will look for different amounts of time at stimuli of different brightnesses; as it gets older, less intensity is needed to produce the pupillary reflex. Even when a newborn is asleep, it will screw up its eyes, frown and tense its muscles if a bright light suddenly shines on its face. But if it is awake and brought near a window but not into bright sunlight, it will often turn towards the light, indicating that it knows where the light is coming from and that it is attracted to it.

According to Bornstein (1988), a baby's sensitivity to brightness is reasonably similar to an adult's.

PERCEPTION OF MOVEMENT

The ability to follow a moving stimulus depends upon a reflex called the optokinetic reflex (or optic nystagmus), which consists of a series of back-and-forth eye movements called visual saccades (you can spot them if you watch the eyes of somebody who is reading; see Chapter 8). This reflex is present soon after birth; for instance, within forty-eight hours of birth, babies can track a slowly moving object. It is only about half as efficient as an adult's at this time, but it improves rapidly during the next three months.

Movement is a powerful dimension of visual stimulation for the human infant. From birth, infants prefer to scan or fixate moving rather than stationary stimuli, although there are preferences for certain types of speeds of movement which change with age (Slater, 1989).

If a series of fine, vertical stripes is passed across the baby's field of vision, they will produce visual saccades; if the stripes are made finer and finer (so that eventually they appear grey) the saccades stop. Babies are more successful at tracking horizontal than vertical movement but even then it will be jerky—they re-fixate often, gazing at the moving object and then shifting their gaze to a different spot. One possible reason for this jerkiness is that *convergence* is absent at birth, although it usually appears two days after birth and is fully developed by two to three months. Convergence is essential for fixation and depth perception (see Chapter 9).

Also essential for efficient vision is *accommodation*. At birth, the eye operates rather like a fixed-focus camera, that is, the baby only sees clear-cut images of objects that are about 20 cm from its face and anything nearer or further will tend to look blurred. (The baby must also be looking directly at the object.) There is no real accommodation at all at first, which is due to the immaturity and weakness of the ciliary muscles which focus the lens by changing its shape.

However, 20 cm, conveniently, is approximately the distance between the baby's face and the face of the person feeding it, which gives the baby plenty of opportunity to examine the adult face and become familiar with it.

By 2 months, the baby is beginning to accommodate to the distance of objects and by 4 months the ability to accommodate has reached adult standards. This improvement, like many of the others we have noted above, seems to be very largely due to maturation.

One of the most basic aspects of the object environment revealed through motion is 'figural coherence' (Bornstein, 1988). A compelling example of this is the 'point-light' walker display which specifies typical human motion: people perceive displays of lights attached to the joints of a human, shown in the dark *not* as an unrelated set of randomly moving dots, but as biomechanical motion giving evidence of figural coherence. Johansson (1975) and Cutting et al (1978) have found that adults shown such a dynamic display can identify the motion and the object in less than 200 m/second, while the same display presented statically is essentially uninterpretable.

What about babies? Bertenthal et al (1984, 1985; cited by Bornstein, 1988) used habituation to study babies and found sensitivity to figural coherence in dynamic light displays as early as three months (and also sensitivity to the 3-D structure of the human form at nine months).

VISUAL ACUITY

Related to the ability to see clear, well-defined images is the efficiency of the baby's vision. The newborn's visual acuity is about 30 times poorer than in the adult. But despite this imperfect vision, the baby likes to see an image in as clear a way as possible. Kalnins and Bruner (1973) found that one- to three-month-olds will learn to operate the focus on a projector in order to make the picture clearer; the focus was connected directly to a nipple and was arranged so that appropriate sucking rates would bring the blurred picture into focus. The babies also looked less at an out-of-focus image than at a clear-cut image.

Visual acuity improves rapidly during the first four to six months and between six and twelve months will come within adult ranges. It may not reach 20:20 until ten or eleven years of age and there are important individual differences as to the eventual attainment of 20:20 vision.

A method of investigating acuity is through visually-evoked potentials (VEPs). Electrodes are attached to the scalp, above the visual cortex, and a visual stimulus is presented. If the electrical activity changes then the baby is judged to be perceiving the stimulus. There is evidence that VEPs exist in newborns, showing that some degree of acuity is present then.

2) STUDYING WHAT THE BABY DOES

What can we tell about the infant's visual perception from studying its behavioural response to stimuli?

PERCEPTION OF PATTERN OR FORM

Fantz (1961) presented thirty babies, aged one to fifteen weeks, with a variety of stimuli and used the time spent looking at each of these as an index of the baby's visual preferences. They were shown, at weekly intervals, pairs of stimuli comprising: bullseyes, horizontal stripes, checkerboards, two sizes of plain square, a cross, a circle and two triangles (of the same area; Fig. 10.8).

There was a distinct preference, at all ages, for the bullseye over the stripes and for the checkerboard over the plain square; the bullseye was

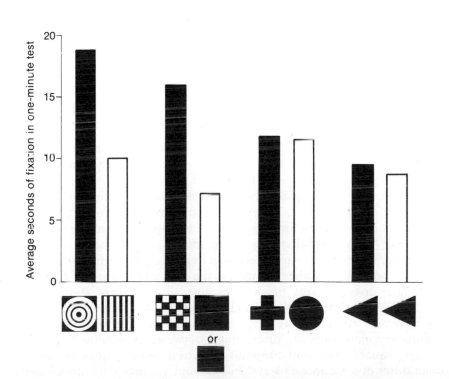

Figure 10.8 The bars indicate looking time for each of the stimulus patterns presented in pairs. (From Fantz, R. L. (1961). The Origin of Form Perception)

most looked at of all the stimuli, and next most popular was the checkerboard.

So, there seems to be a very early, if not inborn, preference for more complex over less complex stimuli, that is, stimuli which contain more information and in which there is more 'going on'. However, this preference for complexity also seems to be a function of age. Fantz's babies, tested weekly, were presented with progressively narrower stripes, and as they got older they could distinguish targets with narrower and narrower stripes.

Other researchers have also found this preference for complexity as a function of age. In another experiment, Fantz (1961) showed that two- to four-month-olds prefer patterns to colour or brightness. Six discs were shown; one was plain red, one plain white and one plain yellow. The others were a face, printed matter and a bullseye. At all ages there was a preference for the face over either the printed matter or the bullseye and all three were preferred to the plain discs (Fig. 10.9).

Figure 10.9 The upper bar of each pair indicates looking time for two- to three-month-olds, the lower bar for babies of four months old. (From Fantz, 1961)

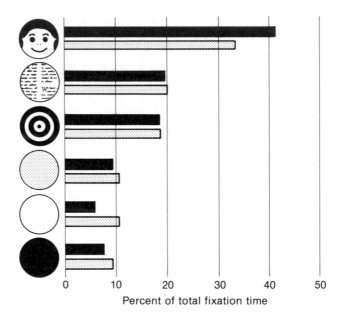

Percent of total fixation time

The preference for increasing complexity seems to indicate that the capacity for differentiation steadily improves, possibly because the ability to scan becomes more efficient and thorough.

Studies of eye movements give precise indications of what subjects are looking at. At first, when a baby finds a stimulus interesting, it continues to scan it but it tends to limit itself to the focus of interest; for example, Salapatek (1975) found that very young infants confine their scanning to one corner of a triangle which seems to indicate a preference for areas of greatest contrast. (Another example is the eyes and hairline of the face.) Only later does the baby begin to explore all around the stimulus and inside it (eg all corners of the triangle or the nose and mouth of a face), ie the baby now attends to the *whole* pattern and not just to specific parts.

Similarly, newborns can discriminate between the outline shapes of a triangle, square, circle and cross but it is not clear *how*, since any two of them differ in a number of ways. For example, if the infant attends only to the bottom of the figures, the square will have a line, but the cross will not. The stimuli differ along other dimensions—orientation of lines and angles, overall size, density of contour, curved versus linear, enclosed versus open, etc. As infants can detect these sorts of lower-order variables, it is very difficult to know whether it is *these* the infant is discriminating rather than the configurations or *gestalt* (ie the triangle, square, etc.; Slater, 1989).

An experiment suggesting a change in how form is perceived in early infancy was conducted by Slater and Morison (1987; cited by Slater, 1989). If infants are made familiar with a number of different instances (exemplars) of the same shape (triangle, square, cross, circle), will they extract the overall shape and learn to disregard the changes to the parts of the stimulus? If so, they should show a novelty preference when a *different* exemplar of the same shape is paired on post-familiarization trials with an exemplar of a different shape (ie they should respond to the latter as a novel stimulus, but show no response to the former).

During the familiarization phase, each newborn and three- to five-month-old saw six exemplars of one stimulus shape, followed by two post-familiarization trials (paired presentation of a different exemplar of the familiar shape and a novel shape). The newborns did not show a preference for the novel shape but the three- to five-month-olds did (the difference was statistically significant):

> ... During the first two months infants can discriminate between shapes, but they probably do so on the basis of differences in lower-order variables, such as orientation, contrast ... and so on. Shortly after this something like true form perception begins and infants respond to higher-order variables ... such as configurational invariance and form categories. (Slater, 1989)

FACEDNESS

It is generally agreed that the human face is probably the most interesting and attractive stimulus experienced by the baby—it is 3-dimensional, contains high-contrast information (particularly, the eyes, mouth and hairline), is constantly moving (eyes, mouth, head), is a source of auditory stimulation (voice) and regulates its behaviour according to the baby's own activities.

So it neatly combines all the stimulus dimensions which babies seem to (innately) prefer (complexity, pattern, movement, etc.). However, does the baby gradually come to prefer faces because they contain all these preferred elements, or is there an inborn predisposition to respond to the face *as a face*, an innate perceptual knowledge of the face?

Fantz takes the latter view. In a famous 1961 study, he presented four-day-olds to six-month-olds with all possible pairs of three stimuli, which were black against a pink background and the approximate shape and size of an adult's head (Fig. 10.10). At all age levels, infants looked more at the schematic representation (a) than they did at the scrambled face (b), while the control stimulus (c) was largely ignored. Even though the difference in the time spent looking at (a) and (b) was slight, Fantz concluded that, 'there is an unlearned, primitive meaning in the form perception of infants', such that there is an innate preference for facedness.

However, Hershenson et al (1965) pointed out that (a) and (b) are both

Figure 10.10 *Looking time for each of three face-like stimuli. (From Fantz, 1961)*

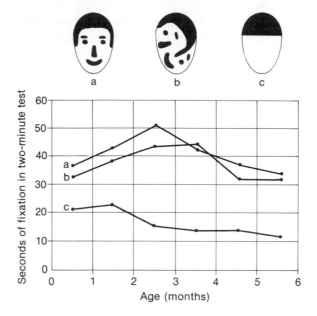

more complex than (c) and that may account for their preference over (c), as opposed to their resemblance to human faces. So they presented newborns with all possible pairs of three equally complex stimuli:

(i)   a real female face;
(ii)   a distorted picture, which retained the outline of head and hair but altered the position of the other features;
(iii) a scrambled face, as in Fantz's experiment (stimulus (b)).

They found no preference for any of these three and concluded that a preference for real faces is not inborn and usually does not appear until about four months of age.

More recently, Kleiner (1987) compared newborns' and two-month-olds' preferences between: (i) two-dimensional face-like patterns; and (ii) abstract patterns and found a clear age difference. Newborns preferred the abstract patterns, while two-month-olds preferred the face-like patterns, the former containing greater contrast. Similar results have been found for six-week-olds and three-month-olds.

Melhuish (1982) showed pictures of the mother's face and female strangers' faces to one-month-olds, one at a time for 30 seconds at a time. Although there was no preference for the mother's face, the infants did look longest at the faces with the highest contrast. Although infants as young as five weeks may be able to discriminate between the photographed face of their mother and a female stranger, it seems that this is based on the outer boundary of the face (hair–face outline), with internal features becoming important only from four to five months.

But what happens if the face-like stimuli are equated for contrast, or in other ways contrast is made irrelevant to the responses and discriminations required? As Slater (1989) points out, people are so important to the infant that it would not be surprising to find that neonates learn quickly to discriminate between them and there is a great deal of evidence that this is so. As we saw earlier, two- to three-week-old breast-fed babies recognize their mother's breast-odour and very quickly show a preference for the mother's voice compared with that of a female stranger (Lipsitt, 1977).

Bushnell and Sai (1987; cited by Slater, 1989) showed newborns their mother's (live) face and the face of a female stranger (matched for overall brightness of face and hair colour). There was a clear preference for the mother's face, indicating a quickly learned visual preference (the babies' mean age was two days, five hours).

But is there any evidence of a *specific* response to the human *face* (as opposed to a more general learning ability)?

Slater (1989) cites a study in which newborns less than an hour old turned their heads and eyes significantly more to track a 2-D schematic face-like stimulus than to track a 'scrambled face', which in turn was preferred to a blank face with no internal detail (thus supporting Fantz's early findings).

Other studies have shown that babies as young as two to three months old show a preference for slides of female faces judged by adults as attractive compared with less attractive faces. Could there be an un-learned aesthetic appreciation of faces? (Slater, 1989).

Instead of taking the view that there is a genetically-determined preference for the human face as such, Rheingold (1961) believes that infants develop a selective responsiveness to it (and things that resemble it) as it embodies all the stimulus dimensions that babies seem, innately, to prefer, conveniently 'packaged' in a very attractive and stimulating form. For this reason, she calls the human face a *supernormal stimulus* (see Chapter 15).

However:

> . . . a growing body of converging evidence—early learning of and prefer-ence for the mother's face, visual following of face-like stimuli, imitation of facial gestures, aesthetic perception of faces—gives strong support to the claim that the human face has special, species-specific visual signi-ficance for the infant from birth onwards. (Slater, 1989)

PERCEPTION OF DEPTH AND 3-D OBJECTS

This has been one of the most researched aspects of infant perception and has perhaps become the focus for the heredity–environment issue. If babies can perceive depth at birth or very soon afterwards, this suggests that the ability is genetically determined; the earlier it develops the more likely it is that learning does not play a very important role.

It has been investigated in rather different ways, but probably the most famous study, and one of the earliest, was carried out by Gibson and Walk (1960) using the 'visual cliff' apparatus. As you can see from Figure 10.11, this consists of a central platform, on one side of which is a sheet of plate glass and immediately below this a black and white checkerboard design (the shallow side). On the other side is another sheet of plate glass, this time with the checkerboard design placed on the floor, a distance of about four feet, giving the appearance of a drop or 'cliff' (the 'deep side'). The baby is placed on the central platform and its mother calls to it and beckons it, first from one side, then from the other.

Gibson and Walk used babies aged six months to fourteen months; most would not crawl onto the 'deep side' and this was interpreted as indicating depth perception (that is, they perceived the visual cliff or

Figure 10.11 The visual cliff. (From Dworetzky, J. P. (1981). Introduction to Child Development. St. Paul, Mn., West Publishing Co.)

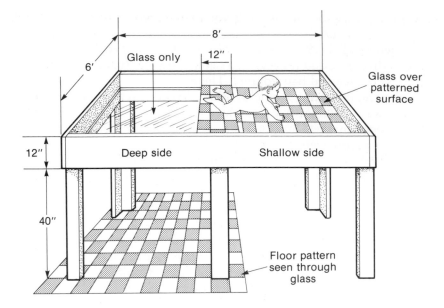

apparent drop and therefore did not venture onto it). The few who did (either by backing onto it or resting one foot on it for support) did so 'accidentally'—their poor motor control was responsible rather than their inability to perceive depth.

But can we be sure that a baby old enough to crawl has not learnt to perceive depth? Gibson and Walk took their findings as strong support for the view that depth perception is (probably) inborn, but since they only used babies who could already crawl, we cannot be certain how early this ability normally appears.

Gibson and Walk also tested other species on the visual cliff and found supporting evidence. Chicks less than one day old never hopped down onto the deep side, goat kids and lambs, tested as soon as they could stand, also avoided it, rats, if they could feel the glass with their very sensitive whiskers, stepped down on either side, and four-week-old kittens avoided the deep side unless they were reared in the dark (in which case they tended to fall down on either side). If forcibly placed on the deep side, these young animals would 'freeze'.

A more direct test of depth perception in infants was conducted by Campos et al (1970). Their subjects were two-, three-and-a-half- and five-month-olds and they used heart rate as the index of depth perception. Even the youngest showed a drop in heart rate, showing interest, when placed on the deep side; they were also less likely to cry and were more attentive to what was underneath them and they clearly were not frightened by what they saw. There were no such changes when they were placed on the shallow side. Therefore it seems that even two-month-olds can perceive depth and that avoidance behaviour is probably learnt (perhaps after the baby has had a few experiences of falling).

Another way of investigating depth perception is to observe how babies react when an object approaches their faces from a distance. Bower et al (1970) found that babies just 20 days show an 'integrated avoidance response', ie they throw back their head, shield their face with their hands and even cry, indicating some very early depth perception. If a large box is moved towards the baby's face, from the visual information that the box is getting larger it seems to understand that it is getting closer and would be harmful and, accordingly, puts its arm in front of its face to protect itself. (This occurs even with one eye closed but not when equivalent pictures were seen on a screen, showing that motion parallax is the critical cue for distance.)

To underline the importance (and inseparability) of both hereditary and environment, Bornstein concludes his review of studies of depth perception by saying:

> ... No matter how early in life depth perception can be demonstrated, the ability still rests on some experience; no matter how late its emergence, it can never be proved that only experience has mattered. (Bornstein, 1988)

The Bower et al study also suggests that the baby sees the box as a solid, 3-D object and Bower (1979) investigated this hypothesis by presenting 'solid' objects which were not solid at all but illusions of 3-D objects created by using special polarizing filters and goggles. Babies aged sixteen to twenty-four weeks old are sat in front of a screen. A plastic, translucent object is suspended between lights and the screen so it casts a double shadow on the back; when the screen is viewed from the front, using polarizing goggles, these double shadows merge to form the image of a single 3-D object (Fig. 10.12).

Virtual object

Figure 10.12 A baby wearing polarizing goggles attempts to grasp a virtual intangible object in front of the screen (Bower, 1979). (From Barnes-Gutteridge, W. (1974). Psychology. London, Hamlyn)

None of the babies showed any surprise when they grasped the real, solid objects but when they reached for the apparent objects and discovered there was nothing solid to get hold of, they all expressed surprise and some even showed distress. Clearly, they expected to be able to touch what they could 'see'. Bower believes that this ability is innate.

THE VISUAL CONSTANCIES

Perceptual constancy represents a major form of *organization* which seems to be a necessary prerequisite for many other types of organization (see Chapter 9). *Empiricists* would argue that constancy is learned and that babies and young children are likely to be 'tricked' by the appearance of things—if something *looks* smaller, for example, (projects a smaller retinal image) then it *is* smaller.

Nativists, on the other hand, would claim that, like all perceptual abilities, constancy is innate, so that the baby can judge the size of an object regardless of the retinal image produced by the object.

Bower (1966) tested these two opposing hypotheses experimentally. Initially, he trained two-month-olds to turn their heads at the sight of a 30 cm cube, at a distance of 1 metre (when they turned their heads in the desired direction, an adult popped up in front of the baby and cried 'peek-a-boo', a very powerful positive reinforcer for babies). When they were looking at the cube consistently, it was replaced by: (i) a 30 cm cube at a distance of 3 metres (this would produce a retinal image one-third the size of the original; (ii) a 90 cm cube at a distance of 1 metre (this would produce a retinal image three times the size of the original); or (iii) a 90 cm cube at a distance of 3 metres (this would produce exactly the same sized image as the original; Fig. 10.13).

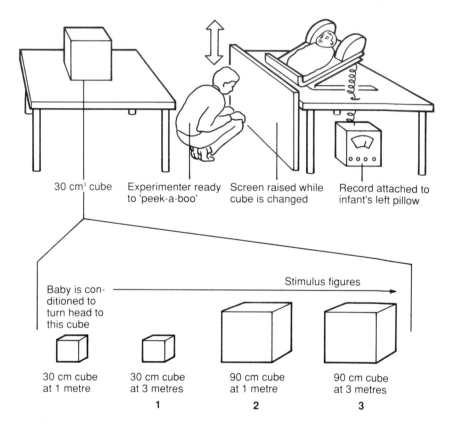

Figure 10.13 Bower's 'peek-a-boo' experiment

How often the baby turned its head towards each of these three cubes could be used as a measure of how similar to the original the baby considered it to be; ie, if the baby generalized its head-turning response mainly to (i), this would be evidence for size constancy. This is what the nativists predict: the baby will respond to the actual size of the cube, regardless of distance. If the head-turning response generalized mainly to (iii), this would be evidence for lack of size constancy: as predicted by the empiricists, the baby at first would 'compare' retinal images and base its perception of similarity on these, regardless of distance.

What Bower found was that, compared with 98 head-turns produced by the original cube, (i) produced 58, (ii) produced 54 and (iii) produced 22. This seems to represent clear support for the nativists: babies responded most to the cube of the same *size*, regardless of distance, next came the cube the same distance away as the original but of a different size, and last of all came the cube of a different size and distance, but giving the same retinal image as the original. It is the difference between (i) and (iii) which constitutes the critical findings.

More recent studies, using recovery from habituation as an index of size constancy, have confirmed that the ability to perceive the true size of an object is present by eighteen weeks (Slater, 1989).

Using a similar procedure to the one described above for size constancy, Bower (1966) studied *shape constancy*. If a two-month-old was trained to turn its head to look at a rectangle, it would continue to do so when the same rectangle was turned slightly (to produce a trapezoid retinal image).

Slater (1989) refers to studies which suggest that newborns are able to extract the constant real shape of an object that is rotated in the third dimension, ie they can recognize object form independently of (transformations in) its orientation in space (shape constancy).

Bornstein (1988), after reviewing recent studies of both shape and size constancy, concludes that, '. . . babies still only in the first year of life can perceive form *qua* form'.

Babies know and like the vertical; two- to four-month-olds prefer the normal vertical orientation of a face compared with upside-down and left and right orientations along the horizontal axis—as measured by their smiling and looking. And before six months they habituate more quickly when presented with a stimulus oriented on the vertical than one on the horizontal axis.

Other perceptual constancies include feature, identity and existence.

Feature constancy is the ability to recognize the invariant features of a stimulus despite some detectable but irrelevant transformations—and this ability is present at birth. If newborns have been habituated to a moving stimulus, they will show a novelty preference when shown the same stimulus paired with a novel shape, both of which are stationary (ie they respond to the new shape, showing that they perceive the familiar stationary stimulus as the same stimulus as when it was moving).

Feature constancy is a necessary prerequisite for *identity constancy*, the ability to recognize a particular object as being exactly the *same* object despite some transformation.

But how could we distinguish *empirically* between identity constancy and (mere) feature constancy?

A study which perhaps comes closest to demonstrating identity constancy is one by Bower (1971) in which babies were seated in front of mirrors which could produce several images of the mother. Babies below twenty weeks old smiled, cooed and waved their arms to each of the 'multiple mothers', whereas older babies became quite upset at seeing more than one mother. This suggests that it is only the older babies who are aware that they have only one mother, and can therefore be said to have identity constancy.

Existence constancy refers to the belief that objects continue to exist even when they are no longer available to the senses, what Piaget called *object permanence* (see Chapter 25). Together, existence and identity constancy comprise the *object concept*, which may appear around the middle of the first year rather than earlier. They are both more sophisticated than shape and size and feature constancies—the object concept may arise out of these 'basic' constancies.

Bower was also interested in how the infant's perception is organized in terms of certain Gestalt principles (see Chapter 9). He wanted to find out if closure is an inborn characteristic (as the Gestalt psychologists claim) by training two-month-olds to respond to a black wire triangle with a black iron bar across it and then presenting them with four triangle-stimuli (Fig. 10.14).

Figure 10.14 The stimulus figures used in Bower's study of closure. (After Bower, 1977)

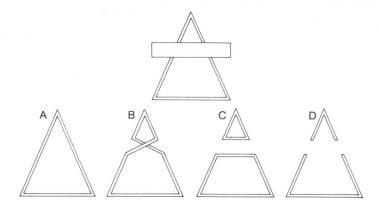

The fact that they generalized their response to a complete triangle suggests that they 'understood' that underneath the black iron bar lay a complete, unbroken triangle and given that they were unlikely to have encountered many triangular stimuli in their lifetime, Bower's findings support the view that closure is an inborn feature of infant perceptual ability.

CONCLUSIONS

As we have said, studies of human infants represent the most direct way of testing the Nature–Nurture controversy with regard to perception but the evidence they provide must be considered in the light of the evidence from the four other major kinds of research—and vice versa.

Because each perceptual ability must be considered separately (eg colour, depth and constancy) there is no simple overall answer to the question: is nature or nurture, heredity or environment, more important, in influencing the course of perceptual development?— except one which makes clear the virtual impossibility of trying to disentangle their effects:

> . . . At present we are only part-way towards a description of the changes in visual competence in early infancy, and the causes of the changes are also poorly understood. Newborns are competent learners and some developments may be a consequence of perceptual experience; others may result from endogenous maturational processes, perhaps linked to the increasing involvement of the visual cortex. (Slater, 1989)

Similarly:

> . . . Some perceptual capacities are given congenitally—even, apparently, in the basic functioning of the sensory systems—whereas other perceptual capacities develop during infancy and maturity. Perceptual development after birth (or whenever the onset of experience takes place) is doubtlessly some complex transaction of these two principal forces [genetic/maturation and experience/environmental influence] . . . basic mechanisms in many cases can impose perceptual structure early in life, but . . . perceptual development is determined and guided by a transaction of these structural endowments in combination with experience. Thus, neither nativism nor empiricism holds sway over perceptual development; rather, innate mechanisms and experience together co-determine how children come to perceive the world veridically. (Bornstein, 1988)

11 ATTENTION

When discussing the topic of perception in Chapter 9, several references were made to the concept of *selection*. For example, one of the major ways in which perceptual set functions is to bias what aspect of a stimulus/stimulus situation we notice. This, in turn, presupposes that we are not capable of noticing everything that is physically available to the senses at any particular moment: in other words, when we describe perception as being a selective process, we are in fact talking about selective attention, the topic of the present chapter:

> The topics of perception and attention merge into each other since both are concerned with the question of what we become aware of in our environment. We can only perceive things we are attending to; we can only attend to things we perceive . . . (Greene and Hicks, 1984)

Much of what arrives at the senses is never perceived, that is, we are not aware of it at any one time. Given the amount of stimulation that surrounds us, and the limited capacity of the brain to process and interpret sensory information, it seems inevitable (and highly desirable) that we should only be able to attend to certain things and not others. Think of how chaotic things would be if, for example, we were constantly aware of the clothes on our body, or the sound of our own breathing, or the sight of our arms and legs as we walk—quite apart from all the stimulation provided by other people and the physical world around us.

Traditionally, the topics of perception and attention have been studied in different ways, the former *assuming* that subjects are attending to particular stimuli presented to them, the latter focusing on just what it is that is 'perceived' and what isn't at any one time. But in Chapter 9 we saw that perception is not always conscious—if subliminal perception is a genuine perceptual process, this suggests that we cannot, after all, see awareness as a factor common to the two topics of perception and attention, as Greene and Hicks (above) suggest.

DEFINITIONS OF ATTENTION

Attention in the sense of selectivity, is, in fact, just one of several senses in which the term has been used. Moray (1970), for example, identified six meanings, but, for our present purposes, two main senses should be stressed (following Wilding, 1982):

(a) Attention as the mechanisms which reject some information and take in others (whether or not the latter enters conscious awareness)—*selective* or *focused attention*.

(b) Attention as some upper limit to the amount of processing that can be performed on incoming information at any one time—*capacity* or *divided attention*.

(Wilding points out that the term has also been used to refer to arousal level, vigilance and the ability to stay alert and concentrate. These were discussed in Chapters 5 and 6.)

METHODS OF STUDYING ATTENTION

Eysenck (1984) identifies two basic experimental techniques used to study attention:

(a) Subjects are presented with two or more simultaneous 'messages' and are instructed to process and respond to only one of these. The most popular way of doing this is to use *shadowing*, whereby one message is fed into the left ear and a different message into the right ear (through headphones) and subjects have to repeat one of these messages aloud as they hear it.

  The shadowing technique is really a particular form of *dichotic listening* (Broadbent, 1954) which refers to the simultaneous reception of two different stimulus inputs, one to each ear. Shadowing was first used by Cherry (1953) who wanted to study the *cocktail party situation*, in which the individual manages to select one or two voices to listen to from the hubbub of numerous conversations taking place at the same time and in the same room. The subject is instructed to select, which can tell us something about the selection process and what happens to unattended stimuli (ie it is used to study *selective attention*). Most studies have studied *auditory* attention.

(b) In the *dual-task* technique, the subject is asked to attend and respond to *both* (or all) the messages. Whereas shadowing focuses attention on a particular message, the dual task method deliberately *divides* the subject's attention and this provides useful information about a person's processing limitations and also about attention mechanisms and their *capacity*. Variables which seem to affect performance on such dual tasks are: (i) task similarity; (ii) task difficulty; and (iii) practice (eg the effects of automaticity).

THEORIES OF SELECTIVE ATTENTION

A number of theories, based largely on the shadowing technique, have tried to account for selective attention by proposing that somewhere in the processing of information there is a 'bottleneck' or *filter* (partly due to neurological limitations), at which point the attended message is passed on for further processing and the non-attended message is either filtered-out altogether (and so has no effect on behaviour) or is processed only to a limited degree.

  These *single channel models* (Broadbent, 1958; Deutsch and Deutsch, 1963; Treisman, 1964; Norman, 1969, 1976) differ essentially over the *position* of the filter and hence how much (and what kind of) processing of the non-attended message takes place.

BROADBENT'S 'FILTER MODEL' (1958)

This model sees the bottleneck occurring very early in processing and is based on the gross *physical* properties of the incoming stimuli. For example, much early research suggested that very little, if any, of the non-attended message could be recalled, except: (i) the speaker's gender; and (ii) whether it consisted of words or pure tones (Cherry, 1953; Treisman, 1964). Subjects were unable to identify its content, the language in which it was spoken, whether it changed from English to German or whether it was English played backwards. Even a word repeated thirty-five times was not recalled (Moray, 1959). The filter is also 'tuned' to other physical characteristics, such as volume, brightness, intensity and novelty.

However, as important as a predisposition to respond to novel stimuli may be, Broadbent's model could not account for a feature of the 'cocktail party situation', whereby we can be engaged in one conversation but can switch our attention if we hear our name mentioned in another. Moray (1959) found this happened about a third of the time in a shadowing task.

Gray and Wedderburn (1960) presented to alternate ears the syllables composing a word plus random digits, so that when a syllable was 'heard' by one ear, the other ear would 'hear' digits. For example:

Left Ear: OB   2   TIVE
Right ear: 6   JEC 9

According to Broadbent, when subjects were asked to repeat what they had heard in one ear (or channel) they should have reported 'ob-two-tive' or 'six-jec-nine'; this is nonsense, of course, but the filter model maintains that it is the physical nature of the auditory signal (ie which ear receives which input) and not meaning which determines what is attended to and, hence, what is recalled.

This was, in fact, demonstrated in one of Broadbent's early (1954) studies. Using a *split-span procedure*, subjects heard six digits, three to each ear in simultaneous pairs, at half-second intervals (261–795). Subjects were asked to recall the digits in either of two ways: (i) pair-by-pair (ie 27/69/15); or (ii) ear-by-ear (261/795). The ear-by-ear method of recall was much easier for subjects and produced more accurate recall. This led Broadbent to suggest that ears act like separate channels which can only be attended to one at a time. The pair-by-pair method of recall is more difficult because it requires subjects to switch continually from one channel to the other—this takes time and so is less efficient. By contrast, the ear-by-ear method requires only one switch of attention from one channel to the other. But as subjects can still successfully report *some* of the items presented to the other ear, these must be held in a temporary buffer store. Broadbent's model is shown in Figure 11.1.

Figure 11.1 Broadbent's filter model

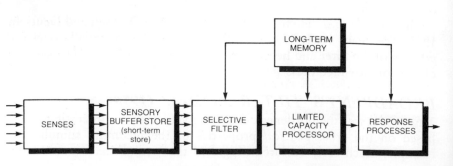

However, Grey and Wedderburn's subjects reported 'objective', thus demonstrating their capacity to switch attention rapidly from channel to channel; Broadbent argued that we can only attend to one channel at a time. Similarly, when the left ear heard 'Dear/5/Jane' and the right heard '3/Aunt/4', subjects tended to report the whole phrase ('Dear Aunt Jane') and so were grouping the bits of the message in terms of meaning.

Treisman (1960) played 'crept out of . . . flowers' as the shadowed message and 'brightly coloured . . . the swamp' as the non-shadowed, and found that subjects often reported 'crept out of the swamp'. In all these examples, the subject's experience with grammatical and semantic aspects of language override the instructions to attend only to one ear.

Again, because subjects are usually not asked about the non-shadowed message until the end of the experiment, it is possible that they have *forgotten* what they have actually noticed during the shadowing task (which would also contradict Broadbent's model). Norman (1969) stopped subjects—without warning—in the middle of a shadowing task and they were able to recall the last few words of the non-shadowed message if questioning occurred within 30 seconds of being interrupted (see Chapter 12).

In the initial shadowing studies, there was a potentially serious limitation, which relates to the point made earlier that, because perception is not always conscious, we cannot necessarily take conscious processing as a measure of attention. The early studies concluded that there is no processing of meaning of unattended messages because of subjects' lack of conscious awareness of their meaning—but what about the possibility of unconscious processing? (Eysenck and Keane, 1990).

A number of studies have shown that when certain words in the shadowed message are followed by electric shock and then later appear in the non-attended message, there is an associated change in GSR (Moray, 1970; Corteen and Wood, 1972; Corteen and Dunn, 1974). Von Wright et al (1975) asked subjects to attend to long lists of words and sometimes an electric shock was received when the Finnish word for 'suitable' was presented. Then they shadowed one auditory word list while a second list was simultaneously presented to the other ear. When the previously shocked word (or a word with a very similar sound or meaning) was presented in the non-shadowed list, there was a noticeable GSR change.

However, in this and the other studies, GSR changes were detected on only a fraction of the trials; therefore, thorough processing of un-attended information presumably only occurred some of the time (Eysenck and Keane, 1990).

TREISMAN'S ATTENUATOR MODEL (1964)

This model retains much of the 'architecture' of Broadbent's, but sees the bottleneck as being much more flexible. Whereas Broadbent's model is an all-or-none model (input is either allowed through or is filtered out, attended to or not attended to), Treisman's stimulus-analysis system proceeds through a hierarchy (Fig. 11.2). First, initial screening evaluates the signal on the basis of gross physical characteristics (much like Broadbent's) but instead of 'irrelevant' messages being excluded, the *attenuator* ('perceptual filter') 'turns their volume down' so that they are still 'available for higher level processing'. 'The channel filter attenuates

Figure 11.2 Treisman's
attenuator model

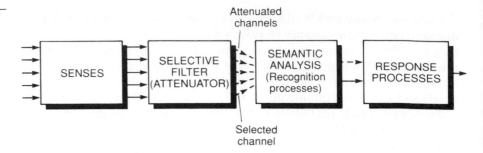

irrelevant messages rather than blocks them completely' (Treisman, 1964). Secondly, further analysis is based on individual words, grammatical structure and word-meaning.

Clearly, Treisman's model can account for the 'cocktail-party situation' (while Broadbent's cannot) and it does seem to provide a logical explanation of how we can 'hear' something while not attending to it and how we attend to the meaning rather than the physical characteristics of the message alone.

However, there remains the problem of how the executive decisions are made: does a simple attenuator have the capacity to analyse the intricate features of a message and check them with some master control to see whether they should or should not pass through and can it do so as quickly as is necessary? (Solso, 1979.)

THE PERTINENCE MODEL
This model, originally proposed by Deutsch and Deutsch in 1963 and revised by Norman in 1969 and 1976, puts the bottleneck much nearer the response end of the processing system by proposing that *all* signals are initially analysed and *then* passed on to an attenuator, which passes on the message for further processing in a to..ed-down form (Fig. 11.3).

Figure 11.3 Norman's late-
selection model

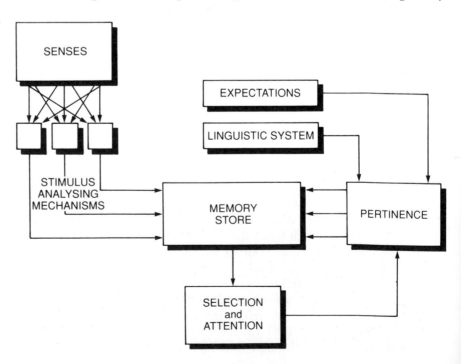

Compared with Treisman's model, the decision as to the *pertinence* or relevance of a message occurs much *earlier*.

If every signal is analysed initially, this would seem to make the model very uneconomical (Solso, 1979) because a great number of irrelevant stimuli need to be checked with long-term memory store before further processing can occur; it also makes it rather rigid and inflexible (Eysenck, 1984). But is there any evidence that *all* incoming information is analysed initially?

Treisman and Geffen (1967) used a shadowing task in which subjects had to repeat the shadowed message aloud but also had to indicate (by tapping) when they heard a certain 'target' word, which could occur in *either* ear. The pertinence model would predict that the target item should be detected and produce a response in whichever ear it appeared while the filter model would predict that it would not be detected if it appeared in the non-shadowed ear. What were the results?

Subjects detected 87 per cent of the target words in the shadowed ear but only 8 per cent in the non-attended ear, which seems to represent unequivocal support for Broadbent. However, Deutsch and Norman (1967) rejected the experiment as a valid test of the pertinence model on the grounds that subjects had to shadow *and* tap in one message but only tap in the other and this made the shadowed target words more important than the non-shadowed ones. However, when Treisman and Riley (1969) removed this bias by telling subjects to stop shadowing and to tap as soon as they detected a target in either message, there was still a greater detection of shadowed target-words than non-shadowed (although it was a less dramatic difference than in the 1967 experiment).

Other studies have also failed to support the pertinence model, (eg Kahneman, 1973; Neisser, 1976).

Johnston and Heinz (1978) have proposed a more flexible model, whereby selection is possible at several different stages of processing and in a 1979 experiment found that the amount of processing of a non-shadowed message varies as a function of task-demand in a way which is more consistent with Treisman's model than that of Deutsch and Deutsch and Norman. Johnston and Wilson (1980) found that non-target words were processed semantically when subjects did not know at which ear target words would arrive (divided attention condition), but they were not semantically processed when they did know (focused attention condition). This suggests that the amount of processing received by non-target stimuli is often only as much as is required to perform the experimental task.

AN EVALUATION OF SINGLE CHANNEL MODELS

Wilding (1982) believes that more is known about non-attended messages than either Broadbent's or Treisman's models can accommodate, but not as much as proposed by the pertinence model.

Many researchers have begun to question whether any filter theory which assumes a single, general purpose, limited-capacity central processor, can, in principle, account for the complexities of selective attention (Norman and Bobrow, 1975; Neisser, 1976; Allport, 1980b) and much of the relevant evidence comes from *dual-task* studies, which are more directly concerned with processing *capacity*.

STUDIES OF DIVIDED ATTENTION

Many of the earlier shadowing experiments overlooked a number of critical variables which can influence performance on these tasks, including practice, degree of similarity between competing tasks, the difficulty of tasks and so on.

According to Hampson (1989), there are more similarities between selective/focused and divided attention than might be thought: factors which make the one easier, also tend to make the other easier, since:

> ...anything which minimizes interference between processes, or keeps them 'further apart' will allow them to be dealt with more readily either selectively or together. (Hampson, 1989)

A clear example of interference in a dual-task situation is an experiment conducted by Shaffer (1975). (Notice that shadowing, used to study selective attention, is often used in dual-task experiments.) A skilled typist performed an audio-typing task (which involved listening to the material to be typed which was presented via headphones to *one* ear). This was combined with each of two concurrent tasks: (i) a shadowing task in which the shadowed message was presented to the ear not receiving the input to be typed; and (ii) a task of reading aloud visually presented material. In both cases, performing the audio-typing task and a concurrent task led to considerably poorer performance on one or both tasks, compared with performance when the tasks were carried out separately. Clearly there was interference between the tasks because of their similarity—the audio-typing task involves the *auditory input* modality (speech via headphones) as did the shadowing task; although here the *output modalities* were different (typing = motor; shadowing = articulatory), the interference caused by the similarity of the input was sufficient to cause decrement in actual performance. The reading aloud task involved visual input (and so was different from the audio-typing auditory) but this time the output modality was the same for both (ie articulatory). The interference here stemmed from what the subject actually had to do.

Eysenck and Keane (1990) summarize some of the research into divided attention using dual-task techniques, in relation to the three variables of task similarity, practice and task difficulty:

(a) *Task similarity*. Allport et al (1972) found that when subjects try to shadow passages of prose while learning auditorily presented words, subsequent recognition-memory performance for the words was no better than chance. But when shadowing was combined with visually presented words to learn, memory was significantly better and it was better still (90 per cent correct) when pictures were the to-be-remembered material.

What different kinds of similarity are relevant in dual-task performance?

Wickens (1984) reviewed the evidence and concluded that two tasks interfere to the extent that they involve the same stimulus modality (visual/auditory), make use of the same stages of processing (input/internal processing/output) and rely on related memory codes (verbal/visual). Response similarity also seems to be important.

Similarity of stimulus modality has probably been the most thoroughly explored. For example, Kolers (1972) invented a headgear with a half-silvered mirror, so that the visual world in front of him and that behind him were both available in the binocular field of view. But he could only attend forwards or backwards—with the unattended scene simply 'disappearing'; he could not attend to both simultaneously.

In addition to their experiments already described, Allport et al (1972) and Shaffer (1975) report findings which demonstrate both a quite astonishing capacity that some people show for handling two inputs simultaneously and also the importance of similarity of modality in influencing that capacity.

Allport et al's (1972) subjects were all skilled pianists. They had to shadow continuous speech while simultaneously sight-reading music which they had not seen before, and in fact performed as well on the sight-reading as they did when there was no concurrent, shadowing task. Shaffer's (1975) subject was a skilled typist who could copy-type prose in German (a language she did not know) presented visually while simultaneously shadowing a prose passage through headphones. Performance on both tasks together was almost as high as when they were done separately:

> It is clear in a general sense that the extent to which two tasks interfere with each other is a function of their similarity. However, what is singularly lacking is any satisfactory measure of similarity . . . (Eysenck and Keane, 1990)

(b) *Practice*. Why might practice make it easier to perform two tasks simultaneously? Firstly, subjects may develop new strategies for performing each of the tasks so as to minimize interference. Secondly, the demands a task makes on attention or other central resources may be reduced as a function of practice. Thirdly, while a task may initially require the use of several specific processing resources, practice may produce a more economical mode of functioning using fewer such resources. (This is discussed further in relation to automatic processing; see below.)

(c) *Task difficulty*. As with similarity, there is a question as to how difficulty should be defined. Sullivan (1976) gave subjects the two tasks of shadowing an auditory message and detecting target words on the non-shadowed message; when the former was made more difficult (by using a less redundant message—ie the subject had to concentrate harder in order to repeat it) fewer target words were detected on the non-shadowed message.

Eysenck and Keane (1990) point out that we cannot just *assume* that the demands for the resources of the two tasks performed together equal the sum of the demands of the same tasks when performed separately because, when they are performed together, fresh demands of co-ordination and avoidance of interference are introduced. For example, Duncan (1979) had subjects respond as quickly as possible to stimuli which followed one another, one requiring a right-hand, the other requiring a left-hand response. The relationship between each stimulus and response was either *corresponding* (for example, the rightmost stimulus required the rightmost finger response) or *crossed* (for example, the rightmost stimulus required the leftmost finger response). Overall, performance was surprisingly poor when the relationship between *one* stimulus and its response was corresponding, and was crossed for the *other* stimulus and *its* response. The errors were mostly those that would be expected if the inappropriate stimulus–response relationship had been selected—this suggests that subjects were confused and found the task complex because of the mixing of two different S–R relationships (corresponding and crossed) which did not exist when only one of the tasks is performed separately.

AUTOMATIC VERSUS CONTROLLED PROCESSING

In cases of people who demonstrate quite remarkable capacity to do two things at the same time (such as Allport et al's pianists and Shaffers' typist, and Japanese abacus operators, who could answer general knowledge questions while operating), the tasks used are very different from each other (eg sight-reading and shadowing prose). This contrasts with the shadowing experiments investigating selective attention, where very similar 'messages' are used (eg digits presented to both ears). Another important difference is to do with the subjects who are often highly skilled and thoroughly practiced in one of the tasks—in Shiffrin and Schneider's (1977) terms, these subjects are displaying *automatic processing* (or *automaticity*).

According to Eysenck and Keane (1990) there is fairly general agreement about what this means: (i) automatic processes are fast; (ii) they do not reduce the capacity for performing other tasks (ie they make *no* demands on the person's attention); (iii) they are not available to consciousness; and (iv) they are unavoidable (such that they always occur when the appropriate stimulus is presented—even if it is outside the field of attention). Automatic processing is contrasted with *controlled processing* (which corresponds to focused attention).

Learning to drive a car clearly results in *automaticity*; at first focused attention is required for each component part of the skill but an experienced driver is able to engage in interaction with the environment in the relative absence of awareness (Norman, 1976).

However, Eysenck and Keane (1990) believe that it is not always easy to demonstrate automaticity empirically. For example, the claim that it makes *no* demands on the person's attention is rarely the case. Again, regarding its 'unavoidability', the *Stroop effect* is usually seen as involving unavoidable and automatic processing. Here, colour words are presented (eg 'blue') in a conflicting coloured ink (eg 'blue' written in red ink) and the subject's task is to name the colour (ie red). The colour *words* usually interfere with the task and the interpretation usually made is that they are processed automatically and unavoidably (even though they are irrelevant to the task).

However, Kahneman and Henik (1979) found that the effect was much greater when the distracting information was in the same *location* as the colour which was to be identified, rather than at an adjacent location within the central fixation area—this suggests that the Stroop effect may *not* be automatic and unavoidable after all.

Shriffin and Schneider (1977) found that attention can be divided among several information sources with reasonable success when automatic processes are used. This is quite different from focused attention, where some sources of information must be attended to and others ignored—controlled processes largely prevent unwanted processing from occurring, whereas automatic processes disrupt performance because of automatic responses to to-be-ignored stimuli (Eysenck and Keane, 1990):

> Automatic processes function rapidly and in parallel but suffer from inflexibility; controlled processes are flexible and versatile but operate relatively slowly and in a serial fashion. (Eysenck, 1982; quoted in Eysenck and Keane, 1990)

While Shiffrin and Schneider's distinction was based on their use of visual tasks, Eysenck and Keane (1990) point out that very similar results have been obtained for auditory tasks.

AUTOMATICITY AND PRACTICE

A central feature of Shiffrin and Schneider's (1977) theory of automatic processing is the claim that some processes become automatic *as a result of practice*. But Eysenck and Keane (1990) point out that this tells us very little about what is actually happening—is it just a speeding up of the process involved or is there a change in the nature of the processes themselves (the latter called 'restructuring' by Cheng, 1985)? Cheng believes that most of Shiffrin and Schneider's findings were in fact based on restructuring.

Norman and Shallice (1980) and Shallice (1982) argue that, instead of automatic versus attentional or controlled processing, it is preferable to identify *three levels of functioning*:

(a) *Fully automatic processing* controlled by schemata (ie organized plans) which occur with very little conscious awareness of the process involved.
(b) *Partially automatic processing*, which involves *contention scheduling* (a way of resolving conflicts between competing schemata) and which generally involves more conscious awareness than (a) but which occurs without deliberate direction or conscious control.
(c) *Deliberate control* by a supervisory attentional system, which is involved in decision making and trouble-shooting and allows flexible responding in novel situations.

Eysenck and Keane (1990) believe this approach is superior to that of Shiffrin and Schneider, which assumes a single control system. The three levels approach provides a more natural explanation for the fact that some processes are fully automatic while others are only partially so. But what exactly happens as automaticity develops through prolonged practice?

According to Logan (1988), Shiffrin and Schneider fail to spell out in any detail *why* practice has the effect it does; like Eysenck and Keane (1990), he argues that their model is largely descriptive and *explains* very little.

As summarized by Eysenck and Keane (1990), Logan makes the following assumptions:

(a) Separate memory traces are stored away every time a stimulus is encountered and processed.
(b) Practice with the same stimulus produces storage of more and more information about the stimulus and what to do with it.
(c) This increase in the knowledge base leads to rapid retrieval of relevant information as soon as the appropriate stimulus is presented.
(d) 'Automaticity is memory retrieval: Performance is automatic when it is based on a single-step, direct-access retrieval of past solutions from memory' (Logan, 1988).
(e) In the absence of practice, the task of responding appropriately to a stimulus requires thought and the application of rules; after prolonged practice, the appropriate response is stored in memory and can be accessed very rapidly.

Novice practice is limited by a lack of knowledge rather than by a lack of resources ... Only the knowledge base changes with practice. (Logan, 1988)

CONCLUSIONS

What seems to emerge from the research and theory which has been discussed above is that some tasks require a greater degree of attention than others. This is why more than one thing can be done at the same time—no one of them requires the full capacity of the attention system (eg audio-typing and shadowing prose). But however skilled one is at a particular activity and, therefore, however much attention can be devoted to some other concurrent task or tasks, surely there is some overall limit to how many things we can do simultaneously? This implies that there is some sort of limited-capacity *central processor*, which co-ordinates and allocates a central (finite) pool of attentional resources to different tasks (like the Treasury allocating resources to different Government Departments) Indeed, *resource allocation* is a term used to describe how attention becomes divided between tasks (and how the money is divided between the Department of Education and Science, Health, Transport, etc.). This view of attention as a flexible process which can be spread across tasks as required seems to fit the facts of everyday observation very well—it seems intuitively right. (You might be having a cup of coffee at this moment as you read, something which you are so skilled at that you hardly need to give it any of your attention—drinking coffee that is!).

A way of saying that a particular task does not require our conscious (focused) attention is to say that it requires little *mental effort*; tasks which require a lot of mental effort make heavy demands on the central, limited-capacity processor.

This concept of mental effort forms an important part of Kahneman's (1973) *theory of attention*, which assumes that there is an overall limit to a person's capacity to perform mental work (Fig. 11.4).

When we are aroused and alert (see Chapters 4, 5 and 6) we have more attentional resources available than when we are tired and lethargic. If we

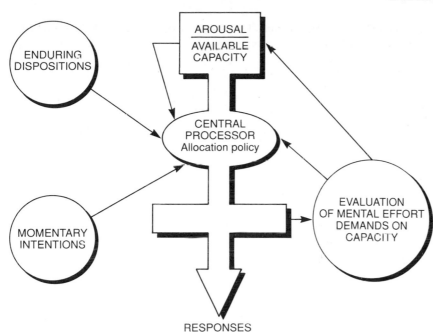

Figure 11.4 Kahneman's model of attention

are both motivated and skilled, we will have attentional capacity 'left over'. It follows that we can attend to more than one thing at a time as long as the total mental effort required does not exceed the total capacity available (we can't 'overspend'). Kahneman believes that allocation of attentional resources depends on a *central allocation policy* adopted by the central processor, which constantly evaluates the level of demand. If level of demand becomes excessive, the central allocation policy must decide which tasks should receive more attention.

The allocation policy is influenced by enduring dispositions (which refer to certain types of external stimuli such as novel stimuli, a suddenly moving object, hearing one's name used in a different conversation) momentary intentions (activities related to current goals) and the overall level of mental effort demand on capacity. The research on attentional capacity strongly suggests that attention is a far more flexible system than is suggested by models of selective attention (particularly Broadbent's filter model). In keeping with this view, Kahneman's model sees attention as a central dynamic process rather than the result of an automatic filtering of perceptual input. Neisser (1976) suggests that attention should be thought of *not* as a mechanism or process but as a skill. Rather than seeing a one-way flow of information from input through to responses, Kahneman sees attention as involving a constant perceptual evaluation of the demands required to produce appropriate responses. Yet Kahneman is not without his critics.

One difficulty is to do with how much of the monitoring of task demand and allocation of attention is an unconscious process, ie how are decisions made to channel our attention to a difficult task, say?

Spelke et al (1976) argue that people's ability to develop skills in specialized situations is so great that it may never be possible to define the general limits of cognitive capacity and so the concept of attention as-capacity is largely redundant.

Allport (1980b) rejects the concept of a general purpose, limited-capacity processor altogether. The concept of attention, he says, is often used synonymously with 'consciousness' with no proper specification of how it is supposed to operate and it has done little, if anything, to increase our understanding of the problems it is meant to explain. Instead, he proposes a number of different specific processing mechanisms; when two simultaneous tasks are highly similar, they compete for the *same* specific mechanisms and this leads to mutual interference but dissimilar tasks involve different mechanisms and so no interference occurs.

However, Eysenck (1984) believes this could lead to chaos; some central control is necessary if behaviour is to be purposeful and co-ordinated. So what is the solution?

One possibility is the proposal by Baddeley (Baddeley and Hitch, 1974; Baddeley, 1986) of two specific systems (an articulatory loop and a visuospatial scratch pad) in addition to a central capacity processor (which is modality-free). This could explain why overt repetition of an over-learned sequence of digits (which uses an articulatory loop) does not interfere with verbal reasoning (which uses the central processor). According to Eysenck and Keane (1990), what is being proposed is a hierarchical structure of processes, with a central processor (attention) at the top and involved in the co-ordination and control of behaviour. Below are specific processing mechanisms which operate relatively separately from each other (ie in a modular fashion). Processes at the bottom tend to be more automatic than those at the top. Without some kind of overall control, chaos would probably result (Eysenck and Keane, 1990). The Baddeley 'solution' relates, in fact, to his model of *working memory*, an attempt to explain what *short-term memory* is for and how it operates.

It is interesting to note that we began this chapter by relating attention to perception; we end the chapter by suggesting an important link between attention and memory, the topic of the next chapter.

12 MEMORY

THE CONCEPT OF MEMORY

As we saw in Chapter 7, learning is defined in terms of relatively permanent changes due to past experience and memory is a crucial part of the learning process—without memory, experiences would be 'lost' and we could not benefit from past experience. Unless, in some way, our prior learning can be 'recorded' it cannot be used at a later date and so we are not in a position to benefit from our past experience. However, trying to define learning and memory independently of each other is very difficult, as they represent two sides of the same coin: (i) learning depends on memory for its 'permanency'; and, conversely, (ii) memory would have no 'content' if learning were not taking place.

Therefore, we could define memory as the *retention* of *learning* or *experience*; this shows how interdependent the two processes are.

In Blakemore's words:

> In the broadest sense, learning is the acquisition of knowledge and memory is the storage of an internal representation of that knowledge ... (Blakemore, 1988)

And again:

> ... without the capacity to remember and to learn, it is difficult to imagine what life would be like, whether it could be called living at all. Without memory, we would be servants of the moment, with nothing but our innate reflexes to help us deal with the world. There could be no language, no art, no science, no culture. Civilization itself is the distillation of human memory. (Blakemore, 1988)

THE STUDY OF MEMORY

As we saw in Chapter 1, memory (like learning) is a hypothetical construct and, as such, is an abstract concept which refers to three distinguishable but interrelated processes: (i) *registration* or (reception); (ii) *storage*; and (iii) *retrieval* (see Fig. 12.1).

Registration can be thought of as a necessary condition for storage to take place but, as we shall see below, it is not a sufficient condition, ie not everything which registers on the sense receptors is stored. The topic of selective attention was discussed in Chapter 11.

Similarly, storage can be seen as a necessary, but not a sufficient, condition for retrieval, ie you can only recover information which has been stored (you cannot remember something you do not know), but the fact that you know it is no guarantee that you will remember it on any particular occasion. This is the crucial distinction between *availability* (whether or not the information has been stored) and *accessibility*

Figure 12.1 *The three processes of memory*

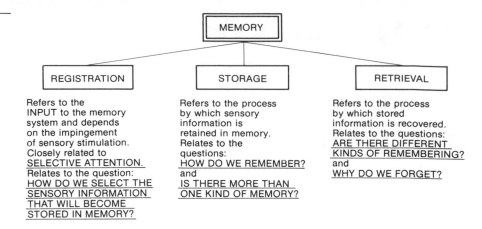

(whether or not it can be retrieved), which is especially relevant in relation to theories of forgetting.

STORAGE

In practice, the way in which storage is studied is through testing the subject's ability to retrieve and this is equivalent to the distinction we made in Chapter 7 between learning and performance: learning corresponds to the storage aspect of memory, while performance corresponds to the retrieval aspect of memory. (This again shows how closely related the two processes of learning and memory are.)

However, there are several kinds of retrieval; so, as tested by recall, for example, storage may seem not to have occurred (no learning) but as tested by recognition, storage (and hence learning) might be demonstrated. In this chapter, we shall be concentrating on memory as storage and memory as retrieval, but it is important to regard memory as a whole as a function of all three.

The distinction between primary memory and secondary memory was originally made by James in 1890, although Ebbinghaus (1885), one of the pioneers of memory research, would have accepted the distinction. Hebb (1949), Broadbent (1958), Waugh and Norman (1965) and many others have also made the distinction but perhaps the most elaborate version is built into Atkinson and Shiffrin's 'Multi-Store Model' or Dual Memory Theory (1968, 1971). Strictly speaking, short-term memory (STM) and long-term memory (LTM) refer to experimental procedures for investigating primary and secondary memory, respectively, which are assumed to underlie them; however, we shall use 'STM' and 'LTM' to refer to both (Fig. 12.2). Although most research and theorizing has concentrated on these second and third stages of the storage process, logically the place to start is with sensory memory (sometimes called 'sensory buffer store' or 'sensory storage').

SENSORY MEMORY

If, after being shown something for a fraction of a second, we did not retain an impression of it in a fairly literal way for a rather long time, in most cases we would not be able to understand or process it adequately and it would not be remembered. It seems that we process information both from the stimulus itself and our subsequent memory of it.

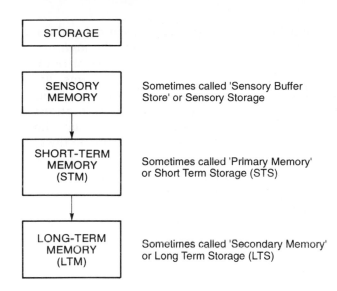

Figure 12.2 *The three forms of storage*

Sensory memory gives us an accurate account of the environment as experienced by the sensory system. When we receive a visual input, for example, its image remains with us for approximately 0.5 seconds in a relatively unanalysed form; after this, any information which is not attended to or processed further is forgotten. So, clearly, sensory memory and registration are very closely related and it is misleading to consider it a form of storage as opposed to a necessary requirement for storage proper (ie STM).

Sensory memory seems to be *modality specific*, that is, the storage (such as it is) occurs *within* the sensory system that received the information, and not at some central location. Additional information entering the *same* sensory channel immediately disrupts the storage. For example, if, shortly after a visual array is presented, a second visual stimulus is flashed, the memory of the initial array may be lost. However, if the second stimulus is a sound or smell it will not interfere with memory of the visual stimulus.

Sperling (1960, 1963) studied the *visual* modality (or the *iconic store*) and showed that more information is available *immediately* after visual stimulation than can be recalled even a few seconds later. He showed subjects an array comprising three rows of four letters in a 4 × 3 matrix for 50 milliseconds (1/20 of a second). When they had to recall as many as possible from the whole matrix (*whole reports* or span of apprehension), subjects recalled, on average, 4.32 letters (out of 12), although they commonly reported having seen more than they could actually remember.

In another condition, subjects were required to recall the top, middle or bottom row, depending on whether they heard a high-, medium- or low-pitched tone. Although subjects could not know in advance which tone would be heard, they succeeded in recalling an average of 3.04 of the letters from each row, which meant that between nine and ten words were available immediately after presentation. Clearly, the information must have been lost rapidly in the first condition: in the time it took to try to recall the whole array approximately five words were lost, and this was supported by the finding that the advantage of *partial reports* (just one row) was lost if the auditory signal was delayed for a second or so.

Similar effects have been reported for the *auditory* modality (what Neisser, 1967, called the *echoic store*) by several researchers, including Broadbent (1958), and Treisman (1964). It seems that iconic memory involves storage of stimuli which have been discriminated in terms of *physical* features only (eg size, shape, colour, location) as distinct from their meaning, and Morton (1970) reported that the echoic store (what he called the pre-categorical acoustic store) works in the same way.

This reference to Broadbent and Treisman highlights the considerable overlap between the areas of attention and memory. For example, Broadbent's Filter Model (see Chapter 11) was in many ways the main precursor of the multi-store approach to memory and there is a definite resemblance between sensory memory (or storage) and Broadbent's sensory 'buffer' store (Eysenck and Keane, 1990; Fig. 11.1).

SHORT-TERM MEMORY (STM)

According to Lloyd et al (1984) probably less than one-hundredth of all the sensory information that impinges every second on the human senses reaches consciousness, and of this, only one-twentieth achieves anything approaching stable storage.

Clearly, if memory ability were limited to sensory memory, our capacity for retaining information about the world would be extremely limited as well as very precarious. However, according to models of memory such as Atkinson and Shiffrin's Multi-Store Model (1968, 1971), some information from sensory memory is successfully passed on to STM, which allows us to store information long enough to be able to *use* it and, for this reason, it is often referred to as 'working memory'. (However, 'working memory' has different connotations as used by Baddeley and Hitch, 1974 and Hitch, 1980—see below.)

We can analyse STM (as we can LTM) in terms of three dimensions: (i) *capacity* (how *much* information can be stored); (ii) *duration* (how *long* the information can be held in storage); and (iii) *coding* (in what *ways* sensory input is transformed or processed so that it can be stored, ie how it is *represented* by the memory system).

i) *Capacity*

Ebbinghaus (1885) and Wundt (in the 1860s) were two of the first psychologists to maintain that STM is limited to six or seven bits of information; but the most famous account is given by Miller in his article *The magical number seven, plus or minus two: some limits on our capacity for processing information* (1956). In this article Miller showed how *chunking* can be used to expand the limited capacity of STM by using already-established memory stores to categorize or encode new information.

If we think of STM's capacity as seven 'slots' (plus or minus two), each slot being able to accommodate one bit or unit of information, then seven individual letters would each fill a slot and there would be no 'room' left for any additional letters. However, if the letters are chunked into a word, then the word would constitute a unit of information and there would still be six free slots.

In the example below, the 25 bits of information can be chunked into (or reduced to) six words, which could quite easily be reduced further to one 'bit' (or chunk) based on prior familiarity with the words:

```
S   A   V   A   O
R   E   E   E   G
U   R   S   Y   A
O   O   D   N   S
F   C   N   E   R
```

To be able to chunk, you have to know the 'rule' or the 'code', which in this case is: starting with *F* (bottom left-hand corner) read upwards until you get to *S* and then drop down to *C* and read upwards until you get to *A*, then go to *N* and read upwards and so on. This should give you 'four score and seven years ago'.

Whenever we reduce a larger to a smaller amount of information we are chunking, and this not only increases the capacity of STM but also makes it more likely that the information will be stored for longer. It also represents a form of encoding information by imposing a *meaning* on otherwise meaningless letters or numbers, etc: (i) arranging letters into words, words into phrases, phrases into sentences; (ii) converting 1066 (four bits of information) into a date (one chunk), so a string of 28 numbers could be reduced to seven dates; (iii) using a *rule* to organize information, eg the series 149162536496481100121 (21 bits) is generated by the rule by which $1^2 = 1$, $2^2 = 4$, $3^2 = 9$ and so on. The rule represents a single chunk and that is all that has to be remembered.

These examples demonstrate how chunking allows us to bypass the seven-bit 'bottleneck'; although the amount of information contained in any one chunk may be unlimited (eg the rule in (iii) above can generate an infinitely long set of digits), the number of chunks which can be held in STM is still limited to 7 plus or minus 2.

ii) *Duration*

It seems that, unaided, we can hold information in STM for between 15 and 30 seconds (according to Atkinson and Shiffrin, 1971), but this can be extended through *rehearsal* or repetition. Rehearsal seems to require some kind of speech (either overtly or mentally) whereby the subject 'says' the information to keep it 'circulating' within STM (eg repeating a telephone number out loud until you dial it), but it is easily disrupted by either external distractions (eg someone asking you for change while you are repeating the number) or internal ones (eg thinking about your own telephone number).

Therefore it seems that in rehearsal information is maintained in the memory system *acoustically* (the *sounds* of the items are repeated and stored); although it *can* be visual, this is likely to be slower than acoustic rehearsal.

iii) *Coding*

As we have seen in relation to rehearsal, coding in STM seems to be primarily acoustic, ie information from sensory memory (including visual) is converted into sound and is stored in this form.

LONG-TERM MEMORY (LTM)

i) *Capacity*

It is usually thought that LTM has unlimited capacity. It can be seen as the repository of all things in memory which are not currently being used but which are potentially retrievable. It enables us to deal with the past and to use that information to deal with the present; in a sense, LTM allows us to live in the past and present simultaneously.

Bower (1975) has identified some of the classes of information contained in LTM. These include: (i) a spatial model of the world around us; (ii) knowledge of the physical world, physical laws and properties of objects; (iii) beliefs about people, ourselves, social norms, values and goals; (iv) motor skills, problem-solving skills and plans for achieving various things; (v) perceptual skills in understanding language, interpreting music, etc.

ii) *Duration*

Information can be held for between a few minutes and several years (which may in fact span the individual's entire lifetime).

iii) *Coding*

There are at least two forms of coding in LTM: (i) *semantic code*, which deals with material in terms of verbal meaning; and (ii) *imagery* or *visual code*, which takes a pictorial form. The former seems to be more common, especially when we have to deal with abstract material for which it is difficult to conjure up appropriate images. However, it has also been suggested that an acoustic code is used in LTM (Table 12.1).

Table 12.1 Summary of major differences between STM and LTM

	CAPACITY	DURATION	CODING
STM	7 bits of information. Can be increased by chunking	15 to 30 seconds (unaided). Can be increased by rehearsal	Acoustic
LTM	Unlimited	From a few seconds to several years (perhaps permanently)	(i) Semantic (ii) Visual (iii) Acoustic

RETRIEVAL

'Remembering' can take many different forms (Fig. 12.3). However, they are all ways of recovering or locating information which has been stored; they also represent different ways of measuring memory in the laboratory.

1) *Recognition* is a sensitive form of remembering, whereby some thing or somebody strikes us as familiar without our necessarily being able to name or otherwise identify it. Or we may recognize certain objects or faces as having been 'present' in a test situation when the 'target' items are present with other 'distractor' items (which were not originally

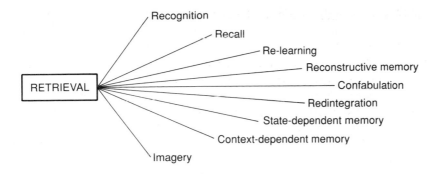

*Figure 12.3 Different forms
of remembering or retrieval*

present). This is the kind of remembering involved in multiple choice
tests—the answers from which you have to choose one can be regarded
as retrieval cues.

2)   *Recall* is a more stringent form of remembering and usually
involves the active searching of our memory stores. When we recall, we
reproduce something learned some time earlier and often the retrieval
cues are missing or very sparse. This is the kind of remembering involved
in timed essays.

3)   *Re-learning* is the most sensitive measure of all—even though
something may seem to be totally 'forgotten', it may be easier to learn
second time around than it was originally. In experiments it is usually
expressed as a

$$Savings\ score = \frac{Original\ trials - Re\text{-}learning\ trials}{Original\ trials} \times \frac{100}{1}$$

4)   *Re-constructive memory* is the kind of remembering involved
when information is passed from one person to another, often by
word-of-mouth, as in the spreading of rumours or gossip. It is not
simple reproduction of the past but interpretation of the past in the light
of our beliefs, schemas, expectations and so on, and so often involves a
distortion of objective truth. (We shall look at this in greater detail
below.)

5)   *Confabulation* refers to a kind of memory error often made under
conditions of high motivation or arousal—if we are unable to recall a
certain item, we may manufacture something that seems appropriate. For
example, the detailed accounts that hypnotized subjects give of their
childhood birthdays often turn out to be confabulations; they seem to
combine several birthdays and 'fill in' the missing details. Patients with
Korsakov's Syndrome are very prone to confabulation.

6)   *Redintegration* is the recollection of past experiences on the basis
of a few cues, which might be souvenirs, particular smells, melodies—
almost anything, in fact, which serve as reminders. Only a portion of the
information is immediately available and a search of memory gradually
leads to the redintegration of knowledge into some kind of coherent
whole. The search is fairly systematic, rather like a detective's investigation, but every so often some item will 'pop up', quite unrelated to what
is currently being consciously thought about. This kind of remembering
is involved in eyewitness testimony and the recollection of childhood
invoved in psychoanalysis (as is reconstructive memory).

7)   *State-dependent memory* and *context-* (or *cue-)dependent*

memory refer to the similarity or difference between the state (eg alcohol or no-alcohol) or the context (eg the room) in which the original learning took place and in which the learning is remembered. Generally, if two different states or contexts are involved, retrieval is poor. We shall return to this in relation to forgetting.

8) *Imagery* is the basis of many kinds of *mnemonic* devices ('memory aids') and there is much evidence that we can remember verbal material better if we can 'hook it' onto some visual image—this relates both to initial learning (how the material is encoded) and retrieval (see Table 12.2).

Table 12.2 Some of the most commonly used mnemonic devices

DEVICE	EXAMPLE
A *Method of loci ('method of places' or the 'house' technique)*	You have to imagine a short walk through a series of locations, perhaps a journey through a familiar street, past well-known buildings or through the rooms in your house or college. Take each of the (unrelated) words to be remembered in turn (eg the items on a shopping list) and associate it with each of your locations. The more bizarre the association, the greater the probability of recalling the words
B *Associations*	You find a relationship between the unrelated words by weaving them into a sensible story
C *Rhyme and rhythm*	Eg 'Thirty days hath September etc.
D *Numeric pegword system ('Pigeonhole technique')*	Numbers are associated with a rhyming object and you picture the items to be remembered in relation to the relevant pegword. Eg One — bun Egg Two — shoe Sausage Three — tree Potatoes The items to be remembered are hooked onto the pegword by constructing an image which includes the first item with the bun, the second with the shoes etc. ('egg on a bun'; 'sausage in a shoe'; 'potatoes growing on a tree')

THE MULTI-STORE MODEL (ATKINSON AND SHIFFRIN, 1968, 1971)

So far, we have been discussing STM and LTM differences without looking specifically at Atkinson and Shiffrin's model (Fig. 12.4). This is sometimes called the Dual Memory Theory (Atkinson et al, 1990) because of the emphasis on STM and LTM in which stored information has been coded, in contrast with sensory memory which holds information from the environment in roughly its original or 'sensory' form.

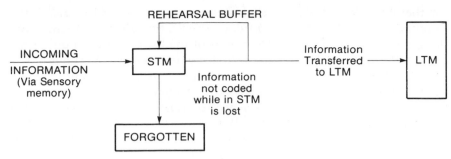

Figure 12.4 The multi-store model of memory. (Based on Atkinson and Shiffrin, 1971)

Sensory memory, STM and LTM are referred to by the model as permanent *structural components* of the memory system and represent intrinsic features of the information-processing system of humans. In addition to these structural components, the memory system comprises relatively transient processes called *control processes*, of which rehearsal is one. Rehearsal serves two main functions: (i) to act as buffer between sensory memory and LTM by maintaining incoming information within STM; and (ii) to transfer information to LTM.

Finally, how does information transfer from sensory memory to STM? According to Atkinson and Shiffrin, it is scanned and matched with information in LTM and if a match occurs (ie *pattern recognition*) the information from sensory memory might then be fed into STM along with a verbal label from LTM. (Pattern recognition was discussed in Chapter 9.)

WHAT IS THE EVIDENCE FOR THE MULTI-STORE MODEL?

TWO-COMPONENT TASKS

In the laboratory, performance on certain memory tasks seems to be most conveniently explained in terms of a STM–LTM distinction; for example, if subjects are shown 20 words in succession and then asked immediately to recall them in any order (*free-recall*), typical results would be as shown in Figure 12.5.

The probability of recalling any word depends on its position in the list (its serial position) and hence the graph shown in Figure 12.5 is called a *serial position curve*. Subjects typically recall those items from the end

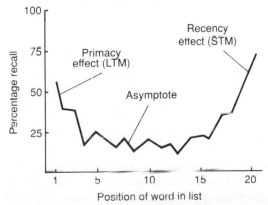

Figure 12.5 A typical serial position curve. (Based on Glanzer and Cunitz, 1966)

of the list first and get more of these correct than earlier items (the *recency effect*). According to Murdock (1962), this is true no matter how long the list. Items from the beginning of the list are recalled quite well relative to those in the middle of the list (the *primacy effect*) but not as well as those at the end. Poorest recall is for items in the middle (and this middle portion of the curve is called the *asymptote*).

The implication is that the recency effect reflects words being retrieved from STM, whereas the primacy effect reflects retrieval from LTM. The last items are only remembered if recalled first and tested immediately, as demonstrated by Glanzer and Cunitz (1966); when recall is delayed by, for example, getting subjects to count backwards in threes (thus preventing rehearsal) the recency effect disappears while recall of earlier items is comparatively unaffected. Two groups of subjects were presented with the same list of words: one group recalled the material immediately after presentation while the other group recalled after 30 seconds. The first group showed a recency effect (indicating STM retrieval) and the second group showed a primacy effect (indicating LTM retrieval; Fig. 12.6).

Figure 12.6 The effect of distraction prior to recall on the serial position curve. (Based on Glanzer, M. and Cunitz, A. R. (1966) Two storage mechanisms in free recall. Journal of Verbal Learning and Verbal Behaviour, 5, 351–60)

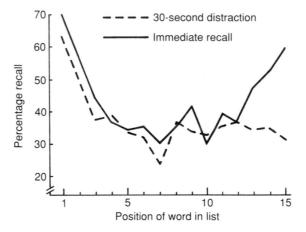

A second kind of task involves what has become known as the *Brown–Peterson* technique (Brown, 1958; Peterson and Peterson, 1959) and is concerned specifically with the effects of the length of the recall interval on recall (Fig. 12.7).

Peterson and Peterson (1959) gave subjects *trigrams*, which are nonsense syllables comprising three consonants (eg CPQ). Only one trigram was to be remembered on each trial, something that would be well within their capabilities if allowed normal rehearsal (ie repeating it over and over to themselves). But this was prevented by getting subjects to count backwards in threes, aloud, for 3, 6, 9, 12, 15 or 18 seconds, or not at all, after which a tone was sounded as a signal for them to stop counting and try to recall the trigram (Glanzer and Cunitz had done this for a period of 30 seconds in their second experiment). Even with very small amounts of information, nearly 70 per cent is forgotten after only a 9-second delay and 90 per cent after 18 seconds. (The remaining 10 per cent is thought to be retained over a longer period and is processed by LTM.)

This rapid loss of information from memory when rehearsal is prevented is usually taken as evidence for the existence of a STM with rapid decay of the memory trace or displacement; the kind of forgetting

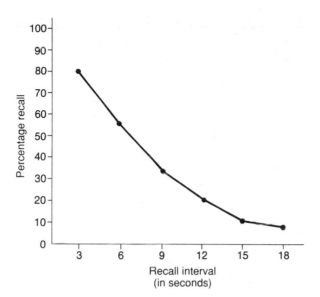

Figure 12.7 The effects of interfering task on recall. (Based on Peterson and Peterson, 1959)

involved in LTM is thought to be different and this difference in forgetting represents further support for the Multi-Store Model (see below). However, not everyone accepts this interpretation of the findings. For example, Gruneberg (1970) argues that they could be a feature of *any* memory system and do not necessarily imply a distinction between two separate stores.

The concept of rehearsal itself, so important in Atkinson and Shiffrin's model, has also been criticized as both unnecessary and too general. Craik and Watkins (1973), for example, asked subjects to remember only certain words (those beginning with a particular letter) from lists presented either rapidly or slowly; the position of critical words relative to non-critical ones determined the amount of time a particular word spent in STM and the number of potential rehearsals given to it. Retention over long periods was found to be unrelated to *either* duration in STM *or* the number of explicit or implicit rehearsals.

An earlier study (Glanzer and Meinzer, 1967) had shown that the apparent effectiveness of rehearsal in enhancing retention may not just be a function of verbal repetition. Subjects who were required to repeat items aloud recalled fewer of them than subjects allowed an equal period of silent rehearsal; perhaps in silent rehearsal the subject is not merely repeating the material but may actually be re-coding it into a different form which enhances recall.

Craik and Watkins (1973) distinguished between: (i) *maintenance* (or rote) *rehearsal*; and (ii) *elaborative rehearsal*. Maintenance rehearsal involves repeating the items in the form in which they are presented and is sufficient to retain them in the short-term. Elaborative rehearsal involves elaboration of the items, for example, semantic recoding (giving them a meaning) or associative linking of words with pre-existing knowledge, and is necessary for long-term retention.

Maintenance rehearsal seems not to be necessary for storage, as illustrated by Jenkin's (1974) study in which subjects showed they could remember material even though they were not expecting to be tested and so were not predisposed to rehearse (this is *incidental learning*).

Therefore it seems that it is the *kind* of rehearsal or processing that is crucial rather than the amount and this idea has been investigated in particular by Craik and Lockhart (1972), in the form of the *Levels of Processing* approach (this will be discussed in detail later in the chapter, see p. 326).

CODING

Many studies have produced results which suggest that STM and LTM code information in different ways.

If we take again the familiar example of trying to remember a telephone number, we keep it in STM by auditory rehearsal (using an acoustic code), that is, we *say* it over and over, regardless of whether we have looked it up in the directory or the operator has given it to us. Experimental findings tend to support this view of STM.

Conrad (1963, 1964) presented subjects with sequences of six consonants and found that the errors they made in trying to remember them were similar in *sound* to the correct item (eg b/d, p/v, m/n) despite the fact that they had been presented *visually*. In fact, they made the same kind of acoustic errors as they did when trying to detect similar spoken consonants against a noisy background.

Wickelgren (1965) asked subjects to read four letters followed by a list of eight letters and then to recall the original four letters. They had more difficulty in doing this when the second list comprised letters of similar *sound* than when they were acoustically different. This was found to be true for digits too.

Baddeley (1966) found that immediate recall of the order of short lists of unrelated words was seriously impeded if the words were acoustically similar (eg caught/short/taut/nought) but not if they were semantically similar (eg huge/great/big/wide). After a delay, however, exactly the opposite effect occurred.

It seems that the phonemic or grammatical features of prose sentences are forgotten almost immediately, while the semantic features are well remembered even after a long delay. Similarly, Craik and Levy (1970) found that material which is highly related conceptually (eg north/south/east/west) is beneficial to LTM but does not affect STM.

Therefore, there is considerable support for the view that STM uses an acoustic code and LTM a semantic code. However, not everyone accepts this view.

When discussing chunking in relation to STM capacity, we used the term 'meaning' to describe what is involved in reducing large amounts of information to smaller and more manageable amounts so as to increase the capacity of STM. According to Miller (1956), chunking represents a linguistic re-coding which seems to be the, 'very lifeblood of the thought process'. He says that it is not surprising that such compression of information can occur when you consider how lexical information is normally processed: our capacity to read and understand is largely based on the chunking of letters into words, words into phrases and phrases into sentences. Therefore, the capability of STM to handle a vast amount of information is facilitated by our ability to chunk information; however, this cannot occur until certain information in LTM is activated and a match made between the incoming items and its representation in LTM.

This is illustrated by an experiment by Miller and Selfridge (1950) in which subjects were presented with a number of 'sentences' (of varying lengths) which represented different approximations to true English sentences. Subjects had to recall the words in their correct order; immediate recall was greater the closer the sentence approximated normal English. This suggests that subjects used knowledge of semantic and grammatical structure (presumably stored in LTM) to facilitate immediate memory.

More recently, Bower and Springston (1970) presented subjects with a letter sequence which they had to recall. In one condition, letters were read so that they did not form a well-known group and so could not be matched with information stored in LTM (fb, iph, dtw, aib, m), while in another they did (fbi, phd, twa, ibm). The latter were more readily recalled; they were clustered along the lines of acronyms familiar to most college students and, in effect, the pause after 'fbi', etc. allowed subjects to 'look it up' in their mental lexicon and so encode the letter in a chunk.

Letter recognition is another way of demonstrating a semantic code in STM. Posner (1970) used response time as a measure of how easy it was to identify two letters as being the same or not. For example, using AA, Aa, Ab and Ab, Aa took longer than AA. Why? Identical letters are judged by physical (or visual) characteristics while letters with the same name but with different visual features (Aa) are compared in terms of their *verbal* characteristics; the latter takes longer.

So, clearly, an acoustic code is *not* the only one used in STM. Equally, you only have to think of all the voices and melodies, for example, which we can remember over long periods of time and which are, presumably, acoustically coded, and of all the faces, scenes, skills and so on which are difficult to process verbally, to recognize that a single, semantic code is *not* the only one used by LTM. Morris (1978) points out that Conrad's study (1964) showed only that the phonetic code is used in STM and the semantic code in LTM, *not* that these are the *only* ones used by each system.

Finally, Wickelgren (1973) says that it could be that the mode of coding reflects the processing which has occurred in a given context, rather than being a property of the memory store itself (see the later section on Levels of Processing, p. 326).

BRAIN-DAMAGED PATIENTS

A third major kind of evidence relevant to the Multi-Store Model is to do with brain damage and its effects on memory: if STM and LTM are indeed distinct, then there should be some kind of brain damage which impairs one without affecting the other.

Such a form of brain damage is *anterograde amnesia* and a famous case that of H.M. (Milner et al, 1978; Box 12.1).

An equally dramatic, but in many ways more tragic case, is that of Clive Wearing (Box 12.2).

The kind of *amnesic syndrome* displayed by H.M. and Clive Wearing has been interpreted by Atkinson and Shiffrin as, 'perhaps the single most convincing demonstration of a dichotomy in the memory system', ie a distinction between STM and LTM:

The general characteristics of the amnesic syndrome indicate that it is not some general deterioration of memory function, but a selective impairment in which some functions such as learning novel information, are

Box 12.1   The Case of H.M. (based on Blakemore, 1988)

H.M. had been suffering epileptic fits of devastating frequency since the age of 16. At 27 he underwent surgery, using a technique never used before, which miraculously cured his epilepsy—but at a terrible cost. The hippocampus was removed on both sides of his brain. He was left with severe anterograde amnesia—he had near normal memory for anything which he had learned *prior* to the surgery but he had severe memory deficits for events which occurred *after* the surgery.

For example, within the first few hours after the operation he was unable to recognize the medical staff and could not find his bedroom.

His STM was generally normal; for instance, he could retain verbal information for about 15 seconds without rehearsal and for much longer with rehearsal. However, he could not transfer information into LTM or, if he could, he could not retrieve it. He seemed entirely incapable of remembering any new fact or event.

He had almost no knowledge of current affairs because he forgot all the news almost as soon as he had read about it; he had no idea what time of day it was unless he had just looked at the clock; he could not remember that his father had died or that his family had moved house; and he would re-read the same magazine without realizing he had already read it.

Although he could recognize friends, tell you their names and relate stories about them, he could do so only if he knew them before the surgery. People he met after the operation remained, in effect, total strangers to him and he had to 'get to know them' afresh each time they came into his house. Brenda Milner has known him for 25 years—yet she is a stranger to him each time they meet.

However, he was able to learn and remember perceptual and motor skills; although he had to be reminded each day just what skills he knew how to do:

> ... But new events, faces, phone numbers, places, now settle in his mind for just a few seconds or minutes before they slip, like water through a sieve, and are lost from his consciousness. (Blakemore, 1988)

severely impaired, while others, including memory span and language, remain normal ... (Parkin, 1987)

What H.M. and Clive Wearing seem to be incapable of doing is *transferring* information from STM into LTM. There is ample evidence that they both retained normally functioning STMs. For example, one observation made by Milner of H.M. was that:

> ... he was able to retain the number 584 for at least 15 minutes, by continuously working out elaborate mnemonic schemes. When asked how he replied: 'It's easy. You just remember 8. You see 5, 8 and 4 add to 17. You remember 8, subtract it from 17 and it leaves 9. Divide 9 in half and you get 5 and 4, and there you are: 584. Easy!' A minute or so later, he could remember neither the number, nor any of his complex mnemonics, nor even that he had been asked to remember a number at all. (Milner, 1971)

Other support for the multi-store model along these lines comes from experimental studies using free recall with amnesic and normal (control) subjects. As we saw in the section on dual-component tasks, serial position curves show a separation of STM (recency effect) and LTM

Box 12.2   The Case of Clive Wearing (based on Blakemore, 1988; Baddeley, 1990)

Clive Wearing used to be the chorus master of the London Sinfonietta and a world expert on Renaissance Music, as well as a BBC radio producer. In March 1985 he suffered a rare brain infection caused by the cold sore virus (*herpes simplex*). The virus attacked his hippocampus and destroyed it—along with other parts of his cortex. Like H.M., he lives in a snapshot of time, constantly believing that he has *just* awoken from years of unconsciousness. For example, when his wife, Deborah, enters his hospital room for the third time in a single morning, he embraces her as if they had been parted for years, saying, 'I'm conscious for the first time' and, 'It's the first time I've seen anybody at all'.

Deborah describes her husband like this:

> Clive's world now consists of a moment, with no past to anchor it
> and no future to look ahead to. It's a blinkered moment.

At first his confusion was total and very frightening to him. Once he held a chocolate in the palm of one hand, covered it with the other for a few seconds till its image disappeared from his memory. When he uncovered it, he thought he had performed a magic trick, conjuring it up from nowhere. He repeated it again and again, with total astonishment and growing fear each time.

He now lives a sort of life, constantly playing patience and obsessively keeping a diary—every few minutes he makes a note that he has *just* woken for the first time.

Like H.M., he can still speak and walk, as well as read music, play the organ and conduct. In fact, his musical ability is remarkably well preserved. Also like H.M., he can learn new skills (eg mirror-reading). Over the course of a few days of testing, the speed of reading such words doubles and it can be done just as well three months later. Yet for Clive it is new every time. But unlike H.M., his capacity for remembering his earlier life was patchy in the extreme. He could still remember general features, including where he had been to school, what Cambridge college he attended, highlights such as singing for the Pope on his visit to London and some particular dramatic musical events he had organized. But in all cases his capacity to recall detail was extremely poor.

He showed considerable impairment in other areas too. He had written a book on an early composer (Lassus) and could still recall just a few relevant features about his life—but with no richness or detail. When shown pictures of Cambridge (where he'd spent four years as an undergraduate and had often visited subsequently) he only recognized King's College Chapel—the best known and most distinctive Cambridge building—but not his own college. He couldn't remember who wrote *Romeo and Juliet* and when shown photos of the Queen and the Duke of Edinburgh he thought they were singers he had known from a Catholic church.

Such amnesic patients' lives are effectively ruined because of a lack of *conscious* recollection; according to Deborah, 'without consciousness he's in many senses dead'. If he goes out alone he gets lost and cannot find his way back—he cannot tell anyone who finds him where he's come from or where he's going. In his own words, his life is, 'Hell on earth—It's like being dead all the bloody time'.

(primacy effect); if amnesics really do have an intact STM, they should show similar recall to normal subjects for items later in the list (ie similar recency effect, based on STM) but poorer recall for items earlier in the list (ie different primacy effect, based on LTM). This is exactly what is found (eg Baddeley and Warrington, 1970). These results have led most psychologists to accept that in the amnesic syndrome, STM function is preserved but LTM function is impaired.

However, there is evidence that the problem in these patients is not one of transfer but one of *retrieval* (Warrington and Weiskrantz, 1968, 1978), ie the information is successfully transferred and stored in LTM but it cannot easily be recovered when required. This interpretation is more consistent with Craik and Lockhart's depth of processing approach (1972)—the amnesic may not be able to process most kinds of new information deeply enough for retrieval from LTM but can do so to allow STM retrieval.

Another implication of these clinical findings is that the idea of a 'unitary' LTM is a gross over-simplification, ie there must be different *kinds* of LTM (see next section).

The other major kind of amnesia is *retrograde amnesia* where the patient fails to remember what happens *before* the surgery or accident which causes it. It can be caused by head injuries, electro-convulsive therapy (ECT), carbon-monoxide poisoning and extreme stress. As in anterograde amnesia, there is typically little or no disruption of STM and the period of memory loss may be minutes, days or even years.

When retrograde amnesia is caused by brain damage it is usually accompanied by anterograde amnesia. Similarly, patients who are suffering from Korsakov's Syndrome (caused by severe, chronic alcoholism involving general brain damage) usually experience both kinds of amnesia. Both H.M. and Clive Wearing suffered only anterograde amnesia.

What seems to be involved in retrograde amnesia is a disruption of the *consolidation process*, whereby, once new information has entered LTM, a consolidation time is needed for it to become firmly established physically in the brain.

ALTERNATIVES TO THE MULTI-STORE MODEL

In this section we shall be discussing three major attempts to modify and revise Atkinson and Shiffrin's multi-store model. None represents an outright rejection of that model; rather, they all share the view that it is an oversimplified account of the highly complex human memory

1) *EPISODIC AND PROCEDURAL MEMORY*

As we saw when discussing H.M. and Clive Wearing, whatever their brain damage prevented them from doing, they were still able to use many basic skills (eg talking and walking, playing the organ, reading) and were even capable of acquiring certain new skills (and retaining these)—but they did not know that they knew them! So, clearly, certain parts of their LTM or certain *kinds* of LTM were still intact, and this makes it necessary to distinguish between different kinds of LTM remembering not allowed for by the multi-store model, which sees 'LTM' as unitary.

Tulving (1972) distinguished between episodic and semantic LTM. *Episodic* memory (EM) is an 'autobiographical' memory responsible for storing a record of our past experiences—the events, people, objects and so on which we have personally encountered. They usually include details about the particular time and place in which objects and events were experienced (ie they have a *spatio-temporal* context). So they relate to questions such as, 'Where did you go on your holiday last year?' and, 'What did you have for breakfast this morning?' They have a subjective (self-focused) reality—but most could, in theory anyway, be verified by others).

Semantic memory (SM) is our store of general, factual, knowledge about the world, including concepts, rules and language:

> ...a mental thesaurus, organized knowledge a person possesses about words and other verbal symbols, their meanings and referents...
> (Tulving, 1972)

The essential feature of SM is that it can be used without reference to where and when that knowledge was originally acquired. For example, we don't remember 'learning to speak' (at least, not our native language but it might apply to learning a foreign language)—we just 'know English'. (Forgetting of words in a free-recall task can be thought of as a failure in our EM, since, clearly, we already know the words as part of our SM but we have failed to remember that they appeared in that particular list just presented to us.) However, SM can also store information about ourselves; for example, when we are asked questions about ourselves (how many brothers and sisters we have, how much we like Psychology, etc.) we do not have to remember specific past experiences in order to answer. Indeed, EM and SM are very closely interrelated. For example, semantic knowledge about clocks is built up from past experiences with particular clocks, through abstraction and generalization (a kind of 'bottom-up' approach) but when a particular clock is personally encountered, we apply our general knowledge in recognizing it, understanding what it is for, etc. (a 'top-down' approach). Everyday memory involves *both* kinds interacting in this way (Cohen, 1986).

According to Eysenck and Keane (1990), there is a growing consensus that the EM/SM distinction is a useful heuristic device (a 'rule of thumb' for guiding research) rather than a description of actually distinctive types of knowledge, since the same item of information (eg meaning of a word) can have *both* semantic characteristics (the meaning itself) and episodic (remembering where you first came across the word).

Similarly, Parkin (1987) sees EM, SM and *procedural* memory (PM) as representing a highly interactive system.

Tulving (1985) (among others, eg Anderson, 1985) defined PM as information from LTM which cannot be inspected consciously. For example, riding a bike is a complex skill which is even more difficult to *describe*. (This corresponds to Bruner's 'enactive' mode of representation, a kind of 'muscle memory', see Chapter 25). Similarly, native speakers of a language cannot usually describe the complex grammatical rules by which they speak correctly (perhaps because they were not learnt consciously in the first place, see Chapter 26). By contrast, EM and SM are both capable of being inspected consciously and the content of both can be described to another person.

A distinction which overlaps with Tulving's is Cohen and Squire's

(1980) distinction between *declarative* and *procedural* memory, which in turn corresponds to Ryle's (1949) distinction between *knowing that* and *knowing how*, respectively. Figure 12.8 shows the relationship between Tulving's and Cohen and Squire's distinctions.

Figure 12.8 Distinctions between different kinds of LTM

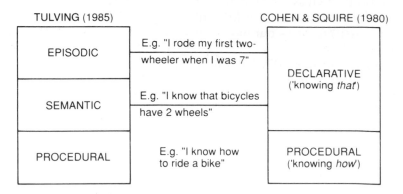

Anderson (1983) argues that when we initially learn something, it is learned and encoded declaratively, but with practice it becomes compiled into a procedural form of knowledge. (This can be seen as corresponding to the distinction between controlled versus automatic processing or focused versus divided attention, discussed in Chapter 11.)

How does all this help us understand the kind of LTM deficiencies patients like H.M. and Clive Wearing suffered? Certainly, most aspects of their PM seemed to be intact (and they could both acquire new skills) but both their EM and SM were partially impaired. Adding to what we have already said about both cases, H.M. was given extensive training (by Gabrieli et al, 1983) in the task of learning the meaning of unfamiliar words which had come into popular use since his operation. He made very little progress, despite extensive practice every day for 10 days. According to Eysenck and Keane (1990), most other amnesics similarly fail to update their SM to take account of changes in the world since onset. For example, Baddeley (1984) reports that many do not know the name of the current Prime Minister or President and have very poor recognition for faces of people who have become famous only quite recently. When new learning did occur, in the cases of H.M. and Clive Wearing, neither patient was aware of having acquired the skill in question, which supports the overall view that it is specifically declarative (ie non-procedural) LTM which is most at risk.

Flashbulb memories refer to a special kind of EM, namely, the kind of vivid and detailed recollections people often have of some major public event (national or international), such as the dismantling of the Berlin Wall or the resignation of Margaret Thatcher. People can usually recall exactly where they were, what they were doing, and with whom, when the news broke (although the detail of peoples' memories and their vividness aren't necessarily signs of their accuracy!).

2) *LEVELS OF PROCESSING (LOP)*
According to Craik and Lockhart (1972) it is not rehearsal as such which is important but what is done with or to the material during rehearsal. It is the attentional and perceptual processes occurring at the time of learning which determine what information is stored in LTM.

The distinction between maintenance and elaborative rehearsal that we noted above is a direct result of the LOP approach (since the latter involves a greater depth of processing) (Baddeley, 1990).

As we have seen, the multi-store model distinghishes between *structural* components (sensory memory, STM and LTM) and *control* processes (eg rehearsal, attention and coding), with the latter being tied to the former and the emphasis on the sequence of stages that information goes through as it passes from one structural component to another when being processed.

The LOP approach, on the other hand, begins with hypothesized processes and then formulates a memory system (the structural components) in terms of these operations. This can be seen as the multi-store model in reverse.

Craik and Lockhart (1972) (and Neisser, 1976) see memory, essentially, as the *by-product* of the processing of information; the durability of memory (or trace persistence) is a direct function of the depth of processing. Incoming stimuli are subjected to a series of analyses, starting with a shallow, sensory analysis, passing through an intermediate, phonetic level and finishing with a deeper, semantic analysis (Table 12.3). Which level is used depends on both the nature of the stimulus and the time available for processing. The general rule is that the deeper the level of processing used, the less likely the material is to be forgotten.

LEVEL	DESCRIPTION
1. *Structural or shallow level*	Is the word written in capital letters—or not? [What does it *look* like?]
2. *Phonetic or phonemic level*	Does the word rhyme with some other word? [What does it *sound* like?]
3. *Semantic level*	Does the word mean the same as some other word? [What does it *mean*?]

Table 12.3 The three levels or depths of processing. (Based on Craik and Lockhart, 1972)

It is important to note that, despite these important differences, Craik and Lockhart still assumed a separate STM. But instead of seeing its main role as the transfer of information to LTM, they emphasized its processing function. However, it is doubtful whether they actually needed to do this. For example, as we saw earlier, STM is traditionally associated with phonological (acoustic) processing and LTM with semantic. But rather than regarding these forms of coding as characteristics of the two stores, Craik and Lockhart regarded the *coding itself* as primary and saw depth of processing as influencing how permanently information is remembered (Baddeley, 1990).

With words, shallow processing corresponds to physical features while deep processing corresponds to meaning.

Craik and Tulving (1975) presented subjects with words via a tachistoscope and were asked one of four questions about each word: (i) is the word in capital letters? (eg TABLE/table); (ii) does the word rhyme with *wait*? (eg 'hate' or 'chicken'), (iii) is the word a type of food? (eg 'cheese' or 'steel'); (iv) would the word fit the sentence 'He kicked the — into the tree'? (eg 'ball' or 'rain').

Of these, (i) corresponds to structural processing, (ii) to phonetic processing and (iii) and (iv) to semantic processing. Subjects had to answer 'yes' or 'no' to each question and were subsequently given an unexpected test of recognition, which involved presentation of the words they had seen intermixed with the same number of words they had not seen; subjects had to say which they had seen before.

There was a significantly better recognition with deeper levels of processing. Also, recognition was superior if the answer was 'yes' than if it was 'no'.

Whilst finding support for the LOP approach, Craik and Tulving (1975) also argued that depth of processing is not the only factor influencing LTM. They found support for the view that *elaboration* of processing is also important, ie the amount of processing of a particular kind. In one experiment they manipulated elaboration by varying the complexity of a sentence frame from *simple* ('She cooked the——') to *complex* ('The great bird swooped down and carried off the struggling ——'). Subjects were given an unexpected cued recall test, whereby they were given the sentence frame and asked to recall the word which had been presented with it.

For those words compatible with the sentence frame, cued recall was twice as high for words accompanying complex compared with simple sentences. Since the same deep or semantic level of processing was involved in both conditions, there must be some additional factor involved, ie elaboration.

However, Craik and Tulving seemed to be assuming that there is a direct relationship between the sheer *number* of elaborations and the probability of recall. But what about the *kind* of elaboration involved?

Bransford et al (1979) found clear evidence for the importance of the nature of the elaboration (eg 'A mosquito is like a doctor because they both draw blood') rather than the number of elaborations (eg 'A mosquito is like a racoon because they both have heads, legs and jaws'). Despite the former involving *fewer* elaborations (it is *minimally* elaborated), such similes were better remembered than the latter which is *multiply* elaborated. Why?

According to Eysenck (1979), Jacoby and Craik (1979) and others, it is encodings which are *distinctive* or unique in some way which are more likely to be remembered. This represents an alternative way of conceptualizing the basic concept of depth—it may be the non-distinctiveness of shallow encodings (as opposed to their shallowness as such) which leads to their poor retention (Eysenck, 1984, 1986).

Is there a proper operational definition of distinctiveness?

One attempt to experimentally test the 'distinctiveness' hypothesis was made by Eysenck and Eysenck (1980), who used nouns with irregular grapheme–phoneme correspondence (ie the nouns are not pronounced in line with normal pronunciation rules). For example, 'glove' would rhyme with 'cove' if it had regular grapheme–phoneme correspondence, and the 'b' in 'comb' would be sounded. Subjects were asked to:

(a) Pronounce such nouns *as if* they had such correspondence, in the belief that this shallow task would nevertheless produce distinctive and unique memory traces (the non-semantic/distinctiveness condition).

(b) Simply pronounce certain other nouns in their normal way (the non-semantic/non-distinctiveness condition).

(c) Process still other nouns in terms of their meaning (the semantic condition).

When later given an unexpected test of recognition, words in (a) were much better remembered than those in (b) and almost as well as those in (c). Similar, though less striking results were found in a test of free recall.

Eysenck (1984, 1986) believes that it is often difficult to choose between LOP, elaboration and distinctiveness because they co-vary (ie occur together). We know that retention cannot be predicted solely on the basis of LOP because more elaborate or distinctive semantic encodings are usually better remembered than non-elaborate or non-distinctive ones. And the Eysenck and Eysenck (1980) study shows that a shallow LOP can cause remembering that is almost as good as a deep LOP, as long as it is also distinctive. It is possible that all three make separate contributions to LTM but distinctiveness, which relates to the *nature* of processing and takes account of relationships between encodings, is likely to prove more important than elaboration, which is only a measure of the *amount* of processing (Eysenck, 1984, 1986).

Evaluation of the LOP Approach

1) According to Eysenck (1984, 1986), LOP was probably the most influential theoretical approach in memory during the 1970s, but it rapidly went out of favour after that. He says that most psychologists believe it contains a grain of truth but is a substantial oversimplification. We should note, though, that Craik and Lockhart themselves claim that their approach does *not* constitute a *theory* of memory but a conceptual framework for memory research; earlier they refer to it as offering a new way of interpreting existing data and as providing a heuristic framework for further research (ie a strategy, empirical rule or 'rule of thumb' which drastically reduces the amount of 'work' that must be done when trying to solve a problem).

According to Parkin (1987), LOP has made a significant contribution to our understanding of memory. Earlier models oversimplified the psychological factors involved in the formation of new memories. Recognizing that acquisition is not a rigid process and that variations in how information is handled can affect how well it is remembered has had an important impact on how psychologists study memory:

> In attempting to explain a wide range of memory phenomena, it is now accepted that changes in the *processing strategy* adopted by the subject may provide the basis for an explanation. (Parkin, 1987)

2) Eysenck (1984, 1986) believes that Craik and Lockhart were absolutely right to argue that perception, attention and memory are interdependent—once it is recognized that memory traces are formed as a result of perceptual and attentional processes, it becomes necessary for memory research to focus on these processes. At this general level, LOP has made a major contribution. Prior to 1972, remarkably few experiments compared the effects on memory of different kinds of processing—it had been implicitly assumed that any particular stimulus will typically be processed in a very similar way by all subjects on all occasions.

3) Probably the most serious problem with LOP is the difficulty of measuring or defining depth *independently* of the actual retention score, ie if 'depth' is defined as 'how many words are remembered' and if 'how many words are remembered' is taken as a measure of 'depth', we are faced with a *circular* definition. Even when the circle is broken into via the kind of orienting task used, the problem may still remain. For example, a famous experiment taken to support the LOP model (Hyde and Jenkins, 1973) used five orienting tasks, meant to vary in the amount of processing of meaning involved. These were: (i) rating words for pleasantness; (ii) estimating the frequency with which the words are used in English: (iii) detecting the number of 'e's and 'g's in the words; (iv) deciding the part of speech appropriate to each word (noun/verb/adjective/'some other'); and (v) deciding whether or not the word fitted various sentence frames ('it is the ———'/'it is ———'). Hyde and Jenkins defined (i) and (ii) as involving semantic (deep) processing and (iii)–(v) as involving non-semantic (shallow) processing. The prediction, of course, was that (i) and (ii) would produce significantly higher retention and this was, indeed, found. However, the assumption that (i) and (ii) involved thinking of the word's meaning while (iv) did not, has been challenged. If it is *no more* than an assumption, we are again faced with the lack of an adequate, independent, measure of 'depth'. According to Baddeley:

> . . . there is no generally accepted way of independently assessing depth of processing. This places major limits on the power of the levels of processing approach. (Baddeley, 1990)

4) Eysenck (1984, 1986) argues that the original theory focused too narrowly on the processing activities occurring at the point of acquisition (operationally defined as the kind of orienting task involved) and virtually ignored all the other determinants of LTM. More specifically, learning and memory are affected by at least four types of factors: (i) the nature of the task; (ii) the kind of stimulus material used; (iii) individual characteristics of the subjects (eg idiosyncratic knowledge); and (iv) the nature of the retention test used to measure memory. In many LOP experiments, several orienting tasks are used but only one kind of stimulus material (usually words), one fairly homogeneous set of subjects and one kind of retention test (eg Hyde and Jenkins, 1973, used only free recall).

However, there are often large interactions between the four factors; an important demonstration of this is the study by Morris et al (1977). They predicted that stored information (whether deep or shallow) will be remembered only to the extent that it is *relevant* to the memory test used; so deep or semantic information would be of little use if the memory test involved learning a list of words and later selecting words that *rhymed* with the stored words, while shallow rhyme information would be very relevant. As an initial orienting task, the experimenter read aloud thirty-two sentences with one word missing from each. Each sentence was followed by vocal presentation of the target word. The subject had to say 'yes' if the target word could be inserted appropriately into the preceding sentence and 'no' if it couldn't (half the target words could, half could not). For half the sentences, the input orienting task was semantic and for the other half it was a rhyme-orienting task. All subjects heard all the sentences.

Half the subjects were given a standard recognition test (the thirty-two original targets were mixed with thirty-two distractors—subjects had to say 'yes' to the targets and 'no' to the distractors) and the other half a rhyming recognition test (new words were presented and subjects had to say 'yes' to the new words which rhymed with the original targets and 'no' to those that didn't). The usual LOP effect was found (ie better retention) in the standard recognition test but the reverse was true for the rhyming recognition test.

This finding represents an experimental disproof of LOP, specifically the idea that deep processing is *intrinsically* more memorable than shallow processing. The results also demonstrate that how memory is tested must be taken into account when we are trying to predict the consequences of some processing activity—LTM is determined by the relevance of stored information to any given retention test. Morris et al (1977) argued that their results supported a *transfer-appropriate processing* view of memory, ie different kinds of processing lead learners to acquire different kinds of information about a stimulus. Whether the information stored as a result actually leads to subsequent retention depends on the *relevance* of that information to the kinds of memory test used. So storing semantic information is basically irrelevant when the memory test requires identifying words which rhyme with list words—what is required here is shallow rhyme information. A form of coding which might be considered shallow for one purpose might be considered deep and meaningful for another (Eysenck and Keane, 1990).

5) The over-emphasis on the processing activities is based on the assumption that the subject's processing of stimuli is determined exclusively by the particular orienting task. However, there is an ever-present danger that the subject will engage in extraneous processing unrelated to the orienting task. For example, one of Hyde and Jenkins's (1973) orienting tasks involved checking for the letter 'e' or 'g' in the word (shallow processing) but they were still able to recall an average of seven words in a subsequent retention test. It seems difficult to explain this just in terms of the orienting task—some additional processing must have occurred. It is impossible to completely control subjects' processing activities (Eysenck, 1984, 1986).

6) While the original LOP model was attractively simple, it always seemed unlikely that depth was the only major factor influencing LTM. Another major problem is that it is more of a description than an explanation—we are not told *why* semantic processing usually produces better retention. Attempts to offer such an explanation were discussed earlier in relation to elaboration and distinctiveness.

7) Finally, a fundamental assumption is that rate of forgetting over time is inversely related to depth of processing. But this can only be tested when the amount of learning at different levels is the same—a requirement not usually fulfilled. Nelson and Vining (1978) manipulated the number of learning trials in order to produce comparable amounts of learning at deep and shallow levels and found that the rate of forgetting was *not* affected by processing depth. It may well be that variations in depth of processing affect *speed* of learning rather than rate of forgetting (Eysenck and Keane, 1990).

3) *WORKING MEMORY*

Just as Tulving's and Cohen and Squire's distinctions challenge the earlier concept of a unitary LTM, so the concept of *working memory* (WM) (Baddeley and Hitch, 1974) challenges the earlier concept of a unitary STM. They adopted a *functional* approach, ie they wanted to answer the question: what is memory *for*? They did not reject the multi-store model's view of STM as rehearsing incoming information for transfer to LTM, but claimed that it is more complex and versatile than this:

> The concept of the short-term store as a *working* memory store empha-
> sizes that it is an *active* store used to hold information which is being
> manipulated. Working memory is the focus of *consciousness*—it holds the
> information you are consciously thinking about now . . . (Cohen, 1990)

The original model has been itself modified and elaborated (Baddeley, 1981, 1986) and in its current form consists of a *central executive*, at the top of a hierarchy, controlling or directing the activities of three other components, the *articulatory loop*, *visuo-spatial scratch pad* and *primary acoustic store* (Fig. 12.9). (The original model did not include the primary acoustic store—this was added by Salame and Baddeley, 1982.)

The *central executive* is the most important component because it is used when dealing with any task which makes cognitive demands. It is so-called because it allocates attention to incoming information (see Chapter 11) and directs the operation of the other components ('slave systems'; Baddeley, 1990). It is a very flexible system that can process

Figure 12.9 *The working memory model. (From Cohen, G., Eysenck, M. W. and Le Voi, M. E. (1986)* Memory—A Cognitive Approach. *Milton Keynes, Open University Press)*

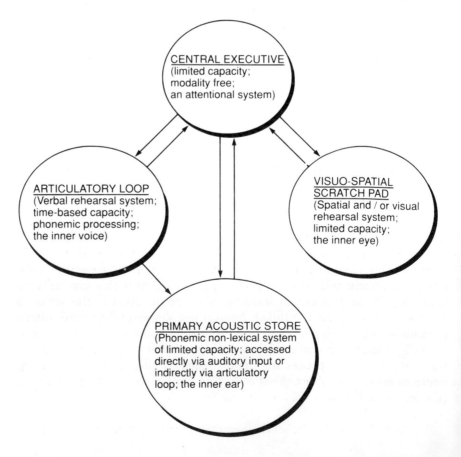

information in any sensory modality (it is modality free) and in a variety of different ways. It can also store information for brief periods of time. According to Baddeley (1981), '. . . the Central Executive is becoming increasingly like a pure attentional system'. The *articulatory* (or *phonological*) *loop* can be regarded as a verbal rehearsal loop that we use when we, for example, try to remember a telephone number for a few seconds by muttering it to ourselves. It is also used to hold the words we are preparing to speak aloud. So it uses an *articulatory/phonological code*, which represents information as it would be spoken (the 'inner voice'). The visuo-spatial scratch pad (or sketch pad) can also rehearse information but deals with visual and/or spatial information, for example, driving along a familiar road approaching a bend and thinking of the spatial layout of the road around the bend (Eysenck, 1986). So it uses a *visual code*, which represents information in the form of visual features, such as size, shape and colour ('the inner eye'). Baddeley describes it as:

> . . . a system especially well adapted to the storage of spatial information, much as a pad of paper might be used by someone trying, for example, to work out a geometric puzzle. (Baddeley, 1986)

The *primary acoustic store* receives auditory input directly; visual input can only enter it indirectly after being converted to a phonological form (ie processed by the articulatory loop). It uses an *acoustic/phonemic code*, which represents information in the form of auditory features such as pitch and loudness (the 'inner ear').

WM has been studied mainly by the use of the concurrent or interference (or dual-) tasks method (very similar in design to dual-task studies of divided attention; see Chapter 11). Assuming that each component of WM has a limited capacity, if two tasks make use of the *same* component(s), then performance of one or both tasks should be *worse* when performed together than when performed separately. If they require *different* components, it should be possible to perform them as well together as separately.

An example involves the use of *articulatory suppression*: the subject rapidly repeats out loud something meaningless (such as 'hi-ya' or 'the') and this uses up the resources of the articulatory loop so that it cannot be used for anything else. If, indeed, this produces poorer performance on another, concurrent, task, then we can infer that this second task also uses the articulatory loop (Eysenck, 1986).

Evaluation of Working Memory

1) Eysenck (1986) believes that it is almost universally agreed that it is much more realistic to assume that WM comprises several relatively independent processing mechanisms than to see STM as a single, unitary, store. It is also useful to treat attentional processes and STM as parts of the same system, mainly because they are probably used together much of the time in everyday life.

2) The notion that any one component of WM may be involved in the performance of a great number of apparently very different tasks is a valuable insight. For example, the articulatory loop seems to play a part in memory span tasks, mental arithmetic, verbal reasoning and reading (Eysenck, 1986).

3) Baddeley (1990) believes that the articulatory loop is far from

being just, '. . . a way of linking together a number of laboratory phenomena . . .' and one reason is that '. . . the articulatory loop, or some similar system plays an important role in learning to read (Jorm, 1983) . . .' (Baddeley, 1990).

He says that if you select a group of children with specific problems in learning to read (despite normal intelligence and supportive family background), one of the most striking features they have in common is an impaired memory span. But they also tend to do rather poorly on tasks which do not directly test memory, such as phonological manipulation and awareness (eg judging whether words rhyme or taking a word and deleting the first phonemes before repeating it, for example, 'spin' becomes 'pin'). So what is it that is causing the difficulty in learning to read? While in the normal development of reading these factors undoubtedly interact, in a minority of children some form of phonological deficit (detectable before the child has even begun to learn to read) seems to prevent that learning:

> It seems likely that this deficit is related to the development of the phonological loop system, although at present we know too little about it to draw any firm conclusions. (Baddeley, 1990)

It would seem, then, that at least certain components of WM have very real (if still only potential) *practical* applications through providing a theoretical framework for the role of STM. This is undoubtedly the component which to date has received the most theoretical and empirical attention (Baddeley, 1986).

4)   It is generally agreed that we know least about the most generally important component, namely, the central executive—and this perhaps is the model's greatest limitation (Eysenck, 1986). It can apparently carry out an enormous variety of processing activities in different conditions which poses obvious problems in terms of describing its precise function—it even suggests that the notion of a single CE may be as inappropriate as that of a unitary STM (Eysenck, 1986).

Baddeley (1981) himself describes his strategy as identifying as many specific processing mechanisms as possible (such as the articulatory loop and scratch pad), in this way progessively 'chipping way' at the CE—the CE then represents whatever is still unknown. Allowing for the problem of how we decide when we have discovered a processing mechanism that is sufficiently important to be added to the list of WM components, Eysenck concludes that:

> . . . we should not abandon the notion of some general Central Executive. If the human mind really consisted of nothing but numerous specific processing mechanisms operating in isolation from each other, it seems likely that total chaos would result. At the very least, some central system seems to be needed in order to co-ordinate the activities of the specific mechanisms, and the Central Executive seems well suited to that role. (Eysenck, 1986)

THEORIES OF FORGETTING

To understand why we forget, we must consider the distinction made earlier between *availability* and *accessibility*; the former refers to whether or not material has been *stored* in the first place, while the latter refers to being able to *retrieve* what has been stored (the question of retrievability). In terms of the multi-store model, since information must be transferred from STM to LTM for permanent storage, availability has to do mainly with STM and the transfer of information from STM into LTM, while accessibility has to do mainly with LTM.

Therefore one way of looking at forgetting is to ask what prevents information staying in STM long enough to be transferred to LTM (some answers are trace decay, displacement and interference) and another is to ask what prevents us from locating the information that is in LTM (some answers being interference, motivated forgetting and cue-dependent forgetting, which are all to do with failure to retrieve).

Other theories of forgetting, which try to explain long-term forgetting, are not concerned with either availability or accessibility as such but are to do with what happens to long-term memories once transfer from STM has occurred—these are trace decay, Gestalt theory and prevention of consolidation (Fig. 12.10).

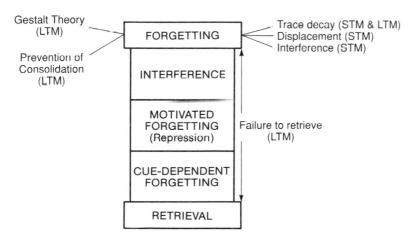

Figure 12.10 Different theories of forgetting, including retrieval failure

TRACE DECAY

Essentially this is an attempt to explain why forgetting increases with time. James (1890) claimed that the limiting factor in STM is simply the passage of time: a stimulus decays from STM as its neural after-effects decay. Modern supporters of this view include Brown (1958), Peterson and Peterson (1959) and Wingfield and Byrnes (1972).

The underlying assumption is that learning leaves a 'trace' in the brain, that is, there is some sort of physical change after learning that was not there before, and forgetting is due to a spontaneous fading or weakening of the neural memory trace over time.

Hebb (1949) argued that the physiological basis of memory is dualistic, that is, there are two phases involved in the formation of memory: (i) a group of nerve cells excite each other, resulting in a very brief memory trace; and (ii) with repeated neural activity, a structural neural change occurs. The first phase corresponds roughly to STM and forgetting is due to neural decay, the second phase corresponds roughly to LTM and forgetting must be due to the intervention of some other information. So, for Hebb, trace decay applies only to STM.

This belief represents a major argument in support of the Multi-store model. However, the idea of trace decay has been extended to LT forgetting, in the form of decay-through-disuse; that is, if certain knowledge or skills are not used or practised for long periods, the memory trace corresponding to them will fade and hence they will be forgotten. Yet a good deal of remembering goes on when we think decay might have eradicated it, especially in the case of motor skills (eg driving, typing, playing the piano) with no intervening practice. The ability of the elderly to recall their youth, or of a delirious person remembering a foreign language not spoken since childhood, also testify against any simple decay-through-disuse explanation. But how satisfactory is trace decay as an account of ST forgetting?

Waugh and Norman (1965) used a *serial probe technique* in which sequences of 16 digits are presented, at the rate of one to four per second and one of the 16 is then selected (the probe) and the subject has to name the digit which *follows* the probe. Simple trace decay would predict much better retention of the rapidly presented digits since there is less time between presentation and test. However, they found no such relationship.

In a famous early study, Jenkins and Dallenbach (1924) found that when subjects were allowed to sleep during the interval between learning and recall of nonsense syllables, they remembered many more of them than subjects who stayed awake for an equivalent period. Two groups of subjects learnt a ten-item list of nonsense syllables either late at night or early in the morning. The night subjects were woken after one, two, four or eight hours and tested for recall (as well as being tested immediately after learning). The day subjects reported back to the lab at the same intervals but continued their daily activities. In both groups, recall declined with time *but* it declined to a greater extent in the day group.

If decay is a natural result of the passage of time alone, then we should have expected equal forgetting in both groups. The results suggest that it is what *happens* in between learning and recall that determines forgetting in STM, not time as such (and this would seem to apply to LT forgetting too). The major alternative to trace decay is *interference* (see below).

DISPLACEMENT

In a limited capacity ST store, new items tend to displace old ones; this, of course, rests on the assumption of a limited number of 'slots' into which new material can be inserted ('the magic number seven, plus or minus two') so that when a new piece of information is to be introduced, one of the existing seven slots would need to release its existing material to make way for it. (In terms of memory traces, new material will have *high* trace-strength and older items *low* trace-strength.) Glanzer et al (1967) tested the trace decay, displacement and interference theories and found displacement to be a *major* factor, but they also found a small effect of time delay, suggesting a possible decay component.

Shallice (1967) found that although rapidly presented digits did show less marked forgetting (suggesting trace decay), elapsed time was *less* important than the number of subsequent items in determining the probability of recall (which suggests displacement).

Finally, Reitman (1971, 1984) found evidence for both trace decay *and* displacement. However, he argues that it is far from clear that displacement refers to a process distinct from either decay, on the one hand, or interference, on the other (or some mixing of the two).

INTERFERENCE

According to this theory, forgetting increases with time *solely* because of increasing interference between competing memories. As our store of information grows, it becomes increasingly difficult to identify or locate a particular item and this constitutes a failure to retrieve from LTM. Near the beginning of the storage process, interference from extraneous material can prevent new information from passing from STM into LTM.

Interference is conceptualized in Stimulus–Response (S–R) terms and is commonly studied experimentally using *paired associate* learning, that is, the first member of the pair is a stimulus for the second member of the pair (the response) and subjects are presented with one list (or more) comprising several such pairs (often nonsense syllables).

The usual procedure for studying interference in the lab is shown in Figure 12.11. Normally, the first member of each pair in list A is the

| RETROACTIVE INHIBITION (Retro = BACKWARD) A ◄——— B | EXPERIMENTAL GROUP | LEARN A | LEARN B | RECALL A |
| | CONTROL GROUP | LEARN A | REST (or Unrelated task) | RECALL A |

Figure 12.11 The usual procedure for studying interference in the laboratory

| PROACTIVE INHIBITION (Pro = FORWARD) A ———► B | EXPERIMENTAL GROUP | LEARN A | LEARN B | RECALL B |
| | CONTROL GROUP | REST (or Unrelated task) | LEARN B | RECALL B |

same as in list B but the second member of each pair is different in the two lists. In *retroactive inhibition* (RI) the learning of a second, later, list (B) interferes with the recall of the original list A (so the interference works *backwards*) while in *proactive inhibition* (PI) list A interferes with the recall of later learned list B (and so works *forwards*).

McGeoch (1942) concluded that the greater the similarity between the two lists, the greater the interference, for example, a list of numbers learned before or after a list of adjectives is likely to interfere very little. However, if the *same* stimulus is associated with a *different* response, interference will be very marked (compare this with negative transfer of learning which we discussed in Chapter 7).

In an early study by McGeoch and McDonald (1931), subjects learned a list of words and then were given an interfering task before being re-tested on the first list—recall of jokes was 43 per cent, of numbers 37 per cent, of nonsense syllables 26 per cent, of unrelated adjectives 22 per cent, of antonyms of the original list 18 per cent and of synonyms of the original list 12 per cent.

Melton and von Lackum (1941), using nonsense syllables, found evidence that the effects of RI were greater than those of PI (using an immediate test of recall). However, Underwood (1948) found that if there was a time interval between the original learning and the recall test, the difference disappeared.

It seems that PI *increases* with time while RI *decreases* with time and Underwood (1957) believes that PI is the more important of the two: the amount of forgetting in any one set of material is an increasing function of the amount of similar material subjects have learned in the past.

But why should RI decrease with time? Underwood (1957) argues that

RI is affected by two factors: first, response competition at recall; and secondly, *unlearning*, that is, a process similar to the extinction involved in conditioning, whereby the responses on the first list are not 'reinforced' during the learning of the second list. But the responses on the first list undergo spontaneous recovery and so RI decreases over time. While RI involves both response competition and unlearning, PI involves only the former—the first list is increasingly able to exert response competition on the second and so PI increases over time.

An interesting study by Ekstrand (1973) investigated the influence of sleep on both kinds of interference. Sleep facilitated recall in both RI and PI but to a greater extent in the former. Ekstrand suggested that the role of sleep is not merely to reduce interference but to facilitate consolidation and dreaming may, in fact, constitute a cause of interference (see Chapter 5).

Evaluation of Interference Theory

Although experimental demonstrations of interference are quite plentiful, real-life situations in which we must learn incompatible responses to the same stimulus are quite rare. Most of the experimental support has used nonsense syllables but interference is much less easy to demonstrate when meaningful material is used.

For example, the subject has to learn the response *bell* to the stimulus *woj*. The word *bell* is not actually 'learned' in the lab but is already part of the subject's semantic memory; what is learned is 'bell-as-a-response-to-woj', events which are dependent on the specific laboratory situation (and which are stored in episodic memory). If studies of RI and PI are largely studying episodic memory, then the 'laws' of interference are also largely based on episodic as opposed to semantic memory and it is likely that, whereas episodic memory is susceptible to interference, semantic memory is much more resistant since it is more stable and structured.

As a complete theory of forgetting, interference faces severe difficulties. For example, in a study by Tulving (1967), each presentation of a list of words was followed by three successive recall trials. Although the number of words recalled on each trial remained fairly constant, the *specific words* recalled change from trial to trial; only about 50 per cent of words recalled were remembered on all three trials.

This is a clear demonstration of storage (or availability) outstripping retrieval (accessibility) which could not be accounted for either by interference (how could a word that was 'unlearned' on trial one be present on trial two or three?) or trace decay (since more time has elapsed by trial three). The best explanation is in terms of different retrieval cues being used on different trials.

Baddeley (1976) regards trace decay as the main cause of forgetting, with interference only a minor contributory factor. He points out that it has been very difficult to demonstrate significant PI outside the lab, one reason being that when learning of potentially interfering material is spaced out over time, interference is greatly reduced and in the lab it is rather artificially compressed in time, thus increasing the probability of interference. So the major problem is generalizing the results to real-life situations.

THE GESTALT THEORY OF FORGETTING

Not surprisingly, the Gestalt account of forgetting is closely related to the Gestalt theory of perception (see Chapter 9). It is the only theory of forgetting which proposes that memories undergo *qualitative* changes over time: complex memories change so as to become more internally consistent in the direction of 'good form'. For example, irregular shapes will increasingly be remembered as more regular and symmetrical. Although there is no convincing evidence of such changes in shape memory, some supporting evidence comes from reconstructive distortions of memory for stories towards greater simplicity and consistency; however, the latter changes are not spontaneous as the Gestalt theory would require (see section on Reconstructive Memory, p. 352).

PREVENTION OF CONSOLIDATION

Once new information has entered LTM, a consolidation time is needed for it to become firmly recorded (this is the *consolidation process*): time-dependent changes occur in the nervous system, as a result of learning.

We saw earlier that patients who have been the victims of concussion or brain injury or who have undergone brain surgery or ECT commonly suffer retrograde amnesia, that is, loss of memory of events which have occurred prior to the accident.

Hudspeth et al (1964) found that retention of a learned response increases with increase in the interval between training and ECT; an hour's delay permits almost perfect retention. McGaugh (1970) reports that certain drugs (strychnine, nicotine, caffeine and amphetamine) given immediately after a learning trial seem to speed up the consolidation process (see Chapter 4).

CUE-DEPENDENT FORGETTING—FAILURE TO RETRIEVE

Tulving (1974) used the term 'cue-dependent forgetting' to refer jointly to: (i) state-dependent; and (ii) context-dependent forgetting. According to Tulving, accessibility (ie retrievability) is governed by *retrieval cues* or *routes* which can either be encoded with the to-be-remembered material (at the time of learning) or can be provided later as prods or pointers which govern where in the memory the search will take place. Psychological or physiological *states* represent internal cues while environmental or *contextual* variables represent external cues.

Goodwin et al (1969) found that memory loss was greater for subjects going from an alcohol to a non-alcohol state, compared with those going from a non-alcohol to an alcohol state. Darley et al (1973) found similar results using marijuana, as did Baddeley (1982) with subjects taking drugs or under hypnotic suggestion to influence mood. Interestingly, Zechmeister and Nyberg (1982) found that these effects can be reduced if subjects are encouraged to re-create imaginatively the conditions of learning.

Regarding context, Abernethy (1940) asked one group of subjects to learn *and* recall in the same room, while a second group learned and recalled in different rooms; the recall of the first group was much better. Godden and Baddeley (1975) had divers learn word lists either on land or

15 feet under water; recall later was either in the same context or a different one and in the latter conditions there was a 30 per cent decrement in recall. They repeated the study in 1980 using recognition as the measure of remembering and found no effect; they concluded therefore, that context-dependent forgetting applies to recall only.

A different kind of contextual variable is that used by Tulving and Pearlstone (1966), which took the form of the category name of words that subjects had to learn. They were read lists of varying numbers of words (12, 24 or 48) containing categories of one, two, or four exemplars per list with the exemplars along with the category name; they were asked only to memorize the exemplars (eg category name = animal, exemplar = dog).

Half the subjects free-recalled by writing the words on a blank piece of paper but the other half were provided with the category names as cues and they recalled more words. However, when the first group were later given the category names, their recall improved, which illustrates very well the distinction between availability and accessibility; the category-name cues helped make accessible what was, in fact, available, so they knew more than they could retrieve under the cue-less conditions.

But how closely related to the recall cue must the encoding cues be in order to operate as effective retrieval cues? Tulving's *encoding specificity principle* (ESP) is one answer to this question (Tulving, 1983) and maintains that cues only help retrieval if they have been encoded *at the time of learning*: in the Tulving and Pearlstone experiment described above, the category names were presented along with the exemplars and so, presumably, were encoded at the time of learning. The ESP, according to Tulving, explains why recall is sometimes superior to recognition (even though recognition is generally considered to be easier than recall).

However, not everyone accepts the ESP. For example, Jones (1979) distinguishes between two kinds of cues: (i) those which may *not* have been encoded in the original learning, and so do not form part of the information to be recalled (based on *extrinsic knowledge*); and (ii) those that *have* been encoded during learning and which do (based on *intrinsic knowledge*). They *both* aid recall but probably work in different ways.

The problem is being able to define a cue encoded at learning independently of its ability to stimulate recall of information. An effective recall cue is inferred to have been encoded while an ineffective one is inferred not to have been and this is rather circular.

MOTIVATED FORGETTING—REPRESSION

As we shall see in Chapter 29, Freud believed that forgetting is motivated, that is, we forget for a reason (or reasons). In the case of repression, painful, disturbing or threatening thoughts or ideas are actively pushed out of our conscious minds and are made unconscious in order to protect ourselves against them. So the unconscious, according to Freud, is largely composed of these repressed memories which are exceedingly difficult to retrieve (are inaccessible) but remain 'in storage' and continue to exert a great influence over us even though we have no awareness of them (and so are available).

Repression and the 'return of the repressed' have been apparently demonstrated in several studies but the interpretation of the evidence is controversial:

In sum, it has not been possible to obtain convincing evidence of repression under laboratory conditions. The main reason is that even the apparently favourable findings are open to a variety of interpretations that have nothing to do with repression. However, there is reasonable evidence for the related phenomenon of *perceptual defence* . . . (Eysenck and Keane, 1990) (see Chapter 9)

However, we should note that Eysenck and Keane agree with Brewin who states:

> The raising of a perceptual threshold is still a long way from the complete absence of a memory for a traumatic event. (Brewin, 1988; cited in Eysenck and Keane, 1990)

According to Baddeley:

> There is no doubt that powerful negative emotions can induce amnesia, although the extent to which the patient is totally unable to access the stressful memories, and to what extent he or she 'chooses' not to is very hard to ascertain. It certainly seems unlikely that in very many of the cases of psychogenic amnesia, the patient is malingering, and simply pretending not to be able to remember. On the other hand, the line between avoiding searching areas of memory that are associated with anxiety . . . and unconscious repression of unwanted memories . . . is hard to draw. Indeed, it is perhaps neither necessary nor desirable to try to draw such a line. (Baddeley, 1990)

We shall consider some of the empirical studies in Chapter 29.

Let us end this section by quoting Baddeley again. He states that, in general, attempts to test the repression hypothesis have declined over recent years, but that in one area there has been an increase in research on the effects of emotion on memory:

> A person who witnesses a violent crime is likely to experience considerable emotion, and this may well influence the reliability of subsequent testimony (Baddeley, 1990).

We shall return to the topic of *eyewitness testimony* in a later section.

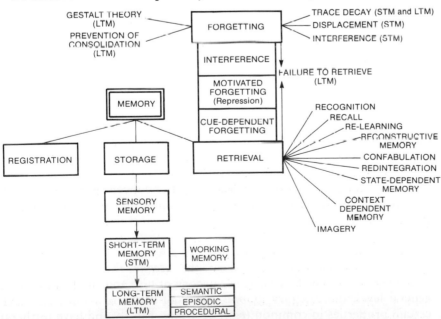

Figure 12.12 A summary of the three components of memory and theories of forgetting

SPECIAL ISSUES

SEMANTIC MEMORY AND KNOWLEDGE

We have discussed Tulving's distinction (1972) between episodic and semantic memory (see p. 324) and have also seen the very close relationship between semantic coding and LTM (p. 319). We shall now explore this aspect of LTM in more depth.

According to Eysenck and Keane (1990), psychologists have, in general, labelled as knowledge information which is represented mentally in a particular format and is structured or organized in some way. This leads to two interrelated questions about the nature of knowledge:

(i)   what format do mental representations take?
(ii) how are these mental representations organized?

Despite its obvious importance, this area was neglected until quite recently when attempts to provide a knowledge-base for computer systems stimulated an interest in how, '...this enormously important but complex facility operates in people (Baddeley, 1990).

1)   Perhaps the best known model of SM, and the one which has generated most research and debate, is the *hierarchical network model* (Collins and Quillian, 1969, 1972), (which in fact began as a computer simulation of how people might actually understand text—'teachable language comprehender' or TLC).

This is concerned with our memory for words and their meanings and the information involved is organized hierarchically, as shown in Figure 12.13. SM is portrayed as a network of concepts which are connected

Figure 12.13 Part of the semantic memory network for a three-level hierarchy. (From Collins and Quillian, 1969)

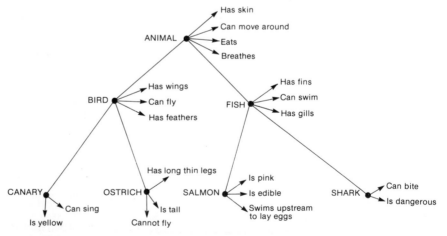

with other concepts by pointers; each word or concept is represented by a particular node in the network. The meaning of a particular word is given by the configuration of pointers that connect that word with other words.

Some pointers indicate the *properties* of a word, eg a canary 'can sing' and 'is yellow'; other pointers indicate the *category* the word belongs to, at a lower, more specific level, the category of *bird* and at a higher, more general level, the category *animal*. Since all birds (or almost all) have certain properties in common (eg have wings, can fly and have feathers) these are stored together with the concept 'bird'; it would be unnecessary (redundant) for them to be stored with each kind of bird. Similarly, the properties shared by canaries, birds and animals need only be stored at the highest level, that of animal—this is the most economical way of storing a great deal of information. Since, by implication, whatever is stored at a higher level (eg animal) applies to lower level words (eg canary), a hierarchical organization involves little redundancy, ie a relatively large amount of information can be stored in a relatively small space.

How does the model explain the way we go about comprehending and verifying simple sentences? If we were asked whether a statement, 'A canary can sing' is true, we would only need to find the word 'canary' and retrieve the properties stored with that word. However, to verify 'a canary can fly' we would first have to find 'canary' and then move up one level to 'bird' before retrieving the property 'can fly'. Assuming that it takes time to move from one level to another, it should take longer to verify 'a canary can fly' than to verify 'a canary can sing' and it would take even longer to verify 'a canary has skin'. The model assumes that the various properties stored with each word are scanned simultaneously so these are not assumed to be a critical variable.

Collins and Quillian presented subjects with various sentences, including the examples given above, which they had to judge as true or false, by pressing an appropriate button as quickly as possible; reaction time was used as a measure of difficulty.

The main finding was that the time taken to decide that a statement is true increased as a function of the number of levels the subject had to go through to verify it. Thus, more time was needed to verify 'a canary is an animal' than 'a canary is a bird', which is what the model, of course, predicts.

However, it is not without its critics. For example, Landauer and Meyer (1972) argue that it takes longer to verify 'a canary is an animal' because there are *more animals* than birds. So the findings of Collins and Quillian could be accounted for in terms of the relationship between category size and reaction time.

Again, some members of a category are judged as more typical than other members, eg 'canary' and 'ostrich' both belong to the category 'bird' but a 'canary' is judged to be a more typical bird than an 'ostrich'. So when determining whether instances belong to a category, subjects respond faster to typical instances ('a canary is a bird') than to atypical ones ('an ostrich is a bird'). That should not happen according to the hierarchical model—presumably the same distance has to be travelled in both cases (Baddeley, 1990).

Conrad (1972) found evidence that response time may reflect the relative frequency with which certain attributes are commonly associated with a particular concept. She presented instances of particular concepts (eg dalmation, dog, shark, fish, animal) and asked subjects to write down as many properties as they could think of for each. Some properties were mentioned very frequently, others very rarely (eg 'salmon are pink' was very much more common than 'salmon have fins'). Then, controlling for frequency, she re-ran Collins and Quillian's experiment and found *no* evidence for longer response times to categories meant to be stored at higher levels. These results strongly suggest that 'semantic relatedness' (what attributes are commonly associated with particular concepts) could fairly easily account for the original findings. The Collins and Quillian model *assumes* that all attributes are equally important or salient in determining the members of a concept—it seems likely that they are not.

Rips et al (1973) and Smith et al (1974) found that subjects took longer to verify 'a bear is a mammal' than 'a bear is an animal' which is the *opposite* of what the hierarchical model predicts, since 'animal' is *higher* up in the hierarchy than 'mammal'. This could be explained partly by claiming that we typically think of bears as 'animals' rather than as 'mammals'. Similarly, we typically think of chickens as 'animals' rather than 'birds' and subjects *do* take longer to verify the latter—the opposite of what the model predicts. *Logically*, results should go the way of the model; *empirically*, the results are rather different.

The findings could be explained in terms of how easy (or difficult) it is to imagine concepts at different levels: the higher up the hierarchy you go, the more abstract the category becomes and the more difficult it becomes to form a mental image of it, eg it is easier to picture a canary than 'an animal'. This could explain the findings at least as well as the distance as such that must be crossed.

2) In the light of these criticisms, Collins and Loftus (1975) proposed a revised network model. The major changes include:

(a) The network is no longer hierarchically organized, making it more flexible.
(b) The new concept of *semantic distance* denotes that highly related concepts are located close together and distance reflects how easily 'excitation' can flow from one node to the next.
(c) A range of different types of link is introduced, such as class membership associations (or *is a* links—eg 'a dog is a mammal', including some negative instances, such as 'a dolphin is not a fish'), *has* links ('an animal has skin'), *can* links ('a bird can fly'), *cannot* links ('an ostrich cannot fly'), etc.

Overall, it uses a much richer and more flexible database, allowing for typicality effects much better than the original model and it also has the advantages that:

(a) It no longer sees the memory network in terms of logical, hierarchical relationships, ie human memory may simply not be as logical and systematic as originally proposed.
(b) It allows for an individual's personal experience and the structure of the environment to which he or she is exposed as, at least, a partial influence on the relationship between concepts.

It also introduced the concept of *spreading activation*, whereby when two concepts are stimulated an activation from each spreads throughout the network until they are linked. This takes time, because semantically related concepts are closer together than semantically unrelated concepts.

But despite the definite improvements compared with the original model, many criticisms have been made of the Collins and Loftus alternative. Baddeley (1990), for example, states that although it can account for most of the available data, this is at the expense of assuming a very complex network and a set of elaborate processing rules. It is not very succinct or parsimonious and does not seem to have provided much more insight into the nature of SM.

A more general kind of criticism is made by Johnson-Laird et al (1984). They argue that in principle network models are so powerful and flexible that they can be made to account for any result and, in this sense, they are more like a modelling language (allowing for the construction of a very large number of models) than a theory. Despite this, there are many phenomena which are difficult to model neatly and convincingly in network terms. There are many examples where the interpretation offered by the network will tend, in actual discourse, to be overridden by the constraints of real-world knowledge; for example, 'the ham sandwich was eaten by the soup'. This would appear to be nonsensical until you put it into the context of a restaurant, where waiters/waitresses sometimes label customers in terms of their order. Johnson-Laird et al call this failure to 'escape from the maze of symbols into the world' the *symbolic fallacy*: you have to know the relationship between symbols and what they refer to. (We shall return to this issue in Chapter 14 in the form of the controversy over whether computers can think.)

3) According to Baddeley (1990), it became increasingly obvious during the 1970s that SM must contain structures considerably larger than the simple concepts involved in network models such as that of Collins and Loftus; this 'larger unit' of SM is the *schema*, a concept which in fact had been used by Bartlett in 1932 and which we shall discuss in depth in the final section of this chapter.

The term 'schema' was borrowed from the neurologist, Henry Head, who used it to represent a person's concept of the location of limbs and body (rather like having a homunculus—little man—inside one's head, keeping track of the position of one's limbs; Baddeley, 1990).

Three major modern schema theories are: (i) Minsky's (1975) concept of a *frame*; (ii) Rumelhart's (1975) theory; and (iii) Schank's (1975) and Schank and Abelson's (1977) theory of *scripts*. We shall concentrate on the second and third here.

There is a good deal of overlap between them and the broad characteristics which they share are summarized by Rumelhart and Norman (1983/85) as:

(a) *Schemas have variables or slots.* Schemas are packets of information which comprise a fixed, compulsory, value plus a variable or optional value. For example, a schema for buying something in a shop would have relatively fixed slots for the exchange of money and goods, while the variable values would be the amount of money and the nature of the goods. In particular cases, a slot may be left unspecified and can often be filled with a 'default' value (a best guess given the available information).

(b) *Schemas can be related together to form systems.* They are not mutually exclusive packets of information but can be overlapping. For example: a schema for a picnic may be part of a larger system of schemas including 'meals', 'outings' and 'parties'.

(c) *Schemas represent knowledge at all levels of abstraction.* For example, abstract ideologies, abstract concepts (eg justice), very concrete schema (eg the appearance of a face).

(d) *Schemas represent knowledge rather than definitions.* Schemas embody knowledge and experience of the world rather than abstract rules.

(e) *Schemas are active recognition devices.* This is very similar to Bartlett's 'effort after meaning', whereby we try to make sense of ambiguous and unfamiliar information in terms of our existing knowledge and understanding (see below).

1) Rumelhart (1975) tried to capture the schematic structure of stories ('story grammar'), using traditional folk tales. Story grammar essentially involves producing a series of rules that capture the structure of stories, allowing them to be analysed and compared.

A number of related grammars were later developed, such as that of Mandler and Johnson (1977). They also looked at folk tales, including the 'War of the Ghosts' (used and made famous by Bartlett). The 'whole story' is shown in Box 12.3, while Table 12.4 shows the story broken down line by line. Figure 12.14 shows Mandler and Johnson's analysis of it.

Box 12.3 The War of the Ghosts

The title of this story is 'The War of the Ghosts'. One night two young men from Egulac went down to the river to hunt seals, and while they were there it became foggy and calm. Then they heard war-cries, and they thought: 'Maybe this is a war-party.' They escaped to the shore, and hid behind a log. Now canoes came up, and they heard the noise of paddles, and saw one canoe coming up to them. There were five men in the canoe, and they said: 'What do you think? We wish to take you along. We are going up the river to make war on the people.' One of the young men said: 'I have no arrows.' 'Arrows are in the canoe', they said. 'I will not go along. I might be killed. My relatives do not know where I have gone. But you', he said, turning to the other, 'may go with them.' So one of the young men went, but the other returned home. And the warriors went on up the river to a town on the other side of Kalama. The people came down to the water, and they began to fight, and many were killed. But presently the young man heard one of the warriors say: 'Quick, let us go home: that Indian has been hit.' Now he thought: 'Oh, they are ghosts.' He did not feel sick, but they said he had been shot. So the canoes went back to Egulac, and the young man went ashore to his house, and made a fire. And he told everybody and said: 'Behold I accompanied the ghosts, and we went to fight. Many of our fellows were killed, and many of those who attacked us were killed. They said I was hit, and I did not feel sick.' He told it all, and then he became quiet. When the sun rose he fell down. Something black came out of his mouth. His face became contorted. The people jumped up and cried. He was dead.

Mandler and Johnson found a number of anomalous features, including the fact that many connections between components which one would normally expect to be *causal* are simply specified *temporally*. Perhaps the clearest example is in lines 26 and 27:

Line 26   Now he thought, 'Oh, they are ghosts.'
Line 27   'He did not feel sick.'

'THE WAR OF THE GHOSTS'

1. One night two young men from Egulac went down to the river to hunt seals
2. and while they were there it become foggy and calm.
3. They heard war cries,
4. and they thought, 'Maybe this is a war party.'
5. They escaped to the shore
6. and hid behind a log.
7. Now canoes came up,
8. and they heard the noise of paddles
9. and saw one canoe coming up to them.
10. There were five men in the canoe,
11. and they said, 'What do you think? We wish to take you along.
12. We are going up the river to make war on the people.'
13. One of the young men said, 'I have no arrows.'
14. 'Arrows are in the canoe,' they said.
15. 'I will not go along.
16. I might get killed.
17. My relatives do not know where I have gone.
18. But you,' he said, turning to the other, 'may go with them.'
19. So one of the young men went,
20. but the other returned home.
21. And the warriors went on up the river to a town on the other side of Kalama.
22. The people came down to the water,
23. and they began to fight,
24. and many were killed.
25. But presently the young man heard one of the warriors say, 'Quick, let us go home; that Indian has been hit.'
26. Now he thought, 'Oh, they are ghosts.'
27. He did not feel sick,
28. but they said he had been shot.
29. So the canoes went back to Egulac,
30. and the young man went ashore to his house and made a fire.
31. And he told everybody and said, 'Behold, I accompanied the ghosts, and we went to fight.
32. Many of our fellows were killed,
33. and many of those who attacked us were killed.
34. And they said I was hit
35. and I did not feel sick.'
36. He told it all,
37. and then he became quiet.
38. When the sun rose he fell down.
39. Something black came from his mouth.
40. His face became contorted.
41. The people jumped up and cried.
42. He was dead.

Table 12.4 Line-by-line breakdown of 'War of the Ghosts' (Mandler and Johnson, 1977)

It is not obvious what the connection is between the two lines—you might *expect* it to be causal but it is difficult to see how it is. This is not helped by the fact that, despite the title, ghosts do not appear until line 26. It is also interesting to note that Bartlett's subjects recalled a mean of 0.61 causally connected episodes compared with 0.48 temporally connected episodes. It would seem that in Western culture, there is an expectation that a story will consist of a series of causally (inter-)related events and the 'War of the Ghosts', from a North American Indian culture, simply does not conform to such expectations.

Figure 12.14 A simplified
analysis of the 'War of the
Ghosts', showing basic nodes,
with violations in boxes
(Mandler and Johnson, 1977)

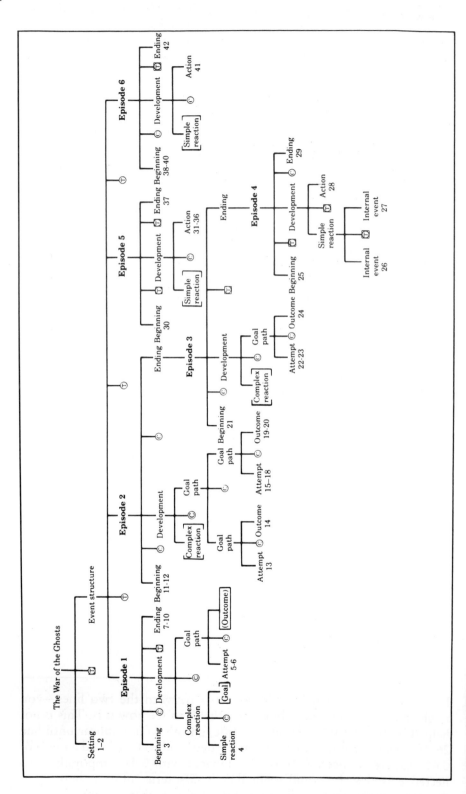

2) Schank (1975) and Schank and Abelson (1977) suggest that we develop schemas or *scripts* which represent commonly experienced social events, such as catching a bus, and going to a restaurant. These allow us to fill in much of the detail not specified in any text that we might read.

For example:

> We had a tandoori chicken at the Taj Mahal last night. The service was slow and we almost missed the start of the play . . .

can only be interpreted by bringing in a great deal of additional information (Baddeley, 1990). We need to have schemas that predict what would happen next and fill in those aspects of the event which are left implicit in the text. Scripts are essential ways of summarizing common cultural assumptions which not only help us to understand text and discourse but also predict future events and behave appropriately in given social situations. Scripts contain the sequences of actions one goes through when carrying out stereotypical events (eg 'catching a bus' or 'eating out') and would also include the sorts of objects and actors we are likely to encounter.

Schank and Abelson (1977) built their scripts into a computer program (SAM) which they claim is capable of answering questions about restaurants and understanding stories about restaurants (see Chapter 14). Table 12.5 shows their script for Eating at a Restaurant.

Bower et al (1979) asked people to list about twenty actions or events, in order, which commonly occur while eating at a restaurant and found considerable agreement. For example, at least 73 per cent mentioned sitting down, looking at the menu, ordering, eating, paying the bill and leaving. Also, at least 48 per cent included entering, giving the reservation name, ordering drinks, discussing the menu, talking, eating salad or soup and ordering dessert, eating dessert and leaving a tip. So there were at least fifteen events which formed part of many peoples' knowledge of what is involved in going to a restaurant. These findings broadly agreed with Schank and Abelson's restaurant script. Interestingly, when such events were incorporated into stories, subjects tended to falsely recall aspects of the passage which were not explicitly included but which were consistent with the script. The order of events was also changed to fit what would 'normally' happen. (This is exactly what Bartlett would have predicted would happen.)

But isn't the concept of a script essentially conservative (and inflexible) since we are only storing what we already know? Surely this cannot be a sufficient account of normal memory? Bower et al's subjects were, in fact, much better at remembering *deviations* from scripts than events which were consistent with them.

This and similar findings led Schank (1982) to propose his *Dynamic Memory Theory*, an attempt, as the name implies, to take account of the more dynamic aspects of memory. (For example, Bower et al's subjects often confused different scripts which, according to the earlier model, should not happen.) Dynamic Memory Theory is a more elaborate version of the original model, comprising *plans, scenes, memory organization packets* (MOPs) and *thematic organization points* (TOPs). It was also an attempt to propose a more flexible, less rigid, model. According to Eysenck and Keane (1990):

> We know a lot about stereotypical situations but we can also deal with the

Table 12.5 A simplified version of Schank and Abelson's (1977) schematic representation of activities involved in going to a restaurant. (From Bower et al, 1979

Name:	Restaurant	**Roles:**	Customer
Props:	Tables		Waiter
	Menu		Cook
	Food		Cashier
	Bill		Owner
	Money		
	Tip		
Entry conditions:	Customer is hungry.	**Results:**	Customer has less money.
	Customer has money.		Owner has more money.
			Customer is not hungry.

Scene 1:	*Entering*	**Scene 3:**	*Eating*
	Customer enters restaurant.		Cook gives food to customer.
	Customer looks for table.		Customer eats food.
	Customer decides where to sit.		
	Customer goes to table.		
	Customer sits down.		
Scene 2:	*Ordering*	**Scene 4:**	*Exiting*
	Customer picks up menu.		Waitress writes bill.
	Customer looks at menu.		Waitress goes over to customer.
	Customer decides on food.		Waitress gives bill to customer.
	Customer signals waitress.		Customer gives tip to waitress.
	Waitress comes to table.		Customer goes to cashier.
	Customer orders food.		Customer gives money to cashier.
	Waitress goes to cook.		Customer leaves restaurant.
	Waitress gives food order to cook.		
	Cook prepares food.		

unexpected. Further, we can act in goal-directed ways in situations where no script could exist. Schank and Abelson argued that scripts are only formed from direct personal experience. So few of us, for example, should be able to understand a bank robbery. *But* clearly we *can*. So we must have a more abstract set of structures which allow us to overcome the rigid structure of scripts and to understand the actions and goals of others in situations we have never experienced personally. While it [schema theory] is and remains one of the most pervasive proposals about the structure and organization of knowledge in long-term memory, it has a number of faults which have led to some disaffection with it. (Eyesenck and Keane, 1990)

ORGANIZATION

We have already mentioned organization when discussing semantic memory and in fact it represents a way of encoding information. For example, Sperling and Speelman (1970) found that some subjects reported actively organizing letters in lists which they had to remember, while others just tried to rehearse them; the latter made acoustic confusional mistakes, whereas the former did not. So the same material can be coded in different ways involving different systems and, hence, different degrees of retention.

According to Meyer (1973), to remember is to have organized. Organization may occur either at *storage* or *retrieval*. At storage, it serves to reduce the amount of material to be remembered by hierarchically grouping or chunking it, while at retrieval, organized items have greater uniqueness and, therefore, an increased number of retrieval routes or 'tags' associated with them.

Organization can either be imposed by the experimenter (EO) or spontaneously by the subject, which Tulving (1980) called 'subjective organization' (SO). He was attempting to account for the findings, from many studies, that in free-recall of randomly selected words, subjects consistently tend to recall groups of words in the *same* order, despite changes in the order of presentation on each trial. The earlier interpretation was that the organization simply reflected pre-existing associations, the results, therefore, being consistent with a passive, associationistic view. Tulving, on the other hand, saw subjects as *actively* imposing their own organization on the lists.

Mandler (1967) found that instructions to organize will facilitate learning, even though the subject is not trying to remember the material. He used a pack of fifty-two cards, with a word printed on each; subjects were told to place the cards into seven columns. Half were told to try to remember the words, but not the other half. After five sorting trials, recall was tested; those instructed to just organize the cards recalled as many words as subjects instructed to remember them, which suggests that organization was equivalent to learning.

A classic study of organization is that of Bower et al (1969). Subjects had to learn a list of 112 words arranged into conceptual hierarchies (Fig. 12.15).

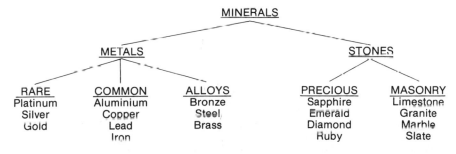

Figure 12.15 An example of a conceptual hierarchy used in Bower et al's (1969) experiment

For experimental subjects, the words were organized in hierarchical form (28 on each of four trials) while control subjects were shown 28 words on each of four trials but they were selected randomly. The experimental subjects recalled a mean of 73 words correctly while control subjects recalled only 21 on average. Clearly, organization can facilitate retention. Restle (1974) proposed the 'degree of organization' principle: the better we can organize new material (relate it to existing knowledge) the better it will be retained. Memory is seen as bound up with our thinking, perception and other cognitive processes;

explanations of memory for digits, letters and other 'bits and pieces' of information are likely to be inadequate as explanations of memory for complex and meaningful material. (This is consistent with Bartlett's theory of Reconstructive Memory and Schema Theories—see below.)

IMAGERY

Imagery is another, much researched, form of organization and, as was mentioned earlier, it plays a very important role in 'memory aids' or *mnemonics*. What they all have in common is either the reduction or elaboration of the way we encode information. We either strip away irrelevant information in order to have as little as possible to remember, or we elaborate the information to be stored (either verbally or through imagery).

An example of (verbal) reduction is the acronym ROYGBIV, an aid to remembering the colours of the spectrum (Red/Orange/Yellow/Green/Blue/Indigo/Violet); of course you must be able to remember the code and also decode it. Alternatively, an elaboration of this acronym is 'Richard of York Gave Battle in Vain', which is decoded in the same way.

According to Paivio (1969), probably the most powerful predictor of the ease with which words will be learned is their 'concreteness', that is, how easily the word evokes a mental image. Richardson (1972) has also stressed the importance of imagery as an aid to memory and regards it as a process of organization, for to produce an image of a single stimulus will not improve recall. In a 1974 experiment, Richardson tested subjects' free recall of a series of 'concrete' and 'abstract' words, and by varying the interval between presenting the stimulus and recalling it, he concluded that the 'effect of imageability lies in secondary memory'; in other words, 'concrete' words were recalled significantly more efficiently from LTM (compared with 'abstract' words) whereas there was no difference with recall from STM.

Bower (1972) showed that asking subjects to form a mental image of pairs of unrelated nouns (eg 'dog' and 'hat') where the two words were interacting in some way, resulted in significantly better recall than when subjects were instructed merely to memorize the words. Bower considers that the more unusual the details of the image the better. Paivio (1971) believes that a general theme or principle, rather than specific content, is more easily retrieved by converting information into visual images. Whenever abstract material can be converted into concrete ideas, recall is enhanced. Exclusive reliance on the verbal system for encoding and retrieving information is a mistake.

A dramatic illustration of the role of imagery is the man with the exceptional memory documented by Luria in *The Mind of a Mnemonist* (1968; Box 12.4).

RECONSTRUCTIVE MEMORY AND EYE-WITNESS TESTIMONY

Because of the large amount of work on the organizational aspects of memory, and because of the need to study meaningful material (as opposed to lists of words, etc.), there has been a 're-discovery' of the work of Bartlett on constructive and inferential memory (*Remembering*,

---

Box 12.4   The Mind of a Mnemonist (Luria, 1968)

S. was a reporter for a Moscow newspaper in the early 1920s. His astounding ability to produce reports, rich in the minutest factual detail without ever taking notes, so amazed the editor that he sent him for psychological evaluation. Luria, who for years had been studying human memory and amnesia caused by various forms of disease, had never encountered anyone like S. There seemed to be no limit either to the capacity of his memory or to the durability of the traces he retained. He could recall, without error, a list of words that increased up to 30, 50 and eventually 70 and he could remember nonsense material after days, months and even years. He could commit to memory, in a few minutes, long lists of numbers and recall them perfectly, hours, days or weeks later. Luria tested him 30 years after they first met and S. could still remember perfectly the numbers of tables he had previously learned!

He seemed to have spontaneously developed mnemonic tricks. For example, he would associate, in his mind's eye, lists of objects he wished to remember with familiar features of a street or some other familiar place. He mentally placed each object at some point on the scene; all he had to do to remember the list was to recall the mental image of the scene and locate each object on display. He would imagine himself walking along a Moscow Street looking in each hiding place for the object he had put there. 'Sometimes I put a word in a dark place and have trouble seeing it as I go by' he wrote (this is the method of loci). His recall was accompanied by extreme synaesthesia, ie sensory information from one modality evokes a sensation in another, for example, colours are associated with tastes. He once said to Luria, 'What a crumbly yellow voice you have.' These synaesthetic components seemed to provide a background for each item to be recalled.

1932). Bartlett used two main methods: (i) *repeated reproduction*; and (ii) *serial reproduction*.

In repeated reproduction, the same subject is presented with a story or argumentative prose passage or a picture and has to recall it some days, weeks or even years later. If the reproductions are given frequently, and at short intervals, they rapidly become fixed and change very little; however, if the intervals are sufficiently long, the material could go on being transformed almost indefinitely.

In serial reproduction, one subject reproduces the original story, a second subject has to reproduce the first reproduction, a third subject has to reproduce the second reproduction and so on until six or seven reproductions have been made. The method is meant to duplicate, to some extent, the process by which rumours or gossip are spread or legends passed from generation to generation.

One of the best-known pieces of material Bartlett used was 'The War of the Ghosts' which, as we saw earlier, is difficult for people from Western culture because of its style and some of its unfamiliar content and underlying beliefs and conventions. Ian Hunter (1972) used 'The War of the Ghosts' (and a serial reproduction method) and found similar characteristic changes to those reported by Bartlett, including:

(a) The story becomes noticeably shorter, eg Bartlett found that after six or seven reproductions, it shrank from 330 to 180 words.

(b) Despite becoming shorter, and details being omitted, the story becomes more coherent; no matter how distorted it might become, it remains a story because the subjects are interpreting the story as a whole, both listening to it and retelling it.

(c) It also becomes more conventional, that is, it retains only those details which can be easily assimilated to the shared past experience and cultural background of the subjects.

(d) It becomes more clichéd, that is, any peculiar or individual interpretations tend to be dropped.

Bartlett concluded that *interpretation* plays a large and largely unrecognized role in the remembering of stories and past events. We *reconstruct* the past by trying to fit it into our existing *schemata*. The more difficult this is to do, the more likely it is that elements are forgotten or distorted so that it fits. Bartlett refers to *efforts after meaning*, ie trying to make the past more logical, more coherent and generally more 'sensible', which involves making *inferences* or deductions about what could or should have happened. Rather than human memory being computer-like, with the output matching the input, Bartlett and Hunter believe that we process information in an active attempt to understand it. Memory is an 'imaginative reconstruction' of experience (Bartlett, 1932).

This view of memory as reconstructive in nature is also taken by Elizabeth Loftus, who has investigated it mainly in relation to *eye-witness testimony*. Loftus argues that the evidence given by witnesses in court cases is highly unreliable; her research strongly suggests that it is the form of questions that witnesses are asked which mainly influences how they 'remember' what they 'witnessed'. 'Leading questions' are of special interest, because they can introduce new information which can alter the witness's memory of an event—by their form or content they suggest to a witness the answer that *should* be given, as in the classic, 'Have you stopped beating your wife?' Lawyers, of course, are skilled at deliberately asking such questions, and undoubtedly, police also use such questioning when interrogating suspects and witnesses to a crime.

Loftus studied the influence of questioning in the laboratory using students as eyewitnesses and films of automobile accidents as the events they had to remember and report. In one study (Loftus and Zanni, 1975), 100 students saw a film of a multiple-car accident and were then asked to complete a 22-item questionnaire, six of which were 'critical' questions. For half the subjects, the critical questions began, 'Did you see *a* (broken headlight)?' and for the other half, they began, 'Did you see *the* (broken headlight)?', the only difference being in the form of the article, *the* or *a*.

Of course, usually when we use the definite article we are assuming the existence of the denoted object, but when we use the indefinite article no such assumption is being made and the influence of the form of question was reflected in the results. When asked about something which had not in fact appeared in the film, 15 per cent in the *the* group said 'Yes' compared with only 7 per cent of the *a* group, who were also more likely to say 'Don't know', both when the object had been present and when it had not.

In another experiment (Loftus and Palmer, 1974), Loftus explored the influence of changing a single word in certain critical questions on the subject's judgement of speed. For some subjects, the critical question was 'About how fast were the cars going when they *hit*?'; for others, 'hit' was replaced by 'smashed', 'collided' 'bumped' or 'contacted'. These different words have very different connotations regarding speed and force of impact and, again, these were born out in the judgements of speed: 'smashed' produced an average speed estimate of 40.8 mph, 'collided' 39.3 mph, 'bumped' 38.1 mph, 'hit' 34.0 mph and 'contacted' 31.8. A different group of subjects was asked to estimate the speed of cars for just 'hit' or 'smashed' with a control group not asked about speed at all.

Loftus wanted to find out if subjects were truly mis-remembering, ie does memory itself undergo change as a result of misleading questions or is the existing memorial representation of the accident merely being supplemented by the misleading questions? Theoretically, this is a very important issue—the idea of *memory as reconstruction* is that memory itself is transformed, at the time of retrieval, that is, what was encoded originally changes when it is recalled.

Loftus tested this by re-testing the 'smashed', 'hit' and control subjects a week later, asking them a new series of questions (without seeing the film again). This time the critical question asked whether the witness had seen any broken glass (although there was none in the film). If 'smashed' really influenced subjects to remember the accident as more serious than it was, then they might also 'remember' details that were not shown but which are consistent with an accident occurring at high speed, such as broken glass.

The results showed that 32 per cent of subjects who had earlier been asked a 'smashed' question reported seeing the non-existent glass compared with 14 per cent of those who had been asked a 'hit' question and 12 per cent of the controls. Clearly, the answer to the question about the glass was determined by the earlier question about speed, which had changed what was originally encoded when seeing the film.

So there would seem to be a good deal of support for the reconstruction hypothesis: eye-witness testimony (EWT) can be easily distorted and modified by information (in the form of questions) which becomes available *subsequent* to the actual event—even to the extent of 're-membering' things which were not actually seen in the original event. This new information becomes incorporated into the memory, updating it and erasing any of the original information which is inconsistent with it. Once this has occurred, the eye-witness cannot distinguish its source—it has become part of the witnessed event:

> Recollection of an event seems to be more fragile and susceptible to modification than might have been expected and this discovery lends weight to attempts by the police and by lawyers to make as little use as possible of leading questions (ie questions suggesting to the witness the desired answer. (Eysenck, 1984)

Similarly:

> It is highly unlikely that eye-witness testimony will ever be eliminated as a form of evidence . . . We might, then, profitably concentrate our efforts on building a research base to guide us in understanding the errors of eye-witnesses and in developing procedures that produce the least amount of error or distortion in eye-witness reports. (Loftus, 1984)

But are these conclusions necessarily valid? Are eye-witnesses really as unreliable as Loftus believes? There are several kinds of evidence which suggest a 'No' reply.

1)   Stephenson (1988) points out that the bulk of the work on EWT has been carried out in laboratories and has concentrated on eye-witness identification of people seen under fairly non-threatening conditions, or even people seen on *films*. In sharp contrast were the subjects of a study by Yuille and Cutshall (1986), described in Box 12.5.

Box 12.5   A Case Study of Eye-Witness Memory of a Crime (Yuille and Cutshall, 1986; cited in Stephenson, 1988)

> The incident involved a gun shooting which occurred on a spring afternoon outside a gun shop in full view of several witnesses [in Vancouver, Canada]. A thief had entered the gun shop, tied up the proprietor, and stolen some money and a number of guns. The store owner freed himself, picked up a revolver, and went outside to take the thief's licence number. The thief, however, had not yet entered his car and in a face-to-face encounter on the street, separated by six feet, the thief fired two shots at the store owner. After a slight pause the store owner discharged all six shots from his revolver. The thief was killed whereas the store owner recovered from serious injury. Witnesses viewed the incident from various vantage points along the street, from adjacent buildings, or from passing automobiles; and they witnessed various aspects of the incident, either prior to and including the actual shooting or after the shots were fired. (Yuille and Cutshall, 1986)

Twenty-one of the witnesses were interviewed by the police shortly after the event and thirteen of them agreed to take part in a research interview, 4–5 months later. In both sets of interviews (police and research), verbatim accounts of the incident were obtained and follow-up questions were asked in order to clarify points of detail. Also, the researchers asked two misleading questions based on Loftus's '*a* broken headlight'/'*the* broken headlight' technique. The sheer volume of accurate detail produced in both sets of interviews is truly impressive. The researchers obtained much more detail than did the police, because they were concerned with memory for details which had no forensic value. Witnesses who were central to the event gave more details than did peripheral witnesses, but there was no overall difference in accuracy between the two groups.

   Regarding the errors in recall, there were few, if any, *inventions* and many of those that were made could plausibly be attributed to perceptual distortion stemming from the disadvantageous viewpoint of one or two peripheral witnesses. Significantly, the wording of the misleading questions had no effect and those who were most deeply distressed by the incident (eg suffered nightmares) were the *most* accurate of the witnesses.

---

2)   Some laboratory research also suggests that subjects will not inevitably be misled by leading questions. Loftus herself (1979), for example, found that if the misleading information is 'blatantly incorrect', it will have no effect—subjects saw colour slides of a man stealing a red purse from a woman's bag; 98 per cent correctly remembered the colour of the purse. When they read a narrative description of the event containing a 'brown purse', all but two continued to remember it as red:

> Thus, memory for obviously important information which is accurately perceived at the time is not easily distorted. (Cohen, 1986)

In the previous example, the purse's colour is the focus of the whole incident, not a peripheral detail. Cohen (1986) believes that people are more likely to be misled if: (i) the false information concerns insignificant details which are peripheral to the main event; (ii) the false information is given after a delay, when the memory of the actual event has had time to fade (but note the accuracy of the recall after 4–5 months in the Yuille and Cutshall study above); (iii) subjects are not aware that they may be deliberately misinformed and so have no reason to distrust the information.

This last point relates to a study by Smith and Ellsworth (1987) which showed that the distorting effect of misleading questions depends on whether subjects believe that the questioner already knows what actually happened—when they believe the questioner is ignorant, misleading questions have *no* effect at all.

Cohen (1986) believes that EWT research has concentrated on the *fallibility* of memory and so gives a rather one-sided picture.

3)   Two other sources of evidence are relevant to the whole issue of the reliability of EWT, firstly the child as a witness (Box 12.6) and, secondly, the relationship between emotional arousal and EWT.

Box 12.6   Children as Witnesses (Davies, 1989)

The special status traditionally accorded by our legal system to child witnesses stems from an implicit psychological conception of the cognitive abilities of the developing child to perceive, remember and recall. They are assumed to be untrustworthy and unreliable witnesses, whose evidence is quantitatively and qualitatively inferior to that of adults. The social consequences of this view and the injustices it perpetuates have come under widespread attack from social workers, psychiatrists, childrens' interest groups and some laywers. There has been much media interest too in the plight of child sexual abuse victims, which represents the most serious, if not the only, role in which a young child may be called before the court. But it is the psychologist who must answer the fundamental question regarding competence; this is an applied problem gaining the attention of social, cognitive and developmental psychologists.

Allegations against using children as witnesses can be categorized under four major headings: (1) inaccuracy of memory; (2) proneness to fantasy and invention; (3) deliberate lying, and (4) receptivity to suggestion.

1)   In a recent study of a *simulated medical inspection*, a stranger in a white coat introduced himself to individual children and interviewed them, noting eye colour, condition of teeth, then weighed and measured them, which required them to remove their shoes and to stand on the scales. He at some point touched each child with his hand. The children were 6–7 and 10–11-year-olds and they were interviewed a week later. 20 per cent of the younger children correctly recalled the stranger's name (compared with 52 per cent of the older ones). But the percentage of mistakes was very similar for both groups (27 per cent). Correct recall of where and when the stranger had touched them was 30 per cent (younger) and 38 per cent (older). There were no wild flights of imagination when asked if the stranger had asked them to take their clothes off. There were no significant age differences when they were asked to choose the stranger from a set of photos—whether he was actually included or not:

It appeared that the greater element of interaction inherent in a personal confrontation between stranger and child led to an increase in accuracy with the younger children, a result encouraging to those who must evaluate the identification competency of younger children who are involved in prolonged face-to-face contact with a stranger during criminal activity. (Davies, 1989)

2) The use of 'anatomically correct dolls' as aids to assist children to demonstrate the behaviour inflicted in sex abuse cases has been controversial (for example, as used in Cleveland). Do they fuel the child's fantasy and imagination? Based on American research and studies at Guy's Hospital, London:

...there seems to be little evidence to support the widespread anxieties over the use of dolls as such as aids to the interrogation of young children. (Davies, 1989)

3) Jones and McGraw (1987) examined 576 cases of alleged sexual abuse reported in 1983 in Denver, Colorado. Only eight seemed to have been fabricated by the child and in four cases the children had been previously abused and transferred their allegation from one adult to another.

4) The most serious charge to consider is that of malleability of memory, ie an adult's suggestion materially alters the child's memory. But, 'true suggestibility in the sense of confabulation concerning the central thread of a witnessed event, is very rare' (Davies 1989):

It is apparent from this representative review of the literature, that differences in competence between younger and older witnesses appear to have been grossly exaggerated . . . younger witnesses differ . . . in terms of the quantity of their testimony rather than in terms of quality . . . Children, like adults, can be misled on detail, but seem just as immovable on the central events of incidents to which they have been a party. (Davies, 1989)

As to the effects of emotional arousal on the reliability of EWT, the empirical evidence seems to be rather mixed (Baddeley 1990). Loftus and Burns (1982), for example, showed subjects a film of a robbery made for bank employees which featured a holdup and the subsequent escape of the gunman. In the *high-arousal condition* a young boy was brutally shot in the face during the escape, while in the *low-arousal condition* there was no such violence. Subjects in the first condition showed poorer recall of detail. But would such findings influence a jury attempting to evaluate the testimony of someone who had undergone a horrifying experience and who states with conviction that they recognize the accused? (Baddeley, 1990). A case in point is 'Ivan the Terrible' (see Box 12.7).

CONCLUSIONS

Loftus et al (1970) believe that people often do little better than guess when trying to identify an alleged criminal in an identity parade. It is evidence such as this which led to the publication of the Devlin Report (1976) which recommends that the trial judge be required to instruct the jury that it is not safe to convict on a single EWT *alone*, except in exceptional circumstances (eg the witness is a close friend or relative) or when there is substantial corroborative evidence. The safeguards recom-

> *Box 12.7 Identifying Ivan (Wagenaar, 1988) (based on Baddeley, 1990)*
>
> John Demjanjuk (Ivan the Terrible) was the operator of the Treblinka gas chambers. The defence case rested on mistaken identity, while the prosecution argued that the horrors would have left an inextinguishable mark, even after 40 years!
>
> Wagenaar, a Dutch psychologist, agreed to act for the defence and claimed that the strength of EWT is weaker than it might seem by drawing on laboratory research. His client was duly convicted.
>
> Wagenaar subsequently collected evidence from the testimony of 78 witnesses involved in the case against Marinus De Rijke, accused of atrocities in Camp Erika, a Dutch concentration camp.
>
> In a personal communication to Baddeley, Wagenaar and Groeneweg report that some witnesses had been questioned shortly after their release (1943–7) and then subsequently (1984–7). The latter questioning was complicated by the fact that many witnesses had seen a TV programme about the camp, including De Rijke's photo, before their re-examination— of these, 80 per cent recognized him compared with 58 per cent who had not seen the programme. But his name was well recalled regardless of seeing the programme or not. Those actually maltreated by him were slightly *more* likely to remember him (80 per cent) than those who had not (74 per cent).
>
> In general, survivors remembered a good deal about their experience, although details had been lost. But however intensely the emotions were felt at the time and however clearly the images were engraved in the victim's memory, in many cases only the bare bones of the experience remains, with the type of detail often so essential in evaluating EWT being largely lost. There is no evidence that the intensity of the experience is a sufficient safeguard against forgetting. Wagenaar and Groeneweg conclude that EWT should not for that reason be discounted, but that, 'the extreme horrors of concentration camp experiences do not dismiss the courts of their task to question the evidence critically'.

mended are much stronger than those of the US Supreme Court but are similar to those of American legal experts (Brown, 1986):

> . . . However, neither the legal profession nor all psychologists, are certain either that acceptance of eye-witness testimony is a dubious practice or that psychologists should testify in court as expert witnesses in cases of disputed eye-witness evidence . . . (Stephenson, 1988)

13 LANGUAGE AND THOUGHT

Clearly, thinking and language both become more complex and sophisticated, although a child's understanding of language usually exceeds its ability to use it. Also, a child may use a word correctly before it grasps the underlying concept. As adults, our thinking often goes on through the medium of imagery and we express our thoughts and feelings through gestures and facial expressions and in other non-verbal ways. Artists 'think' non-linguistically. We have all had the experience of knowing what we want to say but being unable to find the right words to say it (students often do poorly in essays because they cannot put into words what they 'know').

From all of these examples, it would appear that thinking is possible without language. But psychologists differ greatly as to what they believe is the exact relationship between the two; their views fall into three main categories:

(a) Bruner, Sapir, Whorf, Watson, and Bernstein see thought as being dependent on, or caused by language.

It is worth noting here what these very diverse groups of theorists have in common. Sapir and Whorf, the first a linguist and anthropologist, the second a linguist, were both interested in comparing languages, which they saw as a major features of a culture. Individuals, of course, are born into a particular culture and a particular language community, so there was an expectation that language would be the greatest influence—language, because it is shared by all members of a culture (or 'sub-culture') is much more obviously 'public' than the much more private, individual 'thought'.

Watson, the founder of Behaviourism, stressed the role of environmental influences on the individual almost to the exclusion of any 'internal' psychological factors—so, once again, language is the greater influence because it is 'public' and can be studied objectively (at least in its spoken form) while thought is too inaccessible to others to be even worthy of scientific investigation.

Bruner's theory of modes of representation (different forms which our knowledge can take) sees language as being essential if thought or knowledge are not to be limited to what can be learned through actions (the enactive mode) or images (the iconic mode), ie language is crucial for the development of the symbolic mode (Chapter 25).

Finally, Bernstein is a sociologist who sees language codes as a major influence on intelligence, especially in the context of education and social class.

(b) A second view, as represented by Piaget, takes the opposite position, namely that language is dependent on, and reflects, the level of cognitive development. (Piaget's ideas will be discussed in detail, with Bruner's, in Chapter 25.)

(c) A third view regards thought and language as originally quite separate activities which come together and interact at a certain point of development (about two years old) and is associated mainly with Vygotsky, the eminent Russian psychologist.

(The nature of language and language development are discussed in Chapter 26.)

Does Language Determine Thought?

i) *THE LINGUISTIC RELATIVITY HYPOTHESIS*

The philosopher, Ludwig Wittgenstein, claimed that, 'the limits of my language mean the limits of my world;' by this he meant that we can only think about and understand the world through language, so that if our language does not possess certain ideas or concepts, then they cannot exist for us.

Many psychologists argue that language may determine the way we think about objects or events. Others contend that language is not merely a means of expression but actually determines our very ideas, thoughts and perceptions, that is, not simply *how* but *what* we think and perceive depends upon language.

Among those who adopt this latter view are Benjamin Lee Whorf, an amateur linguist, and Edward Sapir, a linguist and anthropologist (someone who studies and compares different societies and cultures). They reached very similar conclusions quite independently of each other, but their theory has become known as the Sapir–Whorf Linguistic Relativity Hypothesis (often their names are dropped and it is understood that Whorf is the major figure whose theory is being discussed). To give a flavour of what this viewpoint entails, let us consider quotes from both men; first Sapir:

> We see and hear and otherwise experience very largely as we do because the language habits of our community predispose certain choices of interpretation. Philosophically, this is very radical, it undermines the possibility of man's access to the real world. (Sapir, 1929)

In the above, Sapir is making a very similar point to Wittgenstein. According to Whorf:

> The categories and types that we isolate in the world of phenomena we don't find there because they stare every observer in the face; we cut nature up, organize it into concepts and describe significances as we do, largely because we are party to an agreement which holds in the pattern of our language. (Whorf, 1941)

What they are both saying is that language determines our concepts and we can think only through the use of concepts (this is *linguistic determinism*). It follows that acquiring a language involves acquiring a world-view (that is, how we 'cut nature up'—it does not come 'ready sliced') and that people with different languages have different world views, that is, they cut nature up differently (this is, strictly speaking, what the *linguistic relativity hypothesis* maintains). We shall be discussing below differences in the way the spectrum is cut up linguistically; the analogy of thin, medium and thick-sliced is not as outrageous as it might first sound!

What sort of thing are Sapir and Whorf describing?

Vocabulary determines the categories we use to perceive and understand the world. For instance, whereas in English we have a single word for snow, the Eskimos have more than twenty specific words (including one for fluffy snow, one for drifting snow, another for packed snow, and so on). The Hopi Indians (whose language Whorf studied for several years) have only one word for 'insect', 'aeroplane' and 'pilot', and the Zuni Indians do not distinguish, verbally, between yellow and orange.

But it is not only the vocabulary of a language that determines how and what we think and perceive but also the grammar. In the Hopi language, no distinction is made between past, present and future; it is a 'timeless language' (compared with English), although it does recognize duration, ie how long an event lasts.

In European languages, 'time' is treated as an objective entity, as if it were a ruler with equal spaces or intervals marked off, and there is a clear demarcation between past, present and future (corresponding to three separate sections of the ruler). We say 'ten days' in much the same way as we say 'ten men', although we cannot experience ten days simultaneously. By contrast, the Hopi Indians do not talk about an objective period of time but only as it appears subjectively to the observer. For example, they say, 'I stayed until the sixth day' or, 'I left on the sixth day' (instead of, 'I stayed for six days').

Again, the Hopi Indians get by without tenses for their verbs and have no words or grammatical forms which refer directly to 'time'. Instead, they use different verb endings according to how certain the speaker is about an event (whether they have actually seen it or have just heard about it), or different voice inflections which express whether the speaker is reporting an event, expecting an event or making a generalization about events.

In English, we think of nouns as denoting objects and events and verbs as denoting actions. But in the Hopi language, 'lightning', 'wave', 'flame', 'meteor', 'puff of smoke' and 'pulsation' are all verbs, as events of necessarily brief duration must be verbs; so, for example, 'it lightened', 'it smoked' and 'it flamed'.

All these differences, according to Sapir and Whorf, determine differences in how native speakers think about, perceive and remember the world: the world *is* different according to what language we speak (or perhaps, more accurately, the language we 'think in').

It is extremely difficult to put the Whorfian hypothesis to direct experimental test. Miller and McNeill (1969) distinguish between three rather different versions, all consistent with Whorf's general theoretical position but varying in the strength of the claims they make. For the sake of simplicity, we shall distinguish between: (i) the *strong version*, which claims that language determines thought; and (ii) the *weak version* (which combines the 'weak' and 'weakest' according to Miller and McNeill), which claims only that language affects perception and memory. By far the most research relates to the weak version.

i) *The Strong Version of the Linguistic Relativity Hypothesis*

Some support for this comes from a study by Carroll and Casagrande

(1958). They compared Navaho children (both those who spoke only Navaho, Navaho-Navaho, and those who spoke English and Navaho, English-Navaho) and American children (of European descent, who spoke only English) on the development of form or shape recognition.

The Navaho language stresses the importance of form. For example, verbs of handling involve different words according to the type of object being handled, so that long and flexible objects (such as string) have one word form, while long, rigid objects (like sticks) have another and flat and flexible objects (like cloth) have still a different word form. It is also known (from other research) that American children of European descent develop object recognition in this order: size, colour and form or shape.

If the Navaho language has influenced cognitive development (as Sapir and Whorf predict it would) then the developmental sequence of the Navaho-Navaho children should differ from that of the American children—they should be superior. And this, indeed, was what Carrol and Casagrande found: the Navaho-Navaho children were best at form recognition and showed it earliest, next came the American children, and last of all the English-Navaho children.

So this seems to lend support to the Sapir–Whorf view. But why did the American children come second and not third? According to the researchers, they were atypical, having had a great deal of experience of shape classification at nursery school.

ii)   *The Weak Version of the Linguistic Relativity Hypothesis*

Several studies have looked at the ways in which different languages 'code' the colours of the spectrum. According to the Linguistic Relativity Hypothesis, if a language does not make certain discriminations in its verbal labels, then native speakers of that language will be unable to make the corresponding perceptual discriminations. In other words, taking a previous example, since the Zuni language does not distinguish between yellow and orange, Zuni speakers should not be able to perceive the difference between these two colours— they would be 'blind' for these two colours. Does this reflect the way things really are?

Brown and Lenneberg (1954) compared English with Shone (a language of Zimbabwe) and Bassa (a language of Liberia), each of which divides up the spectrum very differently. They found that colours (hues) for which there is no single name in the language are not easily recognized by speakers of that language. However, this seems to be a result of storage, or the way that information is coded, rather than a result of the direct influence of language on the perception of colours. When subjects were forced to place greater emphasis on verbal cues when remembering colours they had seen, the colour was more accessible and easily picked out of a large array. That is, by stressing the name of the colour, it became easier to code and hence more easily recognized.

Lenneberg and Roberts (1956) found that the number of errors made by bilingual Zuni-English speakers in distinguishing orange and yellow fell midway between that of monolingual Zuni and monolingual English speakers. This suggests that the two languages do not determine two different sets of perceptions which in some way conflict, but rather two sets of labels for essentially the same colour perceptions.

Other studies show that speakers can learn new labels for colours, indicating that there are no differences in what is actually perceived by native speakers of different languages. Instead, language serves to draw attention to differences in the environment and acts as a label to help store these differences in memory; sometimes the label we apply to what we see may distort our recall of what was seen, since the label determines how we code our experiences into memory storage.

This was well illustrated in a famous experiment by Carmichael, Hogan and Walter (1932). Two separate groups of subjects were given identical stimulus figures but two different sets of labels. After a period of time, both groups were asked to reproduce the figures. The drawings of both groups were distorted in comparison with the original stimulus according to which label had been presented (Fig. 13.1). So there seems to be very little direct evidence to support the original ('strong') form of the Linguistic Relativity Hypothesis, but quite a lot to support the weaker version, which states that language determines how easily we recognize an object or situation, how much attention is paid to it, how codeable certain concepts are and, hence, how 'available' these concepts are to speakers of a language. According to Brown (1956), language merely predisposes people to think or perceive in certain ways, or about certain things—it does not determine these thoughts and perceptions.

Again, is it reasonable to believe that, say, Hopi Indians really think

Figure 13.1 Stimulus figures, word lists and reproduced figures. *(From the experiment by Carmichael et al, 1932)*

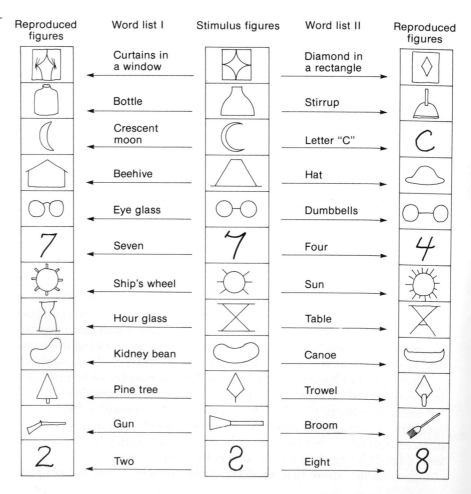

Reproduced figures	Word list I	Stimulus figures	Word list II	Reproduced figures
	Curtains in a window		Diamond in a rectangle	
	Bottle		Stirrup	
	Crescent moon		Letter "C"	
	Beehive		Hat	
	Eye glass		Dumbbells	
	Seven		Four	
	Ship's wheel		Sun	
	Hour glass		Table	
	Kidney bean		Canoe	
	Pine tree		Trowel	
	Gun		Broom	
	Two		Eight	

differently from ourselves? Judith Greene (1975) asks us to imagine a Hopi linguist doing a Whorfian analysis of English: would they think that we have 'primitive' beliefs that ships are really female or that mountains have feet or that 'driving a car', 'driving off in golf' and 'driving a hard bargain' all involve the same activity? Of course not; we do distinguish between the grammar of a language and our perceptual experience. The fact that we can translate from Hopi into English, and vice versa, implies that there is a universally-shared knowledge of the world, which is independent of the particular language in which it is expressed.

Universal Linguistic Structures

A way of countering the Whorfian hypothesis is to look at how thought might influence language. Specifically, the question being asked is: are there universal characteristics of human thought processes that produce universal linguistic structures? (This is much more in line with Piaget's position.)

Berlin and Kay (1969) conducted a survey of a wide variety of languages. Despite a diversity of terms denoting colour, all languages apparently select colour terms from the eleven basic colour categories of black, white, red, green, yellow, blue, brown, purple, pink, orange and grey. In English, all eleven are used. But the Ibibio of Nigeria use only four and the Jalé of New Guinea only two. However, this does not indicate an arbitrary division of the colour spectrum: if a language has fewer than eleven terms, those it lacks come from categories lower down in the list. For example, Jalé names only the first two categories (black and white) and Ibibio the first four (black, white, red and green) and so on down the list. Of course, the smaller the number of terms, the wider the range of colours they apply to. So, for example, green in Ibibio encompasses the English green, yellow and blue. Therefore, according to Whorf, speakers of Ibibio should be unable to perceive the same colour differences that English speakers can. Do the findings bear him out?

Berlin and Kay devised a chart with 320 small squares of colour, comprising virtually all the hues that the human eye can discriminate. They then asked native speakers of dozens of languages to point out the best example of colour terms in their language. The choices were virtually the same from language to language—basic colours seem to correspond across languages.

However, the boundaries of basic colour categories (whether, say, pink is included in the red category or given a separate label) vary according to the number of colour terms a particular language has. It seems that people find certain basic colours more salient or meaningful than others (these are called 'focal colours'). Even when a language does not possess a term for every focal colour, speakers of that language can easily learn the missing ones and can borrow terms for them from other languages. For example, Heider (1972) and Rosch (1973) studied the Dani of Indonesian New Guinea, a Stone-Age agricultural people. Their language has only two basic colour terms—'mola' for bright, warm hues and 'mili' for dark, cold hues. Despite the substantial linguistic differences between the Dani and English speakers, the Dani quickly learnt arbitrary names for eight other focal colours such that both groups showed better recognition memory for focal colours.

Finally, is there any evidence that focal colours are learnt (ie disciminated) *before* any verbal colour labels are learnt, which would represent a very serious contradiction of Whorf?

Bornstein et al (1976) found that 4-month-olds habituated to a light of a single colour and readily noticed when a light of a different hue came on (even when there was no change in brightness). They then habituated to a wavelength of 480 nm (near the boundary between blue and green) and were subsequently shown lights of 450, 480 and 510 nm (all of equal brightness). When shown the 450, the babies treated it the same as 480 but they treated the 510 as different. These and other studies show that:

> ... pre-verbal infants categorize the visible spectrum into relatively discrete hues of blue, green, yellow and red: which are similar to those of adults ... (Bornstein, 1988)

Many psychologists now believe that Whorf overestimated the significance of language differences. The studies of colour 'coding' suggest that:

> ... the similarities between cultures regarding which colours are remembered most easily are far more pronounced than the dissimilarities. This is in spite of the fact that there are considerable differences from one language to the next in the terms available to describe colours. The natural interpretation of this finding is that language does not dictate the way in which colours are perceived and remembered. Indeed, the evidence is more consistent with the notion that thought affects language ... (Eysenck and Keane, 1990)

ii) *PERIPHERALISM*

Another theory which maintains that language determines thought is that of Watson (1912; see Chapter 1). Watson claimed that all thought processes are really no more than the sensations produced by tiny movements of the speech apparatus which are too small to produce audible sounds. In fact, he was trying to deny thought altogether and so 'reduce' it to silent speech. His theory is known as Peripheralism, that is, thinking does not occur centrally in the brain but peripherally in the voice box. In 1912 his theory was very speculative because there were no instruments precise enough to detect such movements. However, movements of the larynx have since been detected. Yet this does not tell us that these movements *are* thoughts or even that they are necessary for thinking to occur, only that they accompany thinking. An experiment by Smith et al (1947) leaves little doubt that, in fact, these movements are *not* necessary. Smith injected himself with a drug (curare) which causes total paralysis of the skeletal muscles and thus causes complete respiratory paralysis, so that he had to be kept breathing artificially. He was later able to report the thoughts and perceptions he had during his paralysis.

Furth (1966) demonstrated experimentally that people who are born deaf and mute, and who do not learn any sign language, are of average ability in thinking and intelligence as adults. Watson would have predicted that such individuals would be incapable of thinking. (It is evidence such as Furth's which lends support to Piaget's view that it is the development of cognitive structures which is of primary importance, with language merely reflecting those structures.)

An important study which suggests that language plays a rather more central role in cognitive development is the Luria and Yudovich study of the Russian twins described in Box 13.1.

Box 13.1   The Case of the Russian Twins (Luria and Yudovich, 1956)

Luria and Yudovich (1956) studied a pair of 5-year-old identical twin boys in Russia, whose home environment was unstimulating and who played almost exclusively together. They had only a very primitive level of speech development, received very little encouragement to speak from adults and made little progress towards a symbolic use of words.

Luria described their speech as *synpraxic*, a primitive form of speech in which the child cannot detach the word from the object or action which it denotes. Their communication with each other consisted of words and actions inextricably mixed. Words on their own had no permanent meanings and could only be understood in a concrete situation; also, their meanings changed according to the situation in which they were used and the tone of voice in which they were spoken. (Usually, words as such are used fairly consistently across different situations—this is really part of the definition of a word, as opposed to a babbled sound. Certainly, adults do have to interpret a child's early speech in light of the context in which it is used but you would not expect to have to do this with a 5-year-old; see Chapter 26.) For example, one of their names (Lioshia) could mean:

'I (Lioshia) am playing nicely' *or*
'Let him (Lioshia) go for a walk' *or*
'Look (Lioshia) what I have done'.

They hardly ever used speech to describe objects or events, or to help them plan their actions, they could not understand other people's speech, and their own represented a private system of communication, a kind of signalling (rather than symbolic) system. However, they were normal in most other ways and did not appear to be mentally retarded, although they never played with other children and when they played with each other the content was always very primitive and monotonous; for example, there was never any attempt to build or construct things. Their language deficiency seemed to underline their backwardness in powers of abstraction and generalization which are so crucial in the organization of planned, complex activity.

The twins were separated and placed in different nursery schools. One was given special remedial training for his language deficiency and the other was not. Although the twin given special treatment did make more rapid progress and, ten months later, was still in advance of his brother, equally significant is the fact that *both* made progress and the synpraxic speech died away. So we must be cautious in drawing any firm conclusions about the effects of the special training that only one twin received.

However, Luria and Yudovich conclude by saying:

The whole structure of the mental life of both twins was simultaneously and sharply changed. Once they acquired an objective language system, the children were able to formulate the aims of their activity verbally and after only three months we observed the beginnings of meaningful play. (Luria and Yudovich, 1956)

Many other studies have shown that retarded children who are given special language training will not only increase their language ability but also their IQ score (see Chapter 28).

iii) *RESTRICTED AND ELABORATED CODES*

As a sociologist, Bernstein was interested in the role of language as a social (rather than an individual) phenomenon, especially as it relates to cultural deprivation.

Essentially, Bernstein (1961) claims that working- and middle-class children speak two different kinds of language (codes)—a restricted code and an elaborated code, respectively. Since the relationship between potential and developed intelligence is mediated through language, the lack of an elaborated code prevents working-class children from developing their full intellectual potential. These language codes, according to Bernstein, underlie the whole pattern of relationships (to objects and people) experienced by middle-class and working-class families, as well as the patterns of learning which their children bring with them to school.

Bernstein studied the effect of social class differences in language on the child's intellectual ability by comparing the performance of boys from lower working-class homes with boys from famous public schools on tests of verbal and non-verbal intelligence (see Chapter 28). Working-class boys who scored high on the non-verbal test scored lower on the verbal test (sometimes there was a difference of up to 26 points) but scores for the public school boys did not show this pattern. These differences in verbal and non-verbal IQ for the working-class boys were attributed to their poor linguistic background, ie their restricted code (or 'public language').

So what are the characteristics of these two codes? The restricted code is grammatically crude, repetitive, rigid, limited in its use of adjectives and adverbs, uses more pronouns than nouns, and involves short, grammatically simple and incomplete sentences. It is context-bound, that is, the meaning is not made explicit but assumes that the listener is familiar with the situation being described. For example, a conversation might start with the words 'He gave me it', when the listener cannot be expected to know who 'he' or what 'it' is. 'I' is rarely used and much of the meaning is conveyed non-verbally. Frequent use is made of uninformative but emotionally reinforcing phrases such as, 'you see', 'you know', 'wouldn't it' and 'don't I'; it tends to emphasize the present, the here and now, is poor at tracing causal relationships, and does not permit the expression of abstract or hypothetical thought.

By contrast, the elaborated code is grammatically more complex and flexible, sentences are longer and more complex. It makes use of a range of subordinate clauses, as well as conjuctions, prepositions, adjectives and adverbs, and allows the expression of abstract thoughts. 'I' is often used, more nouns than pronouns are used, and it is context-independent, so that it does not assume the listener is familiar with the situation being described but makes the meaning explicit (for example, 'John gave me this book'). Also, it emphasizes the precise description of experiences and feelings, as well as the speaker's intentions. Finally, it tends to stress past and future, rather than the present.

Stones (1971) gives examples of imaginary conversations on a bus between a mother and child:

Mother: 'Hold on tight.'
Child: 'Why?'

Mother: 'Hold on Tight.'
Child: 'Why?'
Mother: 'You'll fall.'
Child: 'Why?'
Mother: 'I told you to hold on tight, didn't I?'

This would be a fairly typical restricted code-type of conversation: the words are being used more as signals than symbols, with very little attempt to explain or reason on the mother's part. Now contrast this with an elaborated code mother and her child:

Mother: 'Hold on tight, darling.'
Child: 'Why?'
Mother: 'If you don't you'll be thrown forward and you'll fall.'
Child: 'Why?'
Mother: 'Because if the bus suddenly stops, you'll jerk forward onto the seat in front.'
Child: 'Why?'
Mother: 'Now, darling, hold on tightly and don't make such a fuss.'

Bernstein's theory has important implications for education:

(a) Although lower working-class pupils can achieve a good deal of mechanical learning, they are much more handicapped in attempting academic work. The restricted code acts as a filter to restrict what gets through from the teacher who, by definition, is an elaborated code user; the middle-class child has access to both codes.

(b) Schooling is conducted almost entirely in an elaborated, formal, code. Hence middle-class children merely have to develop their language skills, while working-class children have to change theirs. Put another way, school is *continuous* with the home for middle-class but not for working-class children. The latter may be able to give correct answers but they may not spring from an understanding of the basic concepts involved; instead they may be 'surface' responses which have been learned fairly automatically. The older the child gets, the more difficult it becomes to overcome this disadvantage because the educational system becomes more and more abstract.

(c) The middle-class child is used to attending to long speech sequences (middle-class parents place more emphasis on verbal explanations as part of their disciplinary techniques), while the working-class child, (often used to communicating in a noisy, even chaotic environment) may find concentrating very difficult and may even have learnt how *not* to attend.

(d) Middle-class parents encourage their children to ask questions and if they cannot answer them themselves will consult a book or refer the child to one. The world is presented as rational and knowable—it can be mastered and understood. Working-class parents, on the other hand, are generally less responsive to their child's questions and may be unable or unwilling to 'point the child in the right direction'. The working-class child might then come to regard the world as largely unknowable or only knowable by others. Clearly, asking and answering questions, using books and other reference materials, and generally being inquisitive and wanting to find out about the world are all fundamental parts of formal schooling.

Some support for Bernstein comes from a study by Hess and Shipman (1965). They studied 163 American mothers and their 4-year-olds and found social class-related differences in communication which seemed to influence the child's intellectual development. In particular, they drew attention to, 'a lack of meaning in the mother–child communication system' for low-status families; that is, language was used much less to convey meaning (to describe, explain, express and so on) and much more to give orders and commands to the child. Hess and Shipman claim that, 'the meaning of deprivation is a deprivation of meaning'.

If true, these implications of having only a restricted code are of quite crucial importance. They amount to the impossibility of upward social mobility (moving 'up' from working-class status to middle-class status). How could a working-class child (limited to a restricted code) ever grow up to become a teacher, who is a middle-class elaborated code user? But we know this does happen.

Clearly, any theory formulated in terms of two basic types tends to oversimplify things as they really are, so that a more helpful way of thinking about language codes may be to see restricted and elaborated codes as two ends of a continuum. Perhaps there are some working-class children who are 'stuck' at the restricted code end but many will be able to move varying degrees along the scale. Bernstein himself acknowledges that middle-class children can use the restricted code under appropriate circumstances and perhaps some never reach the elaborated code end of the scale.

Perhaps the most serious criticism of Bernstein's theory is to do with the very terms 'restricted' and 'elaborated': they imply an evaluation of middle-class speech as being in some way 'superior', that is, it resembles 'standard' (or 'the Queen's') English much more than working-class speech does. But this is very difficult to defend on objective grounds.

In a similar fashion, the English spoken by black children and adults, according to Bernstein, is a restricted code, and this makes their thinking less logical than that of white, middle-class, children and adults.

LABOV AND BLACK ENGLISH

Bereiter and Englemann (1966) point out that certain inner-city, black dialects of American English are often called 'substandard' rather than 'non-standard' and are often attacked as illogical. One reason given for this attack is that speakers of these dialects often omit the present tense *copula* (the verb 'to be'), producing such sentences as, 'He a fool' instead of the standard, 'He is a fool'. But which version is more logical?

Labov (1970) showed that speakers of both dialects are, in fact, expressing the same ideas and understand each other equally well. Also, many prestigious world languages, such as Russian and Arabic, like black English, also omit the present tense of the verb 'to be', yet they are never called illogical. This suggests that black English dialects are frowned upon as a matter of convention, or prejudice, and not because they are poorer vehicles for expressing meaning and thinking logically.

Again, the structure of black English (phonology, grammar, etc.), differs in important ways from standard English, and as intelligence tests are administered in standard English, black children are clearly under a linguistic handicap (this also applies to the white, working-class child). Lahey (1973) observed that black English speakers are not making grammatical 'errors' but are correctly using a separate dialect of English; black English is different from standard English but is just as logical. Bernstein based his view of black English on a limited sample; but in addition, many children from low-income black families simply would not or could not speak freely and comfortably in their full language when around whites.

Similarly, Labov has pointed out that the social situation is a powerful determinant of verbal behaviour. He describes the dramatic changes that can take place when the testing conditions are changed. A young black boy, Leon, was shown a toy and asked, by a friendly white interviewer, to tell him everything he could about it. The boy said very little and remained silent for much of the time. In a second situation, Leon was interviewed by a black interviewer. This time, he answered the questions with single words or indistinct sounds. However, when sitting on the floor, sharing a bag of crisps with his best friend, and with the same black interviewer introducing topics in the local dialect, Leon emerged as a lively conversationalist. If the first two situations had been relied upon, Leon would have been labelled 'non-verbal' or 'linguistically retarded'. (In the same way, the nature of the testing situation might be partly responsible for Bernstein's conclusions about the white, working-class, child's restricted code.)

The picture that is emerging is that black children are actually bilingual. At home, in the playground, in their neighbourhoods, they speak an accepted vernacular; but in the classroom, they are forced to use another form of the English language in which they are little practised.

Houston (1970) studied black children in rural northern Florida, USA, and found that they have at least two language 'registers'—one for school and one for out of school. The school register was also used when the children talked to people who seemed to be in authority and only when using the register did they use short sentences, simple grammar and strange intonation; what they said was limited and concealed their thoughts, attitudes and feelings. Once out of school their natural register was easy, fluent, creative and even gifted. It was unquestionably non-standard English (*not* substandard); in fact, it was another language, with its own grammar. Houston's findings certainly do not support the view that such children lack the language needed for abstract thinking.

Williams (1972) devised the BITCH test (Black Intelligence Test of Cultural Homogeneity), a test specifically designed to measure the true ability of black children, written in the dialect in which they are skilled instead of the usual standard English. Significantly, Genshaft and Hirt (1974) found that when white children were tested using black dialect sentences, they did very poorly indeed! Black and white children matched for social class and non-verbal IQ did equally well on tests of standard English sentences.

Many would argue that it is unfair to give white children tests written in black English since they are not skilled in this language register. But it is equally unfair to test black children using standard English because this is often their second language (see Chapter 28).

ARE LANGUAGE AND THOUGHT SEPARATE AND INDEPENDENT?

VYGOTSKY'S THEORY OF THE LANGUAGE–THOUGHT RELATIONSHIP

According to Vygotsky, thought and language start out as separate and independent activities. In very young children (as in animals) thought precedes language (it is pre-verbal, as in sensorimotor intelligence) and language is devoid of thought (for example, when the baby cries or makes other sounds with its vocal apparatus, it is usually expressing feelings or trying to attract attention or fulfilling some other social aim).

Then, at about two years, there is a crucial moment when pre-linguistic thought (actions, perceptions, images, etc.) and pre-intellectual language (crying, babbling, etc.), 'meet and join to initiate a new kind of behaviour ... thought becomes verbal and speech rational' (Vygotsky, 1962).

Vygotsky's theory can be represented as two overlapping circles, one representing pre-linguist thought, the other pre-intellectual language; where they overlap represents verbal thought and rational speech (Fig. 13.2).

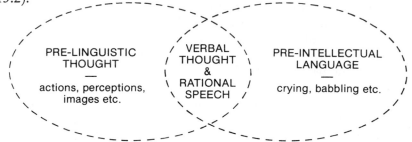

Figure 13.2 Summary of Vygotsky's theory of language and thought

Between the ages of two and seven, language performs two functions: (i) an internal one of monitoring and directing internal thought; and (ii) an external one, namely communicating the results of the child's thinking to others. But the child cannot yet distinguish them, which results in egocentric speech—the child talks out loud about its plans and actions and is neither thinking privately nor communicating publicly to others but is caught somewhere in between. Another way of putting this is that the child cannot distinguish between speech for itself (what Piaget called *autistic speech*) and speech for others (which Piaget called *socialized speech*).

Then at about seven years (when concrete operational thought usually begins) the child starts to restrict its overt language to the purposes of communication, while the thought function of language is now internalized as internal speech or verbal thought. Piaget originally claimed that egocentric speech is just a kind of running commentary on the child's behaviour and that when it declines at around seven it 'disappears' to be replaced by socialized speech (communicative speech). Vygotsky, on the other hand, noted that egocentric speech becomes more and more unlike social speech just as it begins to disappear. His experiments showed that when 6- or 7-year-olds are trying to solve a difficult problem or are thwarted in their attempts to do something (for example, their pencil breaks in the middle of drawing a picture), so that they have to revise their plans, they often revert to overt verbalization. (Adults, too, often 'think out loud' in similar situations; for example, 'Now where did I put it?' or 'Now what am I going to do?' especially if they believe there is no one around who can hear them.)

These findings convinced Vygotsky that the function of egocentric speech is similar to that of inner speech: it does not merely accompany the child's activity but serves 'mental orientation, conscious understanding; it helps in overcoming difficulties, it is speech for oneself, intimately and usefully connected with the child's thinking. In the end it becomes inner speech'.

The positions of Piaget and Vygotsky are summarized in Figure 13.3.

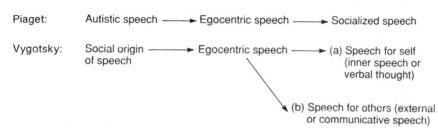

Figure 13.3 Piaget's and Vygotsky's views on egocentric speech

By 1962, Piaget had come to share Vygotsky's view regarding the function and fate of egocentric speech. Both inner speech and egocentric speech differ from speech for others in that they do not have to satisfy the grammatical conventions: they are both elliptical (abbreviated) and incomplete, concerned more with the essential meaning rather than how it is expressed. Inner speech, Vygotsky says, is a, 'dynamic, shifting, unstable thing, fluttering between word and thought'.

It is interesting to note that overt speech can sometimes resemble inner speech, in its abbreviated nature, long after egocentric speech has been replaced. For instance, people who know each other very well, like married couples, may often talk in a kind of shorthand which would not be used with anybody else: 'Tea?' asked with a rising inflection, and perhaps at a certain hour of the day, will be interpreted correctly as, 'Would you like a cup of tea, dear?' (This is reminiscent of the child's one-word sentences or holophrases which adults have to interpret according to the context; see Chapter 26). Friends or colleagues often share a vocabulary which would be meaningless to an outsider; the more familiar we are with others, the more shared experiences we have in common, and the less explicit our speech has to be. In Bernstein's terms, we slip into a restricted code when we are talking to familiar people, in familiar surroundings, whom we assume see things as we do.

CONCLUSION

We have considered different theories about the relationship between language and thought but there are points of overlap between them. If we superimpose them on top of each other we may have a more comprehensive and accurate picture of the nature of that relationship than any one on its own can provide.

Eysenck and Keane (1990) say that it is probably too sweeping to conclude that language has no effect on thought—at the very least, each language may affect certain habits of thought, even if it does not restrict cognitive functioning to a major extent. As thinking certainly begins at an earlier developmental stage than language in the child, it seems reasonable to follow Piaget in arguing that language builds on the cognitive abilities which have developed during the pre-language sensor-imotor stage (see Chapter 26). According to this view, language is shaped, at least partly, by the thought it must communicate:

> . . . It seems intuitively plausible to assume that language is the servant of thought rather than its master . . . (Eysenck and Keane, 1990)

Indeed, it could be argued that the fact that Eskimos have many words to describe snow—some of the most crucial kind of evidence given by Whorf—supports the view that thought influences language and *not* vice versa! Eskimos have developed highly differentiated terms to describe aspects of their environment since this is clearly relevant to their life experience—indeed, to their survival!

According to Eysenck and Keane (1990), renewed interest in the relationship between language and thought was stimulated by Fodor's (1983) *Modularity of Mind*, in which he argued that different cognitive abilities function independently of each other (these are separate modules of the mind or cognitive processors), including one dedicated to language processing. It follows that the process of language comprehension is not influenced by non-linguistic information, including thought.

While Fodor's position is probably too extreme, there is reason to believe that many aspects of language processing are relatively separate from non-linguistic processes. Cognitive neuropsychological evidence indicates that there are processing components devoted to specific aspects of language processing at both the comprehension and the production levels:

> . . . Furthermore, as Harris (1990) pointed out, 'Language processing has to be largely independent of other cognitive activities. For if it were not, we would hear only what we expected to hear and read only what we expected to read'. (Eysenck and Keane, 1990)

14 Thinking, Problem-Solving and Artificial Intelligence

In the earlier chapters of this book we have discussed some basic cognitive processes, in particular perception, attention and memory, and we have also looked at the ways in which all of these might be influenced by language, the latter being what many philosophers and psychologists have argued is unique to human beings (see Chapter 26 for a detailed discussion of this issue).

These basic cognitive processes are all aspects of 'thought' although there is more to thinking than just those particular examples. Another form in which psychologists have chosen to study both human and animal thought is to study problem-solving, a problem being defined as arising whenever a path to a desired goal is blocked, literally in the case of rats running mazes (Greene, 1987).

There is another sense, though, in which:

> ... all thinking involves problem solving, no matter how simple, immediate and effortless it may appear ... (Boden, 1987a)

A good example of this would be perception. You will remember from Chapter 9 that the immediacy and accuracy of perception suggests that there is nothing that needs explaining, that there is no 'vision problem'. But we saw that most psychologists (Gibson being the notable exception) agree in rejecting that view, although they disagree as to how to 'solve the problem'. The scientist who has addressed himself most directly to this issue is Marr, who attempted to provide an answer to the question of how useful information about a scene (some part of the external world) can be extracted from images of that scene, ie what *computations* must be performed.

Much of the work of computer simulation and artificial intelligence (AI) has been centred around problem-solving, ie attempts to produce computer programs which will solve 'human problems' so that we might understand better how *we* solve them. This work is based on the argument that both computers and human problem-solvers are *information-processing machines* (Greene, 1987), whether the problem is of the perception-type (ie a fundamental cognitive process which pervades everything we do and which, of course, we share with animals) or of the puzzle type (ie tasks specially constructed in order to make their solution difficult, from chess, through the missionaries and cannibals puzzle, to Rubik's cube).

Early Studies of Problem-Solving

Some of the earliest research was carried out, and inspired by, the Gestalt psychologists who, based on their theory of perceptual organization (see Chapter 9) saw the essence of problem-solving (PS) as the perceptual re-structuring of the problem resulting in insight. Some of the classic experiments were those performed by Köhler (1925) with chimps (see Chapter 7).

Maier (1931) devised the 'two string and pendulum' problem, in which a room has two strings hanging from the ceiling, plus several other objects (for example, poles, pliers and extension cords). The problem was to tie the two strings together, although they were too far away to be able to reach one while holding the other. Several different solutions were produced but the most 'insightful' and infrequently produced is the 'pendulum' solution: take the pliers and tie them to one of the strings and swing them; holding on to the other string, the 'pendulum' can be caught on its up-swing. Maier demonstrated a striking example of 'problem restructuring', by first allowing subjects to reach a point where they became stuck and then (apparently accidentally) brushing past the string to set it swinging. Soon after this happened they tended to produce the pendulum solution, even though most claimed not to have noticed the 'subtle hint' about how to solve the problem.

Duncker (1926, 1945) performed experiments on *functional fixedness* (or 'fixity'). Subjects were given a candle, box of tacks and several other objects and their task was to attach the candle to a wall over a table so that it did not drip onto the table underneath. Most tried to tack the candle directly to the wall or glue it by melting it. Few thought of using the inside of the tack-box as a candle-holder and tacking *it* to the wall—subjects were 'fixated' on the box's normal function and they needed to re-conceptualize it (to use *lateral thinking*; de Bono, 1967). Their past experience was leading them away from the solution—they needed to look at a familiar object in an unfamiliar way.

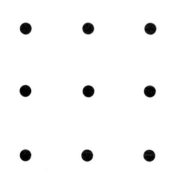

Figure 14.1 *Scheerer's nine-dot problem*

Similar is Scheerer's (1963) nine-dot problem (Fig. 14.1). The problem is to draw four continuous straight lines, connecting all the dots, without lifting the pencil from the paper. Most people fail because they assume that the lines must stay within the square formed by the dots—they 'fixate' on the shape of the dots. (The solution can be found over the page (Fig. 14.2).)

Finally, Luchins (1942) and Luchins and Luchins (1959) devised the water-jug problems. In one version, there are three jugs, A, B and C, which can hold 8, 5 and 3 litres, respectively. A is full, B and C are empty. The subject has to find a way of getting 4 litres into A and 4 litres into B (without any measures on the jugs). Figure 14.3 shows the shortest series of moves to solution (based on Eysenck and Keane, 1990). Luchins also used the jug problems to demonstrate *problem-solving set* (a form of functional fixedness).

In evaluating the Gestalt approach, Eysenck and Keane (1990) claim that the concepts of 'insight' and 'restructuring' are attractive because they are easily understood, especially when accompanied by perceptual demonstrations and, '... convey something of the mysterious dynamism of human creativity.' But as theoretical constructs they are radically under-specified—it is very unclear under what conditions they will occur and exactly what insight involves (see Chapter 7). However, in many ways, the spirit of Gestalt research, with its emphasis on the goal-directed and non-associationist nature of thinking, provide a basis for the information-processing approach. It also left a large body of experimental problems and evidence which any later theory had to be able to re-interpret, '... the legacy of the school was, therefore, substantial.' (Eysenck and Keane, 1990).

CLASSIFYING PROBLEMS—ADVERSARY AND NON-ADVERSARY

Before discussing how AI has helped us understand human problem-solving, it seems useful to categorize different kinds of problem and look at a wider range of problems than those devised by the Gestalt School.

Garnham (1988) distinguishes between two broad classes of problem: *adversary* and *non-adversary*. *Adversary problems* involve two or more people who pit their wits against each other; the prototype example is chess. Garnham says that game-playing is a special kind of PS in which the problem is to find a winning strategy or the best current move. The focus of AI research here has been on two-player games in which each player always has *complete information* about the state of play and in which there is no element of chance. Apart from chess, games used include noughts and crosses (tic-tac-toe) and draughts (checkers). (Compare these with backgammon, which does involve an element of chance, and card games which do not involve complete information because you're not supposed to see your opponent's hand.)

Most problems fall into the *non-adversary* category, in which another person is only involved as the problem-setter. (So the Gestalt problems fall into this category). In addition, some of the most commonly used include:

(a) *The eight-puzzle* (Fig. 14.4).
A 3 × 3 matrix containing the numbers 1–8, with one vacant square, must be moved until the numbers are in order.

(b) *The Missionaries and Cannibals (or 'Hobbits and Orcs') problem* (Fig. 14.5)
The three missionaries and three cannibals must be transported across the river in a single boat which can only hold two people but needs at least one to get it across the river. The cannibals must never outnumber the missionaries on either bank (or they'll be eaten).

(c) *The Tower of Hanoi Problem* (Fig. 14.6)
There are three vertical pegs with four (or more) discs of increasing size stacked on one peg. The problem is to transfer the discs to the second peg, moving only one at a time and never placing a larger disc on top of a smaller one.

(d) *Cryptarithmetic* (Bartlett, 1958)
Given that D = 5 and each letter stands for a digit (0–9), find the digits which make the sum correct.

$$
\begin{array}{r}
\text{DONALD} \\
+\ \text{GERALD} \\
\hline
\text{ROBERT}
\end{array}
$$

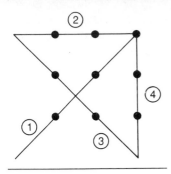

Figure 14.2 The solution to the nine-dot problem. The 'trick' is to draw the lines outside the square of dots

EARLY AI RESEARCH INTO PROBLEM-SOLVING—THE GENERAL PROBLEM-SOLVER, ALGORITHMS AND HEURISTICS

It is almost unanimously agreed among psychologists that cognitive psychology (the 'cognitive revolution') began in 1956. One of the events which occurred in that year was the publication of a paper by Newell and Simon on the Logical Theory Machine (or Logic Theorist) with a further paper by Newell, Shaw and Simon (1958), which was then extended into the General Problem Solver (GPS) by Simon and Newell (1964).

The GPS was a computer program designed to simulate the entire range of human PS and represented the first computational model of psychological phenomena. The GPS was originally based upon records of what people are thinking as they perform some experimental task—usually this meant asking people to report verbally how they are going about the problem they were trying to solve (a kind of running commentary on their own PS performance) called *protocol analysis*. The kind of operations which human subjects indicated they were using were then built into the computer program and, subsequently, the validity of the GPS was tested against further protocol analysis. This new research methodology, however, soon ran into serious difficulties. Garnham

Figure 14.3 The shortest series of moves to the solution of the water-jug problem. The arrows indicate the direction of pouring and the circled numbers indicate how much has been poured

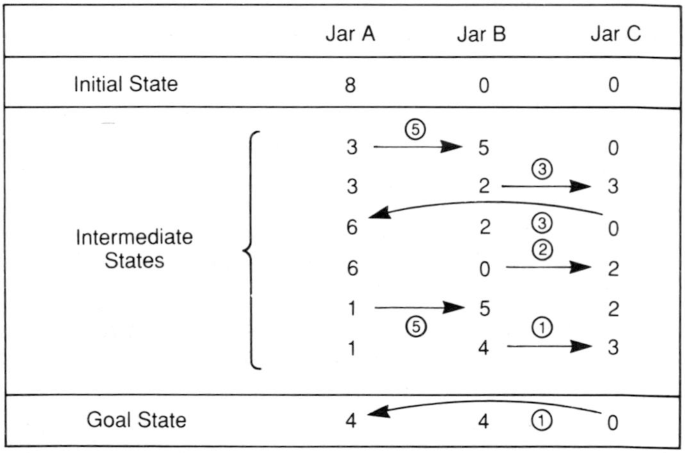

	Jar A	Jar B	Jar C
Initial State	8	0	0
Intermediate States	3 ⑤→	5	0
	3	2 ③→	3
	6 ←	2 ③	0
	6	0 ②→	2
	1 ⑤→	5	2
	1	4 ①→	3
Goal State	4 ←	4 ①	0

(1988) identifies two major problems: (i) it is difficult to measure the goodness of fit between protocol and the so-called 'traces' of a computer program; (ii) it is unclear how peoples' commentary on what they are doing relates to the mental operations actually contributing to the solution of the problem. Even more serious is the fact that in some cases, such as object recognition and language understanding, none of the mental operations which underlie our abilities is available to consciousness at all, making protocol analysis inappropriate.

The Logical Theorist (the forerunner of the GPS) was designed to prove theorems in propositional calculus (as formalized by Whitehead and Russell in *Principia Mathematica*) and in their attempt to simulate

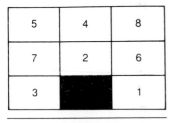

Figure 14.4 The eight-puzzle

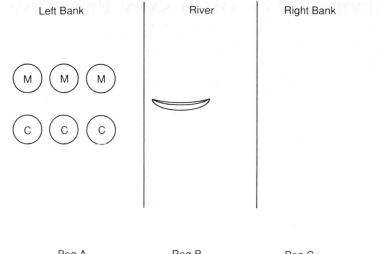

Figure 14.5 *The missionaries and cannibals problem*

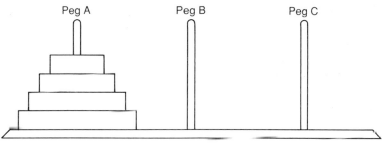

Figure 14.6 *The Tower of Hanoi problem*

this particular ability, Newell et al developed the idea of *heuristics* which are:

> ... procedures that can be used to prove theorems, or solve problems, but which cannot be guaranteed to find a solution, even if there is one. Heuristics are contrasted with *algorithms*, which are procedures that do offer such a guarantee. For many problems, such as finding proofs in propositional calculus, or winning in chess, algorithmic procedures can take unrealistic amounts of time. When people solve such problems they must be using heuristic methods. (Garnham, 1988)

The Logic Theorist used a number of heuristics for finding proofs which, even for simple proofs, speed it up compared with an algorithmic procedure. Even though there were many theorems it could not prove (mainly due to limitations of memory and the amount of time it was allowed to run), the Logic Theorist was important because the idea of heuristics dominated research on theorem proving and PS in the decade following its publication (ie up to the mid-1960s). It was incorporated into the GPS which, as we have seen, was a more direct simulation of human thinking than the Logic Theorist.

People learning geometry have to use their judgement about which steps are likely to prove a theorem, so the GPS had built into it heuristic strategies to help it select from all possible logical steps only those relevant to proving that particular theorem. Heuristics, therefore, are rules of thumb:

> ... guidelines for selecting actions that are most likely to lead a solver towards a goal, but may not always do so. (Greene, 1987)

SOLVING NON-ADVERSARY PROBLEMS

MEANS END ANALYSIS

Simon (1979) describes one general heuristic strategy as incorporating progress tests which indicate whether the solver is 'getting warmer', ie getting nearer to the goal. This was formulated in the GPS and later programs as *Means End Analysis* (MEA). In essence, it involves selecting operations which will reduce the distance between the current situation and the current goal. For example, in a geometry-theorem-solving program, at each point the program selects a method, carries out certain deductions, then tests to see if these have succeeded in narrowing the distance from the current goal. Depending on the outcome, the program either moves on to the next step, tries a different method or gives up altogether. The major aim of any heuristic is to reduce a problem to manageable proportions by increasing the selectivity of the program in choosing which operations to perform:

> . . . The means end heuristic provides a method for evaluating the relevance of actions according to whether they are useful in achieving a current goal. (Greene, 1987)

However, it is often not possible to achieve the main goal all in one step. So another important characteristic of MEA is to break down the main goal into sub-goals (or a problem into sub-problems), each of which has to be solved before the final (main) goal can be reached. (Many real-life situations are of this kind, especially if they involve large amounts of time, eg 'getting to a foreign country' or 'getting to University or Polytechnic'). So the basic procedure would be as shown in Figure 14.7.

Figure 14.7 Outline of major steps involved in sub-goal MEA

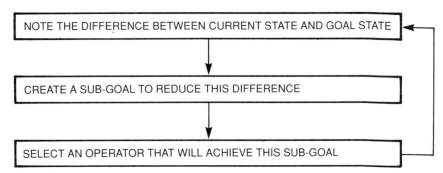

PS programs using MEA have had some success in simulating the verbal protocols of human solvers when the problem has a fairly clear goal or sub-goal structure, for example, the Tower of Hanoi. This particular application of MEA illustrates a major approach to describing the search for problem solution called *problem-reduction representation*. As we have seen, each operator (possible moves) divides one goal into a set of sub-goals, each of which is easier to achieve. For example, in the Tower of Hanoi, the overall goal is to move four discs from A to B, moving one disc at a time and never placing a larger disc on top of a smaller one. This overall goal can be subdivided into three sub-goals:

(i)   transfer the three smaller discs from A—C;
(ii) transfer the largest disc from A—B;
(iii) transfer the three smaller discs from C—B.

(i) and (iii) can be reduced further. (ii) can be achieved directly, assuming that (i) has been achieved. Complete reduction analyses the problem into moves of single discs whose pre-conditions are met; they correspond to the rules (*control strategies*) about only moving one disc at a time and only smaller discs being placed on a larger one (not vice versa).

Problem reduction is what Garnham (1991) calls a 'divide and conquer' approach and he considers it to be a powerful approach. But is it always as clear as this just what the sub-goals are?

The Missionaries problem is a good example of one where the final goal is obvious enough but much less so the sub-goals. Indeed, many puzzles are selected for experiments precisely because the basis for selecting the shortest set of moves to reach the final score is obscure. So how do you measure progress towards the final goal in such problems? It certainly cannot be measured simply by the total number of people transported from the left to the right because if there are too many cannibals the missionaries will get eaten! While it is possible for a computer to work out a sequence of all possible moves and then to plot the quickest path of moves towards a solution, people cannot hold this type of structure in their limited capacity working memories. The water-jug problem poses the same difficulties for human solvers. (If a computer program did systematically check every possible move until the goal-state were reached, it would be using a 'check-every-move' algorithm.)

A further problem with MEA as a heuristic for PS is that it is sometimes necessary to move *further away* from a goal in order to achieve a solution. One reason that the Missionaries and Cannibals problem is so difficult is that at one point it becomes necessary to take a Missionary and a Cannibal back to the left bank from where they started, thus apparently *increasing* the distance from the final goal of getting them all over to the right bank (Greene, 1987).

MEA is a 'top-down' goal-directed strategy for selecting actions which are evaluated in terms of reducing the distance from the final goal. A major drawback of such a strategy is that it grinds on relentlessly, regardless of any changing characteristics of the situation. But:

> . . . problem solvers often have to resort to reacting to the current situation as best they can, hoping that the final goal will take care of itself. (Greene, 1987).

Newell (1973) developed a computer program which simulates the reactive kind of PS, where people react to situations as they arise (as opposed to trying to carry out a pre-planned sequence of actions based on a MEA of the whole problem). It is a more 'bottom-up' approach and its basic form is that of a 'production', which is a rule comprising a condition plus an action: *if* such-and-such a situation, *then* do such-and-such; they are known as *production systems* (Greene, 1987).

STATE-SPACE THEORY

The search-strategy that would be appropriate in cases such as the missionaries and cannibals problem would be *state-space representations*, which are tailored to the use of operators which change one state of the world into another. The basic component is a state of the world or, strictly, a state of that part of the world relevant to the problem. For

Figure 14.8 Two possible states in the missionaries and cannibals problem

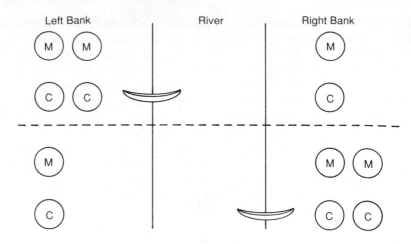

example, in the missionaries and cannibals problem, a typical state of the world might be as shown in Figure 14.8. Operators can change one state into another. So, using the operator which takes one missionary and one cannibal from the left to the right bank in the boat, State (1) can be changed into State (2). From each state it is usually possible to reach several others, using different operators. A map of all states that can be reached from the initial state by applying one or more operators is called the *state-space* (or problem-space), which can be represented by tree diagrams (state-action trees) with the initial state at the top and paths to other states branching beneath it. For many problems, such trees can be extended indefinitely:

> A solution to the problem is, therefore, a sequence of action that gets from the starting state along the branches of the tree to the goal state. (Garnham, 1991)

How does this apply to real-life, everyday problems?

Garnham (1988) believes that in everyday problems, and those requiring a high degree of creative thinking, it is usual for one or more of: (i) the initial state; (ii) the goal state; or (iii) the operators to be ill-defined (ie not made explicit) and this makes AI programs designed to solve such problems difficult to write. But the missionaries and cannibals problem (and the Tower of Hanoi) has all three clearly specified (they are *well-defined* problems) and AI programs are relatively successful in solving them. Is state- (or problem-) space theory a useful way of thinking about how people solve puzzles?

It has proved quite successful for a narrow range of puzzle-like, well-defined problems, but most puzzles people have to solve are not like this. Two major differences between puzzle-problems and real-life problems (according to Greene, 1987) are:

1) Puzzle-problems are unfamiliar problems about which the solver has little knowledge, whereas many everyday problems require considerable amounts of knowledge. The knowledge which is relevant in puzzle-problems is called *general-purpose* or *domain-independent* heuristic knowledge. For example, MEA can be applied in a wide range of different situations (domains). They are generally applicable but not always very efficient, which is why in AI they are often called *universal*,

weak methods. By contrast, everyday problems (which, as we have said, are often ill-defined), require substantial *domain-specific* knowledge—this also applies to skill in adversary problems, such as chess (see below).

2) The knowledge required to solve puzzles is present in the statement of the problem, whereas much of the difficulty with everyday problems is finding the relevant information needed to solve them.

Clearly, people do not construct in their minds potentially infinite state-action trees (but if they did they would be able to read solutions directly from the trees). But peoples' subjective reports do indeed suggest that they do think of puzzles in terms of states and actions. So when people are deciding what action to perform, do they 'look ahead' in their mind's eye and see which sequence of actions gets them nearest to the goal state? To do this they would need to construct *part* of a state action tree in their mind and it looks as though people do *not* do so—at least not in experimental studies where people try to solve unfamiliar puzzles. Instead, they consider only the *immediate* possibilities and choose from these. However, a possible exception to this general rule is the *expert* in their field, for example, the chess master (Garnham, 1991).

Solving Adversary Problems

According to Garnham (1988), two-person games are best described using state-space theory, with states corresponding to board positions and operations to moves by either player. The search tree has the initial board position at the top and different levels of the tree correspond to moves by each player.

Good chess players think through the consequences of a move before making it, which is equivalent to a pattern through a state-action tree. The number of possible sequences of moves is frighteningly large (in computational terms, a *combinatoric explosion* of possibilities—there are an estimated 10^{120} possible games of chess, compared with a mere 10^{16} microseconds per century; Garnham, 1988)—so players only think through a very small proportion. Only rarely can they think through to a win, lose or stalemate situation. It follows that they must have some means of evaluating the intermediate positions they think through to in order to decide which they prefer—these are called 'quiet positions', because there is no imminent danger of losing a piece (except in exchange for the opponent's piece). Clearly, a major consideration in evaluating such a position is the number of pieces left to each player.

Since what is good for one player is bad for the other, players must assume that their opponents will always choose the move which is worst for them. This assumption is the basis of the *minimax procedure* used in computer chess programs: players should *mini*mize the *max*imum loss their opponents can inflict on them. It can in principle be used to choose among all possible moves or among a smaller set initially selected by some other method. Programs used to be like human players—they selected a small number of moves to follow up, then used *minimax* to analyse these in detail. Programs run on small computers still operate in this way. However, top programmers have access to the most powerful machines available and they often revert to a more algorithmic method, for example, examine every possible position that can be reached in the next five moves by each player (which involves comparing hundreds of thousands of positions). While modern computers can perform many millions of operations per second (through 'brute force' methods):

> Unfortunately, it provides few insights for cognitive scientists, since it bears no relationship to the way that people solve difficult problems. (Garnham, 1991)

Even the best human players have an extremely limited *lookahead* compared with such powerful computers (a few hundred board positions).

But how good are those chess-playing programs which do not use brute force methods and which, like human players, set bounds to their lookahead? According to Boden:

> ... They use evaluative functions, embodying knowledge about what moves are likely to contribute to king safety, material balance, centre control, and so on ... some of them can benefit from expert advice. And some of them play very respectable chess: the Greenblatt Chess Program, for instance, wins over 80 per cent of its games against non-tournament players as well as a fair proportion of tournament matches ...
>
> However, there is no prospect of a chess master being beaten by a program in the near future ... Even with heuristics ... there are far too many alternatives to be considered for the program confidently to pick the right one; and as it cuts down the range of alternatives, it is as likely as not to lose the best move, so throwing out the baby with the bathwater ... master chess players develop global perceptual schemata in terms of which they can *see* threats and oppositions on the board much as a lesser mortal can *see* complex emotional response in a cartoon face ... (Boden, 1987a)

A move towards more ecologically valid research is to study how experts solve problems compared with novices (as opposed to powerful computers).

EXPERTS VERSUS NOVICES

According to Greene (1987), what is missing from AI accounts of human PS so far are different experiences people bring to different tasks. MEA, for instance, is meant to be typical of all PS by all problem solvers. Simon presents it as a general characteristic of human thinking which can, in principle, be applied to any problem and the selection of actions to attain the desired goal is considered to be a universal feature of human behaviour. Implicit in this view is the belief that it is only limitations in working memory (WM) capacity that prevents humans from applying MEA in all cases. But the ability to implement a particular PS strategy depends on knowledge—thinking mechanisms may be universal but solvers are categorized as experts or novices in relation to different problem situations. Expertise is more far-reaching than simple knowledge of the rules which apply to a particular problem (otherwise we would all be chess masters!). Chess experts are in fact no better at recalling random arrays of pieces, which suggests there is nothing special about their WM. The gain from expertise is that it places *less* strain on WM since PS strategies are already available, 'the more you know, the less you have to think' (Greene, 1987). (Compare this with controlled vs automatic processing in relation to attention—see Chapter 11.)

> Like problem solving in other ... domains ... chess playing needs more
> than quick thinking and a retentive memory: it requires an appreciation of
> the overall structure of the problem, so that intelligent action can be
> economically planned ... (Boden, 1987a)

De Groot (1965, 1966) compared the performance of five grand masters
and five expert players on choosing a move from a particular board
position. He asked subjects to think aloud and then determined the
number and type of different moves they had considered. Grand masters
did *not* consider more alternative moves, did *not* search any deeper than
experts and yet took slightly less time to make a move. Independent
raters judged the final moves of the masters to be superior to those of the
experts.

His initial explanation for these differences was in terms of knowledge
of different board positions stored in LTM. It is well known that good
players study previous games and can recall their own game in detail; this
use of prior knowledge excludes any need to entertain irrelevant moves
and a host of alternatives. He gave his subjects a five-second presentation
of board positions from actual games and asked them to reconstruct
them from memory—the masters were correct 91 per cent of the time
compared with 41 per cent accuracy for the experts. Clearly the masters
could recognize and encode the various configurations of pieces using
prior knowledge. When pieces were randomly arranged on the board (ie
not in a familiar pattern) both groups did equally badly, ie neither group
had the knowledge available to encode the configuration because they
were (equally) unfamiliar.

Chase and Simon (1973) (amongst others) replicated De Groot's
findings. Experts spent less time, made fewer errors, needed fewer
glances, took in more information per glance than novices when asked to
memorize or reproduce briefly presented, meaningful, board patterns.
But there were no differences when the patterns were random. Better
players also recall clusters often based on attack or defence configurations, implying some sort of abstract knowledge representation:

> ... It appeared, thus, that intelligent systems rely to a great extent on
> stored problem patterns when they face a familiar task. Instead of creating
> solutions from scratch for every problem situation, they make use of
> previously stored information in such a way that it facilitates their coping
> with the current problem. (Sternberg, 1990)

The usefulness of prior knowledge is at least as important in more
natural domains, for instance, language processing. Sternberg says that a
complete understanding of even a very simple sentence pair requires a
memory structure that includes beliefs and expectations about people's
normal behaviour in the world, '... knowledge, thus, is a necessary
ingredient of any intelligent system' (Sternberg, 1990).

EXPERT SYSTEMS (OR INTELLIGENT KNOWLEDGE-BASED SYSTEMS)

Expert Systems (ESs) are important because they promise to be the first
major application of AI research (Garnham, 1991) and the aim is to:

> ... make systems that are cheap enough and reliable enough to augment
> (or, in some cases, replace) human expertise. (Garnham, 1988)

The assumption is made that most kinds of human expertise are in short supply and ESs are aimed at making it more widely available. According to Garnham, 'ES' and 'intelligent knowledge-based system' are amongst the most common terms in AI, especially with respect to its applications; 'knowledge engineering' is the new term for writing ESs.

Basically:

> An E.S. is a program that embodies (some of) the knowledge of a human expert in a domain in which expertise comes with experience... (Garnham, 1988)

In such fields (eg medicine) it is difficult to formulate the knowledge an expert has, since if that knowledge could be explicitly formulated, human experts would be easier to train.

What kind of problems do ESs solve?

Amongst the most successful ESs to date are DENDRAL, which helps organic chemists to establish the structure of complex molecules and XCON, which decides how the various parts of expensive bespoke computer systems should be put together. More controversial are MYCIN and CADUCEUS, both involved in medical diagnosis and discussed further below.

As they are intended to do (some of) the work of human experts, the first condition a problem must satisfy, if it is to be tackled by an ES is that there should be recognized experts at solving it and their performance should be demonstrably better than that of non-experts (eg a medical consultant compared with both the layperson and non-specialist GPs). The case of medical diagnosis illustrates certain other features a problem should have:

(a) There is no simple set of rules a medical expert can follow in diagnosing illness; if there were, diagnosis could be performed by non-intelligent programs (and there would probably be no experts). Instead, consultants draw on wide experience of the connection between *manifestations* of illnesses and underlying causes.

(b) A single manifestation (symptom, sign, test result) may indicate a number of different diseases, but it is unlikely to be associated with any one of them in every case. Further, some of the data diagnosis is based on may be misleading or incorrect, ie reasoning about diagnosis is, in some sense, probabilistic.

(c) Diagnosis does not depend on general knowledge but requires a large but manageable amount of domain-specific knowledge.

What should ESs do?

Apart from the primary goal of solving domain-specific problems (eg medical diagnosis) they should be able to explain how they reached a particular conclusion because they usually interact with people in solving problems and those users often need to know how a decision has been reached.

Where does the ES knowledge come from?

As we have seen, it comes from human experts and the process of encoding it into the system is called *transfer of expertise*. If what differentiates experts from novices is the mastery of a body of knowledge, it might seem to be a relatively straightforward matter to transfer that knowledge by asking them. However, experts cannot always formulate explicitly the knowledge they use, nor can they say how they combine different items of information to make a judgement about a particular case. Lengthy interviews may need to be conducted in which experts are asked to give their opinions on sample cases and this data may have to be supplemented by survey data; for example, patterns of medical symptoms and test results are correlated with eventual diagnosis. This makes the writing of ESs difficult and time-consuming.

Two Examples of ESs—MYCIN and CADUCEUS

MYCIN diagnoses bacterial infections requiring antibiotics and is intended for situations where drugs must be prescribed before the micro-organism responsible for the infection has been properly identified (a laboratory culture may take up to two days to grow). A chronically sick patient needs earlier treatment, so drugs have to be prescribed on the basis of symptoms and the results of quick tests.

MYCIN interacts with a medical expert, requesting information and suggesting treatments. It asks only specific questions related to the hypothesis it is currently considering.

CADUCEUS embodies the knowledge of a single expert (Jack D. Myers, MD), a specialist in internal medicine at the University of Pittsburgh. It knows about many more illnesses than MYCIN, tries to mimic the ways Myers reasons, not just reach the same conclusions, and stores its knowledge about illness in a semantic network (see Chapter 12) as distinct from a set of IF-THEN 'production rules' (which is true of most). It essentially considers related hypotheses in parallel. It also incorporates a preference that medical experts have for formulating at least a partial diagnosis fairly quickly and then use that to give focus to further investigation (Garnham, 1988).

While ESs have now been used in medicine for over twenty years, they are only just beginning to make their appearance in nursing. Two examples are CANDI (Computer-Aided Nursing Diagnosis and Intervention), developed by Chang et al (1988) in the USA based on the diagnosis of patient problems as part of the nursing process, and the Glasgow University Expert Systems in Nursing Group (GUESSING), which has designed experiments to find the cognitive skills of clinically excellent nurses in the area of pressure sore risk and preventative care planning. These were then formalized into a computer program which can be used as both a decision support and a tutoring tool (Jones et al, 1989; both are cited by Eaton, 1991).

Evaluation of ESs

According to Boden (1987a), ESs are much less flexible than their human counterparts and most in actual use are considerably less complex than either MYCIN or DENDRAL, which were the prototypes and both of which took many work-years to build:

> ... In almost every case, their 'explanations' are merely recapitulations of the previous firing of if-then rules ... for they still have no higher-level representations of the knowledge domain, their own problem-solving activity, or the knowledge of their human user. (Boden, 1987a)

Some researchers are trying to provide ESs with causal reasoning, so that they can not only arrive at a conclusion but also explain the reason to the user.

Boden claims that ESs cannot integrate knowledge from distinct domains, using concepts and patterns of inference from one domain to reason (by analogy) in another. Genuine expertise, she argues, requires both high-level knowledge and analogical thinking.

Lenat et al (1986) aim to develop, by 1995, a representation of common sense knowledge and analogical reasoning that could be accessed by *any* AI program, including ESs dealing with indefinitely many domains. Their aim is to, 'represent all the world's knowledge, to a certain level of detail', by representing the knowledge contained in, plus the background and common sense knowledge needed to understand, a one-volume encyclopaedia. This would overcome the 'brittleness' of current ESs, which have the unfortunate tendency to give utterly stupid answers (or none at all) to questions we would regard as only slightly different from those it was specifically designed for (Boden, 1987).

Inevitably, perhaps, ESs raise ethical issues. Those used in the medical domain are especially prone to criticism by virtue of the nature of the domain—patient diagnosis and treatment—and ultimately it is the recipient of the health care who is most affected. But the professionals who come into direct contact with them might see them as both allies and enemies (to anthropomorphize a little), or predominantly as one or the other depending on their status in the hierarchy, how much of an expert one is thought to be:

> It is commonly asserted that knowledge is power. If expert knowledge becomes more accessible, will the balance of power change? There are social consequences to the use and development of these new systems. There is animosity by some as they feel expert systems usurp the human expert. (Eaton, 1991)

WHAT COMPUTERS CAN AND CANNOT DO—THE SCOPE OF AI

So far we have talked about computers as problem-solvers and have looked at some of the important differences between them and human problem-solvers. Also, apart from our discussion of ESs, we have discussed problems of the puzzle variety, ie the non-everyday type of problem, such as the Tower of Hanoi and cannibals and missionaries.

But what about the kind of problem we referred to in the Introduction, such as vision, and language understanding, which humans are 'designed' for? Can computers be programmed to mimic these basic human abilities and, if so, what can we learn about the way we use them?

To try to answer these questions, we need to take a closer look at what computers are, what AI is and some attempts to program computers to do what humans are particularly good at doing—seeing and understanding language.

WHAT IS AI?

According to Garnham (1988) AI is, '...the science of thinking machines...' and, again:

... an approach to understanding behaviour based on the assumption that intelligence can best by analyzed by trying to reproduce it. In practice, reproduction means simulation by computer. AI is, therefore, part of computer science ... (Garnham, 1988)

Newell and Simon originally distinguished the *broad field of AI* from a particular part of it, namely the *computer simulation* of human behaviour. While the former was the attempt to make machines behave intelligently—by whatever means—computer simulation was a particular method for producing intelligent machines, namely, making them reproduce human behaviour and the *goal* of computer simulation was to provide a model of human cognitive functioning.

According to Garnham (1988), most contemporary AI research is influenced more or less by consideration of how people behave—very few researchers simply try to build clever machines disregarding the principles underlying their behaviour. And yet many still have the explicit goal of writing a program which works in the way people do (such as Marr in relation to vision). '... However, the term computer simulation is rarely used these days' (Garnham, 1988).

So cognitive psychologists and workers in AI share an interest in the scientific understanding of cognitive abilities and they should work together to increase that understanding. The majority of AI workers probably do wish to further our knowledge of the mechanisms underlying behaviour and to make general statements about knowledge representation, vision, thinking, language and so on.

These kinds of abilities are all part of 'intelligence' in the broadest sense of that term and Psychology has always had intelligence (in various senses) as one of its central concerns (see Chapters 25 and 28). Just as workers in AI need to have an idea of what intelligence or thinking is before they can make a machine which is intelligent or can think, so AI research can provide insights into human cognitive processes—the relationship between psychology and AI is a reciprocal one. And since the late 1970s (as we saw in Chapter 2), cognitive psychology and AI have both become component disciplines in the new discipline of *cognitive science*, along with Neuroscience, Linguistics, Philosophy and Anthropology. Garnham (1988) believes that:

By the late 1970s cognitive psychologists had more in common with AI researchers than with other psychologists and AI researchers had more in common with cognitive psychologists than with other computer scientists ... (Garnham, 1988)

Boden (1987b) defines AI as, '... the science of making machines do the sorts of things that are done by human minds ...' The 'machines' in question are, typically, digital computers and she is at pains to make clear that AI is *not* the study of computers but:

... it is the study of intelligence in thought and action. Computers are its tools because its theories are expressed as computer programs which are tested by being run on a machine. (Boden, 1987b)

WHAT IS A COMPUTER?

The initial concept of the 'computer' and the first attempts to build the modern digital computer were made by the Cambridge mathematician, Charles Babbage (1792–1871).

The mathematical theory of computability was first developed in the 1930s. It specified what computers can and cannot do and how much time and memory they need for the computations they can perform. A number of mathematicians were independently searching for the smallest set of primitive operations needed to perform *any* possible computation.

One very influential approach was that of Turing (1936) who described an abstract computing device (a *Turing machine*) which performs its calculations with the help of a tape divided into squares, each with a symbol printed on it. Its primitive operations comprise reading and writing symbols on the tape and shifting the tape to the left or right. It uses a finite vocabulary of symbols but the tape is indefinitely long. It only has a finite number of internal states—when it reads the symbol on a square, its state may change, depending on what state it is currently in and on what the symbol is. Additional bits of machinery (eg more tape) do not increase the range of computations but only increase speed. A *universal Turing machine* can mimic the operation of any other Turing machine. To do this it must be given a description of how that machine works, which can be written onto its tape in standard Turing machine format.

Every general-purpose digital computer is an approximation to the universal Turing machine (since no real machine has an indefinitely large memory)—when it runs a program, it behaves as if it were a machine for performing just the task the program performs:

> This special property of digital computers, that they can mimic any discrete machine, is described by saying that they are *universal* machines. The existence of machines with this property has the important consequence that, considerations of speed apart, it is unnecessary to design various new machines to do various computing processes. They can all be done with one digital computer, suitably programmed for each case ... as a consequence of this all digital computers are in a sense equivalent. (Turing, 1950)

The basic active components of *digital* computers are normally in one or two stable states ('on'/'off') making them essentially *binary* in nature, ie they use only two symbols (eg '0'/'1') as in binary arithmetic. They can symbolize indefinitely many things (as can the 26 letters of the Roman alphabet) because they can be grouped together in indefinitely many ways. As described by Turing, they are machines which change according to the problem to be solved (based upon the particular instructions contained within the program). 'Digital' refers to the finger and the fingers can be used as a kind of abacus, a simple form of computing machine. Computers are, in essence, autonomous abaci—working without continuous human intervention (Gregory, 1981).

The other main kind of computer is *analogue*, which are, generally, continuous mechanisms which represent more or less abstract quantities by physical parameters (eg lengths, angles and voltages).

What Can Computers Do? And How Do They Do It?

Strictly, of course, computers are metallic objects (*hardware*) and when we ask what they can do (and, later, when we ask whether they are intelligent) it is not the physical machine, as such, we are interested in but the procedures which they perform, the calculations and other operations they carry out as required by the program (the *software*), ie *the computer-as-an-information-processing device*.

Although originally designed as calculating machines (after all, 'compute' means to 'calculate'):

> a Computer is not a mere 'number cruncher' or supercalculating arithmetic machine ... Computers do not crunch numbers; they manipulate symbols. (Boden, 1987a)

Computers can only 'think' in abstract symbols. In itself, a symbol is meaningless; there need be no intrinsic similarity between a symbol and what it symbolizes. The meaning is assigned by a human user, who interprets it in a particular way. In this way, symbolic representation is said to be *propositional*, ie it represents what is the case in formal language rather than being a physical analogue of something in the world. (An example of an *analogue* process would be a mental image, which bears a much closer relationship to what it is an image of than any symbol, such as a word.) Boden (1987a) points out that some programming languages are more readily amenable than others to symbolizing certain things—ALGOL for example, is similar to albegraic notation and so, not surprisingly, it is much easier to write sensible mathematical programs with it than some 'non-algebraic' programming language. However, just as numbers can be expressed in words (eg 'ten'), so matters usually expressed in words can be expressed in numbers (eg '30120' could be a symbol for a cat, as opposed to 'cat' and so would have no *numerical* meaning).

Computers, therefore, can crunch numbers if specifically programmed to do so—but this is not their essential computational function:

> Digital computers, originally developed with mathematical problems in mind, are in fact general purpose symbol manipulating machines. It is up to the programmer to decide what interpretations can sensibly (that is, consistently) be put to the inherently meaningless ciphers of machine and programming languages ... (Boden, 1987a)

Strong and Weak AI and the Computational Theory of Mind

One of the definitions given earlier of AI was Garnham's (1988) appealingly simple, 'the science of thinking machines'. It is now time to look at that definition a little more closely and to ask whether 'thinking' is to be taken literally or metaphorically. Putting this another way, do computers actually think/behave intelligently (ie are they reproducing or duplicating the human equivalent) or are they merely simulating (mimicking) thought/intelligence?

This distinction corresponds to the one made by Searle (1980) between *strong* and *weak* AI, respectively:

> According to weak AI, the main value of the computer in the study of the mind is that it gives us a very powerful tool, eg it enables us to formulate and test hypotheses in a more rigorous and precise fashion than before. But according to strong AI the computer is not merely a tool; rather, the appropriately programmed computer really is a mind in the sense that computers given the right programme can be literally said to *understand* and have other cognitive states. Further, because the programmed computer has cognitive states, the programs are not mere tools that enable us to test psychological explanations but the programs are themselves explanations... (Searle, 1980)

Searle is a philosopher who is very critical of strong AI, a view advocated by computer scientists, such as Minsky, who defines AI as, '...the science of making machines do things that would require intelligence if done by men'. The implication of such a definition is that machines *must* be intelligent if they can do what humans can do, although this rather begs the question as to what it means to display intelligence.

Underlying strong AI is the *Computational Theory of Mind (CTM)*:

> ...Intelligence may be defined as the ability creatively to manipulate symbols, or process information, given the requirements of the task in hand. If the task is mathematical, then numerical information may need to be processed. But if the task is non-numerical (or 'semantic') in nature... then the information that is coded and processed must be semantic information, irrespective of the superficial form of the symbols used in the information code... (Boden, 1987a)

We have already seen that symbolic representation is *propositional*, ie since a symbol has no inherent similarity to what it symbolizes, it represents something in a purely formal way. Computer programs comprise formal systems, 'a set of basic elements or pieces and a set of rules for forming and transforming the elements or pieces' (Flanagan, 1984). In computer language, symbols stand for whatever objects, relations, or processes we wish—but the computer manipulates the symbols, not their meaning. Programs consist of pure *syntax* (rules for manipulating symbols) and are devoid of *semantic content* (reference to anything in the world). For the computer, there is nothing 'outside' it to which these symbols refer, which is why they have no 'content', only 'form'. It is the human programmer who then attaches the meaning to these symbols.

But, according to CTM, all intelligent systems are defined as symbol-manipulators which, of course, include human minds. So if symbols are meaning-less to a computer, it follows that they are meaning-less also to a human mind. But in that case, how do we account for *intentionality*, which Searle (amongst others) believes is an essential characteristic of genuine mentality or consciousness, ie mental states are *about* things in the world, they have an *external reference* to something outside themselves and this is (part of) what we mean by saying that the world is meaningful to us and that we understand it?

Searle's attack on strong AI and CTM takes the form of a *Gedanken* experiment ('thought experiment') called the Chinese Room, which is described in Box 14.1.

Box 14.1   The Chinese Room (Searle, 1980)

Suppose that I am locked in a room and am given a large batch of Chinese writing. Suppose that I know no Chinese, either written or spoken and that I am not even confident that I could recognize Chinese writing as Chinese writing distinct from, say, Japanese writing or meaningless squiggles. After this first batch of Chinese writing, I am given a second batch together with a set of rules for correlating the second batch with the first batch. The rules are in English and I understand them as well as any other English native speaker. They enable me to correlate one set of formal symbols with another set of formal symbols and all that 'formal' means here is that I can identify the symbols entirely by their shapes. I am then given a third batch of Chinese symbols together with some instructions, again in English, which enable me to correlate elements of this third batch with the first two batches and these rules instruct me how to give back certain Chinese symbols with certain sorts of shapes in response to certain sorts of shapes provided by the third batch. Unknown to me, the people giving me all these symbols call the first batch a 'script', the second batch a 'story', the third batch 'questions', the symbols I give back in response to the third batch, 'answers to the questions' and the set of English rules 'the program'. I am also given stories in English which I understand, questions in English about these stories and I give back answers in English.

After a while I get so good at following the instructions for manipulating the Chinese symbols and the programmers get so good at writing the program that, from the point of view of somebody outside the room, my answers are indistinguishable from those of native Chinese speakers, just as my answers to the English questions are indistinguishable from those of other native English speakers. However, although from the external point of view my answers to the Chinese and the English questions are equally good, in the English case this is because I am a native speaker of English while in the Chinese case this is because I am manipulating uninterpreted formal symbols and in this respect I am simply behaving like a computer, ie performing computational operations on formally specified elements. For the purposes of the Chinese, I am simply a realization of the computer progam.

THE CHINESE ROOM AND THE TURING TEST

Searle believes that he has demonstrated quite conclusively that there is more to intelligence and understanding than mere manipulation of symbols. In particular, he is trying to refute the major *methodological* presupposition of strong AI, namely the Imitation Game (or Turing test) proposed by Turing (1950) as an objective way of trying to answer the question 'Can machines think?' (see Box 14.2, p. 394). According to Garnham (1988) there are no accounts of machines playing the Imitation Game but there are anecdotes about computers being mistaken for people and ELIZA (a program that simulates the speech of a non-directive–client-centred therapist; see Chapter 31) figures in most of them. These stories are rather embarrassing for supporters of CTM, because ELIZA is *not* a very intelligent program (Boden, 1987a).

However, supporters of strong AI claim that it is only a matter of time before computers will pass the Turing Test and once they do so, terms such as thought, understanding, awareness, happiness, pain, etc. could be

---

Box 14.2   The Imitation Game or Turing Test (Turing, 1950)

This is played with three people, a man (A), a woman (B) and an interrogator (C), who may be of either sex. The interrogator stays in a room apart from the other two. The object of the game for the interrogator is to determine which of the other two is the man and which is the woman. He knows them by the labels X and Y, and at the end of the game he says either 'X is A and Y is B' or 'X is B and Y is A'.

The interrogator is allowed to put questions to A and B thus: Will X please tell me the length of his or her hair? Now suppose X is actually A, then A must answer. It is A's object in the game to try to cause C to make the wrong identification. His answer might, therefore, be: My hair is shingled, and the longest strands are about nine inches long.

In order that tones of voice may not help the interrogator, the answers should be written, or better still, typewritten. The ideal arrangement is to have a teleprinter communicating between the two rooms ...

We now ask the question—What will happen when a machine takes the part of A in this game? Will the interrogator decide wrongly as often when the game is played like this as he does when the game is played with a man and a woman? These questions replace our original 'Can machines think?'

... I believe that in about fifty years time it will be possible to program computers, with a storage capacity of about 10^9, to make them play the imitation game so well that, on average the interrogator will not have more than 70 per cent chance of making the right identification after five minutes of questioning ... When this occurs, there is no contradiction in the idea of thinking machines.

---

applied equally to computers and human subjects. Clearly the Turing Test represents an operational, behaviouristic, definition of 'thinking' because it is defined as an appropriate kind of 'output', or performance, regardless of what may be going on 'inside'. Yet this is precisely the definition which the Chinese room is aiming to show is invalid.

But isn't the Chinese room a highly restricted and artificial environment? Gregory (1987) argues that, like us, AI programs must have knowledge of the world in order to deal with the world. Imagine rearing a baby in the Chinese room—how could it learn the meaning of the Chinese (or any other) symbols in such a restricted environment? Years of active exploration in infancy are essential for us to learn to read meanings in the neural signals from our senses; extended to perception as a whole, the Chinese room environment would prevent correlations between symbols and events developing as it has no view of the outside world, provides no opportunity for exploration as a way of building up a store of knowledge and relating these to Chinese (or other) symbols:

> The Chinese Room parable does not show that computer-based robots cannot be intelligent as we are—because *we* wouldn't be intelligent from this school either. (Gregory, 1987)

According to Searle, when we attribute intelligence to people we do so based on all sorts of evidence—behavioural (they act the right way), biological (they have the right sort of bodies) and phenomenological (they have the right sort of experiences). But computers only have to *behave* appropriately in order to pass the Turing Test. However, some of his critics argue that the Turing Test does not discriminate in this way because, in fact, we use exclusively behavioural evidence in the case of people too (Hofstadter, 1981). (Indeed, the whole of cognitive psychology can be seen as relying upon inferences drawn from behaviour.)

By this same argument, supporters of strong AI, by analogy with the computer, analyse human intelligence in terms of the possession and operation of appropriate programs (a form of *'machinomorphism'*). Thus, our bodies—including our brain—are seen as in no way necessary to our intelligence. This is a form of *functionalism* which represents a solution to the mind–body (mind–brain) problem—it is the program (software) that matters (the computational theory of mind) with the brain (hardware) being incidental. This can be seen as a new form of *dualism* (Putnam, 1975; see Chapter 2) which Russell (1984) sees as posing a real dilemma for CTM. On the one hand, CTM is claiming that the 'mind' does not depend on any particular *physical* realization but, on the other hand, computer simulation is meant to be a *realistic* model of how the *brain* carries out information processing.

Flanagan (1984) believes that, while Searle may not have *proved* the impossibility of strong AI, he is certainly correct that merely running a computer program is *not* sufficient for our kind of mentality. So what else is needed?

He finds it implausible that our evolutionary history, genes, biochemistry, anatomy and neurophysiology have nothing essential to do with our defining features (even though it remains *logically* possible). Would an inorganic device which formally operated according to all known biochemical laws about plants be expected to undergo photosynthesis? (Flanagan, 1984).

Searle (1987) believes that mental states and processes are real biological phenomena in the world, as real as digestion, photosynthesis, lactation, etc that they are 'caused by processes going on in the brain' which are entirely internal to the brain. Again, the intrinsically *mental* features of the universe are just higher-level physical features of brains.

Penrose (1987) agrees that there is more to understanding than just carrying out some appropriate program (software) and that the actual physical construction of the brain (hardware) is also important. He argues that a computer designed to follow the logical operations of every detail of the workings of the human brain would itself not achieve 'understanding' even though the person whose brain is being considered would claim to understand.

Searle's view has been referred to as *carbon/protoplasm* chauvinism (Torrance, 1986); ie his only basis for denying that robots think is that they are not made of flesh and blood. His views about the causal properties of the brain have been attacked by many as obscure. Is he proposing that intentionality is a substance secreted by the brain? (Gardner, 1985). Gardner argues that if Searle is claiming that, by definition, *only* the human brain or brain-like mechanisms can display intentionality/understanding, then there is no point to the controversy and the Chinese room loses its force.

A major problem is that we simply do not know what makes the brain conscious and so we cannot design a conscious machine, one that would exactly duplicate its physical nature. Still, the brain *is* a physical entity and it *is* conscious, so it must have *some* design features (presumably physical) which *make* it conscious (McGinn, 1987). This does not mean that a machine could *not* be conscious—only that it would have to be the same kind of machine the brain is, whatever kind that is. In support of Searle, Teichman (1988) states that while we know that the computer hardware does *not* produce (initiate) the program, it is highly probable that the brain does help to produce mental states.

Gregory (1987) believes that intelligence isn't necessarily embodied in living organisms or protoplasm but may occur in a computer system based on silicon (or any other material). The emphasis here is on the process as opposed to the substance—though there must be physical mechanisms to carry out the processes, strong AI claims that *any* physical system capable of carrying out the necessary processes can be described as intelligent—even if it is 'made of old beer cans', in Searle's words.

CONNECTIONISM OR PARALLEL DISTRIBUTED PROCESSING—THE NEW AI

However valid the criticisms of strong AI made by Searle and others may have been at the time that they were made, changes in AI itself have rendered those criticisms less valid and less necessary. The major development which, according to Gordon (1989) could, 'revive the status of the computer as a model [of the mind]' is the *parallel distributed processing* (PDP) approach or *Connectionist Model*. Similarly, Gardner (1987) refers to the PDP approach as representing an alternative 'model view' of cognition, a response to the increasing obvious limitation of the 'serial digital "von Neuman computer"'. The pioneers of this new approach are Rumelhart, Hinton and McClelland (1986).

According to Garnham (1991), the traditional AI approach assumes that what is important about cognition can be described at an abstract level, independent of the machinery (brain or computer) which underlies it. (This, of course, is the software/hardware distinction—CTM sees only the software as of any significance). If cognitive processes are understood as the processing of information, then since it can be encoded in many different physical forms (eg printed in books, recorded on tape), it does not matter whether it is stored and manipulated by the electrical and chemical activity of the brain *or* by the on/off states of transistors in a computer:

> ...So, computers that bear no physical resemblance to brains can be programmed to simulate cognitive abilities. (Garnham, 1991)

However, while connectionist (neural network) models are not actual models of brain processing, Rumelhart et al (1986) describe their work as engaging in, '*neurally inspired* modelling of cognitive processes'.

Ironically, the origins of these modern developments are some of the earliest computers which attempted to develop abstract models of the brain cell and to discover how large networks of cells would work together.

During the 1930s and 1940s Lashley tried to discover the brain sites where learning and memory occurred but his 'search for the engram' (1950) failed. Hebb (1949) proposed that groups of interconnected neurons continue to show increased activity after termination of the stimulus and that clusters of neurons showing *reverberating* activity act as functional units. He further claimed that modifications to such an interacting cluster or network could be the basis of short and long-term learning; he called them 'cell assemblies'.

Both Rosenblatt's *perceptron* (1959) and Selfridge's (1959)/Selfridge and Neisser's (1960) *Pandemonium* (see Chapter 9) tried to model learning phenomena in terms of self-modifying connection strengths between neuron-like elements.

WHAT IS A CONNECTIONIST MACHINE?

A connectionist machine, essentially, comprises a very large number of simple interconnected units. Each unit has a level of activation which it transmits to the units connected to it. Connections between units have numbers (*weights*) attached to them which determine how much activation is passed (Fig. 14.9).

OUTPUT UNITS

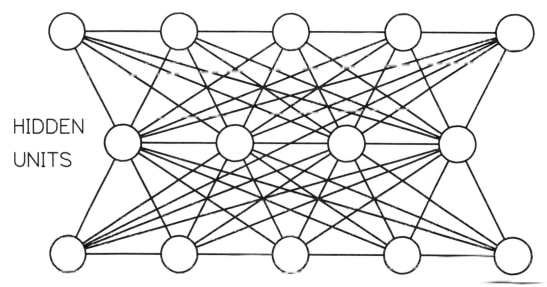

HIDDEN

UNITS

INPUT UNITS

As you can see, there are three layers of units, input, output and hidden.

Input units are activated by something outside the network, and patterns of activation in them represent features of what the model is processing. (This can be compared with, for example, how patterns of activity in retinal cells encode information about a visual scene.) Once input units have been activated, they pass activation, via weighted connections, to the *hidden units*, which in turn pass activation to output units. There may be one or more layers of *hidden units* in between the other two levels, which considerably increase the capabilities of connectionist machines.

Output units indicate, by their pattern of activation, the machine's response to its input. Many different types of responses are possible. For

Figure 14.9 Schematic diagram of a connectionist machine. The circles represent the processing units, and the lines represent the connections along which activation passes from one unit to another. Activation in one unit may either increase or decrease the activation in another unit that it is connected to, depending on whether the connection is positive (faciliatory) or negative (inhibitory). (From A. Garnham, (1991) The Mind in Action. London; Routledge)

example, the machine may classify its input by having two output units, with high activation in one standing for 'yes' (eg it is a dog) and in the other standing for 'no' (it isn't). In a more complex example, the pattern of activation of input units encodes the spelling of a word and the output encodes how the word sounds. The more possible responses to the input, the more output units are needed, with different responses coded by different *patterns* of activation (rather than different *levels* of activation in a single unit).

SO WHAT'S NEW ABOUT CONNECTIONIST MACHINES?

1)   Instead of performing *serial* operations (operations in sequence) or computations on strings of symbols, they comprise thousands of connections among hundreds of units (which, in principle, can be extended to millions or billions of connections). 'Perception', 'action', 'thought', etc. are the consequence of the alteration of the strengths (weights) of the connections between these units. A task is completed (input is processed) when the system finally 'settles' or 'relaxes' (at least tentatively) on a satisfactory set of values or 'stable states' (ie it has reached a solution) (Gardner, 1987).

2)   The network can be set a problem in the form of an input pattern. A successful solution comprises a matching or otherwise acceptable output pattern. Only parts of the output pattern will match at first—the discrepancy between input and output is fed back into the hidden layer, such that connections to outputs which are (nearly) correct are strengthened (according to some pre-determined rule) while others may be left unchanged or even weakened. There is no supervisory control of the network, no central executive guiding the overall flow of information (Gordon, 1989).

3)   PDP models operate in a manner much more reminiscent of the human brain (even if they are not models *of* the brain). It has always been recognized that the brain must operate at least partly via *parallel processing* (as opposed to *serial processing*). Since all knowledge resides in the connections themselves, advocates of PDP models have offered a reconceptualization of major cognitive processes. Memory, for example, instead of a set of facts or events stored in the brain, is viewed as a set of relationships existing between various aspects of facts or events as they are encoded in groupings or patterns of units. What is actually stored, according to this view, are the connections and strengths among units which allow the patterns to be subsequently recreated. Learning involves finding the right connection strengths so that proper patterns of activation are produced under the appropriate conditions (Gardner, 1987).

4)   Many PDP models *learn* to perform tasks as opposed to being programmed to perform them. Although advocates of these models are not claiming that the specific learning methods they have developed are used in the brain, they make general claims about the psychological relevance of how these models learn (Garnham, 1991).

The most important method is a form of *supervised* learning (called *Backwards Error Propagation Using The Generalized Delta Rule* or

GDR—back propagation for short). Briefly, the GDR is a way of using the feedback provided by a teacher to adjust the weights between connections so that actual output becomes more like intended output. 'Back propagation' works backwards from the output layer, through the hidden layer to the input layer.

Very few PDP models exist as machines (Gordon, 1989) but some have been built which claim to be able to perform the complex information processing which is part of language, thinking and problem-solving (Garnham 1991).

One example is Rumelhart and McClelland's English past-tense learning machine, meant to mimic some aspects of how a child learns past-tense endings. Verbs are divided into a number of sub-classes and associated with each sub-class is the change required to produce the past tense from the present. Regular verbs, which followed the -*ed* rule, formed the largest group; other sub-groups comprised irregular verbs that are similar to one another (eg blow/grow/know/throw). Any new verb was assimilated to one of those categories, sometimes producing errors (eg 'grind'→'grind' as opposed to 'ground').

Connectionists argue that, although rules are not explicitly encoded into their machines, those machines can learn to behave as if they were following rules. To the casual observer, Rumelhart and McClelland's machine behaved very impressively but a sophisticated analysis by Pinker and Prince showed that it did *not* know the detailed rules of the English past tense system. Instead of following the complex rules of language, these machines may be following simpler rules which reflect *statistical regularities* ie probabilities of one thing going with another (cited by Garnham, 1991). (This relates to the controversy over the learning of language by chimps! see Chapter 26.)

Even connectionists concede that PDP models deal more effectively with perception and other 'lower level' (subsymbolic) processes than with 'symbol-laden' activities like language.

CONCLUSIONS

1) Gordon (1989) believes that the hardware–software distinction vanishes in the light of PDP models—all units and connections are essentially 'hard-wired' (ie they are physically parts of the system as in hardware) but the connection can be changed (like software). Knowledge is held briefly in the units and for longer in the connections, but there is no special set of places equivalent to the 'memory addresses' of tradition-al computers. Knowledge and memory are not explicit but implicit within each pattern of connections (Gordon, 1989).

Similarly, Sternberg (1990) argues that with the increasing popularity of PDP models, the functionalists' claim that hardware and software are independent might soon have to be modified.

2) Connectionism is basically an *associationist* approach (see Chapter 2) which partly explains why it cannot cope adequately with the complex rule-governed information processing character of much cognition, especially language and reasoning. It can only relate things in terms of 'one thing often goes with another'. And:

> ... the anti-connectionists argue, although associationism is a theory of mind that has been put forward several times in the past, by empiricist philosophers from John Locke onwards, and by behaviourist psychologists such as Watson and Skinner, there are insuperable objections to it. (Garnham, 1991)

(Perhaps it might be more appropriate to put 'because' in place of 'although' in the above quote—see Chapter 2, especially the section on Reductionism.)

3) Finally:

> PDP models are still in their infancy. Thus, although they already offer some interesting insights into the functioning of cognitive systems, it is much too early to offer a concluding statement on the (potentially enormous) impact they might have on our understanding of intelligence in the future. (Sternberg, 1990)

PART 4

Social Behaviour

15 THE ETHOLOGICAL AND SOCIOBIOLOGICAL APPROACH TO THE STUDY OF BEHAVIOUR

EXPERIMENTAL AND NATURALISTIC APPROACHES

In Chapter 1 a distinction was made between the experimental study of animals (comparative or animal psychology) and the ethological approach; while the former is laboratory-based, is associated largely with the behaviourists' attempts to investigate the process of learning and has used 'convenient' species, in particular, rats and pigeons (see Chapter 7), the latter emphasizes the importance of studying animals in their natural habitat, tends to see instinctive (unlearned) behaviour as playing a central role and tries to use as wide a range of species as possible.

Ironically, it was Darwin's theory of evolution which helped to shape behaviourism: if more complex species have evolved from less complex ones so that the differences between them are merely *quantitative*, it made sense to study the simpler ones (eg rats) in order to enhance our understanding of the more complex ones (ie humans). This was conveniently carried out in laboratories and the natural world of Darwinian theory became virtually forgotten—or at least irrelevant.

Ethology also has its roots in evolutionary theory, specifically in the work of the nineteenth and early twentieth century naturalists (Thorpe, 1979), but Lorenz and Tinbergen, two of the key European founders and popularizers of ethology, were trying to redress the 'unnatural' balance created by the study of rats in laboratories by putting behaviour back into its natural context and bringing evolutionary theory back into the centre of the attempt to understand that behaviour.

ETHOLOGICAL QUESTIONS AND METHODS

According to Hinde (1982), when ethologists consider any class of behaviour, they are concerned with four issues (these are, in fact, based on Tinbergen's (1951) *'Four Whys'*):

(a) What immediately causes it. (This would include specific stimuli called *releasers* which trigger instinctive patterns of behaviour, some of these being called *fixed action patterns* —FAPs).

(b) How such behaviour has developed over the animal's life-cycle (*ontogeny*).

(c) What the useful consequences of such behaviour are (its *function*).
(d) How the behaviour has evolved within the species (*phylogeny*).

Clearly, (c) and (d) are directly derived from evolutionary theory: the purpose of behaviour is central to evolution because the basic assumption is that behaviour which has no purpose will disappear and that the behaviour shared by all members of a species (or, for example, all the males or all the females within a species) has been retained because, ultimately, it has helped the species survive. Precisely how it evolved can be at least partly investigated by comparing species which are known to be related morphologically (ie structurally).

The ethologists, as biologists, believe that behaviour can be studied in the same way as any other aspect of life; just as different species have different skeletons, so they have different behaviour, and if species with similar skeletons also display similar behaviour, this is strong evidence in favour of the view that behaviour is *inherited* or *instinctive*.

Although the concept of instinct plays a crucial role in ethology, it does not necessarily exclude learning from the explanation of behaviour; indeed, a great deal of research and theorizing has focused on the learning process called *imprinting* (Lorenz, 1935) which we shall discuss in detail later in the chapter. Again, although ethologists are primarily zoologists, they are not averse to studying animals in the laboratory (especially in relation to question (a)), but the findings are always put back into the animal's natural context of behaviour.

The word *ethology* simply means 'study of behaviour' and, of course, many psychologists are equally interested in this subject-matter. However, ethology represents a special way of studying behaviour, namely treating it as a biological entity, so that it is the study of behaviour as part of zoology (as distinct from social science, for example) (Lea, 1984).

THE EVOLUTION OF ETHOLOGY

According to Smith (1990), there have been three phases which ethology has gone through in its relatively short history: (i) *classical ethology* (1930s–1950s); (ii) *modern ethology* (1950s–1980s); and (iii) *sociobiology* (1970s).

Classical ethology refers to the work of Lorenz (1903–1989) and Tinbergen (1907–1988) on imprinting, releasers, innate releasing mechanisms, fixed action patterns, etc., all of which will be discussed later in the chapter.

Lorenz (1966) applied his ideas to human aggression (see Chapter 16) and to human parental care responses (as triggered by the typical features of a baby's face, such as rounded cheeks and eyes and large forehead). Bowlby was influenced by Lorenz's work on imprinting and incorporated some of these ideas into his theory of human attachment (see Chapter 22).

Eibl-Eibesfeldt (1970, 1971) described ritualized human greeting expressions, most famous being the 'eyebrow flash', a relatively fixed pattern of behaviour, and her work was extended by Desmond Morris, in books such as *The Naked Ape* (1967) and *The Human Zoo* (1969).

Modern ethology evolved out of dissatisfaction during the 1950s with at least the narrower confines of instinct theory and classical ethology. The concepts used were shown to be oversimplified even in the case of those fish and bird species on which many of the earlier studies had been conducted (eg herring gulls and sticklebacks). How much more inadequate would they prove in relation to mammals, especially primates (Hinde, 1959)?

The 1950s and 1960s saw an expansion of the species studied and an expansion of concepts in a broader theoretical framework, plus a unification with comparative psychology, so that learning was seen much more broadly and the laboratory rat was no longer such a central figure.

A good example of this expansion was Harlow's work with rhesus monkeys (see Chapter 23). There was a great increase in primate studies and increased interest in the relationship between social structure and behaviour, on the one hand, and the animal's environment on the other (*sociobiology* or *behavioural ecology*).

However, some ideas from classical ethology were retained, including:

(a) Observation of species in their natural surroundings.
(b) The description of a wide range of behaviours in basic terms (the *ethogram*).
(c) An interest in evolution and the developmental aspects of both causation and function (Tinbergen's *Four Whys*).
(d) A willingness to engage in sensible experimentation. Studying a rat in a Skinner box, for example, is not sensible, since it is an impoverished environment and generalizing to the animal's natural habitat could be misleading. But if experiments are designed to be as natural as possible (eg the pecking response in herring-gull chicks—see below), they can tell us much about causation and function. These kinds of experiments helped bring together ethological and psychological research (Smith, 1990).

Human ethology emerged in the late 1960s and early 1970s and focused mainly on studying children in nurseries, for example Blurton Jones's study of *rough and tumble play*.

Concepts were borrowed from animal—especially primate—studies, such as dominance, territoriality, and effects of density on social behaviour. The International Society for Human Ethology was founded in 1978 and in 1979 the journal *Ethology and Sociobiology* was first published.

Sociobiology was a logical extension of current evolutionary theory but provided a new theoretical paradigm for understanding social structure and behaviour. Smith (1990) says that it can be seen as the realization of the third and fourth of the four questions (see above), ie Tinbergen's function and evolution *Whys*, which had received less than their fair share of attention. Sociobiology is discussed in detail later in the chapter.

Lorenz had always argued that to understand a species you must go through a prolonged period of acclimatization, 'just watching', leaving behind your preconceptions and entering the *Umwelt* (surroundings) of the species being studied. This led to a considerable elaboration of the observational method.

Lea (1984) distinguishes *social ethology*, a field of study, from *sociobiology*, a theoretical system which is applied to social ethology. The basic *method* of sociobiology, he says, is to ask of every behaviour, what would be the evolutionary fate of a gene which produced that behaviour, given the environment in which the organism bearing it must live?

Sociobiology also overlaps with *behavioural ecology*, which is primarily concerned with how behaviour contributes to an animal's equilibrium with its environment; one major point of overlap is the study of *territoriality* (see below and Chapter 16).

ETHOLOGY AND PSYCHOLOGY

As we have seen, both psychologists and ethologists are interested in behaviour, although in different ways and for different reasons. Beyond this, why should psychologists be interested in a biological approach? Lea (1984) believes there are three major reasons:

(a) There have been many attempts to explain human behaviour in terms of the evolutionary history of *Homo sapiens* and so psychologists should take account of such explanations.
(b) An evolutionary explanation is often a good place to begin; it helps us to understand the functions and mechanisms involved which can then provide hypotheses to be tested with human subjects.
(c) We cannot properly understand what it is to be human unless we understand what it is to be non-human.

Lea also points to a number of ways in which ethology may be *applied*: (i) *practically*, to help us breed endangered species, for example; (ii) *methodologically*, particularly in the naturalistic observation of babies and young children; (iii) *conceptually*, by using ideas and concepts from ethology and incorporating them into psychological theory (eg 'personal space', see Chapter 18); and (iv) *empirically*, by direct extrapolation of the results from the study of animals to humans (eg human infants becoming attached to their mother through imprinting as studied in goslings, see Chapter 22).

In terms of our earlier discussion, it could be said that classical ethology contributed mainly conceptually, while modern ethology has contributed both methodologically and conceptually. Sociobiology, by contrast, has contributed largely empirically.

EVOLUTIONARY THEORY

Darwin claimed that all living things are related and that more complex forms of life are derived from the forms which preceded them by a process of adaptation through natural selection, called *evolution*. The earliest of earth's life-forms were single-celled, asexual micro-organisms which reproduced simply by asexual cell division; this meant that offspring were genetically identical to parents so that there was no genetic variability and little room for adaptive selection.

In the course of evolution, the process of *sexual* (diploid) *reproduction* appeared, which enabled offspring to be genetically quite different from either parent or from other offspring, because (except for identical twins) every individual has a unique combination of genes. This greater variability allows more efficient selection, because the greater the variability, the greater the availability of individuals who will survive new or changed environmental conditions. The survivors will then reproduce and pass on to their offspring those genes responsible for the characteristics which enabled them to survive. Gradually, more and more individuals with particular characteristics will emerge and when these individuals can no longer mate with other individuals who have a different set of characteristics, a new species has evolved.

Another crucial evolutionary development was *mobility*: this facilitates adaptation by helping animals:

> ...to cope with the daily cycles of sun, tide and darkness, to protect themselves against seasonal changes by migrating, to seek out new sources of food and shelter, and to colonize new territory. (Latané and Hothersall, 1980)

Lea, (1984) summarizes some of the major terms used in evolutionary theory:

Evolution, of course, implies a gradual rather than a sudden change (and is usually contrasted with 'revolution'); species do not appear 'out of the blue' but emerge from other species by a series of linked steps. However, evolution is not going on at a more or less constant rate: the history of life is characterized by 'punctuated equilibria', long periods during which relatively little is going on by way of new species appearing, followed by 'adaptive radiations' when whole new groups evolve.

Natural selection refers to the natural occurrence of a process performed deliberately by human breeders, perpetuating some lines in preference to others, thus producing new varieties of animal. A *fit* animal is one which leaves more offspring and *adaptedness* means being well-suited to the environment the organism lives in. The precise environment to which an animal is adapted is called its *ecological niche* (and any one ecological niche can only be occupied by one species at any one time).

Selective pressure is any property of the environment (especially of the ecological niche) which tends to favour one form of a species over another, ie it is a factor which makes some animals fitter than others. Finally, a *species* is the range of *gene* exchange and the field within which evolution can operate.

THE CONCEPT OF INSTINCT

As we mentioned earlier, the concept of instinct is central to ethological explanations of behaviour and opposes it to the extreme environmentalism of the behaviourists. Tinbergen's *The Study of Instinct* (1951) represents one of the key landmarks in the history of ethology. So, what is an instinct?

Essentially, it is an inherited behaviour pattern which is common to all members of a species (hence, it is often used synonymously with *species–specific* behaviour). It is innate as opposed to learnt and it tends to be stereotyped, ie it appears in the same form every time it is displayed. An instinct is what motivates behaviour and makes it purposeful and goal-directed and, associated with each instinct (eg hunger, reproduction, aggression), is an *action-specific energy*. This might sound plausible enough, but a major problem with a term like 'instinct' is that it sounds deceptively like an explanation for behaviour when, in fact, it is nothing more than a label, a description.

Partly for this reason, and partly because it is impossible to investigate an instinct without investigating particular manifestations of it, Tinbergen, Lorenz and other ethologists define instincts in terms of *fixed action patterns* (FAPs). These are readily identifiable units of behaviour which break up the stream of behaviour and can be treated like morphological characteristics. Every species has a repertoire of FAPs which are as much characteristic of the species as are its structural characteristics (Hinde, 1982), ie FAPs are species-specific.

FIXED ACTION PATTERNS

Before defining an FAP in more detail, we will look at two commonly-quoted examples: (i) the egg-rolling of the greylag goose (Lorenz and Tinbergen, 1938); and (ii) the begging-response of the herring-gull chick (Tinbergen and Perdeck, 1950):

(a) Whenever an egg rolled away from her nest, a greylag goose always retrieved it in the same way, by turning to face it, stretching out her neck, walking slowly towards it, hooking her beak over it and rolling it slowly back into the nest. This did not seem the most efficient way of going about it—it sometimes took several attempts and on occasions she failed completely.

(b) Herring-gulls nest on the ground and the parents go off to find food at sea, on local rubbish tips or some other distant source. When they return, they land on their small nesting territory and stand close to the chick (or even over it), pointing their beaks at the ground. The chick then pecks at the parents' beak which stimulates the parent to regurgitate the food it has collected, allowing the chick to be fed.

It was from these and numerous other examples (mainly from birds and fish) that the concept of an FAP emerged. Based on Lorenz, Lea (1984) proposes six major characteristics shared by all FAPs (some of which we have already touched on in discussing the concept of 'instinct'):

(a) They are *stereotyped*, ie the behaviour always occurs in the same form.

(b) They are *universal*, that is, they occur in all the members of a species (or at least, all members of a defined class, eg geese as distinct from ganders and goslings), and, therefore, there should be intra-species similarity. FAPs are *species-specific*.

(c) They are *independent of individual experience*, that is, they are unlearnt and so they should occur regardless of an animal's particular history. This can be demonstrated by 'isolation' experiments, where an animal is reared, from birth, entirely on its own, so that its behaviour cannot have been learned through its contact with other members of the species. Any FAPs it displays must, therefore, have been inherited. However, as we shall see below, this does not rule out the role of learning and environmental factors altogether.

(d) They are *ballistic*, that is, they cannot be varied if conditions change once the FAP has been 'launched'. Once triggered, it runs its course.

Although (see (f)) there must be a stimulus which triggers the FAP, its particular characteristics seem to be irrelevant. For instance, Lorenz and Tinbergen presented a greylag goose with a giant, cardboard, Easter egg, painted with the same sort of markings as a real goose egg and in her attempt to roll it in, it got stuck between her beak and her breast and she stayed like that for several seconds. In this sense, the behaviour is totally inflexible (so there is overlap with (a)).

(e) They have a *singleness of purpose*, that is, they have only one function and are only shown in specific situations (eg the greylag goose only uses her FAP for egg-retrieval to retrieve eggs— and for nothing else).

(f) They are *triggered* by *specific stimuli*, which constitute the immediate cause of the FAP. These trigger stimuli can be considered both a necessary and sufficient condition for the appearance of the FAP. The greylag goose will only show her egg-rolling if she sees an egg within reach of the nest and if she does see one will always attempt to roll it in (the egg is an example of a *sign stimulus*).

SIGN STIMULI, RELEASERS AND SUPERNORMAL STIMULI

Just how specific does the trigger have to be? In the above example (d), it would seem that a real goose egg and the giant cardboard Easter egg have enough in common for the latter to 'count' as a trigger for egg-rolling. What seems to be critical is that the trigger has certain characteristics and any others it does or does not have seem to be largely irrelevant. Many famous examples of ethological 'experiments' (often, literally, in the field) involve the presentation of artificial stimuli which resemble the natural trigger stimulus, to a greater or lesser degree, in various ways.

Tinbergen and Perdeck (1950) presented herring-gull chicks with a life-like 3-D model of a gull's head and a simple cardboard cut-out (two dimensional, with just an eye and a beak) and found that both were sufficient to produce the begging response. So what specific features of the parent's head are important?

They tried a number of variations based on three characteristics of the adult herring gull, namely: (i) its white head; (ii) its yellow beak; and (iii) the small red spot one-third of the way from the end of its lower mandible. Three series of cardboard cut-out heads were used, thus manipulating each of three variables:

(a) *Spot Colour*. All models had yellow beaks with spots on The chicks pecked most at the red spot but black, blue and white spots also produced many responses.

(b) *Spot–beak contrast*. All models had medium-grey beaks with the spot colour varying from white through shades of grey to black. Medium-grey spots were the least effective; black and white the most effective.

(c) *Beak colour*. The models were of different colours and all were lacking spots. A yellow beak (the natural colour) was actually *less* effective than a red one and the nearer to red it was, the more effective it was.

Tinbergen and Perdeck concluded that it is the *redness of the beak* (how close to red it is) and the *contrast between the beak and the spot* which are the key features that produce the begging response in herring-gull chicks.

Another example is the size and speckledness of an oystercatcher's eggs. A herring-gull's eggs, in fact, look very much like an oystercatcher's except that they are twice the size. Tinbergen (1948) put a gull's egg near an oystercatcher's nest and found that the returning oystercatcher would choose to brood the outsize gull egg in preference to its own. It would also choose an absurd giant egg (which was as speckled as a real egg) in preference to both its own and the herring-gull's egg.

Herring-gulls themselves also seem to go for size. Baerends and Kruijt (1973) used models to study the egg-rolling of herring-gulls and found that larger models were preferred to smaller, speckled to plain, and green to a variety of other colours; shape seemed to make little difference (Fig. 15.1).

Therefore the most effective stimulus is not necessarily the one which is most like the natural stimulus, and such artificial stimuli are known as *super-normal* stimuli (or *super-releasers*) which Hinde (1982) describes as a kind of caricature of the natural sign stimulus.

Although the terms 'sign stimulus' and 'releaser' are often used interchangeably, there is an important difference, as Lea (1984) points out. Although both the speckles on the oystercatcher's egg and the red spot on the herring-gull's beak are sign stimuli (because they help to trigger particular FAPs), the former seems to have another, more important function, namely, to help camouflage the eggs. The red spot, however, seems to have evolved for the sole purpose of acting as a sign stimulus which makes it a *releaser*. So while all releasers are sign stimuli, not all sign stimuli are releasers and true releasers are often found in one species but not in another, closely related, species.

THE ROLE OF ENVIRONMENTAL FACTORS

Another famous example of a releaser is the bright red underbelly of the male three-spined stickleback studied by Tinbergen but, interestingly the precise FAP it triggers depends on whether the fish is on its own territory or another's. The red belly of an intruder will release *attack* behaviour if the stickelback is on 'homeground' but when it is 'trespassing' the same stickelback will *flee*. (Exactly how it 'knows' whether it is inside or outside its own territory is itself an important and complex issue.)

This tells us that the probability that an FAP will be elicited is *not* determined *solely by* the presence or absence of a releaser (or sign stimulus) which means that it may not, after all, be a sufficient condition (see above).

Apart from territory, what other environmental factors may influence the appearance of FAPs?

When discussing the criteria of FAPs above, we referred to isolation experiments as one way of demonstrating the innateness of such behaviour. One famous isolation experiment is that of Eibl-Eibesfeldt (1975) who took some baby squirrels, still on a liquid diet, and brought them up in bare cages. The cages were quite warm but there was no

Figure 15.1 Herring-gull rolling an egg back into its nest. (From R. A. Hinde (1982) Ethology. London; Fontana)

nesting material to burrow into or hide things in. When they were fully grown, they were given a supply of nuts and, despite having no solid food before and not having seen a nut before (or another squirrel eating one), they ate them quite easily, in much the same way as normally-reared adults. When they had eaten their fill, they attempted to bury the surplus nuts, pushing them into a corner with their noses and stamping them down with their back feet, just as wild squirrels stamp earth over their stores of fruit.

Clearly, the squirrels could not have learned this behaviour—'recognizing' the nuts seems to be part of the squirrels' innate repertoire of behaviour and the nut-burying behaviour an FAP. (This example also seems to demonstrate the stereotyped, species-specific and ballistic nature of FAPs.)

Similarly, female rats reared in isolation developed the normal maternal behaviours of nest-building and retrieval and licking of their pups (Reiss, 1951). However, Reiss also found that if rats were reared so that they were prevented from carrying anything in their paws (eg faeces fell through the floor-grid of the cage and they were given only powdered food instead of pellets), when they came to have litters, they did not build nests, nor did they retrieve their young. It seems that early experience of carrying things is essential for normal maternal behaviour to develop. It also seems that nest-building and temperature are inversely related, so that the higher the temperature, the less the nest-building.

Also, if female rats are prevented from licking their own genital organs (to obtain salt) they fail to lick or retrieve their pups and will actually eat many of them.

Laughing gulls (like herring-gulls) have a red spot on their beak which is a releaser for pecking by chicks. However, the accuracy of pecking improves with time, partly due to learning. One-week-old chicks, for example, have learned to distinguish the shape of the parent's beak and so they peck selectively, whereas, before this, pecking seems to be rather 'hit and miss'.

Another classic study of its kind is Thorpe's study of the chaffinch (Thorpe, 1956, 1963, 1972). Using an acoustic spectograph (which converts sound into a 'sound picture'), Thorpe discovered that only some features of the chaffinch's song are inherited. Birds reared in isolation will only produce the 'basic' song but the 'dialect', ie the full refinements and temporal pattern, are learned from other chaffinches in the locality and this learning has to take place not later than the bird's first spring. Once learned, the dialect remains invariant throughout the bird's life.

Similar findings were reported by Konishi (1965) for the American white-crowned sparrow. Konishi removed the cochlea of fledglings and found that they need to hear their own song in order to produce even the inherited standard song (so acoustic feedback mediates the effects of genetic factors). However, deafening the birds made no difference *after* they had already produced a song.

Evans (1980) likens the inherited, 'basic' song to a *template*—the bird has to use this as a guide and, ultimately, must match its own singing to it. The white-crowned sparrow must receive acoustic feedback to be able to do this.

THE ROLE OF HORMONAL FACTORS AND THEIR INTERACTION WITH THE ENVIRONMENT

Just as the influence of sign stimuli and releasers are mediated by environmental factors, so hormonal factors also help determine their effect.

Achievement of successful reproduction, for example, depends upon a complex series of changes in the endocrine system which are related to changes in the external situation, themselves partly determined by the endocrine and behavioural changes (Hinde, 1982).

In the female canary, for instance, environmental factors, such as long day length and the male canary's song, influence the hypothalamo–pituitary–gonad system and result in gonadal development and the release of oestrogen (see Chapters 4 and 23), which has a positive influence on nest-building behaviour. The external factors themselves also influence the effectiveness of oestrogen in influencing behaviour.

Nest-building results in a nest, and stimuli from the nest produce a change in selection of the nest material (from grass for the outside to feathers for the lining), a decrease in nest-building and further reproductive development; stimuli from the nest are received through the ventral areas of the skin (Hinde, 1965).

Similar findings have come from studies of mammals. For example, stimuli from a female monkey influence the levels of sex hormone in a male and not only does testosterone promote the mating behaviour of male rats, but mating increases testosterone levels.

INNATE RELEASING MECHANISMS

So far we have considered the actual, overt, behaviour (FAPs) and the stimuli which, under certain environmental and hormonal conditions, trigger them (sign stimuli or releasers). Somewhere within the animal's nervous system there must be a mechanism which mediates between the two and this hypothetical 'centre' is known as an *innate releasing mechanism* (IRM).

IRMs, together with the *psycho-hydraulic model* of *motivation*, can help to explain two apparently contradictory findings: (i) that a herring-gull chick that has just eaten will not peck at a cardboard model of a parent gull's head (so clearly the releaser is not sufficient); and (ii) that a whole sequence of behaviour may take place in the absence of any obvious releasing stimulus and so is quite spontaneous (*vacuum activity*), in which case the releaser does not even seem to be necessary.

The IRM has to be sufficiently stimulated for the corresponding FAP to occur and whether or not a releaser will be either necessary or sufficient to produce it will depend on the amount of *action-specific energy* (ASE) which has built up in the hypothetical reservoirs of the psycho-hydraulic model.

For each instinct and FAP there is assumed to be a specific kind of energy which powers or energizes the behaviour (this is the ASE); in the case of the herring-gull chick which has just eaten, all its pecking-ASE has been 'used' up and the releaser is not sufficient to 'switch on' the IRM. By contrast, in the case of vacuum activity, there is such a build-up of ASE that the IRM is activated and the behaviour occurs *without* a releaser being needed. (See Chapter 16 for a discussion of Lorenz's view of human aggression, which sees it as being primarily a form of vacuum activity based on the psycho-hydraulic model.)

So Lorenz's psycho-hydraulic model takes account of both the strength of releasing stimuli and the quantity of accumulated energy; the threshold of response is a changing one, depending on environmental and internal factors (Fig. 15.2).

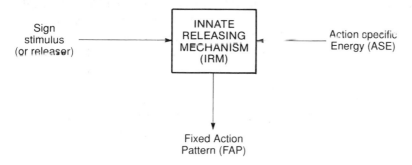

Figure 15.2 *The innate release mechanism (IRM) can be activated either by accumulation of ASE or by a strong stimulus or by the combined effect of both*

CRITICISMS OF THE ETHOLOGICAL APPROACH

1) Although ethologists generally have become increasingly willing to acknowledge the importance of environmental factors in the modification of behaviour patterns, they have always seen instinct as of primary importance. Evans (1975) believes that this has resulted in an over-simplified picture of behaviour, especially when instinct explanations are applied to human behaviour (see Chapter 16).

2) A specific, and famous, example, of a misplaced ethological explanation is Lorenz and Tinbergens' account of the alarm reaction in young turkeys. They found that the most effective alarm-raiser was the silhouette shown in Figure 15.3. However, only when it was moved from right to left did it elicit an alarm reaction; under these conditions the short neck preceded the long tail and so resembled the shadow that would be cast by a bird of prey, such as a hawk; when it was moved from left to right, it resembled a long-necked bird, such as a goose.

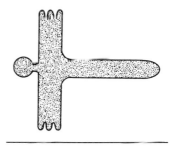

Figure 15.3 *The hawk–goose silhouette used by Lorenz and Tinbergen*

Lorenz and Tinbergen believed that they had demonstrated an IRM especially adapted in the course of evolution to a certain characteristic of birds of prey. However, Schneirla (1965) pointed out that all animals tend to withdraw from any source of stimulation which suddenly changes and even if Lorenz and Tinbergen had used a plain triangle, they would have obtained a similar result: that is, the short neck presented first represents a sudden change while the lock-neck presented first represents a gradual and consequently, less alarming, change in stimulation.

Schneirla is, therefore, arguing that Lorenz and Tinbergens' explanation is more complicated than it needs to be. However, others have subsequently confirmed the original findings.

3) Evans (1980) has criticized the concept of an IRM itself. His reasons are as follows: (i) the very term 'releasing' is itself problematic, because of cases such as young turkey chicks which emit certain specific vocalizations that are designed to *inhibit* a response in the adult bird, not to release one (namely, attacking and killing the chick); (ii) stimuli may orientate behaviour (as in the greylag goose's egg-retrieval) and arouse

the animal, and not just release or trigger responses; and (iii) the sign stimulus is often much more complex than the term 'mechanism' implies (as in the begging-response of herring-gull chicks), and what is needed is a thorough knowledge of how the animal processes information, how stimuli are filtered in the nervous system and how only the key characteristics are selected and attended to.

In defence of the IRM concept, Lea (1984) argues that it is only intended as a *description* of instinctive behaviour (and not an explanation). He suggests that systems which can be described in terms of IRMs should be called 'micro-instincts' (to distinguish them from broad tendencies such as hunger, sex and aggression) and believes that the IRM concept has made instinct a scientifically respectable concept, making it coherent and recognizable.

4) The psycho-hydraulic model has also been criticized, most seriously because it does not fit the facts. The model maintains that energy can only be released through the performance of instinct-related behaviour; if this were so, then *consummatory* behaviour (sequences of responses made when the goal is actually reached, eg drinking) cannot be by-passed, that is, the ASE associated with drinking could only be reduced by actually drinking. However, studies of animals in which water is placed directly into their stomachs shows that they do *not* start drinking (following a 10–15 minute interval to allow the water to be absorbed) which is contrary to what Lorenz's model would predict (see Chapter 6).

Evans (1975) points out that the model has been discredited not only in relation to eating and drinking. In another famous example of FAPs, Tinbergen (1951) describes the courtship behaviour of the stickleback. Normally, when a female swims into a male's territory, he swims up to her in a series of loops called a 'zigzag dance'; she swims round in front of him, then he turns round and swims down the nest (which he has built) and she follows him down. This, in turn, causes him to point his head at the nest entrance; she enters and this releases a quivering response in the male who then thrusts his snout at the female's rump, causing her to spawn eggs. Finally, he fertilizes the eggs, and while he is doing this, she swims away (Fig. 15.4).

However, it seems that merely *seeing* the newly-laid eggs is enough to 'satisfy' the male's mating ASE—actually fertilizing them does not seem to be necessary, contrary to what the hydraulic model would predict.

THE SOCIAL NATURE OF FAPS

In the stickleback's mating behaviour just described, the initial sign stimulus is the female's swollen belly. This sets in motion a series of FAPs, each of which serves as a sign stimulus for the next FAP.

But Lorenz (1950) and Hinde (1982) believe that FAPs often function as *signals*, from one animal to another. While *sign stimulus* implies a selective responsiveness on the part of the responder, *social releaser* 'implies the evolution of especially effective stimulus features, involving movements or structures or both in the signaller' (Hinde, 1982). In other words, in the course of evolution, many FAPs have developed which are triggered by social releasers (which may, themselves, be FAPs triggered by other social releasers, as in the stickleback's mating behaviour) and which are primarily concerned with *communication* between members of

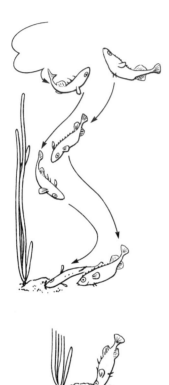

Figure 15.4 The courtship of the three-spined stickleback. In the main diagram, the male is shown on the left, and the female on the right. The male's initial zig-zag dance is elicited by the swollen belly and by the body posture of the female. He then leads her to the nest and she follows. At the nest he shows her the nest entrance. Then (below) she enters and lays her eggs when he stimulates the base of her tail. (From N. Tinbergen (1951) The Study of Instinct. Oxford, Oxford University Press)

the same species; these tend to be either predominantly male–male encounters (as in threat behaviour, territoriality, competition over a female, etc.) or male–female encounters (as in mating and courtship). How have such patterns of social communication evolved?

According to Hinde (1982), there are three main sources: (i) displacement activity; (ii) intention movements; and (iii) the consequences of activity in the autonomic nervous system (eg movements of hair, feathers, urination and defecation, changes in skin colour). We shall concentrate here on (i).

CONFLICT AND DISPLACEMENT ACTIVITY

Animals will sometimes find themselves in a situation where a source of food and a source of threat are in the same place at the same time (eg the food is cheese, the threat is a cat and the animal caught in the middle is a mouse). Alternatively, they may face a conflict between aggression (a rival male should be approached and attacked) and fear (the other male is quite capable of inflicting injury itself).

Another example of *approach–avoidance* conflict is mating in 'distance species' (Hediger, 1951), such as most common garden birds and gulls; members of these species normally like to maintain distance from other members, but, of course, their sexual drive requires that they come into close proximity with another animal. What do animals do when faced with such conflicts?

Often, some third kind of behaviour appears which seems to be entirely irrelevant to the situation. For example, two cocks facing each other and preparing for a fight may suddenly break off and start pulling up the grass, or hungry rats put in an unfamiliar cage may start to wash themselves rigorously (Lea, 1984).

These *displacement activities* often involve preening, washing or other activities associated with care of the body surface (eg the chaffinch wipes its beak or its feathers); alternatively, they may involve nest-building, feeding or even sleeping! They all have in common the fact that they are *readily available* behaviours, that is, they are all behaviours the animal engages in frequently and regularly.

Almost by definition, displacement activities only arise when another animal is involved in some way, which tells us that the conflict involves aggression, fear and sex; they are also generally themselves FAPs, which is important if they are to be used as social signals, since their 'meaning' should be unambiguous for members of the same species.

The psycho-hydraulic model maintains that displacement activity occurs when two mutually incompatible IRMs are released simultaneously and, as a result, inhibit each other; the ASE associated with each overflows into the other, stimulating it and producing some behaviour which is unrelated to either of the original IRMs (*displacement* activity is, therefore, a kind of *vacuum* activity). This implies that the presence or absence, or relative strength, of an appropriate sign stimulus is irrelevant; however, cocks only show displaced feeding or drinking if food or water are available and chaffinch preening is increased if its feathers are sprayed with water. Similar observations have been made in nesting terns.

Often, the inhibition of one activity by the other produces *intention movements*, that is, the incomplete preparatory phases of a movement (for example, a bird crouches before take-off), or there may be a rapid alternation between the two behaviours that are in conflict. Alternatively, elements of both kinds of behaviour may be combined to produce an ambivalent form of behaviour; or, again, one kind of behaviour (eg aggression) may be displayed but with some other animal or object as the target (compare this with displaced aggression described by Freud as a means of ego defence—see Chapter 29).

DISPLACEMENT ACTIVITY, FAPS AND EVOLUTION

According to Lorenz (1950) and, as we have seen, Hinde (1982), many FAPs are social in character and many have probably evolved from displacement reactions. Lea (1984) describes the two stages of evolution involved:

1) The form of displacement reactions would become standardized, so as both to display any relevant body features most effectively and because any animal without such characteristics can be more easily identified and rejected. If a characteristic body structure is involved, there will be a selective advantage for animals who have it in a larger, brighter or exaggerated form or who display it sooner or more vigorously. These structures serve to enhance the signal (eg the stickleback's red belly). The standard form of the displacement reaction is usually exaggerated compared with the original, 'functional' form of the response; this is called *ritualization* (Huxley, 1914).

2) The response, now in full use as a signal, would have lost its connections with its original sign stimuli and motivation; for example, preening becomes attached to the sex drive instead of the care-of-body-surface drive and would be released by some releaser from the female. In effect, a new IRM would have been formed and the process is called *emancipation* (Lorenz, 1950).

Is there any evidence to support Lorenz?

According to Hinde (1982), comparisons across several species often show correlations between the extent to which a signal has been developed and the development of accompanying structures which serve to enhance that signal; they seem to have evolved in parallel.

In zebra finches, beak-wiping is a fairly common displacement reaction to approach–avoidance conflicts. But in two other grass finches (striated and spice), the *same* beak-wiping has become ritualized and emancipated and it functions as an effective courtship response in the male when the female presents herself sexually. (Other examples of ritualization are descibed in Chapter 16 in relation to aggression.)

COURTSHIP AND MATING: HOW DO ANIMALS FALL IN LOVE?

There are many parallels between sexually-motivated postures and appeasement postures. Any behaviour implying subservience is quite likely to be adopted as part of a courtship display. It follows, therefore, that a great deal of courtship ritual involves the *reduction of aggression* necessary for mating to take place. (Conversely, some appeasement displays involve triggering behaviour in the attacker which is incompatible with aggression; for instance, baboons adopt the female sexual presentation posture causing the aggressor to mount them!)

Males and females, of course, are both necessary for reproduction but each contributes a different size and type of sex-cell or gamete; the female ovum contains both genetic information *and* a food store (store of nourishment and energy) for the new organism while the male sperm is a source of genetic information only. Consequently, the female commits more resources to her offspring and this puts her under greater selective pressure to provide care, both pre- and post-natally. This is why, according to sociobiologists, female mammals have evolved so that they retain their offspring inside their bodies for the duration of the pregnancy.

To a great extent, this difference in the size of male and female gametes (*anisogamy*) determines the different roles of males and females. Where fertilization is *internal* (as in birds and mammals), anisogamy has produced physiological adaptations in the female such that she provides food and parental care. As Dawkins (1976) puts it, they have lost the 'race to desert' the offspring long ago in their evolutionary past. Where fertilization is *external* (as in fish), the balance is more equal; the male can be sure of his paternity and so the incentive to desert is weaker. Indeed, the female has to release her eggs first which gives her the opportunity to leave, and in several species (such as the stickleback) it is the male who builds the nest and cares for the eggs until they hatch—or even beyond.

For widely-dispersed, solitary animals, it may not be easy for males and females actually to find each other. To overcome this, many species have evolved auditory signals (such as the cuckoo's call) or chemical communication; for example, many insects and mammals have a wide range of secretory cells which emit substances called *pheromones* into the environment.

However, in most species there are several males and females present in the same vicinity and the problem there becomes how particular males come to mate with particular females. Usually, there are two or more males competing for the attentions of the same female and, as we saw when discussing the evolution of FAPs from displacement activity, the male who shows the appropriate courtship display, in the most exaggerated form and with the greatest persistence, and who also possesses the brightest releasing stimuli, will be chosen.

Once they have 'found each other', what sort of relationship do they form?

Sometimes, copulation is the first and last contact they have with each other (the animal equivalent of a 'one-night-stand', or casual sex), which is what normally happens when no parental care is actually needed; but it may occur when the one-parent family is the normal pattern (eg female cats and male sticklebacks).

Some females (such as chimps) are *promiscuous*, ie they will mate with any and all available males, while in a *pair-bond* (especially common among birds), one male and one female remain more or less 'faithful' to each other for one mating season (or for several) and both may play a substantial part in the care of the offspring. Perhaps more common is for the male and female to play different roles, for instance, the male is the nest-builder and the female does the egg-sitting. In pair-bonds, the male and female are usually similar in size and also in appearance.

In *polygyny*, one male has exclusive access to a group of females (his 'harem') as in red deer, or a small group of males has access to a larger group of females (eg lions). The males tend to be larger than females and often quite different in appearance; care of the young is almost exclusively left to the females. Although not very common, a single female sometimes has access to several males, as in the American jacana or the Tasmanian native hen.

SOCIAL STRUCTURE—WHY DO ANIMALS LIVE IN GROUPS?

According to Lea (1984) there are two ways of trying to answer the question why animals live in groups. Either we can start with simple behaviours which go on between individuals and see how these 'add up' to a social structure (the 'bottom-up' approach) or we can start with whole societies and ask how they influence the behaviour of individuals and how they are produced by natural selection (the 'top-down' approach).

Within non-solitary species, the range of social organization is enormous, varying from flocks of seed-eating birds which form in autumn and are really no more than aggregations of individuals, to *eusocial* insects, where there is a highly structured division of labour—different body structures equip different ants, bees and wasps to perform different but interdependent roles, namely, worker, soldier and queen (these are also among the most altruistic species, see below). According to Lea (1984), there are about 170,000 species of such social insects (*Hymenoptera*) who live in elaborate, differentiated societies.

Living in a group has a number of advantages for an individual animal, in particular, it makes a mate readily accessible. Equally important, finding food may be easier in a group; for instance, members can report to each other where food is available (a famous example being the 'waggle dance' of the honey bee, described by von Frisch (1966), which informs other bees of the exact location of food, who then go in increasing numbers to the food supply to collect it and bring it back to the hive).

A group may also be able to tackle larger prey than an individual animal could (as in lions) and the group has a better chance of spotting a predator and 'sounding the alarm'. Most predators take only one victim (or a very small proportion of the whole group) and so the larger the group the greater the probability that any one individual will survive an attack. However, a large group is more likely to be spotted in the first place.

For groups to remain fairly permanent and stable (and to survive as groups), there needs to be some kind of *dominance hierarchy*, an arrangement whereby some members have precedence over others for such things as access to mates, food, etc. This ensures that at least some members of the group would survive a severe food shortage, because each 'knows its place'; energy is not wasted fighting over scarce resources.

Dominance hierarchies are common among species which live within territories and were originally observed by Schjelderup-Ebbe (1922) who discovered a literal pecking-order among hens; the term 'pecking-order' is now used almost synonymously with *dominance hierarchy*. It represents a simple kind of social structure and has been found in species ranging from red jungle fowl (an ancestor of the domestic chicken) to wild Barbary apes.

Most animal species are more complex than is implied by the dominance hierarchy and even strictly territorial animals usually have at least a minimal social grouping comprising a mother and her young (territoriality will be discussed separately below).

Often a key factor in more complex social groupings is the temporary or permanent nature of sexual relationships between males and females, which we discussed earlier in relation to courtship and mating. However, there are other important kinds of relationship, such as sibling groups and 'matriline'. All the females in a pride of lions or a larger group are, at least, first cousins and in brush turkeys, females are courted by pairs of brothers, only one of which will ultimately mate with her; these are examples of *sibling groups*.

A *matriline* is a group comprising a dominant female, sexually mature daughters (and possibly granddaughters) and the dependent young of all of them, and it is found in almost all primates.

An interesting comparison between different primates is that between chimpanzees and gorillas. Some taxonomists want to put chimps and gorillas in the same genus (*Pan*), others prefer to classify them separately (*Pan* and *Gorilla*). But what is really interesting for the ethologist is that they *behave* very differently from each other, especially in their social and sexual behaviour (Harcourt and Stewart, 1977).

Chimps live in 'loose' communities, where, for much of the time, equal numbers of males and females move around separately. Today, they live scattered in a belt across central Africa in environments varying from dense woodland to relatively open grassland. Males travel over the whole community territory, sometimes alone, sometimes with others, which they defend communally against males from other communities. Not only do they threaten and attack trespassers, but even go on boundary patrols to check for incursions.

A distinctive phenomenon is the fate of maturing males—unlike the young males of most mammals, adolescent male chimps do *not* leave the natal group and spend their reproductive lives with unrelated females. This means that the males within groups are more closely related to each other than they are to males in other communities. But adolescent females do usually leave the home troop to join a neighbouring one. Generally much less is known about female social behaviour. They live in overlapping home ranges about half the size of the males'; many are mothers with young who spend much of their time wandering with their offspring and travelling with other mother-offspring pairs.

Gorillas live in stable groups which forage through dense undergrowth or scattered trees of their leafy home ranges (also in central Africa); neighbouring home ranges may overlap. Each group comprises at least one silverback (fully mature male), one or several adult females (some of whom will have been with the silverback for years) plus their offspring. Here, as with chimps, adolescent females leave the natal group to join other groups. The silverback tolerates young males—probably his sons—who will take over leadership of the group when he dies. Other young males leave the group and wander till they find mates.

TERRITORIALITY

Basically, a territory is an area of space which is held and defended by a solitary animal, or a family group, and in which food is found and the young are reared.

Territoriality is common among birds, many coastal and river fish and many mammals but is less common among invertebrates (Fig. 15.5).

Figure 15.5 Many species compete for territory or for mates, including zebras, elephant seals, red deer and great tits. (From Arak, A. (1984) Playing games is a serious business. New Scientist, February 2nd) (Clockwise from top left: Dr Eckart Pott: Bruce Coleman Ltd; Eric Hosking; Hans Reinhard: Bruce Coleman Ltd; Erwin & Peggy Bauer: Bruce Coleman Ltd)

Territories may vary enormously in size and there is no simple correlation between size of territory and the availability of food (one of the major explanations for the evolution of territoriality). For example, birds of prey have very large territories (about 1 square mile) from which they obtain all their food, while herring-gulls have a limited territory within a colony but they obtain all their food elsewhere (at sea, for instance).

Manning (1973) compares territory to an elastic disc, the centre of which is well-defined as a particular animal's territory and any intruder who enters this space will provoke an extremely aggressive response by the territory owner. As one moves out from the centre, the owner's threat behaviour becomes less pronounced until a point is reached where it becomes quite half-hearted; it is at this peripheral 'no-man's-land' that threat displays are most in evidence, which suggests that they are essentially a compromise when the tendencies to attack and to escape are finely balanced and, as predicted by Lorenz's hydraulic model, displacement activities also commonly occur in this 'border-area'. According to Manning, therefore, territories do *not* have fixed boundaries.

A related concept is that of a *'home range'*, a defined place in which an animal lives but which may overlap with the living space of one or more others. For instance, herring-gulls defend a small area around their nesting sites but their home range also includes various feeding places which they visit in common with many other gulls; at feeding sites *agonistic* encounters (ie attack, threat, fight, flight, submission and appeasement behaviour) may occur over food but *not* over the use of space as such.

Another way in which space may be shared is in terms of time; cats, for example, operate a 'time-share' system, by which the freshness of the urine smell acts as a signal as to whose territory it is at that particular time. Similarly, many primates which live in groups share overlapping home-ranges; by using special vocal signals (as in howler monkeys) groups can avoid each other and, consequently, can avoid disputes over ownership. So the same territory can be owned by several individuals (or groups) but at different times.

Territoriality, therefore, is a much more flexible and varied feature of animal social behaviour than was once thought.

PARENTAL CARE AND IMPRINTING

A large number of instinctive behaviour patterns are concerned with interactions between parents and their young who need to 'know', for instance, what to do in order to elicit food (as in herring-gull chicks). It may also be vital for the young animal's survival that it stay close to its parent(s) if they belong to a *precocial* species, in which the new-born are capable of locomotion and possess well-developed sense-organs. A mobile young animal needs to stay close to its parents and, if it has to *learn* to recognize them, this learning needs to be rapid, and this is one of the characteristics of a form of learning which Lorenz (1935) called *imprinting*.

Lorenz defined imprinting as the learning which occurs in a young bird when following a moving object. Specifically, what the bird learns is the characteristics of the object (which, in the wild, will usually be the mother) so that it discriminates the object from others and, in this

Figure 15.6 Konrad Lorenz with his devoted greylag geese. (Radio Times Picture Library)

way, becomes attached to the imprinted object. This attachment is manifested as a tendency to follow the familiar object, so that following is both a cause and effect of imprinting.

This tendency to become imprinted (*imprintability*) is genetically determined (and species-specific) and the following response is an FAP: the sign stimuli include movement, size and general conspicuousness and since young birds do not innately recognize their mothers, any object which combines these properties can be a potential 'target' for imprinting. Lea (1984) maintains that instinct gives the chick a 'concept' of the mother, but the environment has to supply the details. (This is another 'template' example.)

Indeed, in a very famous ethological experiment, Lorenz took a large clutch of goose eggs and kept them until they were about to hatch out. Half were then placed under the goose mother and the other half Lorenz kept beside him for several hours. After hatching, the first group followed the mother and the second group followed Lorenz. He then put them altogether under an upturned box to allow them to mix and, when the box was removed, the two groups separated to go to their respective guardians (Fig. 15.6).

So what characterizes imprinting as a form of learning?

Lorenz believed that imprinting is unique for the following reasons:

(i) it only occurs during a brief *critical period*, early in the bird's life;
(ii) once it has occurred, it is *irreversible*;
(iii) it is *supra-individual*, that is, it is to do with a *class* of objects (a species) rather than an individual;
(iv) it influences patterns of behavior which have not yet developed in the animal's repertoire (for example, the selection of a sexual partner).

We should add as a fifth characteristic that Lorenz believed that imprinting only occurred in a group of ground-nesting (*nidifugous*) birds called *precocial* (see above), in particular, ducks, geese and chickens. (Precocial species are contrasted with *altricial* species, including human beings, in which newborns are incapable of mobility and are totally dependent on others.)

What is the evidence?

CRITICAL AND SENSITIVE PERIODS

Lorenz borrowed the term 'critical period' from embryology, implying that there are periods in development during which the individual is especially impressionable or vulnerable, that is, when particular experiences exert a profound and lasting influence on later behaviour.

In relation to imprinting, 'critical' implies that *unless* learning occurs during a particular period after hatching, it will *never* occur (it also conveys the second major characteristic of imprinting, namely, irreversibility). Imprintability, according to Lorenz, is genetically 'switched on' and then 'switched off' again at the end of the period; in the case of mallard ducklings the critical period lasts for the first few hours after hatching (Lorenz, 1935) and, more precisely, between 5 and 24 hours after hatching, with a peak between 13 to 16 hours (Ramsay and Hess, 1954). Hess (1958), studying chicks, ducklings and goslings, maintained that although imprinting *could* occur as early as one hour after hatching, the strongest responses occurred between 12 to 17 hours ('critical period peak'); after 32 hours, it was extremely unlikely to happen and it became increasingly difficult after 20 hours. A critical period of 8 to 27 hours (with no peak) has been reported for Peking ducklings.

Are these periods switched on and off in the way Lorenz believed?

Many researchers have shown that if a young bird is kept in isolation, it remains unimprinted (and still imprintable) beyond the end of the normal critical period (for example, Sluckin (1961) and Bateson (1964) with ducklings). Also, if chicks are kept in an unstimulating environment (especially if it is visually unstimulating) they could imprint well after the critical period normally ends (Guiton, 1958). Similar results were found by Moltz and Stettner (1961), who fitted translucent hoods to ducklings, thus preventing perception of patterned light.

In view of this evidence that the young bird's experience can extend the period of imprintability, Lorenz's original proposal that the termination (as well as the onset) of the critical period is under genetic control seemed untenable and this led Sluckin (1965) to coin the term *sensitive period* instead. A sensitive period is one during which learning is most *likely* to happen and will happen most *easily* but it is not as 'critical' or 'once-and-for-all' as the critical period concept suggests. It seems more useful to think in terms of the *probability* that imprinting will occur rather than 'whether-or-not' it will occur.

Hinde (1966) defines a sensitive period as, 'a time during an organism's development when a particular influence is most likely to have an effect', while according to Dworetzky (1981), 'there could be times in our life when we are genetically primed to respond to certain influences and other times when those influences would have little or no effect'.

Hinde (1966) believes that, once imprinting has occurred, the young bird is likely to respond with fear to any other object it encounters and so will avoid them, thus ensuring that no new imprinting occurs.

REVERSIBILITY

Lorenz believed that once imprinting had taken place, it could not be 'undone' or reversed. However, there are many experimental demonstrations of reversibility, such as those of Guiton (1966), Salzen and Sluckin (1959) and Salzen (1967).

Guiton (1966), for example, found that ducklings imprinted on farmyard chickens still tried to mate with other ducks when they became sexually mature, and ducklings imprinted on a pair of yellow rubber gloves showed normal sexual preferences after being familiarized with other ducks. Domestic cocks would only try to mate with a yellow rubber glove if they had been reared alone; early imprinting on the glove was clearly reversed if this was followed by contact with females of the species.

Irreversibility is probably more a feature of imprinting in natural settings than the laboratory.

So what kind of learning is imprinting?

1) As far as the 'following' element is concerned, it seems that even if this is prevented, imprinting will still occur. Baer and Gray (1960) individually exposed 32 domestic chicks to a guinea-pig, separated by a glass wall, thus preventing any bodily contact or overt following. A few

days later, they chose the familiar guinea-pig significantly more often than an unfamiliar one.

Similar results were found by Molz (1960). Baer and Gray (1960) concluded that, 'imprinting is not a learning to follow, but a learning of the characteristics of the parent-object'.

In a similar vein, Sluckin (1965) argues that *'exposure learning'* is the essential process involved; this is similar to the 'perceptual learning' described by Bateson (1966) who found that exposing chicks to a colour pattern in their home pens both subsequently facilitated imprinting to that pattern *and* discrimination learning involving that pattern. Bateson concluded that both perceptual learning and imprinting involve S–S (Stimulus–Stimulus) associations, independent of any Response–Contingent reinforcement. In other words, the young bird is learning *about* the stimulus, to recognize it, not to follow it as such and any following which does occur does so *as a consequence* of this perceptual learning.

Lorenz would certainly agree that imprinting is a different kind of learning altogether from conditioning, but he argued that imprinting is more or less instantaneous. However, it is now clear that the longer a bird is exposed to an object the stronger its preference for that object becomes.

2)   As far as imprinting being *supra*-individual, there can be no doubt that, when a young bird learns the characteristics of its parent and follows it, the learning is of a *particular* parent bird and so cannot be described as supra-individual (characteristic of the species in general).

It seems that learning an attachment to the parent precedes the learning which will determine its sexual preferences when mature. The latter, according to Bateson (1978b), involves learning the characteristics of siblings as well as those of the parent and serves to ensure that the individual will both breed with a mate of the same-species and also *not* breed with a very close relative.

3)   As originally defined by Lorenz, imprinting did not seem to be a very wide-spread phenomenon but was confined to a few species of precocial birds. However, according to Suomi (1982), since the early 1970s there has been a substantial change in how ethologists (and developmental psychologists) have come to view imprinting. Now it is considered to be a very common phenomenon in many species (including many breeds of fish, insects, sheep, deer, buffalo, dogs and goats, higher primates and human beings). For example, a human infant will respond selectively to its own mother's breast-pads by three days after birth (MacFarlane, 1975) and to her voice by thirty days at the latest (Mehler et al, 1978; both cited in Lea, 1984; see Chapter 10). Lea (1984) suggests that imprinting-like processes may be involved in this rapid learning (and may be further examples of the instinctive 'concept' which requires specific experience to 'flesh it out'—see above). However, imprinting is no longer seen as confined to attachment-behaviours but can apply to choice of habitat, preferences for specific foods, learning communications, signals, choice of sexual partner and control of aggression. 'As such, the existence of sensitive phases most likely represents a general psychological principle of development' (Suomi, 1982).

So what are the developmental mechanisms responsible for these sensitive periods? Suomi (1982) believes that these are generally unknown. But he cites some highly suggestive evidence for at least one case of imprinting, namely 'sexual imprinting' in zebra finches. The sensitive phase usually lasts between days 15–45 after hatching and their choice of mate will last the rest of their life. Studies of sexual imprinting (Immelman and Wolff, 1980; cited in Suomi, 1982) have tried to identify possible changes in the structure of the birds' brain which might coincide or overlap with the sensitive period.

On about day 21, there begins a massive cell death in the hyperstriatum. This is followed by a period of secondary growth and synapse formation by the remaining neurons in the hyperstriatum, which is largely completed by day 45. Of course, the evidence is only 'circumstantial' (correlational)—we cannot rule out the possibility that imprinting is 'marked' in other parts of the brain or that the emergence and establishment of imprinting preference is not completely limited to the sensitive period. However, the best current evidence suggests *something* is going on in the zebra finch hyperstriatum at the very same time that the bird establishes a life-partner preference. And the same brain area does *not* change substantially at any time once the sensitive phase has passed.

Suomi (1982) speculates that the zebra finch case represents a specific case of a far more general developmental principle, namely that:

> For any developing brain region, during that period when the greatest neuronal cell death occurs and the most secondary synaptic connections are subsequently found, stimuli that impinge on that brain area will become 'imprinted' in the pattern of emerging synapses. The organism will be especially sensitive to such stimuli during this period, and thereafter it will be able to 'remember' such stimuli as long as the synapses involved remain functional. (Suomi, 1982)

Of course, different brain regions develop at different rates in different species, so you would expect major differences in the sensitive period from region to region and species to species. Where cell death and secondary neuronal growth occur during a short and well-defined period, the sensitive period will correspondingly be short and well defined and the behaviours/preferences established largely permanent (as in filial imprinting in ducks and geese and sexual imprinting in zerba finches). But this would not apply to attachment to the mother in monkeys, apes and humans (Bowlby, 1969). Here the sensitive period is much more drawn out and the resulting behavioural tendencies more easily altered in later life. Again, where secondary synapses continue to be formed throughout life, there is no sensitive period as such—the organism will continue to absorb new information and establish new behavioural tendencies well into maturity (eg some association areas of the human brain).

Finally, although the specific mechanisms underlying phenomena based on sensitive periods no doubt differ from case to case and species to species (Immelman and Suomi, 1981), a general rule seems to be that the *timing* of the sensitive period is nearly always in the genes—the timing of cell migration, orientation, growth, interconnection, etc. in any particular brain region is largely genetically determined. However, *which* nerve cells survive is largely a product of *environmental stimulation*, ie the information which actually gets 'imprinted' in the subject's brain depends entirely on what stimuli it is exposed to during the sensitive phase. It is determined by the subject's environment—it is impossible to separate the two sets of factors; development is a product of both in interaction with each other (Suomi, 1982).

SOCIOBIOLOGY

Perhaps the best way of introducing the sociobiological approach is to consider an example which it seems particularly well suited to explain, namely *biological altruism*.

BIOLOGICAL ALTRUISM (OR: ARE RABBITS REALLY THAT UNSELFISH?)

The animal kingdom abounds with examples of altruistic behaviours that are instantly understandable in human terms. For instance, certain small birds, such as robins, thrushes and titmice, warn others of the approaching threat from a hawk. They crouch low and produce a distinctive thin reedy whistle. Because of its acoustic properties, the source of the whistle is very difficult to locate. Nevertheless, by giving the warning signal an individual is drawing attention to itself in a dangerous situation and a more selfish act would be to keep quiet. Dolphins will often group round an injured individual to push it to the surface where it can breath, rather than abandon it. In African wild dogs, the most social of all carnivorous mammals, one sees altruism in a social context. When there are young in the pack most adults go off on a hunting expedition leaving the pups to be cared for by an adult, usually, but not always, the mother. When the hunters return they regurgitate food for all the animals in the camp, which occasionally also includes sick and crippled individuals. (Wilson, 1976).

Chimps display an interesting form of altruism—they temporarily abandon their normally vegetarian diet and indulge in meat eating. Adult chimps (usually the males) sometimes hunt and catch young monkeys and through a system of elaborate begging gestures other troop members can share with the catch. Curiously, they do not share in this way with leaves and fruit.

Perhaps most striking of all is the altruism of the social insects, who display, '. . . altruistic suicide comparable with that sometimes displayed by man . . .' (Wilson, 1976). A large percentage of ants, bees and wasps are ready to defend the nest with an insane charge against intruders, which may involve inevitable suicide through their heads being ripped off (as in the social stingless bees of the tropics), viscera torn out (honey bee workers) or their whole body being blasted by 'exploding glands' (an African termite).

And, of course, there is the altruistic rabbit.

By drumming its feet on the ground, it increases the chances of other rabbits escaping and, ultimately, producing offspring while at the same time reducing its own chances (by, for example, drawing attention to itself or wasting valuable seconds before it makes its getaway).

THE PARADOX OF ALTRUISM (OR: BUT AREN'T RABBITS NATURALLY SELFISH?)

From the point of view of Darwin's theory of natural selection, it is truly remarkable for members of a species to help each other in such a way and quite the opposite of what could be considered 'natural'. According to

Darwin (*The Origin of Species*, 1859) individual animals survive if they are able to adapt to their environment by virtue of physical (and behavioural) characteristics they possess and which are produced by random genetic variation, or mutation. These better-adapted individuals will, on average, have more offspring and, since those offspring will tend to carry the genes for those adaptive characteristics and behaviours, those genes and characteristics became more and more commonplace in the population.

In this way animal populations become differentiated and when different strains become so different that they can no longer interbreed (because their genotypes are too dissimilar), a new species has evolved. This process of natural selection, therefore:

> ... operates single-mindedly and relentlessy in favour of traits that improve the chances of survival and the number of offspring of the *individual* animal acting. (Brown, 1986)

But surely this is the complete reverse of what happens when an animal acts altruistically? Any animal which regularly acted in a way which benefitted others by risking its own safety and survival would be drastically reducing its own chances of having any offspring at all—these individuals would not last long enough to reproduce successfully! Natural selection predicts that individuals will act to the benefit of themselves alone and *not* their group or species.

The 'paradox of altruism' refers to this apparent contradiction between Darwin's theory of natural selection and observed facts about altruistic behaviour in a number of species. Is it possible for an animal to behave altruistically *and* in accordance with the laws of natural selection at the same time? It seems so, because altruism turns out to be only *apparent*, ie altruistic behaviour is only *selfish behaviour in disguise* and, to understand this, we need to shift our attention away from the individual, self-contained, organism to the *gene* as the fundamental unit of evolution. This is the approach of sociobiology, the selfish gene instead of the selfish rabbit.

THE SOCIOBIOLOGICAL SOLUTION

Sociobiology represents an extension of Darwin's evolutionary theory and was defined by Wilson (1975), one of its most prominent exponents, as 'the systematic study of the biological basis of all social behaviour'. It attempts to understand all types of social behaviour (including altruism, aggression, dominance and sexual behaviour) in evolutionary terms and this extends to human social behaviour.

Hinde (1982), believes that Wilson's 1975 book, *Sociobiology: The New Synthesis*, represents a landmark in biology, integrating population biology, ecology, ethology and related disciplines and helping to bring evolutionary theory and behavioural biology together. However, Hinde is also very critical of Wilson's claims that, eventually, sociobiology would engulf ethology and comparative psychology and that behaviour should be reduced to neurophysiology and sensory physiology. As Hinde points out, altruism for example, can, by definition, only apply to a dyad or larger group and *not* to an individual (see Chapter 2). So how does sociobiology resolve the 'paradox of altruism'?

The most general explanation of apparent altruism is Hamilton's theory of *kin selection* (1964). If we think of an individual animal as a *set of genes* rather than as a separate, 'bounded' organism, then it should be regarded as *distributed across kin*, that is, it shares some proportion of its genes with relatives, according to how close the relationship is. It follows that it is possible for an individual to preserve its genes through its own self-sacrifice—if a mother dies in the course of saving her three offspring from a predator, she will have saved $1\frac{1}{2}$ times her own genes (since each offspring inherits one half of its mother's genes). So, in terms of genes, an act of apparent altruism can turn out to be extremely selfish—surrendering your own life as an individual may reap a net profit as far as the survival of your genes in your relatives is concerned (see *The Selfish Gene* by Dawkins, 1976).

This means that individuals are selected to act *not* to maximize their own fitness (measured in terms of their own survival and reproduction) but to maximize their *inclusive fitness* (measured in terms of their own survival and reproduction *and* that of relatives; Hinde, 1982). Imagine a gene which in some way programmed an individual to give its life for others: one copy of the gene would disappear from the population when the altruist died but if the act saved the life of more than two offspring or siblings (each having 50 per cent of its genes in common with the altruist), then the altruistic gene would *still* increase in frequency.

Thus we seem to have resolved the paradox presented by examples of self-sacrifice; when a male lion defends his mate, or a honey bee dies when stinging an enemy, or a mother bird attracts a predator away from her offspring by feigning a broken wing, we can invoke the principle of inclusive fitness to explain apparently altruistic behaviour which is, fundamentally, selfish:

> . . . how can altruism, which by its nature reduces individual fitness, possibly evolve by natural selection? The answer is kinship, the sharing of common genes by related individuals . . . (Wilson, 1976)

While all the examples of self-sacrifice we noted earlier amongst the social insects involve individuals which are either sterile or of very low reproductive potential:

> . . . by their sacrifice they are (in terms of Darwinian fitness) increasing the reproductive chances of their fertile relatives thus ensuring that their (shared) genes are transmitted to future generations . . . (Wilson, 1976)

However, we are left with another difficulty—what should we make of cases of altruism on the part of animals which are *not* related? Clearly, kin selection cannot accommodate such cases. Trivers (1971) has proposed the principle of '*delayed reciprocal altruism*', by which animals will 'return favours' to other animals which have done them a good turn, or, a good turn is worthwhile because it is likely to be reciprocated. For example, male baboons who do not have a female partner sometimes form a temporary alliance with another solitary male baboon: while the latter attacks a male who is 'courting' a female and so distracts the male's attention, the former mates with the female. Those males who often give this kind of help seem to be more likely to receive help in return, so that reciprocation occurs (Packer, 1977).

Similarly, young baboons direct their grooming behaviour towards individuals who will later benefit them. Young females tend to groom dominant adults females who may be powerful allies in the troop in the future, while young males, who will later leave the troop, tend to groom the more subordinate females, with whom they are likely to be allowed to practise mating.

According to Hinde (1982), other examples are best understood as individuals achieving better results if they make a joint effort (almost a case of 'two heads are better than one'). For instance, it pays two pied wagtails to defend a winter feeding territory, even though they are not related, because in this way then can achieve a higher feeding-rate.

SOCIOBIOLOGY AND HUMAN NATURE

According to Wilson, to understand behaviour we need to look at our evolutionary history—both in the recent period as hominids (ie the past 10 million years or so) and as part of the animal kingdom as a whole:

> ... the role of Sociobiology with reference to human beings ... is to place the social sciences within a biological framework ... constructed from a synthesis of evolutionary studies, genetics, population biology, ecology, animal behaviour, psychology and anthropology ... (Wilson, 1976)

In the last chapter of the original *Sociobiology—The New Synthesis* (1975), and later in *On Human Nature* (1978), Wilson argues that all aspects of human culture and behaviour (like the behaviour of all animals) are coded in the genes and have been moulded by natural selection.

Wilson acknowledges that about 100,000 years ago, *cultural* evolution became more important than biological evolution:

> ... As a result it seems clear that human social evolution is more cultural then genetic. Nevertheless, I consider that the underlying emotion of altruism, expressed powerfully in virtually all human societies, is the consequence of genetic endowment ... (Wilson, 1978)

The critical issue for sociobiology, according to Wilson, is the relative contributions to human behaviour of genetic endowment and environmental experience.

Our overall social behaviour, he says, most closely resembles that of Old World monkeys and apes (our closest relatives biochemically and anatomically)—this is exactly what you would expect if behaviour is not based on experience alone but a result of the interplay between experience and the pattern of genetic possibilities. It is the evolution of this pattern which Sociobiology seeks to analyse.

He includes within the list of human patterns, aggression (including greater aggressiveness of males and their dominance over females), the mother–child bond, language, the incest taboo, the sexual division of labour, altruism, allegiance, conformity, ethics, genocide, indoctrinability, love, spite, territoriality and xenophobia.

These behaviours constitute a universal 'human nature' and are thus shared by *all* human societies; they are the expression of specific genetic structures and are, therefore, the result of evolutionary adaptation through natural selection.

But are these claims justified?

1) One criticism made of Wilson is that the image of society he depicts

is today's European–American capitalist society but clearly many societies do not fit this mould. Any exceptions to his claimed universal human behaviours he calls 'temporary' aberrations or deviations.

2) Is there any direct evidence for the existence of specific genetic structures for the social behaviours listed above?

> ... up to the present time no one has ever been able to relate any aspect of human social behaviour to any particular gene or set of genes, and no one has ever suggested an experimental plan for doing so. Thus, all statements about the genetic basis of human social traits are necessarily purely speculative, no matter how positive they seem to be. (Rose et al, 1984)

3) In some ways a more fundamental criticism is to do with the Sociobiologists use of *metaphors*, which are then mistaken for the 'real thing', while the source of the metaphor is forgotten. The first step is to describe animal societies in terms of human societies. For example, 'slave-making' species of ants capture immature members of 'slave' species; when the captured ants hatch they perform housekeeping tasks with no compulsion, as if they were members of the slave-making species (making 'domestication' a more appropriate term than 'slavery').

The second step is to 'rederive' the human behaviour from the animals', ie human slavery is now seen as a special case of a general phenomenon which has been independently discovered in other species. The error (or perhaps the 'trick') lies in forgetting where the original metaphor came from in the first place!

Using this tactic:

> ... It is a short step to assert that magic, religion, ritual and tribalism are evolutionary genetic adaptations in human societies ... Human institutions thus appear natural, universal and genetically based. (Science as Ideology Group, 1976)

4) Another logical error made by sociobiologists is that they treat categories like slavery, dominance, aggression, tribalism and territoriality as if they were natural objects with a concrete reality:

> ... rather than realizing that these are historically and ideologically conditioned constructs ... (Rose et al, 1984)

Mistaking abstract concepts for concrete objects is called *reification*, a very serious logical error which crops up in various places in psychology (eg intelligence—see Chapter 28).

5) Finally:

> Sociobiology is a reductionist, biologically determinist explanation of human existence ... (Rose et al, 1984)

(See Chapter 2.) Again:

> ... Genetics has as little to tell us about human societies as nuclear physics has to tell us about genetics. In the same way that we do not turn to physics to understand genetics, we should not turn to genetics in order to understand human history and culture. (Science as Ideology Group, 1976)

16 Pro- and Anti-social Behaviour

Kidney donors and rabbits banging their feet on the ground have very little in common at first sight. However, on closer inspection, they do seem to share the element of doing something for the benefit of others. This is self-evident in the case of one person donating a kidney to another person; in the case of the rabbit, banging the feet is used as a warning to other rabbits of some threat or danger (see Chapter 15).

These are both examples of *altruism*, which is really the opposite of selfishness. However, is it possible for an apparently unselfish act to be motivated by basically selfish ends, whether in people or rabbits?

Doing things for others represents a basic social value and so, by definition, is *pro*social. Aggression represents a major form of *anti*social behaviour because, as it is normally defined, it is harmful to, and may even destroy, the person at whom it is directed.

To arrive at a more complete understanding of both altruism and aggression we shall look at them from a number of perspectives, in particular, social psychology, which makes heavy use of laboratory experiments.

Biological and Psychological Altruism

An important distinction is that between biological and psychological altruism, which roughly apply to non-human species and human beings respectively. We could not normally attribute the rabbit which warns its fellow-rabbits of an approaching hunter with altruistic *motives* or *intentions* (we would be guilty of *anthropomorphism* if we did); in a sense this is simply part of its biologically-determined repertoire of behaviour to start banging its feet under certain environmental conditions. So the kind of altruism discussed in the previous chapter is *biological*.

Conversely, in the case of a human kidney donor, we would normally expect the decision to donate to be based on a number of considerations and values; there is certainly no necessity or inevitability about it, and as well as arousing strong feelings, the matter will raise many moral, religious and practical questions. We usually infer altruistic motives and intentions from altruistic acts. Here we are talking about *psychological* altruism.

BIOLOGICAL ALTRUISM IN HUMANS

In terms of *kin selection*, the situation is far more complex among humans than it is with animals. One reason for this, according to Brown (1986), is that the closeness of kinship is construed very differently from one society to another, so there is no simple correspondence between perceived and actual (genetic) kinship. If altruistic behaviour directly reflected actual kinship, rather than learned conceptions of kinship, it would be impossible for adoptive parents to give their adopted children the quality of care they do.

Taking this argument a step further, whole professions and occupations are concerned with helping other, unrelated, people (while at the same time providing a living for those who do the helping). As a species, much of our behaviour is altruistic and kin selection can only account for a small portion of our total behaviour-for-others; some principle such as *delayed reciprocal altruism* is also needed. However, we are still trying to impose a biological explanation on human social behaviour and this may not be the most appropriate way of trying to understand it; as Brown (1986) says:

> Human altruism goes beyond the confines of Darwinism because human evolution is not only biological in nature but also cultural, and, indeed, in recent times primarily cultural. (Brown, 1986)

This brings us to psychological altruism.

PSYCHOLOGICAL ALTRUISM (IS IT POSSIBLE TO BE TOTALLY UNSELFISH?)

Strictly defined, altruism is an act performed for the sake of another person without any personal gain or self-interest. But is there such a thing as a completely unselfish act?

According to Brown (1986), when someone donates a kidney to a relative, they are likely to be rewarded both *extrinsically* (for example, praise and gratitude of the recipient) and *intrinsically* (the satisfaction of having saved a relative's life, for instance) and, to this extent, is not being a true—or pure—psychological altruist (although donating an organ *is* an act of biological altruism).

However, what such donors do is quite extraordinary. About 88 per cent report having made the decision to donate, if asked, immediately upon being notified by the doctor that they might be required to do so and the decision is often made before being informed of the costs or risks. So what about kidney donors to unrelated strangers?

They are clearly biological altruists as is anyone who risks their life for another, but are they psychologically altruistic? Is it possible to donate one of your bodily organs and not feel some sense of pride or satisfaction?

However, Brown (1986) believes that 'rewards' are not all on the same moral level; in general, *extrinsic rewards* (eg money) are considered less morally worthy than *intrinsic ones* (eg satisfaction at doing one's duty):

> We must conclude that cultural evolution, not biological, has produced moral principles that can powerfully reward actions that are in accord with them. (Brown, 1986)

BYSTANDER INTERVENTION—ALTRUISM OR APATHY?

One of the major ways in which social psychologists have investigated altruism is by studying people's readiness to go to the aid of someone who is in danger or has suffered an accident of some kind. Two of the original researchers in this area were Latané and Darley (1968) whose inspiration was a real event involving a murder victim, Kitty Genovese (Box 16.1).

Box 16.1   The Case of Kitty Genovese (From New York Times, *March 27th, 1964)*

37 Who Saw Murder Didn't Call the Police

Apathy at Stabbing of Queen's Woman Shocks Inspector

By Martin Gansberg

For more than half an hour 38 respectable, law-abiding citizens in Queens watched a killer stalk and stab a woman in three separate attacks in Kew Gardens.

Twice the sound of their voices and the sudden glow of their bedroom lights interrupted him and frightened him off. Each time he returned, sought her out and stabbed her again. Not one person telephoned the police during the assault; one witness called after the woman was dead.

That was two weeks ago today. But Assistant Chief Insepctor Frederick M. Lussen, in charge of the borough's detectives and a veteran of 25 years of homicide investigations, is still shocked.

He can give a matter-of-fact recitation of many murders. But the Kew Gardens slaying baffles him—not because it is a murder, but because the 'good people' failed to call the police.

'As we have reconstructed the crime,' he said, 'the assailant had three chances to kill this woman during a 35-minute period. He returned twice to complete the job. If we had been called when he first attacked, the woman might not be dead now.'

This is what the police say happened beginning at 3.20 a.m. in the staid, middle-class, tree-lined Austin Street area:

Twenty-eight-year-old Catherine Genovese, who was called Kitty by almost everyone in the neighborhood was returning home from her job as manager of a bar in Hollis. She parked her red Fiat in a lot adjacent to the Kew Gardens Long Island Rail Road Station, facing Mowbray Place. Like many residents of the neighborhood, she had parked there day after day since her arrival from Connecticut a year ago, although the railroad frowns on the practice.

She turned off the lights of her car, locked the door and started to walk the 100 feet to the entrance of her apartment at 82–70 Austin Street, which is in a Tudor building, with stores on the first floor and apartments on the second.

The entrance to the apartment is in the rear of the building because the front is rented to retail stores. At night the quiet neighborhood is shrouded in the slumbering darkness that marks most residential areas.

Miss Genovese noticed a man at the far end of the lot, near a seven-story apartment house at 82–40 Austin Street. She halted. Then nervously, she headed up Austin Street toward Lefferts Boulevard, where there is a call box to the 102d Police Precinct in nearby Richmond Hill.

'He Stabbed Me!'

She got as far as a street light in front of a bookstore before the man grabbed her. She screamed. Lights went on in the 10-story apartment house at 82–67 Austin Street, which faces the bookstore. Windows slid open and voices punctured the early-morning stillness.

Miss Genovese screamed: 'Oh, my God, he stabbed me! Please help me! Please help me!'

From one of the upper windows in the apartment house, a man called down: 'Let that girl alone!'

The assailant looked up at him, shrugged and walked down Austin Street toward a white sedan parked a short distance away. Miss Genovese struggled to her feet.

Lights went out. The killer returned to Miss Genovese, now trying to make her way around the side of the building by the parking lot to get to her apartment. The assailant grabbed her again.

'I'm dying!' she shrieked.

'I'm dying!'

A City Bus Passed

Windows were opened again, and lights went on in many apartments. The assailant got into his car and drove away. Miss Genovese staggered to her feet. A city bus, Q-10, the Lefferts Boulevard line to Kennedy International Airport passed. It was 3.35 a.m.

The assailant returned. By then, Miss Genovese had crawled to the back of the building where the freshly painted brown doors to the apartment house held out hope of safety. The killer tried the first door; she wasn't there. At the second door, 82–62 Austin Street, he saw her slumped on the floor at the foot of the stairs. He stabbed her a third time—fatally.

It was 3.50 by the time the police received their first call, from a man who was a neighbor of Miss Genovese. In two minutes they were at the scene. The neighbor, a 70-year-old woman and another woman were the only persons on the street. Nobody else came forward.

The man explained that he had called the police after much deliberation. He had phoned a friend in Nassau County for advice and then he had crossed the roof of the elderly woman to get her to make the call.

'I didn't want to get involved,' he sheepishly told the police.

Suspect is Arrested

Six days later, the police arrested Winston Moseley, a 29-year-old business-machine operator, and charged him with the homicide. Mosely had no previous record. He is married, has two children and owns a home at 133–19 Sutter Avenue, South Ozone Park, Queens. On Wednesday, a court committed him to Kings County Hospital for psychiatric observation.

The police stressed how simple it would have been to have gotten in touch with them. 'A phone call', said one of the detectives, 'would have done it.' The question of whether the witnesses can be held legally responsible in any way for failing to report the crime was put to the Police Department's legal bureau. There, a spokesman said:

'There is no legal responsibility, with few exceptions, for any citizen to report a crime.'

Statutes Explained

Under the statutes of the city, he said, a witness to a suspicious or violent death must report it to the medical examiner. Under state law, a witness cannot withhold information in a kidnapping.

Today witnesses from the neighborhood, which is made up of one-family homes in the $35,000 to $60,000 range with the exception of the two apartment houses near the railroad station, find it difficult to explain why they didn't call the police.

Lieut. Bernard Jacobs, who handled the investigation by the detectives, said:

'It is one of the better neighborhoods. There are few reports of crimes.

You only get the usual complaints about boys playing or garbage cans being turned over.'

The police said most persons had told them they had been afraid to call, but had given meaningless answers when asked what they had feared.

'We can understand the reticence of people to become involved in an area of violence,' Lieutenant Jacobs said, 'but where they are in their homes, near phones, why should they be afraid to call the police?'

He said that his men were able to piece together what happened—and capture the suspect—because the residents furnished all the information when detectives rang doorbells during the days following the slaying.

'But why didn't someone call us that night?' he asked unbelievingly.

Witnesses—some of them unable to believe what they had allowed to happen—told a reporter why.

A housewife, knowingly if quite casual, said, 'We thought it was a lovers' quarrel.' A husband and wife both said, 'Frankly, we were afraid.' They seemed aware of the fact that events might have been different. A distraught woman, wiping her hands in her apron, said, 'I didn't want my husband to get involved.'

One couple, now willing to talk about that night, said they heard the first screams. The husband looked thoughtfully at the bookstore where the killer first grabbed Miss Genovese.

'We went to the window to see what was happening,' he said, 'but the light from our bedroom made it difficult to see the street.' The wife, still apprehensive, added: 'I put out the light and we were able to see better.'

Asked why they hadn't called the police, she shrugged and replied, 'I don't know.'

So the concept of the *'unresponsive bystander'* was born and soon after this event, which horrified the American nation, Latané and Darley began their scientific investigation of the phenomenon. Before we look at the research in detail, one major conclusion should be mentioned: while the American media thought it remarkable that out of 38 witnesses not a single one did anything to help, Latané and Darley believed that it was precisely *because* there were so many that Kitty Genovese was not helped.

How does the presence of others contribute to the intervention (or lack of it) of a particular individual in an emergency and what other influences are involved?

There seem to be three major factors which, together, help determine the probability of someone going to the aid of another. There is a logical sequence involved, such that defining the situation as an emergency (one requiring the assistance of another) is necessary for the question of responsibility to arise— which, in turn, is necessary for the costs of intervention to be weighed up. Even then, intervention is not certain to happen.

i) *DEFINING THE SITUATION (WHEN IS AN EMERGENCY NOT AN EMERGENCY?)*

In one of the first of the bystander experiments (Latané and Darley, 1968), subjects were shown into a room in order to complete some questionnaires. In one condition they were alone, in another condition there were two others present. After a while, steam (resembling smoke) began to pour through a vent in the wall. The test was to see how quickly subjects reacted. If no one reacted within six minutes, the experiment was terminated, by which time the steam was so thick is was difficult to see the questionnaires. 75 per cent of subjects working alone reported the smoke, half of them within two minutes, while 62 per cent of those in the three-person groups carried on working for the full six minutes. In only one three-person group was it reported within the first four minutes.

Latané and Rodin (1969) obtained similar results when subjects heard the female experimenter in an adjoining room fall, cry out and moan. Subjects were much faster to react when alone than when others were present. In post-experimental interviews, each subject reported feeling very hesitant about showing anxiety to the other subjects, so they looked to other subjects for signs of anxiety, but since everyone was trying to appear calm, these signs were not found and each subject defined the situation as 'safe'. This is called *pluralistic ignorance*.

In a variation of Latané and Rodin's experiment, 70 per cent of subjects on their own responded within 65 seconds; two friends together responded within a similar time; two strangers together were less likely to react at all, but more slowly if they did; and if a subject was paired with a confederate who had been instructed not to intervene at all, they showed the least and slowest reaction of all.

Can pluralistic ignorance account for the inaction of the witnesses to Kitty Genovese's murder? There seems little doubt that they realized at the time what was going on. Although one woman claimed that she thought it was a 'lover's quarrel', most claimed they were afraid to intervene (they did not deny that help was needed!) and Kitty's second lot of screams (if not the first) must have made the nature of the situation quite unambiguous.

Genuine ambiguity may sometimes account for lack of intervention, as in situations of domestic violence. According to Shotland and Straw (1976) we would be much more likely to help a victim if we believed he/she did not know the attacker than if we believed a relationship existed between the two. Male subjects were shown a staged fight between a man and a woman. In one condition the woman screamed 'I don't even know you', while in another, she screamed 'I don't even know why I married you!' Three times as many subjects intervened in the first condition.

ii) DIFFUSION OF RESPONSIBILITY (WHEN DOES AN EMERGENCY OBLIGE ME TO INTERVENE?

Darley and Latané (1968) recruited college students to discuss some of the problems faced by those attending college in a high-pressure urban environment: instead of face-to-face discussion, they communicated via an intercom system so as to avoid any embarrassment. Each participant would talk for two minutes and then each would comment on what the others had said. The 'other' participants were, in fact, tape recordings. The first voice that was heard said, in a rather embarrassed way, that he was prone to seizures, especially during stressful situations such as exams. When his turn came to give his comments, he began with a few calm, coherent statements and then began to 'experience a seizure'. Darley and Latané were interested in the percentage of subjects who responded within five minutes (by coming out of the small room to look for the victim). Of those who believed they were the only other participant, 85 per cent intervened; of those who believed there were two others (three altogether), 62 per cent intervened; and of those who believed there were five others (six altogether), only 31 per cent intervened. The most responsive group was also the fastest to respond. These findings were confirmed by Latané et al (1981).

How can we explain such findings? While the presence of others may make it less likely that we will define a situation as an emergency in the first place ('if the others look calm and aren't rushing around there can't be anything wrong'), when we do so define it, we may nevertheless decide that somebody else will probably do what is necessary, and the more bystanders that are present (or believed to be present), the lower the probability that any one of them will accept responsibility. This is more likely to happen when the victim is remote, eg can only be 'heard' from some other room in the building (as in the seizure experiment). Kitty Genovese could both be heard and seen (by those who made the effort to look out of their windows) and the second lot of screams must have made it obvious that no one had gone for help after the first lot!

So to pluralistic ignorance we can add *diffusion of responsibility* as a way in which the presence of other people can *inhibit* us and make it less likely that we will intervene and offer help.

Related to diffusion of responsibility, and something which may interact with it, is the *competence* of the bystander to intervene and offer appropriate help (as perceived by the bystander). In the presence of others, one or more of whom you believe are better equipped to offer help, diffusion of responsibility will be even greater. However, if you believe you are the one who is best equipped to help, the presence of others will have relatively little effect on your behaviour.

For example, if a swimmer is in trouble, we will usually let the lifeguard go to the rescue. And even if we were the only other person at the pool, we would be extremely unlikely to dive in if we couldn't swim ourselves! But if we are an excellent swimmer and are trained in life-saving skills, we would be much more likely to help even if others were present (Baron and Byrne, 1991).

Cramer et al (1988) found that, when a bystander was present, registered nurses were more likely to offer help to an accident victim than college students were. When no bystander was present, the college students, despite a lack of medical training, were just as likely to offer help as the nurses.

Piliavin et al (1981) pointed out what they believe is a confusion between *diffusion*, which occurs when responsibility is accepted by the subject but shared by all the witnesses, and *dissolution* which occurs when the behaviour of other witnesses cannot be observed and the subject 'rationalizes' that someone else must have already intervened. However, whichever label is applied, all the studies confirm the original finding that the presence of others inhibits an individual from intervening (Pilivian et al, 1981), and yet there are limits to diffusion of responsibility. Piliavin et al (1969) found that help was offered on crowded subways in New York as frequently as on relatively empty ones. As Brown (1985), suggests, perhaps it is more difficult to refuse help in a face-to face situation and in an enclosed space.

iii) THE COST OF INTERVENTION—WHAT'S IN IT FOR ME?

Studies of bystander intervention have been interpreted in terms of Exchange Theory, which applies the concepts of rewards, costs and profits to social interaction, in particular to bystander intervention and interpersonal relationships (see Chapter 18). To the extent that this is a valid interpretation, people are being shown to be fundamentally selfish—altruism is apparent and not real.

Rewards (R, benefits or positive outcomes) are anything which is desirable and the avoidance of anything undesirable (a negative reinforcement in operant conditioning terms) while costs (C, or negative outcomes) are anything which is undesirable and the deprivation or foregoing of rewards. Profit (P, or net benefit or outcome) is calculated according to the formula $P = R - C$.

According to Exchange Theory, the tendency to engage in a social action will increase as the promise of its profitability increases (relative to alternative actions). A witness to an emergency (whether it is an accident or a crime) finds they are in a situation where there is much to lose and little to gain: costs can include being assaulted, being late for work and having to appear in court to give evidence, (can this help explain the inaction of the Kitty Genovese wtinesses?) while the rewards may amount to little more than a possible 'thank you'. According to Brown (1986), this is a profitless situation from which most of us would want to escape.

THE COST OF TIME

The importance of *loss of time* as a motive for *not helping* was shown in a content analysis of answers given in response to five written traffic-accident scenarios (Bierhoff et al, 1987). We are often in a hurry in many real-life situations and waiting can be very frustrating; hence the willingness to sacrifice time for a person in need can be seen as generous (time is money; Bierhoff and Klein, 1988). The most often mentioned motives for helping were enhancement of self-esteem and moral obligation; also quite common were empathy and reciprocity.

Another relevant—and revealing—study is that of Darley and Batson (1973), whose subjects were students at a theological seminary. They were instructed to present a talk, in a nearby building—for half of them, the talk was to be on the Good Samaritan, for the other half, it was to be about jobs most enjoyed by seminary students. Each subject was then told: (i) he was ahead of schedule and had plenty of time (to get to the other building; (ii) he was right on schedule, or (iii) he was late. On the way to give their speech, all the subjects passed a man slumped in a doorway, coughing and groaning (a confederate). Although the topic given for the talk had little effect on helping, time pressures did—the percentages offering help were 63, 45 and 10 for conditions (i), (ii)) and (iii), respectively.

Ironically, on several occasions, the 'late' students who were on their way to talk about the Good Samaritan literally stepped over the victim!

> This experiment shows that seemingly trivial variables can exert a profound effect on altruistic responses . . . (Bierhoff and Klein, 1988)

By contrast, Bierhoff (1983) asked students to volunteer for a psychology experiment. If they participated without payment, the money would be sent to children in need. They could choose up to 12 half-hour sessions and, on average, students volunteered for 3.71 sessions:

> In summary, these results indicate that the general level of helpfulness is higher than some pessimists might have assumed. The willingness to work two hours for people in need is a substantial contribution which should be taken as an indication that people tend to be altruistic in many situations. (Bierhoff and Klein, 1988)

Certain kinds of low-cost altruism seem to be fairly common, such as giving a stranger directions or telling them the time. Latané and Darley (1970) had psychology students approach a total of 1500 passers-by in New York to ask them such routine, low-cost, favours; depending on the nature of the favour, between 34 and 85 per cent of New Yorkers proved to be 'low-cost altruists'. However, most people refused to tell the student their name.

THE COST OF HELPING DIFFERENT KINDS OF VICTIM

Going to a person's aid (having defined the situation as an emergency and accepted the responsibility) seems to depend to a significant degree on the characteristics of the person needing help, since how the 'victim' is perceived contributes greatly to the net profit (or loss) expected from the intervention.

In the New York subway field experiment (Piliavin et al, 1969) student experimenters pretended to collapse in subway train compartments—they fell to the floor and waited to see if they were helped. Sometimes they would be carrying a cane, sometimes they would wear a jacket which smelled very strongly of alcohol and would be carrying a bottle in a brown paperbag. As predicted by Exchange Theory, help was offered much *less* often in the 'drunk' condition than the 'lame' condition (20 per cent compared with 90 per cent within 70 seconds). In a second study, the person who 'collapsed' bit off a capsule of blood-like dye and this trickled down his chin; the helping rate dropped from 90 per cent to 60 per cent. People were much more likely to get someone else to help, especially someone they thought would be more competent in an emergency (Piliavin and Piliavin, 1972).

These two studies illustrate what we said earlier about the joint effects of diffusion of responsibility and perceived competence to intervene.

Similarly, Piliavin et al (1975) found that when the victim had an ugly facial birthmark, the rate of helping dropped to 61 per cent. Other studies have reported that a stranded motorist who is dressed smartly and is well groomed is far more likely to receive help from passing motorists than one who is casually dressed and has long hair.

In general, it seems that the greater the victim's distress, injury or disfigurement, or the more disapproving we are of them (especially if we blame their plight on their undesirable behaviour—as in the case of drunk victims), the more likely we are to perceive them as being different from ourselves, which, in turn, makes it *less* likely that we will offer them help. The psychological costs of helping someone perceived as being different from ourselves seem to be greater than the same help offered to someone perceived as being similar. On this basis, we would expect help to be offered less often to someone of a different racial group from the bystander; however, the evidence is not as clear-cut as this (Piliavin et al, 1981). They argue that whatever a person's racial attitudes, they may want to project an unprejudiced self-image or may genuinely believe that they are not prejudiced (even if tests suggest otherwise), so that to not offer help because of the victim's race might incur greater psychological costs than to do so. For example in the New York subway experiment, there was no evidence of same-race helping when the victim was apparently ill, but when he appeared drunk, blacks were much more likely to help a black drunk and whites a white drunk.

In terms of the Arousal:Cost-Reward Model (Piliavin et al, 1969; 1981) we can predict the likelihood of someone giving help by comparing the costs of helping and not helping and this has been done by Piliavin et al (1981; Table 16.1). We should be aware that what is high

Table 16.1 *The costs of helping and not helping in emergencies and non-emergencies and the likelihood of help being offered. (Based on Piliavin et al, 1969, 1981)*

COST AND LIKELIHOOD	EXAMPLE
The costs of helping are *low*	(eg you are not likely to be injured yourself, the victim is only shocked).
The costs of *not* helping are *high*	(eg you would feel guilty, others would blame you).
Likelihood of intervention: very high (and direct).	
The costs of helping are *high*	(eg you do not like the sight of blood, you are unsure what to do).
The costs of *not* helping are *high*	(eg it is an emergency, the victim could die).
Likelihood of intervention: fairly high (but indirect, eg phoning for the ambulance or police or asking some other bystander to assist).	
The costs of helping are *high*	(eg 'This drunk could turn violent or over-friendly').
The costs of *not* helping are *low*	(eg 'Who would blame me for not helping?').
Likelihood of intervention: very low (a common response is to turn the other way or change seats or even compartments).	
The costs of helping are *low*	(eg 'It wouldn't hurt me to see this blind man across the street').
The costs of *not* helping are *low*	(eg 'He seems capable of looking after himself and there are plenty of other people crossing anyway').
Likelihood of intervention: fairly high (although people will vary considerably).	

cost for one person may be low cost for another (and vice-versa) and this may differ, for the same person, from one situation to another (and even from one occasion to another, depending on mood, for example).

The Arousal:Cost-Reward Model was first introduced by Piliavin et al (1969) as a 'heuristic device' in attempting to account for the results of the New York subway experiment (see Gross, 1990) and was subsequently revised and expanded to cover both emergency and non-emergency helping (Piliavin et al, 1981).

The model identifies two conceptually distinct but functionally interdependent influences on helping:

(a) *Arousal* in response to the need or distress of others is an emotional response which is the basic *motivational* construct; when attributed to the distress of the victim, it is experienced as unpleasant and the bystander is motivated to reduce it.

(b) *Cost-reward* involves *cognitive* processes by which bystanders assess and weigh up the anticipated costs and rewards associated with both helping and not helping. (This corresponds to the Exchange Theory explanation; the arousal component is what distinguishes the Arousal:Cost-Reward Model from Exchange Theory).

There are five propositions making up the model, all of which have been extensively tested and the results of these studies have been reviewed by Dovidio et al (1991); we shall consider the first four here.

(a) ... People are aroused by the distress of others and exhibit emotionally empathic reactions to the problems and crises of others ... also ... the severity and clarity of another person's emergency and the relationship to the victim systematically influence arousal ... (Dovidio et al, 1991)

(b) ... research demonstrates that emotional reactions to others' distress play an important *causal* role in motivating helping. (Dovidio et al, 1991)

(c) As we have seen, reviews such as that of Piliavin et al (1981) showed that as net costs of helping increase, so intervention decreases. More recent studies have shown that costs may be operationalized in various ways, including psychological aversion based on physical stigma, potential embarrassment, fear of disapproval, relative unfamiliarity with the helping task and pain associated with helping. Conversely, as potential rewards associated with helping increase, so intervention increases. Help is also more likely when it is perceived as effectively improving the victim's condition and when feedback about its effectiveness is possible. Consistent with Piliavin et al's (1981) review, people are generally more helpful when the victim is perceived to be in greater need or distress, seen as more dependent and more deserving of help (eg ill rather than drunk).

A distinction is made between two kinds of costs associated with *not* helping, namely *personal costs* (eg self-blame, public disapproval) and *empathy costs* (eg knowing that the victim continues to suffer):

... In general ... costs for *not* helping affect intervention primarily when the costs *for* helping are low. (Dovidio et al, 1991)

Although *indirect* helping is more likely to occur when the costs for helping are high, it is relatively infrequent when the costs for helping are low. An even more common way of resolving the high-cost-for-helping/high-cost-for-not-helping dilemma is *cognitive reinterpretation* ie redefining the situation as one *not* requiring help, diffusing responsibility, or denigrating (blaming) the victim. These all have the effect of reducing the perceived costs of not helping. (They could be seen as *rationalizations* which reduce the bystander's cognitive dissonance; see Chapter 19.)

(d) Impulsive helping is more likely in emergencies that are clear-cut, more realistic (when staged) and involve a prior relationship between the bystander and the victim. These factors also relate to the bystander's *arousal*—Piliavin et al (1981) speculated that high levels of arousal in impulse-generating situations, through narrowing the focus of attention, could interfere with a broad and rational consideration of costs.

They also hypothesized that trait and state characteristics of the bystander (personality and gender differences) and the nature of the bystander–victim relationship could influence both arousal and cost-reward processes.

Personality Differences

People who are characteristically more sensitive to the needs of others might experience greater arousal in response to another's plight or experience this arousal more negatively or perceive greater costs for *not* helping. Helpers are generally more 'other-oriented' (versus 'self-oriented') than non-helpers.

One particularly interesting study (Oliner and Oliner, 1988) compared 231 non-Jews who helped save Jews in Nazi Europe with 126 non-savers; the former had stronger beliefs in equality and showed greater empathy.

As Table 16.1 shows, individual differences will have their main impact when both the costs for helping and not helping are *low*, and when the situation is ambiguous and 'psychologically weak' or less 'evocative'. But the more emergency-like the situation (and hence the more compelling and evocative it is), the less relevant person variables will be. Indeed, several studies have failed to find personality differences in helping in emergency situations.

Gender Differences

Women may experience greater empathy for others' needs than men and are more attentive to others' needs, which would predict greater helping by women. On the other hand, Eagly and Crowley (1986) reviewed 172 studies and found that men turn out to be significantly more helpful than women. How can these facts be reconciled? One answer is to do with traditional gender roles on the one hand, and the kind of helping required in most experimental studies of bystander intervention on the other.

The female gender role involves *communal* helping—caring for others, providing friends with more personal favours, emotional support, counselling about personal problems, etc. than men. By contrast, the male gender role involves *agentic* helping (Eagly, 1987), namely heroism and chivalry; thus they are more likely to help another when there is an audience present to witness the helping act or other potential witnesses are available. Most studies of bystander intervention (at least those involving emergencies) seem to require *agentic* helping.

We-ness

> This ... connotes a sense of connectedness or the categorization of another person as a member of one's own group ... (Piliavin et al, 1981)

The closer the relationship to the person in need, the greater the initial arousal and costs for not helping, while the costs for helping will be lower. (This would cover both biological *and* psychological altruism; see above.)

Evaluation of the Arousal: Cost Reward Model—Are We Fundamentally Selfish?

Why do we help others? According to Batson and Oleson (1991), we want to know whether helping is *always and exclusively* motivated by the prospect of some benefit for ourselves, however subtle:

> . . . We want to know whether anyone ever, in any degree, transcends the bounds of self-benefit and helps out of genuine concern for the welfare of another. We want to know if altruism exists. (Batson and Oleson, 1991)

Advocates of *universal egoism* claim that everything we do, no matter how noble and beneficial to others, is really directed towards the ultimate goal of self-benefit. Advocates of the *empathy–altruism hypothesis*, while not denying that much of what we do (including much that we do for others) is egoistic, claim that there is much more than just egoism—at least under some circumstances we are capable of a qualitatively different form of motivation, with the ultimate goal of benefiting someone else.

Over the centuries, the most frequently proposed source of altruism has been *empathy*, an other-oriented emotional response associated with the perceived welfare of the other person. Empathic emotions include sympathy, compassion, tenderness and so on, and are associated with *empathic concern*.

These empathic emotions can and should be distinguished from the more self-oriented emotions of discomfort, anxiety and upset which are associated with *personal distress*. (This corresponds to the distinction made above between *personal* and *empathic costs* for not helping.) While *personal distress* produces an *egoistic desire* to reduce *one's own* distress, *empathic concern* produces an *altruistic desire* to reduce the *other's* distress. These are qualitatively different. Let us give the final word to Darley, one of the two pioneers of bystander intervention research, who is clearly a *universal* (or at least a Western-capitalist) *egoist*:

> In the United States and perhaps in all advanced capitalistic societies, it is generally accepted that the true and basic motive for human action is self-interest. It is the primary motivation, and is the one from which other motives derive. Thus it is the only 'real' motivation, a fact that some celebrate and some bemoan but most accept. To use currently fashionable vocabulary, the perspective that asserts the primacy of self-interest, and the ideologies within which that primacy is contained and justified, is now the 'privileged' perspective in our society. To suggest that human actions could arise for other purposes is to court accusations of naïveté or insufficiently deep or realistic analysis. (Darley, 1991)

AGGRESSION

We all seem to recognize aggression when we witness it but defining it often proves much more difficult. When used as a noun, aggression usually conveys some behaviour which is intended to harm another (or at least which has this effect). Yet even this is too broad a definition, since self-defence and unprovoked attack may both involve similar 'amounts' and types of aggression but only the latter would normally be considered 'anti-social' (and the law also recognizes this distinction).

When used as an adjective, aggression sometimes conveys an action carried out with energy and persistence (Lloyd et al, 1984), something which may even be regarded as socially desirable.

It is almost exclusively in the former sense that psychologists have studied aggression and it is also largely aggressive *behaviour* which is the object of study, partly because it is easier to observe and measure than, say, the subjective emotion of aggression.

A number of other important distinctions have been made; eg *hostile* aggression is aimed solely at hurting another ('aggression for the sake of aggression', and so would exclude self-defence) while *instrumental* aggression is a means to an end (and so would include self-defence; Buss, 1961; Feshbach, 1964).

Humanistic psychologists (Maslow, 1968) have distinguished between: (i) *natural* or positive aggression, which is aimed largely at self-defence or combating prejudice and other social injustice; and (ii) *pathological* aggression or violence, which results when our inner nature has become twisted or frustrated.

The distinction between aggression and violence is commonly made. Brown (1985), for example, maintains that, whereas aggression does not necessarily involve physical injury, violence involves the use of great force or physical intensity. Similarly, Moyer (1976) argues that aggression may be no more than verbal or symbolic but violence denotes, 'a form of human aggression that involves inflicting physical damage on persons or property'.

If we combined Moyer's definition with that of Baron and Byrne (1991): '...the intentional infliction of some form of harm on others...', we should have a pretty good idea of what psychologists have in mind when they write about aggression, although they do not always make it clear how they conceptualize the concept (Brown, 1985).

THE NATURE AND NURTURE OF AGGRESSION

The study of aggression represents another example of the nature–nurture issue: the question being asked is whether aggression, as a characteristic of human beings, is biologically determined or the product of learning and environmental influences, and we shall be drawing on a number of theoretical approaches, namely the Ethological, the Neurophysiological, the Psychoanalytic and Learning Theory.

THE ETHOLOGICAL APPROACH

Ethology (and Sociobiology) was discussed in detail in Chapter 15.

As far as aggression is concerned, it is instinctive in all species and is clearly important in the evolutionary development of the species, allowing individuals to adapt to their environment, survive in it and, hence, successfully reproduce. When space or food are scarce, many species limit their reproduction and survive by marking off living space which they defend against 'trespassers'; this is known as *territoriality*. Aggressiveness is clearly important in competing successfully for limited resources, in defending territory and for basic survival. Are there any human parallels?

According to Ardrey (1966), in *The Territorial Imperative*, people strive to acquire land and possessions, form strong attachments to them and are willing to defend (sometimes violently) what they believe is rightfully theirs. However, to infer from these superficial similarities that a fundamentally similar territorial instinct is at work is greatly to over-simply human behaviour, which is vastly more complex than any comparable animal behaviour.

Probably the most famous and most comprehensive ethological account of human aggression is that of Konrad Lorenz in *On Aggression* (1966). He believes that it is legitimate to make direct comparisons between different species, although his theory of human aggression is based on the study of non-primates and mainly non-mammals, in particular, fish and insects. He defines aggression as, 'the fighting instinct in beast and man which is directed *against* members of the same species'. In animals it is basically constructive, but in humans it has become distorted. In what ways?

Probably the major differences between animal and human aggression is to do with *ritualization*, which refers to a way of discharging aggression in a fixed, stereotyped, pattern whereby fights between members of the same species result in relatively little physical harm to either victor or vanquished but at the same time allow a victor to emerge. For instance, the fighting that takes place between stags is highly ritualized and the triumphant one is the male who 'makes his point' rather than the one who kills or incapacitates his opponent. In the same way, wolves will end their fight with the loser exposing its jugular vein—but its exposure is sufficient and no blood is spilled. (This is rather like two sword-fighters, one of whom loses his sword and faces his victor, inviting him to 'run me through' but, by this stage, the fight has already been won and lost.)

Sometimes, antagonists may approach each other in a threatening manner but not actually engage in combat—one will show *appeasement rituals* (or gestures) which prevent the other from engaging in actual conflict. For example, in one species of jackdaws, individuals live in close proximity and to prevent mutually destructive conflict, a very effective appeasement gesture has developed; the nape section at the bottom of the head is clearly marked off from the rest of the body by its plumage and colouring and when one bird 'offers' its nape to an aggressor, the latter will never attack, even if on the verge of doing so. Similarly, in many species a male never 'seriously' attacks a female because the female displays the appropriate appeasement rituals when the male begins to show aggressive 'intent'.

So through these various kinds of ritual, animals avoid destroying each other. But in human beings, according to Lorenz, although aggression remains basically adaptive, it is no longer *under the control* of rituals. This does *not* mean that human appeasement responses are not effective (eg smiling, cowering, cringing, or begging for mercy) and, indeed, Lorenz and Eibl-Eibesfeldt believe that they are normally *very* effective. So what is it about human beings that makes them appear so aggressive?

According to Lorenz, it is their *technololgy*. However naturally aggressive human beings are as a species compared with other species, their superior brains have enabled them to construct weapons which remove combat from the eye-to-eye situation and so the effectiveness of appeasement rituals is reduced. Indeed, the deadliest weapons (as measured by the number of victims who can be killed or injured at one time) are precisely those which can be used at the greatest distance from the intended victims (eg bombs and intercontinental nuclear missles). According to Lea (1984), 'We have developed a technology which enables our intentions to override our instincts.'

Criticisms of Lorenz

1)   In keeping with his belief that humans are naturally highly aggressive, Lorenz maintains that their 'natural condition' is that of 'warrior'. However, he seems to be in a minority of one in this respect. It is generally agreed that early man was not a warrior but a 'hunter–gatherer' (such as the present-day Eskimos, Pygmies of the Ituri forest, Aborigines, Kalahari Bushmen, the Punan of Borneo and so on), who live in small clans which hardly ever come into contact with other groups of people (Siann, 1985).

2)   If early man was, indeed, a warrior, we would expect his close evolutionary relatives to be highly aggressive also. However, the evidence is certainly mixed here. Behaviour within and between groups of primates is predominantly peaceful, and it is not obvious that man's ancestors were any less deadly than other species—even without the most primitive weapons, other primates, including chimps, can and do kill each other.

Goodall (1978) describes warfare between two colonies of chimps which ended in the killing of every male in one of the groups and Lea (1984) points out that infanticide is one of the more common kinds of unrestrained aggression among animals. He cites Hardy's (1977) study of Hanuman langurs, an Indian monkey species, in which incoming males commonly kill infants despite the attempts of females to resist this male aggression.

Infanticide is not confined to primates: male lions that succeed in taking over a 'pride' of females (so displacing other adult males) will often attack and kill any cubs that are present (which then makes the females more available for mating). So Lorenz seems to have greatly overstated the case when he claimed that animal aggression always stops before an animal is killed. Lea (1984) believes that, although there is some truth in Lorenz's claim, it is basically a myth.

According to Leakey and Lewin (1977a), cultural influences are far more important determinants of human aggression than biological factors. Whatever potential for aggression we may have inherited as a species, it is culturally-overridden and re-packaged into forms which fit current circumstances. In most cases, cultural forces teach or support non-aggression but when pro-social aggression is necessary (including disciplining children and wrong-doers, assertiveness, self-defence and even warfare), cultural processes teach and sustain it.

Siann (1985) argues that primates and man are characterized by their responsiveness and adaptiveness to the world around them (eg food, weather, terrain); their behaviour is, typically, not stereotyped and unpredictable and humans are unique in being able to pass on the experience of each generation to future generations through language and customs.

3)   Lorenz's view of aggression, in humans and animals, as being *spontaneous* rather than reactive, has been criticized. Like the other three instincts or drives (namely, hunger, sexuality and flight, which collectively he calls the 'big four'), aggressive behaviour occurs *not* in response to environmental stimuli but spontaneously when instinctive aggressive energy builds up and demands discharge. The evidence for this energy-model is very sparse indeed. According to Siann (1985) it amounts to the male cichlid fish, which attacks its female mate, and an anecdote about Lorenz's maiden aunt! This view of aggression as being inevitable because aggressive energy builds up, unrelated to external events, has come under fire from many contemporary biologists and ethologists, who believe that aggression in animals is reactive and modifiable by a variety of internal and external conditions (Hinde, 1974). (Lorenz's 'hydraulic' model of instinct was discussed in Chapter 15.)

If Lorenz is correct, it should be possible to show specific changes in certain physiological measures before and after aggression (Siann, 1985); but it has proved impossible to do so.

4)   Although it is generally agreed that fighting between animals of the same species is highly ritualized, some critics of Lorenz (Shuster, 1978) have pointed out that he did not take account of how the *goals* of behaviour influence the degree of ritual; for example, antelopes are much more likely to use rituals when fighting over territory than when competing for a sexual partner.

5)   Learning plays no part in Lorenz's theory of aggression which, at least when applied to primates and human beings, makes it inadequate. Cultures differ in the degree and kind of aggression which are permissible and socializing influences can override any innate differences which may exist between males and females (see Mead's study of three New Guinea tribes; Chapter 23).

THE NEUROPHYSIOLOGICAL APPROACH

Much of the evidence for the role of the brain in aggression is based on animal experiments and so any generalization to human beings must be cautiously made.

According to Green (1980), the study of emotion in animals has been concerned almost exclusively with the study of aggression and much of the experimental study of aggression has concentrated on the *limbic system*. The limbic system (see Chapter 4) comprises a number of structures, including the thalamus, hypothalamus, hippocampus, amygdala, septum, cingulate gyrus, olfactory bulbs and mammillary bodies. These are situated in the upper brain-stem and inner surfaces of the cerebral hemispheres, and the limbic system as a whole plays a major role in regulating emotional and sexual behaviour; in vertebrates it is also involved in fight and flight ('emergency') responses.

Early twentieth-century studies showed that if parts of the cortex of cats and dogs are destroyed, '*sham rage*' is produced (so named, by Masserman, because the cat could be stroked and even purr while simultaneously showing all the signs of rage); this suggests that the cortex normally acts as an inhibitor of sub-cortical structures (including the limbic system).

Bard (1928) found in cats that this sham rage, produced by removal of the cortex, largely disappeared if the hypothalamus was also removed (in fact, the rage becomes fragmented, with unsheathed claws but without an arched back). Conversely, the whole of the cerebral cortex could be removed without destroying the rage response and stimulation of the hypothalamus would produce attack behaviour.

So it appears that the hypothalamus is essential for the full expression of aggression (and, indeed, of all emotional behaviour).

Later research has shown that stimulation or destruction of the amygdala can produce either placidity or rage, depending on the precise location. According to Lloyd et al (1984), this suggests that the amygdala plays a controlling or moderating role and that the hypothalamus plays an integrative role. Destruction of the septum produces aggressiveness and hyper-emotionality (lack of emotional control). Papez (1937) claimed that the limbic system includes a set of interconnected pathways and centres (since known as the *Papez circuit*) which play a vital role in aggressive behaviour. His research included post-mortems of the brains of people (who had suffered emotional disorders) as well as rabid dogs.

If the amygdala is removed from the brain of a dominant monkey in a social group, on its return to the colony, it quickly loses its place in the hierarchy having become more docile.

Many studies have confirmed that amygdala damage produces placidity (it has a 'taming effect') which is part of the Kluver-Bucy (1937) syndrome which also includes hypersexuality and hyperorality (putting objects in the mouth).

Moyer (1976) has identified a number of different kinds of aggression (based on ethological studies), including instrumental, inter-male, predatory, fear-provoked, territorial, irritable, maternal and hierarchical. These are meant to apply to both animals and humans and represent related but functionally different behaviours. For each one there is an innate system of neural organization in the brain and an appropriate stimulus which activates the innate system (rather like a sign stimulus triggering a FAP; see Chapter 15). For example, predatory aggression is controlled by the lateral hypothalamus, amygdala and hippocampus and is activated by the animal's natural prey. However, there is no conclusive evidence that 'aggression centres' exist, as Siann (1985) says, and even in rats and cats the elicitation of aggressive behaviour usually depends on aspects of the experimental situation (such as whether or not other animals or objects are present, the strength of the electrical stimulation and the state of the experimental animal itself, such as whether it is hungry or not).

There is no single area in the limbic system of primates which functions autonomously or which directs all the other areas. It is also known that the limbic system of primates is massively interconnected with the brain's thinking and reasoning centres which are located in the cortex (Siann, 1985): those areas involved in aggression are closely related to those which process information from the environment.

Delgado (1967, 1971) implanted electrodes in the brains of several members of a monkey colony and the 'aggression area' of selected monkeys was stimulated (through radio transmission). A monkey's position in the hierarchy had a strong influence on how it behaved when its brain was stimulated. When a dominant male was stimulated, he would attack subordinate males but not females, while when a subordinate male was stimulated, he would show cowering and submissive behaviour in the presence of a dominant male but would attack a submissive partner.

Clearly, these monkeys possess brain mechanisms which allow them to behave aggressively, but the triggering of these mechanisms depends upon other areas of the brain which receive and process information from the environment. What about humans?

Stimulating the limbic system of certain patients can produce fear and anger and, in a study of 46 epileptic patients, it was found that stimulating the amygdala produced fear in just two, while the rest reported confusion or did not respond at all.

Only in a few cases has stimulation of the amygdala actually produced aggressive outbursts or violent attacks of rage and overall the evidence from these kinds of studies is very inconclusive.

There are a number of reports of abnormalities of the limbic system (eg atrophy, tumours and lesions) being associated with abnormal behaviour (including extremely irritable and even explosive behaviour) and there is some evidence that limbic tumours are associated with abnormally aggressive behaviour.

According to Siann (1985), the evidence linking temporal lobe epilepsy and violent behaviour is weak and controversial, as is all the evidence regarding brain abnormalities and aggression or violence. Even if a strong and consistent relationship were found, this would not show that particular abnormalities actually *cause* violent behaviour or that specific brain areas are responsible for the control of aggression—other physical, psychological, social and environmental factors may be involved.

Based on Moyer's ideas, Geen (1990) believes that it is helpful to assume that specific, innate brain systems underlie different kinds of human aggression and that specific stimulus situations are responsible for producing each type of aggression. For example, insults produce angry aggression, promises or rewards for fighting produce instrumental aggression. The innate systems are also linked to a specific pattern of motor behaviour by which the aggression is acted out, thus giving each type its peculiar form. Each system is also connected with the reticular activating system (RAS). In this way, the aroused person is both more attentive to stimuli which provoke the aggression and more aggressive than the less-aroused person.

Siann (1985) also reviews studies of biochemical and genetic influences. She concludes that no particular chemical messenger, neural transmitter, hormone or other substance (such as alcohol or drugs) has been shown to have an, 'invariant specific effect on the predisposition to aggressive emotion or violent behaviour'; the evidence regarding the role of genetic factors is equally weak.

THE PSYCHOANALYTIC APPROACH

Freud's theory will be discussed in detail in Chapter 29, where we shall see that his personality theory is normally regarded as an instinct theory.

It was not until late in his life that Freud recognized aggression as an instinct distinct from sexuality (libido) and it was the horrific carnage of the First World War (1914–18) which provided the impetus for the re-working of his theory of aggression. In *Beyond the Pleasure Principle* (1922) and *The Ego and the Id* (1923) he distinguished between the Life Instincts (or *Eros*), including sexuality, and the Death Instinct (*Thanatos*).

Thanatos represents an inborn destructiveness and aggression, directed primarily against the self. The aim (as with all instincts in Freud's view) is to reduce tension or excitation to a minimum and, ultimately, to its total elimination. This was the idyllic state we enjoyed in the womb, where our needs were met as they arose and, for a while, at our mother's breast, but after this, the only way of achieving such a Nirvana is through death.

However, self-directed aggression conflicts with the Life Instincts (particularly the self-preservative component), so we eroticize it by combining it with libido (producing sadism, masochism and sado-masochism), direct it towards others or take some of this outwardly-directed aggression back into our own personality in the form of the superego (the moral part of personality; see Chapter 27).

Freud believed that we must destroy some other thing or person if we are not to destroy ourselves, so strong is the impulse to self-destruction; paradoxically, conflict with the Life Instinct results in our aggression being displaced onto others. More positively, aggression can be sublimated into sport, physical occupations, and domination and mastery of nature and the world in general.

Like Freud, Lorenz also argued that we need to acknowledge our aggressiveness and to control it through sport (eg the Olympics), expeditions, explorations and so on, especially if international co-operation is involved (activities which Lorenz called 'displacement' activities). Another similarity between them is the view of aggression as *spontaneous* and not reactive, that is, aggressive energy builds up until eventually it has to be discharged in some way.

Some support for Freud (and Lorenz) is provided by studies of people who commit brutal crimes. Megargee (1966), for example, reported that brutally aggressive crimes are often committed by *overcontrolled* individuals; they repress their anger and over a period of time the pressure to be aggressive builds up. Often it is an objectively trivial incident which provokes the destructive outburst, with the aggressors returning to their previously passive state and once more seeming incapable of violence (Box 16.2).

Ultimately, of course, Thanatos always wins its struggle with Eros and sometimes it enjoys a premature victory in the form of suicide.

Unlike his ideas on sexuality, Freud's ideas on aggression made little impact either on the public imagination or on other psychologists (including other psychoanalysts) until the publication of *Frustration and Aggression* by Dollard et al (1939), *Human Aggression* by Storr (1968) and *The Anatomy of Human Destructiveness* by Fromm (1977).

Storr, a psychoanalyst, dedicated his book to Lorenz and in the Introduction to the book, he says:

> That man is an aggressive creature will hardly be disputed. With the exception of certain rodents, no other vertebrate habitually destroys members of his own species. No other animal takes positive pleasure in the exercise of cruelty upon another of his own kind. We generally describe the most repulsive examples of man's cruelty as brutal or bestial, implying

---

Box 16.2   The Over-Controlled Violent Criminal (Megargee, 1966)

In case after case the extremely assaultive offender proves to be a rather passive person with no previous history of aggression. In Phoenix, an 11-year-old boy who stabbed his brother 34 times with a steak knife was described by all who knew him as being extremely polite and soft spoken with no history of assaultive behaviour. In New York an 18-year-old youth who confessed he had assaulted and strangled a 7-year-old girl in a Queens church and later tried to burn her body in the furnace was described in the press as an unemotional person who planned to be a minister. A 21-year-old man from Colorado who was accused of the rape and murder of two little girls had never been a discipline problem and, in fact, his stepfather reported, 'When he was in school the other kids would run all over him and he'd never fight back. There is just no violence in him.' In these cases the homicide was not just one more aggressive offence in a person who had always displayed inadequate controls, but rather a completely uncharacteristic act in a person who had always displayed extraordinarily high levels of control:

> ...the extremely assaultive person is often a fairly mild-mannered, long-suffering individual who buries his resentment under rigid but brittle controls. Under certain circumstances he may lash out and release all his aggression in one, often disastrous, act. Afterwards he reverts to his usual overcontrolled defences. Thus he may be more of a menace than the verbally aggressive 'chip-on-the-shoulder' type who releases his aggression in small doses. (Megargee and Mendelsohn, 1966)

---

by these adjectives that such behaviour is characteristic of less highly developed animals than ourselves. In truth, however, the extremes of 'brutal' behaviour are confined to man; and there is no parallel in nature to our savage treatment of each other. The sombre fact is that we are the cruellest and most ruthless species that has ever walked the earth; and that, although we may recoil in horror when we read in newspaper or history book of the atrocities committed by man upon man, we know in our hearts that each one of us harbours within himself those same savage impulses which lead to murder, to torture and to war.

Storr identified four forms of psychopathology attributable to the inadequate resolution of the aggressive drive, namely depression, schizoid behaviour, paranoia and psychopathy (see Chapter 30).

Fromm, also a psychoanalyst, sees 'aggression' as covering emotions and behaviour motivated to enable the 'aggressor' to preserve or enhance his or her own position. Human beings, like most other animals, have a 'built-in' potential for defensive aggression which is fundamentally harmless; pathological aggression (eg cruelty and destructiveness) are not due to this inbuilt potential but to aggression-producing conditions in the environment. These pathological aspects of aggression can be woven into the individual's character structure by early emotional experiences, as evidenced by intensive explorations of historical figures such as Stalin, Himmler and Hitler.

THE LEARNING THEORY APPROACH

Intended partly to 'translate' some of Freud's psychoanalytic concepts into learning theory terms, Dollard, Doob, Miller, Mowrer and Sears published *Frustration and Aggression* (1939), in which they proposed their *Frustration–Aggression Hypothesis*. According to this:

> . . . aggression is always a consequence of frustration and, contrariwise, . . . the existence of frustration always leads to some form of aggression. (Dollard et al, 1939)

While agreeing with Freud that aggression is an innate response, Dollard et al argued that it would only be triggered by frustrating situations and events.

Some support for this view comes from the displacement of aggression, where a substitute object is found for the expression of aggressive feelings because they cannot be vented openly and directly towards their real target (see Chapter 29). An example of this displacement of aggression is the scapegoating found in prejudice (see Chapter 19) and a study by Barker et al (1941) found that children who were deliberately frustrated by being denied access to attractive toys behaved aggressively towards toys with which they were allowed to play.

However, it soon became apparent that the frustration–aggression hypothesis, in its original form, was an overstatement. Miller (1941) revised it by claiming that frustration is an *instigator* of aggression but situational factors (eg learned inhibition, fear of retaliation) may prevent actual aggressive behaviour from occurring. In other words, although frustration may make aggression more likely, it is far from being a sufficient cause of aggression.

Frustration can produce a variety of responses (of which aggression is but one), including regression (see Chapter 29), depression and lethargy (Seligman, 1975; see Chapter 6). Frustration may also produce different responses in different people in different situations. Kulik and Brown (1979), for example, found that frustration was more likely to produce aggression if it was not anticipated and if subjects believed that the person responsible for frustrating them did so deliberately, and without good reason, showing the importance of cognitive factors as cues for aggressive behaviour. Subjects were told they could earn money by telephoning people and persuading them to make a pledge to charity; some expected that about two-thirds of those contacted would agree to make a pledge, while others expected a very low response rate. All the people telephoned were confederates, none of whom agreed to pledge. The first group of subjects showed more aggression by slamming down the phone, speaking more aggressively, etc. Also, those given reasonable excuses (such as 'I can't afford it') showed less aggression than those given less reasonable excuses (such as 'Charities are a waste of time and a rip-off').

Bandura (1973) argued that frustration might be a source of *arousal*, but frustration-induced arousal (like other types of arousal) could have a variety of outcomes, of which aggression is only one. Whether it actually occurs is more the result of learned patterns of behaviour triggered by environmental cues.

A similar line of argument is that of Berkowitz (1966), who has proposed a number of modifications to the original frustration–aggression hypothesis. His major argument is that frustration produces *anger* rather than aggression; what is important about frustration is that it is psychologically painful and anything which is psychologically (or physically) painful can lead to aggression.

For anger or psychological pain to be converted into actual aggression, certain *cues* are needed; these are *environmental stimuli* associated either with aggressive behaviour or with the frustrating object or person.

In a series of experiments, Berkowitz used the same basic procedure whereby, when subjects arrive, they are told they will be participating with another person (a confederate) in a study concerned with the effects of stress on problem-solving ability. To do this, they will be asked to offer a written solution to a problem. Stress will be introduced by their solution being evaluated by the other subject, who will deliver between 1 and 10 electric shocks to them (according to their evaluation of the solution). After completing their solutions, half the subjects receive a single shock, while the rest receive seven, the lower number of shocks indicating a very favourable evaluation.

Then subjects watch either an aggressive film, depicting a brutal prize fight (starring Kirk Douglas) or a non-aggressive film showing highlights of an exciting track race. Finally, they are presented with a problem solution supposedly written by the confederate and are asked to indicate their evaluation of it by giving an appropriate number of shocks, just as had happened to them. Aggression is measured in terms of both the *number* and *duration* of the shocks the subject delivers.

Berkowitz and Geen (1966) introduced the confederate to the real subject either as *Bob* Anderson or *Kirk* Anderson. As expected, the largest number of shocks were delivered by subjects who were angry (had received seven shocks from the confederate), had witnessed the violent film and believed the confederate's name was Kirk—his name was linked to the witnessed aggression through *Kirk* Douglas.

Berkowitiz and Le Page (1967), in a similar experiment, found that angry subjects delivered more shocks to the confederate if a rifle and revolver were nearby than when neutral objects such as badminton rackets were present. (This is known as the *weapons effect*.)

These, and several other similar studies, seem to suggest that the mere physical presence of weapons, even when not themselves used in the performance of aggressive actions, may none the less increase the occurrence of such behaviour. As Berkowitz (1968) puts it, 'Guns not only permit violence, they can stimulate it as well. The finger pulls the trigger, but the trigger may also be pulling the finger.'

> ... While several experiments undertaken to replicate the original findings ... have succeeded in demonstrating a similar 'weapons effect' ... several others employing virtually identical procedures have failed in this respect ... (Baron, 1977)

There are also, clearly, strong ethical objections which can be made of such studies (see Chapter 3). But, despite these various criticisms:

> ... It is clear that Berkowitz's more general proposal that aggression is 'pulled' or elicited from without by external stimuli rather than merely 'pushed' from within has attained widespread acceptance ... his views in this regard have been highly influential in causing social psychologists to shift their search for the determinants of aggression largely from internal conflict and motives to external environmental factors ... (Baron, 1977)

SOCIAL LEARNING THEORY: THE INFLUENCE OF OBSERVING AGGRESSION

In Chapter 27 we shall look in detail at the work of Bandura and other Social Learning Theorists who believe that *observational learning* (or modelling) is a fundamental form of social learning over and above conditioning (see Chapter 7). A number of different kinds of evidence point towards the importance of models, including laboratory experiments (see Chapter 27) and field (real-life) correlational studies.

Perhaps the most important feature of social learning theory is how it has alerted us to the power of television as a source of modelling, especially for children, including, of course, the modelling of aggression and violence. However, before we can study the *effects* of TV violence, we need to ask: (i) *how much* actual violence is there on TV? and (ii) do viewers *perceive* violence in the same way as it is defined by researchers? Two questions specifically related to the *effects* of TV violence are: (i) *how* is TV supposed to have its effect on attitudes and behaviour? and (ii) *how* have these effects been studied? These questions are discussed in a review of the research literature by Gunter and McAleer (1990).

How Much Violence is there on TV?

> The basic method used by researchers to quantify the amount of violence on television uses simple counting techniques. Violence is defined objectively by researchers who then code samples of TV programmes for any incidents which match their own violence definitions... (Gunter and McAleer, 1990)

Perhaps the largest American study is that by Gerbner et al (1972) and Gerbner and Gross (1976), who monitored samples of all major network prime-time and weekend daytime programmes since 1967. They defined violence as:

> The overt expression of physical force (with or without a weapon) against self or other, compelling action against one's will on pain of being hurt or killed, or actually hurting or killing. (Gerbner and Gross, 1976)

Violent accidents and natural disasters were included.

This analysis of violence provided the framework for British research, beginning with Halloran and Croll (1972) and the BBC's Audience Research Department (1972). The latter was the more extensive of the two, spanning a six-month period and covering dramatic fiction, news, current affairs, documentaries and light entertainment. Both studies agreed that, although a common feature of programming, violence was not as prevalent on British TV as on American TV.

By far the largest and most recent British study to date is that by Cumberbatch (1987), commissioned by the BBC. It analysed all programmes broadcast on all four channels (with the exception of commercials and Open University) on four separate weeks, between May and September 1986. This amounted to 1412 hours of TV, 2076 programmes (930 BBC, 1146 ITV and Channel 4).

'Violence' was defined as:

> ... any action of physical force with or without a weapon against oneself or another person, animal or inanimate object, whether carried through or merely attempted and whether the action caused injury or not. Both intentional and accidental violence were included. Violent accidents and catastrophes were also covered but acts of nature were only included as violence if victims were shown. Verbal abuse and threats were coded separately... (Cumberbatch, 1987)

The primary unit for counting was the *violent act*, '...a coherent uninterrupted sequence of actions involving the same agents in the same role . . .' So, in a violent scene, if A attacked B, B retaliated and C intervened to help A defeat B, this would count as three violent acts.

What did Cumberbatch find?

Thirty per cent of progammes contained *some* violence. The overall frequency was 1.14 violent acts per programme, 1.68 acts per hour, each act lasts, on average, for 25 seconds, and so violence occupies just over 1 per cent of TV time. However, if boxing and wrestling are excluded, the average duration is 13 seconds, (0.5 per cent); if verbal threats are included, the average frequency rises to 1.96 acts per hour.

Top of the list were spy, fantasy, cartoon, war, detective, crime and thriller programmes, and bottom were quiz, game and chat shows, plus (non-contact) sports. However, injuries as such from violent acts were rare—on 26 per cent of occasions, violence resulted in death but in 61 per cent *no* injuries were shown as the victims simply showed pain or were stunned. Again, the portrayal was quite sanitized, with 83 per cent of violence showing no blood at all, while considerable blood and gore featured in only 0.2 per cent of cases. Only 13 per cent of violence was portrayed as retaliation, while aggressors were 50 per cent more likely to be baddies than goodies, taking place more than twice as often in a criminal context than in upholding the law:

> Compared with research carried out in the early 1970s the proportion of programmes containing violence has declined as have overall frequencies. However, within dramatic fiction there was less evidence for this—within specific types of programmes violent acts per hour had increased but the signs are that a marked decrease in potentially violent genres has taken place in the last few years. (Cumberbatch, 1987)

While about 75 per cent of people believe that there is *more* violence now on TV than there was about 10 years ago:

> . . . most people are mistaken. Violence and concerns about violence have clearly increased in society in the last decade but this has not been reflected by a proportional increase on television even in the news. (Cumberbatch, 1987)

He concludes by saying:

> . . . While broadcasters may take some comfort from our data on trends in television violence, they must expect to be continually reminded of their responsibilities in this area and be obliged to acknowledge that a significant minority of people will remain concerned about what's on the box. (Cumberbatch, 1987)

How do Viewers Perceive TV Violence?

Much of their concern, of course, centres on children. Cumberbatch found that, while violence was more likely after 9 p.m., and that generally violence in childrens' TV was rare, the main exception was cartoons. Indeed, much of the public controversy over the harmful effects of TV on children has focused on very popular cartoons such as 'Tom and Jerry' and 'Popeye'. American cartoons are twice as likely to be violent as British ones—but most cartoons are American.

However, do children take cartoons as representing 'reality'?

> . . . Viewers can be highly discriminating when it comes to portrayals of

violence. They do not invariably read into TV content the same meanings as do researchers. Merely knowing how often certain pre-defined incidents occur in programmes, does not tell us how significant these features are for viewers. Thus, viewers' perceptions of how violent TV is may not accord with objective counts of programme incidents. (Gunter and McAleer, 1990)

However, *realism* does appear to be an important element in viewers' perceptions of violence; real-life incidents in news and documentaries are generally rated as more violent than violence presented in fictional settings, thus:

> . . . The closer to everday life the violence is portrayed as being in terms of time and place, the more serious it is judged to be. (Gunter and McAleer, 1990)

Research suggests that children are very similar to adults as far as their judgements of the *amounts* of violent content is concerned. But their *ratings* of violence *do* differ from those of content analyses, ie programmes which are extremely violent according to 'objective' counts of violent acts can be seen by children as 'hardly containing any violence', and this is especially true of cartoons:

> . . . In reflecting the attitudes and perceptions of the audience, research into the amount of violence on TV, therefore, ought to include at least some subjective input from viewers. This would provide an indication of which types of programmes or portrayals viewers themselves regard as violent and with what degree of seriousness. (Gunter and McAleer, 1990)

How does TV Affect Attitudes and Behaviour?

Four specific effects of TV violence have been investigated—*arousal, disinhibition, imitation* and *desensitization.*

1) *Arousal* refers to a non-specific, physiological response, whose 'meaning' will be defined by the viewer in terms of the type of programme being watched (Zillman, 1978; see Chapter 6 on cognitive theories of emotion). Watching TV violence supposedly increases the overall level of emotional arousal and excitement. However, there does not seem to be any strong overall relationship between perceiving a programme as violent and verbal report of emotional arousal, but the more *realistic* the violence is perceived to be, the greater the reported arousal and involvement are likely to be.

2) *Disinhibition* refers to the *reduction of inhibition* about behaving aggressively oneself or coming to believe that aggression is a permitted or *legitimate* way of solving problems or attaining goals. Berkowitz's *aggressive cue theory* which we discussed earlier is relevant here.

3) *Imitation* is perhaps the most direct link between watching TV and the viewer's own behaviour. Bandura's studies of imitative aggression are relevant here and are discussed in detail in Chapter 27. But Social Learning theorists acknowledge the role of cognitive factors as mediating between stimulus and response, so what we have said about how TV violence is perceived and interpreted and the importance of realism are clearly crucial intervening variables (both in children and adults).

4) *Desensitization* refers to the reduction in emotional response to TV violence (an increased acceptance of violence in real life) as a result of

repeated viewing of TV violence. As with drug tolerance, increasingly violent programmes are required to produce an effect (ie an emotional response) in order to satisfy the 'need'.

A study by Drabman and Thomas (1974) supports the desensitization hypothesis. Eight-year-olds saw either a violent or a non-violent programme before witnessing a real (staged) fight between two other children in a playroom. The former were less likely to tell an adult what was happening than the latter.

How have the Effects of TV been Studied?

Most of the research which is related to these four proposed effects has consisted of *laboratory experiments*, designed to demonstrate the *causal* link between watching TV violence and increased viewer aggression. But most studies involve small, unrepresentative samples under highly contrived, unnatural viewing conditions:

> ... Their measures of TV viewing and aggression tend to be so far removed from normal everyday behaviour that whether laboratory findings have any meaning in the outside world is something which can be debated quite strongly. (Gunter and McAleer, 1990)

Much more *ecologically valid* are *field experiments*, in which children or teenagers are assigned to view violent or non-violent programmes for a period of a few days or weeks. Measures of aggressive behaviour, fantasy, attitude, etc. are taken before, during and after the period of controlled viewing. To ensure control over actual viewing, children in group or institutional settings are studied, mostly nursery schools, residential schools or institutions for adolescent boys. Almost without exception they confirm the results of laboratory studies—in general, children who view violent TV are more aggressive than those who do not.

A good example is a study by Parke et al (1977), whose subjects were Belgian and American male juvenile deliquents living in small-group cottages in low security institutions. Their normal rate of aggressive behaviour was assessed (using several measures of physical and verbal aggression) and then the boys in one cottage were exposed to five commercial films involving violence over a period of one week, while boys in another cottage saw five non-violent films during the same period. The former showed significant increases in aggressive behaviour for some of the categories but increases in *other* measures of aggression were confined to boys who were naturally high in aggression (and who saw the violent film).

Field experiments use real TV programmes which are viewed in natural settings and aggression occurs in a situation where naturally-occurring consequences are present.

However, the situation cannot be as well controlled as in the laboratory—we cannot be so sure that the *only* difference between the two groups is the kind of programme viewed, particularly as it is not always possible to assign subjects completely randomly. In the Parke et al study, for example, it was cottages (ie pre-existing groups) which were assigned to violent or non-violent programmes, *not* individuals. Also, by definition, such subjects (juvenile delinquent males) are hardly representative of children or adolescents in general. And when pre-schools are used, *home* viewing is not controlled during the study.

A common alternative to both laboratory and field experiments is the *correlational survey*, in which subjects indicate which programmes they like best and watch most often and the amount of violent content in these choices is then compared with measures of aggression given by peers, teachers, parents, self-reports (or some combination). The evidence from such studies is very inconclusive. The most consistent finding has been that the overall amount of viewing TV violence is related to self-reports of aggressive behaviour (Gunter and McAleer, 1990).

But, of course, it is possible that those who watch more violent television differ in other important respects from those who watch less (for instance, something to do with their personality and/or their family environment may account for their attraction to televised violence in the first place), in which case we cannot be sure that it is the observation of violence which causes their greater behavioural aggression.

Probably the most useful kind of study is the *longitudinal panel study* which, like experiments, but unlike correlational surveys, can tell us about *cause-and-effect* and which normally use sound sampling methods. The aim is to discover relationships which may exist or develop over time between TV viewing and social attitudes and behaviour, and so they are concerned with the *cumulative influence* of TV—the claim is that the link between the two should increase with age. So far, the evidence is mixed.

A major British study was carried out by Belson (1978) in which subjects were not actually studied at different points in time but were questioned *retrospectively* at a single point about their habits over the previous years (and so was a *simulated panel study*). Detailed and extensive interviews with teenage boys revealed a relationship between certain aspects of claimed viewing behaviour and attitudes and tendencies towards the use of violence in their lives—in particular, the more they claimed to watch certain types of dramatic TV (containing violence), the more likely they were to report having used aggression themselves under various circumstances.

However, the validity of these results has been questioned—for example, the boys were trying to recall viewing habits and behaviour for the preceding *ten* years.

However:

> ...The study does indicate usefully that certain types of programming may have a more significant impact than other types on anti-social behaviour among young viewers, and that it is not sufficient to examine only the overall amount of viewing that is done. (Gunter and McAleer, 1990)

In a three-year study of 3200 elementary school children and teenagers by Milavsky et al (1982), measures of verbal and physical aggressive behaviour were obtained by friends (in the case of the children) while the teenagers gave self-reports. The children were interviewed six times, the teenagers five times. They were given check-lists of programmes available on the major networks (pre-classified for violent content), so information was obtained both about general viewing patterns and levels of exposure to violent programmes. Only small associations were found, and:

> ... compared with the influence of family background, social environment

and school performance, the significance of television viewing as an indicator of aggressiveness was very weak. (Gunter and McAleer, 1990)

However, a study by Williams (1986) in Canada presents a very different picture. Naturalistic observation of childrens' behaviour was combined with teacher and peer ratings of their aggression in a community where TV had only recently been introduced for the first time. This community was compared with one in which there was a single TV channel and another which had several. The major finding was that aggressive behaviour in six- to eleven-year-olds increased over a two-year period following the introduction of TV but no such increase was found in those communities where TV was readily available. This was true for verbal and physical aggression, both sexes, and for longitudinal (children aged six to seven prior to TV reception and eight to nine two years later) and cross-sectional (children of the same age at each testing) samples, regardless of the child's initial level of aggression or how much TV they watched:

> In conclusion, the evidence in support of the hypothesis that viewing violence leads to an increase in aggressive behaviour is very strong. (Gunter and McAleer, 1990)

(This study is discussed further in Chapter 23 in relation to TV and sex role stereotyping.)

Conclusions

In their overall evaluation of the evidence, Gunter and McAleer state that:

> ... the measurement of television's effects, and of factors that mediate those effects, is highly complex ... we are still a long way from knowing fully the extent and character of television's influence on childrens' aggressive behaviour. (Gunter and McAleer, 1990)

TELEVISION VIOLENCE AND CATHARSIS

One argument in defence (if not in favour) of watching television violence is that witnessing others being aggressive will help the viewer to 'get it out of their system' (strictly, this is *vicarious catharsis*), thus making the viewer *less* likely to behave aggressively. The argument is based partly on Freud's and Lorenz's theory of aggression but the evidence appears to contradict it.

The basic research paradigm is that used by Berkowitz (see above p. 453).

The results of several such experiments show that: (i) regardless of the level of anger aroused, subjects who witness aggression deliver *more* shocks than those who witness non-violent programmes; (ii) anger-aroused subjects generally respond *more* punitively than non-aroused subjects; and (iii) anger-aroused subjects who witness violence respond *most* punitively of all. This last finding in particular contradicts the vicarious catharsis hypothesis and instead supports a social learning theory explanation.

However, rather than thinking of catharsis as a process which can occur in anybody, researchers are increasingly suggesting that if such a discharge of hostile feelings can occur at all, it is probably restricted to *certain types of personality* or those with high levels of certain cognitive skills, such as fantasizing and day-dreaming:

> ...For some children at least, fictional violence can have positive effects. Their research throws some doubt on the popular view that violence on television and in motion pictures is harmful to all children, even if they view a great deal. It seems that in the case of some youngsters, particularly those who have highly developed imaginations, the effect of these materials might even be beneficial. Violence ... may provide a means through which some children can reduce their angry feelings ... (Gunter and McAleer, 1990)

TELEVISION AND PRO-SOCIAL BEHAVIOUR

If social learning theorists are correct in what they say about the harmful effects of watching television, it follows that watching television can also be beneficial by promoting pro-social behaviour:

> ...These portrayals [of kindness, generosity, being helpful and socially responsible] have been shown to exert both short-term and longer-term influences on similar behaviours among children. Television can have such socially desirable effects not simply through its educational programmes, but also when pro-social portrayals feature in its entertainment and drama productions made for non-popular consumption.
>
> ...It is possible that pro-social content may counteract anti-social content to some extent, and ... may provide valuable alternative programme content control guidelines to simply cutting violence. (Gunter and McAleer, 1990)

AGGRESSION AND DE-INDIVIDUATION

Being in the presence of others may enhance an individual's performance on a task (social facilitation) and this is usually regarded as a positive influence (see Chapter 20). But is it possible that being in the company of other people will have a detrimental influence on a person's behaviour, including the tendency to behave more aggressively?

The concept of *de-individuation* has been used to try to explain why it is that people in groups may behave in an uncharacteristically aggressive way (and in other anti-social ways) relative to their individual behaviour. If people believe that they will be identified, and consequently punished, they will inhibit their aggressive impulses but Gergen and Gergen (1981) suggest that in urban settings identification may be difficult and this may reduce people's fear of punishment, with the effect that they are more 'free' to behave in anti-social ways. When an individual's identity is lost in a mass of people and when the markers of personality are reduced, the individual is said to be de-individuated (Gergen and Gergen, 1981).

One of the earliest studies of crowd behaviour was that of Le Bon (1895) and, based on his work, Festinger et al first introduced the concept of de-individuation, defining it as:

> A state of affairs in a group where members do not pay attention to other individuals *qua* individuals and, correspondingly, the members do not feel they are being singled out by others. (Festinger et al, 1952)

Could this be a motive for becoming a part of certain groups in the first place?

In *Escape from Freedom* (1941), Fromm argued that what makes people free is their individuality, uniqueness and self-awareness but these are the very attributes which may also isolate people from each other so that they come to fear their freedom. However, groups can not only provide people with a sense of identity and belongingness (see Maslow's hierarchy of needs—Chapter 29) but can allow individuals to merge with the group, to forego their individuality and to become anonymous—in other words, to de-individuate. Is there any evidence to support this view?

Most relevant studies have been laboratory experiments but one interesting field-study was conducted by Diener et al (1976), who observed 1300 trick-or-treating children on Halloween night. When they were completely anonymous (for instance, wearing costumes which prevented them from being recognized and going from house to house in large groups) they were most likely to steal money and candy.

In an early experimental study, Festinger et al (1952) ran discussion groups in which male undergraduates were asked to discuss their feelings towards their parents. They found a correlation between how often negative statements about parents were made and the extent to which subjects failed to remember who had said what in the discussion group. This was taken as evidence for the hypothesis that de-individuation produces a lowering of inhibitions.

Festinger et al also found that those groups in which more hostility towards parents was expressed were also more attractive to the participants (as expressed by their willingness to return for a further discussion) which was interpreted as indicating that 'submergence' in a group is one of the attractions of group membership.

However, Brown (1985) believes the study is not a very convincing one. For one thing, rather than de-individuation being the cause of uninhibited behaviour in groups, could it not be caused *by* it, so that the perceived similarity of the members increases and less attention is paid to individuals as they engage in uninhibited behaviour?

Zimbardo (1969) also emphasized the absence of self-awareness and self-evaluation; under certain conditions, an individual changes his/her self-perception and that of others and engages in uninhibited behaviour and this is de-individuation.

Zimbardo regarded *anonymity* as a major source of de-individuation and was the first to operationalize anonymity by having subjects wear hoods and masks. In one study, female students had to deliver electric shocks to another student as an aid to learning. Half the subjects wore bulky lab coats and hoods that hid their faces, were spoken to in groups of four and were never referred to by name; the other half wore their normal clothes, were given large name tabs to wear and were introduced to each other by name and could see each other dimly while giving the shock. The student who received the shock was seen through a one-way mirror and pretended to be in extreme discomfort—writhing, twisting, grimacing and finally tearing her hand away from the strap. The hooded, de-individuated subjects gave twice as much shock as the individuated subjects; if they were told that the student receiving the shock was honest, sincere and warm she did not receive any less shock than those who believed she was conceited or critical; by contrast, the individuated subjects did adjust the shock they administered according to the victim's character.

However, manipulating anonymity has not always proved very easy (Brown, 1985). Some of Zimbardo's (1969) subjects were Belgian soldiers who wore hoods but they did not behave more aggressively; instead they became self-conscious, suspicious and anxious and the apparently individuated controls retained their 'normal' level of de-individuation related to their status as uniformed soldiers.

One of the functions of uniform in the 'real world' is precisely to reduce individuality and hence, at least indirectly, to increase de-individuation. A standard uniform is a clear sign for others, at least, that the wearer belongs to the group or the institution and, to that extent, the uniqueness of the individual is rendered less important or apparent. De-possessing someone of their 'civilian' clothes is a major technique of de-personalizing the inmate in 'total institutions' such as prisons and psychiatric hospitals (Goffman, 1968, 1971).

As Brown (1985) observes, the victims of aggression are often dehumanized by, amongst other things, shaving their heads and dressing them in ill-fitting clothes so that they appear less human and so can be humiliated and abused more easily (see the Prison Simulation Experiment by Zimbardo et al; Chapter 20). While it may be true that the de-individuation produced by wearing military or police uniform increases the likelihood of brutality, it can just as easily work the other way—the anonymity of massed ranks of police or soldiers may make them appear less human and thus make them a more obvious target for a rioting crowd's violence.

Again, is group behaviour always as unreasonable and uncontrolled as Zimbardo and others have proposed? For example, Brown (1988) refers to the US urban riots of the 1960s, where looting and violence were *not* completely random but showed signs of selectivity. Similarly, the St Paul's black–police civil disturbances in Bristol in 1984 were violent but at the same time were relatively controlled—violence was aimed at specific targets and avoided others (such as local shops and houses) and was geographically confined to a small area in the heart of the community. Far from losing their identities, the rioters seemed quite unanimous in a new sense of pride in their community produced by their activities (Brown, 1988).

Just as television need not produce harmful effects, so de-individuation does not necessarily produce anti-social behaviour; under proper circumstances, de-individuation can be liberating. This was well illustrated by the Black Room experiment (Gergen et al, 1973), which involved subjects spending an hour together, either in a completely dark room or in a normally-lit room. In the dark room, subjects at first chatted in a lively manner and explored the physical space and then began to discuss serious matters before conversation faded to be replaced by physical contact; 90 per cent of subjects deliberately touched other subjects, almost 50 per cent hugged and 80 per cent admitted to being sexually aroused. By comparison, control subjects talked politely, in the light, for the whole hour.

It seems that we can become uninhibited in the dark where the usual norms of intimacy no longer prevail—we feel less accountable for our behaviour in such situations but this state of de-individuation can be to the mutual benefit of all participants (Gergen and Gergen, 1981).

17 INTERPERSONAL PERCEPTION

In many ways, it would be quite appropriate to begin a textbook of psychology with a chapter on Interpersonal Perception, as this is concerned with how we all attempt to explain, understand and predict the behaviour of other people. To this extent, we all do in our everyday lives what the professional psychologist does as a scientist (see Chapters 1 and 2), since it is impossible to interact with people and not to try to make sense of their actions and to anticipate how they are likely to behave in the future. So here we shall be examining the key processes involved in our day-to-day attempts to understand and predict the behaviour of others. Probably in no other area of psychology does the unique nature of the discipline as a whole become so apparent, namely, the fact that psychologists are studying 'themselves', they are part of the subject matter, and in order to study human behaviour they must utilize the very same processes they are attempting to explain!

To make this a little more clear, let us think of what the psychologist does when choosing to study a particular aspect of behaviour. First, a *selection* is made from the vast range of behaviour that could be studied. Secondly, the theoretical statements and all the evidence that is collected must be *organized* so that they constitute a coherent whole (eg one theory should be distinguishable from another). Thirdly, there are always elements of *inference* or 'going beyond the information given', that is, making theoretical assumptions about what cannot be directly observed or measured (including generalizing to situations that have not yet been observed and making predictions).

Selection, organization and inference represent three fundamental principles of perception. In any kind of psychological (or other scientific) research, the very same processes are used which some psychologists have chosen to study explicitly; not all psychologists study perception, of course, but they must all engage in the act of perceiving as part of their 'scientific behaviour' (see Chapter 9).

Two important questions have been raised by this discussion:

(a) What is the relationship between perception (in general) and interpersonal perception (in particular)?
(b) What is the difference between the professional psychologist and the amateur (lay person)?

To answer the first question, consider Figure 17.1. As you can see, interpersonal perception is the perception of others (sometimes called 'person perception'), the other component of social perception is the perception of self (see Chapter 21).

As we shall see, the way we perceive others involves: (i) *selection* (eg focusing on someone's physical appearance or on just one particular aspect of their behaviour; (ii) *organization* (eg trying to form a complete,

Figure 17.1 Relationship between general and social perception

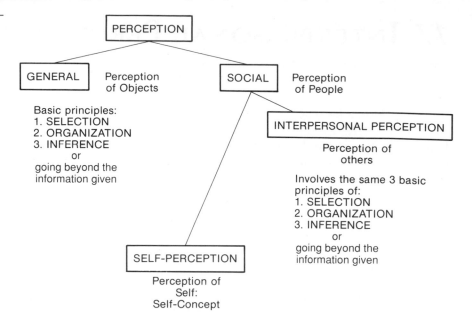

coherent impression of a person); and (iii) *inference* (eg attributing to someone certain characteristics for which there is no direct or immediate evidence, as in stereotyping).

So interpersonal perception, like general (object) perception, is based on these three principles. But, of course, there are also fundamental differences between perceiving inanimate objects and perceiving other people:

(a) People *behave* (but objects do not); it is often behaviour which provides the data for making inferences about what people are like.

(b) People *interact* with other people (but we do not interact with objects or they with each other); one person's behaviour can influence another's, so that each one's behaviour towards the other is at least partly a product of the other's behaviour towards them.

(c) People *perceive* and *experience* (but objects cannot); one person's perception can influence the other's (probably through their behaviour, especially their non-verbal behaviour), so that each person's perception of the other is at least partly a product of the other's perception of them.

Some psychologists (particularly the phenomenological psychologists) regard *experience* as the major source of 'data' (as opposed to behaviour) in social interaction, eg Laing (1967) argued that the task of *social phenomenology* is to relate my experience of your behaviour to your experience of my behaviour, so that it studies the relationship between experience and experience.

In Laing's book *Knots*, (1972), he dramatically (and often humorously) demonstrates (in the form of short prose poems and diagrammatic poems) the kinds of tangles that human relationships can get into. Here are two of the shorter and more straightforward examples:

(a) Jack frightens Jill he will leave her because he is frightened she will leave him.

(b) *Jack:* 'You are a pain in the neck.
To stop *you* giving me a pain in the neck
I protect my neck by tightening my neck muscles,
Which gives me the pain in the neck you are.'
    Jill: 'My head aches through trying to stop you giving me a headache.'

For Laing, 'knots' like these illustrate how my experience of another is a function of the other's experience of me—and vice versa.

As far as the question of how the amateur and professional psychologist differ, let us look at what Judy Gahagan (1975, 1984) has to say on the matter:

(a) The layperson uses his/her theories for pragmatic (or practical) and immediate purposes, as opposed to gaining knowledge for its own sake. (Remember the distinction between pure and applied research discussed in Chapter 1; most research into interpersonal perception is pure research but it sometimes has implications for practical situations, such as interviews.)

(b) The layperson is rarely a disinterested observer of other's behaviour—we usually have a vested interest in what is going on and are usually emotionally involved to some extent. The professional, as a scientist, has to be 'detached' and objective (although complete detachment is impossible: the very fact that a psychologist has chosen one topic to investigate rather than another demonstrates this).

(c) The layperson may be completely unaware of the reasoning he or she has followed when making inferences about others, and this reasoning may change from one situation to another. So the layperson's theories are not spelt out or articulated (hence 'implicit' personality theories) and may not be consistent. But psychologists must try to be consistent and must make their reasoning explicit so that other psychologists can examine it.

DEFINITIONS AND MODELS OF INTERPERSONAL PERCEPTION

Judy Gahagan (1984) defines interpersonal perception as, 'the study of how the layperson uses theory and data in understanding people'. She breaks this definition down further into three main components:

(a) The study of how people perceive others as *physical objects* and form impressions of their physical appearance, actions and the social categories to which they can be assigned. Often the first thing we notice about other people is some aspect of their appearance (eg clothes, hair) and to this extent we are treating them as no more than 'things'. This is usually the first step involved in stereotyping, since it is usually on the basis of their physical appearance that we assign people to groups.

(b) The study of how people perceive others as *psychological entities*— we form impressions of what kind of person they are or we infer what their feelings, motives, personality traits etc, might be (having already identified them as belonging to a particular group—sexual, racial, occupational).

(c) The study of the layperson as a *psychologist*—we have already dealt with this above.

But we could usefully add the claim that:

> We are all psychologists. In attempting to understand other people and ourselves, we are informal scientists who construct our own intuitive theories of human behaviour. In doing so, we face the same basic tasks as the formal scientist . . . (Nisbett and Ross, 1980)

'Intuitive theories' is another way of referring to the 'implicit personality theories' which, as we noted above, represents one of the important differences between the formal and informal psychologist.

According to Cook (1971), interpersonal perception is 'the study of the ways people react and respond to others, in thought, feeling and action'. He goes on to summarize all the research under one of two headings, what he calls the Intuition Model and the Inference Model.

The Intuition Model is mainly concerned with the idea of *global perception*, that is, how we form overall impressions of others and it is based on the work of the Gestalt psychologists, who stressed the importance of perceptual organization (see Chapter 9). Applied to people, it means that we try to perceive people as whole entities, in as complete a way as possible; people are not simply a collection of separate traits or characteristics ('the whole is greater than the sum of its parts').

The Inference Model is mainly concerned with 'implicit personality theories', ie our beliefs, held unconsciously, about how certain traits belong together, so that if a person displays one of these, it is inferred that he/she also has (some of) the others. Stereotypes illustrate such implicit theories. The Inference Model is also concerned with how we make judgements about the causes of people's behaviour (including our own) and whether, therefore, they can be held responsible for it; the study of how people make such judgements is called the Attribution Process.

It is important to note that these two models do *not* represent opposing views of the processes of interpersonal perception. As we have already said, selection, organization and inference are *all* involved in the perception of both people and objects and the two models are best seen as *overlapping* and *complementary*.

The early research tended to be carried out by Gestalt psychologists, such as Asch, who was interested in how traits combine to form an overall impression (gestalt) of the person. But later studies placed more emphasis on how impressions are formed by inferring additional traits from the implicit personality theories which the subject already possesses. Together with the attribution process, the study of the role of cognitive processes involved in impression formation, is part of what is called *social cognition*.

FORMING GLOBAL IMPRESSIONS OF PEOPLE—FITTING THE PIECES TOGETHER

The two major explanations of how global perception takes place are: (i) central versus peripheral traits; and (ii) the primacy-recency effect.

CENTRAL VERSUS PERIPHERAL TRAITS

The basic idea here is that certain information which we have about a person (ie certain traits we believe they possess) is more important in determining our overall impression of that person than any other information.

The classic study is that of Asch (1946), who presented subjects with a list of adjectives describing a fictitious person. One group had the following list: intelligent, skilful, industrious, warm, determined, practical, and cautious. A second group had the same list, except that the word 'cold' replaced the word 'warm'. These lists were called the Stimulus lists.

Both groups were then presented with a second list (the Response list) of eighteen trait words (different to the Stimulus list) and were asked to underline those which described the 'target' person. The two groups chose significantly and consistently different words from the second list. For example, the 'warm' group saw the character as generous, humorous, sociable and popular, while the 'cold' group saw him as having the opposite traits. There were also certain qualities attributed to him equally by both groups, eg reliable, good-looking, persistent, serious, restrained, strong and honest.

The words 'warm' and 'cold' seemed to have a major effect on the overall impression of the target person for the two groups. When Asch used 'polite' and 'blunt' (instead of 'warm' and 'cold') subjects underlined almost identical words in the response list. Asch concluded from this that 'warm–cold' represented a *central* trait or dimension, while 'polite–blunt' represented a *peripheral* trait or dimension. And the central traits which seem to influence our global perception in this way are implicitly *evaluative*, ie they are to do with whether the person is liked or disliked, popular or unpopular, friendly or unfriendly, kind or cruel etc.

Based on Asch's study, Kelley (1950) set out to: (i) check Asch's findings; and (ii) see whether the description of the target person as 'warm' or 'cold' would influence subjects' *behaviour* towards a real (as opposed to hypothetical) person. The subjects were students at the Massachusetts Institute of Technology and the target person was a male member of staff not known to the students. Before he arrived, Kelley explained to the students that their regular teacher would not be coming and they would be having Mr X instead; he also told them that they would be asked to assess him at the end of the session. They were then given some biographical notes about the substitute teacher. For some subjects these included the description 'rather warm' and for others 'rather cold'—otherwise the biographies were identical.

A twenty-minute discussion followed between the teacher and the students, during which Kelley recorded how often each student attempted to interact with the teacher. After he left the room students assessed him on fifteen rating scales (eg 'knows his stuff–doesn't know his stuff', 'good natured–irritable'). It was found that subjects who had read the 'warm' description consistently responded more favourably to him than those who had read the 'cold' description. The two groups also responded differently when asked to write a free description. Fifty-six per cent of the 'warm' group participated in the discussion, compared with 32 per cent of the 'cold' group. So not only had Kelley confirmed

Asch's findings regarding the 'central' nature of the 'warm–cold' dimension, but he had also demonstrated a relationship between how students perceived the target person and their attempts to interact with a real person (as opposed to Asch's fictitious person).

So for Asch, a set of traits produces an integrated impression—a *gestalt*—in which the meaning of one trait has been influenced by the others (with some traits—central traits—exerting a major organizing influence compared with peripheral traits, which have little or no influence) and which can generate inferences about additional traits not given in the set.

By contrast, Bruner and Tagiuiri (1954) argued that both general impressions *and* inferences about additional traits are due to the subject's implicit personality theories. This does not contradict Asch, since he was not opposed to the view that inference is involved, just as Bruner and Tagiuiri were not opposed to Gestalt ideas.

A relevant study here is that of Wishner (1960) who found that the impact of the traits 'warm' and 'cold' on inferences about other traits depends on their prior associations with those traits. So 'warm' and 'cold' affect inferences of traits like 'generous' and 'popular' because these traits are all associated in peoples' implicit personality theories, while 'warm' and 'cold' do not affect inferences of other traits, such as 'reliable' and 'honest'. This suggests that central traits do not *need* to be incorporated into different *gestalten* in order to have the effects on trait inferences which Asch found. Indeed, Asch found only negligible differences in the traits inferred when 'warm' and 'cold' were presented alone and those inferred when they were presented in a list of traits (as in the experiment described above).

However, although the trait associations in peoples' implicit personality theories may account for differing impressions of a warm and cold person, the *meaning* of various traits *may* nevertheless be altered by the context in which they appear, as Asch originally suggested. For example, Zebrowitz (1990) cites studies in which, if someone is described as 'proud', this trait is rated as closer in meaning to 'confident' when it appears in the context of positive traits, but as closer to 'conceited' when it appears in the context of negative traits.

Wishner also showed that whether a trait is central or not is a *relative* matter, ie it depends on what else is known about the person. So, for example, in Asch's study, 'warm'/'cold' was central in relation to generous/humorous/sociable/popular, but peripheral (or at least neutral) in relation to reliable/good-looking/persistent/serious/restrained/strong/honest. So, rather than saying a trait is central or not, we should say, that whether a trait is central in a particular study will depend on the pattern of correlations with other traits in the study.

Asch's original finding that the inclusion of the word 'warm' produces an overall more positive impression compared with the same list including the word 'cold', demonstrates what is called the *halo effect*. If we are told that a person has a particularly favourable characteristic (eg 'warm', which suggests the person is likeable), then we tend to attribute them with other favourable characteristics (a *positive* halo). The reverse is true if we are told the person is 'cold' (and, therefore, unlikeable)—we attribute them with a *negative* halo.

The halo effect seems to illustrate very well two of the principles of perception discussed earlier:

1) We like to see people in as consistent a way as possible. It is simpler to regard someone as having either all good or all bad qualities than a mixture of good and bad. This matches the Gestalt theory of object perception discussed in Chapter 9. Perhaps the most extreme example of this is when lovers regard each other as perfect and faultless—'love is blind' is just an instance of the halo effect.

Similarly, the 'us' and 'them' mentality, when our enemies are seen as personifying evil while we are all good, seems to demonstrate our need to organize or structure our perceptions in as coherent and 'complete' a way as possible (see Chapter 19 on prejudice).

2) The halo effect is a very general form of implicit personality theory, which forms the basis of inferring what someone is like when we have only very limited information about them (a characteristic of all such theories).

THE PRIMACY–RECENCY EFFECT

The other major explanation of global perception concentrates on the *order* in which we learn things about a person: the *primacy effect* refers to the greater impact of what we first learn about someone ('first impressions count') and the *recency effect* refers to the greater impact of what we learn later on.

One of the most famous studies is that of Luchins (1957). Subjects were matched on measures of personality and then allocated to one of four groups: group 1 heard a straightforward description of an extrovert character called Jim; group 2 heard a straightforward introvert description. (These were control groups used to establish that subjects could accurately identify extroverts and introverts—there was a 75 per cent success rate.) Group 3 heard the first half of the extrovert description followed by the second half of the introvert description; and group 4 heard the reverse of group 3 (so for groups 3 and 4 the descriptions were contradictory). The extrovert and introvert descriptions are shown in Box 17.1.

All the subjects were then asked to rate Jim in terms of introversion–extroversion. Group 1 subjects judged him to be the most extroverted and group 2 the most introverted (as you would expect); and, although the judgements of groups 3 and 4 were less extreme, group 3 subjects rated Jim as being more extrovert than group 4 subjects. Remember, they all received the same information about Jim, only the order was different.

Luchins concluded that the earlier elements of the description had a greater impact than the later elements, so he had found evidence for the primacy effect.

Support for this view came in an earlier study, again by Asch (1946). He used two lists of six adjectives describing a hypothetical person (intelligent, industrious, impulsive, critical, stubborn and envious), one in the above order and the other in the reverse order. Subjects given the first list (where the *first* words denoted *desirable* qualities) formed a *favourable* overall impression, while subjects given the second list

---

Box 17.1   The extrovert and introvert descriptions of Jim, used by Luchins (1957)

Extrovert Description
Jim left the house to get some stationery. He walked out in to the sun-filled street with two of his friends, basking in the sun as he walked. Jim entered the stationery store which was full of people. Jim talked with an acquaintance while he waited for the clerk to catch his eye. On his way out, he stopped to chat with a school friend who was just coming into the store. Leaving the store, he walked toward school. On his way out he met the girl to whom he had been introduced the night before. They talked for a short while, and then Jim left for school.

Introvert Description
After school Jim left the classroom alone. Leaving the school, he started on his long walk home. The street was brilliantly filled with sunshine. Jim walked down the street on the shady side. Coming down the street toward him, he saw the pretty girl whom he had met on the previous evening. Jim crossed the street and entered a candy store. The store was crowded with students, and he noticed a few familiar faces. Jim waited quietly until the counterman caught his eye and then gave his order. Taking his drink, he sat down at a side table. When he had finished his drink he went home.

(where the *first* words denoted *undesirable* qualities) formed an *unfavourable* overall impression.

Both the Luchins and Asch studies involved hypothetical people. In Jones et al's study (1968), an actual person was used (a stooge of the experimenters). Subjects watched a student trying to solve a series of difficult multiple-choice problems and were then asked to assess his intelligence. It was arranged so that the student always solved 15 out of 30 correctly; but some subjects saw him get most of the right answers either at the beginning or at the end of the series.

The *common sense prediction* would be that when the student improved as the series went on (ie got most right towards the end) he would be judged as more intelligent than when he seemed to be getting worse as the series went on (got most right towards the beginning)—in the first case he would seem to be learning as he went along, in the second case his early successes could be attributed to guesswork or 'beginner's luck'. Jones et al made the common sense prediction that there would be a *recency effect*. However, the opposite was found—the student under the first condition was judged as being more intelligent—there was a primacy effect. Significantly, subjects' memories were distorted in the same direction—when asked to recall how many problems the student had solved correctly, those who had seen the 15 bunched at the beginning said 20.6 (on average) while those who had seen them bunched at the end said 12.5 (on average), so these over- and under-estimations also reflected the impact of the primacy effect.

How can we account for this?

Luchins himself says that when later information is discrepant with earlier information, people tend to regard the first information as revealing the 'real' person and to explain away or dismiss the later information as not representative or typical. It is discounted because it contradicts what came first. Anderson (1974) maintains that people pay more attention to information that is presented when they are first trying to form an impression about someone and, having formed some initial impression, they pay less attention to any subsequent information.

Asch's explanation is that the first bit of information affects the *meaning* of later information, so that the latter is made consistent with the former and so, effectively, does not contradict it. For example, if you initially find out that someone is courageous and frank, when you later learn that he is also 'undecided', you may take that to mean 'open-minded' rather than 'wishy-washy' (Zebrowitz, 1990). Again, in the sequence 'friendly and ambitious', ambitious means doing the best one can to achieve one's goals, whereas in the sequence 'calculating and ambitious', ambitious means 'unscrupulous'.

But does the primacy effect always prove more powerful than the recency effect? The answer seems to be that it does, but only under certain conditions.

Luchins reasoned that if the primacy effect is due to decreased attention being paid to later information, then it should be possible to destroy the effect by warning subjects against making snap judgements. He found that warning subjects did have this effect and that it was particularly effective if it was given between the presentation of the two inconsistent pieces of information about the same individual.

In a similar vein, Hendrick and Constanini (1970) found that primacy seems to prevail unless subjects are specifically instructed to attend closely to all the information. Also, when subjects performed some irrelevant task in between the two pieces of information, the recency effect proved more powerful and the longer the time-interval between the two, the greater the recency effect proved to be.

Evidence exists that a negative first impression is more resistant to change than a positive one. Why should this be? One explanation may be that negative information carries more weight because it is likely to reflect socially undesirable traits or behaviour and, therefore, the observer can be more confident in attributing the trait or behaviour to the person's 'real' nature. Another explanation may be that it is more adaptive for us to be aware of negative traits than positive ones, since the former are potentially harmful or dangerous to us.

It can be argued that in the Asch and Luchins studies the situation is an extremely artificial one—subjects are obliged to use data selected for them and so are not free to form impressions by selecting information that *they* think is relevant. But Brown (1986) points out that few subjects hesitated to formulate an impression or to answer questions about Jim, even on the basis of very limited information. This supports the view that we characteristically 'go beyond the information given' and seek ways of organizing and structuring our impressions of others using any available 'data'.

Finally, Luchins found that, although the primacy effect may be important in relation to strangers, as far as friends and other people whom we know well are concerned, the recency effect seems to be stronger. For example, we may discover something about a friend's childhood, or something that happened to them before we knew them, which might change our whole perception of them. This raises the fundamental question, 'How well do we (or can we) know anybody?'. This is related to the question of the *accuracy* of our perceptions of others.

little about their underlying dispositions (they are 'just doing their job'). But when they display out-of-role behaviour, we can use their actions to infer 'what they are really like'.

4) *Prior expectations* are based on past experiences with the same actor. The better we know someone, the better placed we are to decide whether their behaviour on a particular occasion is 'typical' and, if it is 'atypical', we are more likely to dismiss it or play down its significance or explain it in terms of situational factors.

KELLEY'S CO-VARIATION MODEL

Also based on Heider's early work, Kelley has investigated the attribution process, concentrating on how we make judgements about internal and external causes. His co-variation model (1967) is intended to explain cases where we have knowledge of how the person being studied usually behaves in a variety of situations and how others usually behave in those situations. *The principle of co-variation* states that, 'an effect is attributed to one of its possible causes with which, over time, it co-varies', ie if two events repeatedly occur together, we are more likely to infer that they are causally related than if they very rarely occur together. If the behaviour to be explained is thought of as an effect, the cause can be one of three kinds and the extent to which the behaviour co-varies with each of these three kinds of possible cause is what we base our attribution upon. So what are the *three kinds of causal information* which Kelley identifies?

To explain this, we will take the hypothetical example of a student, called Sally, who is late for her psychology class:

Consensus refers to the extent to which other people behave in the same way, ie are other students late for psychology class? If all (or most) other students are late then we have *high* consensus, but if Sally is the only one, we have *low* consensus.

Distinctiveness refers to the extent to which Sally behaves in a similar way towards other, similar, 'stimuli' or 'entities', ie is Sally late for other subjects? If she is, then we have *low* distinctiveness, but if she is only late for psychology, then we have *high* distinctiveness.

Consistency refers to how stable Sally's behaviour is over time, ie is Sally regularly late for psychology? If she is, we have *high* consistency, if she is not, then consistency is *low*.

Kelley believes that a combination of *low consensus* (Sally is the only one late), *low distinctiveness* (she is late for all her subjects), and *high consistency* (she is regularly late), will lead us to make a *person attribution*, that is, the cause of Sally's behaviour is 'inside' Sally, eg she is a poor timekeeper. However, any other combination would normally result in an *external* attribution, eg if Sally is generally punctual (low consistency), or if most students are late for psychology (high consensus), then the cause of Sally's lateness might be 'circumstances' in the first case, or the subject and/or the teacher, in the second (Table 17.1).

Is there any empirical support for Kelley?

McArthur (1972) presented subjects with one-sentence descriptions of various responses representing emotions, accomplishments, opinions and actions. For example, 'Sue is afraid of the dog', 'George translates the sentence incorrectly'. Each sentence was accompanied by high or low consensus information, high or low distinctiveness information and high or low consistency information. Subjects had to attribute each response

CAUSAL INFORMATION			
CONSENSUS	DISTINCTIVENESS	CONSISTENCY	CAUSAL ATTRIBUTIONS
Low	Low	High	Person (actor)
Low	High	Low	Circumstances
High	High	High	Stimulus (target)

Table 17.1 Causal attributions based on three different combinations of causal information. (Based on Kelley, 1967)

either to characteristics of the actor, the stimulus (target), circumstances, or some combination of these.

He found strong support for Kelley, as have a number of other studies.

However, not all three types of causal information are used to the same extent by subjects in laboratory studies. For example, Major (1980) found that when subjects are given the option of requesting several instances of consensus, distinctiveness and consistency information before making a causal attribution, most examine all three. However, they sample only a limited portion of the available information and show a marked preference for consistency over the other two, with consensus being the least preferred.

Similarly, Nisbett and Borgida (1975) found surprisingly weak effects of consensus information when they asked university students to explain the behaviour of a participant in a psychology experiment. This participant, like most others, had agreed to tolerate a high level of electric shock. However, subjects who were told that 16/34 participants had tolerated the highest possible shock level were no more likely to make situational attributions than subjects who had been given no consensus information at all. Why?

Nisbett and Borgida argued that peoples' judgements are less responsive to the dull and abstract base rates that consitute consensus information than to the more vivid information regarding the behaviour of one, concrete, target person.

However, what if the available consensus information was contrary to what subjects would expect to be a typical response? Wells and Harvey (1977) replicated Nisbett and Borgida's study but told subjects explicitly that the consensus information was based on a random sample of participants (and, hence, was representative). They found a significant consensus effect. (Of course, by doing this, they made the information about the target person less vivid than in the original experiment and this could have increased the impact of the abstract consensus information; Nisbett and Ross, 1980.)

Further, when given the opportunity, subjects seek additional information about the actor (eg personality) or about the situation (eg norms) as opposed to the types of information suggested by the co-variation model.

Finally, and perhaps most seriously, Kelley seems to have overestimated people's ability to assess co-variation. He originally compared the social perceiver to a naïve scientist, trying to draw inferences in much the same way as the formal scientist draws conclusions from data. More significantly, it is a *normative* model, which states how, *ideally*, people should come to draw inferences about the behaviour of others. However, the actual procedures that people adopt when inferring causality seem to fall short of this idealized picture—we are not as logical, rational and systematic as the model suggests.

More recently, Kelley (1973) has offered an alternative model which is meant to cover those situations (perhaps the majority) in which we do not have information about consensus, distinctiveness and consistency. Indeed, often the only information we have is a single occurrence of the behaviour of a particular individual. In such cases, we must rely on what Kelley calls *causal schemata*, which are general ideas about 'how certain kinds of causes interact to produce a specific kind of effect' (Kelley, 1973). Fiske and Taylor (1984) argue that causal schemata provide the social perceiver with a 'causal shorthand' for accomplishing complex inferences quickly and easily. They are based on our experience of cause–effect relationships, and what we have been taught by others about such relationships, and they come into play when causal information is otherwise ambiguous and incomplete.

A general kind of causal schema is one which corresponds to the pattern in Table 17.1. For example, since *high consensus* is unique to *stimulus* (target) attribution, if all we know is that (to use our earlier example) everyone is late for psychology, then we will attribute Sally's lateness to the subject or teacher or both. Similarly, *low distinctiveness* is unique to a *person* (actor) attribution, so if all we know is that Sally is late for all her lessons (not just psychology), then we will attribute Sally's lateness to her poor time-keeping.

The two major kinds of causal schemata are: (i) *multiple necessary causes*; and (ii) *multiple sufficient causes*.

Experience tells us that, for example, to win a marathon, you must not only be fit and highly motivated, but you must have trained hard for several months beforehand, you must wear the right kind of running shoes, and so on. Even if all these causes are present, success cannot be guaranteed, *but* the absence of any one of them is likely to produce failure; so, in this sense, success is more informative than failure. This is an example of *multiple necessary causes*.

In the case of *multiple sufficient causes*, any one of several causes is sufficient to produce a particular outcome. For example, a film star or sporting personality might promote a particular brand of coffee or aftershave either because they genuinely believe in the product or because of the fee—either is a sufficient cause. Since it is reasonable to assume that it is the fee which accounts for the appearance in the commercial, we discount the other cause (that they 'believe' in the product) according to the *discounting principle* (Kelley, 1973).

SOURCES OF ERROR AND BIAS IN THE ATTRIBUTION PROCESS

We have already seen that perceivers do not always infer causes as prescribed by Kelley's co-variation model. For example, research into sources of error and bias seems to provide a more accurate account of how people *actually* make causal attributions than the normative models which are commonly used to assess their accuracy.

Zebrowitz (1990) defines sources of bias as:

...the tendency to favour one cause over another when explaining some effect. Such favouritism may result in causal attributions that deviate from predictions derived from rational attibutional principles, like covariation...

a) *The Fundamental Attribution Error*

Even though almost all behaviour is the product of *both* the person and the situation, our causal explanations tend to emphasize one or the other. Why should this be?

According to Jones and Nisbett (1971), a possible answer is that it is part of human nature to act in this way: we all want to see ourselves as competent observers and interpreters of human behaviour, and to achieve this end we naïvely assume that simple explanations are better than complex ones. To try to analyse the interactions between personal and situational factors would take time and energy and usually (as we have seen) we seldom have all the relevant information anyway. The *fundamental attribution error* refers to the general tendency to overestimate the importance of personal or dispositional factors relative to situational or environmental factors as causes of behaviour (Ross, 1977).

Why should this happen? In relation to Jones and Nisbett's suggestion that we prefer simple to complex explanations, the preference for internal causes could be understood in terms of making the behaviour of others more predictable which, in turn, enhances our sense of control over the environment as well as making us feel more competent observers.

Heider (1958) believed that behaviour represents the 'figure' against the 'ground', comprised of context, roles, situational pressures and so on, ie behaviour is conspicuous and situational factors are (comparatively) less easily perceived.

Yet under some conditions, people over-emphasize the role of *situational* factors. For example, when subjects are alerted to the possibility of environmental constraints on an actor's behaviour, they perceive these constraints as causing the actor's behaviour even though it is totally explicable in terms of the actor's previously stated attitude (Quattrone, 1982).

For these reasons, Fiske and Taylor (1984) suggest that we should call the fundamental attribution 'error' a 'bias' instead. Similarly, Zebrowitz (1990) argues that:

> ...the fundamental attribution error is best viewed as a bias towards attributing an actor's behaviour to dispositional causes rather than as an attribution error. This bias may be limited to adults in Western societies and it may be most pronounced when they are constrained to attribute behaviour to a single cause... (Zebrowitz, 1990)

It may reflect an efficient, automatic process of inferring dispositions from behaviour which, on average, produces accurate perceptions by perceivers who are too cognitively busy to make conscious corrections based on situational causes (Gilbert, 1989; cited by Zebrowitz, 1990). And how do you establish a standard of accuracy against which to compare peoples' attributions? (Zebrowitz, 1990).

b) *The Actor–Observer Effect*

Related to the fundamental attribution error is the tendency for actors and observers to make *different* attributions about the *same* event (Jones and Nisbett, 1971; Nisbett et al, 1973). Actors usually see their own behaviour as primarily a response to the situation and so quite variable from situation to situation (the cause is *external*), while the observer typically attributes the *same* behaviour to the actor's intentions and dispositions and so quite consistent across situations (the cause is *internal*). (The observer's attribution to internal causes is, of course, the fundamental attribution error.) Nisbett et al (1973) found that students: (i) assumed that actors would behave in the future in ways similar to those they had just witnessed; (ii) described their best friend's choices of girlfriend and college major in terms referring to dispositional qualities of their best friend (while more often describing their own similar choices in terms of properties of the girlfriend or major); and (iii) attributed more personality traits to other people than to themselves.

Why should this occur?

Take the example of a man entering a room full of people, tripping up and spilling his drink. The others will probably be more aware of the behaviour itself, and so judge him to be a 'clumsy clot', while the unfortunate person himself will be more aware of the uneven carpet or the slippery glass. So what is perceptually salient or vivid for the actor (the carpet or the glass) is not what is perceptually salient or vivid for the observer (the tripping and spilling of the drink). This is the figure–ground explanation which we noted when discussing the fundamental attribution error.

According to Zebrowitz (1990), several studies show that when subjects are encouraged to empathize with the actor, attributions become much less dispositional compared with non-empathizing subjects. Also, the actor–observer effect is most pronounced when judging *negative* behaviours and may be absent or even reversed for positive ones. Why?

c) *Self-Serving Attributional Bias*

Naturally, no one wants to admit to being clumsy, so we are more likely to 'blame' tripping over on something external to ourselves. This protects our self-esteem. But we are quite happy to take the credit for our successes. This enhances our self-esteem. This is referred to as *self-serving attributional bias*. A less motivational, more cognitive explanation is that we 'know' that our own failures are unusual whereas our successes are not. There is some evidence that positively valued outcomes (eg altruism) are more often attributed to people, and negatively valued outcomes (eg being late) to situational factors, regardless of who committed them. However, when either the self of someone closely associated with the self has committed the action, credit for positive events (*self-enhancing bias*) and denial of responsibility for negative ones (*self-protecting bias*) are even stronger.

An interesting exception to this general rule is the case of very depressed people. Abramson et al (1978) found that they tend to explain their failures in terms of their own inadequacies and their successes more in terms of external factors, such as luck and chance.

d) *The Importance of the Consequences*

The more serious the *consequences* of the actor's behaviour, the more likely the fundamental attribution error is to be made: the more serious the outcome, the more likely we are to judge the actor as responsible, regardless of the perceived intentions of the actor.

For example, Walster (1966) gave subjects an account of a car accident in which a young man's car had been left at the top of a hill and then rolled down backwards. One group was told that very little damage was done to the car and no other vehicle was involved; a second group was told that it collided with another car, causing some damage; while a third group was told that the car crashed into a shop, injuring the shopkeeper and a small child. When they had to assess how responsible the car owner was, the third group found him more 'guilty' or morally culpable than the second group, and the second group found him more guilty than the first.

If more serious consequences can result in greater blame and responsibility, can the reverse inference occur, ie can belief that an act is intentional affect perception of the seriousness of the consequences?

Darley and Huff (1990) found that subjects' judgements of the damage caused by an action depended on whether they believed it was done intentionally, through negligence, or accidentally. Although the damage done was described in an identical way, subjects who read that the act was done intentionally inflated their estimation of the amount of damage done compared with subjects who believed the damage was caused unintentionally (either through negligence or accident).

Chaikin and Darley (1973) found that if someone spills ink over a large and expensive book, subjects are more likely to hold the person responsible than if it is spilt over a newspaper. Another facet of the consequences of behaviour is how these consequences affect us personally (*personal* or *hedonic relevance*): the more they affect us (the greater the hedonic relevance), the more likely we are to hold the actor responsible. For example, if someone spills ink over *our* large and expensive book, the more likely we are to blame them than if the book belonged to somebody else.

Jones and De Charms (1957) got subjects to participate in an experiment where small groups were engaged in a problem-solving task. In each group was a stooge who behaved quite incompetently at the task; half the subjects in each group were told they would receive prize money based on their individual performance, while the other half were told they would be rewarded according to the group's performance (so if one member failed they would all fail to receive any prize money). Afterwards, each subject had to rate all the other group members: the stooge was rated more negatively if he prevented the subjects from receiving prize money (ie if his behaviour had hedonic relevance for them) even though he behaved identically under both conditions.

Going one step further than hedonic relevance is *personalism*, which is the perceiver's belief that the actor *intended* to harm the perceiver; in terms of Jones and Davis's theory this increases the chances of making a correspondent inference. It seems that hedonic relevance may increase correspondent inferences being made about the *victim* as well as the perpetrator of certain emotionally unsettling acts (unsettling for *us* even if we are not the victim). There is a well-documented tendency to 'blame the victim' who suffers serious consequences more than one who suffers only mildly. How can we account for this? One suggestion is that people want to believe in a *just world* where good things happen to good people

GROUP STEREOTYPES

The basis for applying group stereotypes is similar to that for individual stereotypes: we may infer what qualities a person possesses either by being told what group they belong to (homosexual, Turk, Jew, etc.) or by observing their physical appearance and using one (or more) of these 'clues' to categorize them as belonging to a particular group (policeman, punk, 'old person', etc.). (This last example shows how difficult it sometimes is to make the distinction between group and individual stereotypes.)

The process of stereotyping itself involves the following reasoning: (i) we assign someone to a particular group (eg on the basis of their physical appearance); (ii) we bring into play the belief that all members of the group share certain characteristics (the stereotype); and (iii) we infer that this particular individual must possess these characteristics.

What evidence is there that people do actually apply group stereotypes? Karr (1978) found that homosexual males are usually rated as being more tense, shallow, yielding, impulsive, passive and quiet than men labelled heterosexual; they are also rated as less honest, fair, healthy, valuable, stable, intellectual, friendly and clean as a result of their homosexuality.

The basic method of studying ethnic stereotypes is that used by Katz and Braly (1933) in one of the best known and earliest studies of its kind. One hundred undergraduates at Princeton University, USA were presented with a list of ethnic groups (Americans, Jews, Negroes, Turks, Germans, Chinese, Irish, English, Italians and Japanese) and 84 words describing personality. They were asked to list, for each ethnic group, the five or six traits which were typical of that group. The aim was to find out whether traditional social stereotypes (as typically portrayed in papers and magazines) were actually held by Princeton students. The result showed that, in fact, they showed considerable agreement, especially about derogatory traits. One of the rather disturbing aspects of the findings was that most of the students had had no personal contact with any members of most of the ethnic groups they had to rate. Presumably, they had absorbed the images of those groups prevalent in the media.

In 1951, Gilbert studied another sample of Princeton students and this time found less uniformity of agreement (especially about unfavourable traits) than in the 1933 study. Many expressed great irritation at being asked to make generalizations at all.

In 1967, Karlins et al repeated the study. Again many students objected to doing the task but there was greater agreement on the traits they did assign compared with the 1951 study. There seemed to be a re-emergence of social stereotyping but in the direction of a more favourable stereotypical image.

THE NATURE OF STEREOTYPES

Given that people do use stereotypes, how should they be interpreted? Stereotypes, as a kind of *person schema*, illustrate the general cognitive tendency to store knowledge and experience in the form of simplified, generalized, representations—it would be impossible to store the details of each individual chair, cat or person we encounter (see Chapter 12):

    ... Without schemata and schematic processing, we would simply be overwhelmed by the information that inundates us. We would be very poor information processors. (Atkinson et al, 1990)

So from a cognitive point of view, there is nothing unique about stereotypes—they are universal and inevitable, '... an intrinsic, essential and primitive aspect of cognition ... (Brown, 1986).

But definitions claim that they are *exceptionless generalizations*, ie *every* punk is aggressive, *every* American is materialistic, etc. *without exception*. Can this possibly be the case?

According to Allport (1954), most stereotypes do contain a 'grain of truth'. Clearly, the degree of generalization involved is too great to make a stereotype factually true; no group is completely homogeneous and individual differences are the norm.

And yet the Katz and Braly instructions to list the traits typical of each ethnic/national group was thought to have been understood by subjects as an instruction to list the traits *true of all members* of each group (Brown, 1986). But the early studies never actually found out what subjects did understand by 'typical'. However, we noted that in the 1951 study (and again in 1967), some subjects were objecting to doing what was being asked of them. In fact, fairly substantial numbers actually refused to do it, sensing that characterizing ethnic groups at all would be interpreted as an ignorant or even immoral thing to do.

Brown (1986) cites a very interesting study by McCauley and Stitt (1978), which attempted to find out just what subjects do mean when they say a trait is typical of a group. The group chosen were Germans and three 'typical' traits were selected (efficient/extremely nationalistic/ scientifically-minded), plus two 'a-typical' traits (pleasure-loving/ superstitious).

Junior college students were told they would be asked a series of questions which they would not be able to answer exactly (eg 'What percentage of American cars are Chevrolets?').

Intermixed with these were *critical* questions about Germans—'What percentage of Germans are efficient/extremely nationalistic/ scientifically-minded/pleasure-loving/superstititous?' and, corresponding to these, 'What percentage of people in the world generally are efficient/extremely nationalistic/scientifically-minded/pleasure loving/ superstitious?' The results are shown in Table 17.2.

What do these results mean?

None of these values is even close to 100%, so clearly 'typical' does *not* mean 'true of all' (an exceptionless generalization) and 'Scientifically-

TRAIT	% PEOPLE IN THE WORLD	% GERMANS	DIAGNOSTIC RATIO
Efficient	49.8	63.4	1.27
Extremely nationalistic	35.4	56.3	1.59
Scientifically minded	32.6	43.1	1.32
Pleasure-loving	82.2	72.8	0.89
Superstitious	42.1	30.4	0.72

Table 17.2 The percentage of 'people in the world' and Germans rated as having particular traits (McCauley and Stitt, 1978; cited in Brown, 1986)

minded' is not even attributed to a majority of Germans. What 'typical' seems to mean is 'true of a higher percentage of the group in question than of people in general' (Brown, 1986), ie characteristic. This is what the Diagnostic Ratio is intended to show—it is calculated simply by dividing the percentage for Germans by the percentage for people in the world—anything over 1.00 represents a trait which belongs to the stereotype, anything below 1.00, represents a trait which does not.

So stereotypes, in the light of these results, seem to be schemas about what particular groups are like *relative* to 'people in general': they are *not* meant to be exceptionless generalizations. If this is the case, we should not condemn the fact that stereotypes occur, but condemn:

> . . . taking any serious action, such as hiring or firing an individual on the basis of knowledge of nothing but group membership when more diagnostic information is obtainable. Characterizations of groups are probabilistic in nature and of unknown validity, and so do not provide a rational basis for serious action . . . (Brown, 1986)

So it is not stereotypes themselves which are dangerous or objectionable, but how they affect the way that stereotyped individuals are treated.

STEREOTYPES AND BEHAVIOUR

Another feature of stereotyping is that it can influence how we interpret and classify behaviour we have observed and, in turn, how we recall that behaviour, ie it can determine what we select to notice in the first place and hence what we later remember. Clearly, this has great relevance to eyewitness testimony, that is, what witnesses say about a crime or accident they have witnessed (see Chapter 12).

Duncan (1976) showed subjects a video of a discussion between two males and told them it was a 'live' interaction over closed circuit television; they had to classify various pieces of behaviour. At one point, the discussion became heated and one actor gave the other a shove—the screen then went blank. Duncan wanted to see how subjects classified the shove, and they could choose from 'playing around', 'dramatizing', 'aggressive behaviour' and 'violent behaviour'. Subjects saw a version of the same film which differed only in the race of the two actors, either two whites, two blacks, a white who shoved a black, or a black who shoved a white. Many more subjects classified the black man's shove as violent behaviour, especially if he shoved a white man!

Rothbart et al (1979) found that people often recall better those facts that support their stereotypes (a case of selective remembering); and Howard and Rothbart (1980) found that people have better recall of facts which are critical of the minority than facts which are favourable (a case of negative memory bias). These findings help to explain why prejudices tend to remain fairly stable over time (although stereotypes represent only one component of prejudice—the cognitive or 'belief' component) (see Chapter 19).

Stereotypes may also result in polarized judgements, that is, the tendency to exaggerate the significance of a trait if it does not fit our stereotype of a certain ethnic or other group.

Linville and Jones (1980) gave subjects written descriptions of applications to law school. One group was told that one particularly impressive applicant was black; another group was told that the same applicant was white. Subjects judged the black applicant far more positively than the white—it made him seem all the more exceptional and, therefore, all the more impressive. When the situation was repeated with a particularly poor applicant, the black was judged far more harshly—it made him seem all the more typical and, therefore, unimpressive. Similar results were found when men judged female applicants.

Our expectations of people's personalities or capabilities may influence the way we actually treat them, which in turn may influence their behaviour in such a way that our expectation is confirmed. This is known as the *self-fulfilling prophecy* and is an illustration of how stereotypes can (although unwittingly) influence our behaviour, and not just our perception and memory. As we shall see in Chapter 21, the reactions of others can become a part of our own self-concept and this will be reflected in our actual behaviour. This is particularly dangerous in relation to racial and sexual discrimination. For example, poor housing and education can produce low self-esteem, poor academic achievement, laziness and so on, which are then taken as justification of the continued provision of poor housing and education.

Meichenbaum et al (1969) selected six girls out of a class of fourteen adolescents in a school for juvenile offenders, and their teachers were told they had high academic potential and were late developers. Observers' ratings showed subsequent differences in the teachers' behaviour towards those girls and on later objective examinations the six girls (matched with others on actual potential, classroom behaviour and the amount of attention normally received from teachers) performed significantly better. The teachers' expectations had actually influenced their behaviour towards the 'late developers', which had then influenced the girls' performances.

Finally, according to Campbell (1967) stereotypes can produce serious social problems. They involve: (i) the over-estimation of differences between groups, making groups appear vastly more different from each other than they really are; (ii) the under-estimation of variations within a group, since they regard groups as homogeneous, that is, every single member of the group is the same; (iii) distortions of reality since, like all generalizations, they appear to be factually true; and (iv) so long as the stereotype is in the forefront of consciousness, the individual never has to question it or examine the reasons underlying it—the stereotype can then, through the self-fulfilling prophecy, be used to justify hostility, discrimination and oppression.

Related to (i) is the *illusion of outgroup homogeneity*—the tendency to perceive people belonging to groups other than one's own as all alike. Related to (ii) is the *ingroup differentiation hypothesis*—the tendency to perceive members of one's own group as showing much larger differences from one another than those in other groups (Linville et al, 1989).

INFLUENCING HOW OTHERS SEE US— SELF-PRESENTATION

IMPRESSION MANAGEMENT

It is difficult to think of a social situation in which we are not trying (consciously or otherwise) to influence how others perceive us. This fundamental aspect of social interaction is referred to as *impression management* and is closely related to the concept of *self-presentation*.

Sometimes we may be trying to influence particular people on a particular occasion (eg a job interview) or we may be trying to maintain an image of ourselves which we believe is shared with other people in general (eg that we are caring or competent or attractive). Yet whatever the situation, it does seem that impression management is going on all the time.

Clearly, this is very relevant to *interpersonal attraction*—we can take an *active* role in making ourselves likeable to others; we do not simply sit back and let them be impressed (or not), but attempt to make them form a positive impression of us (Duck, 1988).

Impression management is a manipulation of the public self—it is the public self which is varied, controlled and observed:

> ... Self-presentation is not seen as passive conformity but as an active process of constructing a social identity and self-concept that enables one both to counter the power of others and to control others' actions by manipulating how one is perceived by others ... (Turner, 1991)

According to Turner, a number of studies suggest that concerns with self-presentation may underlie a whole range of phenomena, including bystander intervention, aggression, de-individuation (see Chapter 16), conformity (see Chapter 20) and cognitive dissonance (see Chapter 19).

Because behaviour is the vehicle for conveying impressions, a number of writers have likened the process of impression management to that of *acting*. To create a successful impression requires the right setting, props (eg the way you are dressed), skills and a shared understanding of what counts as 'backstage'. The person who takes *self-disclosure* too far, for instance, may be regarded as bringing onto stage what should be kept 'backstage' and so creates an unfavourable impression. Goffman, a Canadian sociologist, is one of the best-known exponents of this 'dramaturgical' analysis of social interaction, in books such as *Stigma* (1963) and *The Presentation of Self in Everyday Life* (1971).

Impression management requires us to 'take the role of the other' (see Cooley and Mead's theories of self, Chapter 21), ie we must be able, psychologically, to step into someone else's shoes to see how the impression looks from their viewpoint and to adjust our behaviour accordingly.

How do we do it? How do we try to impress another person favourably? Fiske and Taylor (1984), in a review of the literature, identify five major components:

(a) In *behaviour matching*, we try to match the target person's behaviour; an example would be that if they are self-disclosing, we will, too, to a comparable degree.

(b) When we *conform to situational norms*, we use our knowledge of what is appropriate behaviour in a particular situation to adopt that behaviour ourselves. For every social setting, there is a pattern of social interaction which conveys the best identity for that setting—the 'situated identity'. High self-monitors, in this respect, are more likely to be successful in making a favourable impression (see below).

(c) *Appreciating* or *flattering others* can sometimes produce a favourable response from the target person, especially if the appreciation is sincere. But flattery, if seen for what it is, can backfire on the flatterer who will be seen as deliberately trying to achieve his/her own ends.

(d) If we show *consistency among our beliefs*, or between our beliefs and behaviour, we are more likely to impress other people favourably, since inconsistency is generally taken as a sign of weakness.

(e) Our *verbal* and *non-verbal behaviour* should match, which they usually do if we are sincere. However, if we are flattering, for instance, or in some other way being dishonest, the non-verbal channel will often 'leak', giving away our true feelings. When people perceive an inconsistency between what we are saying and what we are conveying with our body, the non-verbal channel is usually taken as conveying the 'true' message (Argyle et al, 1972; Mehrabian, 1972).

Finally, there are certain exceptions to the rule regarding trying to convey positive impressions:

(a) We may feel constrained by the impressions which others already have of us and we act in order to 'muddy the waters'. For instance, if you are continually being told how good a son or daughter you are, the responsibility this places on you might encourage you to behave in the opposite fashion, so that you 'free yourself' from the expectation that you will go on behaving dutifully and respectfully, etc.

(b) You might protect yourself from anticipated failure by blaming, in advance, things about yourself which could explain the failure apart from your lack of competence. For example, teachers at exam time get quite used to students telling them how badly they are going to do, because of lack of sleep, not having been well, having been unable to revise, always getting anxious about exams and so on. These 'excuses' must be plausible, not too damaging and not very easy for anyone else to check out if they are to be successful in terms of impression management. Of course, indirectly they are attempts to convey a positive impression but they make use of negative attributes and these are 'centre stage'. There is a danger that these 'excuses' become internalized and then form part of our self-image, affecting both our behaviour and our self-esteem.

SELF-DISCLOSURE

How accurately others perceive us is determined partly by how much we reveal to them about ourselves, and this special kind of communication is called *self-disclosure*. According to Jourard (1971), we disclose ourselves in many ways—through what we say and do (as well as what we omit to say and do) and this includes facial expressions, gestures and other forms of non-verbal communication (NVC). This means that we have greater control over some aspects of self-disclosure than others, since, generally, we have greater control over verbal than non-verbal behaviour. However, Jourard believes that the decision to self-disclose (or to become 'transparent') is one taken freely and the aim in disclosing ourselves is to, 'be known, to be perceived by the other as the one I know myself to be' (Jourard, 1971).

Jourard believes that we can learn a great deal about ourselves through mutual self-disclosure and our intimacy with others can be enhanced. It is a way of both achieving and maintaining healthy personality (1964) but only if the self-disclosure meets the criterion of *authenticity* (or honesty). People with low self-esteem are often unable or unwilling to be open with others and, if they self-disclose at all, they tend to say things about themselves which they do not mean and which have been chosen more for their impact on how others see them ('impression management') than for their 'truth'.

What factors influence how much we disclose to others? Five major factors have emerged from the research: (i) reciprocity; (ii) norms; (iii) trust; (iv) quality of the relationship; and (v) gender.

(a) *Reciprocity.* The more personal information we disclose to someone, the more personal information they are likely to disclose to us. Sometimes, we might feel the other person is 'overdoing it' and giving too much away but we are still likely to reveal more about ourselves than we otherwise would.

(b) *Norms.* The situation we are in often determines how much (or what kinds of) disclosure are appropriate; for instance, it is acceptable for someone whom we meet at a party to tell us about their job but not to reveal details about medical problems or political beliefs.

(c) *Trust.* Generally, the more we trust someone, the more prepared we are to self-disclose to them.

(d) *Quality of relationships.* Altman and Taylor's 'Social Penetration Theory' maintains that the more intimate we are with somebody, the greater the range of topics we disclose to them and the more deeply we discuss any particular topic. Equally, a high degree of mutual self-disclosure can enhance the intimacy of the relationship and is an excellent predictor of whether couples stay together over a four-year period.

(e) *Gender.* Women generally disclose more than men and Jourard (1971) argues that men's limited self-disclosure prevents healthy self-expression and adds stress to their lives.

As with impression management, self-disclosure is very relevant to the understanding of interpersonal attraction. A key element in developing relationships is that we make ourselves more vulnerable:

> ... We usually tell our new partners increasingly secret or private information about ourselves and we do this as a measure and indication of our liking for them. However, that information—because of its very nature as private, secret, important, and revealing—puts a powerful weapon in his or her hands, if he or she should ever want to harm us. Our vulnerability increases to the extent that we reveal ourselves to the other person—indeed, the paradox of relationships is that increased intimacy and consequent security also increase risk and potential threat. A major concern of persons in dissolving relationships is precisely that the secrets revealed . . . will be used to harm us or gain revenge for the breaking up of the relationship . . . (Duck, 1988)

SELF-MONITORING

This refers to the extent to which people normally attend to external, social, situations as guides for their behaviour, as opposed to their own, internal states.

High self-monitors assess their behaviour with respect to the situation they are in and seem to blend easily into the social situation, knowing exactly what to say and do. If faced with an unfamiliar situation, they will ask, 'What's the ideal person for this situation and how can I be it?'. By contrast, *low self-monitors* remain themselves regardless of the situation and rarely bend or adapt to the norms of the social setting. If faced with an unfamiliar situation, they will ask, 'How can I best be me in this situation?'.

Again, high self-monitors are concerned with behaving in a socially appropriate manner and so are more likely to monitor the situation (rather than themselves), looking for subtle cues as to 'how to behave'. According to Ickes and Barnes, 1977 they are also on the watch for cues as to how others might be trying to manipulate or deceive them. For low self-monitors, the reverse is true: what they are monitoring is their behaviour in relation to their own enduring needs and values and the watch-word is consistency. Perhaps not surprisingly, high self-monitors are found to be more socially skilled; for instance, they learn how to behave in new situations faster, are more likely to initiate conversations and can interpret NVC more accurately compared with low self-monitors (Ickes and Barnes, 1977; Snyder, 1979).

According to Ajzen et al (1982), low self-monitors are more prone to the effect of temporary mood-states or fatigue, ie their behaviour is more likely to reveal their feelings, while highs are better at concealing these sources of internal interference. Because highs are more responsive to the demands of particular situations, their behaviour shows greater cross-situational inconsistency, that is, they behave differently in different situations. In contrast, lows are more consistent in different situations because their behaviour is governed much more by personal characteristics, which are more enduring than the norms associated with different situations.

Finally, highs see themselves as flexible, adaptable and shrewd and point to situational factors when accounting for why they behave as they do (consistent with what we said earlier about the actor–observer effect in attribution) while lows tend to explain their behaviour in terms of personality characteristics, values, principles and so on (clearly an exception to the actor-observer effect).

18 Interpersonal Attraction

According to popular belief, it is love that makes the world go round, but according to Rubin and McNeil (1983) liking perhaps more than loving is what keeps it spinning. How are liking and loving related and how are they different? What determines our choice of friends, partners, lovers and spouses? Is it possible to measure how much we like or love someone and is it possible to predict the kind of choices we are likely to make? Why do relationships go wrong and what causes them to break down?

Interpersonal attraction is really a facet of interpersonal perception. One of the major influences on choice of friends and the permanence of love-relationships seems to be the perceived similarity between oneself and others, another—physical attractiveness—was discussed in Chapter 17 in relation to stereotyping. The other major determinants of attraction are proximity, familiarity, reciprocal liking, complementarity and competence.

Relationships Must be Rewarding— The First 'Law' of Interpersonal Attraction

Before we discuss each of the seven major influences on interpersonal attraction in detail, it is important that we should consider the main overall theoretical approach to attraction, namely Exchange Theory (Thibaut and Kelley, 1959; Blau, 1964; Homans, 1974; Exchange Theory was also discussed in Chapter 16).

In trying to answer the question, 'What do all the important relationships in my life have in common?' you may say something to the effect that they are all rewarding, ie they provide you with security, happiness, contentment, fun and so on and (if you are honest) you will probably also acknowledge that they can be complex, demanding and, at times, even painful. If all relationships involve both positive and negative, desirable and undesirable, aspects, what determines our continued involvement with them (if we have that kind of choice) or how much we value them (if we don't)?

According to Homans (1974), we view our feelings for others in terms of *profits*, ie the amount of reward obtained from the relationship minus the cost—the greater the reward and lower the cost, the greater the profit and the greater the attraction.

According to Blau (1964), our interactions are 'expensive'; they take time, energy, commitment and may involve unpleasant emotions and experiences, and so what we get in return must outweigh what we put in. Similarly, Berscheid and Walster (1978) argue that in any social interaction, people exchange rewards (eg information, affection, status, money, skills and attention) and the degree of attraction or liking will reflect how each person evaluates the rewards they have received relative to those they have given.

But is it appropriate to think of relationships with other people in these economic, even capitalistic, terms? There is no doubt that Exchange Theory sees people as fundamentally selfish and human relationships as based primarily on self-interest. Are we really like this?

Like many attempts in psychology to explain behaviour, Exchange Theory offers a *metaphor* for human relationships and it should not be taken too literally. However, according to Rubin in *Liking and Loving*, although we like to believe that the joy of giving is as important as the desire to receive:

> we must face up to the fact that our attitudes toward other people are determined to a large extent by our assessments of the rewards they hold for us. (Rubin, 1973)

At the same time, he believes that Exchange Theory is not an adequate, complete account:

> Human beings are sometimes altruistic in the fullest sense of the word. They make sacrifices for the sake of others without any consideration of the rewards they will obtain from them in return. (Rubin, 1973)

And altruism is most often and most clearly seen in close interpersonal relationships (see Chapter 16).

Indeed, some psychologists make the distinction between 'true' love and friendship, which are altruistic, and less admirable forms which are based on considerations of exchange (Brown, 1986). Erich Fromm, for instance, in *The Art of Loving* (1956) defines true love as giving, as opposed to the false love of the 'marketing character' which depends upon expecting to have the favours returned. Is there any empirical support for such a distinction?

Mills and Clark (1980) identified two kinds of intimate relationship: (i) the *communal* couple, in which each partner gives out of concern for the other; and (ii) the *exchange* couple, in which each keeps mental records of who is 'ahead' and who is 'behind'. Such a scorekeeping mentality in a close relationship guarantees that both parties will be dissatisfied and Murstein (1978) has designed a scale (the Exchange Orientation Scale) which is intended to identify individuals who are preoccupied with 'getting their "fair" share'. These exchange types are suspicious, fearful, paranoid and insecure compared with the giving and trusting types (Murstein et al, 1977).

EXCHANGE AND EQUITY—RELATIONSHIPS MUST BE FAIR

Exchange Theory is really a special case of a more general account of human relationships, namely *equity theory*. The major extra 'ingredient' which is added to reward, cost and profit is *investment*:

> A person's investments are not just financial; they are *anything at all* that is believed to entitle him to his rewards, costs and profits. An investment is any factor to be weighted in determining fair profits or losses. (Brown, 1986)

Equity does *not* mean *equality*; rather, it refers to a *constant ratio* of rewards to costs or profit to investment:

> . . . Equity offers a rule of fairness more complex than the rule of fairness in Exchange Theory, which simply holds that between a P and O who directly exchange with one another, the profits of P should be equivalent to the profits of O in the more or less long run. (Brown, 1986)

Unlike Exchange Theory, 'equity' is not just in the minds of P *and* O, but comparisons can be made by a third party. Brown believes that Equity Theory captures a profoundly important generalization about social life, namely that:

> . . . Humans in society always acquiesce in some forms of inequality, always find it fair that rewards (or benefits or goods) should be unequally distributed among individuals. (Brown, 1986)

So it is *changes* in the ratios of what you put in and what you get out of a relationship which are likely to cause changes in how you feel about the relationship, rather than the initial ratio. You may believe it is fair and just that you give more than you get but if you start giving very much more than you did and receiving proportionately less, then you are likely to become dissatisfied.

Some versions of Exchange Theory do in fact take account of factors other than the simple and crude profit motives of social interactors. For example, Thibaut and Kelley (1959) introduced the two important concepts of *comparison level* (CL) and *comparison level for alternatives* (CL alt).

CL is basically the average level of rewards and costs that one is used to in relationships; it is the basic level that is expected to be obtained in any future relationship.

So, if my obtained reward:cost ratio in a current relationship falls below my CL, I shall be dissatisfied with the relationship, whereas if it is above my CL, I shall be satisfied.

CL alt is basically my expectation about the reward:cost ratio which *could* be obtained in other alternative relationships. If the ratio in any current relationship exceeds my CL alt, then I am doing better in it than I could do elsewhere, so I should feel satisfied and will probably choose to remain in it.

On this line of reasoning, the endurance of a relationship (as far as one partner is concerned) could be due to the qualities of the (other) partner and the relationship *or* to the negative and unattractive features of the perceived alternatives *or* to the perceived costs of leaving (Duck, 1988).

However, this is still a view of people as fundamentally selfish and some psychologists (Walster et al, 1978; Duck, 1988) prefer to see relationships as being maintained by an equitable distribution of rewards and costs for *both* partners—social actors are seen as being concerned with the equity of outcomes both for themselves and their partners.

THE MATCHING HYPOTHESIS (GETTING THE BEST DEAL WE CAN)

According to Roger Brown (1986), Exchange Theory clearly predicts that individuals who are willing to become romantically involved with each other will be fairly closely matched in their ability to reward one another (the Matching Hypothesis or 'Similarity Hypothesis').

Ideally, we would all have the most beautiful/handsome, charming, generous, and in other ways desirable, partners because we are all perfectly selfish (according to the theory). But, of course, this is impossible and so we have to find a compromise solution. The best general bargain that can be struck is a *value-match*, ie a subjective belief that our partner is the most rewarding we could realistically hope to find.

One of the major ways in which the matching hypothesis has been empirically investigated is the 'computer dance'. Men and women independently buy tickets for a dance (usually at a university or college at the start of an academic year) and complete detailed questionnaires about themselves which the computer, supposedly, uses in order to make ideal matches. The student subjects are rated (without their knowledge, of course) for physical attractiveness and are, in fact, assigned a partner purely randomly.

The earliest study was carried out by Walster et al (1966), who wanted to know how many men would ask their partner for a second date and on what basis. It turned out that the single most important factor that determined how likely it was that a woman would be asked out again was her physical attractiveness—regardless of the man's.

This is contrary to what the matching hypothesis predicts. If we settle for a value-match (as the hypothesis predicts), then only those men who happened to be matched (by chance) with a date whose attractiveness level closely resembled their own would have asked for a second date. But it seems that the men acted on pure selfishness: the more attractive the woman, the greater the probability that she would be asked out again, regardless of the man's own attractiveness. So the matching hypothesis seems to have been contradicted.

In the Walster et al study (as with other early studies), subjects were already sure of a date *before* interacting with their partners and expressed their preference *after* having dated (during the intermission). This, according to Berscheid et al (1971), minimizes the possibility of social rejection as a result of one's choice—the date had already been *assigned* and so there was no risk of choosing a more attractive partner who would rebuff them, hence dampening the aspirations of the unattractive. This implies that a more realistic or valid test of the matching hypothesis is under conditions where one has to *attain* a relationship, to choose a dating partner. So later computer-dance studies have asked subjects to stipulate *in advance* what kind of partners they wish for—here, people rated as high, low or of average attractiveness tended to ask for dates of a corresponding level of attractiveness, thus supporting the matching hypothesis (Dion and Berscheid, 1970; Berscheid and Walster, 1974).

The implication is, then, that the kind of partner we would be satisfied with is one we feel will not reject us, rather than one we positively desire. However, Roger Brown (1986) disagrees. He says the matching phenomenon results from a well-learned sense of what is 'fitting', rather than a fear of being rebuffed, ie we learn to adjust our expectations of rewards in line with what we believe we have to offer others. The computer-dance studies which do support the matching hypothesis also imply that how attractive we see ourselves quite accurately reflects how attractive others see us. Subjects were rated by observers for attractiveness and this attractiveness rating is what was correlated with the preferred level of attractiveness in the date. The significant positive correlation obtained implies a correspondence between the attractiveness rating and the subject's self-rating (although this wasn't actually elicited and is usually probably unconscious).

Despite the more recent support for the matching hypothesis, these studies still only test interpersonal attraction based on, at most, a few hours interaction.

Berscheid and Walster (1974) claim that, 'couples who have formed viable affectional relationships should appear to outside observers to be of approximately equal levels of physical attractiveness'. They cite a study by Silverman (1971) of 'fait accompli' matching (ie matching which has already occurred). Couples were observed in naturalistic dating settings—bars, social events, theatre lobbies. Two males and two females formed the observer team. The observed couples were predominantly eighteen to twenty-two-years-old and unmarried. Each observer independently rated the dating partner of the opposite sex, on a five-point scale. There was an extremely high degree of similarity between the attractiveness of the couple members. Also, the more similar their attractiveness, the happier they seemed to be with each other (as reflected by the degree of intimacy, eg holding hands)—60 per cent of highly similar, 46 per cent of moderately similar and 22 per cent of least similar couples appeared happy.

However, the observers *saw* both dating partners *together*, so a 'halo' emanating from one dating partner might have influenced the observers' rating of the other partner (Berscheid and Walster, 1974), ie the expectation of similarity could have biased the observers' ratings towards a more similar rating of the one member based on the rating of the other. It has also been questioned (Udry, 1971) whether the degree of matching could have occurred by chance, since 85 per cent of the couples were not separated by more than one scale point and no couple by more than 2.5 points. The point here is that the scale did not permit discriminations to be made between individuals because there were only five points on the scale!

A study which gets around the problem of seeing the couple actually together is Murstein's (1972), in which first 99 engaged or steady couples, then a separate sample of 98, were photographed. Judges rated the photographs for physical attractiveness on a five-point scale without knowing who the couples were ('who belonged to whom'). The subjects had to rate their own and their partner's physical attractiveness.

Judges' ratings strongly supported the matching hypothesis—partners received very similar ratings and these were significantly more alike than the same ratings given to 'random couples' (ie the actual couples randomly sorted into couples to form a control group).

How partners rated *themselves* (self-concept for attractiveness) was significantly more similar than self-ratings for random couples, thus also supporting the matching hypothesis, but partners' ratings of *each other* did not prove significant. These results apply (more or less equally) to both samples.

Murstein concludes that:

> Individuals with equal market value for physical attractiveness are more likely to associate in an intimate relationship such as premarital engagement than individuals with disparate values. (Murstein, 1972)

Price and Vandenberg (1979) went a step or two further by studying married couples, aged between 28 and 60. Allowing for age effects on attractiveness (eg young people tend to rate older people as less attractive, everything else being equal), they concluded that, 'the matching phenomenon [of physical attraction levels between marriage partners] is stable within and across generations'.

COMPATIBILITY

As we have seen, physical attraction is the major predictor of liking in the short-term—at least as measured by the wish to date again. But not only is there a matching phenomenon involved in physical attractiveness, according to the matching hypothesis, genuine couples will be more alike than random couples on *any* dimension which enters into a calculation of social value (Brown, 1986) and there is evidence suggesting that matching is an important ingredient of compatibility. Hatfield et al (1978), in a review of the literature, concluded that couples tend to be similar with respect to IQ, education and other characteristics.

Hill et al (1976) studied 231 steadily-dating couples over a two-year period, at the end of which 103 couples had broken up (45 per cent). The surviving couples tended to be more alike in terms of age, intelligence, educational and career plans, as well as physical attractiveness, while those who split up often mentioned differences in interests, background, sexual attitudes and ideas about marriage. Certain other characteristics seemed irrelevant in that they did not distinguish between the couples who split up and those who survived, namely height, religion and father's occupation.

Could the splitting up or staying together have been predicted from the initial questionnaire data? It seems they could to a significant degree: about 80 per cent of the couples who described themselves as being 'in love' at the start stayed together, compared with 56 per cent who did not so describe themselves. Interestingly, whether or not they had had intercourse, and whether or not they were living together, was completely unrelated to whether or not they were still together two years later.

Can the findings throw any light on Exchange Theory?

Of couples in which both members initially reported being equally involved in the relationship, only 23 per cent broke up, but where one member was much more involved than the other, 54 per cent did so. The latter type is a highly unstable couple in which the one who is more involved (putting more in but getting less in return) may feel dependent and exploited, while the one who is less involved (putting less in but getting more in return) may feel restless and guilty (which implies some sense of *fairness*).

Scales have been developed to measure the 'returns' for each member of a couple. The Hatfield Global Measure of Equity–Inequity (Hatfield et al, 1978), for example, attempts to identify individuals who feel that their relationship is *equitable*, that is, they get as much as they give (a scale value of 0), those who feel severely under-benefited, that is, they get much *less* than they give (a scale value of −3) and those who feel extremely over-benefited, that is, they get much *more* than they give (a scale value of +3). (This seems to be a measure of perceived *equality*, which is *not* how we defined equity above.)

Hatfield et al (1978) interviewed 537 college men and women who were dating, either casually or seriously, and asked them if they expected to be together in one and five years time. Those who felt the relationship was equitable were much more likely than either the under- or over-benefited, to believe they would still be together (as predicted by Exchange Theory) and a follow-up $3\frac{1}{2}$ months later confirmed these expectations. Those in equitable relationships were the most happy and contented, the under-benefited felt angry and the over-benefited felt guilty.

Hatfield et al (1979) asked a random sample of newly-weds about their marital happiness and to rate how far they felt they were receiving too much or too little in relation to what they were putting into the marriage. Those who thought they were *under*-benefiting were the least happy but not far behind were those who felt they were *over*-benefiting.

According to Murstein and MacDonald (1983), although the principles of exchange and equity play a significant role in intimate relationships, a great *conscious* concern with 'getting a fair deal', especially in the short term, makes compatibility very hard to achieve, both in friendship and, especially, in marriage. (This corresponds to the 'exchange' couple, described by Mills and Clark (1980), mentioned on p. 493).

What might people do if they believe they are not getting a fair deal in order to restore equity? One course of action is to have an extra-marital affair. Hatfield et al (1978) found that, of 2000 married people they studied, those who felt deprived, cheated or under-benefited had extra-marital affairs sooner into their marriage, and had more of them, than those who felt either fairly treated or over-benefited (Brown, 1986).

SPECIFIC FACTORS INFLUENCING ATTRACTION

PROXIMITY, EXPOSURE AND FAMILIARITY

This really represents a minimum requirement for attraction because it represents a minimum requirement for interaction. Clearly, the further apart two people live, the lower the probability that they will ever meet, let alone become friends or marry each other; and in extreme cases (eg living in different countries) this does not tell us a great deal about why we like some people more than others.

To some extent, our choices about friends and partners are made for us: social circumstances reduce the 'field of availables' (Kerckhoff, 1974), ie the range of people that are *really* available for us to meet (as opposed to those who are *theoretically* available). In any culture, there is considerable pre-selection of the types of people we meet and become aware of and tend to regard or treat as realistic possibilities for relationships. They are mostly from our own racial, religious, social class, and educational groups, and they also tend to be of a similar intellectual level.

These are the *types* of people we tend to find most attractive initially (since similarity of this type makes communication easier, we have something immediately in common with them, as a group), so at this point, attraction has little to do with other peoples' individual characteristics.

However, within these parameters, we will, inevitably, come into contact more often with some members of these groups than others (although this is also something over which we may have little choice or control). For example:

Festinger et al (1950) studied friendship patterns in a university campus housing complex for married students. People were more friendly with those who lived next door (41 per cent), next most friendly with those living two doors away and least friendly with those who lived at the end of the corridor (10 per cent). Families separated by four flats hardly ever became friends and in two-storey blocks of flats, the residents tended to interact mainly with others living on the same floor. On any one floor, people who lived near stairways had more friends than those living at the end of the corridor. Similar friendship patterns have been reported for a new suburban community, student dormitories and residents of a home for the elderly.

Clearly, what all these cases of *proximity* have in common is the increased opportunity for interaction, what Zajonc (1968) calls *exposure*. According to Argyle (1981), the more two people interact, the more *polarized* their attitudes towards each other become, usually in the direction of greater liking which, in turn, increases the likelihood of further interaction, but only if the interaction is as equals. (Equal status interaction has important implications for reducing prejudice; see Chapter 19.)

However, we still have not really explained *why* greater proximity increases attraction: could not increased exposure just as easily decrease attraction? A crucial variable related to exposure is *familiarity*. It seems that we like people and things which are familiar and dislike or mistrust the unfamiliar (and so, to this extent, familiarity does not breed contempt!).

Newcomb (1961) offered male students free board and lodging at a rented boarding house at Michigan University if they participated in a study of the acquaintance process. They were randomly assigned a room and during the first year of the study it seemed that it was similarity of attitudes, beliefs and values which was the strongest determinant of liking. In the second year, using different subjects, Newcomb assigned each student a room-mate who was either highly similar to himself, or as different as possible, on a wide range of attitudes, beliefs and values. It was predicted, based on the first year's results, that similarity would again be the major influence, but it turned out to be familiarity that was the key factor—room-mates became friends far more often than would have been expected on the basis of their characteristics.

Saegert et al (1973) found that female subjects who were 'incidentally' exposed to other women (that is, there was no actual talking or other interaction) on a number of occasions during a 'liquid-tasting experiment' came to prefer these women to those whom they only saw once. Despite having to taste unpleasant laboratory solutions, the mere repeated exposure to other people seems to be a reason for liking them.

Zajonc et al (1971, 1974) asked subjects to evaluate photographs of strangers and those which appeared more often were rated more positively than those which appeared less often. Similar results have been found when female students rated slides of male students for attractiveness, when subjects had to rate paintings, Pakistani music and political candidates. There is also evidence that the amount of exposure given to political candidates by the media was a very reliable predictor of their eventual success in American primary elections.

So it seems that we like what we know and what we are familiar with, perhaps because it is predictable and causes us very little in the way of anxiety. On the other hand, repeated exposure to something or somebody may reveal the less acceptable and desirable qualities, so that familiarity will 'breed contempt'. However, most of the research on familiarity has supported the positive outcome of repeated exposure.

PERSONAL SPACE – CAN PROXIMITY BREED CONTEMPT?

As we have seen, it is not proximity as such which accounts for increased liking but the greater opportunity for interaction with those who are physically accessible to us. In Exchange Theory terms, proximity can bring about rewards at low costs and this interpersonal 'profit' is translated into liking. If we do not have to make great effort to find people whom we like, then we can 'invest' more of ourselves in those who are available, close at hand and 'on tap'.

However, it seems that sometimes mere physical closeness (especially if accompanied by bodily contact) can be unpleasant and cause us to dislike the person concerned, even to the point of physically removing ourselves from their vicinity. If we are sitting in an otherwise empty row of seats in a train, for instance, and someone comes and sits right next to us, we may well feel uneasy and suspicious (especially if the stranger is of the opposite sex), whether or not we do anything about it. In a series of studies by Sommer, the experimenter deliberately sat close to unsuspecting subjects when there was plenty of other available space in order to see how likely they were to react to this invasion of their personal space.

In the Library Study (Felipe and Sommer, 1966), the subjects were female students studying at a large table with six chairs on either side of the table; there were at least two empty chairs on either side of each subject and one opposite, and there were a number of experimental conditions in which, for example, the experimenter: (i) sat next to the subject and moved his chair nearer to hers; (ii) sat two seats away from her (leaving one chair between them); (iii) sat three seats away; and (iv) sat immediately opposite her.

Subjects were more likely to leave, move away, adjust the chair or erect barriers (such as putting a bag on the table between themselves and the 'intruder') when he sat next to them, as in condition (i). Similar results were found for psychiatric patients (Felipe and Sommer, 1966) and for people sitting on park benches (Sommer et al, 1969). In the last study, the experimenter sat six inches away from subjects on an otherwise empty bench and these subjects were much more likely to move away—and sooner—than control subjects who were not joined by the over-friendly stranger.

We have all had the experience of accidentally making body contact with a stranger, which usually produces an immediate apology, and even when forced into very close proximity (such as on a crowded tube train or in a crowded lift) we somehow manage to take 'diversionary action', ie we look away, ensuring that we do not make eye-contact, look down or up, anywhere but *at* the stranger (we may even pretend to cat-nap if there is nowhere or nothing to look at!).

It seems that we are very sensitive to others'—and our own—need for personal space. This term was first used by the anthropologist Edward T. Hall (1959, 1966) to describe the human behaviour which resembled the 'individual distance' of zoo animals (Hediger, 1951), ie the distance which two individuals of the same species try to keep between each other. According to Hall, we learn *proxemic rules*, which prescribe: (i) the amount of physical distance that is appropriate in daily relationships; and (ii) the kinds of situations in which closeness or distance is proper. Our feelings for others may depend on whether these culturally determined rules are followed and these rules are themselves influenced by the nature of the relationship. For instance, relatives and intimate friends are allowed much closer proximity—and bodily contact—than mere acquaintances or strangers. As far as bodily contact is concerned, there are different rules for different relatives, depending on their gender and this applies to friends too.

One famous study by Jourard (1966) asked college students to report which parts of their body were touched by their fathers, mothers, same-sex friends and opposite-sex friends. Not surprisingly, opposite-sex friends turned out to be allowed the most intimate bodily contact, especially in terms of the total body area of contact but also which particular parts of the body are touched (Fig. 18.1).

Hall identifies four main regions or zones of personal space, which are summarized in Table 18.1.

It is important to note that there may be certain exceptions to these proxemic rules and they may be modified under certain circumstances:

(a) We sometimes allow strangers (or near-strangers) to enter our intimate zone, eg doctors, dentists, hairdressers, where bodily contact is expected or necessary as part of our respective roles.

(b) Children are much less sensitive to the rules of proxemics and often embarrass strangers by how freely they enter other people's intimate zone. Clearly, these rules are acquired in the course of socialization although they are usually implicit (like the rules of grammar) and not explicitly taught.

1. *Intimate distance* (0–18 inches)	This may involve actual bodily contact and is reserved for our most intimate relationships	*Table 18.1 Hall's four zones of personal space (1959, 1966)*
2. *Casual-personal distance* (1½ feet–4 feet)	This is the distance in which we usually interact with close friends, trusted acquaintances, at parties, or with those who share special interests with us	
3. *Social-consultative distance* (4 feet–12 feet)	This is the distance commonly found between colleagues at work, and is used for most business and formal contacts	
4. *Public distance* (12 feet and beyond)	This is used for large, public meetings and lectures, and meetings with high-ranking persons	

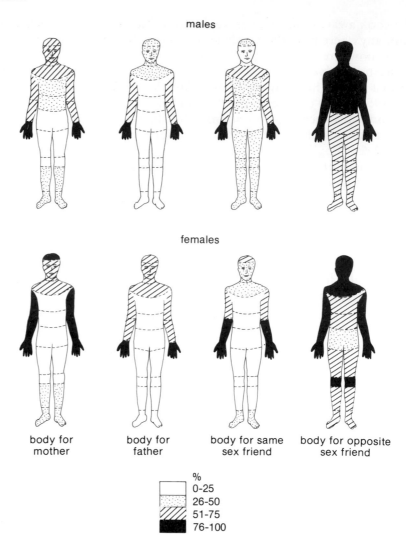

males

females

| body for mother | body for father | body for same sex friend | body for opposite sex friend |

%
0-25
26-50
51-75
76-100

(c) There are important cultural differences regarding proxemic rules. Each zone allows the use of different cues of touch, smell, hearing and seeing, which are more important in some cultures than others. Watson and Graves (1966) observed discussion groups of Americans or those from Arab countries. In the latter there was more direct face-to-face orientation, greater closeness and touching. South Americans and Arabs have been called 'contact cultures', while the Scots and Swedes have been called 'non-contact cultures'.

(d) Proximity is but one kind of social act which makes up the degree of intimacy which exists between two people. According to Argyle and Dean (1965), we all have a tendency to approach others, to be in contact with them, to seek the company of others, and at the same time we have an opposing tendency to avoid others, to remain separate and independent of others. The balance between these two opposing tendencies is 'negotiated', non-verbally, in each social situation in which we find ourselves, so that we try to find a mutually acceptable *level of intimacy*, that is, a level with which we feel comfortable. Clearly, the subjects in the studies of Sommer et al felt uncomfortable when the experimenter sat himself right next to them—he was making the situation too intimate as far as they were concerned. Similarly, when we are squeezed against fellow-passangers in the tube, we look away from those nearest to us to prevent the level of intimacy from increasing any further—it is already psychologically (as well as physically) uncomfortable enough by this stage!

(e) Hildreth et al (1971) found that criminals convicted of violent crimes were much more sensitive to physical closeness with others than non-violent criminals. Nicholson (1977) refers to the concept of a '*body-buffer zone*', defined as the point at which a person begins to feel uncomfortable when approached by another (a concept similar to Hall's 'personal space'). Violent criminals compared with non-criminals (and schizophrenics compared with other kinds of psychiatric patients) tend to have larger body-buffer zones, that is, they more easily begin to feel uneasy when others walk towards them.

Successful friendships may *require* an initial establishment of boundary understandings, ie in Hall's terms, strangers must be 'invited' into our intimate zone and not 'trespass' from an initial casual personal distance, while in Argyle and Dean's 'equilibrium model' of intimacy, strangers who make a situation uncomfortably intimate, too soon, are unlikely to become friends.

SIMILARITY—DO BIRDS OF A FEATHER FLOCK TOGETHER?

We have already discussed this to some extent in relation to the matching hypothesis.

Most studies suggest that the critical similarities are those to do with beliefs, attitudes and values. Newcomb (1943) in a famous study at Bennington College, an expensive American East Coast women's university college with a libertarian tradition amongst the teaching staff and senior students, found that many students coming from conservative backgrounds adopted liberal attitudes in order to gain the liking and acceptance of classmates.

In his 1961 study described above, Newcomb found that similarity of attitudes, values and beliefs was the major determinant of liking among room-mates, at least when they were randomly assigned.

Griffitt and Veitch (1974) paid thirteen males to spend ten days in a fall-out shelter. Those with similar attitudes and opinions liked each other most by the end of the study, particularly if they agreed on highly salient issues. Duck (1973) found that similarity of cognitive constructs used for describing other people was an especially strong determinant of liking (see Chapter 29).

However, it seems that the importance of similarity may depend on how long-standing or otherwise a relationship is. For example, Kerckhoff and Davis (1962) tested and interviewed young couples at college who were contemplating marriage. Those who had been together for less than 18 months tended to have a stronger relationship when the partners' values coincided but with couples of longer-standing, similarity was *not* the most important factor.

This led Kerckhoff and Davis (1962) to propose that relationships pass through a series of 'filters'. At first, similarity of sociological variables will determine the likelihood of individuals meeting in the first place (they determine the 'field of availables'). Then consensus on certain basic values is necessary for the couple to become relatively stable and permanent. Finally, *complementarity* of needs becomes important (see below).

Why should similarity be so important? According to Rubin (1973), similarity is rewarding because:

(a) Agreement may provide a basis for engaging in joint activites.
(b) A person who agrees with us helps to increase our confidence in our own opinions, which enhances our self-esteem. According to Duck (1979) the validation that friends give us is experienced as evidence of the accuracy of our personal constructs.
(c) Most people are vain enough to believe that anyone who shares their views must be a sensitive and praiseworthy individual.
(d) People who agree about things that matter to them generally find it easier to communicate.
(e) We may assume that people with similar attitudes to ourselves will like us—and so we like them in turn (this is called *reciprocal liking*, see below).

COMPLEMENTARITY—DO OPPOSITES ATTRACT?

We have seen that similarity may be especially important during the early stages of a relationship, but that complementary needs may become relatively more important as the relationship persists (Kerckhoff and Davis, 1962).

According to Winch (1955, 1958), happy marriages are often based on each member's ability to fulfill the needs of the other. A classic example is that of a dominant person who would not be likely to choose as a partner someone who was equally dominant, which would probably be a good recipe for disaster and Winch found some empirical support for this view.

Snyder and Fromkin (1980) go so far as to suggest that, because we like to see ourselves as unique individuals, others whom we see as being highly similar to ourselves may be disliked for that reason. However, Rubin and McNeil (1983) disagree. They argue that, although diversity is valuable and enriching and, under certain circumstances we might actively seek it, people with fundamentally different approaches to life are unlikely to become friends. Thus:

> For a human being to adapt to a rapidly changing world, he needs the companionship and support of others with whom he may sometimes disagree, but nevertheless feels a fundamental bond of likemindedness. (Rubin and McNeil, 1983)

RECIPROCAL LIKING (I LIKE YOU BECAUSE YOU LIKE ME)

It is certainly very flattering when someone pays us compliments and generally seems to like us; perhaps it also puts us under a certain obligation to reward the other person in turn.

According to Aronson's *reward–cost principle* (1976), we are most attracted to a person who makes entirely positive comments about us over a number of occasions and least attracted to one who makes entirely negative comments about us. This in itself may seem rather obvious. More interesting, however, is Aronson and Linder's *'gain–loss' theory* of attraction (1965). According to this, someone who starts off by disliking us and then changes their feelings in our favour will be liked *more* than someone who likes us from the start. Equally, someone who begins by liking us and then adopts a negative attitude towards us will be disliked *more* than someone who dislikes us from the start.

Aronson and Linder (1965) told subjects that the experiment was concerned with verbal conditioning and that the learner (a confederate) had to be deceived by being told it was about interpersonal attraction. In fact, the naïve subject believed she was the confederate. She assisted the experimenter by monitoring the learner's performance during seven separate conversations between the experimenter and the learner, in which the latter described her impressions of the subject (whom she had met during the course of the experiment) and then had to rate how much she liked the learner. As predicted, when the learner changed from disliking to liking the subject (*gain condition*), she was liked much more than when she liked the subject from the start; and when the learner changed from liking to disliking (*loss condition*) she was disliked much more than when she disliked the subject from the start.

In a similar study (Clore et al, 1975) subjects had to rate how attracted a woman was to a man in a video on the basis of her non-verbal communication only. As in the Aronson and Linder experiment, the gain condition (in which she first acted rather coolly towards him and then 'warmed up') produced the highest attractiveness rating and the loss condition the lowest.

COMPETENCE

Although we generally admire and respect people who show themselves to be capable and competent, it seems that we prefer competent people who are at the same time fallible: we do not like people who seem perfect and so when their 'human slip' shows, we like them more, not less.

In one famous study, Aronson et al (1966) played tape recordings of a *Quizbowl* (the equivalent of the British *University Challenge* TV programme). Some subjects heard a tape of a 'superior' contestant, who answered 92 per cent of the very difficult quiz questions correctly, was editor of the college yearbook, was a member of the athletics team and so on; while other subjects heard a tape of an average contestant, who answered 30 per cent of the very difficult questions correctly, was a proofreader on the yearbook staff and so on. For each group (superior and average), half the contestants made a 'spilt coffee blunder' and subjects were asked to rate how much they liked the contestant. What were the findings?

Regardless of whether he spilled his coffee, the superior contestant was liked more than the average one *but* the superior contestant who spilled the coffee was the most liked of all; the least-well liked was the clumsy, average contestant.

Showing himself to be fallible (and, to that extent, more human), the competent person may be perceived as more like ourselves and, there-fore, more attractive for that reason. However, this assumes that we regard the competent person as being superior to ourselves in the first place. If we think of ourselves as superior, the clumsiness may then have the effect of making the person seem less like ourselves, and, hence, less likeable.

A critical influence, therefore, on how we respond to the fallibility of other people is our own initial level of *self-esteem*. Aronson et al (1970) repeated the experiment and confirmed that spilling coffee only en-hanced the attractiveness of the superior contestant for subjects of average self-esteem; those with very high *or* very low self-esteem, liked him less. So it is *relative*, rather than absolute, competence or superiority which is related to attraction.

There is some evidence of an interesting sex difference here: while males were attracted to a competent man who made a blunder, women preferred competent people who did not blunder (whether male or female). (What does this suggest to you about the relative self-esteem of men and women?)

Finally, a fascinating real-life example is given by Rubin and McNeil (1983). After President Kennedy had approved the ill-fated Bay of Pigs invasion of Cuba in 1961 (which led to the Cuban missile crisis), an opinion poll taken immediately afterwards showed that his popularity actually *increased*. It seems that we do not like even our national leaders to appear perfect!

PHYSICAL ATTRACTIVENESS

We have said much about this already in relation to the 'matching hypothesis'; but there is a great deal of research which is revealing about the influence of physical appearance on attraction which goes beyond the dimension of similarity.

We saw in Chapter 17, when discussing individual stereotypes, that people who are physically attractive are perceived as being psychologi-cally attractive also, ie they are judged to have a whole host of positive characteristics, even in the absence of any evidence about the kind of person they are, simply on the basis of what they look like. But can it work the other way round, ie if we hear of a person having certain positive qualities, will our rating of their physical attractiveness be increased? It seems that it may well be so.

This represents one way in which perception of physical attractiveness is not objective but is influenced by a number of factors, including culture, gender and context.

CULTURE

Different cultures have different criteria of what constitutes physical beauty. According to Garfield (1982), chipped teeth, body scars, arti-ficially elongated heads and bound feet have all been regarded as beautiful, and even in our own culture definitions change over time, as in the 'ideal' figure for women. Facial beauty is generally regarded as more important in women than men, while in men it is their stature, particularly height, which influences how attractive they are judged to be.

It has been observed that every American President elected between 1900 and 1968 was taller than his major opponent. It is possible, of course, that taller men have other characteristics that make them more desirable than shorter men, but certainly the perception of a man's height is correlated with liking him. Two-thirds of a Californian sample who planned to vote for Kennedy in the 1960 presidential election perceived him as being taller than Nixon and a majority of those planning to vote for Nixon saw him being at least as tall as Kennedy. Kennedy was actually a few inches taller (Hilgard et al, 1979).

However, studies using whole-body silhouettes show that women prefer men with prominent buttocks and large chests. Other evidence suggests that overall body shape is important to both men and women, with upper body shape being most important for men judging women.

GENDER

It seems that men are more responsive to beauty than women; they generally seem to prefer an attractive woman, whether to work with, to date or to marry, whereas women generally consider similarity of interests to be as or more important.

After a dance, men are more likely to report feelings of attraction based on physical appearance than are women (Berscheid and Walster, 1974). These differences seem to be symptomatic of the pervasive difference in gender roles which exist in our society (see Chapter 23), in which, traditionally, a woman has been regarded as the property of a man, whereby her beauty increases his status and respect in the eyes of others (Sigall and Landy, 1973). Again, the reverse does not seem to apply—the attractiveness of a man does not seem to enhance a woman's standing among other women (Bar-Tal and Saxe, 1976).

CONTEXT

Perceived beauty can wax and wane according to circumstances. For example, a person who disagrees with us might suddenly lose their physical appeal—and vice versa.

Several studies have looked at the interaction between a person's physical attractiveness and their chances of being found guilty of a crime. Do good-looking criminals get off lightly?

Monahan (1941) found that beautiful women were less likely to be convicted and Efran (1974) found that we tend to be more lenient when punishing good-looking criminals. However, a criminal's good looks can actually work to their disadvantage depending on the nature of the crime: if it is one in which the criminal's good looks played a part (eg fraud in which a woman charms a man into giving her money for a non-existent cause), they are likely to be *more* severely punished than a less attractive person committing the same crime. When the crime is not related to good looks (eg burglary), an unattractive person is likely to be more severely punished than an attractive one.

Similarly, adults (including parents) may treat children differently according to their physical appeal (quite unconsciously, of course). Adults may also expect that good-looking children will be better behaved than less attractive ones; when the former do behave badly they may have their behaviour excused by adults making situational—as opposed to dispositional—attributions (see Chapter 17).

Dion (1972), in an experimental study, used photographs of seven-year-old children plus accounts of their misbehaviour (either mild or severe) and found that adult subjects were more likely to attribute anti-social tendencies to the unattractive children if the misbehaviour were serious. Subjects also thought that the attractive children were less likely to have behaved badly in the past and were thought less likely to be naughty again (even if the present behaviour were serious). Unattractive girls were evaluated more leniently than unattractive boys, which suggests the interaction of attractiveness and gender role.

Physically attractive children are generally more popular with their peers and they may become friendly and self-confident as a consequence of people's response to their good looks, which may become a source of power over other children (see Influences on Self-Concept, in Chapter 21). Good looks in adults may also become a source of power over other adults.

According to Duck:

> A great deal of research ... confirms that we react more favourably to physically beautiful people than we do to less attractive, ugly or deformed people ... (Duck, 1988)

But rating another person as attractive is hardly the basis for a relationship:

> ... relationships are not created by the mere 'chemistry' of partner attributes, that is they do not spring into life from the mere mixing together of positively valued social attributes, such as physical beauty or an attractive personality. Relating to others involves interaction and social processes that can override the effects of initially positive responses to superficial characteristics ... (Duck, 1988)

LIKING AND LOVING

In *Liking and Loving* (1973), Rubin defines liking as positive evaluation of another and loving as more than an intense liking, being *qualitatively* different and comprising three main components:

(a) *Attachment.* The need for the physical presence and emotional support of the loved one. (On the Love Scale, an attachment item is 'If I could never be with —— I would feel miserable'.)
(b) *Caring.* A feeling of concern and responsibility for the loved one. ('If —— were feeling badly my first duty would be to cheer him/her up'.)
(c) *Intimacy.* The desire for close and confidential contact and communication, wanting to share certain thoughts and feelings with the loved one more fully than with anyone else. ('I feel that I can confide in —— about practically everything'.)

Caring corresponds to Fromm's definition of love (1956) as, 'the active concern for the life and growth of that which we love'.

The Love Scale can also be applied to same-sex friends and Rubin found that females reported loving their friends more than men, but there was no differences in scores on the Liking Scale. Other studies suggest that women's friendships tend to be more intimate than men's, engaging in more spontaneous joint activities and more exchange of confidences. Rubin and McNeil (1983) suggest that loving for men may be channelled into single, sexual relationships while women may be better able to experience attachment, caring and intimacy in a wider range and variety of relationships.

It has been suggested that love is a label that we learn to attach to our own state of physiological arousal (see Chapter 6) but most of the time love does *not* involve intense physical symptoms; love, therefore, is more usefully thought of as a particular sort of attitude that one person has towards another (Rubin and McNeil, 1983).

Berscheid and Walster (1978) agree that love does not usually involve intense physiological arousal by distinguishing between *companionate love* ('the affection we feel for those with whom our lives are deeply entwined', including very close friends and marriage partners) and *passionate* or *romantic love*. ('A state of intense absorption in another. Sometimes lovers are those who long for their partners or for complete fulfilment. Sometimes lovers are those who are ecstatic at finally having attained their partner's love and, momentarily, complete fulfilment. A state of intense physiological arousal.')

These are *qualitatively* different but companionate love is only a more extreme form of *liking* ('the affection we feel for casual acquaintances').

THE BREAK-DOWN OF RELATIONSHIPS

WHY DO RELATIONSHIPS GO WRONG?

We have already touched on some of the contributory causes to relationship breakdown in the sections on compatibility. Here we shall look at some others.

Duck (1988) identifies four antecedents of divorce and marital unhappiness, ie factors making it more likely that the marriage will end in one or both of these:

(a) Marriages where the partners are younger than usual tend to be more unstable. (This can be related to Erikson's concept of intimacy, whereby teenage marriages, for example, involve individuals who have not yet fully established their sense of identity, and so are not ready for a commitment to one particular person; see Chapter 21.) Also:

> There seems to be a link between the rising divorce rate and the increasing trend towards early parenthood which allows young couples little time to adjust to the new relationships and responsibilities of marriage; then financial and housing problems are added with the arrival of a baby. (Kellmer Pringle, 1986)

(b) Marriages between couples from lower socio-economic groups and lower educational levels tend to be more unstable. (These are also the couples which tend to have their children very early into marriage.)

(c) Marriages between partners from different demographic backgrounds (race, religion, etc.) also tend to be more unstable.

(d) Marriages between people who have experienced parental divorce as children or who have had a wider variety of sexual experiences and a greater number of sexual partners than average before marriage, tend to be more unstable.

Clearly, these factors on their own cannot adequately explain why marriage break-up occurs, since only a certain proportion of marriages involving young, lower class individuals or those from different cultural backgrounds, etc. actually end in divorce. Conversely, many divorces will involve couples who do not fit any of these descriptions.

Relationships are highly complex and that is true of the *process* of relationship break-up as much as their formation and maintenance. It applies to the break-up of friendships and sexual relationships and not just marriages:

> ...particularly if the relationship is a long-term one that has embraced many parts of the person's emotional, communicative, leisure and everyday life ... (Duck, 1988)

Duck goes on to discuss six major causes of break-up in addition to those referred to above.

a) *Ineptitude or Lack of Skills in Self-expression*

Lonely, socially isolated people are often lacking in social skills—they are poor conversationalists, poor at indicating their interest in other people, often avoiding eye-contact, smiling little and generally are unrewarding to others in face-to-face interaction. Shy people are often perceived by others as distant, aloof, and even hostile by people who do not know them. This, naturally, puts other people off, which makes the *initiation* of relationships a particular problem. In a sense, their relationships have broken down before they have even got going, but even if they do, they tend to be unsatisfying and short-lived.

A fairly common problem in marriages is that one or other of the partners is over-confident about how accurately they give and receive non-verbal messages, especially those to do with feelings, (this is especially true of husbands). This can lead to 'negativity cycles', where each partner in turn attacks the other for some perceived fault, and where bickering, squabbling and scoring points off each other become commonplace.

b) *Rule-breaking*

The rules in question are 'relationship rules', the *expectations* which each partner has of the other, such as being supportive of their self-esteem and feelings, being loyal and faithful, being honest and open, spending time together, an equitable (relatively even) distribution of effort and resources and the existence of some intangible 'magical quality' in the relationship. Baxter (1986) found that reasons given to him for break-up of romantic relationships usually involved the violation of one of these rules by the former partner—not the person being interviewed!

Argyle and Henderson (1984) also found rule-breaking to be a very important cause of break-up, but usually the 'general rules' of friendship were followed and the ones which were broken were specifically to do with intimacy and support.

c) *Deception*

This represents probably the most important rule that should not be broken. If you cannot *trust* your partner, the relationship is almost certainly doomed.

Since we might be better at detecting lying in people we are *getting to know* (or at least we might be more suspicious of new acquaintances) and since we are better at deceiving people we know well (since we know better how they think), to discover that a friend or lover has deceived us is likely to be even more devastating than deception at the hands of anyone else, especially if the deceit is relevant to the existence or continuation of the relationship (Duck, 1988).

d) *Tiredness, Boredom, and Lack of Stimulation*

> . . . If stimulation is a major consideration in the start and maintenance of relationships, we can be fairly certain that lack of stimulation will be a reason for breaking off relationships . . . (Duck, 1988)

Indeed, a frequently given reason for breaking-off a relationship is boredom or it 'wasn't going anywhere':

> . . . the expectation that a relationship will change and develop is fundamental to its existence, so that its lack of development, particularly in a courtship, is treated as a good enough reason for it to be ended. (Duck, 1988)

e) *'Other' (Relocation and Difficulty of Maintenance)*

When one partner moves away to start a new job or to go to college, strains are inevitably put on the relationship so that the lives of the partners cease to be so 'intertwined' (this is proximity and exposure in reverse). Moving away to start college often presents opportunities to enter new relationships and those temptations may be greater than the wish to continue the now inconvenient, pre-college relationship.

f) *Conflict*

Some kind and degree of conflict is probably inevitable in all relationships and the process of resolving conflicts is often a positive one, promoting growth of the relationship. However, if conflicts recur, indicating a lack of agreement and an inability to resolve the underlying source of conflict, the partners may come to doubt each other as reasonable persons, leading to a 'digging in the heels', a disaffection with each other and, ultimately, a 'strong falling out'.

HOW DO RELATIONSHIPS BREAK DOWN?

The most useful way of looking at the break-down (or break-up) of a relationship is as a *process*, not an event, which takes place over a period of time, often an extended one:

> . . . Breaking up not only is hard to do, but also involves a lot of separate elements that make up the whole rotten experience. (Duck, 1988)

There is a tendency for people who have experienced a break-up to 'rewrite history', to remember the relationship in a way that conforms to a particular viewpoint, one that usually helps to protect the person's self-concept.

Lee (1984) proposed five stages of pre-marital romantic break-ups: (i) *dissatisfaction*, (D) is discovered; then (ii) it is *exposed* (E); (iii) there is some *negotiation* (N) about it; (iv) attempts are made to *resolve* (R) the problem; and finally (v) the relationship is *terminated* (T).

Lee surveyed 112 such break-ups—(E) and (N) tend to be experienced as the most intense, dramatic, exhausting and negative aspects of the whole experience. Those who skipped these stages (by just walking out) felt less intimate with their ex-partner, even while the relationship had been going satisfactorily. Where the whole passage from (D) to (T) is particularly prolonged, people reported feeling more attracted to their ex-partner and experienced greatest loneliness and fear during the break-up.

Table 18.2 *A sketch of the main phases of dissolving personal relationships (Duck, 1982 from Duck, 1988)*

Breakdown—Dissatisfaction with relationship
↓

Threshold: I can't stand this any more

↓

1. INTRA-PSYCHIC PHASE
Personal focus on partner's behaviour.
Assess adequacy of partner's role performance.
Depict and evaluate negative aspects of being in the relationship.
Consider costs of withdrawal.
Assess positive aspects of alternative relationships.
Face 'express/repress dilemma'.

↓

Threshold: I'd be justified in withdrawing

↓

2. DYADIC PHASE
Face 'confrontation/avoidance dilemma'.
Confront partner.
Negotiate in 'Our Relationship Talks'.
Attempt repair and reconciliation?
Assess joint costs of withdrawal or reduced intimacy.

↓

Threshold: I mean it

↓

3. SOCIAL PHASE
Negotiate post-dissolution state with partner.
Initiate gossip/discussion in social network.
Create publicly negotiable face-saving/blame-placing stories and accounts.
Consider and face up to implied social network effect, if any.
Call in intervention teams.

↓

Threshold: It's now inevitable

↓

4. GRAVE DRESSING PHASE
'Getting over' activity.
Retrospective; reformative postmortem attribution.
Public distribution of own version of break-up story.

Duck (1982) proposed a model of relationship dissolution, which is summarized in Table 18.2.

In the *intrapsychic phase*, moaning and complaining is primarily an internal process with little outward display. Beyond a certain threshold, complaints build up so as to produce indirect communication (eg hints) or the 'talking to a wall' style of communication (as if talking to a third party, someone neutral or anonymous, who is not actually present). At this point, the person is really searching for some kind of self-justification, rather than any real action.

In the *dyadic phase*, grievances are now much more out in the open. Partners will probably disagree about the attribution of responsibility for the problems, any revelation of what has been mulled over during the first phase is likely to cause a certain amount of shock and hurt to the other partner. Both will experience pain and distress, which probably explains their hesitation, oscillation, and lack of purpose at this phase.

The *social phase* involves enlisting the support of friends, relatives, etc. as a way of trying to *justify* leaving. Others' involvement helps to sanction the break-up (most obviously in the case of a courtroom where a divorce decree is pronounced).

Social networks serve an important role in recovery from the break-up by giving emotional and other kinds of support.

Finally, in the *grave-dressing phase*, feelings about the relationship, the partner and the break-up must be put into perspective. It is a necessary part of leaving a relationship that each person emerges with an intact reputation for relationship reliability. 'Dressing the grave' involves 'erecting a tablet' which provides a credible, socially acceptable, account of the life and death of the relationship. It helps save face but also serves to keep alive some memories and to 'justify' the original commitment to the ex-partner:

> ... Such stories are an integral and important part of the psychology of ending relationships and cannot be written off as inconsequential. By helping the person to get over the break-up they are immensely significant in preparing the person for future relationships as well as helping them out of old ones. (Duck, 1988)

19 ATTITUDES, ATTITUDE CHANGE AND PREJUDICE

According to Fiske and Taylor (1984), the study of attitudes is the cornerstone of social psychology. Much of the impetus came from attempts to change people's attitudes during the Second World War and the more general concern with the influence of the mass media on the individual. The mass media were becoming an increasingly powerful force in the 1940s, particularly in the United States.

Much of this chapter will be concerned with attitude change, reflecting the context in which the study of attitudes orginally developed. We shall do this in three main ways, by looking at: (i) persuasive communication, that is, study of deliberate attempts to change attitudes; (ii) theories of attitude change, in particular, Festinger's Cognitive Dissonance Theory (1957); and (iii) attempts to reduce prejudice, which is commonly regarded as an extreme attitude.

We shall begin by looking at the nature of attitudes and different ways of measuring them, and we shall also be discussing the nature of prejudice and some theories of its origins.

WHAT ARE ATTITUDES?

There is no single definition on which all psychologists would agree and a sample of definitions is given in Table 19.1. According to Secord and Backman (1964), most definitions comprise three components, namely: (i) the *cognitive*, what a person believes about the attitude object, what it is like, objectively; (ii) the *affective*, what a person feels about the attitude object, how favourably or unfavourably it is evaluated, reflecting its place in the person's scale of values; and (iii) the *behavioural*, how a person actually responds to the attitude object based on (i) and (ii).

Most psychologists would agree with Secord and Backman regarding the three components, although this is not without its problems, in particular, the assumption that they are highly correlated; we shall return to the attitude–behaviour relationship below.

ATTITUDES, BELIEFS AND VALUES: WHAT IS THE DIFFERENCE?

It is easy to use these terms interchangeably and there is no doubt that they are overlapping concepts. However, a distinction is normally made between them and an attitude can be thought of as a kind of blend or integration of beliefs and values (Elms, 1976).

Beliefs represent the knowledge or information we have about the world (although they may be inaccurate or incomplete) and, in them-

Allport 1935	'An attitude is a mental and neural state of readiness, organized through experience, exerting a directive or dynamic influence upon the individual's response to all objects and situations with which it is related'	***Table 19.1*** *Some definitions of attitudes*
Rokeach 1968	'A learned orientation, or disposition, toward an object or situation, which provides a tendency to respond favourably or unfavourably to the object or situation.' [The learning may not be based on personal experience but may be acquired through observational learning and identification]	
Warren and Jahoda 1973	'. . . attitudes have social reference in their origins and development and in their objects, while at the same time they have psychological reference in that they inhere in the individual and are intimately enmeshed in his behaviour and his psychological make-up	
Mednick et al 1975	'An attitude is a predisposition to act in a certain way towards some aspect of one's environment, including other people'	
Bem 1979	'Attitudes are likes and dislikes'	

selves, are non-evaluative. According to Fishbein and Ajzen (1975), 'a belief links an object to some attribute' (eg 'America' and 'capitalist state'). To convert a belief into an attitude, a 'value' ingredient is needed which, by definition, is to do with an individual's sense of what is desirable, good, valuable, worthwhile and so on.

Allport (1935) defined a value as, 'a belief upon which a man acts by preference' and, according to Rokeach (1968), 'a value is an enduring belief that a specific mode of conduct or end-state of existence is personally or socially preferable to an opposite or converse mode of conduct or end-state of existence'. While most adults will have many thousands of beliefs, they have only hundreds of attitudes and a few dozen values.

Rokeach distinguishes between *terminal values* (desirable, end-states or goals, for example, wisdom, an exciting life, equality, peace of mind and brotherhood) and *instrumental values* (desirable attributes, for example, competence, helpfulness and intellectualism); the former are desirable in themselves while the latter are desirable as means to the achievement of the former.

Probably the best known classification of values is that of Allport, Vernon and Lindzey (1951). Their scale of values attempts to measure the relative importance for an individual of six value orientations, namely *theoretical* (truth), *aesthetic* (harmony), *political* (power), *economic* (usefulness), *social* (altruistic love) and *religious* (unity). These value orientations may be regarded as corresponding to Rokeach's terminal values.

Whereas beliefs have an 'is-ness' about them (ie a belief *that* something is so), values have an 'oughtness' about them (ie a belief *in something*). Beliefs are, in themselves, neutral whereas values, by definition, are not: they provide standards and motives which guide our actions towards the achievement of those values.

Finally, it is important to make the point that attitudes, beliefs and values are *hypothetical constructs* and cannot be directly measured or observed but must be inferred from behaviour, including responses to tests and questionnaires. Also, they are all learned through interaction with the social environment.

ATTITUDES AND BEHAVIOUR—HOW ARE THEY RELATED?

Given that attitudes can only be inferred from what a person says and does, once we have established peoples' attitudes, are we then in a position to predict accurately their behaviour? As we saw when discussing the three components of attitudes proposed by Secord and Backman, the behavioural component would seem to be highly correlated with the cognitive and affective components. But is this true in practice? Do peoples' expressed attitudes (cognitive and affective components) coincide with their overt actions (behavioural component)?

An early, classic study which shows the inconsistency of attitudes and behaviour is that of La Piere (1934). He travelled around the USA with a Chinese couple, expecting to encounter anti-Oriental attitudes which would make it difficult for them to find accommodation. But in the course of 10,000 miles of travel they were discriminated against only once and there appeared to be no prejudice. However, when each of the 251 establishments visited was sent a letter six months later asking: 'Will you accept members of the Chinese race as guests in your establishment?', 91 per cent of the 128 which responded gave an emphatic 'No', one establishment gave an unqualified 'Yes', and the rest said their decision would depend on the circumstances. If such inconsistencies are commonplace, how do we account for them?

It is generally agreed that attitudes are only one determinant of behaviour; they represent *predispositions* to behave but how we actually act in a particular situation will depend on the immediate consequences of our behaviour, how we think others will evaluate our actions and habitual ways of behaving in those kinds of situations. In addition, there may be *situational factors* influencing behaviour; for example, in the La Piere study, the high quality of his Chinese friends' clothes and luggage and their politeness, together with the presence of La Piere himself, may have made it more difficult to show overt prejudice, and, besides, to turn away three guests is clearly against the financial interests of a hotel (at least in the short-term). Thus, sometimes we experience a *conflict* of *attitudes* and behaviour may repesent a compromise between them; or, alternatively, the *strength* of one attitude relative to others may dictate a particular course of action. A different kind of conflict situation is where there are pressures on us to *conform*—see Chapter 20.

Again, the same attitude may be expressed, behaviourally, in a variety of ways and in varying degrees; for example, having a positive attitude towards the Labour party does not necessarily mean that you actually become a member or that you attend public meetings. However, if you don't vote Labour in a general election, people may question your attitude. In other words, an attitude should predict behaviour to some extent, even if this is extremely limited and specific.

Indeed, Ajzen and Fishbein (1977) argue that attitudes *can* predict behaviour if and when appropriate attitude-measurement techniques are used; the key to success is to ensure a high degree of *specificity* of attitude and behaviour. For example, if we want to predict whether a person will participate in an anti-litter campaign, we must measure their attitude towards reducing litter, rather than their general attitude towards protecting the environment, that is, the measures of attitude and behaviour must *correspond*.

For example, when married women's attitudes towards birth control were correlated with their actual use of oral contraceptives during the two years following the study, Davidson and Jaccard (1979) found virtually no relationship (0.08); clearly, the correspondence here was very low. However, when 'attitudes towards oral contraceptives' were measured, the correlation rose to 0.32 and when 'attitudes towards oral contraceptives during the next two years' were measured, the correlation rose still further to 0.57; in both these cases, correspondence was much higher.

According to Fazio and Zanna (1981), a number of studies have shown that attitudes which are based on *direct experience* have greater predictive value than those based only on indirect experience. Direct experience, of course, provides us with more information about the attitude object and our attitude may also be more easily retrieved from memory compared with one not based on personal experience.

MEASUREMENT OF ATTITUDES

Many of the problems of attitude measurement are the same as those associated with other kinds of mental measurement, in particular intelligence (see Chapter 28) and personality (see Chapter 29); the general problems of reliability, validity and standardization are discussed in detail there.

However, one or two points should be made here. Most attitude scales rely on verbal reports and usually take the form of standardized statements which clearly refer to the attitude being measured. Such scales make two basic assumptions: (i) that the same statement has the same meaning for all subjects; and, more fundamentally, (ii) that attitudes, when expressed verbally, can be quantified.

One source of bias is *social desirability*, that is, giving answers which the subject thinks are expected or 'proper' rather than giving honest answers; incorporating a *lie scale* can help detect this tendency to give socially desirable answers. Reassuring subjects that their answers will remain anonymous and stressing the importance of giving honest answers can also help reduce social desirability. Similarly, introducing irrelevant items ('red herrings') can help to make the true purpose of the scale less obvious and so less susceptible to distorted responses.

Another source of bias is *response set*, the tendency to agree or disagree with questions consistently or to give answers which are consistently in the middle of the scale (rather than at the extremes).

Both kinds of bias detract from the reliability of attitude scales and, to the extent that a test is not reliable, it cannot be valid (ie actually measure the attitude it claims to measure).

Some of the major methods of attitude measurement are shown in Table 19.2.

	METHOD	DESCRIPTION
Table 19.2 Some major methods used in attitude measurement	*The Bogardus Social Distance Scale (1925)*	This is really a measure of racial prejudice and comprises a series of statements representing degrees of social distance between the subject and a large number of ethnic/national groups which the subject would find tolerable. Statements range from 'to close kinship by marriage' through 'to my street as neighbours' and 'to citizenship in my country' to 'would exclude from my country'. The subject has to tick or cross one or more of these.
	Likert Scale (1932)	This is the most commonly used formal procedure. It comprises a number of statements, for each of which subjects must indicate whether they: (a) strongly agree, (b) agree, (c) undecided, (d) disagree, (e) strongly disagree.
	Thurstone Scale (1929)	This is not itself an attitude scale but a method for devising such a scale. A series of statements, each implying a certain evaluation of the attitude-object, is collected; they must cover a wide range of views and be worded as unambiguously as possible. They are then given to a number of 'judges' who estimate the degree to which each statement (or item) implies a positive or a negative attitude (on an 11-point scale); any items which produce substantial disagreements are discarded, until about 20 remain. Each item will have a numerical rating, assigned by a consensus of judges, ranging from 'extremely favourable' to 'extremely unfavourable' as opposite poles. The questionnaire is then piloted (tested) on subjects who indicate which items they agree with; their responses can then be scored and a mean attitude score calculated.
	Semantic Differential (Osgood, Suci and Tannenbaum, 1957)	This constitutes at least nine pairs of *bipolar* adjectives, for each of which there is a seven-point scale (with a value of seven usually being given to the positive pole, eg good, strong, active, and one to the negative pole). The subject has to tick or cross at some point along the scale for each pair of adjectives. Single words (rather than statements) are used to denote the attitude object, eg *father*. Examples of bipolar scales are: good — — — — — — — bad / strong — — — — — — — weak / active — — — — — — — passive / 'Good-bad' illustrates the *evaluative* factor, 'strong-weak' the *potency* factor and 'active-passive' the *activity* factor; for each factor there would be at least two bipolar scales, with the evaluative factor being the most important.

METHOD	DESCRIPTION	
Sociometry (Moreno, 1953)	This can be used with any 'natural' group (at school, college, work etc.). Each group member is asked to name another who would be their preferred partner for a specific activity or as a friend. The product of these choices is a *sociogram* which charts the friendship groups (sub-groups), who are the popular and unpopular members, who are the isolates, who are the leaders and so on (see diagram). Each circle represents a group member, the arrows indicating direction of preference (ie who prefers whom). Can you identify the most popular (and the most likely leader?) (see Chapter 20).	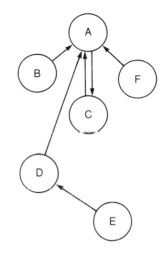*Table 19.2* Continued
Interviews	These can be either: (a) *open-ended* (or unstructured), where the subject is simply asked to express attitudes towards a particular attitude object; or (b) *structured*, where a pre-determined set of questions is asked of each subject (like a verbal questionnaire).	

PERSUASIVE COMMUNICATION

How easy (or difficult) is it to change someone's mind? According to Laswell (1948), in order to understand and predict the effectiveness of one person's attempt to change the attitude of another, we need to know *'who says what to whom and with what effect'*.

In the terms of Hovland and Janis (1959), we need to study: (i) the *source* of the persuasive communication, that is, the communicator (Laswell's 'who'); (ii) the *message* itself (Laswell's 'what'); (iii) the *recipient* of the message, or the audience, (Laswell's 'whom'); and (iv) the *situation* or *context*.

Figure 19.1 shows each of these four factors together with the major

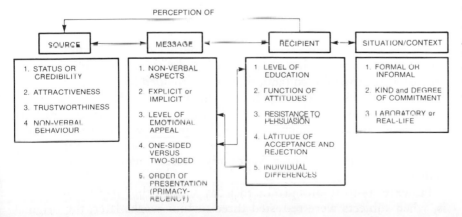

Figure 19.1 The four major factors involved in persuasive communication (arrows between boxes indicate examples of interaction between variables)

aspects of each which have been investigated. Two important points about Figure 19.1 are, first, that as far as the impact of the source is concerned, it is how the recipient *perceives* the source which is crucial (although the experimenter usually assumes that the manipulation of source variables will determine how the source is perceived) and, secondly, that the four factors *interact* with each other and it is quite artificial to investigate them in isolation from each other.

In some studies which we shall be discussing, this interaction becomes evident; for example, the impact of a one- or two-sided message (message-variable) seems to depend on the recipient's level of education (recipient-variable) and, similarly, the effect of a fear-arousing message (message-variable) will depend on the recipients' normal level of anxiety (recipient-variable).

How is attitude change measured? The basic paradigm in attitude-change research involves three steps or stages: (i) measure subjects' (recipients') attitude towards the attitude object (pre-test); (ii) expose subjects to a persuasive communication (manipulate a source, message or situational variable or isolate a recipient-variable as the independent variable); (iii) measure subjects' attitudes again (post-test). If there is a difference between pre- and post-test measures, then the persuasive communication is judged to have 'worked'.

McGuire (1969) sees this dependent variable of 'attitude change' as being too vague and instead proposes that we should be asking about the recipient, have they: (i) *attended* to the message; (ii) *comprehended* it; (iii) *yielded* to it; (iv) *retained* it; and (v) *acted* as a result?

THE SOURCE

1) *Status or credibility*

An important ingredient of status or credibility is whether the source is perceived as being an expert (or at least knowledgeable) in relation to the attitude object; in general, the more expert the source, the more likely we are to be persuaded.

Hovland and Weiss (1951) asked American subjects to read a statement about the practicality of atomic submarines: those who were told it was written by J. Robert Oppenheimer (one of the scientists who helped develop the atomic bomb) were more convinced of its truth than those who were told its source was *Pravda*. A similar effect was found when the article concerned anti-histamine drugs and the source was either the *New England Journal of Medicine* or a mass-circulation magazine.

Hovland and Weiss collected additional questionnaire data which confirmed that subjects saw the medical journal as more credible (in the sense of trustworthy) but there were no differences in how well the articles were remembered (and, therefore, attended to originally).

Kelman and Hovland (1953) found similar results when subjects heard a lecture on juvenile delinquency which advocated a lenient attitude towards juvenile delinquents. When the speaker was a 'juvenile court judge' attitude change was much greater than when the speaker was either a 'dope peddler' or a 'randomly chosen member of the studio audience'.

However both studies produced what is called the '*sleeper effect*', that is, when subjects were re-tested three to four weeks later, the original differences between different sources greatly decreased, so that there was an increasing acceptance of the message from the low-status source and a decreasing acceptance of the high-status source. However, this only occurs if subjects are *not* reminded of the identity and characteristics of the source. So, presumably, the source's identity becomes detached from the actual message with time. According to Hovland, the connection between the arguments and the conclusion of a message is remembered longer than the connection between a 'cue' (such as communicator credibility) and the conclusion. So the sleeper effect represents a *delayed* form of attitude change.

According to Johnson and Scileppi (1969), credibility is only important in relation to attitude issues with which the subject is only mildly involved; when ego involvement is high, the effect vanishes, perhaps because more attention is paid to the content of the message. Also the more important the attitude issue is to our self-concept, the more suspicious we are of attempts to influence us about it (Reich and Adcock, 1975), which points to another interaction between source and recipient variables. (We shall say more about the function of attitudes below.)

In the laboratory, if there is a conflict between a powerful expert figure and the subject's peers, the former is usually more influential, but in real-life situations, the reverse seems to be true. Furthermore, some peers appear to be more influential than others. In a study by Lazarsfeld et al (1948) of voting behaviour in the USA, it emerged that the majority of voters were not being directly influenced by the media but indirectly through peers (relatives, friends, colleagues, etc.) considered to be 'in the know' regarding political matters. These peers were referred to as *opinion leaders* and Lazarsfeld put forward the *'Two-step Flow Hypothesis'*, whereby influences stemming from the media first reach opinion leaders, who, in turn, pass on what they have read and heard to their everyday associates for whom they are influential.

Menzel and Katz (1955) wanted to know how doctors decide to use a new drug and found that doctors who were opinion leaders tended to be influenced by journal articles and professional meetings and conferences, etc. to a greater degree than non-opinion leader colleagues. However, opinion leaders may themselves look to colleagues of even higher status, so that there may be three or four steps between the media and the majority of the target population instead of the two originally proposed by Lazarsfeld.

Another component of credibility is the *similarity* between the source and the recipient (as perceived by the latter) so that the greater the similarity, the greater the credibility (everything else being equal).

2) *Attractiveness*

A source who is charming, humourous and has a pleasant manner is more persuasive (everything else being equal) than one who does not have these qualities. An unattractive or unlikeable source might produce a 'boomerang effect' whereby the audience responds by adopting attitudes which are contrary to those being advocated. This is one reason that politicians (especially in the USA) devote so much effort to enhancing their personal appeal to voters (Baron and Byrne, 1991) and is part of the process of creating a 'media style'.

3) *Trustworthiness*

This relates to the perceived *intentions* and *motives* of the source, in particular, are they *deliberately* trying to influence me and is there an ulterior motive for doing so?

Walster and Festinger (1962) found that if subjects believe they are 'merely overhearing' a message they are more likely to be influenced by it than subjects who hear the same message presented directly to them. This seems to depend on: (i) the subject being interested in the issue to begin with; and (ii) the subject being initially favourably disposed towards the position being advocated.

An overheard source is less likely to be suspected of ulterior motives and, to this extent, is more trustworthy. Also, when the source is perceived as trying to persuade, counter-arguments are provoked in the subject to a greater extent than if the message is 'overheard' and if subjects are actually warned in advance of the source's attempt to change their mind on some issue, the chances of any attitude change occurring are considerably reduced.

Finally, a message is very effective if it is seen as actually being contrary to the source's self-interest. For example, in one study, subjects were presented with arguments advocating more or less power for the courts and which, supposedly, came from either a criminal or a prosecutor. The criminal was less effective when advocating a reduction in the courts' power and more effective when advocating an increase in power, the latter being the opposite of what subjects expected him to advocate. Compared with the prosecutor who argued for an increase in the courts' power, the criminal who did so was seen as both more honest and more persuasive. (If we believe that someone is [sincerely] advocating a position which is opposed to their own self-interest, we may come to regard the argument as worth taking seriously for that reason—this explains the 'sales-talk' technique of *denying* that any pressure is being brought to bear on the would-be customer—the 'soft-sell' is a form of manipulation.)

4) *Non-verbal Behaviour*

This is important largely because of how it contributes to the source being perceived as attractive and trustworthy. One especially relevant dimension of non-verbal behaviour is proximity and personal space (see Chapter 18).

For example, there is evidence that most attitude change is produced when the source stands 14 to 15 feet away and least at a distance of 1 to 2 feet. Subjects in the latter condition probably feel that their intimate zone is being encroached and they resent this.

Abelsen and Zimbardo (1970) advised campaigning candidates and door-to-door canvassers to keep a distance of 4 to 5 feet, a respectful distance when talking to strangers, especially when you are on the stranger's 'territory'; this corresponds to Hall's social–consultative distance (see Chapter 18).

THE MESSAGE

1) *Non-verbal Aspects*

Following on from what we have said about the source, face-to-face communication may be more effective than attempts by the media to change attitudes because when the source receives feedback from the recipient (in the form of facial expressions, eye contact, body posture and so on) they are in a better position to anticipate objections and to modify the message and present counter-arguments.

Maslow et al (1971) found that over-and-above the content of a message, how *confidently* it is presented is a crucial variable. Subjects read details of a law case intended to help them judge whether or not the accused was guilty. Some subjects read a confidently presented argument in favour of the accused (using phrases such as 'obviously', 'I am quite sure', 'I believe'), while others read a much more tentative argument ('I don't know', 'I'm not positive', 'I'm unsure') and, as predicted, significantly more subjects judged in favour of the accused in the former case. In the same study, subjects saw an actor make lip movements to a neutral sounding tape of a non-guilty plea in a confident, neutral or doubtful way (through facial expression, etc.) and similar results were found. (Confidence could just as easily be discussed as a source-variable as opposed to a message-variable.)

2) Explicit or Implicit

The question here is whether the argument should be clearly spelt-out (so that no one is left in any doubt as to the conclusions to be drawn) or whether an implicit message is more effective, leaving the recipient to work out the conclusions on their own.

McGuire (1968) believes that implicit messages may be more effective if the recipient is capable of, and likely to, draw the conclusions; but for recipients of low intelligence or motivation, explicit messages may be preferred.

3) Level of Emotional Appeal

Can subjects be frightened into changing their minds?

One of the most famous attempts to induce attitude change through the manipulation of fear was by Janis and Feshbach (1953). American high-school students were randomly assigned to one of four groups (one control and three experimental). The message was concerned with dental hygiene and degree of fear-arousal was manipulated by the number and nature of consequences of improper care of teeth which were referred to (and shown in colour slides); each message also contained factual information about the causes of tooth decay and some advice about caring for teeth.

The *high fear* condition made 71 references to unpleasant effects, including toothache, painful treatment and possible secondary diseases, including blindness and cancer; the *moderate fear* condition made 49 references and the *low fear* condition just 18. (Control subjects heard a talk about the eye.)

Before the experiment, subjects' attitudes to dental health—and their dental habits—were assessed as part of a general health survey; the same questionnaire was given again immediately following the fear-inducing message and one week later.

As far as how worried subjects were about their teeth (an index of attitude change), it seemed that fear had worked, that is, the stronger the appeal to fear, the more anxious subjects were. However, as far as actual changes in dental behaviour were concerned, the high-fear condition proved to be the least effective; 8 per cent of the high-fear group had adopted the recommendations (changes in toothbrushing and visiting the dentist in the weeks immediately following the experiment), compared with 22 per cent and 37 per cent in the moderate- and low-fear conditions respectively. Similar results were reported by Janis and Terwillinger (1962) when they presented a mild- and strong-fear message concerning the relationship between smoking and cancer.

It would seem that, in McGuire's terms you can frighten people into attending to a message, comprehending it, yielding to it and retaining it but not necessarily into acting upon it; indeed, fear may be so great that action is inhibited rather than facilitated. However, this general conclusion needs to be qualified in three main ways.

First, if the audience is told *how* to avoid undesirable consequences and believes that the preventative action is realistic and will be effective, then even high levels of fear in the message can produce changes in behaviour—and the more specific and precise the instructions, the greater the behaviour change (Fig. 19.2). The presence of such instructions is referred to as the *high availability* factor and a number of studies have demonstrated that while making subjects afraid is in itself counter-

Figure 19.2 Example of
public health campaign poster

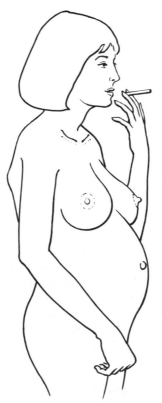

Is it fair to force your baby to smoke cigarettes?

This is what happens if you smoke when you're pregnant.

Every time you inhale you fill your lungs with nicotine and carbon monoxide.

Your blood carries these impurities through the umbilical cord into your baby's bloodstream.

Smoking can restrict your baby's normal growth inside the womb.
It can make him underdeveloped and underweight at birth.
Which, in turn, can make him vulnerable to illness in the first delicate weeks of his life.
It can even kill him.
Last year, in Britain alone, over 1,500 babies might not have died if their mothers had given up smoking when they were pregnant.

If you give up smoking when you're pregnant your baby will be as healthy as if you'd never smoked.

The Health Education Council

productive, if fear-inducement is combined with reassuring recommendations as to how the potential threat can be averted, then behaviour change can take place.

Secondly, in situations of minimal *or* extreme fear, the message may fail to produce any attitude change, let alone any change in behaviour. According to McGuire (1968), there is an inverted U-shaped curve in the relationship between fear and attitude change (Fig. 19.3). In segment 1 of

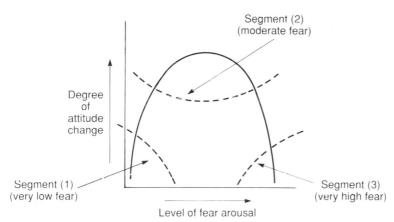

Figure 19.3 Inverted U curve showing relationship between attitude change and fear arousal. (Based on McGuire, 1968)

the curve, the subject is not particularly interested in (aroused by) the message: it is hardly attended to and may not even register. In segment 2, attention and arousal increase as fear increases, but the fear remains within manageable proportions. In segment 3, attention will decrease again but this time because defences are being used to deal with extreme fear, for example, the message may be denied ('it couldn't happen to me') or repressed (made unconscious and, hence, forgotten).

Thirdly, there are important individual differences regarding normal levels of anxiety (either as a personality trait or in connection with the issue in question, which McGuire calls *'initial level of concern'*). Clearly, a person who has a high level of initial concern will be more easily pushed into segment 3 than someone with a low level of intitial concern; the former may be overwhelmed by a high-fear message (in which case defences are used against it) while the latter may not become interested and aroused enough for the message to have an impact. So different degrees of fear will have different effects upon different individuals depending on their initial level of anxiety (another important interaction).

Janis and Feshbach re-analysed their original data and found that high-anxiety subjects (who reported frequent shortage of breath, heart-pounding, etc.) were less influenced by a high-fear message than low-anxiety subjects, but were more influenced by a low-fear message.

Finally, another interesting interaction effect between fear-arousal and recipient-variables is the finding by Insko et al (1965) that moderate fear arousal was more effective for smokers, while a high fear arousal was more effective for strengthening the resolve of non-smokers never to start.

4) *One-sided Versus Two-sided Arguments*

Whether or not advertisers should make any kind of reference to rival products, or politicians to their opponents, seems to depend on the audience: again we have an interaction effect.

Hovland et al (1949) presented two groups of over two hundred soldiers with a series of radio transcripts, arguing that it would take at least two years to end the war with Japan (during the Second World War): one group received a strictly one-sided message and the other a strictly two-sided message.

Overall, the two messages produced the same net change in attitudes. However, when education was taken into account, important differences emerged: those who were better educated (had at least completed high school) were more influenced by a two-sided argument; while those who were less well educated were more influenced by a one-sided presentation. Hass and Linder (1972) suggest that this might be related to the recipients' knowledge of counter-arguments; recipients who are aware of arguments opposed to the speaker's point of view are most persuaded by two-sided messages which explicitly refute these arguments.

Hovland et al also found evidence that soldiers whose initial attitude was similar to the message were more influenced by a one-sided argument (keeping education constant) while the opposite held true for those initially opposed to it. It also appears that a two-sided argument is more effective if subjects are already familiar with the topic.

5) *Order of Presentation (Primacy–Recency)*

Having decided to make a two-sided presentation, which side of the argument should come first—the one you want your audience to hold or the counter-position? This, of course, is another instance of the *primacy–recency* issue which we saw when discussing memory (Chapter 12) and interpersonal perception (Chapter 17).

Early research showed a primacy effect but Hovland et al (1957) thought primacy was more powerful only under certain conditions: (i) if both sides are presented by the same person and the subject is not initially aware that conflicting arguments will be presented; (ii) if the subject makes some kind of public commitment at the end of the first message (eg they agree to their views being published in a magazine).

McGuire (1957) attempted to persuade subjects to accept an educational course by presenting the desirable features first and the undesirable ones second, and found evidence of a primacy effect; if the order of presentation is reversed, the subject 'switches off' from the rest of the message and so the desirable features are not 'heard'.

Rosnow and Robinson (1967) found that when subjects are not very familiar with the issue, or not very interested in it, a recency effect tends to occur, but if the subject is very involved (eg the issue is highly controversial) a primacy effect predominates.

Another important factor is the time interval between the two messages. Miller and Campbell (1959) used material from a simulated jury trial and their findings are shown in Figure 19.4.

If the second sequence of events is taken as representing the summing up in a trial, where the defence lawyer goes first and is followed by the prosecution lawyer, the implication is that the *defence* has an advantage.

Finally, Hass and Linder (1972) advocate that when there are no delays at all, the opposing argument should be given first and then strongly refuted; in this way attention is drawn to the speaker's

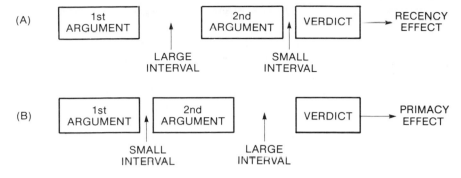

Figure 19.4 The influence of time on primacy-recency in a two-sided argument. (Based on Miller and Campbell, 1959)

viewpoint for most of the presentation. (This, of course, is exactly what the prosecuting lawyer does, except that the opposing argument is presented by another person, ie the defence lawyer.)

THE RECIPIENT

1) Level of Education

We have discussed this already in relation to the Hovland et al study of soldiers (1949) but without saying why the better educated should be more influenced by a two-sided argument. Perhaps they are intellectually better equipped to handle conflicting arguments and are more used to doing so; they might find a two-sided argument more challenging and also may not want to think of themselves as being easily persuaded (as in a one-sided argument).

2) The Function of Attitudes

Given what we have said about attitudes comprising three major components, and given the interconnection between attitudes, values and beliefs, it is perhaps not surprising that many psychologists take the view that not all attitudes have the same significance for the individual and that they serve different functions.

If we accept this, it follows that some attitudes will be harder to change than others and a major classification of the functions of attitudes is that of Katz (1960). He is concerned with the motives which attitudes serve and sees some of these motives as conscious and others unconscious; his approach is probably the closest that modern theories come to a Freudian, psychodynamic view of attitudes.

So what are the psychological needs met by holding and changing attitudes? According to Katz, the two principal functions of attitudes are: (i) they provide a ready basis for interpreting the world and processing new information; and (ii) they provide a way of gaining and maintaining social identification. Beyond this, he proposes four motivational functions, which are summarized in Table 19.3.

Katz's functional approach is especially important in trying to account for prejudice and attempting to reduce it. A similar classification was proposed by Smith et al (1956): (i) *object appraisal* refers to the adaptive function of attitudes in meeting day-to-day problems (corresponding to Katz's knowledge function); (ii) *social adjustment* refers to the usefulness of an attitude in social relationships (corresponding to Katz's adjustive

	FUNCTION	DESCRIPTION
Table 19.3 Four major functions of attitudes (Katz, 1960)	*Knowledge function*	We seek a degree of predictability, consistency and stability in our perception of the world (corresponding to the *cognitive* component of attitudes); attitudes give meaning and direction to experience, supplying frames of reference for judging events and objects.
	Adjustive (instrumental or utilitarian) function	We obtain favourable responses from others by displaying socially acceptable attitudes, so attitudes become associated with important rewards (such as the approval and acceptance of others). These attitudes may be publicly expressed but not necessarily believed, as in compliance (see Chapter 20).
	Value-expressive function	We achieve self-expression through cherished values. The reward may not be gaining social support but confirmation of the more positive aspects of one's own self-concept (of course, self-concept can also be affected by culturally-based stereotypes, eg gender roles). Particularly important for a sense of personal integrity.
	Ego-defensive function	Attitudes help protect us from admitting personal deficiencies. For example, denial permits us to defend our self-concept. Prejudice helps to sustain out self-concept by maintaining a sense of superiority over others. Ego-defence often means avoiding and denying self-knowledge (so this function of attitudes comes closer to being unconscious in Freud's sense). (See Chapter 29.)

function); (iii) *externalization* involves responding to an external event in terms of some unresolved internal conflict, thus distorting it (corresponding to Katz's ego-defensive function); and (iv) *quality* of *expressiveness* which is more concerned with how attitudes reflect an individual's deeper pattern of life, a person's expressive nature or style of operating, and so is not really about functions at all (Reich and Adcock, 1976).

3) *Resistance to Persuasion*

In general, it seems that resistance is strongest when counter-arguments are available and weakest when they are not. According to McGuire and Papageorgis (1961), people can be 'inoculated' against attempts to persuade them: by analogy with medical immunization, the subject is given a mild 'dose' of an argument against their own opinion, sufficient to activate a defensive counter-argument. Subjects were first exposed to an opposing argument and then were given statements countering these arguments and reinforcing their initial attitudes. A week later, they read a different message which also challenged their initial attitude and they were then less likely to be persuaded by it than subjects who had not been inoculated (including some who had received support for their opinion but no attack).

Does simply warning someone in advance help them resist a persuasive message?

According to Kiesler and Jones (1971) the more committed we are to an issue, the more resistant we are likely to be, regardless of any advance warning. When a warning does have an effect it does so by drawing on that commitment and, perhaps, by prompting us to anticipate counter-arguments and prepare arguments against these (a kind of 'self-inoculation'). Also, the better-informed we are about a topic, the more resistant we are likely to be.

Forewarning provides us with extra time to muster our defences (especially if we know about the content of the message) and to recall relevant facts and information which may prove useful in arguing against the persuasive message. According to Baron and Byrne:

> ... to be forewarned *is* to be forearmed, at least in cases in which we care enough about the topic in question to engage in active processing about it. (Baron and Byrne, 1991)

When we feel that another person is trying to exert undue pressure on us, we often react by doing the very opposite of what the other wants us to do or adopting the very opposite attitude (*negative attitude change*). This response to perceived threats to our personal freedom is called *reactance* and represents a strong source of motivation to resist persuasion. Indeed, so strong is the desire to assert one's autonomy that sometimes individuals shift away from the view being advocated, even if it is the one they might normally accept (Baron and Byrne, 1991).

Haas and Mann (1976) warn us against being caught in a situation where we have to defend our attitude but cannot do so intelligently or in an informed way. (An excellent way of learning how to defend a particular viewpoint is, paradoxically, to argue for its *opposite*, that is, to play 'devil's advocate'; in this way, you can discover the weakness in your position and try to prepare defensive arguments. You might like to have a class debate in which you deliberately choose to defend the view which is opposed to your own.)

4) *Latitude of Acceptance and Rejection*

The greater the discrepancy between the attitude a person already holds, and the one which the communicator wants the person to hold, the less likely it is that any shift in attitude will occur. Another way of saying this is that if the persuasive message lies outside a person's *latitude of acceptance* (arguments they are prepared to accept) then it will be rejected (and so will fall within the person's *latitude of rejection*).

Sherif and Hovland (1961) found that unacceptable statements tend to be perceived as even more hostile or unfavourable than they really are (*contrast*) while those which are not so extreme may be gradually incorporated into the person's latitude of acceptance (*assimilation*). The more extreme the person's initial position, and the greater the ego involvement in it: (i) the smaller the latitude of acceptance; (ii) the greater the latitude of rejection; (iii) the greater the contrast effect; and, consequently, (iv) the less the attitude change.

Laboratory experiments normally use issues which are relatively unimportant, together with a high-credibility source; compared with field studies, this has the effect of increasing the latitude of acceptance and hence making attitude change more likely. This throws serious doubt on the *ecological validity* of laboratory studies of persuasive communication.

5) *Individual Differences*

We have discussed anxiety in relation to the impact of messages which appeal to fear, but other important sources of individual differences include gender, self-esteem, persuasibility and intelligence.

Many early studies suggested that women are more easily persuaded but this may simply have been the product of the experimenter's choice of 'male-dominated' issues, such as politics and the economy (Aronson, 1976). Indeed, studies carried out more recently have shown that while women may be more easily persuaded about 'male' issues, men are equally persuasible in relation to 'female' issues, such as home management and family relationships (Sistrunk and McDavid, 1971).

High self-esteem subjects tend to influence others and are less easily persuaded by others compared with low-esteem subjects, at least in the case of men. In women, there is some evidence that low self-esteem subjects may actually move even further away from the message (probably as a form of ego-defence) while women of medium self-esteem are the most persuasible.

Is there a personality factor which can be called persuasibility? McGuire (1968) thinks there is but that it may not manifest itself equally in relation to both comprehension and yielding, and he makes a similar point in relation to intelligence: we would expect a negative correlation between intelligence and persuasibility if the latter is thought of in terms of yielding *but*, because there is a positive correlation between intelligence and comprehension, the overall relationship between intelligence and persuasibility is not a straight-line but a *curvilinear* one (as in the inverted-U curve in Fig. 19.3).

SITUATION OR CONTEXT

Informal situations, such as group discussions, often prove more effective than *formal* situations, such as speeches and lectures, partly because of differences in the perception of who is trying to influence whom and for what motives. Role-play is another kind of informal situation which has been found effective, both in a therapeutic setting (Kelly, 1955) and experimentally (Janis and Mann, 1965). In the latter, subjects who played the role of cancer patients showed significantly greater changes in their attitudes *and* their smoking behaviour than subjects who heard information via a tape-recorder or controls, who did neither.

In a group context, subjects may be obliged to make some kind of public *commitment* to a particular attitude which may initially reflect pressures to conform (see Chapter 20) but which may then bring about genuine attitude change through the reduction of cognitive dissonance (see below). Opinions which are expressed privately or anonymously are far less likely to bring about attitude change.

Finally, as we have already noted, *laboratory* studies are much more likely to produce attitude change than *real-life* situations, for a variety of reasons.

COGNITIVE APPROACHES TO PERSUASIVE COMMUNICATION

So far we have discussed the *traditional approach* and much of the early work was conducted for the US War Department's Information and Education Department, which has provided a great deal of information about the 'when' and 'how' of persuasion (it indicated *when* such attitude change is most likely to occur and *how*, in practical terms, it can be produced). Unfortunately it told us less about the 'why' of persuasion—*why* do people change their attitudes in response to persuasive messages?

A more recent approach is the *cognitive perspective* (eg Chaiken, 1987), which sees the key questions as: (i) what cognitive processes determine whether someone is actually persuaded? (ii) what do people think about when exposed to persuasive appeals? and (iii) how do their various cognitive processes determine whether and to what extent they experience attitude changes? (Baron and Byrne, 1991).

Chaiken's (1987) answer to these questions is in the form of his *heuristic model* of *persuasion*. Heuristics (see Chapter 14) are rules of thumb—mental shortcuts—we use in processing social or any other kind of information. When a situation is personally involving (for example, it involves attitudes which are salient for the individual concerned), careful, cognitive analysis of the input occurs, whereby the degree of attitude change depends largely on the quality of the arguments put forward.

However, when personal involvement is low, individuals rely on various heuristics to determine whether to change their attitudes. Much of the Yale approach, in fact, deals with the content of these heuristics, eg experts are more believable than non-experts and so we are more persuaded by the former, as we are by likeable sources (compared with non-likeable). Other heuristics include: (i) we are more persuaded by a greater than a smaller number of arguments backed up by statistics; and (ii) 'if other people think something is right (or wrong), then I should too'.

To test the last of these, Axsom, Yates and Chaiken (1987) had subjects listen to a recording of what was supposedly a debate about whether probation should be used as an alternative to prison for convicted criminals. Some subjects were given information meant to *increase* their involvement in the issue (eg they were told it was very important), while others were given information meant to *reduce* their personal involvement (eg they were told to just relax while listening to the tape). The quality of the arguments was also varied—some subjects heard high-quality, other low-quality arguments favouring probation. The tape also contained either cheers and enthusiastic clapping by an audience or a few weak claps and cries of derision.

After hearing one version of the tape, subjects indicated their attitudes about probation. As predicted by the heuristic model, under conditions of *low involvement*, subjects felt more favourable towards probation after hearing an *enthusiastic audience response* than an unenthusiastic response—the quality of the argument made little difference. But under conditions of *high involvement*, subjects were influenced primarily by the quality of the argument and the audience reaction made little difference.

The *functions* of attitudes also represent an important feature of the cognitive analysis of persuasion (eg Katz's four functions, see Table

19.2). Sharitt (1990) argues that there is a relationship between attitude function and persuasion, such that persuasive messages that emphasize the appropriate attitude function of a given product should be more successful in changing attitudes than those which focus on other attitude functions. So, for example, a commercial which emphasizes the *utilitarian* (or functional) aspects of, say, air conditioners, should be more successful than one which emphasizes their *social identity function* (ie they allow us to express our identity and project a particular kind of social image), and vice versa for a commercial for perfume.

THEORIES OF ATTITUDE CHANGE (THE NEED FOR CONSISTENCY)

The most influential *theories of attitude change* have concentrated on the principle of *cognitive consistency*, whereby human beings are seen as internally active information processors who sort through and modify a large number of cognitive elements in order to achieve some kind of cognitive coherence. It is really a part of human nature, a basic human need, and so such theories may be seen not just as theories of attitude change but also as theories of *human motivation*—people *need* cognitive consistency (see Chapter 6).

Three of the best known consistency theories are: (i) Heider's *balance theory* (1958), according to which people seek harmony among their various attitudes and beliefs and tend to evaluate in similar ways things that are related to each other; (ii) Osgood and Tannenbaums' *congruity theory* (1955), which maintains that when two attitudes or beliefs are inconsistent with each other, it is the one that is less firmly held which will be the one that changes; and (iii) Festinger's *cognitive dissonance theory* (1957), which we shall now examine in detail.

COGNITIVE DISSONANCE

The central idea is that whenever an individual simultaneously holds two cognitions which are psychologically inconsistent, he/she experiences dissonance, which is a negative drive state—a state of, 'psychological discomfort or tension' which motivates the individual to reduce it by achieving consonance. Attitude change is seen as a major way of reducing dissonance.

Cognitions are, 'the things a person knows about himself, about his behaviour and about his surroundings' (Festinger, 1957) and any two cognitions can be consonant (A implies B), dissonant (A implies not-B, the obverse of A) or irrelevant to each other.

A classic example of when dissonance is likely to arise is if we smoke and also believe that smoking causes cancer: assuming that we would rather not have cancer, the cognition 'I smoke' is psychologically inconsistent with the cognition 'smoking causes cancer'. Perhaps the most efficient (and certainly the healthiest!) way to reduce dissonance is to stop smoking, but most of us will work on the other cognition; for example, we might:

(i)   belittle the evidence about smoking and cancer (eg the human data is only correlational);

(ii) associate with other smokers (eg 'If so-and-so smokes, then it can't be very dangerous');

(iii) smoke low-tar cigarettes;

(iv) convince ourselves that smoking is an important and highly pleasureable activity;

(v) make a virtue out of it by developing a romantic, devil-may-care image and flaunting danger by smoking, etc.

All these possible ways of reducing dissonance demonstrate that dissonance theory regards the human being not as a rational creature but a *rationalizing* one, attempting to *appear* rational both to others and to oneself.

The theory has been tested under three main headings: (i) dissonance following a decision; (ii) dissonance resulting from effort; and (iii) dissonance resulting from counter-attitudinal behaviour.

1) *Dissonance Following a Decision*

If we have to choose between two equally attractive objects or activities, then one way of reducing the resulting dissonance is to emphasize the undesirable features of the one we have rejected; in this way we are trying to add to the number of consonant cognitions and reduce the number of dissonant ones.

This was demonstrated in a study by Brehm (1956) in which female subjects had to rate the desirability of several household appliances on an eight-point scale. When they had done this, they had to choose between two of the items (their reward for participating), which for half the subjects were $\frac{1}{2}$ to $1\frac{1}{2}$ points apart on the scale (*high-dissonance* condition) and for the other half were a full three points apart (*low-dissonance* condition). When subjects were asked to re-evaluate the items they had chosen and rejected, they showed increased liking for the chosen item and decreased liking for the rejected one. So far, so good.

The theory also predicts that we will tend to actively *avoid* information which emphasizes the desirable qualities of the item we have rejected (because that will add to the dissonance) as well as actively *seeking* information which praises the desirable qualities of the item we have chosen (because that will reduce dissonance by increasing consonance). So if we have had a difficult time deciding which new car to buy, we will avoid advertisements for other cars and go out of our way to find advertisements for our own. Is there evidence to support this prediction?

Several studies have suggested that there is a tendency to prefer advertisements showing the car subjects had recently bought but *no* corresponding avoidance of advertisements showing other cars.

Dissonance theory predicts that there will be *selective exposure* to consonant information, ie seeking consistent information which is not present at the time. However, there is more to selective perception then selective exposure: other aspects include *selective attention* (looking at consistent information which is present) and *selective interpretation* (perceiving ambiguous information as being consistent with our other cognitions). Each of these has been investigated and in a review of the literature Fiske and Taylor (1984) conclude that the evidence overall is stronger for selective attention and interpretation than for selective exposure.

2) *Dissonance Resulting from Effort*

In one of the classic dissonance experiments (Aronson and Mills, 1959), female college students volunteered for a discussion on the psychology of sex, with the understanding that the research was concerned with the dynamics of group discussion. Each subject was interviewed individually and asked if she could participate without embarrassment: all but one said yes. If she had been assigned to the *control* condition, she was simply accepted; but for acceptance to the *severe embarrassment* condition she had to take an 'embarrassment test' (reading out loud to a male experimenter a list of obscene words and some explicit sexual passages from modern novels—remember the year was 1959!); and for acceptance to the *mild embarrassment* condition she had to read aloud words like 'prostitute' and 'virgin'. They then all heard a tape-recording of an actual discussion (by a group which they believed they would later join) which was about sex in lower animals and extremely dull. Subjects then had to rate the discussion and the group members in terms of how interesting or dull and intelligent or unintelligent they found them.

As predicted, the *severe embarrassment* subjects gave the *most positive* ratings, because they had experienced the greatest dissonance! These results have been confirmed by several other studies.

So, when a voluntarily chosen experience turns out badly, the fact that we chose it motivates us to try to think that it actually turned out well: the greater the sacrifice or hardship associated with the choice, the greater the dissonance and, therefore, the greater the pressure towards attitude change. (This is called the *suffering-leads-to-liking effect*.)

3) *Engaging in Counter-attitudinal Behaviour*

Probably the most famous of all the dissonance experiments is the one carried out by Festinger and Carlsmith (1959). College students were brought, one at a time, into a small room to work for 30 minutes on two extremely dull and repetitive tasks (stacking spools and turning pegs). Later, they were offered either one dollar or twenty dollars to enter a waiting room and to try to convince the next 'subject' (in fact, a female stooge) that the tasks were interesting and enjoyable. Common sense would predict that the twenty-dollar subjects would be more likely to change their attitude in favour of the tasks (they had more reason to do so) and this is also the predition which would be made by Reinforcement or Incentive Theory (Janis et al, 1965) which maintains that the greater the reward or incentive, the greater the attitude change (liking for the tasks).

However, Festinger and Carlsmith found, as predicted by dissonance theory, that it was, in fact, the one-dollar group which showed the greater attitude change. (This is called the *less-leads-to-more effect*.) Why? The large, twenty-dollar incentive gave those subjects ample *justification* for their counter-attitudinal behaviour and so they experienced very little dissonance; by contrast, the one-dollar subjects experienced considerable dissonance because they could hardly justify their counter-attitudinal behaviour in terms of the negligible reward, hence, the change of attitude to reduce the dissonance.

These findings have been confirmed by several studies in which children are given either a mild or a severe threat not to play with an attractive toy (Aronson and Carlsmith; 1963, Freedman, 1965). If children obey a mild threat, they will experience greater dissonance because it is more difficult for them to justify their behaviour than it is for children who are given a severe threat, and so the mild threat condition produces greater reduction in liking of the toy.

But does counter-attitudinal behaviour always and inevitably produce dissonance and attitude change? It seems not—dissonance only occurs when *volitional* (voluntary) behaviour is involved, that is, when we feel we acted of our own free will: if we believe we had no choice, there is no dissonance and, hence, no attitude change. A study by Freedman (1963) shows that dissonance theory and reinforcement or incentive theory are not necessarily opposed to each other—their respective predictions may *both* be confirmed when applied to the conditions of voluntary or involuntary behaviour.

Freedman asked subjects to perform a dull task after *first* informing them that *either*: (i) the data would definitely be of *no* value to the experimenter, as his experiment was already completed; *or* (ii) that the data would be of *great* value to him. Subjects in (i) enjoyed the task to a much greater extent than those in (ii), because the former experienced greater dissonance (*dissonance effect*). However, in a parallel set of conditions, he withheld information about the value of the task until *after* subjects had completed the task and found the opposite effect, that is, those in (ii) enjoyed the task much more (they received the reward of his gratitude), while those in (i) could reason, 'If I'd only known I wouldn't have done it' and so experienced no dissonance (*incentive effect*).

Another variable which influences dissonance, and which interacts with voluntary or involuntary behaviour, is the degree of *commitment*. Carlsmith et al (1966) used a procedure similar to that of Festinger and Carlsmith's one dollar/twenty dollar experiment and also found that the smaller reward produced the greater attitude change.

However, this dissonance effect was only found under conditions where subjects lied to another person in a highly committing, face-to-face situation (they had to make an identifiable video recording). Where subjects merely had to write an essay and were assured of complete anonymity, then an incentive effect was found (ie the bigger the reward, the greater the attitude change). (In the Festinger and Carlsmith study, this face-to-face variable was not manipulated.)

According to Brehm and Cohen (1962), both volition *and* commitment are necessary for the arousal of dissonance and the greater one of these (or both), the greater the dissonance. Similarly, it seems to be important that we must perceive our behaviour as having serious consequences if we are to experience dissonance. For instance, in the Festinger and Carlsmith experiment, dissonance would only occur if subjects believed they really had convinced the next subject how enjoyable the task was.

Kelman and Baron (1974) distinguish between two *kinds* of dissonance: (i) *moral*, in which counter-attitudinal behaviour is related to a value so that greater reward produces more dissonance (and greater effort produces less dissonance); and (ii) *hedonic*, in which lesser reward produces greater dissonance (and greater effort produces greater dissonance). Hedonic dissonance is involved in the one dollar/twenty dollar experiment.

EVALUATION OF DISSONANCE THEORY

a) *Alternative Explanations*

Not only do dissonance effects occur under certain specified conditions (eg volition and commitment), but some critics have argued that even under those conditions it is possible to explain the findings in other ways.

For instance, in the Aronson and Mills (1959) experiment, the severe embarrassment condition effectively masked the true purpose of the experiment and also seemed to cause genuine embarrassment—blushing, hesitation, looking down at the floor and so on. According to Chapanis and Chapanis (1964), the use of sexual material suggests at least two plausible alternative explanations:

(a) While reciting the material, the female subjects became *sexually aroused* which could have increased the attractiveness of the group.
(b) They felt *relief* (from sexual anxiety) when they discovered how banal the group discussion really was, also increasing the group's attractiveness.

Gerard and Matthewson (1966) tested these alternative explanations by operationalizing 'unpleasant effort' as electric shocks, so that the initiation into the group had nothing to do with sexual arousal or relief from sexual anxiety. What subjects thought would be a discussion about 'college morals' turned out to be one about cheating in exams and, consistent with Aronson and Mills's results, subjects who underwent severe shock rated the discussion far more favourably than mild-shock subjects. Both studies show that dissonance is only experienced when severe initiation is endured *in order* to get into a group which turns out to be dull.

A major critic of dissonance theory has been Bem. He claims that dissonance as such is neither a necessary nor sufficient explanation and he rejects any reference to hypothetical, intervening variables. According to his *Self-Perception Theory* (1965, 1967), any self-report of an attitude is an *inference* from observation of one's own behaviour and the situation in which it occurs. If the situation contains cues (eg offer of a large—$20—incentive) which imply that we might have behaved that way regardless of how we personally felt (we lie about the task being interesting even though it was boring), then we do *not* infer that the behaviour reflected our true attitudes. But in the absence of obvious situational pressures ($1 condition), we assume that our attitudes are what our behaviour suggests they are. In terms of attribution theory (see Chapter 17) the $20 subjects can easily make a *situational attribution* ('I did it for the money') whereas the $1 subjects had to make a *dispositional attribution* ('I did it because I really enjoyed it').

Bem's way of testing his theory is a form of experiment he calls *interpersonal simulation*, in which he presents so-called 'observer' subjects with a summary description of the procedure used in some well-known dissonance experiment (eg the 1 dollar/20 dollar), telling them of the subjects' agreement to perform the counter-attitudinal act requested by the experimenter and then asking them to estimate the original subjects' final attitudinal response. The 'observer's' estimate usually matches the original subjects' responses quite closely and show the predicted effects of different levels of incentive—so when told that subjects were offered $20, they are less likely to assume a match between the subjects' behaviour and their attitude. However, it has not fulfilled its promise as a general alternative to dissonance theory (Eiser and van der Pligt, 1988). Empirically, it is far from clear that Bem's subjects were using the *same* information as the original subjects. On the contrary, when subjects are given further details of the original procedures than contained in Bem's summaries, their estimates tend to be *more* discrepant from the original subjects' responses. Also, the fact that subjects *may* infer their attitudes from their behaviour, does not necessarily mean that they *actually do* (as required by Bem's theory).

Eiser and Van der Pligt (1988) believe that, conceptually, it is very difficult to distinguish between the two theories. Perhaps, as with dissonance and incentive theories, both processes operate but to different extents under different circumstances. Fazio et al (1977), for example, argue that *dissonance* may apply when people behave in a way which is contrary to their initial attitude (*counter-attitudinal behaviour*), while *self-perception* may apply better where their behaviour and initial attitude are broadly consistent (*attitude-congruent behaviour*).

There is no doubt that we do sometimes 'work backwards' from behaviour to 'internal states', eg our stomach rumbles or we have 'second helpings' at a meal and then infer how hungry we must have been, or we shout at someone and infer that we are angry. These would be good examples of attitude-congruent behaviour but are fairly trivial compared with situations in which we experience some kind of *conflict* between what we think and what we do. We should also note that conflict is as often between two attitudes or beliefs as it is between attitudes and behaviour—yet Bem's self-perception theory (based as it is on Attribution) requires some *overt behaviour* from which we then make an inference about our attitudes. However, such behaviour often simply does not occur.

Another general issue is whether what matters is our *own* inferences about the way we behave or the inferences we feel *others* might draw about us ('*impression management theory*'). Tedeschi et al (1971) argue that the effects of many dissonance experiments might not reflect genuine cases of 'private' attitude change but rather an adoption of a public response that protects subjects against the possible accusation of insincerity (ie the need is to *appear* consistent rather than a drive to actually *be* consistent). So subjects in the 1 dollar/20 dollar experiment might *pretend* they really believed the task was interesting so that it wouldn't appear as though they had let themselves be 'bribed'.

Impression-management theorists (Tedeschi and Rosenfield, 1981; Schlenker, 1982) no longer tend to claim that changes in attitude responses are a mere pretence. Instead, much attitude change is seen as an attempt to avoid social anxiety and embarrassment, or to protect positive views of one's own identity. Accordingly, the roots of the 'tension' hypothesized by Festinger may be in peoples' *social* concerns with how others might evaluate them and how they should evaluate themselves. So the 1 dollar subjects' attitude change is genuine but is motivated by *social* (rather than cognitive) factors.

b) *Evidence for a State of Dissonance*

An objection that can be made to experiments like the 1 dollar/20 dollar study is that the reasoning involved is *circular*: (i) the only evidence for the greater dissonance of the $1 subjects is the fact that they rated the task as more interesting; and (ii) the fact that they rated the task as more interesting is evidence of the greater dissonance. Is there any *independent* evidence for the existence of dissonance? What kind of evidence do we require and would we accept? What about physiological evidence? Croyle and Cooper (1983) found evidence for more persistent increase in physiological arousal as measured by GSR (galvanic skin response) in subjects who wrote a *counter-attitudinal* essay under high-choice as compared with low-choice instructions, or with subjects who wrote an essay consistent with their own opinion. However, feelings of un-pleasant tension may also be produced by factors less directly related to the notion of dissonance, eg the belief that a decision subjects have made will have bad consequences (Cooper and Fazio, 1984). According to such an interpretation, attitude change in such experiments should depend both on the amount of arousal experienced by the subject (from whatever sources) *and* on how the subject interprets/explains this arousal.

Support for this notion comes from a study (Zanna and Cooper, 1974) in which subjects wrote a counter-attitudinal essay under instructions which implied either high or low freedom of choice. Consistent with previous findings, the prediction that high-choice subjects change their opinions more than low-choice was confirmed. The novel feature of the experiment was that subjects were also given a placebo pill, which they were either told would make them feel tense or relaxed or told nothing about it at all. The *dissonance theory prediction* was upheld when subjects where given *no information* and even more strongly when they were told it would relax them. But when told the pill would make them feel tense, *no difference* between the high and low choice conditions was found. Why?

If subjects believe the pill will either relax them or have no effect and they also believe they are acting of their own free will, they change their opinions, presumably, because they experience an internal state of dissonance. But if told the pill will make them tense, they will (mis)-attribute their tension to the pill and so little attitude change will occur (as is also true of low freedom of choice subjects). This attribution explanation is consistent with Bem's self-perception theory and so the Zanna and Cooper experiment offers support for both Festinger and Bem. (Compare this with Schachter and Singer's attribution theory of emotion; see Chapter 6.)

c) *Individual Differences*

People seem to differ with regard to their preferred methods of reducing dissonance and also what is dissonant for one person may not necessarily be dissonant for another—self-concept must be taken into account.

It has also been found that chronic anxiety is related to the 'need for balance', so that people rated as highly anxious show behaviour consis-tent with dissonance theory, while those rated low on anxiety show behaviour consistent with reinforcement or incentive theory. The theory also assumes that once a particular threshold of tension or psychological discomfort is reached, the individual will inevitably act to reduce the inconsistency which produced it. However, most people seem to be able to tolerate a great deal of (logical) inconsistency among their actions and beliefs and only a few individuals reveal a strong integration of their belief system (Katz, 1968). Also, dissonant information can sometimes be positively valuable.

d) *Cognitive Dissonance Theory as a Notion*

According to Bannister and Fransella (1980), cognitive dissonance theory is a *notion*, 'the sort of idea which coffee-table conversation amongst psychologists might produce'. They believe it is over-simple and vague and that it functions in psychology in much the same way as folk tales do in literature: it can form the plot for endless experiments but it cannot be legitimately called a theory. However, there is no doubt that it has generated an enormous amount of both research and theorizing.

Prejudice

As an *extreme attitude*, prejudice comprises the components of all attitudes:

(a) The *cognitive* component is the *stereotype* (which, in itself, is neutral, neither favourable nor unfavourable; see Chapter 17).
(b) The *affective* component is a strong feeling of hostility *or* liking (prejudice, as such, is not necessarily prejudice *against* but can also be *for* a particular group or kind of person).
(c) The *behavioural* component can take different forms. Allport (1954) proposed five stages of this component:

   (i)   *anti-locution*—hostile talk, verbal denigration and insult, racial jokes, etc;
   (ii) *avoidance*—keeping a distance but without inflicting any harm;
   (iii) *discrimination*—exclusion from housing, civil rights, employment, etc;
   (iv) *physical attack*—violence against the person and property;
   (v)   *extermination*—indiscriminate violence against an entire group.

As with all attitudes, the cognitive and affective components may not necessarily be manifested behaviourally (as in the La Piere, 1934, study discussed above). But it is just as important to recognize that discrimination does not necessarily imply the presence of cognitive and affective components—people may discriminate if the prevailing social norms dictate that they do so and if their wish to become or remain a member of the discriminating group is stronger than their wish to be fair and egalitarian etc. As far as definitions of prejudice are concerned, almost without exception they stress the hostile, negative, kind (rather than the favourable kind) and the research which tries to identify how prejudice arises, and how it might be reduced, also concentrates on hostile prejudice. Allport defined prejudice as:

> ...an antipathy based on faulty and inflexible generalization directed towards a group as a whole or towards an individual because he is a member of that group. It may be felt or expressed. (Allport, 1954)

According to Baron and Byrne:

... Prejudice is an attitude (usually negative) toward the members of some group, based solely on their membership in that group ... (Baron and Byrne, 1991)

SOME DEMONSTRATIONS OF PREJUDICE

A quite dramatic (and alarming) demonstration of the *creation* of prejudice is the 'blue eyes–brown eyes' field experiment described in Box 19.1.

Box 19.1   The blue eyes–brown eyes experiment (reported by Aronson and Osherow, 1980)

Aronson and Osherow (1980) reported an experiment with third graders (nine-year-olds) in the USA, conducted by their teacher, Jane Elliott.

She told her class one day that brown-eyed people are more intelligent and 'better' people than those with blue eyes. Brown-eyed students, though in the minority, would be the 'ruling class' over the inferior blue-eyed children, given extra privileges and the blue-eyed students were to be 'kept in their place' by such restrictions as being last in line, seated at the back of the class and given less break time. They also had to wear special collars as a sign of their low status.

Within a short time, the blue-eyed children began to do more poorly in their schoolwork and became depressed and angry and described themselves more negatively. The brown-eyed group grew mean, oppressing the others and making derogatory statements about them.

The next day, Elliott announced that she had lied and that it was really blue-eyed people who are superior. The pattern of prejudice and discrimination quickly switched from the blue-eyed as victims to the brown-eyed. She then de-briefed the children: the purpose of the exercise was to provide the children with an opportunity to experience the evils of prejudice and discrimination in a protected environment.

Allport and Kramer (1946) demonstrated an important relationship between racial prejudice and perception. They found that people with strong anti-Semitic prejudice were able to distinguish Jews fron non-Jews more accurately than unprejudiced people. Because of the salience of Jews for the prejudiced subjects, they pay attention to the cues which indicate Jewish-ness (whatever these may be) and ignore other features.

The prejudiced person (or society) must be able to classify everybody as a member of the 'good' or 'bad' race. This can produce ludicrous situations, as in South Africa, where Japanese are classified as white and Chinese as coloured.

The denial of objects at the boundaries of well-defined classes is a feature of normal perception, for, assuming that objects fall into discrete groups, we have an economic (convenient) description of the world. (A relevant study, although not concerned with prejudice, is that of Bruner and Postman (1949) in which subjects were shown unusual playing cards; see Chapter 9.)

Attitudes (like stereotypes; see Chapter 17) often function as *schemas*—cognitive frameworks for organizing, interpreting and recalling information (Fiske and Taylor, 1984). Thus, prejudiced individuals tend to process information about the groups concerned differently from how they process information about other groups. Specifically, information which is consistent with the prejudice may receive more attention, be rehearsed more often and, as a result, tend to be remembered more accurately than information which is not consistent with the prejudice. In this way, prejudice becomes a kind of closed cognitive loop and in the absence of truly dramatic experiences which refute it, can only grow stronger over time (Baron and Byrne, 1991).

Surveys between 1970–76 indicated increasing support for integration in education and housing in the USA. However, many studies of whites' *behaviour* (including that of many college students) in the same period showed that anti-black sentiment remained stronger than the survey data suggest (another example of the inconsistency between the different components of attitudes).

In a study by Benson et al (1976), a completed application to graduate school was 'planted' in an airport telephone booth. Half the time the applicant (shown in a photograph) was white, the other half black. In all cases, a stamped, addressed, envelope, and a note asking 'Dad' to post the form were attached. The context made it clear that 'Dad' had lost the letter in the airport. More of the white subjects who found the application bothered to post it when the applicant was white than when he/she was black.

Crosby et al (1980) found that whites were less likely to help stranded black motorists, less likely to make an emergency phone call for a black, and more likely to report black shoplifters (but see discussion of Bystander Intervention in Chapter 16).

ORIGINS OF PREJUDICE

Theories of the origins of prejudice fall into two major categories: (i) those which see prejudice as stemming from *personality* variables; and (ii) those which emphasize the interaction between personal (individual) and social variables (and which can be called *social psychological theories*).

PERSONALITY THEORIES

a) *The Authoritarian Personality*

In 1950, Adorno, Frenkel-Brunswick, Levinson and Sanford proposed the concept of the authoritarian personality, a type of person who is prejudiced by virtue of specific personality traits which predispose him/her to be hostile towards ethnic, racial and other minority or 'out' groups.

They began by studying anti-semitism in Nazi Germany in the 1940s and drew on Freud's theories to help understand the relationship between 'collective ideologies' (such as Fascism) and individual personality (Brown, 1985). After their emigration to the USA, studies began with 2000 college students and other native-born, white, non-Jewish, middle-class Americans, which involved interviews concerning their political views and childhood experiences and the use of projective tests designed to reveal unconscious attitudes towards minority groups.

A number of scales were developed in the course of their research designed to measure: (i) anti-Semitism; (ii) ethnocentrism (the belief that one's own ethnic—or other membership—group is superior to others and the tendency to judge all other groups from the standpoint of one's own); and (iii) political–economic conservatism. Out of these emerged the famous *F scale* (F for Fascism), which measures anti-democratic tendencies *indirectly* by not mentioning specific minority groups or ideological beliefs; what it reveals is that anti-Semitism is part of a general factor rather than an isolated prejudice, so that the authoritarian personality is prejudiced in a very generalized way. What other characteristics do they have?

Typically, the authoritarian personality is hostile to people of inferior status, servile to those of higher status, contemptuous of weakness, rigid and inflexible, intolerant of ambiguity and uncertainty, unwilling to introspect feelings, and an upholder of conventional values and ways of life (as represented by religion, for example). This belief in convention and intolerance of ambiguity combine to make minorities 'them' and the authoritarian's membership group 'us'; 'they' are by definition 'bad' and 'we' are by definition 'good'.

Authoritarians have often experienced a harsh, punitive, disciplinarian upbringing, with little affection and they often reveal considerable latent hostility towards their parents. Such unconscious hostility may be *displaced* onto minority groups (so that they become the objects of the authoritarian's hostility) and/or *projected* onto these groups (whereby the authoritarian feels threatened *by* them). Is there any evidence to support this account of prejudice?

As far as the relationship between the authoritarian personality and upbringing is concerned, there is some evidence of a correlation between the F-scores of college students and their parents, and Levinson and Huffman (1955) reported that authoritarian parents are more likely to stress discipline, conventionalism and submission in their child-rearing methods compared with non-authoritarian parents. (However, authoritarian parents do not, according to the theory, directly pass on their prejudices to their children, but only *indirectly*, with prejudice being a feature of the authoritarian personality which is a result of a particular kind of child-rearing.)

In the laboratory, authoritarian personalities have been shown to be intolerant of ambiguity, and outside, they show a positive bias towards the police, a negative bias towards pornography, are highly susceptible to social influence, especially in relation to people of higher status (see Chapter 20) and are more likely to give a verdict of guilty and recommend longer sentences when serving on juries. They are also more likely to hold sexist attitudes, vote Conservative and obey the orders of an authority figure to give electric shocks to an innocent stranger (see Chapter 20).

There are a number of problems with Adorno et al's theory, some of which are discussed below in the section on Social Psychological theories. We shall mention two here, as discussed by Brown (1988).

First, the theory cannot explain the widespread *uniformity* of prejudice in certain societies or sub-groups within societies. If prejudice is to be explained in terms of individual *differences*, how can it then be manifested in a whole population or at least a vast majority of that population? In pre-war Nazi Germany, for example (and in many other places since) consistent racist attitudes and behaviour were shown by hundreds of thousands of people who must have differed on most other psychological characteristics.

Secondly, how can the theory account for the sudden rise and falls of prejudice in particular societies at specific historical periods. Again taking the example of anti-semitism in Nazi Germany, this arose during a decade or so which is:

> . . . much too short a time for a whole generation of German families to have adopted new forms of child-rearing practices giving rise to authoritarian and prejudiced children . . . (Brown, 1988)

Even more dramatic was the anti-Japanese prejudice among Americans following the attack on Pearl Habour. Such examples:

> . . . strongly suggest that the attitudes held by members of different groups towards each other have more to do with the objective relations between the groups—relations of political conflict or alliance, economic interdependence and so on—than with the familial relation in which they grew up. (Brown, 1988)

b) *The Open and Closed Mind*

Another criticism made of the Authoritarian Personality is that it assumed that authoritarianism is a characteristic of the political right and so implied that there is no equivalent authoritarianism on the left.

The best known attempt to redress this balance is that of Rokeach (1960), who has developed a *dogmatism scale*; '*ideological dogmatism*' refers to a relatively rigid outlook on life and intolerance of those with opposing beliefs. High scores on the dogmatism scale reveal: (i) closedness of mind; (ii) lack of flexibility; and (iii) authoritarianism, regardless of particular social and political ideology.

So an individual with left-wing or progressive beliefs can espouse them in just as rigid and dogmatic a way as someone with right-wing or reactionary views—they can be equally *extreme* (and closed) regardless of their particular content.

The dogmatic individual tends to accentuate differences between 'us and them' (eg 'The USA and USSR have just about nothing in common'), displays self-aggrandizement (eg 'If I had to choose between happiness and greatness, I'd choose greatness'), a paranoid outlook on life ('I often feel people are looking at me critically') and is uncompromising in his/her beliefs and intolerant of others. These characteristics serve as defences against the dogmatic person's self-inadequacy.

In fact, Rokeach found it difficult to find closed-mindedness in people with left-wing views but, as Brown (1985) points out, such views were generally much more unacceptable in the USA in the 1950s than they are even today and required the people who held them to show open mindedness and cognitive flexibility.

c) *Tough-mindedness and Tender-mindedness*

Similarly, Eysenck (1954) distinguishes between: (i) *Radicalism–Conservatism* (the R factor), corresponding to right/left wing political beliefs; and (ii) *Toughmindedness–Tendermindedness* (the T Factor), corresponding to authoritarianism and dogmatism. A tough-minded person will be attracted to extreme political ideologies, be it Fascism or Communism; the authoritarian person is tough-minded and conservative, while the humanitarian is tender-minded and radical (Fig. 19.5). While the R factor represents social attitudes acquired during one's

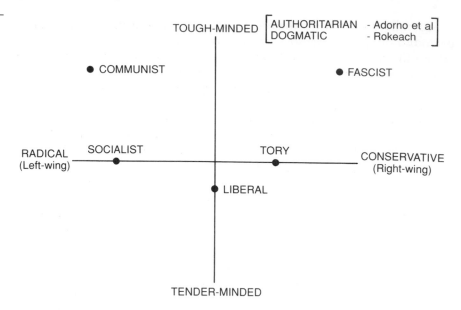

Figure 19.5 *Eysenck's two scales (corresponding to the R and T factors), their relationship to Adorno et al and Rokeach's theories, plus the locations of some 'typical' political attitudes. (Based on Eysenck, 1954)*

lifetime by social and political experience, the T factor is a projection on to the field of social attitudes of certain fundamental personality traits; namely tough-mindedness and extroversion, and tender-mindedness and introversion (see Chapter 29).

SOCIAL PSYCHOLOGICAL THEORIES

Adorno et al recognized that, as important as personality dynamics are, it is *society* which provides the content of attitudes and prejudice and it is society which defines who are the 'out-groups'. Also, as we noted earlier, discrimination does not necessarily imply prejudice, or (by the same token) authoritarianism. According to Brown (1985), 'cultural or societal norms may be much more important than personality in accounting for ethno-centrism, out-group rejection, prejudice and discrimination'.

a) *The Impact of Social Norms—Prejudice as Conformity*

Although research on the authoritarian personality has been valuable, individual bigotry can explain only a small proportion of racial discrimination. For example, even though overt discrimination has been, traditionally, greater in the South of the USA, white Southerners have not scored higher than whites from the north on measures of authoritarianism (Pettigrew, 1959). So, clearly, *conformity to social norms* can prove more powerful as a determinant of behaviour than personality factors.

Minard (1952) found that black and white coal miners in West Virginia followed a pattern of almost complete integration below ground but almost complete segregation above! This only makes sense when viewed in terms of conformity to the norms which operated in those different situations.

Pettigrew (1971) also found that Southern Americans are not more anti-Semitic than those from the North (as the authoritarian personality explanation would require). Again, women are more anti-black than men in the South, but not in the North; those affiliated to a political party are more anti-black in the South than independents, but no such differences exist in the North. These differences cannot be explained in terms of personality differences.

Contrary to the claims of the authoritarian personality, the traditional anti-black attitudes in the southern USA have *not* been combined with anti-Semitism or prejudice against other minority groups, ie prejudice is not the generalized attitude which Adorno et al claim it is

According to Reich and Adcock (1976), the need to conform and to not be seen as different may cause milder prejudices, but active discrimination against, and ill-treatment of, minorities is best seen as reflecting a prejudice which already exists and which is maintained and legitimized by conformity.

If prejudice is *not* a generalized attitude to all out-groups, it suggests that we *learn* to become prejudiced against particular groups in the same way that we learn other kinds of attitudes, eg through observational learning involving parents, peers, the media and so on (see Chapter 23, for example).

b) *Inter-group Conflict*

Campbell (1947) found a strong relationship between dissatisfaction with their financial position and the general political state of the country, on the one hand, and anti-Semitism on the other, on the part of 300 non-Jewish Americans; of those who were generally satisfied, only 22 per cent showed any form of prejudice, while 62 per cent of the dissatisfied were prejudiced against Jews. Also, as prosperity declined between 1880 and 1930 in the USA, the number of lynchings of blacks in the South increased; during the more prosperous years, the lynchings decreased.

These findings are consistent with data from many other nations and historical periods—the greater the competition for scarce resources, the greater the hostility between various ethnic groups; a number of studies have found high levels of racism among lower-class whites who felt that blacks were taking away their jobs:

> ...Thus, it appears that increased competition between various groups during periods of economic decline may indeed be one of the factors contributing to prejudice and interracial violence... (Baron and Byrne, 1991)

Sherif (1966) argues that inter-group conflict arises as a result of a conflict of interests: when two groups want to achieve the same goal but cannot both have it, hostility is produced between them. Indeed, he claims that conflict of interest (or competition) is a *sufficient* condition for the occurrence of hostility or conflict and he bases this claim on one of the most famous field experiments in social psychology, the Robber's Cave experiment, described in Box 19.2, which Brown (1986) describes as the most successful field experiment ever conducted on inter-group conflict.

Box 19.2   The Robber's Cave Experiment (Sherif et al, 1961)

The setting was Robber's Cave State Park in Oklahoma, where 22 white, middle-class, Protestant, well-adjusted boys, spent two weeks at a summer camp; they were randomly assigned to two groups of 11, each occupying a separate cabin, out of sight of each other. None of the boys knew any of the others prior to their arrival at the camp.

During the first stage of the experiment, each group co-operated on a number of activities (eg pitching tents, making meals, a treasure hunt) and soon a distinct set of norms emerged which defined the group's identity; one group called itself the 'Rattlers' and the other called itself the 'Eagles'. Towards the end of the first week, they were allowed to become aware of the other's existence and an 'us and them' language quickly developed.

The second stage began with the announcement that there was to be a grand tournament between the two groups, comprising 10 sporting events, plus points awarded for the state of their cabins and so on; a splendid trophy, medals and four-bladed knives for each of the group members would be awarded to the winning group.

Before the tournament began, the Rattler's flag was burned and the camp counsellors (the experimenters) had to break up a fight between the two groups. With some 'help' from the counsellors, the Eagles won and later the Rattlers stole their medals and knives.

There was a strong preference for the in-group: Rattlers stereotyped all Rattlers as brave, tough, and friendly and (almost) all Eagles as sneaky, stinkers and smart alecks; the reverse was true for the Eagles.

Clearly the competition threatened an unfair distribution of rewards (the trophy, medals and knives) and the losing group inevitably saw the winners as undeserving. Sherif et al's results have been confirmed with adults from industrial organizations meeting for two-week periods.

However, Tyerman and Spencer (1983) challenged Sherif et al's conclusions that competition is a sufficient condition for inter-group conflict by observing scouts at their annual camp. The boys knew each other well before the start of camp and much of what they did there was similar to what the Rattlers and Eagles did at Robber's Cave. They were divided into four 'patrols' who competed in situations familiar to them from previous camps, but the friendship ties which existed prior to arrival at camp were maintained across the patrol groups; competition remained friendly and there was no increase of in-group solidarity. Tyerman and Spencer believe that the four groups continued to see themselves as part of the whole group (a view deliberately encouraged by the leader) and concluded that Sherif et al's results reflect the transitory nature of their experimental group. The fact that the boys knew each other beforehand, had established friendships, were familiar with camp life and had a leader who encouraged co-operation, were all important contextual/situational influences on the boys' behaviour. It seems that 'competition' may not, after all, be a sufficient condition for inter-group conflict and hostility.

If we accept this conclusion, the question arises whether it is a necessary condition. In other words, can hostility arise in the *absence* of conflicting interests?

c)   *Minimal Groups*

According to Tajfel et al (1971), the answer is *yes*. They believe that the mere *perception* of the existence of another group can itself produce discrimination: when people are arbitrarily and randomly divided into two groups, knowledge of the other group's existence is a sufficient condition for the development of pro-in-group and anti-out-group attitudes; this is known as the *minimal* group.

Tajfel et al argue that, before any discrimination can occur, people must be *categorized* as members of an in-group or an out-group (making categorization a necessary condition) but, more significantly, the very act of categorization by itself produces conflict and discrimination (making it also a sufficient condition).

These conclusions are based on the creation of artificial groups among 14- to 15-year-old schoolboys from Bristol. The criteria which were used were arbitrary and superficial and differed from experiment to experiment. They included: (i) chronic 'over-estimators' or 'under-estimators' on a task involving estimating the number of dots appearing on slide projections; (ii) preference for paintings by Klee or Kandinsky; (iii) the toss of a coin.

Once these arbitrary groups had been formed, the boys worked alone in cubicles on a task which required them to allocate points, as in a game, which could be exchanged at the end for one-tenth of a penny each. The points could be allocated: (i) to themselves; (ii) to fellow group-members; or (iii) members of the other group. The only option which was taken up was (ii). The only information each boy had about another boy was whether or not he was a member of the same group or the other group, otherwise he was anonymous, unknown, unseen and unidentified. The allocation of points was always to the advantage of in-group members and to the detriment of out-group members—even when a co-operative strategy would have maximized the outcome for the in-group.

Brown (1986) sees this in-group favouritism as a form of ethnocentrism and cites a number of studies which show that the in-group is always rated as more likeable and fair than the out-group; the work of the in-group is rated more highly and 'good' deeds are attributed to the in-group and 'bad deeds' to the out-group.

In the Tajfel et al experiments, the actual group-assignments were always made randomly whatever the boys believed to be the basis for the categorization. But Billig and Tajfel (1973) and Locksley et al (1980) went even further in the creation of minimal groups by actually *telling* the subjects that they were being randomly assigned, tossing the coin in front of them and giving them obviously meaningless names (such as *A*s and *B*s or 'Kappas' and 'Phis'). These most minimal of all groups *still* showed a strong in-group preference.

These findings have been replicated using a wide range of subjects in a wide range of cultures, including Welsh adults, female undergraduates in California, male and female undergraduates in Oregon and New York, students in Switzerland, soldiers in the then West German army and Maori children in New Zealand:

> Intergroup discrimination in this minimal group situation has proved to be a remarkably robust phenomenon. In more than two dozen independent studies in several different countries using a wide range of experimental participants of both sexes (from young children to adults), essentially the same result has been found: the mere act of allocating people into arbitrary

social categories is sufficient to elicit biased judgements and discriminatory behaviours . . . (Brown, 1988)

However, Wetherall (1982) maintains that inter-group conflict is *not* inevitable. She studied white and Polynesian children in New Zealand and found the latter to be much more generous towards the out-group, reflecting cultural norms which emphasized co-operation. The research has also been criticized on several grounds, especially its *artificiality* (a problem faced by *all* experimental research—see Chapter 2). However:

> . . . the real point of the minimal group experiments is not that they have generated a 'finding' which should then simply be extrapolated wholesole to all groups everywhere. Rather, they should be seen as a further step in discovering not just the shape of one of the pieces of the jigsaw, but how that piece interlocks with all the others. (Brown, 1988)

How can we account for the minimal group effect?

Tajfel and Turner (1979) and Tajfel (1981) offer an explanation in the form of *Social Identity Theory* (SIT). According to SIT: (i) individuals strive to achieve or maintain a positive self-image; and (ii) the self-image has two components, *personal identity* and *social identity* (see Chapter 21). In fact, each of us has several social identities, corresponding to the number of different groups with which we identify and, in relation to each one, the more positive the image of the group, the more positive will be our own social identity and, hence, our self-image. By emphasizing the desirability of the in-group(s) and the undesirability of the out-group(s) and focusing on those distinctions which enable one's own group to come out on top, we help to create for ourselves a satisfactory social identity and this can be seen as lying at the heart of prejudice.

Members of minimal groups in the laboratory (compared with controls who are not assigned to a group) have been found to show higher self-esteem. Lemyre and Smith (1985) confirmed this result and established that it was indeed the opportunity to display *inter-group discrimination* that *increased* self-esteem. Control subjects who were categorized but could only distribute rewards between two in-groupers or two out-groupers or could not distribute rewards at all, showed lower self-esteem than experimental subjects able to make *inter-group* decisions.

SIT is not limited to minimal group experiments. Part of its attraction is its ability to make sense of a wide range of phenomena in naturalistic contexts, including wage differentials (size of wage relative to comparable groups of workers), ethnolinguistic groups (attempts by various ethnic or national groups to maintain the integrity of their native language) and occupational groups (for example, biases in nursing in favour of Registered as opposed to Enrolled Nurses; Brown (1988)).

Some individuals may be more prone to prejudice because they have an intense need for acceptance by others. For such individuals, personal and social identity may be much more interlinked than for those with a lesser need for social acceptance. The need for a sense of security and superiority can be met by belonging to a favoured in-group and showing hostility towards out-groups. This is seen very clearly in majority–minority group relations where, for example, almost any white may feel superior to any black, no matter how well-educated or economically well-off.

Allport (1954) noted that many cases of prejudice are part of the conformity found in 'polite' social chatter. Affiliation needs can readily produce anti-social effects—an otherwise upstanding citizen may feel it necessary to show the strength of his/her affiliation by 'putting down' members of out-groups. This pattern may be especially intense in the case of converts to a new group.

Prejudice can be seen as an adjustive mechanism which bolsters the self-concept of individuals who have feelings of personal inadequacy. It becomes a 'prop' for these individuals (but with potentially undesirable social implications).

d) *Scapegoating*

This theory of prejudice as an outlet for frustration, combines two ideas: (i) Freud's concept of *displacement*, whereby substitute objects or targets for aggression are found when it is impossible to express the hostility towards its real target (see Chapter 29); and (ii) the *frustration–aggression* hypothesis, which maintains that frustration always gives rise to aggression—and aggression is always caused by frustration (see Chapter 16).

The substitute object is, of course, the scapegoat, and there are usually socially-approved (legitimized) groups which serve as targets for frustration-induced aggression. In England, during the 1930s and 1940s the scapegoat was predominantly the Jews, who were replaced by West Indians during the 1950s and 1960s and, during the 1970s and 1980s, by Asians from Pakistan.

Scapegoating can account for the non-experimental findings on inter-group conflict discussed in the previous section, and an interesting laboratory demonstration of this was the experiment by Weatherley (1961). He gave an anti-Semitism scale to subjects and divided them into high and low scorers. Half of each group were subjected to very insulting remarks (while filling in a second questionnaire) and then given picture-story tests and asked to tell a story about each picture. Some pictures showed people with Jewish-sounding names and it was found that high scorers directed more aggression towards 'Jewish' pictures than low scorers *and* this difference was confined to the 'Jewish' pictures. This shows that hostility is not indiscriminate (or 'blind') but requires a target, which is an already-disliked out-group (which tends to contradict the authoritarian personality theory).

THE REDUCTION OF PREJUDICE

According to Brown (1986), two factors seem to be more effective than any others in trying to reduce inter-group conflict and racial (and other kinds of) prejudice: (i) non-competitive contact of an *equal status*; and (ii) the pursuit of common (*superordinate*) goals which are only attainable by co-operation. These are interrelated, as this quote from Allport shows:

> Prejudice (unless deeply rooted in the character structure of the individual) may be reduced by equal status contact between majority and minority groups in the pursuit of common goals. The effect is greatly enhanced if this contact is sanctioned by institutional supports (ie by law, custom or local atmosphere) ... (Allport, 1954)

i) *Equal Status Contact*

It is generally agreed that increased contact by itself is not sufficient to reduce prejudice. Despite what we said in Chapter 18 about preferring people who are familiar, if this contact is between people who are consistently of the same, unequal status, then 'familiarity may breed contempt'. Aronson (1980) points out that many whites (in the USA) have always had a great deal of contact with blacks—as dishwashers, toilet attendants, domestic servants, and so on; such contacts may simply reinforce the stereotypes held by whites of blacks as being inferior.

One early study of equal-status contact was that of Deutsch and Collins (1951), who compared two kinds of housing projects, one of which was thoroughly integrated (blacks and whites were assigned houses regardless of race) and the other segregated. Residents of both were intensively interviewed and it was found that both casual and neighbourly contact were greater in the integrated housing with a corresponding decrease in prejudice among whites towards blacks. So it appeared to be environmental support which was sustaining prejudice in the segregated project.

Similarly, Jahoda (1961) found that, although a majority of American whites stated a preference for residential segregation in a survey, the preference was cut by half where whites had the experience of working with blacks and having them as neighbours. However, was this reduction confined to the black neighbours with whom the whites interacted or was it a more generalized reduction of anti-black prejudice?

The Minard study of miners in West Virginia (1952) suggests that the change was confined to situations in which it was socially permissible to be unprejudiced. Consistent with this are studies by Stouffer (1949) and Amir (1969) which found that inter-racial attitudes improved markedly when blacks and whites served together as soldiers in battle and on ships, although relationship were not so good at base camp.

It might be thought that de-segregation of American schools would provide a major test of the effectiveness of equal-status contact in reducing prejudice and a number of studies have been carried out to this end. However, the results are very discouraging. Gerard and Miller (1975) found in their longitudinal study in Riverside, California, that white, black and Hispanic–American students continued to 'hang-out' together in a clear ethinic stucture.

Stephan (1978) reviewed a number of studies and concluded that de-segregation as such seems *not* to have reduced white prejudice towards blacks, and black prejudice towards whites seems to have increased. Several studies have found that, at first, interaction and friendship are totally governed by group attitudes and then slowly start to take account of personal qualities. However, racial attitudes change very little. If inter-group contact does reduce prejudice, it is *not* because it encourages interpersonal friendship (as Deutsch and Collins would claim) but because of changes in the nature and structure of *inter-group* relationships.

According to Brown and Turner (1981) and Hewstone and Brown (1986), if the contact between groups is *interpersonal* (people are seen as individuals and group memberships are largely insignificant), then any change of attitude may not generalize to other members of the respective groups. At the very least, individuals must be seen as *typical* members of their group if any generalization is to occur.

ii) *Pursuit of Common Goals*

In a co-operative situation, the attainment of one person's goal enhances the chances of attainment of the goals of other group members; and this reverses the situation where competition prevails (Brown, 1986).

One of the few attempts to alter the classroom experience in order to realize equal-status contact *and* mutual co-operation is the *jigsaw classroom* technique of Aronson et al (1978). Children are assigned to small, inter-racial learning groups, in which each member is given material which represents one piece of the lesson to be learned. Each child must learn its part and then communicate it to the rest of the group and, at the end of the lesson, each child is tested on the *whole* lesson and is given an individual score. Each child must, therefore, learn the full lesson but each is dependent on the others in the group for parts of the lesson that can only be learned from them, hence, there is complete mutual interdependence. What are its effects?

Aronson et al (1978) believe that the jigsaw method enhances students' self-esteem, improves academic performance, increases liking for classmates and improves some inter-racial perceptions. However, although the children of different racial groups who had actually worked together came to like each other better as individuals, their reduced prejudice did *not* generalize to those ethnic groups as a whole. However, most experiments of this type are small-scale and relatively short-term interventions. Relating studies of common goals to the failure of desegregation to reduce prejudice, Brown (1986) argues that institutional support from families, school boards and the community is often lacking but, more seriously, equal-status contact in pursuit of common goals is not what actually goes on in desegregated schools. While formal status in the classroom may be equal, the socio-economic status differences still exist, as do differences in achievement status and, far from co-operating in pursuit of common goals, students are competing in pursuit of individual goals.

In the Robber's Cave field experiment, Sherif et al (1961) introduced a third stage in which seven equal-status contact situations were created (including filling out questionnaires together, seeing movies and having meals together). None of these, nor all of them in combination, did anything to reduce friction.

However, it was also arranged that the camp's drinking water supply was cut off and the only way of restoring it was by a co-operative effort by the Rattlers and Eagles. Similarly, in order to afford to hire a movie, the two groups agreed to make an equal contribution and on a trip to Cedar Lake, one of the trucks got stuck and they all had to pull on a rope together to get it started again. Other co-operative tasks involved making meals and pitching tents. In the final few days, the group divisions disappeared and they actually suggested travelling home together in one bus; 65 per cent of their friendship choices now were made from the other group and their stereotypes changed too, becoming much more favourable.

However, the imposition of superordinate goals as a recipe for conflict reduction may not always be effective and, indeed, may sometimes even increase antagonism towards the out-group, if the co-operation fails to achieve its aims. It may also be important for groups engaged in co-operative ventures to have distinctive and complementary roles to play, so that each group's contributions are clearly defined. When this does not happen, liking for the other group may actually decrease, perhaps because group members are concerned with the integrity of the in-group (Brown, 1988).

But what if attempts are made to 're-draw the boundaries' between in- and out-groups?

If, as claimed by minimal group experiments, the mere categorization of oneself as a member of a particular group is sufficient to produce discrimination against other (out-) groups, it follows that *recategoriza-tion* should reduce it, ie people formerly viewed as out-group members come to be viewed as belonging to the in-group and evidence exists to suggest that:

> . . . strategies based on shifting individuals' perceived boundaries between 'us' and 'them' constitute a very promising approach to the problem of intergroup bias. (Baron and Byrne, 1991)

Conclusions

Despite what we have said about the ineffectiveness of mere contact, it none the less provides the opportunity for getting to know members of different racial groups as individuals.

When people are separated and segregated, the stage is set for *autistic hostility*, ie ignorance of others which leads to a failure to understand the reasons for their actions. Lack of contact means there is no 'reality testing' against which to check our own interpretations of others' behaviour.

Autistic hostility can produce a *mirror-image phenomenon* (Bronfen-brenner, 1960), whereby both sides come to see themselves as being in the right and honourable and the other as threatening and unworthy. By increased contact, the out-group loses its strangeness and becomes more differentiated, ie it no longer consists of interchangeable 'units' but a collection of unique individuals. (This represents a reduction in the illusion of *out-group homogeneity*; see Chapter 17.)

If the tendency to form impressions of others on the basis of their membership in various groups or categories (as in *stereotyping*) is a key factor in the occurrence and persistence of prejudice (Fiske, 1989), then interventions designed to reduce the impact of stereotypes might prove highly effective in reducing prejudice.

For example, motivating individuals in some way to pay careful attention to others and to focus on their unique attributes rather than their 'group' attributes can be effective. Relying on stereotypes to form impressions of strangers (*category-driven processing*) represents the least-effortful route, while relying on the unique characteristics of the target person (*attribute-driven processing*) represents the most-effortful route (Fiske and Neuberg, 1990). Conditions which tip the balance in favour of the latter tend to reduce reliance on stereotypes and to this extent can be an important means of reducing several forms of prejudice

(Baron and Byrne, 1991). This might seem to contradict the point made earlier that *interpersonal* contact between individuals may not reduce prejudice because their *group membership* is largely irrelevant (so that there is no *generalization* to the group as a whole). Perhaps the point is that, while people are very skilled at preserving their stereotypes ('You're OK, it's the others') the more often they come into contact with members of a particular group who do not fit the stereotype (through attribute-driven processing), the more likely the stereotype (category-driven processing) is to lose its credibility.

Even when we do not get to know individuals on a personal basis, we may revise our prejudices if we come into contact with people who violate our stereotypes (especially if they seem similar to ourselves). Even contact with a single person who contradicts previous stereotypes may reduce prejudice and the white worker who realizes that their black co-workers may share many of the same aspirations, grievances and attitudes towards the company may begin to discard stereotyped images of blacks (and vice versa).

However, as we have found in a number of studies discussed in this section, changes in prejudice arising from the work situation may not generalize to other situations (eg blacks as parents, or citizens) and until prejudice is reduced in society at large (eg through education and consciousness-raising), particular cases of prejudice-reduction will represent nothing more than what a democratic and just society could be.

Most, if not all, human behaviour can only be properly understood if it is thought of as social in nature, that is, as being directly or indirectly bound up with and influenced by the behaviour of others.

Social influence, as studied by psychologists, can take several different forms. Hollander (1981; cited by Gergen and Gergen, 1981) maintains that it represents the central process of concern in social psychology. He states that social influence occurs whenever an individual responds to the actual or implied presence of one or more others, and that influencing others, for whatever end, is basic to social life.

Simply being in the presence of others will normally affect our behaviour compared with our private behaviour and psychologists have studied this as *social facilitation*. You only have to think of all the things you do in private but would not dream of doing in public to get some idea of how the mere presence of other people can affect our behaviour:

> ...The key idea in understanding what researchers mean by social influence is the concept of a *social norm*. Influence relates to the processes whereby people agree or disagree about appropriate behaviour, form, maintain or change social norms and the social conditions that give rise to, and the effects of such norms... (Turner, 1991)

And again:

> ...A social norm is a generally accepted way of thinking, feeling or behaving that is endorsed and expected because it is perceived as the right and proper thing to do. It is a rule, value or standard shared by the members of a social group that prescribes appropriate, expected or desirable attitudes and conduct in matters relevant to the group... (Turner, 1991)

A more direct form of social influence involves not merely being in the presence of others but interacting with them and making some attempt to change the behaviour of one or more of those involved in a particular direction. This could be a key member of a group exerting influence over the group as a whole in order to solve a problem or complete a task (*leadership*), a group trying to influence its members to adopt a particular attitude or dress code (*conformity*) or an authority figure trying to make someone comply with his/her demands (*obedience*).

SOCIAL FACILITATION

Triplett (1898), carrying out what is widely considered to be the first social psychology experiment, studied the effects of competition on the average time it took children to complete 150 winds of a fishing reel. Each child was tested under two conditions, working alone and working in pairs, each child competing against the other member of the pair; performance was clearly superior in the pairs condition.

However, it seems that it is the mere presence of others which is the crucial variable (*social facilitation*), not the element of competition. F. H. Allport (1924) instructed his subjects not to try to compete against one another (and also prevented any collaboration) while engaging on a variety of tasks, which included crossing out all the vowels in a newspaper article, multiplication and finding logical flaws in arguments. He still found that subjects performed better when they could see others working than when they worked alone and he called this form of social facilitation, the *co-action effect*. Social facilitation can also be seen when an individual performs a task in front of an audience (other people who are not doing what the person is doing)—this is the *audience effect*.

Other studies have shown that social facilitation can occur by simply telling subjects that others are performing the same task elsewhere (Dashiell, 1935).

However, whether or not social facilitation occurs depends on the nature of the task, in particular, how simple and well-learned it is. According to Zajonc (1966), 'an audience impairs the acquisition of new responses and facilitates the emission of well-learned responses'. In other words, things a subject already knows how to do (eg cancelling numbers and letters and simple multiplication) are done better when others are present, but things which are complex or which the subject is required to learn, are done less well when others are present. These findings have been confirmed by others. Why should this be?

According to Zajonc (1966), the presence of others (in whatever capacity) increases the subject's drive level or level of arousal and since, up to a certain level, arousal enhances the performance of well-learned behaviour, the presence of others will facilitate performance on simple tasks. However, when the task is complex, the effect of increased arousal is to make it more likely that incorrect or irrelevant responses will be performed and, hence, more errors are made. The arousal produced by the presence of others, together with that produced by the task itself, produce a level beyond the optimum level for ideal performance (Zajonc's explanation is based on Hull's learning theory; see Chapter 6).

Gahagan (1975) suggests that, strictly, there is no such thing as the *mere* presence of others. She cites a study by Laird (1923) in which the audience was overtly hostile to the subjects. The effect for most subjects was a decline in performance, even on a simple task, although a few actually improved.

LEADERS AND LEADERSHIP

Two of the major approaches to trying to explain what it is that distinguishes leaders from non-leaders are the *trait approach*, which tries to identify the personality traits and the characteristics that make a person a leader, and the *situational approach*, which is concerned with the leader's dependence on the group and views leadership as a complex social process. (These two approaches are also found in discussion of personality; see Chapter 29.)

To an extent, focus on 'the leader' implies a trait approach (ie what is it about leaders as *individuals*, and compared with other individuals, that explains their 'success'?), while to talk about 'leadership' implies a situational approach (eg under what circumstances will an individual assume the role of leader?).

THE TRAIT APPROACH

This represents the earliest major approach, and the broad aim was to determine those personal attributes which make a person a leader. A number of characteristics have been proposed as being advantageous (at least in men) including height, weight, an attractive appearance, self-confidence, and being well-adjusted and intelligent. As far as intelligence is concerned, several studies and reviews have shown that the typical leader is only slightly more intelligent than the average member of the group. Also, leaders are neither extremely authoritarian nor extremely egalitarian but somewhere in between.

The findings overall, however, are inconclusive, ie leaders are not consistently found to be particular kinds of people who differ in predictable ways from non-leaders. According to Brown (1985), for example, although personal qualities are important, it has proved impossible to make a list of attributes or traits which fits a wide range of leaders without considering these leadership qualities, 'in relation to the situations and the problems to be faced by the membership of the group in question'. Similarly, Turner (1991) concludes that early research established that there is no consistent set of personality traits which distinguishes leaders from others—the kinds of traits a leader needs will vary from group to group and problem to problem.

However, 'personality' has been studied in various guises, a major one being that of *leadership style*. An early and famous study of leadership style is that of Lewin, Lippitt and White (1939), which is described in Box 20.1.

Box 20.1   Lewin, Lippit and White's (1939) Study of Leadership Styles

Lewin et al wanted to investigate the effects of three kinds of adult behaviour on a group of 10-year-old boys attending after-school clubs. The clubs were led by adults who acted in one of three ways: *autocratic*, *democratic* or *laissez-faire*.

The Democratic group met two days before the other two groups, and they chose what to do (they were concerned with model-making) the other two groups were told what to do, thus providing a basis for comparing the boys' output, experience and behaviour:

(a) *Autocratic leaders* told the boys what sort of models they would make and with whom they would work. They sometimes praised or blamed them for their work but did not explain their comments and, although friendly, were aloof and impersonal.
(b) *Democratic leaders* discussed various possible projects and allowed the boys to choose work-mates and generally to make their own decisions. They explained their comments and joined in with the group activities.
(c) *Laissez-faire leaders* left the boys very much to their own devices, only offered help when asked for it (which was not very often) and gave neither praise nor blame.

What were the findings?
Boys with an autocratic leader became aggressive towards each other

when things went wrong and were submissive in their approaches to the leader (which were often attention-seeking). If he left the room, the boys stopped working and became either disruptive or apathetic. However, the models they made were comparable, both in quantity and quality, to those of the boys in the democratic group.

Boys with a democratic leader got on much better with each other and seemed to like each other more than the boys who had an autocratic leader. Although slightly less work was actually done, approaches to the leader were usually task-related. When he left the room, the boys carried on working, showing greater independence and they co-operated with each other when things went wrong.

Boys with a laissez-faire leader were aggressive towards each other, although less so than the boys with an autocratic leader. Very little work was done, whether the leader was present or not and they were easily discouraged when things were not going exactly right.

Each leader was then instructed to adopt one of the other kinds of leadership; the boys' behaviour was shown to depend on the style of leadership and *not* on the personality of the leader. Significantly, two of the most aggressive boys from the autocratic group were switched to the democratic group and quickly became co-operative and involved.

Although the findings of the Lewin et al study strongly suggest that it is style of leadership (which is not necessarily a fixed characteristic) rather than personality (which is) that is important, Brown (1985) argues that individuals, their groups and leaders can only be understood in the context of the wider society of which they form a part. The 'democratic' style is, implicitly, the favourable and acceptable one of the three studied by Lewin et al because that was the one prevalent in American society during the 1930s.

Sayles (1966) reviewed both experimental and survey studies of leadership styles in industry. He found that no one style was consistently superior to any other in experimental studies of supervisors; but survey studies showed that democratic leadership was associated with greater productivity, and was more acceptable, than an autocratic style. However, Sayles argued that the tasks used in the experimental studies were so boring and limited that people did not get involved and, consequently, differences in leadership style were not given the chance to show up. He also made the point that democratic supervisors probably also differ in other ways apart from their leadership style (eg intelligence) compared with autocratic colleagues.

THE SITUATIONAL APPROACH

This began to emerge in the 1950s and was an attempt to rectify some of the shortcomings of the trait approach. For instance, the situational approach acknowledges that leadership involves leaders and followers in various role relationships and that there are several paths to becoming validated as a leader.

The question of *validation* is to do with how the leader comes to occupy the role, ie how do they achieve legitimacy as a leader? In a *formal group* structure, the leader is *assigned* by an external authority and is imposed on the group (an *appointed* leader). In an *informal group* structure, the leader *achieves* his/her authority from the group members, who may withdraw their support just as they gave it, and is called an *emergent* leader.

The question, 'Who is leader?' might be better put as, 'What functions are to be fulfilled?'. An appointed leader is one who performs certain kinds of tasks rather than someone who possesses certain characteristics or styles of social interaction, and some leaders may be primarily decision-makers who do not have interpersonal relationships as a major requirement of their role.

This seems to fit Turner's (1991) definition of leaders very well:

> Leaders are persons or social roles who exert more influence in a group than others. They tend to be of high status, to occupy a central position in the communication structure of the group and to display more effective initiative than others in the group, ie they tend to suggest, direct, instruct and advise courses of action that the group actually follows. They play the most important role in directing the group's activities, maintaining its traditions and customs and ensuring that it reaches its goals. (Turner, 1991)

Conversely, even in formal structures there are emergent (or 'informal') leaders who exert influence among their peers by virtue of their personal qualities, especially how verbal they are.

Even in the case of appointed leaders, leadership is a complex social process, involving a transaction or exchange between the group members. The leader is dependent on the rest of the group for liking and approval and their attitudes towards the leader will influence the process of leadership. This was demonstrated in an experiment by Rice et al (1980), whose subjects were military cadets at West Point Academy. Groups of male cadets had to complete tasks under the leadership of either a male or female cadet. The 'followers' were assigned so that half the groups were composed of followers with liberal attitudes towards women's rights and half of followers who held traditional attitudes. The liberal cadets responded in a very similar way to male and female leaders, while the traditionalists preferred the group atmosphere when the leader was male. The latter also attributed the success of the women-led groups to luck and that of the men-led groups to hard work and the co-operation of the group members.

While not ignoring the leader's characteristics, the situational approach stresses their appropriateness to a group in a given situation and a major feature of the situation is the group's *primary task*, ie what the group is in existence to do. So the leader's competence in enabling the group to achieve its purpose is a crucial feature of their role.

FIEDLER'S CONTINGENCY MODEL OF LEADER EFFECTIVENESS

In the 1960s there was a revival of interest in the leader's personality characteristics. However, this was a much more sophisticated approach than the trait approach and also represented an extension of the situational approach.

A major figure in this new approach was Fiedler (1967, 1968, 1971, 1972, 1974), whose *Contingency Model* for the analysis of leadership effectiveness is mainly concerned with the fit or match between a leader's personal qualities or leadership style, on the one hand, and the requirements of the situation, on the other.

Fiedler began by measuring the extent to which leaders distinguish between their most and least preferred co worker (LPC) and developed a scale which gave an LPC score. Someone with a high LPC score still sees their least preferred co-worker in a relatively favourable light and also tends to be more accepting, permissive, considerate and person-oriented in relationships with group members (*relationship-oriented*). By contrast, someone with a low LPC score sees their least-preferred co-worker very differently, regarding them very unfavourably. Low LPC-scorers also tend to be directive, controlling and dominant in relationships with group members (*task-oriented*).

Fiedler then investigated the fit between these two styles of leadership and the needs of the situation; the basic hypothesis is that the effectiveness of a leader is contingent upon the fit between: (i) the leader's style; and (ii) the quality of leader–member relationships, task structure and the position-power of the leader. The *quality* of *leader–member relationships* refers to the extent to which the leader has the confidence of the group and to the general psychological climate of the group. *Task structure* refers to the complexity of the task and the number of possible solutions: the more unstructured the task, the more the leader must motivate and inspire members to find solutions rather than rely on the backing of their superiors. The leader's *position-power* refers to the power inherent in the role, for example, the reward and punishments at their disposal and the organizational support from superiors.

The model predicts varying degrees of effectiveness for different combinations of leader and situational variables and Fiedler tested it in a number of countries and a variety of organizations, including boards of directors, basketball teams and bomber crews. He predicted that task-oriented leaders perform most effectively *either* under very favourable *or* very unfavourable conditions (ie extremes of the three situational variables) while relationship-oriented leaders are most effective under conditions which are neither extremely favourable nor extremely unfavourable. He has reported considerable support for this contingency model.

However, it has not gone uncriticized. For example, some studies have shown that the LPC score is not fixed but changes over time and may be influenced by factors such as the gender of the leader in relation to that of the other group members. Turner (1991) asks what LPC scores actually mean and what is their relationship to the leader's actual behaviour. Fiedler originally saw leadership style represented by LPC score as a relatively fixed personality characteristic but later implied that leaders differ *not* in their access to these styles but in the relative importance they attach to them and that they may be able to use either in appropriate situations. But if this is so, it becomes much less clear what high or low LPC leaders are actually doing to be effective—it seems likely that how they behave will be a function of a complex interaction between their motives, abilities and the specifics of the situation.

LEADERSHIP AND COMMUNICATION NETWORKS

A number of laboratory studies have imposed a particular communication network on a group of subjects (eg a five-person wheel, or 'Y' or chain) in each of which one person is randomly assigned to the central

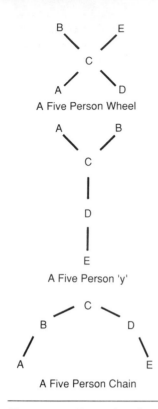

Figure 20.1 Examples of communication networks used in laboratory studies of leadership

position, so that the other group members can only communicate via that central person and not directly with each other (Fig. 20.1).

From studies like these, Brown (1985) concludes that when people are put into positions where the group has to depend on their efforts, they tend to accept the challenge and behave like leaders. Just as crucially, they are recognized as leaders by the rest of the group. Compared with people occupying peripheral positions, they tend to send more messages, to solve problems more quickly, to make fewer errors and to be more satisfied with their own and the group's efforts. Although recognizing that not anyone can fill any role, Brown (1985) concludes that finding oneself in a position of leadership may bring out hidden talents; certainly as far as laboratory studies are concerned it seems to be primarily the position in the network, and not personality, which accounts for the assumption of the leadership role.

Similarly, Turner (1991) concludes that, given certain minimum qualifications, it is probable that *anyone* can act as an effective leader in the right group at the right time. There is no personality type with a mystical, special 'divine right' to lead. Yet people whom we think of as excelling at leadership are probably people who are generally more skilled at being able to vary their actions to suit the group and the moment as a function of real insight into changing group dynamics, *not* persons who cannot change or help the group to change with the times because they are trapped in some rigid, fixed, leadership style. It is surely an elementary requirement of leadership that a leader should be able to see what is needed at any given moment and to adapt his/her behaviour.

For instance, in terms of Lewin et al's democratic/autocratic styles, instead of seeing them as opposites, the ideal leader may be the person who can be both or either as and when the situation demands. In terms of another distinction, namely that between *task specialist* (who 'initiates structure' in relation to the task and ensures that the group achieves its goal) and a *socio-emotional specialist* (who shows 'consideration' towards group members and is relationship-oriented, keeping the group functioning as a cohesive social unit), the person who becomes leader and is an effective leader will be one who looks after the feelings of subordinates and/or organizes in order to get the job done, when the group needs these functions to be served (Sorrentino and Field, 1986).

So how can we conceptualize the personal attributes that predict effective leadership across a variety of situations without falling into the trap of reducing them to rigid consistent traits?

> In general, the data ... are consistent in indicating that groups must believe in people before they will follow them—leaders must prove themselves to be people worth following, who can be trusted, who are not enemies, idiots, incompetent, but people who are skilled, who identify with 'us' and who have the groups' interests at heart. (Kirkhart, 1963; quoted by Turner, 1991)

LEADERSHIP AND POWER

Clearly, leadership and power are closely related concepts, but just as there are different kinds of leader (eg appointed and emergent) so there are different kinds of power. A comprehensive classification has been proposed by French and Raven (1960) and is summarized in Table 20.1.

1. *Legitimate power*	The formal power invested in a particular role (eg President of USA, Prime Minister, headteacher, bank manager) regardless of the personality of the particular occupant	*Table 20.1 Five kinds of power as proposed by French and Raven (1960)*
2. *Reward power*	The power an individual possesses by virtue of his/her control over valued resources ('rewards'), including salary or wages, food, love, respect, co-operation (eg parents, colleagues, bosses, friends, shop-keepers)	
3. *Coercive power*	The power an individual possesses by virtue of his/her control over feared consequences ('punishments'), including the withdrawal of rewards, demotion, dismissal (eg the same as for Reward Power). [In both 2 and 3, the power is to a large extent inherent in the role itself but personality of the role-occupant can play a greater part than in 1]	
4. *Expert power*	The power an individual possesses by virtue of his/her possession of special knowledge, skills and expertise (eg doctors, teachers, plumbers, electricians, car mechanics). [Related to this is *informational power* which is to do with *access* to important sources of information, such as that available through the media]	
5. *Referent power*	The power an individual possesses by virtue of his/her personal qualities (eg charm, magnetism, ability to persuade and 'win' people over). The *charismatic* leader has great referent power (which may be more important than his/her legitimate power) but parents, teachers, friends and others may also possess this kind of power.	

In the context of the trait approach, might we have inadvertently stumbled across a characteristic which is consistently displayed by every leader, namely the lust for power? If we accept Adler's theory of the 'will to power', ie the tendency in each of us to overcome our fundamental feeling of inferiority (see Chapter 28), then leaders could be seen as satisfying their will to power in that particular way and this would lend further support to the notion of desire for power as a characteristic of all leaders.

However, Gergen and Gergen (1981) warn us against this conclusion: although leadership does imply power, it would be a mistake, they argue, to assume that everyone who possesses power is highly motivated to achieve it. They claim that many political leaders, for example, are recruited and encouraged by others who promote them to powerful positions and their needs for affiliation may be far stronger than their needs for power.

CONFORMITY

Crutchfield (1962) defined conformity simply as, 'yielding to group pressures'. Aronson (1976) defined it as, 'a change in a person's behaviour or opinions as a result of real or imagined pressure from a person or group of people'. Mann (1969) said that, 'the essence of conformity is yielding to group pressures but it may take different forms and be based on motives other than group pressure'. We shall consider these motives later in the chapter.

What these definitions have in common is the reference to group pressure. They do not specify particular groups with particular beliefs or practices but any group which is important for the individual at the time. The group may be composed of people who are significant others for the individual, for example, family or peers, or it may be a reference group, whose values the individual admires or aspires to but which does not involve actual membership.

So conformity does not imply adhering to any particular set of attitudes or values, for instance, traditional middle class or bourgeois, but yielding to the pressures of a group, regardless of its majority or minority status.

EMPIRICAL STUDIES OF CONFORMITY

An early study by Jenness (1932) could be regarded as one of the very first empirical studies of conformity, although it is usually discussed in the context of social facilitation. Jenness asked individual students to estimate the number of beans in a bottle and then had them discuss it to arrive at a group estimate. When they were asked individually to make a second estimate, there was a distinct shift towards the group's estimate.

Sherif (1935)

Using a similar procedure to Jenness, Sherif used a visual illusion called the autokinetic effect, whereby a spot of light seen in an otherwise dark room appears to move.

He told his subjects that he was going to move the light and that their task was to say how far they thought the light moved. They were tested individually at first, being asked to estimate the extent of movement several times. The estimates fluctuated to begin with but then 'settled down' and became quite consistent. However, there were wide differences between subjects. Subjects then heard the estimates of other subjects—this represented the group situation (there were usually three per group). Under these conditions, the estimates of different subjects *converged*, ie they became more alike; a group norm developed.

To illustrate what happened, let us suppose that when tested individually, four subjects gave fairly consistent estimates of 8, 6, $3\frac{1}{2}$ and $2\frac{1}{2}$ inches, respectively. In the group situation, when hearing the estimates of the other three, the estimates of the four subjects changed to 6, 5, 4, and 5 inches—much closer to each other than their original, individual estimates. (In this hypothetical example, the average or mean score is 5 inches, both for the individual and the group estimates, but the first set of scores differs from each other much more than the second set. So when subjects are tested in a group, scores converge towards the average of their individual scores. In practice, it did not always work out quite as neatly as this.)

Just as different individuals produced different estimates, so did different groups. This happened both under the conditions already described and also when subjects were tested in small groups right from the start. Two further points need to be made: (i) subjects were not in any way instructed to agree with the others in the group, yet their estimates still converged, even when there were wide differences to begin with between individuals; (ii) when subjects were tested again individually, their estimates closely resembled the group estimate or norm (rather than their original, individual, estimates).

Comparing Sherif's and Jenness's experiments, whereas Jenness's subjects were instructed to arrive at a group estimate, there were no such instructions for Sherif's subjects, who were quite unaware of being influenced. Indeed, in interviews they hotly denied being affected by the others' estimates. Even though they did not think of themselves as being engaged in a common task, Sherif's subjects none the less adjusted their judgements to bring them into line with those of others.

According to Brown (1985), at least in Western culture, to be in agreement with others satisfies an important psychological need, especially in situations where people are uncertain. Clearly, in an ambiguous situation such as the autokinetic effect represented, subjects were only too willing to validate their own estimates by comparing them with those of other subjects, 'and through such a "social comparison" process (Festinger, 1954) a common social reality is established and validated' (Brown, 1985):

> . . . It seems that subjects made use of each others' judgements to develop a shared frame of reference in the same way that they had earlier used their own judgements. It appears too that subjects were relatively unaware of being influenced by the other judges. They appear to be largely unconsciously adjusting their judgement in the light of others' reports to arrive at a stable, agreed picture of a shared but initially unstructured world. (Turner, 1991)

Asch (1951, 1952, 1956)

While Sherif believed that he had shown that conformity does indeed take place, others, notably Asch, were very critical of his findings. According to Asch, the fact that the task used by Sherif was ambiguous (ie there was no right or wrong answer) made it difficult to draw any definite conclusions about conformity: conformity should be measured in terms of the individual's tendency to agree with other group members who unanimously give the wrong answer on a task where the solution is obvious or unambiguous. If people yield to group pressure when the answer is obvious, this is a much stricter test of conformity than where there is no correct or incorrect answer to begin with, as in Sherif's autokinetic effect (where the light does not actually move at all!).

In a series of experiments, beginning in 1951, Asch gave subjects the simple perceptual task of matching one line (a standard line) with another (a comparison line), each presented on a separate card (Fig. 20.2).

The subject has to say which of A, B or C is the same length as the standard line.

A group of 36 control subjects, who were tested individually, made only three mistakes when tested 20 times each (using different standard and comparison lines), showing that the task was simple—the answer was obvious and unambiguous!

In the original experiment, students were tested in groups of seven to nine, in which only one person was a 'real' (naive) subject, the others being confederates or accomplices of Asch, who had been instructed

Figure 20.2 Stimulus cards used in Asch's conformity experiments (1951, 1952, 1956)

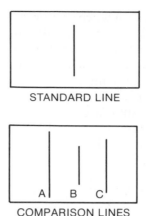

STANDARD LINE

COMPARISON LINES

beforehand to give the same wrong answers on certain trials ('critical' trials).

They were seated either in a straight line or round a table and it was arranged so that the real subject was always the last to answer (or the last but one). On the first two trials, the confederates all gave the right answer, as did the real subject (these were *neutral* trials). However, on the third trial, all the confederates agreed on the 'wrong' answer. During the next twenty minutes, there were eleven more critical trials (making twelve in all) plus four more neutral trials (making six in all.) What were the findings?

The basic conformity rate was 32 per cent, ie on average, subjects gave wrong answers on one-third of the critical trials by agreeing with the confederate majority. This is a staggeringly high figure considering how unambiguous the task was and how few mistakes were made by the control subjects:

> The results reveal the tremendous impact of an 'obviously' incorrect but unanimous majority on the judgments of a lone subject... (Van Avermaet, 1988)

However, the overall figure of 32 per cent conceals large individual differences. About 25 per cent of subjects showed no conformity at all and remained independent throughout the critical trials; about 28 per cent gave eight or more incorrect answers; about 47 per cent gave between one and seven incorrect answers, making about 75 per cent who conformed at least once. Only about 5 per cent conformed on every single critical trial.

When interviewed at length following the experiment, the real subjects said that they had been influenced to some extent by the opposition of the rest of the group. But there were more specific reasons that subjects gave for conforming. Some wanted to act in accordance with the experimenter's wishes and wanted to convey a favourable impression of themselves by not 'upsetting the experiment', which they believed they would have done by disagreeing with the majority; they thought some obscure 'mistake' had been made. Others said that they wanted to be like everyone else, did not want to 'appear different', 'be made to look a fool', a 'social outcast' or 'inferior'.

So, for many subjects there was a discrepancy between what answer they gave in the group and what they privately believed: they knew the 'wrong' answer was wrong but went along with it none the less. Contrast this with the subjects in Sherif's experiment, for whom there was no conflict between the group's estimate and their own, individual, estimates (Fig. 20.3).

Figure 20.3 *A minority of one faces a unanimous majority. (Courtesy William Vandivert and Scientific American, November 1955)*

However, some of Asch's subjects seemed to believe that the majority opinion was actually correct on the critical trials (and that the majority is usually correct, regardless of the issue in question). A few, who had no reason to believe that there was anything wrong with their eye sight, genuinely doubted the validity of their own judgements by wondering if they were suffering from eye strain or if their chairs had been moved so that they could not see the cards properly. So the reasons for conforming can be several, yet whatever the particular reason(s), the kind of conformity here (for the majority of subjects, anyway) is different from that involved in Sherif's experiment, where there was no majority wrong answer to conflict with the individual's, privately-held, right answer.

It was clear that many subjects did experience a good deal of stress as a result of the conflict and a subsequent study by Bogdonoff et al (1961) actually measured the physiological stresses associated with the Asch experiments. They found that increase in the level of plasma-free fatty acid (an indicator of central nervous system arousal) was correlated with the subjects' state of conflict when they realized that there was a discrepancy between their judgement and that of the majority. This high level was maintained for those who stuck to their judgement but dropped sharply if they conformed.

So far, we have described the original, basic, experiment. Asch subsequently varied the basic situation and manipulated different variables in order to see what the crucial influences on conformity were:

1) Does the rate of conformity go on increasing as the size of the majority goes on increasing?

It seems not. Where there is a real subject and just one confederate, the conformity rate is very low indeed, as you might expect ('it's my word against yours'). Where there are two confederates and one subject, conformity begins to increase (about 13 per cent), and with three confederates it reaches the 32 per cent which, as we have seen, was the overall conformity rate. But beyond three, conformity does not continue to rise. So, for example, sixteen confederates to one real subject does not produce more conformity than a ratio of three to one. This finding suggests that it is the *unanimity* of the group which is important (ie the confederates all agree with each other) rather than the actual size of the majority (the number of confederates)—it is consensus, not numbers, that matters:

> . . . a unanimous majority of three is, under the given conditions, far more
> effective than a majority of eight containing one dissenter . . . (Asch, 1951)

However, Gerard et al (1968) and Latané and Wolf (1981) have questioned this conclusion—adding more confederates *will* increase conformity although the *rate* of increase falls with each extra majority member. However, adding more members will only produce more conformity if the majority members are perceived as *independent* judges and not as sheep following each other or as members of a group who have jointly reached a judgement.

Wilder (1977) found that two independent groups of two people had more impact than four people who present a group judgement. Similarly, three groups of two have more impact than two groups of three, who in turn have more impact than a single group of six.

2) What is the effect of having another member of the group agree with the real subject?

It is to reduce conformity from 32 per cent to 5.5 per cent, whether the member who agrees is another real subject or a confederate. Significantly a *dissenter* who disagrees *both* with the real subject *and* the majority has almost as much effect on reducing conformity as one who gives the correct answer (ie agrees with the real subject).

What seems to be crucial in both cases is *breaking the unanimity* of the majority. However, this seems to apply only to unambiguous stimulus situations (like Asch's perceptual task)—with opinion statements only a genuine social supporter will reduce conformity rate (Allen and Leume, 1968). A social supporter provides the subject with an *independent* assessment of reality, sufficient to outweigh the potential informational value of the majority's answers.

3) What happens when the real subject has a 'supporter' at the beginning and then loses that support?

In one situation, the fourth confederate to answer gave the correct answer on the first half of the critical trials but then switched to the incorrect majority answer for the second half. Under these conditions, conformity increased from 5.5 to 32 per cent, ie the conformity rate is that which would have occurred if there had been no supporter to begin with.

4) In the original experiment, were subjects justified in fearing that they would be ridiculed by the rest of the group if they gave the answer they believed to be correct?

It seems they were. A group of sixteen naïve subjects participated with a single confederate, who gave the wrong answer on the critical trials as happened in the original experiment. The dramatic reaction of the naïve subjects was sarcasm, exclamations of disbelief and ridiculing laughter!

5) Will task difficulty affect conformity?

When Asch made the comparison lines more similar in length, so that the task was more difficult, subjects were more likely to yield to the incorrect majority answer, and this is especially true when subjects feel confident that there is a right answer. When tasks are more ambiguous, in the sense that they involve expressing opinions or stating preferences (so there is no objectively correct answer), conformity actually decreases. (Although there are some interesting, if not alarming, exceptions to this—see below.)

6) If we think we are in some way less competent than the other group members in relation to the task at hand, are we more likely to conform?

Imagine that the naïve subject is thinking, 'If I didn't know better, I'd think these guys were blind or crazy. But if they all agree, they'll think *I'm* blind or crazy if I disagree.' So the subject conforms in order to avoid being labelled in that way.

But now imagine that the confederates are all wearing dark glasses. The subject can now easily 'understand' their errors and if they believe that the others know that they can see perfectly well, the subject will have no qualms about reporting the right answer. So, if the difference between the answers of the majority and the real subject can be attributed to some clear difference in ability, or to a difference in perspective, the pressure to conform will be greatly reduced (provided, of course, that subjects believe it is *they* who have the greater ability).

7) Is conformity rate affected by giving answers in private?

Critics of Asch's experiment have pointed out that the subjects may conform because they are reluctant or too embarrassed to expose their private views in face-to-face situations. If so, the level of conformity should decrease if subjects are allowed to write their answers down, or where there is no face-to-face contact between the group members, or where subjects remain anonymous in some other way.

For example, Deutsch and Gerard (1955) used partitions which shielded subjects from the other participants whose reponse showed up on a light panel in front of them—the real subject had to press one of three buttons. Under these conditions, conformity was lower than in Asch's face-to-face situation. Indeed, when Asch himself allowed the naïve subject to answer in writing (while the confederates still gave their answers publicly), conformity dropped to 12.5 per cent.

However, it must be remembered that the participants in the Asch experiments were complete strangers to the real subjects, with no special claim to their loyalty or affection. The subjects, therefore, had little reason to fear the social repercussions of not conforming. Yet conformity occurred despite this *and* when the correct answers were so obvious.

Would we expect conformity to be higher still among friends because the social cost of being different is greater? Or might it be lower since we are not so afraid of losing face or looking silly with people we know and trust?

Replications of Asch's Experiments

The Asch studies have stimulated a great deal of research, including many fairly recent attempts to replicate the original findings, and some very interesting results have emerged.

Larsen (1974) found significantly lower conformity rates than Asch had found among groups of American students and suggested that this was because of a changed climate of opinion in America in the 1970s towards independence and criticism and away from conformity. However, in a later (1979) study, Larsen found results very similar to those of Asch. Perhaps the pendulum had begun to swing back again.

Perrin and Spencer (1981) found very low rates of conformity (one out of 396 trials) for a group of British students; but they were engineering, maths and chemistry students and so were perhaps better able to resist conformity pressure because of their special knowledge and experience. Significantly, in the same study, young offenders on probation showed very similar rates of conformity to Asch's; the confederate majority consisted of probation officers and the experimenter was an 'authority figure'.

Brown (1985) makes the interesting suggestion that it may not be just students who have changed since the 1950s but the experimenters too, that is, they may not *expect* so much conformity:

> Even when Asch's paradigm is apparently faithfully replicated, the experimenter may, unwittingly, convey to the subjects certain expectations as to the outcome of the experiment. (Brown, 1985)

(See Chapter 2 on 'experimenter effects'.)

What can we conclude about Asch's research?

> ... Asch's experiment, with its astonishing results, provided the groundwork for a rich tradition of theoretical speculations and empirical studies ... (Van Avermaet, 1988)

Despite a minority of subjects remaining totally independent and a majority remaining independent most of the time:

> ... Nevertheless, the pervasive inference drawn from these studies has been of the weakness of the individual in face of the group and the strength of spontaneous pressures for conformity inherent in the group context. (Turner, 1991)

Crutchfield (1954)

Crutchfield criticized Asch's experiments for being time-consuming and uneconomical, since only one subject could be tested at a time. He therefore, changed the experimental situation so that several (usually five) real subjects could be tested at the same time. Altogether, he tested over 600 subjects.

Each subject sat in an open cubicle which had a panel with an array of lights and switches; subjects could not see neighbouring panels. Questions, pictures and other kinds of stimuli were projected on to the wall in front of the subject and each believed that they were the last to respond. The subject was also told that the lights on the display panel indicated the answers of the other subjects; in fact, each subject saw an identical display and so received the same information. The answers were wrong on approximately half the trials.

Crutchfield presented a variety of tasks, and conformity to the wrong answers differed according to the type of task involved:

(a) On the Asch-type perceptual judgement, he found 30 per cent conformity.

(b) When asked to compete a series of numbers (as in IQ tests) he also found 30 per cent conformity.

(c) When he presented a star which was obviously smaller in area than a circle (by about one-third, in fact), there was 46 per cent agreement that the circle was smaller than the star.

(d) Some of his subjects were army officers attending a three-day assessment programme. 37 per cent of them agreed with the statement, 'I doubt whether I would make a good leader' when it was presented in the booth but, significantly, none of them agreed with it when tested privately.

(e) A substantial proportion of college students agreed with statements which, under more 'normal' circumstances, they would not be expected to. For example: (i) 60 to 70 per cent of the population of the USA is aged 65 or over; (ii) American males are, on average, taller than American females, by eight or nine inches; (iii) the life expectancy of American males is only about 25 years; (iv) Americans sleep four to five hours per night, on average, and eat six meals a day; (v) free speech being a privilege rather than a right, it is proper for a society to suspend free speech when it feels itself threatened.

Some subjects conformed to all of the above tasks, others did not agree to any; most conformed to some.

(f) Apart from these individual differences, it was found that individuals were more prepared to conform to difficult items (as in the Asch experiment).

For most of the different kinds of tasks, the tendency to conform dropped considerably when subjects were re-tested individually. However, there were differences in how much it dropped between submissive and self-confident subjects. For the former, when they were assured that the majority of judgements were false, conformity dropped only by 15 per cent and when assured that the majority judgements were correct, conformity actually rose by 25 per cent.

INDIVIDUAL DIFFERENCES IN CONFORMITY

Is there a conforming personality?

Crutchfield (1955) found that people who tend to conform have the following characteristics: they are intellectually less effective, have less ego strength, less leadership ability, less mature social relationships, have feelings of inferiority, tend to be authoritarian, are less self-sufficient, are more submissive, narrow-minded and inhibited and have relatively little insight into their own personalities compared with those who tend not to conform.

But can we say that there is a conforming personality, ie is a person who conforms in one situation also likely to conform in other situations?

McGuire (1968) concluded that consistency across situations is not high. The authoritarian personality (Adorno et al, 1950) is perhaps as close to such a personality type as can be found (see Chapter 19). Elms and Milgram (1966) described the authoritarian personality as having an 'unquestioning respect for convention'.

Men of low self-esteem tend to conform more often than those who are self-assured, suggesting that the former may be motivated by the need for acceptance and security. People with a high need for social approval conform more readily than those with a low need. Again, conforming seems to be a way of gaining the approval of others.

These latter findings suggest that conformity is a means of fulfilling a variety of psychological needs: if approval or acceptance is the real motive underlying conforming behaviour, then instead of talking about a conforming personality, we should talk about conformity as a means to an end, a means of satisfying certain needs which are more important to some people than to others.

CONFORMITY AND NON-CONFORMITY

Are all non-conformers alike? To counter-balance the emphasis that has been placed so far on conformity, it is important that we now look at non-conformity.

According to Willis (1963), two dimensions are necessary in order to construct an adequate representation of conformity and non-conformity, namely: (i) *dependence–independence*; and (ii) *conformity–anti-conformity*. Taken together, these produce three major patterns of behaviour over a series of interactions:

(i) *conformity*, which involves a consistent movement *towards* social expectancy;
(ii) *independence*, which involves a *lack* of consistent movement either towards or away from social expectancy;
(iii) *anti-conformity*, which involves a consistent movement *away* from social conformity.

Both (ii) and (iii) represent *non-conformity* but they differ, particularly in relation to the dimension of independence. Whereas (i) and (iii) both reveal dependence on others, (ii), as the word 'independent' implies, is (relatively) free of such dependence, and (iii) is still tied to the norms of some minority group which they put forward in opposition to those of the majority.

Willis saw conformity and non-conformity *not* as personality characteristics but as the outcomes of interaction in a particular situation. The degree of independence, for example, is not fixed, even for the same individual. Just as there are different cultural valuations made of different kinds of leadership style, so anti-conformity has a more negative valuation in our culture than independence, 'independence is probably seen as a more authentic, self-motivated, form of response than is the negativism of anticonformity' (Hollander, 1981).

Hollander and Willis (1964) found that subjects responded differently to co-workers (when jointly engaged on a task) according to whether they behaved in a conforming, independent or anti-conforming way. Even when co-workers were presented as being more competent than the subject with respect to the task, subjects were more influenced by the independent, competent co-worker than by the anti-conforming and equally competent co-worker. This lends empirical support to Willis's argument that independence and anti-conformity represent essentially different kinds of non-conformity.

According to Brown (1985), it is virtually impossible to classify behaviour at all as conformist or independent unless we understand the *meaning* the situation has for the individual and the implications it has for their self-image. She concludes that, 'both a person's disposition and situational variables would appear to determine the *degree* of an individual's dissent from or agreement with a group' (Brown, 1985).

THEORIES OF CONFORMITY—WHY DO PEOPLE CONFORM?

Now that we have looked at some of the major studies of conformity and the factors which influence it, we are in a better position to look at the mechanisms underlying conformity. How do groups influence the decisions, beliefs and attitudes of their members?

> . . . We know groups constrain and direct the actions of their members, but there is considerable controversy as to how, and under what conditions, various forms of influence operate. (Abrams et al, 1990)

One very influential and widely accepted account of group influence is Deutsch and Gerard's (1955) distinction between *informational influence* and *normative influence*.

A major motive underlying *informational influence* is the need to be right, to have an accurate perception of reality. So when we are uncertain, when we face an ambiguous situation, we look to others to help us perceive the stimulus situation accurately (or define the situation; see Chapter 16). This involves a *social comparison* with other group members (Festinger, 1954) in order to reduce the uncertainty.

Underlying *normative influence* is the need to be accepted by other people and to make a favourable impression on them. We conform in order to gain social approval and avoid rejection—we agree with others because of their power to reward, punish, accept or reject us.

How does this basic distinction relate to the major conformity experiments?

1) When discussing Sherif's experiment, we noted that the autokinetic effect is an ambiguous situation (there is no actual movement of the light and so there cannot be any right or wrong answers). Under these conditions, subjects very readily used the estimates of others to help them modify their own initial estimates (in the form of *convergence*). Others' opinions were seen as being at least as valid as the subject's own and Sherif's results support the *social reality hypothesis*, which states that '. . . The less one can rely on one's own direct perception and behavioural contact with the physical world, the more susceptible one should be to influence from others . . . (Turner, 1991).

Clearly, then, *informational influence* was involved.

2) In Asch's experiment (and to a large extent in Crutchfield's too), most subjects were not uncertain about the correct answer but were faced with a *conflict* between two sources of information which normally coincide, namely their own judgement and that of others. In opting for their *own* judgement, they risked rejection (ridicule, etc.) by the majority and so *normative influence* was involved.

Related to those two kinds of influence are two major *kinds* of *conformity*: Sherif's subjects used others' judgements to help them attain a more accurate perception of reality, so that when tested again individually following the group situation, their answers were closer to the group norm than to their own initial (individual) judgement. This illustrates *internalization* (Kelman, 1958), whereby our private belief or opinion coincides with our *public* belief or opinion, ie we believe what we say and we say what we believe (Mann (1969) preferred to call this *true conformity*). It can be thought of as a *conversion* to other peoples' point of view.

By contrast, Asch's subjects, as we have said, faced a conflict and a *compromise* was reached in the form of *compliance*, whereby the answer they give publicly (in the group) is *not* the one which is privately believed—what they say they don't believe and what they believe they don't say.

The relationship between the two kinds of influence and the two kinds of conformity is summarized in Figure 20.4.

While the informational–normative influence distinction has proved very influential, like all distinctions it faces the problem of false dichotomy, ie are they really separate, opposite forms of influence or are they complementary?

A study by Insko et al (1983) suggests that they can indeed operate

Figure 20.4 The relationship between different kinds of influence and different kinds of conformity

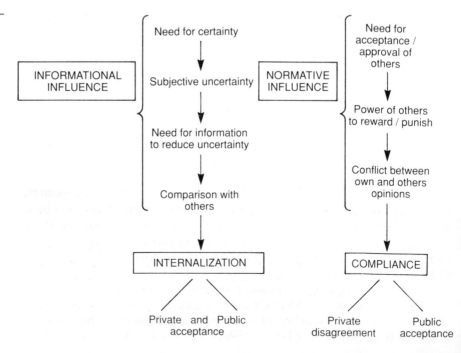

together. Subjects, in groups of six, had to judge whether a colour shown on a slide was more similar to another colour shown to the left or to another colour shown to the right.

On critical trials, four confederates who answered before the naïve subject, and another who answered last, gave answers which deviated from those given by most subjects in a control condition who were tested alone. There were two independent variables: (i) subjects answered either publicly or privately; and (ii) the experimenter could or could not determine which response was more correct (in the '*determined*' condition, the experimenter referred to an apparatus through which he could accurately measure which response was more correct; in the '*undetermined*' condition, this was said to be impossible).

Two hypotheses were tested: (i) there will be greater conformity in the *public* than the private condition due to *normative influence*; and (ii) there will be greater conformity in the *determined* than the undetermined condition due to *informational influence*.

Both hypotheses were confirmed. Also, the determined condition produced greater conformity in *both* private and public conditions and all four conditions produced greater conformity than the control condition.

> Hence, even with 'objective stimuli', informational influence can add to the effect of normative influence! (Van Avermaet, 1988)

Remember that when Asch made the three comparison lines much more similar, and hence the task more difficult, conformity increased and this seems to be confined to situations in which subjects believe there *is* a correct answer. Clearly, informational influence is involved here (whereas normative influence is the predominant form of influence in Asch's experiment). If we believe there is a correct answer and we are uncertain what that answer is, it seems quite logical to expect that an individual will be more influenced by a *unanimous majority*. This is why having a supporter or the presence of a dissenter has the effect of reducing conformity—by breaking the group consensus the subject is shown both that disagreement is possible and that the group is fallible:

> In sum, the more consensual the group and the more isolated the individual (ie the less others agree with the deviant), the greater the power of the group to define reality, induce self-doubt in the deviant as to both her competence and social position, and threaten her with ridicule and rejection for being different. (Turner, 1991)

This clearly shows how both informational and normative influence can operate in conjunction with each other and should not be seen as opposed processes of influence.

Finally, a second broad approach to explaining conformity sees both normative and informational influence as stemming from a single process:

> ...When others disagree with one's opinion they exert influence by undermining the subjective validity of that opinion. But the social world is filled with dissenting voices and the question is which of these will create uncertainty? According to Turner (1985), uncertainty arises only from disagreement with those with whom one expects to agree. In particular, it is those who are regarded as members of the same category or group as oneself in respects which are relevant to judgements made in a shared

stimulus situation who exert influence. Hence, social influence results from a process of self-categorization whereby the person perceives him or herself as a group member, and thus as possessing the same characteristics and reactions as other group members. Turner (1982) terms this mode of influence when group membership is salient, referent informational influence. (Abrams et al, 1990)

According to this view, Sherif's subjects were influenced by their assumption that the illusion is objectively real, and by their expectation to agree.

Indeed, once subjects discover that the autokinetic effect is only an illusion, mutual influence and convergence cease (Sperling, 1946; cited in Abrams et al, 1990):

> ...Uncertainty is a social product of disagreement between people categorized as identical to self. The perception of others as an appropriate reference group for social comparison creates the shared expectations of agreement necessary for the arousal of uncertainty and mutual influence. (Turner, 1985)

Abrams et al (1990), using the Sherif paradigm, but manipulating categorization (ie subjects saw others as either belonging to the in-group or to the out-group) found that ambiguity results in informational influence mostly from those who are categorized as being equivalent to self (ie member of the in-group). So self-categorization may set limits on informational influence.

It should also set limits on normative influence, since individuals will presumably have a stronger desire to receive rewards, approval and acceptance from those categorized in the same way as oneself than from those categorized differently. Using the Asch paradigm, but again manipulating categorization, Abrams et al (1990) found that conformity exceeded the usual level of 32 per cent in the in-group condition but was greatly below this level in the out-group condition.

CRITICISMS OF CONFORMITY EXPERIMENTS

1) They fail to isolate the *motive* underlying the conformity behaviour, ie is it informational or normative, or the related *kind* of conformity, ie internalization or compliance.

2) There is the implicit assumption that independence is 'good' and conformity is 'bad'. Asch (1952) in fact made this value judgement quite explicit. However, as Gahagan (1975) points out, conformity can be highly functional, facilitating the satisfaction of social and non-social needs; it is also necessary, to some extent, for social life to proceed at all.

3) Their relevance to everyday life is questionable, to say the least. Again, Gahagan (1975) explores this criticism. She says that there are two main questions that need to be asked:

(a) To what extent, if any, is our knowledge of the world defined in terms of other people's beliefs and opinions? Many kinds of knowledge that we take for granted, as 'facts', are actually culturally determined so that different cultures define 'the truth' differently. It is all the more likely that where there is room for disagreement and shades of opinion, as in politics, religion, sport, etc. that we will take note of others' reactions and assess 'the truth' accordingly. In practice, the majority opinion is often the one that individuals identify as 'fact'.

(b) Should we view the naïve subject in the Asch experiment as the individual fighting for 'the truth' against the social pressure of the majority (as, for example, some scientists have had to fight to get their views accepted, such as Darwin and Freud) or in some other way?

Moscovici and Faucheux (1972) advocate that we think of the naïve subject as embodying the 'conventional', self-evident opinion of the majority (for example, the conviction that the earth is flat or that man was created in the Garden of Eden), while the confederates giving false answers represent unorthodox, unconventional, eccentric and even outragous viewpoints or theories (for example, the earth is round, man evolved from apes). Looked at in this way, the conformity experiments seem to provide evidence relating to the question 'How do new ideas come to be accepted?' rather than, 'What processes operate to maintain the status quo?'

OBEDIENCE

We have defined conformity as yielding to group pressure; obedience can be defined as complying with the demands of an authority figure. Hedy Brown (1985) sees both conformity and obedience involving an abdication of personal responsibility, but there are important differences between these. Conformity has to do with the psychological 'need' for acceptance by others and entails going along with one's peers in a group situation; obedience has to do with the social power and status of an authority figure in a hierarchical situation. While we may deny that we conform (because this seems to detract from our sense of individuality), most of us would be willing to make excuses for ourselves by saying that we were 'obeying orders'.

Roger Brown (1986) makes a similar distinction; he says that conformity behaviour is affected by *example* (from peers or equals) while obedience is affected by *direction* (from somebody in higher authority).

MILGRAM (1963, 1965, 1974)

In the conformity experiments of Sherif, Asch and Crutchfield, subjects showed conformity by giving a verbal response of some kind or pressing buttons representing answers on various tasks. In what is the most famous and controversial obedience experiment, Milgram's subjects were required to 'kill' another human being.

Milgram was attempting to test the 'Germans are different' hypothesis. This hypothesis has been used by historians to explain the systematic destruction of millions of Jews, Poles and others by the Nazis during the 1930s and 1940s. It maintains that: (i) Hitler could not have put his evil plans into operation without the co-operation of thousands of others; and (ii) the Germans have a basic character defect, namely a readiness to obey authority without question, regardless of the acts demanded by the authority figure, and that it is this readiness to obey which provided Hitler with the co-operation he needed. It is really the second part of the hypothesis which Milgram was trying to test. He had originally planned to take his experiment to Germany, once it was completed at New Haven, Connecticut, but, as we shall see, that proved unnecessary.

The subjects in the original experiment were 20- to 50-year-old men, from all walks of life. They answered advertisements in local newspapers, or that came by post, which asked for volunteers for a study of learning, to be conducted at Yale University. It would take about one hour and there would be a payment of $4.50 (see Fig. 20.5).

Figure 20.5 Announcement placed in a local newspaper to recruit subjects. (From Milgram, 1974)

Public Announcement

WE WILL PAY YOU $4.00 FOR ONE HOUR OF YOUR TIME

Persons Needed for a Study of Memory

*We will pay five hundred New Haven men to help us complete a scientific study of memory and learning. The study is being done at Yale University.

*Each person who participates will be paid $4.00 (plus 50c carfare) for approximately 1 hour's time. We need you for only one hour: there are no further obligations. You may choose the time you would like to come (evenings, weekdays, or weekends).

*No special training, education, or experience is needed. We want:

Factory workers	Businessmen	Construction workers
City employees	Clerks	Salespeople
Laborers	Professional people	White-collar workers
Barbers	Telephone workers	Others

All persons must be between the ages of 20 and 50. High school and college students cannot be used.

*If you meet these qualifications, fill out the coupon below and mail it now to Professor Stanley Milgram, Department of Psychology, Yale University, New Haven. You will be notified later of the specific time and place of the study. We reserve the right to decline any application.

*You will be paid $4.00 (plus 50c carfare) as soon as you arrive at the laboratory.

- -

TO:
PROF. STANLEY MILGRAM, DEPARTMENT OF PSYCHOLOGY, YALE UNIVERSITY, NEW HAVEN, CONN. I want to take part in this study of memory and learning. I am between the ages of 20 and 50. I will be paid $4.00 (plus 50c carfare) if I participate.

NAME (Please Print). . . . .

ADDRESS . . . .

TELEPHONE NO. . . . . Best time to call you . . . .

AGE . . . . OCCUPATION. SEX . . . . . .
CAN YOU COME:

WEEKDAYS . . . . EVENINGS . . . . . . WEEKENDS. . . . .

The Basic Experiment

When subjects arrived at Yale University Psychology Department, they were met by a young, crew-cut man in a laboratory coat, who intro-

duced himself as Jack Williams, the experimenter. Also present was a Mr Wallace, supposedly another subject, in his late fifties, an accountant, a little overweight and generally a very mild and harmless-looking man (Fig. 20.6). In fact, Mr Wallace was an assistant of Milgram, and everything that happened after this was pre-planned, staged and scripted: everything, that is, except the degree to which the real subject obeyed the experimenter's instructions. It was as if the whole experiment were a play with the script of the leading character left unwritten—each successive subject wrote his/her own script as the drama unfolded. The irony is that the subject was the only character who did not know that they were in a play at all!

The subject and Mr Wallace were told that the experiment was concerned with the effects of punishment on learning and that one of them was to be the teacher and the other the learner. Their roles were determined by each drawing a piece of paper from a hat: both, in fact, had 'teacher' written on them. Mr Wallace drew first and called out 'learner', so, of course, the real subject was always the teacher.

They all went into an adjoining room where the learner (Mr Wallace) was strapped into a chair with his arms attached to electrodes which would deliver a shock from the shock generator situated in an adjacent room. The teacher (subject) and experimenter (Mr Williams) then moved next door where the generator was situated; the teacher was, in fact, given a 45-volt shock to convince him that it was real, for he was to operate the generator during the experiment. However, that was the only real shock that either the teacher or the learner was to receive.

The generator (which Milgram himself had built and which looked authentic) had a number of switches, each clearly marked with voltage levels and verbal descriptions, starting at 15 volts and going up to 450 in intervals of 15:

15– 60	*slight shock*
75–120	*moderate shock*
135–180	*strong shock*
195–240	*very strong shock*
255–300	*intense shock*
315–360	*intense to extreme shock*
375–420	*danger: severe shock*
435–450	*XXX*

The teacher had to read out a series of word pairs (eg 'blue–girl', 'nice–day', 'fat–neck') and then the first of one pair (the stimulus word) followed by five words, of which one was the original paired response. The learner had to choose the correct response to the stimulus word by pressing one of four switches, which turned on a light on a panel in the generator room. Each time he made a mistake, the teacher had to deliver a shock, and each successive mistake was punished by a shock 15 volts higher than the one before.

Milgram had asked fourteen psychology students to predict what would happen for 100 subjects in this situation. They thought that a few would break off early on, most would stop somewhere in the middle and a few would continue right up to 450 volts. The highest single estimate for those who would go right to the end was three. He also asked forty

Figure 20.6 1 Shock generator used in the experiments. Fifteen of the 30 switches have already been depressed. 2 Learner is strapped into chair and electrodes are attached to his wrist. Electrode paste is applied by the experimenter. Learner provides answers by depressing switches that light up numbers on an answer box. 3 Subject receives sample shock from the generator. 4 Subject breaks off experiment. On right, event recorder wired into generator automatically records switches used by the subject. (Copyright 1965 by Stanley Milgram from the film Obedience, *distributed by the Pennsylvania State University, Audio Visual Services.) (From Milgram, 1974)*

psychiatrists, who predicted that less than one per cent would administer the highest voltage. These estimates were based on what Milgram called the *'remote' victim* experiment, which was the first of a series of eighteen different experiments, all variations on the same basic theme. In this particular experiment, Mr Wallace was heard to pound loudly on the wall at 300 volts and, after 315 volts, no further answers were given and no further pounding was heard.

The frighteningly high figure for those subjects who actually went on giving shocks up to and including 450 volts was 65 per cent, with all subjects giving shocks up to at least 300 volts. Those who continued after 300 volts either refused to carry on somewhere between 315 and 375, or went all the way up to 450 volts.

In the second experiment (*voice-feedback*), subjects heard a tape-recorded series of verbal responses, which they believed were the spontaneous reactions of Mr Wallace to the increasing shock levels:

At 75 volts, he made a little grunt (as he did at 90 and 105 volts).

At 120 volts, he shouted to the experimenter that the shocks were becoming painful.

At 135 volts, he made painful groans.

At 150 volts, he cried out, 'Experimenter, get me out of here! I won't be in the experiment any more! I refuse to go on!' This continued with rising intensity until

At 180 volts, he shouted, 'I can't stand the pain.'

At 270 volts, he let out an agonized scream. [He continued to insist on being released.]

At 300 volts, he shouted desperately that he would no longer provide answers.

At 315 volts, he let out a violent scream, reaffirming vehemently that he was no longer participating.

After 330 volts, ominous silence!

(The teacher was instructed to treat no response as if it were an incorrect response, so the shocks could continue beyond 300 volts.) In addition, the experimenter had a script prepared for whenever the teacher refused to continue or showed any resistance or reluctance to do so:

Prod 1: 'Please continue' or 'Please go on.'
Prod 2: 'The experiment requires that you continue.'
Prod 3: 'It's absolutely essential that you continue.'
Prod 4: 'You have no other choice, you *must* go on.'

There were also 'special prods' to reassure the subject that he was not doing the learner any permanent harm:

'Although the shocks may be painful there is no permanent tissue damage, so please go on.

If the subject claimed that the *learner* didn't want to go on, the experimenter would say,

'Whether the learner likes it or not, you must go on until he has learned all the word pairs correctly. So please go on.'

In this second (voice-feedback) condition, 62.5 per cent of subjects went on giving shocks up to 450 volts.

Before the impression is given that a large percentage of subjects quite callously gave shocks of such high intensities to an innocent 'victim' through blind obedience, we should note that many subjects displayed great anguish, verbally attacked the experimenter, twitched nervously, or broke out into nervous laughter. Many were observed to, 'sweat, stutter, tremble, groan, bite their lips and dig their nails into their flesh. Full-blown, uncontrollabe seizures were observed for three subjects.' One experiment had to be stopped due to the subject having a violently convulsive seizure.

Why was there such a high level of obedience?

Milgram tried to answer this crucial question by devising some variations to the basic experiment in order to identify the critical variables.

Variations of the Basic Experiment

1) In post-experimental interviews, many subjects said that they had continued giving shocks because the experiment was being carried out at Yale, a very prestigious and highly respected American university. Milgram therefore transferred the experiment to a run-down office building located in downtown Bridgeport, Connecticut (Experiment 10). In this setting, the obedience rate was 47.5 per cent (for those continuing up to 450 volts), indicating that the awe-inspiring nature of the original location was not a crucial factor, although it clearly played some part.

2) The proximity of the teacher to the learner proved to be of greater significance than the physical setting. Remember that in the original experiment the teacher and learner were in separate but adjoining rooms, so that the teacher heard the learner (via a tape-recorder) but could not see him.

When they were in the same room (about $1\frac{1}{2}$ feet apart), so that the teacher could see as well as hear the learner, the obedience level dropped to 40 per cent (Experiment 3). It dropped further still to 30 per cent when the teacher was required to force the learner's hand onto the shock plate (Experiment 4). Clearly, it became much more uncomfortable to see the effects of their obedience, so that considerably fewer subjects were prepared to go all the way. However, these figures of 40 and 30 per cent are still alarmingly high.

3) Another variation involved giving the teacher social support for refusing to obey (Experiment 17). The real subject was teamed with two other 'teachers' (confederates of Milgram). After 150 volts, one of the accomplices announced that he was not going to continue and moved to another part of the room.

After 210 volts, the second one also refused. In all cases, the experimenter continued to order the real subject to proceed as described above.

Only 10 per cent of real subjects then continued all the way to 450 volts—they stopped obeying either immediately after one of the confederates did so or very shortly afterwards. The real subject made very revealing remarks afterwards, such as, 'I didn't realize I could' (ie refuse to obey). So the 'demands of the situation' seem to be crucial, that is, how the subject interprets and defines what is possible or permissible (see Chapter 2).

4) When the teacher was paired with another, confederate, teacher, and the real subject had only to read out the word-pairs—the confederate threw the switches—there was 92.5 per cent obedience. Clearly, it was easier to shift responsibility from themselves to the confederate for what the learner was suffering since, 'their hand was not on the button' (Experiment 18).

5) The proximity of the experimenter to the teacher was also found to be crucial. When the experimenter left the room, having given the initial instructions, and issued subsequent instructions by telephone, the obedience level dropped to 20.5 per cent (Experiment 7).

An interesting finding was that subjects often pretended to press the shock button or pressed the button for a lower voltage than they were meant to. This suggests that they were trying to compromise between what their conscience was telling them to do and what the experimenter was telling them to do; in his absence, it was easier to disobey him and to obey the dictates of conscience!

SO WHY DO PEOPLE OBEY IN THE MILGRAM EXPERIMENT?

1) In the experimenter's absence, subjects are forced to accept responsibility for their own actions, while in his presence, with all the prods and prompts, it was much easier to deny personal responsibility (they were merely 'doing what they were told').

But clearly it was not as cut and dried as this. We saw earlier that many subjects showed obvious signs of distress and conflict. The experimenter was, it seems, being seen as a legitimate authority in that situation, which was totally convincing and very real for the subjects. The conflict is between two opposing sets of demands, the external authority of the experimenter, who says, 'Shock' and the internal authority of the conscience, which says, 'Don't shock'. The point at which conscience triumphs is, of course, where the subject (finally) stops obeying the experimenter—at that point, the experimenter, in a sense, ceases to be a legitimate authority in the eyes of the subject. Thirty-five per cent of subjects in the original experiment reached that point somewhere before 450 volts; for many of those subjects, the crucial 'prod' was when the experimenter said, 'You have no other choice, you *must* go on'. They were able to exercise the choice which, of course, they *did* have and so at that point they stopped obeying.

The most common mental adjustment in the fully obedient subject is to see himself as an agent of external authority, (the 'agentic state'), a typical response being: 'I wouldn't have done it by myself, I was just doing what I was told', *as if* he had no choice (this is similar to the concept of de-individuation; see Chapter 16).

This agentic state (the opposite of autonomy) is what allows humans to function in an organized, hierarchical, social system—for the group to function as a unified whole, individuals must be able to give up responsibility and defer to others of higher status in the social hierarchy. Legitimate authority replaces the individual's own self-regulation (Turner, 1991).

2) In these studies the experimenter wore a grey, not a white,

laboratory coat, which was meant to be ambiguous (eg a white might have suggested a medical technician) but which indicated his position as an authority figure. Other studies have shown that the fact that someone is wearing a uniform is often reason enough for them to be obeyed. For example, in a study by Bickman (1974), researchers approached people on the streets of New York and ordered them either to pick up a paper bag or give a coin to a stranger. Half of the researchers were dressed in neat street clothes and half in a guard's uniform. Under 40 per cent obeyed the civilians but more than 80 per cent obeyed the 'guard', even when he walked off after giving the order so that, as far as the 'subjects' were concerned, he could not see whether they had complied or not.

Milgram concludes this way:

> A substantial proportion of people do what they are told to do, irrespective of the content of the act and without limitations of conscience, so long as they perceive that the command comes from a legitimate authority. (Milgram, 1974)

CRITICISMS OF MILGRAM

1) The main criticisms are to do with the *ethics* of Milgram's experiments. These were discussed in some detail in Chapter 3.

However, we should note here that Milgram asks whether the ethical criticisms are based as much on the nature of the (unexpected) results as on the procedure itself. Aronson (1988) asks if we would question the ethics if none of the subjects had gone beyond the 150 volt level, which is the point at which most people are expected to stop according to Milgram's students and the forty psychiatrists he consulted. Aronson has manipulated the results experimentally and finds that this *does* affect subjects' ratings of the 'harmlessness' of the procedure, ie the higher the percentage of subjects going right up to 450 volts, the more harmful the effects of the experiment are judged to be.

2) The charge that the subjects were atypical of the American population seems to be unjustified. Altogether, 636 subjects were tested (in the eighteen separate experiments as a whole), representing a cross-section of the population of New Haven, thought to be a fairly typical small American town. However, Milgram admits that those who went on obeying up to 450 volts were more likely to see the learner as responsible for what happened to him and not themselves! They seemed to have a stronger authoritarian character and a less advanced level of moral development. But this was a matter of degree only. As Rosenthal and Rosnow (1966) and others have found, people who volunteer for experiments are considerably *less* authoritarian than those who do not.

Also, Mantell (1971) repeated the experiment in Germany and found an even higher obedience rate than Milgram (85 per cent); 80 per cent obedience has been found in Jordan, and high levels have also been found in Italy and Australia.

3) Only forty women were included in Milgram's sample. They showed a 65 per cent obedience rate, just like their male counterparts.

4) Finally, it has been claimed that what happened to Milgram's subjects cannot be generalized to real-life outside the laboratory. So, in Aronson's terms, do Milgram's experiments have *mundane realism*?

Milgram defends himself by maintaining that the essential process involved in complying to the demands of an authority figure is the same, whether the setting is the artificial one of the laboratory or a naturally occurring one outside it.

In discussing the relationship between subject and experimenter, Colman (1987) says that, although it possesses a special quality of implicit trust and dependency:

> the further implication that only the subject–experimenter relationship possesses this quality is not merely gratuitous, but blind to the reality of social life, which is replete with hierarchical structures . . . the occasion we term a psychological experiment shares its essential structural properties with other situations composed of subordinate–superordinate roles. (Colman, 1987)

Milgram himself acknowledges the differences (some more obvious than others) between his laboratory studies of obedience and Nazi Germany:

> . . . The difference in the two situations are, of course, enormous, yet difference in scale, numbers and political context may turn out to be relatively unimportant as long as certain essential features are retained. The essence of obedience consists in the fact that a person comes to view himself as the instrument for carrying out another person's wishes, and he, therefore, no longer regards himself as responsible for his actions. Once this critical shift of viewpoint has occurred in the person, all the essential features of obedience follow. (Milgram, 1974)

A study of great relevance to this issue was conducted by Hofling et al (1966), which aimed to discover whether nurses would comply with an instruction which would involve them having to infringe both hospital regulations and medical ethics (Box 20.2).

Box 20.2   Obedience in a Natural Setting (based on Hofling et al, 1966)

Identical boxes of capsules were placed in twenty-two wards of both public and private psychiatric hospitals in the USA. The capsules were, in fact placebos (consisting of glucose). But the containers were labelled '5 mg capsules of Astrofen'; the labels also indicated that the normal dose is 5 mg with a maximum daily dose of 10 mg.

While the nurse was on duty, a 'doctor' (a confederate 'Dr Smith from the Psychiatric Department') instructed the nurse, by telephone, to give 20 mg of Astrofen to his patient, a Mr Jones, as he was in a desperate hurry and the patient needed the capsules. He said that he would come in to see Mr Jones in 10 minutes time and that he would sign the authorization document for the drug when he got there.

To comply with this request, the nurse would be breaking three basic procedural rules:

(i)   the dose was above the maximum daily dose of 10 mg;
(ii)   drugs should only be given after written authority has been obtained;
(iii) the nurse must be absolutely sure that 'Dr Smith' is a genuine doctor.

A real doctor was posted nearby, unseen by the nurse, and observed what the nurse did following the telephone call—did she comply, did she refuse, or did she try to contact another doctor?

Whatever her course of action, the observer-doctor then revealed to her what was really going on.

Twenty-one out of twenty-two nurses complied unhesitatingly! Eleven later said that they had not noticed the dosage disrepancy.

In interviews, twenty-two graduate nurses who had not participated in the actual experiment were presented with the same situation as an issue to discuss; twenty-one said that they would not have given the drug without written authorization, especially as it exceeded the maximum daily dose. This brings to mind the predictions of the psychology students and psychiatrists that very few subjects would go on giving shocks up to 450 volts in Milgram's experiments. How many of the subjects themselves would have said that they would do so? Rather fewer than 65 per cent, no doubt!

There is, of course, an important difference between the two situations. Milgram's subjects were being asked to inflict pain upon another human being, while the nurses in the Hofling study were being asked to do something quite consistent with their role and, presumably, in the patient's best interests. Or was it?

The twenty-one nurses who complied probably did not question that it was, since the request came from a Dr Smith from the Psychiatry Department.

In a way, because of the real-life setting of the experiment, and because of the implications of what would transpire were it not an experiment, these results are more disturbing than Milgram's. Admittedly, the sample was much smaller than Milgram's and, since 1966, the role of the nurse may have become less 'obedient' and deferential towards doctors and more questioning and critical. But it seems that built into our social roles is a polarity (pair of opposites) which might be expressed as domineering–servile, powerful–powerless, dominant–submissive. Rather than asking what makes some people more obedient than others, or how we would have reacted if we had been one of Milgram's subjects, we should be asking how we would behave if we were put into a position of authority ourselves. How easily could we assume the role and use the power that goes with it? And if we could, how might we explain our ability to do so?

An intriguing but also rather frightening experiment by Zimbardo et al (1973) explored these questions. Their famous Prison Simulation Experiment is described in Box 20.3.

Box 20.3   The Prison Simulation Experiment (Zimbardo et al, 1973)

The subjects were recruited through advertisements placed in a city newspaper asking for student volunteers for a two-week study of prison life. They would be paid 15 dollars a day (210 dollars in all, quite a lot of money for a poor student) and over 100 volunteers came forward initially.

They were given clinical interviews and 25 were eventually selected. They were judged to be emotionally stable, physically healthy, 'normal to average', on the basis of extensive personality tests, and also law-abiding (they had no history of convictions, violence or drug-abuse). They were told that their assignment to the role of either prisoner or prison-guard would be determined by the toss of a coin. They all stated a preference for being prisoners.

So at the start of the study there were no measurable differences between those who were to be assigned to one or other role; they were a relatively homogeneous sample of white, middle-class college students from all over the USA and Canada. They all had an equal chance of being either prisoner or guard.

The intention was not to make a literal copy of a real prison setting but to achieve some equivalent psychological effects; the 'mock prison' represented an attempt to simulate functionally some of the significant features of the psychological state of imprisonment.

The basement of Stanford University in California was converted into a mock prison and the experiment began one Sunday morning when the students who had been allocated the prisoner role were 'arrested', by the Palo Alto police, charged with a felony, told their constitutional rights, searched, handcuffed and taken in the back set of a squad car to the police station to be booked. After being fingerprinted and having identification forms prepared for his 'jacket' (central information file), the prisoner was taken, blindfold, to 'Stanford County Prison' (the basement of Stanford University), where he was stripped naked, skin-searched, deloused, issued a uniform, bedding, etc.

Prisoners wore a loose-fitting smock, with an identification number, front and back, plus a chain bolted around one ankle; they also wore a nylon stocking to cover their hair (instead of being shaved). The guards wore military khaki-style uniforms, silver reflector sunglasses (which made eye-contact impossible) and they carried clubs, whistles, handcuffs and keys to the cells and main gate.

Orders were shouted and the guards pushed the prisoners around if they did not comply quickly enough, but any other physical contact was forbidden. There were visits from a former prison chaplain, a public defender, and relatives and friends of some of the prisoners, as well as disciplinary and parole hearings before a board comprising a group of 'adult authorities'.

Although the guards worked eight-hour shifts, the prisoners were imprisoned in their cells around the clock, allowed out only for meals, exercise, toilet privileges, head-counts and work.

In a remarkably short time, a perverted relationship developed between the prisoners and guards. After an initial rebellion had been crushed, the prisoners reacted passively as the guards stepped up their aggression each day, which made the prisoners even more passive and dependent, and made them feel helpless, that they were no longer in control of their life. In less than 36 hours, one prisoner had to be released because of uncontrolled crying, fits or rage, disorganized thinking and severe depression. Three more developed similar symptoms and had to be released on successive days. A fifth prisoner developed a rash over his whole body which was triggered when his 'parole' had been rejected.

The entire experiment, planned to run for two weeks, was stopped after six days because of the pathological reactions of the prisoners who had originally been selected for their normality.

Social power became the major dimension on which everyone and everything was defined. The primary forms of interaction on the part of the guards were commands, insults, degrading comments, verbal and physical aggression and threats. The counterpart by the prisoners were resistance, giving information when asked questions, questioning and (initially) insulting the guards.

Every guard at sometime or another behaved in an abusive, authoritarian way; many seemed positively to enjoy the new-found power and the almost total control over the prisoners which went with the uniform.

For example, Guard A said:

I was surprised at myself—I made them call each other names and clean the toilets out with their bare hands. I practically considered the prisoners cattle and I kept thinking I have to watch out for them in case they try something.

Guard B (preparing for the visitors' first night):

> I made sure I was one of the guards on the yard, because this was my first chance for the type of manipulative power that I really like—being a very noticed figure with complete control over what is said or not.

Guard C:

> Acting authoritatively can be fun. Power can be a great pleasure.

How can we account for such behaviour?

As we have already noted, we cannot attribute the behaviour to any pre-existing personality traits, such as 'psychopathic' or 'sadistic' guards or 'criminal, weak impulse–control' prisoners.

As Zimbardo and Ruch (1977) point out, the abnormal behaviour of both groups is best viewed as a product of transactions with an environment that supports such behaviour. As they were randomly assigned their roles, showed no prior personality pathology and received no training, how was it that the subjects assumed their roles as quickly and completely as they did?

First, presumably, they had learned stereotypes of guard and prisoner roles from the mass media as well as from social models of power and powerlessness (for example, the parent–child, teacher–student, employer–employee relationships). We are able to draw on our experience and knowledge of other role relationship whenever we are faced with new ones, whether we are called upon to be 'in charge' or to be the submissive or powerless one.

Secondly, environmental conditions facilitate role-playing. A brutalizing atmosphere, like the 'mock' prison, produces brutality and perhaps this kind of aggression is potential in all of us. Had the roles been reversed, those who suffered as the prisoners may just as easily have inflicted suffering on those who were randomly chosen as guards. (In contrast to the Milgram experiment, there seemed to be no conflict for the guards, quite the reverse, in fact. Clearly the role of teacher and the requirement that he should deliver painful electric shocks were seen by the subjects as inconsistent with each other. But a guard is someone who is meant to behave in an aggressive and brutal way; hence, no conflict.)

Zimbardo and Ruch conclude by saying that:

> This research illustrates not only what a prison-like environment can bring out in relatively normal people, but also how they have been socialized by their society. (Zimbardo and Ruch, 1977)

Conclusions

Zimbardo et al, like Milgram, have come under severe criticism for the ethics of their research. Savin, for example asks:

> ... Is the degradation of thirty-two young men justified by the importance of the results of this research? ...
> ... Most of the psychologists whose experiments involve mistreatment of human subjects are university professors and most of their subjects are university students. Professors who, in pursuit of their own academic interests and professional advancement, deceive, humiliate and otherwise mistreat their students are subverting the atmosphere of mutual trust and

intellectual honesty without which . . . neither education nor free enquiry can flourish. (Savin, 1973)

Yet, however valid these criticisms might be, is it possible that underlying them is a rather different response which is more difficult to articulate, namely the shock and horror at what Arendt called, 'the banality of evil' (the sub-title of her book, in 1963, about the Israeli trial of Adolf Eichmann, the Nazi war criminal)? To believe that 'ordinary people' could do what Eichmann did, or what Milgram's or Zimbardo's guard-subjects did, is far less acceptable than that Eichmann was an inhuman monster or that experimental subjects have been put under immorally high levels of stress.

Following the trial of William Calley for the Mi Lai massacre during the Vietnam war, a national survey was made of the reaction of the American public to the trial: 51 per cent said that they would follow orders if commanded to shoot all inhabitants of a Vietnamese village. Kelman and Lawrence (1972), who conducted the survey, concluded that many Americans regard Calley's actions at Mi Lai as, 'normal, even desirable, because [they think] he performed them in obedience to legitimate authority'.

As Brown (1985) observes, both Milgram's and Zimbardo's research shows how easily people can come to behave in 'uncharacteristic' ways when placed in new physical and social situations and given the chance to assume new roles, even temporarily. Both studies testify to, 'the power of social, institutional forces to make good men engage in evil deeds'. (Zimbardo, 1973.)

PART 5

Developmental Processes

21 CHILDHOOD AND ADOLESCENCE— DEVELOPMENT OF PERSONALITY AND THE SELF-CONCEPT

All the chapters in this section of the book could be thought of as dealing with various aspects of personality development, if personality is defined as the totality of ways in which individuals function as people. So this would include the development of our first relationships with other human beings (and how these affect our later relationships), how we develop a sense of our own sexual identity (and how that relates to our actual behaviour as males and females), the development of our knowledge and understanding and ability to use and understand language and, finally, the development of our sense of right and wrong (and how this relates to our actual moral behaviour).

However, some of the theories to be discussed in these later chapters are concerned with fairly specific aspects of development, and for this reason are not usually thought of as theories of *personality* development. Similarly, certain other theories, such as Learning Theory or Social Learning Theory, although always included in chapters on development, are not strictly *developmental* theories at all, as they are not primarily (or, sometimes, even at all) concerned with explaining psychological *change* (which is in the nature of development).

Two theories which certainly meet both these 'conditions' (ie they are theories of *personality* and theories of *development*) are Freud's *Psychoanalytic Theory* (which has already been referred to in earlier chapters) and Erikson's *Psychosocial Theory*. As we shall see, Freud emphasized development during the first five/six years of life, while Erikson saw development as a life-long process, spanning childhood, adolescence and adulthood. Consequently, Freud's is perhaps more accurately described as a theory of *childhood development* than Erikson's, while Erikson is best known for his views on *adolescent development*.

We shall also be discussing the *self-concept* and how this changes during childhood and adolescence.

FREUD'S PSYCHOANALYTIC THEORY

Freud's theory of personality development is closely related to the other aspects of his theory, in particular his theory of the structure of personality and his motivational theory. His theory as a whole is also closely tied to his work as a psychotherapist and it is quite common to refer to all of these as 'psychoanalysis'. However, it might be helpful to reserve that term to denote Freud's form of psychotherapy and to use the term 'psychoanalytic theory' when discussing his theories.

The sheer volume of Freud's work, the fact that his theories were intended to cover all aspects of human behaviour, together with the great influence his work has had within psychology as a whole, makes it impossible to do him justice in part of one chapter, so here we shall be concentrating on his stages of psychosexual development. Chapters 24 and 27 will discuss other aspects of his developmental theory, while in Chapter 29 we shall look at more general aspects of his personality theory. Chapter 31 will discuss psychoanalysis.

BIOGRAPHICAL SKETCH

In 1856 Sigmund Freud (see Fig. 1.4) was born in Moravia, which was then part of the Austrian Empire and is now in present-day Czechoslovakia. He spent most of his life in Vienna, from where he fled, in 1937, when the Nazis invaded. Neither Freud himself, being Jewish, nor his theories, were very popular with the invaders and he escaped to London, where he died in 1939. He had wanted to be a research scientist but anti-Semitism forced him to choose a medical career instead and he worked in Vienna as a doctor, specializing in neurological disorders (disorders of the nervous system). He constantly revised and modified his theories right up until his death but much of his psychoanalytic theory was produced between 1900 and 1930. Most of what is discussed in this chapter represents the 'final version' of the theory.

INFLUENCES ON FREUD'S THOUGHT

Freud originally attempted to explain the workings of the mind in terms of physiology and neurology and he thought in the manner of a natural scientist. Helmholtz, one of the leading physicists of his day, had formulated the law of Conservation of Energy, which states that energy (like mass) can be transformed but not destroyed. In 1874, Brücke, an eminent physiologist, argued that the living organism is a dynamic system to which the laws of physics and chemistry apply. Freud was to put these two principles together and extend them by applying them to the (non-physical) personality.

Quite early in his treatment of neurological patients, Freud realized that symptoms which had no organic or bodily basis could imitate the 'real thing' and that they were as real for the patient as if they had been neurologically caused. So began Freud's search for psychological explanations of these symptoms and ways of treating them.

In 1885 he spent a year in Paris learning hypnosis from the neurologist Charcot; he then started using hypnosis with his patients in Vienna. However, he found its effects to be only temporary, at best, and it did not usually get to the root of the problem; nor was everybody a suitable subject.

An alternative approach was being developed by Breuer, another Viennese doctor. Breuer was using the cathartic method, where patients would talk out their problems; Freud adopted Breuer's method and called it 'free association' which became one of the three fundamental tools of psychoanalysis (see Chapter 31).

Freud began his self-analysis during the 1890s and in 1900 published *The Interpretation of Dreams*, in which he outlined his theory of the mind, followed by *The Psychopathology of Everyday Life* (1901), *A Case of Hysteria* and *Three Essays on the Theory of Sexuality* (1905).

Two of Freud's closest colleagues, Carl Jung and Alfred Adler, helped him form the psychoanalytic movement and the first International Psychoanalytic Congress was held at Salzburg in 1908. The *Journal of Psychoanalysis* was first published in 1909 and, in that year, Freud and Jung made a lecture tour of the USA. (Jung's and Adler's theories are described in Chapter 29.)

THE STRUCTURE OF PERSONALITY

Freud believed that the personality or 'psychic apparatus' consists of three parts (which must not be thought of as parts of the brain or in any way physical), the *id*, the *ego* and the *superego*.

The Id

Although part of the personality, the id responds directly to the instincts, those demands arising from within the body itself, for instance, the biologically-based needs for food, warmth, sexual gratification and so on.

For Freud, the human organism is a complex energy system and the kind of energy needed to fuel or operate the psychic apparatus is *psychic energy*, which performs psychological work: the source of psychic energy is the id:

> It contains everything that is inherited, that is present at birth, that is laid down in the constitution—above all, therefore, the instincts ... (Freud, 1964)

The wishes and impulses arising from the body's needs build up a sort of pressure or tension (excitation) which demand immediate release or satisfaction. When this happens, we experience pleasure but when it is prevented, we experience pain or frustration. Since the id is in closer touch with the body than with the outside world, and since it is not affected by logic or reason, and its sole aim is to reduce excitation to a minimum, it is said to be governed by the *pleasure principle* (seeking pleasure and avoiding pain). For this reason, the id can be thought of as the infantile part of the personality, what we are before the social environment has begun to exert any influence over us (including other people), the *pre-socialized* part of our make-up.

At birth, we are 'bundles of id' and the id retains its infantile character throughout our lives. Whenever we act on impulse, selfishly, or demand something 'here and now', it is our id controlling our behaviour (it is 'the spoiled child' of the personality).

In its earliest, most primitive form, the id acts in a reflex way to release tension, for example, blinking the eye or the eye watering to remove dust or dirt, sneezing to remove an irritation from the nostril and automatic opening of the bladder when pressure on its reaches a certain level. However, not all tension can be released in this reflex way, for instance, hunger does not automatically produce food but only irritability and crying, etc. These signals have to be interpreted by another person if the baby is not to starve to death.

Indeed, if the id were capable of satisfying the body's needs in a reflex way, there would be no need for psychological development—so not only is some degree of frustration and discomfort inevitable, they are also necessary for development beyond the reflex level:

> It is the dark, inaccessible part of our personality . . . We approach the id with analogies: we call it a chaos, a cauldron full of seething excitations . . . It is filled with energy reaching it from the instincts, but it has no organization . . . but only a striving to bring about the satisfaction of instinctual needs subject to the observance of the pleasure principle. The logical laws of thought do not apply to the id . . . there is no recognition of the passage of time . . . (Freud, 1933)

The main development that occurs in the id is the *primary process*, a form of thinking in which an image of the object needed to reduce tension is produced. So, for example, through repeated association of food and hunger-reduction, the hungry baby, if not fed immediately, may conjure up an image of food. However, the id is incapable of distinguishing between the subjective memory-image and the real thing—that is left to the ego.

The Ego

The ego is:

> . . . that part of the id which has been modified by the direct influence of the external world through the medium of conscious perception. (Freud, 1923)

It gradually develops (starting at a few months) as psychic energy is 'borrowed' from the id and directed outwards towards external reality.

The ego can also be described as the 'executive' of the personality, the planning, decision-making, rational and logical part of us, which engages in *secondary process thinking*, which is roughly equivalent to the cognitive processes of perception, attention, memory, reasoning, problem-solving and so on. It enables us to distinguish between a wish and reality, inside from outside, subjective from objective and so on, and is governed by the *reality principle*.

While the id demands immediate gratification for some need arising within the body, the ego will postpone its satisfaction until the appropriate time and place ('deferred gratification'). However, this does not imply any kind of moral code—what the ego considers 'right' or 'correct' is what others would find acceptable or what is objectively possible in the situation—it is the *consequences* of the act rather than the act itself which is the ego's priority. For example, whereas the id would have us scratch wherever and whenever an itch arises, the ego takes reality into account by deciding that scratching in public might offend others and may lead to our being ostracized, which most of us would not like to happen. So the ego, like the id, is amoral, but the feelings, needs, reactions and so on of other peole *are* taken into account; again, while the id is concerned only with *what* it wants, the ego is equally concerned with *how* to get it:

> The ego seeks to bring the influence of the external world to bear upon the id and its tendencies, and endeavours to substitute the reality principle for the pleasure principle which reigns unrestrictedly in the id. For the ego, perception plays the part which in the id falls to instinct. The ego represents what may be called reason and common sense, in contrast to the id, which contains the passions . . . (Freud, 1923)

The Superego

Not until the superego has developed can we describe the person as a moral being. Morality involves the internalization of a set of moral values which determine that certain behaviour is good or bad, right or wrong, *in itself*. So the superego represents the moral or judicial branch of the personality and its development is discussed in detail in Chapter 27. It comprises two components: (i) the *conscience*, which threatens the ego with punishment (in the form of guilt) for bad behaviour; and (ii) the *ego-ideal*, which promises the ego rewards (in the form of pride and high self-esteem) for good behaviour:

> The long period of childhood, during which the growing human lives in dependence on its parents, leaves behind it . . . the formation in his ego of a special agency in which the parental influence is prolonged. It has received the name of *superego*. In so far as this superego is differentiated from the ego or is opposed to it, it constitutes a third power which the ego must take into account . . . (Freud, 1940)

CONFLICT AND THE EGO

As shown in Figure 21.1, the ego can be viewed as 'located' squarely in the middle of the psychic apparatus, the point of convergence of

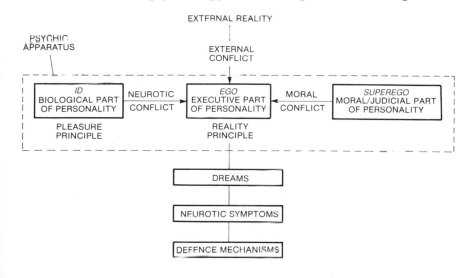

Figure 21.1 The psychic apparatus, showing sources of conflict and ways of resolving it

conflicting demands from three sources—external reality, the id and the superego. Where external reality makes demands on the ego (eg someone threatening you with a knife) the resulting conflict is called *external* or *reality conflict*. When the ego fears being overwhelmed by the power of the id's demands for instinctual gratification, the result is *neurotic conflict*. Where the ego feels threatened by punishment from the conscience, the result is *moral conflict*.

Freud believes that conflict is inevitable; we live in society which, for its own survival, cannot allow us to give free expression to our id impulses and our ego develops in order to ensure that the individual acknowledges social and material reality. The superego develops in order to assist the ego in keeping the very powerful id in its place but it can only do so by making demands on the ego—there is no direct 'contact' between the id and the superego. Consequently, the ego, part of which constitutes our conscious self, is caught in the middle of opposing sets of demands, it is the battleground on which three opposing factions (reality, the id and the superego) fight for supremacy. But the ego is, at the same time, the arbitrator and has to find ways of keeping all the factions 'happy', of satisfying all their demands and not responding to some at the expense of others! How is this achieved?

For Freud, all behaviour is a *compromise* which can take three major forms—dreams, neurotic symptoms and defence mechanisms (these will be discussed in Chapter 29).

FREUD'S INSTINCT THEORY

Psychoanalytic theory is often described as an instinct theory. From what we have said about the id, it should be evident that Freud believed that personality is based on biological drives, mainly sexual and aggressive in nature, rooted in the body with its unalterable hereditary constitution.

However, this needs to be qualified in two main ways. First, although he saw personality development as largely bound up with development of the sexual instinct (libido) which passes through a maturational, biologically determined sequence of stages, Freud also stressed the influence of the reactions of significant others (especially parents) on the child's behaviour as it passes through the stages. As we shall see below, Freud's theory of how adult personality types arise is directly linked to experiences the child has had at a particular developmental stage. Secondly, Freud's concept of an instinct was very different from the earlier view of unlearned, largely automatic (pre-programmed) responses to specific stimuli (based on instincts in other species). He saw instincts as relatively undifferentiated energy, capable of almost infinite variation through experience; indeed, instead of using the German *Instinckt*, he used *Trieb* which is most accurately translated as 'drive'.

Although Freud emphasized the role of the sexual instinct in personality development, this was by no means the only one he identified. In *Beyond the Pleasure Principle* (1920), he distinguished two main groups of instincts: (i) the Life Instincts (*Eros*) which include libido (sexual energy); and (ii) the Death Instincts (*Thanatos*), comprising, primarily, aggression. Libido later came to refer to *all* kinds of psychic (drive) energy, the principal components of which are sexual. However, Freud never maintained that no other instincts exist or that 'everything is sex' (see Chapter 16).

PSYCHOSEXUAL DEVELOPMENT

One of the most radical aspects of Freud's theories is the notion of *infantile sexuality*, the view that babies and young children (and not just adolescents and adults) have sexual experiences and are capable of sexual pleasure. As a way of trying to illustrate how revolutionary this part of the theory was, Table 21.1 compares the Victorian concept of sexuality (the 'official' view) with Freud's in terms of the four major components of an instinct, namely, source, impetus or force, aim and object.

According to Freud, sexuality is not confined to adults but is evident

COMPONENTS OF AN INSTINCT	THE VICTORIAN VIEW OF SEXUALITY	FREUD'S VIEW (INFANTILE SEXUALITY)
Source Where in the body does it arise?	Arises exclusively in the genital area, and so does not appear before puberty	Present at birth and passes through a series of pre-determined stages, each one focused on a different part of the body (*erogenous/erotogenic zone*): Stages of psychosexual development { Oral (0–1) Anal (1 3) Phallic (3–5/6) Latency (5/6 to puberty) Genital (puberty to maturity)
Impetus or *force* How much excitement is produced?	It varies, in adults, from one time to another; gratification reduces it to a minimum. Frustration increases the impetus. In children it is absent so there is zero impetus	It can be as strong in a baby (oral stage) as in an adult (genital stage). In itself, one kind of sexuality is no more or less strong than any other. Difference between stages is *qualitative*
Aim What is it for? What is its purpose?	*Primary aim:* Procreation (reproduction) *Secondary aim:* Release of tension	*Primary aim:* Release of tension (ie pleasure) Procreation is almost incidental
Object What or whom is needed in order to satisfy it?	Legal spouse	At first, ourselves, eg sucking, later masturbation (ie auto-erotism). From the genital stage onwards, we need an adult of the opposite sex

Table 21.1 *Comparison between Freud's theory of infantile sexuality and the Victorian view of sexuality*

from the moment of birth. In order to understand Freud's theory of infantile sexuality we must understand his use of the term sexuality: he used it to describe the desire for physical, sensuous, pleasure of any kind and, far from being a highly specific drive towards heterosexual gratification (ie genital stimulation), sexuality can be satisfied in a variety of ways. The essence of sexual pleasure lies in the rhythmical stroking or stimulation of virtually any part of the body and, accordingly, he describes the baby as 'polymorphously perverse'.

Why did he define sexuality in this unusual way?

(a) In sexual perversions, adult behaviour may be directed towards persons of the same sex, the individual, him/herself, animals, inanimate objects, etc. so sexual desire is not necessarily aimed exclusively at adult members of the opposite sex.

(b) Even with adult members of the opposite sex, genital intercourse is not the only form of sexual behaviour enjoyed.

(c) Infants often show behaviour similar to adult perverts, eg interest in urination and defecation, thumb-sucking, exposing their naked body and enjoying seeing others naked.

Freud believed that current (adult) neuroses are the result of inadequate solutions to the problems experienced in childhood at one or more psychosexual stage. Each stage (the sequence being maturationally determined) involves a particular mode or means of achieving gratification and the degree and kind of satisfaction which the child experiences at each stage will depend on how the child is treated by its parents (in particular).

According to Freud, both excessive gratification and extreme frustration can produce permanent consequences for the individual (*fixation*) and the nature of these consequences is a function of the particular stage at which it occurs and the form it takes. The most satisfactory balance is between gaining enough pleasure to be willing to move on to the next stage but not so much that the individual is content to stay there!

Development for Freud is a complex interaction between a biologically-programmed timetable of change and the environmental or social context in which it happens, and if we want to understand the adult we need to retrace his/her childhood, hence, 'the child is father to the man'.

ORAL STAGE (0 TO 1 YEAR)

It is through the mouth that the newborn must obtain life-sustaining nourishment; the nerve endings in the lips and mouth are particularly sensitive so that the baby derives pleasure from sucking quite independently of the feeding process (non-nutritive sucking). The mouth is also important for finding out about objects.

The oral stage is divided into two: the earlier, *receptive or incorporative sub-stage* (lasting for the first few months), and the later, *biting or aggressive sub-stage*. In the former, the baby is passive and almost totally dependent and the major oral activities are sucking, swallowing and mouthing. In the latter, gums are hardening and teeth erupting and biting and chewing become the most important activities. Biting the breast, or fingers, etc. can express the baby's *ambivalence*, its experience of both loving and hating the same object (ie the mother) at the same time.

ANAL STAGE (1 TO 3 YEARS)

The most sensitive and pleasurable body zone is now the anal cavity, the sphincter muscles of the lower bowel and the muscles of the urinary system (because the urinary functions are involved as well as the anal, it is sometimes called the anal–urethral stage). The primary concern is with expelling and retaining faeces; the stage divides into two sub-stages: (i) the earlier, *expulsion* and; (ii) the later, *retention*, sub-stages. In the former, the child experiences its first encounter with external restrictions on its wish to defecate where and when it pleases, in the form of parents trying to potty-train it. This represents a crucial time for the child to learn to earn praise and approval—love from parents is no longer unconditional but now depends on how the child *behaves*. It is also a crucial time for developing (general) attitudes towards authority. In the latter, the child has learned to retain faeces and urine at will and now sensuous pleasure can be derived from holding in or holding onto these bodily 'products' or 'creations'.

PHALLIC STAGE (3 TO 5 OR 6 YEARS)

Sensitivity now becomes concentrated in the genitals and masturbation (in both sexes) becomes a new source of pleasure. The child becomes aware of anatomical sex differences, which sets in motion the conflict between erotic attraction, resentment, rivalry, jealousy and fear, which Freud called the *Oedipus Complex*. The word 'phallic' comes from the Greek 'phallus' which means penis and Freud chose this word to imply: (i) that the penis and the clitoris are equivalent; and (ii) that females do not experience their vaginas as a source of pleasure until puberty. When girls compare their 'phallus' with that of boys, they feel inferior, resentful and jealous or envious.

Oedipus Complex—Boys

In the case of boys (who, like girls, take the mother as their first love-object), beginning at about 3, their love for their mother becomes increasingly passionate and this brings them into conflict and rivalry with their father. The little boy does not want to share his mother with anyone and so he is jealous of the father who already 'possesses' her and he wants him dead (which, for a 3-year-old, means 'out of the way').

However, his father is bigger and more powerful and eventually he comes to fear that he may lose the thing he values most in the world, namely, his penis. Partly because he has been punished for masturbating, and may actually have been threatened with all its nasty consequences, and partly because he has observed the absence of a penis in girls, the boy comes to fear that his father will cut off his penis (*fear of castration* or *castration anxiety*).

This situation of jealousy, fear and love Freud called the Oedipus complex, after the mythical King of Thebes, Oedipus, who unwittingly killed his father and married his mother. (When he discovered what he had done, Oedipus blinded himself by gouging out his eyes.)

To resolve the dilemma, the boy represses his desire for his mother (ie makes it unconscious) and identifies with his father, ie he comes to think, feel and act as if he were his father. This way, at least, he keeps his male organ and can have the mother vicariously, since by becoming like his father, he can indirectly have what his father has.

Oedipus Complex—Girls

The equivalent situation for girls is often referred to as the *Electra Complex*, a term first used by Jung. But having originally used the term, Freud rejected it because he felt it gave the misleading impression that the experience of boys and girls is very similar. As we shall see, it clearly is not.

While the boy's Oedipus complex *ends* with fear of castration, the girl's *begins* with the belief that she has already been castrated, since little boys have something she does not, namely, a penis. The situation is more complex for girls than boys: while boys have to make one 'move', from a romantic attachment to their mother to identification with their father, girls, who take their mother as their first love-object, become romantically attached to their father before finally identifying with their mother. Why does the girl become attracted to her father?

Freud's answer is *penis envy*. Following her discovery of anatomical sex diferences, and her consequent belief that she has already been castrated (for which she blames her mother), a girl feels inadequate for not having a penis. Eventually realizing that it is unrealistic to hope for one, she substitutes the wish for a penis with the wish for a baby and she turns to her father as a love-object, hoping that he will provide her with this replacement for her anatomical deficiency. At this point according to Freud, '. . . the girl has turned into a little woman' (Freud, 1925).

But why does she identify with her mother?

Freud admitted that he was much less clear about the girl's motive for identifying with the mother than he was about the boy's motive for identifying with the father: if boys fear castration at the hands of their more powerful father, then surely this is sufficient reason to repress desire for the mother and to try to become like the father! It is referred to as *identification with the aggressor* ('If you can't beat them, join them') and the essential motive, therefore, is fear. But what do girls have to fear if they believe they have already been castrated? The girl may fear the loss of her mother's love if the 'family romance' continues and so, for girls, *anaclitic identification* may be the more important kind in her moral development.

To ease the pain that results from the fear of loss of love (or its threatened withdrawal), she internalizes the images of the mother and this entails being the 'good' child that her mother would wish her to be ('If I'm not what she wants me to be she'll stop loving me'). This process of internalization is known as anaclitic identification and, like identification with the aggressor, is defensive, since it keeps the mother 'alive' inside the child.

What Freud did seem quite sure about was that the girl's identification is much weaker and less complete than the boy's with his father, and this has significant implications for their psychological development, particularly in relation to the superego ('the heir to the Oedipus Complex'; see Chapter 27).

LATENCY (5 OR 6 TO PUBERTY)

Freud uses the term 'latency' to indicate that only quantitative changes occur in the libido during these few years prior to puberty— there are no new qualitative changes as in the earlier stages. But this does *not* mean that the child is asexual: it falls 'victim' to 'infantile amnesia' and represses the sexual preoccupations of the earlier years, allowing social and intellectual development to proceed. Much of the child's energies are channelled into developing new skills and acquiring new knowledge and play becomes largely confined to other children of the same gender (helping the child to control sexual thoughts). Freud's theory of play is summarized in Box 21.1.

In relative terms, the balance between the id, ego and superego is greater during latency than at any time in the child's life; indeed, latency represents the calm before the storm of puberty, which marks the beginning of the *genital stage*. The relative harmony within the child's

---

Box 21.1   Freud's Theory of Play (based on Millar, 1972)

1) Like *all* behaviour, play is motivated behaviour (ie caused by the child's feelings and emotions, both unconscious and conscious).

2)   In common with dreams and fantasy, play is determined by *wishes*. The child *can* distinguish play from reality but uses objects and situations from the real world to create a world of its own in which to *repeat* pleasant experiences at will and to order and alter events in the way that it finds most pleasing. For instance, children want to be grown up and do what adults do—in play this is possible.

3)   But how does this account for the frequency with which *unpleasant* experiences are repeated in play? For example, children who hate taking medicine dose their dolls or they graphically re-enact a frightening accident or event. Given that we try to keep excitation to a minimum, so that all increases in excitation are felt as unpleasant and all decreases as pleasurable, repeating distressing or upsetting experiences in play is, in fact, an attempt to feel pleasure, since repetition *reduces* the excitation associated with them.

4)   This impulse to repeat (*repetition compulsion*) is part of the urge to return to an earlier, more stable, tension-free state (ie death). (See section on Freud's Instinct Theory and Chapter 16.)

5)   Through play the child can *master* disturbing experiences by *actively* bringing them about rather than being a passive and helpless victim; this view contributed to the development of *play therapy* and the use of *projective* tests of personality (see Chapters 30 and 31)

6)   *Play* and the *Defence mechanisms* (see Chapter 29). Given that conflict and frustration are inevitable, then much play can be seen as the special use of:

(i)   *projection*—dolls, imaginary companions, evil witches, etc. behave maliciously;
(ii) *displacement*—immersing doll-baby or toy in water or throwing it about helps relieve a jealous sibling's feelings without harming the new baby brother or sister;
(iii) *regression*—blowing bubbles may represent a return to oral over-indulgence or frustration;
(iv) *sublimation*—sand and water play are acceptable, while playing with faeces is not.

7)   Different kinds of play will be associated with different psychosexual stages, eg the example of sublimation above, or playing roles reflecting identification with same-sex parents during phallic stage.

---

personality is now disrupted and the id begins to make powerful new demands in the form of heterosexual desires, so that members of the opposite sex are now needed to satisfy the libido (see below).

EVIDENCE FOR THE OEDIPUS COMPLEX

Is there any evidence to support Freud's account of the Oedipus complex?

One criticism is that, even if true for western cultures, the Oedipus complex may not be universal, ie it may not apply to all cultures and to all historical periods. For instance, Malinowski (1929), studied the Trobriand Islanders in the South Pacific, a culture in which the mother's brother, not the child's father, is the figure of authority. Thus, repressive discipline does not originate in the man who sexually monopolizes the child's mother and the father–son relationship is deprived of the ambivalent love–hate features (Eysenck, 1985).

Walters and Thomas (1963) showed that, at least in the laboratory, both adults and children readily imitate aggressive models who pose no threat to them whatsoever; assuming that imitation is some kind of index of identification, this suggests that being in conflict with the model and fearing some kind of punishment from him is neither a necessary nor a sufficient condition for identification to occur.

Kagan and Lemkin (1960) found no evidence of a shift amongst 5- to 6-year-old boys away from their mothers towards their fathers; but Fisher and Greenberg (1977), in one of the major reviews of empirical studies of Freudian theory to date, concluded that children do have to cope with erotic feelings towards the opposite-sex parent and feelings of hostility towards the parent of the same sex.

In the same review, Fisher and Greenberg report that fear of castration (expressed indirectly as concern about physical injury, fear of death, fear of bodily harm or attack) is relatively common in men and is intensified when they are exposed to erotic heterosexual stimulation. Women do seem to be more motivated by fear of loss of love.

Freud's own evidence was clinical, based on case studies of his patients who, with one exception, were adults. A common criticism of his theories is that no valid theory of development in children can be based on studies of adults (see Chapter 29) and so the case of little Hans assumes even greater significance (Box 21.2).

Box 21.2 Analysis of a Phobia in a 5-Year-Old Boy—the Case of Little Hans (Freud, 1909)

Hans had a phobia of being bitten by a horse and was especially afraid of white horses with black around the mouth and wearing blinkers; he tried to avoid horses at all costs. [Freud's interpretation: fear of being bitten represented Hans's fear of castration.]

Hans was particularly frightened when he once saw a horse collapse in the street. [Freud's interpretation: seeing the horse collapse reminded him, unconsciously, of his death wish against his father, which made him feel guilty and afraid.]

Is there any reason to believe that Hans saw the horses as symbolizing his father?

(a) Hans once said to his father as he got up from the table: 'Daddy, don't *trot* away from me'.
(b) On another occasion, Hans said: 'Daddy, you are lovely, you're so white'. This suggests he may have thought his father resembled a white horse (as opposed to a dark one).
(c) Hans's father had a moustache ('the black on the horses' mouth').
(d) His father wore glasses, which resembled blinkers as worn by horses.
(e) Hans had played 'horses' with his father, with Hans usually riding on his father's back.

Hans claimed that his fear stemmed from the time he saw a horse collapse in the street: 'When the horse in the bus fell down it gave me such a fright really; that was when I got the nonsense (ie the phobia)'. This was confirmed by Hans's mother. But his father, and Freud, paid little attention to this plausible explanation of the phobia.

Freud believed Hans was a 'little Oedipus', loving to be in bed with his mother and going to the bathroom with her, and regarding his father as a rival and wanting him out of the way. But rather than the father being 'the aggressor', it seemed to be the mother who made explicit threats of castration:

(a) 'If you do that [touch his penis] I shall send for doctor A to cut off your widdler. And then what'll you widdle with?' (Mother).
(b) She threatened to abandon him; Hans said, 'Mummy's told me she won't come back.'
(c) 'It's only in the big bath that I'm afraid of falling in' (Hans).
    'But Mummy baths you in it. Are you afraid of Mummy dropping you in the water?' (Father).
    'I'm afraid of her letting go and my head going in' (Hans).

It seems very difficult for at least two reasons to regard the case of little Hans as evidence for the Oedipus theory: (i) Freud had already made up his mind what was wrong with him and interpreted all the data accordingly; (ii) Hans's psychoanalysis was conducted primarily *by the father* (not Freud) a follower of Freud's ideas. The two men conferred and consulted each other but Freud himself only met Hans on one or two occasions. (By the way, Hans's mother had been a patient of Freud's before her marriage.)

As far as (i) is concerned, Little Hans was seen by Freud as confirming the Oedipal theory which had already been proposed in the *Three Essays on the Theory of Sexuality* (1905)—Freud saw Hans as a 'little Oedipus'.

As far as (ii) is concerned, Freud himself was aware of the methodological objections which could be raised—how could the father be objective in his observations and psychoanalyse someone with whom he was so emotionally involved? Also, the child will be susceptible to his father's suggestions. Doesn't this immediately invalidate the case study as an *independent* confirmation of Freud's Oedipal theory?

Freud himself seems to agree with this criticism by saying that Hans's father did put into words things Hans could not himself say and present Hans with thoughts which he had not previously shown signs of possessing, etc., all of which detracts from the evidential value of the analysis. (This, and other issues dealing with the scientific nature of Freud's theory will be dealt with in Chapter 29.)

One of the most serious problems faced by much of Freud's theory in general, and Little Hans in particular, is that of *alternative explanations*. Is Freud's interpretation of Hans's phobia the only reasonable, feasible one? Amongst those who offer alternative interpretations are two very eminent psychoanalysts, Erich Fromm and John Bowlby.

According to Fromm (1970) (Fig. 21.2), Freud wanted to find support for the theory of sexuality based on adults by directly reviewing material drawn from a child. He considered that Hans's parents had raised their son with as little coercion as possible and generally treated him in a very positive way. But what about the threats of castration from the mother, her threats not to come back, the lies they told (eg about the stork bringing his sister, Hanna, who was born when Hans was 3½, and his mother telling him that she too had a penis, a lie confirmed by the father)?

Figure 21.2 Erich Fromm (1900–1980) (UPI/Bettmann Archive, Inc.)

While Freud claims that the dread of castration came from 'very slight allusions', Fromm believes that there were clear, strong threats—made by the mother. Freud's extreme patriarchical attitude prevented him from conceiving that the woman *could* be the main cause of fear. Indeed:

> . . . clinical observation amply proves that the most intense and pathogenic fears are indeed related to the mother; by comparison, the dread of the father is relatively insignificant. (Fromm, 1970)

It would seem that Hans needed his father to protect him from a menacing mother. Fromm believes that the successful outcome of the therapy was due not so much to the interpretations made of Hans's fear, as the protective role of the father and the 'super-father' (Freud). He believes the fear of horses has two origins: (i) fear of the mother (due to her castration threat); and (ii) fear of death (he had witnessed a funeral and then later a fallen horse which he thought dead). To avoid both fears he developed a fear of being bitten which protects him both from horses and from experiencing (consciously) both types of anxiety.

According to Freud, the boy's incestuous desire for the mother is 'endogenous', ie *not* the result of maternal seduction. But is it as intense, exclusive and spontaneous as Freud believed? Fromm points out that Hans's mother liked to have him in bed with her and to take him with her to the bathroom. But Hans wanted to sleep with Mariedl (the landlord's 13-year-old daughter) and once said he preferred her company to his mother's.

Finally, Fromm suggests that rather than being directed towards his father (as the Oedipus theory states), Hans's hostility is aimed at his mother (based on her castration threats, her 'treason' at giving birth to Hanna and his desire to be free from fixation on her).

Fromm believes that Hans's yearning to take his father's place was *not* necessarily an expression of hate or desire for the father's death but the universal tendency to want to be grown up and no longer be subjected to adult power. Indeed, there is much evidence of great warmth and friendship in their relationship.

Fromm concludes this way:

> Finally, this was a slight phobia, such as occurs in many children, and it would probably have disappeared by itself without any treatment and without the father's support and interest. (Fromm, 1970)

Bowlby's (1973) re-interpretation of Little Hans is in terms of attachment theory (see Chapter 22). He asks whether Hans's anxiety about availability of attachment figures played a larger part than Freud realized. Agreeing with Fromm, Bowlby argues that most of Hans's anxiety arose from threats by the mother to desert the family. The main evidence comes from: (i) the sequence in which the symptoms developed and statements made by Hans himself; and (ii) evidence in the father's account that the mother was in the habit of using threats of an alarming kind to discipline Hans, including the threat to abandon him.

The symptoms did not come out of the blue; Hans had been upset throughout the preceding week. They began when Hans had woken up one morning in tears. Asked why he was crying he said to his mother, 'When I was asleep, I thought you were gone and I had no Mummy to coax with.' ('coax'=cuddle).

Some days later his nursemaid had taken him to a local park, as usual.

But he started crying in the street and asked to be taken home—so he could 'coax' with his mother. During that evening he became very frightened and cried, demanding to stay with his mother. The next day, his mother, eager to find out what was wrong, took him to Schonbrunn, when the horse phobia was first noticed. But the week preceding the onset of the phobia was *not* the first time Hans had expressed fear his mother might disappear. Six months earlier he made remarks such as, 'Suppose I was to have no Mummy', 'Suppose you were to go away'.

When Hanna was born, Hans was kept away from his mother. The father stated that Hans's, 'present anxiety, which prevents him leaving the neighbourhood of the house, is in reality the longing for [his mother] which he felt then.'

Freud endorses this by describing Hans's 'enormously intensified affection' for his mother as, 'the fundamental phenomenon in his condition':

> Thus, both the sequence of events leading up to the phobia and Hans's own statement make it clear that distinct from and preceding any fear of horses, Hans was afraid his mother might go away and leave him. (Bowlby, 1973)

Did she actually threaten, implicitly, or explicitly, to leave the family?

One conversation between Hans and his father in the father's bed one morning is very revealing:

> Hans, 'When you're away, I'm afraid you're not coming home.'
> Father, 'And have I ever threatened you that I shan't come home?'
> Hans, 'Not you, but Mummy. Mummy's told me she won't come back.'
> Father, 'She said that because you were naughty?'
> Hans, 'Yes.'

Even the fear of being bitten by a horse is consistent with the view that fear of the mother's departure is the main source of anxiety. During the summer holiday of the previous year, Lizzi, a little girl staying in a neighbouring house, had gone away. The luggage was taken to the station in a cart pulled by a white horse. Lizzi's father was there and had warned her: 'Don't put your fingers to the white horse or it'll bite you.'

So, fear of being bitten was closely linked in Hans's mind to someone's departure.

A fascinating postscript to this case study (Freud, 1922) lends support to various aspects of both Fromm and Bowlby's interpretations. Hans's parents had divorced (but we are not told exactly when) and each had re-married. At age 19, he was living on his own, was on good terms with both parents and only regretted that as a result of the family break-up he had been separated from Hanna of whom he was so fond.

OEDIPUS COMPLEX, SEDUCTION THEORY AND CHILD ABUSE

In 1896 (prior to publication of his theory of infantile sexuality), Freud gave a lecture called 'The Aetiology of Hysteria' in which he described his findings that in eighteen cases of previously unexplained hysteria referred to him, each patient had been sexually abused in childhood—either by an adult or by an older sibling. None had been aware of this when they first consulted him and it only emerged during the course of therapy.

The lecture caused such an outcry that he abandoned the *seduction theory* in 1897 and replaced it with what came to be called the Oedipus complex. In other words, having originally believed that children were the victims of actual abuse, he claimed, instead, that the 'abuse' was in the mind of the child, it happened in the child's fantasy. According to Search:

> . . . Children who claimed to have been sexually abused by someone they knew were making it up. If there was incontrovertible physical proof that they weren't—a sexually transmitted disease or a pregnancy, for example—the view generally was that the fantasies were so powerful that they had spilled over into reality and the children had initiated the sexual contact themselves. (Search, 1988)

And again:

> From the experience of rape crisis centres and Incest Crisis Line, it is clear that although many people have never told anyone what had happened to them, those who *had* tried to tell were usually not believed—not simply by parents or other trusted adults, but by professionals. (Search, 1988)

The reason, primarily, was Freud's theory of infantile sexuality and the Oedipus complex (Search, 1988).

According to Fromm (1970), the Oedipus complex was a much less radical alternative than the Seduction Theory (however controversial the former might be) and Freud has been accused of cowardice, even by other psychoanalysts (and particularly by Masson (1985)).

PSYCHOSEXUAL DEVELOPMENT AND PERSONALITY TYPES

We noted earlier that both excessive gratification *and* extreme frustration (especially during the oral stage) could produce long-lasting consequences, notably, the kind and combination of personality that the adult possesses. The process by which these traits are determined is *fixation*. However, fixation is not an all-or-none thing, it can vary in degree. There are many examples of how commonplace oral fixation is: for example, smoking, nail-biting, pen-sucking and kissing are all 'oral' activities, while many swear words make reference to anal–urinary activities ('crap', 'shit', 'piss', for example). These examples show that the early stages of development all leave their mark or imprint to varying degrees.

Freud was equally interested in more extreme examples of fixation and identified two major personality types—the oral and the anal. Some of the major traits associated with these, together with traits and activities resulting from the use of defence mechanisms, are shown in Box 21.3.

IS THERE ANY EVIDENCE TO SUPPORT FREUD?

Kline and Storey (1977) found evidence for two oral characters, one in which dependency, fluency, sociability, liking of novelty and relaxation clustered together (*oral optimistic*) and one in which independence, verbal aggression, envy, coldness and hostility, malice, ambition and impatience clustered together (*oral pessimistic*). Storey (1980) found a relationship between these scores and smoking, food preferences and nail-biting.

Fisher and Greenberg (1977) concluded that people who are unusually

Box 21.3 *Relationship between fixation at psychosexual stages and adult personality*

Oral (0–1)	*Incorporative*	Fixation through over-indulgence	Passive—	1. Cheerful, unrealistically optimistic; 'life is easy.' 2. 'I am the centre of the universe'; self-centredness. 3. Dependent—can't bear others' disapproval.
				Through *sublimation*: interest in languages, compulsive talker, ventriloquist, 'thirst for knowledge'.
		Fixation through frustration	Dependent	1. Greedy, acquisitive. 2. Envious, pessimistic. 3. Addict, parasite. 4. Gluttonous. 5. Thumb-sucker. 6. Smoker.
	Aggressive	Fixation through over-indulgence	Active—	
		Fixation through frustration	Biting	1. Cynical. 2. Verbally, 'biting', sarcastic, scornful, disdainful, contemptuous. 3. Nail-biter.
Anal (1–3)	*Expulsive*	Orderliness could represent a *Reaction formation* against the wish to mess.		
		a) Orderliness	1. Pre-occupation with punctuality, routine; everything must be in its proper place. 2. Obsessive-compulsive behaviour (in extreme cases). *'Performing'* for others, giving presents, donating to charity etc, could be *sublimations* of wish to 'perform on the potty' for parents. Sculptors, potters, gardeners are all *sublimating* the wish to smear.	
	Retentive	b) Parsimony c) Obstinacy	1. Miserly, thrifty. 2. Wilfully hoarding	*Reaction formation* against this could be feeling compelled to give things away or lose them through gambling or speculation on stock market.
Phallic (3–5/6)		1. Homosexuality 2. Curiosity 3. Exhibitionism 4. Exploitation of others	5. Excessive displays of masculinity/femininity 6. Extreme self-centredness 7. Excessive ambition 8. Narcissism (self-love)	A surgeon may be *sublimating* hostile feelings towards same-sex parent. Writer of pornography may be *sublimating* sexual preoccupations.
Latency (5/6–puberty)		1. Never feeling comfortable with members of the opposite sex; may avoid heterosexual relationships. 2. May perform sexual activities in an emotionally-detached or aggressive way.		

preoccupied with oral themes tend to crave approval and support from significant others. Also, 'oral people' (eg those sensitive to oral images or dependency themes) use submission and passivity to maintain contact with potential supporters; they also tend to over-eat, smoke and drink a lot of alcohol.

What about the evidence for the anal personality?

Kline (1972), Fisher and Greenberg (1977) and Pollak (1979) found evidence for the clustering of three major character traits, namely *orderliness*, *parsimony* and *obstinacy*. But some of the studies reviewed by Kline as supporting the anal character have been criticized for having major methodological weaknesses.

Better support comes from studies where a questionnaire and behavioural measures of anal anxiety have been correlated with specific behavioural measures of the three main anal traits. For example, Rosenwald (1972) found that the amount of anxiety experienced about anal matters predicted how carefully subjects arranged magazines when asked to do so by the experimenter and subjects' obstinacy in shifting their opinion was predicted by the difficulty they experienced in solving a puzzle which involved immersing their hands in a faecal-like substance.

Fisher (1978) found that racial prejudice based on skin colour can be predicted by subjects' attitudes to cleanliness and thrift, implying that colour prejudice is at least partly the consequence of an unconscious connection between skin colour and faeces. As Fonagy (1981) points out, these predictions certainly seen highly counter-intuitive and difficult to account for except in psychoanalytic terms.

However, the fact that there is substantial evidence for the *existence* of oral and anal personality types does not, of course, mean that these traits come about in the way Freud believes. So what is the evidence that these personality variables are related to early oral/anal experiences?

Fisher and Greenberg (1977) found that the evidence is often contradictory. For example, some studies have found a correlation between orality and length of breast-feeding and others that dependency is related to severity of weaning. However, still others have found no relationship between dependency and duration of breast-feeding.

However, the measures of feeding-styles used in these studies do not do justice to the complexities of mother–infant interaction and when these are taken into account, the evidence tends to be favourable to Freud.

Laboratory studies also tend to suggest that the oral person is rather dependent, eg positive correlations have been found between orality and responsiveness to *verbal reinforcement*, *verbal advice* and *social support* under stress. However, not only do these studies *not* show cause-and-effect but they all use different measures of orality (eg number of mouth movements, number of ice-creams eaten, etc.) and how valid are such measures?

As to the anal character, most studies have failed to verify that the anal person differs from other types in age of initiation or completion of toilet training or in severity of training procedures.

DEVELOPMENT OF THE SELF-CONCEPT

So far in this chapter, we have discussed Freud's theory of personality development. The self-concept can be thought of as the individual's *beliefs* about his/her personality—how the individual *perceives* his/her personality. (Self-perception has been discussed elsewhere, eg in Chapter 19 in relation to Cognitive Dissonance.)

CONSCIOUSNESS AND SELF-CONSCIOUSNESS

When you look in the mirror at your face, you are both the person who is looking and that which is looked at. In a less tangible or concrete way, when you think about the kind of person you are, or something you have done, you are both the person doing the thinking and what is being thought about. In other words, you are both *subject* (the thinker or looker) and *object* (what is being looked at or thought about). We use the personal pronoun 'I' to refer to us as subject and 'me' to refer to us as object and this represents a rather special relationship that we have with ourselves, namely *self-consciousness* or *self-awareness*.

While other animal species have consciousness (ie they have sensations of cold, heat, hunger, thirst, and can feel pleasure, pain, fear, sexual arousal, etc.) only humans have self-consciousness. The term 'self-conscious' is often used to mean embarrassment or shyness and certainly we do feel like this in situations where we are made to feel object-like, or exposed in some way, eg if we get on the bus in the morning to discover we are wearing odd socks or have our sweater on back-to-front. But this is a secondary meaning—the primary meaning refers to this unique relationship whereby the same person, the same *self*, is both subject and object, knower and known, thinker and thought about, seer and seen, etc.

WHAT IS THE SELF?

There are many 'self' terms, which are often used interchangeably but which have fairly distinct meanings (eg 'self-image', 'self-esteem', 'ideal self', 'self-identity'). 'Self' and 'self-concept' are used interchangeably to refer to an individual's overall self-awareness. According to Murphy (1947), 'the self is the individual as known to the individual', and Burns (1980) defines it as, 'the set of attitudes a person holds towards himself'.

Certainly, in our everyday interactions with others, it is a great advantage to know something about their self-concept, as this makes their behaviour both more understandable and more predictable. When we say we know someone well, part of what we mean is that we know what they think of themselves; behaviour that is apparently the same may have two different meanings if performed by two individuals with different self-concepts. For example, if two children both choose very difficult problems to solve instead of easier ones, it could reflect the genuine self-confidence of one child, while for the other child it could be a defence against fear of failing at easier problems (since the child could not be criticized for failing on very difficult ones). So we cannot fully understand a person's behaviour unless we also understand what that behaviour means for the person.

COMPONENTS OF THE SELF-CONCEPT

The self-concept is a general term that traditionally refers to three major components: (i) self-image; (ii) self-esteem; and (iii) ideal-self.

SELF-IMAGE (EGO IDENTITY)

This refers to the way in which we would describe ourselves, the kind of person we think we are (whether we like what we are or not). One way of investigating self-image is to ask people to answer the question, 'Who am I?' twenty times (Kuhn and McPartland, 1954). This, typically, produces two main categories of answers—social roles and personality traits. Social roles are usually quite objective aspects of our self-image (eg son, daughter, brother, sister, student, etc.); they are 'facts' and can be verified by others. Personality traits, on the other hand, are more a matter of opinion and judgement and what we think we are like may be different from how others see us (eg we may think we are quite friendly but others may see us as cold or a little aloof). But, as we said earlier, the better we know someone, the more we know how they see themselves and so the more likely it is that our perception of them and their perception of themselves coincide.

As well as social roles and personality traits, people often make reference to their physical characteristics in response to the 'who am I?' question, such as tall, short, fat, thin, blue-eyed, brown-haired, etc. These are part of our *body image* or *bodily self*, the bodily *me*, which also includes bodily sensations (usually temporary states) of pain, cold, hunger and so on.

A more permanent feature of our body image is concerned with what we count as part of our body (and hence belonging to *us*) and what we do not. Gordon Allport (1955), a very eminent self-theorist, gives two rather dramatic and vivid examples of how intimate our bodily sense is and just where we draw the boundaries between 'me' and 'not me':

(a) Imagine swallowing your saliva—or actually do it! Now imagine spitting it into a cup and drinking it! Clearly, once we have spat out our saliva, we have disowned it—it no longer belongs to us.

(b) Imagine sucking blood from a cut in your finger (something we do quite automatically, assuming the cut is relatively slight). Now imagine sucking the blood from a plaster on your finger! Again, once it has soaked into the plaster it has ceased to be part of ourselves.

Interestingly this rule does not always apply. For example, we might feel we have lost part of ourselves when we have very long hair cut off and lovers often keep a lock of each other's hair as a constant (and tangible) reminder that the other exists.

Clearly, whenever our body changes in some way, so our body image changes. In extreme cases, where a limb is lost, or a person is scarred due to an accident, or undergoes cosmetic surgery to, say, change the shape of their nose, we would expect a correspondingly dramatic change in body image, sometimes favourable, sometimes not.

But, throughout our lives, as part of the normal process of maturation and ageing, we all experience growth spurts, changes in height, weight and the general appearance and 'feel' of our body, and each time we have to make an adjustment to our body image. Later we shall look at puberty and how the bodily changes involved affect the adolescents' body image and, hence, their self-concept; and in Chapter 24 we shall be discussing how the physical (as well as the social and intellectual) changes involved in ageing can influence the self-image of the ageing individual.

Another fundamental aspect of body-image is to do with our biological sex. As we will see in Chapter 23, gender is the social equivalent or the social interpretation of sex, and our gender, or gender identity, is another part of the central core of our self-image.

SELF-ESTEEM (SELF-REGARD)

While the self-image is essentially descriptive, self-esteem is essentially evaluative: it refers to the extent to which we like and accept or approve of ourselves, how worthwhile a person we think we are. Coopersmith (1967), whose important study of self-esteem we shall be describing in detail later on, defined it as, 'a personal judgement of worthiness, that is expressed in the attitudes the individual holds towards himself'.

How much we like or value ourselves can be an overall judgement or it can relate to specific areas of our lives. For example, we can have a generally high opinion of ourselves and yet not like certain of our characteristics or attributes, such as our wavy or curly hair (when we want it straight) or our lack of assertiveness (when we want to be more assertive). Alternatively, it may be impossible or certainly very difficult to have high overall esteem if we are very badly disfigured or are desperately shy. Again, we may regard ourselves highly as far as our academic abilities are concerned but not think we are 'up to much' when it comes to athletics.

Our self-esteem can be regarded as how we evaluate our self-image, ie how much we like the kind of person we think we are. Clearly, certain characteristics or abilities have a greater value in society generally and so are likely to influence our self-esteem accordingly, for example, being physically attractive as opposed to unattractive (see Chapters 17 and 18). But, of course, there are degrees of attractiveness, and physical appearance will be more important to some individuals than to others.

Also, certain characteristics or abilities will have differing values according to the society we live in or the particular groups we belong to, whether we are male or female, young or old, working-class or middle-class, and so on. Thus, being tall may be an advantage if you are male but not if you are female, being intelligent may have a positive 'loading' if your peer group is academically orientated but not if your peers think that being 'cool' and having fun are what matter in life.

Our self-esteem will also be partly determined by how much our self-image differs from our ideal-self, the third component of the self-concept.

IDEAL-SELF (EGO IDEAL OR IDEALIZED SELF-IMAGE)

If our self-image is the kind of person we think we are, then our ideal-self is the kind of person we would like to be. Again, this can vary in extent and degree—we may want to be different in certain aspects or we may want to be a totally different person. (We may even wish we were someone else!)

We might be very dissatisfied with what we are like and want to be different for this reason, or we may basically like ourselves and want to develop and extend ourselves along essentially the same lines.

Generally, the greater the gap between our self-image and our ideal-self, the lower our self-esteem (see Roger's Self Theory in Chapter 29).

THEORIES OF SELF

One of the earliest and most influential theories of self was proposed by Mead (1934) who was influenced both by James's distinction between 'I' (self as knower) and 'Me' (self as known) and by Cooley's (1902) theory of the 'looking-glass self'.

Cooley's theory maintains that the self is reflected in the reactions of other people, who are the 'looking-glass' for oneself, ie in order to understand what we are like, we need to see how others see us, and this is how children gradually build up an impression of what they are like. At first, the infant is not aware of self and others and makes no distinction between 'me' and 'not me': it simply experiences a 'stream of impressions' which gradually become integrated and discriminated so that the distinction is finally made.

Mead also believed that knowledge of self and others develops simultaneously, both being dependent on social interaction; self and society represent a common whole and neither can exist without the other. According to Mead, the human being is an organism with a self and this converts him into a special kind of actor, transforms his relation to the world and gives his actions a unique character. The human being is an object to himself, that is, he can perceive himself, have conceptions about himself, communicate with himself and so on. In summary, he can interact with himself (address himself, respond to the address and address himself anew). This self-interaction is a great influence upon his transactions with the world in general and with other people in particular.

Mead stresses that the self is a *process* and not a structure (it is not equivalent, for example, to Freud's ego, nor is it an organized body of needs and motives, nor a collection of attitudes, norms and values). What makes a self what it is, is a *reflexive* process, whereby it acts upon and responds to itself. (This is Mead's way of making the 'I'/'Me' distinction—the experiencing 'I' cannot be an object, it cannot itself be experienced, since it is the very act of experiencing; what we experience and interact with is our 'me'.)

An important feature of interaction is language, which represents a fundamental means by which we come to represent ourselves to ourselves. But the key process by which we come to represent ourselves to ourselves (ie develop a concept of self) is *role-taking*. By placing ourselves in the position of others we can look back on ourselves. The idea of self can only develop if the individual can 'get outside himself (experientially) in such a way as to become an object to himself' (Mead, 1934), ie to see ourselves from the standpoint of others.

Initially, the child thinks about his conduct as 'good or bad only as he reacts to his own acts in the remembered words of his parents' (Mead, 1934); 'me' at this stage is a combination of the child's memory of his own actions and the kind of reaction they received.

In the next stage, the child's pretend play, in particular 'playing at mummies and daddies', or 'doctors or nurses', helps the child to understand and incorporate adult attitudes and behaviour. Here, the child is not merely imitating, but also, 'calls out in himself the same response as he calls out in the other', ie he is being, say, the child *and* the parent and, as the parent, is responding to himself as the child. So, in playing with a doll, the child, 'responds in tone of voice and in attitudes as his parents respond to his cries and chortles' (Mead, 1934). Play is distinguished from *games*, which involve *rules*:

> ... The child must not only take the role of the other, as he does in the play, but he must assume the various roles of all the participants in the game, and govern his action accordingly ... (Mead, 1934)

Games are a later development than play (see Piaget's theory; Chapter 25).

In this way, the child acquires a variety of social viewpoints or 'perspectives' (mother, father, nurse, doctor, etc.) which are then used to accompany, direct and evaluate its own behaviour. This is how the socialized part of the self (Mead's 'Me') expands and develops. At first, these viewpoints or perspectives are based upon specific adults but, in time, the child comes to react to itself and its behaviour from the viewpoint of a 'typical mother', a 'typical nurse' or 'people in general'. Mead called these the perspectives of the *generalized other* and the incorporation of the generalized other marks the final, qualitative change in 'the me'. To quote Mead again:

> It is this generalized other in his experience which provides him with a self. (Mead, 1934)

Grammatically, our 'Me' is third person (like 'she' or 'he') and it is an image of self seen from the perspective of a judgemental, non-participant observer. By its very nature, 'Me' is social, because it grows out of this role-playing, whereby the child is being the other person.

As to *how* we get to know ourselves, there seems little doubt that this is a developmental process. Bannister and Agnew (1977) made tape-recordings of groups of children answering a variety of questions about their school, home, favourite games and so on. Tapes were transcribed and then re-recorded in different voices so as to exclude circumstantial clues (such as name, parents' occupation) as to the identity of the children. Four months after the original recording, the children were asked to identify their own statements, to point out statements that were definitely not theirs and to give reasons for their choice.

The children's ability to recognize their own statements increased steadily with age and the strategies used became more complex. At five, they relied heavily on their (often inaccurate) memory or used simple clues such as whether they themselves participated in the kinds of activity mentioned in the statement. By nine, they were using psychologically more complex methods of identifying which statements they had made and which they had not.

Any theory or attempt to explain how we come to be what we are and how we change, involves us in the question of what kind of evidence we use. Kelly (1955), in a similar vein to Cooley and Mead, believes that we derive our picture of ourselves through the picture we have of other people's picture of us. So the central evidence is the reaction of others to us, both what they say of us and the implications of their behaviour towards us; we filter others' views of us through our view of them. We build up a continuous and changing picture of ourselves out of our interaction with others.

In relation to change, and the fear of change, Fransella (1972) explored the way in which stutterers who seem to be on the verge of a cure, often suddenly relapse. They know how to live as 'stutterers' and understand how people react and relate to them in that role; nearing cure, they are overwhelmed by fear of the unknown and the strangeness of being a fluent speaker, a non-stutterer. (This can probably be extended to other cases where people continue to play familiar roles despite their apparent—or indeed real—suffering and hardship. It is a case of, 'better the devil you know . . .'.)

The paradox of self-knowing is that, if I come to learn something about myself, then that knowledge immediately changes me, to some degree or other: we can never be exactly the same again because we know something we did not know before!

FACTORS INFLUENCING THE DEVELOPMENT OF THE SELF-CONCEPT

Argyle (1969, 1983) believes that there are four major factors which influence the development of the self-concept, namely: (i) the reaction of others; (ii) comparison with others; (iii) social roles; and (iv) identification.

We should note that the importance of these factors extends beyond childhood—our self-concept is constantly being revised—but probably the most significant 'change' is the time when it is originally being formed.

i) REACTION OF OTHERS

We have already seen in the theories of Cooley and Mead how central the reactions of others are in the formulation of our self-concept and there is considerable support.

Guthrie (1938) told the story of a female student, a dull and unattractive girl. Some of her classmates decided to play a trick on her by pretending she was the most desirable girl in the college and drawing lots to decide who would take her out first, second and so on. By the fifth or sixth date, she was no longer regarded as dull and unattractive—by being treated as attractive she had, in a sense, *become* attractive (perhaps by wearing different clothes and smiling more, etc.) and her self-image had clearly changed; for the boys who dated her later, it was no longer a chore!

> Before the year was over, she had developed an easy manner and a confident assumption that she was popular. (Guthrie, 1938)

During the pre-school years children are extremely concerned with how adults view them and few things are more relevant than how significant others react to them, ie parents, older siblings and other people whose opinions the child values. Strictly speaking, it is the child's *perception* of others' reactions that makes such an important contribution to how the child comes to perceive itself. After all, the child has no frame of reference for evaluating parental reactions—parents are all-powerful figures as far as the pre-schooler is concerned, so what they say is 'fact'. If a child is consistently told how beautiful she is, she will come to believe it, it will become part of her self-image; similarly, if a child is repeatedly told how stupid or clumsy he is, this too will become accepted as the 'truth' and the child will tend to act accordingly. The first child is likely to develop high self-esteem, and the second low self-esteem.

Argyle explains this in terms of *introjection* (a process very similar to identification) whereby we come to incorporate into our own personalities the perceptions, attitudes and reactions to ourselves of our parents, and it is through the reactions of others that the child learns its conditions of worth, ie which behaviours will produce positive regard and which will not (see Rogers' theory; Chapter 29).

When the child starts school, the number and variety of significant others increases, to include teachers and peers. At the same time, the child's self-image is becoming more differentiated, ie it has more parts to it, and significant others then become important in relation to different parts of the self-image. For example, the teacher is important as far as the child's academic ability is concerned, parents as far as how lovable the child is, and so on.

A good deal of research has been conducted in connection with self-esteem and the reaction of others and the study by Coopersmith (1967) is one of the most important. He assessed hundreds of nine- and ten-year-old boys for their level of self-esteem by combining their scores on his Self-Esteem Inventory (comprising 58 questions about peers, parents, school and personal interests), with teachers' evaluations of the boys (their reactions to failure, self-confidence in new situations, sociability with peers and need for encouragement and reassurance) and with their scores on the Thematic Apperception Test (TAT), in which the subject is shown a standard series of pictures, in a definite sequence, and is asked to invent a story for each picture. The stories can then be analysed for such things as need for achievement and self-esteem (see Chapter 6).

Of the large original sample, Coopersmith selected five groups, including those who scored high on all three measures of self-esteem and those who scored low on the three measures (17 per group). They were studied in depth, using a variety of tests, and it was found that the high-esteem boys were confident about their own perceptions and judgements, expected to succeed at new tasks and to influence others, and readily expressed their opinions. They were also doing better in school and were more often chosen as friends by other children than the low-esteem boys; they had a realistic view of themselves and their abilities, were not unduly worried by criticism and enjoyed participating in things. By contrast, the low-esteem boys were a 'sad little group', isolated, fearful, reluctant to join in, self-conscious, over-sensitive to criticism, consistently underrated themselves, tended to underachieve in class and were pre-occupied with their own problems.

Interestingly, there were no measurably significant differences in intelligence or physical attractiveness between the two groups; they were all white and from middle-class homes and were free from any obvious emotional disturbance. So how did Coopersmith account for their differences in self-esteem?

He gave the boys' mothers a questionnaire to complete, gave them in-depth interviews, and the boys were also asked about their parents' child-rearing methods; he found significant differences between the two sets of parents (Table 21.2).

The optimum conditions for the development of high self-esteem seem to involve a combination of firm enforcement of limits on the child's behaviour plus a good deal of acceptance of the child's autonomy and

Table 21.2 The main characteristics of parents in Coopersmith's 1967 study of self-esteem

PARENTS OF HIGH-ESTEEM BOYS	PARENTS OF LOW-ESTEEM BOYS
1. Also had high-esteem	(No corresponding findings)
2. Were emotionally stable, self-reliant and resilient	(No corresponding findings)
3. Had clear definitions of each parent's areas of authority and responsibility	(No corresponding findings)
4. Had high expectations of their children but also provided sound models for them and gave consistent encouragement and support	4. Seemed unclear what their standards and expectations for their children were and so could not enforce them in any systematic way
5. Regarded their children as important and interesting people and respected their opinions. Indeed, they often sought the child's opinion and stressed his rights and encouraged discussion. Reasoning was strongly valued as a method of obtaining co-operation and compliance	5. They seemed to consider their sons as not being very significant and not deserving the respect owed to adults. They tended to use autocratic measures and stressed their rights and powers as parents
6. They tended to punish promptly and consistently	6. Their discipline was very unpredictable and inconsistent and so their sons were not sure where they stood
7. They were neither very punitive nor very permissive, tended not to use physical punishment, gave rewards for good behaviour and occasionally withdrawal of love or approval for bad behaviour	7. They fluctuated between over-strictness and over-permissiveness, preferred punishment to reward, did use physical punishment, and were more likely to use love-withdrawal as punishment
8. They were more accepting of their children and expressed this through specific everyday concern, physical affection and close rapport. They also seemed to know a great deal about their children (eg interests, friends' names)	8. They tended to withdraw from their children, were inattentive and neglectful, were relatively harsh and disrespectful towards them, and provided a physically, emotionally and intellectually rather impoverished environment. They knew significantly less about their children and treated them almost as if they were a burden
9. They were regarded by their sons as being 'fair' towards them	9. They were often regarded as being 'unfair' by their sons

freedom within those limits. Firm management helps the child to develop firm inner controls, and a predictable and structured social environment helps the child to deal effectively with the environment and hence to feel 'in control' of the world (rather than controlled by it). Clear and firmly enforced rules help the child to establish clear self-definitions—the child is forced to acknowledge powers outside itself and to recognize the needs and rights of others, thereby learning to distinguish between wish and reality, self and others, me and not-me. Also, parental restrictions (although sometimes frustrating) prove to the child that they are concerned about its welfare.

Coopersmith followed the boys through into adulthood and found that the high-esteem boys consistently out-performed the low-esteem boys and proved more successful educationally and vocationally.

But we must be careful not to infer from Coopersmith's findings that certain kinds of child-rearing methods actually *produce* different levels of self-esteem in the child. Coopersmith's data are only correlational, ie he found an association between the two variables, and so we cannot be sure that one is the cause of the other. Remember, too, that his subjects were white middle-class boys and therefore were not representative of the American population as a whole—what about working-class, black and female children?

Research has shown that, generally, working-class children suffer from lower self-esteem, as do delinquent groups; the latter's 'toughness' and anti-social behaviour are often an attempt to protect self-esteem by demonstrating their power to destroy what society values and so to prove that they do matter after all.

Girls, generally, have lower self-esteem than boys. For instance, when paired with boys in problem-solving tasks, they sometimes artificially depress their performance so as not to outshine their male partners (boys very rarely do this!). Some girls seem to feel uncomfortable in the superior role, as if this is inconsistent with their 'true' position in life (see Chapter 6). They also tend to rate themselves less highly than boys on written tests of self-esteem, set themselves lower goals in life and are more inclined to under-estimate their abilities than boys, even in primary school, where in reading and language skills they often tend to surpass boys.

However, Sears (1970), studying boys and girls, confirmed Coopersmith's results for boys—but not for girls; children with at least one warm and accepting parent had higher self-esteem than children with cold and unaccepting parents.

An interesting contrast with the parents of high-esteem boys in Coopersmith's and Sear's studies is the study of interaction between parents and their schizophrenic children. These parents tend to deny communicative support to the child, and often do not respond to the child's statements and demands for recognition of its opinions. When the parents do communicate with the child it is often in the form of an interruption or an intrusion, rather than a response to the child. In fact, they respond selectively to those of the child's utterances which they themselves have initiated rather than those initiated by the child. At the same time, interaction proceeds in a rather stereotyped way—making spontaneity almost impossible.

Laing (1971) suggests that these kinds of communication patterns within the family make the development of ego boundaries in the child very difficult, ie there is a confusion between self and not-self (me and not-me). This impaired autonomy of the self (or self-identity) and impaired appreciation of external reality are often found to be fundamental characteristics of schizophrenic adolescents and adults (see Chapter 30).

ii) *COMPARISON WITH OTHERS*

According to Bannister and Agnew (1976), the personal construct of 'self' is intrinsically *bipolar*, ie having a concept of self implies a concept of not-self. (This is similar to what Cooley and Mead say about self and society being unable to exist without each other—they are really two sides of the same coin.) So one way in which we come to form a picture of what we are like is to see how we compare with others.

Indeed, there are certain parts of our self-image which only take on any significance at all through comparison with others. For example, 'tall' and 'fat' are not absolute characteristics (like, say, 'blue-eyed'), and we are only tall or fat in comparison with others who are shorter or thinner than ourselves. This is true of many other characteristics, including intelligence.

Part of the reaction of parents and other adults to a child often takes the form of a comparison between the child and other siblings (or unrelated children). If the child is told repeatedly that she is 'less clever than your big sister', she will come to incorporate this as part of her self-image and will probably have lower self-esteem as a result. This could adversely affect her academic performance so that she does not achieve in line with her true ability. A child of above average intelligence who has grown up in the shadow of a brilliant brother or sister may be less successful academically than an average or even below average child who has not had to face these unfavourable comparisons.

Rosenburg (1965) studied large numbers of adolescents and found that those with the highest self-esteem tended to be of higher social class, to have done better at school and to have been leaders in their clubs, all of which represent the basis for a favourable comparison between self and others.

This seems to make sense in terms of our everyday experience. If we are trying to assess our ability or our improvement in some skill, we would normally, and most usefully, compare ourselves with others who are comparable, those who are 'in the same league' as ourselves(eg other A-level students rather than degree-level students). And, if we play tennis, although we may fantasize about being Wimbledon champion, a realistic comparison would be with others who belong to our tennis club or with players we compete against. Our ideal-self (as far as tennis is concerned) should then involve becoming a player who wins more matches than are lost or whose back-hand is reasonably good (when at present it is non-existent). Anything else (such as wanting to be best in the world) is likely to create the conditions for disappointment and low self-esteem.

iii) *SOCIAL ROLES*

As mentioned earlier when discussing the central core of the self-image, social roles are what people commonly regard as part of 'who they are'. Kuhn (1960) asked seven-year-olds and undergraduate students to give twenty different answers to the question, 'Who am I?'. The seven-year-olds gave an average of five answers relating to roles, while the undergraduates gave an average of ten.

Clearly, individuals incorporate more and more roles into their self-image as they grow up; and this is what we would expect since, as we get older we assume an increasing number and variety of roles. The pre-schooler is a son or daughter, perhaps a brother or sister, and has other familial roles, and may also be a friend to another child, but the number and range of roles are limited compared with the older child or adult. As we grow up and venture into the 'big wide world', our duties and responsibilities, as well as our choices, involve us in all kinds of roles and relationships with others (eg occupational roles, groups and organizations we belong to and so on). (Social Roles were discussed in some detail in Chapter 17.)

iv) IDENTIFICATION
We have already discussed this in relation to Freud's psychosexual stages of personality development and will return to it in Chapters 24 and 27.

DEVELOPMENTAL CHANGES IN THE SELF-CONCEPT
As we have said, at first the infant cannot differentiate between self and not-self and the self-concept (or sense of self) is something acquired gradually during childhood as the result of experience. But does this mean that the baby does not have any sense of self at all?

Maccoby (1980) maintains that babies do have ample basis for making a distinction between themselves and others on two counts: (i) their own fingers hurt when bitten (but they do not have any such sensations when they are biting their rattle or their mother's fingers); and (ii) probably quite early in life they begin to associate feelings from their own body movements with the sight of their own limbs and the sounds of their own cries. These sense impressions are bound together into a cluster that defines the bodily self so this is probably the first aspect of the self-concept to develop.

Other aspects of self-concept develop by degrees, but there do seem to be fairly clearly-defined stages of development. Young children may know their own names, understand the limits of their own bodies, and yet be unable to think about themselves as coherent entities—so self-awareness or self-consciousness develops very gradually. According to Piaget, an awareness of self comes through the gradual process of adaptation to the environment (see Chapter 25) As the child explores objects and accommodates to them (thus developing new sensorimotor schemas) it simultaneously discovers aspects of its self, for example, trying to put a large block into its mouth and finding that it will not fit is a lesson in self-hood as well as a lesson about the world of objects.

SELF-RECOGNITION
One way in which the development of bodily self has been studied is through self-recognition and this involves more than just a simple discrimination of bodily features. To determine that the person in a photograph, or a film, or the reflection in a mirror, is oneself, certain knowledge seems to be necessary. First, at least a rudimentary knowledge of oneself as continuous through time (necessary for recognizing ourselves in a photograph or movie) and space (necessary for recognizing ourselves in mirrors); and secondly, knowledge of particular features (what we look like).

This means that recognizing a visual representation of oneself presupposes at least some kind of knowledge of self. Although other kinds of self-recognition are possible (eg one's voice or feelings), only *visual self-recognition* has been studied extensively, both in animals and humans.

SELF-RECOGNITION IN NON-HUMAN SPECIES

Many animals (including fish, birds, chickens and monkeys) react to their mirror-images as if they were other animals, ie they do not seem to recognize it as their reflection at all. But self-recognition has been observed in the higher primates—chimpanzees and other great apes.

Gallup (1977), working with pre-adolescent, wild-born chimps, placed a full-length mirror on the wall of each animal's cage. At first they reacted as if another chimp had appeared—they threatened, vocalized or made conciliatory gestures; but this quickly faded out and by the end of three days had almost disappeared. They then used the image to explore themselves, eg they would pick up a piece of food and place it on their face, which could not be seen without the mirror.

After ten days exposure, each chimp was anaesthetized and a bright red spot was painted on the uppermost part of one eyebrow ridge and a second spot on the top of the opposite ear, using an odourless, non-irritating dye. When the chimp had recovered from the anaesthetic, it was returned to its cage, from which the mirror had been removed, and it was observed to see how often it touched the marked parts of its body. The mirror was then replaced and each chimp began to explore the marked spots 25 times more often than it had done before.

The procedure was repeated with chimps which had never seen themselves in the mirror and they reacted to the mirror-image as if it were another chimp (they did not touch the spots). So it seems that the first group had learned to recognize themselves, supporting Cooley's and Mead's theories which stress interaction with others and the reactions of others as crucial to the development of self-concept.

Lower primates (monkeys, gibbons and baboons) are unable to learn to recognize their mirror-image, whether they are raised in isolation or normally.

SELF-RECOGNITION IN HUMAN INFANTS

a) Mirrors

A number of researchers (Lewis and Brooks-Gunn, 1979) have used modified forms of Gallup's technique with 6–24-month-olds. The mother applies a dot of rouge to the child's nose (while pretending to wipe the baby's face) and the baby is observed to see how often it touches its nose. It is then placed in front of a mirror and again the number of times it touches its nose is recorded. At about 18 months, there is a significant change: touching the dot was never seen before 15 months; between 15 and 18 months, 5 to 25 per cent of infants touched it, while 75 per cent of the 18–20-month-old did.

In order to use the mirror-image to touch the dot on its nose, the baby must also have built up a schema of how its face should look in the mirror before it can notice the discrepancy created by the dot, and it seems this does not develop before about 18 months. This is also about the time when, according to Piaget, object permanence is completed, so object permanence would seem to be a necessary condition for the development of self-recognition (see Chapter 25).

b) *Photographs*

Self-recognition in photographs is usually confined to the face (even adults have trouble with their bodies, let alone infants and young children). Pre-verbal children's ability to recognize their faces is best inferred by comparing their response to photographs of themselves with their response to photographs of others (making the photographs as similar as possible).

Lewis and Brooks-Gunn (1979) studied 9–24-month-olds with 35 mm slides of themselves, same-sex peers and opposite-sex peers, with only the faces and shoulders showing. Under 24 months (and in some cases under 12 months), babies reacted differently to themselves (by, for example, smiling more). Some of the youngest differentiated between photos of themselves and those of opposite-sex infants but *not* between photos of themselves and infants of the same sex.

 ## SELF-DEFINITION

Piaget, Mead and many others have pointed to the importance of language in consolidating the early development of self-awareness by providing labels which permit distinctions between self and not-self ('I', 'you', 'me', 'it' and so on). These labels can, of course, then be used by the toddler to communicate notions of selfhood to others.

Before we look at the development of personal pronouns 'I' and 'you', it is worth mentioning a very important label which, at first, is applied by others to the child but which the child then uses to label itself and which is part of the central core of the self-image, ie the child's *name*. Names are not usually chosen arbitrarily—either the parents particularly like the name, or they want to name the child after a relative or famous person and so on; certainly, names are not neutral labels in terms of how people respond to them and what they associate with them. (We may, for example, be more or less favourably disposed to people by virtue of their name alone; see Chapter 17.)

Jahoda (1954) described the naming practices of the Ashanti tribe of West Africa. Children born on different days of the week are given names accordingly, because of the belief that they have different personalities. Police records showed that among juvenile delinquents, there was a very low percentage of boys born on Monday (believed to have a quiet and calm personality) but a very high rate of Wednesday-born boys (thought to be naturally aggressive).

This is an example of the *self-fulfilling prophecy*, whereby, on the basis of some label that is applied, people are treated in such a way that they actually develop the characteristics and behaviour which the label says they (should) have. It is reasonable to believe that these Ashanti boys were treated in a way consistent with the name given to them and that, as a result, they 'became' what their name indicated they were 'really' like. In English speaking countries, days of the week (eg Tuesday) and months of the year (April, May and June) are used as names and they have associations which may influence others' reactions. (For example, 'Monday's child is fair of face, Tuesday's child is full of grace . . .'.)

When children refer to themselves as 'I' (or 'me') and others as 'you', they are having to reverse the labels that are normally used to refer to them by others ('you','he', 'she'). Also, of course, they hear others refer to themselves as 'I' and not as 'you', 'he', 'she'. This is a problem of *shifting reference*.

But, despite this, most children do not invert 'I' and 'you' and this requires the child to decide on a working rule of usage, in order to solve the problem of shifting reference (Clark, 1976).

'I' sometimes refers to the child's mother, father or assorted others, and the child may use one of two hypotheses:

(i)   'I' means an adult who is speaking and 'you' means the child;
(ii) 'I' means whoever is speaking and 'you' whoever is spoken to.

Only the second takes into account the shifting reference. Some children adopt the first but then discard it after a few months.

It seems that some kind of rule must be involved since, if the child's use of pronouns were based on imitation of the speech it hears, it would almost certainly refer to itself as others do, namely 'you', 'he' or 'she'. Admittedly, most children do go through a stage of referring to themselves by their name but it seems that toddlers focus on the consistencies in speech and use 'you' and 'I' appropriately at a time when the tendency to imitate is still very strong.

An interesting observation is that autistic and blind children often use personal pronouns incorrectly, using 'I' for others and 'you' for self. (This may be associated with the abnormal interactions and relationships that these children experience which, in turn, would further support Cooley and Mead.)

THE PSYCHOLOGICAL SELF

Maccoby (1980) has asked what exactly children mean when they refer to themselves as 'I' or 'me'. Are they referring to anything more than a physical entity enclosed by an envelope of skin?

Flavell (1978) investigated development of the psychological self in $2\frac{1}{2}$- to 5-year-olds. In one study, he placed a doll on the table in front of the child and explained that dolls are like people in some ways—arms, legs, hands and so on (pointing as he did so). Then the child was asked how dolls are different from people, whether they know their names and think about things, etc. Most children said a doll does not know its name and cannot think about things, but people can. They were then asked, 'Where is the part of you that knows your name and thinks about things?' and 'Where do you do your thinking and knowing?'. Fourteen out of twenty-two children gave fairly clear localization for the thinking self, namely, 'in their heads', while others found it very difficult. The experimenters then looked directly into the child's eyes and asked, 'Can I see you thinking in there?'. Most children thought not.

These answers suggest that by $3\frac{1}{2}$ to 4 years, children have a rudimentary concept of a private, thinking self that is not visible even to someone looking directly into their eyes; they can distinguish this from the bodily self which they know is visible to others (see Chapter 25 on Egocentrism).

THE CATEGORICAL SELF

We have already noted that age and gender are parts of the central core of the self-image; they represent two of the *categories* regarding the self which are also used to perceive and interpret the behaviour of others.

Age is probably the first social category to be acquired by the child (and is so even before a concept of number develops). Perceptual factors like facial, vocal and size changes, language usage, dress and body movements, make age a fairly obvious way of categorizing and classifying people (and hence of discriminating between them). Social factors related to age (eg status, control, roles) may also be perceived by the young child.

Lewis and Brooks-Gunn (1979) found that 6- to 12-month olds can distinguish between photographs, slides and papier-maché heads of adults and babies. By 12 months, they prefer interacting with strange babies to strange adults. Also, as soon as they have acquired labels like 'mummy' and 'daddy' and 'baby', they almost never make age-related mistakes.

Before the age of seven, children tend to define the self in physical terms—hair colour, height, favourite activities—while inner, psychological, experiences and characteristics are not described as being distinct from overt behaviour and external, physical characteristics. During middle childhood, descriptions shift gradually to more abstract descriptions of facts and from 'physicalistic' to psychological.

ADOLESCENCE AND THE SELF-CONCEPT

Body-image

Just as the bodily self is the first aspect of the self-concept that emerges in the baby, so the bodily-self undergoes a dramatic change with the onset of puberty, which marks the beginning of adolescence.

Prior to the onset of puberty, most children have felt very much at home in their bodies and have been relatively unaware of their bodies as such; they have been more concerned with what their bodies can *do* (or what they can do with the help of their bodies) than what their bodies are like.

But the growth spurt of puberty, together with the dramatic changes in the shape and appearance of the body, plus the new sexual feelings and other sensations that accompany these changes, put an end to all that! Inevitably, it seems, the adolescent has a much stronger and more clearly defined body-image.

Arnoff and Damianopoulos (1962) showed that 20-year-olds, just beyond adolescence, had a more definite body-image than 40-year-olds. They were all shown a set of six photographs of men dressed only in shorts and with faces blacked out, one of which was themselves; the younger subjects were better at recognizing their own photograph than the older subjects. (When you think of how much time adolescents spend admiring and examining themselves in front of the mirror, these findings do not seem very surprising. But we should also be aware of important individual differences which cut across age differences.)

Jersild (1952) found that when adolescents were asked what they did not like about themselves, very few mentioned their abilities but about 60 per cent referred to some aspect of their physical appearance, especially facial defects like skin problems.

The time at which the adolescent growth spurt occurs may have an important effect on the adolescent's self-concept, especially self-esteem. Physical growth can be a source of great anxiety; is it too fast or too slow, too little or too much, etc.? The rate of physical development often becomes an important basis for adolescents making comparisons between themselves and other adolescents.

The behavioural and emotional effects of early and late maturation on the self-concept seem to be different for boys and girls. Jones and Bayley (1950) picked the most advanced and retarded 14- to 18-year-old boys and studied their personalities and how adults and peers reacted to them. Early maturers were usually seen as more attractive, less childish and less talkative than the late maturers, they showed more interest in girls at 15 and were more likely to be popular and hold positions of responsibility; the later maturers were more childish and attention-seeking. At 17, the early maturers were still more self-confident and less dependent; the later maturers had very strong desires for contact with girls and were more aggressive.

Eichorn (1963) followed up these adolescents when they were 33. The late maturers were more likely to seek aid and encouragement from others, were more impulsive and touchy but showed more insight into the problems of others.

Weatherley (1964) found that boys who developed at an average age were very similar to those who matured early, and both groups differed from the late maturers, who scored significantly lower in self-esteem. This suggests that it is only late maturation that causes difficulties (while early maturation does not necessarily confer any advantage).

In the case of girls, the effects of rate of maturation, whether early or late, seem to be much less marked than with boys. Mussen and Jones (1957) compared early and late maturing 17-year-old girls in terms of self-concept, motivation and interpersonal attitudes. Early maturers had more favourable self-concepts and less dependency needs than the late maturers, but the differences were far less clear-cut than for boys. However, an interesting finding reported by Argyle (1973) is that girls who are taller than average at 13 still see themselves as tall later in life, even though they are only average by the time they have stopped growing.

The gender differences may be accounted for by the fact that females in our culture are expected to make themselves look attractive and are judged according to how they look; they can 'manipulate' their appearance in various ways (eg make-up). Males, on the other hand, are expected to be strong and to perform athletic and other physical feats and it is much more difficult to manipulate these. Their appearance is relatively less important than for females and it is generally more difficult for males in our culture to alter their appearance. A number of studies all show that a large or strong stature is a central part of the male's ideal bodily self. (This does not necessarily indicate what females regard as an ideal male physique!)

Females are generally more sensitive to obesity in others and they take more notice of this in themselves, expressing more concern over body shape and wanting to lose weight more often than males. It seems highly probable that we learn what kind of a body we 'should' have and then judge our bodily-self in terms of these cultural ideal-types. The advertising media is largely responsible for presenting particular ideal face and body types and, in the main, these have been aimed at females.

Support for this view comes from a study by Garner et al (1980) who found a trend towards thinner female figures since 1970 both in magazine dieting articles and in other media. Furnham and Alibhai (1983) believe that Western ideals of physique play a large part in the greater self-consciousness of girls regarding overweight. They found that predominantly slim and borderline anorexic shapes were often rated as highly attractive, and desirable personality traits were more often associated with slim as opposed to obese figures.

Davies and Furnham (1986), in a study of 182 11- to 18-year-olds, reported that, although comparatively few at any age were actually overweight, nearly half in each age group wished to lose weight—and considerably fewer wished to put on weight. Dissatisfaction with their weight was also found to increase with age and this was particularly marked between 14 and 16. Further, the numbers wishing to lose weight (at all ages) far exceeded the numbers classifying themselves as overweight, which seems to represent very powerful evidence of the influence of cultural pressures. Indeed, Davies and Furnham noted a trend towards exercising as against dieting as a way of losing weight, reflecting the recent 'aerobics revolution'.

ANOREXIA NERVOSA

The pressure to conform to ideal bodily types may partly account for the illness *anorexia nervosa* (literally, 'nervous lack of appetite'), which is suffered mainly by 16- to 19-year-old girls. One study of nine secondary schools in London (Crisp et al, 1976) found that one out of every 100 16- to 18-year-olds had anorexia.

However, according to Richards (1982), the number of young people diagnosed as having anorexia has doubled in each decade over the last 30 years.

Anorexia is commonly understood to be a steady loss of weight, associated with dieting, which, if untreated, will be fatal. But what exactly is it and what causes it?

One long-held theory is that it is a rejection of womanhood and that adolescent girls use it as a way of warding off maturity, of preventing bust growth, menstruation and, thereby, conception. But this is arguable—are all girls aware that their periods will stop when they practice self-starvation? And how long is it before they realize that the bust is less affected by weight loss than other parts of the body?

It is true that women are more prone than men to being teased about puppy fat and obesity and are more likely to be advised or pressurized to diet. One Australian study did, indeed, find these to be among the stresses which precede anorexia.

Dieting itself is not the cause of anorexia but it can act as a trigger. Many may start by wanting to lose a few pounds but carry on if the results are rewarding—an upper limit may then be set and movement towards this causes great distress and guilt. Self-starvation becomes very satisfying and all the girl's energy is channelled into losing weight so that everything else loses its meaning. Another stress that can lead to anorexia is parental pressure to do well at school or university. Significantly, anorexia is highest in the private sector of education and the fathers of anorexics are usually in professional or managerial jobs. Many anorexic girls are often very intelligent and feel that their identity is linked with achievement. When they go to university or college, they might find themselves to be 'a small fish in a big pool' and they have to face greater competition and experience greater stress as a result.

The onset of anorexia may also be a reaction to pressures at home, such as hostility towards one or both parents, a change or disruption in family relationships or a history of psychiatric illness in the family.

Certainly, what all anorexics seem to have in common is a distorted body-image, a belief that they look and are greatly overweight, when, in fact, they are severely underweight. They are also particularly vulnerable to ordinary life events, have rather obsessive personalities and tend to avoid situations they fear. They have low self-esteem and seem incapable or afraid of managing their own lives as an adult—it is easier to remain a child and they both want and fear autonomy.

Some anorexics cannot control their desperate need to eat and find a solution in starving, then going on a binge of eating and then, finally, making themselves vomit. (This is known as 'secondary anorexia' or *bulimia*.)

Figure 21.3 *Erik Erikson (born 1902). (Olive Pierce: Black Star)*

ERIKSON'S PSYCHOSOCIAL THEORY OF DEVELOPMENT

Apart from representing a significant contribution to psychological theory in its own right, Erikson's theory represents an important way of assessing Freud's theory and putting it into perspective.

Born in Germany in 1902 to Danish parents, Erikson (Fig. 21.3) trained as a Montessori teacher and took a teaching post in Vienna in 1927, where he undertook psychoanalytic training with Anna Freud, Sigmund Freud's daughter. She was much more interested in child analysis than her father had been and this influenced Erikson. He fled from the Nazis in 1933 and went to the USA, setting up private practice as a child analyst in Boston, where he came into contact with such famous anthropologists as Ruth Benedict and Margaret Mead, whose discipline was to have such an impact on his theory.

SIMILARITIES BETWEEN ERIKSON AND FREUD

(a) Erikson accepted Freud's tripartite theory of the structure of personality (id, ego and superego).
(b) He accepted Freud's three levels of consciousness (conscious, preconscious and unconscious; see Chapter 29).
(c) He accepted Freud's psychosexual stages as basically valid—as far as they went (but he thought that, as they stood, they did not go far enough).

DIFFERENCES BETWEEN ERIKSON AND FREUD

(a) Erikson saw development as proceeding throughout the life-cycle, with Freud's last stage—the genital—constituting the pre-adult (adolescent) stage, and a subsequent three stages spanning adulthood (early, middle and late). (His *Eight Ages of Man* were first proposed in 1950.)

(b) He believed (as did many other neo-Freudians) that Freud under-emphasized the role of socialization of the individual, particularly the various patterns of behaviour which different cultures consider desirable and which individuals need to adopt in order to be accepted by their cultural or sub-cultural group.

(c) Erikson believes that the interaction between the individual and the social environment produces eight *psychosocial stages* (as opposed to Freud's psycho*sexual* stages), each of which centres around a developmental *crisis*, involving a struggle between two opposing or conflicting personality characteristics.

(d) Erikson was much more concerned than was Freud with *mental health*. This is reflected in his concept of *ego identity* which is achieved by resolving the specified psychological crisis at each developmental stage.

(e) Erikson is an *ego* psychologist (whereas Freud is an *id* psychologist), believing, for example, that conflict *within* the ego itself (as against conflict between the ego and the id or superego) could produce emotional disturbance and this, in turn, is related to his greater emphasis on social and cultural factors. Indeed, the individual (psychological) aspect of each developmental stage is inseparable from the social and cultural—they are opposite sides of the same coin. At each stage, a new dimension of 'social interaction' becomes possible, and this denotes the person's interaction both with the self and the social environment.

However, Erikson agreed with Freud that there is a biological basis to development—the sequence of stages is genetically determined and so is universal, the same for members of all cultures. Yet even here there is a crucial difference between the two theories: whereas for Freud, the baby begins life as a 'bundle of id' and only gradually becomes socialized, acquiring in turn an ego and superego, for Erikson, the human being is at *all times* an organism (id), an ego and a member of society (superego) and the individual must be biologically, psychologically and socially *ready* to move from one stage to the next. This, in turn, is matched by society's readiness. Although the order of stages is biologically based, the stages constitute the *ego's* timetable and mirror the structure of the relevant social institutions; in this sense, individuals and society are interdependent.

Erikson's belief in the fixed, pre-determined sequence of the stages is expressed in his *epigenetic principle*, based on embryology, which maintains that the entire pattern of development is governed by a genetic structure common to all humans, whereby the genes dictate a timetable for the growth of each part of the unborn baby. (This biological principle can be seen in post-natal development too, for example, crawling, walking and puberty.)

Erikson extended this principle to social and psychological growth and proposed that personality seems to develop according to steps:

> ... predetermined in the human organism's readiness to be driven toward, to be aware of, and to interact with, a widening radius of significant individuals and institutions. (Erikson, 1968)

So Erikson believed that it is human nature to pass through a pre-determined sequence of psychosocial stages which are genetically determined. However, the social–cultural environment has a significant influence on the psychosocial modalities (dominant modes of acting and being), 'the radius of significant individuals and institutions' with which the individual interacts, *and* the nature of the crisis which arises at each stage (Table 21.3).

Erikson's theory of play is outlined in Box 21.4.

Box 21.4   Erikson's Theory of Play

The great emphasis given to play by psychotherapists is based on their recognition that young children are limited in their ability to communicate their problems in the way adults may. So in therapy, play situations are opportunities for the child to *externalize* its problems, work them through and come to terms with them; they are also, of course, opportunities for the therapist to observe and understand those problems.

Play deals with life experiences which the child attempts to repeat, master or negate in order to organize its inner world in relation to the outer one. It also involves self-teaching and self-healing:

> The child uses play to make up for defeats, sufferings and frustrations, especially those resulting from a technically and culturally limited use of language. (Erikson, 1950)

'Playing it out' becomes the child's means of reasoning and allows the child to free itself from the ego boundaries of time, space and reality but maintain a reality orientation because it and others know it is 'just play'.

Play, too, is an important form of self-expression for the ego and helps the child towards new mastery and new developmental stages. For example, play provides a safe island where the child can develop a sense of autonomy within its own boundaries or laws. Doubt and shame can be conquered here:

> The small world of manageable toys is a harbour which the child establishes to return to when he needs to overhaul his ego. (Erikson, 1950)

But just as Freud defined sexuality in a very broad way, so Erikson defined play very broadly. In *Toys and Reasons* (1977) he makes it clear that play is not limited to childhood but is pursued throughout the life-cycle. Play is not simply what we do when we are not working, not just a non-serious pastime or diversion but rather is often an attempt by the individual to resolve the psychosocial crisis he/she is currently experiencing. So, for Erikson, the child is playing when it builds a structure with bricks or when it acts out the family drama with dolls and the physicist, too, is playing when putting forward a model of the universe.

Play also has a crucial social quality or dimension: it cannot help us resolve our psychosocial crises unless we can try out possible solutions on others and see how they respond.

Erikson believes that anatomical differences contribute to personality differences between males and females. The 'inner space' or a woman's ability to bear children is a pervasive force in female gender identity. His position is based on observations of the miniature play constructions of boys and girls from 10 to 12 years. Typically, girls construct an interior scene, while boys construct an exterior scene with elaborate walls of facades and protrusions or high towers (contrast the internal and external sex organs of females and males respectively).

Table 21.3 *Comparison between Erikson's and Freud's stages of development. (Based on Thomas, 1985/Erikson, 1959)*

NUMBER OF STAGE	NAME OF STAGE (PSYCHO-SOCIAL CRISIS)	PSYCHO SOCIAL MOD-ALITIES (DOMINANT MODES OF BEING AND ACTING)	RADIUS OF SIGNIFICANT RELATION-SHIPS	HUMAN VIRTUES ('QUALITIES OF STRENGTH')	FREUD'S PSYCHO-SEXUAL STAGES	APPROXI-MATE AGES
1	Basic trust versus Basic mistrust	To get, To give in return	Mother or mother-figure	Hope	Oral-Respiratory Sensory-Kinaesthetic	0–1
2	Autonomy versus Shame and doubt	To hold on, To let go	Parents	Willpower	Anal-Urethral Muscular	1–3
3	Initiative versus Guilt	To make (going after), To 'make like' (playing)	Basic family	Purpose	Phallic Locomotor	3–6
4	Industry versus Inferiority	To make things (completing), To make things together	Neighbourhood and school	Competence	Latency	7–12
5	Identity versus Role confusion	To be oneself (or not to be), To share being oneself	Peer groups and outgroups, models of leadership	Fidelity	Genital	12–18
6	Intimacy versus Isolation	To lose and find oneself in another	Partners in friendship, sex, competition, co-operation	Love		20s
7	Generativity versus Stagnation	To make be, To take care of	Divided labour and Shared houschold	Care		Late 20s–50s
8	Ego integrity versus Despair	To be, through having been, To face not being	'Humankind', 'my kind'	Wisdom		50s and beyond

ERIKSON'S PSYCHOSOCIAL STAGES

As we have said, at each stage a conflict arises which centres around two possible and opposing outcomes of the attempt to resolve the problems inherent in that stage. Each stage is named by reference to these two opposite outcomes, the first referring to the positive or functional (adaptive) outcome, eg trust, and the second referring to the negative or dysfunctional (maladaptive) outcome, eg mistrust.

However, it is important to stress that these are extremes and it is not an either/or situation but rather every personality represents some mixture of trust and mistrust (and similarly for the other seven stages). Trust and mistrust, etc. are relative terms and healthy development involves trust outweighing mistrust, etc.

Although the optimum time for developing a sense of trust is during infancy, Erikson believes it is possible to make up for unsatisfactory early experiences at a later stage, although it becomes increasingly difficult to do so. Conversely, a sense of trust developed during infancy could be shattered or at least shaken if later deprivation is experienced. Either way, Erikson presents a much less deterministic view than Freud: the issue of trust–mistrust is not resolved once and for all during the first year but recurs at each successive stage of development, so there are 'second chances' as well as the danger of positive early outcomes turning out badly later on.

BASIC TRUST VERSUS BASIC MISTRUST (0–1)

The quality of care the baby receives determines how it comes to view its mother and other people in particular and the world in general (see Chapter 22)—is it a safe, predictable, comfortable place to be or is it full of hazards? This is linked to the infant's sense of its ability to influence what happens to it and hence to its trust in itself. If the infant's needs are met as they arise and its discomforts quickly removed, if it is cuddled and fondled, played with and talked to, it develops a sense of the world as a safe place to be and of people as helpful and dependable. However, if its care is inconsistent, it develops a sense of mistrust, fear and suspicion, which reveal themselves as apathetic or withdrawn behaviour, a sense of being controlled rather than being able to control. A sense of trust allows the baby to accept new experiences and fear of the unknown is accepted as part and parcel of having new experiences.

AUTONOMY VERSUS SHAME AND DOUBT (1–3)

The child's cognitive and muscle systems are maturing and it is becoming more mobile so that its range of experience and choices is expanding. The child is beginning to think of itself as a person in its own right, separate from the parents, and this new sense of power is the basis for its growing sense of autonomy and independence. The child wants to do everything itself and parents have to allow it to exercise these new abilities while simultaneously ensuring that the child does not 'bite off more than it can chew'—repeated failures and ridicule from others can lead to a sense of shame and doubt. The child must be allowed to do things at its own pace and in its own time; parents should not impatiently do things for it 'to save time' or criticize the child for its failures and the inevitable accidents. These 'accidents', and the whole conflict between autonomy and shame and doubt, may have become focused on toilet-training. If this is too strict or starts too early, the child may be faced with a 'double rebellion and a double defeat', feeling powerless to control its bowels and its parents' actions. This may result in regression to oral activities (eg thumb-sucking), attention-seeking or a pretence at having become autonomous by rejecting the help of others and becoming very strong-willed. But firm and considerate training helps the child to develop a sense of 'self-control without a loss of self-esteem'.

INITIATIVE VERSUS GUILT (3–5/6)

The child's development proceeds at a rapid pace, physically, intellectually and socially, and the child is keen to try out its developing abilities and skills to achieve all sorts of new goals. If the child is encouraged to ask questions and in other ways express its natural curiosity, and is given the freedom to run and jump, ride a bike and to indulge in fantasy and other kinds of play, its sense of initiative will be reinforced. However, if parents tend to find the child's questions embarrassing, difficult intellectually or a nuisance, its motor activity dangerous and its fantasy play silly, then the child may come to feel guilty about intruding into others' lives and activities, which may inhibit its initiative and curiosity.

This guilt can be exaggerated by the Oedipus complex, but whereas for Freud this is the central feature of this stage, for Erikson it is but one feature of a much wider theme.

INDUSTRY VERSUS INFERIORITY (7–12 OR SO)

Industry refers to the child's concern with how things work, how they are made and their own efforts to make things. This is reinforced when the child is encouraged by adults, who now are no longer confined to the parents. Teachers begin to assume a very real significance in the child's life and society requires them to help the child to develop all sorts of new skills valued by society. The peer group also assumes increasing importance relative to that of adults and is a major source of self-esteem; children begin to compare themselves with other children as a way of assessing their own achievements.

Self-esteem and the esteem of others stem largely from the successful completion of realistic tasks, being allowed to make things and being given the necessary guidance and encouragement by adults. A child may have potential abilities which, if not nurtured during this period, may 'develop late or never'.

IDENTITY VERSUS ROLE CONFUSION (12–18)

Throughout life the individual has to try to maintain a balance between the constant (or invariant) and the changing (or variant) aspects of the self. But across the life-span there are periods when the self-concept undergoes quite dramatic and extensive change, for example, during toddlerhood or the 'terrible twos' (1½ to 3 years), when starting school (4 to 5) and adolescence (starting with puberty), and at these times the balance is much more difficult to maintain.

Recall that at all stages, Erikson believes that the individual exists and develops on three planes and levels simultaneously: (i) the biological (organism); (ii) the social (member of society); and (iii) the psychological (individual).

1) We have already looked at how the *body image* changes in adolescence but a few of Erikson's observations are worth noting. He says that the rapid body growth disturbs the previous trust in the body and mastery of its functions that were enjoyed in childhood. So adolescents have to learn to 'grow into' their new body, but for a long time it will not feel comfortable and will not seem to 'fit' properly.

Sexual maturity implies the need for other people to fulfil new sexual needs and feelings. Masturbation is very common, especially among boys, in early adolescence, and is often accompanied by sexual fantasy, but it can never be totally fulfilling.

The social and psychological counterpart of this is having to decide on a sexual identity, that is, deciding about one's sexual preference or orientation, whether to be heterosexual or homosexual.

2) At the *social* level, Western culture has invented adolescence as a *moratorium*, an authorized delay of adulthood (in the form of extended formal education, certain laws relating to marriage, voting and so on) which is aimed at helping the young person to make the difficult transition from childhood to adulthood.

Yet it often creates confusion and conflict at the same time as it reduces them. For example, social and biological abilities and status may not be compatible, as in the case of the 'gym-slip mother' or the teenager who is married and still at school. Teenagers are expected to make decisions about their future (by parents and teachers) but are not allowed to vote and generally they are being kept dependent on adults, while being expected to behave like adults, in an independent and responsible way.

If adolescents make their choices too early (what Erikson calls a 'premature foreclosure' of the moratorium), this may be regretted and they are especially vulnerable to identity confusion in later life. Catholic confirmation and the Jewish bar-mitzvah may limit young people, forcing them into a narrow, negative, identity.

Marcia (1966, 1968, 1970), inspired by Erikson and based on his own research, identified four states of adolescent identity formation. The two essential factors in the attainment of a mature identity are: (i) the individual must experience several *crises* in choosing among life's alternatives; and (ii) they must finally arrive at a *commitment*, an investment of the self in those choices.

The four states or statuses are:

(a) *Identity diffusion*. The person is in crisis and is unable to formulate clear self-definition, goals and commitments; it represents an inability to 'take hold' of some kind of adult identity.
(b) *Identity foreclosure*. The person has avoided the uncertainties and anxieties of crisis by rapidly committing him/herself to safe and conventional goals without exploring the many options open to the self.
(c) *Identity moratorium*. Decisions about identity are postponed while the person tries out alternative identities without being committed to any particular one.
(d) *Identity achievement*. The person has experienced a crisis but has emerged successfully with firm commitments, goals and ideology.

Unlike Erikson's eight stages, these four states of identity are not sequential (they are not stages), with the exception that identity moratorium is a prerequisite for identity achievement.

Traditionally, the 'world of work' and the 'adult' world have been virtually synonymous and this is what most young people aim at, either through gaining relevant qualifications or by wanting to leave school at the earliest opportunity in order to assume adult status and to earn money and become self-supporting. With unemployment at the level it is, the purpose of schooling and young peoples' expectations regarding their entry into the adult world must be much more blurred than ever before (see below).

Quite clearly, there is no well-defined initiation into adulthood in our culture as there is in many non-Western cultures where, at a certain age, ritualized puberty rites or initiation ceremonies take place, marking the end of childhood and the start of adulthood. In these other cultures, adolescence, as such, does not exist, and while puberty is a biological fact, adolescence is very much a socially constructed phenomenon.

3) At the *psychological* level, the adolescent re-experiences the conflicts of early childhood, particularly the early encounter with parents as authority figures (focused around toilet training) and the Oedipus complex.

Related to this are the typical adolescent mood swings and *ambivalence*, whereby they are sometimes very co-operative with parents and other adults and at other times 'dig in their heels' and disobey, almost for the sake of it (this ambivalence is also typical of the 3-year-old). This is very difficult for parents to cope with, especially when they need to remain stable, firm and predictable for the sake of their adolescents.

As we shall see when discussing Piaget in Chapter 25, adolescents, having obtained formal operational thought, can think in abstract and hypothetical terms about what might be (and not just about what does exist), about other people's thinking and, particularly, what others think about them. They can conceive of ideal families, religions and societies, which can then be compared with what they have themselves experienced. They can also construct theories and philosophies designed to bring all the varied and conflicting aspects of society into a working, harmonious and peaceful whole. To quote David Elkind (1970), the adolescent is, 'an impatient idealist, who believes that it is as easy to realize an ideal as it is to imagine it'.

Elkind also draws a very significant and intriguing parallel between the child and the adolescent in terms of egocentrism: even though adolescents are cognitively able to understand that their view of things is not the only possible view of things:

> Since he fails to differentiate between what others are thinking about and his own mental preoccupations ... he assumes that other people are as obsessed with his behaviour and appearance as he is himself. It is this belief that others are preoccupied with his appearance and behaviour that constitutes the egocentrism of the adolescent. (Elkind, 1967)

Piaget and Inhelder (1958) make similar comments. Elkind goes on to say that adolescents are forever playing to (imaginary) audiences, think they are special, have a sense of immortality and 'personal fable', a story which they tell themselves but which is not true.

The major developmental task of adolescence is to develop a sense of identity, ie to bring together all the things we have learned about ourselves as a son/daughter, brother/sister, friend, student and so on, plus all our past experiences, thoughts and feelings, to integrate these different and varied images of ourselves into a whole which makes sense and which has continuity with the past while preparing for the future. If young people are successful, they will emerge from this developmental stage with a sense of psychosocial identity (the positive component), a sense of who they are, where they have been and where they are going.

The influence of parents is much more *indirect* than it has been in previous stages; it is more a question of how they influenced earlier stages (trust versus mistrust, initiative versus guilt, industry versus initiative), rather than how they directly influence the search for identity. So, the more positive the outcome of the earlier stages, the more likely it is that the adolescent will achieve an integrated psychosocial identity.

David Elkind (1970) points out that this will also depend on the social milieu in which the adolescent grows up. For example, in a society where women are second-class citizens, it may be more difficult for females to arrive at a sense of psychosocial identity. Likewise, at times of rapid social and technological change, such as the present, where there is a breakdown of many traditional values, it may be more difficult for young people to find continuity between what they learned and experienced as children and what they learn and experience as adolescents. This may lead them to seek causes (political, religious, humanistic) which give meaning and direction to their lives.

Typically, the adolescent will experiment with several different identities which may involve taking very extreme views on certain issues: whereas children merely play at social roles, the adolescent actually tries them out.

Identity confusion (or diffusion) has four major components:

(a) *Intimacy*. Fear of commitment to, or involvement in, close relationships out of fear of losing one's own identity. This can result in stereotyped, formalized relationships, isolation, or the young person may, '... in repeated hectic attempts and dismal failures, seek intimacy with the most improbable partners' (Erikson, 1968).

(b) *Time-perspective*. Inability to plan for the future or retain any sense of time, associated with anxieties about change and becoming an adult and often, '... consists of decided disbelief in the possibility that time may bring change and yet also of a violent fear that it might' (Erikson, 1968).

(c) *Industry*. Difficulty in channelling resources in a realistic way in work or study, both of which require commitment. As a defence the adolescent may find it impossible to concentrate or become frenetically engaged in a single activity to the exclusion of all others.

(d) *Negative identity*. Not knowing what you are, where you belong or to whom you belong. A negative identity (eg delinquent, punk), although clearly the exact opposite of what parents and other important adults would approve of, is *not* an act of rebellion but a way of achieving *an* identity—a negative identity may be better than having no identity at all.

Whatever the final outcome of this stage Erikson believes that some form of stress or turmoil or disturbance of identity is inevitable (the *normative crisis* or *identity crisis*). He says, 'at no other phase of the life-cycle are the pressures of finding oneself and the threat of losing oneself so closely allied'.

Failure to establish a clear sense of personal identity at adolescence does not necessarily mean perpetual failure; equally, the person who attains a greater sense of identity than role confusion will inevitably encounter challenges and threats to that identity as they move through life.

Erikson stresses that life is constant change and that confronting problems at one stage of life is no guarantee against the re-appearance of these problems at later stages, or against the finding of new solutions to them. As far as a sense of identity is concerned, the optimum time to achieve it is during adolescence. To have a sense of self-identity is to have a 'feeling of being at home in one's body, a sense of knowing where one is going and an inner assurance of anticipated recognition from those who count'.

WORK AS A SOURCE OF IDENTITY

Given that definitions of adolescence emphasize the part played by work in marking the end of adolescence and the achievement of an adult identity, it is important to consider the influence on identify formation of the inability to find work—or the loss of a job for those who have been working. Although the importance of leisure time has been growing in the last few decades, Erikson (1968) believes that the jobs people choose still play a major role in their representation of themselves to society.

According to Kelvin (1981), if work is crucial to an individual's self-concept, it will also be crucial to their relationships with others. In introducing the subject of psychology at the beginning of Chapter 1, I suggested a scenario in which two people meet at a party and one asks the other 'What do you do?'. People normally understand that this means 'what job do you do?', and the reason why this is often one of the first bits of information we try to obtain about another is that it is highly illuminating. According to Brown (1978), a person's work (or the fact that they do not or cannot work) tells us so much else about their social situation and likely life experiences:

> An occupation is a socially recognized set of work activities ... it, therefore, implies ... a place in the social division of labour. (Brown, 1978)

Garraty (1978) maintains that to be unemployed places a person outside the accepted, taken-for-granted, system and sets them apart from those who are in work. Kelvin (1981) argues that the unemployed generally withdraw from much of their previous network of wider social activities, partly for financial reasons but also partly because of a subjective sense of inadequacy, a feeling, 'that one is not quite a full member of society in which social life takes place'. The outcome is 'retreatism' (Merton, 1968). In losing our job, we lose much of our social identity (Kelvin, 1981).

Erikson claims that a state of acute identity confusion usually manifests itself at a time when the young person is faced with a combination of experiences which demand simultaneous commitment, including occupational choice. If such a choice is denied the school-leaver, the opportunity to engage in other activities vital to the development of a sense of personal identity may be denied as well. Failure to achieve identity may prevent the development of intimacy (along with work, the other major criterion of adulthood).

According to Hill (1977), one of the main problems for the young person out of work might be that unemployment extends the period of stay at home and increases dependence on parents at a time when the main psychosocial task is to achieve independence. For many young people, therefore, unemployment may represent an enforced and prolonged moratorium. What are the psychological consequences?

In a survey of 15-year-olds, Porteous (1979) found that not being able to find a job was one of the main concerns of this age-group. Other studies have reported a significant association between economic conditions and psychological well-being, and unemployment is related to both depressed mood and stressful life events.

Jahoda (1979) believes that a change of economic status is not the only consequence of unemployment; a loss of *structured* activity, social contacts and a sense of identity and purpose are also suffered. Indeed, the young school-leaver is unlikely to experience a significant change of economic status at all (if anything they will be better off by becoming eligible for social security benefits) and yet their distress may be as great as that of any adult faced with redundancy.

This lack of structure, etc. is, according to Kelvin (1981), a problem of 'not being in work' (as opposed to being unemployed as such) and its ill-effects are also found amongst the retired (see Chapter 24). Leisure activities are usually no substitute for the *interdependence*, on a continuing basis, which is the essence of most work relationships (Kelvin, 1981).

Stafford et al (1980) studied school leavers in the north of England and found that those who did not find work showed higher levels of minor psychiatric problems. Similar results were found by Banks and Jackson (1982). Youngsters were studied while still at school and after leaving and finding (or not finding) work and, while there were no significant differences between them prior to leaving school:

> ... the experience of unemployment (is) more likely to create increased symptoms rather than the other way round. (Banks and Jackson, 1982)

Donovan et al (1985) compared 800 15-year-olds while still at school and then again six to eight months after leaving school. Of the 131 who were studied on the later occasion, 45 were employed, 43 were unemployed and 43 were participating in a government training scheme. Based on a general health questionnaire and measures of anxiety and depression, present life satisfaction, self-esteem and self-adjustment, the unemployed were found to show the greatest number of psychological symptoms, to have the lowest degree of satisfaction with their lives and to experience poorer family and social relationships, and these differences held good after allowance was made for individual differences, gender, socio-economic status and educational attainment.

EVALUATION OF ERIKSON'S THEORY

As we saw earlier, Erikson has emphasized the healthy personality in contrast to Freud, who stressed conflict and the neurotic personality. This difference stems largely from the importance of the ego and id in their respective theories. For Erikson, 'growing up' is a process of achieving Ego Identity which comprises: (i) an *inner focused* aspect; and (ii) an *outer-focused* aspect. The former is the individual's recognition of his/her own unified, 'self-sameness and continuity in time' (Erikson, 1959), knowing and accepting oneself; while the latter is the individual's recognition of, and identity with, the ideals and essential pattern of the culture and includes sharing 'some kind of essential character with others' (Erikson, 1968).

A healthy mature person combines individual happiness and responsible citizenship. This is similar to Adler's belief in the need for a suitable adjustment to be made in the areas of love, work and society, and Freud's 'Lieben und Arbeiten' (love and work). Again, a healthy person actively masters the environment, shows a unity of personality and is able to perceive the world and self correctly—the newborn displays none of these, the healthiest adult displays them all (Erikson, 1968).

In 1964, Erikson expanded his basic, 1959, picture of positive ego development by describing a set of *human virtues* or *qualities of strength*, meant to express an integration of psychosexual and psychosocial growth schedules. As can be seen from Table 21.3 (p. 627), they are based on the positive outcomes of each of the eight stages of psychological development.

The criticisms made of Freud's methods of study and his biased and and limited samples (see Chapter 29) cannot be made so easily against Erikson; he did not confine his studies to small numbers of neurotic adults from one particular culture but included much larger numbers of both disturbed and healthy individuals of all ages from a variety of cultures. Erikson was a psychoanalyst and teacher in Europe, a child analyst in Boston, he studied normal adolescents in California and spent time living among the Sioux Indians of South Dakota and the Yurok Indians of Northern California.

It was while working with the Indians that Erikson began to notice syndromes which he could not explain within the terms of Freudian theory. Central to many of the Indians' emotional problems was their sense of being uprooted and a lack of continuity between their present lifestyle and the one portrayed in the tribal history. This sense of a break with the past, and an inability to identify with a future requiring assimilation of white cultural values, is an *ego-related* and *culture-related* conflict and has little to do with sexual drives.

These impressions were reinforced during the Second World War when Erikson worked at a war-veterans' rehabilitation centre. He saw many soldiers who did not seem to fit the traditional 'shell shock' or 'malingerer' cases of the First World War; instead they seemed to have lost a sense of who and what they were. They suffered an 'identity confusion'—they could not reconcile what they had felt and done as soldiers with what they had known before the war.

One of Erikson's major innovations is his method of *psychohistory*, in which he applies his theory of the human life-cycle to the study of famous historical figures; after essays on Gorky, Shaw and Freud, he devoted whole books to Martin Luther (*Young Man Luther*, 1958) and Gandhi (*Gandhi's Truth*, 1969).

According to Elkind (1970), teaching of Erikson's concepts is on the increase in psychology, psychiatry, education and social work. However, although researchers have found his theory rather difficult to test and not everyone agrees with the details of the theory, it is generally agreed that Erikson has inspired the 'life-span' approach in developmental psychology.

OTHER THEORIES OF ADOLESCENCE

The word 'adolescence' comes from the Latin *adolescere* meaning 'to grow into maturity'. Traditionally, this stage has been regarded as a prelude to, and a preparation for, adulthood, a transitional period of life between immaturity and maturity.

Probably the earliest theory of adolescence was that of G. Stanley Hall in his book *Adolescence* (1904) and he is generally regarded as the father of adolescent psychology; he was also one of the pioneers of developmental psychology as a whole. Heavily influenced by Darwin's evolutionary theory, Hall believed that each individual's psychological development recapitulates the evolution of the human species, both biological and cultural. In the case of adolescence (12 to 25 years), he saw it as a time of *storm and stress* (or *Sturm und Drang*) which mirrors the volatile history of the human race during the past 2000 years.

Although the 'Recapitulation Theory' is only of historical interest, parts of it are consistent with modern theories, in particular, the notion of 'storm and stress', important ingredients of which are the violent swings of mood and other 'contradictory tendencies', such as: (i) energy and enthusiasm versus indifference and boredom; (ii) gaiety and laughter versus gloom and melancholy; and (iii) idealistic altruism versus selfishness.

While adolescence is generally taken to *begin* with puberty (which itself is a lengthy process which passes through stages) to say when it ends is more problematic. Usually, the criteria are psychological (rather than physical) and they constitute the beginning of adulthood, for example: (i) the development of a sense of personal identity (Erikson, 1950); (ii) the ability to engage in a truly intimate relationship with another person (Erikson, 1950; Dacey, 1982); (iii) the achievement of employment, a relatively permanent relationship with another, or both (Abbott, 1981).

Psychoanalytic Theories

Both Sigmund Freud and his daughter, Anna, saw adolescence as a stage in which the balance within the personality of the child becomes disturbed. During the latency period (5 to 6 to puberty), the id, ego and superego are in relative harmony but the new id urges which arise at puberty are very powerful and the suprego is 'in the melting pot', that is, there is a bid for independence (whereby the identification with the same-sex parent is weakened) but at the same time there is a renewed dependence on the opposite-sex parent.

So there is a re-emergence of strong Oedipal feelings and the adolescent's task is to restore the psychic balance. Anna Freud (*The Ego and the Mechanisms of Defence*, 1937) believed that her father had over-emphasized the development of sexuality early in life and neglected its adolescent manifestation. She also regarded the ego defence mechanisms (see Chapter 29) which were used prior to puberty as no longer adequate to deal with the upsurge of instincts and she identified two new adolescent defences: (i) *asceticism*, whereby adolescents deprive themselves of pleasurable experiences and activities (particularly sexual ones); and (ii) *intellecualization*, whereby anxiety-provoking subjects are discussed and read about at great length (typically, adolescents spend more time talking about sex than enjoying it).

More recently, Blos (1967) has described adolescence as a 'second individuation process', ie the process of becoming a separate person (the first individuation process having occurred at the end of the child's third year).

Adolescents *disengage*, ie renounce their dependency on the family and loosen early childhood ties which, until puberty, were the main source of emotional sustenance. This, in turn, produces 'affect and object hunger', a means of coping with the 'inner emptiness' which results from the breaking of childhood ties. Affect and object hunger are satisfied by: (i) group experiences (a family substitute); (ii) doing exciting things 'just for kicks'; (iii) frequent and abrupt changes in relationships; and (iv) drug-induced and mystical experiences.

Disengagement also produces regression, which can take the form of 'hero worship' (of rock stars, sporting personalities, etc.) and the 'homosexual crush' (on a same-sex teacher or friend of the parents—both involving the search for substitute parents), absorption in politics, religion and philosophy, etc., and ambivalence. Ambivalence underlies relationships with parents in early childhood and involves a fluctuation between loving and hating, dependent and independent, co-operative and un-co-operative and so on. According to Blos, ambivalence is reactivated in adolescence in an extreme form and accounts for much of the aggressive, negative and generally unpredictable behaviour which parents in particular, and adults in general, find so hard to understand.

Blos believes that regression is actually necessary for progress to take place and the non-conformity of adolescents is, in fact, a very adaptive defence against the temptation to become dependent again on the parents and other adults. He also sees transient maladaptive behaviour (what Erikson calls the 'psychopathology of everyday adolescence') as inevitable.

Cultural Relativism: the Contribution of Cultural Anthropology

The theories of Ruth Benedict (1934, 1954) and Margaret Mead (1942, 1944, 1961) were partly a reaction against the instinct theories of Freud, any conflict, stress or problem experienced by young people cannot usefully be understood in isolation from the cultural norms and institutions to which they are related.

While it is universal for children to move from a state of dependence upon older people to relative independence, how this takes place varies greatly from one society to another. In some (such as the Cheyenne Indians studied by Benedict in 1934) the transition is smooth, gradual and continuous, eg a Cheyenne boy's hunting prowess is recognized by adults and his contribution to the feast is valued alongside the father's.

However, in Western culture, many adult activities are forbidden to children and a great deal of behaviour which is thought appropriate for children must be 'unlearned' when we 'grow up'. We make fairly sharp distinctions between 'being mature' and 'being immature' and the unlearning which this involves produces inevitable strain which lies at the root of adolescent difficulties.

Specifically, there are three types of *discontinuity* in Western culture, namely those centring around: (i) responsible and non-responsible roles; (ii) dominant and submissive roles; and (iii) sexual roles. Related to these are three kinds of unlearning: (i) play attitudes when moving into the world of work; (ii) submissive attitudes when assuming positions of authority; and (iii) the taboo on sex when moving into marriage.

Although Mead (like Erikson) acknowledged the part played by biological changes at puberty, she believed that adolescent problems are mainly due to social factors, in particular, the wide range of choices open to the individual in a rapidly changing world. If the primary task of adolescence is to establish a meaningful identity, the obstacles to doing this are greater now than ever before; there is no enduring frame of reference, no single set of values (religious, political, ideological, etc.) by which the adolescent can make sense of the world.

Coleman's Focal Theory of Adolescence (1978, 1980)

The 'classical' picture of adolescence which emerges from the theories we have considered (and many which we have not) has three main components: (i) *storm and stress*; (ii) *identity crisis*; and (iii) *generation gap*. However, Coleman believes that the actual empirical data paint a very different picture.

i) Storm and Stress

Several studies have concluded that adolescence is *not* a period which typically involves stress, tension and emotional turmoil.

In a study of adolescents on the Isle of Wight, Rutter et al (1976) found hardly any difference in the number of 10-year-olds, 14-year-olds and adults who were judged as having psychiatric disorders (10.9 per cent, 12.5 per cent and 11.9 per cent, respectively) and a substantial proportion of these 14-year-olds with problems had had problems since childhood. Again, when difficulties did first appear during adolescence they were mainly associated with stressful situations, such as the parents' marital discord. Only 20 per cent of teenagers agreed with the statement, 'I often feel miserable or depressed'.

The National Children's Bureau study (1976) of all the 16-year-olds born in a single week in 1958 in England, Scotland and Wales (over 14,000 of them) concluded that it is a 'difficult' age, at least for parents. Parents most often described their 16-year-olds as solitary, then came irritable ('quick to fly off the handle'), then 'fussy or overparticular'. Very few were described as destructive or aggressive to others or frequently disobedient; 12 per cent were thought to be untruthful on some occasions; 2 per cent still sucked their thumbs; 3 per cent suffered emotional problems; 15 per cent were nail-biters; 11 per cent suffered from migraine or recurrent headaches; 3 per cent had a stammer or stutter and 1 per cent were still wetting the bed (Fogelman, 1976):

> The transitional period of adolescence does present the adolescent with a special burden, a challenge and an opportunity. He has to individualize, build up confidence in himself and his abilities, make important decisions

concerning his future, and free himself of his earlier attachments to his parents ... the majority of the teenagers in our sample coped with these tasks successfully. They lack the turmoil of the disturbed adolescent precisely because their ego is strong enough to withstand the pressures ... (Offer, 1969)

But critics (of studies like Offer's) have implied that lack of turmoil is a bad prognostic sign and inevitably prevents the adolescent from developing into a mature adult:

... All of our data, including the psychological testing, point in the opposite direction. The adolescents not only adjusted well, they were also in touch with their feelings and developed meaningful relationships with significant others. (Offer, 1969)

Similarly:

In this study some 33.5 per cent of adolescents surveyed reported *no* symptoms of psychological distress and another 39 per cent reported five or fewer symptoms (a mild level of distress) ... a significant 27.5 per cent reported higher levels of psychological distress. For the majority the adolescent transition may be relatively smooth; however, for a minority it does indeed appear to be a period of stress and turmoil ...

The large majority of adolescents appear to get on well with adults and are able to cope effectively with demands of school and peer groups. They use their resources to make adjustments with environmental stressors with hardly visible signs of psychological distress. (Siddique and D'arcy, 1984)

ii) *Identity Crisis*

Many of Erikson's notions surrounding identity crisis are difficult to translate into empirically meaningful terms but many researchers have used measures of the self-concept (in particular, self-esteem) as indicators of crisis.

We have already discussed self-esteem in relation to *body image*, including early and late maturation and satisfaction with body weight, particularly in girls. And we have also discussed the effects of being out of work on self-esteem and general mental health.

Simmons and Rosenberg (1975) found that lowered self-esteem is more common during early adolescence than either late childhood or later adolescence, and this was more evident in girls than boys. For example, 32 per cent of 12- to 14-year-old girls had lower self-esteem (26 per cent of boys) and 43 per cent of girls had a more unstable self-image (30 per cent of boys). (The sample comprised nearly 2000 school-age children.) Half the pre-pubescent girls were satisfied with their physical appearance, compared with only one-quarter of the early adolescents.

However, most studies seem to paint a rather different picture. For example, based on the use of the Offer Self-Image Questionnaire, Offer et al (1981) concluded that there seems to be no increase in the disturbance of the self-image during early adolescence.

Coleman and Hendry take the view that while such disturbance is more likely in the early adolescent years than later on in adolescence:

... only a relatively small proportion of the total adolescent population are likely to have a negative self-image or to have very low self-esteem. (Coleman and Hendry, 1990)

While it is around puberty that there is the greatest chance of some form of disturbance:

... It seems probable ... that for the majority of adolescents the most viable course will be to avoid any sudden identity crisis, adapting very gradually over a period of years to the changes in identity experienced by them. (Coleman and Hendry, 1990)

iii)   *The Generation Gap*

Bandura (1972) found no support for the 'classical' view that adolescents are trying to emancipate themselves from parental ties. However he did find that independence from the parents is more or less completed by 13 or 14 years (*not* just beginning) and that the autonomy of adolescents seems to pose more problems for adults than the adolescents themselves.

Instead of parents becoming more restrictive and controlling, Bandura found the reverse; relationships were seen by both as becoming easier with more mutual trust. He also found that adolescents were very selective in their choice of reference groups and there was little evidence of the 'slavish conformity' to the peer group which is another feature of the 'classical' view. In general, peer group values and parental values were *not* in direct opposition and peer group membership did not necessarily generate family conflict. Similarly, Offer and Offer (1975) conclude that peer group values are likely to be extensions of parental values.

In the National Children's Bureau study, for example, the majority of parents and 16-year-olds reported harmonious family relationships; only 3 per cent of the teenagers were totally against marriage, and the vast majority believed the ideal age for getting married is between 20 and 25 with two children as the ideal family.

Parents were given a list of issues on which it is commonly thought that adults and 16-year-olds might disagree. The results indicated a situation which was, from the parents' point of view, a harmonious one (Table 21.4).

The 16-year-olds confirmed their parents' attitudes—appearance and evening activities were sometimes issues of disagreement in the home, but otherwise the atmosphere was free from major conflict (Table 21.5).

Table 21.4 Disagreement between parents and study child (parents' report) (N = 11 521)

	OFTEN %	SOMETIMES %	NEVER OR HARDLY EVER %
Choice of friends of the same sex	3	16	81
Choice of friends of opposite sex	2	9	89
Dress or hairstyle	11	35	54
Time of coming in at night or going to bed	8	26	66
Places gone to in own time	2	9	89
Doing homework	6	18	76
Smoking	6	9	85
Drinking	1	5	94

	VERY TRUE %	TRUE %	UN-CERTAIN %	UNTRUE %	VERY UNTRUE %
I get on well with my mother	41	45	8	4	1
I get on well with my father	35	45	13	5	2
I often quarrel with a brother or sister	23	43	10	19	5
My parents have strong views about my appearance (eg dress, hairstyle, etc.)	15	33	19	27	6
My parents want to know where I go in the evening	27	51	8	11	3
My parents disapprove of some of my male friends	9	19	18	37	16
My parents disapprove of some of my female friends	5	15	18	40	22

Table 21.5 Family relationships (children's report) (N = 11 045)

About two-thirds of those with siblings said they quarrelled between themselves, yet:

> Many wrote a qualifying note to the effect that although they might often quarrel with a brother or sister, or disagree with their parents, this did not mean there was anything wrong with the underlying relationship. (Fogelman, 1976)

According to Offer et al:

> Throughout the ages adults have created a 'generation gap' by systematically distorting the adolescent experience. This has clearly been a disservice to normal teenagers, since distortion forestalls effective communication. But it is also a disservice to deviant and disturbed teenagers, since they are denied needed help by adults who blithely assert that 'adolescents are just going through a stage'. (Offer et al, 1981)

So what conclusions can be drawn about the 'classical' view of adolescence in the light of the evidence?

> Broadly speaking ... research provides little support for current theories, and fails to substantiate much of what both psychoanalysts and sociologists appear to believe ... while there is certainly some change in the self-concept, there is no evidence to show that any but a small minority experience a serious identity crisis. In most cases relationships with parents are positive and constructive, and young people, by and large, do not reject adult values in favour of those espoused by the peer group. In fact, in most situations peer group values appear to be consistent with those of important adults, rather than in conflict with them. Fears of promiscuity among the young are not borne out by the research findings,

nor do studies support the belief that the peer group encourages anti-social behaviour . . .

Lastly, there is no evidence to suggest that during the adolescent years there is a higher level of psychopathology than at other times . . . although a small minority may show disturbance, the great majority of teenagers seem to cope well and to show no undue signs of turmoil or stress. (Coleman and Hendry, 1990)

So if the 'classical' view and empirical data present two contradictory pictures, how can we reconcile them?

Coleman's solution, essentially, is to see the truth as lying somewhere between these two versions:

(a) Psychoanalytic theories have tended to be built upon clinical data, so that a distorted picture of the 'typical' adolescent emerges from an atypical sample of emotionally disturbed patients.

(b) Sociologists must disentangle concepts of 'youth'/the youth movement from notions about young people themselves:

> . . . youth is frequently seen by sociologists as being in the forefront of social change. Youth is, as it were, the advance party where innovations or alteration in the values of society are concerned . . . it is but a short step to use youth as a metaphor for social change and thus to confuse radical forces in society with the beliefs of ordinary young people. (Brake, 1985; quoted in Coleman and Hendry, 1990)

(c) Certain adolescent behaviours (eg vandalism/drugs/hooliganism, etc.) are extremely threatening to adults. The minority involved in such activities, therefore, attain undue prominence in the public eye, especially through the mass media. This sensationalism makes those behaviours seem very much more common than they really are.

(d) Large-scale surveys tend to neglect the possibility that individual adolescents may be either unwilling or unable to reveal their innermost feelings. It is very difficult for a shy, resentful or anxious teenager to share fears, worries or conflicts with a strange interviewer. This kind of inhibition may result in an *underestimation* of the degree of stress experienced by young people. So there may be methodological causes of the widening of the gap between theory and research, ie research workers are missing more subtle indications of emotional tension.

Coleman and Hendry (1990) go on to discuss the *need* for a theory of adolescence. Both psychoanalysis *and* sociology have contributed theories which are still relevant:

> . . . they have provided the foundation for an understanding of young people with serious problems and a greater knowledge of those who belong to minority or deviant groups . . . [but] adolescence needs a theory, not of abnormality, but of normality. Any viable theoretical viewpoint . . . must not only acknowledge the fact that, although for some young people adolescence may be a difficult time, for the majority it is a period of relative stability. None the less, there is general agreement that during the teenage years major adaptation has to occur. The transition between childhood and adulthood cannot be achieved without substantial adjustments of both a psychological and social nature; and yet most young people appear to cope without undue stress. How do they do it? (Coleman and Hendry, 1990).

The Focal Theory

The *focal model* (1974, 1978, 1979, 1980) was based on a study of 800 boys and girls at ages 11, 13, 15 and 17. They were given a set of identical tests dealing with self-image, being alone, heterosexual relationships, parental relationships, friendships, and large group situations. Attitudes towards all these issues changed as a function of age. But, more importantly, concerns about different issues reached a *peak* at different ages for *both* sexes (Fig. 21.4, which only shows data for boys).

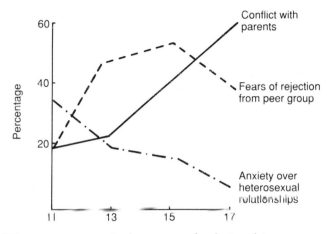

Figure 21.4 Peak ages for the expression of different themes (boys only)

At different ages, particular sorts of relationship patterns come into focus (ie they are the most prominent) but no pattern is specific to one age only. Patterns overlap and there will also be individual differences, so that just because an issue is not the predominant feature of a particular age, this does not mean that it will not be critical for some individuals.

So, to adjust to so much potentially stressful change and at the same time to do this with relative stability, the adolescent copes by dealing with one issue at a time:

> They spread the process of adaptation over a span of years, attempting to resolve first one issue, and then the next. Different problems, different relationship issues come into focus and are tackled at different stages, so that the stresses resulting from the need to adapt to new modes of behaviour are rarely concentrated all at one time. It follows from this that it is precisely in those who, for whatever reason, do have more than one issue to cope with at a time that problems are most likely to occur... (Coleman and Hendry, 1990)

Evaluation of Focal Theory

It is directly based on empirical evidence and helps to reconcile the apparent contradiction between the 'classical' and empirical views. While it needs further testing, some writers regard it as an important contribution to the theoretical understanding of adolescence (Siddique and D'arcy, 1984; Meadows, 1986).

Kroger (1985) replicated Coleman's (1974) research on large US and New Zealand samples, and found almost identical patterns of development in the three countries. Despite obvious cultural differences:

> ... the same proportions of adolescents appear to face the same interpersonal issues in much the same way in each of the three national settings. (Coleman and Hendry, 1990)

Simmons and Blyth (1987) tested the hypothesis that those who adjust less well during adolescence are likely to be those facing more than one interpersonal issue at a time, and found strong support for Focal Theory:

> ... There is evidence of detrimental effects if change occurs at too young an age, if it causes the individual to be extremely off-time in development, if the transition places the person in the lowest ranking cohort in the environment, if change is marked by sharp discontinuity, and if many significant changes cumulate and occur close together in time. (Simmons and Blyth, 1987)

A way of coping is to see certain issues as residing in the future, so that they do not have to be dealt with now. Porteous (1985) showed that for 12- to 16-year-olds living in the north of England and Eire problems which are prevalent in early adolescence (eg about rules, permissiveness, adult criticism, bullying and friendships) decline and are replaced by worries about employment and, in some cases, worries about their worth as an individual. Porteous also found that with increasing age self-awareness increases and there is a growing tendency to be self-critical and to make comparisons between self and others, particularly in the case of girls:

> ... We believe that most young people pace themselves through the adolescent transition. Most of them hold back on one issue, while they are grappling with another. Most sense what they can and cannot cope with, and will, in the real sense of the term, be an active agent in their own development. (Coleman and Hendry, 1990)

22 ATTACHMENT AND SEPARATION: THE EFFECTS OF EARLY EXPERIENCE

THE NATURE OF ATTACHMENT

CONCEPT OF ATTACHMENT

The concept of attachment is central to any discussion of the role of parenting (or what, traditionally, has been referred to as 'mothering') and so it is necessary to begin by asking why this is considered to be of such importance in the individual's development.

John Bowlby, writing in 1951, maintained that, 'mother love in infancy and childhood is as important for mental health as are vitamins and proteins for physical health'. More recently (1969, 1971) he has gone so far as to suggest that individuals with any kind of psychiatric disorder *always* show a disturbance in their social relationships (affectional bonding) and that, in many cases, this has been caused by disturbed bonding (selective attachment) in childhood.

The first relationship is generally regarded as crucial for healthy development because it acts as a model (or prototype) of all later relationships, ie a 'good' mother–child relationship teaches the child what it can expect from, and what it must give to, any future relationship. Erikson believes that what the infant learns through its interaction with its mother is a 'basic trust' or a 'basic mistrust' of the world in general and other people in particular.

But does an attachment always and inevitably develop between every mother and child, or does it depend, at least to some extent, on the *quality* of the mothering the child receives? When it does occur, does it happen immediately or over a period of time? Can a child be attached to only one person at a time (ie the mother) or can it have multiple attachments and how important are fathers as attachment figures? Are there different degrees of attachment or are they all equally strong? Is there a critical or sensitive period for the development of attachments or can they develop at any time during childhood (or even beyond)? These are the major questions which we shall be trying to answer in the first part of this chapter.

THE GRADUAL DEVELOPMENT OF ATTACHMENTS

In *Mothering* (1977), Rudolph Schaffer describes the three stages involved in social development in infancy:

(a) The first stage is marked by the infant's attraction to other human beings in preference to inanimate features of the environment.
    As we saw in Chapter 10, it is initially the complexity of a stimulus

which attracts babies, rather than its 'human-ness'. But about six weeks after birth, babies begin to smile more at human faces and voices, which embody all the qualities of objects (including complexity) in an exaggerated and particularly attractive way. The first 'social smile', therefore, occurs at about six weeks.

(b) The second stage is reached when the infant learns to distinguish different human beings, so that the parent is recognized as familiar and strangers as unfamiliar, as shown by its smiling, for example.

However, the baby still allows other people to handle and look after it without becoming noticeably upset; people are still largely interchangeable (ie equivalent) so long as they provide adequate care. This ability to tell strangers from non-strangers appears, on average, at three months.

(c) The third stage is reached when the baby is capable of forming a lasting, emotionally meaningful bond or attachment with certain specific individuals whose company and attention it actively seeks.

This represents the culmination of a process which began at about six weeks, and the major indications that a bond has been formed are: (i) first, the ability to miss the mother when she is absent, so that fretting will occur if she is out of the room (and, therefore, out of sight) even for a few minutes; and (ii) the appearance of the fear response to strangers, whereby being picked up and talked to by an unfamiliar person causes crying and general distress, sometimes even in the mother's presence. However, the mere presence of a stranger is not usually sufficient to induce this fear response—some direct contact is usually necessary. (By contrast, the mere presence of the mother may offer the young child enough security for it to explore and investigate a strange environment.) These two events (actively missing the mother and showing a fear of strangers) mark the establishment of an attachment and occur, on average, at six or seven months.

THE OTHER SIDE OF ATTACHMENT

This gradual development of attachments has important implications for understanding how any separation that has to take place between mother and child may affect not only the child but also the mother herself—and the relationship between them.

Psychologists have studied the attachment almost exclusively from the point of view of the child, with the important exception of Klaus and Kennell (1976), who look at the bonding process from the point of view of the caregiver. Based on studies of premature babies, they concluded that the amount of physical contact ('skin-to-skin') is important, but even more crucial is the *timing* of such contact. Kennell et al (1979) propose that six to twelve hours after birth constitutes a critical period for the mother's emotional bonding to her infant, ie the contact must take place during that time or the attachment may fail to develop!

However, others disagree. For example, Rutter (1979) stresses that the bonding process builds up slowly over a period of months (rather than hours) just as the baby's does: the idea of a 'maternal instinct' can blind us to the gradual development of the mother's attachment to her infant, which is by no means automatic or immediate.

ATTACHMENT, ATTACHMENT BEHAVIOUR AND BONDS

Babies show a general tendency to want to be close to people, to seek attachments, and at first this is directed towards anyone who happens to be around; if familiar figures are absent, babies will soon seek new attachments to other people (Robertson and Robertson, 1971). However, this general tendency is built on to form selective attachments or *bonds*, ie attachments to particular individuals which persist over time, even during a period of no contact with the attachment figure.

Maccoby (1980) defines an attachment as, 'a relatively enduring emotional tie to a specific other person'. In infancy and early childhood, attachment is shown primarily by four kinds of behaviour: (i) seeking to be near the other person; (ii) showing distress on separation from that person; (iii) showing joy or relief on reunion; and (iv) being generally oriented towards the person, even when not in close proximity, through, for example, listening for the person's voice, watching what they do, getting their attention by showing them toys and so on.

DIFFERENT KINDS OF ATTACHMENT

Despite this general tendency to seek attachment and the gradual development of selective attachments, there are important differences in the strength and security of children's bonds.

The *strength* of an attachment refers to the intensity with which attachment behaviours are displayed, while the *security* of an attachment refers to how confident the child is of the attachment figure being there when needed and being able to use her (or him) as a safe 'base' from which to explore in a strange environment. How are strength and security related?

There are certain examples of how they are *inversely* related. First, a child may be very 'clingy' because it has returned home from hospital or its mother has been in hospital to have another baby. Secondly, Tizard and Rees (1974) found that four-year-old children reared in institutions showed more clinging and following behaviour than family-reared children but were less likely to show selective attachment or deep relationships: although they seemed to be closely attached to someone, they did not seem to care at all when the person left, which seemed to be a defensive reaction to many experiences of loss. When these children were two, they were very clinging, would run and climb on the lap of anybody they knew even slightly, and in this respect were much more like twelve- to eighteen-month-olds. When first meeting strangers, they were very shy and frightened but were much more affectionate to a much wider range of people whom they knew just a little compared with most two-year-olds.

To look at a third case, Rosenblum and Harlow (1963) found that rejected infant monkeys showed very strong attachments to rejecting 'mothers'—the monkeys were isolated at birth and reared in a cage with a 'cloth mother' which at random intervals blasted the clinging baby with a strong current of compressed air. These 'blasted' infants spent more time clinging to the surrogate (substitute) mother than controls whose cloth mothers did not abuse them in this way. Similar results were found when infant monkeys were abused by their mothers (who themselves had been 'reared' from birth with surrogate mothers).

It seems that the very act of 'rejection' results in more clinging which, in turn, results in more rejection and this pattern of interaction can be seen in the strength of attachment and loyalty of many abused children.

Fourthly, Hinde and Spencer-Booth (1970) studied infant monkeys and found that those which showed most distress after separation were those which had experienced most rejection from their mothers and for whom there was the most tension in the infant–mother relationship. So anxiety appears to increase attachment behaviour regardless of the response of the attachment-object.

There are also examples of a *positive* relationship between strength and security, for instance, Stayton and Ainsworth (1973) found that children of sensitive, responsive mothers showed *more* positive greeting on reunion and *more* following (suggesting *stronger* attachments) than those shown by children of insensitive, unresponsive mothers, but that the former showed *less* crying and distress on separation (suggesting *more secure* attachments; (see below).

The whole purpose of bonding is to enable the child to feel secure in strange environments, to move further away from the mother, both literally and emotionally, so that attachment behaviours (eg clinging and following) are reduced and exploration and independence increase; this is known as *detachment*. Normally, we would expect attachment behaviour to be at its peak between twelve and eighteen months, (although, according to Maccoby (1980) it is quite common up to twenty-four months) and to decline gradually after that. According to Rutter (1981), the aim of attachment is detachment but for this to happen the bonds must be secure.

THE STUDY OF ATTACHMENTS: 'THE STRANGE SITUATION'

Ainsworth and her colleagues (Ainsworth, Bell and Stayton, 1971, Ainsworth et al, 1978) have devised a method of studying attachments called 'The Strange Situation', which consists of a sequence of eight episodes in which the mother (and/or the father) and a stranger come and go from the room, each episode lasting about three minutes. The sequence of comings and goings is pre-determined and is the same for all the children and so the method used is controlled observation: one or more trained observers record the child's attachment behaviour in the mother's presence, when she leaves, when she returns, how the child responds to the stranger and how the child's play is affected throughout.

It has been mostly one-year-old white middle-class children who have been studied and Table 22.1 summarizes the major findings.

THE STABILITY OF ATTACHMENTS

Ainsworth et al's classification system is generally regarded as very reliable and has been used in a large number of studies in which attachment has been the major dependent variable. (Types A and C are sometimes grouped together as Anxiously or Insecurely attached but Type A seems to suggest the absence of any kind of emotional relationship at all, ie *indifference*, while type C suggests *ambivalence*).

Several studies have shown this pattern of attachment to be a stable characteristic. However, Vaughn et al (1970) studied mother–infant pairs

Table 22.1 Behaviour associated with three types of attachment in one-year-olds, based on the 'strange situation' (Ainsworth et al, 1978)

CATEGORY	GENERAL DESCRIPTION	PERCENTAGE OF SAMPLE	RESPONSE TO MOTHER LEAVING	RESPONSE TO MOTHER RETURNING	RESPONSE TO STRANGER
Type A	Anxious-avoidant	15	Show little or no distress. Play is little affected by mother's presence or absence or her whereabouts in the room when present. Generally, they don't seek closeness or contact with her; when she initiates it, they neither resist it nor attempt to maintain it	They avoid closeness to or interaction with her. Typically, they ignore her or only casually greet her. If they make any approach at all, it is tentative, eg after starting to approach they may turn or look away	Usually they show no distress and play is little affected. Distress comes from being alone (rather than being left by mother) and they are as easily comforted by stranger as by mother. In fact, in general, they treat both adults in a similar way
Type B	Securely-attached	70	Play happily with toys. They don't stay particularly close to mother before she leaves but they do try to maintain contact. They will often resist being put down. Obviously distressed during her absence and play is considerably reduced	They go to her immediately, seeking contact. Quickly calm down in her arms and then able to resume play	They usually react happily to strangers (in mother's presence) but are distressed by her absence (and not only being alone). The stranger can provide some comfort but not as much as the mother. Generally, they treat mother and stranger very differently
Type C	Anxious-resistant	15	They are generally either angrier or more passive than types A or B. Fussy and wary in pre-separation episode; they cry a lot more and explore much less than types A or B. Have difficulty using mother as secure base for exploration	Seek contact with her but simultaneously resist contact and show their anger. Eg they may approach her quickly and reach out to be picked up but, once picked up, struggle to get down. They do not return readily to play but remain uninvolved, glancing frequently at mother	They actively resist the efforts of strangers to make contact during the pre-separation episodes

living in poverty and experiencing frequent changes of accommodation; they were all single-parent families. At twelve months, 55 per cent were assessed as securely attached (the rest evenly distributed between types A and C) while at eighteen months, 66 per cent were securely attached. Significantly, 38 per cent were classified differently on two occasions and this seemed to be related to changes in the family's circumstances. For example, those who were securely attached at first, but were anxiously attached by eighteen months, had the most stressed mothers and those who shifted from anxious to secure or who were anxious on both occasions had mothers who experienced an intermediate amount of stress.

Children's early attachment patterns, then, are not necessarily permanent characteristics; if important aspects of their life situation change, children can shift from secure to insecure attachments or vice versa.

ATTACHMENT AND SOCIAL COMPETENCE

Many studies have shown that there is a positive correlation between attachment as assessed by the 'Strange Situation' and later social behaviour with adults and peers; there is also a correlation with motor and language development and problem-solving skills.

Arend et al (1979) concluded that at eighteen months, the competent infant actively and effectively finds comfort when needed and uses the attachment figure as a secure base for exploring and mastering the physical world. At twenty-four months, they confront problems enthusiastically and persistently and enjoy mastery. Although much more independent now, the child can still use the parents as and when they are needed. Finally the competent pre-schooler is enthusiastically involved with school tasks and age mates and can deal with problems in an organized, persistent and flexible way (the findings can be seen as lending support to Erikson's theory of psychosocial development; see Chapter 21).

However, as Fishbein (1984) points out, we cannot be certain that the early attachment is directly responsible for the later competence of the child—the latter might simply reflect a continuation of the healthy relationship with the parents.

THEORIES OF ATTACHMENT

a) CUPBOARD LOVE THEORIES

Until the mid- to late 1950s, the dominant view of why babies become attached was the *Cupboard Love Theory*—babies become attached to the mother who feeds them! There are two theoretical strands to this view, which normally are diametrically opposed, namely Freud's Psychoanalytic Theory and Learning Theory.

According to Freud:

> The reason why the infant in arms wants to perceive the presence of its mother is only because it already knows by experience that she satisfies all its needs without delay. (Freud, 1926)

And again:

> Love has its origin in attachment to the satisfied need for nourishment. (Freud, 1940)

So, for Freud, the primary drive is for food, and through associating the mother with satisfaction of this primary drive, the child acquires a secondary drive for the mother—she eventually becomes desired in her own right.

It is in these terms (Drive–Reduction or Secondary Drive Theory) that Dollard and Miller (1950), Sears et al (1957) and other learning theorists explain the development of attachments. The baby's primary hunger drive is reduced (satisfied) by the mother and, through a process of classical conditioning, the baby acquires a secondary (dependency) drive for the mother herself. While food is a primary reinforcer, the mother is a secondary reinforcer (see Chapter 7).

How adequate is the cupboard love explanation of attachment?

A number of studies and theoretical developments have helped to expose its shortcomings:

Figure 22.1 *Harlow's rhesus monkeys*

1) Harlow and Zimmerman (1959) raised rhesus monkeys from birth with two surrogate mothers—a wire 'mother' and a 'mother' covered in terry-towelling. Half the infants were supplied with milk by the wire mother and the other half by the cloth mother. Regardless of who fed it, all the infants became attached to the cloth mother—they used her as a safe base for exploring a new cage and would seek comfort from her when they were frightened by a mechanical toy. The warmth and 'contact comfort' provided by the cloth mother seemed to be a more powerful contributor to the attachment than the milk she supplied (although the cloth mother who also supplied milk represented an even more powerful combination; Fig. 22.1).

2) In a longitudinal study of Scottish infants, Schaffer and Emerson (1964) found that infants become attached to people who do not perform caretaking activities (notably the father) and, conversely, in 39 per cent of cases, the person who typically fed, bathed and changed the child (typically the mother) was *not* the child's primary attachment object.

Schaffer and Emerson concluded that the two features of an attachment figure's behaviour which best predicted the character of the infant's attachment to them were: (i) responsiveness to the infants' behaviour; and (ii) the total amount of stimulation provided (eg talking, touching and playing).

3) Both Rheingold and Eckerman (1970) and Schaffer (1971) see the infant as an active seeker of stimulation and not a passive recipient of food and drink (which is the image portrayed by the cupboard love approach). Much of the infant's social interaction, even in the first few months, takes place when it is fed, clean and generally free from obvious 'biological' needs. The need for stimulation, which Schaffer believes is inborn, becomes selective (the infant comes to prefer human sources of stimulation) and eventually focuses on particular individuals (the infant comes to prefer specific attachment figures). According to this view, babies do not 'live to eat' but 'eat to live'.

4) The work of ethologists, beginning with Lorenz's famous studies of imprinting in goslings (1935), found that attachment of young birds

(and various mammals too) takes place through mere exposure, without any feeding taking place (see Chapter 15). Although there is no direct comparison between imprinting and human attachments, Bowlby (1969), who originally trained as a psychoanalyst, was greatly influenced by the ethological approach. In particular he emphasized: (i) the *instinctive* nature of attachment behaviour, whereby babies are born with the tendency to display certain behaviours which help ensure proximity and contact with the mother or mother-figure (eg crying, smiling, crawling, etc.); (ii) the importance of parental responsiveness to these innate behaviours; and (iii) a critical or sensitive period early in the child's life when attachments must develop. From an evolutionary point of view, attachment behaviour makes very good sense. During the evolution of the human species, it would have been the babies who stayed close to their mothers who would have survived to have children of their own and Bowlby hypothesized that both infants and mothers have evolved a biological need to stay in constant contact with each other.

b) *BOWLBY'S MONOTROPY THEORY*

Bowlby (1951) claimed that, in general, mothering is almost useless if delayed until after two-and-a-half to three years and, for most children, if delayed till after twelve months, ie there is a *critical period* for the development of attachments. Bowlby also (1969) claimed that the infant displays a strong innate, tendency to become attached to *one* particular individual (*monotropy*), although this need not be the natural or biological mother, and also that this attachment is different in kind (qualitatively different) from any subsequent attachment the child might form. Although the evidence supports the view that not all the child's attachments are of equal strength or intensity, ie that there is a persisting hierarchy (Schaffer and Emerson, 1964), Bowlby seems to be arguing that the relationship with the mother is, somehow, of a different order altogether from other relationships.

Is there any evidence to contradict Bowlby's monotropy theory?

i) *The Display of Attachment Behaviour*

Rutter (1981) points out that each of several indicators of attachment (protest or distress if the attached person leaves the child, reduction of anxiety and increase in exploration in a strange situation when the attachment figure is present, and following or seeking contact with the person) has been shown for a variety of attachment figures: siblings, peers, fathers and even inanimate objects (as in Harlow and Zimmermann's cloth mothers), as well as mothers. Significantly, these attachment responses to others occur even in children who have developed their bonds with their mothers—but they are not shown towards strangers.

ii) *Attachments with More Than One Person*

If the development of multiple attachments is not something Bowlby would dispute, he might still contend that the attachment to the mother is unique in that it is the first to appear and remains the strongest of all. However, on both these counts, the evidence seems to suggest otherwise.

In the Schaffer and Emerson (1964) longitudinal study, referred to above, four-weekly visits were made to the family home during the baby's first year, followed by another visit at eighteen months. As their measure of attachment they used the amount of protest the baby showed when separated from a familiar person; they also asked mothers whether the baby cried or fussed when left in its crib, outside a shop in its pram or in a room by itself.

At about seven months, 29 per cent had already formed several attachments simultaneously; in fact, 10 per cent had formed five or more. At ten months, 59 per cent had developed more than one attachment and by eighteen months, 87 per cent had done so (a third had formed five or more). Although there was usually one particularly strong attachment, the majority of the children showed multiple attachments of varying intensity and only half of the eighteen-month-olds were principally attached to the mother; in nearly a third of cases the main attachment was to the father, and 75 per cent were attached to the father at eighteen months. Although the infants, when young, tended to protest more when the mother left than when the father left, this tendency was short lived and by eighteen months most children protested equally at the departure of either parent.

iii) *Fathers as Attachment Figures*

These findings suggest that there is more to 'parenting' than 'mothering'. However, both Bowlby and Freud believed that the father is a less important and secondary attachment figure than the 'primary' mother. Bowlby argued that the father is of no direct (emotional) significance to the young child but is only of indirect value as an emotional and economic support for the mother.

Margaret Mead, the anthropologist, regarded the father as a 'biological necessity but a social accident' (1949), again implying the relative unimportance of the father as an attachment figure. Traditionally, the influence of parenting on the child's development has been equated with the influence of 'mothering', hence the term 'maternal deprivation' (coined by Bowlby) to refer to failure to form an attachment with a mother-figure or, once formed, an interruption of that attachment.

It is very unusual to hear psychologists discuss 'paternal' or even 'parental' deprivation and the notion of a 'paternal instinct' is even more improbable. However, a number of studies (including the Schaffer and Emerson study) reveal a very real role that fathers play in the social and emotional development of their young children.

Despite the increasing trend towards fathers taking a more equal, or even an exclusive, share of the upbringing of young children, it seems that fathers make a different kind of contribution from mothers and that the attachments that develop are correspondingly different (although not in the way or for the reasons that Bowlby suggests).

Fathers often relate to their children in an intense and exclusive manner. For instance, they may play together for half an hour or so when he gets home from work and before the child goes to bed. During that time, the child receives the father's undivided attention in a way that is often very difficult or even impossible for most busy mothers.

Clarke-Stewart (1978) found that most children between seven and thirty months chose their fathers as playmates in preference to their mothers. Parke (1981) reports that even when the mother's and father's style of play are compared, there are important differences. The father usually engages in more vigorous, physically stimulating, games or unusual and unpredictable types of play (which babies seem to enjoy the most) while the mother plays more conventional games (eg pat-a-cake), joins in the child's play with toys and reads to the child.

Similar results were found by Lamb (1977) who observed seven- to thirteen-month-olds at home. Mothers and fathers hold their babies for basically different reasons, mothers for caretaking and restricting, fathers for playful purposes or because the baby wants to be held.

Mothers seem to be preferred as sources of comfort when the infant is distressed, although this is more likely in unfamiliar surroundings (eg the 'Strange Situation'); fathers are preferred as playmates and someone to have fun with! Maccoby (1980) maintains that more than one kind of satisfaction can be derived from an attachment figure and a given child will develop qualitatively different attachments with several significant people in its life, who include, of course, the father.

According to Parke (1981):

> Both mother and father are important attachment objects for their infants, but the circumstances that lead to selecting mum or dad may differ.

The father is not just a poor substitute for the mother—he makes his own unique contribution to the care and development of infants and young children. This is true, of course, in situations where *both* parents are available to the child. Mothers and fathers may appear to be more comparable as *single* parents.

FACTORS INFLUENCING ATTACHMENT

So far, we have seen that: (i) there is no foundation for the belief that the biological mother is uniquely capable of caring for her child (the 'blood bond' myth); (ii) the 'mother' does not even have to be female; (iii) multiple attachments rather than a distinct preference for a mother-figure is the rule rather than the exception for even young infants; and (iv) attachment is unrelated to the amount of physical caretaking the baby receives from the attachment figure.

So what does determine the number and intensity of a young child's attachments?

a) INTENSITY OF INTERACTION

As we have seen, Schaffer and Emerson (1964) believe that the total amount of stimulation provided is one of two major predictors of attachment. The evidence relating to infants' attachments to their fathers demonstrates that the sheer amount of time spent with someone is, in itself, no guarantee that an attachment will develop—it is what happens during the interaction that matters.

Similarly, observations of child–parent relationships from Israeli kibbutzim suggest that it is the intensity of the contact, rather than the amount, that is important (quality not quantity). In the kibbutzim, babies are often brought up in communal nurseries from when they are four days old and thereafter the parents spend two or three hours per day with them. The significant feature of this interaction is that there are none of the distractions of housework and demands from other children to 'dilute' the quality of contact—parents can devote all their energies and attention to their child for the time they are together. (Of course, a certain minimum amount of time spent in interaction is necessary for any attachment to develop at all, but beyond this it is quality that matters.)

b) SENSITIVITY AND THE MOTHER'S PERSONALITY

Ainsworth and her colleagues (eg Ainsworth et al, 1971) have proposed that the crucial feature of the mother's behaviour towards her child is her sensitivity. For example, waking in the middle of the night to hear the baby crying in the next room is an example of the intent awareness of the baby and anticipation of its needs which facilitate their satisfaction.

The sensitive mother can see things from her baby's point of view and correctly interpret its signals, she responds to her baby's needs and wishes as and when they arise and she is also accepting of the baby, co-operative with it and accessible or available for it.

By contrast, the insensitive mother interacts with the baby almost exclusively in terms of her own wishes, moods and activities. She may distort the implications of the baby's signals and communications or may even ignore them altogether.

Using the 'Strange Situation', Ainsworth et al have concluded that: (i) sensitive mothers have secure babies who can explore strange environments, using the mother as a safe base, and who can also tolerate brief occasional, separations from her; and (ii) babies of insensitive mothers are so insecure that either they become very angry when she leaves or they seem almost indifferent to her presence or absence and do not use her as a safe base (see Table 22.1).

Similar results were found by Clarke-Stewart (1973) who used three categories of maternal behaviour, which overlap with Ainsworth et al's sensitivity: (i) expression of positive emotion (affectionate, touching, smiling, praise and social speech); (ii) contingent responsiveness (the proportion of the baby's cries and so on to which the mother responds); and (iii) social stimulation (coming close to the baby, smiling, talking and imitating it).

In general, then, attachments probably develop most readily to *people* (not just mothers) who can adapt their behaviour to the specific needs—and personality—of the individual child; parental apathy and lack of responsiveness tend to inhibit the bonding process.

c) CONSISTENCY

Given that the parent-figure is responsive to the child's needs and that the interaction is reasonably intense, he or she must still be a *consistent* figure in the child's world; people must be *predictable* parts of the child's environment. This predictability and regularity of contact are conspicuously absent in long-stay institutions, such as residential nurseries (Tizard and Rees, 1974).

d) SOCIAL RESPONSIVENESS AND THE CHILD'S PERSONALITY

Just as adults differ (with respect to sensitivity, predictability and so on), so there is evidence that babies also differ in their need for physical contact and comfort.

Schaffer and Emerson (1964) found that some babies liked cuddling while others preferred not to be cuddled. Several actively resisted being embraced or hugged or held tight, even when they were tired, frightened or ill and these babies were much more active and restless generally and much more intolerant of physical restraints, such as being dressed. By contrast, the 'cuddlers' were quite placid, slept more and showed more interest in cuddly toys.

These differences were evident during the early weeks and did not seem to be related to how much the mother handled them—they were probably part of the baby's temperament. However, the mother was still a 'haven of safety' for the 'non-cuddlers'—they tried to establish visual contact with her or held on to her skirt when frightened but would not cuddle up.

Although these babies were still attached to their mothers, it is interesting to ask whether the mothers of non-cuddlers had more difficulty becoming attached to their infants and whether the non-cuddlers would have difficulties in their adult relationships, particularly their sexual relationships and their relationships with their own children.

THE EFFECTS OF SEPARATION: BOWLBY'S MATERNAL DEPRIVATION HYPOTHESIS

Bowlby argued that:

> ... an infant and young child should experience a warm, intimate and continuous relationship with his mother (or permanent mother-figure) in which both find satisfaction and enjoyment. (Bowlby, 1951)

This, together with his monotropy theory, led during the 1950s and 1960s to criticism of the 'latch-key child' phenomenon and the general insistence, from many quarters of society, that mothers with young children should not go out to work but devote twenty-four hours of every day to child care. Bowlby, in fact, never advocated such a policy but, if a mother is away from her child regularly (even if she works part-time), this could be interpreted as not fulfilling the requirements that the mother–child relationship be continuous.

Is there any relevant evidence?

Bowlby's (1951) claim that the maternal bond could not be broken in the first few years of life without serious and permanent damage to social, emotional and intellectual development, was based largely on the study of children brought up in orphanages, residential nurseries and other large institutions, conducted during the 1930s and 1940s.

For instance, Goldfarb (1943a) compared one group of fifteen children raised in institutions from about six months until three-and-a-half years of age, when they were fostered (the institution group), with another group of fifteen children who had gone straight from their mothers to foster homes (the fostered group).

Although they were matched for genetic factors, mothers' education and occupational status, they might have differed in other important respects which may have determined whether they were fostered or placed in an institution initially, for example, how bright or easy-going they seemed, how withdrawn or prone to illness they were. Clearly, they were not assigned randomly.

The institutions were very clean but lacked human contact or stimulation. Babies below nine months were kept in separate cubicles, intended to prevent the spread of infection, and their only contact with other people occurred during feeding and changing. After nine months, they were put into groups of fifteen to twenty and were supervised by a single nurse. They lived 'in almost complete social isolation during the first year of life' and their experience in the following two years was only slightly better.

At three years they were given intelligence tests, tests of abstract thinking and social maturity, and their ability to follow rules and make friends was also assessed. Not surprisingly, the institution group fell behind the fostered group on all these measures. For example, all fifteen in the fostered group were average in language development compared with only three in the institution group, and the latter were characterized by an inability to keep the rules, a lack of guilt, craving for affection and an inability to make lasting relationships.

When they were assessed later, between the ages of ten and fourteen, the institution group performed more poorly on tests of intelligence (average IQ was 72 compared with 95 for the fostered group), social maturity, speech and ability to form relationships. Goldfarb attributed all these differences to the time spent in the institutions.

Classic studies by Spitz (1945, 1946) and Spitz and Wolf (1946) concentrated more on the emotional effects of institutionalization. Spitz visited some very poor orphanages in South America where infants, who received only irregular attention from the staff, became extremely apathetic and displayed high rates of 'anaclitic depression', a severe disturbance which involves symptoms such as poor appetite and morbidity. After three months of unbroken deprivation, recovery is rarely, if ever, complete, and they painted a horrifying picture of developmental retardation and progressive dehumanization. A similar syndrome, which Spitz called 'hospitalism', involving physical and mental deterioration, is caused by prolonged hospitalization, when separation from the mother takes place.

What both these studies, and Bowlby himself, failed to recognize is that the institutions, which were clearly of a very poor quality, not only failed to provide adequate maternal care, but they were also extremely unstimulating environments in which to grow up. Consequently, we cannot conclude that it was 'maternal deprivation' that was responsible for the developmental retardation—we must distinguish between different *kinds* of deprivation and try to relate these to different kinds of retardation (Rutter, 1981).

Also, by using the general term 'maternal deprivation', Bowlby failed to distinguish between the effects of being separated from an attachment figure and the effects of never having formed an attachment to begin with. As Rutter (1981) points out, the term *deprivation* (de-privation) refers to the *loss* (through separation) of the mother-figure; the effects are usually *short-term* and can be summarized as *distress*. Bowlby was concerned mainly with *deprivation*. *Privation*, by contrast, refers to the *absence* of any attachment; the effects are usually *long-term* and can be summarized as *developmental retardation*.

In the remainder of this chapter we shall look at some of the most important effects of deprivation and privation, and conclude by asking how permanent the long-term effects are.

EFFECTS OF DEPRIVATION (SEPARATION)

i) SHORT-TERM

Typical examples of a short-term separation is a child going into a residential nursery while its mother goes into hospital to have another baby, or a child itself having to go into hospital. It is difficult to define precisely how short a short-term separation is but, as a rough guide, it is days or weeks, rather than months.

Bowlby has found that the term *distress* characterizes the kind of response which young children typically manifest when they go into hospital; it comprises three components or stages:

(a) *Protest*. The initial and immediate reaction takes the form of crying, screaming, kicking and generally struggling to escape or clinging to the mother to prevent her leaving. This is an outward and direct expression of everything the child feels—anger, fear, bitterness, bewilderment, etc.

(b) *Despair*. The struggling and protest eventually give way to calmer behaviour; the child seems to become apathetic. But internally the child still feels all the anger and fear that were previously displayed to the world; these are now kept locked inside and the child wants nothing to do with other people. The child may appear depressed and sad and may no longer anticipate the mother's return. It barely reacts to offers of comfort from others and prefers to comfort itself—by rocking, thumb-sucking, etc.

(c) *Detachment*. If the separation continues, the child begins to respond to people again but will tend to treat everybody alike and rather superficially. However, if reunited with the mother at this stage, the child may well have to 're-learn' the relationship with her and may even 'reject' her (as she 'rejected' her child).

But clearly not every child goes through these stages of distress and the degree of distress is not the same for all children. So what factors mediate to determine the kind of experience the separation is for a child?

a) Age of the Child

Separations are likely to be more distressing between six and seven months (when attachments have just developed) and three years, reaching a peak between twelve and eighteen months (Maccoby, 1980). One of the crucial variables associated with age is the ability to hold in the mind an image of the absent mother (ie to think of her). Also, the child's limited understanding of language, especially concepts like 'tomorrow' and 'only for a few days', makes it very difficult to explain to the child that the separation is only temporary (and why it has to take place). Young children, therefore, may believe that they have been abandoned altogether, that their mother no longer loves them, and that they may in some way be to blame for what has happened ('Because I'm naughty'). This makes it essential to try to compensate for the limitations of the child's understanding by, eg giving the child a photograph of the mother, even a tape-recording of her voice, or some article of her clothing, indeed, anything to keep alive the child's memory of her.

b) *Gender and Temperament*

Boys are generally more distressed and vulnerable than girls (everything else being equal). But boys vary a great deal in how they react to separations, as indeed do girls, ie some cope better than others. For both genders, any behaviour problems existing prior to separation are likely to become accentuated. For example, those who make poor relationships (with adults and/or children), or who are socially inhibited, uncommunicative or aggressive, are the most likely to be disturbed by admission to hospital.

c) *Existing Relationship with Mother and Previous Separations*

In general, the more stable and less tense the relationship before separation, the better the child appears to cope. For example, there is less chance that the child will blame itself in any way for the separation taking place.

On the other hand, an extremely close and protective relationship, where the child is rarely or never out of its mother's sight for more than a few minutes and where it is unused to meeting new people (children or adults), may cushion the child against separations to its disadvantage, ie the present separation will be more traumatic because the child has never experienced anything like it before!

Indeed, there is evidence that 'good' previous separations may not only help the child cope with subsequent separations but that they help the child become more independent and self-sufficient generally.

Stacey et al (1970) studied four-year-old children in Wales who went into hospital to have their tonsils removed. They stayed four days and their parents were not able to stay overnight. Some coped very well and it was discovered that they had experienced separations before, mostly staying overnight with their grandparents or a friend.

Multiple attachments should also make any separation less stressful because the child is, by definition, not totally dependent upon any one individual. Kotelchuck (1976), using the 'Strange Situation', found that when fathers are actively involved as caretakers, children are more comfortable when left alone with strangers and the period during which children strongly protested at separation was shorter if they were cared for by both parents (as opposed to mainly the mother).

d) *Unfamiliarity and Stimulating Quality of the Environment*

Bowlby's work and that of the Robertsons, who made a series of films in the 1960s on 'children in brief separation', helped bring into effect the policy of allowing mothers to stay with their children in hospital. Quite clearly, young children (and many adults) are distressed by a strange building, a strange bed, a different routine, strange sounds and smells, and unfamiliar faces which are always coming and going.

Many institutions in the past have proved very unstimulating places for young children. Jolly (1969) believes that boredom resulting from under-stimulation can itself cause distress, so adequate play facilities must be provided by trained workers.

A factor which can offset the effects of separation in general, and strangeness of the environment in particular, is the presence of persons familiar to the child, but not necessarily who provide any kind of substitute mothering, in particular a sibling, even if the sibling is too young to take on a caretaking role. Strangeness can also be offset by taking a familiar toy or blanket into hospital and visits before actual admission.

e) *Quality of Substitute Care*

In the total absence of the mother, the person or persons who take over the care of the child will determine to a large extent how distressed the child becomes. Multiple attachments will make the situation less stressful, especially if the child remains in its own familiar home environment or stays in another setting it knows well. Even institutions can provide high-quality substitute care, a famous example being the Hampstead nursery run by Burlingham and Anna Freud (1942–44), where stability, affection and active involvement were encouraged.

However, many institutions are run in such a way that it is virtually impossible for any kind of substitute attachment to develop. Staff rotas and turnover, a large number of children all competing for the attention of a few adults, and sometimes a deliberate policy of no special relationships in order to avoid claims of favouritism and resultant jealousies (eg the residential nurseries studied by Tizard and Rees (1974)) contribute to this (see below).

Effects of Day-care on Attachment

A number of American studies have compared the attachments of children (both working and middle-class, from one- and two-parent families) who have experienced day-care (usually a day-care centre) with those of children who have not. There seems to be general agreement that what matters is *not* whether or not the child experiences day-care but: (i) the quality of that substitute care, eg how well staffed the institutions are; and (ii) the stability of the arrangement.

Although there may be disturbance to the child's social and emotional development, this is usually only temporary and reflects the child's adjustment to being away from the mother (Vaughn et al, 1980). Indeed, there may be long-term benefits for the child who experiences day-care; for instance, Rubinstein and Howes (1979) found that infants placed in high quality centres were more socially adept with peers than comparable home-reared infants.

In one of the biggest longitudinal studies, Kagan et al (1980) studied children who experienced day-care for seven hours a day, five days a week, over five years. They were thoroughly tested from three-and-a-half to twenty-nine months for intellectual growth (eg language development), social development (eg relationships with other children) and attachment to the mother, and were compared with children raised at home. No significant differences were found between the two groups in any aspect of development, provided that the day-care facility was well staffed and well equipped; but poor centres can be harmful.

Another crucial factor is the role of work in the mother's life as a whole and whether she enjoys what she is doing. Hoffman (1974) reviewed 122 studies of working mothers and concluded that the dissatisfied mother, whether working or not, and regardless of social class, is less likely to be an adequate mother. Working mothers who enjoy their job are more affectionate and less likely to lose their tempers, and their children are likely to have higher self-esteem.

Studies of child-minders (Mayall and Petrie, 1977; Bryant et al, 1980) and day-nurseries in Britain (Garland and White, 1980) tend to confirm the American findings, especially in relation to quality and stability of the substitute care. However, the variety of quality of care, especially among child-minders, and the different beliefs about their function, especially among day nurseries, are perhaps greater than the American studies reveal and direct comparisons with children who do not receive regular substitute care have not been made.

ii) *LONG-TERM*

Long-term separation includes the permanent separation resulting from the death of a parent and the increasingly common separation caused by divorce. Possibly the most common effect of long-term separation is what Bowlby calls *separation anxiety*, namely the fear that separations will occur again in the future.

Psychosomatic reactions are one way in which separation anxiety may manifest itself. Others include: (i) increased aggressive behaviour and greater demands towards the mother; (ii) clinging behaviour—the child will not let the mother out of its sight; (iii) detachment—the child becomes apparently self-sufficient because it cannot afford to be let down again; and (iv) some fluctuation between (ii) and (iii).

Separation anxiety, expressed as clinging in the child, may generalize to relationships in general so that, for example in marriage, a man who experienced 'bad' separations in childhood may be very dependent on and demanding of his wife.

Bowlby regards *school phobia/refusal* as an expression of separation anxiety—the child fears that something dreadful will happen to its mother while it is at school and stays home in order to prevent it. Two major sources of such fears are: (i) actual events (eg the recent illness of the mother or the death of a relative); and (ii) threats by the mother that she will leave home or 'go mad' or 'kill herself' if things do not improve. (Recall that Bowlby interpreted Little Hans' fear of horses in terms of separation anxiety; see Chapter 21.)

The Effects of Death and Divorce

The total number of children under sixteen affected by divorce in England and Wales has increased steadily during the 1970s and 1980s, so that in 1986, 20 per cent of children will have been affected before their nineteenth birthday. About 60 per cent of all divorces involve children and of those affected, 25 per cent are under four years old. More than half of them will lose touch with the non-custodial parent within two years.

Both death and divorce can be misleadingly and inaccurately described as *events*, rather than *processes*, but only by regarding them as processes will we gain an understanding of how children are affected by them. Having said that, Richards (1987) points out that research shows that the consequences of divorce are more serious than those following the death of the father (children are much more likely to lose their father than their mother this way), a rather puzzling finding from the perspective of attachment theories like Bowlby's (which see the mother–child relationship as the critical one). How can this be explained?

Richards attempts to answer this by comparing the two situations as processes:

1) It is commonly found that children experiencing parental divorce show separation anxiety (eg by refusing to be left at nursery or school, insisting on having their bedroom light left on at night)—it is not surprising that they may begin to question the security of their remaining relationship, since if the father can leave, why not the mother too? (This could occur after a parent's death too but is less likely given the other differences below.)

2) Children usually deeply resent their parents' separation and may retain fantasies of reunion for many years to come. They experience the separation as a course that has been *chosen* by the parents in the knowledge that they (the children) do not want it. This makes them feel powerless, disregarded and angry.

By contrast, when a parent dies the child does not have to contemplate an act which was chosen by others against the child's wishes.

3) It is, sadly, commonplace for children to be given a very negative picture of the departing parent by the one who remains. When the father dies, however, he is often idealized. Also, the custodial parent is less likely to visit school to discuss the child's progress, etc. while widows usually become *more* involved. And, not surprisingly, divorce has a far greater negative effect on the child's school work than the death of a parent.

4) Especially if the departing parent loses regular touch with the child, the child may also lose contact with *all* the relatives on that side of the family.

The opposite seems to happen following a death—usually members of the whole kinship network are expected to play an active part in the funeral and grieving process. After divorce, however, there is a tendency to take sides and in-laws may cut off (or be cut off from) all future relationships.

5) Re-marriage is more likely after divorce and the interval is much briefer. This can create new stresses for children (eg having to get used to a step-parent and maybe step-siblings too), although it can also produce financial benefits (financial problems are usually more severe following divorce).

As a result of all these factors, the relationship between the child and the custodial parent is bound to suffer, at least temporarily. Hetherington et al (1978) studied four-year-olds living with their mothers following divorce and who were in regular contact with their fathers.

During the first year, mothers became more authoritarian, increasing the number of demands and restrictions and becoming less affectionate. The children (especially the boys) became more aggressive and inflexible.

Domestic routines became disrupted. Fathers tended to become less disciplinarian and more indulgent, treating the child and buying presents more often (the *crisis phase*).

By two years after the divorce, the balance was beginning to be restored—mother had become more patient and communicative and domestic life was more structured with both parents. The children's behaviour settled down accordingly (the *adjustment phase*).

Richards (1987) concludes that the best arrangement as far as the child's short- and long-term psychological well-being is concerned, is a good relationship with *both* parents following the divorce.

The essential point of difference between death and divorce is the degree of *conflict* which is typically involved—it is this, rather than divorce as such which seems to be damaging. This is consistent with the view that a bad marriage is *worse* for the children than divorce.

Similarly, it is very difficult in practice to separate the effects of the death itself from a whole host of factors associated with it, for example, break-up of the family, grief of the remaining parent and their ability to take over the role of the deceased, the actual circumstances of the death (long illness or accident) and so on.

Rutter (1970) studied nine- to twelve-year-old boys living on the Isle of Wight and in London. He came across several who had been separated from their mothers when young but who seemed quite well-adjusted. Although they had suffered difficulties at the time, they had overcome them when family life returned to normal; however, some were later rated as maladjusted. What differences were there between the two groups?

Rutter discovered that those who became maladjusted had been separated due to family discord, caused, for instance, by the psychiatric illness of one or both parents. Those who did not become maladjusted had been separated because of physical illness, housing problems or holidays, and not disturbance of social relationships as such—even the death of a parent had little lasting effect. Clearly, it is *not* separation, as such, which is harmful but the *reasons* for the separation and, the longer the family disharmony lasts, the greater the risk for the child.

EFFECTS OF PRIVATION

As we noted earlier, privation refers to the failure to develop an attachment to any individual and is usually, but not necessarily, associated with children reared from birth (or shortly after) in institutions. Dwarfism (failure to grow properly), for example, may result from inadequate diet, but also from maternal rejection (privation in a family setting). As we noted earlier, the studies of Spitz, Wolf and Goldfarb confused the effects of maternal and other kinds of privation, namely sensory and intellectual (all of which are normally referred to as forms of deprivation).

Prior to these studies, Skeels and Dye (1939) had shown a dramatic difference in intellectual functioning between an experimental group of children moved from a state orphanage in the USA to a state school for the mentally retarded, and a control group who stayed behind.

A total of twenty-five children were raised in an orphanage, where they experienced a minimum of social interaction and stimulation, until they were almost two years old (average age nineteen months); thirteen of them (average IQ, 64.3) were then transferred to a school for the mentally retarded where they received individual care from older, subnormal girls. They also enjoyed far superior play facilities, intellectual stimulation, staff–child ratios and so on. The other twelve children (average IQ 86.7) stayed behind and were the control group.

When they were about three-and-a-half years old, the experimental group of children either returned to the orphanage or were adopted; their average IQ had risen to 92.8 while that for the control group had dropped to 60.5. When they were seven years old, the average gain for the experimental group was 36 IQ points and the average loss for the control group was 21 points.

Skeels (1966) followed them up into adulthood. All the experimental subjects had more education than the controls, they had all finished high school, about one-third had gone to college, had married, had children of normal intelligence and had been self-supporting through their adult lives. The control subjects had mostly remained in institutions and were unable to earn enough to be self-supporting; they were still mentally retarded.

So what can we conclude about the effects of maternal privation?

a) *AFFECTIONLESS PSYCHOPATHY*

In the light of what we said earlier about the importance of the child's first relationship, it would not be unreasonable to expect that a failure to develop an attachment of any kind early on in life would adversely affect all subsequent relationships.

The Harlow 'socially deprived' infant monkeys, especially if they were brought up only with surrogate mothers (and not with other infants) were very disturbed in their later sexual behaviour, and unmothered females themselves become very inadequate mothers. (They have to be artificially inseminated because they will not mate naturally.) But what about human infants?

Bowlby's original contention was that maternal deprivation caused affectionless psychopathy, ie the inability to have deep feelings for other people and the consequent lack of meaningful interpersonal relationships. But his evidence for this is rather unconvincing.

In 1946, Bowlby studied forty-four juvenile delinquents who were attending a clinic, having been found guilty of theft. They were compared with a control group, similar in number, age and gender and who, like the first group, were emotionally disturbed (but were not guilty of theft).

Bowlby claimed that affectionless psychopathy was strongly linked to separation experiences in early childhood; fourteen of the forty-four thieves (but none of the control group) showed many characteristics of the affectionless character (including an inability to experience guilt) and seven of them had suffered complete and prolonged separation from their mothers, or established foster-mothers, for six months or more, during the first five years of life. Two others from among the fourteen affectionless characters had spent nine months in hospital, unvisited, during their second year (when attachments are normally being consolidated). Only three of the thirty other, non-affectionless, thieves had suffered comparable separations.

This suggests that *privation* rather than deprivation was the major cause of the affectionless character: the general picture is of multiple changes of mother-figure and home during the early years making the establishment of attachments very difficult (Rutter, 1981).

However, even if we accept this conclusion, there are still problems with the study. It was a *retrospective* study, which means that the delinquents and their mothers had to remember past events and we know that human memory is far from reliable (especially about very emotive experiences). Also, how does Bowlby account for the remainder of the juvenile thieves (the majority) who had *not* suffered complete and prolonged separations?

A further study carried out by Bowlby et al (1956) involved sixty children (forty-one boys and nineteen girls) aged between seven and thirteen, who had spent between five months and two years in a tuberculosis sanatorium, at various ages up to four years; about half of them had been separated from their parents before they were two. No substitute mothering was provided in the sanatorium, where forty to sixty children were in residence at any one time.

Compared with a group of non-separated control children from the same classes at school, few signficant differences emerged. For instance, the average IQ score of the sanatorium children was 107, compared with 110 for the controls, and teachers' ratings were only a little less favourable for the sanatorium children. Although the separated children did more daydreaming, showed less initiative, got over-excited, were rougher in their play, less able to concentrate and less competitive, the overall picture was of two groups who were more similar than different. There was certainly no evidence of the sanatorium children showing more signs of affectionless psychopathy than the controls, regardless of whether the separation had occurred before or after two years of age. Referring to the fact that illness and death were common in the families of the sanatorium children (10 per cent of the mothers had died by the time of follow-up), Bowlby et al themselves admit that:

> ... part of the emotional disturbance can be attributed to factors other than separation. (Bowlby et al, 1956)

Therefore, Bowlby's claim for a link between affectionless psychopathy and *separation* (bond disruption) seems largely unsubstantiated but, indirectly, he may have provided evidence to support the view that *privation* (failure to form bonds) may be associated with the affectionless character; Rutter too would support this latter view.

According to Rutter, it is possible that a failure to form bonds in early childhood is likely to lead to:

> An initial phase of clinging, dependent behaviour, followed by attention-seeking, uninhibited, indiscriminate friendliness and finally a personality characterized by lack of guilt, an inability to keep rules and an inability to form lasting friendships. (Rutter, 1981)

b) *DEVELOPMENTAL RETARDATION*

The Skeels and Dye (1939) and Skeels (1966) studies suggest that a crucial variable for intellectual development is the amount of intellectual stimulation the child receives, and not the amount of mothering (as Spitz, Goldfarb and Bowlby claimed).

In general, poor, unstimulating environments are associated with mental subnormality and retarded linguistic development (language is crucial for intellectual development generally). Also, Down's syndrome children make less progress in institutions than at home, and boys again seem more vulnerable than girls to the effects of most kinds of privation. There are very important individual differences within the sexes too.

One difficulty in trying to identify the effects of privation is to be able to pinpoint which type of privation (eg sensory, intellectual, social or emotional) produces which particular long-term effect. A possible solution is to try to identify critical or sensitive periods.

c) CRITICAL OR SENSITIVE PERIODS

It seems that the first six to eight months are critical for the rhesus monkey's social development and the first three years for the development of affectionless psychopathy in humans. As we noted earlier, Bowlby went even further and said that mothering is useless for most children after twelve months. Dennis (1960), based on his study of orphanages in Iran, concluded that there is a critical period for intellectual development before two years of age: children adopted from orphanages after two years, unlike those adopted earlier, seemed to be incapable of closing the gap in average IQ between themselves and the average child. Again post-natal brain growth is most rapid in the first two years of life and susceptibility to damage (eg from an inadequate diet) is greatest during periods of most rapid development (see Chapter 4).

So what is the evidence that critical or sensitive periods actually exist? In general, the more difficult it is to *reverse* the effects of privation, the stronger the belief in such crucial early developmental periods.

d) REVERSIBILITY OF LONG-TERM EFFECTS

Clarke and Clarke (1976), in a review of the relevant studies, came to the conclusion that the effects of early privation are much more easily reversible than has been traditionally thought.

For example, as far as Dennis's critical period for intellectual development is concerned, they argue that a later age of adoption makes adapting to the new home a totally different process from that experienced by the early-adopted child. Also, the child has had longer in which to develop habits which may interfere with adjustment; the child may be more withdrawn and disturbed and this may have a reciprocal effect on the family. Looked at in this way, the time spent in the institution has not had a direct, irreversible effect on intellectual functioning, but has had effects which may interfere with future learning and development. Again, though, the early-adopted child may have been brighter to begin with, which may have influenced their selection!

e) STUDIES OF ADOPTION

Barbara Tizard in *Adoption—a Second Chance* (1977) and Tizard and Hodges (1978), report their findings on children in care throughout their early years who, on leaving care, were either adopted or returned to their own families. (This was a continuation of the Tizard and Rees (1974) study referred to earlier.)

The children (first studied at age two; Tizard and Tizard, 1971) received good physical care in their institutions, which also appeared to provide adequately for their cognitive development—by four-and-a-half, the mean IQ score of the institution children was 105 (above the average of 100) and earlier signs of some language retardation were no longer evident.

However, staff turnover and an explicit policy against allowing too strong an attachment to develop between the children and the nurses who looked after them had given the children little opportunity to form close, continuous relationships with an adult. By the age of two, an average of twenty-four different caregivers had looked after them for at least a week; by age four, the average was fifty. This seems to fit Bowlby's (1951) description of maternal deprivation as, 'not uncommonly almost complete in institutions ... where the child aften has no one person who cares for him in a personal way and with whom he feels secure'. As a result, the children's attachment behaviour was very unusual. As we saw earlier, at two, they seemed to be attached to a large number of adults, ie they would run to be picked up when anyone familiar entered the room and cry when they left. At the same time, they were more fearful of strangers than a home-reared comparison group (Tizard and Tizard, 1971). By age four, 70 per cent of those still in institutions were said by the staff 'not to care deeply about anyone' (Tizard and Rees, 1974). It seems likely that generally the children's first opportunity for a close reciprocal long-term attachment came when they left the institutions and were placed in families, at ages ranging from two to seven years.

Although most formed attachments to their parents, the ex-institution children showed a number of atypical features in social development. At four, they were no longer shy of strangers. About one-third were markedly attention-seeking and over-friendly to strangers and a few were indiscriminately affectionate to all adults. Although these traits were shown only by a minority of the children, they did set the ex-institution children off as a group from comparison, non-institution children.

By age eight, the majority of adopted children and some of the restored children had formed close attachments to their parents, despite their lack of early attachments in the institutions. The adoptive parents very much wanted a child and put much time and energy into building up a relationship. The biological parents, by contrast, were more likely to be ambivalent about having the child back and often had other children, plus material difficulties, competing for their attention. According to their parents, the ex-institutional children did not present more problems than a comparison group who had never been in care; but according to their teachers more of them showed problems, notably attention-seeking behaviour, especially from adults, restlessness, disobedience and poor peer relationships—they were quarrelsome and unpopular (as they had been at age four). Their earlier over-friendliness also persisted (Tizard and Hodges, 1978). These difficulties are very similar to those reported by Goldfarb but, whereas he found many other problems in his ex-institutional group, including poorer cognitive and language skill, this was not the case with the present sample—presumably because the care offered in institutions has improved considerably since the 1940s.

Hodges and Tizard (1989) followed these children up again at age sixteen.

The family relationships of most of the adopted sixteen-year-olds seemed satisfactory, both for them and their parents and differed little from non-adopted comparisons who had never been in care. In contrast, the restored group still suffered difficulties and poor family relationships much more often than either the adoptees or their own comparison group. They and their parents were less often attached to each other and where there were siblings their mothers tended to prefer them to the restored child. Restored sixteen-year-olds showed less affection to their parents than did any other groups (as they had when aged eight) and their parents, equally, found it difficult showing affection to them; they seemed to identify less with their parents and wanted less involvement in family discussions. Restored adolescents also had more difficulty with siblings than did adoptees, probably because the former had entered their families to find younger siblings already there; the problems remained at mid-adolescence.

Although good relationships were not universal in the adoptive families, these families differed very little from their comparison group but contrasted greatly with the restored group. Early institutional care had not necessarily led to a later inability to form a close attachment to parents and to become as much a part of the family as any other child. Where the parent wanted the child and put a lot into the relationship, attachments were encouraged to develop and the adoption was successful; where this was lacking, the adoption 'situation' broke down.

In contrast, the two ex-institution groups showed very similar relationships to peers and adults outside the family. Although the indiscriminate 'over-friendliness' of some eight-year-olds was no longer a problem at sixteen, the ex-institution group was still more often oriented towards adult affection and approval than comparison adolescents. They were also more likely to have difficulties in peer relations, less likely to have a special friend or to see peers as a source of emotional support and more likely to be friendly to any peer, rather than choosing their friends:

> In conclusion, the study suggests that children who are deprived of close and lasting attachments to adults in their first years of life can make such attachments later. But these do not arise automatically if the child is placed in a family, but depend on the adults concerned and how much they nurture such attachments. Yet despite these attachments, certain differences and difficulties in social relationships are found over 12 years after the child has joined a family; these are not related to the kind of family, but seem to originate in the children's early institutional experience. Since they affect relationships with peers, as well as with adults outside the family, they may have implications for the future adult relationships of these 16 year-olds ... (Hodges and Tizard, 1989)

If their major relationship difficulties are with peers, would we expect this to apply to heterosexual relationships as much as to same-sex friendships? We need to know whether the ex-institution adolescents will be able to form stable, long-term relationships (Erikson's *intimacy*) and, in turn, be able to nuture children of their own (*generativity*).

Ideally, follow-up for another twenty to thirty years should be carried out (Gross, 1990).

Tizard (1977) believes that adoption is the best solution to children's needs, compared with the alternatives of continued institutionalization, long-term fostering or return to the natural family.

Kadushin (1970) in the USA followed up ninety-one children adopted between the ages of five and twelve years. The vast majority were perfectly successful when studied at age fourteen and the outcome was much better than expected on the basis of their early history of neglect, multiple changes of foster parents and late age of adoption.

Triseliotis (1980) followed up forty people born during 1956 and 1957 who had experienced long-term fostering (between seven and fifteen years in a single foster home before the age of sixteen) and interviewed them when they were twenty to twenty-one years old. He concluded that if the quality and continuity of care and relationships are adequate, the effects of earlier disruptions and suffering can be reversed and normal development can be achieved.

f) STUDIES OF CHILDREN SUFFERING EXTREME PRIVATION

Some very dramatic evidence comes in the form of studies of children who have been discovered after enduring years of extreme privation and isolation. Among the most famous are Anna (Davis, 1940, 1947), Isabelle (Mason, 1942), the Czech Twins (Koluchova, 1972, 1976), Genie (Curtiss, 1977) and the concentration camp survivors (Freud and Dann (1951). Less well known is the study by Skuse (1984) of Mary and Louise (see Gross, 1990).

Genie is briefly described in Chapter 24. Here, we shall look in some detail at the Freud and Dann Study (Box 22.1), the case of the Czech Twins (Box 22.2) and at Mary and Louise (Box 22.3).

Box 22.1   Childhood Survivors of the Holocaust (Freud and Dann, 1951)

Anna Freud and Sophie Dann studied six German–Jewish orphans rescued from a concentration camp at the end of the Second World War. They had all been orphaned when a few months old and thereafter kept together as a group in a deportation camp (Tereszin) and cared for by camp inmates who were successively deported to Auschwitz. One of the inmates who survived later said, 'We looked after the bodily welfare of the children as much as possible . . . but it was not possible to attend their other needs' (Moskovitz, 1985, cited in Tizard, 1986).

They had been subjected to many terrifying experiences, including witnessing camp hangings. On release, at age three, all were severely malnourished, normal speech had hardly developed, and they had developed the same kind of intense attachment to each other that children normally have for their parents and an absence of the jealousy and rivalry usually found among siblings. They refused to be separated even for a moment, and were extremely considerate and generous to each other. Towards adults they showed cold indifference or fearful hostility.

A month after the liberation of the camp by the Russians they were flown to England to a special reception-camp in Windermere, in the Lake District. Subsequently they were moved to Bulldogs Bank.

The children's positive feelings were centered exclusively in their own group. They obviously cared greatly for each other and not at all for anybody or anything else.

They refused to be separated, even for short moments. This insistence on being inseparable made it impossible at first to treat them as individuals. But gradually they began to form attachments to specific adult caretakers and, despite being jealous and possessive of each other's relationships, this lessened and they showed a spurt in social and language development.

Within the next two years, five of the six children were adopted. The exception was Berli, who was a very mischievous child, often getting into trouble at school and the children's home until early adolescence, when he began to settle down. At eighteen he went to live with an uncle in the USA. He spent a year in Vietnam, was a sergeant and teacher in the National Guard, and had a long and troubled marriage, which ended in bitter court battles.

Judith married and had children, as did Jack, a London taxi-driver, who talked of great feelings of aloneness which came in bursts every so often.

Leah married and had four children. She had migraines since childhood, very low self-esteem and was unsuccessful at school. She became a devout Christian. She had a fear of hospitals, had trouble sleeping and had received psychiatric care from age seven-and-a-half.

Gadi was a history teacher in the USA, having obtained a Master's Degree in Education. He had trouble adjusting to school and was prone to temper tantrums and locking himself in the bathroom. He died in 1980.

Finally, Bella married and had children, having met her husband while training to be a (Hebrew) Sunday class teacher. She believes strongly that:

... If children come from good [group] homes, where they have the companionship of other children, I think sometimes they're better off [there] than being isolated individually into families that don't really know how to cope with them.

All six were traced and interviewed by Sarah Moskovitz during 1979 and 1980 and described in her book *Love Despite Hate—Child Survivors of the Holocaust and their Adult Lives* (1983).

The Freud and Dann study suggests that it is bond formation which is important for the development of social and emotional relationships in later childhood and adulthood, rather than *with whom* the bond is formed:

Box 22.2   The Case of the Czech Twins (Koluchova, 1972, 1976)

Koluchova (1972) reported the case of two identical twin boys in Czechoslovakia, who were cruelly treated by their stepmother and found in 1967 at about seven years of age. They had grown up in a small, unheated closet, had often been locked in the cellar and were often harshly beaten. After their discovery, they spent time in a children's home and a school for the mentally retarded, before being fostered in 1969. At first they were terrified of many aspects of their new environment and communicated largely by gestures; they had little spontaneous speech. They made steady progress, both socially and intellectually.

A follow-up in 1976 reported that, at fourteen (seven years after discovery), the twins showed no psychopathological symptoms or unusual behaviour. In a personal communication to Clarke (reported in Skuse, 1984), Koluchova reported that by twenty they had completed quite a demanding apprenticeship (in the maintenance of office machinery), were above average intelligence, still had very good relationships with their foster mother and her relatives and their adopted sisters, and they had developed normal heterosexual relationships, both recently experiencing their first love affairs.

... This study provides ... evidence of the protective function of attachments in development, even when they are not directed to the mother, or indeed to an adult. (Tizard, 1986)

Similarly, the case of the Czech twins seems to highlight the fundamental importance of having *somebody* (not necessarily a mother-figure) with whom to form an emotional bond, as well as showing that the effects of long-term, extreme privation can be reversed.

Box 22.3   *The Case of Mary and Louise (Skuse, 1984)*

In 1977, Mary, almost nine, was referred to the Children's Department at a large post-graduate teaching hospital. During the previous year she had shown increasingly disruptive behaviour in the small children's hospital where she had lived the previous six years with her sister Louise (fourteen months older). Their early lives were spent in a remarkably deprived environment with a mentally retarded and microcephalic mother, who may have also been schizophrenic. Upon their discovery by the Social Services, they were described as '... very strange creatures indeed'.

Aged three-and-a-half and two-and-a-third, they took no notice of anyone, except to scamper up and sniff strangers, grunting and snuffling like animals. Both still sucked dummies, and no attempt had been made to toilet train them (so they were still in nappies). Neither had any constructive play but picked up objects, handled, smelt and felt them. Mary had no speech at all and made no hearing responses—she made just a few high pitched sounds. It later came to light that they had been tied on leashes to the bed, partly as a way their mother could ensure the flat stayed spotless and partly to ensure they would not fall off the balcony. If they became too noisy or active, they were put onto a mattress and covered with a blanket. They were subsequently taken into care.

---

g)   *STUDIES OF ISOLATED RHESUS MONKEYS*

In a similar vein, Harlow found that the rhesus monkeys which had been reared without a mother but with other baby monkeys grew up to be more-or-less normal adults, while those reared only with surrogate mothers developed abnormally, being unable to mate properly and, in the case of females, rejecting their offspring. However, this latter finding is hardly surprising; as Morgan (1974) points out, surrogate-only infants are being brought up without a society, apart from any other monkeys, which is a very abnormal state of affairs. Other monkeys, brought up with a mother only (no other babies), were less well adjusted than those reared normally with peers and a mother which is a much more informative finding.

As far as the reversibility of this early privation is concerned, Suomi and Harlow (1972), Novak and Harlow (1975) and Novak (1979) all found that whereas previously isolated monkeys (reared with surrogates) would completely ignore their first offspring, they would care for their second baby in a quite normal fashion. It appears that the first baby acts as a kind of monkey 'therapist' and as a consequence of this observation, previously isolated monkeys (for six months) were reared with younger, three-month-old female monkeys, chosen because they were less likely to be upset or aggressive when faced with an isolate's aggression or lack of response. The younger monkeys were also likely to approach and play on an elementary, rather than a sophisticated, level with the isolates.

After twenty-six weeks of 'therapy', the isolates' behaviour was virtually indistinguishable from that of a normally-reared monkey. Follow-up of these 'rehabilitated' monkeys showed their behaviour to be perfectly normal two years later (Cummins and Suomi, 1976).

Of course, we must not generalize from animals to humans. However, the general principle may be the same, namely, that only a deliberate programme of adequate and well-organized compensation will tell us if the effects of privation are reversible or not.

CONCLUSIONS: EARLY EXPERIENCE AND LATER DEVELOPMENT

Studies of maternal (de-)privation should be seen in the wider context of the effect of early experience on later behaviour and development. According to Rutter (1989), in recent years there has been something of a return to the view that development involves both *continuities* (consistencies of personality and behaviour) and *discontinuities* (inconsistencies).

The process of development is concerned with *change* and it is not reasonable to suppose that the pattern will be set in early life. Physiological changes (eg puberty) and new experiences will both serve to shape psychological functioning. But continuities will also occur because children carry with them the results of earlier learning and of earlier structural and functional change (Rutter, 1989).

The studies of adoption and extreme privation that we have discussed represent a major source of data regarding the whole continuity–discontinuity debate. What they seem to demonstrate is that theories which stress the overriding importance of early experience for later growth (ie critical periods) are inadequate (Clarke, 1972). Adverse early life experiences may, but not necessarily, have serious lasting effects on development in some circumstances (Rutter, 1981). Individuals show much resilience to such events and circumstances and there is no straightforward connection between cause and effect in most cases. Further, according to Skuse (1984), there is an increasing tendency to see the child as *part of a social system* in which they are in a mutually modifying relationship, with the mother no longer playing such a pivotal role. 'Maternal deprivation' is too general and heterogeneous and its effects too varied to be of continuing value (Rutter, 1981):

> There is now a need to focus instead on the particularities of specific early experience in order to understand better the various mechanisms by which they operate.
>
> Not only must variation in outcome relate to the specific deprivations and disortions of early experience, but the vulnerability of the individual to such adversity will itself vary. (Skuse, 1984)

Skuse (1984) asks if there is a characteristic clinical picture of the victim of such deprivation upon discovery? And do certain aspects of development seem more vulnerable than others?

The answer is 'Yes, there is a pattern': motor retardation, absent or very rudimentary vocal and symbolic language, grossly retarded perceptuomotor skills, poor emotional expression, lack of attachment behaviour and social withdrawal. (This combination is unlikely to be found in any other condition, except, perhaps, profound mental retardation and childhood autism.)

Language is undoubtedly the most vulnerable cognitive faculty—it was profoundly retarded at first in all cases (even where other features of mental development are apparently unaffected). By contrast, perceptuomotor skills are relatively resilient to lack of stimulation, as is gross motor development. The early combination of profound language deficit and apathy/withdrawal from social contact leads to special difficulties in developing a normal range and quality of relationships later on.

The evidence suggests that if recovery of normal ability in a particular faculty is going to occur, rapid progress is the rule.

However, further progress may be made several years after discovery, even in cases where the obstacles to success were thought to be genetic/congenital—in the case of Mary and Louise, both received speech therapy after discovery but this was abandoned with Mary due to poor progress. Her relative lack of social communication and language at age nine were reminiscent of autism. But four years later a remarkable transformation had occurred—she had made tremendous progress in both areas and such autistic features vanished. Despite having been placed in a variety of children's homes over that period, she did receive some consistent, intensive speech therapy (Skuse, 1984). Most human characteristics (with the possible exception of language) are strongly 'canalized' (Scarr-Salapatek, 1976) and hence virtually resistant to obliteration by even the most dire early environments:

> Fortunately the evidence reviewed suggests that, in the absence of genetic or congenital abnormalities, victims of such deprivation have an excellent prognosis. Some subtle deficits in social adjustment may persist. (Skuse, 1984)

23 SEX AND GENDER

It would probably be true to say that one of the first things we notice about somebody, if not *the* first thing, is whether they are male or female; it almost seems as if we need to have this information about a person if we are to be able to interact with them properly.

We also expect people to be able to identify us correctly as male or female and if they cannot, or do not, we would probably be most offended. Our name, age and sex are standard pieces of information on all official forms and our sex, of course, is one of the facts which appears on everyone's birth certificate.

Our sex, therefore, is a fundamental part of our self-concept and of our interactions with others. So, given its importance, it is perhaps surprising that there is so much confusion over the terms used to refer to it—sex, gender, sexual identity, sex role and so on. Many of these terms are used interchangeably, but there are crucial differences between them.

In this chapter, we will examine these terms and explore some of the misconceptions and confusions surrounding them. We will also discuss the major theories of sex and gender development: not surprisingly, these theories will once again be those which recur throughout this book, including Psychoanalytic, Learning, and Social Learning Theory.

TERMS RELATING TO SEX AND GENDER

1) Of all the terms used, *sex* is the only one which refers to some biological fact about a person. Our sex is our actual physical status, although it is much more complex than it is often taken to be. For example, there are many ways of defining it apart from our external sexual (genital) organs (we shall return to this in a moment).

Sexual identity is an alternative way of referring to our biological status as male or female.

2) Corresponding to our sex (or sexual identity) is our *gender* or *gender identity*, which refers to our classification of ourselves (and others) as male or female, boy or girl, etc. A continuous and persistent sense of ourselves as male or female, gender is something which develops gradually through a number of distinct stages. It is the social equivalent, or the social interpretation, of sex.

For most of us, sex and gender correspond, but an important exception is the transsexual (see below). So 'sex' is a biological term and is usually denoted by the terms 'male' and 'female' (which is how we are classified on our birth certificate) while 'gender' is a psychological or cultural term, which does not necessarily reflect biological sex.

3) *Gender role* (often called sex role) refers to the behaviours, attitudes, values, beliefs and so on, which a particular society expects from, or considers appropriate to, males and females on the basis of their

biological sex. So to be *masculine*, a male must conform to the male gender role; similarly, for a female to be *feminine*, she must conform to the female gender role.

4) The idea or belief which embodies these expectations is called a *gender role stereotype* (or sex role stereotype). It is a belief about what males and females are supposed to be like, as well as what they are 'naturally' like. Gender role stereotyping, therefore, gives rise to beliefs about *gender differences* (more commonly called *sex differences*).

We shall consider later whether there is any foundation for these stereotypes: are there any significant *psychological* differences between males and females and, if so, how do these differences arise? (Are they biologically or culturally determined—or both?)

5) If stereotypes refer to what males and females are meant to be like, *gender role behaviour* refers to what they are actually like. So we shall be trying to answer the question of whether gender role behaviour and gender role stereotypes bear any relationship to each other.

6) *Gender role identity* (or sex role identity) refers to the understanding and acceptance of gender roles, ie understanding and accepting that males and females are expected to be different from each other and to behave in different ways.

7) *Sex typing* refers to the differential treatment of children according to their (biological) sex. If gender differences do exist, then sex typing may be a major determining factor.

8) *Sexual orientation* or *preference* refers to an individual's tastes or preferences in sexual partners: this can be *hetero*sexual (preference for a partner of the opposite sex, 'hetero' meaning 'different'), *homo*sexual (preference for a partner of the same sex, 'homo' meaning 'same'), or *bi*sexual (a choice of both kinds of partner, although there may be a stronger preference for one or the other).

Homosexuals are anatomically normal males or females, whose gender identity is, usually, quite consistent with their biological sex and sex of rearing.

9) The *transsexual* is an anatomically normal person who genuinely and very firmly believes that he or she is a member of the opposite sex ('trapped' inside an 'alien' body). Consequently, there is a fundamental inconsistency between their biological sexual identity and their gender identity.

BIOLOGICAL CATEGORIES

Biologically, sex is *not* a unidimensional variable, ie there are at least five separate biological categories which can be distinguished, each constituting a (partial) definition:

(a) *Chromosomal sex*. XX female and XY male.
(b) *Gonadal sex*. The sexual or reproductive organs (ovaries in females and testes in male).
(c) *Hormonal sex*. The male hormones are the *androgens*, the most important of which is *testosterone* (secreted by the testes); the ovaries secrete two distinct types of female hormone, namely *oestrogen* and *progesterone*. While the number and range of hormones produced by males and females are virtually the same, females

usually produce a preponderance of oestrogen and progesterone, while males usually produce a preponderance of testosterone and androgen, ie we all produce both male and female hormones, but males usually produce more male hormones and females more female hormones.

(d) *Sex of the internal accessory organs.* The wolffian ducts in males and the mullerian ducts in females. These are the embryonic forerunners of the reproductive structures (namely, the prostate gland, sperm ducts, seminal vesicles and testes in males and the fallopian tubes, womb and ovaries in females).

(e) *Function and appearance of the external genitalia.* The penis and scrotum in males, the outer lips of the vagina (labia majora) in females (Fig. 23.1).

Figure 23.1 Pre-natal differentiation of male and female genitalia. From a relatively undifferentiated state, development proceeds by means of the relative enlargement of structures that have analogues in members of the other sex. (From Unger, R. K. (1979) Female and Male, *New York: Harper and Row)*

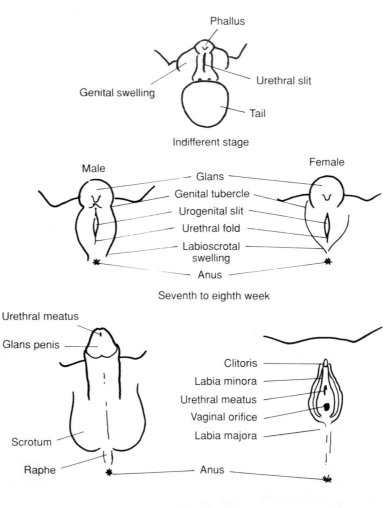

All five of these sexual categories are usually highly correlated, ie an individual tends to be either male in all these respects or female in all these respects. They also tend to be correlated with non-biological aspects of sex, including the sex to which the baby is assigned at birth, how the child is brought up, gender identity, gender role identity and so on.

However, there are certain disorders which arise during pre- and post-natal development resulting in an inconsistency or lack of correlation between the five sexual categories described above. From these we can learn a great deal about the development of gender identity, gender role and gender role identity; collectively, individuals with such disorders are known as hermaphrodites.

HERMAPHRODITISM

This term is currently used to refer to any discrepancy or contradiction between any of the various components of sexual anatomy and physiology, although, strictly the term hermaphrodite (from the mythical Greek god/goddess, who had attributes of both sexes) denotes a person who has functioning organs of both sexes (either simultaneously or sequentially).

So included under this heading are:

(a) Chromosome abnormalities, where there is a discrepancy between chromosomal sex and external appearance, including the genitalia (the best known are Turner's syndrome (XO) and Klinefelter's syndrome (XXY).
(b) Testosterone insensitivity or testicular feminizing syndrome.
(c) Adrenogenital syndrome.
(d) True hermaphroditism (the others are, strictly, pseudo-hermaphrodites) (Box 23.1).

Both (b) and (c) are the effects of hormones (or lack of them) on the process of sexual differentiation, and we shall concentrate on them now.

Box 23.1   The Case of Mr Blackwell

In an article called 'The Fight to be Male' (*The Listener*, May 1979), Edward Goldwyn cites the case of Mr Blackwell, only the 303rd patient in all of medical history to be a true hermaphrodite. He is described as a handsome and rather shy eighteen-year-old Bantu. Although he had a small vaginal opening as well as a penis, he was taken to be a boy and brought up as such. But when he was fourteen he developed breasts and was sent to hospital to discover why this had happened. It was found that he had an active ovary on one side of his body and an active testicle on the other. He expressed the wish to remain male and so his female parts were removed.

Goldwyn points out that if his internal ducts had been differently connected, Mr Blackwell could have actually fertilized himself without being able to control it.

TESTOSTERONE INSENSITIVITY (TESTICULAR FEMINIZING SYNDROME)

(See Box 23.2, p. 683—the Batista family.)

At least in the case of the Batista family the eventual sexual status is quite unambiguous—by the age of twelve they are, unequivocally, male.

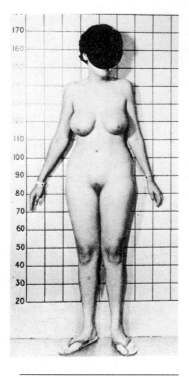

Figure 23.2 Adult with testicular feminization (XY, but with an insenstivity to androgen). These individuals are usually taller than the average female and tend to have a very attractive 'female' physique. (From Money, J. and Ehrhardt, A. (1972) Man and Woman, Boy and Girl. Baltimore: Johns Hopkins Press. Copyright 1972 by the Johns Hopkins Press. Reprinted by permission)

But there are many individuals who never complete the route to maleness and end up as neither fully male nor fully female.

Goldwyn describes the case of Daphne Went, a motherly-looking woman, who possessed two testes where most women have ovaries. She is one of 500 or so 'women' in Britain who have this condition called Testosterone Insensitivity (or Testicular Feminizing Syndrome).

This woman's development began along the male route but it was never finished. The egg was fertilized by a Y sperm and two normal testes developed. They secreted their first hormone, which absorbed the female parts, but when they produced testosterone her body did not respond to it. So, apart from the womb, which had gone, everything developed along female lines. When at puberty she developed no pubic hair and did not menstruate (despite breast development and female contours—as a result of the action of oestrogen), there was clearly something wrong! Hormones did not bring on her periods because she had no womb. Chromosomally, Mrs Went is male, in terms of her gonads she is also male (she has testes), but her external appearance is female. She is married, has adopted two children and leads an active and successful life as a woman.

This insensitivity to testosterone is due to a recessive gene and is often diagnosed when a hernia (lump in the abdomen) turns out to be a testis. There is a high probability that the testes will become malignant and so these are usually removed surgically. A 'blind' (very short) vagina is present so that little or no plastic surgery is needed for the adoption of a female appearance and gender role. The Y chromosome tends to give these individuals extra height, which is more typical of males than females (Fig. 23.2).

ADRENOGENITAL SYNDROME

This is more common than the Testicular Feminizing Syndrome and is really the converse of it. It is caused by an excessive amount of a testosterone-like substance during the development of a chromosomally normal female. It can happen in one of two ways: either (i) *endogenously* (originating from within), where androgens (male hormones) are produced by excessive activity of the mother's adrenal glands during pregnancy (the adrenal glands produce oestrogens and androgens in both sexes); or (ii) *exogenously* (originating from without), where the mother takes progesterone (which is chemically very similar to testosterone) in the form of an artificial hormone preparation called 'progestin', or other steroids, in an attempt to prevent miscarriage.

However it is caused, the adrenogenital syndrome involves the female's external genitalia bearing varying degrees of resemblance to the male external genitalia. There is usually an enlarged clitoris and fusion of the labioscrotal folds, producing a rather ambiguous genital appearance. Some individuals have even had a complete closure of the urethral groove and a penis capable of becoming erect. The internal organs do not appear to be affected, however.

Until fairly recently, sex at birth was assigned on the basis of inspection of the genitalia, so that two individuals with equivalent ambiguities might have been classified differently. More recently, information about the structure of the gonads and the chromosomal make-up of the individual has been acquired, so that females with the syndrome are usually raised as females. The internal structure is usually female and many such individuals are fertile. Therefore, a relatively small amount of cosmetic surgery is all that is required to bring their external appearance into line with other components of their sexual identity (Fig. 23.3).

Those whose adrenals are over-active must also take cortisone to prevent early virilization or masculinization at puberty.

GENDER ROLE DIFFERENCES (WILL BOYS BE BOYS AND GIRLS BE GIRLS?)

So far, we have been looking at some of the key concepts involved in sex and gender as well as some very important biological aspects of sex, which we shall draw on when discussing the more directly psychological issues. One of these is to do with gender role differences (or *psychological sex differences*). There are at least two distinct but related questions involved here:

(a) Is there any evidence that boys and girls do actually behave in accordance with gender roles? That is, are boys in fact more masculine than girls and girls more feminine than boys? This is the issue of *psychological sex differences*.

(b) If such differences do exist, how do we account for them? This is another example of the *heredity–environment issue*.

Probably the best way of answering the first question is to summarize the conclusions of Maccoby and Jacklin in one of the largest reviews of the literature, *The Psychology of Sex Differences* (1974). They set out to show that many of the popular stereotypes about males and females are not borne out by the evidence and concluded that there is a great deal of myth in both popular and scientific views regarding male–female differences (as well as some degree of truth). They spent three years compiling, reviewing and interpreting over two thousand books and articles on sex differences in motivation, social behaviour and intellectual ability. (The terms 'sex' and 'gender' will be used interchangeably when discussing Maccoby and Jacklin's work.)

What are some of the myths?

(i)   girls are more 'social' than boys;
(ii)   girls are more suggestible than boys;
(iii)   girls have lower self-esteem than boys;
(iv)   girls lack achievement motivation relative to boys;
(v)   boys are more 'analytic' than girls;
(vi)   girls are more affected by heredity and boys by environment;
(vii)   girls are 'auditory' while boys are 'visual'.

What are the some of the differences for which Maccoby and Jacklin did find evidence?

Males are More Aggressive than Females

In all cultures where aggression has been observed, boys are more aggressive than girls, both physically and verbally. They engage in

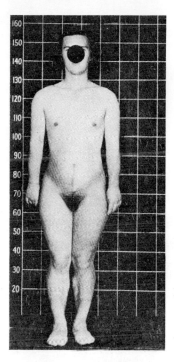

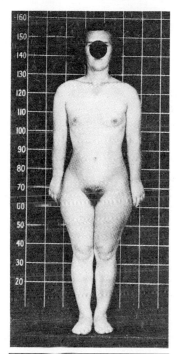

Figure 23.3 Above, *the masculinized body contours of a female with untreated adrenogenital syndrome. Below, the beginning of feminization induced by treatment. (From Money, J. and Ehrhardt, A. (1972).*

mock-fighting and aggressive fantasies, as well as in direct forms of aggression more often than girls.

The difference manifests itself as soon as social play begins, at about two-and-a-half years. From an early age the primary victims of male aggression are other males, not females. Although both sexes become less aggressive with age, boys and men remain more aggressive during the college years. Little information is available for older adults (see Chapter 16).

Girls have Greater Verbal Ability than Boys

Girls' verbal abilities probably mature somewhat more rapidly in early life, although a number of studies have found no sex differences. From pre-school to adolescence, the sexes are very similar in their verbal abilities. But at about eleven, they begin to diverge and female superiority increases during adolescence and possibly beyond.

Girls score higher on tasks that involve understanding and producing language and on 'high level' verbal tasks (analogies, comprehension of difficult written material, creative writing) as well as 'lower level' measures (fluency and spelling).

Boys Excel in Visual–Spatial Ability

This involves the visual perception of figures or objects in space and how they are related to each other, eg jigsaw puzzles require this sort of ability. Male superiority does not appear in childhood but is fairly consistent in adolescence and adulthood. The sex differences are roughly equal on analytic and non-analytic tasks.

Boys Excel in Mathematical Ability

The sexes are similar in the early acquisition of number concepts and the mastery of arithmetic during the primary school years. But beginning at about 12 or 13, boys' mathematical skills increase faster than girls'. Different studies tend to reveal differences of varying sizes, but overall they are not as great as for spatial ability.

On some issues, Maccoby and Jacklin found ambiguous or inconclusive findings or too little evidence on which to base any definite conclusions—a lot more research is clearly needed into the following areas:

(i)   are there differences in tactile sensitivity?
(ii)   are there differences in fear, timidity and anxiety?
(iii) is one sex more active than the other?
(iv)   is one sex more competitive than the other?
(v)   is one sex more compliant than the other?

There has been a steady stream of research since Maccoby and Jacklin's review was published in 1974. For example, some studies show that boys are more active than girls, more willing to take risks, more demanding and less likely to comply with parental requests.

Maccoby (1980) suggests that perhaps there is, after all, some truth in the popular belief that boys are harder to bring up than girls.

Maccoby and Jacklin concluded in 1974 that, from their survey of all the data, many popular, widely held, gender-role stereotypes have little or no basis in fact; yet people continue to believe them and to be influenced by them. Why should this be?

One explanation is that our perception is selective—we see what we expect to see—and so myths live on that would otherwise die out under the impact of negative (counter) evidence. Maccoby (1980) argues that even if group gender differences are found in a given area of behaviour (physical, cognitive, emotional or social), the behaviour of individual members of the two genders is often very similar. Men and women, boys and girls, are more *alike* than they are different.

GENDER ROLE IDENTITY

Before we turn to the question of how we can explain the differences that are found between males and females, we should consider the evidence that children understand and accept gender role differences.

Kuhn et al (1978) found that even two-and-a-half- to three-and-a-half-year-olds categorize certain behaviours as 'boy' or 'girl' behaviours and Kohlberg (1966) reported that toddlers know that crossing these gender role lines is to be avoided at all costs.

Maccoby (1980) concluded that boys are more likely to avoid 'sissy' behaviours than girls are to avoid 'tomboy' behaviours. This seems to support, and to reflect, the different valuations that these two labels have: to be a 'sissy' (ie to behave in a feminine way if you are a male) is a greater sin than to be a 'tomboy' (ie to behave in a masculine way if you are female), implying that masculine behaviour in general is somehow more desirable than feminine behaviour. (We shall return to this issue at the end of the chapter when we consider the concept of *androgyny*.)

Maccoby and Jacklin (1978) found that, by the age of three, children play more with same gender playmates than those of the opposite gender. Parish and Bryant (1978) found that children aged five to eleven tend to be more positive about their own gender and more negative about the opposite gender. They also give higher ratings to male and female peers who excel in subject areas that their gender is known to do well in, eg girls who did well in reading and boys in mathematics received higher ratings from their eleven- and twelve-year-old peers than boys who did well in reading and girls in mathematics.

We will now return to the second question, ie if psychological sex differences do exist, how can we account for them?

There are a number of competing (and sometimes conflicting) theories that try to explain gender differences and gender role identity, in particular: (i) the biological approach (Hutt, 1972); (ii) Biosocial Theory (Money and Ehrhardt, 1972); (iii) Freud's Psychoanalytic Theory; (iv) Social Learning Theory (Bandura, 1977); (v) cultural relativism (Mead, 1935); and (vi) Cognitive–Developmental Theory (Kohlberg, 1966).

i) THE BIOLOGICAL APPROACH

This does not represent a unitary theory (as do the others that we shall be discussing) but rather a way of trying to account for gender differences by concentrating directly on biological aspects of sex differences, such as genetic differences, the process of sexual differentiation, hormonal differences and so on.

As far as sexual differentiation is concerned, Alfred Jost proposed in the

1950s that the natural form of the human is female. This was based on his observation (in rats) that even if the ovaries are removed at the earliest stage of embryonic development, growth still follows a female route, while if the testicles are removed early on, development reverts to the female route. (This was confirmed by Jost in 1970 using rabbits.) So Jost saw male development as the result of interference with the natural (female) developmental course; if a Y chromosome is present, the gonad becomes the testis and male development proceeds, while in the absence of a Y chromosome an ovary is produced and the embryo becomes a female (see Fig. 23.1).

Not only does the presence or absence of a Y chromosome determine the course of sexual differentiation, it also seems to be correlated with the biological vulnerability of the sexes, both before and after birth. Although in theory there is a 50:50 chance of a male or female being conceived, in fact there is a preponderance of males: approximately 120 males are conceived for every 100 females, but this ratio reduces to 110:100 for fetuses that survive to full-term (40 weeks of pregnancy), and reduces still further to 106:100 for live births.

This means that more male foetuses are spontaneously aborted and more of them are stillborn or die of birth trauma (including congenital deformities). In fact, throughout life, the male is more vulnerable than the female. For example, in the first year of life, 54 per cent of all deaths involve boys, at the age of twenty-one the figure rises to 68 per cent, and by fifty-five it is still as high as 64 per cent. Between sixty-five and seventy this difference diminishes and after seventy-five, the ratio of women to men is higher—more women survive to older ages, ie their average life-expectancy is higher (see Chapter 24). Males are also more susceptible to asphyxiation, cerebral palsy, convulsions, virus infections, ulcers, heart disease and some kinds of cancer, and the smaller Y chromosome makes the male more vulnerable to various kinds of inherited diseases and disorders (eg haemophilia).

There is no doubt that males are, biologically, the weaker sex!

Genetic and hormonal differences are responsible for a number of sex-linked characteristics which are apparent at birth or shortly after. For instance, several studies have shown that female infants are hardier, more regular in their sleeping and eating patterns, more socially responsive, mature faster and are more sensitive to pain, while larger, more muscular males tend to sleep less, cry more, be more active, more irritable and harder to pacify.

Could it be that, if these sex differences are innate, males and females are biologically programmed for certain kinds of activities that are compatible with male and female roles? For instance, might boys be predisposed towards aggression, assertiveness, rough-and-tumble play, etc. by virtue of higher pain thresholds, higher activity levels, a more muscular physique and their more irritable and demanding temperament? And might docile, undemanding and highly verbal females be ideally suited for adopting nurturant, co-operative, compliant roles? Is there any evidence to support the biological view?

The case of the four Batista boys (Box 23.2), who were raised as girls from birth and who at puberty suddenly 'became' males seems to support the biological view; inside each female body was a brain which had been masculinized by the testosterone present before birth and which was then activated by another surge at puberty. They have all taken on male roles, do men's jobs, have married women and are accepted as men in spite of the fact that they were reared as girls and, presumably, thought of themselves as girls for the first 10 years or so of their lives (ie had a female gender identity). However, they may have made the transition as easily as they did because their environment supported their new identity.

Box 23.2   The Case of the Batista Family (Imperato-McGinley et al (1974))

Imperato-McGinley et al (1974) studied a remarkable family who live in Santo Domingo in the Dominican Republic (in the Caribbean). Of the ten children in the Batista family, four of the sons have changed from being born and growing up as girls into muscular men. These four children were born with normal female genitalia and body shape but, when they were twelve, their vaginas healed over, two testicles descended and they grew full-size penises.

The Batistas are just one of twenty-three affected families in their village in which thirty-seven children have undergone this change. All these families had a common ancestor, Attagracia Carrasco, who lived in the mid-eighteenth century. She passed on a mutant gene which only shows when carried by both parents.

What happens to these children in the womb?

The egg is fertilized by a Y sperm and it first develops into a fetus with normal testes. The female parts are absorbed in the normal way and testosterone preserves the male ducts. But the body misses a critical chemical step and so the external anatomy does not change. The step that is missed is the production of the hormone dihydrotestosterone which, it is now known, is responsible for creating the male external anatomy.

The change that occurs at puberty is due to the flood of testosterone which, in turn, produces enough dihydrotestosterone to give the normal male appearance (which would normally happen ten to twelve years earlier).

Brecher (1970) reports findings for a group of women who had developed a defect of the adrenal gland which causes secretion of male hormones, both before and after birth. If untreated, this can speed up the rate of sexual development and may bring puberty forward to the age of five or six. Cortisone therapy in the 1950s enabled the adrenals to be partially switched off. But, compared with a control group matched for age, intelligence and social class, these women were much more tomboyish

The claim that the Batista boys could so easily assume male roles because the testosterone had pre-programmed masculinity into their brains itself implies that male and female brains are different. Is there any evidence that they are?

Dorner (1968), who worked with rats, thinks so. He identified a sex centre in the brain such that when a small part of this was destroyed in a newborn male, it would behave as a female. In his terms, it became homosexual. Dorner argues that the same basic differences exist in human brains and that male homosexuals have a female brain. This happens, he claims, due to unusually low levels of testosterone in the womb. In turn, low levels of the male hormone can be induced by high levels of stress in the pregnant mother. But again, this relationship is based on studies of rats. Clearly, generalizing from rats to humans must be done with great caution.

The case of Mrs Went (see p. 678) certainly does nothing to support Dorner's hypothesis, nor is there any convincing evidence that there are hormonal differences between homosexual and heterosexual adults.

Another case, that of Mr Blackwell (see Box 23.1), also detracts from the biological view. He has a female brain—his hormones used to go through a complete female menstrual cycle and he used to ovulate once a month. Yet, despite his female brain, he wanted to remain a male and does not display the female behaviour predicted by Dorner's theory.

A different kind of evidence relating to brain differences is to do with hemispheric specialization (see Chapter 4). As measured by brainwave patterns, it appears that men have a greater degree of such specialization than women. For example, when performing spatial tasks, a man's right hemisphere tends to be more active while with women both hemispheres are activated. In fact, the right hemisphere is generally the dominant one in men and the left in women, which could explain why men are *generally* superior at spatial and mathematical tasks and women at verbal tasks.

Ornstein (1986) refers to the work of De Lacoste and her colleagues, who are beginning to be able to identify the male and female corpus collosum by sight alone. They are, it seems, as 'diamorphic' as are male and female arms: womens' are larger overall and longer towards the back of the brain.

But Bogen (1969) believes that we must not let the 'rich diveristy of natural phenomena obscure our recognition of the common and representative types', ie the similarities still outweigh the differences (see Chapter 4).

Maccoby (1980) too argues that the similarities are greater than the differences between men and women; in other words, the differences *within* each gender are at least as great as the differences *between* them.

ii) *BIOSOCIAL THEORY*

Biosocial Theory, as the name suggests, takes social factors into account in relation to biological ones. Specifically, it focuses on how babies of different temperaments contribute to their own development by influencing how others treat them; it is the *interaction* between biological and social factors that is important rather than the influence of biology directly.

Intuitively, it is easy to see how these constitutional differences can be reinforced by interaction with adults. Adults prefer to spend time with babies who respond to them in 'rewarding' ways, and more demonstrative babies (or 'demanding' ones) tend to receive the adult attention they seek while the more passive baby is more easily 'forgotten'.

However, the baby's sex is just as important as its temperament as far as others are concerned. For instance, Moss (1967) found that even at three weeks after birth, boys are more irritable than girls but, significantly, mothers become relatively less responsive to boys who are crying compared with girls; perhaps they find that attempts to comfort their sons are less effective, or perhaps they believe that boys should not be 'pampered' as much as girls. Whichever of these is true (or even if both apply), we can once again see the reciprocal nature of the parent–child relationship—babies influence their parents at least as much as parents influence them and this is an ongoing process throughout childhood.

Money and Ehrhardt (1972) have concentrated on the very *fact* of a child's sexual identity in their Biosocial Theory. For them 'anatomy is destiny' in the sense that how the infant is labelled sexually determines how the infant is raised or socialized. This, in turn, determines the child's *gender identity* and from this follow gender-role, gender-role identity and sexual orientation or preference.

Money and Ehrhardt believe that at first there is considerable flexibility in the process by which the child categorizes itself as a boy or girl: the 'sex of rearing' can be changed within the first two and a half to three years without any undue psychological harm being done. However, once a child has developed a gender identity, being reassigned to the opposite sex can result in extreme psychological disturbance. Thus the first two-and-a-half to three years of life are seen as a *critical* or *sensitive period* for the development of gender identity.

Money and Ehrhardt (1972) studied girls who were suffering from the adrenogenital syndrome and who were raised as boys. If the mistake was discovered, their genitals surgically corrected and they were reassigned and reared as girls before the age of three, then they easily accepted the gender change; but when this happened after three years there were many adjustment problems.

Based on their studies of hermaphrodites and pseudo-hermaphrodites, Money and Ehrhardt, Hampson and Hampson, and others, conclude that, despite disparities between an individual's genetic sex, hormonal sex, internal and external organs and the sex of rearing, in the vast majority of cases the individual assumes the gender role consistent with the sex of rearing. In their view, *psychologically*, sexuality is undifferentiated at birth and it becomes differentiated as masculine or feminine in the course of various experiences of growing up.

Money and Ehrhardt (1972) studied ten individuals with the Testicular Feminizing Syndrome (who, remember, are genetically male but who are invariably reared as female because of their female external appearance). These ten showed a high preference for the female role: eight preferred the role of homemaker over an outside job and all reported dreams or fantasies of raising a family. Eight had played primarily with dolls and other typically female toys. They rated themselves high on affection and were fully content with the female role. From other studies it has been shown that such people often find employment in jobs that put a high premium on an attractive female appearance and feminine behaviour, eg modelling, acting and even prostitution.

The case of Mrs Went, discussed earlier, also tends to support the view that sex of rearing is more important than biological sex.

Money, Hampson and Hampson (1957) studied matched pairs of individuals with the adrenogenital syndrome, the members of each pair having a very similar external genital appearance. The crucial difference between them was that they had been assigned to a different sex. They concluded that psychosexual identity is established more in accordance with the sex of rearing than on the basis of any biological factors. Money (1971) pointed out that requests for sexual reassignment are very rare amongst such individuals. The conformity of most hermaphrodites to their early sex of assignment is so strong that it can withstand ugly virilization in a 'girl' at puberty or breast development and difficulties in having an erection in a 'boy'. In *Man and Woman, Boy and Girl* (1972) Money and Ehrhardt maintain that the human central nervous system is so amenable to the effects of learning that biological contributions to psychosexual identity can be moulded and even reversed by the social influences of early childhood.

However, Diamond (1965, 1968) points out that to demonstrate that human beings are flexible in their psychosexual identity does not in itself disprove that 'built-in biases' still have to be overcome. Money et al's subjects have been hermaphrodites and, therefore, atypical, not representative of the population as a whole. Is it valid to generalize from an abnormal sample to the 'normal' population? The fact that individuals of ambiguous sex are flexible in their psychosexual orientation and identity does not necessarily mean that the same is true of people in general.

How could we settle the controversy? (Box 23.3).

Box 23.3   The Circumcision that Went Wrong (Money, 1974)

A classic piece of evidence relevant to the issue was reported by Money in 1974. It involves a pair of monozygotic (identical) twins whose embryonic and fetal development were that of a normal male. An accident during circumcision (by cautery) caused one of the twins to lose his penis. Assuming that gender is primarily a social phenomenon, and that identity is learned, it was decided to raise the unfortunate 'penectomized' boy as a girl.

This would seem to be a decisive way of choosing between the learning versus biological arguments, by letting rearing 'compete' with biology, and it would have been a true test case had not as much as possible been done to 'defeat' the male biological realities and to enhance female biological maturation.

At seventeen months, 'he' was castrated, ie the androgen-secreting testes were removed, and was given oestrogen (female hormone); a vaginal canal was constructed at this time. Much earlier than this, the parents changed 'his' clothes and hairstyle. By the age of four, 'he' preferred dresses to trousers, took pride in 'his' long hair and was much neater and cleaner than 'his' brother. 'He' sat while urinating, in the usual female fashion, and was modest about exposing 'his' genitals (in contrast to the other twin, for whom an incident of public urination was described by the mother with amusement). 'He' was encouraged to help the mother with the housework, while the brother 'couldn't care less about it'.

At five years, 'he' had many tomboyish traits, but was encouraged to be less rough and tough than the other twin, and was generally quieter and more 'ladylike', while the normal twin was physically protective of his 'sister'. At nine years, although 'he' had been the dominant one since birth, 'he' expressed this by being a 'fussy little mother' to 'his' brother. The brother continued to play the traditional protective, male role.

This seems to support the view that gender identity (and gender role) is learnt. The reversal of original sexual assignment is possible if it takes place early enough and is consistent in all respects, which includes the external genitalia conforming well enough to the new sex. However, the castration and use of oestrogen clearly contributed to the ease of reassignment and probably also accounts for the normal twin being taller.

iii) *FREUD'S PSYCHOANALYTIC THEORY*

We have discussed Freud's theory of psychosexual development in great detail in Chapter 21.

You will recall that, according to Freud, sexual identity and sex role are acquired (along with a superego) when the Oedipus complex is resolved, at five or six years of age. The role of the traditional mother and father family unit (two-parent family) is, therefore, of crucial importance in Freud's theory of sexual development, whereby the child must identify with the same-sex parent.

So what would Freud have predicted about the psychosexual development of a child who grows up in an 'abnormal', atypical family, which is becoming increasingly commonplace in contemporary society: for example, single-parent families, including lesbian and heterosexual women who have become pregnant by artificial insemination, and lesbian couples with children (eg the lesbian mother is given custody of the child or children after a divorce)? Indeed, according to Rutter (1979), the non-traditional family may have become the norm. Is there any evidence that psychosexual development is adversely affected as a result of growing up in an 'un-Freudian' family?

According to Lamb (1977, 1979), fathers, at the beginning of the child's second year, begin to pay special attention to their sons and withdraw from their daughters. As this happens, boys channel their attention towards their father's behaviour and girls towards their mother's. Through this channelling, children prefer to interact with the same-gender parent and this makes it more likely that identification will occur. So preference for the same-gender parent does seem to be a major factor in the child's acquisition of gender role identity. Research on father absence, for example by Hetherington (1966, 1972), supports the idea that gender role identity develops within the first two or three years and that fathers are important in this process. If the father is absent before the boy's fourth birthday, he is apt to be less 'masculine', in the sense of being more dependent on his peers, less assertive and less involved in competitive and physical contact sports. However, after the age of four, absence of the father has little effect on the boy's gender role identity. In the case of girls, the effect does not usually show up until adolescence; the most common outcome of father absence for girls is difficulty in adjusting to the female role and in interacting with men. More about fathers when we discuss androgyny.

The biggest single fear expressed in relation to unconventional families is that if the children are exposed to any combination other than a 'feminine' mother and a 'masculine' father then they are considerably more 'at risk' of becoming homosexual. However, just as exposure to heterosexual relationships between parents does not prevent the child becoming homosexual (indeed, the vast majority of homosexuals grow up in heterosexual families), so exposure to homosexual models seems unlikely to have a decisive impact on sexual orientation either. The evidence suggests that homosexuality, in so far as it is shaped by early life experience, is more likely to be influenced by *poor* relationships with parents, perhaps especially with the same-sex parent.

Hoeffer (1981) and Kirkpatrick et al (1981) compared children raised in homosexual and heterosexual single-mother households and found normal levels of heterosexual development in both groups. Green (1978) studied thirty-seven children (eighteen males and nineteen females), aged between three and twenty (average age eleven), all of whom were being raised by either a female homosexual or by parents who had undergone sex reassignments (twenty-one by homosexual mothers, sixteen by transsexual parents); most of the children of the latter were aware that their parents had at one time been a member of the opposite sex. The study was conducted over a two-year period. Green evaluated the younger children's sexual preferences by asking them what toys and games they preferred, about their peer preferences, the roles they chose during fantasy play, their clothing preferences and vocational desires. They were also given the Draw-a-Person Test—children usually draw a person of their own gender before one of the opposite gender. For the adolescents, Green obtained information about their sexual desires and their fantasies about sexual partners as well as about their overt sexual behaviour.

All thirty-seven (with the questionable exception of one child) developed heterosexual preferences and showed a marked desire to conform to the gender roles provided by their culture. None had homosexual or transsexual fantasies. All the young children wanted to play with others of the same gender. Boys wanted to be doctors, firemen, policemen, engineers or scientists, while the girls wanted to be nurses, teachers, mothers or housewives.

Finally, Golombok et al (1983) compared thirty-seven five- to seventeen-year-olds reared in twenty-seven lesbian households (ie lesbian couples) with thirty-eight of the same age-range raised in twenty-seven heterosexual single-parent households. There were systematic, standardized interviews with the children and the mothers, plus questionnaires given to teachers and the mothers. The two groups did not differ in terms of gender identity, sex role behaviour or sexual orientation, nor did they differ on most measures of emotions, behaviour and relationships (although there was some indication of more frequent psychiatric problems in the single-parent group). It was concluded that rearing in a lesbian household as such did *not* lead to atypical psychosexual development or constitute a psychiatric risk factor.

iv) *SOCIAL LEARNING THEORY*

As we have seen elsewhere (Chapter 7) social learning (SL) theorists emphasize the crucial role played by: (i) observational learning (learning from *models*); and (ii) reinforcement. Bandura et al (1961) found that boys were more likely to imitate aggressive male models than girls were (based on perceived similarity and relevance; see Chapter 27). But how representative are these findings? Are children more likely to imitate same-sex models?

Overall, the evidence is inconclusive. Maccoby and Jacklin (1974), for example, concluded that there is very little evidence that children do actually imitate same-sex models more than opposite-sex models.

It is sometimes found that children are more likely to imitate a same-sex model than an opposite-sex model even if the behaviour is sex-inappropriate. But other studies have found the reverse to be true, namely, that children preferred to imitate behaviour that is appropriate to their own sex, regardless of the sex of the model!

Perhaps children imitate same-sex models more than opposite-sex ones when there is no information regarding the sex-appropriateness of the modelled behaviour. However, when there is such information, then the sex of the model seems to become relatively unimportant. It could be that children *attend* equally to *all* models but *imitate* same-sex models more because they are reinforced for doing so. However, while it does appear that children recall more of a model's behaviour when they have previously been reinforced for imitating that model, there is little evidence that children are actually rewarded for imitating models of the same sex.

Starting at about six or seven years, children *do* begin to pay more attention to same-sex models. Significantly, this is when *gender constancy* develops (we shall discuss this in relation to Kohlberg's cognitive theory).

Effects of the Media on Gender-role Sterotypes

Parents, of course, are not the only models that children are exposed to and SL theorists are particularly interested in the way that males and females are portrayed on TV, in books, films, etc. Gender-role stereotyping is the belief that it is only natural and fitting for males and females to adhere to traditional gender-role patterns. There is a great deal of evidence that gender-role stereotypes are held by parents, pre-school teachers, and the media, including both TV and books.

According to the official viewing figures for the UK (published by the Broadcasters Audience Research Board—BARB), four- to seven-year-olds watched an average of 2.8 hours of TV per day during 1987, while eight- to eleven-year-olds watched an average of 3.3 hours per day. These figures compare with 2.4 and 2.9 hours, respectively, for 1982.

Before we can properly evaluate studies of the effects of TV watching, it is important to adopt a valid view of the person who is watching:

> ... To assume that television can impact upon a passively receptive child audience with messages about sex stereotyping, thus moulding innocent young viewers' conceptions of gender, is largely accepted as an over-simplistic picture of what really goes on. Viewers exhibit a degree of activity in selecting what to watch ... what to pay attention to, and what to remember of the things they see ... Even children respond in a selective fashion to particular characters and events ... and their perceptions, memories and understanding of what they have seen may often be mediated by dispositions they bring with them to the viewing situation. (Gunter and McAleer, 1990)

Also, studies of the effects of TV assume that TV content is actually sex-role stereotyped. There is substantial evidence to suggest that it is. So what about the influence of TV on sex-role stereotypes?

Gunter (1986) reports a small number of surveys which report significant links between personal or parental estimates of children's TV viewing and their sex-role perceptions—these have been taken as evidence for a TV *influence*. Youngsters who were categorized as heavy viewers were found to hold stronger stereotyped beliefs than lighter viewers. However, much of this research failed to produce precise measures of what programmes were actually watched (Gunter and McAleer, 1990).

Frueh and McGhee (1975) interviewed four- to twelve-year-olds (forty boys and forty girls) about their viewing, along with their parents, and then gave the children a projective measure of sex stereotyping (a paper and pencil test which examined choice of sex-typed toys). A clear relationship was found between the amount of reported TV viewing and choice of toys—the heaviest viewers were the ones who chose toys in the most stereotyped way.

So does this mean that children learn about traditional sex roles from TV?

Gunter and McAleer believe that a number of critical questions remain unanswered about the Frueh and McGhee study—eg why were boys and older children more traditional in their attitudes? Was it their more traditional attitudes that made them heavier viewers in the first place? What role did parents play, not only in teaching children about sex-roles, but also in helping them to interpret what they watched? How accurate was parental monitoring of actual viewing among the youngest children? Was the sample representative? Was the projective test valid?

This and other similar studies all provide only a 'snapshot' of links between increased TV viewing and sex stereotypes at one point in time (ie they are *cross-sectional* studies).

Morgan (1982) conducted a *longitudinal* study of a large sample of teenagers over a two-year period. His results support the view that TV cultivates certain sex-role attitudes, but these effects are confined to girls. The heavier female viewers became more likely over time to think that women are less ambitious than men and are happiest among children. The effect was strongest of all among middle-class girls—both lower-class girls and boys were generally more sexist *regardless* of viewing levels.

However, Gunter and McAleer (1990) point out a number of difficulties in interpreting these results, including the small size of the correlations.

A study in Canada (Williams, 1986) investigated the effects of the introduction of TV on an essentially TV-naïve community (ie one which previously had not had TV reception). Three towns were compared ('Notel', 'Unitel' and 'Multitel') which at the start of the study had no TV, one channel only and four channels, respectively. By the end of the study (two years later) Notel had one channel, Unitel had two and Multitel still had four. Children in Notel were assessed for their sex-role attitudes at the start of the study and then two years later.

Initially, children in Unitel and Multitel were found to be much more stereotyped in terms of how appropriate or frequent they believed certain behaviours are for their peer group. Two years later, Notel children had become significantly more stereotyped but the change did not extend to how they rated their own parents' frequency of performing certain tasks.

Williams concluded that, in the longer term, TV had the potential to shape children's sex-role attitudes and recommended that special attention should be given to how women are presented on TV. It appeared that any sex-stereotyped messages that were being broadcast were being absorbed, especially by boys. A recent British survey (Wober et al, 1987) explored children's perceptions of whether on TV different occupational activities were seen to be done primarily by males or by females. The children were 334 members of a national UK viewing panel, aged between five and twelve.

From a list of fourteen jobs, 'serving customers in a shop', 'attending to patients in a hospital', 'taking care of baby children' and 'typing in an office' were principally done by girls or women on TV, while 'working a big machine in an office', 'piloting an aeroplane', 'laying bricks to build a house', 'manning a fire engine and putting out a fire' and 'repairing TVs and electric machines' were very much male occupations. Some were seen as being done by both males and females (eg 'being in charge of curing a sick animal' and 'driving a police car').

Girls were more likely to notice female activities and boys male activities. When asked which occuptation they would like themselves, three more from the entertainment industry were added to the list ('to be in a TV serial', 'work the camera in a TV studio' and 'be a singer in a pop group'). All were relatively popular choices, with girls much more likely than boys to want to be soap stars or pop singers, and boys more likely to want to be camera operators.

The kinds of jobs females do on TV corresponded closely with the kinds of things the girls said they wanted to do in the future; the same was true for boys and TV portrayals of males.

Sex-typing

The SL theorists are also interested in child-rearing methods and how differences in those may contribute to gender differences. An important dimension of child-rearing is how parents (and other adults) treat and react to the child by virtue of the child's biological sex, ie *sex-typing*.

Sears et al (1957) found that the greatest and most consistent differences between boys and girls was in the area of aggression, with boys being allowed more aggression in their relationships with other children, while this was discouraged in girls. Boys were also allowed to express aggression towards their parents more than girls were. For some mothers, being 'boylike' meant being aggressive and boys were often encouraged to fight back.

While there do not appear to be any differences at birth (although baby boys may be more restless and less socially responsive than baby girls), by the age of four or five these differences have become quite clear-cut.

Condry and Condry (1976) asked a group of adults to rate the emotional behaviour of nine-month-old infants. One half of the group was told the infant was a boy, the other half that it was a girl. The same baby was thought to display different emotions and different levels of emotional arousal depending on whether the adults had been told it was a boy or girl. When the infant was presented with a 'jack-in-the-box', 'girls' were judged to be showing 'fear', while the 'boys' were judged to be showing 'anger'.

Frisch (1977) observed adults interacting with fourteen-month-olds. In one session, each child was introduced as a boy, in a second session, the same child was introduced as a girl. The adults encouraged more activity and tended to choose male toys when playing with children they thought were boys. When they thought the babies were girls, the adults interacted in a more interpersonal and nurturant way.

It seems that from the moment of birth boys and girls are seen as different by their parents, girls being seen as smaller, weaker and prettier, boys as firmer, better co-ordinated, stronger and more alert. (Boys do, in fact, tend to be longer and heavier at birth and they also tend to be stronger—but the crucial finding is that they are *perceived* as being different.)

Parents tend to provide vehicles, educational materials, sports equipment, machines, toys or real animals and military toys for their sons and decorate their rooms with pictures of animals. Daughters are given dolls, dollshouses, housekeeping toys, and their rooms are decorated with lace, ruffles, fringes and floral designs. While sons are encouraged to achieve and compete, daughters are encouraged to be sociable. Like peers, parents tend to discourage 'sissy' behaviour in their sons much more than they discourage 'tomboy' behaviour in their daughters.

Several studies have revealed an interesting social class difference. In England and the USA, lower socio-economic status (SES) children commonly show stronger preferences for sex-typed behaviours and also hold more stereotyped views about gender roles than children from higher SES backgrounds. So, in this sense, parents of different SES backgrounds may provide different kinds of models for their children.

Despite all the evidence that sex-typing does go on, we cannot be sure that there is a cause-and-effect relationship between this and the gender differences that have been found to exist. That is, we cannot be absolutely certain that, for example, because boys are allowed to be more aggressive, and are given more aggressive-type toys, than girls, that this actually makes boys more aggressive. The evidence is only correlational.

v) *CULTURAL RELATIVISM*

This really represents the most direct challenge to the biological approach. If gender differences do reflect biological differences, then we would expect to find the same differences occurring in different cultures. Any differences that exist between different cultures in relation to gender roles would tend to support the view that gender role is culturally determined (*cultural relativism*), that is, learned.

One of the most famous and influential of all anthropologists has been Margaret Mead (who died in 1980) who, in her *Sex and Temperament in Three Primitive Societies* (1935), concluded that the traits which we call masculine and feminine are completely unrelated to biological sex. Just as the clothing, manner and head-dress that are considered to be appropriate in a particular society, at a particular time, are not determined by sex, so temperament and gender-role are not biologically but culturally determined.

Margaret Mead studied three New Guinea tribes, who lived quite separately from each other within about a 100-mile radius.

The Arapesh, who lived on hillsides, she described as gentle, loving and co-operative; boys and girls were reared in order to develop these qualities, which in Western society, are stereotypically feminine ones. Both parents were said to 'bear a child' and men took to bed while the child was born.

The Mundugumor were riverside dwellers and ex-cannibals. Both males and females were self-assertive, arrogant, fierce and continually quarrelling, and they both detested the whole business of pregnancy and child-rearing. Sleeping babies were hung in rough-textured baskets in a dark place against the wall and, when they cried, someone would scratch gratingly on the outside of the basket.

The Tchambuli, who lived on the lakeside, represented the reversal of traditional Western gender-roles. Girls were encouraged to take an interest in the tribe's economic affairs while the boys were not. The women took care of trading and food gathering while the men, considered sentimental, emotional and incapable of making serious decisions, spent much of the day sitting around in groups, gossiping and 'preening' themselves.

But Tony Booth (1975) proposes that the conclusions which Mead drew from her research may have been influenced by things going on in her private life. She had always been very keen to have a child but was told she was unable to have children, and Booth believes that her perception of the aggressive, arrogant Mundugumor, who did not seem to place great value on children generally, may have been coloured by her own sadness and frustration. Significantly, perhaps, she described the Arapesh after the colonial period (before colonization, the Arapesh had been quite warlike; according to Fortune (1939), half of the older men claimed to have killed at least one person), yet referred to the Mundugumor as if they still practised their old forms of warfare—this exaggerated the differences between them.

By 1949 (in *Male and Female—a Study of the Sexes in a Changing World*), after she had studied four other cultures (Samoa, Manus, Iatmul and Bali), Mead had rather dramatically changed her views about gender-roles. From a rather extreme 'cultural determinism' in the original 1935 book, she now concluded that women were 'naturally' more nurturing than men, expressing their creativity through childbearing and childbirth, and are superior in intellectual abilities requiring intuition. While motherhood is a 'biological inclination', fatherhood is a 'social invention': the implication is that societies which encourage a gender-role division other than that in which dominant, sexually energetic men live with passive, nurturant women, are 'going against nature'. Significantly, by this time she had given birth to a child of her own!

A finding which may seem to support Mead in her search for 'natural' differences is that there is no known society in which the female does the fighting in warfare, and this includes the Tchambuli and the Arapesh (Fortune, 1939). However, to define aggression in this way is extremely limited—aggression can be expressed in many, more subtle, ways which it is often difficult to measure (see Chapter 16).

Furthermore, Malinowski (1929), studying the Trobriand Islanders, reported that, in order to foster their tribe's reputation for virility, groups of women would catch a man from another tribe, arouse him to erection and rape him! This 'gang rape' was carried out in a brutal manner and the women often boasted about their achievement.

There are also accounts of many cultures where women do the heavy work because men are thought to be too weak.

These findings, of course, tend to detract from the view that there are biologically (probably hormonally) determined psychological gender differences. Further evidence that gender roles are learned rather than 'natural' comes from a study of the Sakalavas in Madagascar. There, boys who are thought to be pretty are raised as girls and readily adopt the female gender role.

The Aleutian Islanders in Alaska also raise handsome boys as girls. Their beards are plucked at puberty and they are later married to rich men; they too seem to adapt quite readily to their assigned gender role.

Studies of certain North American Indian tribes reveal the possibility of *more* than two basic gender roles. For example, the 'berdache', a biological male of the Crow tribe, are males who simply choose not to follow the ideal role of warrior. Instead, they might become the 'wife' of a warrior but they are never scorned or ridiculed by their fellow Crows. (Little Horse in the film, *Little Big Man*, starring Dustin Hoffman, was a 'berdache').

The Mohave Indians recognized *four* distinct gender roles: (i) traditional male; (ii) traditional female; (iii) 'alyha'; and (iv) 'hwame'. The 'alyha' was a male who chose to live as a woman (to the extent of mimicking menstruation by cutting his upper thigh and undergoing a ritualistic pregnancy) and the 'hwame' was a female who chose to become a man.

These exceptions to the general rule of two fundamental gender roles provide further evidence for the shortcomings of the biological approach.

vi) COGNITIVE–DEVELOPMENTAL THEORY

We could sum up the social learning theory approach in this way: I want rewards, I am rewarded for doing boy/girl things, *therefore*, I want to be a boy/girl.

Using the same form of argument, we could sum up Kohlberg's Cognitive–Developmental Theory like this: I am a boy/girl, I want to do boy/girl things, *therefore*, the opportunity to do boy/girl things (and gain approval) is rewarding.

For Kohlberg (1966, 1969) the child first comes to think of itself as a boy or girl and only then will it selectively attend to (or identify with) same-sex models, ie the child first develops a *gender identity* which determines who it will imitate, which is the *reverse* of the SL Theory view. As we shall see below, gender identity develops in stages and reflects the child's general cognitive development.

According to Kohlberg, the child actively constructs its own conception of gender, based on both physical and social sources; the crucial organizer of gender roles, gender role identity and, therefore, gender differences, is the child's categorization of itself as a 'boy' or 'girl'.

Once the child has acquired its gender label, it comes to value behaviours, objects and activities which are consistent with it—rewards stem from behaving consistently with one's gender label rather than from what other people consider appropriate.

STAGES OF GENDER IDENTITY

i) Basic Gender Identity (Two/Three to Five Years)

Kohlberg (1966) found that a two- or three-year-old boy may be able to tell you that he is a boy, but that he believes he *could* become a girl, or a mummy, if he wanted to, eg by playing girls' games or wearing dresses or growing his hair long: he lacks gender consistency. Similar results were found by Marcus and Overton (1978) and Slaby and Frey (1975) for three to five-year-olds. All the three-year-old subjects could identify the gender of dolls on the basis of hair and clothing cues, but only 12 per cent of them could do so on the basis of genitals. However, 31 per cent of four-year-olds, 51 per cent of five-year-olds and 70 per cent of six-year-olds could use genital differences to classify male and female dolls.

ii) *Gender Stability (Four/Five to Six Years)*

This involves understanding that you stay the same gender throughout your life, ie basic gender identity is seen as stable over time, as reflected in the answers to questions such as, 'When you were a little baby, were you a little boy or a little girl?' and, 'When you grow up will you be a mummy or a daddy?'.

iii) *Gender Constancy or Consistency (Six to Seven Years)*

The child now grasps that gender identity is stable over time *and* across situations, eg someone remains the same gender even though they may appear to change by wearing different clothes or a different hairstyle.

Gender constancy represents a kind of conservation (see Chapter 25) and, significantly, appears shortly *after* the child has mastered conservation of quantity (Marcus and Overton, 1978). The child has to learn that gender is not like other personal characteristics that do change, such as age and size.

Slaby and Frey (1975) found that children at a higher stage of gender constancy were more likely to attend to same sex models in a film compared with lower-stage children. This supports Kohlberg's belief that gender constancy is a *cause* of imitation of same-sex models rather than an effect (as the SL theorists would argue).

However, a major problem for Kohlberg's theory is that sex-typing is already well underway before the child acquires a mature gender identity. For example, two-year-old boys prefer masculine toys before they have even become aware that these are more appropriate for boys, and Kuhn et al (1978) and Maccoby (1980) found that three-year-olds have learned many gender-role stereotypes and already prefer same-sex activities or playmates long before they begin to attend selectively to same-sex models.

Finally, Money and Ehrhardt's claim (1972) that gender reassignment is very difficult after three years of age (which is when, according to Kohlberg, the child is only just beginning to develop a stable and constant sense of its status as boy or girl) seems to pose serious problems for Kohlberg's theory.

ANDROGYNY

This term is a convenient way of drawing together many of the findings and controversies regarding how gender roles are determined and the stereotypes which reflect them.

In *Fluffy Women and Chesty Men* (1975) Sandra Bem points out that the masculine–feminine pair of opposites had traditionally been taken as evidence of psychological health. This is reflected in psychological tests of masculinity and femininity, where a person scores as either one or the other—they do not permit a person to say that he or she is both.

The word 'androgynous' (from '*andro*' meaning male and '*gyne*' meaning female) is used to refer to the possession and expression of characteristics, behaviours, abilities, values, etc. that are both 'masculine' and feminine', by the same person, regardless of biological sex.

Bem, together with a growing number of psychologists and feminists, believes that we need a new standard of psychological health, one that frees us from the strait-jacket of stereotypes and which allows people to be more flexible in meeting new situations, in what they can do and how they do it. Usually, we tend to suppress parts of our personality which might be thought 'unmasculine' or 'unfeminine', eg men being afraid to be gentle or to cry, and women being afraid to be assertive. In brief, men are reluctant to do 'women's work' and women are afraid to enter the 'man's world'. Bem points out that there is considerable evidence that traditional sex-typing is unhealthy.

In order to 'discover' androgyny, it was necessary to see masculinity and femininity as not mutually exclusive but as two *independent* dimensions and to incorporate this into a new sort of test which would produce two logically independent scores. Bem developed such a test (1974), the Bem Sex Role Inventory (BSRI) which consists of a list of sixty personality characteristics, twenty traditionally masculine, twenty traditionally feminine and twenty neutral. The subject has to rate each of the sixty characteristics in terms of the extent to which they apply to them personally. If masculinity and femininity scores are approximately equal, the individual is judged to be androgenous. (The neutral characteristics constitute a Social Desirability Scale, ie a measure of the general tendency to endorse socially desirable traits; see Table 23.1).

Table 23.1 Items on the masculinity, femininity and social desirability scales of the BSRI (Bem, 1974)

MASCULINE ITEMS	FEMININE ITEMS	NEUTRAL ITEMS
49. Acts as a leader	11. Affectionate	51. Adaptable
46. Aggressive	5. Cheerful	36. Concerted
58. Ambitious	50. Childlike	9. Conscientious
22. Analytical	32. Compassionate	60. Conventional
13. Assertive	53. Does not use harsh language	45. Friendly
10. Athletic	25. Eager to soothe hurt feelings	15. Happy
55. Competitive	20. Feminine	3. Helpful
4. Defends own beliefs	14. Flatterable	48. Inefficient
37. Dominant	59. Gentle	24. Jealous
19. Forceful	47. Gullible	39. Likeable
25. Has leadership abilities	56. Loves children	6. Moody
7. Independent	17. Loyal	21. Reliable
52. Individualistic	26. Sensitive to the needs of others	30. Secretive
31. Makes decisions easily	8. Shy	33. Sincere
40. Masculine	38. Soft spoken	42. Solemn
1. Self-reliant	23. Sympathetic	57. Tactful
34. Self-sufficient	44. Tender	12. Theatrical
16. Strong personality	29. Understanding	27. Truthful
43. Willing to take a stand	41. Warm	18. Unpredictable
28. Willing to take risks	2. Yielding	54. Unsystematic

Note: The number before each item refers to the position of each adjective as it actually appears on the Inventory.

The BSRI is the most widely used measure of sex-role stereotyping in adults (Hargreaves, 1986) but is not the only fairly recent test of androgyny. Quite independently of Bem, Spence et al (1975) devised the Personal Attributes Questionnaire (PAQ), which comprises instrumental (masculine) and expressive (feminine) trait terms and produces two essentially independent scores.

However, the PAQ did not assess androgyny in the same way as the BSRI and this underlined a major problem with the BSRI, to do with the very concept of androgyny itself. By defining androgyny as the difference between a person's masculinity and femininity scores, Bem (unwittingly, of course) allowed for the same androgyny score to be obtained in two very *different* ways—either by an individual who scores *high* on both scales or *low* on both. But surely two such individuals are likely to be very different kinds of persons, in which case what do their same androgyny scores mean?

By contrast, PAQ allowed for four categories of person: (i) the highly sex-typed male—*high* masculinity, *low* femininity; (ii) the highly sex-typed female—*low* masculinity, *high* femininity; (iii) the androgynous person—*high* masculinity and *high* femininity; and (iv) the 'undifferentiated' person—*low* masculinity and *low* femininity. The crucial difference is that Bem confounded (iii) and (iv). Consequently, she compared her original (1974) results with those of Spence et al and concluded that the four categories (2×2) were superior; androgyny was now defined as only high in both masculinity and feminity (not low in both too). Her revised, and shortened, version of the BSRI (1977) is considered to be equivalent to PAQ.

Does the empirical research support the predictions made on the basis of the BSRI? Essentially, there are two: (i) scores on the BSRI will predict certain kinds of behaviour preference; and (ii) androgyny is a good predictor of psychological well-being/mental health.

1) Bem's research strategy is to assess sex-typing by means of the BSRI, then to relate this to behaviour in real-life situations. For example, Bem and Lenney (1976) asked subjects to indicate which of a series of paired activities they would prefer to perform, for payment, while being photographed. Twenty activities were stereotypically masculine (eg nail two boards together), twenty were sterotypically feminine (eg iron cloth napkins) and twenty were neutral (eg play with a yo-yo). Sex-typed subjects expressed a clear preference for sex-appropriate as opposed to sex-inappropriate activities, even though such choices paid less money than cross sex-typed activities.

2) Bem (1975) found that androgynous subjects show sex-role adaptability across situations, ie they will behave as the situation requires, even though this means behaving in a sex-inappropriate way. Lubinski et al (1981) reported that they express greater subjective feelings of emotional well-being and Spence et al (1975) found that they show higher levels of self-esteem. However, it is by no means clear that androgyny is a good predictor of psychological well-being. Indeed, a review by Taylor and Hall (1982) suggests that masculinity in both males *and* females may be a *better* predictor than certain measures of androgyny, and Taylor (1986) makes the point that traditional sex roles are, on the whole, advantageous for men but disadvantageous for women. This

asymmetry between males and females is expressed by Hefner et al like this:

> ... both men and women are trapped in the prisons of gender ... but the situation is far from symmetrical; men are the oppressors and women are the oppressed. (Hefner et al, 1975; quoted in Taylor, 1986)

Psychological well-being (measured by, for example, self-esteem, adjustment, relative absence of anxiety, depression, psychosomatic symptoms) is generally more strongly related to masculinity than femininity on the BSRI and seems not to distinguish reliably between sex-typed and androgenous individuals (Taylor, 1986).

The BSRI does distinguish between male and female test-takers (Bem, 1974, 1977) as does the PAQ (Spence and Helmreich, 1978; Storms, 1979) and, although the differences in means are usually small, they are significant. As might be predicted, samples of homosexual male students (at the University of Texas), when compared with unselected male students, were found to be significantly lower on masculinity and higher on femininity and the reverse pattern was found for lesbians, using PAQ (Spence and Helmreich, 1978). Larson (1981) found similar results using the BSRI.

Bem (1984) has reformulated her ideas as *Gender Schema Theory* (see Chapter 12). She believes that the BSRI (and PAQ) *are* adequate measures of sex typing and androgyny, despite criticisms that it is measuring characteristics rather more narrow than 'masculinity' and 'femininity'. Sex-typing essentially involves spontaneously thinking of things in sex-typed terms, whereas androgyny is a disposition to process information in accordance with relative non-sex principles. In deciding whether a particular attribute on the BSRI is or is not self-descriptive, the sex-typed person does not reflect on individual behaviour but quickly 'looks up' the attribute in his/her gender schemas and responds accordingly. The essential difference between these two kinds of people is one of *cognitive* style. It no longer seems reasonable to expect androgynous *behaviour* in a sex-typed culture to be a mode of mental health but Bem still believes that information-processing freed of the tyranny of sex-typing (androgyny) is desirable (Brown, 1986).

Coincidental with the 'discovery' of androgyny, during the 1970s, was the 're-discovery' of the father as an important figure in the socialization process. Before then, the father was almost totally ignored in the research literature and the use of terms such as 'mothering' and 'maternal deprivation' reflected this bias towards the mother as the major influence in the development of the child's personality (see Chapter 22). But now the father has come into his own as a parent and it is much more common to read about 'parenting' and the effects of the father's absence, etc. than it ever was before the mid-1970s.

The amount of father participation in child-rearing is related to how androgynous the father is. Bem (1974), and others have found that androgynous fathers are more nurturant, more involved in everyday child activities and generally interact with their children more than 'masculine' fathers.

Finally, what would be the consequences of Bem's goal of an androgynous society? If a society were to give meaning to behaviour in a way which ignored the actor's gender, the very notions of masculinity and femininity would cease to have significance. To the extent that we are currently able to specify the limits of masculinity and femininity, then we are able to measure androgyny. As Bem says:

> When androgyny becomes a reality the *concept* of androgyny will have been transcended. (Bem, 1979)

But Archer and Lloyd (1985), amongst others, are very sceptical of the probability of an androgynous society—it will not be realized, they say, because some form of group differentiation seems essential to human social organization. They argue that it is difficult to imagine a completely androgynous society. Awareness of one's gender develops very early and is essential to the development of self and it is difficult to imagine an individual functioning adequately in society as we understand it without a firm sense of self. Thus early gender awareness aids the child in organizing the social world and reflects the child's understanding of it. Gender awareness arises not only from the infant's experience of his/her own body but through interaction with adults in his/her society who are themselves moulded by their membership of gender groups. Nurture becomes second nature and gender identity becomes an important schema in mental life.

While advocating the retention of gender roles, Archer and Lloyd express the hope that change in their *content* (and that of gender stereotypes) will continue as they have over the last 50 years. But they firmly expect gender categories to continue to exist in some form.

One final point is worth making: gender roles and gender differences have to be understood not only in a culturally relative way but also in a historically relative way, ie ideas about what is masculine and feminine change within the same society at different times in its history—the very concept of androgyny is an example of this. Not only does androgyny challenge traditional Western gender-roles and gender-role stereotypes, it also proposes a new way of being a person, where biological sex is no longer one of the fundamental determinants of one's identity, personality, behaviour and relationships with others.

24 ADULTHOOD AND OLD AGE— DEVELOPMENT OF PERSONALITY AND THE SELF-CONCEPT

According to Levinson et al (1978) adulthood is, 'one of the best kept secrets in our society and probably in human history generally'. By this they mean that, while adulthood is the longest phase of the life-cycle (ie we spend most of our lives as adults—assuming we enjoy a normal life-span) until recently very little was known about it in terms of psychological theory and research.

Traditionally, the focus of developmental psychology has been on infancy and childhood and Freud's emphasis on the formative nature of the first five years of life has probably had much to do with the neglect of the study of adulthood. Equally, Erikson has had much to do with the reversal of that trend, or at least with the view that development is a life-long process (the *life-span approach*).

So what does it mean to be an adult?

1) One criterion of psychological adulthood is the concept of *maturity* which, according to Whitbourne and Weinstock (1979) involves the ability to shoulder responsibilities, make logical decisions, empathize with others, cope with minor frustrations and accept one's social role.

Turner and Helms (1989) define it as, '... a state that promotes physical and psychological well being...'. In most cases, they say, a mature person possesses a well-developed value system, an accurate self-concept, stable emotional behaviour, satisfying social relationships, intellectual insight and a realistic assessment of future goals.

This might sound like a rather tall order, something which most of us would not expect to achieve. But maturity is not a unitary concept (there are many features which comprise maturity) nor is it an all-or-none phenomenon, ie we can achieve varying *degrees* of maturity.

What many writers agree about is that being mature means being able to deal with failures and frustrations as well as accepting triumphs and successes. Also, maturity implies accepting *responsibility* for one's choices and decisions.

2) A second way of trying to define adulthood is in terms of successful handling of the developmental tasks which characterize adulthood.

While discussing adolescence in Chapter 21 we unavoidably touched on adulthood and mentioned *intimacy* as a criterion of having attained the psychosocial state of adulthood. For Erikson, the attainment of identity by the end of adolescence is a pre-requisite for the ability to become intimate with another person. By this, he means not simply making love but the ability to share with, and care about, another person, 'without fear of losing oneself in the process' (Elkind, 1970). It is the essential ability to relate our deepest hopes and fears to another person and to accept another's need for intimacy in turn (Dacey, 1982). Indeed, intimacy need not involve sexuality at all and describes the relationship between friends as much as that between husband and wife.

Our personal identity only becomes fully realized and consolidated through sharing ourselves with another and if a sense of intimacy is not established with friends or a marriage partner, the result, in Erikson's view, is a sense of *isolation*, of being alone without anyone to share with or care for.

Intimacy is normally achieved, according to Erikson, in our twenties (young adulthood), after which we enter middle age (our thirties, forties and fifties) which brings with it either *generativity* or *stagnation* (self-absorption). Generativity means that the person begins to be concerned with others beyond the immediate family, with future generations and the nature of the society and world in which those generations will live. Generativity is not confined to parents but is displayed by anyone who is actively concerned with the welfare of young people and with making the world a better place for them to live and work, such as teachers, youth workers, community workers and so on.

Failure to establish a sense of generativity results in a sense of stagnation in which the individual becomes pre-occupied with their personal needs and comforts. Such people indulge themselves as if they were their own (or another's) only child.

Many writers believe that most adults never attain generativity and that men get 'stuck' in Erikson's industry stage (7 to 12) and women in the adolescent stage.

According to Gould (1978), the major task of women during their mid-forties is to deal with the persisting assumption that they need a 'protector' to survive. It is a time for women to reach full independence for the first time.

Sanguiliano (1978) interviewed women in depth and concluded that they achieve identity and intimacy in *reverse* order. Agreeing with Gould, she found that a full occupational identity is not achieved until much later than is typical for men. Indeed, the typical life course for women is to pass directly into a stage of intimacy without achieving personal identity; most women submerge their identity into that of their partner and only at mid-life do they emerge from this to search for their own, separate, identity.

However, Sanguiliano's sample was very small and unrepresentative and there are some important qualifications that need to be made to her conclusions. In particular, there are major *social class* differences, which apply to men and women.

Working-class men and women tend to marry earlier and their careers may 'top out' sooner; this may change the *pace* of the sequence of stages compared with middle class men and women.

Neugarten (1975) found that working-class men see an early marriage as part of the normal or 'good' life pattern. Their young adulthood (twenties) is a time for settling down, having a family and working steadily. In contrast, middle-class men and women see their twenties as a time for explorations, trying out different occupations; marriage comes later and settling down is postponed until the thirties.

Therefore it seems necessary to describe developmental patterns for gender and social class-groups separately. It is more difficult to describe universal stages for adults than it is for children and even adolescents and adult development seems to be very much influenced by *social* definitions of roles (Bee and Mitchell, 1980). Nevertheless, some stage theories of adulthood have been proposed in the last decade or so.

STAGE THEORIES OF ADULTHOOD

What such theories represent is a third approach to defining adulthood, namely defining it by asking, *'How is adulthood experienced?'* (Sugarman, 1986). The two major theories to be described here are those of Levinson et al (1978) and Gould (1978) both based on detailed, in-depth accounts given by adults of what it is like to be adults in the USA in the 1970s.

LEVINSON ET AL'S (1978) 'SEASONS OF A MAN'S LIFE'

During 1969, forty men (business executives, university biologists, industrial workers and novelists) aged between 35–45, were studied primarily through 'biographical interviewing'—five to ten interviews per subject were conducted, each lasting 1–2 hours, over a 2–3 month period. These were tape-recorded and then transcribed (producing an average of 300 pages per subject).

The pivotal concept of the theory is the individual's *life structure*—'the underlying pattern or design of a person's life at a given time'. It is used to explore:

> ... the interrelationships of self and world—to see how the self is in the world and the world is in the self. (Levinson et al, 1978)

Life structure evolves through a series of alternating *stable (structure building)* and *transitional (structure changing)* phases which give overall shape to the course of adult development ('the seasons of a man's life'). Each transitional period has features in common with all other transitional periods (and similarly with the stable periods) *but* each has specific tasks reflecting its place in the life-cycle and distinguishing it from the other periods (see Fig. 24.1).

i) *EARLY ADULT TRANSITION (17–22 YEARS)*

This represents the developmental bridge between the adolescent (pre-adult) and adult worlds. One key theme is *separation* (especially from the family of origin) which is both *external* (moving out of the family home, increasing financial independence, entering new, more independent and responsible, roles and living arrangements) and *internal* (increasing differentiation between self and parents, greater psychological distance from family, less emotional dependence on parental support and authority). A second theme is the forging of initial *attachments* to the adult

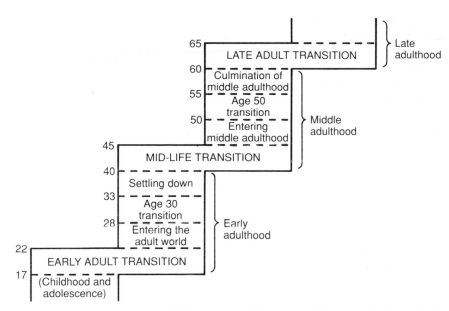

Figure 24.1 Developmental periods in early and middle adulthood. (Based on Levinson et al, 1978)

world—exploring its possibilities, imagining oneself as a participant in it, making and testing some preliminary identities and choices for living.

Separation and attachment are both a matter of *degree* (the process is never complete). The first phase forms the basis for living in the adult world before becoming fully part of it. The major task is to reappraise the sense of self developed during adolescence and to obtain further training and to learn more about the self and world in general. More clearly defined options for adult living must be made, specific life goals planned and a higher measure of self-definition as an adult gained.

ii) *ENTERING THE ADULT WORLD (22–28 YEARS)*

This represents the first structure-*building* (as opposed to *changing*) phase and the overall goal is:

> ... to fashion a provisional structure that provides a workable link between the valued self and adult society. (Levinson et al, 1978)

The young person enters a *novice phase*, in which they shape important dimensions of what may become a more permanent fixture of the life-structure. They must begin to define themselves as an adult and make and live with initial choices regarding occupation, love relationships, peer relationships, lifestyle and values. *But* they must also keep their options open and so not commit themselves prematurely to a given course. Hence there must be a balance between: (i) exploring possibilities ('*keeping one's options open*'); and (ii) creating a stable life structure ('*putting down some roots*').

If the emphasis on (i) is stronger, the young person's life will have a transient/rootless quality; a stronger emphasis on (ii) creates the risk of commitments based on insufficient exploration of alternatives.

These decisions are made within the context of one's *dream*, 'a vague sense of the self-in-the-adult-world', what one wants to do with one's life. The young adult must overcome disappointments and setbacks and learn to accept and profit from successes so that the 'thread' of the dream isn't lost in the course of 'moving up the ladder' and revising the life-structure.

Looking to older, more experienced, others for guidance and direction, helps young adults in their efforts at self-definition.

iii) *AGE THIRTY TRANSITION (28–33 YEARS)*
This:

> ... provides an opportunity to work on the flaws and limitations of the first life structure and to create the basis for a more satisfactory structure with which to complete the era of young adulthood. (Levinson et al, 1978)

Most subjects experienced an *'age 30 crisis'*, involving high or moderate stress, considerable self-doubt, feelings that life is losing its provisional quality, is becoming more serious, of time pressure, ie if we want to change, we must do so now! But a minority experienced a 'smooth process of change', with growth continuing smoothly without overt disruption or crisis. Their relationships with family and friends remain satisfactory and occupational pursuits progress quickly.

iv) *SETTLING DOWN (33–40 YEARS)*
This represents consolidation of the second life-structure, which began to take shape at the end of the previous phase. There is a shift away from tentative choices regarding family and career towards more permanent, almost irreversible ones. There is a strong sense of commitment to a personal, familial and occupational future. The individual begins to map out a path for success in work, husband and father roles. ('I am a responsible adult now', as opposed to 'I'm just beginning to find out what's important to me or what my opinions are'.)

The major goal is:

> ... to settle for a few key choices, to create a broader structure around them, to invest oneself as fully as possible in the various components of the structure (such as work, family, community, solitary interests, friendships) and to pursue long-range plans and goals within it. (Levinson et al, 1978)

There are two sub-stages:

(a) *Early settling down (33–36)*. The task here is to establish a niche in society, to 'dig in', 'build a nest'. This contributes to the stability of a defined structure.

(b) *Becoming one's own man [BOOM] (36–40)*. The task is to work at advancement and strive to succeed onwards and upwards, build a better life, improve and use one's skills, become more creative and in general contribute to society. We want recognition, affirmation from society, but we also want to be self-sufficient and free of social pressure and control; this may produce a 'boy–man' conflict but can represent a step forward.

We may assume a *mentor* role for someone younger who is just beginning to work on his/her own life structure. Mentors can fulfil a *formal*, more *external* guiding, teaching, function in helping the novice to define their Dream *or* a more *informal, internal*, advisory, emotionally supportive function (like a parent). Like active parenting, the mentor role will be shed (willingly or not) as the young adult reaches their own BOOM period (where he/she will serve as someone else's mentor).

v) MID-LIFE TRANSITION (40–45 YEARS)

The three main tasks here are: (i) termination of one life structure; (ii) initiation of another; and (iii) continuation of the process of individuation started during BOOM:

> ... the person forms a clearer boundary between self and world. He forms a stronger sense of who he is and what he wants and a more realistic, sophisticated view of the world and what it is like, what it offers him and demands from him. Greater individuation allows him to be more separate from the world and to be more independent and self-generating. But it also gives him the confidence and understanding to have more intense attachments in the world and to feel more fully a part of it. (Levinson et al, 1978)

It is a time of soul-searching, questioning and assessing the real meaning of the achievements of the life-structure ('mid-life crisis'). For some, the change is gradual and fairly painless, for others it is full of uncertainties and has an 'either/or' quality to it—either one starts anew or perceives that one has failed in some way to define what's important, in which case several years may be needed 'to form a new path or to modify an old one'.

Most of Levinson et al's subjects had not reached the age of 45.

Follow up interviews were conducted with most subjects two years later and four men were chosen for more intensive study. Altogether, data was obtained on their lives after 45 for 15 subjects aged 42–45 at the start of the study. Consequently, the evidence for the remaining phases is much sketchier than that for earlier ones. (None was actually in his 50s.) These will therefore be outlined only briefly.

vi) ENTERING MIDDLE ADULTHOOD (45–50)

Having resolved (more or less satisfactorily) whether what one has committed oneself to is really worthwhile, choices must again be made regarding a new life structure. Sometimes these choices are defined by *marker events* (divorce, illness, change in occupation, death of someone close); sometimes by less obvious but significant changes, such as subtle shifts in enthusiasm for work or in the quality of one's marriage. As before, the resulting life structure varies in how satisfying it is, how connected it is to the self—it may or may not be intrinsically happy and fulfilling. The re-structuring comprises many steps and may face many setbacks; options may have to be abandoned ('back to the drawing board').

vii) AGE FIFTY TRANSITION (50–55)

> It is not possible to get through middle adulthood without having at least a moderate crisis in either the midlife transition or the age 50 transition. (Levinson et al, 1978)

viii) CULMINATION OF MIDDLE ADULTHOOD (55–60)

This is a relatively stable period, analogous to the settling down phase, where life structure is consolidated.

ix) *LATE ADULT TRANSITION (60–65)*
We will be discussing Retirement and Ageing later in the chapter.

Clearly, Levinson et al's theory is based on an extremely limited and biased sample, both in terms of gender and the occupation of the subjects. Also, occupation is very much at the centre of the theory—but this is not the be-all and end-all of life. A much broader view of adulthood (although from a particular theoretical perspective) and based on a much more representative sample, is Gould's Theory.

GOULD'S (1978, 1980) THEORY OF THE EVOLUTION OF ADULT CONSCIOUSNESS

Gould's ideas derived from his work as a psychiatrist but were tested on over 500 non-patients aged 16–50. They represent perhaps the most significant extension of Freud's theory to adulthod. Gould sees growth and maturity as more or less boiling down to a complete resolution of *separation anxiety* in childhood.

While Levinson et al talk about evolving life structures, Gould talks about, 'the evolution of adult consciousness as we release ourselves from the constraints and ties of childhood consciousness'. The thrust of adult development is towards the realization and acceptance of ourselves as creators of our own lives and away from the assumption that the rules and standards of childhood determine our destiny. We have to free ourselves of the *illusion of absolute safety*. This involves *transformations*, giving up the security of the past to form our own ideas. This is necessarily a troublesome task.

These false assumptions often embody the concept of parental dependency and this must be replaced by a sense of personal autonomy, of owning one's self. But this is very hard because these ideas are a normal feature of childhood—indeed, they represent beliefs ('convenient fictions') which keep children secure and without which childhood might resemble a nightmare! But to 'grow up', you have to 'give up' these basic assumptions about the self and the world (the details of the four major false assumptions are shown in Table 24.1). This is a gradual process and continues throughout adulthood (at least up to age 50), both intellectually and emotionally.

Alongside the shedding of childhood consciousness, there is change in the individual's *sense of time*:

(a) Until we leave our family of origin (at around 18), we are protected by parents, but we are also constrained by them, never quite believing that we shall escape from our family world. It is like being in a timeless capsule, 'the future is a fantasy space that may possibly not exist'. But we begin to glimpse an endless future, an infinite amount of time ahead of us *provided* we're not suddenly snatched back into the restricted world of our childhood.

(b) Once into our 20s, we are more confident that we have separated from the family; but we have not yet formed a coherent early-adult life structure (in Levinson et al's terms):

Because of all the new decisions and novel experiences that come with

AGE	FALSE ASSUMPTIONS AND THEIR COMPONENT PARTS
Late teens, early 20s	I will always belong to my parents and believe in their version of reality. (i) If I get any more independent, it'll be a disaster. (ii) I can only see the world through my parents assumptions. (iii) Only they can guarantee my safety. (iv) They must be my only family. (v) I don't own my body
20s. Apprenticeship period of life. We need to look outward and develop competency in roles outside the family	Doing it my own way with will power and perseverence will bring results but when I am frustrated, confused, tired, or unable, they will step in and show me the way (i) Rewards will come automatically if we do what we are supposed to do. (ii) There is only one right way to do things. (iii) My loved ones are able to do for me what I haven't been able to do for myself. (iv) Rationality, commitment and effort will always prevail over all other forces
Late 20s, early 30s Return to inner selves, confronting parts suppressed. Disillusionment and confusion about what life is all about	Life is simple, not complicated. There are no significant unknown inner forces within me; there are no multiple coexisting, contradictory realities present in my life (i) What I know intellectually, I know emotionally. (ii) I am not like my parents in ways I don't want to be. (iii) I can see the reality of those close to me quite clearly. (iv) Threats to my security aren't real
35–50. Ending of illusion of absolute safety	There is no evil or death in the world. The demonic has been expelled (i) My work (for men) or my relationship with men (for women) grant me immunity from death and anger. (ii) There is no life beyond the family. (iii) I am innocent

Table 24.1 Gould's *(1978/ 1980) theory of the evolution of adult consciousness. (Based on Sugarman, 1986/Hayslip and Panek, 1989)*

setting up new adult enterprises, our time sense, when we're being successful, is one of movement along a chosen path that leads linearly to some obscure prize decades in the future. There is plenty of time, but we're still in a hurry once we've developed a clearer, often stereotyped, picture of where we want to be by then'. (Gould, 1980)

(c) By the end of our 20s, our sense of time incorporates our adult *past* as well as future. The future is neither infinite nor linear—we must choose between different branches because there isn't time to take them all.

(d) From our mid-30s to mid-40s there develops a sense of urgency that time is running out. We also have an emotional awareness of our own mortality which, once attained, is never far from consciousness. How time is spent becomes a matter of great importance. We also begin to question whether our 'prize' (freedom from restrictions by the persons who have formed us—our parents) has been worth it (or even if it exists). (This is similar to Levinson's 'Dream').

When we replace child with adult consciousness, we replace 'I am theirs' with 'I own myself'. This frees us from the struggle for status; we are free to acknowledge our mysterious, indelible 'me' as the core of the rest of our life, allowing us to face disappointment, ill-health, and pain with greater strength.

Old people who haven't made this contact with their inner core have no recourse against the feeling that they are losing the battle with life—finding no meaning in their own life, they attack life itself as meaningless (in Erikson's terms, they've lost the battle between integrity and despair).

AN EVALUATION OF STAGE THEORIES OF ADULTHOOD

Fiske (1980) conducted a longitudinal study of several hundred adults and found that many of the mainstream working and middle-class population do *not* 'grow' or change in systematic ways; instead of an ebb and flow of stability followed by transition, followed by a further period of stability and so on, Fiske observed many rapid fluctuations, depending on the individual's relationship, work demands and other life stresses at each moment. To talk about stages, which are sequential and predictable, would seem inappropriate in the light of such data.

Others see considerable *continuity* of personality during adult life and do not accept the existence of developmental stages of any kind. This is consistent with the popular stereotype which sees middle adulthood as a time when the person is responsible, settled, contented and at the peak of their achievement (Hopson and Scally, 1980). As with other stereotypes, the experience of being adult is affected by these age stereotypes and people who find that they simply do not conform to expectations tend to blame themselves rather than seeing the stereotype as simply wrong (Schlossberg et al, 1978).

Schlossberg et al (1978) suggest that a 'social clock' is used by adults to judge whether or not they are on time with respect to a particular life event (marriage, having children, etc.). To be 'off-time' (either early or late) is to be an age-deviant and, like other forms of deviancy, can result in social penalties.

IS THE 'MID-LIFE CRISIS' A DEVELOPMENTAL STAGE?

In *Passages—Predictable Crises of Adult Life* (1976), Gail Sheehy describes a shift in our forties when men begin to explore and develop their more 'feminine' selves (eg they become more nurturant, affiliative and intimate) while women are discovering their more 'masculine' selves (eg they become more action-oriented, assertive and ambitious). This passing-by, in opposite directions, produces distress and pain which is the 'mid-life crisis' (compare this with Bem's concept of *androgyny*; see Chapter 23).

Hopson and Scally (1980) argue that it is *not* a stage through which everyone must pass; it can stem from a number of sources, including the ineffective adjustment to the normal stresses of growth and transition in middle age, and the reaction of a particularly vulnerable person to these stresses. They prefer not to talk about stages or cycles, seasons or passages, at all. Because of the diversity of adult experience, these terms are too restrictive and instead they describe *themes*; these include the changing nature of roles, adaptation to life transitions, adjustment to biological ageing and so on. More specifically, they might refer to concepts such as 'mid-life crisis', the 'empty nest syndrome' and 'age-30 transition'.

Bee and Mitchell (1980) suggest that, in any particular society, there are particular ages at which a large number of stressful life-changes (biological, social and psychological) are likely to happen together, so that most people will experience a transition or crisis at roughly the same time in their life-cycle. Individuals will differ in how much stress they can tolerate before a 'crisis' is experienced and in how they respond to it when it does occur. One potential response is personal growth, so that another piece of 'childhood consciousness' is removed (in Gould's terms); another response is to change major 'external' aspects of one's life, such as change jobs, get divorced, move house (which are emphasized by Levinson et al).

A limitation of both Levinson et al and Gould's theories is that they both presuppose the full availability of employment and a full range of choices across different social class groups. However, any adequate theory of adult development must take into account: (i) the changing pattern of gender roles including female employment; and (ii) the very real impact of unemployment. It is to the latter that we now turn.

THE EFFECTS OF UNEMPLOYMENT

Raphael (1984) distinguishes between sudden, unanticipated loss of work (unemployment) and anticipated loss of work (retirement). She claims that loss of work is in many ways similar to other kinds of loss, such as bereavement. The initial response may be shock, numbness, disbelief. If other similar work is easily available, these feelings may be transient and soon replaced by rationalizations that it was 'all for the best anyway' and blame directed at the employer. Even so, there is likely to be some sense of loss—of workmates, security, self-esteem. Where the job was valued and cannot be easily replaced, the bereavement response is likely to be much more intense.

Like the bereaved person who desperately goes over the events leading up to and surrounding the loss, the unemployed person tries to make sense of what has happened and gain mastery over the situation—the ultimate aim is to undo the helplessness and prevent its recurrence:

> . . . with the loss of work, interactions and behaviours that were geared to that end become meaningless. There is no motivation to initiate activities and behaviour may take on the same purposelessness and disorganization found in other bereaved people whose actions have no significance now that their object is gone. (Raphael, 1984)

Anger towards employers must be held in if the unemployed person is to seek further work, but this increases depression; many men affected this way (especially if they lack deep, satisfying family relationships) pass into bitter, apathetic and chronic depression (they 'give up'). According to Argyle (1989), 'the unemployed have higher rates of mental ill health and distress of several kinds':

(a) Depression is usually higher among the unemployed and the level increases with the period of unemployment (Warr, 1984). After a long period of unemployment, people increasingly blame themselves, get into a state of 'learned helplessness', where aspects of themselves are seen as the main cause of their unemployment and can't be changed. (They make an *internal* (self-)attribution in a situation that has gone badly, which is a fairly typical 'depressive' response; see Chapter 17).

(b) Depression (together with poverty, reduced social support and alcoholism) is a factor contributing to suicide, which is more common among the unemployed. For example, attempted suicides in Edinburgh were eight times more common among the unemployed, the highest rates being during the first month and after 12 months of unemployment (Platt, 1986).

(c) General emotional disturbance is lower for those at work than for *all* categories of unemployed (including retired people); it usually takes some time for the effects of unemployment on mental health to appear (Argyle, 1989).

(d) While some studies have found that total consumption of alcohol doesn't change, the unemployed seem to drink faster and more at a single session and so are more likely to get drunk. But other studies have found more 'heavy drinkers' among the unemployed. The unemployed certainly have more 'unstructured' time (watching TV, chatting, reading the paper and 'hanging about').

What about physical health?

According to Argyle (1989) health usually suffers as a *result* of unemployment (rather than being a cause). However, Warr (1984) studied 954 British unemployed men and found that although 27 per cent said their health deteriorated, 11 per cent said it actually improved (due to less work strain and more relaxation and exercise).

The mortality rate is higher for the unemployed. A 10-year census study of British men who had lost their jobs in 1971 found that the death rate was 36 per cent higher than for the whole population of males aged 15–64, and 21 per cent higher if age and social class are held constant. Their wives were also 20 per cent more likely to die, with the risk greater in the second half of the decade, both results suggesting stress, as opposed to previous illness, as the cause (Moser et al, 1984).

WHAT SPECIFIC FACTORS RELATED TO UNEMPLOYMENT CAUSE DISTRESS?

In addition to the material hardships of low income there is loss of self-esteem through ceasing to be the breadwinner and through becoming the recipient of unemployment benefit. Financial strain is likely to be greater when there are dependent children to feed, clothe and educate and financial problems are a major source of emotional distress. (Warr, 1984; quoted in Argyle, 1989)

Apart from the financial effects of unemployment, Argyle (1989) identifies *five major causes of distress*:

(i)   length of unemployment;
(ii)   commitment to work;
(iii)   social support from the family;
(iv)   level of activity;
(v)   perceived causes of unemployment.

Length of Unemployment

Some claim there is a series of regular reactions to loss of a job (as it is claimed there is to bereavement; Kelvin and Jarrett, 1985): (i) the initial response is *shock*, anger and incomprehension; (ii) the first stage is followed by *optimism*, a feeling of being between jobs, a kind of holiday with active job searching; (iii) this is replaced by *pessimism* as job searching fails—people see themselves as unemployed and become worried about money and the future; and finally (iv) *fatalism*—hopelessness and apathy set in and job hunting is abandoned. (But there are many exceptions to this sequence, as there are to the sequence of 'stages' of bereavement; see p. 733).

Studies using the General Health Questionnaire (GHQ) have shown that scores fall during the first 3–6 months of unemployment and then tend to level off, or may even improve.

Commitment to Work

Those most attached to their jobs are more distressed by losing them. This probably explains why unemployment is more distressing for middle-aged men than for young people or married women (Warr, 1987).

Social Support

Social support, especially from the family, 'buffers' the effects of stress:

Family support is important since unemployment results in a serious loss of social relationships. There is a loss of all relationships at work, ie loss of a co-operative network of friendships. At work, people are part of a complex set of complementary relationships which convey identity and status. All of this is lost in unemployment.

There is usually some withdrawal from friendships during unemployment partly because the unemployed often cannot afford to pay for drinks, entertainment or to go on outings. They may feel inferior and stigmatized and may withdraw from the company of employed people, thinking rightly or wrongly that they are being ostracized. The bonds between unemployed people are weak: it is a group to which they do not want to belong. (Argyle, 1989)

Level of Activity

A minority undertake unpaid work, pursue hobbies, do gardening, and keep active in other ways (Argyle, 1989). GHQ scores are worse for those whose time is not fully occupied or have problems filling time, with correlations as high as 0.55 (Warr, 1984). After a long period out of work, some individuals adapt by staying in bed late, killing time, watching a lot of TV and they give up bothering to look for work:

> ... In order to provide satisfaction similar to that of work, leisure should have certain properties, such as commitment to long-term goals, co-operation in a group and use of skills ...
>
> It is clear that there are plenty of things for the unemployed to do with their time, just as there are for the young, retired and the many women who choose to stay at home. If they succeed in working out an organized pattern of life, they enjoy a greater sense of well-being. (Argyle, 1989)

Perceived Causes of Unemployment

During periods of full employment, to be out of work was mainly due to personal incompetence. To be out of work may *still* be seen as a sign of failure—it is a social stigma, a form of deviance (Kelvin, 1981):

> Unemployment has now become very widespread, however, and includes people from all sections of society, including many who are highly qualified and who have held responsible jobs in the past. Among the young, very large proportions cannot find work in some areas. Among the middle-aged, unemployment can be seen as 'early retirement'. The result is that many of the unemployed now feel less responsible for their plight, and more accepting of it. If you know many other people who are also out of work, this part of the identity problem is greatly eased. It is found that satisfaction with the self is higher when the local level of unemployment is high. (Warr, 1984; quoted in Argyle, 1989)

RETIREMENT

Retirement is an *anticipated loss of work* and:

> ... many make this transition in a careful, measured way without undue psychological upheaval ... (Raphael, 1984)

But even in the most positive of situations, some *loss* is inevitable:

> Losses accompanying retirement may include those of finances, personal identity, meaning to life, and sources of gratification, among others. Even though it is seen as inevitable by most pepople, retirement may feel very unacceptable at a particular stage in life when, for instance, a person sees himself as 'too young' to stop work ... (Raphael, 1984)

Perhaps the most serious loss is of everyday, regular, ritualized patterns of behaviour. The comfortable familiarity of the workplace and colleagues, the times of day spent there and the tasks all contribute to the fabric of the individual's existence. When these are gone, there will be a great emptiness, at least for a while, '... the work and all it meant will be gradually mourned ...' (Raphael, 1984). While shock and disbelief are uncommon, some people use denial and realize what retirement means only on the first days at home—its full meaning 'hits' them only then. For most, the early weeks are full, freedom is celebrated, and only as the months go by do frustration and a sense of 'uselessness' set in. There may be an angry and irritable response to the world.

Many couples face the problem of adjusting to increased time together; many compound the crisis of retirement by moving to a new house which involves loss of familiar surroundings, friendships and neighbourhood networks:

> . . . retirement entails the transition from an economically productive role, which is clearly defined, to an economically non-productive role, which is often vague and ambiguous. This ambiguity in the retirement role is because of its relative newness and unique social position, for which there is no precedence. In the past, people worked for pretty much their entire lives. Today, people retire and live out their remaining years doing other things. (Harris and Cole, 1980; quoted in Turner and Helms, 1989)

> . . . when retirement takes place, functions must be reintegrated if life is to continue fruitfully and harmoniously. Since retirement as a stage of life is such a new developmental phenomenon, however, our culture has yet to prescribe suitable behaviour for this period. Consequently, each of us may react differently. (Turner and Helms, 1989)

And again:

> Leaving the world of work and relinquishing a significant part of one's identity is a difficult psychological adjustment. For many, such a transition brings about a major loss of self-esteem. The ability to deal with this stage of life depends to a considerable extent on past adjustment patterns. Those who adjust well to retirement are typically able to develop a lifestyle that provides continuity with the past and meets their long-term needs. Successful adjustment is also characterized by the harmonious resolution of demands and tasks throughout the course of one's life. (Turner and Helms, 1989)

Atchley (1982, 1985) and Atchley and Robinson (1982) see retirement as a *process* and a *social role* which unfold through a series of six phases, at each of which an adjustment is required. These phases are difficult to relate to chronological age, occur in no fixed order and are not necessarily *all* experienced by every individual (Box 24.1).

Box 24.1 The six phases in the process of retirement (based on Atchley/ Atchley and Robinson (1982))

(a) *Pre-retirement phase:* (i) In the *remote* sub-phase retirement is seen as in a reasonably distant future; (ii) the *near* sub-phase may be initiated by the retirement of older friends/colleagues and there may be much anxiety about how lifestyle will change, especially financially.

(b) *Honeymoon phase* (Immediate post-retirement): typical euphoria, partly due to new-found freedom, often a busy period (which may be long or short).

(c) *Disenchantment phase:* involves a slowing down after (b), feelings of being let down and even depressed. Degree of disenchantment is related to declining health, finances. Eagerly anticipated post-retirement activities (eg travel) may have lost their original appeal. Disenchantment may be produced by unrealistic pre-retirement fantasies or inadequate anticipatory socialization (ie preparation for retirement).

(d) *Reorientation phase:* time to develop a more realistic view of life alternatives. May involve exploring new avenues of involvement, sometimes with the help of community groups (eg special voluntary/paid jobs for the retired)—helps decrease feelings of role loss, is a means of achieving self-actualization and of voicing political concerns.

(e) *Stability phase:* involves the routinization of criteria for dealing with change, well-established criteria for making choices, allowing the individual to deal with life in a fairly comfortable and orderly way. They know what's expected of them, what their strengths and weaknesses are, allowing mastery of the retirement role.

(f) *Termination phase:* usually illness and disability make housework and self-care difficult or impossible, leading to the assumption of sick or disabled (as opposed to retirement) role.

An important distinction here is between *voluntary* and *involuntary retirement.* Those who retire voluntarily usually have little or no difficulty adjusting. But those forced to because they have reached compulsory retirement age, tend to be dissatisfied at first (but eventually adapt). The least satisfied are those whose health is poor (though health very often improves after retirement):

> Retirement signifies the loss of job-related social contacts, although many compensate for this by establishing new friendships. The retiree must adjust to the fact that a work-related reference group is now gone ... individuals need to establish who they are beyond the work they used to perform each day ... (Turner and Helms, 1989)

According to Argyle (1989) satisfaction with and adjustment to retirement depends on a number of factors (although several are predictors of satisfaction for everybody): (i) health; (ii) finance; (iii) purpose in life; (iv) having strong interests; (v) education and social class; (vi) voluntary and planned retirement; (vii) gender—married women have the least difficulty in adjusting to retirement:

> ... given reasonable physical health and financial resources, the average retired man or woman soon adapts to the changed circumstances and shows an improvement in physical health and outlook. It is the transition that creates problems of adjustment. (Bromley, 1988)

For many working men, release from exacting physical labour over long hours in unsatisfactory conditions is followed not by frustration and idleness but by more enjoyable leisure time activity, closer family relationships and better physical health. Men do not feel very different from before, despite the 40 hours per week spent not working—these are easily absorbed by extra rest and sleep, slower pace of work, family and domestic activities and more and more prolonged leisure activities.

We can no longer think of retirement as a sudden enforced dislocation of a working life, almost inevitably causing feelings of rejection and physical and mental ill health. A substantial proportion of men choose early retirement. After 65, an even larger proportion don't actively seek paid work, even though the generally low levels of income in later life constitute a strong incentive to work.

Women are increasingly entering the workforce (although a majority only part-time)—they represent about 40 per cent of the total workforce and about 50 per cent of adult women are in paid employment. Although women live longer on average than men, they retire at 60. Until recently, it has been unusual to think of women as 'retired', as their social condition was defined in terms of their marital status and continuing domestic activities. However a large number of older women are retired from paid employment and so have to face not only that problem but also their husband's retirement and, for many, widowhood. But home and family still occupy a major part of a working woman's time—so retirement is seen as less of a change in life-style compared with men (Bromley, 1988).

DIFFERENCES BETWEEN RETIREMENT AND UNEMPLOYMENT

Argyle (1989) compares the effects of retirement and unemployment and these are summarized in Table 24.2.

SIMILARITIES	DIFFERENCES
1. Both involve being out of work 2. Both involve a drop in income 3. Both involve increased leisure time	1. The retired don't go job-hunting 2. The retired get out and about less 3. The retired are happier. Some feel bored, lonely and useless but the unemployed are depressed and generally in poor mental health 4. The unemployed are in poor general health

Table 24.2 Comparison of the effects of retirement and unemployment. (Based on Argyle, 1989)

Why the difference?

... It must be because retirement is an accepted and honourable social status, while unemployment is not. Retirement is seen as a proper reward for a hard life's work, while unemployment has the implication of failure, being unwanted, a scrounger living on charity. 'For most men, being retired seems to be a rather benign condition of life; being unemployed is a disturbing and often degrading experience' (Campbell, 1981). (Argyle, 1989)

... The people most satisfied in retirement are those scientists, writers, and other academics who can simply carry on working with little loss of continuity from very satisfying jobs. Another group are those who discover really satisfying leisure activities, which in most cases have some of the characteristics of work. (Argyle, 1989)

... The retiring person's problem is to find satisfactory ways of disengaging from employment without suffering economic hardships or emotional deprivations such as loneliness and boredom. The problems can only be met by long-term planning ... but many people enter retirement inadequately prepared. Preparation means ... putting money aside ... attending to health needs, getting information and advice about leisure-time interests and gradually changing the balance between disengagement and activity ... People need to acquire new skills, new attitudes and interests, and new social relationships if they are to make the most of their retirement. (Bromley, 1988)

AGEING

While 'growing up' is normally taken to be something desirable and almost an end in itself, 'growing old' has, traditionally, had very negative connotations. This negative view of ageing is based on the *Decrement Model*, which sees ageing as a process of decay or decline of our physical and mental health, our intellectual abilities and our social relationships.

In contrast, the *Personal Growth Model* stresses the potential advantages of old age and this much more positive attitude is the way in which ageing is studied within the life-span approach. For example, Kalish (1979, 1982) emphasizes the increase in leisure time, the reduction in many day-to-day responsibilities and the ability to pay attention only to matters of high priority among the elderly. Older people respond to the reality of a finite and limited future by ignoring many of the inconsequential details of life and channelling their energies into what is really important.

AGEISM

It will take time for the balance between the decrement and personal growth models to shift; our prejudice against ageing and the aged (*ageism*) runs very deep (reflecting, perhaps, our deep-seated fear of death) and is mirrored in our language and our behaviour.

In an article called *"Old" is not a Four-Letter Word* (1978), Anderson claims that old people face a painful wall of discrimination that they are often too polite or too timid to attack. They are not hired for new jobs, and are eased out of old ones (because they are considered rigid or feeble-minded), they are shunned socially (because they are considered 'senile' or boring) and they are edged out of family life (because their children often regard them as sickly or parasitic).

There is evidence that children and young people are much more likely to associate old age with negative qualities than other periods in the life-cycle. Similarly, studies have found a preference among workers in the caring professions to work with children or younger adults and in hospital emergency rooms old people are less likely to receive a thorough examination or to elicit the fullest efforts of the medical staff; they are also more likely to be declared 'dead on arrival' than younger age-groups.

Even those psychologists who study ageing and try to present the positive features of growing old may, inadvertently, be guilty of ageism. For example, Kalish (1975) defined 'successful ageing' as continuing to behave as we did when we were younger (ie middle-aged). This assumes that one age group's pattern of behaviour is somehow inherently superior to that of another and is, therefore, a value-judgement (rather than an objective observation) which merely reinforces the idea of 'younger' being more desirable than 'older'.

Our prejudices against the elderly are built into everyday expressions (as are our racial, religious and gender-related prejudices), such as 'dirty old man' and 'old hag', which we often use without being aware of the attitudes on which they are based.

Undoubtedly, the elderly enjoy a very low status compared with both children and younger adults, and this inevitably influences the self-concept of those who are nearing the latter part of their lives. In turn, this change in self-concept may partly determine the behaviour of the older person. But how much are these changes an inherent part of the ageing process itself?

(a) Is there any foundation for our very negative attitude towards growing old?

(b) How much evidence, if any, is there to support the decrement model?

(c) Is growing old inevitably and necessarily a period of decay and decline?

(d) Are our fears of and resistance to growing old justified?

(e) Just what are the facts of ageing (as far as they are known) and how can we account for them?

These are some of the major questions investigated by *gerontology* (from the Greek words *geron* and *ontos*, meaning 'old man') which is a multi-disciplinary field of scientific research concerned with the ageing process and which we shall be discussing in the remainder of this chapter.

THE AGES OF ME

Can 'age' have more than one meaning? Can we be more than one age at the same time? These may seem rather strange questions to ask until you begin to think about them a little more carefully.

If age is an important part of our self-concept and if society generally seems to value 'younger' much more positively than 'older', then how old (or young) we perceive ourselves as being is going to have a significant effect on how we value ourselves (ie our self-esteem).

Robert Kastenbaum, in *Growing Old—Years of Fulfilment* (1979) has devised a questionnaire (called 'The Ages of me') which assesses how we see ourselves at the present moment in relation to our age.

My *chronological* age is my actual or official age, dated from the time of my birth. (Interestingly, this is not a universal method—in some cultures, a year is added on so that we are one when we are born.) Again, different people (according to their actual age) will define what is— chronologically—old very differently; children will probably see anyone over 16 as old, while the 70-year-old will regard those over 80 as old, and not themselves! Chronological age itself, therefore, is a very unreliable measure of 'old-ness'; what is old is a very relative matter!

My *biological* age refers to the state and appearance of my face and body (on the questionnaire, this is indicated by the item: (i) 'In other people's eyes, I *look* as though I am about ____ years of age'; and (ii) 'In my own eyes, I judge my body to be like that of a person of about ____ years of age').

Subjective age is indicated by, 'Deep down inside, I really feel like a person of about ____ years of age'. This corresponds, of course, to the popular expression 'you're as old as you feel'.

My *functional* age, which is closely related to my *social* age, is the kind of life I lead, what I am able to do, the status I believe I have, whether I work, have dependent children, live in my own home, etc. Thus: (i) 'My thoughts and interests are like those of a person of about ____ years of age'; and (ii) 'My position in society is like that of a person of about ____ years of age'.

Of course, because of official retirement, society makes it very difficult for people over 60 or 65 to be in work, even if they are fit and willing to go on working. This contributes to what is probably a fairly high correlation between functional, social and chronological age (ie there is quite a high correspondence between them, so that the older we are—at least beyond 60 or 65—the lower our social status, for example). If people were allowed to go on working until they decided to stop, or until they become physically unfit to do so, the correlation would be much lower. Some people may decide to stop working in their fifties, others not until they were in their seventies or even beyond. One of the features of mass unemployment is the trend towards early retirement, which probably serves to reduce the correlation even further (see above).

In practice, few people, at any chronological age, describe themselves consistently (ie give the same answer to all the items). One of the most typical differences occurs between subjective and chronological age: people in their twenties and above usually *feel* younger than their official age (and this includes many in their seventies and eighties) and also *prefer* to be younger, that is to say, they consider themselves to be *too* old. Very few people say they want to be older, which seems to confirm the aversion to old age that we have already discussed.

Two people of the same chronological age may behave quite differently and have very different subjective, biological, functional and social ages. The range of individual differences between people in their sixties and above is probably as great as that between children and younger adults, and knowing a person's chronological age tells us really very little about them. Yet one of the dangerous aspects of ageism is that actual age is taken as an accurate indicator of all the others, so that we tend to infer that people over 60 all have certain characteristics which, together, make up the decrement model ('past it', 'over the hill', etc.). Recognizing the different 'ages of me' should help us to break down this idea of ageing as decaying and to look more analytically and more positively at old age.

LIFE-SPAN AND LIFE-EXPECTANCY

There is no doubt that people are living longer, that is, life-expectancy is increasing. For example, in 1900, the average life-expectancy (at birth) was 49 years, while in 1976 it was 73; females can expect to live a little longer than males (75 versus 69 years, respectively).

Clearly, these gains are the result of advances in the prevention and treatment of childhood and other killer diseases; only 41 per cent of the babies born in 1900 reached 65 compared with 74 per cent in 1974. Further, a man who reaches 65 today can expect to live to almost 79 and a woman to 83. But these gains in life-expectancy after 65 are quite modest compared with the gains made in the chances of surviving as far as 65.

Nevertheless, it means that the elderly represent an increasingly large proportion of the population. For example, they made up 4 per cent of the total American population in 1930, 10 per cent in 1980 and will be an estimated 13 per cent in 2020. In Britain, there were one million people aged 80 and over in 1961 (representing 2 per cent of the population), 1.6 million in 1981 (representing 3 per cent of the population) and an expected 2.2 million in 1991 (almost 4 per cent of the population). The projected figure for 2001 is 2.5 million or 4 per cent of the population).

But is there an upper limit to how long human beings can live? This is the question of *life-span* (as distinct from *life-expectancy*).

All forms of life have some upper limit to how long they live; for example, ten to twenty days for the house-fly and up to 2000 years for some trees. Our increasing longevity (long life) reflects the fact that we are now able to live out a greater portion of our intrinsic life-span, ie our life-expectancy has increased and has moved close to the life-span of our species. Life-span itself—the inherent length of life of a particular species—has remained unchanged for humans during this century and, apparently, throughout recorded history. Humans live longer than other mammals; Medvedev (1975) estimates a maximum life span of 110 years.

Perhaps life-expectancy has increased to the detriment of the quality of those extra years. Society seems not to have been prepared for the increased life-expectancy of this century and, as a result, too many elderly people have spent their 'golden years' poor, dependent and sick.

According to Aschoff (1938), natural death in humans never occurs, or only in rare instances; the majority of deaths, he claimed, are caused by pathological factors (disease, etc.). As we learn to prevent or treat more and more diseases which are commonly associated with old age, we move closer to the point where ageing, and not disease, becomes the limiting factor in life-expectancy.

PHYSICAL ASPECTS OF AGEING

According to Bee and Mitchell (1980), because growth essentially comes to an end in the late teens and early twenties, we are inclined to think that body change and development also stop. But all the organ systems in the body show normal and predictable changes in structure and function during the adult years. Yet much less is known about these changes compared with what is known about infancy, childhood and adolescence and it is also more difficult to specify the age at which changes can be expected to occur. In adults, physical changes are less tied to chronological age and maturation and more to social and interpersonal factors.

It is interesting to note that *geriatrics* (from the Greek words *geras* meaning 'old age' and *iatros* meaning 'physician') which is the branch of medicine concerned with the diseases and care of the elderly, is more recent, has much less money spent on it and is generally less attractive and respected than paediatrics, which is concerned with the diseases of childhood. (This is another example of ageism.)

Bee and Mitchell summarize the major physical changes that occur in old age under five headings: (i) smaller; (ii) slower; (iii) weaker; (iv) lesser; and (v) fewer.

i) SMALLER

Height tends to decrease, due not to the long bones of the body (arms and legs) becoming smaller but rather to the connective tissues that hold them together (tendons, ligaments and muscles) becoming compressed and flattened (this is especially true of the bones of the spine). Related to these spinal changes is the stooped posture of the elderly.

Weight also decreases. Calcium tends to be lost from the bones (especially in women) so that they account for a smaller percentage of total body weight than in younger people.

Muscle mass is also reduced and some body organs get smaller, eg the uterus and vagina may shrink to their pre-adolescent size and the testes get smaller, as does the bladder.

ii) SLOWER

Electrical nerve impulses travel more slowly to and from the brain (about 15 to 20 per cent slower in an 80-year-old than in a 20-year-old); this partly accounts for slower response or reaction time. Some basic reflexes (eg bladder control) may also slow down.

As far as homeostasis is concerned (maintenance of the body's internal environment), there is no substantial difference between younger and older people under normal conditions but, under stress, older people show much slower recovery.

Fractures may also take longer to heal in the elderly (partly due to the loss of calcium) and a simple break may result in a serious or complicated disability. The rate of renewal of liver and skin cells also slows down.

iii) WEAKER

Bones become more brittle and break more easily, partly due, again, to the loss of calcium and partly to wear and tear. This applies to all bones, including the small bones of the middle ear (the ossicles) which can result in impaired hearing, especially the ability to hear high-pitched sounds (see Chapter 8).

Muscles also become weaker, including those of the arms, legs, chest, diaphragm (crucial for breathing), face (crucial for chewing and facial expressions), and bladder (crucial for bladder control). After about 30, there is a gradual reduction in the speed and power of muscles and decreased capacity for sustained muscular effort. Generally, the senses become less efficient. In the case of vision, convergence becomes less efficient, the iris fades, the cornea thickens and loses its lustre and becomes less transparent, thus making the projection of light from objects onto the retina more difficult and the image less clear. The retina also receives a poorer blood supply (see Chapter 8).

iv) LESSER

The gradual lessening of the elastic tissue in the skin causes wrinkling and sagging. The eardrum loses some of its elasticity, which mainly affects hearing high frequency sounds, as does the lens of the eye, which produces poor accommodation to short distances and hence a tendency towards farsightedness (see Chapter 8).

Blood vessels also become less elastic, which can give rise to circulatory problems. In women, the ovaries stop producing eggs and so reproductive ability (fertility) is totally lost. This represents the most dramatic change associated with the menopause (or climacteric) and, of course, means the end of menstruation. For most women, this occurs sometime during the late forties and early fifties but there is considerable variation, depending on a number of factors, including ethnic origin, living standards, whether or not the woman has had any children, when she started menstruating and her weight.

The major cause of all the changes related to the menopause (including the 'hot flushes', depression and weight gain) is the reduced level of oestrogen.

Men too show 'menopausal' symptoms during middle age, such as insomnia, depression and weight gain. Although the production of testosterone declines, there is no equivalent in men to the cessation of menstruation. In fact, they never stop producing sperm and are usually capable of reproducing right up until their death.

v) FEWER

Body hair becomes more sparse and the number of teeth and taste-buds is reduced; hence different foods tend to taste rather more alike.

After 30, neurons die at an estimated rate of 30 per minute within the central nervous system, but we do have an estimated 10 billion of them! Loss of brain weight is about 20 per cent between the ages of 20 and 80.

When the rate of brain cell death reaches certain proportions, senile dementia occurs, but this applies to only a small minority of old people and it is not an inevitable part of ageing. However, the normal changes in the brain may account for changes in memory, intelligence and reaction time (see p. 722).

Most of these physical changes have been taking place, gradually, since about 30, but we are more likely to become aware of them after about 60. Also, the range of individual differences in ageing is very great and ageing generally is not a process of rapid and drastic physical decline.

The specific factors that may increase human life-expectancy have been suggested by studies of communities where it is not uncommon for people to live to extreme old age, even to 120 and above. This, of course, challenges the figure of 110 which Medvedev takes to be the human life-span. So can the kind of life we lead increase not just out life-expectancy but also the life-span of the species too?

The communities that were studied were Vilcabamba, an Andean village in Ecuador, a village in Kashmir, and a village in Georgia (in what was the USSR). In Vilcabamba, out of a population of 819, nine were over 100 years old (0.01 per cent compared with 0.003 per cent in the American population).

What did these three villages all have in common which might account for the unusual longevity of their inhabitants?

(a) They were all located at high altitudes, in rugged mountainous areas, where the air was clean and bracing.

(b) The work done was very rugged and went on mainly outdoors.

(c) Men and women continued to work well into their eighties and sometimes beyond, which gave them a sense of usefulness and purpose —there was no such thing as compulsory retirement.

(d) The elderly enjoyed a high social status, mainly related to their being seen as a repository of wisdom. (This is quite common in societies which undergo relatively little change from one generation to the next, unlike Western culture.)

(e) The elderly belonged to an extended family and were cared for (if necessary) within the family structure. (There were no institutions specially set up for the purpose.) There was also the expectation of longevity.

(f) All the centenarians had at least one parent and/or one sibling who had also lived to 100 or more. This suggests that there is some genetic predisposition towards long-life, although there is no known 'long-life' gene; it is more likely to be an absence of 'bad' ones. (This is probably also true of the greater life-expectancy of women in our society—they are more resistant to heart disease and certain forms of cancer.)

(g) As far as diet is concerned, in Vilcabamba and the Kashmir village, meat and dairy produce represented a very small percentage of the overall diet. Protein and fat were derived mainly from vegetable sources and there was little obesity or under-nutrition. So the inhabitants were mainly vegetarians and they also drank river-water.

(h) In the Georgian village, some of the oldest amongst them smoked, drank and showed an interest in the opposite sex. Extreme old age was attained only by the married.

It seems, then, that there are a number of factors which are related to longevity.

However, the study has been criticized. For example, it has been maintained that those people claiming to be centenarians in Vilcabamba were, in fact, not. When naming patterns, the frequency of age exaggeration, population migration patterns and civil and church records were investigated, it turned out that the oldest person born before 1900 was a mere 96!

It seems that much of the confusion stems from the custom of passing a family name from one generation to the next. Because of this, the actual recorded birth dates of these people living in Valcabamba are often confused with those of their parents and grandparents. Another common practice is to give a surviving child the same name as that of a sibling who has died; consequently, a person's age is often the sum total of more than one family member.

There was also a tendency to exaggerate age once the inhabitants reached 60 and the world-wide attention which has been focused on the village has made this even more likely to happen. Apparently, one woman told an Italian television crew that she was 146 and that she had had her last child when she was 115!

However, more reliable data relating to geographical, ethnic and racial variations in life-expectancy, especially in the USA, suggest that more research into the interplay between biology, social status and environment in longevity could prove very valuable, both practically and scientifically.

Having discussed some of the possible social and other environmental factors that may extend our *life-expectancy*, more fundamental questions of *life-span* require attention (but no attempt to answer it will be made here).

Is ageing inevitable? Are we programmed to die? What are the mechanisms which underlie our growing old, and is it possible (and desirable) to interfere with those mechanisms, so that our life-span can be extended, if not indefinitely, then at least significantly beyond the 110 years suggested by Medvedev?

INTELLIGENCE, IQ AND AGEING

Until recently, psychologists believed that our intellectual capacity reaches a peak in our late teens or early 20s, levels off (reaches a plateau) in our 20s and 30s and then starts to decline fairly steadily during middle age and more rapidly in old age.

This general picture of decline seems to be based upon a number of factors, in particular:

(i)   the way that intelligence is defined;
(ii) the type of tests used to measure intelligence and the way the results are analysed;
(iii) the kind of study used to compare intelligence at different ages (cross-sectional versus longitudinal).

THE DEFINITION OF INTELLIGENCE

This has always been a matter of disagreement and controversy among psychologists and will be looked at in detail in Chapter 28. Psychologists cannot agree on a single definition of intelligence, and whether intelligence tests reliably and validly measure intelligence is still hotly debated. Suffice it to say here that intelligence (at any age) is best understood as multi-dimensional, that is, it is composed of a number of different abilities and each of us has a different pattern or profile, so that we are better at some than at others (compared with ourselves and with others). Also, this pattern may change over time, both for individuals and for age-groups as a whole. This way of thinking about intelligence makes it possible that, as far as certain abilities are concerned, the traditional picture of decline may be fairly accurate, but as far as others are concerned intelligence may actually go on increasing.

One way of classifying these various abilities is in terms of *fluid* and *crystallized intelligence*, a distinction made by Cattell. Fluid intelligence refers to the ability to solve novel and unusual problems (ones which the individual has not come across before) and involves memory span and mental agility, ie the speed of thought needed, for example, to find the pattern in a string of letters, visualizing an object in space or doing jigsaws. So it is not based on specific knowledge or any particular previous learning. It can also be thought of as the capacity or aptitude to learn.

Crystallized intelligence, on the other hand, refers to knowledge and skills acquired through living in society and includes the ability to define words, verbal skills in general, and the effective use of the skills and knowledge which formal education is primarily concerned with.

Since fluid intelligence is thought to be more sensitive to changes in the central nervous system, and since ageing involves such changes, we might expect it to decline with age, and since crystallized intelligence is more dependent on ongoing experience, we might expect that it will go on improving. This is exactly what has been found.

Most people show decline in fluid intelligence during the second half of their lives—it seems to reach a peak in adolescence and then drop fairly sharply afterwards; it has been estimated that the average 30-year-old has already lost about 50 per cent of the measurable fluid intelligence that they will have lost by age 65.

A test which attempts to measure these two different kinds of intelligence is the Primary Mental Abilities (PMA) test, based on the work of Thurstone (1938). Fluid intelligence is measured by response speed (for example, writing down, within a specific time limit, all words beginning with a particular letter), memory span and non-verbal reasoning. These do show a decline with age. Crystallized intelligence is measured by reading comprehension and vocabulary and these show no decline with age.

Botwinick (1978), for example, found that fluid intelligence begins a gradual decline in middle age and may drop more sharply for many people in later adulthood, while Nesselroade et al (1972) found that crystallized intelligence remains the same or actually improves at least until the early eighties (see Fig. 24.2).

Figure 24.2 Changes in fluid and crystallized intelligence with age

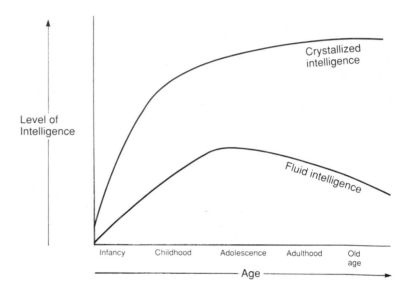

INTELLIGENCE TESTS

The most widely used test of adult intelligence is the Wechsler Adult Intelligence Test (WAIS), designed by Wechsler in 1958. It consists of two separate scales, a *verbal* scale and a *performance* scale, and each of these produces a separate IQ (Intelligence Quotient); the scales can be combined to produce a third, total or overall IQ (see Chapter 28).

The test was originally standardized on 2000 men and women, aged 16 to 75 years, ie it was given to these subjects in order to determine how people typically score at different ages. The highest overall scores were obtained by 25- to 29-year-olds and the younger subjects tended to have an overall IQ that was more evenly determined by the verbal and performance scales compared with older subjects, whose verbal ability contributed a much larger proportion of their total IQ. Another way of putting this is to say that, while total IQ seems to decline with age, verbal IQ does not (at least not until after 60); performance IQ seems to follow the pattern for total IQ. (This is equivalent to the findings for fluid and crystallized intelligence.)

However, there are certain important differences within each scale. As far as digit span (one of the verbal sub-tests) is concerned, while there is very little deterioration for recalling digits in the order in which they are presented, there is more when they have to be remembered in reverse order (especially for people over 45 years). There is usually more decline for mental arithmetic, where marks are given for speed and accuracy.

There is some decline on similarities, even though speed is not important here. On the digit symbol test, what is mainly needed are speed of writing and of eye movements, as well as the ability to hold information in short-term memory. The ability to concentrate is important too and in all these respects older people tend to be at a disadvantage.

CROSS-SECTIONAL VERSUS LONGITUDINAL STUDIES

These findings for the WAIS and those referred to earlier for the PMA, are based mainly on *cross-sectional* studies, which involve studying different age-groups at the same time, so that, say, 20-year-olds are a different group from the 50-year-olds, who are a different group from the 70-year-olds, and so on.

The traditional view of intelligence as declining steadily with age has emerged from these cross-sectional studies, in which an overall IQ on the WAIS or the PMA is compared for different age-groups, or where group tests (pencil-and-paper tests, often computer-marked, giving just an overall IQ) have been used. But there are serious problems associated with this method of study, in particular, what is known as the *cohort effect*. This refers to the fact that differences between, say, 20-year-olds and 80-year-olds, are not confined merely to age, but include all those features of their upbringing and experience (eg wars, poverty and education). The two age-groups represent different *cohorts* and so we cannot draw any simple conclusions about how intelligence changes with age on the basis of differences in IQ between the two groups—we know how a whole range of environmental and social factors can influence the development of intelligence, and, hence of IQ. For example, younger subjects were born in a time of greater educational opportunity, which almost certainly contributes to their higher scores on IQ tests.

We should also note that younger subjects are more likely to have already been given an IQ test while many of the elderly subjects will be doing one for the first time. Also, the elderly are likely to be less confident and less motivated; the test will probably have little meaning or relevance for them and they tend to take fewer risks and so take longer over any one test item. Yet the test has no way of measuring these effects separately from the effects of intellectual ability.

Longitudinal studies do not face this difficulty: since the same individuals are tested and re-tested at various times during their lifetime, we are always comparing them with themselves (ie there is only one cohort involved).

However, it is practically very difficult to carry them out: the study has to last at least 60 years in the case of intelligence and ageing, and so, not surprisingly, there are very few covering the full adult life-span. However, those that have been conducted, according to Botwinick (1978), show less decline in intelligence with age than cross-sectional studies and the decline tends to occur late in life.

However, there is a kind of compromise method of study (the *cross-longitudinal method*), which attempts to combine the advantages of both while reducing the disadvantages; groups of subjects, of different ages, are followed up over as long a period of time as possible.

One study of this kind was reported by Schaie and Strother (1968) and Schaie and Labouvie Vief (1974). In 1956, Schaie gave the PMA test to a large group of subjects, aged 20 to 70, and in 1963, and again in 1970, he retested as many as possible (161 in all). They were divided into age-groups (on the basis of their age at the start of the study), ranging from 25, 32, 39 and so on up to 67. Each group was a cohort and test scores for each cohort can be viewed as a small longitudinal study of a particular 14-year-long 'slice' of adulthood. These overlapping slices could then be combined.

On verbal meaning (vocabulary) for the 25- and 32-year-old groups, scores actually got better; for the oldest groups (60 and 67) the scores got worse. Overall, scores increased or remained stable up to 60 and then began to decline. Fluid intelligence (eg measured by word fluency) showed a decline for all age-groups.

COGNITIVE CHANGES IN ADULTHOOD AND OLD AGE

Some fascinating research in the USA during the 1970s has attempted to answer the question as to whether there might be a fifth stage of cognitive development.

According to Piaget (see Chapter 25), although adults may become increasingly knowledgeable and skilful in the use of logical thinking, there is no new *kind* of thinking that develops after about 15 years of age. Indeed, many adults never attain *formal operational thinking* (see p. 754) at all and, of those who do, many do so only in relation to their own particular area of expertise and experience.

But many psychologists have pointed out that the mental abilities related to formal operational thought are all focused on problem-solving of one kind or another, whereby several pieces of information must be brought together to find the solution to a problem; this is known as *convergent* thinking (it is the kind of thinking assessed by IQ tests; see Chapter 28).

Yet many problem situations in real life require *divergent* thinking, whereby for example, a solution is found by approaching the problem in an original and unconventional way and where a number of possible solutions may be required and not just one. This kind of approach is not covered by Piaget's theory.

Patricia Arlin (1975/1977) has suggested that there is a fifth stage of development, corresponding to this ability to think divergently, which she calls *problem-finding*.

Riegel (1973), on similar lines to Arlin, advocated that we should de-emphasize formal thought and study *mature* thought in adults instead: mature thought is the acceptance that some things can be both true and not true at the same time. For example, to the person using *concrete operations*, it would mean understanding that two lumps of plasticine are simultaneously the same (quantity) *and* different (shape). But in Piaget's *conservation tasks*, only one or other can be true, ie they are either judged to be the same (despite their different appearance), in which case the individual displays conservation, or they are judged as being different (despite the fact that nothing has been added ot taken away), in which case the individual does not display conservation.

In Piaget's theory, the emphasis is on how the child tries to resolve the contradiction by building new cognitive structures. But Riegel suggests that, instead of resolving the contradiction, the child needs to learn to accept it—concrete operations can be used skilfully and flexibly.

But can cognitive performance be affected by environmental and situational factors?

Many institutions for the elderly are similar to orphanages, residential nurseries and other institutions for children as far as social deprivation is concerned: residents are given very little individual attention by the staff and receive little physical affection, stimulation or social interaction of any kind. This kind of atmosphere could impair cognitive functioning in the same way as it does in infant development.

The degree to which the older person has the opportunity to be physically active and intellectually stimulated, to use their minds and bodies, is as crucial as for other stages of development, if not more so. Why it may be *more* important is because of what we said earlier about ageism and the popular stereotype of ageing, which regards the elderly as not needing to think or to be stimulated, since they have reached the 'end of the road'.

At least we recognize that children can be helped to develop and so we provide what they need: the elderly may have to look after themselves in this respect! (This is another instance of 'growing up' versus 'growing old'.) In adults, as in children, depression, despair, and a sense of worthlessness can all detrimentally affect physical and mental well-being.

AGEING AND MEMORY

It seems that, as we get older, the co-ordination between STM and LTM deteriorates (see Chapter 12). Each part of the memory system may be all right in itself but we are unable to transfer information from STM to LTM as efficiently as we could when younger. Tasks in which there is a time limit, or which require information to be retrieved from memory quickly, are especially difficult.

Also, STM in the elderly is likely to be hindered by a task requiring a division of attention. For example, older people have more difficulty performing two tasks at the same time, as when having to sort triangles according to colour, say, and circles according to size. Here, you have to keep a lot of information in your head at the same time (see Chapter 11).

As far as LTM is concerned, the popular belief that the elderly have little trouble recalling events from their youth and early adult life has some empirical support. But Warrington and Sanders (1971), for example, found that older adults had rather more difficulty recalling news events from the distant past compared with younger adults, although the differences were not dramatic.

When questioned about major news events from 1 to 24 months earlier, subjects of all age-groups recalled less information as the number of months that had elapsed since the event increased. Perhaps the elderly have relatively less trouble remembering incidents that occurred in their own lives, and since they have so much more to remember and the time-span is so much greater than for younger people, this feat seems all the more impressive!

SOCIAL CHANGE IN OLD AGE

SOCIAL DISENGAGEMENT THEORY

The process of *disengagement* is the central concept in Social Disengagement Theory (Cumming and Henry, *Growing Old—The Process of Disengagement*, 1961), perhaps the most influential account of what happens to us socially as we grow old. It was based on a five-year study of 275 50 to 90-year-olds in Kansas City.

Social disengagement refers to the mutual withdrawal of society from the individual (compulsory retirement, children growing up and leaving home and starting families of their own, the death of spouse and friends, etc.) and of the individual from society (reduced social activities and a more solitary life). The theory also considers that this mutual withdrawal is the most appropriate and successful way to age.

Cumming and Henry also claim that most people, regardless of their attitudes towards retirement before the event, will, in practice, feel fearful and rejected when it actually happens to them. Since our lives usually revolve around our work and colleagues, our social relationships are much more difficult to maintain after retirement. It also becomes more difficult physically to travel in order to see family and friends and so in this way also the number of friends begins to decrease.

The disengaging person retreats from the social world as if preparing for their eventual death and it is a process resulting from both external (economic and social) and internal (physical and developmental) factors. The latter include decreased pre-occupation with the self and decreased emotional investment in other people and objects and, to this extent, disengagement is a natural process rather than an imposed one. The older person who has a sense of psychological well-being will usually have attained a new equilibrium characterized by greater psychological distance, altered types of relationahips and decreased social interaction.

Bromley (1988) defines disengagement as a '... systematic reduction in certain kinds of social interaction ...' and:

> In its simplest and crudest form, the theory of Disengagement states that the diminishing psychological and biological capacities of people in later life necessitates a severance of the relationships that they have with younger people in the central activities of society, and the replacement of these older individuals by younger people. In this way society renews itself and the elderly are free to die (Bromley, 1988).

But is this process of disengagement inevitable? And is it the one which most accurately describes and accounts for what happens?

Bromley proposes three main criticisms of the theory, practical, theoretical and empirical. The *practical* criticism is that such a view of ageing encourages a policy of segregation, even indifference to the elderly and a very destructive belief that old age has no value. The *theoretical* criticism claims that Disengagement is not a true theory but more of a 'proto-theory': a collection of loosely related arguments and assumptions. Most serious is the *empirical* criticism; this is the one which Bromley and other critics have focused their objections on.

The Empirical Criticism of Social Disengagement Theory

While there *are* losses in social relationships following retirement, children leaving home, death of spouse and so on, relationships with other relatives (in particular, grandchildren), friends and neighbours go some way to make good these losses. The activities and relationships of later life may be more important in nature (quality may become more important than quantity). Contrary to expectations, engagement and activity are more likely to be sought by older people:

> On the whole it is more accurate to speak of 'industrial disengagement and increased socio-economic dependence' than of 'social disengagement'; in this way, the origins and circumstances of retirement are kept in focus and the theory ties in more closely with the empirical evidence and common-sense impressions. (Bromley, 1988)

Havighurst, Neugarten and Tobin (1968) followed-up the 1961 sample but only 55 per cent of the original 275 were included. It showed that, although increasing age *is* accompanied by increasing disengagement, some elderly people who remained active and engaged reported relatively high levels of contentment. On the whole, the most active were the happiest. This point represents the most serious single criticism of the theory—the theory assumes that the tendency to withdraw from mainstream society is *natural*, that it is an *inherent* part of the ageing process.

As Turner and Helms (1989), for example, point out, many of the past societal conditions forcing adults into restricted environments have changed improved health care, earlier retirement age, higher educational levels, etc. have opened up new areas of pursuit for the elderly and have made possible more active life-styles:

> ... The current view among gerontologists is that Disengagement represents only one of many possible paths of ageing. It has no blanket application to all old people. (Kennis, 1984; quoted in Turner and Helms, 1989)

It has also been suggested that Disengagement may be *cohort-specific*, ie it may have been adaptive to withdraw from an ageist society in the 1950s but may not be so in a more enlightened culture. Not only are there important individual differences, but individuals rarely disengage from all roles to the same degree and *psychological* disengagement may not coincide with disengagement from *social* roles.

As Bromley (1988) points out, the disposition to disengage is a *personality dimension* as well as a characteristic of ageing. The Havighurst et al (1968) follow-up identified a number of different personality types, including three kinds of Integrated person—reorganizers, focused and disengaged. *Reorganizers* are involved in a wide range of activities and re-organize their lives to substitute for lost activities, while the *disengaged* have voluntarily moved away from role commitments and so have low activity levels *but* have high life satisfaction (thus supporting disengagement theory).

Reichard et al (1962) studied 87 men, aged between 55 and 84 and identified five major personality types: (i) *mature* (constructive); (ii) *rocking-chair* (dependent); (iii) *armoured* (defensive); (iv) *angry* (hostile); and (v) *self-haters*.

ACTIVITY (OR RE-ENGAGEMENT) THEORY

The major alternative to Social Disengagement theory is Activity Theory (Havighurst, 1964; Maddox, 1964). Except for the inevitable changes in biology and health, older people are the same as middle-aged people, with essentially the same psychological and social needs.

Decreased social interaction in old age results from the withdrawal by society from the ageing person and happens against the wishes of most elderly people—so the withdrawal is not mutual, as maintained by social disengagement theory.

Optimal ageing, therefore, involves staying active and managing to resist the 'shrinkage' of the social world by maintaining the activities of middle age for as long as possible and then finding substitutes for work or retirement and for spouse and friends upon their deaths. In particular, it is important for the old person to maintain their 'role count', ie to ensure that they always have several different roles to play.

However, there are many exceptions to the rule that the greater the level of activity the greater the degree of satisfaction. By the same token, as we have seen, there are some elderly people who seem satisfied with disengagement and this suggests that activity theory on its own is not an adequate theory of successful ageing. So what else is involved?

Personality seems to play a crucial role in determining the relationship between levels of activity and life satisfaction. According to Neugarten et al (1972) people will select a style of ageing that is best suited to their personality and past experience or lifestyle—there is no single way to age successfully.

Some people may actually develop new interests or pursue in earnest those for which they did not have enough time during their working lives, many will be developing relationships with grandchildren (or even great-grandchildren), some will be re-marrying (or even getting married for the first time) and some will go on working part-time or in a voluntary capacity in their local community.

As a counterbalance to Disengagement Theory, Activity Theory asserts that the natural tendency of most elderly people is to associate with others, particularly in group and community affairs, but that this is often blocked by present-day retirement practices. According to Bromley:

> ... The former [Disengagement] enables or obliges older people to relinguish certain social roles, namely those which they cannot adequately fulfill; the latter [Re-engagement] prevents the consequences of Disengagement from going too far in the direction of isolation, apathy and inaction. (Bromley, 1988)

Not only has Activity Theory probably oversimplified the issues involved but there is little empirical support for it—activity can decline *without* adversely affecting morale and a more leisurely lifestyle, with fewer responsibilities, etc. can be seen as one of the *rewards* of old age. This idea is at the centre of Social Exchange Theory (not to be confused with the theory of human relationships and helping behaviour discussed in Chapters 16 and 18).

SOCIAL EXCHANGE THEORY

Dyson (1980) has criticized both Disengagement and Activity Theories for not taking sufficient account of the physical and economic factors which might limit the individual's choice of how they age. Both theories are, therefore, *prescriptive*, ie they say what the elderly should be doing during this stage of life rather than accounting for how most people do, in fact, age. Again, they involve value-judgements about what it is to *age successfully* (Hayslip and Panek, 1989).

Dyson suggests that a more useful approach is to see the process of adjusting to retirement in particular, and ageing in general, as a sort of *contract* between the individual and society. Dowd (1975), for instance, proposed that we give up our role as an economically active member of society when we retire but, in exchange, we receive increased leisure time, less responsibility and so on. The contract is, for the most part, unwritten and not enforceable, but most people will probably conform to the expectations about being elderly which are built-in to social institutions and stereotypes.

An Evaluation of Theories of Ageing

According to Hayslip and Panek (1989), each theory may refer to a *legitimate* process by which *some* individuals come to terms with a multitude of changes which may accompany ageing. In this sense, they are options.

Just as Disengagement may be involuntary (for instance, through poor health or having to move house), so an individual may face involuntarily high levels of activity (for example, through *having* to work) and both may be equally maladaptive. Arguably, Disengagement Theory under-estimates, and Activity Theory over-estimates, the degree of control people have over the 'reconstruction' of their lives and both see ageing as being essentially the same for all elderly people. However:

> . . . personality is the pivotal factor in determining whether an individual will age successfully, and . . . Activity and Disengagement theories, alone, are inadequate to explain successful ageing . . . (Turner and Helms, 1989)

Again:

> . . . no one pattern of ageing guarantees satisfaction in the later years. Satisfaction, morale, and adaptations in later life generally appear to be closely related to a person's lifelong personality style and general way of dealing with stress and change. In this sense, the past is prologue to the future. While the personality changes somewhat in response to various life events and changes, it generally remains stable throughout all of adult life. (Reedy, 1983; quoted in Turner and Helms, 1989)

Erikson's Psychosocial Theory

Perhaps a more valid and useful way of looking at what all elderly people have in common is to look at the psychological importance of old age as a stage of development, albeit the last that we shall go through, indeed, this is precisely where its importance lies. This brings us, alost full circle, to the Personal Growth Model, which stresses the advantages and positive aspects of ageing. The original and perhaps still the most influential representative of this view is Erikson. In old age ('maturity') there is a conflict between *Ego Integrity* (the positive force) on the one hand and *Despair* (the negative force) on the other and the individual's task is to end the stage, and hence his/her life, with greater ego integrity than despair. The achievement of this represents, for Erikson, successful ageing.

But as with all the other seven stages, we cannot avoid the conflict which is an unavoidable outcome of biological, psychological and social forces. The important thing is how successfully we resolve it. The task of ageing is to take stock of one's life, to look back over it and assess and evaluate how worthwhile and fulfilling it has been.

What exactly does Erikson mean by ego integrity?

(a) The conviction that, in the long-term view, life does have a purpose and a meaning and does make sense.

(b) The conclusion that, within the context of one's life as a whole, what happened was somehow inevitable and could only have happened when and how it did.

(c) The belief that all life's experiences offer something of value, ie there is something to be learned from everything that happens to us, including the bad times. Looking back, we are able to see how we have grown psychologically as a result of life's ups and downs, triumphs and failures, calm and crisis.

(d) Coming to see our own parents in a new light and being able to understand them better because we have lived through our own adulthood and probably have raised children of our own.

(e) Coming to see that what we share with all other human beings, past, present and future, is the inevitable cycle of birth and death. Whatever the differences, historically, culturally, economically, etc. all human beings have this much in common; in the light of this, 'death loses its sting'.

Lack or loss of this ego integrity is signified by a fear of death, which is the most conspicuous symptom of despair. Despair expresses the feeling that it is too late to undo the past, to put back the clock, in order to do what one has omitted to do or to put right the wrongs. Life is almost over and it is the only chance you get! This despair is, in fact, a form of basic mistrust, a fear of the unknown which follows death. (This mistrust is also the negative component of the conflict involved in infancy, the first of Erikson's eight Ages of Man, and so here is an important link between infancy and old age within Erikson's psychosocial theory; see Chapter 21.)

BEREAVEMENT, GRIEF AND MOURNING

As we have seen, a feature of growing old is that it becomes increasingly likely that we will suffer the loss, through death, of loved ones, parents, husbands and wives, siblings and friends, even children.

Suffering such losses is referred to as *bereavement*, while *grief* is the complex set of psychological and bodily reactions commonly found in people who suffer bereavement. Parkes and Weiss (1983) define grief as, 'a normal reaction to overwhelming loss, albeit a reaction in which normal functioning no longer holds'; they distinguish between *grief* and *mourning*, the latter being the, 'observable expression of grief'. (Mourning is also used in a different sense to refer to the social customs and conventions surrounding death, such as funerals, wearing dark clothes, cancelling social engagements and so on; we talk about a 'period of mourning' in which grieving is 'official' and largely public.) What constitutes a normal pattern of grieving?

A number of writers (including Freud, Engel and Parkes) have described the characteristic stages or phases of the grieving process. Engel (1962), for example, uses the concept of *grief work* to refer to the process of mourning through which a bereaved person readjusts to loss; it comprises three phases:

(a) *Disbelief and shock*. The initial reaction to the loss, which can last for up to a few days and involves the refusal to accept the truth of what has happened.
(b) *Developing awareness*. The gradual realization and acknowledgement of what has happened, often accompanied by pangs of grief and guilt. Apathy, exhaustion and anger are also common, the last being closely related to self-blame and guilt and at this time it is important that there are people around who are willing simply to listen and tolerate the expression of all these feelings.
(c) *Resolution*. This involves the establishment of a new identity, the full acceptance of what has happened, and marks the completion of grief work. The bereaved person takes a realistic view of their situation and resolves to cope without the loved one and begin a new life.

All grief theorists agree that grief must be worked through—there is some sort of natural progression and blending of feelings which must be experienced if a healthy adjustment to the loss is to be achieved.

However, some prefer to talk about *components of grief* instead of stages: the latter implies a clear-cut, orderly, pre-determined set of events which is the same for everyone. Yet this is not the case—the 'stages' are not separate, may not be successive and it is not certain that everyone has to experience each and every one of them.

Ramsay and de Groot (1977) describe nine components, some of which tend to appear earlier in the grief process, some of which come later (see Table 24.3).

Parkes (1965), in a study of a number of bereaved people who needed psychiatric treatment, found that one-quarter showed considerable animosity towards the doctor or clergy, making wild accusations of neglect or incompetence, which were usually quite unjustified.

In a later study (1970), Parkes reported that most widows experiencing apparently normal reactions to bereavement had periods of irritability and bitterness, tending to blame others, God and sometimes the deceased themselves.

Marris (1958) interviewed widows and found that many spoke of feeling that their husbands were still present; about half a sample of bereaved psychiatric patients had a similar impression (Parkes, 1962). Similarly, Rees (1971) reported that one in eight widows and widowers had hallucinations of hearing their dead spouse speak and a similar

Table 24.3 Ramsay and de Groot's nine components of grief	1. *Shock*	Usually the first response, most often described as a feeling of 'numbness'. However, feelings can include pain or calm, apathy, depersonalization and derealization. It is as if the feelings are so strong that they are 'turned off' and this can last from a few seconds to several weeks
	2. *Disorganization*	The bereaved person may be unable to do the simplest thing or, alternatively, may be able to organize the entire funeral—and then collapses
	3. *Denial*	Usually an early feature of grief but this defence against feeling too much pain at once may recur at any time throughout the entire process. A common form of denial is searching behaviour, eg waiting for the deceased to come home, looking for them in the street and having hallucinations of seeing or hearing them. In denial, the bereaved behaves as if the deceased were still alive
	4. *Depression*	Emerges as the denial breaks down and can also occur throughout the entire grieving process but it tends to become less frequent and intense. Two forms of this are: (i) 'desolate pining', an active feeling and yearning and longing, an emptiness 'interspersed with waves of intense psychic pain', and (ii) 'despair', a feeling of helplessness and hopelessness, the blackness of the realization of powerlessness to bring back the dead
	5. *Guilt*	Can be both real and imagined, for actual neglect of the deceased when they were still alive or for angry thoughts or feelings
	6. *Anxiety*	May take the form of fear of losing control of one's feelings, of going mad, or more general apprehension about the future (changed roles, increased responsibilities, financial worries, etc.)
	7. *Aggression*	Can range from irritability towards family and friends to outbursts of anger towards God or fate, doctors and nurses, the clergy or even the person who has died
	8. *Resolution*	As the emotions die down, an acceptance of the death emerges; a 'taking leave of the dead and an acceptance that life must go on'
	9. *Re-integration*	Acceptance is put into practice and the bereaved reorganizes their life in which the dead person has no place. (However, pining and despair and other components may re-appear on occasions, eg anniversaries, birthdays, etc.)

proportion claimed to have seen the deceased. They also referred to a general sensation of the presence of the dead person, which could continue for years, and they found it helped them; significantly, this was reported more often by those who had been happily married.

NORMAL AND ABNORMAL GRIEVING

One problem involved in trying to distinguish normal from abnormal or pathological grief is the enormous variation in the grieving patterns of different individuals (even though the components may be similar). As far as the duration of grieving is concerned, Hinton (1975) claims that the more severe mental pain will have largely eased within one, two or perhaps a few more weeks and that it is generally assumed that the grief will have largely abated within six months.

However, several studies have found that widows may well continue to experience some psychological or physical ill-health a year after their husband's death.

Parkes believes that prolonged, incapacitating grief ('chronic grief') is the most common variant of the usual pattern of grieving and that people who at first do not show their grief may later show this disturbed, chronic, form of mourning.

What are some of the other abnormal patterns of grieving?

Hinton (1975) identifies three: (i) exaggeration of the *numbness* associated with the shock of the loss; (ii) shading of some of the more immediate responses into *neurotic forms of emotional distress*; and (iii) the appearance of *physical symptoms*, sometimes merely accompanying, sometimes over-shadowing, the emotional disturbance.

Looking at these in more detail:

(a) Some bereaved people continue going about their everyday business for many days or even weeks as if the fact of the loss had never really registered. If it does lie hidden for a while, it may finally erupt some weeks later or may appear on a much later but emotionally salient occasion, such as the anniversary of the death or the dead person's birthday. There is also some evidence that a psychological illness is likely to develop when a person reaches, for example, the age at which their parent died or when their own child reaches the age at which they themselves suffered a bereavement and it is also quite common for people to experience anxiety about not living beyond the age at which one of their parents died.

(b) According to Parkes (1970), occasional feelings of panic are so common-place that it could be considered a normal reaction. Other illogical fears may include being alone, claustrophobia, dirt and death. Feelings of depersonalization among the bereaved, a sense of being unreal or unfamiliar to oneself, and obsessions too may become more likely.

(c) Fatigue, insomnia, loss of appetite, weight loss, headaches, breathlessness, palpitations, blurred vision and exhaustion are among the many physical symptoms of which widows complain to their doctors. Parkes (1964) found that widows needed to consult their GPs much more often than usual during the first six months of widowhood, both for physical and psychological symptoms.

Elderly people who suffer bereavement are especially likely to experience their distress as predominantly physical.

Widows and widowers, for some time after the death of their spouse, in fact run a greater risk of suffering serious illness and themselves dying than married people of similar age, with widowers being at a relatively greater risk.

Parkes et al (1969) believe this risk is largely confined to the first six months after the bereavement and identify three main factors that are responsible: (i) self-neglect; (ii) suicide; and (iii) cardiac disease ('broken heart') and (in the case of widowers) death through a disease similar to that of the wife.

Interestingly, it is younger adults (up to their mid-thirties), especially men, who are most at risk.

THE CAUSES OF PATHOLOGICAL GRIEF

According to Parkes and Weiss (1983) most of the psychological symptoms that bring the bereaved into the care of their doctors can be seen as distortions or exaggerations of the normal process of grieving and this leads us to look more closely at the day-to-day factors which normally influence the course of grief. Given the range of individual differences in the intensity, duration and pattern of grieving, and that most of these variations are within the range of normality, it may well be that the pathological variations are simply the extreme responses to particularly unfavourable circumstances.

Parkes and Weiss identify two main groups of factors which are likely to complicate the course of the grieving process: (i) those which discourage the *expression* of grief; and (ii) those which discourage the *ending* of grief.

(a) The mode of death is of particular importance; a sudden and untimely death will produce greater shock and set in motion more psychological defences (which probably explains why younger widows and widowers are especially susceptible).

The immediate family may encourage or discourage the bereaved to express or inhibit their grief, and society at large may also influence grieving through religious and other rituals.

Parkes (1970) describes seven widows who expressed very little distress during the first week of bereavement, did not wear mourning dress and failed to visit their husband's grave. They were significantly more distressed three months later than eighteen other widows who had expressed grief and mourned actively from the start.

(b) Grief is not only a psychological reaction to bereavement but a duty to the dead. Some may feel that to engage in perpetual mourning is a tribute to the dead. It may also be a way of making restitution for some failure or neglect of the dead.

Parkes (1962), in a study of 98 bereaved psychiatric patients, found that 21 per cent of those whose illness was evidently a pathological form of grief had mixed feelings of fondness and hostility towards the decreased, compared with 6 per cent of those who showed little evidence of problematic grief at the time of admission. Parkes also found a high incidence of previous depressive illness among the bereaved psychiatric patients.

Family and friends may put pressure on the bereaved to come out of mourning, even though grieving continues, and some may fear social ostracism if they continue to be seen as 'in mourning' and so conceal their grief.

Finally, the more unsatisfactory the relationship with the decreased while they were alive, the more disturbed the grieving process will be. As Krupp (1962) put it, 'if one can learn how to live with the living, then one can manage to live with the dead'.

DEATH OF THE SELF

Much of what we have said about ageing has been to do with *loss* of various kinds—loss of work, loss of financial status, loss of social status, loss of relationships through death and so on:

> As life draws to its end, the ageing person faces another death. He experiences even more clearly the knowledge of his own death—the death of the 'self'. There may be many partial deaths along the way. The loss of sexuality may seem the death of a vital part of the self. The failing of the brain with its dementing processes is another partial death of self that may have to be endured . . . (Raphael, 1984)

The older person becomes increasingly preoccupied with death, which starts to be thought of personally—when and how will it come? There is an *ambivalence* in attitudes to death—sometimes shutting it out and trying to deny it, sometimes a desperate wish to talk about it, share one's fears and find out more about the unknown. This is a process of *anticipatory grief* (a term coined by Kübler-Ross (1969) to describe how the terminally ill come to terms with their own, imminent, death)

A common feature of anticipatory grief is *reminiscing*.

According to Butler (1963), much of the reminiscing common in later life may be a valuable way of 'sorting out' the past and the present. Prompted by the recognition of impending death, the elderly re-examine old conflicts, consider how they have treated others and come to some conclusion about themselves and their lives. This *life review* may result in a new sense of accomplishment, satisfaction and peace (equivalent to Erikson's ego integrity).

It represents, at least partly, grieving for the life and the self which will be relinquished with death:

> . . . For life is very sweet and not easily relinquished even for those to whom it has brought much pain. (Raphael, 1984)

Coming to terms with our own death is a crucial *task* of old age (what Peck, 1968, calls *ego transcendence* versus *ego preoccupation*):

> . . . Through children, through contributions to the culture, through friendships—these are ways in which human beings can achieve enduring significance for their actions which goes beyond the limit of their own skins and their own lives. It may, indeed be the only *knowable* kind of self-perpetuation after death. (Peck, 1968)

Some individuals review their lives privately or internally, others share their memories and reflections with others. For the latter, this serves a double purpose: (i) it helps them to organize a final perspective on their lives for themselves; (ii) it leaves a record that will live on with others after their death.

Clearly, however we may go about it, one task of life, especially during our 'twilight years', is to prepare for death

25 COGNITIVE DEVELOPMENT

Figure 25.1 *Jean Piaget (1896–1980). (Yves De Braine from Black Star)*

In this chapter we shall be concentrating on the work of Jean Piaget (1896–1980; Fig. 25.1) who, like Freud and Skinner, has made a massive contribution to psychology as a whole and child development in particular.

Born in Neuchâtel, Switzerland, Piaget was trained as a zoologist and, as such, he was especially interested in the question of how animals adapt to their environment. It was in this context that he become involved in the study of human intelligence. He was also very interested in philosophy, particularly the branch that deals with general questions about the nature of knowledge, called epistemology, and he came to combine these two areas of interest in *genetic epistemology*, the study of how knowledge develops in human beings.

We shall also be discussing the theories of Jerome Bruner and Lev Vygotsky.

PIAGET'S THEORY

INTELLIGENCE: TRAIT OR PROCESS?

Ironically, Piaget's early involvement with intelligence tests, which attempt to compare individuals on what is assumed to be a fixed trait, was to lead him towards his lifelong study of intelligence as a process. He was not concerned with individual differences but with what is common to all individuals as they pass through the same stages of intellectual or cognitive development.

While working in Binet's Paris laboratory (Binet developed the first recognized intelligence test), on the standardization of Burt's IQ test for use with French children (see Chapter 28), Piaget became intrigued by the unusual and unexpected replies that children often gave and wanted to discover the processes by which these wrong answers were arrived at. He believed that children's mistakes were a much better indicator of how they think than their correct answers ever could be; he also became convinced that their errors were not random but systematic, that there was a pattern to them which revealed the underlying mental structures that generated them. Whereas IQ tests are concerned with the *what* of the child's answers (how many are right or wrong), Piaget was concerned with the *how* (especially as suggested by their mistakes).

THE NATURE OF INTELLECTUAL DEVELOPMENT

To Piaget, intelligence is the whole system of cognitive adaptations in humans; intelligence consists of knowledge and the cognitive functions integral to the form of knowledge representation. This entails a theory of knowledge known as 'constructivism', which distinguishes it from 'rationalism' (the theory that knowledge is innate) and 'associationism' (the theory that knowledge consists of passive registration of associations in the world) . . . (Richardson, 1991)

As we have seen, Piaget regarded intelligence as a *process*, something which changes over time; it also represents a fundamental means by which human being *adapt* to their environment. The process essentially involves the individual trying to *construct* an understanding of reality through *interacting* with it; knowledge does not come 'ready-made' but has to be discovered actively (or even 'invented'). It consists:

> . . . neither of a simple copy of external objects nor of a mere unfolding of structures preformed inside the subject, but rather . . . a set of structures progressively constructed by continuous interaction between the subject and the external world. (Piaget, 1970)

These structures develop in a predictable fashion and can be summarized as four *stages* which all children pass through in the same sequence.

How does development occur?

Underlying these changes are certain *functional invariants*, ie fundamental aspects of the developmental process which remain the same and work in the same way throughout the various stages, in particular, *assimilation, accommodation* and *equilibration*. But before we can properly understand these unchanging features of development, we need to understand exactly what it is that changes, namely schemas (or schemata; see Chapters 9 and 12).

A *schema* (or scheme) can be thought of as the basic unit or building-block of intelligent behaviour. More formally, it is a way of organizing experience which makes the world more simple, more predictable and more 'know-able'. The baby's schemas are largely confined to inborn reflexes, such as sucking, and they tend to operate quite independently of other reflexes; a sucking schema is also a physical, overt, action. But, in the course of development, individual schemas become co-ordinated and integrated into more inclusive structures and it is these larger structures which constitute the typical abilities and understanding of each developmental stage.

> Each stage is characterized by an overall structure in terms of which the main behaviour patterns can be explained. (Piaget and Inhelder, 1969)

Also, the baby's physical (motor) behaviour comes more and more under its voluntary control and schemas gradually become more and more internal or 'interiorized', ie they become mental and the child starts to *think* in something like the adult sense of the word. But if at birth we are limited to a few, simple, unrelated, reflexes, how do our schemas change in these ways? This is where assimilation, accommodation and equilibration come in.

At first, the baby will suck anything that touches its lips or is put into its mouth, whether this is its mother's nipple (which produces nourishment) or its father's finger (which does not). The baby is applying a schema that it already possesses by (in this case, literally), fitting objects into it, sucking them in more or less the same way, ie *assimilating* them.

However, while the baby is still very young, it will gradually change the shapes of its lips according to whether it is sucking a nipple or a finger. Later on, when it is given a cup to feed from, it must change the way it sucks (and swallows) yet again; this will not occur without a lot of spilt milk but eventually a 'drinking-out-of-a-cup' schema will have developed and this illustrates *accommodation*. So in assimilation we apply the schemas we already possess and try to fit the environment into them; it can be thought of as a generalized use of what we can already do. Schemas are not just physical actions or skills but include ideas, concepts, bits of knowledge, verbal labels and so on. In accommodation, we change already-existing schemas to match the requirements of the environment, which brings us to equilibration.

As long as the child is able to deal with all (or most) new experiences by assimilating them, it will be in a comfortable state of balance or equilibrium (brought about by *equilibration*). However, if already-existing schemas are inadequate to cope with new situations, the child is pushed into a less comfortable state of disequilibrium and, to restore the balance, it must change one or more of its schemas, ie it must accommodate.

So it is through this process of equilibration that development proceeds, a continuous series of assimilations and accommodations, equilibrium and disequilibrium, an ongoing process throughout life but with the most significant developments taking place during the first fifteen years or so (Fig. 25.2).

Figure 25.2 Relationship between assimilation, equilibrium, disequilibrium and accommodation in the development of schemas

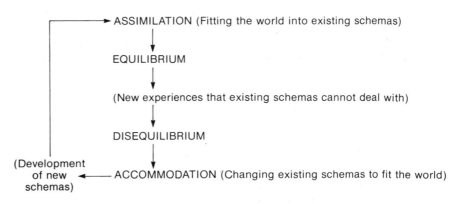

When a schema has recently developed, assimilation ensures that the new learning, which the schema represents, is consolidated, ie it is practised repeatedly until it can be used easily and even automatically. But assimilation alone would make behaviour very rigid and inflexible and, indeed, very little development would actually take place—this can only happen through accommodation. So assimilation and accommodation are both necessary and complementary and together they constitute the fundamental process of *adaptation* (adaptation equals assimilation plus accommodation).

STAGES OF COGNITIVE DEVELOPMENT

Having discussed how schemas change and develop in general, we are in a position to look at the characteristic changes that take place during the four major stages that Piaget describes, namely:

(i) the *sensorimotor* (0 to 2 years);
(ii) the *pre-operational* (2 to 7 years);

(iii) the *concrete operational* (7 to 11 years);
(iv) the *formal operational* (11 to 15 years).

Each stage represents a stage in the development of intelligence (hence 'sensorimotor intelligence', 'pre-operational intelligence' and so on) and is really a way of summarizing the various schemas the individual has at any particular time. But two notes of caution are necessary.

First, the ages corresponding to each stage are only approximations or averages. Children move through the stages at different speeds, often due to environmental factors, although the *sequence* of stages is invariant and universal (the same for all human beings) and is based on biological maturation. Secondly, the concept of a 'stage' of development is often interpreted to indicate that development is discontinuous, ie not a gradual process of change but broken up into 'segments' (the stages). This was not the impression Piaget wanted to create and, from 1970, he preferred to think of development as a spiral, implying a continuous process. However, later stages build on earlier ones and entail *reconstructing* at a new level what was achieved at the earlier stage:

> ... cognitive stages have a sequential property, that is, they appear in a fixed order of succession because each one of them is necessary for the formation of the following one. (Piaget, 1970)

For instance, the operational intelligence of the seven- to eleven-year-old originates in the sensorimotor intelligence of the newborn to two-year-old but they are qualitatively different, ie different kinds of intelligence. (We shall discuss the concept of a stage again when we evaluate Piaget's theory as a whole.)

i) *THE SENSORIMOTOR STAGE (BIRTH TO TWO YEARS)*

The baby's intelligence is essentially *practical*, ie its interactions with the environment consist of overt actions, either *sensory* (seeing, hearing, etc.) or *motor* (grasping, pulling, etc.). The baby 'thinks' through acting upon objects and/or perceiving them—a rattle *is* its colour when looked at, its texture when touched or sucked, its sound when shaken—and when it is not being perceived or acted upon in any of these ways, it no longer exists as far as the baby is concerned. This is referred to as a lack of *object permanence*.

This lack of object permanence is part of the baby's profound *egocentrism*, ie it makes no distinction between itself and the rest of the world, so that nothing (including itself) has any separate, independent, existence. (This should not be confused with egocentrism as it has been studied in the two- to seven-year-old, where the child cannot distinguish between its own viewpoint and other people's; see below.)

The development of object permanence is one of the major achievements of the sensorimotor period so we shall discuss it in some detail (see Chapter 10).

Object Permanence

Between one and four months, when the baby sees its bottle, for example, it begins to suck, apparently for the pleasure of it, even if the teat does not touch its lips. This suggests that the baby has learned to *recognize* its bottle; but this hardly constitutes understanding that the bottle exists independently of the baby itself. The infant will look at a toy if it is within visual range, follow it with its eyes and, between three and four months, try to grasp it. But as soon as it has moved out of sight, the baby acts as if it had ceased to exist; there is no attempt to search for it, with eyes or hands. (It is a case of 'out of sight, out of mind'.)

However, some psychologists believe that Piaget may have been misjudging what babies can do. For example, Bower and Wishart (1972) found that the way an object is made to disappear influences a baby's response, while Piaget believed that it should not make any difference at all. If babies were looking at an object and reaching for it when the lights were turned off, Bower and Wishart found that they would continue to reach for it for up to $1\frac{1}{2}$ minutes (they used infra-red cameras to observe the babies in the dark). This strongly suggests that the baby remembers that the object is still there and Bower (1977) believes that the baby's initial difficulty is to do with understanding concepts of location and movement and *not* the object-concept as such.

Also during this stage, according to Piaget, the *whole* object must be visible if the baby is to respond to it at all. However, Bower (1977) claims that if a month-old baby is shown a toy, then a screen is put between the baby and the toy, and the toy is removed and then the screen, the baby shows some surprise, or even a startled response, indicating that it expected the toy still to be there. Piaget may have been observing immature motor skills in the infant's failure to 'search' rather than an immature object-concept.

By six to seven months, says Piaget, the baby will reach for a familiar object if only a *part* of it is visible, suggesting that it realizes that the rest of it is attached to the part that is showing. (Bower, 1977, believes this will happen as early as four months.) However, if you cover up the object completely, even if the baby sees you do it, it will not search for it.

A good illustration of this is one of the many accounts Piaget gives of his own three children. See Box 25.1 for an account of Jacqueline when she was 7 months, 28 days old.

Box 25.1   An Illustration of Lack of Object Permanence (Piaget, 1963)

At 0,7 (28) Jacqueline tried to grasp a celluloid duck on top of her quilt. She almost catches it, shakes herself, and the duck slides down beside her. It falls very close to her hand but behind a fold in the sheet. Jacqueline's eyes have followed the movement, she has even followed it with her outstretched hand. But as soon as the duck has disappeared—nothing more! It does not occur to her to search behind the fold of the sheet, which would be very easy to do (she twists it mechanically without searching at all) . . . I try showing it to her a few times. Each time she tries to grasp it, but when she is about to touch it I replace it very obviously under the sheet. Jacqueline immediately withdraws her hand and gives up . . . Everything occurs as though the child believed that the object is alternately made and unmade . . .

Not until eight months will the baby search for a completely hidden object, but even then, and for a few months after that, the baby will still be 'deceived' by the physical conditions of the search. So, if you hide a toy under a cloth (A) the baby can retrieve it with no difficulty. But if, in full view of the baby, you then place it under a second cloth (B), it will continue to search under cloth (A) (Fig. 25.3). Not until about twelve months will the baby search under the cloth where it last saw the toy hidden and can do this even when three or four cloths are used. (Others have suggested that this ability appears as early as nine months.)

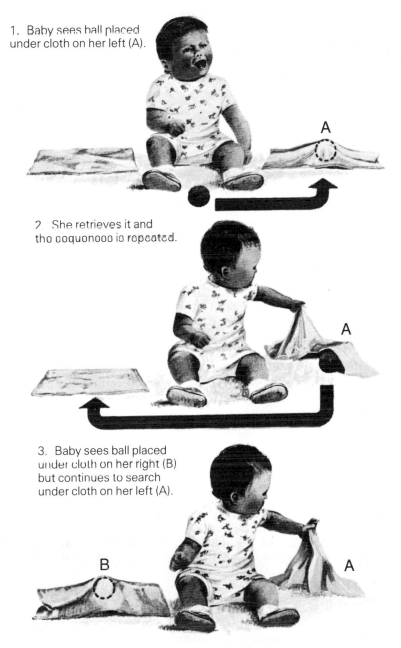

1. Baby sees ball placed under cloth on her left (A).

A

2. She retrieves it and the sequences is repeated.

A

3. Baby sees ball placed under cloth on her right (B) but continues to search under cloth on her left (A).

B   A

Figure 25.3 Piaget's demonstration of the limited object permanence of babies below twelve months—they can retrieve a hidden object only from its original hiding place (not where it was last hidden). (From Barnes-Gutteridge, W. (1974) Psychology. London: Hamlyn)

Another way of testing object permanence is to observe the baby's eye movements to see if it follows a moving object and continues to look along its path even after it has vanished, for example behind a screen. If the baby looks at the other side of the screen where the object would re-appear, the visual search suggests that the baby expects it to re-appear which, in turn, indicates object permanence. (Bower et al (1971) found that this visual tracking of objects begins between four to eight months.)

Between eight and twelve months, the concept of a person as a permanent 'object' develops rapidly and, according to Bell (1970), 'person permanence' may develop at a faster rate than 'physical object permanence', especially in babies whose mothers spend a great deal of time with them in a warm and close relationship. (It is likely that through realizing the individuality and permanence of the mother, the baby begins to appreciate the permanence of physical objects.)

Even when the baby can successfully retrieve a hidden object from where it was last hidden, object permanence is still not fully developed. For instance, the baby watches you place a toy in a matchbox, after which you place the matchbox under a pillow. When the baby isn't looking, you slip the toy out of the box and leave it under the pillow. Next, you put the now empty box in front of the baby who quickly searches it; on finding no toy inside, it does not search for the missing toy under the pillow.

Before about eighteen months, the young child cannot take into account the possibility that something it has not actually seen might have happened; Piaget refers to this as a *failure to infer invisible displacements* and, once the child can do this, the development of object permanence is complete.

The General Symbolic Function

Apart from object permanence, the sensorimotor stage is important mainly for the development of the *general symbolic function*, one manifestation of which is *language*. But rather than regarding language as the *source* of thought Piaget saw it as *reflecting* thought that originates in *action*. (We shall return to the issue of the relationship between language and thought later, but also see Chapter 13.)

Piaget distinguishes between *symbols*, which resemble the things they represent (eg mental images), and *signs*, which stand for things in a quite arbitrary way and are merely conventional; and language in fact falls into the latter category. When the child begins to represent objects to itself in the form of mental images, it is no longer so dependent on physical exploration and the manipulation of objects; it is now beginning to *think*, working things out in its head. Schemas are now 'interiorized' and this can lead to sudden, insightful solutions. For example, the child might put a cup down on the floor in order to have both hands free to open a door. After looking at the door and then at the cup, it 'realizes', through a mental image of the door opening, that the cup is in the way. So it decides to move the cup to a safer place before trying to open the door.

The other major manifestations of the general symbolic function are: (i) *deferred imitation*, the ability to imitate or reproduce something seen or heard when the 'model' is no longer present, indicating an important advance in the child's capacity to remember; and (ii) *representational* or *make-believe play*, where one object is used as if it were another and this too depends on the child's growing ability to form mental images of things and people in their absence. These developments usually become apparent between eighteen and twenty-four months.

ii) THE PRE-OPERATIONAL STAGE (TWO TO SEVEN YEARS)

Probably the main difference between this and the sensorimotor stage is the continued development and use of internal images, symbols and language, which is especially important for the child's developing sense of self-awareness. At the same time, the child's world is still fundamentally concrete and absolute—things *are* very much as they *seem* and the child tends to be influenced by how things look rather than by logical principles or operations (hence 'pre-operational': the child lacks the logical operations characteristic of later stages).

Piaget in fact subdivided the stage into two: (i) the pre-conceptual (two to four years); and (ii) the intuitive (four to seven years).

i) Pre-conceptual

The *absolute* nature of the child's thinking makes it very difficult for it to understand relative terms, such as 'bigger' or 'stronger', and things tend to be 'biggest' or just 'big'.

Classification

If you ask a two- to four-year-old to divide apples into 'big red apples' and 'small green apples', the child will *either* put all the red apples together or all the green apples together (regardless of size) *or* all the big ones together or all the small ones together (regardless of colour). In other words, a child of this age can only classify things on the basis of a *single* attribute at a time—in our example, either colour or size but not both at the same time.

Piaget called this *centration*; until it can de-centre, the child will be unable to classify things in any kind of logical or systematic way.

The unsystematic nature of the pre-conceptual child's thinking is well illustrated by what Piaget calls *syncretic thought* (what Vygotsky called 'complexive thinking', see p. 766), ie the tendency to link together any neighbouring objects or event on the basis of what individual instances have in common. For example, if a three-year-old is given a box of wooden shapes, of different colours, and is asked to pick out four that are alike, the child might pick the shapes shown in Figure 25.4. Here, the

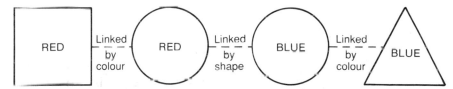

Figure 25.4 Simple example of syncretic thought

characteristic the child focuses on changes with each second shape that is chosen: a *red* square is followed by a *red* circle which is followed by a *blue* circle which is followed by a *blue* triangle, so that only the first and second, second and third, and third and fourth objects have anything in common—there is no one characteristic that all four have in common. A five-year-old would be able to select four of the same shape or four of the same colour—and say what they have in common.

In *transductive reasoning*, the child draws an inference about the relationship between two objects based on a *single* attribute. For example, if A has four legs and B has four legs, then A must be B. If A happens to be a cat and B a dog, the child will call both cats and dogs by the one name with which it is most familiar. This kind of reasoning can lead to what Piaget calls *animistic thinking*, the belief that inanimate objects are alive. For example, because the sun (seems to) follow us when we walk, it must be alive, the reasoning being that if people move and if the sun moves, then the sun is the same as people, ie they are both alive (some other examples of animism are given in Box 25.2).

Box 25.2   Examples of children's animism during the pre-operational stage (From Piaget, J. (1973) The Child's Conception of the World. *Paladin)*

CLI (3 years 9 months) speaking of a motor in a garage: *'The motor's gone to bye-byes. It doesn't go out because of the rain* [elle fait dodo, elle sort pas . . .].

BAD (3 years): *'The bells have woken up, haven't they?'*

NEL (2 years 9 months) seeing a hollow chestnut tree: *'Didn't it cry when the hole was made?'* To a stone: *'Don't touch my garden! . . . My garden would cry.'* Nel, after throwing a stone on to a sloping bank, watching the stone rolling down said: *'Look at the stone. It's afraid of the grass.'*

Nel scratched herself against a wall. Looking at her hand: *'Who made that mark? . . . It hurts where the wall hit me.'*

DAR (1 year 8 months to 2 years 5 months) bringing his toy motor to the window: *'Motor see the snow.'* Dar stood up in bed, crying and calling out: *'The mummies* (the ladies) *all on the ground, hurt!'* Dar was watching the grey clouds. He was told that it was going to rain. *'Oh, look at the wind!—Naughty wind, smack wind.'*

Do you think that would hurt the wind?

Yes.' A few days later: *'Bad wind.—No, not naughty—rain naughty. Wind good.*

Why is the rain naughty?

Because Mummy pushes the pram and the pram all wet.' Dar couldn't go to sleep, so the light was left on at his demand: *'Nice light'* [gentille]. On a morning in winter when the sun shone into the room: *'Oh, good! the sun's come to make the radiator warm.'*

The pre-conceptual child also has difficulty with *seriation*, ie arranging objects on the basis of a particular dimension, such as increasing height. Piaget and Szeminska (1941, 1952) asked children to put a number of sticks in order of decreasing length and found that even five- and six-year-olds tended to do this by trial-and-error. They had particular difficulty understanding that a stick (B) can be both smaller than one stick (A) and larger than another stick (C), and once they have completed the series they are unable to insert an extra stick. The two- to four-year-old also cannot easily perceive actions as following a particular order or sequence through time, as in the falling-stick cards test, shown in Figure 25.5.

Figure 25.5 The falling-stick card test

ii) *Intuitive*

While four- to seven-year-olds may have developed the kinds of thinking described above, they are still very limited in their ability to think logically. Let us look at classification again, this time at what are known as *class-inclusion tasks*.

Class-Inclusion Tasks

Imagine a child is presented with several wooden beads, mostly brown but a few white, and is then asked:

(a) 'Are they all wooden?' The child will answer 'Yes'.
(b) 'Are there more brown or more white beads?' 'Brown'.
(c) 'Are there more brown beads or more beads?' 'Brown'.

According to Piaget, what the child is failing to understand is the relationship between the *whole* (the class of wooden beads) and the *parts* (the classes of brown and white beads); these are referred to as the *superordinate* and the *subordinate class(es)* respectively. The child is still influenced by what it perceives; it can *see* the brown beads, which are more numerous than the white, in a more immediate and direct way than the wooden beads (despite being able to answer the first question correctly).

Piaget took this to be another example of the child's inability to de-centre, but others have challenged his interpretation. Donaldson (1978), for example, asks if the difficulty the child experiences is to do with what is expected of it and how the task is presented. She cites a study by McGarrigle et al which involved four toy cows, three black and one white; they were laid on their sides and children (average age of six) were told they were 'sleeping'. Of those children asked the standard form of the question ('Are there more black cows or more cows?'), 25 per cent answered correctly; while of those asked, 'Are there more black cows or more *sleeping* cows?' 48 per cent answered correctly, the difference being statistically significant.

Piaget's interpretation of his own findings assumes that the child's understanding of 'more' is the same as an adult's. But is it? Donaldson and McGarrigle (1974) carried out a study which suggests it is not. It involved toy cars and garages, arranged on two shelves, one above the other (Fig. 25.6). At first, the children saw the cars *without* garages and

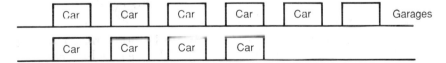

Figure 25.6 *Toy cars and garages as used by Donaldson and McGarrigle (1974)*

were asked, 'Are there more cars on this shelf or more cars on this shelf?' Most of the four- to six-year-olds answered readily and correctly. When the garages were placed over the cars, and the question repeated about one-third of the children changed their judgements, saying that now the shelf with four cars had *more* cars than the shelf with five! Why? Donaldson (1978) suggests that, when the garages are present, the children tend to interpret the situation in terms of the full set of cars which would be appropriate to the garages, so that the row of five cars with six garages is seen as *lacking* a car, ie the children seem to think they are meant to attend to *fullness*.

Although not a class-inclusion study, the cars and garage experiment underlines the importance of making the experimental situation as unambiguous for the child as possible—both linguistic and social factors will affect the child's performance over and above the child's actual abilities and Piaget has been criticized for under-estimating their influence. This is probably most clearly seen in his study of *egocentrism* and *conservation*.

Egocentrism

Another predominant feature of the whole pre-operational period is the child's *egocentrism*. The child, according to Piaget, is literally *self-centred*, sees the world totally from its own standpoint and cannot understand that other people might see things differently. Essentially, what the child is unable to do is put itself, psychologically, in other people's shoes in order to realize that they do not know everything that it knows, do not perceive what it perceives, do not feel what it feels. One amusing example (Phillips, 1969) is of a four-year-old who is asked, 'Do you have a brother?' to which he replies 'Yes'. Then he is asked, 'What's his name?' to which he replies, 'Jim'. Finally, in response to the question, 'Does Jim have a brother?', he says, 'No'.

One of Piaget's most famous demonstrations of egocentrism involved a three-dimensional model of a Swiss mountain scene (Piaget and Inhelder, 1956; Fig. 25.7). The three mountains were of different colours

Figure 25.7 Piaget and Inhelder's three-mountain scene, seen from four different sides. (From Smith, P. K. and Cowie, H. (1988) Understanding Children's Development. *London: Basil Blackwell)*

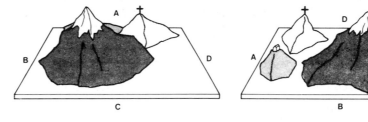

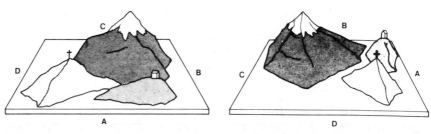

with snow on top of one, a house on another and a red cross on the third. The child could walk round and explore the model and then sat on one side while a doll was placed at some different location: the child was shown a set of ten pictures showing different views of the model and asked to choose the one that represented how the doll saw it.

Four-year-olds were totally unaware of different perspectives from their own and instead chose a picture which matched how they themselves saw the model; six-year-olds showed some awareness but often chose the wrong picture, and only seven- to eight-year-olds consistently chose the one that represented the doll's view. According to

Piaget, children below seven are bound by the *egocentric illusion*; they fail to understand that what they see is relative to their own position and instead take it to represent 'the world as it really is'.

However, several more recent studies have disputed the conclusion that Piaget drew. Borke (1975), for instance, believes that the three-mountain scene is an unusually difficult way of presenting the problem. She allowed the child to move a second three-dimensional model on a turntable and, under these conditions, even three-year-olds (42 per cent of the time) and four-year-olds (67 per cent of the time) were able to see things as the doll 'saw' them (the doll was Grover, a character from *Sesame Street*).

Borke demonstrated clearly that the *task itself* has a crucial influence on the child's performance of perspective-taking skills, and she concluded that even three- and four-year-olds are not as egocentric as Piaget has claimed.

Donaldson (1978) cites a study by Hughes using a piece of apparatus meant to be equivalent to the three-mountain scene, comprising two 'walls' intersecting to form a cross (Fig. 25.8).

At first, the policeman doll is placed where he could see areas B and D but not A and C (he isn't tall enough to 'see' over the wall). Then the boy doll is put into area A and the child is asked if the policeman can see him, and this is repeated by putting the boy doll in areas B, C and D. Next the policeman is placed where he could see A and C and the child is asked to 'hide the boy so that the policeman can't see him'. If the child makes any mistakes at this stage they are pointed out and the question repeated until the correct answer is given; but very few mistakes were made. The test proper begins with the introduction of a second policeman and the child is now asked to hide the boy from both policemen; this is repeated three times so that each time a different area becomes the only possible hiding place left. For example, with one policeman at the right end of the cross and the other at the top end, the only hiding place for the boy is C. Piaget would predict that children would hide the boy from themselves, ie where they, the child, could not see him.

However, three-and-a-half- to five-year-olds hid the boy successfully 90 per cent of the time (including 88 per cent of the three-and-a-half- to four-year-olds), even when this meant the boy doll being clearly visible to the child. Even when Hughes used up to six sections of wall and a third policeman, four-year-olds were successful 90 per cent of the time; three-year-olds found it more difficult but still managed 60 per cent success.

How can we account for this discrepancy between Hughes's results and those of Piaget? According to Donaldson, the policeman and boy doll situation enables the child to understand what is being asked of it because there is a meaningful context: it makes 'human sense', even to a three-year-old, because the child can relate to the idea of 'hiding from someone'. By contrast, she thinks the three-mountain situation has no meaningful context, is 'disembedded' (taken out of context), does not make 'human sense' and is 'cold blooded'. Donaldson compares this situation with that in which an American Indian was asked to translate into his native tongue, 'the white man shot six bears today'. 'How can I do that?' he protested, 'No white man could shoot six bears in a day.' It just did not make 'human sense'.

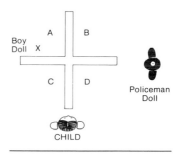

Figure 25.8 *Apparatus used by Hughes to test egocentrism. (From Donaldson, 1984)*

Finally, an intriguing study by Flavell (1978, cited by Maccoby), tested Piaget's egocentric interpretation of the young child who, with its hands covering its eyes, says, 'Now you can't see me'. According to Flavell, children may think of their eyes as 'the window of the soul', so that when somebody is not looking directly into their eyes, they cannot see the child's real self (see Chapter 21).

Flavell tested these two hypotheses by giving two-and-a-half to five-year-olds a series of tests concerning what they thought others could see. The experimenter and the child sat on opposite sides of a table on which sat a Snoopy doll. In the simplest procedure, the child was asked to close or cover both eyes and the experimenter said, 'Now your eyes are closed and mine are open', and then asked a series of questions— 'Do I see you?', 'Do I see Snoopy?', 'Do I see your head?' and so on.

The youngest children (below the age of three-and-a-half) often said that the experimenter could not see them but, without exception, they said that he could see Snoopy and most believed that he could see their head or arm. So the egocentric explanation was ruled out—the children understood that the experimenter could see something which they themselves could not.

Conservation

The other major feature of the pre-operational stage is the child's inability to *conserve*: the child fails to understand that things remain the same (constant) despite changes in their appearance (how they look). It is the perceptual appearance of things that still dominates—things *are* what they *seem* and this is what 'intuitive' is meant to convey.

Piaget's conservation experiments are probably his most famous and have been replicated many times. Let us start with the conservation of *liquid quantity* (or continuous quantity). (Incidentally, this is often referred to as *volume* conservation, but this is incorrect.)

In the situation represented in Figure 25.9, although the child agrees that there is the same amount of liquid in A and B, when the contents of B are poured into C, the appearance of C sways the child's judgement so that C is now judged to contain more than A ('it looks more' or 'it's taller'). Although the child has seen the liquid poured from B into C and agrees that none has been spilled or added in the process (Piaget called this *identity*), the appearance of the higher level of liquid in the taller, thinner, beaker C is compulsive.

According to Piaget, this is yet another example of *centration*; here the pre-seven-year-old is centring on just one dimension of the beaker C, usually its height, and so fails to take width into account. What the concrete operational child will be able to understand is that as C gets taller it also gets narrower and that these cancel each other out. Piaget calls this *compensation*.

If the water is poured back from C into B, the child will again say that there are equal amounts in A and B; but what it cannot do (which the concrete operational child can) is perform this *operation* mentally, in its head. The ability to perform this mental operation is called *reversibility*.

Other kinds of conservation include number, quantity or substance (discrete quantity), weight and volume. To test number conservation, two rows of counters are put in a one-to-one correspondence and then one row is pushed together, as shown in Figure 25.10. The pre-

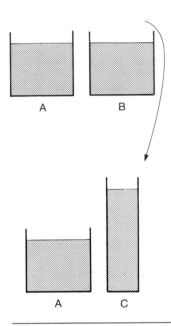

Figure 25.9 The conservation of liquid quantity

Figure 25.10 Number
conservation using counters

operational child usually thinks that there are more counters in A than in C because A is 'longer', despite being able to count correctly and agreeing that A and B have equal numbers. In conservation of quantity or substance, two equal-sized balls of plasticine are used, one of which is rolled into a long sausage and the child typically judges the sausages to have more than the ball (Fig. 25.11).

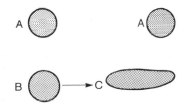

Figure 25.11 Substance
conservation using plasticine

Weight conservation is tested by putting two balls of plasticine on measuring scales and then transforming one of them as in conservation of quantity; and volume conservation involves dropping plasticine into water, and seeing how much is displaced before and after transformation.

As with Piaget's test of egocentrism, many other psychologists have been critical of his methods and, consequently, of his conclusions regarding the pre-operational child's lack of conservation.

Donaldson (1978) has argued that the experimenter may be unwittingly forcing children to produce the wrong answer against their better judgement by the mere fact that they ask the same question twice, once before and once after the transformation. 'If the experimenter pours the liquid from one beaker into another or pushes one row of counters together, they must be doing it for a reason and probably want me to give a different answer,' is how the child's reasoning might run, suggesting that, 'contextual cues might override purely linguistic ones'. How could we test these hypotheses?

One method, used by Rose and Blank (1974), was to drop the pre-transformation question and only ask the child to compare two rows of counters *after* the transformation: under these conditions six-year-olds often succeeded compared with those tested on the standard form of the task. Significantly, they made fewer errors on the standard task when re-tested a week later. Samuel and Bryant (1984), testing 252 boys and girls aged between five and eight-and-a-half years, confirmed Rose and Blank's findings for conservation of number, quantity and volume (the latter tested by different sized beakers of liquid, so, strictly, liquid quantity).

Another alternative to Piaget's method was devised by McGarrigle and Donaldson (1974). It was concerned with number and length conservation. In the case of number conservation, the procedure begins in the usual way up to the point where the child agreed that there is an equal number of counters in the two rows. Then 'Naughty Teddy' emerges from a hiding place and sweeps over one of the rows and disarranges it, so that the one-to-one correspondence is disrupted. The child is invited to put Teddy back in his box (usually accepted with glee) and the questioning resumes: 'Now, where were we? Ah, yes, is the number in this row the same as the number in that row?' and so on.

Fifty out of eighty four- to six-year-olds conserved, compared with thirteen out of eighty tested using the standard version. According to Piaget, it should not matter *who* re-arranges the counters (or *how* it happens) but it seems to be relevant to the child. The point is that the transformation caused by Naughty Teddy is meant to be seen as *accidental* (not intentionally made by the experimenter).

Light et al (1979) replicated the 'Naughty Teddy' experiment (using only conservation of length) with five-year-olds. The overall conserving rates were lower than McGarrigle and Donaldson had found in both conditions, but their findings confirmed a significantly higher success rate in the 'Naughty Teddy' condition.

However, they were at the same time critical of the basic assumption made in the original study, namely that Naughty Teddy represents an *accidental* transformation of the materials—while the children were clearly willing to play along with the experimenter in attributing responsibility (agency) to the teddy, they clearly also knew that it was the experimenter who was responsible for both introducing and manipulating it (Light, 1986):

> The extent to which the child holds separate the intentions of the tester and those of the teddy bear must remain in doubt. As any parent knows, children at this age have an unnerving tendency to 'step outside' role-playing situations of this kind just when the adult has been drawn in most deeply. (Light et al, 1979)

So Light et al (1979) created an *incidental* condition in which five- and six-year-olds were tested in pairs. In the *standard* condition they watched as two identical beakers were filled to the same level with pasta shells. When both the children had judged the quantities to be equal, the experimenter introduced a further, larger, container, and tipped into it the contents of one of the beakers. The children were then asked (in turn) to judge whether or not the amounts of shells were still the same.

In the *incidental* condition, the pairs of children were first shown grids into which the pasta shells could be inserted, one per cell, and it was explained to them that they would be playing a game in which the first child to get all his or her shells into the grid would be the winner. So when the shells were put into the two identical beakers, the children understood this to be a preparation for the competitive game. When they had judged the two beakers to contain equal amounts (ie the game was fair), as the second child was about to receive his/her beaker, the experimenter 'noticed' with some alarm that the rim was chipped, making it too dangerous to use and 'found' another container which was then filled with the shells from the chipped beaker. The usual conservation question followed. The results were that 5 per cent of the children conserved in the standard condition compared with 70 per cent in the incidental condition.

This finding has been replicated by others, including Hargreaves et al (1982), using five-year-olds and number conservation. They had an *accidental* condition (featuring a naughty monkey glove puppet and also two experimenters, one of whom controlled the monkey while the other asked the questions, etc.), thereby replicating the Naughty Teddy experiment, and an *incidental* condition, in which a second adult came into the room to 'borrow' some of the counters, taking them from the table. The experimenter protested that the counters were needed, and they were duly returned, but of course they had become disarranged. Conservation rates under this condition were close to 90 per cent.

In both the Light et al and the Hargreaves et al studies, the transformation was successfully embedded within a socially intelligible sequence of events. Children who fail on the standard version of the task certainly do seem to be able to conserve under these more meaningful conditions.

However, it is possible that in the accidental and incidental conditions the child is being (unwittingly) misled into making the *correct* judgement (ie being right for the wrong reasons) just as Donaldson believes that the child is being led to make the *incorrect* judgement in the standard condition? In Piaget's version, there may be an implicit message: 'take note of the transformation—it is relevant' (ie give a *different* answer), while in the accidental/incidental conditions, the implicit message might be: 'this transformation makes no difference—ignore it' (ie give the *same* answer; Light, 1986).

It follows that if some change *actually* takes place, the implicit message to *ignore* the transformation would make children give an *incorrect* conservation answer. The standard Piaget task involves an *irrelevant* perceptual change (nothing is being added or taken away) but where a *relevant* perceptual change occurs, children tested under the accidental or incidental condition should do *worse* than those tested in the standard way. This prediction was supported by Light and Gilmour (1983) and Moore and Fry (1986).

Other criticisms of Piaget deal with the actual words used in the conservation-task questions. For example, when the liquid is poured from beaker B to beaker C and the child is asked, 'Which contains more or are they the same?', how does the pre-operational child interpret 'more'?

Berko and Brown (1960) and Bruner et al (1966) found that some children used 'more' or 'less' when they were really referring to height and length, so in the conservation task they might be quite correct in pointing to beaker C because it is 'taller' than beaker A. As Dworetzky (1981) points out, when a child asks for 'more milk', it observes the level in the glass rise and there may be other similar examples which explains why 'more' is understood as 'tall' or 'taller', and also why children of up to six or seven regard the vertical dimension as so important when judging the overall size of something. Donaldson and Wales (1970) also observed that children have trouble with words such as 'less', 'more', 'same', 'different from', 'more than', but they claimed that the linguistic bias of the task as a whole creates difficulties for children. Another relevant study here is the Donaldson and McGarrigle (1974) study using toy cars and garages (see above).

iii) *THE CONCRETE OPERATIONAL STAGE (SEVEN TO ELEVEN YEARS)*

In this stage, children develop the mental structure called an *operation*, which is, essentially, an action, performed mentally, comprising: (i) *compensation*; (ii) *reversibility*; and (iii) *identity* (see above) and is best seen in the ability to conserve. However, they can only perform the operation in the presence of actual objects—they must be looking at or manipulating the materials (beakers of water, counters, etc.), hence the name of the stage (ie *concrete*).

Also, some types of conservation are mastered before others: the order in which they appear tends to be invariant (as in the order of the four major stages), namely: (i) *number* and *liquid quantity* (continuous quantity) at six to seven; (ii) *substance* or *quantity* and *length* at seven or eight; (iii) *weight* at eight to ten; and (iv) *volume* at eleven to twelve.

This step-by-step acquisition of new operations is called *décalage* (displacement or 'slips in level of performance'); in the case of conservation it is *horizontal* (eg a seven-year-old can conserve number but not weight), so that inconsistencies exist *within* the same kind of ability or operation. *Vertical* décalage refers to inconsistencies *between* different abilities or operations, eg a child may have mastered all kinds of classification but not all kinds of conservation.

With regard to classification, the concrete operational child can now understand the relationship between super- and sub-ordinate classes, ie the part–whole relationship. This is closely related to addition and subtraction, eg adding the parts to make the whole and then subtracting the parts (a form of reversibility).

Further examples of the child's growing ability to de-centre include: (i) sorting objects on the basis of two or more attributes; and (ii) a significant decline in egocentrism and the growing relativism of the child's viewpoint.

One remaining problem for the child is concerned with *transitivity* tasks. For example, 'If John is taller than Susan and Susan is taller than Charlie, who is taller, John or Charlie?' Not until the age of eleven or so will the child be able to solve this entirely in its head; the concrete operational child is usually limited to solving the problem using real objects (eg dolls).

iv) *THE FORMAL OPERATIONAL STAGE (ELEVEN TO FIFTEEN YEARS)*

While the concrete operational child is still concerned with manipulating *things* (even if this is done 'in the mind'), the formal operational thinker can manipulate *ideas* or propositions and can reason solely on the basis of verbal statements ('first order' and 'second order' operations, respectively). *Formal* refers to the ability to follow the *form* of an argument without reference to its particular content. In the case of transitivity problems, for example, 'If A is taller than B, and B is taller than C, then A is taller than C', is a form of argument such that the conclusion is logically true, and will always be true, regardless of what A, B or C might refer to.

Adolescents can also think *hypothetically*, ie think about situations they have not actually experienced before—or about things which *nobody* has experienced before. For example, Dworetzky (1981) notes that if you asked formal operational individuals what it would be like if people had tails, they might tell you:

(a) 'Lovers could secretly hold tails under the table.'
(b) 'People would leave lifts in a great hurry.'
(c) 'Dogs would know when you were happy.'

By contrast, a concrete operational child might tell you not to be so silly, or would tell you where on the body a tail might be, or how funny it would look, showing its dependence upon what has actually been seen.

This ability to imagine and discuss what has never been encountered before is evidence of the continued de-centration that occurs beyond concrete operations. The formal operational person can, therefore, deal with *possibilities* and not just with *actualities*, with 'what is not and what could be', with alternatives to existing (concrete) reality as well as inconsistencies and contradictions in other people's behaviour (especially that of their parents).

Similarly, adolescents can ask questions about themselves which would have been impossible earlier, such as, 'What or who can I become?'. These kinds of questions form part of the 'identity crisis' of adolescence discussed by Erikson (see Chapter 21).

Finally, adolescents can experiment and search systematically and methodically in order to find the solution to a problem. They can consider all the possible combinations of factors likely to have an effect and through careful reasoning eliminate the irrelevant ones. For example, in the beaker problem (Inhelder and Piaget, 1958), there are four beakers of colourless, odourless liquid (1, 2, 3 and 4) plus a smaller bottle (g) also containing a colourless, odourless liquid; the problem is to find the liquid, or combination of liquids, which will turn yellow when a few drops from bottle g are added to it (the actual combination is 1 plus 3 plus g). Concrete operational children often begin randomly trying various combinations of pairs of liquids, while adolescents systematically consider all the possible combinations.

However, several studies have found that even well-educated adults make all sorts of mistakes on formal reasoning problems and that only about one-third of average adolescents and adults ever attain formal operations.

According to Dasen (1977), formal reasoning does not appear at all in some cultures and even where it does occur it may not be the typical mode of thought; and Flavell (1977) concludes that, while formal operational thinking may emerge during adolescence, it cannot be regarded as the 'characteristic mode of thought for that developmental period'. How can we account for this?

Piaget (1972) suggests that all normal individuals attain formal operations, if not by the age of fifteen then by twenty, but they do so in different areas according to their aptitudes and areas of experience and expertise. Piaget seems to be saying that the specific knowledge and training people have are as important to their cognitive performance as is their general level of cognitive development, which seems to be a rather different position from the one he adopts regarding the first three stages.

PIAGET ON PLAY

Piaget (1951) saw play as an *adaptive* activity, which begins early in the sensorimotor period when infants start to repeat actions which they find satisfying or pleasurable. He called these reptitions of actions 'circular reactions' and distinguished three major kinds corresponding to three sub-stages of the sensorimotor period: (i) *primary circular reactions* (one to four months) which are centred on the baby's own body; (ii) *secondary circular reactions* (four to eight months) which are centred on external objects; and (iii) *tertiary circular reactions* (twelve to eighteen months) where the child experiments in order to find new ways to solve problems or to reproduce interesting outcomes.

As an adaptive activity, play involves both assimilation and accommodation. However, assimilation is often the more important and evident of the two processes and a great deal of play (especially up to the end of the pre-operational period) is 'pure assimilation', whereby the child attempts to fit the world of reality into its own needs and experience. (By contrast, imitation is an action of almost 'pure' accommodation.) Following on from this, Piaget made a distinction between play, on the one hand, and 'strictly intellectual activity' on the other. In the latter, there is 'adaptation of the schemas to an external reality which constitutes a problem', ie there is an external aim or purpose. But in play, the child, 'repeats his behaviour not in any further effort to learn or investigate but for the mere joy of mastering it and of showing off to himself his own power of subduing reality' (Piaget, 1951), ie it is done for its own sake. So play allows children to practise their competencies in a relaxed and carefree way.

This distinction between play and intellectual activity applies to all three major kinds of play, although it is arguably more difficult to make in the case of *mastery play* than it is in *symbolic* or *make-believe* and *play with rules*. But throughout development, play serves to consolidate recently acquired abilities and also aids the development of additional cognitive and social skills.

These three major kinds of play correspond to the major stages of cognitive development:

(i)   sensorimotor stage (0 to 2 years):   Mastery (or practice play)
(ii) pre-operational stage (2 to 7 years): Symbolic (or make-believe play)
(iii) concrete operational stage (7 to 11 years) ⎫
      formal operational stage (11 to 15 years) ⎬ Play with rules

Mastery (or Practice) Play

Essentially this involves repeating new motor schemas in one new context after another and, in a sense, this theme of 'play as mastery' runs through the other kinds of play too: whenever a new skill has been acquired, it tends to be used at almost every opportunity, for the sheer pleasure of doing so, and represents 'pure assimilation'. So play involves the repetition of a schema that has already been mastered, while investigation or exploration involve accommodation to reality and constitute ways in which new schemas develop.

Symbolic (or Make-Believe) Play

This type of play involves the child transforming itself or some object into somebody or something else. It begins between one-and-a-half and two years and is usually at its height up until about the age of five.

An important feature of make-believe play is role-taking (or role play) which may serve an important function in helping the child to cope with emotional crises and reducing interpersonal conflicts, eg having rules which it does not fully understand imposed by parents. Piaget and Inhelder (1969) observe that a child may discipline its doll or teddy as the child itself had been disciplined (so *inverting* or reversing roles) or it might re-enact a scene and produce a happy ending. So through make-believe play the child can change the world, internally, into what it wants it to be. (Compare this with Freud's theory of play; see Chapter 21.)

Many psychologists (Garvey, 1977) have pointed out the vital role of language in the development of symbolic play. This is shown when children speak to their doll in the way their parents talk to them and (usually from four onwards) when 'collective symbolism' appears, eg children playing together and all assuming complementary roles (eg cowboys and indians). (See Mead's theory of self, Chapter 21.)

Play with Rules

As the child's thinking becomes more logical, so its games begin to incorporate and be governed by rules. But the child's understanding of rules itself goes through certain developmental changes (see Chapter 27 on moral development).

EVALUATION OF PIAGET'S THEORY

1) Is Piaget's theory really a *stage* theory at all? And how useful is the concept of a stage?

We saw earlier that from 1970 Piaget proposed that development should be thought of as a spiral (implying a continuous process) rather than as a step-by-step, discontinuous process (as implied by a stage theory proper). Indeed, the individual may 'straddle' more than one stage at any one time (*décalage*), which means that cognitive structures do not have to change all at the same time (and to the same extent), which again is implied by a stage theory. Clearly, intellectual development may not be as 'stage-like' as Piaget at first thought.

There is no doubt that the concept of 'stage' implies a degree of consistency of thought and understanding across a range of different content areas. However, some inconsistency is to be expected, particularly while concrete, or formal operations are in the process of developing (ie during 'transitional' periods). For example, some new ability usually appears first in the content areas most familiar to the child, and only later in more unfamiliar, abstract areas. But the question then arises: how *much* consistency is needed to warrant categorizing a child as, say, 'pre-operational' or 'concrete operational'?

According to Meadows (1988), the research tends to show *less* consistency between different aspects of concrete operations than Piaget's theory would predict and, although he did acknowledge the existence of décalages, he was more interested in how children manage the general principle underlying operational thought. Even though Flavell (1971), for example, argues that it is not necessary in a stage theory to predict abrupt, all-or-nothing, changes, Sternberg (1990) wonders whether it might be better to abandon (at least temporarily) the idea of stages and to focus instead on the development of individual processes and strategies. He believes that we cannot just *assume* that there is only one strategy for solving a particular problem (as Piaget does, eg children give correct answers in conservation tasks because they have mastered reversibility and compensation); what is needed is an analysis of the *information-processing* requirements of the task (ie exactly what cognitive processes are involved/needed to succeed).

These have been ignored by Piaget, as have differences in ability between children within a common stage and Sternberg believes that this reduces the value of Piaget's theory in explaining and predicting many aspects of performance. Piaget acknowledged that the *rate of progress* through the stages does vary to some extent between individuals (due to differences in environmental stimulation) but Meadows (1988) says that he was concerned with the idealized 'normal' epistemic subject rather than with individual differences (ie with common structures of knowledge). He ignored factors known to affect performance such as impulsiveness, conscientiousness, persistence and creativity. In all these ways he has been criticized for not offering an *explanation* but an *elaborate description* of cognitive development.

2)   A different way of evaluating the stage concept is to look at attempts to train children; ie *can the rate of development be deliberately speeded up?* According to Piaget this should not be possible—the child's current level of cognitive functioning will set limits on learning, since:

> . . . The child cannot assimilate or accommodate to events which are too incompatible with his or her whole coherent system of understanding, and instructions can at best produce only a limited and possibly temporary advance isolated in the area being trained. (Meadows, 1988)

However:

> . . . contrary to the predictions of the Piagetian account, training does produce improvement in performance which can be considerable, long-lasting and pervasive. A variety of training methods have been seen to succeed . . . (Meadows, 1988)

For example, pre-schoolers have successfully been trained on concrete operational tasks (the focus of most such attempts), three or four years ahead of 'schedule' and their performance following training seems to be as competent as that of untrained eight-year-olds (Brainerd, 1983). Any speeding-up of development which might occur would, according to Piagetians, have to involve the use of learning experiences which resemble those which occur outside the experimental training situation, namely *active self-discovery*. This is contrasted with the traditional methods of teaching whereby the teacher imparts information ('ready-made knowledge') to a passively receptive child (*'tutorial' training*). However, the successful attempts at training which Meadows and Brainerd refer to have all used some kind of 'tutorial' methods. Since the early 1970s studies have shown that, '. . . although self-discovery training can produce learning, it is generally *less* effective than tutorial training' (Brainerd, 1983).

3)   How has Piaget contributed to educational theory and practice?

Brainerd (1983) believes that there are three main implications of Piaget's theory for education, which should be seen not as explicit recommendations but more like how others have interpreted Piaget's relevance for education (particularly preschool and primary). Piaget himself had no 'theory of instruction' (Ginsberg, 1981). These are: (i) the concept of *readiness*; (ii) curriculum (*what* to teach); and (iii) teaching methods (*how* to teach).

As far as (i) is concerned, much of what we said above about limits set on learning by the child's current stage of development relates to the concept of readiness. The apparent success of attempts to train concepts suggests that this is not a particularly helpful or valid concept.

Regarding (ii), appropriate concepts to teach will be logic (eg transitive inference), maths (eg numbers), science (eg conservation) and space (eg Euclidean geometry). Whatever the particular concepts, teaching materials should comprise *concrete objects* of some sort that can be easily *manipulated*.

However:

> ... an attempt to base education on the teaching of Piagetian stages is an unfortunate misapplication of the theory. A more useful approach is the modification of the curriculum in line with knowledge of the Piagetian stages, without, however, placing undue emphasis on them and without allowing them to circumscribe one's approach ... (Ginsberg, 1981)

Yet Piaget's theory seems to suggest that certain concepts should be tackled in a definite sequence. For example, conservation of substance naturally precedes conservation of weight, which naturally precedes conservation of volume, but traditional schools often do not base their teaching on such sequences in development (Elkind, 1976).

(iii) As we saw earlier, central to Piaget's vew of the educational process is *active self-discovery* (or discovery-learning) whereby the child is at the centre of his/her learning—and not the teacher:

> ... From the Piagetian standpoint, children learn from actions rather than from passive observations ... The teacher must recognise that each child needs to construct knowledge for himself; active learning results in deeper understanding. (Smith and Cowie, 1988)

So what is the teacher's role in the Piagetian classroom?

(a) It is essential for the teacher to assess very carefully each individual child's current stage of cognitive development. (This relates to the concept of readiness). The child can then be set tasks which are tailored to his/her needs and so are intrinsically motivating.

(b) The teacher must provide the child with learning opportunities which enable the child to advance to the next developmental step. This is done by creating disequilibrium, whereby the child's current schemas are not quite sufficient to deal with the reality he or she is confronted with, leading to accommodation and equilibrium.

This means that the teacher does not just provide the appropriate materials and equipment and let the child 'Get on with it':

> ... Instead, the teacher is expected to achieve a proper balance between actively guiding and directing children's thinking patterns and providing opportunities for children to explore by themselves. (Thomas, 1985)

(c) The teacher is concerned with the *process* rather than the end-product of learning. This entails encouraging the child to ask questions, experiment, explore and so on, looking for the reasoning behind the child's answers, particularly the child's *mistakes*.

(d) The teacher's role is also to encourage children to learn from each other, to hear other (often conflicting) views, which can help break down egocentrism. Peer interaction can have *cognitive*, as well as *social* value, so small-group activity is as important as individual work.

(e) Finally:

> ... The teacher is the guide in the child's process of discovery, and the curriculum is adapted to each child's individual needs and intellectual level ... (Smith and Cowie, 1988)

In evaluating the Piagetian contribution to education, Ginsberg (1981) believes that the two great deficiencies are: (i) the ignoring of individual differences (referred to earlier); and (ii) the emphasis on discovery learning to the exclusion of *academic* or *school* knowledge. For example, to what extent can concrete operations *explain in detail* the child's performance in algebra or in reading?

> If education is in good measure concerned with acculturation—the transmission of the accumulated wisdom of a culture—then Piaget's theory is limited in its explanatory power with respect to academic knowledge. At the very least ... it is not clear that there is a strong relation between the Piagetian structures and the kinds of thought processes involved in school learning ... (Ginsberg, 1981)

4) Is there any evidence that the *sequence* of stages is as Piaget has described it?

There is a great deal of *cross-cultural* evidence to support Piaget's claim that the stages are invariant and universal, at least up to and including the concrete operational stage. For instance, Cowan (1978) and Flavell (1977) both conclude that the order of stages originally observed in Piaget's Swiss sample also describes the course and content for children in hundreds of countries, cultures and sub-cultures.

Conservation tasks have been the most commonly used cross-culturally. For example, Nyiti (1976) tested the Meru of Tanzania, Kamara and Easley (1977) the Themne of Sierra Leone, Kiminyo (1977) the Kamba of Kenya and Nyiti again (1982) compared English-speaking Canadians and the Micmac Canadian Indians. These groups (seven- to twelve-year-olds) were all tested on conservation of substance, weight and volume and the average ages at which these were correctly solved were highly comparable with those for the USA, Canada and Europe. Significantly, there was some tendency for eleven- to twelve-year-olds who had never attended school to have more difficulty in volume conservation than their peers who had attended school, but this would be consistent with Piaget's theory.

Fishbein (1984) concludes that the cross-cultural studies seem to indicate that Piaget has identified important, and perhaps universal, aspects of cognitive development.

5) One final point to do with stages is the question of whether there are any stages of cognitive development beyond formal operations. This was discussed in Chapter 24.

6) How scientific are Piaget's methods?

We have already seen how many of his basic ways of testing children's abilities (eg classification, egocentrism, conservation) have been criticized and seem to have resulted in the under-estimation of what children can do at particular ages.

But his general *clinical method* has been criticized on other grounds. Basically, it comprises a question-and-answer technique: the child is presented with a problem of some sort and then invited to respond; once the child answers, the investigator will ask a second question or introduce a variation of the original problem in order to clarify the child's reasoning. All children are asked the same questions to begin with, but how each child responds to these initial probes determines what the investigator does next. The essential problem with this approach is that if the questions and tasks are tailored to individual subjects, how can we compare the answers of different children to identify general trends? How reliable are the data when the procedures are basically un-standardized (ie different for different subjects)?

Additional criticisms are that Piaget often did not give details regarding the numbers and ages of his subjects and usually did not present any kind of statistical analysis.

Although aware of some of these shortcomings, Piaget did stress the need for a flexible methodology, ie one which enables the investigator to probe the child's thinking without distorting it by imposing their own views on the child:

> ... Piaget's clinical method is deliberately unstandardized since that is a superior way to explore the subtleties of the child's cognitive structure ... Tapping the child's competence requires subtle and sensitive procedures, tailored to the peculiarities of each individual child ... (Ginsberg, 1981)

7) Some critics claim that Piaget over-emphasized cognitive aspects of development to the exclusion of the emotional (and others would say the reverse is true for Freud). But he was familiar with Freud's work and thought it provided valuable clues as to the *content* of children's thinking if not about *how* they think, which was Piaget's prime concern.

However, in 1972, Piaget expressed his belief that:

> There will be a time when the psychology of the cognitive functions and psychoanalysis will have to blend into a general theory which will improve both by correcting each. (Piaget, 1972)

Elkind (1971) has drawn an interesting parallel between Piaget and Freud by remarking how they both stressed the qualitative differences between children and adults. Elkind says that, relative to adults, the child is a 'cognitive alien' (Piaget) and an 'emotional alien' (Freud).

8) There is no doubt that Piaget's theory has stimulated more research than any other single theory of child development, including a great deal which suggests that he under-estimated the abilities of young children:

> ... It seems likely that, as far as the school years are concerned, the difference between younger and older children will turn out to be that the former can do what the latter can; but only sometimes, only under favourable conditions, only with help, only without distractions, only up to a point, without so much efficiency ... self control ... awareness of the implications ... certainty ... It seems likely also, that ... our emergent theory of cognitive development will be proud to have Piaget's theory as an ancestor. Given the scope of his work, it will be several generations of thinking yet before 'new' ideas about cognitive development cannot be greeted by Piagetians with a true claim that 'Piaget said that'. (Meadows, 1988)

Despite all the criticisms:

> . it is certainly true that, whether we agree with the theory or not, Piaget has changed the way we think about children's thinking ... (Sternberg, 1990)

9) Another way of evaluating Piaget's theory is to compare it with other developmental theories and that is what we shall do in the rest of this chapter, by discussing the views of Bruner and Vygotsky.

BRUNER'S DEVELOPMENTAL THEORY

Bruner has been greatly influenced by Piaget and they share certain basic beliefs, in particular:

(a) Children are born with a biological organization that helps them to understand their world, and their underlying cognitive structure matures over time, so that they can think about and organize their world in an increasingly complex way.

(b) Children are actively curious and explorative and capable of adapting to their environment through interaction with it.

Bruner's (1966) theory, however, is *not* about stages of development as such but rather about three ways or *modes* of representing the world, ie forms that our knowledge and understanding can take, and so he is not concerned exclusively with cognitive growth but also with knowledge in general. The three modes are the *enactive*, *iconic* and *symbolic*, and they develop in this order in the child.

i) *ENACTIVE*

At first, babies represent the world through actions; any knowledge they have is based upon what they have experienced through their own behaviour (this corresponds to Piaget's sensorimotor stage). Past events are represented through appropriate motor responses; many of our motor schemas, eg 'bicycle riding, tying knots, aspects of driving, get represented in our muscles, so to speak,' and even when we have the use of language it is often extremely difficult to describe in words *how* we do certain things. Through repeated encounters with the regularities of the environment (ie the same events and conditions repeating themselves) we build up these virtually automatic, abbreviated, patterns of motor activity which we 'run off' as units in the appropriate situation.

Like Piaget, Bruner sees the onset of object permanence as a great leap, a qualitative change in the young child's cognitive development.

ii) *ICONIC*

An icon is an image, so this form of representation involves building up a mental image of things we have experienced. Such images are normally composite, ie made up of a number of past encounters with similar objects or situations. This mode, therefore, corresponds to the last six months of the sensorimotor stage (where schemas become interiorized) and the whole of the pre-operational stage, where the child is at the mercy of what it perceives in drawing intuitive conclusions about the nature of reality. For example, in the conservation of liquid quantity test, it is the image of the higher level in the taller, thinner, beaker which, according to Piaget, dictates the child's answer.

iii) *SYMBOLIC*

Bruner's main interest was in the transition from the iconic to the symbolic modes. He and Piaget agree that a very important cognitive change occurs at around six or seven years. While Piaget describes it as the start of logical operations (albeit tied to concrete reality), Bruner sees it as the appearance of the symbolic mode, with language coming into its own as an influence on thought (see Chapter 13).

The transition from iconic to symbolic modes was demonstrated by Bruner and Kenney (1966). They arranged nine plastic glasses on a 3×3 matrix, as shown in Figure 25.12.

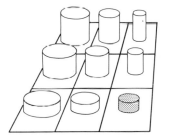 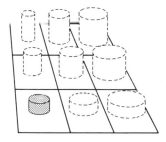

Figure 25.12 The two arrangements of glasses used by Bruner and Kenney (1966)

Three- to seven-year-olds were familiarized with the matrix. The glasses were then scrambled and the children were asked to put them back the way they had been before; this was the *reproduction task*.

In the *transposition task*, the glasses were removed from the matrix and the glass which had been in the bottom right hand square was placed in the bottom left-hand square; the child had to rebuild the matrix in this transposed manner.

Children generally could reproduce it earlier than they could transpose it: the reproduction task involved the iconic mode (60 per cent of the five-year-olds could do this, 72 per cent of the six-year-olds and 80 per cent of the seven-year-olds); while the transposition task involved the symbolic mode (the results were nil, 27 and 79 per cent, respectively). Clearly, the five-year-olds were dominated by the visual image of the original matrix, while the six- and seven-year-olds translated their visual information into the symbolic mode. They relied upon verbal rules to guide them, such as, 'it gets fatter going one way and taller going the other'. So a child using images but not symbols can reproduce but not restructure.

However, the major difference between Bruner and Piaget is to do with the role that language plays in cognitive development.

LANGUAGE AND COGNITIVE DEVELOPMENT

We discussed the views of both Bruner and Piaget on the role of language in Chapter 13.

Bruner believes that the leap from the iconic to the symbolic mode is due to the development of language; Piaget, on the other hand, believes that the development of logical thought is due to the acquisition of operations—language is not the cause of cognitive development but a tool to be used in the course of operational thinking. So for Bruner, language and logical thinking are inseparable; without language, human thought would be limited to what could be learned through actions or images. For Piaget, language merely reflects and builds on cognitive structures which have already developed through interaction with the environment. It follows that Bruner believes that cognitive development can be significantly speeded up by training children in the use of symbols; as far as Piaget is concerned, it would make no difference.

Does the available evidence help us to choose between these two conflicting views? Two experiments which seem to support Bruner are those conducted by Sonstroem (1966) and Bruner et al (1966).

Sonstroem (1966) tested six- and seven-year-olds for conservation of substance; those who failed were divided into four groups:

(a) Group A reshaped the plasticine ball themselves and had to describe the new shape—they *manipulated* and *labelled*, using their *enactive*, *iconic* and *symbolic* modes.

(b) Group B saw the experimenter reshape the ball and were asked to describe the new shape—they *labelled* without manipulating, using their *iconic* and *symbolic* modes.

(c) Group C *manipulated* but did not label—using their *enactive* and *iconic* modes.

(d) Group D neither manipulated nor labelled—using only their *iconic* mode.

They were then re-tested. Group A showed a significant improvement while none of the other three groups did. Why?

Inability to conserve is a characteristic of children using the iconic mode—they are dominated by the appearance of the plasticine, but if they are encouraged to use their language skills (symbolic mode), especially in combination with the enactive, the appearance of the plasticine ceases to dominate and they can give a correct conservation response.

In a study of conservation of liquid quantity, Bruner et al (1966) gave four- to seven-year-olds the orthodox Piagetian task (pre-test): almost all the four- and five-year-olds said that there was more liquid in the taller, thinner, beaker, as did about half the six- and seven-year-olds.

The children were then shown two standard beakers and a third, wider, beaker and all three were *screened*, so that when the contents of one of the standard beakers was poured into the wider one, the children could not see the level of the liquid but only the tops of the beakers. They were asked which had the most liquid with the screen still covering the liquid level and almost all the five- to seven-year-olds answered correctly, as did about half the four-year-olds. When the screen was removed, all the four-year-olds reverted to their pre-screening answer but all the others stuck to the answer given while the screen was in place.

Finally, in the post-test situation, two standard beakers and a taller, thinner, one were used in the orthodox Piagetian way (without a screen): the four-year-olds were unaffected by having seen the beakers screened but the five-year-olds' success rate rose from 20 per cent (pre-test) to 70 per cent (post-test) and for the six- and seven-year-olds the figures were 50 (pre-test) and 90 (post-test). What do these results mean?

Activating their speech (symbolic mode) by having them 'say' their judgement when the screen was covering the liquid levels prevented the children of five and over—who normally fail to conserve on the standard Piagetian task—being dominated by the iconic mode. However, the four-year-olds were, clearly, not ready to benefit from this symbolic training and, to this extent, Piaget's view that the mental structures must have already developed before training can help seems to have been supported. Yet the five-year-olds did benefit, contrary to what Piaget would have predicted, and so this finding also seems to support Bruner.

Indirect support for Piaget comes from studies of the deaf, who are as capable of operational thinking as the hearing although its appearance is often greatly delayed. Furth (1966) conducted several studies of the development of thinking in the deaf using Piaget-type tasks and concluded that language does not appear to be necessary.

In contrast, according to Hatwell (1966), the blind, who are in full possession of normal language but are impaired in their sensorimotor experiences, are severely delayed in their operational thought development. Piaget takes this as a particularly convincing demonstration that language is not the source of operational thought.

However, studies of the deaf seem to have under-played the delay of operational thought and Cromer (1973) believes that the blind may not, after all, be delayed. Thus the evidence here is mixed.

So what about the more directly relevant question of the effectiveness of language training?

Two studies by Sinclair-de-Zwart seem to support Piaget. In 1967, children were taught the verbal expressions used by other children who had been able to describe how two pencils, two balls of clay and two rows of beads differed. The training sessions, which exposed the children to comparative terms such as 'long', 'thin', 'short', 'fat', 'more' and 'less', proved largely unsuccessful. Although children appeared to understand the language instructions and how to use the words, it was concluded that their level of cognitive maturity prevented them from solving the Piagetian tasks. In a 1969 study, it was shown that children who displayed conservation of volume understood the meaning of words like 'bigger', 'more', 'as much as' and 'same', whereas those who lacked conservation showed no improvement in their ability to use these words correctly after language training. What the latter needed was a grasp of the *concept* of conservation and until this developed the words would remain relatively meaningless, however well they were taught.

Interestingly, Piaget himself and other Piagetian researchers (Inhelder and Karmiloff-Smith, 1978) believe that linguistic interaction with other young children may help the child to advance intellectually, even though verbal training does not. They consider that children's attempts to convince their peers of their own points of view, and the ensuing disputes and conflicts generated by being made aware of contradictions, are all necessary steps in cognitive growth (see the section on Piaget and education, p. 758).

What about formal operational thought?

Furth and Younis (1971) believe that language has a 'direct facilitating effect' on formal operational thought, 'precisely because of the close relationship between formal operations and symbolic functioning'. Piaget himself seems to take the view that, while language might be necessary for formal operations, it is not sufficient. Indeed, the language of the formal operational individual does not seem to differ significantly from what it was at some earlier stage.

In conclusion, Piaget believes that:

> . . . language and thought are links in a genetic circle . . . in the last analysis, both depend on intelligence itself, which antedates language and is independent of it.

Vygotsky's Developmental Theory

Vygotsky (1896–1934) (Fig. 25.13) is, '... arguably the greatest Russian psychologist of all time and one of the greatest psychologists of any country ...' (Sternberg, 1990). Born in the same year as Piaget, he died of tuberculosis at the age of 38, but not before he had made a considerable and lasting contribution to psychology.

We discussed his views on the relationship between language and thought in Chapter 13. Remember that one of the major differences between his ideas and those of Piaget was to do with the origins of language—for Vygotsky, all speech is *social* in nature, ie it is about communication and human interaction. This theme runs right through his developmental theory.

Our ability to think and reason by ourselves and for ourselves (inner speech or verbal thought) is the result of a fundamentally *social* process. We *start out* as social beings, capable of interacting with others but able to do little by or for ourselves (either practically or intellectually) and gradually move towards self-sufficiency and independence. This process of internalization is the reverse of how Piaget (originally) saw things—for Vygotsky, intelligence does not begin 'inside the head' but in human relationships. *Internalization* is the internal reconstruction of an external operation: we observe those around us acting in certain ways and we internalize their actions so that they become a part of ourselves. For example, learning how to speak, ride a bike, read a book and raising our children (by observing how our parents raised us).

A specific example he gives (1978) is that of *pointing*. Initially, pointing is nothing more than an unsuccessful attempt to grasp something beyond the baby's reach. When the mother sees the child trying to grasp it, she comes to its aid and is likely to point to the object. The baby learns to do the same. It is the social mediation, *not* the object itself, which provides the basis for the child's learning to point.

The transformation of an *inter*personal process into an *intra*personal one, the internalization of socially based and historically developed activities, represents the essential difference between human and animal intelligence.

Another feature of Vygotsky's theory which makes it distinctive is his belief in the convergence of speech and practical activity. Instead of seeing the origin and development of speech as independent of how the child organizes its practical activities ('sign use' as opposed to 'tool use'), Vygotsky claims that:

> ... the most significant moment in the course of intellectual development, which gives birth to the purely human forms of practical and abstract intelligence, occurs when speech and practical activity, two previously completely independent lines of development, converge. (Vygotsky, 1962)

This is closely related to the idea that pre-linguistic thought (practical activity) and pre-intellectual language come together at about two years of age to produce verbal thought (see Chapter 13). Children's intelligence is rather similar to that of animals' (especially apes') right up to the point where the convergence of speech and practical activity occurs. This produces a qualitative leap. Speech is as important as acting in attaining goals (problem-solving) and, in general, the more complex the solution required, the more important speech will be.

Figure 25.13 *L. S. Vygotsky (1896–1934). (From Vygotsky, L. S. (1978)* Mind in Society *(ed. M. Cole et al). Cambridge, Massachusetts: Harvard University Press)*

Linking the two ideas of internalization and convergence is Vygotsky's famous concept of the *Zone of Proximal* (or *potential*) *Development*. Since children move from being able to do things with others to being able to do them by themselves, the development of this ability is seen in terms of what the child could do when given help:

> It is the distance between the actual developmental level as determined by independent problem solving and the level of potential development as determined through problem solving under adult guidance or in collaboration with more capable peers. (Vygotsky, 1978)

We need to be *prospective* (what *could* the child *do*) as well as retrospective (what *has* the child *done*) in our understanding and assessment of intelligence:

> The zone of proximal development defines those functions that have not yet matured but are in the process of maturation, functions that will mature tomorrow but are currently in an embryonic state. These functions could be termed the 'buds' or 'flowers' of development rather than the 'fruits' of development. The actual developmental level characterizes mental development retrospectively, while the zone of proximal development characterizes mental development prospectively. (Vygotsky, 1978)

Consider the investigation of two ten-year-olds, both with a mental age of eight—can we necessarily be sure that they will subsequently develop and succeed academically to the same degree? Of course not, because there are non-intellectual factors which influence school achievement. But what if we assume these are comparable for the two children—could we now make comparable predictions about each child? The predictive validity of IQ tests is based on this very assumption (see Chapter 28) but Vygotsky believes it is a mistaken view.

Suppose a teacher-examiner provides guided assistance to each child in order to help them solve a given problem. With this help Child A can deal with the problem up to a twelve-year-old level but Child B can only go up to a nine-year-old level. Would we still want to say that they are mentally the same? No, because Child A's *zone of proximal development* is the difference between a mental age of twelve and eight and child B's is the difference between nine and eight:

> ... what is the zone of proximal development today will be the actual developmental level tomorrow—that is, what a child can do with assistance today she will be able to do by herself tomorrow. (Vygotsky, 1978)

So much of our everyday lives, so many of our interactions with other people, so much of our learning, goes on through the medium of language (spoken and written), that it is almost impossible to discuss any aspect of human behaviour or thinking without taking the role of language into account when studying psychology.

As our brains seem especially designed to enable us to use speech, it is perhaps not surprising that language should play such a central part in our lives. Many psychologists and philosophers have claimed that it is language which makes us unique as a species—that it is almost what makes us human.

There are a number of separate but interrelated questions that we need to ask, some of which will be given more emphasis than others in this chapter:

(a) What is language? How can it be defined and what are its major components?
(b) How does language develop and what is the course of language development in the child? Here, we shall be looking mainly at the *stages* of development that have been identified in an attempt to describe it.
(c) Why does language develop in the way it does? Here, we shall be looking at the major *theories* of language acquisition.
(d) What can be learnt about the uniqueness of language ability to human beings by attempts to teach language to non-humans, particularly chimpanzees?

WHAT IS LANGUAGE?

In order to understand language development and to discuss whether language is unique to human beings, we must first ask what language *is*, what precisely it is which develops in the child and which only appears spontaneously in our species.

Until fairly recently, the study of language was undertaken largely by *linguists*, who are concerned primarily with the *structure* of language— the sounds that compose it, how these relate to words and sentences, and the rules which govern the relationships between all of these.

But in the last twenty years or so, psychologists have become interested in language not so much for its own sake, but for how it is acquired, whether it is a human species-specific behaviour, how it affects learning, memory, thinking in general, and so on. The 'marriage' of psychology and linguistics is called *psycholinguistics*, which can be defined as the study of how language is acquired, perceived, understood and produced.

Roger Brown, an eminent American psycholinguist, defines language as an arbitrary system of symbols:

> ... which taken together make it possible for a creature with limited powers of discrimination and a limited memory to transmit and understand an infinite variety of messages and to do this in spite of noise and distraction. (Brown, 1965)

It is, perhaps, this 'infinite variety of messages' that makes human language unique; other species may be able to communicate with each other but it is a very limited system. Attempts to teach chimpanzees language (which we shall be considering later, see p. 789) have, until recently, involved deliberate training: contrast this with children's spontaneous and quite easy mastery of human language within about five years after birth.

In another definition of language, Brown (1973) points out that people do not simply acquire a repertoire of sentences but, 'acquire a rule system that makes it possible to generate a literally infinite variety of sentences, most of them never heard from anyone else'. This rule system is what psycholinguists call *grammar*, but grammar is much more than the parts of speech that we learn about in English at school. It is concerned with the description of language, the rules which determine how a language works, and it comprises *phonology*, *semantics* and *syntax* (see Fig. 26.1).

PHONOLOGY

Phonology refers to the *sound system* of a language—what counts as a sound, what is an acceptable sequence of sounds. Humans are capable of producing many different speech sounds (called *phones* or phonetic segments). By convention, phones are denoted by enclosing symbols inside square brackets, for example [p] is the initial phone in the word 'pin'. The linguistic analysis of a language typically begins with a description of the phones used in that language.

Different languages consist of different numbers and combinations of these basic sounds. English, for example, uses approximately forty distinguishable sounds, some languages use as few as fifteen and others as many as eighty-five. When we say that someone speaks English with a foreign accent, we are really saying that they have not yet mastered all the phones of English. Similarly, when we recognize a foreign language as, say, French, without being able to speak it or even understand it ourselves, we are recognizing the phones as those which 'define' French

Although all phones are different, only some of the differences matter, namely those which affect the meaning of what is being said. For example, the [p] phone can be articulated (pronounced) slightly differently each time it is uttered without changing the perception of 'pin'. But the difference between [p] and [d] does matter because that difference alone can lead to two words with different meanings (eg 'pin' and 'din', 'pot' and 'dot'). So [p] and [d] cannot be interchanged without changing the meaning of the words, so that they belong to different *functional* classes of phones.

The classes of phones which are functionally important in a language are called *phonemes* (phonological segments). So [p] and [d] belong to the different phonemes /p/ and /d/. Just as different languages differ with

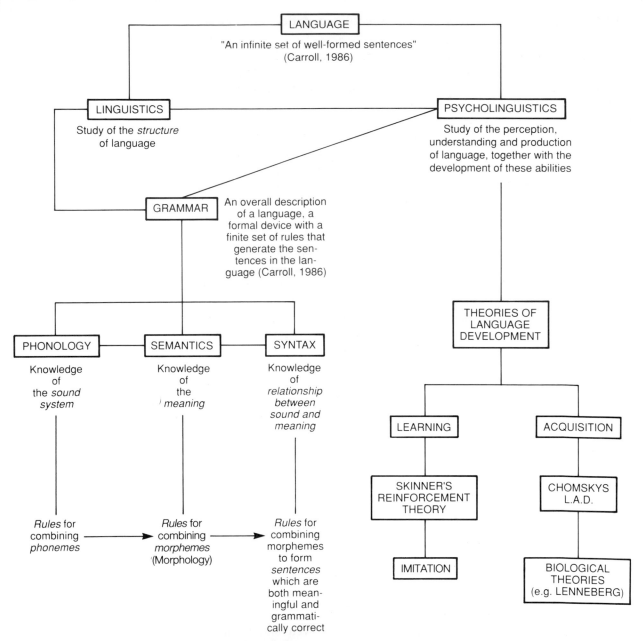

Figure 26.1 The major components of grammar and the relationship between linguistics and psycholinguistics

respect to phones, so they differ in terms of their phonemes, eg [l] and [r] belong to different phonemes in English but not in Japanese.

Phonological rules also constrain the permitted sequences of phonemes, eg 'port' is an *actual* sequence, 'plort' is a *possible* sequence, but 'pbort' is an illegal (ungrammatical) sequence in English.

These examples show that phonemes are devoid of meaning—they are just sounds. They correspond roughly to the vowels and consonants of the alphabet but, as there are only twenty-six of these in English, the same vowel, for example, can represent more than one phoneme (eg the 'o' in '*hop*' is pronounced very differently from the 'o' in '*hope*' and so constitutes a different phoneme). However, although meaningless in themselves, phonemes are, as we have seen, important for meaning, which brings us onto semantics.

SEMANTICS

Semantics is the study of the *meaning* of language and can be analysed at the level of *morphemes* and at the level of *sentences* (which is where *syntax* comes in). *Morphology* refers to the rules for combining phonemes into *morphemes* which are the *basic units of meaning* in a language and consist mainly of words. Other morphemes are prefixes (letters attached to the beginning of a word, such as 'de' or 're') and suffixes (letters attached to the end of a word, such as 's' to make a plural—adding 's' to 'dog' clearly changes the meaning, since we now know there is more than one animal). Some morphemes are 'bound' (like the plural 's'), ie they only take on meaning when attached to other morphemes. But most morphemes are 'free', ie they have meaning when they stand alone, as most words have. However, single words have only a limited meaning and we usually combine them into longer strings of phrases and sentences.

SYNTAX

Syntax refers to the rules for combining words into phrases and sentences (and is often taken to be the same as grammar but, as we have seen, syntax is only one part of grammar). For example, in the sentence 'the dog chased the ____' we know that only a noun can complete it; this is an example of a *syntactic* rule.

Another important syntactic rule is *word order*, which has great significance for understanding language development and for evaluating studies which claim that chimps and other non-human primates can be taught language. Clearly, 'John loves Mary' has a very different meaning from 'Mary loves John'. Again 'the academic lecture attracted a limited audience' and 'the academic liquid became an odourless audience' are both equally correct (grammatically) but it is difficult to know what the second one means. 'Liquid the an became audience odourless academic' breaks all the rules of syntax *and* is also incomprehensible.

These examples show that syntax and semantics are very closely interrelated—but they are distinct.

We should also note that sentences have sounds *and* meanings and syntax refers to the *structure* which relates the two.

LINGUISTICS AND PSYCHOLOGY— PSYCHOLINGUISTICS

As shown in Figure 26.1, while both linguists and psycholinguists are interested in the structure of language and the rules which govern that structure (ie grammar), the focus of interest is very different—linguists are interested largely in *language itself* (almost disembodied from the human beings who use it), while psycholinguists attempt to understand language *as it is used by people* (the *language-user* rather than the language itself).

Why psychologists are interested in the grammars proposed by linguists is because:

> Grammars represent the tacit knowledge that native speakers have about their language, which includes knowing how to form grammatically acceptable sentences, knowing what they mean and knowing how to pronounce them ... (Carroll, 1986)

What psycholinguists want to know is: do grammatical rules have any 'psychological reality', ie do people actually use the linguist's rules when producing and understanding everyday language? (Plunkett, 1981). An adequate psychological model of language will need to represent the language user's knowledge of the language and to specify the process by which this knowledge is translated into actual performance (Carroll, 1986). Also, it must be consistent with what is known about cognitive processes in general—although language is a very special skill, it is only *one* of the ways in which we get things done in the world (Plunkett, 1981). Not quite so important is the requirement that any model should be compatible with what we know about the neurophysiology of the brain.

As far as this present chapter is concerned, the most important criterion is that any adequate psychological model of language must be able to account for how children acquire complex linguistic skills.

A linguist whose model of language promised to meet these criteria is Noam Chomsky, who has undoubtedly had the greatest impact on psychology in recent times. His *Syntactic Structure* (1957) caused a revolution in thinking about language. In that book he outlined his theory of *transformational grammar* (TG), at the heart of which is a set of rules called *phrase structure rules*. When applied systematically, these rules generate sentences in English or any other language. Some examples are given in Figure 26.2.

Figure 26.2 Examples of Chomsky's phase structure rules

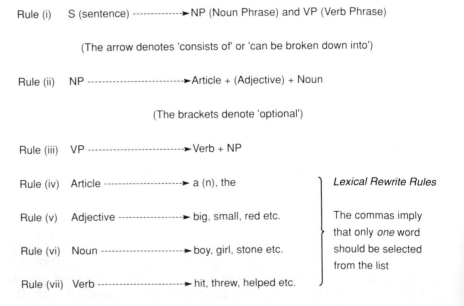

Rule (i)   S (sentence) -------------➤ NP (Noun Phrase) and VP (Verb Phrase)

(The arrow denotes 'consists of' or 'can be broken down into')

Rule (ii)   NP -----------------------➤ Article + (Adjective) + Noun

(The brackets denote 'optional')

Rule (iii)   VP -----------------------➤ Verb + NP

Rule (iv)   Article ---------------------➤ a (n), the   *Lexical Rewrite Rules*

Rule (v)   Adjective -----------------➤ big, small, red etc.   The commas imply that only *one* word should be selected from the list

Rule (vi)   Noun ----------------------➤ boy, girl, stone etc.

Rule (vii)   Verb ----------------------➤ hit, threw, helped etc.

Applied to a particular example, a tree diagram can be drawn to represent the structure of the sentence, as in Figure 26.3.

While *phrase structure rules* replace *single symbols* by different sets of symbols, *transformational rules* rearrange *strings of symbols* and often add to them: the sentence in Figure 26.3 is an *active* sentence and from it, using transformational rules, more complex sentence forms can be derived (eg *passive*, *interrogative* and *negative*). If we take the original sentence:

A   small   boy   helped the   girl
(Article)+(adjective)+(noun)+(verb)+(article)+(noun)

and now apply a transformational rule (rule viii), we obtain the *passive* form of the sentence:

Article+noun+was+verb+ by+article+adjective+noun
The   girl   was   helped by a   small   boy

If the above account is correct, then simple active sentences occupy a special place in the language: they are the only ones where phrase structures do not undergo any transformation (they are called *kernel sentences*) and should, therefore, be the easiest sentences for native speakers to produce and understand. We would also expect them to appear earlier developmentally than more complex sentences (see below).

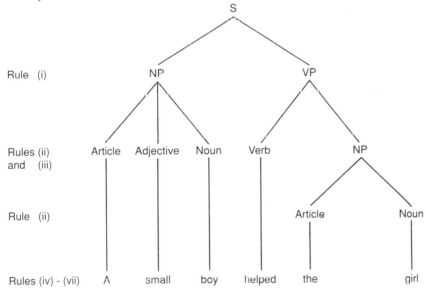

Figure 26.3 A sentence produced by Chomsky's phrase structure rules

Chomsky not only proposed a grammar which is one of the most adequate ever written (Plunkett, 1981) but he proposed how such an extremely complex grammar could be acquired by the child, in the form of *universal grammar, linguistic universals* and a *language acquisition device*. We shall return to Chomsky's theory of language acquisition later in this section but we should have said enough already to indicate why psychologists were so interested in Chomsky's ideas, particularly during the 1960s and 1970s.

DESCRIBING LANGUAGE DEVELOPMENT

Many psychologists have pointed out that there seems to be a universal timetable for language development, ie all children pass through the same stages, regardless of the particular language, culture, geography, cognition or training involved, and at more or less the same age. So *maturation* seems to play a very important part but, of course, environment is equally necessary—the child comes to speak the language it does because that is the one it is exposed to.

Children seem to be programmed by nature to learn language if they are exposed to it and, as we shall see later, sometimes even when they are *not* (for example, children of deaf–mute parents or congenitally deaf children) they still seem to create some kind of non-verbal language.

Thus language is acquired by every normal person in a predictable, sequential fashion, although the rate of development may differ from child to child.

The major stages that we shall be examining are: (i) the pre-linguistic; (ii) the one-word stage; and (iii) the stage of two-word sentences, which comprises two sub-stages, stage 1 grammar and stage 2 grammar.

i) *PRE-LINGUISTIC STAGE (UP TO ONE YEAR)*

The first year of life is really a pre-linguistic phase; the baby makes various sounds with its vocal organs, including crying, long before it can talk. Crying tends to dominate the first month or so, with the baby having different kinds of cries, which the parents learn to discriminate.

At about six weeks babies begin to coo, producing sounds which seem to be associated with pleasurable states. The vowel sounds that are produced during these early weeks are different from those that will later be made and out of which the first words will be built. During the first six months, the baby's oral cavity and nervous system are not sufficiently mature to enable it to produce the sounds necessary for speech.

The major development to occur during the first year is *babbling*, which usually begins somewhere between six and nine months; the baby now produces phonemes, which take the form of combinations of vowels and consonants (eg *ma*, *ba*, *ga*, *da*). Sometimes these are repeated to produce *reduplicated monosyllables* (*mama*, *gaga*) and although very different from the earliest cooing sounds, these babbled sounds still have no meaning—it will be another few months before we can say the baby is actually talking.

Two of the main differences between babbling and pre-babbling vocalization are: (i) the baby spends more time making noises, especially when alone in its cot, and seems to enjoy exercising its voice for the sake of it; (ii) babbling has intonational patterns, like speech, with rising inflections and speech-like rhythm.

By eleven or twelve months, the baby often repeats syllables over and over again (*dadadada*) and this is called *echolalia*; the baby seems to be echoing itself (the term is also used to refer to the repeating back of other people's speech, in autistic children for example).

At first, only a few phonemes are produced in the baby's babbling. But then *phonemic* (or phonetic) *expansion* occurs, whereby almost every available phoneme is produced. The onset of babbling and phonemic expansion both seem to be based on maturation, independent of experience or learning. Babbling occurs roughly at the same time all over the world, and even deaf babies, or those born to deaf–mute parents (and who, therefore, hear very little speech, if any) babble—and, on average, at the same time as normal babies.

However, by nine or ten months, phonetic or phonemic *contraction* begins to take place, whereby phonemes become restricted to those used in the baby's native tongue. This seems to be based on the baby's sampling of the phonemes used in the language environment to which it is exposed. At this age, therefore, it would be possible to distinguish babies of different nationalities—an English, Chinese and French baby would no longer all sound alike; a speech expert or linguist could correctly identify the baby's native tongue, even though the baby is still only babbling and not yet producing meaningful sounds. Significantly, deaf babies normally stop babbling at around nine or ten months, presumably because of lack of feedback from their own voice.

Although the baby is now only using phonemes which are 'useful' (those necessary for speech) it will be several years more before *all* the phonemes are mastered. For example, by two and a half years, most children have mastered twenty-seven of the forty or so phonemes of English (all the vowels and about two-thirds of the consonants); three-, four- and five-year-olds commonly have trouble pronouncing at least one phoneme. But by seven years, most English-speaking children have mastered them all.

It seems that the ability to perceive the difference between different speech sounds is innate. Eimas (1975) conditioned two-day-old infants to suck a dummy in order to operate the repeated presentation of 'ba'. Habituation occurred after about 30 seconds (ie the baby stopped sucking). If a new sound was presented (eg 'pa'), sucking picked up to its original rate. He also systematically varied the voice onset time (VOT) of 'b' in 'ba' as it was repeated; VOT refers to the interval between the time the lips move and the time the vocal cords are set in motion, so that for 'b' VOT is 0 milliseconds (there is no measurable delay) while for 'p' it is 40 milliseconds. The babies' sucking continued to drop off as 'ba' was repeated until VOT reached about 30 milliseconds, when it picked up again, indicating that the baby had perceived a different sound.

It seems, then, that babies do not need to *learn* the 'p'/'b' difference; similarly, with 'd'/'t' and 'g'/'k'. Without such inborn abilities, the sound of language would seem very confusing. In Chomsky's terms, these phonetic discriminations may be thought of as the first *linguistic universals* which the baby discovers, ie the first grammatical rules to be acquired are *phonetic* rather than syntactic.

Pre-linguistic Communication

One of the influences which Chomsky's theory had on the study of language development was to focus on the emergence of *syntactic rules*, which do not usually appear before eighteen months, with the beginning of the two-word stage. But during the 1970s there was a shift in the study of language development to what goes on during the first twelve to eighteen months, which is clearly a great deal:

> ... Not only are they [infants] interesting in their own right, but the basic skills acquired during the first 18 months of life may contribute substantially to the syntactic skills characteristic of adult language. (Plunkett, 1981)

How do children 'discover' their language, ie how do they learn that there is such a thing as language which can be used for communicating, categorizing, problem-solving and so on? A purely syntactic analysis cannot possibly provide answers to these kinds of questions.

According to Smith and Cowie (1988) the *language and social interaction* approach sees language as being used to communicate needs and intentions and as an enjoyable means of entering into a community—the baby initially masters a *social* world onto which it later 'maps' language. How is this achieved?

Snow (1977), for example, observes that adults tend to attach meaning to the baby's sounds and utterances—burps, gurgles, grunts, etc. are interpreted as expressions of intent and feeling, as is their non-verbal communication (smiling, eye-contact, etc.). This represents a kind of primitive conversation (*proto-conversation*) which has a rather one-sided quality: it requires a 'generous' adult attributing some kind of intended meaning to the baby's sounds and non-verbal behaviour. From this perspective, the infant is an inadequate conversational partner.

According to Ryan (1974), the *function* of pre-linguistic interactions is to *prepare* the baby for language. Infants and adults together create a range of *formats* (habitual exchanges or routines) which form the basis for interpreting what both mean. In the course of these 'dialogues' or 'pre-speech conversations', the baby is developing the skills which are:

> . . . as essential to speaking and understanding language as the mastery of grammar is supposed to be. (Ryan, 1974; quoted in Smith and Cowie, 1988)

These skills are extended by ritualizing games, such as peek-a-boo and joint picture-book reading.

Bruner (1975) also cites games like peek-a-boo as exchanges which stress the need for turn-taking and so help the baby to discover the *social* function of communication. He later (1983) refers to such exchanges as being part of the *language acquisition support system* (LASS). By as early as four months, the adult can direct the baby's attention to an object by simply looking at it and, later, by pointing. In these, and various other ways, mother and baby are very finely 'tuned-in' to one another.

So far, we have looked at the 'partnership' between adult and infant mainly from the adult's point of view or, at least, with the adult being portrayed as the 'senior partner'. A way of looking at things more from the baby's viewpoint and at the baby as a more 'active' partner is the view of language as a *cause–effect analytic device*:

> . . . the fundamental function of words is to bring about changes in the speaker's environment and . . . linguistic understanding consists in a grasp of these causal relations. (Gauker, 1990)

Bates (1979) stresses that language should be viewed as a form of *tool use*, a tool being a symbol or set of symbols whose use results in a change of behaviour in the listener.

This use of words as a '*communicative tool*' can be seen during the '*emergence of communicative intentionality*' (Bates, 1979; Bruner, 1983). During the pre-linguistic stage, the child at first has no awareness that one can gain a desired effect *indirectly* by changing somebody else's behaviour (through behaviours such as words, gestures or glances)—he/she may cry and reach for something but *not* look back at the caretaker nor direct the cry towards the caretaker. The cry is a mere expression of frustration, *not* a communicative signal designed to affect the other's behaviour. (This 'analysis' of means–end relationships—ie what causes what—solely as the product of one's own actions is called *first order causality*).

But the emergence of communicative intentionality involves *second order causality*, the awareness of the ability to bring about a desired goal through the means of using *another person* as a tool. Pointing gestures and glances now rapidly proliferate as a means of asking others to look at or act upon an object. The child is beginning to understand, in a general sense:

> . . . that it is possible to 'cause' others to engage in desired actions, through the mechanism of communications about these actions. (Savage-Rumbaugh, 1990)

This use of *animate tools* (other people) parallels the child's use of *inanimate tools* (physical objects) which is an important feature of sensorimotor intelligence (see Chapter 25). Some kinds of *instrumental understanding* (what-leads-to-what) seems to underlie both activities.

Savage-Rumbaugh (1990) claims that another important component a language acquisition system (whether a neural network, child or chimp) must have is *observational learning* or *goal-directed imitation*, ie the capacity for learning cause-effect sequences without ever experiencing either the cause or the effect directly. Bates (1979) agrees that such observational learning is critical in the language acquisition of normal children.

However, as important as this cause-effect analysis of language function may be, language *comprehension* cannot so easily be analysed in this way as language *production* (the former preceding and outstripping the latter)—what is one causing to happen by *understanding* the things said to one? Based on work with chimps, Savage-Rumbaugh concludes that:

> . . . Language comprehension is . . . clearly becoming the driving force underlying the language acquisition process. Language production is but one outcome of the development of language comprehension. Language production, without comprehension, is not characteristic of the child and when it does occur, it reflects a pathological condition. . . (Savage-Rumbaugh, 1990)

i) ONE-WORD STAGE (TWELVE TO EIGHTEEN MONTHS)

While there is considerable variability in the age at which infants produce their very first word (anywhere from nine to sixteen months), on average it occurs at twelve months. (It is interesting to note that the word 'infant' comes from the Latin word *infans*, which means 'without speech' or 'not speaking'; so perhaps when individuals begin to use words for the first time, they can no longer be considered babies.)

Of course, the baby does not wake up on its first birthday and decide that it is about time it stopped babbling like a baby and started speaking like a child: babbling merges and overlaps with patterned speech (words). Non-word sounds continue for up to another six months (and are called *jargon*; again note that we often criticize experts in various fields for using jargon or technical language which only they seem to understand—we might describe anyone whom we cannot understand as 'babbling on').

Lenneberg believes that the shift from babbling to words occurs as a result of fundamental developments in the brain; certainly the one-word stage is universal. Since the baby's first words (or articulate sounds) come soon after phonemic contraction, it is not surprising that they involve only a few phonemes. They are often 'invented', not very much like 'adult words' at all to begin with. For example, Scollon (1976) studied the first words of Brenda, a one-year-old. 'Da' was used only when referring to a doll; 'awa', though used in several different situations, always meant something like 'I don't want'; and 'nene' was used to refer to a whole collection of objects or people who had something to do with nurturing or comfort.

Scollon defines a word as, 'a systematic matching of form and meaning'—the baby consistently uses the *same* sound to label the *same* thing or kind of thing and there is now a clear intent to communicate. However, this does not necessarily imply that the words are being used *referentially* (to *refer* to the same thing regardless of the context):

> ... the infant's earliest words are usually context-bound in nature, their predominant characteristic being that they are produced only in very limited and specific situations or contexts in which particular actions or events occur... (Barrett, 1989)

For example, Bloom (1973) reports the case of one child who initially began to use the word 'car' at nine months only while she was looking out of the living room window at cars moving on the street below. It was *not* used to refer to stationary cars, pictures of cars or while actually sitting in a car.

Similarly, Bates et al (1979) reported on one infant who only ever said 'bye' (when it was *first* acquired) while putting a telephone receiving down, and Barrett (1986) found that 'duck' was produced (at first) by a particular infant only while hitting a toy duck off the edge of the bath and never in any other context.

What all these examples have in common is that the words, when first used, are tied to a specific situation or context, characterized by a frequently occurring event which involves behaviours which have often acquired a ritualized or standardized format (which relates to what we said earlier about pre-linguistic conversation).

These context-bound words are typically used simply as *accompaniments* to the occurrence of particular actions or events and, to this extent, they are not serving a communicative purpose as such—they function as pure 'performatives', ie their utterance is more like the performance of a ritualized action than the expression of a lexical meaning to another person (Barrett, 1989). However, *some* of the infant's first words do seem to be concerned with communicating either internal states, such as pleasure or distress, or reactions to objects, such as surprise, recognition or rejection (the *expressive function*) or with directing the behaviour of other people (the *directive function*), such as ordering, requesting, obtaining attention and directing their attention (eg 'see' and 'go'; this is a further development of *second order causality*).

These two functions of speech are mirrored by the infant's *pre-linguistic gestures*, for example, arm-waving, hand-flapping, and object rejection are often used to express internal states, while open-handed reaching, arm-raising, pointing and direct physical contact are often used to direct others' behaviour:

> ... Thus, there would appear to be considerable functional continuity

between pre-linguistic and very early linguistic communication. (Barrett, 1989)

Another characteristic of this stage is that single words are often used to convey a much more complex message, sometimes a whole sentence, in which case they are known as *holophrases*. So, 'milk' might, on one occasion, mean, 'I want some more milk', on another occasion, 'I don't want to finish my milk' and on a third, 'I've just spilt my milk'.

Greenfield and Smith (1976) see holophrases as precursors of later, more complex, sentences: the child uses gestures, tone of voice, and the situation, to add the full meaning to the individual word. Of course, they are still very much dependent on the adult making the 'correct' interpretation (older siblings, too, often take on this interpreter 'role' on behalf of their younger brother or sister).

Nelson (1973) studied eighteen babies and found that it took anywhere from thirteen until about nineteen months to acquire a ten-word vocabulary (the average being fifteen months), but after that vocabulary builds quite quickly, so that by nineteen or twenty months, babies had a fifty-word vocabulary. Despite individual differences, all eighteen babies showed this 'vocabulary explosion' after the initial ten words. What kinds of words are they?

Nelson identified six categories and calculated the percentage of the babies' first fifty words that each category represented in her eighteen-baby sample:

Category 1: *specific nominals*. Names for unique objects, people or animals (14 per cent).
Category 2: *general nominals*. Names for classes of objects, people or animals, eg 'ball', 'car', 'milk', 'doggie', 'girl', 'he', 'that' (51 per cent).
Category 3: *action words*. Describe or accompany actions or express or demand attention, eg 'bye-bye', 'up', 'look', 'hi' (13 per cent).
Category 4: *modifiers*. Refer to properties or qualities of things, eg 'big', 'red', 'pretty', 'hot', 'all gone', 'there', 'mine' (9 per cent).
Category 5: *personal–social words*. Say something about the child's feelings or social relationships, eg 'ouch', 'please', 'no', 'yes', 'want' (8 per cent).
Category 6: *function words*. Have only a grammatical function, eg 'what', 'where', 'is', 'to', 'for' (4 per cent).

So the nouns (specific and general nominals) compose 65 per cent and action words another 13 per cent, making 78 per cent altogether. Interestingly, even the nouns were related in some way to things the child could do, for example, the names of toys and food. It seems that it is not just the amount of exposure to objects and words that matters but whether the child can play with it, manipulate it, eat it and so on; *active involvement* with its environment will help determine many of the child's first words.

While the child is continuing to acquire new context-bound words, he/she is at the same time beginning to de-contextualize many of these words as the single-word stage progresses (but this occurs at different times for different words).

In addition, the child also acquires many new *referential* words for labelling objects, ie words which are used from the start in a decontextualized way. However, the exact point at which they first begin to use words in this way probably varies (Barrett, 1989).

Finally, as the single-word stage progresses, new communicative functions begin to emerge, namely, answering questions, asking questions and providing comments on the people and objects in their immediate environment. These abilities enable children to participate in very simple conversations with other people.

iii) TWO-WORD STAGE (STARTING AT ABOUT EIGHTEEN MONTHS)

This stage, like the earlier one, is universal, but individual differences in the rate of development become increasingly conspicuous.

Like the transition from babbling to one-word sentences, the move from the one-word to the two-word stage is also gradual. Initially, two-word sentences are produced relatively infrequently and children still rely primarily on single-word utterances. Multi-word utterances begin to predominate only at about twenty-four months.

Bee and Mitchell (1980) point out that as well as the continued development of the child's vocabulary, what becomes important now is the growth of understanding of grammar. They subdivide this third stage into two: between eighteen and thirty months they call stage 1 grammar, and from thirty months onwards, stage 2 grammar.

Stage 1 Grammar (Eighteen to Thirty Months)

The child's speech is typically *telegraphic* (Brown, 1965)—very much like the words found in telegrams. The essence of a telegram, of course, is that as much information as possible is conveyed in as few words as possible, so the words must be very economical. This is exactly what the child's speech is like:

(a) Only key words are used, those that contain the most information (Brown calls these *contentives*).
(b) Purely grammatical terms, eg the verb *to be*, plurals, possessives, are omitted (these are known as functional words or *functors*).
(c) There is a *rigid word order*, which seems to preserve the grammatically correct order and so helps preserve the meaning of the sentence. For example, if a child is asked, 'Does Tanya want to go to sleep?' she might say, 'Tanya sleep' (or, later on, 'Tanya go sleep').

By contrast, adults do not rely *exclusively* on word order to express meaning; the passive form of a sentence is a good example ('Joelle ate the banana' and, 'The banana was eaten by Joelle' both convey the same meaning, although the word order of each sentence is different).

Again, the child's imitations of adult sentences are simple but retain the word order of the original sentence, eg 'Jessica is playing with the dog' is imitated as 'Play dog'. This is an example of *imitation by reduction*. Complementary to this is *imitation with expansion*, which is the adult's imitation of the child's utterances and involves inserting the 'missing' *functors*, eg 'Baby highchair' becomes 'Baby is in the highchair'. The rigid word order of the child's utterances make it easier to interpret their meaning but with gestures and the context still providing important clues (as in the one-word stage).

Adults also simplify their speech when addressing children (*motherese* or *baby-talk register*) in order to achieve a mutual understanding with children who have not yet mastered the full complexity of language. This continues long after children have acquired all the basic syntactic rules.

Sensitivity to a child's vocabulary and intellectual and social knowledge is an example of a *pragmatic rule* for ensuring a degree of shared understanding (Greene, 1990).

Clearly, the child's two-word utterances are not random combinations of words, but are systematic expressions of specific semantic relations. Some examples are shown in Table 26.1.

TWO-WORD UTTERANCE	SEMANTIC RELATION EXPRESSED	COMBINATORIAL RULES INVOLVED
that book	nomination (of object, action or attribute)	
hi belt	notice (of object, action or attribute)	
more milk	recurrence (of object, action or attribute)	Pivotal rules
allgone juice	non-existence (of object, action or attribute)	
big train	attribute—object	
mommy lunch	possessor—possessed	
book table	object—location	
walk street	action—location	Categorical rules
Adam put	agent—action	
mommy sock	agent—object	
hit ball	action—object	

Table 26.1 Examples of two word utterances, and the semantic relations expressed by them. (Based on Barrett, 1989; Brown, 1970)

Brown distinguishes two main types of semantic relations: (i) those expressed by combining a single constant term or *pivot word* (eg 'more', 'all gone') with another word which refers to an object, action or attribute; (ii) those which do *not* involve the use of constant or pivot words. The appearance of two-word utterances can, therefore, be attributed to the child's acquisition of two different types of combinatorial rule, namely *pivotal* and *categorical* rules.

There is considerable individual variation in the type of two-word utterances which different children produce, with some relying largely on pivotal rules and others relying primarily on categorical rules instead (Barrett, 1989).

Word order in two-word utterances seems to reflect the child's pre-linguistic knowledge. According to the *cognition hypothesis* (Cromer, 1974) language structures can only be used correctly when our cognitive structures enable us to do so. Children form *schemas* to understand the world and *then* talk about them. *Object permanence* is a necessary prerequisite for understanding that words can represent things—if the child didn't already understand the relationships between objects, people and events in the real world, its first words would be like random, unconnected, lists. These are important concepts in Piaget's developmental theory and are consistent with his view of language development *reflecting* the child's stage of cognitive development (see Chapters 13 and 25).

Stage 2 Grammar (from about Thirty Months)

This second stage lasts perhaps until four or five years of age, and although it may be different for different languages, the rule-governed behaviour in language development is universal.

Vocabulary is growing rapidly but also sentences are becoming longer and more complex. The increase in *mean length of utterance* (MLU) is due largely to the gradual inclusion of the *function words* that are left out of the telegraphic speech of stage 1 grammar. So stage 2 grammar really begins with the first use of purely grammatical words and continues for several years.

Brown (1973) has found that there is a distinct regularity among English-speaking children in the order in which the grammatical complexities are added.

A study by deVilliers and deVilliers (1973) found that children the world over seem to acquire functional words in the same general order but at different rates. Each function word corresponds to a *syntactic rule* but when children begin to apply these rules, for example plurals, how do we know that they have actually learned a rule and are not just imitating what they have heard others say?

This is a wug

Now there is another one.
There are two of them.
There are two ———

Figure 26.4 Berko's (1958) method of testing children's use of the rule for forming plurals

One demonstration of children's rule-learning ability was carried out by Berko (1958), who showed children a picture of a fictitious creature called a *wug* and told them, 'This is a wug' (Fig. 26.4). The children were then shown a second picture in which there were two of these creatures and were told, 'Now there is another one. There are two of them.' They were asked to complete the sentence 'There are two ———'. Children three and four years old could successfully supply the correct answer 'wugs', although they had never seen one of these creatures before and certainly could not have been imitating anybody else's speech. Clearly, they were applying a rule about how to form plurals.

Again, in their spontaneous speech, children show that they apply rules that they have inferred or deduced from all the speech going on around then. It is often through their grammatical mistakes (which adults find so amusing) that children demonstrate this rule-governed behaviour, eg 'sheeps', 'geeses', 'mans', 'goed', 'wented'. Since it is extremely unlikely that the child has actually heard these words spoken (by adults), the child could not be simply imitating them. What the child seems to be doing is *over-generalizing* the rule or *over-regularizing* the English language; children from thirty months to about five years make language more regular than it really is. This is one of the outstanding characteristics of the child's language development in stage 2 grammar.

A significant fact is that the child is not consciously aware that it has acquired these rules and could not say what the rule is. The rules have not been deliberately taught by parents and yet the child's language is governed by rules.

According to Miller (1951) by the age of four or five years basic grammatical rules have been learned and by five or six a child's language is remarkably like that of an adult. But typically, a five-year-old will have difficulty understanding passive sentences. If asked to act out 'The horse is kissed by the cow', the child will reverse the meaning, making the horse do the kissing.

There are also a great number of irregular words still to be learned and this aspect of grammatical development will take several more years. However, all the basic skills have been acquired.

THEORIES EXPLAINING LANGUAGE DEVELOPMENT

In trying to answer the question *why* children develop language in the way thay do, we are once again involved in the heredity and environment (or nature–nurture) issue.

One type of theory regards language as being *learned* through essentially the same processes as other behaviour and centres around the concepts of selective reinforcement, shaping and imitation (see Chapter 7). Another kind of theory sees language as an inherent, biologically-determined capacity of human beings and the process of language development is essentially one of *acquisition* (as distinct from learning).

SELECTIVE REINFORCEMENT AND IMITATION

In *Verbal Behaviour* (1957) Skinner applied the principles of operant conditioning to explain language development in children. In essence, he claimed that adults shape the baby's sounds into words and its words into sentences (ie correct grammar is reinforced and incorrect grammar is not), through selective reinforcement. Sometimes, the positive reinforcement comes in the form of the child getting what it asks for, 'May I have some water?' produces a drink which then reinforces that form of words ('*mands*'):

> The basic processes and relations which give verbal behaviour its special characteristics are now fairly well understood. Much of the experimental work responsible for their advances has been carried out on other species but the results have proved to be surprisingly free of species restrictions. Recent work has shown that the methods can be extended to human behaviour without serious modifications. (Skinner, 1957)

Parents may provide reinforcement by becoming excited, poking, touching, patting and feeding children when they vocalize. A mother's delight upon hearing her child's first real word is exciting for the child and so acquiring language becomes reinforcing in itself.

Skinner also refers to the imitation (*echoic responses*) of verbal labels ('*tacts*') which receive immediate reinforcement in the form of the approval of parents, etc. to the extent that they resemble the correct word.

But what is the evidence that parents do actually shape their children's speech? And even if parents are found to reinforce selectively in the way Skinner claims, does it necessarily have any influence on the child's grammar?

Brown et al (1969) wanted to discover whether mothers' responses to their children's language depended on its grammatical correctness or on its presumed meaning. In most cases it was the *truth value* and *not* the grammatical correctness or complexity which the mothers responded to: they extract meaning from and interpret the child's incomplete and sometimes primitive sentences.

Braine (1971) and Tizard et al (1972) found that trying to correct grammatical mistakes or teach grammar has very little effect. Indeed, Nelson (1973) found that the children of mothers who systematically corrected their child's poor word pronunciation and rewarded good pronunciation actually developed vocabulary more slowly.

Slobin (1975) found that children learn grammatical rules *despite* their parents, who usually pay little attention to the grammatical structure of their child's speech and often, in fact, reinforce incorrect grammar. He claims that, 'a mother is too engaged in interacting with a child to pay attention to the linguistic form of his utterance'. So, while parents usually respond to (reinforce) true statements and criticize or correct false ones, they pay little regard to their grammatical correctness, and even if they did it would have little effect.

As for the role of imitation, it clearly has to be involved in the learning of accent and vocabulary. But when it comes to the complex aspects of language, namely syntax and semantics, the role played by imitation is much less obvious.

When children do imitate adult sentences, they tend to reduce or convert them to their own, currently-operating grammar. As we saw before, between eighteen and thirty months the child's imitations are as telegraphic as its spontaneous speech (*imitation by reduction*). Again, a good deal of adult language is, in fact, ungrammatical, so that imitation alone could not explain how we ever learn 'correct' English. Even if we do not always speak grammatically ourselves, we still know what is good grammar and what is not.

Lenneberg (1967) cites the case of a boy, who was totally dumb but who could hear and was quite normal mentally; he could understand language and obey verbal instructions, etc. but, of course, he could not imitate.

What selective reinforcement and imitation both fail to explain are:

(a) Why native speakers of a language have the capacity to produce and understand an indefinitely large number of sentences that they have never heard before and which, indeed, may never have been uttered before by anyone. This is referred to as the *creativity* of language (or its 'openendedness', in contrast to the 'closed' nature of the vast majority of animal communication; see Chapter 15):

> The normal use of language is innovative, in the sense that much of what we say in the course of normal language use is entirely new, not a repetition of anything that we have heard before . . . (Chomsky, 1968)

(b) The distinction between *competence* (understanding or implicit knowledge of the language) and *performance* (actual use of language on particular occasions). For Skinner, there is only performance. Competence is what underlies the creativity of language and for Chomsky it comprises knowledge of *syntactic rules*.

(c) The spontaneous use of *grammatical rules*, which have never been explicitly heard or taught. These rules, as we have seen, are often over-generalized, resulting in linguistic mistakes, but they are clearly not the product of imitation or reinforcement. Indeed, we have also seen that children are largely impervious to parental attempts to correct their grammatical errors.

(d) The child's ability to understand the meaning of sentences, as opposed to word meaning. The meaning of a sentence is *not* simply the sum of the meaning of individual words. As Neisser (1967) points out, the structure of language is comparable to the structure of perception as described by the Gestalt psychologists (see Chapter 9). Skinner may be able to account for how the child learns the meaning of individual nouns and verbs (since they have an obvious reference) but what about the meaning of grammatical terms ('functors')?

(e) The universal sequence of stages of language development.

LANGUAGE ACQUISITION AND THE BIOLOGICAL ASPECTS OF LANGUAGE

The major alternative theory also has two main strands: (i) Chomsky's (1965, 1968) and McNeill's (1970) innate *language acquisition device* (LAD); and (ii) biological aspects of language.

Chomsky's central idea is that children are born already programmed in some way to learn language. LAD is a hypothetical model (ie an attempt to explain language development by inferring what must be going on in the child's brain but without being able to observe it directly). It is based on the theory that individuals are born with the ability to formulate and understand all types of sentences even though they have never heard them before.

To understand properly what Chomsky is proposing, let us look at one of the major criticisms he made of Skinner's theory. He argued that Skinner fundamentally misunderstands the *nature* of language. It is infinitely more complex and less predictable than Skinner believes. For example, it uses *structure-dependent operations*. Aitchison (1983) points out that sometimes language does involve simple *slot-filling operations* (which corresponds to Skinner's simplistic view); for example:

(a) Bees/love/Honey.
(b) I/want/my/tea.
(c) My brother/has hit/me.

In these examples, each sentence is allocated a number of 'slots' and then units are slotted into each hole.

But there is a lot more going on than this:

> It is evident that more is involved in sentence structure than insertion of lexical items in grammatical frames. (Chomsky, 1959)

For example:

(d) Performing fleas/can be/amusing.
(e) Playing tiddlywinks/can be/amusing.

have the same superficial structure but rather different meanings. In (d) 'performing' describes the fleas, but in (e), 'playing' is a verb. As soon as we try to find other words to fit into the second slot, we run into problems: 'are' fits in with (d), but not (e) and vice versa with 'is'. Even more ambiguous are the following:

(f) Cleaning ladies can be delightful.
(g) The missionary was ready to eat.

It was examples like these which led Chomsky to distinguish between the *deep* and *surface* structure of a sentence.

When we hear a spoken sentence, we do not 'process' or retain the grammatical structure, the actual words or phrases used (ie the *surface structure*) but instead we transform it into another form, which more or less corresponds to the meaning of the sentence (ie *deep structure*). This understanding or knowledge of how to transform the meaning of a sentence into the words that make up the sentence, and vice versa (ie *transformational grammar*), is what Chomsky believes is innate, and it is this innate ability which enables us to produce an infinite number of meaningful sentences.

For example, the *same* surface structure can have *different* deep structures, as in examples (f) and (g). Can you work out the two meanings of each sentence? Conversely, *different* surface structures can have the *same* deep structure, eg:

(h) The dog chased the cat.
(i) The cat was chased by the dog.

Our ability to understand *both* meanings of (f) and (g) and the *single* meaning of (h) and (i) is based on *transformational grammar*, which is essentially what LAD comprises. Children are equipped with the ability to learn the rules that transform deep structure into various surface structures (transformations). This is done by looking for certain kinds of linguistic features (*linguistic universals*) which are common to all languages. For example, all known languages make use of consonants and vowels, syllables, subject-predicate, modifier and noun, verb and object. Collectively, these universals provide the *deep structure*.

Chomsky argues that these features *must* be universal because all children can learn any language to which they are exposed with equal ease: a child born in England of English parents, if flown over to China soon after birth and brought up by a Chinese family, will learn to speak Chinese just as efficiently as any native-born Chinese (and just as efficiently as it would have learnt English).

Only some kind of LAD, Chomsky argues, can account for the child's learning and knowledge of grammatical rules, in view of the limited and often ungrammatical and incomplete samples of speech that a child hears.

(We should note, as does Lyons (1970), that transformational grammar is *not* intended as a psychological model of how people construct and understand utterances. The grammar of a language, as seen by Chomsky, is an *idealized description* of the *linguistic competence* of native speakers of the language; any model of how this competence is applied in actual performance must take into account certain psychologically relevant facts such as memory, attention, the workings of the nervous system and so on.)

Is there any evidence to support Chomsky?

Much of the supporting evidence which does exist comes from study of the biological aspects of language:

1) We have already seen that many of the stages of language development are universal, which suggests the role of maturation. We also saw that deaf babies babble at the same time, and in the same way, as hearing babies—this too implies a maturational underpinning. And the ability to discriminate different speech sounds seems to be innate.

2) Our vocal organs, breathing apparatus, auditory systems and brain are all highly specialized for spoken communication.

3) As we noted above, adult languages all over the world have certain important features in common (linguistic universals) and transformational grammar is acquired in some form by all human beings, regardless of culture. This universality of language features may reflect the fact that all human brains are 'built' in a certain way and this matching of language structures and brain structure could account for the ease with which babies learn their native tongue.

4) Lenneberg (1964, 1967) studied normal and Down's syndrome children and found a consistently strong correlation between *motor* milestones (eg sitting, crawling, standing, walking) and *language* milestones (eg babbling, one-word sentences, two-word sentences). This correlation is much higher than that between language development and age which, in fact, is lacking altogether in Down's syndrome children. Although the *rate* of motor and language development is much slower in Down's syndrome children, the correlation between them is as high as it is for normal children. This again strongly suggests the role of maturation in language development, which Lenneberg says is much more like learning to walk than learning to read.

5) The built-in tendency to develop language in some form or other is dramatically illustrated by the case of four congenitally deaf children (Goldin-Meadow and Feldman, 1975). These children developed what looked like stage 1 grammar in their gestures, although their parents did not know how to use sign language, they were not exposed to any sign language and they could hear no speech.

The children were observed from the time they were eighteen months old and it was found that they created a sign language, first for individual objects and actions (comparable to holophrases) and then later combined them into two-gesture sentences. Although confined to things that were immediately present, they were beginning to use the language process on their own with no encouragement or training from parents. So it seems that LAD may be applied to gestural language as well as to speech. Language is very difficult to suppress, even in adverse environmental circumstances.

As adults combine all the pieces of the transformation together, it makes sense that the child goes through stages that are not reflected in adult speech. The child only learns transformational rules one at a time and only gradually do the child's rules come to resemble those of the adult.

6) Lenneberg also points out that almost all human beings acquire language, regardless of IQ. The only exceptions (apart from individuals who are severely retarded) are 'wild' or 'wolf' children, who are thought to have been raised by wild animals. However, it has been suggested that

such children may have been abandoned at birth because they were brain-damaged in some way.

7) Lenneberg believes that the years leading to puberty (ten to eleven) constitute a *critical period* for language development. His argument centres around the relative lack of specialization of the brain while it is still developing, so that brain-damaged children who lose their language abilities can relearn at least some of them as other, non-damaged, parts of the brain seem to take over the language function. By contrast, adults or adolescents, suffering an equivalent amount of damage, will be unable to regain abilities corresponding to the site of the injury because their brains have already 'set', ie become specialized. For most of us, our left hemisphere is dominant for language (see Chapter 14). However, many of these claims have been disputed. For example, several researchers have suggested that specialization or localization of brain function may be present at birth.

Studies of children reared in conditions of extreme (de)privation also suggest that the first ten or so years may not necessarily be the critical period that Lenneberg maintains (Box 26.1).

Box 26.1   The Case of Genie (Curtiss, 1977; based on Skuse, 1984)

One of the most extraordinary cases of severe deprivation yet reported is that of Genie, who was born in USA in April 1957. She was found aged thirteen years seven months, a painfully thin child who appeared six or seven years old. From the age of twenty months she had been confined to a small room under conditions of extreme physical restraint. In this room she received minimal care from a mother who was herself rapidly losing her sight. Genie was physically punished by her father if she made any sound. Most of the time she was kept harnessed into an infant's potty-chair but at night she was confined in a home-made sleeping bag fashioned like a strait jacket and lay in an infant's crib covered with wire mesh. She was fed only infant food. Genie's father was convinced that she would die; he was positive that she would not live past the age of twelve and promised that the mother could seek help for the child if she did so. But when the age of twelve had come and gone and she survived, the father reneged on his promise. It was not until Genie was thirteen and a half years old that her mother managed to get away, leaving home and husband, to seek help for the child. At this time Genie could not stand erect and could walk only with difficulty, shuffling her feet and swaying from side to side. Having been beaten for making any noise she had learned to suppress almost all vocalization save a whimper. She salivated copiously, spitting onto anything at hand, and was incontinent of urine and faeces. Curtiss comments 'Genie was unsocialized, primitive, hardly human'.

On her discovery she could understand a few words ('rattle'. 'bunny', 'red', 'blue', 'green' and 'brown') to which she always responded in the same way. But essentially she had to learn her first language at thirteen. Genie never developed normal language, it remained constrained and lacked the spontaneity of normal speech. However, she could develop new sentences of her own design. She had to be taught the rules of language long after they are normally (and spontaneously) picked up and so it proved much more difficult for her than for younger children.

The fact that it was possible for Genie to learn any language at all tends to detract from Lenneberg's idea of a critical period (see also Chapter 22).

AN EVALUATION OF CHOMSKY'S THEORY

According to Aitchison:

> Chomsky is substantially correct when he assumes that children are 'wired' with an innate hypothesis-making device. They automatically 'know' that language is rule-governed and they make a succession of hypotheses about the rules underlying the speech they hear around them. (Aitchison, 1983)

However, he goes on to claim that a child's brain naturally contains a considerable amount of specific information about language (transformational grammar)—LAD comprises *both* a hypothesis-making device *and* transformational grammar.

Aitchison rejects this second claim (what she calls 'Content Cuthbert') and, in preference, opts for 'Process Peggy' a *process* approach whereby children are seen as having an inbuilt *puzzle-solving* equipment which enables them to *process* linguistic data.

She cites Sampson (1980), according to whom no special advance knowledge of what language is like is necessary because children are highly efficient puzzle-solvers in all areas of human behaviour— language is just *one* type of puzzle which their high level of general intelligence enables them to solve fast and well.

By contrast, Chomsky believes that an innate language ability exists *independently* of other innate abilities—the mind is 'constituted of "mental organs" just as specialized and differentiated as those of the body' (1979) and, 'language is a system ... easy to isolate among the various mental faculties' (1979; see Gardner's Theory of Multiple Intelligences; Chapter 28).

An alternative explanation of the rule-bound nature of children's speech is that it arises from the child's *pre-linguistic knowledge*, which we discussed earlier on. This represents a move away from the *grammatical competence* approach inspired by Chomsky and McNeill.

TEACHING LANGUAGE TO NON-HUMANS

Another way of investigating the nature nurture issue is to look at attempts that have been made to teach language to non-humans. Until recently, it was generally believed that language ability is confined to humans. Lenneberg, for instance, claims that it represents a species-specific behaviour, common to all humans and found only in humans. But clearly if non-humans can be taught to use language, then they have the capacity for language (although it does not appear spontaneously, it must be potential in them) and so we would have to revise our ideas as to what makes us different from other species. (Chomsky also believes that language is unique to human beings.)

The obvious subjects for such language training are our closest evolutionary relatives, chimpanzees and gorillas, the non-human primates. But before considering the findings, we should look again at what defines or characterizes language. Clearly, speech and language are not identical (although we often equate them)—parrots can 'talk' but they are not capable of language because there is no meaning or understanding in the sounds they produce. (This is why we call rote learning 'parrot-fashion' learning, because it does not require understanding, just recall.)

In Chomsky's terms, the parrot displays no linguistic *competence*. Conversely, a child may display competence without being able to speak (no linguistic *performance*).

So how can we define language in a way that will prove useful for evaluating the results of studies where humans have tried to teach it to non-humans (who do not speak)?

Hockett (1960) proposed thirteen 'design features' of language (Fig. 26.5). Based on these, Aitchison (1983) proposes that ten criteria should be sufficient (not all of these are included in Hockett's list), namely:

(i)   use of the *vocal–auditory channel*;
(ii)   *arbitrariness* (use of neutral symbols—words—to denote objects, etc.);
(iii)   *semanticity* (use of symbols to mean or refer to objects/actions, etc.);
(iv)   *cultural transmission* (handing down the language from generation to generation);
(v)   *spontaneous usage* (freely initiating speech, etc.);
(vi)   *turn-taking* (conversation is a two-way process);
(vii)   *duality* (organization into basic sounds plus combinations/ sequences of these);
(viii) *displacement* (reference to things not present in time or space);
(ix)   *structure-dependence* (the patterned nature of language and use of 'structured chunks, eg word-order);
(x)   *creativity* (what Brown (1972) calls productivity—the ability to produce and understand an infinite number of novel utterances).

By analysing human and animal language in terms of all ten criteria, Aitchison concludes that four are unique to humans, namely (iii), (viii), (ix) and (x). It is in terms of these four criteria that we shall evaluate attempts to teach language to non-human primates.

Early attempts to teach chimpanzees to speak were almost totally unsuccessful.

1)   Kellogg and Kellogg (1933) raised Gua with their own child and treated them exactly alike. Although she could understand a total of 70 words or commands, Gua failed to utter a single word.

2)   Hayes and Hayes (1951) used operant conditioning in what was the first deliberate attempt to teach human language to a non-human— Viki, a baby chimp. By age three, she could say 'up' and 'cup' and (less convincingly) 'mama' and 'papa'.

It became obvious that chimps' vocal apparatus is unsuited to making English speech sounds, but this does not rule out the possibility that they may still be capable of learning language in some non-spoken form. This is precisely what several psychologists have tried to demonstrate since the 1960s (Table 26.2).

3)   The Gardners (1969) took advantage of the fact that chimps are extremely nimble-fingered (they can groom themselves and others, peel fruit, make simple tools, use a screwdriver, wind watches, thread needles and so on) to teach Washoe *American sign language* (ASL or Ameslan). This is the sign language used by many deaf people in the USA and is

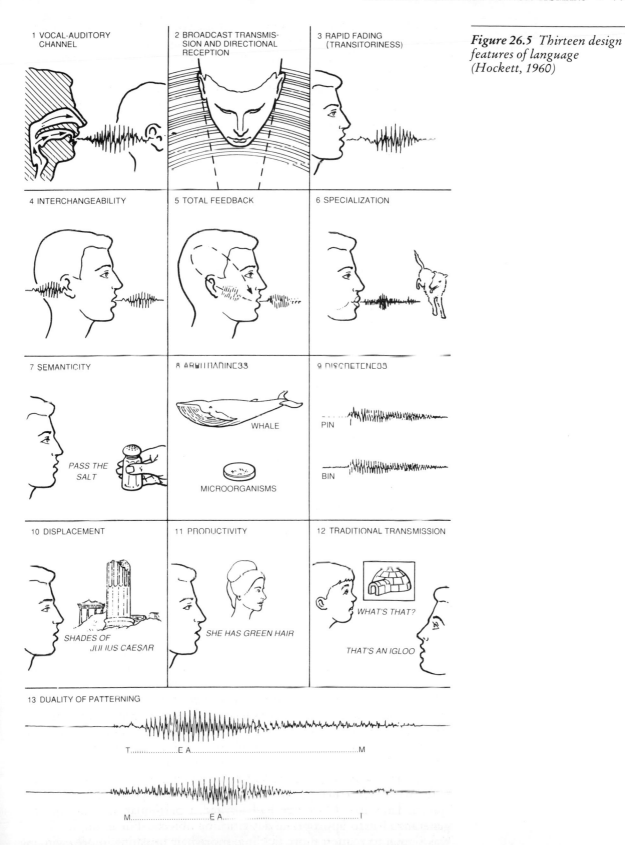

Figure 26.5 *Thirteen design features of language (Hockett, 1960)*

Table 26.2 *The major studies which have attempted to teach language to non-human primates*

STUDY	SUBJECT	METHOD OF LANGUAGE-TRAINING
Gardner and Gardner (1969)	Washoe (female chimp)	American sign language (A.S.L. or Ameslan). Based on a series of gestures, each corresponding to a word. Many gestures visually represent aspects of the word's meaning
Premack (1971)	Sarah (female chimp)	Small plastic symbols of various shapes and colours, each symbol standing for a word; they could be arranged on a special magnetized board. Eg a mauve △ = 'apple'; a pale blue ☆ = 'insert'; a red □ = 'banana'
Rumbaugh et al (1977)/ Savage-Rumbaugh et al (1980)	Lana (female chimp)	Special typewriter controlled by a computer. Machine had 50 keys, each displaying a geometric pattern representing a word in a specially devised language ('Yerkish'). When Lana typed, the pattern appeared on a screen in front of her 'Lana' 'Eat'
Patterson (1978, 1979, 1980)	Koko (female gorilla)	American sign language
Terrace (1979)	Nim Chimpsky (male chimp)	American sign language

Operant conditioning is used in all these studies when signs etc. are correctly used.

based on a series of gestures, each of which corresponds to a word. Many gestures visually represent aspects of the word's meaning. ASL also has devices for signalling verb tense and other grammatical structures and it is fully adequate for expressing everything that can be spoken.

Washoe's training began when she was about one year old. The Gardners created for her as human an environment as possible (her 'house' was a house trailer), with social companions, objects and daily play activities, including word or sign games. They signed to Washoe and to one another in her presence (just as deaf parents might) and whenever she made a correct sign, she was positively reinforced. Sometimes her natural gestures were close enough to the correct signs to permit shaping and her fingers were placed in the correct position. After four years of training Washoe had about 130 signs.

In many ways her progress was similar to a young child learning spoken language. Once she had learned a particular sign she quickly generalized it to appropriate activities or objects. For example, 'more' was signed to request more tickling, more hair brushing, more swinging and a second helping of food. She also over-generalized, as we have seen young children typically do.

Significantly, as soon as Washoe had learned eight to ten signs, she spontaneously began to combine them, forming sentences such as, 'more sweet', 'listen dog', and 'Roger come'. Later she combined three or more. By age five her command of language was roughly equivalent to that of a three-year-old child. It seemed that she did acquire syntax and could combine signs in various ways.

But in other respects, Washoe's progress was quite different from a child's. She was not exposed to sign language until she was a year old and the Gardners had only just acquired ASL as a 'second language'. More recently, they have been working with chimps that have been exposed since birth to people who are fluent in ASL, and the chimps seem to be learning much faster.

Fouts (1972), one of the Gardners' former assistants, has been trying to study how chimps might use ASL with each other and whether chimp mothers teach it to their offspring. It was hoped that Washoe might spontaneously teach her own babies but, unfortunately, they both died soon after birth.

Since then, Washoe has adopted a baby chimp called Loulis. Experiments began in 1979 and Washoe began signing to Loulis daily. Loulis has imitated a number of Washoe's signs, but it is not yet clear if he understands what they mean.

4) Premack (1971) taught Sarah a language based on *small plastic symbols* of varying shapes and colours; each plastic symbol stood for a word. She learned to construct sentences by arranging symbols on a special magnetized board. (This is easier than learning ASL because the symbols were all in front of her and so she did not have to remember them. But she was 'mute' when she did not have her symbols with her.)

Sarah was raised in a cage and had much less contact with humans than Washoe. Once again, operant conditioning was used, eg if she correctly chose the symbol for a banana, she would receive the banana as a reinforcement. In this way, she developed a small but impressive vocabulary, making compound sentences and answering simple questions. However, she was unable to generate new sentences of her own.

5) Rumbaugh et al (1977) used a different kind of approach again, with Lana. They taught her to operate a *special typewriter* controlled by a computer. The machine had fifty keys, each displaying a geometric configuration or pattern representing a word in a specially devised language called *Yerkish*. When Lana typed a configuration it appeared on a screen in front of her. She spontaneously learned to correct herself by checking the sequence of configurations on the screen—she learned to read! Not only did Lana respond to humans who 'conversed' with her via the computer, but she initiated some of the conversations. And when confronted with an object for which she had not been taught a word, she created one. For example, when seeing a ring for the first time she labelled it as a 'finger bracelet' (combining two words she already knew).

6) Finally, Patterson (1978, 1979, 1980) trained Koko, a female gorilla. She used ASL and, after seven years of training, Koko has mastered almost 400 signs. She also understands many equivalent English words for these signs. She has developed syntax and a number of novel sentences; she has also invented twenty of her own combinations

of signs for 'nail file', 'eye make-up', 'runny nose' and 'obnoxious'!

Koko's hearing is excellent and she can make subtle auditory language discriminations. For example, one day in a 'discussion' about time, she signed 'lemon'. Her thumb is too short to make the sign for 'eleven', so instead she signed 'lemon o'clock', a like-sounding word: eleven o'clock happens to be the time she has her morning snack!

Dworetzky (1981) claims that speaking to a gorilla is like glimpsing inside the mind of an alien who sees some things in a different way, sometimes a metaphorically beautiful way (see Table 26.3). Koko can use language to express anger ('red mad gorilla') and she has even lied by blaming others, claiming events which never happened and deliberately describing acts differently from how they were. This represents a quite sophisticated use of language.

7) Terrace (1979) after five years of working with his own chimp, Nim Chimpsky, concludes that although chimps can acquire a large vocabulary, they are not capable of producing original sentences.

Terrace argues that the great apes have been operantly conditioned to make certain signs in order to get what they want and that they are often inadvertently cued by their trainers to produce these signs in sequence; the apes are not really aware of what the signs mean.

Table 26.3 Summary of major findings of primate studies in relation to four criteria of language

SUBJECT OF STUDY	CRITERIA OF LANGUAGE			
	SEMANTICITY	DISPLACEMENT	STRUCTURE-DEPENDENCE	CREATIVITY (PRODUCTIVITY)
Washoe	After 4 years, about 130 signs. Could generalize from one situation to another (eg 'more').	Some evidence of this eg could ask for or refer to absent objects/people ('more milk', 'allgone cup').	Didn't always care about sign-order. Eg as likely to sign 'sweet go' as 'go sweet'. But in later reports (1971/75/78/), it's claimed she eventually became consistent.	Once 8–10 signs learned, spontaneously began to combine them. Eg "gimme tickle'=(come and tickle me), 'listen eat'=(listen to the dinner gong), 'go sweet'=(take me to the raspberry bushes), 'open food drink'=(open the fridge), 'hurry gimme toothbrush', 'Roger Washoe tickle'.
Sarah	Over 100 'words', including complex ideas, eg 'colour of', 'some', 'different', 'if . . . then'.	No evidence	Trained to use a fixed word order—no reward if order incorrect. Could obey instructions and	Could re-produce compound sentences previously rewarded. BUT couldn't

SUBJECT OF STUDY	CRITERIA OF LANGUAGE			
	SEMANTICITY	DISPLACEMENT	STRUCTURE-DEPENDENCE	CREATIVITY (PRODUCTIVITY)
			answer simple instructions.	spontaneously produce new sentences. Didn't hold 'conversation' like Washoe.
Lana	Over 100 symbols. Could generalize	Had been taught 'PUT' and 'IN' in connection with putting a ball into a box. Soon after, one of her trainers, Tim, was late with her morning milk. She spontaneously requested: 'Tim put milk in machine'.	Trained to use a fixed word order (as with Sarah). But could distinguish between 'Lana groom Tim' and 'Tim groom Lana'.	'Apple which is orange' (orange), 'Banana which is green' (cucumber).
Koko	After 7 years of training, nearly 400 signs. (Also understands many equivalent English words for those signs.) Generalization, eg 'straw' (drinking straw) generalized to cigarettes/plastic tubing/car radio aerial.	She supposedly apologized for a biting incident 3 days before. When shown bite mark on Penny's arm, she signed: 'Sorry bite scratch wrong bite' (Koko). 'Why bite?' (Penny). 'Because mad' (Koko). 'Why mad?' (Penny). 'Don't know' (Koko).	No evidence	'Cookie rock'=sweet or roll. 'Penny toilet dirty devil' (when angry with her trainer). 'Bottle match' = cigarette lighter. 'White tiger ' = zebra. 'Quiet chase' = hide-and-seek. 'Look mask' = viewmaster 'False mouth' = nose 'Elephant baby' = Pinnochio doll. 'Eye-hat' = mask.
Nim Chimpsky	Acquired many signs—but not used to make longer sentences as time passed.	No evidence	Had a statistical preference for putting certain words in certain order (eg 'more' verbs taking an object). No evidence of rules.	Only 12% of utterances were spontaneous.

EVALUATION

Looking at Table 26.3, the most consistent evidence seems to be for *semanticity* and *creativity*, while the least convincing evidence relates to displacement and structure-dependence. How might we explain these findings?

As far as Washoe's apparent failure to show *structure-dependence*, Aitchison (1983) suggests four reasons: (i) the Gardners' over-eagerness may have led them to reward her every time she signed correctly (regardless of order) so that the idea that order was important may never have been learnt; (ii) it may be easier to preserve order with words than with signs, eg deaf adults are also inconsistent in their word order; (iii) this may have been a temporary intermediate stage before she eventually learnt to keep to a fixed order (the Gardners in fact claim (1971, 1975, 1978, 1980) that she did so); (iv) she did not and could not understand the essentially patterned nature of language.

Both Sarah and Lana were *trained* to use a fixed order (and were not rewarded if they deviated from this). However, Sarah could obey instructions and answer simple instructions, while Lana could distinguish between 'Lana groom Tim' and 'Tim groom Lana'. Koko does not seem to have kept to any particular sign order, while Nim Chimpsky showed a statistical preference for putting certain words in a certain order (ie they were more likely to appear in one position rather than another) but no evidence of understanding any *rules*.

Petitto and Seidenberg (1979) conclude that, 'repetitive, inconsistently structured strings are in fact characteristic of ape signing'. Nim's longest recorded utterance is: 'Eat drink eat drink, eat Nim eat Nim, Drink eat Drink eat, Nim eat Nim eat, Me eat Me eat.'

IS THE LANGUAGE OF CHILDREN AND CHIMPS QUALITATIVELY DIFFERENT?

If we evaluate these studies by comparing chimps with children, then even semanticity turns out to be problematical. Is the correct use of signs to refer to things a sufficient criterion of semanticity? When compared with how it is displayed by young children, major doubts arise. Savage-Rumbaugh et al (1980) seriously doubt whether any of the apes (including their own, Lana) used the individual elements of their vocabularies as words. Terrace (1987) suggests that a strong case can be made for the hypothesis that the deceptively simple ability to use a symbol as a name required a cognitive advance in the evolution of human intelligence at least as significant as the advances that led to grammatical competence.

The function of much of a child's initial vocabulary of names is to inform another person (usually the adult) that he/she has *noticed something* (MacNamara, 1980). Often the child refers to the object spontaneously, showing obvious delight from the sheer act of *naming*. And it is precisely this aspect of uttering a name which has *not* been observed in apes. Could any amount of training produce an ape with such ability? MacNamara thinks not for the simple reason that the act of referring is not learnt but is a 'primitive of cognitive psychology' (and is a necessary precursor of naming). By contrast, chimps usually try to 'acquire' an object (approach it, explore it, etc.) and show no signs of trying to communicate the fact that it has noticed an object as an end in itself (Terrace, 1987).

This, in turn, relates to something we discussed earlier regarding the pre-linguistic stage of development, namely the *'emergence of communicative intentionality'* and *second order causality*. Remember that this is to do with the child's learning to bring about changes in its environment through influencing the behaviour of other people (via the child's use of gesture, etc.). This is a view of communication as having an *instrumental* function(ie it helps to get things done).

How does this tie in with the chimp studies?

Several critics have claimed that the linguistic abilities of chimps amount to a wholly 'instrumental use' of symbols. Referring to Savage-Rumbaugh's work with Kanzi (a pygmy chimp, supposedly spectacularly intelligent), Seidenberg and Petitto (1986) claim that Kanzi, 'may not know what the symbols mean' but only, 'how to produce behaviours that others can interpret'.

However, Gauker argues that:

> ... we might do well to view 'knowing what symbols mean' as nothing other than an understanding of more or less sophisticated instrumental uses of symbols ... even in human beings linguistic understanding consists in a grasp of the causal relations into which linguistic signs may enter ... (Gauker, 1990)

As we saw earlier, the use of words as a *communicative tool* can be seen during the *'emergence of communicative intentionality'*.

HELPING CHIMPS BE MORE LIKE CHILDREN

During the 1980s, Savage-Rumbaugh, at the Yerkes Primate Center and Georgia State University, has been working with chimps in a way which is much more like how children acquire language (and in certain respects more like the pioneers in this field, the Kelloggs and the Hayes). Instead of putting the chimps through rote learning of symbols, gradually building up a vocabulary a symbol at a time (*production-based training*), she aimed to use a large vocabulary of symbols from the start, using them as language is used around human children. This way, they might pick up language as children do.

The shift in questions asked was away from an emphasis on grammatical structure (at least in the beginning) and towards *comprehension*:

> It seemed reasonable to me—obvious even—that comprehension was an important element of language, that language is first acquired through comprehension, and that production flows from that. (Savage-Rumbaugh; quoted in Lewin, 1991).

This new approach was applied on a limited scale with Austin and Sherman, two common chimps. But it really got going with some pygmy chimps (bonobos), which are slightly smaller than common chimps and said to be more vocal and more communicative through facial expressions and gestures.

Work with Matata began in 1981. But Matata did not come alone—six months earlier she had kidnapped a newborn infant and kept it as her own. This was Kanzi. While Savage-Rumbaugh and her colleagues were working with Matata, Kanzi ran around, generally playing about and getting into mischief. Instead of ASL, Savage-Rumbaugh used an

Figure 26.6 Kanzi and Savage-Rumbaugh

extensive 'lexigram', a matrix of 256 geometrical shapes on a board. Instructors touch the symbols, which represent verbs and nouns, to create simple requests or commands. At the same time, the sentence is spoken, with the aim of testing comprehension of spoken English.

Although she was clearly intelligent in many ways, Matata was a poor learner and only used about six symbols. However, despite no attempt to teach Kanzi anything, he had picked up the symbols Matata knew, as naturally as human children do. From that point onwards, an even greater effort was made to place language learning in a naturalistic context.

Kanzi acquired a sister, Mulika, when he was two-and-a-half years old and the two siblings grew up together.

By age ten (1991), Kanzi has a vocabulary of some 200 words, but it is not the size of his vocabulary but what the words apparently mean to him that is impressive. He was given verbal requests to do things, in sentence form, by someone out of his sight. Savage-Rumbaugh's assistants in the same room with Kanzi wore earphones so they could not hear the instructions and so could not cue Kanzi, even unconsciously. None of the sentences was practiced, and each one was different. 'Can you put the raisins in the bowl' and 'Can you give the cereal to Karen' posed no problems for Kanzi. Nor did 'Can you go to the colony room and get the telephone' (There were four or five objects in the colony room, which were not normally there. Already, these kinds of abilities went beyond what Austin and Sherman could do; for one thing, they had been unable to learn and understand *spoken* English.)

More testing still was the instruction 'Go to the colony room and get the orange' with an orange in front of Kanzi. This caused him confusion about 90 per cent of the time. But if asked to 'Get the orange that's in the colony room', he did so without hesitation:

> This suggests to me that the syntactically more complex phrase is producing better comprehension than the simple one... (Savage-Rumbaugh; quoted in Lewin, 1991)

Kanzi could show this level of comprehension when he was nine years old, but not when he was younger than six.

He also showed understanding of the syntactical rule that in two-word utterances, action precedes object and, significantly, he went from a random ordering initially to a clear, consistent preference:

> Language training that is production-based as was the case for Sherman and Austin, is sufficiently detrimental that it may be said to disrupt the 'normal course' of language acquisition in the ape.
>
> When the environment is structured in a way that makes it possible for the chimpanzee to acquire language much as does the normal child, by coming to understand what is said to it before it elects to produce utterances, the perspective of language acquisition and function that emerges is very different from that seen by Sherman and Austin. (Savage-Rumbaugh, 1990)

Kanzi was the first to demonstrate that *observational exposure* is sufficient to provide for the acquisition of lexical and vocal symbols. Three other chimps (two pygmy and one common) have also learned symbols without training (so Kanzi's ability is neither unique to him nor his species):

> There is little doubt that observational learning is a more powerful method of language acquisition than is symbol training, given that the ape can manage to imitate the movements required to produce the symbols. When words are learned observationally it is difficult to offer an explanation of how the behaviour was acquired and what served as the reward... (Savage-Rumbaugh, 1990)

For example, how can a chimp (or a child, for that matter) know where one word ends and the next begins, ie what the units are, if it is only '*exposed to language*' and *not* deliberately taught it?

> Symbol acquisition in the chimpanzee in the current comprehension-based programme appears to begin with the learning of routines. These are not explicitly planned routines but rather routines which emerge out of daily

> life that has been constructed for the chimpanzees . . . (Savage-Rumbaugh, 1990)

A typical day (for Kanzi and two other chimps, Panbanisha and Panpanzee) is like a field-based pre-school for apes. Food can be found throughout a 50-acre forest. They have much time off for social play with different companions, interesting places to visit, plus time devoted to structured testing, during which the chimp is asked to sit quietly and apply itself as fully as possible. Caretakers' only instructions are to communicate with them much as one would with very young children, except that they must accompany their speech with pointing to lexical symbols. They talk about things which are concrete and immediate and clarify their intent with gestures and actions. More input focuses on where they and the chimps are going, what they're both going to do next, and what just happened to them. There is no insistence that the chimps 'talk' but they respond if they do so spontaneously. 'Conversations' move from topic-to-topic with the natural flow of the day and *routines* include nappy changing, getting ready to go outside, bathing, riding in the car, looking at a book, blowing bubbles, putting things in the backpack, visiting other apes, playing games of tickle and travelling down various forest trails.

Apes move from passive observer of routine towards active participant, to primitive initiator to a communicator symbolically announcing its intentions to another party. At first, symbols are only understood within an established routine; later it will be understood and used beyond the routine itself:

> . . . The driving force that moves the ape from symbol comprehension to symbol production is the desire to *exert some control* over what happens or is done next . . . (Savage-Rumbaugh, 1990)

CONCLUSIONS

Almost all the criticisms of ape studies and the conclusions drawn from them are based on the *production-based* studies (as summarized in Tables 26.2 and 26.3). Most psychologists seem to take the view expressed by Aitchison and Carroll:

> Even though intelligent animals seem *capable* of coping with some of the rudimentary characteristics of human language, they do not seem *predisposed* to cope with them. (Aitchison, 1983)

And again:

> The apparent ease with which humans acquire language, compared with apes, supports the suggestion that they are innately programmed to do so. (Aitchison, 1983)

> . . . although these chimps have grasped some of the rudiments of human language, what they have learned and the speed at which they learn it . . . is qualitatively different from those of human beings. (Carroll, 1986)

Savage-Rumbaugh believes that it is only a *quantitative* difference (ie one of degree). Referring to criticisms by Terrace that Kanzi still only uses his symbols to get things done, to ask for things, rather than to share his perception of the world, she acknowledges that Kanzi uses his symbols for these purposes, but so do young children. In fact, the predominant symbol use of normal children is 'requesting':

> Kanzi's percentage is higher, but he can reliably tell you some things, such as when is he going to be 'good' or 'bad', when he has just eaten or where he is headed while travelling. Terrace has consistently refused to acknowledge this. (Savage-Rumbaugh; quoted in Lewin, 1991)

Kanzi's capacity for comprehension far outstrips his capacity for producing language using the lexigram and this makes him extremely frustrated, at which times he often becomes very vocal, making high-pitched squeaks. Is he trying to speak?

> And if Kanzi were to talk, what would he say? Maybe the first thing he'd say is that he is fed up with Terrace claiming that apes don't have language. (Lewin, 1991)

27 MORAL DEVELOPMENT

As scientists, psychologists who study moral development are not interested in morality as such (ie those rules and principles for distinguishing right from wrong conduct) or in particular moralities or moral codes, but in the process by which the individual acquires those rules. The *processes* are assumed to be the same for all, regardless of the particular moral code the individual acquires.

Roger Brown (1965) compared a morality with the grammar of language, the latter being a set of rules for forming well-formed as opposed to badly-formed sentences (see Chapter 26).

Eleanor Maccoby (1980) defines moral development as the child's acquisition of rules which govern behaviour in the social world and, in particular, the development of a sense of right and wrong, how the child begins to understand the values that guide and regulate behaviour within a given social system.

As implied by Maccoby's definition, morality has more than one dimension: it is not merely a matter of acquiring an intellectual understanding of society's rules, ie knowing what is right and wrong (*cognitive* component), but also of behaving in accordance with those rules, ie our actual moral conduct (*behavioural* component). Clearly, we often say one thing and behave in a contradictory way—we may know what is right or wrong but we do not necessarily translate this into action. There is also a third component, the feeling aspect, ie guilt, shame, pride and so on (*affective* component). We may behave in a way that most people would judge to be immoral and yet feel no guilt or remorse or, conversely, we may be troubled by a guilty conscience and yet be a law-abiding citizen.

These examples suggest that the three components of morality are, indeed, distinct and that the exact relationship between them is complex and worthy of empirical investigation by psychologists. In practice, psychologists have tended to concentrate on one of the three components, often to the exclusion of the other two. Consequently, no one theory or approach is comprehensive in the sense that it tries to show how moral knowledge, behaviour and feelings are actually interrelated, but rather three or four major theoretical approaches each emphasizes one component and presents a very different views of what moral development involves:

(a) *Freud's psychoanalytic theory* focuses on the *affective* component; in particular, guilt or moral anxiety, on the one hand, and pride or self-esteem on the other.

(b) *Learning theory*, based on classical and operant conditioning, emphasizes the *behavioural* component (but one version—Eysenck's—is concerned with the acquisition of guilt).

(c) *Social Learning Theory* is also concerned largely with the *behavioural* component.

(d) The *cognitive–developmental theories of Piaget and Kohlberg* concentrate on the *cognitive* component, ie moral knowledge, understanding and reasoning.

They all have in common the assumption that the acquisition of morality is part of the wider process of socialization, ie it develops according to the same principles which govern the development of other aspects of socialized behaviour. It follows that, in order to understand moral development in particular, we must understand the process of development in general.

FREUD'S PSYCHOANALYTIC THEORY

According to Freud, our moral behaviour is controlled by the superego, which comprises the conscience and the ego-ideal. As we saw in Chapter 21, the conscience is that part of our personality which punishes us when we have committed some wrong-doing and so is the source of feelings of guilt. It represents the 'punishing parent' within our personality and is composed of all the prohibitions imposed on us by our parents, the 'thou shalt nots'.

The ego-ideal rewards us when we have behaved in accordance with our basic moral values ('thou shalts'); it is the source of our feelings of pride and self-satisfaction and represents the 'rewarding parent' within our personality.

Each part of the superego is acquired through a different process of identification (the conscience through identification with the aggressor, the ego-ideal through anaclitic identification) and the process is completed by age five or six.

PSYCHOSEXUAL AND MORAL DEVELOPMENT

To appreciate Freud's theory of moral development, it must be seen in the context of personality development which, you will remember from Chapter 21 proceeds through five *psychosexual stages*: the oral stage (up to one year), the anal stage (one to three years), the phallic stage (three years to five or six), latency (age five or six to puberty) and the genital stage (puberty to maturity). It is the third of these—the phallic stage—which is the important one as far as moral development is concerned because the Oedipus complex occurs during this stage and the outcome is the acquisition of the superego, through the process of identification.

You will remember from Chapter 21 that Freud admitted he was much less clear about the girl's motive for identifying with the mother than he was about the boy's motive for identifying with the father: the boy's fear of castration is a very powerful motive but:

> The fear of castration being thus excluded in the little girl, a powerful motive also drops out for the setting up of a superego . . . (Freud, 1924)

Freud was quite sure, however, that whatever the girl's motive may be her identification with her mother is bound to be weaker than that of the boy's with his father. For boys:

> ... the authority of the father ... is introjected into the ego and there it forms the nucleus of the superego, which takes over the severity of the father and perpetuates his prohibition against incest. (Freud, 1924)

But this only happens partially in the girl to whom, in any case, the father is something less of an authority figure. He has always been more interested in 'seducing' her affection ('daddy's little girl') and so she remains in a state of hostile attachment to her mother. The girl's love for her father does not have to be as thoroughly abandoned (repressed) as the boy's for his mother—she does not have to shatter her Oedipus complex so completely (Mitchell, 1974).

ARE MALES MORALLY SUPERIOR TO FEMALES?

If we follow Freud's account through, it would seem that the boy's conscience will be stronger than the girl's because: (i) the conscience represents the punishing parent; (ii) it is acquired through identification with the aggressor; and (iii) the boy's motive for identifying is much stronger than the girl's (ie the fear of castration). Similarly, we would expect a girl's *ego-ideal* to be more pronounced than a boy's since: (i) the ego-ideal represents the rewarding parent; (ii) it is acquired through anaclitic identification; and (iii) the girl's motive for identifying is stronger than the boy's (ie fear of loss of mother's love).

Freud did, in fact, maintain that women have weaker superegos than men (although he did not specifically differentiate between the conscience and ego-ideal in this context). Because her identification with the mother is less complete, the girl relies more on *external* authority figures throughout her childhood, has to be more compliant, less 'naughty' (there is no equivalent of 'boys will be boys'). It is through his strong identification with the father that the boy achieves independence which the girl will have to try to achieve in adolescence:

> ... Many women, though nominally they leave home, understandably, never make it ... (Mitchell, 1974)

But there is *no* evidence to support this view. For example, Hoffman (1975) reviewed a number of studies where children are left alone and tempted to violate a prohibition. There are not usually any overall gender differences but, where they *are* found, they tend to show girls being the *better able to resist temptation*.

Freud also saw females as being *sexually inferior*—they have to make do with babies as a poor substitute for a penis—and he may reasonably be regarded as the father of male chauvinism. Many feminist writers (including Karen Horney (1924) and Clara Thompson (1943), two eminent psychoanalysts) have pointed out that what girls (and women) envy is *not* the penis but the superior status that men enjoy in our society. It is the penis as a *symbol* for that superior status which is envied, not literally the penis as such, and it is men, not women, who equate lack of a penis with inferiority. Horney and Sherman (1971) both report 'womb envy' in men.

There is little evidence that women have more difficulty achieving gender identity than men or that they have an inferiority complex about their bodies although Horney (1924) 'concedes' that since the woman's genitals are hidden and so cannot be displayed she later displays her whole body instead, and is liable to turn inward on herself in greater subjectivity.

IS A GUILTY CONSCIENCE THE SIGN OF A MORAL OR AN IMMORAL PERSON?

Turning now to the relationship between our moral behaviour and our experience of guilt (which has its source in the conscience), Freud's view is counter-intuitive. The common sense view is that the greater the wrong-doing, the greater the guilt, ie the more wrong-doing we do, the more reason we have to feel guilty. But Freud claims that the greater the wrong-doing, the *less* the guilt, or the less the wrong-doing the *greater* the guilt.

How can this be?

The conscience causes us to renounce many of our basic impulses or instinctual wishes, especially our aggressive and sexual urges, and the energy from these renounced desires then becomes available to the conscience. Aggression that is not expressed and directed outwards towards others is instead directed inwards, against the self, a form of self-punishment which is experienced as guilt. So a severe, punitive, conscience is one which has a lot of energy at its disposal to keep in check our basic impulses; hence the more severe our conscience (ie the more guilt we are prone to) the *less* will be our objectively immoral behaviour (in other words, they are *inversely* related).

How severe or punitive the conscience is depends on the intensity of the child's aggression felt towards the parent (especially the father) and which does not find an outlet on its original target. It is inevitable that the child will be frustrated and feel hostile towards the parent who punishes it but if the child openly expresses this hostility it is likely to come in for even more severe punishment. So the child turns this aggression in on itself, punishing itself and in this way taking over the parental role—and it is through this process of identification with the aggressor that conscience is acquired.

Strength of conscience, as we have seen, depends on the child's unexpressed hostility towards the punishing parent and this is only partly determined by the actual severity of the parent's punishment. So the relationship between parents' methods of discipline and the strength of the child's conscience will only be indirect: it is how hostile the child *perceives* the parents to be that is of direct importance and this, in turn, is largely a reflection of the child's own hostility towards the parents.

It follows that a child treated very leniently *could* acquire a very severe conscience and that a son who is brutally beaten by his father *could* have a very weak one.

Is there any evidence to support Freud's belief that guilt and objective wrong-doing are inversely related? And is there any evidence that different kinds of parental discipline are related to strength of conscience?

A relevant study was undertaken by MacKinnon (1938), in which ninety-three subjects were given a series of problems to solve, working alone in a room which contained answer books, some of which they were allowed to use, others not. It was found that forty-three cheated; the other fifty did not.

Four weeks later, those who had cheated (and who did not know they had been found out) were asked if they had, in fact, cheated; about 50 per cent of them confessed, while the rest denied it. Those who confessed were asked if they felt guilty about what they had done and those who denied were asked if they *would have* felt guilty—25 per cent said they did or would have felt guilty. Of those who had not cheated, 84 per cent said they would have felt guilty.

They were also asked, 'Do you in everyday life often feel guilty about things you have done or not done?' 75 per cent of the non-cheaters said 'Yes', compared with 29 per cent of the cheaters. This seems to confirm Freud's predictions that guilt is not directly proportional to wrong-doing and that, indeed, they are inversely related.

MacKinnon also recorded the incidental behaviour of subjects when they were working on the original problems: nine of the cheats swore out loud or otherwise cussed at the problem (eg 'You bastard' or, 'These are the God-damnedest things I ever saw') but none of the non-cheats did this. Of the cheats, 31 per cent also performed restless acts such as pounding their fists or kicking the leg of the table, compared with only 4 per cent of the non-cheats.

Could it be that the aggressive energy expressed by the cheats was 'subtracted' from the energy available to the conscience, while the energy unexpressed by the non-cheats could be used to 'fuel' the conscience, as Freud would have suggested?

Sometime after the original experiment, MacKinnon managed to track down twenty-eight of the original subjects, all males, thirteen of the cheats and fifteen of the non-cheats. They were asked to check on a list of common forms of punishment, those most often used by their parents. Seventy-eight per cent of the cheaters checked physical punishments (including beatings and loss of privileges), compared with 48 per cent of the non-cheats; while 22 per cent of the cheats ticked psychological punishments (eg making the child feel that it has fallen short of some standard or had hurt the parents and lost some of their love) compared with 52 per cent of the non-cheats (the results are summarized in Table 27.1).

Table 27.1 The percentage of cheats and non-cheats who had been punished, physically or psychologically in MacKinnon's (1938) study	TYPE OF PUNISHMENT	
	PHYSICAL	PSYCHOLOGICAL
Cheats (13)	78%	22%
Non-cheats (15)	48%	52%

However, MacKinnon's data are, of course, only *correlational*, so we cannot be sure that the differences in the strength of conscience were caused by differences in child-rearing. For instance, parents who used psychological methods may have differed in other important respects from those who preferred physical methods and these other differences may have been the critical ones.

Again, the direction of causation could have been the other way round—the children may have forced their parents to use physical methods as a last resort when more psychological methods failed. For instance, it is probably easier to use psychological methods of discipline with children who are relatively passive, placid or 'undemanding' by nature.

MacKinnon's subjects had to recall their childhood experiences and make judgements about how to classify the kinds of punishment used by their parents; memory is notoriously unreliable, particularly with regard to such emotionally salient matters as this.

Perhaps the distinction between physical and psychological punishment is rather artificial. From what we have said about identification with the aggressor, it would seem that it is how the child perceives the punishment that is critical, including the intensity of feeling with which it is carried out.

Can we be sure that the behaviour of MacKinnon's subjects was typical of their moral behaviour in general? This is an issue which we shall come back to shortly.

There is, in fact, a good deal of additional evidence which supports the view that a strong conscience and psychological methods of punishment are positively correlated.

One famous study was carried out by Sears, Maccoby and Levin (1957), who interviewed 379 mothers of five-year-olds in Boston, USA, both middle- and working-class. Two main kinds of child-rearing techniques emerged: (i) *love-oriented*, more psychological techniques, which made use of praise and affection as rewards for good behaviour, and isolation and love-withdrawal as punishments for bad behaviour; and (ii) *object-oriented*, more physical techniques, which used tangible rewards, deprivation of privileges and actual physical punishment.

The love-oriented parents tended to have children with a more highly developed conscience compared with the children of object-oriented parents. However, the associations were not strong; the strongest were with physical punishment, so that of parents who used it a great deal, 15 per cent had children with a strong conscience compared with 32 per cent of those who used it very little.

Sears et al also found that the mothers most likely to have children with a strong conscience were generally warm and used love-withdrawal as a major disciplinary technique. This is consistent with Danziger's (1971) claim that it may be fear of loss of love, rather than love itself, which motivates the child to behave in socially approved ways (and hence with Freud's notion of anaclitic identification).

According to Hoffman (1970), excessive use of power-assertive techniques of punishment (physical punishment, withdrawal of privileges, or the threat of either) is associated with low levels of moral development. Reasoning or explaining tends to be associated with high levels of moral development (as measured by consideration for others, moral reasoning and guilt), verbal explanations are more effective than physical punishment and children seem to learn best how to control their own behaviour if parents explain what they have done wrong, what led up to the misdeed or what the consequences of the misdeed were for the child and others.

Glueck and Glueck (1950) found that severe punishment is one of the major factors associated with delinquency in young boys.

Bandura and Walters (1959) compared the attitudes of parents of twenty-six highly aggressive boys with those of twenty-six normal boys, matched for intelligence and socio-economic status. Most of the former had been in trouble with the law, felt less guilt and had parents who used physical punishment, compared with the latter; the aggressive boys were also more likely to have been rejected by their parents.

If it is method of punishment which determines the strength of conscience, how does it actually work to produce the effect it does?

One suggestion is that different responses are required in the child in order to end the punishment:

(a) In the case of psychological methods, there must be some kind of *symbolic renunciation*—an apology, a promise not to do it again, etc. In time, these responses become organized into what is normally called conscience.

(b) When the child is punished physically, the response is often more aggression or, at least, feelings of hostility, and the parent may, in fact be unwittingly providing the child with a model of aggressive behaviour to imitate; this does not encourage the inner control implied by conscience (see Chapter 7).

AN EVALUATION OF FREUD'S CONCEPT OF CONSCIENCE

Freud defined the superego like this:

> This new psychical agency continues to carry on the functions which have hitherto been performed by the people in the external world: it observes the ego, gives it orders, judges it and threatens it with punishments, exactly like the parents whose place it has taken. (Freud, 1938).

This way of characterizing the superego serves to reinforce a common way of referring to it in everyday language (or, at least, to a part of it, the conscience). White (1975) points out that we usually tend to personalize conscience (eg we say, 'My conscience would not let me do it' or, 'My conscience got the better of me') as if it had an independent life of its own and existed in its own right.

The word 'conscience' (*con* plus *sciens*) means 'knowing with someone else' and it is often used as if it were an independent witness of our behaviour, an internal judge (as Freud says) of whether our behaviour conforms with our moral code.

Many psychologists have become dissatisfied with the term in recent years, partly for the reasons outlined above and partly also because of the particular form it takes in Freud's theory. One major criticism (Kohlberg, 1969; Hoffman, 1976) has been that conscience does not suddenly come into existence at five or six years old, but rather moral development is a gradual process which begins in childhood and extends into adulthood.

Another criticism is that the belief in an internalized conscience implies that moral behaviour should be consistent across different situations, that is, if our moral conduct is determined by a part of our personality which is unchanging, then the details of the moral situation should be largely irrelevant as far as how we act is concerned. It also follows that people will display 'moral traits', such as honesty, whereby someone who is honest on one occasion, in one type of situation, will be honest on another occasion in other types of situation. But is this what people are like?

GENERALITY VERSUS SPECIFICITY IN MORAL CONDUCT

The classic study which set out to investigate this issue was the 'Character Education Inquiry', begun in 1928 by Hartshorne and May. They studied 12,000 eleven- to fourteen-year-olds who were given the opportunity to cheat, lie and steal under conditions in which they were confident of not being found out.

They were observed in a variety of situations—in the classroom, playground, after-school activities, in sports, during party games, and at home. They were also given twenty pencil and paper tests designed to measure moral knowledge (where the questions had objectively right answers) and moral opinions (where they did not). These tests were sometimes scored against adult consensus (what a majority of adults believed) and sometimes against a kind of ideal code supplied by the researchers.

It came as quite a surprise to Hartshorne and May that the results were very inconsistent, so that a child who, say, cheated in one situation (eg an arithmetic test) would often not cheat in another (eg a spelling test). The overall correlation between bad behaviour in one setting and bad behaviour in another situation was 0.34, much lower than had been expected. Even *within* the same situation (eg school tests in the classroom) children behaved inconsistently, although the consistency was relatively higher than it was *between* situations (eg playground and classroom). So it would appear that a child does not have a uniform, generalized, code of morals to determine behaviour in a variety of situations, but rather the situation is at least as much responsible for the child's moral actions as conscience.

Hartshorne and May concluded that honesty was largely situation-specific and not a general personality trait, ie we cannot say that some people are more honest than others, because this implies consistency across situations which they did not find ('*Doctrine of Specificity*').

However, subsequent re-analysis of the data showed a significant, if small, tendency for children who were honest on one test to be so on others. And subsequent studies of different measures have tended to confirm that they are positively correlated, including resistance to temptation and altruism.

Therefore, in conclusion, it appears that personality, as well as the situation, determines several important aspects of moral behaviour and this represents some measure of support for Freud's concept of the superego (see Chapter 29 for a discussion of the influence of personality and situational variables in general behaviour).

Freud's approach also limits the child's moral learning to the family which, admittedly, was a much greater influence on the child at the turn of the century, when Freud was first formulating his theories, than it is now. Today's child is exposed to many moral influences in addition to the family, both before and after starting school, including the media, teachers and peers.

Other criticisms have come from learning theorists who, as well as being generally critical of Freud's theories, believe that conscience can be accounted for in terms of the principles of conditioning.

LEARNING THEORY APPROACH

The Learning Theory (or S–R) approach maintains that moral behaviour is learned according to exactly the same principles of classical and operant conditioning as any other behaviour (see Chapter 7).

THE CONTRIBUTION OF CLASSICAL CONDITIONING

Psychologists such as Eysenck believe that what we normally call conscience is no more and no less than a conditioned response of an emotional type (conditioned emotional response, CER) or, more precisely, a collection of such CERs. How might these CERs come about?

The short answer is, by exactly the same procedure by which salivation becomes a conditioned response (CR) to a bell. If, for example, a child is frequently disciplined for being naughty, the negative feelings (mainly anxiety) which the child associates with punishment become associated with the wrong-doing. So the child comes to feel anxious when contemplating doing something naughty and this eventually happens even when the parents are not present.

For instance, if the child is smacked (unconditioned stimulus, UCS), which produces pain and anxiety (unconditioned response, UCR), for stealing, and the child is told, 'You must not steal' (conditioned stimulus, CS) just before it is smacked, eventually the words, 'You must not steal' will come to produce anxiety in the child (CR) and, finally, when the child even thinks about stealing, this CR will be produced.

This anxiety builds up at the thought of doing wrong and reaches a climax just before the wrong-doing, and is a far more effective deterrent than the thought of being caught (which may or may not happen), hence Hamlet's 'Thus conscience does make cowards of us all'. In this sense, the self is generally a better deterrent against law-breaking than police or magistrates.

These feelings of anxiety (CERs) represent our ability to resist temptation. But conscience, according to Eysenck, also refers to our susceptibility to feelings of guilt, ie what we feel *after* we have committed some wrong-doing. It seems to be the *timing* of the punishment which determines whether the resistance-to-temptation component or the guilt component of conscience is affected.

A famous experiment by Solomon et al (1968) with puppies tends to support the view that resistance to temptation and guilt are not functionally equivalent components of conscience (although they are subjectively the same). Puppies were 'punished' (swatted with a newspaper) either just before they began to eat forbidden food or just after they had started to eat it. After being trained in one of these two ways, they were all tested by being made hungry and left alone in a room with the forbidden food. Those puppies punished just before eating, held out much longer against the temptation to eat than those punished just after they had eaten a little during training sessions.

However, once the early-punished puppies had started to eat, they showed little sign of anxiety, in sharp contrast to the second group, which showed all the usual signs of 'doggy guilt'. These differences are explained by assuming that the first group were classically conditioned to respond with anxiety to all those stimuli which occurred during the approach to food, while the second group were conditioned to those stimuli occurring after food had been eaten.

So, 'punishment' that is consistently given *before* a misdeed will result in high resistance to temptation but weak guilt when wrong-doing does occur, and the reverse will be true when punishment consistently *follows* the misdeed. (We should note that the anxiety experienced when contemplating some misdeed is reduced if the temptation is actually resisted; in this way, through *negative reinforcement*, resistance to temptation can be strengthened—through operant conditioning.)

Several studies have found similar effects to those found with puppies when children are the subjects. For example, Aronfreed (1963) punished a group of young boys verbally for touching attractive toys, while still in the act of reaching (as the transgression was about to occur), while boys in a second group were punished a few moments after picking up the toys. They were then left in a room with the toys and told not to touch them. As predicted, the first group were better able to resist than the second group.

However, even in the relatively simple case of a child who is conditioned to feel anxiety when about to steal, *cognitive factors* are clearly involved. For example, if children are given a rationale for not touching a particular toy (it is fragile and might break or it belongs to another child who did not want them to touch it), together with a mild punishment, they are significantly less likely to touch it than if given just punishment. Equally important is the finding that, when reasons are given, the timing of punishment becomes irrelevant.

Parke, in a review of several studies (1972, 1977), concluded that, when a rationale accompanies punishment:

(i) mild forms of punishment become just as effective as severe punishment at producing resistance to temptation;
(ii) delayed punishment becomes as effective as early punishment;
(iii) punishment from an aloof and impersonal adult becomes as effective as that from a warm, friendly adult;
(iv) resistance to temptation is much more stable over time.

There are also interesting developmental factors involved. For instance, Parke (1974) found that three-year-olds were quite effectively inhibited from touching by being told the toy was fragile and might break (*object-oriented rationale*) but telling them it belonged to another child (*person-oriented rationale*) had very little effect. However, five-year-olds did respond to appeals based on property rights.

Parke concludes that long-term (internalized) moral controls may require cognitively-oriented training procedures as opposed to those which rely solely on the conditioning of anxiety responses.

THE CONTRIBUTION OF OPERANT (INSTRUMENTAL) CONDITIONING

This takes a more active view of the learner; what is being conditioned is not an automatic, physiological response like anxiety but some behaviour of the child which is essentially voluntary. So, while classical conditioning is concerned primarily with the affective or emotional components of morality, operant conditioning is concerned with trying to explain how *moral behaviour* is acquired. The assumption made is that moral behaviour, like all other operant behaviour, can be made more or less likely to occur depending on its *consequences*, ie whether it is reinforced or punished. Let us look at some of the evidence.

The Role of Reward and Punishment

Several studies have used a variety of positive reinforcements for increasing a range of morally desirable behaviours, including bubble-gum, praise, hugs and sharing marbles, giving sweets to other children and co-operating with others. However, several researchers have also pointed out that reward cannot be applied mechanically. If a parent is not warmly attached to their child, then reward may be of little value in altering the child's behaviour. (This parallels the point we made earlier that the threat of withdrawal of love is only effective if the relationship between parent and child is a warm and close one.)

Similarly, the effect of punishment depends on the relationship between the punisher and the child; if there is already a warm and affectionate relationship between them, the child is much more likely to inhibit unacceptable behaviour than if the same punishment is given by a cold, unaffectionate agent (Sears et al, 1957; Parke, 1969).

The Relative Effectiveness of Reward and Punishment

1) Reward (or positive reinforcement) provides information about which of the many alternatives for action are likely to bring 'happiness' or pleasant outcomes; but punishment only tells us what we should *not* do, not what we should. So while reward can produce morally acceptable behaviour, punishment, at best, produces an inhibition of morally unacceptable behaviour (ie it does not 'eradicate' it).

2) Reward may be especially useful in creating high morale or a sense of joy and well-being, while punishment often produces hostility and resentment towards the punisher.

3) The punisher may under-estimate the severity and intensity of the punishment and thus abuse it. This is especially likely to occur when an adult physically punishes a child, 'I didn't know my own strength' may be used as an excuse (and sometimes, perhaps, a genuine reason) for a case of child abuse. Also the child may well get used to certain levels of physical punishment, so that the adult has to step up the intensity of the punishment ('smack a bit harder') for it to have any effect.

4) As we have noted in relation to modelling and observational learning (see Chapter 7), each time the child is punished (either by an adult or an older child) it is witnessing the meaning of 'social power'. The punisher, by virtue of age, gender, strength or status, is seen as having the right to define what is and what is not 'desirable behaviour' and to perform acts against the powerless child (which, in turn, are condoned by society). So the child learns to follow this model and may well use punishing strategies for controlling the behaviour of others.

5) Punishment often occurs in a social situation involving people other than the punisher and the punished. The presence of these others may add to the humiliation felt by the person being punished and they may even 'join in' (as when both parents tell the child off, one after the other). Alternatively, the presence of others may bias the behaviour of the punisher who may be concerned about his/her image and use punishment to impress the onlookers in some way or to 'keep up

appearances' (especially if they are adults) or to teach the others a lesson (if they are children). In the latter case, how effective is the punishment likely to be as far as the originally punished child is concerned?

O'Leary et al (1970) made a study of the spontaneous use of punishment by schoolteachers. Two children from each of five classes were observed for a four-month period. They were quite disruptive in the classroom and were often reprimanded for it publicly by their teacher, usually loudly enough to be heard by the rest of the class but with little effect on the disruptive behaviour. The teachers were asked to use soft reprimands, audible only to the child being disruptive. In almost all cases, disruptive behaviour decreased when soft reprimands were directed only at the child in question. When the earlier method was reintroduced, disruptive behaviour again increased, only to fall again when the 'soft' approach was retried.

6) Punishments may, inadvertently, increase the very behaviour they are intended to stop. For example, if children find that adults will pay attention to them only when they are being naughty, then they are more, rather than less, likely to be naughty, since even a smack or a telling off is preferable to being ignored! So what may be intended as a punishment by the adult, may be a reinforcement as far as the child is concerned.

7) Is it possible for rewards to decrease the behaviour being rewarded?

The answer is 'yes', when *extrinsic* (external) rewards are offered for activities which are already intrinsically rewarding, that is, activities which are rewarding in themselves. This is known as the *paradox of reward*.

Extrinsic rewards may cause people to change their explanation for their own behaviour. So, from explaining their behaviour in terms of intrinsic rewards (eg 'I enjoy it'), they may come to believe that they were motivated by the desire for the extrinsic reward, and if that is then withdrawn they may decide that the activity is no longer worth doing (Bem, 1972; Lepper and Greene, 1978).

Children's spontaneous motivation to engage in certain kinds of activities is not necessarily facilitated by the knowledge that someone else wants them to do these things. For example, Lepper et al (1973) studied children in nursery school who spent most of their time in a large room with tables set out with a variety of toys (eg puzzles, clay, picture books, letter games and beads).

The children had free choice and could spend as much time as they wished with each one. For several days before the experiment, a set of magic markers (which the children did not previously have access to in the school) was put on one of the tables. Records were kept of how long each child spent using them. The children were then taken individually into an adjoining room where they participated in one of three experimental conditions.

One group sat at a table with a set of magic markers. They were shown an impressive-looking 'good player award' and were told they could earn it if they did a good job of drawing with the markers. When they had worked on drawings for a standard length of time, they were given the award.

A second group worked with the markers for a time equal to the first group. But they were not shown the reward before they started drawing and nothing was said about a reward. At the end of the session, however, they received an award and were told they had done well.

A third group spent an equivalent time using the markers but were neither promised an award nor given one.

About two weeks later, the markers were set out in the classroom again and the researchers recorded the children's spontaneous interest in them. It was found that the first group had lost interest compared with the other two groups. Why should this have happened?

Lepper et al's explanation is that an expected reward robs an activity of its intrinsic interest value and makes it seem like a means to an end (not an end in itself).

To support this, they showed that, although the first group of children produced more pictures, the pictures were of lower quality (less detailed, thoughtful and original) than those produced by the children in the other two groups.

These results have been confirmed, using different rewards, by others.

8) Finally (and in support of Skinner), Perry and Parke (1975) found that a combination of punishment (a loud buzzer that sounded whenever eight-year-old boys touched an attractive but forbidden toy) and reward (praise for playing with an unattractive and permitted toy) was more effective than either the reward alone or the punishment alone (the latter being the least effective). It is important that the rewarded behaviour is incompatible with the punished behaviour.

SOCIAL LEARNING THEORY

We discussed in Chapter 7 some of the major differences between Social Learning (SL) Theory and Conditioning Theory, one of them being the importance of observational learning (or modelling), another being the role of cognitive factors intervening between stimulus and response. We also said that the SL Theory arose partly as an attempt to 'translate' Freud's theories, in particular his concept of identification, into learning theory terms and has been studied largely through the laboratory study of imitation (see Chapter 16).

Bandura (1977) believes that the development of self-control is heavily influenced by the *models* children observe *and* by patterns of direct reinforcement they encounter (ie the disciplinary measures used by adults).

WHAT CHARACTERISTICS OF MODELS ARE IMPORTANT FOR IMITATION?

Evidence from everyday observation tells us that it is not necessary for the model to be known, personally, to the child; and, indeed, the model may not even be a person at all. Although for most children it is parents and siblings who are the most important and frequently imitated models, dogs and cats (and other animals), cartoon super-heroes and even inanimate objects, such as cars and aeroplanes, may all be found sufficiently novel and stimulating for the child to want to reproduce their sounds, movements and actions.

Older children and adolescents choose pop stars, sporting personalities, film stars and other 'remote' people as models. So, clearly, it is not necessary that a model be a human being (although most are) nor that the child has ever actually interacted with the model. But, obviously, observation of the model is necessary for imitation to occur.

Clearly, however, this is not sufficient; if it were, children would spend all their time imitating everything they see (assuming that they can remember and are physically capable of reproducing what they see). But they do not. So who is likely to be imitated?

1)   One important factor seems to be the *appropriateness* of the model's behaviour, as perceived by the child. This was demonstrated in an experiment by Bandura et al (1961).

They found that aggressive male models were more readily imitated than aggressive female models.

One probable reason for this is to do with sex roles: it is more acceptable in Western culture for men to be aggressive as compared with women, and even by three or four years of age children are learning the dominant stereotypes that relate to sex-role differences (see Chapter 23). So aggressive male models are more likely to be imitated since this is seen by the child as more fitting or appropriate for men (in general) than for women (in general).

2)   The same experiment (Bandura et al, 1961) showed that the *relevance* of the model's behaviour, again as perceived by the child, is another important variable. Boys were more likely to imitate the aggressive male model than were girls: the greater relevance of the male model's behaviour for boys lies in the fact that boys perceive the *similarity* between themselves and the model.

3)   Therefore, *similarity* between the model and the child represents another important factor. Perception of this similarity is based upon development of the child's gender identity, ie the ability to classify itself (and others) as a boy or girl, male or female (again, see Chapter 23). The first stage of this ability is not usually reached until two-and-a-half to three years of age and certainly before that there is no preferential imitation of same-sex models.

4)   Nurturant (warm and friendly) adults are more likely to be imitated than unfriendly ones.

In an interesting and instructive demonstration of this, Yarrow et al (1973) exposed children to a model in an attempt to teach them altruism (what might be done to help others in distress). What they learned from the model would only be used in real-life situations if the model had previously established a warm, friendly relationship with them.

5)   Bandura et al (1963) shows children films of adults behaving in striking, novel, unusual or aggressive ways. Those who were rewarded for any of these kinds of behaviour were more likely to be imitated than those who were not.

6)   They also found that more *powerful* models were more rapidly imitated than less powerful ones.

7)   The *consistency* of a model's behaviour also seems to be a factor that will determine how likely they are to be imitated.

Consistency is also important outside the laboratory. Many psychologists have observed that inconsistency is one of the consistent characteristics of human behaviour and parents may be as guilty of this as anybody. So what happens when they do not practise what they preach, when they tell their children to behave one way (eg 'You must not shout') and then behave themselves in a contradictory way (eg raising their own voices while telling children not to shout)? (This is an example of how we can, inadvertently, model the very behaviour which we wish to discourage in others.)

Research suggests that talking is not enough: children tend to imitate adults exactly, in a rather 'literal' way. So 'do as I say, not as I do' (parent) becomes 'I'll say as you say and do as you do' (child). If the adult's behaviour is at odds with their preaching, then children's behaviour tends to copy this inconsistency.

LEARNING VERSUS PERFORMANCE AND THE ROLE OF REINFORCEMENT

In a study by Bandura (1965), three groups of children were shown a film of an adult who behaved aggressively towards a bobo doll. Group A (the *control group*) saw the adult kicking, pummelling and punching the bobo doll.

Group B (the *model-rewarded group*) saw the same adult performing exactly the same aggressive acts, but this time a second adult entered the scene, towards the end of the film, who complimented the model on his aggressive behaviour and gave him helpings of sweets and lemonade to restore his lost energy.

Group C (the *model-punished group*) saw the same aggressive model as the other two groups but this time a second adult came on at the end of the film and scolded the model and warned him not to be aggressive again.

Thus, the only difference between the three groups was the *consequences* of the model's behaviour: for group A nothing happened (neither reward nor punishment), for group B the model was rewarded, and for group C the model was punished.

After the film, all the children (one by one) went into a playroom which contained a great number of toys, many of which had not been seen in the film, but which included a bobo doll and a mallet. They were left for 10 minutes in order to see how many acts of imitative aggression each performed (Fig. 27.1). As might be expected, group C children showed significantly less imitative aggression than those in the other two groups.

However, there was no difference between groups A and B. According to the principle of vicarious reinforcement, group B children, who had seen the model rewarded, should have shown much more imitative aggression than group A children, who saw the model neither rewarded nor punished. So it appears that seeing someone else being reinforced is much less powerful an influence than seeing someone else being punished.

But more significant still are the findings from a second stage of the experiment. Each child (from all three groups) was asked to reproduce as much as possible of the model's behaviour and was directly rewarded for each act of imitative aggression. Under these conditions, there was no difference between any of the three groups—they all showed the same high level of imitative aggression. What this means, of course, is that the children in the model-punished group had attended to, and remembered,

Figure 27.1 *After watching films of an aggressive model who punched, pummelled and hurled a bobo doll, these children spontaneously imitated the model's aggression*

the model's behaviour (ie learned from the model) to the same extent as those in the other two groups; however, this had not been manifested in their behaviour at first. So the original difference between group C and the other two groups was one of *performance* (imitation) and *not* one of *learning* (acquisition).

Thus, rewarding the child's performance was more crucial than whether or not the model had been rewarded. Reinforcing the child for imitating the model merely brought out what the child had already learned through earlier observation of the model—it was *not* the agent or cause of the original learning (as Skinner would maintain).

This means that it is possible for learning to occur but not actually to show up in the child's overt behaviour at the time. The experiment therefore demonstrated the crucial distinction between learning and performance. For learning to occur, mere *exposure* to the model is sufficient, but whether this learning actually reveals itself in the child's behaviour depends upon factors such as the consequences of the behaviour (both for the model and the child), the child's anticipation of reward or punishment, whether the child is instructed or encouraged to produce the model's behaviour and so on.

It would appear, then, that children may *learn* equally from all kinds of models (male or female, nurturant or unfriendly, rewarded or punished and so on) but are more likely to *imitate* models who possess certain characteristics.

EVALUATION OF EXPERIMENTAL STUDIES OF IMITATION

Bronfenbrenner (1973) has been one of the most outspoken critics of laboratory studies of imitation. He points out that the basic situation involves the child and an adult model, which is a rather limited social situation and is treated as if it existed in isolation from all other social relationships. Also, there is no actual interaction between the child and the model at any point; certainly, the child has no chance to influence the model in any way.

Finally, the model and the child are complete strangers and the model is often seen on film and not in the flesh at all. This, of course, is quite unlike 'normal' modelling which takes place within the family.

Bandura would probably reply that television, movie and sporting stars are often important models and are also complete strangers, at least in the sense that there is no interpersonal contact between the child and the model (see Chapter 16).

This last point can be considered in terms of a distinction made by Danziger (1971) between two kinds of models, namely personal and positional models. A *personal model* is imitated because of his/her personal qualities or characteristics, while a *positional model* is imitated because of the social role that he/she represents (eg gender, age, occupation).

In the kind of laboratory experiment that Bandura and his colleagues have conducted, a male model represents not only himself but men in general. So, not surprisingly, the aggressive behaviour of a male model is more readily imitated than that of a female model. (We have already discussed this as an example of the appropriateness factor.) Taking over aggressiveness from a female model would involve a more personal kind of imitation and is much less likely to occur in the laboratory where there is no familiarity with the model as a person.

Familiarity, based on previous interaction with the model, may be crucial for personal modelling but clearly is not for positional modelling, where the child need only be familiar with the social role in general (for example, in the case of aggressive behaviour, the child has to have some knowledge of the sex-role stereotype which maintains that, among other things, it is appropriate for men to be aggressive but not for women).

Clearly, personal modelling is much more closely related to the process of *identification* than it is to imitation.

IMITATION AND IDENTIFICATION

An interesting finding reported by Baer and Sherman (1964) is that when children are directly rewarded for imitating a model's behaviour, imitation often generalizes to other aspects of the model's behaviour; such *generalized imitation* may play an important part in the learning processes included under the concept of identification. This generalized (spontaneous) imitation may be seen as an important area of overlap between the two concepts of imitation and identification.

The major similarities and differences between imitation and identification are summarized in Table 27.2.

Table 27.2 The major similarities and differences between imitation and identification

Similarities between imitation and identification
1. They are both types of learning.
2. They both involve the reproduction of somebody else's behaviour (the model).
3. They are both examples of observational learning.

Differences	
Imitation	*Identification*
1. Involves fairly specific and overt aspects of the model's behaviour	1. Involves the child coming to think, feel and act as if it were the model, and so is not confined to overt behaviour but includes the model's attitudes, motives, values, idiosyncrasies, tastes etc
2. Usually occurs soon after observation of the model's behaviour (minutes or hours rather than days or weeks)	2. Is a process which takes place over an extended period of time, usually years
3. Does not depend upon any prior interaction or familiarity with the model, who may be a total stranger and who need not even be a person (eg a cartoon character)	3. Depends upon the existence of a personal relationship between the child and the model, based upon previous interaction. The relationship often takes the form of a strong emotional involvement between them (eg parent and child)
4. Involves *positional modelling*. The emphasis is on *what* is being imitated, that is, the behaviour itself rather than the model as a person. What the model represents is a social role (eg men in general)	4. Involves *personal modelling*. The emphasis is on *who* is being identified with, that is, the model as a unique individual. Who the model is, is what the child is trying to be
5. May be conscious or unconscious	5. By definition, is an unconscious process

SL theory represents an S–O–R approach to learning, where 'O' stands for 'organism' and acknowledges the role of cognitive and other intervening variables (between stimulus and response). Identification is seen as one of these intervening variables which:

> ... very early in life enables the child to learn without the parents having to teach and which creates a self-reinforcing mechanism that competes effectively in some instances with external sources of reinforcement. (Sears et al, 1965)

Sears et al (1965) derived a series of hypotheses about how different sorts of parents might influence children through the models they provide and they tested these through the study of child-rearing practices. We discussed some of these when discussing Freud's theory earlier in the chapter (see p. 807).

Figure 27.2 Walter Mischel

ROLE OF COGNITIVE VARIABLES

In Chapter 7, we considered some of the important cognitive factors involved in observational learning (attention, memory, etc.). In this chapter we have also seen the importance of the child's perception of the model and how the model's behaviour is interpreted by the child.

Mischel (1973) (Fig. 27.2) describes five kinds of cognitive variables which he called *person variables*, which are:

(a) *Competencies.* Intellectual abilities, social skills, physical skills and other special abilities.

(b) *Cognitive strategies.* Habitual ways of selectively attending to information and organizing it into meaningful categories.

(c) *Expectancies.* About the consequences of different behaviours, about the meaning of different stimuli and about the efficacy of one's own behaviour.

(d) *Subjective outcome variables.* The value we place on the expected outcome or consequences of our behaviour. For example, what may be a punishment for one child may actually be reinforcing for another (as in the attention-seeking child for whom a smack represents the giving of attention). So rewards and punishments cannot be 'objectively' defined, ie without taking into account the individual concerned.

(e) *Self-regulatory systems and plans.* Self-imposed standards or rules which people adopt for regulating their own behaviour.

This last person variable relates to an important distinction that SL theorists make between *external* and *internal reinforcement* and *punishment* (for Skinner, they are external only; see Fig. 27.3).

Figure 27.3 Different sources of reinforcement and punishment as seen by Social Learning Theory

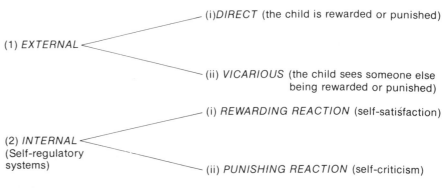

(1) EXTERNAL
  — (i)DIRECT (the child is rewarded or punished)
  — (ii) VICARIOUS (the child sees someone else being rewarded or punished)

(2) INTERNAL (Self-regulatory systems)
  — (i) REWARDING REACTION (self-satisfaction)
  — (ii) PUNISHING REACTION (self-criticism)

Internal reinforcement and punishment can be seen as the SL theory equivalent of Freud's superego (ego-ideal and conscience respectively). Both theories agree that, eventually, the child no longer needs an outside agency (parents or other adults) to administer rewards and punishments—the child can reward itself (through feelings of pride) and punish itself (through guilt).

Just as both parts of the superego develop through identification, so, as you might expect, self-reinforcement and self-punishment are acquired through observation and imitation of the parents' rewards and punishments. The child's own actions, previously rewarded or punished by the parents, can be reinforced or punished when performed alone, by the child's own *imitative self-approval* ('good girl') and *imitative self-disapproval* ('bad boy').

We set our own standards of conduct and evaluate or respond to our behaviour in the light of these. External reinforcement may only be effective when it is consistent with self-reinforcement, that is, when society approves behaviour which the individual already values highly.

This idea of self-regulation is very similar to that of conscience as an internal judge or policeman, making sure that we 'keep to the straight and narrow'. The ability to reward or punish oneself is an important kind of cognitive or mediating variable.

Whatever the advantages of SL theory compared with orthodox learning theory, one limitation of both approaches is the fact that they say nothing about moral *progress*. Although SL theorists accept that children learn more as they get older and, in that sense, become 'more' moral, they do not see development as having certain laws of its own and so do not see children as changing in similar ways as they get older—the changes that occur are quantitative rather than qualitative.

Again, although SL theorists take cognitive factors (including cognitive development) into account, they represent but one set of factors amongst several (including the situation itself) which determine the child's moral behaviour, and it is still, primarily, behaviour which is of interest.

The Cognitive–Developmental Approach

This fourth and final major approach is the only one which focuses on the cognitive aspect of morality and, hence, on *moral development* as such, since moral development and overall cognitive development go very much hand in hand. The cognitive–developmental approach, therefore, is the only one which does offer a *progressive* view of morality: disagreeing with Freud, it sees morality as developing gradually during childhood and adolescence, into adulthood, and disagreeing with the Learning Theory and SL Theory approaches, it maintains that there are *stages* of moral development which, like all developmental stages, are qualitatively different (different in kind).

PIAGET'S THEORY

Just as Piaget's theory of cognitive development is concerned with how the child's knowledge and understanding change with age, so his theory of moral development is concerned with how the child's moral knowledge and understanding change with age. More specifically, in the *Moral Judgement of the Child* (1932), Piaget investigated: (i) the child's ideas about the rules of the game of marbles; (ii) the child's moral judgements; and (iii) the child's conception of punishment and justice:

> Children's games constitute the most admirable social institutions. The game of marbles, for instance, as played by boys, contains an extremely complex system of rules, that is to say, a code of laws, a jurisprudence of its own ... All morality consists in a system of rules, and the essence of all morality is to be sought for in the respect which the individual acquires for these rules. (Piaget, 1932)

1) So, for Piaget, morality is any system of rules which governs interaction between people, and that includes the game of marbles. By

studying how moral knowledge is acquired in games, he believed he could discover how children's moral knowledge in general develops.

He also thought that by studying rules in the context of a game he could by-pass the influence of adult teaching and study the child's spontaneous thought directly; this way, he could observe how the child's conception of rules related to its conformity to those rules.

He played the game with a child and pretended not to know the rules. He asked the child to explain them to him and in the course of the game he probed the child's understanding by asking questions such as: 'Where do rules come from?', 'Who made them?' and, 'Can we change them?'.

The idea was to pose the child a problem which it had not had to face before and so throw the child on its own resources. What were his findings?

Children of five to about nine years tended to believe that rules came from the semi-mystical authority of older children, adults, or even God; they are sacred and inviolable and have always existed in their present form and cannot be changed in any way. But in their actual play, children unashamedly bent the rules to suit themselves and saw nothing contradictory in the idea of both players winning.

Children of ten years and over understood that the rules are invented by children themselves, so that they can be changed. However, as rules are needed to make a game possible, and to prevent quarrelling and to ensure fair play, they can only be changed if all the players agree to the change. At the same time, the older children kept meticulously to the rules, becoming 'lawyers' of the game, discussing the finer points and the implications of any changes that might be made:

> ... the rule of a game appears to the child no longer as an external law, sacred insofar as it has been laid down by adults, but as the outcome of a free decision and worthy of respect in the measure that it has enlisted mutual consent. (Piaget, 1932)

2) To assess changes in the child's *moral judgements*, Piaget told children pairs of hypothetical stories about children who tell lies or steal or break something. For example:

> A little boy called John is in his room. He is called to dinner. He goes into the dining room. But behind the door there is a chair and on the chair there is a tray with fifteen cups on it. John couldn't have known that there was all this behind the door. He goes in, the door knocks against the tray, bang go the fifteen cups, and they all get broken.

And:

> Once there was a little boy called Henry. One day, when his mother was out, he tried to get some jam out of the cupboard. He climbed up onto a chair and stretched out his arm. But the jam was too high up and he couldn't reach it and have any. But while he was trying to get it he knocked over a cup. The cup fell down and broke.

or:

> There was once a little girl who was called Marie. She wanted to give her mother a nice surprise and cut out a piece of sewing for her. But she didn't know how to use the scissors properly and cut a big hole in her dress.

And:

> A little girl called Margaret went and took her mother's scissors one day when her mother was out. She played with them for a bit. Then, as she didn't know how to use them properly, she made a little hole in her dress.

The child is asked 'who is naughtier?' and 'who should be punished more?'.

Piaget was interested in the *reasons* the children gave for their answers, rather than the answers themselves. Typically, five- to nine-year-olds said that John or Marie were naughtier, because John broke fifteen cups (compared with Henry's one) and Marie made a big hole in her dress (compared with Margaret's little one). Although able to distinguish between intentional and unintentional actions, younger children based their judgement on the *severity of the outcome*, the sheer amount of damage done (*objective* or *external responsibility*).

Children of ten years and over, on the other hand, chose Henry and Margaret, because they were both doing something they should not have been and, although the damage done was not deliberate in either case, older children based their judgement on the motive or intention behind the act that resulted in the damage (*internal responsibility*).

What happens when children are asked to make a judgement between a small amount of deliberate damage and a large amount of accidental damage?

This situation was studied by Armsby (1971), who found that even six-year-olds say that a small amount of deliberate damage is naughtier. However, the answers depend partly on the extent and nature of the damage. For example, if the choice is between the deliberate breakage of a cup and the accidental damage of a television set, 40 per cent of six-year-olds and under 10 per cent of ten-year-olds said the latter was more deserving of punishment. This suggests that young children *can* understand intention (in the sense of deliberate naughtiness) and that they are aware that damage to valued objects is something to be avoided, but also that they have problems weighing up their *relative* importance. As we get older, it becomes easier to weigh up the *relative importance* of intentions and the damage done, as it does to infer what others' intentions actually are.

For example, according to Karniol (1978) and Keasey (1978), for all children aged six and over, bad intended acts are morally worse than accidents, *regardless* of the amount of damage done. But six- and seven-year-olds (not older children) base their moral judgement on the amount of damage when the actor's intentions are *good*. This implies that: (i) children learn about the importance of *bad* intentions before good ones; and (ii) for young children the consequences of an act determine its moral value *either* when the actor's intentions are positive *or* when the damage is accidental.

A similar pattern of results is found when the consequences involve parents' approval or disapproval. Constanzo et al (1973), for example, read stories to six-, eight- and ten-year-olds about a boy who emptied a box of toys on the floor *either* so he could sort them out (good motive/intention) *or* to make a mess (bad intention). His mother, not knowing his intentions, entered the room and either approved or disapproved. When she *disapproved*, the six-year-olds (but *not* the others) judged him naughty *regardless* of his actual intention. Why?

Karniol (1978) suggests that parents are particularly likely to punish on the basis of how much damage is done, which teaches children that the amount of *damage* and the amount of *wrong-doing* are connected:

> Additionally, parents tend to be more concerned with inhibiting undesirable behaviour, than with promoting commendable behaviour and are, therefore, more likely to punish than reward. Since ill-intended acts are likely to lead to punishment and well-intended acts are less likely to be rewarded, children will have greater experience with the social consequences of ill-intentional acts than with . . . well-intentional acts. (Karniol, 1978)

Nelson (1980) found that even three-year-olds can make judgements about intentions regardless of consequences *if* the information about intentions is made explicit. In Piaget's stories, this information was *not* made explicit while the consequences were. Nelson found that in this kind of story three-year-olds assume that actors who bring about negative consequences must have had negative motives. In this way they are less proficient than older children at discriminating intentions from consequences and using these separate pieces of information to make moral judgements.

Leon (1982) looked at how children's moral judgements are influenced by story-characters giving a rationale following certain accidental or intentional behaviour: six- and seven-year-olds seem to *add together* the intention and damage dimensions (one does not replace the other) but the rationale seems to be *more* important than either.

All of these studies suggest that the child's understanding of intention is much more complex than Piaget believed.

What do children understand by a *lie*? Piaget found that an unintentional falsehood which has serious consequences is judged as naughtier by younger children than a deliberate lie that does not. This too suggests the difficulty that younger children have in weighing up the relative importance of intention, on the one hand, and damage or consequences on the other.

For younger children, the seriousness of a lie is measured by the degree of literal departure from the truth. So, for example, a wild and totally unconvincing fantasy is worse than a realistic and successful deceit. A child who claims to have seen a 'dog as big as an elephant' is naughtier than one who claims to have seen a 'dog as big as a horse' (since elephants are bigger than horses). For the younger child, lies are wrong because they are punished by adults and lying to adults is worse than lying to other children. For the older child, lying is wrong because it betrays the trust without which fruitful and worthwhile social interaction is impossible; lying to adults is not necessarily worse than lying to one's peers.

3) The young child feels the need for misdeeds to be punished in some way, but the form of the punishment can be quite arbitrary. What matters is that people should pay for their crime with some kind of suffering and, generally, the greater suffering the better (Piaget called this *expiatory punishment*, 'expiatory' meaning 'making amends for' or 'paying the penalty of'). Punishment is decreed by authority and is accepted as just because of its source. So, for example, it is acceptable for a whole class of children to be punished for the misdeed of a single child

if the latter does not own up and the others refuse to identify the offender.

A misfortune that closely follows some misdeed that has gone undetected or unpunished is often construed as a punishment, as if natural forces are 'in league' with people in authority to ensure that the disobedient suffer in the end (this is known as *immanent justice*, 'immanent' meaning 'inherent'). So, if a child tells a lie and gets away with it then later trips and breaks an arm, this is taken by the younger child as a punishment, almost as if God (or some equivalent force) were keeping a constant eye on one's deeds. (Compare this with the concept of 'conscience'.) The older child, by contrast, sees punishment as bringing home to the offender the nature of the offence and as a deterrent from future misdeeds. Also the 'punishment should fit the crime'. For example, if one child takes another's sweets, the former should be deprived of his/her sweets or should make it up to the victim in some other appropriate way (the principle of *reciprocity*). There is currently a trend in Britain, following a lead from the USA, whereby criminals make amends for their crimes in a fairly literal way, by, for example, repairing damage to property, paying for stolen or damaged goods, instead of going to prison. (Part of the philosophy behind 'community service' is a 'giving back' to society.) Some older children go further and say that punishment should take into account the circumstances and needs of the offender (a mild punishment for one person may be severe for another) and some believe that no punishment may be necessary at all if the offender can be reformed without it.

Justice is no longer tied to authority, there is less belief in immanent justice, and punishing innocent persons for the misdeeds of only one is now thought to always be wrong.

Summary of Piaget's Theory

The morality of the five- to nine/ten-year-old is *heteronomous* ('being subject to another's laws or rules') and that of the child of ten and over is *autonomous* ('being subject to one's own laws or rules').

The younger child's moral knowledge and understanding are objective and absolute: laws, rules, punishment, right and wrong, etc. exist almost as 'things'. They emanate from external sources and either exist or do not exist, and obedience is a virtue and is good in itself (*moral realism*).

The older child, however, gradually comes to realize that morality is not a matter of obeying external authorities but of evolving and agreeing about principles for achieving mutually agreed and valued ends, ie moral rules grow out of human relationships and we must respect people's differing points of view (*moral relativism*).

However, the moral thinking of any child is always a mixture of heteronomous morality/moral reality and autonomous morality/moral relativism—it is a matter of which one predominates and they are not mutually exclusive. Also, many elements of the latter can be detected in adults' moral thinking (see the discussion of errors in the Attribution Process in Chapter 17).

How did Piaget account for the shift from heteronomous to autonomous morality?

1)   It happens partly because of the move from egocentric to operational thought (see Chapter 25), which enables the child to see things from the point of view of others. According to Piaget, remember, this decline of egocentrism usually happens at around seven years, so cognitive development seems to be a *necessary* condition for moral development, but not a sufficient condition; moral development lags at least a year or two behind cognitive development and the latter is no guarantee of the former. So what else is involved?

2)   There is also a progressive change in social relationships from *unilateral* respect (ie unconditional, absolute and one-way obedience to parents and other adults) to *mutual* respect, within the peer group, where disagreements and disputes between equals have to be negotiated and resolved and a compromise reached. Although they must appear in this order, mutual respect can be delayed or prevented, either by slow cognitive development or by social experience in which unilateral respect predominates. Although adults may be capable of operational thinking, when their relationships have been, and still are, mainly unilateral, they will show marked traces of moral realism.

Is there any evidence to support Piaget?

There is quite a lot of cross-cultural support for the existence of general age trends as Piaget described them (ie a general shift from heteronomous to autonomous morality at about nine or ten years). There is also some evidence to support the relationship between intelligence and the maturity of moral judgement: the more intelligent the child, the more mature its moral judgement is likely to be, whether an IQ test or a Piaget-type test is used.

But as to *why* the shift from one type of morality to the other occurs, the evidence is less encouraging for Piaget.

Kohlberg (1963) concluded that, overall, the evidence regarding the association between heteronomous morality and unilateral respect on the one hand, and autonomous morality and mutual respect on the other, is very inconclusive.

According to Wright (1971), Piaget's theory is really intended to explain how *practical* morality develops, ie how we conceive those situations in which we are actively involved and which demands a moral response, a moral decision. Yet the evidence which Piaget drew on were samples of the child's *theoretical* morality, ie how an individual thinks about moral problems, real and hypothetical, one's own and others', when not immediately or directly involved. So how are the two related?

According to Piaget, they are related via the concept of *conscious realization*—theory is the conscious realization of the moral principles on which we actually operate, ie we can already *do* things by the time we come to think about them and reflect on them. (A good example is the fact that a child learns to talk according to the rules of grammar long before the realization that there are such things as grammatical rules—as we saw in Chapter 26.)

It follows that there is always a time-lag between practical and theoretical morality, a delay before a developmental change at the practical level is registered at the theoretical level; this implies that theoretical morality is shaped by practical morality (and not the other way round). It follows that adult theorizing (tuition) will *not* affect the child's practical morality. At best, it can only help theoretical morality to catch up with practical morality (Wright, 1971).

KOHLBERG'S THEORY

The other major cognitive-developmental theorist is Lawrence Kohlberg, who in 1955 began to redefine and elaborate Piaget's theory, both longitudinally and cross-sectionally. He has also studied moral development right through to middle age.

Kohlberg was critical of both the concept of a superego or conscience and of the Learning Theory and SL Theory approaches to morality. He believed that the learning theory approach, in particular (which emphasizes overt behaviour) largely ignores or underplays the importance of the way the individual construes the situation and thinks about the issues raised by it, as well as how these cognitive processes change with age. SL Theory also fails to show developmental changes which even common sense suggests do, in fact, occur.

Kohlberg also believes that research has failed to show any consistent relationship between different patterns of child-rearing and different kinds of moral behaviour. The only way to find any underlying consistency in an individual's moral behaviour and any evidence of developmental trends, Kohlberg believes, is to study the philosophy, logic or reasoning implicit in the cognitive structure which underlies both an individual's thinking and acting (corresponding to Piaget's theoretical and practical morality, respectively). He believes that only the cognitive–developmental approach provides a satisfactory *conceptual* integration of such phenomena as resistance to temptation, pro-social behaviour and so on.

The way Kohlberg has studied moral development is to present subjects with moral dilemmas (nine in all), each involving a conflict between two (or more) moral principles and where the subject has to choose between them. Like Piaget, he is interested not in the actual judgement or choice itself but in the reasons the subject gives for making the choice—*how* people think rather than *what* they think. The reasons represent the structure of the judgement and centre around ten universal moral issues or values, namely: (i) punishment; (ii) property; (iii) law; (iv) roles and concerns of affection; (v) roles and concerns of authority; (vi) life; (vii) liberty; (viii) distributive justice; (ix) truth; and (x) sex.

The most famous of the Kohlberg dilemmas is the one involving Heinz:

> In Europe, a woman was dying from cancer. One drug might save her, a form of radium that a druggist in the same town had recently discovered. The druggist was charging 2000 dollars, ten times what the drug cost him to make. The sick woman's husband, Heinz, went to everyone he knew to borrow the money, but he could only get together about half of what it cost. He told the druggist that his wife was dying and asked him to sell it cheaper or let him pay later. But the druggist said 'No'. The husband got desperate and broke into the man's store to steal the drug for his wife.

Should Heinz have done it? Why? Was it actually right or wrong? Why?
What if he didn't love his wife—would that change anything?
Is it a husband's duty to steal the drug for his wife if he can get it no other way?

Would a good husband do it?

Did the druggist have the right to charge that much where there is no law actually setting a price limit? Why?

What if the dying person were a stranger? Should he have stolen the drug anyway?

Based on the logic or reasoning revealed by their answers, subjects are classified according to their *level* of moral development (ie which of the six stages their answers best illustrate; see Table 27.3). Two people at the same level and stage could still give two opposing answers: one could say 'Yes, Heinz should have stolen the drug', the other could say 'No, Heinz should not have stolen it'. Remember, it is the underlying *reasons* that determine how mature is a person's moral development.

Table 27.3 Kohlberg's three levels (six stages) of moral development	**Level 1: Pre-Conventional**	*Stage 1 (Punishment and Obedience Orientation)* What is right and wrong is determined by what is punishable and what is not—if stealing is wrong it is because authority figures say so and because they will punish stealing ('might makes right'). So moral action is essentially the avoidance of punishment; things are not right or wrong, good or bad, in themselves
		Stage 2 (Instrumental–Relativist Orientation) What is right and wrong, good and bad, is now determined by what brings reward and what people want (rather than the more negative avoidance of punishment). Other people's needs and wants come into the picture but only in a reciprocal sense ('You scratch my back, I'll scratch yours')
	Level 2: Conventional	*Stage 3 (Interpersonal Concordance or 'Good boy—nice girl' Orientation)* Good behaviour is whatever pleases others, and being moral is being 'a good person in your own eyes and those of others'. There is emphasis on conformity to stereotyped images of 'majority' or 'natural' behaviour—what the majority thinks is right is right by definition. Intentions begin to be taken into account too. But primarily, behaving morally is pleasing and helping others and doing what they approve of
		Stage 4 ('Law and Order' Orientation) Being good now comes to mean 'doing one's duty'—showing respect for authority and maintaining the social order (status quo) for its own sake. Concern for the common good has gone beyond the stage 3 concern for the good of the family—society protects the rights of individuals and so society must be protected by the individual. Laws are automatically and unquestionably accepted and obeyed
	Level 3: Post-Conventional	*Stage 5 (Social Contract–Legalistic Orientation)* Apart from what is constitutionally or democratically agreed upon, what is right is a matter of personal 'values' and 'opinions'. Consequently, there is emphasis on the 'legal point of view'—since laws are established by mutual agreement, they can be changed by the same democratic process.

> Although laws and rules should be respected, since they protect the rights of the individual as well as those of society as a whole, individual rights can sometimes supersede these laws if they become too destructive or restrictive. The law should *not* be obeyed at all costs, eg life is more 'sacred' than any principle, legal or otherwise

> *Stage 6 (Universal–Ethical Principle Orientation)*
> Moral action is determined by our inner conscience and may or may not be in accord with public opinion or society's laws. What is right or wrong is based upon self-chosen, ethical principles which we arrive at through individual reflection—they are not laid down by society as such. The principles are abstract and universal, such as Justice, Equality, the sacredness of human life and respect for the dignity of human beings as individuals, and only by acting in accordance with them do we ultimately attain full responsibility for our actions

The central conflict in the Heinz dilemma is between preserving life and upholding the law. Others involve: (i) obeying authority figures and the value of social contract (a promise); and (ii) upholding the law and extenuating circumstances.

Let us see how Kohlberg's stages would apply to a particular moral dilemma (*not* one of Kohlberg's):

> John is seven and has recently been beaten up by an older boy who attends his brother Alan's school. Alan is a very protective older brother and they are very close; Alan decides to avenge John's victimization and to beat up the older boy. But his parents strongly disapprove of physical aggression and he could get into serious trouble with them (as well as the school authorities). One day, after school, Alan waited for the boy and gave him a thorough beating.

Should he have done it? Why?

In Table 27.4 are some typical pro and con answers at each of the six stages. Can you identify the central conflict involved?

PRO	CON
Stage 1	
It is not really bad to beat him up—so long as he doesn't do him any serious injury. After all, he is only doing what the boy did to John and no one else need find out. He might be called a coward if he didn't do it	You can't go round beating people up—he might cause him serious injury. If he gets caught he'll be in real trouble—he could be expelled. Even if he's not caught he'll always be afraid of getting beaten up himself or of John being victimized again
Stage 2	
If he wants to show he really cares for John and can look after him then he should have beaten the boy up. Wouldn't the punishment be worth it	The boy must have had his reasons for beating up John—perhaps he was provoked. What good would it do John anyway? Perhaps he'd prefer

Table 27.4 Responses to a moral dilemma at each of Kohlberg's six stages

PRO	CON
if you've proved you can play 'big brother'?	Alan to do nothing

Stage 3

Physical violence is bad but the whole situation is a bad one. He's doing what is natural for a good older brother. You can't blame him for doing something out of caring for and wanting to protect his younger brother. He would have been blamed for not doing it	If your younger brother gets beaten up, you can't blame yourself for it. Alan showed he cared by *wanting* to beat up the boy—it's the older boy who is the guilty party, not Alan. Alan couldn't have prevented what happened to John and if he gets expelled, this will bring disgrace on the whole family

Stage 4

The older boy can't get away with bullying younger boys. So it is Alan's duty to look after John and he would always reproach himself for not doing so. But nor can Alan go round beating up people and he must accept the consequences of his actions, even if this means being expelled. Two wrongs don't make it right	It is natural for Alan to want to avenge John but it is always wrong to be violent. You have to follow the rules regardless of your feelings or special circumstances

Stage 5

Before you say what Alan did was wrong, you must consider the whole situation. Of course, if an adult were to commit the same act of violence as Alan, they could be prosecuted for assault—the law is quite clear. But it would be quite reasonable for anyone in Alan's situation to do what he did. People will respect him for what he did	Alan would feel better, and so would John, if the culprit was punished for what he did. but it's not Alan's place to do the punishing—the ends don't justify the means. You can't say categorically it's wrong but even in the circumstances you can't (fully) justify it either. Alan might reproach himself later for acting impulsively

Stage 6

When you have to choose between acting in a caring and protective way towards someone close to you and behaving in a violent way towards a person who aggressed against them, the higher principle of caring and protecting makes it morally right to behave violently—so the end justifies the means. Alan had to choose between his own standards of conscience and the dictates of external (social) rules	The only correct course of action is one that is 'right' for all the parties concerned. Alan's behaviour is the same as the behaviour he is avenging. Others might understand Alan's behaviour but he might condemn himself later on. Alan's behaviour should be determined by what he thinks an 'ideally just person' would do in the situation

Cognitive and Moral Development

Like Piaget, Kohlberg believes that cognitive development is a necessary, but not a sufficient, condition of moral development, ie cognitive development does not guarantee a particular level of moral development.

Another way of expressing this relationship is to say that cognitive development sets a limit on maturity of moral reasoning and usually moral development lags behind cognitive development. Table 27.5 shows the relationship between these two aspects of development.

When discussing cognitive development in Chapter 25, we noted that many adults do not attain formal operations (about 50 per cent in fact) and if this is a necessary condition for reaching the post-conventional level of moral development (stages 5 and 6), then it is not surprising that only about 10 per cent (Kohlberg, 1975) to 15 per cent (Colby et al, 1983) of adults attain the highest level of moral reasoning (according to the latter, not before their mid-30s).

KOHLBERG'S THEORY OF MORAL DEVELOPMENT	AGE–GROUP INCLUDED WITHIN KOHLBERG'S LEVELS	STAGE OF COGNITIVE DEVELOPMENT (PIAGET)	STAGE OF MORAL DEVELOPMENT (PIAGET)
1. Pre-conventional level (Stages 1 and 2)	Most 9-year-olds and below Some over 9	Pre-operational (2 to 7 years)	Heteronomous (5 to 8 or 9 years)
2. Conventional level (Stages 3 and 4)	Most adolescents and adults	Concrete operational (7 to 11 years)	Heteronomous (eg respect for the law and authority figures) *plus* Autonomous (eg taking intentions into account)
3. Post-conventional level (Stages 5 and 6)	10–15 per cent of adults not before mid-30s	Formal operational (11 years plus)	Autonomous (10 years and above)

Table 27.5 The relationship between Kohlberg's and Piaget's theories of moral development and Piaget's stages of cognitive development

What Evidence is there to Support Kohlberg?

In 1957, Kohlberg began a twenty-year longitudinal study of 58 boys in the Chicago area, both working class and middle class. They were initially interviewed when aged ten and sixteen years, then at three-yearly intervals up to age 30–36; more than half of their thinking was always at the same stage and the rest was at the next adjacent stage (up or down). The stages were confirmed up to stage 4 (Colby et al, 1983).

Kohlberg also conducted a small, six-year longitudinal study of Turkish village and city boys of the same age which confirmed the Chicago findings. On every re-test, individuals were either at the same stage as three years earlier or had moved up.

Rest (1983) in a twenty-year longitudinal study of men from early adolescence to their mid-thirties, found that the stages do occur in the order Kohlberg described, but change is very gradual. Over the twenty-year period, these men changed, on average, less than two stages.

Researchers, including Kohlberg himself, have failed to uncover any stage 6 reasoning in the responses of 'ordinary' subjects and considerably less stage 5 reasoning then Kohlberg originally reported. In 1978, he reviewed his theory and concluded that there may not after all be a separate sixth stage—his studies of American and Turkish young people provided no evidence for it. It seems that universal ethical principles guide the reasoning of only a few, very exceptional individuals, such as Martin Luther King, who devote their lives to humanistic causes.

Only 10–15 per cent of adults show level 3 reasoning as we have seen and according to Atkinson et al (1990), it cannot be considered part of the normal or expected course of development but a philosophical ideal. However, Colby et al (1983) argue that the dilemmas and interviewing techniques are unable to differentiate between stages 5 and 6 and do not rule out the possibility that stage 6 may still exist as a 'natural psychological stage in the moral developmental sequence'.

What determines movement from one stage to the next?

We have already noted that *cognitive development* is a *necessary* condition for moral development, and that educational and other socio-economic factors can influence the rate of moral development and how far it will actually progress. Kohlberg also believes that new and challenging social experience is important.

As cognitive development is partly under the control of maturation, it follows that moral development is too and, in this sense, morality also has biological roots. This does not mean that specific kinds of moral behaviour or thinking are innate, or that morality is not a cultural phenomenon transmitted across generations, but only that the child is biologically predisposed to acquire this form of thinking in relation to its social experience. (You can compare this with the child's predisposition to acquire language; the actual language the child learns is, of course, the one it is exposed to.)

Compared with Piaget, Kohlberg puts more emphasis on maturation as a determinant of movement through the stages.

He describes children as 'moral philosophers' who develop moral standards of their own. These do not necessarily reflect those of their parents or peers but emerge from cognitive interaction between the child and the social environment. Movement from one stage to the next involves an internal cognitive re-organization rather than a simple acquisition of moral concepts prevalent in the culture.

Evaluation of Kohlberg's Theory

1)   Some critics have pointed to the dilemma stories themselves, saying they are unfamiliar to most subjects—children might show more mature reasoning if asked about issues relevant to their day-to-day experience. They are also *hypothetical* and do not involve any serious personal consequences. Would subjects necessarily reason at the same level if they had to think about practical moral issues that could have negative implications for themselves?

Sobesky (1983) presented the Heinz dilemma to high school and college students who were told either that the consequences of stealing the drug were severe (Heinz would definitely be caught and sent to prison) or mild (Heinz could take such a small amount it would not be missed). They were asked to imagine themselves in Heinz's position and describe what they would do and why. In the severe condition, subjects were less likely to advocate stealing and levels of reasoning were lower.

2) Underlying the dilemmas is what is called *Ethical Rule Theory*, which places universal principles at the centre of moral judgement—for Kohlberg *justice* is the fundamental principle underlying moral development. This theory assumes that one must have a moral rule in order to make a justified moral judgement and this rule is needed for identifying the relevant facts of a case *before* the judgement is made.

An alternative view is *Ethical Act Theory*—relevant facts may be identified *without* moral rules and may over-ride moral generalizations. Moral rules are 'summaries' to which there may be exceptions and so morality is situation-specific.

For example, Rosen (1980) asks us to suppose that Heinz's wife has contemplated suicide for years and wants to die with dignity now. What if Heinz wants to keep her alive because they live off interest from a trust fund in her name? Again, suppose the druggist is the wife's brother, knows her wishes and prices the drug so that Heinz will not be able to afford it.

Do these details of the case change it from a moral point of view? Meadows, for one, thinks it does:

> . . . Moral dilemmas are real problems, faced by people in a real setting. It is no test of an ethical theory, or of the moral reasoning of people . . . to pose artifical problems. The problems . . . are not artificial primarily because they are fictional. They are artificial because they do not represent realistic situations with all their complexity. Perhaps we should let poets and the novelists describe the moral problems for the tests and not philosophers and psychologists. The problems would be more difficult to solve, but at least they would be relevant to the real problems that human beings have. (Meadows, 1986)

3) Some critics believe that Kohlberg has over-emphasized justice to the exclusion of other aspects of morality.

Why should *justice* be elevated to the most important theme of moral development? What about the principle of caring for others, sympathy, courage, integrity, autonomy (Peters, 1974; Gilligan, 1977)?

There is evidence that even very young children are aware of and often behave sympathetically towards other peoples' feelings; a model of moral development focusing on sensitivity to others would be much more positive about young children than Kohlberg's justice model (Meadows, 1986).

4) It would also reverse the *sexist bias* of Kohlberg's theory. According to Gilligan (1977, 1982), the essence of morality for women is not the same as for men. Kohlberg's stages are fundamentally flawed because they are based on a *male* concept of morality.

The very traits which have traditionally defined 'goodness' for women (ie their care for, sensitivity to others, responsibility towards others) aren't especially valued by men.

Kohlberg has often reported women to be at stage 3 ('good-boy—nice-girl') and interpreted this as 'lower' than men's and both 'functional and adequate for them!'

Indeed, morality is defined in interpersonal terms at stage 3, relationships are subordinated to rules at stage 4 and at stages 5/6 rules are subordinated to universal principles of justice:

> ... Gilligan's criticisms are telling and it is hoped that they will stimulate others to look more closely at the interplay of values and cognition inherent in theories of moral development. (Coleman and Hendry, 1990)

According to Peters (1974) and others, it is not enough to know what is 'right' and 'wrong'—one also has to care:

> It is this neglect of feeling and of actions that is one of the most serious reasons why Kohlberg's theory must not be taken as a complete account of moral development. (Meadows, 1986)

5) The theory doesn't look closely enough at the relationship between judgement and behaviour. The little evidence there is suggests that level of moral judgement *doesn't* predict behaviour well (Kurtines and Greif, 1974). Although Blasi (1980) found that juvenile delinquents show lower levels of moral judgements than non-delinquents of the same age and intelligence, in general, correlations are low (Mischel and Mischel, 1976; Rest, 1983). Kohlberg himself admits that:

> ... a stage of judgements of justice is a necessary but not a sufficient condition for moral action. (Kohlberg, 1981)

If Freud seems to over-emphasize the emotional aspects of morality Kohlberg seems to *under-emphasize* them—or even totally ignore them. Most of our moral responses seem to be more a matter of intuition and feeling than of reasoning and logical deduction—we are not always the rational creatures we would like to be.

6) According to Turiel (1978), Kohlberg has failed to make a basic distinction between *social rules* or *conventions* (arbitrary rules of conduct sanctioned by custom and tradition), eg etiquette and the rules of a game, and *moral rules* (general principles relating to justice, fairness and the welfare of others), eg 'it is wrong to steal'. At least within a given culture, conventional rules can be changed but moral rules cannot—the latter seem to be right in themselves.

Turiel asked American sixteen- and seventeen-year-olds, 'If a country has no rule against stealing, would it be right for a person to steal in that country?'. Most said it would still be wrong. But they said the rules of a game could be changed if everyone agreed. They also agreed that calling teachers by their first name would be all right if there were no rules forbidding it. Turiel goes as far as to claim that social and conventional thinking are two distinct conceptual systems.

Weston and Turiel (1980) found that four- to six-year-olds could recognize the difference. They also read five- to eleven-year-olds two kinds of hypothetical stories, one about a school in which there were no rules about hitting (representing a moral rule) and the other about a school where children were allowed to take their clothes off (representing a social convention); a majority of children at all ages said a school should not allow hitting but it could allow undressing.

Kohlberg views moral judgement and social understanding as one and the same (the 'socio-moral perspective'). (Although Piaget studied children's conceptions of the rules of marbles, this criticism applies equally to him.)

7) Finally, Hoffman (1977) believes that Kohlberg's is the best

available approach to understanding the progression from a child's sense of morality (based on the consequences of actions) to the abstract moral code of adults.

Kohlberg's theory has stimulated a great deal of research (especially cross-cultural) and has opened up a number of perspectives on moral growth (Thomas, 1985):

> ... whatever its shortcomings, it remains the most stimulating and potentially fertile model of children's moral growth in current psychological and philosophical circles ... (Meadows, 1986)

PART 6

Individual Differences

28 INTELLIGENCE

The concept of intelligence is probably one of the most elusive in the whole of psychology: to try to pin it down and provide a definition which all (or even most) psychologists can agree on seems almost impossible and attempts to measure it are fraught with difficulties (not least of which is not knowing what it is).

Intelligence represents one of the most researched sources of individual differences but it is not just of academic interest—the intelligence test (in one form or another) has impinged on the lives of most of us, whether it is for educational selection, occupational selection or selection for Mensa, the high IQ society. According to Vernon (1979), over 2000 million tests of intelligence or achievement are given every year in the USA alone.

The near-obsession of Western culture with measuring and categorizing people is also highly emotionally charged and politically sensitive, particularly in relation to the question of racial differences in intelligence, which represents another instance of the heredity–environment issue.

Yet, unlike the discussion of language or perception, or even personality, the nature–nurture debate in intelligence has become equated with extremes of political viewpoints and the issue highlights the impossibility of completely divorcing the social from the scientific functions of psychology.

DEFINITIONS OF INTELLIGENCE

So diverse are the definitions of intelligence, that Vernon (1960) thought it necessary to identify three broad groups of definition, namely biological, psychological and operational.

1) *Biological* definitions see intelligence as related to adaptation to the environment. As we saw in Chapter 25, Piaget studied intelligence as a process and not as a set of capacities, so that he was not interested in how individuals differ from one another but rather in what stages of development all individuals go through.

For Piaget, intelligence is:

> . . . essentially a system of living and acting operations, ie a state of balance or equilibrium achieved by the person when he is able to deal adequately with the data before him. But it is not a static state, it is dynamic in that it continually adapts itself to new environmental stimuli.

And again:

> . . . intelligence constitutes the state of equilibrium towards which tend all the successive adaptations of a sensory, motor and cognitive nature. (Piaget, 1950).

So Piaget represents the *qualitative* approach to intelligence, where the focus is on intelligence itself and not differences in intelligence between individuals.

2) *Psychological* definitions, by contrast, represent the *quantitative* or *psychometric* approach, where the emphasis is very much on the measurement of intelligence to compare and differentiate between individuals. There are many psychological definitions and some of the best known and most influential are shown in Table 28.1.

Table 28.1 Some psychological definitions of intelligence	RESEARCHER	DEFINITION
	Binet (1905)	'It seems to us that in intelligence there is a fundamental faculty, the impairment of which is of the utmost importance for practical life. This faculty is called judgement, otherwise called good sense, practical sense, initiative, the faculty of adapting one's self to circumstances. To judge well, to comprehend well, to reason well . . .'
	Terman (1921)	'An individual is intelligent in proportion as he is able to carry on abstract thinking'
	Burt (1955)	'Innate, general, cognitive ability'
	Wechsler (1944)	'The aggregate of the global capacity to act purposefully, think rationally, to deal effectively with the environment'
	Heim (1970)	'Intelligent activity consists in grasping the essentials in a situation and responding appropriately to them'
	Vernon (1969)	'The effective all-round cognitive abilities to comprehend, to grasp relations and reason'

The definitions of Terman, Burt and Vernon all stress the purely intellectual aspects of the concept, while Binet's and Wechsler's definitions are much broader and perhaps closer to commonsense understanding.

According to Heim, however intelligence may be defined, 'it is complex and not simple, facets are many and varied' and, consequently, to speak of an individual's 'true' intelligence is meaningless. (We shall take up this point again later when we discuss intelligence tests.)

Heim objects to the use of intelligence as a noun because, she says, it smacks of an 'isolable entity or thing', which is opposed to her belief that intelligence should be regarded as part of personality as a whole (combining cognitive, affective and conative dimensions, the last referring to the 'striving, doing, aspect of experience'), which is an integrated unit. Consequently, she prefers to talk about 'intelligent activity' rather than 'intelligence'.

3) The third kind of definition identified by Vernon—*operational*—simply defines intelligence in terms of tests designed to measure it, ie 'intelligence is what intelligence tests measure' (Boring, 1923). While such a definition is intended to get round the problem of the multiplicity of definitions that exists, it fails to tell us exactly what it is that

intelligence tests measure and is, in fact, *circular*, ie the concept being defined is part of the definition itself (see Chapter 2). Miles argues that if we substitute the names of particular tests, then we can break into the circle, but Heim is not convinced, pointing out that this merely decreases the circumference of the circle!

Like Heim, Ryle (1949), believes that 'intelligence' does not denote an entity or an engine inside us causing us to act in particular ways; instead, he argues that any action can be performed more or less intelligently, so it should be used as an adjective and not as a noun.

One attempt to 'solve' the problem of defining intelligence was made by Neisser (1979):

> There are no definitive criteria of intelligence, just as there are none for chairness, it is a fuzzy-edged concept to which many features are relevant. Two people may both be quite intelligent and yet have very few traits in common—they resemble the prototype along different dimensions ... [Intelligence] is a resemblance between two individuals, one real and the other prototypical.

Perhaps most of our concepts are like this and trying to define something so precisely that it accommodates every single instance is doomed to failure—intelligence is a 'natural' concept which is too 'loose' to be adequately defined by any single definition.

So Neisser advocates that intelligence should be viewed in terms of *prototypes* ('best instances' or ideal cases)—we imagine a prototypically intelligent person and compare particular individuals with the imagined person.

However, different social groups may have somewhat different prototypes, in which case which one do we choose? And while Neisser's approach seems to be an excellent way of discovering what people mean by 'intelligence', it does not help us discover what 'intelligence' means— for Neisser there is no difference, but for Sternberg (1987), for example, there is.

Factor Analytic Theories of Intelligence: One Factor or Many?

Having looked at some of the major definitions of intelligence, we now turn to more detailed accounts of the nature of intelligence. Not surprisingly, there are sharp divisions of opinion here too but they all have in common the basic assumption that intelligence is a characteristic of a person that can be measured by intelligence tests which, in turn, implies that individuals differ with respect to that characteristic. This describes the *psychometric* ('mental measurement') approach.

We shall be discussing tests later in the chapter and all we need to understand for the moment is that theories of intelligence are based upon analysis of scores of large numbers of individuals on various intelligence tests using a statistical technique called *factor analysis* (FA; see Chapter 29).

FA involves correlating the scores of a large sample of subjects to determine whether scores on certain tests are related to scores on certain other tests, ie whether some, or any, of the tests have something in common. The basic assumption made is that the more similar the scores on two or more tests (ie the higher the correlation), the more likely it is that these tests are tapping the same basic ability (or factor).

If we find, for example, that people's scores on tests A, B, C, D and E are highly correlated (ie if they score high on one they tend to score high on the others or low on all five) then it could be inferred that all five tests are measuring the same ability and individuals differ according to how much or how little of that particular ability they have. However, if there is very little relationship between scores on the five tests, then each test may be measuring a distinct ability and when comparing individuals we would have to look at each ability separately (Table 28.2).

Table 28.2 *Average correlations between WAIS-R subtests*

SUBTEST	INFOR-MATION	DIGIT SPAN	VOCA-BULARY	ARITH-METIC	COMPRE-HENSION	SIMILAR-ITIES	PICTURE COMPLE-TION	PICTURE ARRANGE-MENT	BLOCK DESIGN	OBJECT ASSEMBLY	DIGIT SYMBOL
Information	—										
Digit span	0.46	—									
Vocabulary	0.81	0.52	—								
Arithmetic	0.61	0.56	0.63	—							
Comprehension	0.68	0.45	0.74	0.57	—						
Similarities	0.66	0.45	0.72	0.56	0.68	—					
Picture completion	0.52	0.37	0.55	0.48	0.52	0.54	—				
Picture arrangement	0.50	0.37	0.51	0.46	0.48	0.50	0.51	—			
Block design	0.50	0.43	0.52	0.56	0.48	0.51	0.54	0.47	—		
Object assembly	0.39	0.33	0.41	0.42	0.40	0.43	0.52	0.40	0.63	—	
Digit symbol	0.44	0.42	0.47	0.45	0.44	0.46	0.42	0.39	0.47	0.38	—

(Source: data adapted from Wechsler, 1981.)
(From Colman, A. M. (1990) in Roth, I. (ed.) Introduction to Psychology, Open University and LEA.)

These two hypothetical outcomes roughly correspond to two theories of intelligence, the first of which is sometimes referred to as the 'London Line' and is associated with Spearman (1904, 1927), Burt (1949, 1955) and Vernon (1950), in contrast with the mainly American approach of Thurstone (1938) and Guilford (1959). However, as we shall see, there are important differences within each of these approaches.

SPEARMAN'S TWO-FACTOR THEORY

Spearman factor-analysed the results of children's performance on various tests and found that many tests were moderately positively correlated, concluding that all the tests had something in common (a general factor) as well as something specific to each test (a specific factor). Spearman believed that every intellectual activity involves both a general factor (which he called g or general intelligence) and a specific factor (s) and differences between individuals are largely attributable to differences in their g. (This g is, in fact, an abbreviation for *neogenesis*, which refers to the ability to 'educe relations', as in a common kind of test item which asks 'A is to Y as B is to ?'). Although g accounts for why people who are good at one mental ability also tend to be good at others, people also differ according to their specific abilities. g is entirely innate:

All branches of intellectual activity have in common one fundamental function ... whereas the remaining or specific elements seem in every case to be wholly different from that in all the others ... This g, far from being confined to some small set of abilities whose inter-correlations have actually been measured and drawn up in some particular table, may enter into all abilities whatsoever. (Spearman, 1904, quoted in Gould, 1981)

Spearman himself believed that he had discovered the elusive entity that would make psychology a true science. He had found, he thought, the innate essence of intelligence, the reality underlying all the superficial and inadequate measures devised to search for it:

> Spearman's g would be the philosopher's stone of psychology, its hard, quantifiable 'thing'—a fundamental particle that would pave the way for an exact science as firm and as basic as physics. (Gould, 1981)

If this was to prove to be a rather exaggerated claim, it was still a major landmark in psychometrics:

> No single event in the history of mental testing has proved to be of such momentous importance as Spearman's proposal of his famous two-factor theory. (Guilford, 1936; quoted in Gould, 1981)

BURT AND VERNON'S HIERARCHICAL MODEL

Burt (who was a student of Spearman) agreed that there is a g factor common to all tests but also thought that the two-factor model was too simple. He and Vernon elaborated and extended Spearman's model by identifying a series of group factors (major and minor) in between g and s factors (Fig. 28.1).

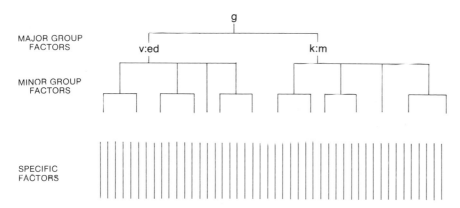

v:ed = Verbal-educational ability

k:m = Spatial-mechanical ability

MAJOR GROUP FACTORS

MINOR GROUP FACTORS

SPECIFIC FACTORS

Figure 28.1 The hierarchical model of intelligence. (After Vernon, 1950)

According to this model, g is what all the tests are measuring, the major groups factors (*v:ed* and *k:m*) are what some tests are measuring (some to a greater extent than others), the minor group factors are what particular tests measure whenever they are given, while specific factors are what particular tests measure on specific occasions (Burt, 1970).

An important educational implication of this view is that, given the dominance of g in the hierarchy, each child can be ranked on a single scale of (innate) intelligence. General ability can be measured early in life and children sorted according to their intellectual promise. (This is the thinking behind the 11-plus examination.)

THURSTONE'S PRIMARY MENTAL ABILITIES

Using fourteen-year-olds and college students as his subjects, Thurstone (1938, 1947) found that not all mental tests correlate equally but appear to form seven distinct factors or groupings, which he called *Primary Mental Abilities* (or PMAs), namely:

Spatial (S)—the ability to recognize spatial relationships.
Perceptual speed (P)—The quick and accurate detection of visual detail.
Numerical reasoning (N)—the ability to perform arithmetical operations quickly and accurately.
Verbal meaning (V)—understanding the meaning of words and verbal concepts.
Word fluency (W)—speed in recognizing single and isolated words.
Memory (M)—the ability to recall a list of words, numbers or other material.
Inductive reasoning (I)—the ability to generate a rule or relationship that describes a set of observations.

Thurstone sometimes referred to these mental abilities as 'mental faculties' or 'the vectors of mind' (the title of his 1935 book). He saw g as a grand average of positive correlations for a particular battery of tests. This means that g can change according to the particular battery of tests used and so it:

> ... has no fundamental psychological significance beyond the arbitrary collection of tests that anyone happens to put together ... We cannot be interested in a general factor which is only the average of any random collection of tests. (Thurstone, 1940; quoted in Gould, 1981)

So the PMAs are independent and uncorrelated—these corresponded to the group factors in the hierarchical model but there was no general factor to which they were all related. As there is no general ability, the overall ranking of pupils is inappropriate—some children will be good at some things, others at other things. He advocated the use of individual *profiles* of all PMAs.

Many researchers have questioned Thurstone's conclusions, pointing out that people who score high on a test of one PMA also tend to score high on most of the others. Indeed, Thurstone himself later (1947) admitted that g seems to be involved in all PMAs (having carried out a 'second-order' factor analysis on the results of the first).

Jensen (1980), a key figure amongst the psychologists who argue that intelligence differences are largely inherited or genetic, believes that this change of mind by Thurstone proves that Spearman and Burt were right all along. Jensen is a 'pure Spearman-ian' (Gould, 1981)—he based his 800-page defence of IQ (*Bias in Mental Testing*) on the reliability of g. Intelligence is 'the g factor of an indefinitely large and varied battery of mental tests'; 'we identify intelligence with g' and, 'to the extent that a test orders individuals on g, it can be said to be a test of intelligence' (Jensen, 1980).

But Gould (1981) disagrees that Thurstone eventually came to accept g. It was still of *secondary* importance to the PMAs and, mathematically, he seems to have been correct—a 'second order' g rarely accounts for more than a small percentage of the total information in a matrix of tests (compared with *Spearman's g*, which often accounts for more than half).

Even after he admitted a second-order *g* (when he revised his *Vectors of Mind* in 1947), Thurstone continued to contrast himself with the British school.

GUILFORD'S 'STRUCTURE OF INTELLECT' MODEL

This represents the most extreme alternative to Spearman's two-factor theory and totally rejects the notion of a general intelligence factor.

Guilford first classified a cognitive task along three major dimensions: *content* (what must the subject think about?); *operations* (what kind of thinking is the subject being asked to perform?); and *products* (what kind of answer is required?'). He identified four kinds of content, five kinds of operation and six kinds of product which, multiplied together, yields a total of 120 distinct mental abilities. Guilford's model is presented in more detail in Figure 28.2.

Guilford set out to construct tests to measure each of the 120 abilities; according to Shaffer, writing in 1985, tests have been devised to assess more than 70. However, the scores people get are often correlated, which suggests that the number of basic mental abilities is much smaller than Guilford assumed (Brody and Brody, 1976).

However, the multi-factorial approach of Guilford (and to a lesser extent that of Thurstone) represents an important counter-balance to the much more restricted model of Spearman. Vernon (1950) concluded that intelligence is *neither* a single general mental ability *nor* a number of more specific, independent, abilities—but both; general intelligence plays a part in all mental activities but more specific abilities are also involved in producing performance. Shaffer (1985) believes that this combined approach is the currently held viewpoint amongst most psychologists.

CRITICISMS OF FACTOR ANALYSIS

How can we account for the conflicting models of intelligence to have emerged from the work of different psychologists, all of whom have used factor analysis?

1) The simple answer is that there is more than one way of factor analysing a set of data and there is no 'best' way. As we have seen above, Thurstone re-analysed his original data by using a 'second-order' FA which produced a very different pattern of factors. Originally, he had used a form of FA which gives a 'simple structure' solution in contrast to the 'principal component' solutions resulting from Spearman's and Burt's analyses. Shackleton and Fletcher (1984) say that these two alternatives are mathematically equivalent and the same data from the same sample can produce a number of different patterns of factors depending on which alternative is used. (But doesn't this contradict what Gould says about Thurstone being correct?—see above.)

2) In practice, however, it seems that the split between the British and American models of intelligence is as much a reflection of the type of subjects used as of the form of FA employed. Thurstone and Guilford used mainly college students, while Spearman, Burt and Vernon used mainly schoolchildren; the former are much more alike in terms of their all-round intelligence than the latter, and are a much more self-selected and therefore homogenous group and so differences between them are

Figure 28.2 *A summary of Guilford's 'structure of intellect' model. (After Shaffer, 1985)*

CONTENT		OPERATIONS		PRODUCTS	
1. FIGURAL	- the properties of stimuli we can experience through the senses e.g. colour, loudness, shape, texture.	1. COGNITION	- recognizing and discovering.	1. UNITS	- a single number, letter or word.
2. SYMBOLIC	- numbers, letters, symbols, designs.	2. MEMORY	- retaining and recalling the contents of thought.	2. CLASSES	- a higher order concept (e.g. men + women = people)
3. SEMANTIC	- the meaning of words, ideas.	3. DIVERGENT PRODUCTION	- producing a variety of ideas or solutions to a problem.	3. RELATIONS	- a connection between concepts.
4. BEHAVIOURAL	- the actions and expressions of other people.	4. CONVERGENT PRODUCTION	- producing a single best solution to a problem.	4. SYSTEMS	- an ordering or classification of relations.
		5. EVALUATION	- deciding whether intellectual contents are positive or negative, good or bad etc.	5. TRANS-FORMATION	- altering or restructuring intellectual contents.
				6. IMPLICATION	- making inferences from separate pieces of information

likely to reflect differences in particular abilities which are relatively independent of each other.

3) The type and number of tests used (in conjunction with type of subjects) can also determine the pattern of factors that emerges. Shackleton and Fletcher (1984) maintain that if a few, similar tests are used with subjects who vary widely in age, education, cognitive abilities and so on, a picture of intelligence comprising one dominant, general ability, is likely to emerge, while a large number of different types of tests given to a homogenous sample is likely to produce a larger number of independent factors without a general intelligence factor being involved.

4) Even without these problems, there is still the fundamental issue of interpreting the factors which do emerge. All that FA achieves is a cluster of inter-correlations between different tests and parts of tests— it is then up to the researcher to scan these patterns of inter-correlations and to label them. As Radford (1980) says, factors do not come 'ready-labelled' and the labels that are attached to the factors are only 'best guesses' about the psychological meaning of the factors—they may or may not reflect 'psychological reality'. (This could be compared with the debate in Artificial Intelligence about whether computers really think and have intelligence: if computers manipulate symbols but symbols are meaningless in themselves, it needs a human to give them meanings. In the same way, clusters of inter-correlations (the product of FA) are meaningless until they are given an interpretation by the psychologist.)

5) Surely a technique that leaves so much room for subjective interpretation and, hence, disagreement, amongst different researchers, is hardly very objective and several writers have questioned the relevance of the whole technique in providing an account of the structure of intelligence (eg Block and Dworkin, 1974).

Vernon (1979) has attempted to defend FA by arguing that the differences between various models are more apparent than real. However, it is still true that how factors are labelled is an arbitary act on the part of the researcher, 'merely to label a factor in one way or another is not necessarily to advance our understanding of the nature of intelligence' (Lloyd et al, 1984).

6) Once a factor has been labelled (eg 'verbal ability') there is the danger of believing that it exists in some objective way (this is called *reification*) whereas a factor is merely a statistic. In Gould's (1981) terms they are '... by themselves, ... neither things nor causes; they are mathematical abstractions...'. And according to Gillham:

> Factors, like human beings, are born with no name although there is usually one waiting for them, which may not fit their character very well. But as with their human counterparts they soon become assimilated to their name...
>
> Human beings, however, have the advantage over factors in that their meaning does not reside just in their name. Factors, like correlation coefficients, have no intrinsic psychological significance: meaning is ascribed to them by a psychologist with his preferences and presuppositions... (Gillham, 1978)

ALTERNATIVE MODELS OF INTELLIGENCE

1) Although still working within the FA approach, Cattell (1963) and

Horn and Cattell (1967/1982) have proposed a model which can to some degree reconcile the different models discussed above. They argue that the *g* factor can be sub-divided into two major dimensions—*fluid* and *crystallized* intelligence (see Chapter 24).

Fluid intelligence ('gf') is the ability to solve abstract relational problems of the sort that are not taught and which are relatively free of cultural influences. It increases gradually throughout childhood and adolescence as the nervous system matures, then levels off during young adulthood and after that begins a steady decline.

By contrast, *crystallized* intelligence ('gc') increases throughout the life-span and is primarily a reflection of one's cumulative learning experience. It involves understanding relations or solving problems which depend on knowledge acquired as a result of schooling and other life experiences (eg general knowledge, word comprehension and numerical abilities).

2) Apart from Piaget's qualitative approach, the other major theoretical approach to the study of intelligence is that known as the *information processing approach*. According to Fishbein (1984), this approach sees intelligence as the steps or processes people go through in solving problems; one person may be more intelligent than another because they move through the same steps more quickly or efficiently or are more familiar with the required problem-solving steps.

Advocates of this view (eg Sternberg, 1979) focus on: (i) how information is internally represented; (ii) the kinds of strategies people use in processing that information; (iii) the nature of the components (eg memory, inference, comparison) used in carrying out those strategies; and (iv) how decisions are made as to which strategies to use.

Regarding (iii), Sternberg (1987) identifies five major kinds of components:

(a) *Meta-components.* Higher-order control processes used in planning how a problem should be solved in making decisions regarding alternative courses of action during problem-solving, and in monitoring one's progress during the course of problem-solution.
(b) *Performance components.* Processes used in the actual execution of a problem-solving strategy.
(c) *Acquisition components.* Processes used in *learning* (acquisition of knowledge).
(d) *Retention components.* Processes used in *remembering* (retrieval of previously acquired information).
(e) *Transfer components.* Processes used in *generalizing* (transfer of knowledge from one task or task context to another).

He gives the example of how these five kinds of components might be applied in the solution of an arithmetical problem:

> Mrs Smith decided to impress Mrs Jones. She went to a costume jewellery shop and bought three imitation diamonds of equal value. She received £4 in change from the £10 note she gave the assistant. (But as Mrs Smith was receiving her change, Mrs Jones walked into the shop!) How much did each imitation diamond cost?

Metacomponents would be used in setting up the equations for solving the problem, eg in deciding that the problem can be solved by subtracting £4 from £10 and dividing the difference by 3. They must also decide what information is relevant and what is not. *Performance* components would be used in the actual solution of these equations as to obtain first £6 as the price of the imitation diamonds and, then, £2 as the price of each item. *Acquisition* components were used in the problem-solver's past to learn how to set up the equation, how to subtract, divide and so on. *Retention* components are used to retrieve this information from memory when it is needed and *Transfer* components are used to draw an analogy between this problem and previous ones of a similar kind.

How does this relate to the various factorial theories of intelligence (such as Spearman's and Thurstone's)?

According to Sternberg, the *g* factor results from the operations of components which are general across the range of tasks represented on IQ tests. These are mainly meta-components, for example, deciding which particular components to use in the solution of a problem, deciding on a strategy for solving it and monitoring whether the chosen strategy is leading to a solution, plus deciding how quickly the strategy can be executed and still achieve a satisfactory result. Burt and Vernon's major group factors and Thurstone's PMAs are the result of the operation of the other four kinds of component.

We noted earlier that Sternberg believes Neisser's 'prototype' view of intelligence is unsatisfactory partly because different social groups will have different prototypes. While the components involved in the solution of the 'same' problem would overlap regardless of the particular culture, the kinds of problems needing solution will differ widely from one culture to another:

> Hence, the kinds of persons who are considered intelligent may vary widely from one culture to another, as a function of the components that are important for adaptation to the requirements of living in the various cultures. (Sternberg, 1987)

Like Piaget, those who adopt an information-processing approach are trying to develop a theory of intelligence which is universal (and so which applies equally to everyone) but like the factor analytic theorists, they are interested in individual differences in information processing. As Fishbein puts it, they see intelligence as neither an 'it' (for example *g*) nor a 'them' (for example, primary mental abilities) but as everything the mind does in processing information.

3) Sternberg's *Triarchic Theory of Human Intelligence* (1985, 1988) incorporates what we said about which components are involved in information—processing but is far broader. It comprises three sub-theories which attempt to explain, in an integrative way, the relationship between: (i) intelligence and the internal world of the individual ie the mental mechanisms which underlie intelligent behaviour (the *Componential Sub-Theory*); (ii) intelligence and the *external* world of the individual, ie how these mechanisms are used in everyday life in order to attain an intelligent fit to the environment (the *Contextual Sub-Theory*); and (iii) intelligence and experience, ie '. . . the mediating role of one's passage through life between the individual's internal and external worlds' (*the Experiential Sub-Theory*).

All I shall add here to what we have already said about the components is that one of the most interesting classes of *performance* components are those found in inductive reasoning, the kind of thinking required in series completion tasks and analogies for example, 'A is to B as Y is to —'). Sternberg believes that identifying these performance components can provide insight into the nature of *g*:

> . . . But understanding the nature of the components of intelligence is not, in itself, sufficient to understand the nature of intelligence, because there is more to intelligence than a set of information-processing components. One could scarcely understand all of what it is that makes one person more intelligent than another by understanding the components of processing on, say, an intelligence test . . . (Sternberg, 1990)

The other two sub-theories address some of the other aspects of intelligence which contribute to individual differences in observed performance—both inside and outside test situations.

Intelligent thought is directed towards one or more of three behavioural goals—*adaptation* to an environment, *shaping* of an environment and *selection* of an environment. These are the functions towards which intelligence is directed:

> . . . Intelligence is not aimless or random mental activity . . . Rather it is purposefully directed toward the pursuit of these three global goals [adaptation to, shaping and selection of, an environment] . . . (Sternberg, 1990)

As far as *adaptation* is concerned, '. . . what is intelligent in one culture may be viewed as unintelligent in another', and:

> . . . To understand intelligence, one must understand it . . . in terms of how thought is intellectually translated into action in a variety of different contextual settings . . . (Sternberg, 1990)

Sternberg believes that *shaping* may represent the essence of intelligent thought and behaviour:

> . . . Perhaps it is this skill that has enabled human kind to reach its current level of scientific, technological, and cultural advancement . . . In science, the greatest scientists are those who set the paradigms (shaping), rather than those who merely follow them (adaptation) . . . (Sternberg, 1990)

> According to the experiential sub-theory, intelligence is best measured at those regions of the experiential continuum that involve tasks or situations that are either relatively novel, on the one hand, or in the process of beoming automatized on the other . . . (Sternberg, 1990)

To test how far children's understanding extends, you might give them problems which are just at the limits of their current understanding (this relates to Vygotsky's zone of proximal development; see Chapter 25). Several sources of evidence suggest that the *ability to deal with relative novelty* is a good way of measuring intelligence (and is a characteristic of intellectually gifted children). (Compare with Cattell's *fluid* intelligence, see p. 848.)

Equally, a key aspect of intelligence is the ability to *automatize information processing* (eg as in a skilled reader), because this makes more resources available for dealing with novelty. (This relates to the distinction between controlled/automatic processing; see Chapter 11.)

According to Bee (1989), standard IQ tests have omitted many of the kinds of abilities included under the contextual and experiential sub-theories—in the world outside school, these may be required at least as much as those included under the componential sub-theory. Clearly, traditional IQ tests do *not* measure *all* significant aspects of intellectual skill.

4) Gardner proposed his *Theory of Multiple Intelligences* in his book *Frames of Mind* (1983). It is based on three fundamental principles: (i) intelligence is not a single, unitary, thing but a collection of multiple intelligences, each one a system in its own right (as opposed to merely separate aspects of a larger system, ie 'intelligence'); (ii) each intelligence is independent of all the others; (iii) the intelligences interact, otherwise nothing could be achieved. An intelligence is defined as:

> . . . an ability or set of abilities that permits an individual to solve problems or fashion products that are of consequence in a particular cultural setting. (Walters and Gardner, 1986; quoted in Sternberg, 1990.)

Gardner's seven intelligences are summarized in Table 28.3.

Table 28.3 Gardner's Theory of Multiple Intelligence (1983)

INTELLIGENCES	DESCRIPTION
1. Linguistic	Includes skills involved in reading, writing, listening and talking
2. Logical—mathematical	Involved in numerical computation, deriving proofs, solving logical puzzles and most scientific thinking
3. Spatial	Used in marine navigation, piloting a plane, driving a car, working out how to get from A to B, figuring out one's orientation in space. Important also in the visual arts and playing chess, recognizing faces and scenes
4. Musical	Includes singing, playing an instrument, conducting, composing and to some extent, musical appreciation
5. Bodily—kinaesthetic	Involves the use of one's whole body or parts of it, to solve problems, construct products and displays. Used in dance, athletics, acting, surgery
6. Interpersonal	Includes understanding and acting upon one's understanding of others—noticing differences between people, reading their moods, temperaments, intentions etc. Especially important in politics, sales, psychotherapy and teaching
7. Intrapersonal	Self-understanding—symbolized in the world of dreams

Gardner identifies eight different criteria for distinguishing an independent intelligence, including: (i) potential isolation by brain damage (he believes that each intelligence resides in a separate region of the brain, so that a given intelligence should be isolable by studying brain-damaged patients; (ii) an identifiable core operation or set of operations; (iii) support from psychometric findings (patterns of inter-correlations/FA) and (iv) the existence of idiot savants, prodigies, and other exceptional individuals. A discussion of studies of idiots savants appears in Box 28.1.

Box 28.1 *The Study of Idiots Savants (based on Howe, 1989 and O'Connor and Hermelin, 1988)*

'Idiots savants' is a term applied to certain mentally handicapped individuals who, despite their disabilities, are capable of remarkable feats. But how is it possible for certain people to possess abilities which seem to demand high levels of intelligence which they obviously do not have? Such cases certainly challenge the view that human intelligence is unitary or controlled by some general intelligence. A substantial minority of idiots savants are also autistic but they constitute a very varied group with little in common.

Harriet (Viscott, 1970) was a mentally handicapped woman with an overall IQ of 73; she had very poor general knowledge and was also strikingly socially inadequate. But she was a superb pianist. She could transcribe from memory, make different key changes in the middle of playing a piece, fill in parts from the full orchestra version not included in her piano score and could name each of the component notes of a four-note chord held for just half a second. When talking about music she often used words that she never otherwise used and had an encyclopaedic knowledge of classical music. There are other cases similar to hers.

Sacks (in *The Man Who Mistook His Wife For a Hat*, 1985) described a profoundly retarded, autistic man, with no speech, who made realistic drawings of natural objects, showing humour and imagination not otherwise even glimpsed.

Other cases of extraordinary artistic abilities include a young autistic boy, Stephen Wiltshire, who draws buildings and has sold some of his drawings and has been commissioned by large corporations to do drawings for them.

Nadia (Selfe, 1977), a young autistic girl who had no speech and was profoundly retarded, produced, from the age of three, drawings of animals of an outstanding technical standard. Selfe (1983) reports on eleven others with similar talents—all abnormal in some way, mostly mentally handicapped.

About one-third of all published cases are of *calendar counting*—at its simplest, the ability to state the day of the week on which a specified date falls—some calendar counters can solve problems of this kind for spans of dates extending several hundred years into the past and future.

Clearly, calendar counting makes substantial demands on memory and many of the accomplishments of idiots savants are essentially memory feats. But how are these skills acquired? Case studies are largely descriptive and no serious attempt is made to answer this question. However such abilities develop, these cases show that it is quite possible for complex intellectual skills to exist in relative isolation—and that different abilities in people of all ability levels may be largely autonomous, thus supporting theories such as Gardner's multiple intelligences.

INTELLIGENCE TESTS

A BRIEF HISTORY OF INTELLIGENCE TESTS

In 1904, Binet and Simon were commissioned by the French government to devise a test which would identify those children who would not benefit from ordinary schooling because of their inferior intelligence. The result was the Simon–Binet (1905) test, generally accepted as the first intelligence test.

The sample of children used for the development of the test (the standardization sample) was very small and it was subsequently revised twice, in 1908 and 1911, with much larger samples.

In 1910, Terman began adapting the Simon–Binet test for use in the USA and, as he was working at Stanford University, the test became known as the 'Stanford–Binet' test, and is still referred to in this way. The first revision was published in 1916 and was designed to measure normal and superior intelligence as well as subnormal. In 1937, the Terman–Merrill revision appeared, comprising two equivalent forms of the test (L and M) and in 1960 the most useful questions from the 1937 revision were combined into a single form (L–M) and an improved scoring system was used.

Prior to 1960, the Stanford–Binet test was designed for individuals up to age sixteen (starting at two-and-a-half to three) but this was extended to eighteen in the 1960 revision. A further revision was published in 1973 and the most recent in 1986.

Another major figure in intelligence testing is Wechsler, who developed the most widely used test of adult intelligence, the Wechsler Adult Intelligence Scale (WAIS; 1944), revised in 1958 and again in 1981 (WAIS-R). (It was originally published in 1939 as the Wechsler–Bellvue Intelligence Scale.) Wechsler has also constructed the Wechsler Intelligence Scale for Children (WISC), first published in 1949 and revised in 1974 (WISC R), designed for children between five and fifteen years, and the Wechsler Pre-School Primary Scale of Intelligence—WPPSI—first published in 1963 and designed for four- to six-and-a-half-year-olds.

An important impetus to the development of intelligence testing was America's involvement in the First World War; a fairly quick and easy method of selecting over one million recruits for suitable tasks was needed and the result was the 'Army Alpha' and 'Army Beta' tests.

The most recent new individual British test is the British Ability Scales (BAS), (1979), which consists of twenty-four sub-scales designed to measure twenty-four distinct aspects of intelligence in two-and-a-half-to seventeen-year-olds, which relate to five major 'mental processes', including retrieval and application of knowledge and speed of information processing. The latter is meant to underlie performance on all the other sub-scales and is one of the novel features of the test, reflecting the influence of the information-processing approach.

One way of testing this is to present a page of a 5×5 block of numbers. The child has to strike out the largest number in each row and total time is measured. Difficulty is increased from item to item by increasing the number of digits in each number (from three to five).

Like the Wechsler scales, the BAS gives three IQ scores—a verbal, a visual and an overall (general) IQ. And, in keeping with Thurstone's PMA model:

> From the start ... the original research team had in mind the construction of an intelligence scale which would provide a profile of special abilities rather than merely produce an overall IQ figure ... (Elliot, 1975; quoted in Richardson, 1991)

INDIVIDUAL AND GROUP TESTS

Although all the tests mentioned above are tests of intelligence, an important difference between them is that some are given to one person at a time (eg the Stanford–Binet and Wechsler tests and the BAS) and so are known as Individual Tests, while others are given to groups of people at a time (eg the Army Alpha and Beta tests) and so are referred to as Group Tests. Related to this distinction are other important differences:

1) Individual tests are used primarily as diagnostic tests in a clinical setting, for example, they are used to assess the ability of a child who has learning difficulties in school and the Stanford–Binet and Wechsler are the tests most widely used by educational psychologists both in the UK and the USA. Group tests, by contrast, are used primarily for purposes of selection and research; for example, in Britain until the mid-1960s, all children aged eleven sat an examination (the 11-plus), which would determine the kind of secondary schooling they would receive and this consisted largely of a group test of intelligence. (It was designed largely to assess g.) (Despite the introduction of comprehensive schools, there are many parts of the UK where selection at eleven still takes place.) Again, when large groups of people are being studied as part of a research project, it is very likely that their intelligence will be assessed by using one or other group test.

2) Because the individual test involves a one-to-one situation, it is clearly more time-consuming than a group test, which, in theory, can be given to as many individuals as can be comfortably accommodated in a particular room.

3) Although individual tests require that instructions are standardized (the same for all testees) and that the same questions are asked and in the same sequence, there is some degree of leeway on the part of the tester as to exactly how the test is conducted; for example, the child must be put at its ease before the test proper can begin and it is important that a good rapport be established between the child and the tester. How the tester achieves this will probably vary on each occasion; no face-to-face situation can be made totally uniform or predictable, and the psychologist's training will help prepare them for this. Groups tests, on the other hand, are presented in the form of written questions, the group is read out a set of standardized instructions and the test is timed; the person administering the test need not be a psychologist and, indeed, may have no special training or familiarity with the particular test and the marking can either be done by using a special marking key or by computer. In this respect, then, group tests are more objective, that is, only one answer is accepted as correct and there is no room for interpretation on the part of the marker.

4) Individual tests usually involve some *performance* items, ie the testee has to *do* something (eg a jigsaw puzzle) as well as answer questions about the meaning of words and do some mental arithmetic, etc. By contrast, the group tests are 'pencil-and-paper' tests and in that respect are much like other, written, exams.

MENTAL AGE AND IQ

The Stanford–Binet test is based on the assumption that mental ability is developmental, ie it increases with age through childhood and so consists of a number of age-related scales; each scale comprises a series of questions which are normally answered correctly by a majority of children of that age. So, for example, the five-year-old scale is what most five-year-olds could pass comfortably (as well as all children over five) but which most four-year-olds could not; hence, a child passing the five-year-old scale has a *mental* age of five, that is, the child can do what the average five-year-old can do (some examples of questions from different age-scales are given in Table 28.4).

Table 28.4 Some items from the Stanford–Binet (1973) test and the two scales of the WAIS-R (1981)

Stanford-Binet

Children of 3 should be able to:
Point to objects that serve various functions (eg 'goes on your feet'). Repeat a list of 2 words or digits (eg 'can' and 'dog').
Children of 4 should be able to:
Discriminate visual forms (eg squares, circles and triangles). Define words (eg ball and bat). Repeat 10-word sentences, count up to 4 objects, solve problems (eg 'In daytime it is light, at night it is . . .').
Children of 9 should be able to:
Solve verbal problems (eg 'tell me a number that rhymes with tree'). Solve simple arithmetical problems and repeat 4 digits in reverse order.
Children of 12 should be able to:
Define words (eg 'skill' and 'muzzle'). Repeat 5 digits in reverse order. Solve verbal absurdities (eg 'One day we saw several icebergs that had been entirely melted by the warmth of the Gulf Stream.' What is foolish about that?).

Wechsler Adult Intelligence Scale (WAIS-R)

Verbal Scale (None of sub-tests is timed)

1. *Information*—general knowledge.
2. *Comprehension*—ability to use knowledge in practical settings (eg 'What would you do if you were lost in a large, strange, town?').
3. *Arithmetic*.
4. *Similarities*—Conceptual and analogical reasoning (eg 'In what ways are a book and TV alike?').
5. *Digit span*—STM (eg repeating a string of digits in the same or reverse order).
6. *Vocabulary*—word meaning.

Performance Scale (All sub-tests are timed)

1. *Picture completion*—assessment of visual efficiency and memory by spotting missing items in drawings.
2. *Picture arrangements*—assessment of sequential understanding by arranging a series of pictures to tell a story.
3. *Block design*—ability to perceive or analyse patterns by copying pictures using multicoloured blocks.
4. *Object assembly*—jigsaw puzzles.
5. *Digit symbol*—ability to memorize and order abstract visual patterns.

In practice, a child is started off on the scale immediately below its chronological age (to determine its *basal age*) and then the scale corresponding to its chronological age and so on, until the child fails to answer any questions correctly on a particular scale.

The concept of Mental Age is useful in that it gives an *absolute* assessment of the child's level of intellectual development, but by itself it does not tell us how bright, average or dull the child is; to establish this we must compare the child's Mental Age with its Chronological (actual) Age (CA). Imagine two children, both of whom do equally well on the test and attain a Mental Age (MA) of ten; can we regard them as equally intelligent? The answer is 'No', because one of them is ten years old while the other is only nine, and nine-year-olds are not expected to do as well on the test as ten-year-olds. So, when we take CA into account, we are thereby making a *comparison* with other children.

For these reasons, Stern introduced the notion of an Intelligence Quotient (IQ) in 1912, in which the MA is expressed as a ratio of CA, multiplied by 100 to produce a whole number. The first IQ was, therefore, a *ratio* IQ, such that where MA and CA are the same, IQ is 100 (which, by definition, is average) where MA is greater than CA, IQ is over 100 (and, therefore, above average) and, where CA is greater than MA, IQ is below 100 (and ,therefore, below average).

It should be clear from these examples that for IQ to remain stable over time, the MA must increase in step with the CA. However, the concept of MA does not apply beyond eighteen, since intellectual ability is usually fully developed by that time (according to the 1960 version of the Stanford–Binet, anyway) and consequently, the test IQ is not meaningful beyond a chronological age of eighteen. (The measurement of adult IQ was discussed in Chapter 24.)

The WAIS–R is the most widely used test of adult intelligence (sixteen- to seventy-four-year-olds) and is structured in a similar way to the WISC–R. The test comprises two separate scales (a verbal scale and a performance scale) each comprising a number of sub-tests, and each producing a separate IQ, which can then be combined to yield an overall IQ. By contrast, the Stanford–Binet test includes performance items only for the youngest children (up to age four or five) when verbal abilities are still relatively underdeveloped (see Table 28.4).

A second important difference between them is that the same items are given to all children (or adults) on the Wechsler tests, so that age-related scales are not used. The questions become progressively more difficult and the testing usually continues until the testee has failed on a predetermined number of items in successsion.

In the 1986 revision of the Stanford–Binet, items are grouped into four broad areas of intellectual ability; (i) *verbal reasoning*; (ii) *abstract/visual reasoning*; (iii) *quantitative reasoning*; and (iv) *short-term memory*. A separate score is obtained for each area (whereas previously a single overall IQ score was given).

THE RELATIONSHIP BETWEEN INTELLIGENCE AND IQ

The Wechsler tests do not use the concept of MA in the way that the Stanford–Binet test did and instead uses a *deviation* IQ, which expresses the test result as a *standard score*, ie it tells the tester how many standard deviations (SDs) above or below the mean of the testee's age-group the score lies.

Before 1960, it was very difficult to compare scores on the two tests because of the difference in the way the IQ was calculated—the ratio IQ of the Stanford–Binet and the deviation IQ of the Wechsler test are not equivalent. However, in the 1960 revision of the Stanford–Binet, the ratio IQ was replaced by the deviation IQ, making scores on the two tests more comparable. However, although all tests are designed in such a way as to produce a normal curve, ie a symmetrical distribution of IQ scores, with a mean of 100, the standard deviation (or dispersion of the scores around the mean) can differ from test to test.

Fontana (1981) gives the example of two tests, A and B, test A having a SD of 10 and test B having a SD of 20. In both cases, 68 per cent (approximately) of children would be expected to have scores one SD below or above the mean (ie between 90 and 110 in Test A and between 80 and 120 in Test B). So a particular child might have a score of 110 on test A and 110 on test B and yet the scores would be telling us the same thing (Fig. 28.3).

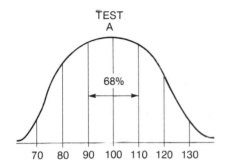

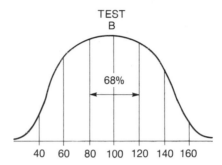

Figure 28.3 *Normal curves for two hypothetical IQ tests, each with a different standard deviation*

This suggests that while *intelligence* is a *psychological concept*, that of *IQ* is purely *statistical*. Put another way, if it is possible for the same characteristic of a person (intelligence) to be assigned different values according to which test is used to measure it, then instead of asking, 'How intelligent is this individual?' we should ask, 'How intelligent is this individual as measured by this particular test?'. Since the IQ score of the same individual can vary according to the standard deviation of the particular test being used, we cannot equate 'IQ' with 'intelligence': whereas we can (and usually do) enquire about somebody's height without taking the particular measuring rod or tape measure into account, we cannot do this in the case of a person's intelligence.

The very relationship between 'intelligence' and 'IQ' is problematic in a way that the one between 'height' and 'feet and inches' is not. Normally, we are prepared to accept an operational definition of someone's height, that is, height is the number of feet and inches as measured by a tape measure and there is no debate as to the 'true nature of height'. However, as we have seen, an *operational definition* of intelligence is not satisfactory precisely because there is such a variety of definitions and we feel that IQ is an unwarranted 'reduction' of intelligence, something very diverse and complex, to a single number (see Chapter 2).

In agreeing with Heim that to name the particular test used is merely to reduce the circumference of the circle represented by an operational definition, we could perhaps take this a step further by saying that for each separate test there exists a separate circle.

In *IQ—The Illusion of Objectivity* (1972), Joanna Ryan points out that because intelligence is expressed as a number, the impression is created that IQ tells us in some absolute way about an individual's intellectual ability, in the same way as feet and inches tell us about someone's height. However, there is a fundamental difference between the two measuring scales being used. IQ scores are not 'free-standing' scores in the way that somebody's height is: we can measure a person's height without having to take anybody else's height into account, but IQ only derives its meaning *as a comparison* with other people's scores. This is because intelligence is measured on an *ordinal* scale, which tells us whether one person is more or less intelligent than another but little else. For instance, the difference between an IQ of 100 and 105 *appears* to be the same as the difference between scores of 105 and 110 and leads some to argue that intelligence tests involve an interval scale (as in temperature); however, Ryan (1972) argues that this sort of arithmetical move is unjustified.

Interestingly enough, the BAS claims to give 'direct estimates of ability' as opposed to a mere relative ordering of subjects, ie it claims to provide direct estimates of ability (as if by a dipstick or linear rule) (Richardson, 1991). Richardson doubts that this claim to interval scaling is valid.

THE CRITERIA OF AN INTELLIGENCE TEST: WHAT MAKES A TEST A 'GOOD' TEST?

According to Kline (1982) all psychological tests must fulfil three criteria if they are to be considered good or efficient tests: (i) discriminatory power; (ii) reliability; and (iii) validity; to these we can add a fourth—standardization.

i) *Discriminatory Power and Standardization*

Good psychological tests should be discriminating, ie they should produce a wide distribution of scores. If everyone scored equally well (or badly) on a particular test it would not be discriminating, ie it would not reveal differences between people with respect to the characteristic or ability being measured.

This requirement of a test is a practical and a statistical one, but it is not a logical one. For example, we want tests to be discriminating because we want to use test scores as a basis for categorizing and selecting people and if our society did not run this way, there would be no problem involved in most people scoring very high (or very low); indeed, in such a society, there might be no need for tests at all. Quite clearly, what is considered a 'good' test depends to a very large extent on the purposes to which the test is put.

The statistical side of the requirement that a good test be discriminating is related to the kind of distribution of scores that is expected, and here we return to the normal curve and the standard deviation. The assumption is made that intelligence is normally distributed, so that fixed proportions of the population will score so many standard deviations above or below the mean. (This idea is based on the further assumption that intelligence is largely biologically determined—since other characteristics such as height and weight, which are also largely biologically determined are found to be normally distributed, then it is expected that intelligence will also be.)

Starting out with this assumption, when testers are standardizing their tests, ie trying to establish a set of norms for a particular population against which any individual's score can be compared, they modify the test items to fit the requirements of a normal distribution.

For example, if a particular item is passed by all testees it would be considered too easy and probably dropped from the test; similarly, if an item is so difficult that it is passed by nobody, then it too will be dropped. The items that are retained should then discriminate between testees so as to conform with the normal curve.

Of course, once a test has been standardized so as to produce a normal distribution, the tester can use this as evidence that intelligence is, indeed, a biological property. However, many writers have criticized this view of intelligence, including Hilary and Steven Rose in an article called 'The IQ Myth', in which they point out that not all biological properties are normally distributed and that tests reveal, 'as much about the assumptions of their designers and users as about the individuals to whom they are applied'. We have stumbled upon another circle!

Standardization also requires testing a large, representative sample of the population for whom the test is intended, otherwise the resulting norms cannot be used legitimately for certain groups of individuals. Classic examples of improper standardization involve the two most widely-used individual tests of intelligence, the Stanford–Binet and the Wechsler scales, both of which were originally standardized in the USA. In the 1960 revision of the Stanford–Binet, Terman and Merrill took only the population included in the census as their reference group, which excluded many migrant and unemployed workers. More seriously, both tests were standardized on whites only (without any explanation for this from the authors) and yet they would be used with both black and white children; as Ryan (1972) says, these tests are, therefore, tests of white abilities and although we can still compare black and white children, we must be aware that in doing so we are not comparing black and white intelligence 'but instead how blacks do on tests of white intelligence'. In the 1973 revision of the Stanford–Binet, the 2100 strong standardization sample did include black children but it remains to be seen how this will affect the race and IQ controversy in the future (see below).

Heather (1976) also points out the ideological significant of IQ as illustrated by re-standardization of tests. Before 1937, the mean score of women on the Stanford–Binet was ten points lower than that of men and it was decided to eliminate this discrepancy by modifying the items so that average scores for men and women were the same. Heather asks why this has not been done with blacks and answers his own question in terms of the *predictive efficiency* (a measure of validity) of the test: tests are meant to predict future education and occupational success, so changing a test so as to eliminate racial differences, while not at the same time changing social inequalities (a much longer process, of course), would render the test a less efficient predictive tool. As Heather notes, removing the male–female bias did, in fact, make the test less efficient as a predictor of gender differences in educational and occupational success.

ii) *Reliability*

This refers to how consistently the test measures whatever it is measuring. Consistency can refer either to: (i) the test itself (*internal consistency*); or (ii) consistency over time. In (i), each item on the test should be measuring the same variable and to the same extent, ie they should all contribute equally to the overall test score. One way of assessing internal reliability is the *split-half* method where, for example, scores on the odd-numbered questions are correlated with scores on the even-numbered questions. If the test is reliable, there should be a significant, positive, correlation.

These two sets of scores can be thought of as two forms of the same test and, indeed, there is a method of assessing reliability called *Alternate or Parallel Forms* (as in the 1937 version of the Stanford–Binet) where scores on one form should correlate very highly with scores on the other. Finally, the *Kuder–Richardson method* refers to all possible ways in which a test can be split in half.

In (ii), consistency over time, the most commonly used method is *Test–Re-test* reliability, where the same subjects are given the same test on more than one occasion; a reliable test is one which produces very similar scores when repeated.

In relation to intelligence tests, IQ is expected to be stable across time, not just because a good test must be reliable but also because the predominant view of intelligence underlying most tests is that it is largely genetically determined and, hence, unlikely to fluctuate in an individual over time. However, the evidence suggests a rather different picture, which we shall discuss later in relation to the heredity–environment issue.

Reliability is not only important in itself but is a prerequisite for validity: if a test produces different scores on different occasions, it cannot possibly be valid; yet a test's reliability is no guarantee of its validity.

iii) *Validity*

A test is valid if it measures what it claims to measure, and there are several ways of assessing it. In relation to intelligence tests, the question is, do they measure intelligence?

1) *Face* (or *content*) *validity* is a rather superficial type of validity, which refers to whether or not the test seems to be testing what it claims to test by looking at the kind of questions it contains. In a sense, this begs the question of just what intelligence is; whereas we can fairly easily determine whether a test measures knowledge of history, for example, and know that it is not a valid history test if the questions deal with geography, the situation is far more complex in the case of intelligence tests precisely because of the failure by psychologists to agree on what intelligence is.

2) *Concurrent validity* involves trying to correlate scores on an intelligence test with some other, independent, measure or criterion at the same point in time. One method is to correlate scores on a new test with scores on another, well-established test (in practice, this is very often the Stanford–Binet). The circularity of this attempt should be obvious: what independent proof do we have that the well-established test is itself a valid test of intelligence? Even if we could get around this problem, the question would arise as to what value the new test has, since, if the correlation between the two tests is very high, they would seem to be measuring the same thing! (Kline, 1982). Other criteria that might be used include teachers' ratings and the child's current academic performance, both of which seem to create as many problems as they

solve and which are most usefully discussed in relation to predictive validity.

3) *Predictive validity* (which, together with 2, is known as *external validity*) refers to the correlation of a test with some future criterion measure and is the more commonly used method of establishing validity.

Probably the most common and powerful external criterion is educability or educational success, and Binet started the trend by establishing that scores on his test differentiated between children thought to be bright or dull based on classroom performance. Many studies show that well-established tests do, in fact, predict school achievement with considerable accuracy.

However, to conclude from these findings that intelligence tests therefore measure some 'pure', cognitive ability called 'general intelligence' is unjustified. Many writers have pointed out that all the variables (including cognitive ability) that contribute to school success also contribute to performance on IQ tests and a high correlation would be expected for this reason. Heather (1976), for example, argues that 'general intelligence' can be called 'school intelligence', the ability to do well at school. Similarly, Richardson (1991) asks whether the correlation with school performance makes IQ tests valid tests of educational prediction rather than valid tests of intelligence. Ryan (1972) maintains that to the extent that tests do measure educability, they are measuring something which is influenced to a considerable extent by various social and motivational factors. Although tests are intended to measure only cognitive ability or potential, by trying to validate them against educational success, 'many important social influences are thereby implicitly introduced'. Again, 'IQ tests do not, and could not, assess only the cognitive, as opposed to social and motivational, determinants of school success' (Ryan, 1972). Heim (1970), who advocates a view of intelligence as a part of personality as a whole, would agree.

As we saw when discussing standardization, the predictive validity of tests is closely related to the practical and social purposes to which they are put—so validation is not a purely objective, scientific, process.

The other major external criterion used is occupational success. According to Jensen (1975), 'Intelligence tests have more than proved themselves as valid predictors of scholastic performance and occupational level.' But this is precisely what they are designed to predict—so might not predictive correlations be self-fulfilling? (Richardson, 1991).

4) *Construct validity* is defined, 'by taking a large set of results obtained with the test and seeing how well they fit in with our notion of the psychological nature of the variable which the test claims to measure' (Kline, 1982). So it embraces both concurrent and predictive validity and normally involves formulating hypotheses about what kind of test results we would expect if the test really does measure intelligence. For example: (i) scores on the test will correlate highly with educational attainment (both currently and in the future); and (ii) scores on the test will correlate highly with scores on other, well-established, tests (concurrent validity).

To the extent that such hypotheses are supported, the construct validity of the test has been demonstrated, and Kline (1982) concludes that most well-known tests of intelligence, 'have now accumulated so much evidence relating to validity that there is no dispute about them'.

Similarly, Heim (1970) concludes that, 'a reputable test is still the best single means of assessing an individual's intelligence, whatever definition is used. It is more objective, consistent and valid as a first approximation than any of the validatory criteria against which tests may be calibrated.'

However, we should also remind ourselves of the diversity of definitions and (perhaps more importantly) theories of intelligence which abound in psychology, and the logical problem of measuring something if we cannot first agree *what* it is that we are measuring:

> ... the absence of a clear theory about the intelligence we claim to be measuring [makes] construct validity ... not one of the strengths of most IQ tests ... (Richardson, 1991)

THE CULTURAL NATURE OF INTELLIGENCE AND INTELLIGENCE TESTS

One of the major criticisms of intelligence tests has been that they are biased in favour of white middle-class children and adults; it follows that it is both unfair and meaningless to compare groups which differ substantially in their social and cultural experience.

However, defenders of tests would appeal to the distinction between attainment and aptitude tests, ie two kinds of ability tests. *Attainment* (or achievement) *tests* are concerned with how much a person knows about a specific subject (eg geography) or with a person's current level of performance (eg reading) and are unambiguously related to actual learning and educational experiences.

Aptitude tests, by contrast, are intended to measure somebody's capacity or potential ability to succeed in a particular task or job of work or academic subject, and are designed to reduce to a minimum the influence of specific learning and experience. Intelligence tests have always claimed to be aptitude tests and, to this extent, test constructors have argued, they are culture-fair or culture-free.

But is the attainment–aptitude distinction a valid one and is it possible to design a test which is completely culture-free?

Aren't aptitude tests merely attainment tests in disguise? Group tests, in particular, rely on reading and arithmetic which are taught in all schools and so, in practice, at least, it is very difficult to separate aptitude from attainment. It is somewhat easier to distinguish between them in terms of their purpose and ways of trying to validate them; aptitude tests, by definition, are trying to assess some future performance and so involve predictive validity, but we have already seen the problems that this entails.

Ryan (1972) accepts that intelligence tests are very different in content from school attainment tests and to this extent they do eliminate some specific aspects of differing educational experiences. However, they do not and cannot minimize the more general effects of education and upbringing: 'the cumulative effects of different social histories are extremely complex and pervasive and an individual's behaviour will always reflect this'.

She also makes a different kind of criticism, which seems to strike at the heart of the attainment–aptitude distinction, namely that it is logically impossible to measure potential separately from some actual behaviour, ie some of the skills that individuals have developed during their lifetime must be used when they do an intelligence test. 'There is nothing extra "behind" the behaviour corresponding to potential that could be observed independently of the behaviour itself' (Ryan, 1972). She concludes that the notion of 'innate potential' itself makes no sense.

Given the breakdown of the attainment–aptitude distinction, a number of attempts have been made to produce culture-free tests, which usually consist of non-verbal questions; traditionally, the emphasis on language has been one of the more obvious sources of bias in intelligence tests. An example of the kind of questions involved is shown in Figure 28.4 and is based on Raven's Progressive Matrices, one of the most widely held culture-free tests.

Even without any written intructions, you can probably infer what you have to do. However, the very nature of the task is something which is likely to reflect particular cultural experiences: questions must be formulated in words or symbols of some kind and the testee's familiarity with these will depend on their life experience. According to Brian Simon (1971), 'the suggestion that human intelligence might be measurable by the development of a new kind of test which actually eliminates all words and symbols is an absurdity', and Owen and Stoneman (1972) believe that because the influence of language is so pervasive, any attempt to devise a culture-fair test by removing 'overt language structures' is doomed to failure. Vernon (1968) argues that, 'we must give up the notion of intelligence as some mysterious power or faculty of the mind which everyone, regardless of race or culture, possesses in varying amounts, and which determines his potentiality for achievement'. He concludes by stating that, 'there is no such thing as a culture-fair test and never can be' and Bruner agrees by maintaining that, 'the culture-free test is the intelligence-free test, for intelligence is a cultural concept' (quoted by Gillham, 1975).

Finally, Gillham (1975) concludes that any attempts to 'define' intelligence which do not involve identifying 'specially valued cultural attainments' must fail. The concept of intelligence only derives its meaning within a particular cultural and social context (see Sternberg's criticism of Neisser and his contextual sub-theory).

PSYCHOPHYSIOLOGICAL APPROACHES TO MEASURING INTELLIGENCE

A fairly recent attempt to avoid some of the difficulties discussed above (although not usually discussed in the context of 'culture-free' tests) is to correlate IQ test scores with certain physiological measures, such as electroencephalograms (EEGs), evoked potentials (EPs) and reaction time (RT). Some of the early investigators found only moderate correlations between average evoked potentials (AEPs) and IQ but more recently much higher correlations have been reported.

But how should such findings be interpreted? Do the EPs somehow *cause* intelligent cognition? Equally plausible is the claim that intelligent cognition produces certain patterns of EP:

> ... Despite the striking magnitude of some correlations, we are far from understanding the neural mechanisms that are actually responsible for them ... Until we understand the relationship better, I am unenthusiastic about using EPs as some kind of 'culture-free' intelligence test ... (Sternberg, 1990)

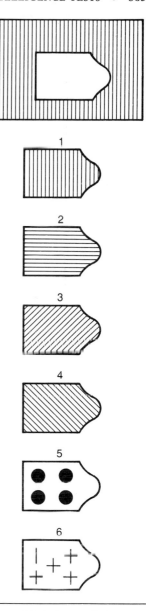

Figure 28.4 A sample item from the Raven's progressive matrices test

Also, despite these promising findings, the use of IQ tests as a validating criterion throws up all the difficulties which we have encountered already.

THE HEREDITY–ENVIRONMENT ISSUE: WHY ARE SOME PEOPLE MORE INTELLIGENT THAN OTHERS?

Along with gender differences, the debate about the source of intelligence differences must be the most controversial and divisive in the whole of psychology. Before we begin to consider the relevant evidence, there are a number of preliminary points that should be made.

First, intelligence tests are, in practice, assumed to be valid measures of intelligence, so 'IQ' is used synonymously with 'intelligence' in discussion of the heredity–environment issue.

Secondly, the heredity–environment issue is about how we account for intelligence differences *between* individuals (and, even more controversially, between groups, particularly working-class, middle-class and black–white differences). The impression is sometimes created that the heredity–environment issue is about how much of an individual's intelligence is determined by genetic factors and how much by environmental factors, but this is logically absurd. Hebb (1949) likened it to asking how much of the area of a rectangle is contributed by its width, a meaningless question, since area, by definition, is width times length.

According to McGurk (1975), there are four interrelated propositions which seem to follow from the genetic theory (the belief that IQ differences are largely determined by genetic factors), namely:

Proposition 1 The closer the genetic relationship between any two individuals, the greater should be the correspondence (concordance) between them with respect to intelligence.
Proposition 2 As the genetic inheritance of each individual is a constant, there should be a high degree of continuity in IQ throughout an individual's life-span.
Proposition 3 Individual differences in early experience should have no fundamental effect on the development of individual differences in intelligence.
Proposition 4 Deliberate attempts to increase the level of intelligence by special enrichment-experience should have no effect.

What is the evidence for and against these propositions?

PROPOSITION 1

Table 28.5 shows the results of Bouchard and McGue's (1981) review of 111 studies of IQ correlations between relatives from the world literature. It updates the Erlenmeyer-Kimling and Jarvik (1963) review and the findings are generally consistent with it.

First, we need to understand the difference between MZ and DZ twins. MZ stands for 'monozygotic' meaning 'one egg'. So MZs are identical twins who have developed from the same, single, fertilized ovum and are usually regarded as being genetically identical and are, by

Table 28.5 *Familial correlations for IQ. The vertical bar in each distribution indicates the median correlation; the arrow, the correlation predicted by a simple polygenic model. From Bouchard and McGue (1981)*

Relationship	No. of correlations	No. of pairings	Median correlation	Weighted average
Monozygotic twins reared together	34	4672	0.85	0.86
Monozygotic twins reared apart	3	65	0.67	0.72
Midparent–midoffspring reared together	3	410	0.73	0.72
Midparent–offspring reared together	8	992	0.475	0.50
Dizygotic twins reared together	41	5546	0.58	0.60
Siblings reared together	69	26 473	0.45	0.47
Siblings reared apart	2	203	0.24	0.24
Single parent–offspring reared together	32	8433	0.385	0.42
Single parent–offspring reared apart	4	814	0.22	0.22
Half-siblings	2	200	0.35	0.31
Cousins	4	1176	0.145	0.15
Non-biological sibling pairs (adopted/natural pairings)	5	345	0.29	0.29
Non-biological sibling pairs (adopted/adopted pairings)	6	369	0.31	0.34
Adopting midparent–offspring	6	758	0.19	0.24
Adopting parent–offspring	6	1397	0.18	0.19
Assortative mating	16	3817	0.365	0.33

definition, of the same sex. DZ stands for 'dizygotic', meaning 'two-egg', so DZs are non-identical (or fraternal) twins who have developed from two quite separately fertilized ova; they are no more alike than ordinary siblings (ie they have roughly 50 per cent of their genes in common) and can be either of the same or different sex.

Secondly, we can see fairly easily that the closer the kinship relation (and, hence, the greater the genetic similarity), the higher the correlation for IQ. Can we take this as support for the genetic theory? Unfortunately, it is not as simple as this. Notice what else is happening as the genetic similarity increases—the environments are also becoming more similar!

Take the case of MZs reared together: not only are they as similar genetically as any two humans can get, but they are much more likely to be treated in the same way than DZs or ordinary siblings. Kamin (1981), for example, points out that even MZs vary in their physical likeness and this seems to be a factor in determining how similarly they are treated; significantly, the more alike physically they are, the more similar their IQ. He also claims that DZs of the same sex are treated more alike than opposite sex Dzs and both are treated more alike than ordinary siblings; even though all these groups are similar genetically, same-sex DZs are most alike in IQ scores.

This is borne out by the Bouchard and McGue data. Table 28.5 does not give separate figures for DZs of same and different sex but they were, in fact, 0.62 and 0.57, respectively. (The figure used here is the *weighted average*, ie a figure which takes sample size into account to make different studies more comparable.)

So it is difficult to draw any conclusions from the fact that MZs reared together are most alike in IQ (0.86) since this would be predicted from both a genetic theory *and* an environmentalist theory. Yet how would an environmentalist explain the finding that separated MZs are more alike than like-sex DZs reared together (0.72 and 0.60, respectively)? Taken at face value, this would certainly seem to support the genetic argument and, indeed, is generally regarded as the strongest single piece of evidence. But we need to look at studies of separated twins in more detail.

The Rationale of Twin Studies

Why do we need to study separated twins?

As we have seen, MZs reared together do not tell us about the relative importance of genetic and environmental factors, although even here environmental factors must be playing some role, since if only genetic factors were involved in IQ, the correlation would be perfect (ie 1.00). If the differences in IQ due to environmental difference (MZs reared apart) are *smaller* (ie the correlation is higher) than IQ differences due to genetic differences (DZs of the same sex reared together), then we can conclude that environmental factors are *less* important than genetic factors in causing differences in IQ. So the crucial comparison is between MZs reared apart and DZs of the same sex reared together; in the former case, genetic factors are held constant while environmental factors vary and in the latter the situation is reversed; so twin studies represent an important kind of natural experiment (see Chapter 2).

The four major studies of separated MZs are Newman et al (1937), Burt (1955, 1958, 1966), Shields (1962) and Juel-Nielsen (1965). A summary of the main findings appears in Table 28.6. As can be seen, MZs reared apart turn out to be more alike than DZs of like-sex brought up together (and in the Shields study, they were actually more alike than MZs reared together—a rather strange finding which neither theory

Table 28.6 The findings from the four major studies of separated identical twins

NAME OF STUDY	IQ CORRELATIONS (NUMBERS OF PAIRS ARE SHOWN IN BRACKETS)		
	MZS REARED TOGETHER	MZS REARED APART	DZS (SAME SEX) REARED TOGETHER
Newman, Freeman and Holzinger (1937)	0.91(50)	0.67(19)	0.64(50)
Burt (1955)*	0.944(83)	0.771(21)	
Burt (1958)	0.944(?)	0.771('Over 30')	
Conway (1958)	0.936(?)	0.778(42)	
Burt (1966)	0.944(95)	0.771(53)	0.552(127)
Shields (1962)	0.76(34)	0.77(40)	0.51
Juel-Nielsen (1965)		0.62(12)	

*The Burt data are not included in the Bouchard and McGue review (see text).

would predict). So is the genetic theory proven? According to Kamin (1977, 1981) the answer is a resounding 'No'. Why?

Criticisms of Twin Studies

1) Perhaps the most damaging criticism is that the 'separated' MZs turn out not to be separated at all. For instance, in the Shields study, the criterion of separation was that the twins should have been reared in different homes for at least five years, even though in some cases the separation did not occur until seven, eight or nine years (and very few separations occurred at birth). Out of forty separated pairs twenty-seven were actually raised in related branches of the parents' families and attended the same school. The most common arrangement was for one twin to stay with the natural mother and the other to go to the maternal grandmother or aunt; the correlation for these twenty-seven pairs was 0.83. The remaining thirteen pairs were, in fact, raised in unrelated families (although these often were friends of the mother) and their correlation was 0.51.

Jessie and Winifred were eight-years-old when studied and had been 'separated' at three months, but they were:

> ... brought up within a few hundred yards of each other ... told they were twins after the girls discovered it for themselves, having gravitated to one another at school at the age of 5. They played together quite a lot ... Jessie often goes to tea with Winifred ... They were never apart and wanted to sit at the same desk. (Shields, 1962)

Similar cases are reported in the Juel-Nielsen (1965) study.

2) When twins have to be split up, the agencies responsible for placing them will try to match the respective families as closely as possible, which can account for much of the similarity found between the separated MZs. However, when the environments are substantially different, very marked IQ differences are found.

For example, one of the pairs in the Newman et al (1937) study experienced very contrasting upbringings: one girl was raised in a good farming region, went to college and became a teacher and her IQ was 116; her sister was reared in the backwoods, had only two years of regular schooling and, although she later worked in a big city as a general assistant in a printing firm, her IQ was only 92. This twenty-four-point difference was the largest difference found for any of the nineteen pairs, which also included differences of nineteen and seventeen points. Three other pairs had very different educational experiences and the average difference for these was thirteen IQ points. Using a rating scale to estimate the educational difference between all nineteen pairs, there was an overall correlation of 0.79 between educational difference and IQ difference.

3) These findings also demonstrate the large *absolute* differences which may exist between pairs of separated MZs. This is important because the use of correlation coefficients tends to emphasize the *relative* similarities of MZs compared with DZs.

4) Experimenter bias is another problem, especially in the Newman et al and Shields studies. In the Newman et al study, when the twins were tested, the investigators knew which were MZs and which were not. Similarly, Shields tested both members of thirty-five out of the forty

pairs of separated MZs himself and the overall correlation was 0.84 (with a mean difference of 8.5 points); this compared with 0.11 (and a mean difference of 22.4 points) for the remaining five pairs (one member of which was tested by Shields and the other by another tester).

5) The twin samples were often biased. For instance, in the Newman et al study, volunteers responded to newspaper and radio appeals and then had to send in a questionnaire and a photograph of themselves. When a pair who looked so alike that they were mistaken for each other gave very different answers on the questionnaire, they were judged not to be MZs and were excluded from the study; so it is possible that amongst those who were excluded were MZs who happened to have developed very different personalities. This is a particularly serious criticism since, in 1937, there was no reliable medical test of zygosity (ie whether twins are MZ or DZ) and the reliability of the case histories is very dubious (eg regarding when they were separated).

6) The intelligence tests used differed from study to study, which makes it very difficult to compare different studies. There are also problems with the tests used in particular studies; for example, Newman et al used the 1916 version of the Stanford–Binet which, as we have seen, was designed for people up to age sixteen and, since the nineteen pairs of MZs were mostly adults (age range eleven to fifty-nine), the similarity of their IQs was artificially increased.

Similarly, Shields used two tests, the Dominoes Test (a test of non-verbal intelligence) and the Mill Hill Vocabulary Scale, neither of which had been standardized on females, a significant fact when you consider that two-thirds of his sample of MZs were female!

The Danish translation of the WAIS used by Juel-Nielsen had never been standardized on a Danish sample.

7) As can be seen from Table 28.6, the largest number of separated MZs was gathered by Burt, and Eysenck and Jensen have based their genetic theory largely on Burt's findings. However, it is now generally accepted that Burt actually invented some of his data. Kamin (1977) pointed out, 'a number of puzzling inconsistencies' as well as 'a number of astonishing consistencies' (there are correlation coefficients, expressed to three decimal places, despite differences in the number of twin pairs). Some of his data was published under the names of fictitious co-workers (eg the Conway, 1958, paper) and Kamin (1977) concludes that, 'the numbers left behind by Professor Burt are simply not worthy of our current scientific attention'.

An Evaluation of Twin Studies

Do they provide a *heritability estimate for intelligence?*

Based on twin studies in general, and Burt's study in particular, Eysenck and Jensen have proposed that 80 per cent of the variance between the IQ scores of individuals is attributable to genetic differences; this is referred to as a *heritability estimate* (of 80 per cent).

In view of all the shortcomings of twin studies, they would appear to be an extremely unreliable basis for drawing such a conclusion, particularly (as pointed out by Kamin and others) when a heritability estimate applies only to a *particular population* at a *particular time*. What does this mean? All the twin studies used white middle-class Americans, Britons or Danes and so we are not justified in applying the heritability estimate to blacks or to working-class populations (something of which both Eysenck and Jensen are guilty); if they tell us anything at all, they tell us about differences *within* the white middle-class population of those particular countries. We have also seen that where environmental differences between separated MZs are quite substantial, there is a correspondingly large difference in their IQs, which means the heritability will be smaller and, indeed, the three studies produce different heritability estimates. So, clearly, the amount of 'room for manoeuvre' that genetic factors have depends very much on the kind of environmental conditions in which they find themselves (Herrnstein (1982) has observed that heritability estimates vary from 0.50 to 0.80.)

Even within the white middle-class populations that have been studied, Kamin argues that twin studies could be used as a basis for a heritability estimate *only* if:

(a) The twins were genetically representative of the population.
(b) The range of environments to which the twins were exposed was also representative.
(c) There was no tendency for the environments to be systematically correlated (or matched).

According to Bodmer (1972), for example, the difference between members of a DZ pair represents only a fraction of the genetic difference that can exist between any two individuals taken at random; like siblings, they have half their genes in common. MZs, of course, have all their genes in common, and so are even less representative of the population as a whole.

As far as their environments are concerned, Bodmer again argues that the environmental differences between members of a twin pair represent only a fraction of the total environmental differences that can exist between two individuals chosen at random. Even within the same family, the environment of twins (MZ or DZ) will be more similar than for ordinary siblings, as we have seen. We have already seen how similar the environments of separated MZs were, partly because of deliberate matching by the agencies responsible and partly because of the more informal arrangements made by the family.

In the light of this, Kamin concludes that none of the three conditions has been met and so twin studies are not a reliable source of data regarding a heritability estimate for intelligence. Regarding the exposure of Burt's fabrication of his results, Jensen (1974) claims that there is other evidence which is equally supportive of the genetic theory, Scarr and Weinberg (1977) believe that estimates of heritability should be scaled downwards, but not drastically, and Vernon (1979) agrees. This other evidence which Jensen alludes to are Fostering and Adoption studies.

Fostering and Adoption Studies

The average correlation of 0.19 between fostered/adopted children and their foster/adoptive parents compared with 0.50 between natural children and their parents would seem to indicate a strong genetic component.

The early studies (Burks, 1928; Leahy, 1935; Skodak and Skeels, 1949) have been criticized on methodological grounds.

Both Burks and Leahy found a correlation of 0.15 between adoptive parents and adopted children. This compared with a correlation of 0.48 between biological parents and biological children in a 'matched control group' of ordinary families. But how were they matched?

The two groups of children were matched for age and sex, the two groups of families were matched for parental occupation, educational levels and 'type of neighbourhood'. But the adoptive parents were considerably older (having tried to have a child of their own for some time before adopting—so there were fewer siblings in the adoptive families), had incomes that were 50 per cent higher, larger and more expensive homes and, like all adoptive parents, actively wanted children and were carefully screened by the adoption agencies for their suitability as parents.

So not only did they turn out to be more 'successful' as a group than the control group but they also represent a more homogeneous group providing very little *variation* in the richness of their environment—the statistical consequence of this is that there cannot be a very high correlation between adopted children's IQ and environmental measures, such as the adoptive parents' IQ (Rose et al, 1984).

McGurk (1975) and others also point out that in terms of *absolute* level of IQ, adopted children move towards the level of the adoptive parents and, on average, they score significantly above those of the natural parents, ie the adoptive environment raises the child's IQ above what it probably would have been if the child had remained with the natural parents.

The obvious improvement on this 'classical' design is to study adoptive parents who also have a biological child of their own. Here the two children will have been reared in the same environment by the same parents—although they will be genetically unrelated to each other and of course, the adopted children will be genetically unrelated to the adoptive parents.

Two such studies are those of Scarr and Weinberg (1977, 1983) and Horn et al (1979).

Scarr and Weinberg studied transracial adoptions, ie in almost all cases the mother and her biological child were white while the adopted child was black.

In both studies, there was no significant difference between: (i) the correlation of the mother's IQ and her biological child's IQ; and (ii) the correlation of her IQ with the adopted child's IQ (although Horn et al found a slightly greater correlation between the mother and *adopted* child while for Scarr and Weinberg it was slightly greater with the *natural* child):

> The child's race, like its adoptive status, had no effect on the degree of parent–child resemblance in IQ. These results appear to inflict fatal damage to the notion that IQ is highly heritable . . . children reared by the same mother resemble her in IQ to the same degree, whether or not they share her genes. (Rose et al, 1984)

Many of these black children (and many of those in the Skodak and Skeels study) came from disadvantaged homes where the biological parents were poorly educated and were below average in IQ. By age four to seven, the adopted children were scoring well above average on IQ tests (about 110 in the Scarr and Weinberg study and 112 in Skodak and

Skeels), scores that are considerably higher than would have been expected on the basis of the natural parents' IQ and education levels or the IQs of other children from disadvantaged backgrounds. Since the adoptive parents are known to be highly educated and above average in IQ, it seems reasonable to assume that they provide an enriched, intellectually stimulating, home environment which facilitates the cognitive development of the adopted children.

Finally, Schiff et al (1978) in France, studied thirty-two children, born to parents of low social status, who were adopted before they were six months old by parents of high social status. Compared with the IQs of their biological siblings reared by the natural mother, the average IQ of the adopted children was far superior (95 and 111, respectively).

Reaction Range: An Example of Gene–Environment Interaction

A way of summarizing these studies is by reference to the concept of *reaction range*. This refers to the range of possible responses by an individual to the particular environment he/she encounters; it is unique to that individual and is related to genetic make-up. So, for instance, your genes might dictate that you grow to be six feet tall but this will only happen if you receive an adequate diet.

As far as IQ is concerned, Scarr-Salapatek (1971) maintains that, assuming the individual is not severely retarded, he/she has a reaction range of 20–25 IQ points, ie any individual's IQ score can vary by as much as 25 points (almost two standard deviations) depending on the kind of environment to which he/she is exposed.

Another classic example of gene–environment interaction is the disease phenylketonuria (PKU), which involves the inheritance of two recessive genes, one from each parent, which prevent the body's production of an enzyme, whose function is to metabolize phenylalanine (a common constituent of many foodstuffs, particularly dairy produce). If untreated, phenylalanine builds up in the bloodstream and poisons the nervous system, causing severe mental retardation and, eventually, death. However, by putting the baby on a low-protein diet (for at least its first ten to twelve years), these effects can be prevented and normal intelligence will develop. This suggests that any talk of 'high or low IQ genes' is meaningless—how particular genes contribute to high or low intelligence depends upon the environment in which they express themselves; in themselves they are neither 'bright' nor 'dull'.

PROPOSITION 2

To evaluate studies of the stability of IQ, we should note that IQ is not normally used as a measure of intelligence below two years of age; instead a Developmental Quotient (DQ) is used and perhaps the most widely used is the Bayley Scales of Infant Development (Bayley, 1969); designed for two- to thirty-month-olds, it assesses a child's rate of development compared with the 'average' child of the same age.

Generally, the younger a child is when given a developmental test, the lower the correlation between its DQ and its later performance on an IQ test (Anderson, 1939; Honzik, 1976).

Once IQ begins to be measurable, it becomes a better predictor of adult IQ (compared with DQ). However, the evidence is still very mixed. Honzik et al (1948) studied over 250 children in California, testing them at regular intervals between two and eighteen years. Some of the important findings are shown in Table 28.7.

AGE OF CHILD	CORRELATION WITH IQ AT AGE 10	CORRELATION WITH IQ AT AGE 18
4	0.66	0.42
6	0.76	0.61
8	0.88	0.70
10		0.76
12	0.87	0.76

Table 28.7 Correlations for IQ at ages 4–18 for the same individuals. (After Honzik et al, 1948)

Clearly, the closer in time the IQ scores are taken, the higher the correlation and the overall picture is one of little fluctuation over time. However, there were many fluctuations in the short-term, often related to disturbing factors in the child's life, and the 'stability coefficients' are based on large groups of subjects, obscuring important individual differences.

The Fels Longitudinal Study of Development (McCall et al, 1973) studied 140 middle-class children from two-and-a-half to seventeen years. The average change in IQ during that period was twenty-eight points and even the 'most stable' changed an average of ten points. About 15 per cent shifted fifty points or more (in either direction) and one child increased by seventy-four points!

Bee et al (1982) studied 193 families from before the birth of their first child until the child was eight. The Bayley Infant Development Scales were given at one and two years, the Stanford–Binet at four and the WISC–R at eight. The results are shown in Table 28.8.

IQ TESTS	INFANT SCORES (BAYLEY)	
	12 months	24 months
4 years (Stanford–Binet)	0.21 (stat. sig.)	0.53 (stat. sig.)
8 years (WISC-R)	0.15 (stat. sig.)	0.39 (stat. sig.)

Table 28.8 Correlations between IQ scores at 12 and 24 months and 4 and 8 years. (From Bee, 1989)

These results are consistent with previous studies in showing that the closer in time the two measures are taken, the higher the correlations will be. However, fluctuations in score seem to be much greater than a simple genetic theory would predict:

> Thus, caution must be exercised in drawing conclusions about later-life IQ from early performance data because intelligence is not as fixed as the original theories assumed. (Rebok, 1987)

A different approach to studying the continuity of IQ is Kagan's study of a Guatemalan village (Box 28.2).

PROPOSITION 3

A much-cited study (which could just as easily be discussed in relation to

> *Box 28.2 Kagan's (1973) Study of Guatemalan Children*
>
> Kagan conducted some research in a small, remote, farming village in Guatemala, where infants typically spend their first year in an isolated state, in a dark and tiny hut. They are not played with or spoken to and are poorly nourished, experiencing continuous gastrointestinal and respiratory illness; compared with American babies of the same age, they are mentally retarded.
>
> By their second year, conditions change; they are allowed to move about outside the hut and they begin to develop an interest in people, animals and objects. By four or five years they are playing with other children and at eight or nine assume some responsibilities in the family farm and domestic chores. Yet until ten they remain inferior intellectually to their American counterparts; they also do more poorly on tests of perception, memory and reasoning compared with other Indian children from a nearby village who are not so completely isolated during their first year. However, by the time they reach adolescence, they do almost as well as Americans on intelligence tests; any remaining differences are likely to be due to relatively poor schooling and general cultural deprivation.

proposition 4) is that of Skeels and Dye (1939), and the follow-up by Skeels (1966); these were described in detail in Chapter 22. Perhaps the most directly relevant studies here are those which are concerned with factors which adversely affect intellectual development. Table 28.9 summarizes some of the major variables.

GENETIC	ENVIRONMENTAL	
(i) *Down's syndrome* (extra 21st chromosome). (ii) *Klinefelter's syndrome* ('Apparent Males' XXY). (iii) *Turner's syndrome* ('Apparent Females' XO). (iv) *Phenylketonuria* (PKU) (2 recessive genes)	*Biological (Pre-natal)* 1. Maternal diseases (eg rubella, syphilis) 2. Rh incompatibility 3. X-rays and other radiation 4. Toxic agents (eg lead poisoning, carbon monoxide) 5. Drugs (eg thalidomide, cigarettes, alcohol, barbiturates, heroin) 6. Maternal stress during pregnancy 7. Mother's age 8. Multiple pregnancies→ Family size 9. Birth order 10. Birth difficulties 11. Prematurity 12. Mother's diet and malnutrition	*Socio-cultural (Post-natal)* Many of these pre-natal variations are correlated with socio-economic status (SES) and race. In USA, SES and race are more highly correlated than in UK

Table 28.9 Major variables, genetic and environmental, which adversely influence intellectual development

PROPOSITION 4

Two books which first appeared in the early 1960s contributed to the deliberate attempt in the USA to close the educational gap between white middle-class children and those from socially disadvantaged backgrounds, particularly those from black and other ethnic minorities.

J. McVicker Hunt's *Intelligence and Experience* (1961) summarized all the evidence showing that intelligence was not a fixed attribute of a person but depended very heavily on environmental experience. Bloom's 1964 *Stability and Change in Human Characteristics* also argued that intellectual ability could be increased by circumstances and that it was essential to give disadvantaged children enriched opportunities early in life.

The first of these compensatory pre-school programmes was Operation Headstart, begun in 1965. Initially this took the form of an eight-week summer programme and shortly afterwards became a full year's pre-school project. The aim was, literally, to give an educational headstart, but the first follow-up studies (conducted one or two years after starting school) were discouraging: IQ gains, when they did occur, were short-lived and educational improvement was minimal.

However, Hunt (1969, 1972) was critical of Headstart, claiming that it was inappropriate to the needs of the children involved, not providing them with the skills that they had failed to develop at home during their first four years and which are developed by most middle-class children. There was also too much emphasis on IQ as a criterion of success.

Yet these criticisms were, themselves, to prove premature, since the impact of early intervention has been shown to be cumulative, not showing up for several years. One major follow-up of Headstart by Collins (1983) suggests there is a 'sleeper effect'; compared with non-participants:

(a) Participants tend to score somewhat higher on tests of reading, language and maths and this 'achievement gap' tends to widen between the ages of six and fourteen.
(b) Participants are more likely to meet the school's basic requirements, ie they are less likely to be assigned to special education/remedial classes, to repeat a year in the same grade, or to drop-out of high school.
(c) Participants are more likely to want to succeed academically.
(d) Participants' mothers are more satisfied with their children's school performance and hold higher occupational aspirations for their children.

The gains in IQ, which lasted for up to four years after the programme ended, were not sustained and by age eleven to twelve there were no differences between those who had and those who had not participated.

Ironically (in view of these subsequent findings for Headstart participants), other compensatory programmes in the 1960s and 1970s tried to provide a more appropriate pre-school education, including Bereiter and Engelmann (1966), Blank and Solomon (1965), Klaus and Gray (1968) in Tennessee, Karnes et al (1970) and Garber and Heber (1977) in Milwaukee. In a review of eleven early intervention programmes, Lazar and Darlington (1982) reached similar overall conclusions to those of Collins.

Atkinson et al (1990) refer to a number of follow-up studies (up to age fifteen) of various early education programmes which all tend to show the same basic pattern of findings as reported by Collins. Citing Darlington (1986), they conclude that:

> Headstart programs have shown that early intellectual stimulation can have a significant impact on later school performance. But the specific method used appears to be less important than parental involvement. Programs that actively involve the parents, that interest them in their children's development and show them how to provide a more stimulating home environment, tend to produce the greatest gains . . . (Atkinson et al, 1990)

CONCLUSIONS: NATURE, NURTURE OR AN INTERACTION

Much of what we have discussed in relation to each of the four propositions implied by the genetic theory seems to suggest that environmental factors are considerably more important than a heritability estimate of 80:20 suggests.

As long ago as 1949, Hebb suggested that the whole nature–nurture controversy was a result of the 'double reference' to the term 'intelligence'. One meaning of the term (*intelligence A*) is an 'innate potential, the capacity for development, a fully innate property that amounts to the possession of a good brain and a good neural metabolism'; in this sense, intelligence is not measurable. *Intelligence B* is a product of the interaction between intelligence A and the environment and is defined as, 'the functioning of a brain in which development has gone on, determining an average level of performance or comprehension by the partly grown or mature person'. To ask about difference in intelligence is to ask about intelligence B. We can never, in principle, compare people's intelligence A or know how much of their innate potential is reflected in their intelligence B.

However, despite Hebb, the controversy has raged on, particularly since the mid to late 1960s. Vernon, who in 1969 added *intelligence C* to Hebb's A and B (to refer to IQ test scores, really a sample of B), believes that there are certain observed phenomena which represent very strong arguments in favour of the genetic theory:

(a) The difference in IQ between siblings, sometimes of up to thirty points.
(b) Very bright children being born to relatively dull parents.
(c) Very dull children being born to highly intelligent parents.

He believes that an environmentalist would find it very difficult to explain these while a genetic theorist would predict such phenomena. Reviewing the evidence in all its forms, Vernon (1979) concludes that it demonstrates a strong genetic component in the development of individual differences in intelligence. Although environment has an important role to play, measurable IQ seems to, 'depend more on genetic endowment than on favourable or unfavourable environmental opportunities and learning, at least within white culture'. However, both heredity and environment, 'are essential and neither can be neglected if we are to plan children's upbringing and education wisely'.

The idea that differences in IQ are inherited is deeply built into the theory of IQ testing itself because of its commitment to the measurement of something intrinsic and unchangeable.

From the very beginning of the American and British mental testing movement, it was assumed that IQ was biologically heritable (Rose et al, 1984). Spearman, for example, believed that *g* is a physical property of the brain, a form of mental energy pervading the entire brain: the strength of a person's *g* reflects heredity alone (while *s* factors reflect the influence of education). So IQ, as a measure of *g*, records an innate general intelligence.

However, according to Rose et al (1984), psychometricians often use the term 'heritable' mistakenly compared with how the geneticist uses it and this contributes to false conclusions about the consequences of heritability: (i) genes do *not* determine intelligence: there is no one-to-one correspondence between the genes inherited from one's parents and even *physical* characteristics. What we inherit is the *genotype*, the genes which are involved in the development of a particular trait; the *phenotype* is the actual trait itself as it manifests itself in the organism. While the former is fixed, the latter develops and changes constantly. The first principle of developmental genetics is that every organism is a unique product of the *interaction* between genes and environment at every stage of life; (ii) even allowing that genes alone do not determine the phenotype, it is claimed that they determine the effective limits of the phenotype, ie genes determine capacity or potential. We considered earlier Ryan's (1972) rejection of the concept of potential.

Gould (1981) makes a similar point:

> Genes do not make specific bits and pieces of a body, they code for a range of forms under an array of environmental conditions. Moreover, even when a trait has been built and set, environmental intervention may still modify inherited defects . . . (Gould, 1981)

The 'hereditarian fallacy', as Gould calls it, rests on two false assumptions. First, that 'heritable' *means* 'inevitable' (which he and Rose et al clearly believe it does not). Second, that *within-group* heredity can be applied to *between-group* heredity (see below).

RACE AND IQ (ARE SOME RACIAL GROUPS NATURALLY MORE INTELLIGENT THAN OTHERS?)

The figure at the centre of the race and IQ controversy is the American psychologist Arthur Jensen. In 1969, in the *Harvard Educational Review*, he published an article called 'How much can we boost IQ and scholastic achievement?', in which he reviewed all the literature which compared black and white IQ scores.

The basic findings, namely that, 'on average, Negroes test about one standard deviation (fifteen IQ points) below the average of the white population in IQ' is not itself a matter of dispute; it is Jensen's explanation of these findings that constitutes the controversy:

> Genetic factors are strongly implicated in the average Negro–white intelligence differences. The preponderance of the evidence is, in my opinion, less consistent with a strictly environmental hypothesis than with a genetic hypothesis . . . (Jensen, 1969)

Eysenck (1971) and Herrnstein (1971) agree with Jensen.

Some of the evidence upon which Jensen based his genetic theory was the apparent failure of compensatory pre-school programmes, such as Headstart, which, as we have seen, was a rather premature conclusion. Perhaps the most fundamental criticism of Jensen is that he bases his view of black–white differences (*between-group* differences) on the heritability estimate of 80:20 which, as we have seen, is based on studies of the white population (and is about *within-group* differences). Several writers, including many biologists (eg Bodmer, 1972) have pointed out the illegitimacy of making this logical jump.

As an example here, suppose we take a bag of seed collected from a wheat field and sow one handful on barren ground, and another on fertile ground. Those sown on fertile ground will clearly grow taller and give a much higher yield per plant than those sown on barren ground. Within each crop there will be differences, which clearly must be related to genetic differences, but which have nothing to do with the overall differences between the two crops, which have grown in two very different environments (Bodmer, 1972).

Relating this to intelligence, it is perfectly possible that individual differences in IQ (*within-group* differences) are heavily influenced by genetic differences, while group differences (*between-group* differences) are largely or entirely the result of environmental differences.

Jensen's response to this criticism is to appeal to studies in which environmental factors are controlled. For example, Shuey (1966) compared middle- and working-class blacks and whites and found the same average fifteen-point difference. But is social class (measured largely in terms of occupation and income) a sufficiently sensitive measure of 'environment' to be very helpful? Should we expect the experience of working-class and middle-class blacks to be equivalent to that of their white counterparts, given the history of slavery and continuing prejudice and discrimination? According to Bodmer (1972), 'measuring the environment only by standard socio-economic parameters is a little bit like trying to assess the character of an individual by his height, weight and eye colour'.

Tobias (1974) points out a further problem with Jensen's argument—when he says that environment has been controlled, he means controlled at the moment in time when the investigation began. Yet the study of a ten-year-old child, for example, when the family may have attained a reasonable status, tells us nothing about the family's position when the child was passing through its critical, formative period (both pre- and post-natally), such as mother's diet, illnesses, emotional stress and other adverse influences on intellectual development (see Table 28.9).

We have already discussed the cultural nature of IQ tests, which represents another stumbling block to Jensen's argument. It is certainly easier to devise tests which are patently biased than to construct a culture-fair or culture-free test. This was demonstrated by Dove, a black American sociologist, who in 1968 published the Dove Counterbalance General Intelligence Test ('Chitling Test'), a parody of the white bias in traditional tests. It draws freely on black language and culture and whites would be expected to emerge as inferior to blacks on such a test. (See Chapter 13 for a discussion of Black English.) Significantly, the gap between American whites and blacks is almost non-existent in the pre-school years (using, for example, the Gesell developmental test for newborns to two-year-olds). Both African and American black children show the highest mean scores of any group tested, while Western whites score lowest of all. It is only at school age, when IQ tests come to rely much more heavily on verbal items, that the gap begins to widen—in the opposite direction.

Mercer (1972) argues that, 'IQ tests are Anglocentric: they measure the extent to which an individual's background matches the average cultural pattern of American society', ie white, middle-class society. Her conclusions, based on studies in Riverside, California, led to legislation in that state making it illegal to determine that a child is retarded on the sole basis of its score on an IQ test; Massachusetts, Washington DC, Philadelphia and New York have gone even further and have banned the use of tests in the school system altogether.

Finally, the whole concept of race itself is problematic. Like intelligence, there are various definitions and criteria, but whichever is used (eg blood types) the extent of genetic variation *within* any population is usually far greater than the average difference *between* populations (eg Bodmer, 1972). The same is true of IQ scores and to emphasize average group differences (as Jensen does) is to overlook the considerable overlap between whites and blacks as well as the even greater differences within each population:

> ... *Homo sapiens* is tens of thousands, or at most a few hundred thousand, years old, and all modern human races probably split from a common ancestral stock only tens of thousands of years ago. A few outstanding traits of external appearance lead to our subjective judgement of important differences. But biologists have recently affirmed—as long suspected— that the overall genetic differences among human races are astonishingly small. Although frequencies for different states of gene differ among races, we have found no 'race genes'—that is, states fixed in certain races and absent from all others ... (Gould, 1981)

CONCLUSIONS

On the basis of their adoption studies, Scarr and Weinberg (1983) believe that genetic differences do not account for most of the IQ differences between racial groups. Loehlin et al (1975) explain racial differences in terms of three interacting, factors:

(i)   the inadequacy and bias of tests;
(ii) environmental differences;
(iii) genetic differences.

It is *how* these factors contribute to racial differences, rather than how much, which is perhaps the crucial question.

29 PERSONALITY

INTRODUCTION

As we saw in Chapter 1, 'personality' is one of the terms which, while commonly used in everyday language, has been given a special technical meaning by psychologists which is why, in any psychological discussion, it makes no sense to say that a person has 'lots of personality'.

We also saw in Chapter 1 that 'personality' is a hypothetical construct, something which cannot be directly observed but only inferred from behaviour in order to make sense of it.

In Chapter 17 we discussed the ways in which our perception of other people (and, to that extent, our interaction with them) is influenced by 'implicit personality theories', in particular stereotypes, ie our beliefs about which characteristics or traits tend to cluster together in individuals. If, indeed, we predict how someone is going to behave on the basis of what we believe they are like, and if our behaviour towards that person is likewise influenced, then this suggests that personality is not merely an abstraction which helps to explain an individual's behaviour in isolation but a concept which has real meaning in the context of interpersonal behaviour.

Another interesting connection with other topics is that of self-concept. You will remember from Chapter 21 that one of the major categories to emerge from studies of people's self-image is personality traits and we also saw how important the reaction of others and comparison with others are in the development of the self-concept. To this extent, personality is not something a person 'has' (it is not a 'thing') but rather is to do with *how* we relate to other people and generally deal with the world.

THE PLACE OF PERSONALITY IN PSYCHOLOGY AS A WHOLE

The study of personality is, probably, what many potential students of psychology imagine the subject to be about and, up to a point, they are right: personality does enter into other topic areas (as we have noted above), some of the major theoretical schools of psychology (in particular, psychoanalytic theories) are mainly concerned with personality, and the largest single group of psychologists are clinical psychologists, whose work brings them into contact with a wide range of personalities, many of which are regarded as abnormal or pathological (see Chapter 30).

Fontana (1982) goes so far as to claim that, 'of all the areas of psychology, the study of personality is the most important', although many would disagree. However, even if we did accept Fontana's claim, it would still be true that personality is conceptualized and studied in a variety of different ways according to the persuasion of the psychologist.

HOW DO THEORIES OF PERSONALITY DIFFER?

Because of the diversity of theories, it is virtually impossible to find a definition which all psychologists would accept. However, if our aim is to highlight some of the dimensions along which different theories differ, then a useful definition of personality would be:

> ... Those relatively stable and enduring aspects of individuals which distinguish them from other people, making them unique, but which at the same time permit a comparison between individuals.

The definition brings into focus two central issues: (i) does personality consist of *permanent traits* or *characteristics*? and (ii) is the study of personality the study of *unique individuals* or is it aimed at *comparing* individuals and discovering the factors which constitute *personality in general*? (Table 29.1).

Table 29.1 A classification of personality theories

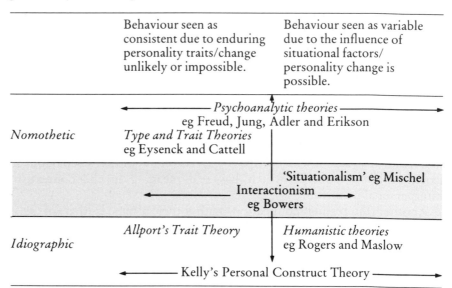

1)   Those psychologists who answer 'yes' to the first question and who are interested in personality in general belong to the *psychometric* tradition and are known as *type* and *trait* theorists. They make great use of personality questionnaires and the results from these are analysed using a statistical technique called *factor analysis*. In trying to establish factors in terms of which everyone can be compared, they adopt a *nomothetic* approach and the major figures are Eysenck and Cattell.

2)   Those who believe in the uniqueness of every individual represent the *idiographic* approach, but beyond this it is not easy to say what else they have in common. For example, they may or may not see personality as permanent or may differ as to how much or what kind of change is possible. But they are concerned with the *whole person* whereas psychometric theorists want to rank or order individuals with respect to *particular* aspects of personality. Allport is probably the most ardent advocate of the idiographic approach, although, paradoxically, he puts forward a trait theory of personality (but one that is very different from that of Cattell, for example).

Kelly's Personal Construct Theory is perhaps the most radical of all in so far as it is not so much a theory of personality as a total psychology:

according to Fransella (1981), 'Kelly sought to incorporate within the same theoretical framework those areas in psychology usually coming under separate chapter headings' (learning, cognition, motivation, emotion, psychophysiology) and, to this extent, the theory provides a total psychology about the total person.

The other major representations of the idiographic approach are the Humanistic psychologists, in particular Maslow and Rogers.

What they share is a concern for those characteristics of people which make us distinctively human, including our experience of ourselves as persons.

The kinds of methods used include case studies, biographical studies, rating scales, the Rep Grid (developed by Kelly) and the Q-Sort, developed by Stephenson in 1953 and used extensively by Rogers in his study of the effects on the self-concept of his client centred therapy (see Chapter 31). The Rep Grid is also used to evaluate the progress of therapy (see Chapter 31).

3)   The psychoanalytic theories of Freud, Jung, Adler and Erikson are clearly idiographic in that they are based on case studies of patients in the clinical context of psychotherapy and they are not attempting to measure personality in any sense. However, they are concerned with the nature of personality in general, and Freud and Jung especially are also trying to account for individual differences. It was Jung, for example, who first distinguished between introverts and extroverts, which Eysenck later investigated in depth and measured in his personality questionnaires.

As far as the enduring nature of personality is concerned, the psychoanalytic theorists all allow for the possibility of change, primarily through psychotherapy, although at any point in time behaviour is essentially the reflection of a person's characteristics and habitual ways of dealing with the world.

THE NOMOTHETIC VERSUS IDIOGRAPHIC APPROACH: INDIVIDUAL DIFFERENCES OR UNIQUE INDIVIDUALS?

According to Kluckhohn and Murray (1953), 'every man is in certain respects like all other men, like some other men and like no other men'. What we have in common with *all* other human beings is the subject-matter of experimental or 'general' psychology, which studies cognitive and physiological processes and learning; much of developmental and social psychology too are concerned with discovering 'universal norms' which apply equally to all individuals.

What we have in common with *some* other human beings is what the area of psychology known as individual differences (or differential psychology) has traditionally concentrated on: personality differences represent one kind of 'group norm', others being age, gender, ethnic and cultural background and intelligence. It is the study of 'how and how much a particular individual is similar to or differs from others' (Shackleton and Fletcher, 1984) which constitutes the factor-analytic/ psychometric approach; as we have seen, this is also a nomothetic approach.

Finally, what we have in common with *no* other human beings is what

Figure 29.1 *Gordon W. Allport (1897–1967). (UPI/ Bettmann Archive)*

makes us unique and, of course, this is an expression of the idiographic approach which attempts to discover 'idiosyncratic norms'.

ALLPORT'S TRAIT THEORY (1961)

Allport (Fig. 29.1) defined personality as:

> ... The dynamic organization within the individual of those psychophysical systems that determine his characteristic behaviour and thoughts. (Allport, 1961)

Allport and Odbert (1936) found over 18,000 terms describing personal characteristics and, even after omitting evaluative terms and transient states, there remained between four and five thousand. Allport believed that this large number of trait words could be reduced further, in fact, to two basic kinds:

(a) *Common traits*. These are basic modes of adjustment which are applicable to all members of a particular cultural, ethnic or linguistic background. For instance, since we must all interact in a competitive world, we must each develop our own most suitable level of aggression and each of us can be placed somewhere along a scale of aggressiveness.

(b) *Individual traits*. These are a unique set of personal dispositions based on unique life experiences and are unique ways of organizing the world; they are *not* dimensions which can be applied to all people. They cannot be measured by a standardized test and can be discovered only by careful and detailed study of individuals.

Individual traits can take one of three forms:

(a) *Cardinal traits*. These are so all-pervading that almost all of an individual's behaviour is dictated and directed by that cardinal trait. For instance, someone who is consumed by greed, ambition or lust. However, such traits are quite rare and most people do not have one, predominant, trait.

(b) *Central traits*. These are the basic building-blocks which make up the core of personality and which constitute the individual's characteristic ways of dealing with the world (eg honest, loving, happy-go-lucky). A surprisingly small number of these is usually sufficient to capture the essence of a person.

(c) *Secondary traits*. These are less consistent and less influential than central traits and refer to tastes, preferences, political persuasions, reactions to particular situations and so on.

Clearly, *common traits* are the subject-matter of the *nomothetic approach* and *individual traits* the subject matter of the *idiographic approach*.

Allport believed that the unique individual cannot be studied scientifically because science deals with the general (see Chapter 2). The nomothetic approach, for example, ignores the 'novelty' that results from an interaction of an individual's traits and an individual cannot be reduced to a combination of numerous, unrelated attributes. However, are the idiographic and nomothetic approaches necessarily opposed in this way?

In terms of Popper's (1945) distinction between the *descriptive sciences* (which include history and biography) and the *generalizing sciences* (which are the natural sciences—physics and chemistry), Allport's argument does not appear to be valid: only if *all* science were of the generalizing kind would the study of the individual *per se* be inconsistent with scientific methods. According to Kirby and Radford (1976), Allport was engaged in a different activity from the study of 'individual differences', which, as Bannister and Fransella (1971) correctly point out in their criticism of the nomothetic approach, is, in fact, the study of *group sameness* Allport was concerned with 'idiography' or 'idiodynamics', the study of *individual norms.*

Perhaps a more incisive criticism is that of Holt (1962) who argues that the idiographic–nomothetic issue is based on a false dichotomy: all description involves some degree of generalization, so that to imagine that we can describe an individual in terms which make no reference to any other individual is a fallacy. To describe a person *as* a person, we must use descriptive terms which apply to others as well, hence, in principle, assimilating the individual to the general. As Kirby and Radford (1976) argue, a 'truly unique individual would be incomprehensible, in fact not recognizable as an individual'.

Holt also argues that Allport's so-called idiographic methods are just more or less nomothetic ones applied to individual cases. Conversely, Kline (1981) believes that the existence of personality scales or question naires is not incompatible with the notion of uniqueness: in any one sample individuals will have very different profiles across a range of scales, but this does not mean that they will not share certain characteristics or groups of characteristics in common with other members of the sample.

BEHAVIOUR—IS IT THE PRODUCT OF PERSONALITY OR THE SITUATION, OR BOTH?

Most definitions of traits focus on their stability and permanency which, in turn, implies that an individual's behaviour is *consistent* over time and from one situation to another.

Indeed, Baron and Byrne define personality as:

> ... The combination of those relatively enduring traits which influence behaviour in a predictable way in a variety of situations ... (Baron and Byrne, 1991)

Guilford (1959), for example, defined a trait as, 'any relatively enduring way in which one individual differs from another' and Hall and Lindzey (1957) defined it as, 'a determining tendency or predisposition to respond'.

When discussing the attribution process (Chapter 17) we noted that there is a tendency to attribute other people's behaviour primarily to their dispositional qualities (including personality traits) as opposed to situational factors (fundamental attribution error) while we tend to see our own behaviour primarily as a response to the situation (actor–observer effect). It follows from this that we are likely to regard the behaviour of others as more consistent (and, hence, more predictable) and to regard our own as more variable from situation to situation (and, hence, less predictable).

Seeing behaviour as primarily caused by personality traits (the *trait approach*) is usually opposed to what has become known as *situationalism* (Mischel, 1968)—the view that behaviour is largely determined by situational factors.

Mischel, a social learning theorist (see Chapters 7 and 27), threw doubt on the validity of the trait approach by reviewing a large number of studies which showed that correlations between scores on personality tests and measures of behaviour in various situations rarely exceeded 0.3. This lack of cross-situation consistency was taken by Mischel to indicate the importance of the situation in determining behaviour. For example, if people have been reinforced for behaving in particular ways in particular kinds of situation, or if different kinds of models have been available, then we would expect people to behave differently in different situations and there is no longer any need to appeal to traits since they are used to account for consistency which Mischel believed is lacking.

However, intuitively there seems to be something wrong with situationalism, at least in its extreme form. Surely different people behave differently even *within* the same situation and, conversely, are we not recognizably the *same* person from one situation to another?

Eysenck and Eysenck (1980) and Kline (1983) cite a number of studies which demonstrate consistency between scores on questionnaires and rating scales on the one hand and behaviour on the other, with average correlations of around 0.8 and Bowers (1973) criticized the social learning theorists for favouring an experimental design which is intended to emphasize the role of situational determinants of behaviour (situation-specificity) relative to behavioural consistency or stability.

A number of writers have pointed out that to regard behaviour as being caused *either* by situational factors *or* by personality traits is an oversimplification of a complex issue. Bowers (1973), Endler (1975) and Pervin and Lewis (1978) all advocate an *interactionist* position, which stresses the mutual influence of situational *and* dispositional variables.

Bowers, for instance, reviewed eleven studies covering a wide range of behaviour including aggression in young boys, anxiety in students and resistance to temptation in children and concluded that 13 per cent of the variance in subjects' behaviour was due to *person* variables, 10 per cent to *situational* variables and 20 per cent to an *interaction* between the two.

Mischel has himself moved towards a more interactionist position (eg 1973) but prefers to talk about 'person' variables (as we saw in Chapter 27) as opposed to traits, the former being more cognitive, the latter being more related to temperament. Mischel believes that the 'same' situation can have different meaning for different individuals, depending on past learning experiences. This determines how we select, evaluate and interpret stimuli and, in turn, how particular stimuli will affect behaviour. It follows that situational factors cannot account adequately for human behaviour on their own because they do not exist *objectively*, independently of the actor. Based on a study of children's ability to resist temptation when looking at attractive sweets, Mischel concluded that:

> The results clearly show that what is in the children's heads—not what is physically in front of them—determines their ability to delay. (Mischel, 1973)

Bem and Allen (1974), while recognizing the validity of Mischel's criticisms of trait theory, also stressed the considerable importance of trait theory. They argued that our intuitions are not entirely wrong—each person will show consistent behaviour as far as a few traits are concerned but which traits they are will vary from person to person.

Students were asked to rate themselves on their consistency of 'friendliness' and 'conscientiousness' and for each trait they were divided into two groups, one which rated themselves as consistent and one which rated themselves as quite inconsistent. These self-ratings were then compared with ratings from subjects' parents and friends and with the ratings of two independent observers who rated their behaviour in group discussions and other situations.

The crucial finding was that subjects who rated themselves as consistent on one or other trait were also rated as being consistent by others on that trait (for instance, for friendliness, the correlation was 0.73) while those who described themselves as inconsistent were rated in this way by others too (0.3).

Not only were subjects quite accurate in assessing their own behaviour, but subjects who showed consistency on one trait were not necessarily consistent on the other, showing that people vary in their consistency on different traits. As Hilgard et al (1979) point out, if a random selection of subjects is taken in an attempt to demonstrate high cross-situational consistency (as would be predicted by a trait theorist), this is bound to fail, because some subjects will be highly consistent on that trait while others will be low on consistency. The claim that some people behave consistently with respect to certain traits while other people behave consistently on others, is called the *metatrait hypothesis* (Baron and Byrne, 1991). (We should also note that those traits on which individuals rate themselves as consistent—and on which they are consistent as rated by others—are likely to be an important part of their self-image and, in Allport's terms, are likely to be central traits.)

Bem and Allen (1974) conclude that we must take internal and external forces into account, the former including the person's perception of the situation. Similarly, to predict behaviour we must assess people *and* situations, as what is taken to be subjects' behavioural inconsistency may be due as much to the investigator's ignorance of how they perceive or construe situations as to their ratings on particular traits.

When situational factors are very powerful, personality factors are relatively weak in explaining people' behaviour. Milgram's classic study of obedience and Zimbardo et al's Prison Simulation experiment (see Chapter 20) are good examples of how the 'demands of the situation' can largely 'over-ride' individual traits and dispositions, so that knowing what these demands are is a fairly accurate predictor of how people will behave (*inter-individual consistency*). However, even here not all subjects behave in an identical way. In general, when situational factors are numerous and complex, or weak, personality variables are more likely to operate and knowing how particular individuals usually behave in a variety of situations will be a much better predictor of how they will behave in the current situation (*intra-individual consistency; see* Sources of Error in the Attribution Process, Chapter 17).

THE TYPE AND TRAIT APPROACH— EYSENCK AND CATTELL

To understand the similarities and differences between these two psychometric theorists, we need to say something about Factor Analysis (FA) which is an essential part of this approach.

THE USE OF FACTOR ANALYSIS

Factor analysis is a statistical technique, based on correlation, which attempts to reduce a large amount of data (scores on personality questionnaires, objective tests and other measuring devices) to a much smaller amount. Essentially, the aim is to discover which test items correlate with one another and which do not and then to identify the resulting correlation clusters (or factors). Put another way, what is the smallest number of factors which can adequately account for the variance between subjects on the measures in question?

Assuming that the tests are 'good' tests, the researcher is trying to discover the fundamental components of personality which apply to everyone and in terms of which everyone can be compared. As measured by the tests, individuals will differ in the degree to which they display these components. But what is meant by a good test?

(a) A good test should have *discriminatory power*, ie it should produce a wide distribution of scores.

(b) A good test should be properly *standardized*, ie it should have been tried out with a large, representative, sample of the population for whom the test is intended so that the resulting norms (typical scores or distribution for the groups) can be legitimately used when assessing an individual's score.

(c) A good test should be *reliable*, ie should consistently measure the variable it measures.

(d) A good test should be *valid*, ie it should actually measure what it claims to measure.

(These components were discussed in relation to intelligence tests in Chapter 28.)

Just as there are different kinds of reliability and validity, so there are different kinds of FA. One of the most important distinctions is between *orthogonal* and *oblique* methods. An *orthogonal* method aims to identify a small number of powerful factors which are independent of each other (uncorrelated), and this is the method preferred by Eysenck. An *oblique* method aims to identify a larger number of less powerful factors which are not independent (ie they are correlated to some degree), and this is the method preferred by Cattell.

Since it is possible to carry out a further FA of oblique factors, they are referred to as *first-order factors* and the resulting re-grouping of the oblique factors as *second-order factors*. In fact, Cattell has discovered a small number of second-order factors which correspond closely to Eysenck's three major second-order factors (see below).

Eysenck's second-order factors are referred to as *types* (what Cattell calls *surface traits*) and Cattell's first-order factors as *traits* (what Cattell calls *source traits*). The differences between the two theorists are summarized in Table 29.2.

	EYSENCK	CATTELL
Preferred method of Factor Analysis	Orthogonal	Oblique
Level of analysis	Second order	First order
Description of Factors	Types ('Surface Traits')	Traits ('Source Traits')

Table 29.2 Differences between Eysenck and Cattell regarding factor analysis

What is it that determines which method is chosen by a particular researcher? Is one superior to the other?

Ultimately, the method used depends on the taste or preference of the researchers. Both Cattell and Eysenck believe that their method is the one which best reflects the psychological reality of personality, but there is no objective way of establishing that one is right and the other wrong.

Because there is an infinite number of possible solutions, Heim (1975) believes that FA should not be used at all. However, Thurstone (1947) had argued that *rotation to simple structure* could overcome this difficulty and Cattell (1966) and Cattell and Kline (1977) support this view. *Simple structure* means that each factor will have a few high loadings (ie correlate quite highly with a few other factors) and a large number of low or nil loadings (very little or no correlation with a large number of factors), making each factor simple to interpret. The rationale behind simple structure is the law of parsimony, the most economical solution to the problem. As Kline (1981) suggests, if each FA solution is regarded as a hypothesis accounting for the correlations, the most simple is to be preferred. Cattell argues that an orthogonal technique prevents the attainment of simple structure.

Guilford (1959), on the other hand, believes that a set of uncorrelated factors is more simple than a set of oblique or correlated ones, which is why Eysenck opts for an orthogonal technique (again, see Chapter 28).

According to Kline (1981), most factor analysts, in practice, prefer oblique factors.

EYSENCK'S TYPE THEORY

The use of the term 'type' (since it is based on second-order FA) to describe Eysenck's theory is, in fact, a misnomer, since Eysenck (Fig. 29.2) proposes major *dimensions* of personality which represent continuums along which everyone can be placed. By contrast, a true type theory places people in categories so that any individual can only belong to one or another.

Figure 29.2 Hans J. Eysenck (born 1916)

One of the earliest type theories (and, indeed, one of the first theories of personality of any kind) was Galen's theory of the four Humours (put forward in the second century AD); these are included in the inner circle of Eysenck's diagram, shown in Figure 29.3.

Eysenck's dimensions in fact constitute the highest level of a *hierarchy* (Cattell's 'surface' traits) with a number of traits at the next level down (Cattell's 'source' traits), and below that a set of habitual responses (typical ways of behaving) linked to a particular trait. At the lowest level is a specific response (a response on one particular occasion; see Fig. 29.4). This hierarchical model is similar to Vernon's (1950) model of intelligence, to which Eysenck subscribes (see Chapter 28).

Figure 29.3 Dimensions of personality. (From Eysenck, 1965)

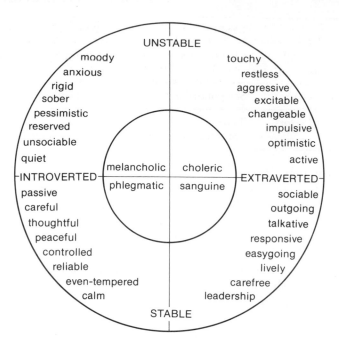

Figure 29.3 Dimensions of personality. (From Eysenck, 1965)

Figure 29.4 Eysenck's hierarchical model of personality in relation to the introversion dimension. (After Eysenck, 1953)

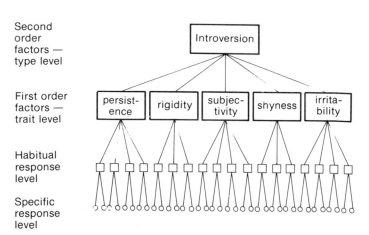

INTROVERSION–EXTROVERSION, NEUROTICISM AND PSYCHOTICISM

Eysenck (1947) factor analysed thirty-nine items of personal data for each of 700 neurotic soldiers, screening them for brain damage and physical illness; the items included personality ratings. Two orthogonal (uncorrelated) factors emerged, introversion–extroversion (E) and neuroticism or emotionality–stability (N). These two dimensions are assumed to be normally distributed so that most people will score somewhere in the middle of the scale and very few at either extreme. The following descriptions are of 'typical' introverts and extroverts, and are 'idealized extremes' (or ideal types):

The typical introvert is a quiet, retiring sort of person, introspective, fond of books rather than people; he is reserved and distant except to intimate friends. He tends to plan ahead, 'looks before he leaps' and distrusts the impulse of the moment. He does not like excitement, takes matters of everyday life with proper seriousness, and likes a well-ordered mode of life. He keeps his feelings under close control, seldom behaves in an aggressive manner, and does not lose his temper easily. He is reliable, somewhat pessimistic, and places great importance on ethical standards. (Eysenck, 1965)

The typical extrovert is sociable, likes parties, has many friends, needs to have people to talk to, and does not like reading or studying by himself. He craves excitement, takes chances, often sticks his neck out, acts on the spur of the moment, and is generally an impulsive individual. He is fond of practical jokes, always has a ready answer, and generally likes change; he is carefree, easy-going, optimistic and likes to 'laugh and be merry'. He prefers to keep moving and doing things, tends to be aggressive and lose his temper quickly; altogether his feelings are not kept under tight control, and he is not always a reliable person. (Eysenck, 1965)

As regards neuroticism, the typical high N scorer could be described as:

. . . an anxious, worrying individual, moody and frequently depressed; he is likely to sleep badly and to suffer from various psychosomatic disorders. He is overly emotional, reacting too strongly to all sorts of stimuli and finds it difficult to get back on an even keep after each emotionally arousing experience. (Eysenck, 1965)

By contrast, the stable individual:

. . . tends to respond emotionally only slowly and generally weakly and to return to baseline quickly after emotional arousal; he is usually calm, even-tempered, controlled and unworried.' (Eysenck, 1965)

Since the original 1947 study, the existence of E and N has been supported by further research involving literally thousands of subjects.

In 1952, a study of psychiatric patients uncovered a third dimension—psychoticism (P)—also unrelated to E and N. However, P is less well-established than the other two dimensions:

A high scorer, then, may be described as being solitary, not caring for people; he is often troublesome, not fitting in anywhere. He may be cruel and inhumane, lacking in feelings and empathy, and altogether insensitive. He is hostile to others, even his own kith and kin, and aggressive, even to loved ones. He has a liking for odd and unusual things, and a disregard for danger; he likes to make fools of other people, and to upset them. (Eysenck and Eysenck, 1975)

Unlike E and N, P is not normally distributed—both normals and neurotics score low on P. Eysenck also believes that P overlaps with (other) psychiatric labels, in particular with 'schizoid', 'psychopathic' and 'behaviour disorders' (see Chapter 30). However, there is only a *quantitative* difference (ie a difference of *degree*) between normals and psychotics (and this applies equally to differences between normals and neurotics).

PERSONALITY QUESTIONNAIRES

The original questionnaire was the Maudsley Medical Questionnaire (MMQ), first used in 1952, which only measured N. This was replaced in 1959 by the Maudsley Personality Inventory (MPI), which measured both E and N. The Eysenck Personality Inventory (EPI) added a Lie

Scale, which measures a person's tendency to give socially-desirable answers and which Eysenck believes is a stable personality dimension (Eysenck and Eysenck, 1964). Finally, the Eysenck Personality Questionnaire added a P scale (Eysenck and Eysenck, 1975). There are also junior versions of these questionnaires for use with nine-year-olds and over.

The scales all comprise items of a 'yes/no' variety. They are essentially intended as research tools (as opposed to diagnostic tools for use in clinical settings) and, as such, they are generally regarded as acceptable, reliable and valid (Kline, 1981; Shackleton and Fletcher, 1984), the main exception being the P scale, which Eysenck himself admits is psychometrically inferior to other scales.

An important way in which Eysenck has attempted to validate his scales is through *criterion analysis*. This involves giving the questionnaires to groups of individuals who are known to differ on the dimensions in question. For example, although the test is not meant to diagnose neurosis, we would still expect diagnosed neurotics to score very high on N compared with non-neurotics, and generally this is found to be the case. Eysenck also believes that criterion analysis overcomes the problem of the arbitrary nature of the labels given to the factors that emerge from FA (see Chapter 28).

THE BIOLOGICAL BASIS OF PERSONALITY

Eysenck's theory attempts to explain personality differences in terms of differences in the kinds of nervous system that individuals possess. In turn, these nervous system differences are inherited. As far as E is concerned, it is the balance between *excitation* and *inhibition* processes in the central nervous system that is crucial, specifically the Reticular Activating System (RAS; see Chapter 4.) The RAS is located in the central core of the brain-stem and its main function is to maintain an optimum level of alertness or 'arousal': it can do this either by enhancing the incoming sensory data to the cortex through the excitation of neural impulses or it can 'damp them down' through inhibition.

In these terms, extroverts have a 'strong nervous system'; their RAS is biased towards the inhibition of impulses, inhibition builds up quickly and strongly and it dissipates only slowly, with the effect of *reducing* the intensity of any sensory stimulation reaching the cortex (they are *chronically under-aroused*).

For introverts, the bias is in the opposite direction; for them, excitation builds up strongly and rapidly and inhibition develops slowly and weakly, with the effect of *increasing* the intensity of any sensory stimulation reaching the cortex (they are *chronically over-aroused*).

As far as N is concerned, it is the reactivity (or *lability*) of the Autonomic Nervous System (ANS) that determines a person's standing on the scale and, in particular, differences in the limbic system, which controls the ANS. Especially important is the sympathetic branch of the ANS, which is activated by frightening or stressful experiences ('fight or flight syndrome'), resulting in increases in heart-rate, breathing rate, blood pressure, sweating, adrenaline production and so on (see Chapter 4).

The person who scores high on N has an ANS which reacts particularly strongly and quickly to stressful situations compared with less emotional or more stable individuals.

Finally, regarding P, the biological basis is much more uncertain but Eysenck (1980) has suggested that it may be related to levels of the male hormone, androgen, and/or other hormones.

Is there any evidence to support this part of Eysenck's theory?

Eysenck (1967) linked the concepts of inhibition and excitation to *psychical fatigue*, so that extroverts (who are characterized by *low arousal*) 'tire' more easily (eg become bored more easily and persevere less) than introverts (who are characterized by *high arousal*). According to Kline (1983), there should be clear differences between introverts and extroverts on long and tedious jobs: extroverts should start better than introverts, do worse in the middle and then improve again towards the end, while introverts would work much more steadily throughout. Evidence to support these hypotheses comes from Eysenck (1967 and 1971) and Harkins and Green (1975), who found that introverts do better at vigilance tasks, which require prolonged periods of concentration.

Wilson (1976) points out that we would expect introverts to be more difficult to sedate using a drug such as sodium amytal because they are supposed to be more aroused. He cites a study by Claridge and Herrington (1963) in which introverted neurotics (*dysthymics*) were more difficult to sedate than extroverted neurotics (*hysterics*), the latter being more easily sedated than normal subjects.

Again, regardless of an individual's normal position on the scale, stimulant drugs should shift behaviour in an *introverted* direction while depressant drugs should have the opposite effect, pushing behaviour in an *extroverted* direction and Eysenck (1967) claims to have found considerable support for these hypotheses.

According to Eysenck (1970), the greater sensitivity of introverts to stimuli is matched by their relative dislike of strong stimuli; everyone has an optimum level of stimulation but this is *lower* for the more highly aroused introvert. Introverts have lower pain thresholds and extroverts are more susceptible to the adverse effects of sensory deprivation. For example one demonstration of the 'stimulus-hunger' of extroverts is their willingness to go to great lengths to obtain a 'reward' of loud jazz music or bright lights which introverts work hard to *avoid*.

However, Claridge (1967) could not find a simple relationship between E and physiological arousal; instead, there seems to be a complex interconnection between arousal and the individual's position on E and N (as shown by the Claridge and Herrington (1963) study).

THE RELATIONSHIP BETWEEN PERSONALITY AND CONDITIONABILITY

From a strictly psychological point of view, the importance of the biological aspects of Eysenck's theory is how they are related to individual differences in *conditionability*. Because extroverts require a stronger stimulus to make an impact (they are 'stimulus-hungry') compared with the more easily stimulated introvert, and because the learning of S–R connections is best achieved by a strong and rapid build-up of excitation in the nervous system (which is characteristic of introverts), introverts are more easily conditioned than extroverts. Does the evidence support Eysenck?

Despite Eysenck's strong claims to the contrary, the evidence is equivocal; for instance, about half the studies he reviewed in 1967 support his predictions while the other half do not. Eysenck seems to regard conditionability as a *unitary* trait, ie if introverts are easily conditioned to one kind of stimulus, they will also condition easily to a range of other stimuli. However, such a general trait has never been demonstrated and the experimental evidence mainly involves three conditioned responses—the GSR (galvanic skin response), the eye-blink and simple verbal conditioning. According to Kline (1983), until such a general dimension is discovered, this part of the theory remains weak and, in addition, extrapolation from laboratory studies to real-life situations is a dangerous business.

PERSONALITY AND CRIMINALITY

In view of the criticisms of conditionability, it becomes all the more important to 'test' the theory in the 'real world' and one way in which Eysenck has done this is by advancing a theory of criminality. For Eysenck, the criminal is a *neurotic extrovert*: because the extrovert is more difficult to condition, and because 'conscience' is nothing more than a series of conditioned anxiety responses (see Chapter 27), the neurotic extrovert is under-socialized and has an under-developed conscience.

Cochrane (1974) reviewed a number of studies in which prisoners and control groups were given EPI questionnaires. Although prisoners are generally higher on N, they are *not* higher on E and, indeed, several studies have shown criminals to be *less* extroverted (and so *more* introverted) than controls. Given the crucial part played by conditionability in Eysenck's theory, these findings would appear to seriously undermine it. However, Eysenck (1974) retorted by claiming that the EPI largely measures the 'sociability' component of extroversion rather than the 'impulsivity' component, which is more relevant to conditionability; here, he is certainly changing his earlier position whereby he equated 'sociability' (ie capacity for socialization) and 'conditionability'. Cochrane concludes that, at least in its original form, the theory has been discredited.

Even if prisoners were uniformly more extroverted and neurotic than non-prisoners, it could still be possible to explain these differences by reference to factors other than personality. For example, offenders who are caught (or found guilty) might differ in certain significant ways from those who are not (or who are not found guilty), such as the nature of the offence and the 'offender's' social status.

Hampson (1982), in a review of the research, concludes that, although there is some evidence that criminals are highly neurotic, the neurotic–extrovert theory is not supported (thus agreeing with Cochrane) and any attempt to identify any personal trait or dimension which differentiates criminals from non-criminals has been singularly unsuccessful.

A final criticism comes from Heather, who argues that:

The notion that such a complex and meaningful *social* phenomenon as crime can ever be explained by appealing to the activity of individual nervous systems would be laughable were it not so insidious. (Heather, 1976)

What makes the theory insidious, he says, is that it, 'places the fault inside individuals rather than in the social system where it almost always belongs' (see the discussion of Reductionism in Chapter 2).

PSYCHIATRIC DIAGNOSIS

Eysenck argues for a dimensional (as opposed to a categorical or classificatory) approach to psychiatric diagnosis, with two independent dimensions of N and P each forming a continuum from extreme abnormality to normality.

However, the whole status of P as a separate dimension has been seriously questioned. There is some evidence that P is a normal personality dimension (ie continuous between normals and psychiatric patients) but there is also considerable overlap between low N subjects and high P subjects on several psychological and physiological measures.

Within the broad group of neurotic disorders, Eysenck distinguishes between *dysthymic* disorders, such as depression, obsessions and phobias (related to high N and low E scores) and *hysterical* disorders (related to high N and high E scores). Patients who are high on P and low on E are likely to develop a psychotic, schizophrenic, disorder. According to McGuire et al (1963), hysterics tend to be rather lower on N than dysthymics but normal on E, that is, neither highly introverted nor highly extroverted.

Although the theory hinges on the differences in conditionability between different groups of neurotic patients (a phobia, for instance, being seen as a conditioned anxiety response to a previously neutral stimulus through classical conditioning), and despite the major contribution which Eysenck himself has made to behaviour therapy (see Chapter 31), most behaviour therapists do not seem to use the concepts of E and N at all. According to Peck and Whitlow (1975), lack of evidence has led to a general disillusionment with standardized tests (such as the EPI and EPQ) as predictors of response to treatment or as a measure of change.

AN EVALUATION OF EYSENCK'S THEORY AS A WHOLE

1) One of the most serious weaknesses seems to be the failure to produce any convincing evidence that introverts do, in fact, condition more easily than extroverts. Conditionability is a vital part of the overall theory because it 'points inwards' towards the biological (including genetic) basis of personality and 'outwards' towards the socialization experiences of different individuals (behaviour always being the product of an interaction between a nervous system and an environment).

2) Heim (1970) has criticized the EPI (and, by implication, the EPQ) because of its forced-choice ('yes/no') form; she argues that a few, simple yes/no questions can hardly be expected to do justice to the complexities of human personality and she has criticized the Lie Scale for its lack of subtlety (again, see Reductionism, Chapter 2).

3) Validation of the scales, as we have seen, has involved the use of criterion groups, for instance, groups of neurotics who tend to score at

Figure 29.5 *Raymond B. Cattell (born 1905). (From Ewen, R. B. (1988)* An Introduction to Theories of Personality *(3rd edn). Hillsdale, New Jersey: Lawrence Erlbaum Associates, Inc.)*

the extreme ends of the scale. But can we assume that the scale is 'valid' for the majority of people who lie somewhere in the middle? Gibson (1971) tried to overcome this by asking students to complete the EPI to rate an unselected group of their friends and he found significant overall correlations between these ratings and their friends' self-ratings on the E and N scales. This offers some support for the validity of the EPI when used with unselected subjects who may score at any point along the scale.

4)   Shackleton and Fletcher (1984) have pointed out the vast amount of research Eysenck's theory has generated, 'whilst the theory as it now stands is not adequate, some aspects of it, maybe even most, may well survive the test of time'.

CATTELL'S TRAIT THEORY

As we have seen, Cattell's (Fig. 29.5) factors are first-order, oblique, source traits, which he believed to be the fundamental dimensions of personality, the underlying roots or causes of clusters of behaviour that are surface traits. Whereas surface traits may correspond to common sense ways of describing behaviour, and may sometimes be measured by simple observation, they are, in fact, the result of interactions among the source traits; valid explanations of behaviour must concentrate on source traits as the structural factors which determine personality.

Cattell identified three sources of data relevant to personality, L-data (L for 'Life'), Q-data (Q for 'Questionnaire') and T-data (T for 'Tests').

1)   *L-data* refer to ratings by observers which Cattell regarded as the best source but which he also recognized are notoriously difficult to make; great skill and time are needed to make accurate ratings. His research began by identifying all the words in the English language which describe behaviour (trait elements), including the more technical terms from psychology and psychiatry, and after removing all the synonyms, a small sample of students was intesively studied for six months by trained personnel who rated each subject on all the trait elements.

The resulting data was factor analysed, producing fifteen first-order traits or source traits (also called primary traits by Cattell).

2)   *Q-data* refers to scores on personality questionnaires. Based on the original fifteen source traits, a large number of questionnaire items were assembled and given to large numbers of subjects. When their scores were factor analysed, sixteen source traits emerged, composed of twelve of the original L-data factors plus four new ones. These sixteen factors were measured by the widely used Cattell 16PF (Personality Factor) Questionnaire, which is intended for adults. As shown in Table 29.3, the first twelve factors are found in L-data and Q-data, while the last four (Q1–Q4) are based on Q-data only.

The Pre-School Personality Quiz (PSPQ) is designed for four- to six-year-olds, the Child's Personality Quiz (CPQ) for six- to eleven-year-olds and the High School Personality Questionnaire (HSPQ) for twelve- to fifteen-year-olds.

From Table 29.3 you will notice that there is no D-factor (excitability versus undemonstrativeness) or J-factor (individuality versus liking for group action): these are adolescent factors which appear in the HSPQ

DESCRIPTION	NAME OF TRAIT	DESCRIPTION
Warm-hearted, outgoing, easygoing, sociable	A Affectia v. Sizia	Reserved, cool, detached, aloof
High score: abstract-thinker, intellectual interests	B Intelligence	Low score: concrete-thinker, practically-minded
Emotionally stable, calm, mature, stable	C Ego-strength v. Dissatisfied emotionality	Emotionally unstable, easily upset, immature
Assertive, aggressive, dominant, competitive	E Dominance v. Submisiveness	Submissive, modest, mild, accommodating
Happy-go-lucky, enthusiastic, unworrying	F Surgency v. Desurgency	Pessimistic, subdued, sober, cautious, serious, taciturn
Persevering, conscientious moralistic, straight-laced } High score	G Super-ego strength	Expedient, disregards rules, feels few obligations, law to onself } Low score
Adventurous, gregarious, uninhibited, socially bold	H Parmia v. Threctia	Shy, restrained, timid, diffident, inhibited
Tender-minded, sensitive, gentle, clinging	I Premsia v. Harria	Tough-minded, self-reliant, practical, realistic, no-nonsense
Suspicious, jealous, self-opinionated	L Protension v. Alexia	Trusting, understanding, adaptable, easy to get along with
Unconventional, imaginative, strong subjective life, bohemian	M Autia v. Praxernia	Conformist, conventional, influenced by external realities
Shrewd, calculating, worldly, penetrating	N Shrewdness v. Naivety	Simple, artless, natural, unpretentious, lacking insight
Insecure, worrying, self-reproaching	O Guilt proneness	Self-assured, confident, complacent, spirited
Liberal, free-thinking	Q1 Radicalism v. Conservatism	Conservative, traditional
Prefers own decisions	Q2 Self-sufficiency v. Group dependence	Group dependent, a follower
High score: Controlled socially precise	Q3 Self-sentiment strength	Low score: Undisciplined, careless of social rules
High score. Relaxed, composed	Q4 Ergic tension	Low score: Overwrought, tense, frustrated

Table 29.3 The sixteen source traits measured by Cattell's 16PF questionnaire. (After Cattell, 1965)

but not in the 16PF (conversely, Factors L, M and Q1 appear in the 16PF but not in the HSPQ). There is also a Clinical Analysis Questionnaire (CAQ) designed for use with psychotic patients.

Unlike Eysenck's questionnaires, Cattell's scales are not exclusively of the 'yes/no' variety; for instance, there may be three choices—yes/occasionally/no. However, there is the problem of social desirability (which Eysenck tries to measure by inclusion of an L-scale) and also acquiescence, a kind of 'response set' in which the subject tends to put 'yes' rather than 'no' or to agree with the questionnaire items.

Although intended mainly as a research instrument, the 16PF has been used in clinical work, as well as occupational selection and assessment. However, its validity for use as a diagnostic tool in a clinical setting has been seriously questioned.

Five alternative forms of the 16PF have been developed (Cattell et al, 1970) of which A and B are the most widely used; alternative forms are very important when the realiability of the test is being investigated (see Chapter 28).

3) *T-data* refer to objective tests specially devised to measure personality; for instance, the Objective–Analytic (O–A) test battery measures, amongst other things, GSR, reaction time, body-sway and suggestibility. T-data are objective primarily in the sense that the purpose of the test is concealed from the subject. Factor analysis of these has yielded twenty-one factors altogether (the O–A battery measuring just twelve of these) and some of these correspond to a number of second-order factors obtained from Q-data.

FIRST- AND SECOND-ORDER FACTORS: CATTELL AND EYSENCK COMPARED

As we have seen, first-order (oblique) factors correlate with each other to some degree and, indeed, Cattell argues that overlapping factors are what would be expected since, for example, an intelligent person (B-factor) is also likely to be shrewd and worldly (N-factor). We should note here that whereas Eysenck does not include intelligence amongst his three major personality dimensions, Cattell does include it in his sixteen primary factors, although it assumes a rather different meaning in the 16PF than it does in his distinction between fluid and crystallized intelligence (see Chapters 24 and 28).

However, Cattell has carried out a second-order factor analysis of his sixteen primary factors which yields a number of surface traits, the two most important being *exvia–invia* and *anxiety*, which seem to correspond to Eysenck's E and N respectively (Fig. 29.6). Others include *radicalism* (aggressive and independent), *tendermindedness* (sensitivity, frustration and emotionality) and *superego* (conscientious, conforming and preserving).

Another important difference is that Cattell believes that there is a fundamental *discontinuity* between normals and, say, schizophrenics, ie there is a *qualitative* difference and not merely a quantitative one, as Eysenck maintains. For instance, Q-data used with psychiatric patients produce twelve factors which discriminate psychotics as a group (eg paranoia, suicidal disgust, schizophrenia and high general psychosis),

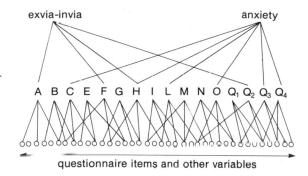

Second order factors — type level

First order factors — trait level

Figure 29.6 The hierarchical organization of personality resulting from a second-order analysis of the first-order 'source of traits'. (After Cattell, 1965)

who score very high on these compared with normals. A second-order FA of Q-data from psychiatric patients yields three factors, one of which resembles Eysenck's P.

Altogether, using L and Q-data, Cattell has identified twenty-three primary factors, although the sixteen shown in Table 29.3 are still the best established, plus eight surface traits in normal subjects, as well as the twelve source and three surface traits in abnormal subjects (Cattell and Kline, 1977).

EVALUATION OF THE 16PF

As far as test/re-test reliability is concerned (ie how consistently subjects score when they do the test on a subsequent occasion), no data are presented, as Cattell assumes that normal variations in traits occur over time and so low test/re-test correlations are only to be expected.

As for its validity, this has been challenged by several researchers, including Eysenck and Eysenck (1969), and Browne and Howarth (1977), all of whom found a smaller number of source traits than Cattell.

Again, Howarth and Browne (1971) failed to find any kind of clear-cut factor structure using a sample of over 500 students. However, Kline (1981) has pointed out that different investigators have used different techniques and so it is not always possible to make meaningful comparisons.

As we have already seen, the agreement between Cattell and Eysenck as far as certain second-order factors are concerned tends to enhance the validity of the 16PF and Cattell believes that many of these criticisms no longer apply to the improved 1974 version of the questionnaire.

PERSONALITY AND BEHAVIOUR

Although clearly belonging to the nomothetic approach which sees behaviour as reflecting a relatively enduring personality (see Table 29.1) Cattell, much more than Eysenck, acknowledges the way that behaviour can fluctuate in response to situational factors.

His definition of personality as 'what determines behaviour in a defined situation and a defined mood' (Cattell, 1965) implies that behaviour is never totally determined by source traits: although personality factors remain fairly stable over time, they constitute only one kind of variable influencing overt behaviour. So what other kinds are there?

Cattell distinguishes between: (i) *mood and state factors* (eg depression, arousal, anxiety, fatigue and intoxication); and (ii) *motivational factors*. He distinguishes two kinds of motivational factors: (i) *ergs*, which are the innate, biological, drives (the ten so far identified are food-seeking, gregariousness, mating, narcissism, acquisitiveness, parental, pugnacity, security, exploration and assertiveness); and (ii) *sentiments*, which are culturally acquired drives.

Cattell also identifies seven main components of a motive, three of which are: *alpha*, the 'id' component, coresponding to 'I want'; *beta*, the 'ego' component, concerned with knowledge and information; *gamma*, the 'superego' component, corresponding to 'I ought'.

Although an ardent behaviourist, Cattell was influenced by Freud's psychoanalytic theory, at least to the extent that three of the 16PF names are derived from Freudian terminology (C—ego strength, G—superego strength and Q4—ergic or id tension) together with the three components of a motive which we have just discussed.

We shall discuss the relationship between Freud's theory and factor-analytic concepts later in the chapter.

Figure 29.7 George A. Kelly (1905–1966). (From Ohio State University Photo Archives)

KELLY'S PERSONAL CONSTRUCT THEORY

As Table 29.1 shows, Kelly's (Fig. 29.7) Personal Construct Theory (PCT) is an *idiographic* approach, stressing the uniqueness of each individual; it is also a *phenomenological* approach, in that it attempts to understand the person in terms of his/her experience and perception of the world, a vew of the world through the person's own eyes and not an observer's interpretation or analysis which is imposed on the person.

Kelly's dissatisfaction with both Freudian and behaviourist theories led him to propose a model of the human being which was radically different from any model previously proposed, namely *man the scientist*. (This was a notion we discussed in relation to interpersonal perception; see Chapter 17.) What does Kelly mean?

We are all scientists in the sense that we put our own interpretation (or theories) on the world of events and from these personal theories we produce hypotheses, which are predictions about future events. Every time we act we are putting our hypotheses to the test and, in this sense, behaviour is the Independent Variable—it is the experiment. Depending on the outcome, our hypotheses are either validated—or not—and this will determine the nature of our subsequent behavioural experiments (Fransella, 1981). But what exactly are these personal theories from which we derive our hypotheses?

To answer this question, we need to discuss Kelly's philosophy of *constructive alternativism*. Although a real world of physical objects and events does exist, no one organism has the privilege of 'knowing' it; all we can do is place our personal constructs upon it and the better our constructs 'fit' the world, the better will be our control over our own, personal world. To quote Kelly:

> Man looks at his world through transparent patterns or templates which he creates and then attempts to fit over the realities of which the world is composed. The fit is not always very good. Yet without such patterns the world appears to be such an undifferentiated homogeneity that man is unable to make any sense of it. (Kelly, 1955)

In other words, there is no way of getting 'behind' our interpretations of the world to check if it matches what the world is *really* like: all we have are our own interpretations (compare this with Gregory's definition of perception; see Chapter 9) and so we necessarily see the world 'through goggles', which cannot be removed. However, these goggles or *constructs* are not fixed once and for all; the person as scientist is constantly engaged in testing, checking, modifying and revising his/her unique set of constructs which represent these working hypotheses.

Each person's construct system is organized in a hierarchical way, with some broad constructs (superordinate) subsuming other, narrow constructs (subordinate). The theory basically comprises a *fundamental postulate* ('A person's processes are psychologically channelized by the ways in which he anticipates events') plus eleven corollaries, meant to explain how we use our personal constructs to predict the future.

THE REPERTORY GRID TECHNIQUE

The original test used for eliciting personal constructs was the Role Construct Repertory Test ('Rep Test'), which was designed for individual use by a clinical psychologist. This has been succeeded by the Repertory Grid Test ('Rep Grid') which is used as a major research instrument (Box 29.1).

The Rep Grid is a very flexible instrument and there are different ways in which it can be used. Kelly himself suggested that twenty-four role titles (elements) might provide a representative sample of 'significant others' and eight different ways in which triads of role titles can be compiled. However this may be done, the Rep Grid is an attempt to help the individual discover the fundamental constructs he/she uses for perceiving and relating to others.

The grid can be factor analysed, and this often reveals that many constructs overlap, ie they mean more or less the same thing: probably between three and six major constructs cover most people's construct system. It can be used nomothetically, as Bannister and Fransella have done with thought-disordered schizophrenics. Their Grid Test of Thought Disorder (Bannister and Fransella, 1966, 1967) contains standardized elements and constructs (ie they are supplied by the researcher) and the test has been standardized on large numbers of similar patients so that an individual score can be compared with group norms. However, this is probably rather far removed from how Kelly intended the technique to be used. It has also been used to study how patients participating in group psychotherapy change their perception of each other (and themselves) during the period of therapy, where the group members are themselves the elements and a number of constructs are supplied (Fransella, 1970). Fransella (1972) has used it extensively with people being treated for severe stuttering.

However, its uses are not confined to clinical situations. Elements need not be people at all, but could be occupations, religions, cars and so on, and Shackleton and Fletcher (1984) argue that the Rep Grid stands on its own as a technique, that is, you do not have to believe in Kelly's PCT in order to use it.

AN EVALUATION OF PCT

Some of the most common criticisms have been to do with the reliability

Box 29.1 *Constructing a Repertory Grid (based on Kelly, 1955)*
The basic method involves the following steps:

(a) Write a list of the most important people in your life (*elements*).
(b) Choose three of these elements.
(c) Ask yourself, 'In what ways are two of these alike and different from the third?' The descriptions given (eg 'My mother and girlfriend are affectionate, my father is not') constitute a *construct* which is expressed in a *bipolar* way, ie 'affectionate–not affectionate'.
(d) This construct is applied to all the remaining elements. Remember, constructs are bipolar opposites (*either* affectionate *or* not affectionate).
(e) Then another set of three elements is selected and the whole process is repeated. It continues until either you have produced all the constructs you can (which is usually no more than twenty-five with one set of elements) or until a sufficient number has been produced as judged by the investigator.

All this information can be collated in the form of a *grid*, with the elements across the top and the constructs down the side and a tick or cross indicating which pole of the construct is applicable (for example, a tick indicates 'affectionate' and a cross indicates 'not-affectionate').

Constructs	Elements							
	Mother	Father	Brother	Sister	Boy-friend	Girl-friend	Psychology lecturer	etc.
Affectionate (√) Not affectionate (×)	√	×	×	√	×	√	√	
Intelligent (√) Unintelligent (×)								
Sense of humour (√) No sense of humour (×)								
etc.								

and validity of the Rep Grid. Gathercole et al (1970), for example, studied 'parallel-form' reliability (in which different persons were put into the same role titles) as well as test/re-test reliability of various types of Rep Grid in general use. They concluded that generalizations about individuals based on single grids, especially if the constructs are elicited from the subject, should only be made with extreme caution because the results are likely to be unreliable.

However, Bannister and Mair (1968) believe that the concepts of reliability and validity are not strictly relevant or applicable since the Rep Grid is primarily a methodology rather than a standardized test.

Unfortunately, we have only been able to scratch the surface of Kelly's very complex and challenging theory. An excellent summary is Bannister and Fransella's, *Inquiring Man* (1980) and Fransella (1981). They point out that the theory is deliberately stated in very abstract terms so as to avoid the limitations of a particular time and culture; it is an attempt to redefine psychology as a psychology of persons and is 'content-free'. As we noted earlier, PCT is not so much a personality theory, more a total psychology: Kelly is not concerned with separate sub-divisions of psychology as dealt with in most textbooks because he belives these can all be dealt with by the fundamental postulate and eleven corollaries.

For instance, Kelly believes that the traditional concept of *motivation* can be dispensed with. We do not need concepts like drives or needs or psychic energy (see Chapters 6 and 21) to explain what makes people 'get up and go'—man is a form of motion and a basic assumption about life is that 'it goes on', 'It isn't that something *makes* you go on, the going on is *the thing itself*' (Kelly, 1962).

However, he implicitly assumes that we all seek a sense of order and predictability in our dealings with the external world—the overriding goal of anticipating the future represents a basic form of motivation. We achieve this through (as we have already seen) behaving much like a research scientist. 'The scientist's ultimate aim is to predict and control . . .'

Various aspects of *emotion* are dealt with in terms of how an individual's construct system is organized and how it changes; for instance, 'anxiety' is the awareness that what you are confronted with is not within the framework of your existing construct system—you do not know *how* to construe it (this is discussed in Chapter 31). For some, this is far too cognitive and rational an approach; what about the subjective experience (the gut feeling) that we call anxiety? It is almost as if emotional experiences and 'behaviour' itself are being drowned in a sea of constructs.

Peck and Whitlow (1975) believe that Kelly trivializes important aspects of behaviour, including learning, emotion and motivation, as well as neglecting situational influences on behaviour; PCT, they say, appears to place the person in an 'empty world'.

However, they conclude by saying that, 'Personal Construct Theory constitutes a brave and imaginative attempt to create a comprehensive, cognitive, theory of personality' (Peck and Whitlow, 1975).

HUMANISTIC THEORIES

'Humanistic' is an umbrella term (first coined by Cantril in 1955) referring to a group of theories which all share the belief that scientific attempts to study human beings are misplaced and inappropriate, because:

> . . . to see man at second hand through his behaviour as against his experience is ultimately to see ourselves at second hand and never be ourselves. (Evans, 1975)

Maslow introduced the notion of a 'third force' in psychology in 1958—Behaviourism and Psychoanalytic theory being the first and second forces—and it is he and Rogers who are the best known humanistic psychologists.

Humanistic theories (and Kelly's PCT) have their philosophical roots in phenomenology and existentialism and, some would say, they justify the label 'philosophical' more than they warrant the label 'psychological'. They are concerned with characteristics that are distinctively and uniquely human, in particular, experience, uniqueness, meaning, freedom and choice; we have first-hand experience of ourselves as persons and Rogers's particular theory is centred around the self-concept.

Figure 29.8 *Abraham H. Maslow (1908–1970). (From Brandeis University Photo)*

What Rogers and Maslow have in common is their positive evaluation of human nature, a belief in the individual's potential for personal growth, what they call *self-actualization*.

MASLOW'S HIERARCHY OF NEEDS

Self-actualization represents the top-most level of a hierarchy of human needs, which Maslow (Fig. 29.8) first proposed in 1954 (Fig. 29.9). Because he is describing 'needs', Maslow's hierarchy is often discussed in the context of motivation.

According to Maslow, we are subject to two quite different sets of motivational state or forces: (i) those that ensure *survival* by satisfying basic physical and psychological needs (physiological, safety, belongingness and love and esteem needs); and (ii) those that promote the persons's *self-actualization*, ie realizing one's full potential, 'becoming everything that one is capable of becoming' (Maslow, 1970), especially in the intellectual and creative domains:

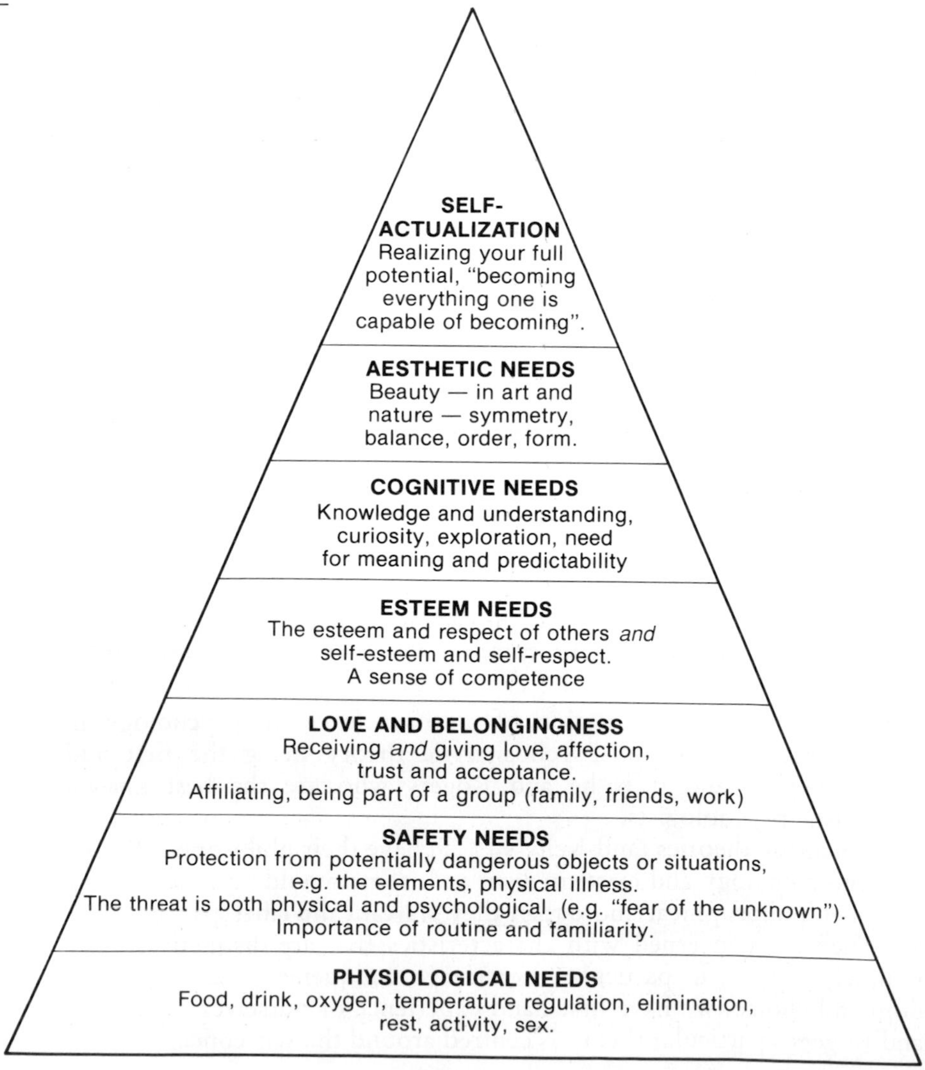

Figure 29.9 *Maslow's hierarchy of needs. (Based on Maslow, 1954)*

SELF-ACTUALIZATION
Realizing your full potential, "becoming everything one is capable of becoming".

AESTHETIC NEEDS
Beauty — in art and nature — symmetry, balance, order, form.

COGNITIVE NEEDS
Knowledge and understanding, curiosity, exploration, need for meaning and predictability

ESTEEM NEEDS
The esteem and respect of others *and* self-esteem and self-respect. A sense of competence

LOVE AND BELONGINGNESS
Receiving *and* giving love, affection, trust and acceptance. Affiliating, being part of a group (family, friends, work)

SAFETY NEEDS
Protection from potentially dangerous objects or situations, e.g. the elements, physical illness. The threat is both physical and psychological. (e.g. "fear of the unknown"). Importance of routine and familiarity.

PHYSIOLOGICAL NEEDS
Food, drink, oxygen, temperature regulation, elimination, rest, activity, sex.

> We share the need for food with all living things, the need for love with (perhaps) the higher apes, [and] the need for Self-Actualization with [no other species]. (Maslow, 1970)

While behaviours that relate to survival or deficiency needs (deficiency or D-Motives) are engaged in because they satisfy those needs (a means to an end), those that relate to self-actualization are engaged in for their own sake, because they are intrinsically satisfying (growth, being or B-Motives):

> Growth is, *in itself*, a rewarding and exciting process. [Examples include] the fulfilling of yearnings and ambitions, like that of being a good doctor; the acquisition of admired skills, like playing the violin or being a good carpenter; the steady increase of understanding about people or about the universe, or about oneself; the development of creativeness in whatever field; or, most important, simply the ambition to be a good human being ... It is simply inaccurate to speak in such instances of tension-reduction, implying thereby getting rid of an annoying state. For these states are not annoying. (Maslow, 1968)

The hierarchical nature of Maslow's theory is intended to emphasize the following points:

1) Needs lower down in the hierarchy must be satisfied before we can fully attend to needs at the next level up; for instance, physiological needs must be met before we concentrate on safety needs. If you are trying to concentrate on what you are reading while your stomach is trying to tell you it is lunchtime, you probably will not absorb much about Maslow; similarly, if you are very tired or in pain.

Yet it is possible to think of exceptions: the starving artist who finds inspiration despite hunger or the mountain-climber who risks his/her life for the sake of adventure (what Maslow would call a 'peak' experience—pun intended!).

2) Higher-level needs are a later evolutionary development, that is, in the development of the human species (*phylogenesis*), self-actualization is a fairly recent need to have appeared. This applies equally to the development of individuals (*ontogenesis*): clearly, babies are much more concerned with their bellies than their brains. However, it is never a case of one need being present and another being absent but rather one predominating over another; this applies at any stage of development.

3) The higher up the hierarchy we go, the more the need becomes linked to life experience and the less the biological character of the need. Individuals will achieve self-actualization in different ways, through different activities and by different routes and this is related to experience, not biology:

> Self-actualization is idiosyncratic, since every person is different ... The individual [must do] what *he*, individually, is fitted for. A musician must make music, an artist must paint, a poet must write, if he is to be ultimately at peace with himself. What a man *can* be, he *must* be. (Maslow, 1968)

4) Following on from 3), the higher up the hierarchy we go, the more difficult the need is to achieve. Many human goals are remote and long-term, and can only be achieved in a series of steps. This pursuit of ends that lie very much in the future is one of the unique features of human behaviour and individuals differ in their ability to set and realize such goals.

WHO ACHIEVES SELF-ACTUALIZATION?

Although we are all, theoretically, capable of self-actualizing, most of us will not do so, or only to a limited degree. Maslow was particularly interested in the characteristics of people whom he considered to have achieved their potential as persons: his list included Einstein, William James, Eleanor Roosevelt, Abraham Lincoln, Spinoza, Thomas Jefferson and Walt Whitman. Some of the characteristics of self-actualizers and some of the behaviours leading to self-actualization are shown in Table 29.4. Although individuals achieve self-actualization in their own,

Table 29.4 Characteristics of self-actualizers and behaviour leading to self-actualization. (After Maslow, 1962/70)

Characteristics of self-actualizers

(i) They perceive reality efficiently and can tolerate uncertainty;
(ii) Accept themselves and others for what they are;
(iii) Spontaneous in thought and action;
(iv) Problem-centred (not self-centred);
(v) Unusual sense of humour;
(vi) Able to look at life objectively;
(vii) Highly creative;
(viii) Resistant to enculturation, but not purposely unconventional;
(ix) Concerned for the welfare of mankind;
(x) Capable of deep appreciation of basic life-experience;
(xi) Establish deep satisfying interpersonal relationships with a few people;
(xii) Peak experiences;
(xiii) Need for privacy;
(xiv) Democratic attitudes;
(xv) Strong moral/ethical standards.

Behaviour leading to self-actualization

(a) Experiencing life like a child, with full absorption and concentration;
(b) Trying new things instead of sticking to safe paths;
(c) Listening to your own feelings in evaluating experiences instead of the voice of tradition or authority or the majority;
(d) Avoiding pretence ('game playing') and being honest;
(e) Being prepared to be unpopular if your views do not coincide with those of the majority;
(f) Taking responsibility and working hard;
(g) Trying to identify your defences and having the courage to give them up.

unique, way, they tend to share certain characteristics. However, self-actualization is a matter of degree, 'There are no perfect human beings' (Maslow, 1970).

EMPIRICAL STUDIES OF SELF-ACTUALIZATION

One way of measuring self-actualization is to study people's *peak experiences*, moments of ecstatic happiness when people feel most 'real' and alive. Maslow (1962) interviewed several people, many of whom were successful in their chosen field. His view was confirmed that at such moments, the person is concerned with 'being' and is totally unaware of any deficiency needs or the possible reactions of others.

Czikszentmihalyi (1975) interviewed a wide variety of prominent sportsmen and reported experiences, similar to those reported by Maslow, of ecstatically losing themselves in the highly skilled performance of their sport.

Such peak experiences cannot, normally, be consciously planned and yet, for many, the growth of humanistic psychology is almost synonymous with *deliberate* attempts to enhance personal growth through encounter groups and other short, intensive, group experiences. (This is associated more with Rogers's theory than with Maslow's.)

Whatever the empirical support or otherwise for Maslow's theory, there is no doubt that it represents an important counterbalance to the nomothetic approach of Cattell and Eysenck by attempting to capture the richness of the personal experience of being human. Also:

> [My goal] is to integrate into a single theoretical structure the partial truths ... in Freud, Adler, Jung ... Freud is still required reading for the humanistic psychologist ... [yet] it is as if [he] supplied to us the sick half of psychology, and we must now fill out with the healthy half ... (Maslow, 1968)

ROGERS'S SELF-THEORY

Rogers (Fig. 29.10), like Maslow, rejected the *deterministic* nature of psychoanalysis (behaviour is a response to *unconscious* forces) and behaviourism (behaviour is a response to *external stimuli*), believing, rather, that behaviour is a response to the individual's perception/interpretation of external stimuli. As no one else can know how we perceive, we are the best experts on ourselves.

Related to this emphasis on how we perceive and interpret reality is the importance of a person's current, moment-to-moment experience, what we are thinking and feeling *now*, in contrast to Freud's belief that our present behaviour is largely determined by our past, in the form of repressed childhood experiences. Freud also believed that human nature is fundamentally destructive and irrational and he took a very pessimistic view of human beings. Rogers (like Maslow), on the other hand, sees human nature in a very positive and optimistic light, 'there is no beast in man; there is only man in man'.

The forces that direct behaviour reside within us and when social conditions do not block or distort them, these forces direct us towards *self-actualization*, which Rogers defines as, 'the inherent tendency of the organism to develop all its capacities in ways which serve to maintain or enhance the organism'. Like Maslow, Rogers believes that self-actualization is an innate tendency, a basic motivating force which makes us different from other animal species and therefore peculiarly human.

Central to Rogers's theory (and to his form of psychotherapy, known as client-centred therapy) is the *concept of self*. The self is an 'organized, consistent set of perceptions and beliefs about oneself'. It includes my awareness of 'what I am', 'what I can do', and influences both my perception of the world and my behaviour; we evaluate every experience in terms of it and most human behaviour can be understood as an attempt to maintain consistency between our self-image and our actions (see Chapter 21).

But this consistency is not always achieved and our self-image (and related self-esteem) may differ quite radically from our actual behaviour and from how others see us. For example, a person may be highly successful and respected by others and yet regard himself as a failure! This would be an example of what Rogers calls *incongruence*—being told you are successful is incongruent or inconsistent with the fact that you

Figure 29.10 Carl Rogers (1902–1987), (The Bettmann Archive)

do not hold this view of your self. Incongruent experiences, feelings, actions and so on, because they conflict with our (conscious) self-image, and because we prefer to act and feel in ways that are consistent with our self-image, may be threatening and so are denied access to awareness (they may remain *unsymbolized*) through actual denial, distortion or blocking.

These defence mechanisms prevent the self from growing and changing and widen the gulf between our self-image and reality (ie our actual behaviour or our true feelings). As the self-image becomes more and more unrealistic, so the incongruent person becomes more and more confused, vulnerable, dissatisfied, and, eventually, seriously maladjusted.

The self-image of the congruent person is flexible and realistically changes as new experiences occur; the opposite is true of the incongruent person.

When your self-image matches what you really think and feel and do, you are in the best position to realize your potential (self-actualize); the greater the gap between self-image and reality, the greater the likelihood of anxiety and emotional disturbance. Similarly the greater the gap between self-image and ideal-self, the less fulfilled the individual will be.

To show how two different examples of a rigid and inflexible self-image may work, let us suppose that a young man's self-image requires that every woman he meets will find him irresistible and fall head-over-heels in love with him. He meets a woman whom he finds attractive but she shows no interest in him; this represents an incongruence between his self-image and his experience. How does he deal with the threat this represents for him? He might say, 'She's just playing hard to get' or, 'She has no taste' or, 'She must be crazy—thank goodness I found out before she fell hopelessly in love with me'.

Now let us look at the opposite extreme, a young man who believes that he is totally unattractive to women. If an attractive women shows an interest in him, this will produce incongruence and hence threat and he might deal with it by rationalizing that, 'She's just feeling sorry for me' or he might deliberately do something (eg be rude to her) to sabotage the relationship and so remove the threat.

Of course, most of us will not have such an extreme self-image as either of these two hypothetical young men, whether positive or negative, and most of us are sufficiently flexible and realistic to recognize that just as we are not 'God's gift to the opposite sex' nor are we sexually hopeless cases—indeed, our self-image regarding our sexual appeal has been learned from our past successes *and* failures ('you win some, you lose some').

How does our self-concept develop?

Many of Rogers's therapeutic clients had trouble accepting their own feelings and experiences; they seemed to have learned during childhood that in order to obtain the love and acceptance of others (particularly their parents), they have to feel and act in distorted or dishonest ways, ie they had to deny certain parts of themselves. (Rogers calls this *conditional positive regard*.)

This applies, in varying degrees, to almost every child—love and praise are withheld until the child conforms to parental and social standards of conduct. So the child (and later the adult) learns to act and feel in ways that earn approval from others, rather than in ways which may be more intrinsically satisfying and more 'real'. To maintain conditional positive regard, we suppress actions and feelings that are unacceptable to others who are important to us (significant others), instead of using our own spontaneous perceptions and feelings as guides to our behaviour. Rogers says that we develop *conditions of worth* (those conditions under which positive regard will be forthcoming) which become internalized—we perceive and are aware of those experiences that coincide with the conditions of worth but distort or deny those that do not. This denial and distortion leads to a distinction between the *organism* and the *self*, whereby the organism is the whole of one's possible experience (everything we do and feel and think) and the self is the recognized, accepted and acknowledged part of a person's experience. Ideally, the two would refer to one and the same thing, but, for most of us, they do not.

Corresponding to the need for positive regard (the universal wish to be loved and accepted by significant others) is the need for *positive self-regard*, the internalization of those values and behaviour of which others approve, so that we think of ourselves as good and lovable and worthy. (This corresponds to high self-esteem, while negative self-regard corresponds to low self-esteem).

To experience positive self-regard, our behaviour and experience must match our conditions of worth; the problem here is that this can produce incongruence through the denial of our true thoughts and feelings. But since the need for positive regard and positive self-regard is so strong, these conditions of worth can supersede the values associated with self-actualization. Consequently, we come to behave and think and feel in particular ways because others want us to and many adult adjustment problems are bound up with an attempt to live by other people's standards instead of one's own.

Congruence and self-actualization are enhanced by substituting organismic values for conditions of worth, so that the distinction between the self and organism becomes more and more blurred. The greater the *unconditional positive regard*, the greater the congruence between: (i) self-image and reality; and (ii) self-image and ideal-self. It is precisely this unconditional positive regard that the therapist offers the client in Rogers's client-centred therapy, ie the therapist creates an atmosphere of total acceptance and support, regardless of what the client says or does, and which is non-judgemental, so that the client, in turn, comes to accept certain feelings and thoughts as their own, instead of denying, distorting and disowning them (illustrated by such responses as, 'I don't know why I did that' or 'I wasn't feeling myself'). Finally, positive self-regard is no longer dependent upon conditions of worth (see Chapter 31).

PSYCHOANALYTIC THEORIES

We have already discussed at length the developmental aspects of Freud's theory (Chapters 21, 23 and 27) as well as some of the more general features, such as the structure of the personality (id, ego, superego). We have also discussed Erikson's psychosocial theory in Chapters 21, 22 and 24. Two of the other major psychoanalytic or *psychodynamic* theories are those of Jung and Adler. *Psychodynamic* implies the *active* forces within the personality, the inner causes of behaviour, which include feelings, conflicts, drives and a variety of unconscious motivational factors. Freud's was the first of this kind of theory and all psychodynamic theories stem, more or less directly, from Freud's work. Collectively, they are known as *depth psychology*.

FREUD'S PSYCHOANALYTIC THEORY

You will recall from Chapter 21 that Freud believed that conflict within the personality is unavoidable, because the ego is being 'pulled' in two opposing directions: on one side is the id, wanting immediate satisfaction of its instictual wishes, on the other is the superego, which threatens the ego with punishment (in the form of guilt) if it gives in to the id. So what is the ego to do? Freud's answer is to describe three forms of *compromise*, namely dreams, neurotic symptoms and defence mechanisms.

DREAMS

'A dream is a (disguised) fulfilment of a (suppressed or repressed) wish' (Freud, 1976/1900) and so is another example of the id's *primary process* thinking; it represents a compromise between forbidden urges and their repression. What we dream about and are conscious of upon waking (what we report) is called the *manifest content*, while the meaning of the dream (the wish being fulfilled) is the *latent content*.

The manifest content is often the product of the weaving together of certain fragments from that day's events (*day residues*) and the forbidden wish and is, essentially, a hallucinatory experience (predominantly visual for most people). It often appears disjointed, fragmentary and sometimes bizarre and nonsensical; dream interpretation (a major technique involved in psychoanalysis) aims to make sense of the manifest content by 'translating' it into the underlying wish fulfilment.

Dreams come into being through *dream work*, which converts the underlying (latent) wish into the manifest content and comprises displacement, condensation and concrete representation; it is controlled by the ego.

Displacement refers to the role of *symbols* in dreams, whereby something (eg a king) appears in the manifest dream as a substitute for something or somebody involved in the wish (eg the dreamer's father).

Condensation involves the same part of the manifest dream representing different parts of the latent wish. For example, a king may represent not only the dreamer's father but authority figures in general or very wealthy and powerful people. So more than one dream idea may be 'condensed' into a single manifest image and Freud would say the manifest image is 'over-determined' (see below).

Concrete representation refers to the expression of some abstract idea in a very concrete way; the concrete image of a king, for example, could represent the abstract notion of authority, power or wealth.

The importance of dream work as a whole is that it permits the expression of a repressed (and, therefore, forbidden and disturbing) wish and at the same time allows the dreamer to go on sleeping. The compromise involved in dreaming takes the form of disguising the true nature of the dream (ie wish-fulfilment), for if the wish were not disguised, the dreamer would wake up in a state of shock and distress. Hence, 'the dream is the guardian of sleep'.

Dream interpretation is also the 'royal road to the unconscious'; reversing the dream work and unravelling the wish from the manifest content can provide invaluable information about the unconscious mind in general and about the dreamer's in particular. (Interpreting his own dreams was a major part of Freud's self-analysis.) Two examples of dreams as diagnosed with-fulfilment are given in Box 29.2.

Box 29.2 Dreams reported by two of Freud's patients (from 'The Interpretation of Dreams', 1900/1976)

1) A young woman who had been orphaned at an early age, spent her adolescence in the home of her older sister, who had two sons, Otto and Charles. The patient adored Otto and treated him like her own son. To her great sadness, Otto died. She eventually went to live on her own.

When in therapy with Freud she dreamt:

> ... That I saw Charles lying dead before me. He was lying in his little coffin, his hands folded; there were candles all about; and, in short, it was just as it was at the time of Little Otto's death, which gave me such a shock. Now tell me, what does this mean? You know me—am I really so bad as to wish that my sister should lose the only child she has left? Or does the dream mean that I wish that Charles had died rather than Otto, who I liked so much better?

Freud knew that when the patient was living with her sister, she had fallen in love with a friend of the family, a professor of literature. For various reasons, the courtship ended and thereafter he avoided the house. She turned her affections to Otto but she continued to be in love with the professor and she found various ways of seeing him without his knowing (for example, she would attend his public lectures).

When asked if she connected the professor in any way with Otto's death, she said, 'Of course, the professor returned then after a long absence and I saw him once more beside little Otto's coffin'.

This was just as Freud expected and he interpreted the dream as follows:

> ... if now the other boy were to die, the same thing would happen again. You would spend the day with your sister, the professor would certainly come to offer his condolences and you would see him once more under the same circumstances as before. The dream signifies nothing more than this wish of yours to see him again—a wish against which you are fighting inwardly'.

The scene of death is the ego's way of 'slipping' the erotic wish-fulfilment past the superego. A child's funeral is the last thing one would (consciously) associate with sexual yearning and so it offered excellent 'cover' or disguise.

2) A 'typical example of a disguised Oedipus dream' is that of a man who dreamt that he had a secret liaison with a lady whom someone else wanted to marry. He was worried in case this other man might discover the liaison and the proposed marriage come to nothing. He, therefore, behaved in a very affectionate way to the man. He embraced him and kissed him (see Chapter 21).

So what happens when we have a nightmare (or 'anxiety dream')? Freud says that the ego normally acts as a 'censor' of what is consciously experienced but is less alert and on guard when we are asleep. Occasionally, the dream work is less effective than usual in disguising the repressed wish so that it becomes too clear and, therefore, too dangerous; consequently, the dream awakens the sleeping ego and brings the undisguised wish-fulfilment to an abrupt end.

NEUROTIC SYMPTOMS

Symptoms have much in common with dreams; they are essentially the expression of a repressed wish (or memory) that has become disguised in ways that are very similar to those involved in dream work:

(a) The symptom in some way *symbolizes* the wish to which it is linked. For example, one of Freud's patients (cited by Wollheim, 1971) suffered from hysterical hand-twitching, which was related to her memories of being badly frightened while playing the piano (*displacement*).

(b) A symptom can be over-determined, for example, this same patient's hand-twitching was traced to two other memories—receiving a disciplinary strapping on the hands as a schoolgirl and being forced to massage the back of a detested uncle (*condensation*).

(c) The symptom is often something 'physical', while the underlying cause is something 'mental' (*concrete representation*).

Most of Freud's patients were suffering from 'hysterical conversion neurosis', whereby emotional energy is converted into physical energy, so that the manifest problem is paralysis, blindness, deafness, headaches and a whole variety of other 'physical' symptoms. Through displacement and concrete representation in particular, the symptom deflects the patient's attention (and that of others) away from the repressed material—it is acceptable to consult a doctor about the symptom but not about the unconscious wish. It is in this way that symptoms, like dreams, are compromises—every symptom must comply with the demands of the ego or it too would be repressed. Freud and Breuer (1895) called these underlying wishes and memories *pathogenic* ('disease-producing') *ideas*, and Freud later reached the conclusion that *all* symptoms are caused by pathogenic ideas of a *sexual* nature (although not every dream).

DEFENCE MECHANISMS

These represent the third major form of compromise used by the ego in the face of inevitable conflict. The defence mechanisms of the ego are, by definition, unconscious, and this is partly how they derive their effectiveness: if we knew about them (at the time) we would, in most cases, be unable to go on using them. They also share the characteristic of involving some degree of *self-deception* (which is linked to their being unconscious) and this, in turn, is related to their distortion of 'reality', both the internal reality of feelings, etc. and the external reality of other people and the physical world.

Partly because of this distortion and deception, and partly despite it, the defences help us deal with anxiety; they prevent us from being overwhelmed by temporary threats or traumas and can provide 'breathing space' in which to come to terms with conflict or find alternative ways of coping. As short-term measures, they are advantageous, necessary and 'normal', but as long-term solutions to life's problems they are usually regarded as unhealthy and undesirable. Some of the major defence mechanisms are shown in Table 29.5.

NAME OF DEFENCE	DESCRIPTION	EXAMPLE(S)
1. *Repression* (Motivated Forgetting see Chapter 12)	Forcing a dangerous/ threatening memory/ idea/feeling/wish, etc out of consciousness and making it unconscious. Often used in conjunction with one or more other defences; one of the first used by the child	A 5 to 6-year-old child repressing its incestuous desire for the opposite-sex parent as part of the Oedipus complex (see Chapter 21)
2. *Displacement*	Choosing a substitute object for the expression of your feelings because you cannot express them openly towards their real target. You transfer your feelings onto something quite innocent, or harmless, because it is convenient in some way	Anger with your boy/ girl friend is taken out on your mother/father/ brother/sister, or you slam the door (or kick the cat). Phobias (see Chapters 30 and 31). Prejudice (see Chapter 19)
3. *Denial*	Refusing to acknowledge certain aspects of reality, refusing to perceive something because it is so painful or distressing	Refusing to accept that you have a serious illness or that a relationship is 'on the rocks' or that you have an exam tomorrow. Common component of grieving (see Chapter 24)
4. *Rationalization*	Finding an acceptable excuse for something which is really quite unacceptable, a 'cover story' which preserves your self-image or that of someone close to you. Justifying your own and others' actions to yourself—and believing it!	'Being cruel to be kind.' 'I only did it for you.' 'It was in your best interests.' 'I did so badly because I didn't revise properly'
5. *Reaction formation*	Consciously feeling or thinking the very opposite of what you (truly) unconsciously feel or think. The conscious thoughts or feelings are experienced as quite real	Being considerate/ polite to someone you cannot stand, even going out of your way to be nice to them. This 'display' may be quite suspicious to an observer.

Table 29.5 Some of the major ego defence mechanisms

Table 29.5 Continued	NAME OF DEFENCE	DESCRIPTION	EXAMPLE(S)
			Obsessive-compulsive neurosis, eg compulsive cleanliness as an attempt to cancel out an obsession with dirt (see Chapter 30)
	6. *Sublimation*	A form of displacement where a substitute activity is found to express an unacceptable impulse. The activity is usually socially acceptable—if not desirable. One of the most positive/ constructive of all defences	Playing sport to re-channel aggressive impulses. Doing sculpture or pottery or gardening to re-channel the desire to play with faeces. All artistic and cultural activities (see Chapter 16)
	7. *Identification*	The incorporation or *introjection* of an external object (usually another person) into one's own personality, making them a part of oneself. Coming to think, act and feel as if one were that person. Involves imitation and modelling	A young boy's assumption of the male role and acquisition of a conscience in order to avoid castration (*Identification with the aggressor*) (see Chapters 21 and 27). A common component of grieving (see Chapter 24)
	8. *Projection*	Attributing your own unwanted, feelings and characteristics onto someone else. The reverse of Identification	Suspecting or accusing someone of dishonourable motives based on your own (unconscious) dishonourable motives. 'I hate you' becomes 'You hate me'. The basis of paranoia (see Chapter 30)
	9. *Regression*	Engaging in behaviour characteristic of an earlier stage of development. We normally regress to the point of fixation (see Chapter 21)	Taking to your bed when upset, crying, losing your temper, eating when depressed, wetting yourself if extremely frightened
	10. *Isolation*	Separating contradictory thoughts or feelings into 'logic-right' compartments so that no conflict is experienced. Separating thoughts and emotions which usually go together. A form of dissociation	Calmly and clinically talking about a very traumatic experience without showing any emotion (or even giggling about it, as in schizophrenia) (see Chapter 30)

FREUD'S THEORY OF THE MIND (LEVELS OF CONSCIOUSNESS)

Freud believed that thoughts, ideas, memories and other psychic material could operate at one of three levels: conscious, pre-conscious and unconscious. These levels of consciousness do not correspond to areas or layers of the mind or brain but refer to how accessible the thought, etc. is to the thinker.

What we are consciously aware of at any one time represents the mere tip of an iceberg—most of our thoughts and ideas are either not accessible at that moment (pre-conscious) or are totally inaccessible (unconscious), at least without the use of special techniques such as free association and dream interpretation (see Chapter 31). The ego represents the *conscious* part of the mind, together with some aspects of the superego, namely those moral rules and values that we are able to express in words.

The ego also controls the *pre-conscious*, a kind of 'ante-room', an extension of the conscious, whereby things we are not fully aware of right now can become so fairly easily if our attention is directed to them. For example, you suddenly realize that you have been in pain for some time or you notice a ticking clock that has been ticking away all the time. The pre-conscious also processes ill-defined id urges into perceptible images and part of the superego may also function at a pre-conscious level.

The *unconscious* (the most contentious part of Freud's theory of the mind) comprises: (i) id impulses; (ii) all repressed material; (iii) the unconscious part of the ego (the part which is involved in dream work, neurotic symptoms and defence mechanisms); and (iv) part of the superego, for example, the free-floating or vague feelings of guilt or shame which are difficult to account for, and behaving in ways which seem to reflect parental standards but not being able to say what these standards are.

Freud depicted the unconscious as a *dynamic* force and not a mere 'dustbin' for all those thoughts, etc. which are not important or too weak to force themselves into awareness; this is best illustrated by the process of repression, whereby what is threatening is actively forced out of consciousness by the ego (Thomas, 1985).

'OUR REASONS' VERSUS 'THE REASONS'

We discussed *overdetermination* earlier in relation to dream work and neurotic symptoms. Freud also used the term in a more general way to refer to the fact that much of our behaviour (and our thoughts and feelings) has multiple causes, some conscious, some unconscious. By definition, we only know about the conscious causes and these are what we normally take to be *the* reasons for our actions. However, if the causes also include unconscious factors, then the reasons we give for our behaviour can never tell the whole story and, indeed, the unconscious causes may be the more important.

This view of the individual as never being fully aware of all the reasons for his/her behaviour is one of *irrational man*—we do not know ourselves as well as we would like, or as well as we think we do.

Overdetermination is one aspect of *psychic determinism*, the view that all behaviour is purposive, or goal-directed, and that everything we do, think and feel has a *cause* (often unconscious). It follows that what we often call 'accidents' (implying a chance occurrence, something which 'just happens'), do have a cause after all and, taking this a step further, that the cause (or contributory cause) may actually turn out to be the 'victim'. For instance, the 'accident-prone' person is *not*, according to Freud, an unfortunate victim of circumstances but is, unconsciously, bringing about the accidents—perhaps in an attempt to punish themselves in some way. Freud did not deny the existence of events which lie beyond the control of the victim but these are rare occurrences; it is more common for an 'accident' to be the consequence of our own, unconscious, wishes and motives.

THE PSYCHOPATHOLOGY OF EVERYDAY LIFE

We have seen how the unconscious reveals itself through dreams and neurotic symptoms and the major aim of psychoanalysis is to make the unconscious conscious. But Freud believed that there is another important way in which our everyday behaviour provides us with glimpses of the unconscious at work and that is what he called *parapraxes*, the all-too-common slips of the tongue, slips of the pen, forgetting things (including words and people's names), leaving things behind and 'accidents'. Parapraxes have come to be known as 'Freudian slips', an indication of how Freud's theories have permeated our everyday language and thinking. Some examples are given in Box 29.3.

Box 29.3 Some examples of Parapraxes ('Freudian slips') (from 'The Psychopathology of Every Day Life', 1901)

1) 'A patient consulted me for the first time and from her history it became apparent that the cause of her nervousness was largely an unhappy married life. Without any encouragement she went into details about her marital troubles. She had not lived with her husband for about six months, and she saw him last at the theatre, when she saw the play "Officer 606". I called her attention to the mistake, and she immediately corrected herself, saying that she meant to say "Officer 666" (the name of a recent popular play). I decided to find out the reason for the mistake, and as the patient came to me for analytic treatment, I discovered that the immediate cause of the rupture between herself and her husband was the disease which is treated by "606".' [ie venereal disease]

2) 'I was to give a lecture to a woman. Her husband, upon whose request this was done, stood behind the door listening. At the end of my sermonizing, which had made a visible impression, I said, "Good-bye, sir!" To the experienced person I thus betrayed the fact that the words were directed towards the husband; that I had spoken to oblige him.'

3) 'While writing a prescription for a woman who was especially weighted down by the financial burden of the treatment, I was interested to hear her say suddenly, "Please do not give be *big bills*, because I cannot swallow them". Of course she meant to say *pills*.'

EVALUATION OF FREUD'S THEORY

a) *EMPIRICAL STUDIES OF FREUD'S THEORIES*

There have been literally thousands of empirical studies of various aspects of Freud's theories.

Two of the major reviews of this research have been carried out by Kline (1972, 1982) and Fisher and Greenberg (1977), the latter being perhaps the most comprehensive to date. They conclude that Freud was right in some areas, wrong in others and too vague to be tested at all in still others. Psychoanalytic theory cannot be accepted or rejected as a total package, 'it is a complex structure consisting of many parts, some of which should be accepted, others rejected and the rest at least partially re-shaped' (Fisher and Greenberg, 1977).

Three basic kinds of study have been carried out: (i) *validational*, which try to test directly various parts of the theory, mainly in the laboratory; (ii) those which try to investigate some of the *underlying mechanisms* involved but which are not direct tests of the theory, again mainly laboratory experiments; (iii) those which study the *effects* of *psychoanalysis* as therapy (these will be discussed in Chapter 31).

Fonagy (1981) asks whether it is conceivable that laboratory studies could 're-create' the clinical concepts and experience that Freud describes and, therefore, questions the usefulness of validational studies. He also queries the relevance of studies of treatment-effectiveness as a way of 'testing' the theory—he says it is equivalent to the relevance of the effectiveness of aspirin to a theory of headaches!

Validational Studies

Many of these have been concerned with Freud's theory of personality types, especially the Oral and Anal. These have been discussed in Chapter 21.

Defence Mechanisms

We discussed *repression* in relation to theories of forgetting, in Chapter 12.

A very famous study of repression in the laboratory is that by Levinger and Clark (1961), who required subjects to produce associations to a total of sixty words, some relatively neutral (window/cow/tree), others with more emotional connotations (quarrel/anger/fear). As predicted, the latter produced higher GSRs. When asked to give free associations to the words, the emotive words also produced a longer response latency (ie it took longer to come up with an association). When they were given the cue words again and asked to recall the association they had previously given, subjects were particularly poor at remembering the associations they had given to the emotional words. They took this as evidence in support of Freud's concept of repression.

However, Eysenck and Wilson (1973) offered an alternative interpretation. They argued that Levinger and Clark only examined *immediate recall*: if the items are being repressed, then they should *continue* to be repressed, whereas if *arousal* is the crucial variable, then the effect should reverse.

Baddeley (1990) refers to an experiment designed to choose between these two opposing interpretations. He replicated the original study but half the subjects returned after twenty-eight days and were given a cued recall list. On *immediate* recall, the Levinger and Clark effect was found. But, after twenty-eight days, the effect reversed strongly. The words included were associated with both positive and negative emotions—repression should only occur with the negative associations. Arousal, on the other hand, should accompany both and, indeed, both pleasant and unpleasant—arousing words were poorly recalled at first, further supporting the arousal hypothesis. This study was replicated and extended by Parkin et al (1982).

Perhaps rather stronger evidence in support of Freud comes from the study by Speisman et al (1964) who demonstrated *intellectualization* by measuring subjects' GSR as they watched a stressful film with commentaries intended either to increase or decrease stress (see Chapter 6).

However, Fonagy (1981) points out that in some of these studies the thinking and feeling involved were conscious, while defence mechanisms, as Freud defined them, are unconscious. But these difficulties aside, he believes that much more relevant is the second kind of study, namely those that go beyond trying to replicate clinical phenomena and which instead attempt to identify basic mechanisms or processes which may underlie unconscious phenomena.

Relationship Between Freudian and Factor-analytic Concepts
Although not validation studies as such, the factor-analytic studies of Eysenck and Cattell provide some indirect support for Freud. In a review of these, Kline (1983) argues that studies of Eysenck's N, showing a continuum, indirectly support Freud's view that neurotics are only different in degree from non-neurotics.

As far as psychotics are concerned, Freud (1924) argued that they deny reality and obey their instinctual urges compared with neurotics who deny their urges and obey reality, in other words, there is a discontinuity between psychotics on the one hand and neurotics and normals on the other (hence, a qualitative difference). Eysenck's findings that both normals and neurotics score low on P seems to confirm Freud's view (although for Eysenck this is only a matter of degree).

As far as Cattell is concerned, we noted that he was influenced by Freud in the labels he attached to some of his primary factors: Factor C (ego-strength), Factor G (superego) and Factor Q4 (id tension). According to Freud, neurotics have weak egos: either they feel threatened by id impulses (neurotic conflict) or they have a very strong superego (moral conflict), and this picture has been confirmed by Cattell. For example, on the 16PF, diagnosed neurotics score low on C and high on Q4 and as far as Factor O is concerned (guilt proneness), neurotics also score high.

Studies of Underlying Mechanisms Involved in Unconscious Phenomena

A concept which is closely related to that of repression is *perceptual defence*, whereby stimuli which are threatening or anxiety-provoking in some way are more difficult to perceive at a conscious level (than those which are not). In turn, perceptual defence is linked to the more general and less defence-oriented-concept of *subliminal perception*, ie perception which takes place below the threshold of conscious awareness.

In Chapter 9 we discussed a number of relevant studies and found considerable support for both concepts. This is perhaps the best example of the investigation of an *underlying mechanism* involved in unconscious phenomena which Fonagy (1981) sees as being much more relevant than direct tests of Freud's theory.

A further source of evidence is neurophysiological psychology. Penfield (1958) directly stimulated the temporal cortex and patients reported phenomenal experiences of 'bygone days', including the entire spectrum of emotions and visual/acoustic components. The central nervous system seems to preserve a record of past experience and perceptions of astonishing detail, which is not normally available to consciousness. Perhaps these perceptions, encoded as memories, form the basis of pre-conscious and unconscious systems.

Bogen (1969), Galin (1974) and McKinnon (1979) have all equated the function of the dominant hemisphere of the brain (the left for most people) with secondary process thinking and that of the minor hemisphere with primary process thinking.

Other support for Freud comes from studies of *split-brain* patients (whose left and right hemispheres are no longer physically connected; see Chapters 4 and 5). Several studies have found that, as the ability to speak is localized in the left (dominant) hemisphere, all phenomenal experiences these patients report refer to the left hemisphere: their dreams are free from primary process distortions and bizareness and lie much closer to ordinary modes of thinking of awake adults. This suggests that dreams and primary process thinking as a whole are normally controlled by the right side of the brain.

b) *IS THE THEORY SCIENTIFIC?*

We have seen how much research Freud's theories have generated and, in the light of this, it seems very difficult to accept Popper's criticism (see Chapter 2) that they are unfalsifiable and, therefore, unscientific. The theory as a whole (or, at least, many parts of it) does seem testable (even if it is not always shown to be true), although we should note Fonagy's (1981) warning that many validational studies may not be very relevant to an understanding of the clinical phenomena as Freud described them. Perhaps more relevant to Popper's criticism are rather specific parts of the theory, in particular, the defence mechanism of *reaction formation*.

Scodel (1957) predicted, based on Freud's theories, that highly dependent men would prefer big-breasted women. (Dependency, is an oral trait and the breast can be regarded as a symbol of a state of dependency.) Scodel in fact found the opposite to be true —dependent men tended to prefer *small*-breasted women, so Freud's theory, in this respect, seems to have been falsified (on this occasion, at least). However, Kline (1972) invoked the concept of reaction formation in order to show that Scodel had *confirmed* the theory, since a fixation (unconscious) with big breasts may show up as a preference (conscious) for small breasts! According to Kline then, *either* outcome (preference for big *or* small-breasted women) would have shown Freud to be right!

As we saw in Chapter 2, another important scientific criterion is to do with predictability and, at least as far as the concept of reaction formation is concerned, Freud's theory is very bad at predicting particular outcomes; it is very good, however, at accounting for what has already happened in the past. Is there, at least in principle, any way of testing the hypothesis that someone's affection towards another person is, in fact, a reaction formation against their repressed hostility? At the worst, the Freudian would only have to concede (if it was somehow shown that the affection was genuine) that the person's behaviour was 'overdetermined' (ie motivated by conscious affection *and* unconscious hostility).

Eysenck (1973) also points to reaction formation to demonstrate the low status of psychoanalytic theory as a scientific theory: he argues that for the Freudian *all* behaviour can be explained, even if none can be predicted, and this is largely because of the retrospective nature of data-collection involved in the case study method which Freud used (see (c) below).

However, it would be a serious mistake to regard reaction formation as typifying Freudian theory; the sheer volume of research suggests that it cannot be dismissed as lightly as Popper and Eysenck would like on the grounds of being 'unscientific'.

According to Kline (1989), the view adopted by almost all experimental psychologists involved in the study of Freud's theory is that it should be seen as a *collection of hypotheses*.

Agreeing with Fisher and Greenberg (1977), this view holds that some of these will turn out to be true, others false, when put to Popper's test of falsifiability. Certainly some are more critical to the overall theory than others. For example, if no evidence could be found for repression, this would alter considerably the nature of psychoanalysis but if it was found that the Oedipus complex was more pronounced in small as opposed to large families, this would *not* radically affect the theory.

c) *HOW VALID IS THE CASE STUDY METHOD?*

Relying as it does on the re-construction of childhood events, the case study, as used by Freud, is generally considered to be the least scientific of all empirical methods used by psychologists; it is open to many types of distortion and uncontrolled influences. Not only were the memories of his patients part of the basic data but Freud himself made no notes during the treatment sessions themselves but only several hours later—the distortions involved in remembering are notorious (see Chapter 12).

Fisher and Greenberg (1977) point out the tendency to select or emphasize material which supported particular interpretations and nowhere is this more clearly illustrated than in the case of Little Hans (Chapter 21).

As we saw, Freud recognized that there was a problem of objectivity by virtue of the fact that it was Little Hans' *father* actually conducting the psychoanalysis. But he goes on to say that this case was no different from the analysis of adults:

> ... For a psychoanalysis is not an impartial scientific investigation, but a therapeutic measure. Its essence is not to prove anything but merely to alter something. (Freud, 1909)

But doesn't this condemn the whole of Freud's work to the realm of 'non-science', since his theories are all constructed from his case studies? Isn't the consulting room his 'laboratory', his patients his 'subjects', what they say about themselves (especially their childhood) the data? (Gross, 1990).

This point is answered by Storr (1987), a leading popularizer of psychoanalytic theory and himself a trained psychoanalyst. He claims that although some of the hypotheses of psychoanalytic theory can be tested scientifically (ie are refutable), this applies only to a minority—the majority are based on observations made in the course of psychoanalytic treatment, which cannot be regarded as a scientific procedure. Such observations are inevitably contaminated by the subjective experience and prejudice of the observer, however detached he/she tries to be, and so cannot be regarded in the same light as observations made during, say a chemistry or physics experiment. It is certainly possible, he goes on, to study human beings as if they were objects merely responding to the stimuli impinging on them (ie experimental psychology). But it is *not* possible to conduct psychoanalysis (or any form of psychotherapy) in this way.

So do we have to accept Storr's conclusion that psychoanalytic theory can never be thought of as scientific? One defence of Freud may be that to study people as objects responding to stimuli is not truly scientific because that is not what people are actually like and so to study them in this way is not only immoral but inaccurate. Perhaps Freud is much closer to treating people *as* people and, to that extent, perhaps more of a scientist than most experimental psychologists!

In a similar vein, Thomas (1990) argues that:

> Sigmund Freud is probably the most famous of all psychologists. His work has had an important influence on the development of psychology and, perhaps, an even more fundamental impact on western culture . . . His ideas and development of them by other people have influenced our conception of morality, family life and childhood and thus perhaps the structure of our society; and they have changed our attitudes to mental illness. Freudian assumptions are now part of the fabric of literature and the arts . . . (Thomas, 1990)

Finally:

> . . . Freudian theory is still a powerful intellectual force. To claim that it is dead, as do many experimental psychologists—at least by implication for it rarely influences their thinking—must be either ignorance or wishful thinking. (Kline, 1989)

d) HOW REPRESENTATIVE WERE THE SUBJECTS STUDIED BY FREUD?

One of the standard criticisms made of Freud's database is that his patients were mainly wealthy, middle-class Jewish females, living in Vienna at the turn of the century, and therefore hardly representative of the population to whom his theories were generalized. If these people were also neurotic, how can we be sure that what Freud discovered about them is true of normal individuals? However, as we have seen, Freud regarded neurosis as continuous with normal behaviour, that is, neurotics are suffering only from more extreme problems experienced by all of us.

More serious, perhaps, is the criticism that Freud studied only adults (with the very dubious exception of Little Hans) and yet he put forward a theory of personality *development*. How many steps removed were his data from his theory? According to Thomas (1985): the analyst interprets, through his theoretical 'lens', ostensibly symbolic material derived from the reported dreams/memories, etc. of neurotics about ostensible experiences stemming from their childhood one or more decades earlier. However, this in itself does not invalidate the theory—it merely makes the study of children all the more necessary.

Significantly, although Freud described most of his patients as neurotics, many writers have subsequently concluded that many of them would today be diagnosed as psychotic (see Chapter 30).

e) *BIOLOGICAL FACTORS*

A key issue which divides Freudians and other psychodynamic theorists is the role of biological factors in personality development. While none of the neo-Freudians denied that biological factors are important, or that all psychic energy must ultimately be rooted in the body, they did deny that all behaviour is directed towards the satisfaction of biological needs in the way Freud believed. For example, although it may be true that hoarding is a trait associated with the anal stage, it is absurd to claim that hoarding is *always* the manifestation of anal fixation (Brown, 1963; see Chapter 21).

It was Freud's emphasis on the role of sexuality which ultimately led to the split with Jung and Adler, and neo-Freudians such as Erikson stressed the role of socio-cultural influences almost as a counter-balance to Freud's pre-occupation with biological factors.

f) *REIFICATION*

Several writers have criticized terms like the id, ego and superego as bad metaphors; they do not correspond to any aspect of psychology or neurophysiology and they encourage *reification*, ie treating metaphorical terms as if they were 'things' or entities.

However, Bettelheim (1985) points out that much of Freud's terminology was mistranslated and this has led to a misrepresentation of those parts of his theory. For example, Freud himself never used the Latin words *id*, *ego* and *superego*; he used the German *das Es* ('the it'), *das Ich* ('the I') and *das Über-Ich* (the 'over-I'), which were intended to capture how the individual relates to different aspects of the self, whereas the Latin terms tend to depersonalize these and give the impression that there are three separate 'selves' which we all possess! The Latin words (chosen by his American translator to give greater scientific credibility) turn the concepts into cold technical terms which arouse no personal associations; whereas the 'I' can only be studied from the inside (through introspection), the 'ego' can be studied from the outside (as behaviour). In translation, Freud's 'soul' became scientific psychology's 'psyche' or 'personality' (Bettelheim, 1985).

More positively, there is no doubting the tremendous impact that Freud has had, both within psychology and outside. The fertility of psychoanalytic theory, in terms of the debate, research and theorizing it has generated, makes it one of the richest in the whole of psychology:

He [Freud] has provided us with a set of ideas and concepts which, both in literature and everyday conversation, have helped us to formulate questions about ourselves, our inner experience and our social conditioning. He helped explode the myth of 'rational Man' and has brought us face to face with our irrational selves, a new image of ourselves as least as valid as any other major image-of-man that Social Science has offered and perhaps as challenging and disturbing as any it is ever likely to offer. (Clift, 1984)

JUNG'S ANALYTICAL PSYCHOLOGY

Jung 'broke ranks' with Freud in 1913 to form his 'Analytical Psychology'; because he disagreed with Freud over a number of fundamental issues. It is these disagreements that I shall emphasize here.

Figure 29.11 Carl Gustav Jung (1875–1961). (From Bettmann Archive Inc.)

STRUCTURE OF THE PERSONALITY AND LEVELS OF CONSCIOUSNESS

For Jung (Fig. 29.11) the personality as a whole is the *psyche*, the totality of all psychic processes, conscious and unconscious; it embraces all thought, feeling and behaviour and helps the individual adapt to the social and physical environment. The term psyche also includes what is normally called 'soul'. The person is seen as a whole almost from the moment of birth: personality is not acquired piece-by-piece (the 'jigsaw' concept) through learning and experience but it is already there, so that instead of striving to achieve wholeness, our aim in life is to *maintain* it and to prevent the splitting or dissociation of the psyche into separate and conflicting parts. Jung saw the role of therapy as helping the patient recover this lost wholeness and to strengthen the psyche so as to resist future dissociation. The psyche comprises three major, interacting, levels: (i) *consciousness*, (ii) the *personal unconscious*, and (iii) the *collective unconscious*. The distinction between (ii) and (iii) represents one of the major differences between Jung and Freud.

i) *Consciousness*

This is the only part of the mind known directly by the individual; it appears early in life through the operation of four *basic functions*: (i) *thinking* (which tries to understand the world through cognition); (ii) *feeling* (which tries to evaluate things in terms of 'pleasant–unpleasant', 'acceptable–unacceptable'); (iii) *sensing* (which comprises all conscious experiences produced by stimulation of the sense organs—internal and external); and (iv) *intuiting* (which is 'knowing something without knowing how you know it' or 'perception via the unconscious'). While all four functions are constitutionally present in each person, they are not all used to the same degree and one usually predominates; this is what makes the basic character of one person different from that of another.

In addition to these four functions there are two attitudes which determine the orientation of the conscious mind: (i) *extroversion*; and (ii) *introversion*. The extrovert's *libido* (Jung's term for psychic energy as a whole or life-force) is directed outwards towards the external, objective world of physical objects, people, customs and conventions, social institutions and so on and they are preoccupied with *interpersonal* relationships and are generally more active and outgoing. By contrast, the introvert's libido is directed inwards towards the internal, subjective world of thoughts, feelings and so on and they are preoccupied with *intra*personal matters, are introspective and withdrawn and may be seen by others as aloof, reserved and antisocial. Jung believed that a person is predominantly one or the other throughout life, although there may be occasional inconsistencies in different situations; so for Jung, extroversion–introversion represents a *typology* (Eysenck's 'adoption' of Jung's terms took the form of personality *dimensions*, with extreme extroversion at one end and extreme introversion at the other).

Jung believed that the development of consciousness is also the beginning of *individuation*, the process by which a person becomes, psychologically 'in-dividual', ie a separate, indivisible unity or whole, and from this process emerges the *ego*. The ego refers to how the conscious mind is organized and consists of conscious perceptions, memories, thoughts and feelings. Although it represents only a small part of the psyche as a whole, it plays the essential role of 'gatekeeper to consciousness', ie it selects important sensations, feelings, ideas, etc. and allows them through into conscious awareness (much as Freud's preconscious does); this prevents us from becoming overwhelmed by the mass of stimulation going on around (and inside) us.

The ego provides a sense of identity and continuity for the individual and it is the central core of the personality.

ii)   *The Personal Unconscious*

The Freudian unconscious, in Jung's terms, is predominantly 'personal', ie composed of the individual's particular and unique experiences which have been made unconscious through repression. For Jung, repressed material represents only one kind of unconscious content. The personal unconscious also includes things we have forgotten because they were irrelevant (or seemed unimportant) at the time or because they have lost some of their 'energetic value' since they happened, as well as all those things which we think of as being 'stored in memory', and things which may not be accessible to conscious recall at a particular time but which are available and could become accessible (see Chapter 12). In these respects, Jung's personal unconscious resembles Freud's pre-conscious.

A major feature of the personal unconscious is that associated groups of feelings, thoughts and memories may cluster together to form a *complex*, which represents a quite autonomous and powerful 'mini-personality' within the total psyche. It is from Jung that the term has been 'borrowed' and become a commonly used one in everyday language, together with synonyms such as 'hang-up' (Hall and Nordby, 1973). Freud's Oedipus Complex illustrates this constellation of thoughts and feelings. Although not necessarily detrimental, complexes often prevent the complete individuation of a person from taking place and one aim of therapy is to free the patient from the grip of such complexes.

In looking for the origin of complexes, Jung eventually turned to the collective unconscious.

iii)   *The Collective Unconscious*

This part of Jung's theory sets him apart from Freud probably more than any other, as Jung was acknowledging the role of evolution and heredity in providing a blueprint for the psyche just as they do for the body.

Freud's id is, of course, part of each individual's 'personal' unconscious and represents our biological inheritance. (Ironically, in view of the criticism of Freud that he overemphasized the role of biological factors, Jung could be seen as having given inherited factors an even greater role than Freud by virtue of his collective unconscious.) According to Jung, the mind (through the brain) has inherited characteristics which determine how a person will react to life experiences and what type of experiences these will be.

Whereas for Freud our childhood is of critical importance in making us what we are as adults, Jung attached relatively little importance to our individual past in relation to the personal unconscious but saw the evolutionary history of human beings as a species as being all-important in relation to the collective (or *racial*) unconscious.

The collective unconscious can be thought of as a reservoir of latent images, called *primordial images*, which relate to the 'first' or 'original' development of the psyche, stemming from our ancestral past, both human, pre-human and animal (Hall and Nordby, 1973). These images are not literally pictures in the mind but are predispositions or potentialities for experiencing and responding to the world in the same way that our ancestors did. For example, we do not have to learn to fear the dark or snakes through direct experience because we are naturally predisposed to develop such fears through the inheritance of our ancestors' fears. (Interestingly, support for Jung comes from studies of conditioning, which, as we saw in Chapter 7, show that it is much easier to induce a fear of snakes, for example, than to induce a fear of flowers. Similarly, clinical psychology shows that naturally acquired phobias of snakes and spiders are the most common amongst adults and of the dark in children; see Chapters 30 and 31.)

The contents of the collective unconscious are known as *archetypes* (a prototype or 'original model or pattern'), which, according to Hall and Nordby (1973), are more like a negative (which has to be developed through experience) than an already-developed and clearly recognizable photograph, 'forms without content', potential ways of perceiving and feeling and acting.

Jung identified a large number of archetypes, including birth, re-birth, death, power, magic, the hero, the child, the trickster, God, the demon, the wise old man, earthmother and the giant. Although universal, archetypes are expressed differently by different individuals, within and between racial and cultural groups; they also form the nucleus of a complex. Jung paid special attention to four archetypes: the Persona, Anima/Animus, the Shadow and the Self and these are featured in Box Box 29.4.

Box 29.4 The Four Major Archetypes of the Collective Unconscious

The Persona ('Mask')
This is the outward face we present to the world, both revealing and concealing the real self; it allows us to play our part in social interaction and to be accepted by others. It is the 'packaging' of the ego, the ego's PR man or woman, a kind of cloak between the ego and the objective world. It is very similar to the notion of a social role, which refers to the

expectations and obligations associated with a particular social position; Jung describes it as the 'conformity' archetype.

Normally, we play a variety of roles and personality as a whole cannot be reduced to any one of them, or to the entire set. However, we sometimes become dominated by a particular role, which can take over our entire personality; when the ego identifies with the persona, Jung says that *inflation* is happening.

Anima/Animus

This refers to the unconscious mirror-image of our conscious ('official') gender—if we are male, our *anima* is our unconscious female side and if we are female, our *animus* is our unconscious male side. We all have qualities of the opposite sex/gender—both biologically and psychological-ly—and in a well-adjusted person both sides must be allowed to express themselves in thought and behaviour.

The anima has a preference for all things vain, helpless, uncertain and unintentional; the animus prefers the heroic, the intellectual, the artistic and athletic. These would be expressed in different ways in different cultures but are universal characteristics (compare them with gender role stereotypes as discussed in Chapter 23). Jung believed that repression of the anima/animus is very common in Western culture, where the persona predominates. (What about androgyny? Again see Chapter 23.)

The Shadow

This contains more of our basic animal nature than any other archetype and is similar to Freud's id. Like the id, it must be kept in check if we are to live in society but this is not achieved easily and is always at the expense of our creativity and spontaneity, depth of feeling and insight. So the shadow represents the source of our creative impulses—but also of our destructive urges; if it is too severely repressed it will seek revenge, as in war. When the ego and shadow work harmoniously, the person is full of energy—both mentally and physically. The shadow of the highly creative person may occasionally overwhelm the ego causing temporary insanity (confirming the popular belief that genius is akin to madness).

The Self

This is the central archetype ('the archetype of archetypes'), which unites the personality, giving it a sense of 'oneness' and firmness. The ultimate aim of every personality is to achieve a state of selfhood and individuation (similar to Maslow's Self-actualization); this is a life-long process, attained by very few individuals, Jesus and Buddha being notable exceptions. It is commonly represented as a *Mandala*, an age-old symbol of wholeness and totality, found all over the world.

What did Jung base his theory of archetypes on, and what is the evidence for their existence?

According to Brown (1963) there are three major sources of evidence: (i) the 'extraordinary' similarity of themes in the mythologies of various cultures; (ii) the recurring appaearance, in therapy, of symbols which have become divorced from any of the patient's personal experiences and which become more and more like the primitive and universal symbols found in myths and legends; (iii) the content of fantasies of psychotics (especially schizophrenics) which are full of themes such as death and re-birth, which are similar to those found in mythology.

Many writers do not accept the theory of a collective unconscious. For example, Brown (1963) argues that members of all cultures share certain common experiences and so it is not surprising that they dream or create myths about archetypal themes. The deeper the interpretation, he says, the more likely we are to come up with universal explanations which seem to have an innate or biological basis. Less deep, ego interpretations, however, are more likely to reveal the specific features of different cultures, ie cultural differences (Brown (1963); see Fig. 29.12 for a diagrammatic representation of the psyche as a whole).

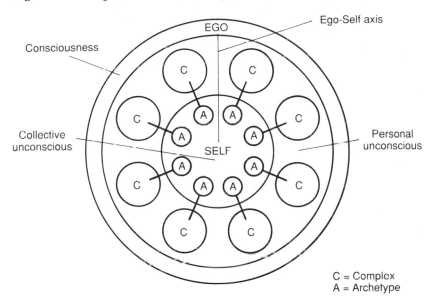

Figure 29.12 Schematic diagram of Jung's model of the psyche. (Based on Stevens, 1990)

OTHER SIMILARITIES AND DIFFERENCES BETWEEN JUNG AND FREUD

1) Dream Theory

Jung shared Freud's belief that dreams are the 'royal road to the unconscious'. However, he certainly disagreed with Freud that all dreams are wish-fulfilments; rather, Jung saw dreams as an important way of attaining self-knowledge which, in turn (together with religious or spiritual experiences) is a path to achieving individuation. However, not all dreams are equally significant in this respect.

The great function of dreams is to restore our psychological balance and to re-establish 'the total psychic equilibrium' and they are just as likely to point to the future (eg by suggesting a solution to a conflict) as to the past. He also believed that Freud's 'disguise' was far too elaborate and preferred to take the dream at face value. Dream symbols do not have a fixed meaning (as they very largely did for Freud) and he also advocated the study of *dream series*, ie several dreams recorded over a period of time by the same individual.

2) Stage of Development

Jung's theory of personality development is, as we have seen, much less tied up with sexual development than Freud's. Jung identified four major life stages: (i) childhood (birth to puberty); (ii) youth and young adulthood (puberty to 35–40); (iii) middle age (35–40 to old age); and (iv) old age. To the extent that he recognized developmental stages beyond young adulthood (Freud's genital stage), Jung's theory has more in common with Erikson's than Freud's (see Chapter 21).

3) *Neurosis and Therapy*

Repression plays very little part in Jung's theory of neurosis; more important is the conflict between different parts of the personality which have developed unequally. Jungian therapy is much more concerned with future goals than past history and the present situation is the key to neurosis; therapy aims to bring the patient into contact with the healing collective unconscious, largely through dream interpretation. Free association is also important but the Jungian analyst, compared with the Freudian, plays a much more active role and therapy is seen as a co-operative venture between patient and therapist.

ADLER'S INDIVIDUAL PSYCHOLOGY

Adler (Fig. 29.13) broke from Freud two years earlier than Jung—in 1911. Although he agreed with Freud about the importance of unconscious forces, he, like Jung, rejected Freud's emphasis on sexuality as the major influence on the personality and, instead, saw people as being motivated primarily by the drive towards affirmation of their personality, the tendency towards self-preservation, the *will to power* or striving for superiority.

Adler was much more interested than Freud in the social nature of human beings and, like Jung, he saw the individual as an indivisible unity or whole; any event must be considered in the light of its effect on the whole person if we are to understand it properly.

Adler was impressed by the body's capacity to compensate for organic damage, for example, damage to a kidney or lung may be followed by increased compensatory functioning of the undamaged one, and an undamaged part of the brain may take over the job normally carried out by the damaged area (see Chapter 4). To this extent, the strictly biological basis of Freud's theory was attractive to Adler and he believed that similar processes could be observed in the psychological sphere, for example, painters with imperfect vision, musicians and composers who are deaf, might be compensating for their defect in such a way that their inferiority actually becomes transformed into superiority. Adler saw feelings of inferiority as not only inevitable but as the key to understanding the whole of mental life.

THE ORIGINS OF INFERIORITY

Every child spends its early years in a state of dependence on others and experiences all kinds of desires which cannot be satisfied; by comparison, adults seem happier and have more power. As a result, children come to experience their dependence and powerlessness as a state of *inferiority* relative to adults and, in reaction to this, an unconscious drive emerges towards superiority, the *will to power*.

FACTORS CONTRIBUTING TO INFERIORITY

Against this common background of inferiority, Adler identified several factors which could influence the degree of inferiority an individual might experience:

Figure 29.13 *Alfred Adler (1870–1937). (From Bettmann Archive Inc.)*

1) Any kind of *physical deformity*, either congenital (eg harelip) or environmental (scarring as the result of an accident), to the extent that it is experienced psychologically.

2) *Gender*—Adler recognized the inequality of men and women in society and believed that the equation between 'masculine' and 'strong and superior' and 'feminine' and 'weak and inferior' is made at an early age. Some boys may be unable to live up to these gender role stereotypes, especially if their fathers attribute them with masculine qualities which they do not possess and this may be at the root of homosexuality and other sexual 'deviations'. The Don Juan character, for example, is continually trying to convince himself of his masculinity (which he equates with sexual prowess); it is usually the 'conquest' rather than the actual sexual experience that matters since his behaviour is motivated not by an insatiable sexual appetite as such but by his underlying sense of inferiority. Women may try to compensate for their inferiority by wishing to be a man (the 'masculine protest') or by exploiting their 'weakness' and their feminine charms.

3) *Birth order*, the *social and economic status* of the family and the length and quality of *education* can all contribute to a sense of inferiority.

4) The way parents in particular, and adults in general, react to the *child's successes and failures* are vitally important; pressure to succeed may be too great and unrealistic for a particular child and its failures can produce anxiety in the parents which, in turn, cause extra pressure and anxiety in the child (see Erikson's stage of 'initiative versus doubt and shame'; Chapter 21).

5) A *neglected, spoilt or hated child* is likely to have very low self-esteem.

How do people cope with inferiority?

In general, the more the original feelings of inferiority develop into the unconscious form of an inferiority complex, the greater the drive towards compensation. Each child develops early on in life its own particular strategy for dealing with the family situation as it is perceived; this strategy essentially comprises a set of attitudes which, collectively, form the 'lifestyle' upon which the adult personality is based. The traits we adopt have functional value for us in the earliest days—they were the traits which seemed to give us the best results in terms of power.

In addition, Adler identified three major techniques by which people try to overcome inferiority:

(a) *Successful compensation* involves compensating in a positive and constructive way which is socially advantageous for the individual, for example, intellectual achievement as a compensation for some physical handicap. In general, it refers to a successful adjustment to life's three challenges—society, work and sex.

(b) *Overcompensation* involves trying too hard, so that the underlying motive becomes obvious, ie aiming for extraordinary achievements and settling for nothing less. Such goals may be achievable only in fantasy and this can result in maladjustment. Less extreme examples are the bumptious little man, or the small man who smokes a huge cigar or drives an enormous car or lives in an enormous house, or the coward who becomes a bully.

(c) *Escape from combat* is essentially a way of ensuring that failure is impossible (or is reduced to a minimum)—but at the price of any real success. For example, physical symptoms can be 'used' to deflect attention away from the real reasons for opting out, which may be fear of failure (very often the fear of failing to achieve impossibly high standards). This retreat into illness or adoption of the sick role can become a way of life and a means of gaining power over others.

Another form this can take is for the individual to go about things so casually that other people form the impression that they are not really trying or doing their best. This 'covers' the person in the event of failure, as the best way of never experiencing a real failure is never to have given yourself completely to the task in the first place.

NEUROSIS AND THERAPY

According to Adler, 'every neurosis can be understood as an attempt to free oneself from a feeling of inferiority in order to gain a feeling of superiority'. The neurotic is a person who is unable to gain superiority by legitimate means and so develops symptoms, either as an excuse to avoid situations in which they might be exposed as a failure or as a means of gaining control over others by a sort of emotional blackmail (as we saw in escape from combat).

The essential aim of therapy is to help the patient to understand their secret psychic processes and to gain the courage and self-confidence necessary to exist and develop in a normal way; the analyst points out the patient's style of life with its *fictive goals* (unrealistic goals) and gives some practical advice regarding a more sensible alternative future lifestyle.

EVALUATION

Adler's emphasis on social factors in personality development, his view of the person as a unity, the de-emphasis on sexual influences, and his relative emphasis on the conscious ego (as opposed to unconscious forces) are all significant modifications of Freud's theory which helped to inspire the theories of the neo-Freudians, such as Erikson (born 1902), Horney (1885–1952) and Fromm (born 1900).

However, he seems to have over-emphasized the role of inferiority; as Brown (1963) points out, it is difficult to believe that *all* the non-organic nervous disorders (neuroses) are produced by a 'feeling of inferiority' or that psychoses are the result of complete failure to conquer inferiority, which leads the psychotic to 'refuse to play' the game of life.

According to Brown (1963), Adler's individual psychology has almost ceased to exist as a distinct, independent theory but its influence lives on (although this is not always acknowledged) in the theories of neo-Freudians.

30 PSYCHOPATHOLOGY

So far, the emphasis in this book has been on normal psychological processes and development. However, we have also had occasion to qualify what we have said in two ways: first, by considering examples of abnormality (which often serve to illuminate the normal); and, secondly, by considering individual differences. In discussing psychopathology, we are bringing these two issues together, since psychological disorders represent a major source of individual differences.

Psychopathology also constitutes the point of contact between psychiatry (a branch of medicine) and psychology, most clearly and importantly in the shape of clinical psychology (see Chapter 1).

Here, and in Chapter 31, we shall be looking at the contributions of both disciplines to the understanding and alleviation of psychological disorders and we shall see how radically different their theories and methods are. (This difference is only to be expected in view of the very different training each discipline provides.)

However, within clinical psychology itself there are various approaches which correspond to those we have already discussed throughout the book, namely, the Psychoanalytic, the Behavioural, the Humanistic–Existential, the Neurobiological and the Cognitive; each defines psychological abnormality differently and, accordingly, favours a different way of dealing with it. Before we consider each in detail, we must discuss the concept of abnormality itself.

THE CONCEPT OF ABNORMALITY

Implicit within each psychological theory of abnormality is the assumption that it is possible, and meaningful, to draw the line between normal and abnormal. How, if at all, can the line be drawn?

THE STATISTICAL CRITERION

This represents the literal sense of abnormality, whereby any behaviour which is not typical or usual (ie infrequent) is, by definition, abnormal. Again, 'normal' is 'average', it is what most people do or are like. However, this does not help to distinguish between atypical behaviour which is desirable (or, at least, acceptable) and that which is undesirable and unacceptable. For example, creative genius (such as that possessed by Picasso) and megalomania (such as that possessed by Hitler) are both statistically rare (and to this extent, abnormal) but the former would be rated as much more desirable than the latter.

Again, there are certain types of behaviour and experience which are so common as to be normal in the statistical sense but which are regarded as constituting psychological disorders, such as anxiety and depression. So the statistical criterion would seem to be neither necessary nor sufficient as a way of defining abnormality.

DEVIATION-FROM-THE-NORM CRITERION

If the statistical criterion is insufficient, it is because it is essentially *neutral*, ie the statistical average is neither good nor bad, desirable nor undesirable (abnormal is defined as deviation-from-the-average). Deviation-from-the-*norm*, however, implies not behaving or feeling as one *should*: 'norm' has an 'oughtness' about it whereby behaviour is expected from individuals occupying particular roles and if those expectations are not met or are positively 'transgressed', a judgement of 'bad' or 'sick' may be passed.

For example, as far as many people are concerned, homosexuality is abnormal not because it is statistically less common than heterosexuality but because the latter represents the 'normal' state of sexual affairs, ie the 'natural' form of sexual behaviour in human beings (and, they would argue, in other species too) is heterosexual. From a religious–moral perspective, homosexuality might be judged as 'bad', 'wicked', 'sinful', etc. (implying, perhaps, the element of choice) while from a more biological–scientific perspective, it might be labelled 'sick', 'perverse', 'deviant', etc. (implying perhaps lack of choice and responsibility). Either way, even if it was found that a majority of men and women engaged in homosexual relationships (making *hetero*sexuality abnormal according to the statistical criterion), this would still be considered a deviation from the norm and, therefore, abnormal. (This point is discussed further in relation to the next criterion of Mental Health.)

There is a further implication, which is that what is 'normal' is also 'desirable'; unlike the statistical criterion, deviation-from-the-norm does not allow for deviations which are also desirable.

THE ADEQUACY OR MENTAL HEALTH CRITERION

One way of 'fleshing out' the notion of desirability is to identify characteristics and abilities which people should possess for them to be considered normal; by implication, any lack or impoverishment of these characteristics and abilities constitutes abnormality or disorder.

Jahoda (1958) identified several ways in which mental health has been (or might be) defined, including:

(a) The absence of mental illness (clearly, a very negative definition).
(b) Being able to introspect about ourselves, being aware of what we are doing and why.
(c) Growth, development and self-actualization (as emphasized by Rogers and Maslow; see Chapter 29).
(d) Integration of all the processes and attributes of the individual (eg balance between the id, ego and superego in Freud's theory and the achievement of ego identity in Erikson's theory, see Chapters 21 and 24).
(e) The ability to cope with stress (see Chapter 6).
(f) Autonomy (a concept which appears in many theories; eg Maslow and Erikson).
(g) Seeing the world as it really is (part of Erikson's concept of ego identity).
(h) Environmental mastery—the ability to love, to be adequate in love, work and play, to be satisfactory in our interpersonal relationships

and the capacity for adaptation and adjustment (Erikson's ego identity again, Adler's belief in the need for an adjustment in the areas of love, work and society and Freud's 'lieben and arbeiten'— love and work).

While many or all these criteria of mental health may seem valid and are intuitively appealing, that they are intended to be universal and absolute raises three serious problems.

1)   According to these criteria, most of us would be considered maladjusted or disordered, for example, Maslow himself argues that most of us do not achieve self-actualization and so there is a fundamental discrepancy between these criteria and the statistical criterion (Mackay, 1975).

2)   Although there is some overlap between these criteria, and many psychologists would subscribe to them, they are essentially value-judgements, reflecting what is considered to be an *ideal* state of being human. By contrast, there is little dispute as to the precise nature of physical health. According to Szasz (1960), 'the norm is the structural and functional integrity of the human body' and if there are no abnormalities present, the person is considered to be in good health. Judgements about physical health do *not* involve making moral or philosophical decisions, 'what health is can be stated in anatomical and physical terms' (Szasz, 1960) and ideal and statistical criteria tend to be roughly equivalent (Mackay, 1975).

3)   If follows from 2) that what is considered to be psychologically normal (and, hence, abnormal), depends upon the society and culture in which a person lives; psychological normality and abnormality are *culturally* defined (unlike physical normality–abnormality which ,Szasz believes, can be defined in universally applicable ways).

Take the example of homosexuality again: for 23 years (up to 1974), homosexuality was defined as a mental disorder by the American Psychiatric Association's official diagnostic manual. Clearly, nothing happened to homosexuality itself after that period—what changed were attitudes towards it, which then became reflected in its official psychiatric status. Put another way, homosexuality *in itself* is neither normal nor abnormal, desirable nor undesirable, and this can be extended to all behaviour.

Again, within the same culture or society, a particular instance of behaviour may be considered normal or abnormal depending on the *situation* or *context*. For example, taking your clothes off is fine if you are about to step into a bath, but not in the middle of a supermarket, and what determines judgements of normality/abnormality are the norms (expectations) associated with those situations. Behaviour, of course, always does occur (and can only occur) within particular situational contexts and so can never be judged except in terms of situational norms; behaviour is inherently *social*.

We should also note that situational norms are not the only ones we apply; there are also *developmental* norms, whereby particular behaviour may be judged as normal or abnormal depending on the developmental age of the person. For instance, regardless of where they occur, we accept temper tantrums as perfectly normal in a two-year-old but decidedly abnormal in a thirty-two-year-old (even in the privacy of their own home).

Smith et al argue that people with behaviour disorders:

> are unable to modify their behaviour in response to changing environmental requirements. Thus, their behaviour is maladaptive because it is inflexible and unrealistic. It is also likely to be statistically uncommon and socially deviant, although neither of these characteristics is always present. People whose behaviour is abnormal may or may not seen unhappy about their failure to adapt. (Smith et al, 1986)

ABNORMALITY AS PERSONAL DISTRESS

Following on from the last part of Smith et al's definition, Atkinson et al (1990) propose that subjective feelings of *personal distress* may sometimes be the only symptom of abnormality. Most people who are diagnosed as mentally ill often feel acutely miserable, anxious, depressed and agitated and may suffer from insomnia, loss of appetite and a variety of aches and pains. As far as their public behaviour is concerned, they may be perfectly normal. (But the converse is also sometimes true—someone whose behaviour is obviously 'mad' as far as others are concerned, may be oblivious of how others see them and may experience no subjective distress. This is sometimes referred to as lack of insight and is a feature of psychotic illness; see below.)

ABNORMALITY AS MALADAPTIVENESS

People may be judged as abnormal if their behaviour adversely affects either their own well-being, or that of others, or both, either physically, psychologically, or both. The concept of being a risk to one's own or other's health and/or safety is the basis of compulsory detention in a psychiatric hospital; see below.

THE MENTAL ILLNESS CRITERION— ABNORMALITY AS MENTAL ILLNESS

The influence of the *medical model* extends beyond psychiatry and many psychological theories of abnormality or disorder represent a rejection of and alternative to the medical model or, in the case of the neurobiological approach, an attempt to find empirical support for it.

Many writers have pointed out that the vocabulary we use to refer to psychological disorder is borrowed from medical terminology: deviant behaviour is referred to as psycho*pathology* (the title of this chapter), is classified on the basis of *symptoms*, the classification being called a *diagnosis*, the methods used to try to change the behaviour are called *therapies* and these are often carried out in mental or psychiatric *hospitals*. If the deviant behaviour ceases, the *patient* is described as *cured* (Maher, 1966).

It is the use of such vocabulary which reflects the pervasiveness of a 'sickness' model of psychological abnormality (together with terms such as 'syndrome', 'prognosis', 'in remission' and so on); in other words, whether we realize it or not, when we think about abnormal behaviour we think about it *as if* it were indicative of some underlying *illness*. How valid is the medical model?

THE CONCEPT OF MENTAL ILLNESS: THE CASE FOR AND AGAINST

1) Many defenders of the medical model have argued that it is more *humane* to regard a psychologically disturbed person as sick (or mad) than plain bad, ie it is more stigmatizing to be regarded as morally defective (Blaney, 1975). However, when we label someone as sick or ill we are removing all *responsibility* from them for their behaviour; just as we do not normally hold someone responsible for having cancer or a broken leg, so 'mental illness' implies that something has happened to the person who is a victim and who is, accordingly, put in the care (and often the custody) of doctors and nurses who will take over responsibility. (We should note that stigma may be attached to physical illness, even if responsibility is not—as with cancer—but with AIDS part of the stigma seems to be the *blame* attached to the patient.)

It could be argued that the stigma attached to mental illness is actually greater than that attached to labels of 'bad' because our fear of mental illness is even greater than our fear of becoming involved in crime or other immoral activities due to our belief that the former is something that 'happens to people' while the latter is chosen in some way.

While it may be considered more humanitarian to care for people in hospitals than to torture them for witchcraft, exorcize their evil spirits or lock them up in prisons, there is a sense in which these past practices were more honest than some of the current abuses of psychiatry. When people were imprisoned, society was saying quite unambiguously, 'We do not approve of your behaviour and will not tolerate it', making its values clear but also not removing responsibility from the person whose behaviour was being condemned. However, when (until recently) Soviet political dissidents were diagnosed as suffering from schizophrenia (the most 'serious' form of mental illness), society was saying, 'No one in their right mind could hold the views you express, so you must be out of your mind', thereby bypassing the actual issues raised by the dissident's beliefs and removing responsibility for those beliefs from the 'patient'.

2) As we have seen in discussing criteria of normality–abnormality, defining psychological health is much more problematic than defining physical health; not only do norms differ between cultures but they change within the same culture from one historical period to another and, for this reason, Heather (1976) believes that the criteria used by psychiatry to judge abnormality must be seen in a *moral* context and *not* a medical one. The fact of cultural relativity, he argues, makes psychiatry an entirely different kind of enterprise from legitimate medicine: psychiatry's claim to be an orthodox part of medical science rests upon the concept of mental illness, but far from being another medical speciality, psychiatry is a 'quasi-medical illusion' (Heather, 1976).

3) Probably the most radical critic of the concept of mental illness is Szasz; the titles of his books give an indication of his position, for example, *The Myth of Mental Illness* (1962), *The Manufacture of Madness* and *Ideology and Insanity* (1974).

According to Szasz, the basic assumption made by psychiatrists is that 'mental illness' is caused by diseases or disorders of the nervous system (in particular, the brain) which are revealed in abnormal thinking and behaviour. If this is the case, it would be better to call them 'diseases of the brain' or neurophysiological disorders; this would then get rid of the confusion between any physical, organic, defect (which must be seen in an anatomical and physiological context) and any 'problems in living' the person may have (which must be seen in an ethical and social context).

The vast majority of cases of 'mental illness' are, according to Szasz, actually cases of problems of living and they should be referred to as such. It is the exception to the rule to find a 'mentally ill' person who is actually suffering from some organic brain disease (as in senile dementia, alcoholic poisoning, etc.) and this fact is recognized by psychiatrists themselves when they distinguish between *organic psychosis* and *functional psychosis*; 'functional' means that there is no demonstrable physical basis for the abnormal behaviour and that something has gone wrong with the way the person functions in the network of relationships which make up their world (Bailey, 1979).

Although this distinction between organic and functional psychosis is made, organic psychiatrists believe that medical science will, in time, identify the physical causes of the latter (which include schizophrenia and psychotic depression). However, as Heather (1976) points out, this belief does not constitute evidence and even if such evidence were forthcoming it would still leave major categories of mental disorder (in particular, neurosis and personality disorder) which even the organicists admit are *not* bodily diseases in any sense!

If it is not the brain which is diseased, we are left asking in what sense can we think of the mind as being diseased? Szasz answers this by saying that only *metaphorically* can we attribute disease to the mind; in a literal sense, it is logically impossible for a non-spatial, non-physical, mind to be suffering from a disorder of a physico-chemical nature (unless, of course we identify the mind with the brain; see the discussion of reductionism in Chapter 2).

According to Bailey (1979), medicine began by classifying such things as syphilis, tuberculosis, carcinoma and typhoid as illnesses, all sharing the common feature of reference to a state of disordered structure and/or functioning of the human body as a physico-chemical machine; the mistake was to keep adding to this list additional items which are *not* illnesses in this sense. Agreeing with Szasz, Bailey maintains that: (i) *organic* mental illnesses are *not* mental illnesses at all but *physical* illnesses in which mental symptoms are manifested and which aid diagnosis and treatment; (ii) *functional* mental illnesses are *not* illnesses but *disorders* of *psychosocial* or *interpersonal functioning* (Szasz's 'problems in living') in which mental symptoms are important in deciding the type of therapy the patient requires.

4) An important difference between diagnosis in general medicine and psychiatry is to do with the role of *signs* and *symptoms*. While a doctor looks for *signs* of disease (ie the results of objective tests, such as blood tests, X-rays and so on and physical examination) as well as *symptoms* (the patient's report of pain, etc.), they tend to attach more weight to the former when forming a diagnosis. (This has implications for classification; see later.)

By contrast, the psychiatrist is much more at the mercy of symptoms; although psychological tests are the psychiatric equivalent of blood tests and X-rays, they are nothing like as reliable and valid (see Chapters 28 and 29) and, in practice, the psychiatrist will rely to a large extent on the patient's own description of the problem.

Whether or not the patient's claim that he is Napoleon, for example, will be judged by the psychiatrist to be a symptom depends on whether the psychiatrist believes that the patient means it or not, their overall impression of the patient, their comparison of the patient's statement with their *own* beliefs and their interpretation of the norms of the society in which they live (Fransella, 1975).

In trying to describe the *norms* from which the mentally ill are thought to deviate, Szasz (1962) found that they have to be stated in psychological, ethical and legal terms and yet the remedy is sought in terms of *medical* measures. For this reason, Szasz believes that the concept of mental illness has replaced beliefs in demonology and witchcraft; 'mental illness thus exists or is "real" in exactly the same sense in which witches existed or were real' (Szasz, 1962) and serves the same political purposes. What might these be?

In *Ideology and Insanity* (1974), Szasz argues that whenever people wish to exclude others from their midst, they attach to them *stigmatizing labels* eg 'foreigner', 'criminal', 'mentally ill', etc.).

Unlike people suffering from physical illness, most people considered to be mentally ill (especially those 'certified' or 'sectioned' and so legally mentally ill) are so defined by others (relatives, friends, employers, police, etc.), *not* by themselves. They have upset the social order (by violating or ignoring social laws and conventions) and so society labels them as mentally ill and (in many cases) punishes them by commitment to a mental hospital.

However, punishment is the last thing that psychiatrists would admit to giving their patients. As doctors, they must believe that what they give is help, care, treatment, etc., which are all in the patients' best interest. The patient soon learns that until they change their behaviour (in the way required by the hospital) they will remain segregated from society. However, even if this happens and the patient is 'let out', their 'record' goes with them (much like a criminal record); stigmatizing labels become very firmly attached!

Because of the over-emphasis on the therapeutic potentialities of psychiatry, and the under-emphasis of its punitive functions, Szasz believes that there has developed a distorted relationship between psychiatry and the law (in the USA at least). People accused of serious crimes used to be advised to *plead insanity* (which would reduce their prison sentence or require them to receive psychiatric help rather than imprisonment) but now they are often being *charged* with it and being branded 'insane' may result in incarceration for *life* in a psychiatric institution. This is what happened to a filling-station operator whom Szasz calls Joe Skulski:

When he was told to move his business to make way for a new shopping centre, he stubbornly resisted eviction. Finally the police were summoned. Joe greeted them with a warning shot in the air. He was taken into custody and denied bail, because the police considered his protest peculiar and thought he must be crazy. The district attorney requested a pre-trial psychiatric examination of the accused. Mr Skulski was examined, pronounced mentally unfit to stand trial, and confined in the state hospital for the criminally insane. Through it all, he pleaded for the right to be tried for his offence. Now in the mental hospital, he will spend years of fruitless effort to prove that he is sane enough to stand trial. If he had been convicted, his prison sentence would have been shorter than the term he has already served in the hosptial. (Szasz, 1974)

(Psychiatry and the Law is discussed in Box 30.2, p. 959.)

Underlying the labelling process, according to Szasz, is the need to *predict* other people's behaviour: people who are labelled 'mentally ill' are far less easy to predict and others find this disturbing. Attaching a diagnostic label represents a *symbolic recapture* and this may be followed by a *physical capture* (hospitalization, drugs, etc.). (Laing also observes that it is usually *we* who are disturbed by the patient's behaviour, rarely the patient.) While medical diagnosis usually focuses only on the damaged or diseased parts of the body (eg someone has a broken leg or lung cancer), psychiatric diagnosis describes the *whole person*—someone does not have schizophrenia but is *schizophrenic*; this represents a new and total identity, which not only describes the person but describes how they should be regarded and treated by others.

Psychiatric diagnosis, therefore, is a form of *action*. But in what ways are schizophrenics unpredictable and what kinds of rules are they breaking?

According to Scheff (1966), they are breaking *residual rules*, the 'unnameable' expectations we have regarding such things as 'decency' and 'reality'. Because these rules are themselves implicit, taken-for-granted and not articulated, behaviour that violates them is not easily understood and is also difficult to articulate; hence, it is found strange and frightening.

According to Becker (1963), the values on which psychiatric intervention is based are, generally speaking, middle-class values regarding decent, reasonable, proper behaviour and experience and which are applied to working-class patients, who constitute the vast majority of the inmates of psychiatric hospitals. In *Asylums* (1968), Goffman describes the 'career' of psychiatric patients, by which he means any social strand in a person's journey through life: the progress of an individual from being a member of society with a full range of rights and privileges to a patient dispossessed of almost all of those rights and privileges can be thought of as a developing career. Related to this is the patient's *moral* career, by which he means the changes in the patient's view of themselves and others.

Psychiatric hospitals (like prisons and boarding schools) are *total institutions*, ie they encompass all aspects of an inmate's life and like all institutions, they have an overt, official purpose as well as a covert, unofficial, purpose: the former is to help the mentally ill recover from their illness, while the latter is to destroy the patient's previous personal identity and to re-mould it into a form required by the institution.

In this way, psychiatric hospitals operate as agencies for *social control*. As Szasz (1970) observes, persons who have not broken the law are deprived of their civil liberties.

5)   An integral part of the medical model is the *classification* of *mental illness* and the related process of diagnosis.

All systems of classification stem from the work of Emil Kraepelin (1913) who claimed that certain groups of signs and symptoms occur together sufficiently often to merit the designation 'disease' or syndrome; he then described the diagnostic indicators associated with each syndrome.

Kraepelin's classification is embodied in the 1959 Mental Health Act, although the latter is much broader and, in fact, is concerned with mental *disorders* (including mental illness). The classification system currently used in the UK is the Mental Disorders Section of the Tenth Revision of the International Classification of Diseases (ICD-10) published by the World Health Organization in 1987.

In the USA, the American Psychiatric Association's official classification system is the Diagnostic and Statistical Manual of Mental Disorders (DSM); DSM-1 was published in 1952, DSM-II in 1968 and DSM-III, in 1980. DSM-III was revised in 1987 (DSM-III-R). Table 30.1 shows the

DSM-III-R (1987)	ICD-IO (1987)
1. Organic mental disorders	1. Organic mental disorders
2. Schizophrenic disorders	2. Schizophrenia, schizotypal states and delusional disorders
3. Delusional (paranoid) disorders	
4. Psychotic Disorders not elsewhere classified	
5. Psychoactive substance use disorders	3. Mental and behavioural disorders due to psychoactive substance use
6. Affective (mood) disorders	4. Mood (affective) disorders
7. Anxiety disorders	5. Neurotic, stress related and somatoform disorders
8. Somatoform disorders	
9. Dissociative disorders	
10. Adjustment disorders	
11. Disorders usually first evident in infancy, childhood or adolescence (Axis II)*	6. Behavioural and emotional disorders with onset usually occurring in childhood or adolescence
	7. Mental retardation
	8. Developmental disorders
12. Personality disorders (Axis II)*	9. Disorders of adult personality and behaviour
13. Psychological factors affecting physical conditions	10. Behavioural syndromes and mental disorders associated with physiological dysfunction and hormonal disturbances
14. Psychosexual disorders	
15. Sleep disorders	
16. Factitious disorders	
17. Impulse control disorders	

Table 30.1 Major categories of mental disorder

*See Table 30.2.

major categories of both ICD-10 and DSM-III-R. Figure 30.1 shows eight major categories, with examples of specific disorders based on both classification schemes.

COMPARISON BETWEEN DSM-III-R AND ICD-10

1) Table 30.1 shows how the two systems overlap, such that they have the following categories in common: Organic Mental Disorders, Psychoactive Substance Use Disorders, Affective Disorders and Personality Disorders plus categories 13 (DSM-III-R) and 10 (ICD-10).

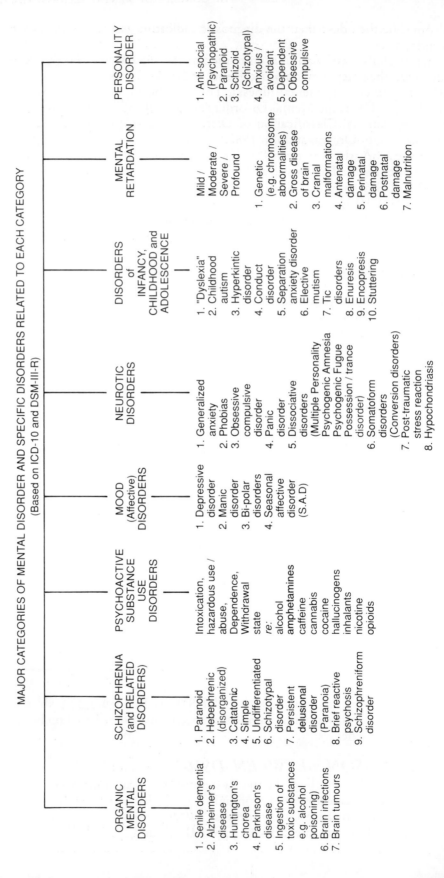

Figure 30.1 *Major categories of mental disorder and specific disorders related to each category. (Based on ICD-10 and DSM-III-R)*

2)   Neither uses the term *mental illness*, which is ironic in view of the earlier discussion about the term, which has traditionally been at the centre of the controversy over the medical model. Instead, they use the term *mental disorder*, which is defined by DSM-III-R as:

> A clinically significant behaviour or psychological syndrome or pattern that occurs in a person and that is associated with present distress (a painful symptom) or disability (impairment of one or more important areas of functioning) or with a significantly increased risk of suffering death, pain, disability, or an important loss of freedom. In addition, this syndrome or pattern must not be merely an expectable response to a particular event, for example, the death of a loved one.

3)   DSM-III (1980) had, in fact, been based to a large extent on ICD-9 (1978) and one of the major changes which was made compared with DSM-II (1968), to bring it in line with ICD-9, was the introduction of a *multi-axial system of classification*.

Whereas DSM-II required only a simple diagnostic label (eg 'schizophrenia' or 'anxiety neurosis') DSM-III (and, similarly, DSM-III-R) instructs the psychiatrist to evaluate the patient on five different *axes*, which represent different areas of functioning. (The inclusion of the axes reflects the assumption that most disorders are caused by the interaction of biological, psychological and sociological factors.) The five axes are shown in Table 30.2. Instead of simply placing someone in a single

AXIS	DESCRIPTION
Axis 1: *Clinical syndromes* (diagnostic category)	The patient's specific psychological disorder at the time they come for assessment (eg paranoid schizophrenia);
Axis 2: *Personality disorders* and specific developmental disorders	A set of deeply ingrained, inflexible and maladaptive traits which significantly impair an individual's psychological and social functioning; may occur quite independently of the Axis 1 syndrome and may affect response to treatment (eg paranoid personality)
Axis 3: *Medical disorders* which seem relevant	Eg heart attacks
Axis 4: *Severity of psychosocial stressors*	Stressful events which have occurred within a year of the current problem which are judged to be a possible contributory factor and which might influence the course of treatment (eg divorce or death of a parent); these are rated on a scale of 1 to 7 (from 'none' to 'catastrophic');
Axis 5: *Highest level* of *adaptive functioning*	How well the patient has performed during the previous year in social relationships, occupational activities and leisure time. Again a 7-point scale is used ('superior' to 'grossly impaired') and the rating gives an indication of the patient's potential for recovery (prognosis).

Table 30.2 The five axes of DSM-III-R and appropriate sub-classes

category (eg schizophrenia), the patient is assessed much more broadly, giving a more global and in-depth picture. However, while axes 1–3 are compulsory, 4 and 5 are optional.

4) Both have dropped the traditional distinction between *Neurosis* and *Psychosis*, although ICD-10 retains the term 'neurotic' (Category 5) and DSM-III-R retains the term 'psychotic' (Category 4). According to Gelder et al (1989) there are four major reasons for getting rid of the distinction: (i) there are exceptions to all the criteria used to distinguish them (Table 30.3); (ii) disorders included under the broad categories of

Table 30.3 The major criteria for making the traditional distinction between neurosis and psychosis

NEUROSIS	PSYCHOSIS
Only a *part* of the personality is involved/affected	The *whole* personality is involved/affected
Contact with reality is *maintained*	Contact with reality is *lost*—inability to distinguish between subjective experience and external reality (eg hallucinations and delusions)
The neurotic has *insight* (ie recognizes that they have a problem)	The psychotic has *no* insight
Neurotic behaviour is understandable as an exaggeration of 'normal' behaviour (so there is only a *quantitative* difference).	Psychotic behaviour is discontinuous with 'normal' behaviour (so there is a *qualitative* difference)
Often begins as a response to a stressor	There is usually *no* precipitating cause
The neurotic disturbance is related to the person's personality prior to their 'illness' (the pre-morbid personality)	The psychotic disturbance is *not* related to the person's personality prior to their 'illness'
Treated mainly by *psychological* methods	Treated mainly by *physical* methods (particularly early on)

'neurosis' or 'psychosis' have little in common; (iii) it is less informative to classify a disorder as neurotic or psychotic than it is to classify it as a particular disorder *within* that very broad category (eg 'schizophrenic' is more informative than 'psychotic'); (iv) DSM-III wanted to remove the psychoanalytic influence in the way 'neurotic' was used and understood (based on Freud's theories). However, Gelder et al say that in everyday psychiatric practice they are convenient terms for disorders which cannot be given a more precise diagnosis and also the terms are still in general use (as in 'antipsychotic drugs' and when referring to symptoms).

5) Both have introduced explicit operational criteria for diagnosis (based on Spitzer et al's (1978) Research Diagnostic Criteria). For each category, there is a specified list of symptoms, all or some of which must be present, for a specified period of time. The aim is to make diagnosis more reliable and more valid (see later) by laying down rules for the inclusion or exclusion of cases (DSM-III-R has made rather greater use of these than ICD-10).

6) One of the major differences between DSM-III-R and ICD-10 is the number of major categories, as shown in Table 30.1. Most differences arise because DSM-III-R uses a larger number of discrete categories to classify disorders that appear under a small number of more general categories in ICD-10. Two such differences are shown in Figure 30.2.

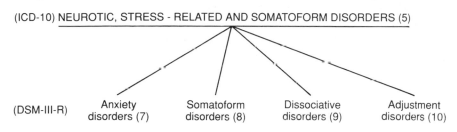

(ICD-10) NEUROTIC, STRESS - RELATED AND SOMATOFORM DISORDERS (5)

(DSM-III-R)   Anxiety disorders (7)   Somatoform disorders (8)   Dissociative disorders (9)   Adjustment disorders (10)

Figure 30.2 Two examples of how a general ICD-10 category incorporates three or more DSM-III-R categories

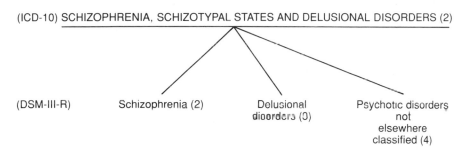

(ICD-10) SCHIZOPHRENIA, SCHIZOTYPAL STATES AND DELUSIONAL DISORDERS (2)

(DSM-III-R)   Schizophrenia (2)   Delusional disorders (0)   Psychotic disorders not elsewhere classified (4)

Another important difference is that ICD-10 distinguishes Mental Retardation (7) both from Behavioural and Emotional Disorders with Onset Usually Occurring in Childhood or Adolescence (16) (eg hyperkinesis, ie 'hyperactivity') and Developmental Disorders (8) (eg autism). But DSM-III-R includes Mental Retardation under the general category of Disorders Usually First Evident in Childhood or Adolescence (11).

While DSM-III-R includes *eating disorders* (such as anorexia nervosa and bulimia) under category 11, ICD-10 would classify them under category 10 (Behavioural Syndromes and Mental Disorders associated with Physiological Dysfunction and Hormonal Disturbances). *Sleep disorders* would also be classified under 10 but in DSM-III-R there is a separate category for Sleep Disorders (15). The same applies to Psychosexual Disorders (DSM-III-R-14). Before considering questions about the need for clasification, its reliability and validity, etc., let us look at some of the major disorders themselves. We shall do this within the framework of Figure 30.1.

NEUROTIC DISORDERS

ANXIETY NEUROSIS (GENERALIZED OR 'FREE-FLOATING' ANXIETY)

The person experiences a generalized, diffused, anxiety which is not aroused by any particular situation or object and in the absence of any realistic threat or danger. The person is typically jumpy, irritable, finds it difficult to concentrate and make decisions, has trouble sleeping, a poor appetite and may experience a whole range of physical symptoms.

The person may experience occasional *anxiety attacks* (which may last from fifteen minutes to an hour) in which there are feelings of inescapable danger which can leave them feeling exhausted. An extreme form of anxiety attack are *panic reactions*, which may last for days, producing a state of disorganization and disorientation.

PHOBIAS

A phobia is defined as an extreme, irrational, fear of some specific object or situation. Typically, the phobic acknowledges that the object of fear is harmless but the fear is experienced none the less (this is the irrational element) and trying to hide the phobia from others may induce further anxiety, guilt and shame. The phobic will try to avoid the feared object or situation at all costs, and it is this avoidance behaviour which can interfere with the person's normal functioning and which distinguishes a phobia from a milder fear or mere dislike of something.

Almost anything may become the object of a phobia but some phobias are much more common than others. The most common of all is *agoraphobia* (usually defined as fear of open spaces), accounting for about 60 per cent of all phobic patients (and about 6 per 1000 of the general population), followed by *social* phobias, including fear of having to eat or drink in public, talking to members of the opposite sex or having to speak or write in front of others, which account for another 8 per cent, and *animal* phobias or zoophobia (with some much more common than others, eg snakes and spiders) accounting for a further 3 per cent (Marks, 1970; see Chapters 7 and 31 for a discussion of 'preparedness'.)

Marks (1970) conducted a ten-year retrospective study of out-patients seen at the Maudsley Hospital in London and found that phobic disorders represented 5 per cent of all cases seen; this compares with the figure of 2 to 3 per cent of all neurotic patients seen in both the UK and the USA (Torgersen, 1979). Because of its common occurrence, much attention has been given to agoraphobia. According to Mitchell (1982), although some patients are terrified of being alone in wide open spaces (such as fields, deserted moorland and so on), what all agoraphobics share is a fear of being alone *anywhere* and they are probably suffering from a form of separation anxiety, fearing that something unpleasant will happen to them because there is no one there who could come to their assistance.

The *primary* fear, says Mitchell, is leaving the safety and security of home and/or companions; fear of being in public places (shops, on buses, in the street, etc.) represents a *secondary* fear but, significantly, the patient is usually aware only of the latter.

Agoraphobia occurs predominantly in women, while most other phobias tend to be fairly evenly divided between the sexes. Other phobias include *acrophobia* (fear of heights), *school phobia* or 'school-refusal', *algophobia* (fear of pain), *astraphobia* (fear of thunder and/or lightning), *hydrophobia* (fear of water), *nyctophobia* (fear of darkness, which is quite normal in young children), *xenophobia* (fear of strangers) and, would you believe, *phobophobia* (fear of fear!).

OBSESSIVE–COMPULSIVE DISORDER

Obsessions are recurring irrational thoughts or ideas over which the person has no control, while compulsions are actions which the victim feels compelled to repeat over and over again (a common example being compulsive hand-washing).

Obsessions and compulsions are often related, the latter representing an attempt to counteract the former; for example, compulsive hand-washing may be an attempt to remove the obsessive pre-occupation with contamination by dirt or germs, either as agent or victim (hence obsessive compulsive neurosis). Howard Hughes was a well-known neurotic of this kind.

An example, of an obsession occurring without compulsive behaviour is sexual jealousy, an extreme case of which is described by Stuart Sutherland in *Breakdown* (1976). Sutherland was a well-known British experimental psychologist who had been happily married for several years when his wife suddenly revealed that she had been having an affair (but had no wish to end their marriage). At first, he was able to accept the situation and, indeed, found that the increased honesty and communication actually improved their marriage. However, after asking his wife for further details of the affair, he became obsessed with vivid images of his wife in moments of sexual passion with her lover and he could not remove these thoughts from his mind, day or night. Finally, he had to leave his teaching and research duties and it was only after several months of trying various forms of therapy that he managed to reduce the obsessive thoughts sufficiently to be able to return to work.

SOMATOFORM (CONVERSION) DISORDERS

In the *conversion type* of hysterical neurosis (which was the 'model' of neurosis on which Freud based his psychoanalytic theory) a simulation of physical symptoms occurs, ie the person experiences physical symptoms for which there is no detectable physical or bodily cause. According to Mackay (1975), these are usually one of three kinds:

(a) *Sensory symptoms*. Anaesthesia (complete loss of sensation to pain) or paraesthesia (tingling or other unusual sensation), hysterical blindness or deafness.

(b) *Motor symptoms*. Paralysis, aphonia (inability to talk above a whisper) and mutism (complete inability to talk).

(c) *Visceral symptoms*. Psuedo-appendicitis, malaria, tuberculosis, pregnancy, coughing fits, black-outs, severe headaches.

There are usually three 'tell-tale' signs. First, a lack of concern about the symptoms ('la belle indifférence'), second, the selective nature of the dysfunction (for example, the patient is mute only in the presence of certain people), and third, the inconsistency in the symptomatology (for example, the paralysed arm which does not atrophy or wither). Symptoms can also appear and disappear quite suddenly (unlike genuine symptoms). These apparently physical symptoms will still demand a great deal of attention from doctors and relatives, etc. and they may also ensure that the person will avoid certain unpleasant situations; these advantages of being 'ill' are known as 'secondary gain' (see Chapter 31).

DISSOCIATIVE DISORDERS

In the *dissociative type* of hysterical neurosis, psychological rather than physical dysfunction occurs and takes the form of a separation, or dissociation, of one part of the self from the other parts. (This has led to the common confusion between multiple personality, one kind of dissociative disorder, and schizophrenia, in which a splitting occurs but is different in character from dissociation—we shall return to this point later.)

In *somnambulism* (sleepwalking), one part of the personality takes over control of behaviour while the 'ordinary' personality becomes inactive or sleeps; these daze-like states occur during the day or night, with the eyes open or closed.

Amnesia often appears 'out of the blue' (with nothing to account for it, such as a blow to the head) and may disappear just as suddenly. The forgetting is very selective and the forgotten material can often be recovered under hypnosis or will be recognized when presented (which would not be true of a brain-damaged patient). *Fugue* ('flight') may be thought of as an extension of amnesia, in which the patient flees from home and self by wandering off on a journey, not knowing how they got there and unable to recall their true identity. The person assumes a new identity but, unlike many amnesic patients, does not experience confusion and disorientation. It is usually a brief episode, lasting from hours to days rather than weeks. Like amnesia, it may often be triggered by severe psychological stress and in both cases recovery is usually rapid and complete and recurrence is rare.

Multiple personality involves two or more integrated personalities 'residing' within the same body, each dominating at different times. The 'original' personality is usually not aware of the other(s) although these others may be (at least partly) aware of the first. Often, the other personalities embody parts of the first personality which have become repressed and so have remained unexpressed; for example, a shy and sexually inhibited person may develop a second personality who is flirtatious and sexually promiscuous. Shifts from one to the other may be sudden and dramatic and multiple personality may be accompanied by fugue.

The 'original' case was Robert Louis Stevenson's fictional *Dr Jekyll and Mr Hyde*. True-life cases (which are very rare) include 'The Three Faces of Eve' (Thigpen et al, 1957) and the truly staggering 'Sybil' (Schreiber, 1973) who had sixteen separate personalities—the case must be read to be believed! (For a detailed discussion of 'Eve', see Gross, 1990.)

PSYCHOSOMATIC (OR PSYCHOPHYSIOLOGICAL) DISORDERS

These are not always included under the general category heading of neurotic disorders, but it is convenient to do so here because of the part played by anxiety which is really the 'hallmark' of neurosis in general. The symptoms involved here (unlike those of hysterical conversion neurosis) are real and are confirmed by medical examination ('signs'); they include ulcers, high blood pressure, asthma, migraine, headaches, heart attacks, etc., and are clearly stress-induced or stress-related (see Chapter 6).

ORGANIC MENTAL DISORDERS

Organic disorders are the only kind of mental disorder in which there are known, identifiable, organic causes.

Brain infections include general paresis ('general paralysis of the insane'), a major psychiatric disorder caused by untreated syphilis and which is terminal. *Brain tumours* may sometimes give rise to psychiatric symptoms (eg the first indication may be that relatives detect a 'changed personality' in the patient) and their effects will always depend on their precise location.

Acute brain damage is caused by high fevers, hormonal disturbances, excessive drug intake and severe nutritional deficiencies and is usually only temporary. Chronic brain damage, however, is more severe and is basically irreversible. Some of the clinical signs of brain damage include: (i) memory dysfunction (eg confabulation, see Chapter 12); (ii) affective changes (eg an increase in emotional instability); (iii) general intellectual impairment (eg less capable of abstract thought, understanding new ideas or making decisions); (iv) disorders of attention (eg more easily distracted and less able to concentrate); (v) personality changes (which are usually related to the pre-morbid personality); and (vi) epileptic fits.

Degeneration of the nervous system includes senile dementia, Huntington's Chorea, Pick's Disease, Alzheimer's Disease and Parkinson's Disease.

SCHIZOPHRENIA AND RELATED DISORDERS

SCHIZOPHRENIA

What we now call schizophrenia was originally called *dementia praecox* ('senility of youth') by Kraepelin (1902), who believed that the typical symptoms (namely, delusions, hallucinations, attention deficits and bizarre motor activity) were due to a form of mental deterioration which began in adolescence.

Bleuler (1911) observed, however, that many patients displaying these symptoms did *not* go on deteriorating and that illness often begins much later than adolescence. Consequently, he introduced the term *schizophrenia* instead (literally 'split mind' or 'divided self') to describe an illness in which 'the personality loses its unity'.

According to Clare (1976), the diagnosis of schizophrenia in the UK relies greatly on what Schneider (1959) called *first rank symptoms*; in the presence of one or more of these (and in the absence of brain disease, etc.) a diagnosis of schizophrenia is usually made. But even in their absence the diagnosis may still be made as, in the very early and acute stages of the illness, and in the chronic 'defect' state of the severely disturbed patient, first rank symptoms are often not apparent (Clare, 1976). Schneider's first rank symptoms are shown in Table 30.4.

Slater and Roth (1969) regard hallucinations as the least important of all the major symptoms because they are not exclusive to schizophrenia; in addition to Schneider's first rank symptoms, they identify: (i) thought process disorder; (ii) disturbances of affect; (iii) psychomotor disorders;

Table 30.4 Schneider's (1959) first rank symptoms of schizophrenia	1. *Passivity experiences and thought disturbances*	Thoughts, emotions, impulses or actions are experienced as under external, alien, control, including 'made' experiences which the patient believes are imposed on them or in which their will seems to be taken away. Certain thought-control disturbances are included: *Thought insertion* (thoughts are inserted into one's mind from outside and are under external influence); *Thought withdrawal* (thoughts are removed from one's mind and are under external control); *Thought broadcasting* (thoughts are broadcast to—or otherwise made known to—others). External forces may include the Martians, the Communists and 'the Government' and such experiences are sometimes referred to as *delusions* (see below)
	2. *Auditory hallucinations (in the third person)*	Hallucinatory voices are heard discussing one's thoughts or behaviour as they occur (a kind of 'running commentary') or they are heard arguing about one in the third person (or using one's name) or repeating one's thoughts out loud or anticipating one's thoughts. 'True' hallucinations involve the voices being experienced as alien or under the influence of some external source. (Hallucinations experienced by patients with organic psychoses tend to be visual.)
	3. *Primary delusions*	Delusions are false beliefs which are maintained in the face of contradictory evidence. Two major kinds are delusions of *grandeur* (eg 'I am Napoleon' or, 'I am God') and delusions of *persecution* (eg 'my mother is trying to poison me' and the beliefs regarding thought-control). A 'primary' delusion appears suddenly and in a moment of clear consciousness and is accompanied by a strong feeling of conviction; it is often of the grandiose type

and (iv) lack of volition as the key symptoms. These are described in Table 30.5.

DSM-III-R requires that there should be continuous signs of disturbance for at least six months before a diagnosis of schizophrenia is made. ICD-10 requires only one month's duration and relies more heavily on Schneider's first rank symptoms than does DSM-III-R.

Simple Schizophrenia

This often appears during late adolescence and has a slow, gradual onset. The main symptoms are gradual social deterioration, withdrawal of interest from the environment, an increase in apathy, difficulty in making friends and a decline in academic or occupational performance. Such people may become drifters or tramps and are often regarded by others as idle and 'layabouts'. Clear symptoms are absent and so diagnosis is unreliable.

Hebephrenic or Disorganized Schizophrenia

This is probably the nearest thing to many people's beliefs about what a

1. *Thought process disorder*	The inability to keep to the point, being easily distracted and side-tracked, especially in the form of *clang associations* (eg 'big', 'pig', twig'), where words are 'thrown' together by virtue of their sounds rather than their meaning (producing an apparently incoherent jumble of words, or 'word salad'), being unable to finish a sentence and sometimes stopping in the middle of a word ('thought-blocking'). Also making up new words (neologisms) and interpreting language very literally (eg proverbs)	*Table 30.5 Other major-symptoms of schizophrenia. (Based on Slater and Roth, 1969)*
2. *Disturbances of affect*	A 'flattening of affect', in which they may appear insensitive, inconsiderate or indifferent to other people's feelings and experiences and 'incongruity of affect', a loss of appropriate emotional responses, such as laughing or getting angry without any apparent reason, changing very suddenly from one mood or emotional state to another, feeling happy but non-verbally (eg through facial-expressions) conveying dejection and misery, or giggling when given bad news	
3. *Psychomotor disorders*	Catelepsy (muscles in a state of semi-rigidity), grimacing of facial muscles, twitching of limbs, stereotyped behaviours (such as constant pacing up and down) or catatonic stupor (assuming a fixed position for long periods of time—several years in some cases)	
4. *Lack of volition*	Inability to make decisions or carry out a particular activity, loss of will power or drive, loss of interest in the environment and a loss of affection for loved ones	

'mad' or 'crazy' person is like and typically makes a gradual appearance between 20 and 25 years of age. The hebephrenic will typically display many of the symptoms described in Tables 30.4 and 30.5, including hallucinations, delusions, thought process disorder and disturbances of affect. Behaviour is often silly or mischievious, childish or bizarre and sometimes may be violent (if, for example, the patient is approached while hallucinating).

Catatonic Schizophrenia

This is characterized by excited, sometimes violent, motor behaviour or mute, unmoving, stupors; some patients alternate between these two states but usually one or other dominates. Another symptom which is sometimes displayed is negativism—doing the opposite of what is asked. Hallucinations and delusions, etc. are usually less obvious.

Paranoid Schizophrenia

This is characterized by either delusions of persecution *or* grandeur (or both). In other respects, the person is less disturbed (the personality is better preserved) than in the other three kinds. It is the most homogeneous of the four categories (ie paranoid schizophrenics are more alike than are catatonics, etc.).

With the possible exception of paranoid, these 'sub-categories' are of doubtful validity. Some patients present symptoms of one sub-group at one time, then symptoms of another sub-group later. Catatonic symptoms are much less common now than 50 years ago (perhaps because of improvement in the social environment in which patients are treated). The four sub-groups cannot be clearly distinguished in clinical practice (Gelder et al, 1989), and the fifth sub-group (undifferentiated) is meant to accommodate patients who cannot be easily placed elsewhere.

THEORIES OF SCHIZOPHRENIA

Not only is schizophrenia the single most commonly diagnosed form of mental disorder—some 40 to 50 per cent of all psychiatric patients are labelled schizophrenic and 1 per cent of the whole population will be hospitalized at some point in their lives as schizophrenic—but it has become the focus for the whole controversy surrounding the medical model; many of its most articulate critics, such as Szasz and Laing, have directed their critique towards schizophrenia as the example par excellence of what the medical model sees as *mental illness*.

Part of the controversy surrounds the *causes* of schizophrenia and we shall now consider some of the various theories regarding aetiology.

1) *The Genetic Theory*

A great deal of research has gone into trying to demonstrate a genetic component in schizophrenia. As with intelligence (Chapter 28), the two major kinds of study are those involving twins and adopted children. Just as those studies discussed in Chapter 28 presuppose that IQ tests are a valid measure of intelligence, so the studies discussed here presuppose that schizophrenia is a distinct syndrome which can be reliably diagnosed by different psychiatrists; this presupposition has been seriously questioned.

Some of the major twin studies are summarized in Table 30.6.

	STUDY	COUNTRY	CONCORDANCE RATE (%)—MZS	CONCORDANCE RATE (%)—DZS
Table 30.6 Concordance rates for schizophrenia for MZs and DZs	Luxenburger (1935)	Germany	58	0
	Rosanoff et al (1934)	USA	61	13
	Essen-Moller (1941)	Sweden	64	15
	Kallmann (1946)	USA	69	11
	Slater (1953)	England	65	14
	Inouye (1961)	Japan	60	18
	Gottesman and Shields (1966, 1972)	England	54	18
	Kringlen (1968)	Norway	38	10
	Hoffer et al (1968)	USA	15.5	4.4
	Fischer (1978)	Denmark	48	20
	Tienari (1968)	Finland	43	9

In most cases, the MZs have been reared together and we saw in Chapter 28 how this tends to confound the relative influence of genetic and environmental factors. Furthermore, the concordance rate for MZs in different studies ranges from 15.5 to 69 per cent (for DZs it is 0 to 20), which suggests that different countries use different criteria for diagnosing schizophrenia (and there is evidence that they, in fact, do—see below). By the same token, if the highest concordance rate for MZs is 69 per cent, this still leaves plenty of scope for the role of environmental factors. Of course, if schizophrenia were totally genetically determined, then we would expect to find a 100 per cent concordance rate for MZs, ie if one member of an MZ pair has schizophrenia, the other twin should also have it in every single case.

However, on the genetic side, the average concordance rate for MZs is five times higher than that for DZs (50 per cent and 10 per cent, respectively; Shields, 1976, 1978).

A more precise estimate for the relative importance of genetic and environmental factors comes from studies where MZs reared apart are compared with MZs reared together (a rather different comparison from that made in the area of intelligence). According to Shields (1976, 1978), the concordance rates are quite similar for the two groups, suggesting a major genetic contribution. (For a detailed critique of all these twin studies, see Rose et al, 1984.)

In *adoption studies*, children born to parents, of whom one or both are schizophrenic, are adopted early in life into a normal family and these children are compared either with biological children of the adoptive parents or other adopted children whose biological parents are not schizophrenic.

In one such study, Heston (1966) studied forty-seven adults who had been born to schizophrenic mothers and separated from them within three days of birth. As children they had been reared in a variety of circumstances, though not by the mother's family. They were compared (average age thirty-six) with controls who were matched for circumstances of upbringing, but where mothers had not been schizophrenic. Five of the experimental group but none of the controls were diagnosed as schizophrenic. There was also an excess of antisocial personality and neurotic disorders among the children of schizophrenic mothers, ie children of schizophrenic parents run a greater risk of developing *some* kind of mental disorder even if it is not schizophrenia. Rosenthal et al (1971) began a series of studies in 1965 in Denmark, which has national registers of psychiatric cases and adoptions. They confirmed Heston's findings, using children separated from schizophrenic mothers, on average at six months.

The major study (Kety et al, 1975) uses a different design. Two groups of adoptees were identified: thirty-three who had schizophrenia and a matched group who did not. Rates of disorder were compared in the biological and adoptive families of the two groups of adoptees—the rate was greater among the biological relatives of the schizophrenic adoptees than among those of the controls, a finding which supports the genetic hypothesis. Further, the rate of schizophrenia was not increased among couples who adopted the schizophrenic adoptees, suggesting that environmental factors were not of crucial importance (Gelder et al, 1989). The reverse situation was studied by Wender et al (1974) who found no increase among adoptees with normal biological parents but with a schizophrenic adoptive parent.

Gottesman et al (1982), reviewing adoption studies, conclude that they show a major role for heredity and Gottesman (1977) believes that twin studies and adoption studies have provided sufficient support for the genetic theory to enable researchers to turn their attention to the *environmental stressors* which activate the genetic predisposition.

Zubin and Spring (1977) conclude that what we probably inherit is a degree of vulnerability to exhibit schizophrenic symptoms; whether or not we do will depend on environmental stresses. This very important point is relevant to the equally important distinction between *reactive* and *process* schizophrenia. Reactive schizophrenia appears quite suddenly and usually later in life (not before adolescence) and is normally seen as a response to extreme stress, while in process schizophrenia pathological symptoms have been evident for many years before the 'breakdown' occurs and genetic factors seem to play a relatively greater role (Rosenthal et al, 1971).

A number of studies have shown that where there is an identifiable precipitating factor, onset is acute, there is no family history of schizophrenia, a stable personality prior to onset, warm personal relationships, stable family relationships and prompt treatment, the chances of recovery are greatly enhanced (reactive schizophrenia) compared with process schizophrenia (Clare, 1976).

There is also evidence that people who are later going to develop schizophrenia are disadvantaged educationally, occupationally and in their capacity to make and sustain social and sexual relationships. While it is generally agreed that the lower the social status the higher the incidence of schizophrenia, this can be interpreted in one of two ways—schizophrenia may either be seen as a *cause* of social disadvantage (the *social drift hypothesis*) or an *effect* (the *social causation hypothesis*).

2) *The Biochemical Theory*

It has been proposed that what directly causes schizophrenic symptoms is an excess of the neurotransmitter dopamine (the *dopamine hypothesis*).

The evidence for this hypothesis comes from three main sources: (i) post-mortems on schizophrenics show unusually high levels of dopamine, especially in the limbic system (Iversen, 1979); (ii) the belief that anti-schizophrenic drugs (such as chlorpromazine) work by binding to dopamine receptor sites; and (iii) the observation that high doses of amphetamines and L-dopa (used in the treatment of Parkinson's Disease), both of which enhance the activity of dopamine, can sometimes produce symptoms very similar to those of schizophrenia (see Table 4.2, p. 80).

Although there is strong evidence that dopamine is central to the action of antipsychotic drugs, the evidence that dopamine metabolism is abnormal in schizophrenia is weak. Positron emission tomography (PET) scans provide a way of studying dopamine receptor binding in the brain of living patients (untreated), but the evidence to date is very inconclusive and more work is needed before definite conclusions can be reached (Gelder et al, 1989; see Chapter 4).

A word of caution: even if schizophrenics do have higher natural levels of dopamine, this could as easily be a *result* of schizophrenia as its cause. Even if dopamine were found to be a causative factor, this could turn out to be indirect, such that abnormal family circumstances give rise to high levels of dopamine which, in turn, trigger the symptoms (Lloyd et al, 1984).

3) *Laing and Existential Psychiatry*

During the 1950s and 1960s, several British psychiatrists, notably R. D. Laing, David Cooper and Aaron Esterson, united in their opposition to existing conditions in state mental hospitals. They rejected the medical model of mental disorder and were hostile to the exclusively organic and genetic explanations of schizophrenia. Like Szasz, they denied the existence of schizophrenia as a disease entity and instead saw it as a metaphor for dealing with people whose behaviour and experience fails to conform to the dominant model of social reality; they thus spearheaded the *anti-psychiatry* movement (Graham, 1986).

Heather (1976) identifies three major landmarks in the development of Laing's thought, corresponding to the publication of three major books.

First, in *Divided Self* (1959), Laing tried to make sense of schizophrenia by 'getting inside the head' of a schizophrenic, by trying to see the world as the schizophrenic sees it. This *existentialist* analysis retained the categories of classical psychiatry but proceeded from the assumption that what the schizophrenic says and does are intelligible if you listen carefully enough and relate to their 'being-in-the-world'.

What Laing found was a split in the patient's relationship with the world and with the self. The schizophrenic (and the schizoid personality, who may well develop full-blown schizophrenic symptoms) experiences an intense form of *ontological insecurity* and everyday events may threaten the schizophrenic's very existence.

Specifically, ontological insecurity comprises engulfment, implosion and petrification or depersonalization. *Engulfment* refers to the dread of being swallowed up by others if involvement becomes too close and common expressions of this are, 'being buried, drowned, caught and dragged down into quicksand', being 'on fire, bodies being burned up', feeling 'cold and dry—dreads fire or water'. To be loved is more threatening than to be hated; indeed, all love is a form of hate.

Implosion refers to the fear that the world, at any moment, will come crashing in and obliterate their identity; schizophrenics feel empty, like a vacuum, and they *are* the vacuum; anything ('reality') can threaten that empty space which must be protected at all costs.

Petrification or *depersonalization* involves fear of being turned to stone (catatonia), fear of being turned into a robot or automaton (thought-control) and fear of turning others into stone. To consider another person as a free agent can be threatening, because you can become an *it* for them; in order to prevent the other depersonalizing you, you may have to depersonalize the other.

Secondly, in *Self and Others* (1961), Laing maintained that 'schizophrenia' does not refer to any kind of entity (clinical, existential or otherwise) but rather refers to an *interpersonal ploy* used by some people (parents, doctors, psychiatrists, etc.) in their interactions with others (the schizophrenic). According to the *family interaction model*, schizophrenia can only be understood as something which takes place *between* people (and not *inside* them, as maintained by the psychoanalytic model of *Divided Self*).

To understand individuals we must study not individuals but interactions between individuals and this is the subject-matter of *social phenomenology* (see Chapter 17 on Interpersonal Perception). The family interaction model was consistent with research in America, especially that of Gregory Bateson et al (1956), which showed that schizophrenia arises within families which use 'pathological' forms of communication, in particular, contradictory messages (*double-binds*) in which, for example, a mother induces her son to give her a hug but when he does so tells him 'not to be such a baby'.

In *Sanity, Madness and the Family* (1964), Laing and Esterson presented eleven family case histories, in all of which one member becomes a diagnosed schizophrenic, in order to make schizophrenia intelligible in the context of what happens within the patient's family and, in so doing, to further undermine the disease model of schizophrenia.

Finally, in *The Politics of Experience* (1967), two new models emerged, the conspiratorial and the psychedelic. The *conspiratorial model* maintains that schizophrenia is a *label*, a form of violence perpetrated by some people on others. The family, GP and psychiatrists conspire against schizophrenics to keep them in check; to maintain their definition of reality (the status quo) they treat schizophrenics as if they were sick, imprison them in a mental hospital where they are degraded and invalidated as human beings.

Laing now sees the schizophrenic as, in fact, an exceptionally eloquent critic of society and schizophrenia is, 'itself a natural way of healing our own appalling state of alienation called normality'. Again, 'madness need not be all breakdown ... it may also be breakthrough'; in Bateson's words, the 'patient embarks on a voyage of discovery (death) and returns (rebirth) to the normal world with new insights'. Schizophrenia is seen as a voyage into 'inner space', a 'natural healing process'. Unfortunately, the 'natural sequence' of schizophrenia is very rarely allowed to occur because, says Laing, we are too busy *treating* the patient.

This represents the *Psychedelic Model* of schizophrenia.

Brief reactive psychosis refers to a syndrome which does not last more than a month, it is apparently precipitated by stress with prominent emotional turmoil.

Schizophreniform psychosis is a syndrome similar to schizophrenia, lasting less than six months.

Schizotypal disorder refers to eccentric behaviour and unusual thinking and affect which resemble those seen in schizophrenia but without definite and characteristic schizophrenic abnormalities.

Persistent delusional disorder (paranoia) is characterized by persistent single or multiple delusions without other symptoms.

Mood (Affective) Disorders

MANIC DISORDER (MANIA)

Mania is a sense of intense euphoria or elation, which may manifest as anything from infectious humour to wild excitement. A characteristic symptom is a 'flight of ideas': ideas come rushing into the person's mind with little apparent logical connection and there is a tendency to pun and play with words. Manics have a great deal of energy and rush around, usually achieving little and not putting their energies to good use. There is *disinhibition*, which may take the form of a vastly increased sexual appetite (usually out of keeping with their 'normal' personality). They often go on spending sprees, getting through a lot of money, building up large debts. They are constantly talking, on the move, have little need for sleep and may appear excessively conceited ('grandiose ideas').

DEPRESSIVE DISORDER

The depressive is the complete reverse of the manic: they experience a decreased sex drive and loss of appetite (which can lead to serious malnutrition), a slowing down of thought processes, a sense of hopelessness and despair, worthlessness and ugliness, a general lack of appetite for life and loss of initiative. There may be delusions of physical decay, an expectation of severe punishment and suicide may seem the only way out of a hopeless situation. This describes what traditionally was called *psychotic* or *endogenous* depression, as opposed to *neurotic* or *reactive* depression. But the distinction is controversial.

BI-POLAR DISORDER (MANIC DEPRESSION)

In about 20 per cent of cases, patients experience alternating periods of mania and depression. It is thought that depression may be caused by low levels of dopamine, noradrenaline and serotonin in certain brain areas, while mania is associated with excessively high levels (Iversen, 1979).

These neurotransmitter imbalances seem to be inherited (Kety, 1979).

SEASONAL AFFECTIVE DISORDER (SAD)

Some patients repeatedly develop a depressive disorder at the same time of year and it has been suggested (Rosenthal et al, 1984) that they might be related to the changes in the seasons, specifically, the length of daylight. The most common pattern is onset in autumn or winter, with recovery in spring or summer and the most common form of treatment is exposure to bright artificial light. Rosenthal et al (1984) report that symptoms are reduced after 3–4 days of such treatment, though they generally relapse soon after it is stopped. According to Gelder et al (1989), the hypothesis that the improvements are related to the known effect of light in suppressing the nocturnal secretion of melatonin is not well supported by the evidence (see Chapter 5).

PERSONALITY DISORDERS

ANTI-SOCIAL (SOCIOPATHIC/PSYCHOPATHIC) PERSONALITY

Psychopaths are often of above average intelligence and are charming and socially skilled; their charm can be very disarming and enables them to manipulate and exploit others for their own gain. Whether or not they engage in criminal activities, they are amoral (cannot experience guilt), insensitive to others' feelings, impulsive, stimulus-seeking (needing excitement) and have a low tolerance of frustration. They are unable to develop or maintain meaningful interpersonal relationships because they are incapable of giving—or receiving—love and affection (affectionless psychopathy—see Chapter 23). Sexual activity is carried on without evidence of tenderness. Marriage is often marked by lack of concern for the partner and sometimes by physical violence. Many marriages end in separation or divorce. The characteristic impulsiveness often leads to frequent dismissals from jobs and is often reflected in a lack of any overall purpose in life. The combination of impulsiveness and lack of guilt is often associated with repeated crime, which may be violent and usually shows a callous lack of concern for others.

OBSESSIVE–COMPULSIVE PERSONALITY

Such people are unable to adapt to new situations, rigid in their views and inflexible in their approach to problems. They are upset by change and prefer a safe and familiar routine. They are inhibited by their perfectionism which makes ordinary work a burden and gets them bogged down in trivial detail. Exaggerated moral standards become painful, and result in a guilty preoccupation with wrongdoing, which prevents enjoyment. They are also often humourless, judgemental, mean, indecisive and sensitive to criticism.

PARANOID PERSONALITY

The central traits are suspiciousness and sensitivity. Such people may be constantly on the lookout for attempts by others to get the better of them, deceive them, or play tricks on them and they doubt others' loyalty and trustworthiness. They do not make friends easily and may avoid involvement with groups—they may be perceived by others as secretive, devious and self-sufficient to a fault, as well as argumentative and stubborn. But they also show a strong sense of self-importance, a powerful inner conviction of being unusually talented and capable of great things—but others have prevented them from realizing their potential!

Their sensitivity takes the form of being easily made to feel ashamed and humiliated; they take offence easily and appear prickly, unreasonable and 'difficult'.

SCHIZOID PERSONALITY

Such people are introspective and prone to engage in fantasy rather than take action, emotionally cold, self-sufficient and detached from others. The term was originally used by Kretschmer (1936), who believed that schizoids were likely to become schizophrenic—but this is certainly not always so and the term does *not* imply a causal relationship with schizophrenia (Gelder et al, 1989).

They seem incapable of expressing affection or tenderness, are unable to make intimate friendships and often remain unmarried. They pursue a lonely course through life and their usually solitary habits tend to be intellectual rather than practical.

RETARDATION

The 1959 Mental Health Act introduced the terms 'subnormality' and 'severe subnormality' to replace the terms 'idiocy', 'imbecility' and 'feeble-mindedness' (used by the 1944 Education Act). Severe subnormality is usually associated with brain damage (genetic, eg Down's syndrome, or otherwise), while subnormality is usually associated with gross under-stimulation during infancy and childhood. However, the distinction is ultimately one of clinical judgement (according to the 1983 Mental Health Act).

According to Gelder et al (1989), there are four main categories of mental retardation:

i) Mild Retardation (IQ 50–70)

Such people account for 80 per cent of all mentally retarded people. Their appearance is usually normal and any sensory or motor deficits are slight. Most develop more or less normal language and social behaviour during the pre-school years and their retardation may never be formally identified. As adults, most can live independently in ordinary surroundings but they may need help with housing and employment or when under some unusual stress.

ii) Moderate Retardation (IQ 35–49)

Such people account for about 12 per cent of all mentally retarded people. Most can talk or at least communicate and most can learn to care for themselves with supervision. As adults, they can usually undertake simple routine work and find their way around.

iii) Severe Retardation (IQ 20–34)

Such people account for about 7 per cent of all mentally retarded people. In the pre-school years their development is usually greatly slowed. Eventually many can be trained to look after themselves with close supervision and to communicate simply. (See the discussion of 'idiots savants' in Chapter 28.)

iv) Profound Retardation (IQ below 20)

Such people account for less than 1 per cent of all mentally retarded people. Few learn to care for themselves completely and some achieve some simple speech and social behaviour.

PROBLEMS WITH THE CLASSIFICATION OF MENTAL DISORDER

One of the most famous studies criticizing basic psychiatric concepts and practices is that of Rosenhan (1973), which is described in Box 30.1.

Box 30.1 'On Being Sane in Insane Places' (Rosenhan, 1973)

Eight psychiatrically 'normal' people (a psychology student, three psychologists, a paediatrician, a psychiatrist, a painter–decorator and a housewife) presented themselves at the admissions offices of eight different psychiatric hospitals in the USA, complaining of hearing voices saying 'empty', 'hollow' and 'thud' (auditory hallucinations). These symptoms, together with their name and occupation, were the only falsification of the truth that was involved at any stage of the study.

All eight were admitted and once this has occurred they stopped claiming to hear voices; they were eventually discharged with a diagnosis of 'schizophrenia in remission' (ie without signs of illness). The only people to have been suspicious of their true identity were some of their 'fellow' patients.

In a second experiment, members of a teaching hospital were told about the findings of the original study and were warned that some pseudo-patients would be trying to gain admission during a particular three-month period. Each member of staff was asked to rate every new patient as an impostor or not. During the experimental period, 193 patients were admitted, of whom forty-one were confidently alleged to be an impostor by at least one member of staff, twenty-three were suspected by one psychiatrist and a further nineteen were suspected by one psychiatrist *and* one other staff member.

All were genuine patients.

If Rosenhan's findings are valid, it appears that psychiatrists are unable to distinguish the 'sane' from the 'insane' and that the traditional psychiatric classification of mental disorders is unreliable, invalid and harmful to the welfare of patients (Spitzer, 1976). But just how valid is the Rosenhan study?

RELIABILITY

Diagnosis is the process of identifying a disease and allocating it to a category on the basis of symptoms and signs. Clearly, any system of classification will be of little value unless psychiatrists can agree with one another when trying to reach a diagnosis (Gelder et al, 1989).

Early studies consistently showed poor diagnostic reliablility: psychiatrists varied widely in the amount of information they elicit at interview and in their interpretation of that information and variations were found between groups of psychiatrists trained in different countries. For example, the US–UK Diagnostic Project (Cooper et al, 1972) showed American and British psychiatrists the same video-taped clinical interviews and asked them to make a diagnosis. New York psychiatrists diagnosed schizophrenia *twice* as often, while the London psychiatrists diagnosed mania and depression *twice* as often. (This led some wit to recommend that American schizophrenics should cross the Atlantic for a cure—presumably, the same advice should be given to British manic-depressives! However, New York was subsequently shown not to be typical of North America.)

The International Pilot Study of Schizophrenia (WHO, 1973) compared psychiatrists in nine countries—Columbia, Czechoslovakia, Denmark, England, India, Nigeria, Taiwan, USA and USSR—and found substantial agreement between seven of them, the exceptions being USA and USSR which both seemed to have unusually broad concepts of schizophrenia (thus confirming, after all, the Cooper et al results).

So what can be done to improve reliability?

Differences in eliciting symptoms can be reduced if psychiatrists are trained to use standardized interview schedules, such as the Present State Examination (PSE; Wing et al, 1974) and Endicott and Spitzer's (1978) Schedule of Affective Disorders and Schizophrenia (SADS). These are intended to: (i) specify sets of symptoms which must be enquired about;

and (ii) define the symptoms precisely and to give instructions on rating their severity.

Also, we noted earlier that both DSM-III-R and ICD-10 have introduced explicit operational criteria to be used in making a diagnosis, so that diagnosis may be more objective and hence more reliable. These are basically rules for deciding whether a particular patient is to be included within a particular diagnostic category or excluded from it. The Feighner Criteria (Feighner et al, 1972) and the Research Diagnostic Criteria (Spitzer et al, 1978; Williams and Spitzer, 1982) both helped to shape DSM-III(1980).

Fonagy and Higgitt (1984) believe that the use of operational criteria now leaves relatively little room for subjective judgement when diagnosing a patient—the use of checklists, for example, has helped to increase reliability, whereby the patient must show a specified number of observable symptoms before being diagnosed in a particular way:

> Classifications are needed in psychiatry, as in medicine, in order that doctors and others can communicate easily about the nature of patients' problems and about prognosis and treatment, and in order that research can be conducted with comparable groups of patients... (Gelder et al, 1989)

Gelder et al believe that critics of psychiatric classification are usually *psychotherapists* who argue that: (i) allocating a patient to a diagnostic category detracts from understanding his/her unique personality difficulty; and (ii) individual patients do not fit neatly into the available categories. (The critics seem to be saying that psychiatrists are using a *nomothetic* approach when an *idiographic* approach is more suitable.)

However, Gelder et al say that these are only arguments against the *improper use* of classification (rather than classification per se):

> ... The use of classification can certainly be combined with consideration of a patient's unique qualities, indeed it is important to combine the two because these qualities can modify prognosis and need to be taken into account in treatment... (Gelder et al, 1989)

The multi-axial approach of DSM-III-R can be regarded as a way of providing a much more detailed and rounded picture of the patient than was ever possible prior to 1980:

> In psychiatry, classification attempts to bring some order into the great diversity of phenomena encountered in clinical practice. Its purpose is to identify groups of patients who share similar clinical features, so that suitable treatment can be planned and the likely outcome predicted... (Gelder et al, 1989)

Kendall (1983) claims that every psychiatric patient has attributes at three levels: (A) those shared with *all* other psychiatric patients; (B) those shared with *some* other psychiatric patients; (C) those that are unique to them. Classification is feasible providing that there are attributes at level (B) (the shared attributes are what constitute one category as distinct from another). The value of classification rests on the relative size in importance of the attributes at (B) compared with (A) and (C):

> It is certainly the conventional view of most psychologists and psychiatrists that there are important attributes at level B. (Miller and Morley, 1986)

VALIDITY

As we saw when discussing IQ tests (Chapter 28), reliability is a pre-condition for validity; if a test (or a classificatory system) is not reliable is cannot be valid. However, there are other grounds for doubting the validity of the classification of mental disorder.

The primary purpose of making a diagnosis is, surely, to enable a suitable programme of treatment to be chosen; treatment cannot be selected randomly but is aimed at eliminating the underlying cause of the disorder (where it is known). However, in psychiatry, as Heather (1976) argues, very few 'causes' are known (except the organic disorders) and he maintains that there is only a 50 per cent chance of correctly predicting what treatment a patient will receive on the basis of diagnosis. Bannister et al (1964) statistically analysed the relationship between diagnosis and treatment in one thousand cases and found that there simply was no clear-cut relationship. One reason for this seems to be that factors other than diagnosis may be equally important in deciding on a particular treatment.

If the label applied to a patient does not allow the psychiatrist to make a judgement about the causes of the disorder, or a prediction regarding prognosis and response to treatment, how can that diagnostic process be a valid one? (Mackay, 1975).

Mackay concludes:

> The notion of illness implies a relatively discrete disease entity with associated signs and symptoms, which has a specific cause, a certain probability of recovery and its own treatments. The various states of unhappiness, anxiety and confusion which we term 'mental illness' fall far short of these criteria in most cases. (Mackay, 1975)

However, to put psychiatric diagnosis into perspective, we should compare it with *medical diagnosis in general*. In one survey, Falek and Moser (1975) found that agreement between doctors regarding angina, emphysema and tonsillitis (diagnosed without a definitive laboratory test) was no better (and sometimes actually worse) than that for schizophrenia.

Clare (1980) argues that the nature of physical illness is *not* as clear-cut as the critics of the medical model claim; while agreeing with criticisms of psychiatric diagnosis, he believes they should be directed at psychiatrists and not the process of diagnosis in general.

Clare (1980) and Clarke (1975) agree that there is a false dichotomy between body and mind: physical suffering is never without psychological aspects and psychological suffering is often expressed physically. Clarke (1975) also argues that treatment does *not* always aspire to 'cure' the patient but often aims simply to alleviate the suffering; knowledge of the cause does not always or necessarily determine treatment and disorders rarely have *single* causes. People are neither mindless bodies not bodyless minds, he says, and many organic illnesses require psychological treatment.

CONCLUSIONS: TO CLASSIFY OR NOT TO CLASSIFY?

As fundamental as the questions raised by Rosenhan's study might be,

Box 30.2   Criminal Responsibility—Was the Yorkshire Ripper Mad or Bad?

Forensic psychiatry is that branch of psychiatry which deals with assessment and treatment of mentally abnormal offenders and there are several clauses within the 1983 Mental Health Act which provide for compulsory detention of prisoners (either while awaiting trial or as part of their sentence) in hospital. Psychiatrists, as expert witnesses, can play an important role in advising the Court about: (i) fitness to plead; (ii) mental state at time of the offence; (iii) diminished criminal responsibility.

The defence of diminished responsibility (for murder) was introduced in England and Wales in 1957 and has largely replaced the 'Not guilty by reason of insanity', which was based on the so-called *McNaughton Rules*: In 1843, Daniel McNaughton shot and killed Edward Drummond, Private Secretary to the then Prime Minister, Sir Robert Peel. He shot Drummond by mistake; he intended to shoot Peel. In the Old Bailey Trial, the defence of not guilty by reason of insanity was made on the grounds that McNaughton had suffered delusions for many years—his paranoia focused on the Tory Party and he decided to kill Peel. In accordance with the judge's summing up, he was found not guilty on the grounds of insanity but was admitted to Bethlem Hospital and subsequently to the Criminal Lunatic Asylum, Broadmoor, soon after it opened.

There was a public outcry at the decision, which was debated in the House of Lords, resulting in the McNaughton Rules which, although having no statutory basis, were given the same status by the courts as an actual law. However, they were considered to present far too narrow a concept of insanity (working to the disadvantage of the mentally ill) and the 1957 Homicide Act introduced the plea of *diminished responsibility* for murder charges, so that, if accepted, there is no trial but a sentence for manslaughter is passed. If not, a trial is held and the jury must decide whether at the material time the accused was suffering from an abnormality of mind and, if so, was it such as to *substantially impair his/her responsibility*.

The Yorkshire Ripper

Peter Sutcliffe was a rather sickly child but as a teenager he developed physically and also began to come out of his shell. He started work as a grave-digger in 1964, in Bingley, Yorkshire and this place was to figure very prominently in his trial. Accused of murder and attempted murder, he told the jury that it was in Bingley Cemetery, in 1967, when he was nearly twenty-one, that he first heard 'the voice', which eventually instructed him that he had been chosen as the instrument of God's will. He was dismissed from his cemetery job that same year. The voice at first was benign and 'reassuring' but later started instructing him on his mission:

> This is what I believed was the voice of God saying it was prostitutes who were responsible for all these problems . . . It kept saying I was to remove the prostitutes. To get rid of them.

Peter Sutcliffe was found guilty of the murder of thirteen women and the attempted murder of seven more. He was sentenced to twenty concurrent terms of life imprisonment. The trial had turned on the question of his mental state and the prosecution had successfully argued that he was responsible for his actions. He went to prison but was later transferred to Broadmoor Special Hospital, like McNaughton before him. However, unlike his predecessor, he had been found guilty of his crimes.

the study itself has been criticized, notably by Spitzer (1976).

As a professor of law and psychology, Rosenhan should know that the terms 'sane' and 'insane' are *legal*, not psychiatric, concepts and that no psychiatrist makes a diagnosis of 'sanity' or 'insanity' (Box 30.2).

Perhaps more seriously, Spitzer notes that the diagnosis 'schizophrenia in remission' is extremely rare; in addition to his own New York hospital, he examined the records of discharged schizophrenic patients for twelve other US hospitals and found that in eleven cases, 'in remission' was either never used or used for only a handful of patients each year. Spitzer concluded from this that Rosenhan's pseudo-patients were given a discharge diagnosis which is rarely given to *real* patients with an admission diagnosis of schizophrenia and that, therefore, the diagnoses were a *function* of the pseudo-patients' behaviours and *not* of the setting (psychiatric hospital) in which the diagnoses were made (as Rosenhan claimed).

Further, there is a serious problem in generalizing from these eight pseudo-patients to genuine psychiatric patients in general; as Spitzer argues, they are two different populations. And if Rosenhan's pseudo-patients had tried to get themselves admitted once DSM-III(1980) had been introduced, they would almost certainly have failed.

Finally, evidence regarding the unreliability of medical diagnosis, even when tests are used does not mean that medical diagnosis is of no value—similarly, with psychiatric diagnosis (Spitzer, 1976).

A CLASSIFICATION OF TREATMENTS AND THERAPIES

It is more difficult to say what different treatment approaches have in common, and so classify them in some meaningful way, than it is to describe the aims and techniques of particular approaches. One of the problems is the sheer diversity of therapies and obviously in one chapter we can only attempt to discuss the major ones. So how can we begin to categorize different forms of therapy?

1) As you can see from Figure 31.1, all the major theoretical approaches which have been discussed throughout this book are represented and we have touched on aspects of their methods of therapy in earlier chapters. Table 1.1 (p. 17) indicates the position of the five major theoretical approaches regarding the causes of disorder, methods of treatment and the goals of treatment; it should be clear by now that the way each approach defines abnormality is logically related to how it defines normality (and this will be further reinforced in this chapter). The relationship between theory and therapy, however, is not quite so straightforward.

Where theory has grown out of clinical practice (ie work with psychiatric patients), theory and therapy are intimately connected (eg Freud's psychoanalysis and Rogers' client-centred therapy). By contrast, behavioural therapies (of which there are many different kinds) are not always directly derived from learning theory, which is sometimes unable to account for therapeutic outcomes and certain aspects of abnormal behaviour. (This is especially true in the case of phobias, which we shall discuss in detail.)

2) Some forms of therapy are not directly related to any particular theory (eg Psychodrama and Transactional Analysis) and, in practice, treatment is often 'eclectic', ie it combines different techniques from different approaches.

3) A major distinction is between *physical* (organic) and *psychological* treatments—what the latter all share is a rejection of the medical model. For example, although Freud distinguished between 'symptoms' and 'underlying pathology', the latter is conceived in psychological terms (not genetic or biochemical) and he was concerned with the individual and not the 'disorder'. Although he used diagnostic labels, he did so as linguistic conveniences rather than as an integral part of his theories and he focused on understanding his patient's problems in their life context rather than on clinical labelling (Mackay, 1975).

4) All psychological therapies are sometimes, misleadingly, referred to as 'psychotherapy' but I prefer to reserve the term for methods based

Figure 31.1 *Major approaches to treatment and therapy*

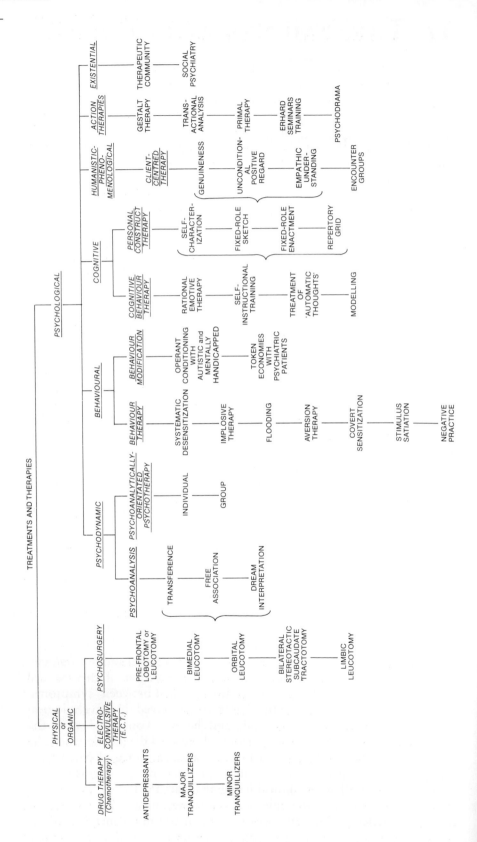

on Freudian psychoanalysis (psychodynamic treatments). Similarly, 'behavioural psychotherapy' is sometimes used to refer to what I will call 'behaviour therapy'.

5) What do different forms of therapy have in common?

According to Oatley (1984), the major common element is that they all take place within a *human relationship*. One aspect of 'technique' which is profoundly important in the therapeutic relationship is whether or not the therapist makes suggestions and gives advice to the patient (or client). In *directive* therapies, concrete suggestions are made and the client is often instructed to do certain things, for example, they may be given 'homework' in between sessions or may have to perform specific exercises under the therapist's supervision. Directive therapy is best illustrated by behaviour therapy, cognitive behaviour therapy, personal construct therapy and Gestalt therapy.

Non-directive therapies, on the other hand, concentrate on making sense of what is going on in the relationship between therapist and client and on understanding the meanings of the client's experience; the best examples are psychoanalysis (and psychodynamic or 'insight' therapies in general) and client-centred therapy.

Directive therapies are generally easier to describe because they seem to comprise procedures which the therapist suggests and which the client either goes along with or not. What distinguishes different directive therapies is *what* they suggest the client does and *how* this leads to the desired change (which, in turn, of course, depends upon what the therapist sees as 'the problem' in the first place). For example, behaviour therapy concentrates directly upon changing people's *behaviour* (and any desired changes in thoughts and feelings will 'look after themselves') while cognitive–behaviour therapy is aimed directly at thoughts and feelings, so that clients are instructed to talk to themselves in different ways, to give themselves instructions for behaviour, to write down their distressing and negative thought patterns and so on.

Non-directive therapies are, by comparison, more difficult to describe because the therapist plays a more passive role and generally does not suggest things to the client but, 'rather listens and takes part with the client in exploring and experiencing what is going on between them' (Oatley, 1984). But as with directive therapies, there are important differences, in particular, how the therapist contributes to that process of exploring and experiencing which, in turn, reflect the therapist's theoretical assumptions about what is wrong.

6) Another important way in which therapies differ is whether they are conducted between a therapist and a client (*individual*) or with several clients at a time, with one or more therapists or leaders (*group*); most of the major approaches to be described in this chapter are individual but some less well-known therapies are, by definition, group therapies (eg psychodrama, encounter groups and therapeutic communities). We should also note that psychodynamic and client-centred therapies may be individual or group but they will be described here in their individual form.

7) A major development in psychotherapy in the late 1970s and early 1980s was the emergence of *family therapies* and *marital/couple therapy*, which seems to reflect the growing awareness by therapists of the important role played by the client's relationships in the development

and maintenance of their problems (Dryden, 1984).

This change seems to have been inspired by Laing's *family interaction model* of schizophrenia, which has been applied to less 'serious' problems that commonly occur in families and between partners. Generally, where the problem is seen as interpersonal, family, marital/couple or group therapy is likely to be recommended. However, where the problem is seen as 'residing' within the client (*intrapsychic*), individual therapy would be recommended.

Of course, the separation of intrapsychic processes and interpersonal processes is quite artificial as these processes are always mutually influencing one another but Dryden (1984) sees them as separate, independent dimensions, so that both can have a high or low impact (at extreme points on each continuum) on a client's psychological problems. It is not unusual for a client to be involved in some form of individual *and* group or family or marital/couple therapy at the same time.

We will now consider in more detail the seven main approaches, as outlined in Figure 31.1.

Physical or Organic Approaches

DRUG THERAPY (CHEMOTHERAPY)

Table 4.2 (p. 80) shows the three major groups of *psychoactive* drugs used in the treatment of mental illness: (i) the *anti-depressants*, (ii) the *major tranquillizers* (phenothiazines or 'anti-schizophrenic drugs'); and (iii) the *minor tranquillizers* (benzodiazepines, 'anti-anxiety drugs' or anxiolytic sedatives).

Anti-depressants

Anti-depressants were discovered accidentally in 1952 when tuberculosis patients were being treated with ipronazid and it was found to produce euphoria in some patients.

Imipramine (Tofranil®), one of the tricyclic anti-depressants, is the most studied and is often used as a standard for comparing other anti-depressants. It is probably most effective with psychotic (endogenous) depression but has also been used successfully with obsessives and patients with bizarre states of pain (Wright, 1976).

The monoamine oxidase (MAO) inhibitors (eg phenelzine or Nardil®) are less effective than the tricyclics and can cause cerebral haemorrhage by causing the bodily accumulation of amine chemicals. Interestingly, Nardil® has been used with agoraphobic patients (and various social phobias) and was found to be comparable to other treatments, especially the minor tranquillizers Valium® or Librium®.

Lithium carbonate (Lithane or Lithonate) is used to treat manic disorder and manic-depressive disorder and can help to restore emotional equilibrium, but there is the risk of kidney poisoning.

Major Tranquillizers

These were first introduced in the early 1950s and are considered to have revolutionized psychiatry by permitting the most disturbed schizophrenic patients to live outside a psychiatric hospital or to reduce their average length of stay. However, re-admission rates have increased and many critics have called these drugs (in particular, chlorpromazine (Largactil®)) 'pharmacological straitjackets' replacing the kind with straps, with the 'zombie-like' state which they produce.

Chlorpromazine becomes concentrated in the brain-stem and is secreted only very slowly, so that the effect on the brain is prolonged. At first there is a striking sedation effect, which wears off after a few days; it reduces responsiveness to external stimulation and gross motor activity but without reducing motor power or co-ordination. It has been shown to be superior to placebos in controlling hallucinations, excitement, thought disorder and delusions, but this is often at the expense of a dry mouth, blurred vision, low blood pressure (which may cause fainting attacks) and neuromuscular effects (identical to those seen in Parkinson's Disease), most serious being tardive dyskinesia, whose existence 'should be a deterrant to the long-term prescribing of antipsychotic drugs in large doses' (Gelder et al, 1989).

Many believe that the combination of these drugs with psychotherapy is the most productive way of treating severely disturbed patients; drugs cannot produce a 'cure' but can only alleviate some of the symptoms which may enable the patient to benefit from other forms of treatment or therapy.

Minor Tranquillizers

These reduce anxiety and cause drowsiness by depressing neural activity, especially in the brain-stem and the limbic system. They are quite ineffective in the treatment of psychosis and are used mainly for neurotic disorder where anxiety is usually the central symptom. Whereas only psychiatrists would prescribe a major tranquillizer, minor tranquillizers are commonly prescribed by GPs (far too commonly, many would say) for all kinds of anxieties and diazepam (Valium®) has been described as the most prescribed drug in the world.

ELECTRO-CONVULSIVE THERAPY

During 1935–6, Cerletti and his colleagues began to use electro-convulsive therapy (ECT) on the assumption that schizophrenia and epilepsy do not occur together in the same person; if a grand mal epileptic fit is induced (artificially) this should reduce or eliminate the symptoms of schizophrenia. This is the logic behind ECT historically, but it is now used mainly with depressive patients. What happens?

First, the patient is made comfortable on a bed, clothes loosened and shoes and dentures removed; atropine is given as a routine pre-anaesthetic medication (to dry up salivary and bronchial secretions) and then thiopentone, a quick-acting anaesthetic, is given, followed by a muscle relaxant.

An 80–110 volt shock lasting a fraction of a second is then given through electrodes placed on the temples, producing a generalized convulsion (which is detected by facial and limb twitching). Many psychiatrists believe that for severe depression, *bilateral* ECT (one electrode on each side of the head) is preferable as it acts more quickly and fewer treatments are needed. In *unilateral* ECT, an electrode is applied to the non-dominant hemisphere side (the right side for most people) and is intended to reduce the side-effects, particularly memory disruption (Benton, 1981).

SIDE-EFFECTS OF ECT

Memory disruption includes retrograde amnesia and impaired ability to acquire new memories (see Chapter 12); however, depression is associated with impaired memory function and so it is not clear how much ECT itself is responsible (Benton, 1981). The patient is normally confused for up to forty minutes following treatment but recall of events prior to treatment gradually returns, although some degree of memory loss may persist for several weeks.

The mortality rate is now quite low, somewhere between 3.6 and 9 per 100 000 treatments (a figure very similar to those resulting from anaesthetics for minor surgery). According to Smith (1977), the Registrar General's figures for deaths during the 1960s in the UK made ECT one of the safest medical treatments there is (an average of 3 per cent for the whole country) and when the number of suicides resulting from depression are taken into account (one estimate being that, without treatment, 11 per cent of depressives will die from suicide or other causes over a five-year period), ECT emerges as very low-risk indeed.

However, the possibility of death is only one of the objections made to ECT by, for example MIND (the National Association for Mental Health) and PROMPT (Protect the Rights of Mental Patients in Therapy) in the UK and NAPA (Network Against Psychiatric Assault) in the USA. The main objections are *ethical*, one of them being that since we do not know how it works (and *if* it works) it should not be used, another being to do with *consent*.

IS ECT EFFECTIVE?

One problem with trying to measure its effectiveness experimentally is, ironically, also ethical, namely, the problem of the placebo effect or simulated ('dummy') ECT, in which the patient undergoes all aspects of the ECT procedure except that no electrical current is passed through the brain (so no seizure is produced).

Fink (1978) reviewed the literature on ECT, comparing it with a variety of other treatments, including psychotherapy, chemotherapy and simulated ECT and concluded that, for psychotic-depressive patients (and manic patients), success rates were from 60 to 90 per cent. One measure of success is the suicide rate for depressive patients—several studies found that suicide was less frequent in ECT-treated patients than among those who received only psychotherapy.

Several studies have shown that ECT is effective when antidepressant drugs have failed and that ECT is generally unsuitable for non-depressed patients.

HOW DOES ECT WORK?

Benton (1981) identifies three proposed explanations:

(a) Patients learn that treatment is recommended because of their pathological behaviour and so ECT is seen as a *punishment* which extinguishes the undesirable behaviour. However, equally unpleasant but *sub*-convulsive shocks (ie they do not produce a convulsion) are not effective, which seems inconsistent with the punishment explanation.

(b) *Memory loss* allows the restructuring of the patient's view of life. However, unilateral ECT is intended to minimize memory disruption and so it seems possible to dissociate memory loss from therapeutic advantage.

(c) The shock produces a wide range of *biochemical changes* in the brain (eg the stimulation of noradrenaline) and this effect is more widespread than that produced by antidepressant drugs.

Clearly, there is no generally accepted explanation, only very tentative hypotheses; however, Benton (1981) believes that this does not constitute a reason for not using it since many medical treatments fall into this category (eg aspirin getting rid of headaches).

Clare argues that, because it is relatively quick and easy to administer, ECT is much abused and over-used:

> Psychiatrists who persist in so abusing it have only themselves to blame if the public conclude that the treatment is a fraud and an anachronism and demand its abolition. (Clare, 1980)

Again, 'it is easier for a psychiatrist, overwhelmed by the sheer number of patients, to reach for the ECT machine than to use more time-consuming and different approaches.'

PSYCHOSURGERY

Psychosurgery began with Moniz, a Portuguese professor of neurology, in 1935. It represents the most drastic form of physical intervention and is by far the most controversial of the medical approaches, partly because it is irreversible.

Between 1935 and 1949, Moniz performed about one hundred *pre-frontal lobotomies* or *leucotomies* in which tissue connecting the frontal lobes of the cortex with sub-cortical brain areas is cut, on both sides of the cortex. (Moniz was awarded the Nobel Price for Medicine in 1949).

Freeman and Watts pioneered psychosurgery in the USA and it has been estimated that 40 000 to 50 000 pre-frontal lobotomies have been performed in that country alone since the late 1930s.

In the UK, about 10 000 operations were carried out between 1942 and 1952, two-thirds of which involved schizophrenics and about one-quarter depressives, with the latter responding much more favourably.

Since the 1950s and the widespread use of antischizophrenic drugs, schizophrenics have rarely been treated in this way and psychosurgery has become much more sophisticated, with very small amounts of brain tissue being destroyed in very precise locations ('fractional operations'). Some of these include: (i) *bimedial leucotomy* (first used at the Maudsley Hospital in London in 1951), used mainly with depressive or obsessional patients; (ii) *orbital leucotomy*, used with depressives, obsessionals and patients with extreme anxiety; (iii) *bilateral stereotactic subcaudate tractotomy*, used mainly with patients suffering from severe and intractable depression; and (iv) *limbic leucotomy*.

The first two (together with the original pre-frontal lobotomy) involved serious side-effects, including death and significant personality changes. The third technique (iii) is considered much safer; for example, the risk of post-operative epileptic fits is about 1 per cent, which is no higher than for any operation inside the skull.

Limbic leucotomies involve the destruction of tissue in a variety of sites; when used with patients who are abnormally aggressive, the neural circuit connecting the amygdala and the hypothalamus is destroyed (based on Kluver and Bucy's work with cats; see Chapter 16). This is perhaps the most controversial of all psychosurgical techniques, partly because the patient is not usually suffering, partly because it is often used with subnormal aggressive patients (so informed consent is unlikely to be given) and partly because, although the surgery has a 'marked calming effect' in 95 per cent of cases, it cannot entirely eliminate episodes of terror and outbursts of violence.

PSYCHODYNAMIC APPROACHES

FREUD'S THEORY OF PSYCHOLOGICAL DISORDER

In Chapter 29, neurotic symptoms were described as compromises (as were dreams and defence mechanisms) between the opposing demands made on the ego by the id and the superego; symptoms, dreams and defences are all expressions of the inevitable conflict which arises from these opposing demands and are, at the same time, attempts to deal with it.

When the person experiences anxiety, the ego is signalling that it fears being overwhelmed by an all-powerful id (neurotic anxiety) or superego (moral anxiety) and so must mobilize its defences. Anxiety is the hallmark of most neurotic disorders but, except in 'freefloating anxiety' it becomes redirected or transformed in some way (depending on which particular defence is used), so that the resulting symptom makes it even less likely that the true nature of the problem (ie the underlying conflict) will be spotted.

Phobias, for example, involve *repression* (as do all neuroses) plus *displacement* and *projection*. Little Hans, for example (see Chapter 21), had a phobia of being bitten by a horse, which could be explained in terms of: (i) repressing his jealous anger and hatred felt towards his father; (ii) projecting these feelings onto his father, thus seeing him as a threatening, murderous man; and (iii) displacing this perception of his father onto a 'safer' target, namely, horses. Phobic objects, according to Freud, are not arbitrarily chosen but in some way symbolically represent the object for which they are a substitute.

Neuroses, therefore, are maladaptive solutions to the problems faced by the person, that is they do not help them resolve the conflict but merely help to avoid it (both in thought and behaviour). So neurotics adopt self-defeating strategies; far from solving problems, the neurotic's behaviour usually creates its own distress and unhappiness (the 'neurotic paradox'). How can we account for such paradoxical behaviour? One answer is that it permits *immediate* tension release, even if it only adds to the neurotic's problems in the long-term. (This is an explanation that easily fits the learning theory principle of reinforcement, which we shall discuss in detail in the next section.)

Psychoneurotic symptoms, therefore, are indicative of deep-seated, unresolved, unconscious conflicts, usually of a sexual and/or aggressive nature, which stem from childhood feelings, memories, wishes and experiences which have been repressed and defended against in other ways; however, these defences are not effective ways of dealing with the conflict and they create their own distress and anxiety.

THE AIMS OF PSYCHOANALYSIS

The basic goal of psychoanalysis is to make 'the unconscious conscious', to undo unsatisfactory defences and through a 'therapeutic regression' (Winnicott, 1958) to re-experience repressed feelings and wishes, which have been frustrated in childhood, in a safe context and to express them, as an adult, in a more appropriate way, 'with a new ending' (Alexander and French, 1946).

Again, the aim of therapy is to provide the client with *insight*, self-knowledge and self-understanding.

THERAPEUTIC TECHNIQUES: HOW ARE THE AIMS ACHIEVED?

1) In classical psychoanalysis, the analyst is meant to remain 'anonymous', ie he/she should not show any emotion, should not reveal any personal information and should not make any value-judgements regarding anything the client might say or do. Instead, the analyst tries to become an 'ambiguous object' onto which the client can project and displace repressed feelings, in particular, those concerning parents.

The anonymity of the analyst is aided by the client lying on a couch with the analyst sitting behind, out of the client's (*analysand's*) field of vision (Fig. 31.2); the client's projection and displacement onto the analyst is called *transference*. According to Sandler et al (1970), Freud viewed transference as, 'the displacement of libido from the memory of the original object to the person of the analyst, who becomes the new

Figure 31.2 Sigmund Freud's couch (© Freud Museum Publications Ltd)

object of the patient's sexual wishes, the patient being unaware of this displacement from the past.'

Transference can be positive, manifesting as childlike dependence, a passionate, erotic attachment, an overestimation of the therapist's qualities or jealousy of the therapist's family (Thomas, 1990) or negative (anger, hostility and so on):

> ... Over the years it has become increasingly clear to practising analysts that the process of transference ... is one of the most important tools they have. It has become so central to theory and practice that many, though not all, analysts believe that making interpretations about transference is what distinguishes psychoanalysis from other forms of psychotherapy. When attention is focused on the transference and what is happening in the here and now, the historical reconstruction of childhood events and the search for the childhood origins of conflicts may take second place. (Thomas, 1990)

There is also the related process of *counter-transference*, which refers to the therapist's feelings of irritation or dislike, or sexual attraction, towards the client:

> ... In Freud's time, counter-transference feelings ... were considered to be a failing on the part of the analyst. These feelings were to be controlled absolutely ... Now, counter-transference is considered an unavoidable outcome of the analytic process, irrespective of how well prepared the analyst is by analytic training and its years of required personal analysis ... most modern analysts are trained to observe their own counter-transference feelings and to *use* these to increase their understanding of the patients' transference and defences. (Thomas, 1990)

2) To enable the client to understand the transference and how it relates to childhood conflicts, the analyst must *interpret* it, ie tell the client what it means, its significance in terms of what has already been revealed about the client's childhood experiences. Because this is likely to be painful and distressing clients use another form of defence called *resistance*, an attempt to escape from, or avoid, these self-revelations; it may take the form of 'drying up' when talking, changing the subject, dismissing some emotionally highly significant event in a very flippant way, even falling asleep or arriving late for therapy. All forms of resistance are extremely significant items and themselves require interpretation.

3) Despite what we have said about the analyst's anonymity, it is essential that there is a 'working alliance' with the client, whereby the client's ego is strengthened sufficiently to be able to cope with the anxiety caused by the return to consciousness of repressed feelings and memories. According to Jacobs (1984), the working alliance consists of two adults co-operating to understand the 'child' in the client; the analyst adopts a quiet, reflective, style, intervening when they judge the client to be ready to make use of a particular interpretation. This is an art, says Jacobs, and does *not* involve fitting the client into psychoanalytic theory, as some critics suggest. Throughout the process of analysis, the analyst remains a real person; the client moves from transference relationships to forming an accurate perception of the analyst as a person in his/her own right (Guntrip, 1971).

4) Apart from transference, the two other major techniques used to reveal the client's unconscious mind are *dream interpretation* (which we discussed in Chapter 29) and *free association*, in which the client says

whatever comes to mind, no matter how silly, irrelevant or embarrassing it may seen. (These may both lead to resistance which, like transference, will in turn be interpreted by the analyst.)

THE CONCEPT OF CURE—HOW DO YOU KNOW WHEN TO STOP?

According to Jacobs (1984), the goals of therapy are limited by what clients consciously want to achieve and are capable of achieving, together with their motivation, ego strength, capacity for insight, ability to tolerate the frustration of gradual change, financial cost and so on. These factors, in turn, will determine how a cure is to be defined and assessed.

In practice, psychoanalysis ranges from *psychoanalytical first aid* (Guntrip, 1968) or symptom relief to different levels of more intense work. However, Storr (1966) believes that a quick, complete 'cure' is very much the exception rather than the rule and the majority of people who present themselves for psychoanalysis cannot expect that their symptoms will easily disappear or, even if this should happen, that they will be freed of emotional problems. This is because of what we have already noted about the distinction between symptoms and underlying pathology: neurotic symptoms are merely the outward and visible signs of an inner, less visible, distortion of the client's total personality, and exploration and analysis of the symptoms inevitably lead to an analysis of the whole person.

In trying to assess the effectiveness of psychoanalysis, the usual practice is to assess the extent to which clients experience relief of their symptoms, but Storr believes this is an inappropriate way of thinking of 'cure', partly because of symptom analysis being only the *start* of the analytic process and also because a majority of clients do not have clear-cut symptoms anyway. (We shall return later on to the debate about the effectiveness of psychoanalysis compared with other approaches.)

PSYCHOANALYTICALLY-ORIENTED PSYCHOTHERAPY

Classical psychoanalysis requires the client to attend five 50-minute sessions per week for several years which, for many people, is far too expensive, as well as too time-consuming.

In a modified form of analysis, therapist and client meet once or twice a week for a limited period. For example, Malan (1979) at the Tavistock Clinic in London uses *brief focal therapy* (one session per week for about thirty weeks), in which the focus is on fairly specific psychological problems, such as a single conflict area or relationship in the client's current life.

Although all the basic techniques of psychoanalysis may be used, there is considerably less emphasis on the client's past and client and therapist usually sit in armchairs face-to-face; this form of psychotherapy is practised by many clinical psychologists (as well as psychiatrists and social workers) *without* receiving a full-blown psychoanalytic training (Fonagy and Higgitt, 1984).

Finally, another form of this is psychoanalytically-orientated *group psychotherapy*.

Behavioural Approaches

Treatment methods based on classical learning theory (ie conditioning) are often referred to interchangeably as 'behaviour therapy' and 'behaviour modification'. However, I shall distinguish between them in the way proposed by Walker (1984), namely:

(a) *Behaviour therapy* refers to techniques based on *classical conditioning* and developed by psychologists such as Wolpe and Eysenck in order to extinguish maladaptive behaviours and substitute adaptive ones.

(b) *Behaviour modification* refers to techniques based on *operant conditioning* and developed by psychologists such as Allyon and Azrin to build up appropriate behaviour (where it did not previously exist) or to increase the frequency of certain responses and decrease the frequency of others.

MODELS OF PSYCHOLOGICAL DISORDER

(a) Both behaviour therapy and modification regard *all* behaviour, whether adaptive or maladaptive, as acquired by the same principles of classical and operant conditioning respectively (see Chapter 7).

(b) The medical model is completely rejected, including any distinction between 'symptoms' and underlying pathology; according to Eysenck (1960), if you 'get rid of the symptom . . . you have eliminated the neurosis', ie what you see is what there is! However, Mackay (1975) observes that some behaviour therapists make use of the formal diagnostic categories or 'syndromes' and try to discover which techniques are most effective with particular diagnostic groups; key figures in this *nomothetic* approach are Eysenck, Rachman and Marks, and Mackay refers to it as *behavioural technology*.

   Other behaviour therapists, however, believe that therapists should isolate the stimuli and consequences that are maintaining the inappropriate behaviour in each individual case and that, accordingly, any treatment programme should be derived from such a 'behavioural analysis' (or 'functional analysis'). Mackay calls this *idiographic* approach, associated with Yates, Meyer and others, *behavioural psychotherapy*.

(c) Part of the functional analysis is an emphasis on *current* behaviour–environment relations, in contrast to the Freudian emphasis on past events (particularly early childhood ones) and unconscious (and other internal) factors. Psychological problems are behavioural problems which need to be *operationalized* (ie described in terms of observable behaviours) before we attempt to change them.

(d) According to Eysenck and Rachman (1965), the case of Little Albert (Chapter 7) exemplifies how *all* abnormal fears are acquired (ie through classical conditioning):

   . . . any neutral stimulus, simple or complex, that happens to make an impact on an individual at about the time a fear reaction is evoked, acquires the ability to evoke fear subsequently . . . there will be generalization of fear reactions to stimuli resembling the conditioned stimulus. (Wolpe and Rachman, 1960)

Evidence to support this view comes from many sources, for example, phobics often recall an earlier traumatic experience associated with the onset of their phobia (eg a dog phobic recalling being attacked by a large Alsatian) and laboratory studies with humans and animals have shown that if the UCS is highly traumatic, a single pairing of the CS and UCS may be sufficient to induce a long-lasting CR (eg Garcia's *taste aversion studies*; see Chapter 7).

However, there is also considerable evidence *against* Eysenck and Rachman. Several studies have shown that phobics are often unable to recall any traumatic experience involving the object of their fear and, conversely, people may experience profound traumas without developing any obvious phobias (eg the concentration camp survivors, studied by Freud and Dann, 1951; see Chapter 22, and evidence from civilians who were continually bombed during the Second World War).

We noted in Chapter 7 that some phobias are easier to induce in the laboratory (in subjects who do not already have them) and it is well-known that certain naturally-occurring phobias are more common than others. For example, rats, jellyfish, cockroaches, spiders and slugs are consistently rated as frightening and rabbits, ladybirds, cats and lambs as non-frightening, and the crucial perceptual qualities seem to be ugliness, sliminess, speed and suddenness of movement (Bennett-Levy and Marteau, 1984).

These and similar findings are consistent with the concept of *preparedness* (Seligman, 1970; Ohman et al, 1979), which was discussed in Chapter 7. However, these findings have not always been replicated. For example, induced phobias of snakes and corpses are no harder to extinguish through treatment than phobias of chocolate and, in a review of the literature, McNally and Reiss (1982) concluded that there is little evidence to support the concept of preparedness.

Rachman (1977) himself now believes that direct conditioning of any kind accounts for relatively few phobias. Instead, he claims that many phobias are acquired on the basis of information transmitted through observation and instruction. Some support for this comes from a study by Murray and Foote (1979) who conclude by saying that although preparedness for direct conditioning does not seem to be relevant, a preparedness for observational and instructional learning is possible. Others agree; for example:

> It appears then that phobias are not acquired by the chance association of a stimulus with a fearful situation, but can be learned by imitation and tend to be associated with certain objects rather than others ... (Baddeley, 1990)

It is the persistence of naturally-occurring phobias (ie their failure to extinguish) that poses one of the greatest difficulties for the classical conditioning explanation and the major theoretical attempt to account for this phenomenon has been the *two process/two factor model*, whereby the reduction of fear brought about by escaping or avoiding the feared object or situation negatively reinforces the escape or avoidance behaviour so that it tends to be repeated (this is the operant conditioning factor). The fear may have been acquired initially through classical conditioning (the other 'factor') but, on its own, classical conditioning cannot explain its persistence (see Chapter 7).

The persistence of neurotic behaviour may also be accounted for in terms of what Freud (1926) called 'secondary gain', whereby other people may, inadvertently, *positively* reinforce it; because of the role of positive and negative reinforcement in maintaining neurotic behaviour, Ullman and Krasner (1975) refused to accept that neurosis is, in any sense, paradoxical.

We should note that the 'two-process/factor' model has itself come in for criticism. One important alternative to it is the *safety-signal hypothesis*, which maintains that avoidance is motivated *not* by the reduction of anxiety but by the *positive* feeling of safety. According to Rachman (1984), agoraphobia is motivated by seeking signals of safety and the safety-signal hypothesis provides a better explanation of why agoraphobics find it easier to go out with, or be driven by, someone they trust and to take certain routes to their destination than the 'two process/factor' model—perhaps trusted individuals and certain streets and situations, etc. act as safety signals. It may also explain why the loss of a close relative so often marks the onset of a phobia (Fonagy and Higgitt, 1984).

BEHAVIOUR THERAPY

Systematic Desensitization

As we saw in Chapter 7, the case of Little Peter represents perhaps the earliest attempt to remove a phobia using systematic desensitization (SD) (and, indeed, the earliest attempt at any kind of behavioural treatment).

Wolpe (1958) defined behaviour therapy as a whole as 'the use of experimentally established principles of learning for the purpose of changing unadaptive behaviour' and he is perhaps best known for his use and development of SD.

Wolpe was very much influenced by the theory of Hull (see Chapter 6) and the key concept in SD is that of *reciprocal inhibition* (taken from Sherrington's work on the spinal cord). As applied to phobias (for which SD is mainly used), this maintains that it is impossible for two opposite emotions (eg anxiety and relaxation) to exist together at the same time. Accordingly, a patient with, for example, a spider phobia, is taught to relax through deep muscle relaxation in which different muscle groups are alternately relaxed and tensed (alternatively, hypnosis or tranquillizers might be used) so that relaxation and fear of the object or situation 'cancel each other out' (this is the 'desensitization' part of the procedure).

The 'systematic' part of the procedure involves a gradual, step-by-step, contact with the phobic object (usually by *imagining* it) based on a *hierarchy*, running from the least to the most feared possible contact, drawn up together by the therapist and the patient. Starting with the least feared contact, the patient, while relaxing, imagines it until this can be done without feeling any anxiety at all; then, and only then, will the next most feared contact be dealt with, in the same way, until the *most* frightening contact can be imagined with no anxiety.

For example, imagining the word 'spider' on a printed page may cause very little anxiety while imagining a large, hairy, spider running all over your body might be very frightening indeed!

Rachman and Wilson (1980) and McGlynn et al (1981) believe that SD is, beyond doubt, effective, although it is most effective for the treatment of *minor* phobias (eg animal phobias) as opposed to say, agoraphobia and for patients who are able to learn relaxation skills and have sufficiently vivid imaginations to be able to conjure up the sources of their fear. Another limitation of SD is that some patients may have difficulty transferring from the imaginary stimulus to real-life situations.

Again, there is some debate as to whether or not either relaxation or the use of a hierarchy is actually necessary at all. For instance, it has been found that snake phobias are effectively dealt with by relaxation *plus* a hierarchical presentation of 'snake scenes' but relaxation *alone* proves ineffective. However, other studies have found no difference between the use of a hierarchy with or without relaxation (suggesting that relaxation is not necessary) or no difference when a hierarchy was presented in the standard way (least to most frightening), in reverse (most to least frightening) or randomly (suggesting that a hierarchy is not necessary). These studies combined suggest that what is probably the essential ingredient is *exposure* to the feared object. According to Kazdin and Wilcoxin (1976), neither reciprocal inhibition nor relaxation is necessary for therapeutic benefit and the use of real objects makes the use of a graded hierarchy unnecessary.

Implosive Therapy (or Implosion) and Flooding

The essence of *implosion* is to expose the patient to what, in SD, would be at the top of the hierarchy; there is no gradual exposure accompanied by relaxation but the patient is 'thrown in at the deep end' right from the start. This is done by getting the patient to imagine their most terrifying form of contact (the big, hairy spider let loose, again) with vivid verbal descriptions by the therapist (*stimulus augmentation*) to supplement the patient's vivid imagery. How is it meant to work?

(a) The patient's anxiety is maintained at such a high level that eventually some process of exhaustion or stimulus satiation takes place—the anxiety level can only go down!

(b) Extinction occurs by preventing the patient from making their usual escape or avoidance response (Mowrer, 1960) and so implosion— and flooding—represent 'a form of forced reality testing' (Yates, 1970).

Flooding is exposure that takes place *in vivo* (eg with an actual spider). Marks et al (1971) compared SD with flooding and found flooding to be superior and Gelder et al (1973) compared SD with implosion and found no difference. These findings suggest that it is *in vivo exposure* which is crucial, and several writers consider flooding to be more effectve than implosion (Emmelkamp and Wessels, 1975).

Emmelkamp and Wessels (1975) and Marks et al (1981) used flooding with agoraphobics very successfully and other studies have reported continued improvement for up to nine years after treatment without the appearance of 'substitute' problems. Wolpe (1960) forced an adolescent girl with a fear of cars into the back of a car and drove her around continuously for four hours; her fear reached hysterical heights but then receded and, by the end of the journay, had completely disappeared.

Marks (1981), in a review of flooding studies, found it to be the most universally effective of all the techniques used to treat fear.

Aversion Therapy and Covert Sensitization

In *aversion therapy* some undesirable response to a particular stimulus is removed by associating the stimulus with another, aversive, stimulus. So, for example, alcohol is paired with an emetic drug (which induces severe nausea and vomiting) so that nausea and vomiting become a conditioned response to alcohol, ie:

(UCS) Emetic drug (Antabuse
    or apomorphine) ⟶ Nausea/vomiting (UCR)
(CS) Alcohol+(UCS) emetic drug ⟶ Nausea/vomiting (UCR)
(CS) Alcohol ⟶ Nausea/vomiting (CR)

The patient would, typically, be given warm saline solution containing the emetic drug; immediately before the vomiting begins, they are given a four-ounce glass of whisky which they are required to smell, taste, and swill around in the mouth before being swallowed. (If vomiting has not occurred, another straight whisky is given and, to prolong nausea, the patient is given a glass of beer containing emetic.) Subsequent treatments involve larger doses of injected emetic or increases in the length of treatment time or a widening range of hard liquors (Kleinmuntz, 1980). (Between trials, the patient may sip soft drinks to prevent generalization to all drinking behaviour and to promote the use of alcohol substitutes.)

Meyer and Chesser (1970) found that about half their alcoholic patients abstained for at least one year following treatment and that aversion therapy is better than no treatment.

More controversially, aversion therapy has been used with homosexuals, fetishists, male transvestites and sadomasochists, and Marks et al (1970) reported desired changes for up to two years after treatment. In a typical treatment, slides of nude males are presented to male homosexuals and then quickly followed by electric shocks; the conditioned response to the slides is intended to generalize to homosexual fantasies and activities outside the treatment sessions. More recently, attempts have been made to replace homosexual responses with heterosexual ones by showing slides of naked females; any sexual response will terminate the shock.

Covert sensitization is a variant of aversion therapy which also includes elements of SD. 'Covert' refers to the fact that both the behaviour to be removed and the aversive stimulus to be associated with it are *imagined* by the patient, who has to visualize the events leading up to the initiation of the undesirable behaviour: just as this happens they have to imagine nausea or some other aversive sensation. 'Sensitization' is achieved by associating the undesirable act with an exceedingly disagreeable consequence (Kleinmuntz, 1980). The patient may also be instructed to rehearse an alternative 'relief' scene in which the decision *not* to drink or whatever is accompanied by pleasurable sensations. (This is generally preferred to aversion therapy on humanitarian grounds.)

Stimulus Satiation

In stimulus satiation, a patient who hoards things would be *given* as many of the hoarded objects as they can 'tolerate' until they begin to refuse them (Allyon, 1963). *Negative practice* (Meyer and Chesser, 1970) is often used with nervous tics where the patient is told to produce the tic deliberately, as accurately and frequently as possible for several minutes at a time; eventually (it is hoped) fatigue will prodice extinction.

BEHAVIOUR MODIFICATION

According to Baddeley (1990), most behavioural programmes follow a broadly similar pattern involving a series of steps:

Step 1.   Specify the behaviour to be changed. It is important to choose small, measurable, achievable goals.

Step 2.   The goal should be stated as specifically as possible.

Step 3.   A baseline rate should be measured over a period of several days—ie how does the person 'normally' behave with respect to the selected behaviour. This may involve detailed observation which can suggest hypotheses as to what is maintaining that behaviour.

Step 4.   Decide on a strategy, for example selectively reinforce non-yelling behaviour (through attention) and ensure that yelling behaviour is ignored.

Step 5.   Plan treatment. It is essential that everyone coming into contact with the patient behaves in accordance with the chosen strategy.

A design which is commonly used to check the effectiveness of treatment is the AB–AB design, where A is the baseline condition and B is the experimental treatment. So, if treatment is working, the level of yelling should be reduced during the initial B-phase (compared with the initial A phase) and should increase again when treatment is stopped (the second A-phase); when treatment is reintroduced (second B-phase), yelling should once more reduce.

Step 6.   Begin treatment.

Step 7.   Monitor progress.

Step 8.   Change the programme if necessary.

Operant Conditioning with Autistic Children and the Mentally Handicapped

Lovaas et al (1967) pioneered operant conditioning with autistic children who normally have little or no normal speech. They used a shaping technique:

1)   The first step was to pair verbal approval with a bit of food whenever the child made eye-contact or merely attended to the therapist's speech or behaviour (which is also unusual for autistic children); this reinforces attention and associates a positive social gesture with food so that verbal approval eventually becomes a conditioned reinforcer.

2)   The next step was to reinforce the child with food and praise whenever it made any kind of speech sound or even tried to imitate the therapist's actions.

3)   Once this occurred without prompting, the therapist gradually withheld reinforcement until the child successfully imitated complete actions or uttered particular vowel or consonant sounds, then syllables, then words and, finally, combinations of words.

Sometimes hundreds or even thousands of reinforcements were necessary before the child began to label objects appropriately or imitate simple phrases and even when children have received extensive training they are likely to regress if returned to a non-supportive institutional setting. Even under optimum conditions, they never achieve the creative use of language and broad range of social skills of normal children (Thomas, 1985). However, Lovaas et al (1976) believe that many therapeutic gains can be retained (and even some modest improvements shown) at home if parents have been trained to use the shaping techniques.

There are many striking examples of successful modification programmes with the mentally handicapped, both adults and children. In one large-scale study, Matson et al (1980) reported substantial improvements in the eating behaviour of profoundly impaired adults; they used peer and therapist modelling (see below), social reinforcement, verbal prompts to shape eating, the use of utensils, table manners, etc. Reinforcers included going to meals early and having one's own table-mat and there was a significant improvement in the treated group even four months after the end of treatment, compared with an untreated control group.

Azrin and Foxx (1971) and Foxx and Azrin (1973) produced a toilet-training 'package' in which: (i) the client is taken to the toilet every half hour and given extra fluids, sweets, biscuits, praise and attention when it is used successfully; (ii) the client is strapped into a chair for half an hour, away from other people, if they have an accident (this is *not* a punishment procedure but '*time out*', ie a time away from positive reinforcement).

As with speech training in autistic children, there are problems of generalizing from hospital-based improvement to the home situation but if parents continue the programme at home, there can be short- and long-term benefits.

A form of behaviour often displayed by autistic and mentally handicapped individuals is self-mutilation by biting, scratching, head-banging and so on, all of which can be life-threatening. Baddeley (1990) describes a case of self-mutilation which was successfully treated by use of operant techniques (Box 31.1).

Box 31.1 Self-mutilation treated by operant conditioning (Bull and LaVecchio, 1978)

A boy suffering from Lesch–Nyhan syndrome, a rare genetic disorder which involves neurological disorders, psychomotor retardation and often self-mutilation, began showing self-injurious behaviour at about age three. He was eventually confined to a wheelchair, his arms were constrained by splints, he wore a helmet and shoulder pads. At night, he slept in a jacket and safety straps to stop him biting. He held his breath, removed his finger and toe nails, spat, displayed projectile vomiting and head-banging, screamed and used foul language. Despite the restraints, he could still inflict wounds on various parts of his body and while doing so, would often shout 'I hate myself'. His abnormal behaviour seemed to be associated with periods of anxiety and agitation and was sometimes provoked by the removal of his restraining devices about which he felt very ambivalent (he didn't want them on but nor did he want them off!).

Treatment was aimed at: (i) allowing him to tolerate being without his restraints; and (ii) extinguishing the self-injurious behaviour. Initially, removal of even a peripheral part of the protective equipment could only be achieved using nitrous oxide as a relaxant. It was also observed that treating his self-inflicted wounds was reinforcing so this was then done under anaesthetic to avoid any association between self-injury and reward.

He was then put in a room on his own (containing a one-way mirror) and his self-injurious behaviour stopped, suggesting it was motivated by the need for attention. Consequently, attention was used as a reinforcer, being withheld during self-mutilation and given at other times.

Over the course of fifteen one-hour sessions, withdrawal of attention during self-injury led to the reduction and ultimate extinction of biting behaviour. The process was repeated for the other abnormal behaviours.

Eighteen months later, the improvement had clearly been maintained. He had no restraints, could feed himself, was learning to walk with crutches, was attending a special class in a normal school and was interacting and communicating with other children.

Token Economy Programmes with Chronic Psychiatric Patients

The *token economy* (Allyon and Azrin, 1968) is based on the principle of *secondary reinforcement*, whereby tokens (conditioned reinforcers) are given for socially desirable/acceptable behaviours as they occur; the tokens can then be exchanged for certain 'primary' reinforcers. (For example, making one's own bed is worth one token, brushing teeth once a day, one token, and washing up for ten minutes, six tokens; twenty tokens can 'buy' a private consultation with the ward psychologist and three tokens a favourite TV programme.)

If the introduction of chlorpromazine and other antischizophrenic drugs in the 1950s marked a revolution in psychiatry, the introduction of token economy programmes during the 1960s was, in its way, equally revolutionary, partly because it drew attention to the ways in which nursing (and other) staff were inadvertently maintaining the psychotic, 'mad' behaviour of many chronic schizophrenics by giving them attention, thus reinforcing unwanted behaviour.

There seems little doubt that well-run token economy programmes do produce behaviour change, in the required direction, even among chronic, institutionalized schizophrenics (Walker, 1984). However, a number of doubts have been raised and questions asked:

1)   There is the problem of transferring the control of behaviours from tokens to social reinforcers both within and, ultimately, outside the hospital; the former is normally achieved by gradually 'weaning' patients off the tokens and the latter by transferring patients to halfway houses and other community live-in arrangements. However, there tends to be a high re-hospitalization rate for such patients.

2)   Baddeley (1990) argues that when used in an educational setting (eg in a home for emotionally disturbed children), a token economy can produce a very mercenary approach to learning, (token economies lead to token learning) ie children may only read or indulge in any educational activity if directly rewarded for it. This may be effective within the confines of the token economy itself, but will be:

> ... quite unproductive in the outside, where it is necessary to learn to operate on a subtler and less immediate reward system. (Baddeley, 1990)

But is it possible for patients' behaviour to become more 'natural', ie less dependent on the token economy itself?

3) Within the hospital, a recent preoccupation has been with maintaining new behaviours once the formal token economy programme is finished. One study did find long-term behaviour change for those patients whose newly acquired behaviours were 'trapped' by natural social reinforcers. For example, some patients were so incapable of behaving in a socially appropriate way that they were avoided by staff prior to the start of the programme but the programme produced such marked changes in their behaviour that they were actually invited home to tea by the staff! Such reinforcement was sufficient to maintain the newly acquired social behaviour (Wood et al, 1984).

4) What this study suggests is that a crucial factor in the effectiveness of token economies might be the changes that take place at the *staff* level as opposed to the patients themselves! The use of behaviour modification to change staff behaviour can be very effective, for example, and Burgio et al (1983) found that selectively reinforcing staff for verbal interaction with residents produced a reliable improvement in the residents' behaviour.

Feedback that staff receive about their own effectiveness seems to be another crucial factor. For instance, if ward staff know how well they are doing with their patients' behaviour, then they will tend to keep up the kind of interaction with these patients which will maintain the acceptable behaviours.

5) What these studies suggest is that the fact that token economies work does not in itself prove that they work because of reinforcement. Other, confounding, variables may include improvement in nurse–patient ratio, increase in staff morale and an overall more optimistic and enthusiastic approach to patients. Any one of these could, on its own, account for at least some of the improvements commonly found, so that, as with other successful behavioural interventions, the reason for the effectiveness of token economy programmes may be quite unrelated to learning theory principles (Fonagy and Higgitt, 1984).

Finally, the use of token economy programmes (and other forms of behaviour modification) have raised serious ethical issues, some of which were discussed in Chapter 3:

> I suspect that behaviour modifcation will fail in so far as it attempts to induce habits that go consistently against the long term motivations and aims of the subject. This does not have to be so, mankind could be infinitely directable and malleable. Behaviour modification appears to offer a technology by which we can help people, but we cannot dominate them. Long may that state of affairs continue! (Baddeley, 1990)

COGNITIVE APPROACHES

COGNITIVE–BEHAVIOUR THERAPY: MODEL OF PSYCHOLOGICAL DISORDER

According to Mahoney (1974) and Meichenbaum (1977), many (if not the majority) clinical problems are best described as disorders of thought and feeling; and since behaviour is to a large extent controlled by the way we think, the most logical and effective way of trying to change maladaptive behaviour is to change the maladaptive thinking which lies behind it.

Wessler (1986) defines cognitive–behaviour therapy (CBT) as a 'collection of assumptions about disturbance and a set of treatment interventions in which human cognitions are assigned a central role'. It is derived from various theoretical and therapeutic sources and the way that cognition is defined and operationalized differs according to particular approaches. However, Wessler stresses that the attempt to change cognition (*cognitive restructuring*) is always a *means* to an end, that end being the 'lasting changes in target emotions and behaviour' (Wessler, 1986).

Rational Emotive Therapy (Ellis, 1962, 1973)

Ellis believes that *irrational thoughts* are the main cause of all types of emotional distress and behaviour disorders. Irrational thinking leads to a self-defeating internal dialogue, comprising negative self-statements and these are seen as 'covert' behaviours which are subject to the same principles of learning as overt behaviour. Phobias, for example, are linked to *catastrophizing self-statements* and, as with other disorders, the aim of therapy is to replace these irrational, unreasonable, beliefs and ideas with more reasonable and realistic ones.

In its simplest form, patients are told to look on the bright side, stop worrying, pull themselves together and so on. As Walker (1984) observes, 'rational' should not be taken too literally as sometimes counter-productive thoughts and beliefs may be replaced by more positive and helpful but equally irrational ones. For instance, it is not necessarily more rational to be an optimist than a pessimist but it is usually more productive and should be encouraged in depressed patients (Walker, 1984).

Ellis (1962) identified eleven basic irrational beliefs or ideas which tend to be emotionally self-defeating and which are commonly associated with psychological problems, including, 'I must be loved and accepted by absolutely everybody', 'I must be excellent in all possible respects and never make mistakes—otherwise I'm worthless' and 'I am unable to control my emotions'. In rational emotive therapy (RET), the patient is challenged to *prove* that they are worthless because they make mistakes, etc., or to say exactly *how* making mistakes makes one a worthless person. Patients may be explicitly directed to practise certain positive/optimistic statements and are generally urged to 'look for the "musts" when they experience inappropriate emotions' (Wessler, 1986).

Self-Instructional Training (Meichenbaum, 1973)

Meichenbaum believes that neurotic behaviour is due, at least partly, to *faulty internal dialogues* (internal speech), in which the patient is failing to *self-instruct* successfully. The underlying rationale for self-instructional therapy (SIT) is a study by Meichenbaum and Goodman (1971) in which impulsive and hyperactive children were trained to administer self-instructions for tasks on which they had previously made frequent errors, first by talking aloud, then covertly, without talking, but still moving their lips and, finally, without any lip movements. This 'silent speech' is the essence of verbal thought (see the discussion of Vygotsky's theory of thought and language in Chapter 13).

Patients are made aware of the maladaptive nature of their self-statements and are then helped to develop coping skills in the form of coping self-statements, relaxation and plans for behaviour change. For instance, a patient might write down a strategy for dealing with a particular social interaction (eg asking someone to dance at a disco) and then role-play it with a continuous commentary on self-statements before actually doing it 'for real'; as well as these advance preparations, the patient may give on-the-spot self-warnings and self-debriefings once it is over.

Wolpe (1978) argues that these techniques are not very useful in cases of severe anxiety because many strong neurotic fears are triggered by objects and situations which the patient *knows* are harmless—this is why phobias are irrational! So Wolpe has used a technique called *thought-stopping* (mainly with obsessive–compulsive patients) in which the patient is told to dwell on their obsessive thoughts and, while this is happening, the therapist shouts *'Stop!'* The patient then repeats the command out loud and eventually repeats it sub-vocally (in thought only).

(Covert sensitization, which we discussed in the section on Aversion Therapy (p. 976), is a form of self-instruction or self-training.)

Treatment of 'Automatic Thoughts' (Beck, 1963)

Beck believed that depressives see themselves as victims (based largely on interpretation of their dreams). The key elements in depression are negative thought about oneself, the world and the future (the *cognitive triad* of depression) and these thoughts seem to come automatically and involuntarily. The source of such thoughts are logical errors based on faulty 'data' and, once negative thinking has been identified, it can be replaced by collecting evidence against it. Accordingly, Beck sees the client as a colleague of the therapist who researches verifiable reality (Wessler, 1986).

For example, if a client expresses the negative thought, 'I'm a poor father because my children are not better disciplined', Beck would take the second part of the statement and seek factual evidence about its truth; he would also focus on the evaluative conclusion that one is a *poor* father because one's children sometimes misbehave. In these and other ways, clients are trained to distance themselves from things, to be more objective, to distinguish fact from fiction and fact from evaluation, to see things in proportion and not to see things in such extreme terms.

Modelling (Bandura, 1968, 1977)

Modelling, of course, is a direct application of Social Learning Theory (discussed in Chapters 7 and 27). In a famous demonstration of therapeutic modelling (Bandura and Menlove, 1968), forty-eight nursery school children with dog phobias were divided into three groups:

Group 1—the *single model condition*—saw eight three-minute films (two per day for four days) in which a five-year-old boy engaged in progressively bolder interactions with a cocker spaniel.
Group 2—the *multiple model condition*—saw similar films, but several

boys and girls were seen interacting with a number of dogs ranging in size from very small to quite large.

Group 3—the *control group*—saw a film about Disneyland and Marineland.

The day after the final film, the children were asked to perform fourteen acts as a test of their fear of dogs. Compared with a pre-test performance, the control group showed no fear reduction, but Groups 1 and 2 were much more willing to approach and interact with a real dog and, one month later, the differences remained. (Group 2 children were much more willing to initiate very intimate contact than Group 1 children.)

Bandura argues that: (i) modelling is more effective for treating phobias than counter-conditioning (based on classical conditioning); (ii) symbolic modelling (films) is *less* powerful than live demonstrations; and (iii) the age of the model seems to be irrelevant. Bandura (1969) claimed a 90 per cent success rate in curing snake phobias and similar success for dog phobias. However, it seems to be mainly effective with children (although it may form part of behaviour therapy with adults) and with simple (eg animal) phobias; it may work simply by persuading the child to *expose* itself to the object of its fear (Marks, 1978).

According to Kazdin and Wilcoxin (1976), the crucial ingredients of therapy (whatever techniques are involved) are: (i) the patient is influenced to *expect* success; and (ii) the patient's *self-concept* changes, whereby they come to believe (through supervised practice) that the previously feared object or situation *can* be coped with. Bandura (1977) has integrated a number of findings into the proposal that the central element in psychological therapy is the cognitive change towards *self-efficacy*, ie the belief that one can perform desired behaviour effectively and this is brought about best through actual experience in facing previously feared or avoided situations.

PERSONAL CONSTRUCT THERAPY (KELLY, 1955): MODEL OF PSYCHOLOGICAL DISORDER

Kelly's concept of disorder is directly related to his view of normality (his Personal Construct Theory (PCT) was discussed in Chapter 29).

Kelly completely rejects the medical model and with it all notions of 'illness' and 'health'. Instead, he uses the concept of *functioning*: a person who is functioning fully is able to construe the world in such a way that predictions are, most of the time, confirmed or validated but, when they are not validated, they can change his/her personal construct system accordingly (things are put down to 'experience'; Fransella, 1984).

If our constructs are repeatedly invalidated, we may consider we have 'a problem' and a psychological disorder is defined as 'any personal construction which is used repeatedly in spite of consistent invalidation' (Kelly, 1955). Symptoms serve to give structure and meaning to the chaotic experience which arises out of the use of invalidated constructs. For instance, anxiety is an indication that an individual's personal construct systems are inadequate for, or inappropriate to, the events to which they are applied, ie those events lie outside its *range of convenience*. One response to anxiety is to *loosen* our constructs, so that more events can be accommodated by them—our predictions become less specific and so there is less chance of our being wrong.

According to Bannister (1963, 1965), schizophrenia represents an extreme form of loosening—constructs which are normally interlinked come to 'hang together' in an almost random way. Obsessive–compulsive symptoms represent the opposite way of dealing with anxiety, namely an extreme *tightening* of the construct system, an attempt to ensure that predictions are never invalidated.

THE AIMS OF THERAPY

The basic aim of PCT is to change the client's way of construing the world in order to make better sense of it and predict it more accurately: the constructs of a loose construer need to be tightened and those of a tight construer loosened.

THERAPEUTIC TECHNIQUES

It is much more difficult to identify specific techniques than it is in most other approaches and the therapist may well use techniques from other approaches. For example, if a client is a tight construer, free association, dream interpretation, Gestalt therapy and some aspects of Rogers' client-centred therapy may be used (see below) while a loose construer may undergo behaviour therapy (Mackay, 1975). More specifically, the client–therapist relationship, self-characterization and fixed role therapy (sketch and enactment) constitute the basic ingredients of PCT.

1) The *relationship* between client and therapist is seen, essentially, as comparable to that between a PhD student and his/her supervisor; together, they struggle to understand why one of them is failing to solve the problems that they encounter in life. The therapy room is a laboratory and the therapist is a *validator* of the client's behavioural experiments; they can help the client to see alternative ways of construing the world (Fransella, 1984).

2) A client's problem is that their construct system has not adapted to deal with certain vital aspects of life; therefore, 'diagnosis' involves trying to understand the problem *as the client sees it* and a method of trying to achieve this is *self-characterization* (which, together with Fixed Role Therapy, is the only really original treatment device, according to Mackay, 1975).

The client is asked to write a character sketch about themselves, in the third person:

> . . . just as if she were the principal character in a play. Write it as if it might be written by a friend who knew her *intimately* and very *sympathetically*, perhaps better than anyone ever really could know her . . . (Fransella, 1984)

3) The therapist then writes a second version of the client's original self-characterization (called a *fixed role sketch*) which, ideally, lies somewhere between the client's self-portrait and its exact opposite, eg if the client uses the construct 'aggressive–submissive' in relation to their boss, the therapist will use 'respectful' (Fransella, 1984). The client and therapist discuss the fixed role sketch together and modify it until it describes a person the client feels it is possible to be. The client then goes away and lives the life of that person for a few weeks (*fixed role*

enactment) with frequent meetings during this period *in the prescribed role*.

The purpose of fixed role enactment is to show the client that we can, indeed, change ourselves.

4)   The *repertory grid* (see Chapter 29), may be used in a variety of ways: (i) to measure the client's construct system; (ii) to measure the therapist's construct system, eg how they construe the client; and (iii) to monitor the therapeutic process, for example, the client can provide a series of self-ratings and the selves as rated can form the elements of a grid which can then be combined to make a grid which can provide a summary of the change, through time, of the therapeutic process (Ryle, 1975).

HUMANISTIC–PHENOMENOLOGICAL APPROACHES

CLIENT-CENTRED THERAPY: MODEL OF PSYCHOLOGICAL DISORDER

As we saw in Chapter 29, when a person is aware of a lack of *congruence* between their experience and self-concept, *threat, anxiety or depression* is experienced. Because of our need for positive regard, we may behave in ways which are discrepant with the values of our self, and feeling threatened anxious or depressed is the price we pay. As defences against these unpleasant feelings, we use *denial* and *distortion*, whereby part of reality is prevented from entering consciousness and is, consequently, unable to contribute to our self-concept. As a result, our self-concept becomes increasingly incongruent with reality which, in turn, increases anxiety and makes the need for defences all the greater—a vicious circle has been created.

Where the incongruence is severe and/or persistent, the resulting threat, anxiety or depression may interfere with the person's life in a *neurotic* way; where it is so great as to defy denial and distortion, the incongruent experience is accurately symbolized at a conscious level and this leads to the disintegration of personality (characterized by bizarre, crazy, behaviour) which is commonly called *psychotic*.

However, Rogers regards individuals as *unique* and human personality is so complex that no diagnostic labelling of persons can ever be fully justified; indeed, Rogers rejects all diagnostic labelling.

THE AIMS OF THERAPY

Client-centred therapy (CCT) is a process where the individual has the opportunity to re-organize his/her subjective world so as to integrate and actualize the self; the key process, therefore, is facilitation of the experience of becoming a more autonomous, spontaneous and confident person (Graham, 1986).

People have within themselves an inherent capacity for, and tendency towards, self-understanding and self-actualization *but* the conditions for facilitating its development reside in the *relationship* between the client and the therapist. The word 'client' is used to emphasize the person's self-responsibility (while 'patient' implies the opposite) and 'client-centred' implies that the client is encouraged to direct the whole therapeutic process—any changes which occur during therapy are brought about by the client.

THE THERAPEUTIC PROCESS

The therapist's main task is to create a *therapeutic atmosphere* in which clients can become fully integrated again. This can only be achieved if clients reduce their conditions of worth and increase their unconditional positive self-regard.

The therapist's job is to create a situation in which clients can change themselves, and this is aided by an emotionally warm, accepting, understanding and non-evaluative relationship in which the person is free from threat and has the freedom to be 'the self that he really is' (Graham, 1986).

There are three particularly significant qualities to the realtionship or *attitudes* on the part of the therapist who must effectively communicate them to the client as both a necessary and sufficient condition for therapeutic change:

1) *Genuineness* (authenticity or congruence). The therapist must show him/herself to be a *real* person, with feelings which should be expressed where appropriate. The client needs to feel that the therapist is emotionally involved and not hiding behind a facade of professional impersonality; the therapist must be 'transparent'. This is the most important of the three qualities or attitudes.

2) *Unconditional positive regard*. The therapist must show complete acceptance of, and regard for, the client, as a separate person in their own right. The therapist must have a deep and genuine caring for the client *as they are now* in a non-judgemental way.

3) *Empathic understanding*. The therapist must try to enter the client's inner world through a genuine, attentive listening, which involves intense concentration. This may involve re-stating what the client says as a way of trying to clarify its emotional significance (rather than its verbal content) and this requires the therapist to be sensitive to what is currently going on in the client and of meanings which are just below the level of awareness.

Thorne (1984) believes that this is the most 'trainable' of the three therapist attitudes but is at the same time remarkably rare. He also suggests that a fourth attitude, *tenderness*, could be added to Rogers' three.

If these therapeutic conditions are established, clients will talk about themselves more honestly and this will bring about a re-establishment of congruence which will be sufficient to produce changes in behaviour (Fonagy and Higgitt, 1984).

Unlike most other humanistic therapists, Rogers has attempted to validate his therapy empirically (and has encouraged others to do so). A form of assessment used by Rogers is the *Q-sort*, which comprises a number of cards with statements referring to the self (eg 'I am a domineering person'); the client is asked to arrange them in a series of ten piles ranging from 'very characteristic of me' to 'not at all characteristic of me' (describing the self-image) and the process is repeated so as to describe the ideal self. The two Q-sorts are then correlated to determine the discrepancy between self-image and ideal self—the lower the correlations, the greater the discrepancy. The whole procedure is repeated at various intervals during the course of therapy (in a similar way to the use of the Repertory Grid in Kelly's PCT).

One way of assessing the importance of the three qualities or attitudes of the therapist is to give trained judges transcripts or tape-recordings of therapy sessions which they have to rate. Truax and Mitchell (1971) found that therapists who were rated high were much more likely to be associated with desirable changes in their clients and low-rated therapists actually worsened their clients' condition. But others have found that the therapists' personal characteristics are likely to be no more important than any specific techniques used.

CCT AND COUNSELLING

Despite their questionable empirical basis, Rogers' ideas about ideal therapeutic relationships and attitudes have become part of the accepted clinical wisdom of psychologists of all theoretical orientations. Essentially, Rogerian therapy provides a situation in which the client learns to be free and, as such, it is an *educational* process, which Rogers believes can be as effective in the classroom as in the clinic (*Freedom to Learn*, 1969). He is generally regarded as having inspired the *counselling* movement, especially in the UK, which is a product of his involvement with therapy *and* education (Graham, 1986).

ENCOUNTER GROUPS

Another spin-off of CCT is the encounter or personal growth movement, originally very much an American (particularly Californian) phenomenon of the 1960s and 1970s. These were originally developed by Rogers, 'as a means whereby people can break through the barriers erected by themselves and others in order to react openly and freely with one another' (Graham, 1986).

Participants (not 'clients') are encouraged to act out their emotions (not just talk about them) through body contact and structured activities and 'games'; the leader (or facilitator) attempts to create a climate of mutual trust in which people (usually between eight and eighteen in number) feel free to express their true feelings—both positive and negative—thereby reducing defensiveness and promoting self-actualization (Rogers, 1973).

Variants of encounter groups include T-groups or Sensitivity Training Groups (Maslow, 1969); how effective these actually are in bringing about change is very unclear and, indeed, many writers have warned against the dangers of such groups. For example, it has been claimed that they can cause—or at least precipitate—various sorts of psychological disturbance. Aggressive and highly charismatic, authoritarian, leaders are the most likely to have casualties in their groups.

One of their destructive characteristics is the pressure to have some ecstatic or 'peak' experience, which is seen as necessary for continuing mental health; but Maslow would say that such experiences are relatively uncommon and certainly cannot be produced 'on demand' (see Chapter 29).

ACTION THERAPIES

These refer to a diverse set of therapeutic approaches which are derived from an equally diverse set of theoretical perspectives. Encounter groups are, of course, action-based and are quite closely related to Rogers' theory of self. The others that I shall briefly describe in this section are Gestalt Therapy, Transactional Analysis, Primal Therapy, Erhard Seminars Training (EST) and Psychodrama.

GESTALT THERAPY (PERLS, 1969)

Based on the Gestalt theory of perception (see Chapter 9), Gestalt therapy helps people to become *whole* by putting them in touch with their *entire* selves and their surroundings. We tend to block awareness of aspects of ourselves and only by acknowledging every part of ourselves can the self emerge as a unified *figure* against its environmental *ground* or field.

The client is required to play *all* the roles of a drama alone, either by acting each part in turn or in the form of dialogues between the various parts (including physical props); one popular method is the 'empty chair technique' in which the client projects into an empty chair any part of the drama in order to confront it (eg aspects of the client's self which are normally unexpressed, or other people—real or imagined). The overall aim is, by bringing these elements into the open, to enable people to identify and integrate the various diverse parts of themselves and, thereby, to achieve an individual *gestalt* (Graham, 1986).

TRANSACTIONAL ANALYSIS (BERNE, 1968)

Influenced very much by psychoanalytic theory, transactional analysis (TA) sees personality as comprising three ego-states—*parent*, *child* and *ego*, corresponding to the Superego, Id and Ego respectively.

Through role-play, an individual's ego states are identified as they are used in various personal transactions; this 'structural analysis' enables the person to understand their behaviour and change it in a way which will give them greater control over their life. This is usually conducted on an individual basis initially, after which the person is free to participate in group transactions or TA proper.

In the group, participants are encouraged to experiment by enacting more appropriate ego states and observing their effects on themselves and others. The focus is on the individual's tendency to manipulate others in destructive and non-productive ways. Berne (*The Games that People Play*, 1968) identified a number of distinct games and strategies which are commonly used in interpersonal relationships and which prevent spontaneous and appropriate behaviour; TA involves analysing an individual's characteristic games and strategies.

PRIMAL THERAPY (JANOV, 1973)

In *The Primal Scream* (1973), Janov describes how birth represents the primary trauma in an individual's life from which all others stem and which, therefore, is the source of all anxiety; the aim of primal therapy is to help the person overcome the defences built up against the intolerable pain associated with birth by experiencing the pain while re-enacting the birth process. This is facilitated by careful 'staging'; for example, the client assumes a fetal position, is covered in pillows (representing the birth canal), is encouraged to scream (the 'primal scream') and so on.

'Re-birthing' may symbolically represent the person's desire to make a fresh start in life; it is cathartic, releasing blocked emotions and the pain associated with the birth experience.

ERHARD SEMINARS TRAINING

During the early 1970s, Erhard Seminars Training (EST) became the fastest growing and most controversial enlightenment programme in the USA (Graham, 1986). It is very eclectic, drawing on techniques used in many religious and therapeutic disciplines, including Gestalt, psychodrama, encounter groups and sensitivity training.

The aim is to encourage people to take responsibility for themselves. Paradoxically, this is achieved by means of manipulative techniques, including various kinds of deprivation, sensory overload and shock tactics. One of the original and most publicized features is work with *crowds*: spanning two weekends (lasting over sixty hours altogether), 250 people are assembled to be shouted at, bossed around, humiliated, lectured at and coaxed into performing a highly structured programme of exercises and procedures designed to help people realize what life is actually like and to accept it for what it is! (Graham, 1986.)

PSYCHODRAMA

Jacob Moreno was a Viennese psychiatrist and a contemporary of Freud who sought alternative approaches to the predominantly verbal nature of orthodox psychoanalysis but which would facilitate powerful emotional release or catharsis.

He believed that most human problems arise from the need to create and maintain social roles which may conflict with each other and the person's essential self; this conflict is the source of anxiety. Starting in the 1920s, Moreno proposed that within the relative safety of psychodrama, groups of individuals (usually seven to eight but up to twelve) could explore role conflicts, together with those aspects of self which are not expressed through any existing roles, in order to bring about integration and balance within the personality.

The principal actor who is dramatizing his/her conflicts and problems is the *protagonist*, who is helped to create the atmosphere and circumstances of the situation and 'sets the scene' at a physical level by describing it in words and with the aid of very simple props. The interpersonal events are then recreated by role-play; the protagonist chooses other members of the group to represent the key figures and they are briefed by being given a full description of the role (they are known as *auxiliary egos*). They try to 'feel their way' into the part, *not* by aiming for dramatic excellence but by trying to discover the possible feelings and perceptions that the person they are playing might have in the situation.

Another technique is *role-reversal* in which the protagonist switches roles with the auxiliary egos. In *doubling*, the leader (or some other member) stands with the protagonist and suggests to them feelings, perceptions, motives, etc., which may be operating within them (but which have not yet been identified); and *mirroring* involves group members mimicking or exaggerating the protagonist's behaviour in order to provide effective feedback. The group leader generally directs proceedings, often intervening with suggestions (eg role-switching) and directions designed to enable the protagonist to stop and explore his/her feelings and perceptions.

EXISTENTIAL APPROACHES

The Therapeutic Community

As we saw in Chapter 30, psychiatrists such as Laing, Cooper and Esterson championed the *anti-psychiatry* movement during the 1950s and 1960s. They advocated the removal of all diagnostic labels and categories as well as all role distinctions between therapists and clients/patients and the provision of an informal, unstructured environment where schizophrenics could discover themselves through genuine encounters with others (Graham, 1986).

This was first attempted by Cooper in 1962. 'Villa 21' was an experimental therapeutic ward within a conventional mental hospital and was specifically geared towards the problems of young, recently labelled, schizophrenics. Although short-lived, Villa 21 showed that such radical alternatives to conventional psychiatric care could be established outside the larger institution; such *therapeutic communities* should be somewhere that people *choose* to go, an *asylum* (safe refuge) in the true meaning of the term.

Laing, Cooper and Esterson founded the Philadelphia Association in 1964, a charity which set up the famous Kingsley Hall in the East End of London in 1965. Perhaps the most famous resident was Mary Barnes who, with the support of her therapist, Joseph Berke, 'went down' into her own madness (she had been diagnosed as schizophrenic twelve years earlier and had been given ECT during a year-long stay in hospital), regressed to infancy and acted out the anger which had been repressed by her family. From a demanding, obsessive child, there emerged a whole, creative, adult human being. Her story is told in *Mary Barnes—two accounts of a journey through madness* (Barnes, M. and Berke, J. 1973, Harmondsworth, Penguin).

Although Kingsley Hall closed in 1970, the Philadelphia Association now has a network of similar households in London and offers training in psychotherapy and community therapy. Joseph Berke has helped to establish the Arbours Association, a mental health charity to assist those in emotional distress. It sponsors four long-term communities and a short-stay crisis centre, psychotherapy training and training in social psychiatry.

Social Psychiatry

This essentially means the treatment of psychological disorder outside mental hospitals, in the community; apart from therapeutic communities such as those run by the Philadelphia and Arbours Associations (and other mental health charities), community care facilities include small selective units specializing in alcoholism and drug addiction, day-care units, local authority hostels and halfway houses for the rehabilitation of drug addicts and newly-released psychiatric patients (and prisoners). Any crisis-intervention facilities, such as telephone hot-lines (eg the

Samaritans) also form an important part of the community care/social psychiatric alternative to psychiatric hospitals.

TREATMENT EFFECTIVENESS: DOES THERAPY WORK?

We have discussed some of the evidence relating to treatment effectiveness as we have examined particular approaches; we need now to refer to some other studies of effectiveness.

Probably the most famous (and controversial) is that of Eysenck (1952) in which he reviewed five studies of the effectiveness of psychoanalysis and nineteen studies of the effectiveness of 'eclectic' psychotherapy. He concluded that only 44 per cent of psychoanalytic patients improved and 64 per cent of those who received the 'mixed' therapy. However, since roughly 66 per cent of patients improve without *any* treatment (*spontaneous remission*), Eysenck concluded that psychoanalysis in particular, and psychotherapy in general, simply do not work—they achieve nothing which would not have happened anyway without therapy! (Table 31.1).

By 1960, Eysenck was arguing that behaviour therapy is the *only* kind of therapy worth rational consideration and he inspired an enormous amount of research on therapy outcomes (Oatley, 1984). However:

(a) If the many patients who drop out of psychoanalysis are excluded from the 44 per cent quoted by Eysenck (they cannot legitimately be counted as 'failures' or 'not cured'), the figure rises to 66 per cent;

(b) Bergin (1971) reviewed some of the papers included in Eysenck's review and concluded that, by choosing different criteria of 'improvement', the success rate of psychoanalysis could be raised to 83 per cent. He also cited studies which showed only a 30 per cent spontaneous remission rate.

   The two studies which Eysenck used to establish his spontaneous remission rate of 66 per cent were Landis (1938) and Denker (1946). Basically, Landis compared patients who had received psychotherapy ('experimental group') with a control group who had been hospitalized for 'neurosis' in state mental hospitals, while Denker's control group had been treated only by their GPs with sedatives, tonics, suggestion and reassurance.

   Landis himself pointed out a number of differences between his psychotherapy group and the hospital patient controls and concluded that these differences 'all argue against the acceptance of [this] figure ... as a truly satisfactory baseline, but in the absence of any other better figure this must serve'.

(c) Bergin and Lambert (1978) reviewed seventeen studies of untreated 'neurotics' and found a median spontaneous remission rate of 43 per cent. They also found that the rate of spontaneous remission varies a great deal depending on the disorder—generalized anxiety and depression, for example, are much more likely to 'cure themselves' than phobias or obsessive–compulsive disorders.

(d) Smith and Glass (1977) reviewed 400 studies of a wide variety of therapies (including psychodynamic, Gestalt, CCT, TA, SD and eclectic) and concluded that all were more effective than no treat-

Table 31.1 Summary of Reports and the Results of Psychotherapy (from Eysenck, 1952)

	N	CURED; MUCH IMPROVED	IMPROVED	SLIGHTLY IMPROVED	NOT IMPROVED; DIED; LEFT TREATMENT	% CURED; MUCH IMPROVED; IMPROVED
(A) *Psychoanalytic*						
Fenichel (1920–1930)	484	104	84	99	179	39
Kessel and Hyman (1933)	34	16	5	4	9	62
Jones (1926–1936)	59	20	8	28	3	47
Alexander (1932–1937)	141	28	42	23	48	50
Knight (1941)	42	8	20	7	7	67
ALL CASES	760	335		407		44
(B) *Eclectic*						
Huddleson (1927)	200	19	74	80	27	46
Matz (1929)	775	10	310	310	145	41
Maudsley Hospital Report (1931)	1721	288	900	533		69
Maudsley Hospital Report (1935)	1711	371	765	575		64
Neustatter (1935)	46	9	14	8	15	50
Luff and Garrod (1935)	500	140	135	26	199	55
Luff and Garrod (1935)	210	38	84	54	34	68
Ross (1936)	1089	547	306	236		77
Yaskin (1936)	100	29	29	42		58
Curran (1937)	83	51		32		61
Masserman and Carmichael (1938)	50	7	20	5	18	54
Carmichael and Masserman (1939)	77	16	25	14	22	53
Schilder (1939)	35	11	11	6	7	63
Hamilton and Wall (1941)	100	32	34	17	17	66
Hamilton et al (1942)	100	48	5	17	32	51
Landis (1938)	119	40	47	32		73
Institute Med. Pscyhol. (quoted Neustatter)	270	58	132	55	25	70
Wilder (1945)	54	3	24	16	11	50
Miles et al (1951)	53	13	18	13	9	58
ALL CASES	7293	4661		2632		64

ment. For example, the 'average' client who had received therapy scored more favourably on the outcome measures than 75 per cent of those in the untreated control groups.

Smith et al (1980) extended the 1977 study to include 475 studies (an estimated 75 per cent of the published literature). Strict criteria for admission into their 'meta-analysis' included the comparison between a treated group (given a specified form of therapy) with a second group (drawn from the same population) given either no therapy, put on a waiting list or given some alternative form of therapy. As with the 1977 results, the effectiveness of therapy was shown to be highly significant—the average client was better off than 80 per cent of the control groups on the outcome measures.

Different therapies had different kinds of effects: (i) the largest overall effects were produced by *cognitive* therapies and *cognitive–behaviour* therapies, which were particularly effective with single, simple phobias, fear and anxiety; (ii) psychodynamic therapies did best with psychotics; (iii) CCT did best with low self-esteem clients; (iv) dynamic eclectic therapy did best with work and school adjustment; and (v) neither behaviour therapy nor psychodynamic therapy emerged as superior to the other.

CONCLUSIONS

1) The whole concept of 'cure' is highly complex and is itself defined differently from different theoretical and therapeutic perspectives. For example, as we noted earlier, as far as psychoanalysis is concerned, a 'cure' cannot be defined in terms of symptom removal because the 'real' problem is an underlying conflict and not the symptoms themselves; consequently, if the underlying conflict is not successfully dealt with, other symptoms will replace those which have been removed (*symptom substitution*).

Behaviour therapists, on the other hand, believe that symptom removal constitutes a cure, since symptoms *are* the disorder (and so, no symptom substitution will occur).

However, this way of presenting the issue is probably an oversimplification. Bandura (1969), for instance, argues that behaviour therapists (as well as psychoanalysts) may talk about 'merely treating the symptom', implying that the therapist has been too narrow in his/her perception of the number of different situations in which the deviant behaviour is used. What may appear to be symptom substitution (as judged by a psychoanalyst) may be the substitution of a response lower down in the person's hierarchy of responses for that situation but which is also socially unacceptable (ie the person has already acquired a hierarchy of *possible* responses).

According to Beech (1972), symptom substitution probably does occur in some cases but is relatively uncommon. Sometimes symptoms might be seen in too simple a way (and lead to inappropriate treatment) as when a 'superficial' symptom (eg writer's cramp and stammering) might be related to a more basic and meaningful 'symptom' (eg fear of dealing with people in authority); it is the latter which needs treatment (and, in a way, is equivalent to the 'underlying conflict' of psychoanalysis).

Sometimes, what may be considered the 'opposite' of symptom substitution can occur.

In the case of treating enuresis ('bed-wetting') in children, behavioural treatment often appears to lead to a general overall improvement in their functioning, since these children often have numerous problems resulting from their 'symptoms' (eg children making fun of them, their mother getting angry with them, lower self-esteem) (Shwartz and Johnson, 1981).

2) The crux of Eysenck's (1952) review is how the effectiveness of

psychotherapy should be assessed. He uses Denker's criteria, namely: (i) return to work and ability to carry on well in economic ajustments for at least five years; (ii) complaint of no further or very slight difficulties; and (iii) making successful social adjustments.

These are all fairly tangible indicators of improvement, and even more so are the behaviour therapists' criteria that cure is achieved when patients no longer manifest the original maladaptive behaviour (eg the fear of spiders is eliminated). If these more stringent (or more easily measured) criteria of actual behaviour change are required before the therapist can be viewed as successful, then behaviour therapists *do* seem to be more effective than psychoanalysts or humanistic therapists (with cognitive approaches in between) (Rachman and Wilson, 1980, Shapiro and Shapiro, 1982).

But are those kinds of criteria necessarily appropriate to assessing 'cure' or improvement as applied to psychoanalysis? Surely, they are *not*.

Again, psychoanalytic therapists may answer the question 'does therapy work?', by saying it is a misleading question, like asking whether friendship 'works'. It is an activity that people take part in, which is important to them, affects, moves, even transforms them (Oatley, 1984).

But for Eysenck, if it cannot be empirically demonstrated that it has well-defined beneficial effects, then it is worthless. Because he is interested in comparing recovery rates (measured statistically), his assessment of the effects of therapy is purely *quantitative*, while psychoanalysts and those from other non-behavioural approaches (eg Rogers' client-centred therapy) are likely to be much more concerned with the *qualitative* aspects of therapy—*how* does it work, what is the nature of the therapeutic process, the role of the relationship between client and therapist, important qualities of the therapist, etc.

The point here is that there are different *kinds* of questions one can ask when trying to assess the effects of psychotherapy.

3)   Outcome studies in general indicate the effectiveness of *both*: (i) specific factors due to the *particular* form of therapy used; *and* (ii) some non-specific factors, the most important of which might well be the *relationship* with the therapist and the *expectation* of improvement (Oatley, 1984).

4)   To ask, 'Does therapy work?' or, 'Is one form of therapy more effective than another?' is to ask the wrong sorts of questions. According to Ryle (1975), there are two fundamental questions which need to be kept separate: (i) 'What kinds of patient can change in what kinds of ways through what kinds of therapy?' (research into *outcome*); and (ii) '*How* does therapy effect these changes?' (research into *process*). In a similar vein, Altrocchi suggests that we ask:

> What therapeutic techniques used by what kinds of therapists, under what conditions, produce what kinds of behaviour changes, in what recipients, with what other effects? (Altrocchi, 1980)

5)   Finally, psychotherapy:

> ... may not educate as well as schools; it may not produce goods and services as well as management science; it may not cure illnesses as well as medicine; but it reaches a part of life that nothing else touches as well. (Smith et al, 1980; quoted in Oatley, 1984)

REFERENCES AND FURTHER READING

Abrams, D., Wetherell, M., Cochrane, S., Hogg, M.A. & Turner, J.C. (1990) Knowing what to think by knowing who you are: Self-categorization and the nature of norm formation, conformity and group polarization. *British Journal of Social Psychology*, 29 (part 2), 97–119.

Abramson, L.Y. & Martin, D.J. (1981) Depression and the causal inference process. In J.H. Harvey, J. Ickes & R.F. Kidd (Eds.), *New directions in attitude research, Vol. 3*. Hillsdale, New Jersey: Lawrence Erlbaum Associates Inc.

Abramson, L.Y., Seligman, M.E.P. & Teasdale, J.D. (1978) Learned helplessness in humans: Critique and reformulation. *Journal of Abnormal Psychology*, 87, 49–74.

Adler, A. (1927) *The practice and theory of individual psychology*. New York: Harcourt Brace Jovanovich.

Adler, A. (1936) The neurotic's picture of the world. *International Journal of Individual Psychology*, 2, 3–10.

Adorno, T.W., Frenkel-Brunswick, E., Levinson, D.J. & Sanford, R.N. (1950) *The authoritarian personality*. New York: Harper & Row.

Ainsworth, M.D.S., Bell, S.M.V, & Stayton, D.J. (1971) Individual differences in strange-situation behaviour of one-year-olds. In H.R. Schaffer (Ed.), *The origins of human social relations*. New York: Academic Press.

Ainsworth, M.D.S., Blehar, M C, Waters, E. & Wall, S. (1978) *Patterns of attachment: A psychological study of the strange situation*. Hillsdale, New Jersey: Lawrence Erlbaum Associates Inc.

Aitchison, J. (1983) *The articulate mammal* (2nd ed.) London: Hutchinson.

Azjen, I. & Fishbein, M. (1977) Attitude–behaviour relations: A theoretical analysis and review of empirical research. *Psychological Bulletin*, 84, 888–918.

Alexander, F. & French, T.M. (1946) *Psychoanalytic therapy*. New York: Ronald Press.

Allport, D.A. (1980a) Patterns and actions: Cognitive mechanisms are content specific. In G. Claxton (Ed.), *Cognitive psychology: New directions*. London: Routlege, Kegan, Paul.

Allport, D.A. (1980b) Attention and performance: In G. Claxton (Ed.), *Cognitive psychology: New directions*. London: Routledge, Kegan, Paul.

Allport, D.A., Antonis, B. & Reynolds, P. (1972) On the division of attention: A disproof of the single channel hypothesis. *Quarterly Journal of Experimental Psychology*, 24, 225–35.

Allport, F.H. (1924) *Social psychology*. Boston: Houghton Mifflin.

Allport, G.W. (1954) *The nature of prejudice*. Reading, Massachusetts: Addison-Wesley.

Allport, G.W. (1955) *Becoming— basic considerations for a psychology of personality*. New Haven, Connecticut: Yale University Press.

Allport, G.W. (1961) *Pattern and growth in personality*. New York: Holt Rinehart Winston.

Allport, G.W. & Odbert, H.S. (1935) Attitudes. In C M. Murchison (Ed.), *Handbook of social psychology*. Clark University Press.

Allport, G.W. & Odbert, H.S. (1936) Trait names: A psycho-lexical study. *Psychological Monographs: General and Applied*, 47, (Whole No. 211).

Allport, G.W. & Pettigrew, T.F. (1957) Cultural influences on the perception of movement: The trapezoidal illusion among Zulus. *Journal of Abnormal and Social Psychology*, 55, 104–13.

Allport, G.W., Vernon, P.G. & Lindzey, G, (1951) *Study of values*. Boston: Houghton-Mifflin.

Allyon, J. & Azrin, N. (1968) *The token economy*. New York: Appleton-Century-Crofts.

Altman, I. & Taylor, D.A. (1973) Social penetration: The development of interpersonal relationships. New York: Holt, Rinehart & Winston.

Altrocchi, J. (1980) *Abnormal behaviour*. New York: Harcourt Brace Jovanovich.

American Psychiatric Association (1980) *Diagnostic and statistical manual of mental disorders* (3rd ed.). Washington, DC: American Psychiatric Association.

American Psychiatric Association (1987) Diagnostic and statistical manual of mental disorders (3rd ed. revised). Washington, DC: American Psychiatric Association.

Anderson, A. (1978) 'Old' is not a four-letter word. *Across the Board*, May.

Anderson, J.R. (1983) *The architecure of cognition* (2nd ed.). Cambridge, Massachusetts: Harvard University Press.

Anderson, J.R. (1985) *Cognitive psychology and its implications*. New York: Freeman.

Anderson, J.R. & Reder, L. (1979) An elaborate processing explanation of depth of processing. In L.S. Cermak & F.I.M. Craik (Eds.), *Levels of processing in human memory*. Hillsdale, New Jersey: Lawrence Erlbaum Associates Inc.

Anderson, N.H. (1974) Cognitive algebra: Integration theory applied to social attribution. In L. Berkowitz (Ed.), *Advances in experimental social psychology, Vol. 7*. New York: Academic Press.

Annett, M. (1991) Laterality and cerebral dominance. *Journal of Child Psychology and Psychiatry*, 32(2), 219–32.

Antaki, C. (1984) Core concepts in attribution theory. In J. Nicholson & H. Beloff (Eds.), *Psychology Survey 5*. Leicester: British Psychological Society.

Archer, J. & Lloyd, B. (1985) *Sex and gender*. New York: Cambridge University Press.

Argyle, M. (1989) *The social psychology of work* (2nd ed.). Harmondsworth, Middlesex: Penguin.

Argyle, M. & Dean, J. (1965) Eye contact, distance and affiliation. *Sociometry*, 28, 289–364.

Argyle, M. & Henderson, M. (1984) The rules of friendship. *Journal of Social and Personal Relationships*, 1, 211–37.

Arlin, P.K. (1975) Cognitive development in adulthood: A fifth stage? *Developmental Psychology*, 11, 602–6.

Arlin, P.K. (1977) Piagetian operations in problem finding. *Developmental Psychology*, 13, 297–8.

Armsby, R.E. (1971) A re-examination of the development of moral judgement in children. *Child Development*, 42, 1241–8.

Aronfreed, J. (1963) The effects of experimental socialization: para digms upon two moral responses to transgression. *Journal of Abnormal & Social Psychology*, 66, 437–8.

Aronfreed, J. (1969) The concept of internalization. In D.A. Goslin (Ed.), *Handbook of socialization theory and research*. Chicago: Rand McNally.

Aronfreed, J. & Reber, A. (1965) Internalised behavioural suppression and the timing of social punishment. *Journal of Personality & Social Psychology*, 1, 3–17.

Aronson, E. (1968) The process of dissonance. In N. Warren &

M. Jahoda (Eds.), *Attitudes*. Harmondsworth, Middlesex: Penguin.

Aronson, E. (1980) *The social animal* (3rd. ed.). San Fransisco: W.H. Freeman.

Aronson, E. (1988) *The social animal* (5th ed.). New York: Freeman.

Aronson, E. & Carlsmith, J.M. (1963) Effect of the severity of threat on the devaluation of forbidden behaviour. *Journal of Abnormal and Social Psychology*, 6, 584–8.

Aronson, E. & Linder, D. (1965) Gain and loss of esteem as determinants of interpersonal attractiveness. *Journal of Experimental & Social Psychology*, 1, 156–71.

Aronson, E. & Mills, J. (1959) The effect of severity of initiation on liking for a group. *Journal of Abnormal and Social Psychology*, 59, 177–81.

Aronson, E. & Osherow, N. (1980) Co-operation, prosocial behaviour and academic performance: Experiments in the desegregated classroom. In L. Bickman (Ed.), *Applied social psychology annual, Vol. 1*. Beverly Hills, California: Sage Publications.

Aronson, E., Willerman, B. & Floyd, J. (1966) The effect of a pratfall on increasing interpersonal attractiveness. *Psychonomic Science*, 4, 227–8.

Aronson, E., Bridgeman, D.L. & Geffner, R. (1978) The effects of a cooperative classroom structure on student behaviour and attitudes. In D. Bar-Tal & L. Saxe (Eds.), *Social psychology of education*. New York: Wiley.

Asch, S.E. (1946) Forming impressions of personality. *Journal of Abnormal and Social Psychology*, 4, 258–90

Asch, S.E. (1952) *Social psychology*. Englewood Cliffs, New Jersey: Prentice Hall.

Asch, S.E. (1951) Effect of group pressure upon the modification and distortion of judgements. In H. Guetzkow (Ed.), *Groups, leadership and men*. Pittsburg, Pennsylvania: Carnegie Press.

Asch, S.E. (1956) Studies of independence and submission to group pressure: 1: A minority of one against a unanimous majority. *Psychological Monographs*, 70, (9) (Whole No. 416).

Aserinsky, E. & Kleitman, N. (1953) Regularly occurring periods of eye mobility and concomitant phenomena during sleep. *Science*, 118, 273.

Atchley, R.C. (1982) Retirement: leaving the world of work. *Annals of the American Academy of Political and Social Science*, 464, 120–31.

Atchley, R.C. (1985) *Social forces and ageing: An introduction to social gerontology*. Belmont, California: Wadsworth.

Atkinson, R.C. & Shiffrin, R.M. (1968) Human memory: A proposed system and its control processes. In K.W. Spence & J.T. Spence (Eds.), *The psychology of learning & motivation, Vol. 2*. London: Academic Press.

Atkinson, R.C. & Shiffrin, R.M. (1971) The control of short-term memory. *Scientific American*, 224, 82–90.

Atkinson, R.L., Atkinson, R.C., Smith, E.E. & Bem, D.J. (1990) *Introduction to Psychology* (10th ed.). New York: Harcourt Brace Jovanovich.

Attneave, F. (1954) Some informational aspects of visual perception. *Psychological Review*, 61, 183–93.

Baddeley, A.D. (1966) The influence of acoustic and semantic similarity on long term memory for word sequences. *Quarterly Journal of Experimental Psychology*, 18, 302–9.

Baddeley, A.D. (1978) The trouble with levels: A re-examination of Craik and Lockharts' "Framework for Memory Research". *Psychological Review*, 85, 139–52.

Baddeley, A.D. (1981) The concept of working memory: A view of its current state and probable future development. *Cognition*, 10, 17–23.

Baddeley, A.D. (1982) Domains of recollection. *Psychological Review*, 89, 708–29.

Baddeley, A.D. (1986) *Working memory*. Oxford: Oxford University Press.

Baddeley, A.D. (1990) *Human memory*. Hove, East Sussex: Lawrence Erlbaum Associates Ltd.

Baddeley, A.D. & Hitch, G. (1974) Working memory. In G.A. Bower (Ed.), *Recent advances in learning and motivation, Vol. 8*. New York: Academic Press.

Baddeley, A.D. & Warrington, E.H. (1970) Amnesia and the distinction between long- and short-term memory. *Journal of Verbal Learning & Verbal Behaviour*, 9, 176–89.

Baer, D.M. & Sherman, J.A. (1964) Reinforcement control of generalized imitation in young children. *Journal of Experimental Child Psychology*, 1, 37–49.

Baerends, G.P. & Kruijt, J.P. (1973) *Constraints on learning: Limitations and predispositions*. London: Academic Press.

Bailey, C.L. (1979) Mental illness—a logical misrepresentation? *Nursing Times*, May, 761–2.

Bandura, A. (1965) Influence of model's reinforcement contingencies on the acquisition of imitative responses. *Journal of Personality and Social Psychology*, 1, 589–95.

Bandura, A. (1973) *Aggression: A social learning analysis*. London: Prentice Hall.

Bandura, A. (1974) Behaviour theory and models of man. *American Psychologist*, 29, 859–69.

Bandura, A. (1977) Self-efficacy: Toward a unifying theory of behaviour change. *Psychological Review*, 84, 191–215.

Bandura, A. & Walters, R. (1959) *Social learning and personality development*. New York: Holt.

Bandura, A. & Walters, R. (1963) *Adolescent aggression*. New York: Ronald Press.

Bandura, A., Ross, D. & Ross, S.A. (1963) Imitation of film-mediated aggressive models. *Journal of Abnormal and Social Psychology*, 66, 3–11.

Bannister, D. (1963) The genesis of schizophrenic thought disorder: A serial invalidation hypothesis. *British Journal of Psychiatry*, 109, 680–8.

Bannister, D. (1965) The genesis of schizophrenic thought disorder: A retest of the serial invalidation hypothesis. *British Journal of Psychiatry*, 111, 377–82.

Bannister, D. & Agnew, J. (1976) The child's construing of self. In J.K. Coal & A.W. Landfield (Eds.), *Nebraska Symposium on Motivation*. Lincoln, Nebraska: University of Nebraska Press.

Bannister, D. & Fransella, F. (1967) *A grid test of schizophrenic thought disorder*. Barnstaple: Psychological Test Publications.

Bannister, D. & Mair, M.J.M. (1968) *The evaluation of personal constructs*. London: Academic Press.

Bannister, D., Salmon, P. & Leiberman, D.M. (1964) Diagnosis—treatment relationships in psychiatry: a statistical analysis. *British Journal of Psychiatry*, 110, 726–32.

Barber, T.X. (1969) *Hypnosis: A scientific approach*. New York: Van Nostrand.

Barfield, R.E. & Morgan, J.N. (1978) Trends in satisfaction with retirement. *Gerontologist*, 18, 19–23.

Baron, R.A. (1977) *Human aggression*. New York: Plenum.

Baron, R.A. & Byrne, D. (1991) *Social psychology* (6th ed.). Boston: Allyn and Bacon.

Barrett, M.D. (1986) Early semantic representations and early word usage. In S.A. Kuczaj & M.D. Barrett (Eds.), *The development of word meaning*. New York: Springer Verlag.

Barrett, M. (1989) Early language development. In A. Slater & G. Bremmer (Eds.), *Infant development*. Hove, East Sussex: Lawrence Erlbaum Associates Ltd.

Bar-Tal, D. & Saxe, L. (1976) Perception of similarity and dissimilarity in attractive couples and individuals. *Journal of Personality and Social Psychology*, 33, 772–81.

Bartlett, F.C. (1932) *Remembering*. Cambridge: Cambridge University Press.

Bates, E., Benigni, L., Bretherton, I., Camaioni, L. & Volterra, V. (1979) *The emergence of symbols: Cognition and communication in infancy*. New York: Academic Press.

Bateson, P.P.G. (1964) Effect of similarity between rearing and testing conditions on chicks' following and avoidance responses. *Journal of Comparative and Physiological Psychology*, 57, 100–3.

Batson, C.D. & Oleson, K.C. (1991) Current status of the empathy–altruism hypothesis. In M.S. Clark (Ed.), *Prosocial behaviour, review of personality and social psychology, 12*. Newbury Park, California: Sage Publications.

Baumrind, D. (1964) Some thoughts on ethics of research: after reading Milgram's behavioural study of obedience. *American Psychologist, 19*, 421–3.

Bayley, N. (1969) *Bayley scale of infant development*. New York: Psychological Corporation.

Beaumont, J.G. (1988) *Understanding neuropsychology*. Oxford: Blackwell.

Beck, A.T. (1963) Thinking and depression. *Archives of General Psychiatry, 9*, 324–33.

Bee, H. (1989) *The developing child* (5th ed.). New York: Harper & Row.

Bee, H., Barnard, K.E., Eyres, S.J., Gray, C.A., Hammond, M.A., Spietz, A.L., Snyder, C. & Clark B. (1982) Prediction of IQ and language skill from perinatal status, child performance, family characteristics and mother–infant interaction. *Child Development, 53*, 1135–56.

Bekerian, D.A. & Bowers, J.M. (1983) Eye-witness testimony: Were we misled? *Journal of Experimental Psychology, Learning, Memory, and Cognition, 9*, 139–45.

Bell, S. (1970) The development of the concept of object as related to infant–mother attachment. *Child Development, 41*, 291–311.

Beloff, J. (1973) *Psychological sciences*. London: Staples.

Belson, W.A. (1978) *Television violence and the adolescent boy*. Farnborough: Saxon House.

Bem, D.J. (1965) An experimental analysis of self-persuasion. *Journal of Experimental and Social Psychology, 1*, 199–218.

Bem, D.J. (1967) Self-perception: An alternative interpretation of cognitive dissonance phenomena. *Psychological Review, 74*, 183–200.

Bem, D.J. (1970) *Beliefs, attitudes and human affairs*. Belmont, California: Brooks Cole.

Bem, S.L. (1974) The measurement of psychological androgyny. *Journal of Consulting and Clinical Psychology, 42* (2), 155–62.

Bem, D.J. & Allen, A. (1974) On predicting some of the people some of the time: A search for cross-situational consistencies in behaviour. *Psychological Review, 81*, 506–20.

Benedict, R. (1934) *Patterns of culture*. Boston: Houghton Mifflin.

Benedict, R. (1954) Continuities and discontinuities in cultural conditioning. In W.E. Martin & C.B. Stendler (Eds.), *Readings in child development*. New York: Harcourt Brace Jovanovich.

Bennett-Levy, J. & Marteau, T. (1984) Fear of animals: What is prepared. *British Journal of Psychology, 75*, 37–42.

Benson, P.L., Karabenick, S.A. & Lerner, R.M. (1976) Pretty pleases: The effects of physical attractiveness, race and sex on receiving help. *Journal of Experimental and Social Psychology, 12*, 409–15.

Bereiter, C. & Engelman, S. (1966) *Teaching disadvantaged children in pre-school*. Englewood Cliffs, New Jersey: Prentice Hall.

Bergin, A.E. (1971) The evaluation of therapeutic outcomes. In A. Bergin & S.L. Garfield (Eds.), *Handbook of psychotherapy and behaviour change: An empirical analysis*. New York: Wiley.

Bergin, A.E. & Lambert, M.J. (1978) The evaluation of therapeutic outcomes. In A.E. Bergin & S.L. Garfield (Eds.), *Handbook of psychotherapy and behaviour change (2nd ed.): An empirical analysis*. New York: Wiley.

Berko, J. (1958) The child's learning of English morphology. *Word, 14*, 150–77.

Berkowitz, L. (1962) *Aggression: A social psychological analysis*. New York: McGraw Hill.

Berkowitz, L. (1968) Impulse, aggression and the gun. *Psychology Today, September*, 18–22.

Berkowitz, L. (1969) The frustration–aggression hypothesis revisited. In L. Berkowitz (Ed.), *Roots of aggression: A re-examination of the frustration–aggression hypothesis*. New York: Atherton Press.

Berkowitz, L. & La Page, A. (1967) Weapons as aggression-eliciting stimuli. *Journal of Personality and Social Psychology, 7*, 202–7.

Berne, E. (1968) *Games people play*. Harmondsworth, Middlesex: Penguin.

Bernstein, B. (1961) Social class and linguistic development. In A.H. Halsey, J. Flaud & C.A. Anderson (Eds.), *Education, economy and society*. London: Collier–Macmillan Ltd.

Berscheid, E. & Walster, E.M. (1974) Physical attractiveness. In L. Berkowitz (Ed.), *Advances in experimental social psychology, Vol. 7*. New York: Academic Press.

Berscheid, E. & Walster, E. (1978) *Interpersonal attraction*. Reading, Massachusetts: Adison-Wesley.

Berscheid, E., Dion, K., Hatfield, E. & Walster, G.W. (1971) Physical attractiveness and dating choice: A test of the matching hypothesis. *Journal of Experimental and Social Psychology, 7*, 173–89.

Berthenthal, B.I., Proffit, D.R. & Cutting, J.E. (1984) Infant sensitivity to figural coherence in biomechanical motions. *Journal of Experimental Child Psychology, 37*, 1072–80.

Berthenthal, B.I., Proffitt, D.R., Spetner, N.B. & Thomas, M.A. (1985) The development of infant sensitivity to biomechanical motions. *Child Development, 56*, 531–43.

Bickman, L. (1974) The social power of a uniform. *Journal of Applied Social Psychology, 1*, 47–61.

Bierhoff, H.W. & Klein, R. (1988) Prosocial behaviour. In M. Hewstone, W. Stroebe, J.P. Codol & G.M. Stephenson (Eds.), *Introduction to social psychology*. Oxford: Basil Blackwell.

Billig, M. & Tajfel, H. (1973) Social categorization and similarity in intergroup behaviour. *European Journal of Social Psychology, 3*, 27–52.

Bishop, D.V.M. (1977) The P scale and psychosis. *Journal of Abnormal Psychology, 86*, 127–34.

Blakemore, C. (1988) *The mind machine*. London: BBC Publications.

Blakemore, C. & Cooper, G.F. (1970) Development of the brain depends on the visual environment. *Nature, 228*, 477–8.

Blank, M. & Solomon, F. (1968) A tutorial language programme to develop abstract thinking in socially disadvantaged pre-school children. *Child Development, 39*, 379–89.

Blasi, A. (1980) Bridging moral cognition and moral action: A critical review of the literature. *Psychological Bulletin, 88*, 1–45.

Blau, P.M. (1964) *Exchange and power in social life*. New York: John Wiley & Sons.

Bleuler, E. (1911) *Dementia praecox or the group of schizophrenias*. (J. Avikin, trans.). New York: International University Press.

Block, N.J. & Dworkin, G. (1974) I.Q.: Heritability and inequality. *Philosophy and Public Affairs, 3*, 331–407.

Bloom, B.S. (1964) *Stability and change in human characteristics*. New York: Harcourt Brace Jovanovich.

Bloom, L. (1973) *One word at a time*. The Hague: Mouton.

Blos, P. (1967) The second individuation process of adolescence. *The psychoanalytic study of the child, Vol. 22*. New York: International University Press.

Boas, F. (1927) *Primitive art*. Oslo: Institute for Sammenlignende Kulturforskning.

Boden, M. (1972) *Purposive explanation in psychology*. Cambridge, Massachusetts: Harvard University Press.

Boden, M. (1987a) *Artificial intelligence and natural man* (2nd ed.). Cambridge, Massachusetts: Harvard University Press.

Boden, M. (1987b) Artificial intelligence. In R. Gregory (Ed.), *Oxford companion to the mind*. Oxford: Oxford University Press.

Bodmer, W.F. (1972) Race and I.Q.: The genetic background. In K. Richardson & D. Spears (Eds.), *Race, culture and intelligence*. Harmondsworth, Middlesex: Penguin.

Bogardus, E.S. (1925) Measuring social distance. *Journal of Applied Sociology, 9*, 299–308.

Bogdonoff, M.D., Klein, R.F., Estes, E.H., Shaw, D.M. & Back, K. (1961) The modifying effect of conforming behaviour upon lipid responses accompanying CNS arousal. *Clinical Research, 9*, 135.

Bogen, J.E. (1969) The other side of the brain. In R. Ornstein (Ed.), *The psychology of consciousness* (2nd ed., revised 1986). Harmondsworth, Middlesex: Penguin.

Bolles, R.C. (1980) Ethological learning theory. In G.M. Gazda &

R.J. Corsini (Eds.), *Theories of learning: A comparative approach.* Itaska, Illinois: Free Press.

Booth, T. (1975) *Growing up in society.* London: Methuen.

Borke, H. (1975) Piaget's mountains revisited: Changes in the egocentric landscape. *Developmental Psychology, 11*, 240–3.

Bornstein, M.H. (1976) Infants are trichromats. *Journal of Experimental Child Psychology, 19*, 401–19.

Bornstein, M.H. (1988) Perceptual development across the life cycle. In M.H. Bornstein & M.E. Lamb (Eds.), *Perceptual, cognitive and linguistic development.* Hove, East Sussex: Lawrence Erlbaum Associates Ltd.

Botwinick, J. (1978) *Aging and behaviour* (2nd ed.). New York: Springer.

Bouchard, T.J. & McGue, M. (1981) Familial studies of intelligence: A review. *Science, 22*, 1055–9.

Bousfield, W.A. (1953) The occurrence of clustering in the recall of randomly arranged associates. *Journal of General Psychology, 49*, 229–40.

Bower, G.H. (1972) Mental imagery and associative learning. In L. Gregg (Ed.), *Cognition in learning and memory.* New York: Wiley.

Bower, G.H. (1975) Cognitive psychology: An introduction. In W. Estes (Ed.), *Handbook of learning and cognitive processes, Vol 1.* Hillsdale, New Jersey: Lawrence Erlbaum Associates Inc.

Bower, G.H. & Karlin, M.B. (1974) Depth of processing pictures of faces and recognition memory. *Journal of Experimental Psychology, 103*, 751–7.

Bower, G.H., Clark, M., Lesgold, A. & Winzenz, D. (1969) Hierarchical retrieval schemes in recall of categorized word lists. *Journal of Verbal Learning and Verbal Behaviour, 8*, 323–43.

Bower, G.H., Black, J.B. & Turner, T.J. (1979) Scripts in memory for text. *Cognitive Psychology, 11*, 177–220.

Bower, T.G.R. (1966) The visual world of infants. *Scientific American, 215* (6), 80–92.

Bower, T.G.R. (1971) The object in the world of the infant. *Scientific American, 225* (4), 30–8.

Bower, T.G.R. (1976) Repetitive processes in child development. *Scientific American, 235* (5), 38–47.

Bower, T.G.R. (1979) *Human development.* San Francisco: W.H. Freeman.

Bower, T.G.R., Broughton, J.M. & Moore, M.K. (1970) Infant responses to approaching objects: An indicator of response to distal variables. *Perception and Psychophysics, 9*, 193–6.

Bower, T.G.R. & Wishart, J.G. (1972) The effects of motor skill on object permanence. *Cognition, 1* (2), 28–35.

Bowers, K. (1973) Situationism in psychology: An analysis and critique. *Psychological Review, 80*, 307–36.

Bowlby, J. (1946) *Forty-four juvenile thieves.* London: Balliére, Tindall and Cox.

Bowlby, J. (1951) *Maternal care and mental health.* Geneva: World Health Organization.

Bowlby, J. (1969) *Attachment and loss. Vol. 1: Attachment.* Harmondsworth, Middlesex: Penguin.

Bowlby, J. (1973) *Attachment and loss. Vol. 2: Separation.* Harmondsworth, Middlesex: Penguin.

Brady, J.V. (1958) Ulcers in 'executive monkeys'. *Scientific American, 199*, 95–100.

Brainerd, C.J. (1978) Learning research and Piagetian theory. In L. Siegel & C.J. Brainerd (Eds.), *Alternatives to Piaget: Critical essays on the theory.* New York: Academic Press.

Brainerd, C.J. (1983) Modifiability of cognitive development. In S. Meadows (Ed.), *Development thinking.* London: Methuen.

Bransford, J.D., Franks, J.J., Morris, C.D. & Stein, B.S. (1979) Some general constraints on learning and memory research. In L.S. Cerack & F.I.M. Craik (Eds.), *Levels of processing in human memory.* Hillsdale, New Jersey: Lawrence Erlbaum Associates Inc.

Brehm, J.W. (1956) Post-decision changes in the desirability of alternatives. *Journal of Abnormal and Social Psychology, 52*, 384–9.

Brehm, J.W. (1966) *Theory of psychological reactance.* New York: Academic Press.

Brehm, J.W. & Cohen, A.R. (1962) *Explorations in cognitive dissonance.* New York: Wiley.

British Broadcasting Corporation (1972) *Violence on television: Programme content and viewer perceptions.* London: BBC Publications.

British Psychological Society (1978) Ethical principles for research with human subjects. *Bulletin of the British Psychological Society, 31*, 48–9.

British Psychological Society (1983) *Guidelines for the professional practice of clinical psychology.* Leicester: British Psychological Society.

British Psychological Society (1985) A code of conduct for psychologists. *Bulletin of the British Psychological Society, 38*, 41–3.

British Psychological Society (1990) Ethical principles for conducting research with human participants. *The Psychologist, 3* (6), June.

British Psychological Society and Committee of the Experimental Psychological Society (1985) *Guidelines for the use of animals in research.* Leicester: British Psychological Society.

Broadbent, D.E. (1954) The role of auditory localization in attention and memory span. *Journal of Experimental Psychology, 47*, 191–6.

Broadbent, D.E. (1958) *Perception and Communication.* London: Pergamon.

Broadbent, D.E. (1961) *Behaviour.* London: Eyre & Spottiswoode.

Brody, E.B. & Brody, N. (1976) *Intelligence: Nature, determinants and consequences.* New York: Academic Press.

Bromley, D.B. (1988) *Human ageing: An introduction to gerontology* (3rd ed.). Harmondsworth, Middlesex: Penguin.

Bronfenbrenner, U. (1960) Freudian theories of identification and their derivatives. *Child Development, 31*, 15–40.

Brown, H. (1985) *People, groups and society.* Milton Keynes: Open University Press.

Brown, J.A.C. (1961) *Freud and the post-Freudians.* Harmondsworth, Middlesex: Penguin.

Brown, R. (1958) *Words and things.* Glencoe, Illinois: Free Press.

Brown, R. (1986) *Social psychology* (2nd ed.). New York: Free Press.

Brown, R. (1988) Intergroup relations. In M. Hewstone, W. Stroebe, J.P. Codol & G.M. Stephenson (Eds.), *Introduction to social psychology.* Oxford: Basil Blackwell.

Brown, R.J. & Turner, J.C. (1981) Interpersonal and intergroup behaviour. In J.C. Turner & H. Giles (Eds.), *Intergroup behaviour.* Oxford: Basil Blackwell.

Bruce, V. & Green, P.R. (1990) *Visual perception* (2nd ed.). Hove, East Sussex: Lawrence Erlbaum Associates Ltd.

Bruner, J.S. (1966) On the conservation of liquids. In J.S. Bruner, R.R. Olver & P.M. Greenfield (Eds.), *Studies in cognitive growth.* New York: Wiley.

Bruner, J.S. (1966) *Towards a theory of instruction.* Cambridge, Massachussets: Harvard University Press.

Bruner, J.S. (1975) The ontogenesis of speech acts. *Journal of Child Language, 2*, 1–21.

Bruner, J.S. (1983) *Child's talk: Learning to use language.* Oxford: Oxford University Press.

Bruner, J.S. & Goodman, C.C. (1947) Value and need as organizing factors in perception. *Journal of Abnormal and Social Psychology, 42*, 33–44.

Bruner, J.S. & Kenney, H. (1966) *The development of the concepts of order and proportion in children.* New York: Wiley.

Bruner, J.S. & Postman, L. (1949) On the perception of incongruity: A paradigm. *Journal of Personality, 18*, 206–23.

Bruner, J.S. & Tagiuri, R. (1954) The perception of people. In G. Lindzey (Ed.), *Handbook of social psychology, Vol. 2.* Reading, Massachusetts: Addison-Wesley.

Brunswick, E. (1955) Representative design and probabilistic theory in a functional psychology. *Psychological Review, 62*, 193–217.

Brunswick, E. (1956) *Perception and the representative design of psychological experiments.* Berkeley, California: University of

California Press.

Burgio, L.D., Whitman, T.I. & Reid, D.H. (1983) A participative management approach for improving direct-care staff performance in an institutional setting. *Journal of Applied Behaviour Analysis*, 16, 37–52.

Burks, B.S. (1928) The relative influence of nature and nurture upon mental development: A comparative study of foster parent–foster child resemblance and true parent–true child resemblance. *Yearbook of the National Society for the Study of Education*, 27, 219–316.

Burns, R.B. & Dobson, C.B. (1984) *Introductory psychology*. Lancaster: MTP Press.

Burt, C.L. (1966) The genetic determination of differences in intelligence: A study of monozygotic twins reared together and apart. *British Journal of Psychology*, 57, 137–53.

Burton, R.V. (1963) Generality of honesty reconsidered. *Psychological Review*, 70, 481–99.

Buss, A.H. (1961) *The psychology of aggression*. New York: Wiley.

Buss, A.H. (1963) Physical aggression in relation to different frustrations. *Journal of Abnormal and Social Psychology*, 67, 1–7.

Buss, A.H. (1966) Instrumentality of aggression, feedback and frustration and determinants of physical aggression. *Journal of Personality and Social Psychology*, 3, 153–62.

Butler, R.A. (1954) Curiosity in monkeys. *Scientific American*, February, 70–5.

Byrne, D. (1971) *The attraction paradigm*. New York: Academic Press.

Byrne, D. & Buehler, J.A. (1965) A note on the influence of propinquity upon acquaintanceships. *Journal of Abnormal and Social Psychology*, 51, 147–8.

Bryne, D. & Griffitt, W. (1973) Interpersonal attraction. *Annual Review of Psychology*, 24, 317–36.

Campbell, D.T. (1967) Stereotypes and the perception of group differences. *American Psychologist*, 22, 817–29.

Campos. J.J., Langer, A. & Krowitz, A. (1970) Cardiac responses on the cliff in pre-locomotor human infants. *Science*, 170, 196–7.

Cannon, W.B. (1927) The James–Lange theory of emotions: A critical examination and an alternative. *American Journal of Psychology*, 39, 106–24.

Cannon. W.B. (1929) *Bodily changes in pain, hunger, fear and rage*. New York: Appleton-Century-Crofts.

Cannon, W.B. & Washburn, A.L. (1912) An explanation of hunger. *American Journal of Psychology*, 29, 441–54.

Carlsmith, J.M., Collins, B.E. & Helmreich, R.L. (1966) Studies in forced compliance: 1. The effect of pressure for compliance on attitude change produced by face-to-face role playing and anonymous essay writing. *Journal of Personality and Social Psychology*, 4, 1–13.

Carmichael, L., Hogan, P. & Walter, A. (1932) An experimental study of the effect of language on the reproduction of visually perceived forms. *Journal of Experimental Psychology*, 15, 1–22.

Carrol, D.W. (1986) *Psychology of language*. Monterey, California: Brooks/Cole Publishing Co.

Carroll, J.B. & Casagrande, J.B. (1958) The function of language classifications in behaviour. In E.E. Maccoby, T.M. Newcombe & E.L. Hartley (Eds.), *Readings in social psychology* (3rd ed.). New York: Holt, Rinehart & Winston.

Cattell, R.B. (1963) Theory of fluid and crystallized intelligence: A critical experiment. *Journal of Educational Psychology*, 54, 1–22.

Cattell, R.B. (1965) *The scientific analysis of personality*. Harmondsworth, Middlesex: Penguin.

Cautela, J.R. (1967) Covert sensitization. *Psychology Reports*, 20, 459–68.

Cernoch, J.M. & Porter, R.H. (1985) Recognition of maternal axillary odors by infants. *Child Development*, 56, 1593–8.

Chaiken, S. (1987) The heuristic model of persuasion. In M.P. Zanna, J.M. Olsen & C.P. Herman (Eds.), *Social influence: The Ontario symposium*, Vol. 5. Hillsdale, New Jersey: Lawrence Erlbaum Associates Inc.

Chaikin, A.L. & Darley, J.M. (1973) Victim or perpetrator? Defensive attribution of responsibility and the need for order and justice. *Journal of Personality and Social Psychology*, 25, 268–75.

Chase, W.G. & Simon, H.A. (1973) Perception in chess. *Cognitive Psychology*, 4, 55–81.

Cheng, P.W. (1985) Restructuring versus automaticity: Alternative accounts of skill acquisition. *Psychological Review*, 92, 414–23.

Cherry, E.C. (1953) Some experiments on the recognition of speech with one and two ears. *Journal of the Acoustical Society of America*, 25, 975–9.

Chomsky, N. (1957) *Syntactic structures*. The Hague: Mouton.

Chomsky, N. (1959) Review of Skinner's *Verbal Behaviour*. *Language*, 35, 26–58.

Chomsky, N. (1965) *Aspects of the theory of syntax*. Cambridge, Massachusetts: MIT Press.

Chomsky, N. (1968) *Language and mind*. New York: Harcourt Brace Jovanovich.

Chomsky, N. (1979) *Language and responsibility*. Sussex: Harvester Press.

Chapanis, N.P. & Chapanis, A. (1964) Cognitive dissonance—5 years later. *Psychological Bulletin*, 61 (1), 1–22.

Clare, A. (1976) What is schizophrenia? *New Society*, May 20, 410–12.

Clare, A. (1980) *Psychiatry in dissent*. London: Tavistock.

Claridge, G.S. (1967) *Personality and arousal*. Oxford: Pergamon Press.

Claridge, G.S. & Chappa, H.J. (1973) Psychoticism: A study of its biological basis in normal subjects. *British Journal of Social and Clinical Psychology*, 12, 175–87.

Clarke, A.M. & Clarke, A.D.B. (1976) *Early experience: Myth and evidence*. London: Open Books.

Clarke, P.R.F. (1975) The medical model defended. *New Society*, January 9, 64–5.

Clarke, R. (1979) Assessment in psychiatric hospitals. *Nursing Times*, April 5, 590–2.

Clarke-Stewart, K.A. (1973) Interactions between mothers and their young children: Characteristics and consequences. *Monograph of the Society for Research into Child Development*, 38 (6–7, Serial No. 153).

Clarke-Stewart, K.A. (1978) And daddy makes three: The father's impact on mother and young child. *Child Development*, 49, 446–78.

Clift, S.M. (1984) Should we still teach Freud? *Psychology Teaching*, December, 8–14.

Cochrane, R. (1974) Circadian variations in mental efficiency. In W.P. Colquhoun (Ed.), *Biological rhythms and human performance*. London: Academic Press.

Cohen, G. (1975) Cerebral apartheid: A fanciful notion? *New Behaviour*, 18, 458–61.

Cohen, G. (1986) Everyday memory. In G. Cohen, M.W. Eysenck & M.E. Le Voi (Eds.), *Memory: A cognitive approach*. Milton Keynes: Open University Press.

Cohen, G. (1990) Memory. In I. Roth (Ed.), *Introduction to psychology*, Vol. 2. Hove, E.Sussex/Milton Keynes: Open University/Lawrence Erlbaum Associates Ltd.

Cohen, N.J. & Squire, L.R. (1980) Preserved learning and retention of pattern-analyzing skills in amnesia: Dissociation of knowing how from knowing that. *Science*, 210, 207–10.

Colman, A.M. (1987) *Facts, fallacies and frauds in psychology*. London: Unwin Hyman.

Coleman, J.C. (1980) *The nature of adolescence*. London: Methuen.

Coleman, J.C. & Hendry, L. (1990) *The nature of adolescence* (2nd ed.). London: Routledge.

Collins, A.M. & Loftus, E.F. (1975) A spreading-activation theory of semantic processing. *Psychological Review*, 82, 407–28.

Collins, A.M. & Quillian, M. (1969) Retrieval time for semantic memory. *Journal of Verbal Learning and Verbal Behaviour*, 8, 240–7.

Condry, J. & Condry, S. (1976) Sex differences: A study in the eye of the beholder. *Child Development*, *47*, 812–19.

Conrad, C. (1972) Cognitive economy in semantic memory. *Journal of Experimental Psychology*, *92*, 148–54.

Conrad, R. (1963) Acoustic confusions and memory span for words. *Nature*, *197*, 1029–30.

Conrad, R. (1964) Acoustic confusion in immediate memory. *British Journal of Psychology*, *55*, 75–84.

Constanzo, P.R., Coie, J.D., Grumet, J.F. & Farnill, D. (1973) Re-examination of the effects of intent and consequence on children's moral judgements. *Child Development*, *44*, 154–61.

Cook, M. (1971) *Interpersonal perception*. Harmondsworth, Middlesex: Penguin.

Cook, S.W. & Selltiz, C.A. A multiple indicator approach to attitude measurement. *Psychological Bulletin*, *62*, 36–55.

Cooley, C.H. (1902) *Human nature and social order*. New York: Shocken.

Coolican, H. (1990) *Research methods and statistics in psychology*. Sevenoaks: Hodder & Stoughton.

Coon, D. (1983) *Introduction to psychology* (3rd ed.). St Paul, Minnesota: West Publishing Co.

Cooper, J.E., Kendall, R.E., Gurland, B.J., Sharple, L., Copeland, J.R.M. & Simon, R. (1972) Psychiatric diagnosis in New York and London. *Maudsley Monograph No. 20*. London: Oxford University Press.

Cooper, J. & Fazio, R.H. (1984) A new look at dissonance theory. In L. Berkowitz (Ed.), *Advances in experimental social psychology*, *Vol. 15*. New York: Academic Press.

Corteen, R.S. & Wood, B. (1972) Autonomic responses to shock-associated words in an unattended channel. *Journal of Experimental Psychology*, *94*, 308–13.

Corteen, R.S. & Dunn, D. (1974) Shock-associated words in a non-attended message: A test for momentary awareness. *Journal of Experimental Psychology*, *102*, 1143–4.

Corter, C.M. (1973) A comparison of the mother's and a stranger's control over the behaviour of infants. *Child Development*, *44*, 705–13.

Cox, T. (1975) The nature and management of stress. *New Behaviour*, *September 25*, 493–5.

Craik, F. & Lockhart, R. (1972) Levels of processing. *Journal of Verbal Learning and Verbal Behaviour*, *11*, 671–84.

Craik, F. & Tulving, E. (1975) Depth of processing and the retention of words in episodic memory. *Journal of Experimental Psychology: General*, *104*, 268–94.

Craimer, R.E., McMaster, M.R., Bartell, P.A. & Dragna, M. (1988) Subject competence and minimization of the bystander effect. *Journal of Applied Social Psychology*, *18*, 1133–48.

Crick, F. & Mitchison, G. (1983) The function of REM sleep. *Nature*, *304*, 111–14.

Cromer, R.F. (1974) The development of language and cognition: The cognition hypothesis. In B. Foss (Ed.), *New perspectives in child development*. Harmondsworth, Middlesex: Penguin.

Cromer, R.F. (1980) Normal language development: Recent progress. In L.A. Hersov, M. Berger & A.R. Nicol (Eds.), *Language and language disorders*. Oxford: Pergamon Press.

Crosby, F., Bromley, S. and Saxe, L. (1980) Recent unobtrusive studies of black and white discriminations and prejudice: A literature review. *Psychological Bulletin*, *87*, 546–63.

Croyle, R.T. & Cooper, J. (1983) Dissonance arousal: Physiological evidence. *Journal of Personality and Social Psychology*, *45*, 782–91.

Crutchfield, R.S. (1954) A new technique for measuring individual differences in conformity to group judgement. *Proceedings of the Invitational Conference on Testing Problems* (pp. 69–74).

Crutchfield, R.S. (1955) Conformity and character. *American Psychologist*, *10*, 191–8.

Cumberbatch, G. (1987) *The portrayal of violence on British television*. London: BBC Publications.

Cumming, E. & Henry, W.E. (1961) *Growing old: The process of disengagement*. New York: Basic.

Cummins, M.S. & Suomi, S.J. (1976) Long-term effects of social

rehabilitation in rhesus monkeys. *Primates*, *17*, 43–51.

Curtiss, S. (1977) *Genie: A psycholinguistic study of a modern-day 'wild child'*. London: Academic Press.

Cutting, J.E., Proffitt, D.R. & Kozlowski, L.J. (1978) A biomechanical invariant for gait perception. *Journal of Experimental Psychology: Human Perception and Performance*, *4*, 357–72.

Dacey, J.S. (1982) *Adolescents today* (2nd ed.). Glenview, Illinois: Scott, Foresman & Co.

Dallos, R. & Cullen, C. (1990) Clinical psychology. In I. Roth (Ed.), *Introduction to psychology*, *Vol. 2*. Hove, E.Sussex/Milton Keynes: Open University Press/Lawrence Erlbaum Associates Ltd.

Danziger, K. (1971) *Socialization*. Harmondsworth, Middlesex: Penguin.

Darley, J.M. (1991) Altruism and prosocial behaviour research: Reflections and prospects. In M.S. Clark (Ed.), *Prosocial behaviour, review of personality and social psychology*, *12*. Newbury Park, California: Sage Publications.

Darley, J.M. & Batson, C.D. (1973) From Jerusalem to Jericho: A study of situational and dispositional variables in helping behaviour. *Journal of Personality and Social Psychology*, *27*, 100–8.

Darley, J.M. & Huff, C.W. (1990) Heightened damage assessment as a result of the intentionality of the damage-causing act. *British Journal of Social Psychology*, *29* (2), 181–8.

Darley, J.M. & Latané, B. (1968) Bystander intervention in emergencies: Diffusion of responsibility. *Journal of Personality and Social Psychology*, *8*, 377–83.

Dasen, P.R. (1977) *Piagetian psychology: Cross-cultural contributions*. New York: Gardner Press.

Davidson, A.R. & Jaccard, J. (1979) Variables that moderate the attitude–behaviour relation: Results of a longitudinal survey. *Journal of Personality and Social Psychology*, *37*, 1364–76.

Davies, G. (1989) Children as witnesses. In A.M. Colman & J.G. Beaumont (Eds.), *Psychology Survey* (No. 7). Leicester: British Psychological Society/Routledge.

Davis, K. (1940) Extreme isolation of a child. *American Journal of Sociology*, *45*, 554–65.

Davis, K. (1947) Final note on a case of extreme isolation. *American Journal of Sociology*, *52*, 432–7.

Dawkins, M.S. (1980) The many faces of animal suffering. *New Scientist*, *November 20*.

Dawkins, R. (1978) *The selfish gene*. Oxford: Oxford University Press.

de Bono, E. (1967) *The use of lateral thinking*. Harmondsworth, Middlesex: Penguin.

Deese, J. (1972) *Psychology as a science and art*. New York: Harcourt Brace Jovanovich.

Dement, W. (1960) The effect of dream deprivation. *Science*, *131*, 1705–7.

Dement, W. (1972) *Some must watch while some must sleep*. Stanford, California: Stanford Alumni Association.

Dement, W. & Kleitman, N. (1957) The relation of eye movements during sleep to dream activity: An objective method for the study of dreaming. *Journal of Experimental Psychology*, *53* (5), 339–46.

Dennis, W. (1960) Causes of retardation among institutional children: Iran. *Journal of Genetic Psychology*, *96*, 47–59.

Department of Health and Social Security (1983) *Mental Health Act, 1983*. London: HMSO.

Deregowski, J. (1968) Pictorial recognition in subjects from a relatively pictureless environment. *African Social Research*, *5*, 356–64.

Deregowski, J. (1969) Preference for chain-type drawings in Zambian domestic servants and primary school children. *Psychologia Africana*, *82*, 9–13.

Deregowski, J. (1970) A note on the possible determinants of split representation as an artistic style. *International Journal of Psychology*, *5*, 21–6.

Deregowski, J. (1972) Pictorial perception and culture. *Scientific American*, *227*, 82–8.

Deregowski, J., Muldrow, E.S. & Muldrow, W.F. (1972) Pictorial recognition in a remote Ethiopian population. *Perception, 1,* 417–25.

Dermer, M. & Thiel, D.L. (1975) When beauty may fail. *Journal of Personality and Social Psychology, 31,* 1168–76.

Deutsch, J.A. & Deutsch, D. (1963) Attention: Some theoretical considerations. *Psychological Review, 70,* 80–90.

Deutsch, M. & Collins, M.E. (1951) *Interracial housing: A psychological evaluation of a social experiment.* Minneapolis, Minnesota: University of Minnesota Press.

Deutsch, M. & Gerard, H.B. (1955) A study of normative and informational social influences upon individual judgement. *Journal of Abnormal and Social Psychology, 51,* 629–36.

de Villiers, P.A. & de Villiers, J.G. (1979) *Early language,* Cambridge, Massachusetts: Harvard University Press.

Devlin Report (1976) Report to the Secretary of State for the Home Department of the Departmental Committee on Evidence of Identification in Criminal Cases. London: HMSO.

Dewey, J. (1922) *Human nature and conduct: An introduction to social psychology.* New York: Modern Library (1957).

Diagram Group (1982) *The brain—a user's manual.* New York: G.P. Putnams & Son.

Diamond, M. (1978) Sexual identity and sex roles. *The Humanist, March/April.*

Dicara, L.V. & Miller, N.E. (1968) Changes in heart rate instrumentally learned by curarised rats as avoidance responses. *Journal of Comparative and Physiological Psychology, 65,* 8–12.

Dion, K.K. (1972) Physical attractiveness and evaluation of children's transgressions. *Journal of Personality and Social Psychology, 24,* 207–13.

Dion, K.K. & Berscheid, E. (1974) Physical attractiveness and peer perception among children. *Sociometry, 37,* 1–12.

Dion, K.K., Berscheid, E. & Walster, E. (1972) What is beautiful is good. *Journal of Personality and Social Psychology, 24,* 285–90.

Dixon, N.F. (1971) *Subliminal perception: The nature of the controversy.* London: McGraw Hill.

Dixon, N.F. (1981) *Preconscious processing.* London: Wiley.

Dollard, J. & Miller, N.E. (1950) *Personality and psychotherapy.* New York: McGraw Hill.

Dollard, J., Doob, L.W., Miller, N.E., Mowrer, O.H. & Sears, R.R. (1939) *Frustration and aggression.* New Haven, Connecticut: Harvard University Press.

Donaldson, M. (1984) *Childrens' minds.* London: Fontana.

Donaldson, M. & Wales, R.J. (1970) On the acquisition of some relational terms. In J.R. Hayes (Ed.), *Cognition and the development of language.* New York: Wiley.

Donovan, A., Oddy, M., Pardoe, R. & Ades, A. (1985) Employment status and psychological well-being: A longitudinal study of 16-year-old school leavers. *Journal of Child Psychology and Psychiatry, 27,* 65–76.

Donvan, E.A. & Adelson, J. (1966) *The adolescent experience.* New York: Wiley.

Dovidio, J.F., Piliavin, J.A., Gaertner, S.L., Schroeder, D.A. & Clark, R.D. (1991) The arousal: Cost–reward model and the process of intervention. In M.S. Clark (Ed.), *Prosocial behaviour: Review of personality and social psychology, 12.* Newbury Park, California: Sage Publications.

Downing, D. (1988) *Day-light robbery.* London: Arrow Books.

Drabman, R.S. & Thomas, M.H. (1974) Does media violence increase children's toleration of real-life aggression? *Developmental Psychology, 10,* 418–21.

Dryden, W. (1984) Therapeutic arenas. In W. Dryden (Ed.), *Individual therapy in Britain.* London: Harper & Row.

Duck, S. (1988) *Relating to others.* Milton Keynes: Open University Press.

Duncan, H.F., Gourlay, N. & Hudson, W. (1973) *A study of pictorial perception among Bantu and white primary school children in South Africa.* Johannesburg: Witwatersrand University Press.

Duncan, J. (1979) Divided attention: The whole is more than the sum of its parts. *Journal of Experimental Psychology: Human Percep-*tion, *5,* 216–28.

Duncan, S.L. (1976) Differential social perception and attribution of intergroup violence: Testing the lower limits of stereotyping of blacks. *Journal of Personality and Social Psychology, 34,* 590–8.

Duncker, K. (1926) A qualitative (experimental and theoretical) study of productive thinking (solving of comprehensible problems). *Journal of Genetic Psychology, 68,* 97–116.

Durkin, K. (1985) *Television, sex roles and children.* Milton Keynes: Open University Press.

Dutton, D.C. & Aron, A.P. (1974) Some evidence for heightened sexual attraction under conditions of high anxiety. *Journal of Personality and Social Psychology, 30,* 510–17.

Dworetzky, J.P. (1981) *Introduction to child development.* St Paul, Minnesota: West Publishing Co.

Eagly, A.H. (1987) *Sex differences in social behaviour: A social-role interpretation.* London: Lawrence Erlbaum Associates Ltd.

Eagly, A.H. & Crowley, M. (1986) Gender and helping behaviour: A meta-analytic review of the social psychological literature. *Psychological Bulletin, 100,* 282–308.

Eaton, N. (1991) Expert systems in nursing. *Nursing Standard, 5* (38), 32–5.

Ebbinghaus, H. (1885/1913) *Memory.* New York: Teachers' College Press (Original work published 1885).

Efran, M.G. (1974) The effect of physical appearance on the judgement of guilt, interpersonal attraction and severity of recommended punishment in a simulated jury task. *Journal of Experimental Research in Personality, 8,* 45–54.

Eibel-Eibesfeldt, I. (1970) *Ethology: The biology of behaviour.* New York: Holt, Rinehart & Winston.

Eibel-Eibesfeldt, I. (1971) *Love and hate.* London: Methuen.

Eimas, P.D. (1975) Speech perception in early infancy. In L.B. Cohen & P. Salapatek (Eds.), *Infant perception: From sensation to cognition, Vol. 2.* New York: Academic Press.

Eiser, J.R. & van der Pligt, J. (1988) *Attitudes and decisions.* London: Routledge.

Ekman, P., Friesen, W.V. & Simons, R.C. (1985) Is the startle reaction an emotion? *Journal of Personality and Social Psychology, 49,* 1416–26.

Elkind, D. (1970) Erik Erikson's eight ages of man. *New York Times Magazine, April 5.*

Elkind, D. (1971) *Children and adolescents: Interpretative essays on Jean Piaget.* New York: Oxford University Press.

Elkind, D. (1976) *Child development and education: A Piagetian perspective.* New York: Oxford University Press.

Elliot, C. (1976) The British Intelligence Scale: final report before standardisation, 1975–6. Papers presented at the Annual Conference of the British Psychological Society, 1975. *Occasional Papers of the Division of Education and Child Psychology of the British Psychological Society, 10, Spring 1976.*

Ellis, A. (1962) *Reason and emotion in psychotherapy.* Secaucus, New Jersey: Lyle Stuart.

Ellis, A. (1973) *Humanistic psychotherapy.* New York: McGraw Hill.

Elms, A.C. (1976) *Attitudes.* Milton Keynes: Open University Press.

Emmelkamp, P.M.G. (1982) *Phobic and obsessive–compulsive disorders.* New York: Plenum.

Emmelkamp, P.M.G. & Wessels, H. (1975) Flooding in imagination versus flooding in vivo: A comparison with agoraphobics. *Behaviour Research and Therapy, 13,* 7–15.

Empson, J. (1989) *Sleep and dreaming.* London: Faber & Faber.

Endicott, J. & Spitzer, R.L. (1978) A diagnostic interview: The schedule for affective disorders and schizophrenia. *Archives of General Psychiatry, 35,* 837–44.

Erdelyi, M.H. (1974) A new look at the new look: Perceptual defence and vigilance. *Psychological Review, 81,* 1–24.

Erikson, E.H. (1965) *Childhood and society.* Harmondsworth, Middlesex: Penguin.

Erikson, E.H. (1968) *Identity: Youth and crisis.* New York: Norton.

Erikson, E.H. (1980) *Identity and the life cycle.* New York: Norton.

Erikson, M. (1968) The inhumanity of ordinary people. *International*

Journal of Psychiatry, 6, 278–9.

Erlenmeyer-Kimling, L. & Jarvik, L.F. (1963) Genetics and intelligence: A review. *Science*, 142, 1477–9.

Etzioni, A. (1968) A model of significant research. *International Journal of Psychiatry*, 6, 279–80.

Evans, P. (1980) Ethiological studies I and II, In J. Radford & E. Govier (Eds.), *A textbook of psychology*. London: Sheldon Press.

Evans, P.D. (1990) Type A behaviour and coronary heart disease: When will the jury return? *British Journal of Psychology*, 81 (2), 147–57.

Eysenck, H.J. (1952) The effects of psychotherapy: An evaluation. *Journal of Consulting Psychology*, 16, 319–24.

Eysenck, H.J. (1954) *The psychology of politics*. London: RKP.

Eysenck, H.J. (1970) *Crime and personality*. London: Paladin.

Eysenck, H.J. (1971) *Race, intelligence and education*. London: Temple-Smith.

Eysenck, H.J. (1974) Crime and personality reconsidered. *Bulletin of the British Psychological Society*, 27, 23–4.

Eysenck, H.J. (1976) The learning theory model of neurosis: A new approach. *Behaviour Research and Therapy*, 14, 251–67.

Eysenck, H.J. & Eysenck, S.B.G. (1975) *Manual of the Eysenck personality questionnaire*. London: Hodder & Stoughton.

Eysenck, H.J. & Rachman, S. (1965) *The cause and cure of neurosis*. London: RKP.

Eysenck, H.J. & Wilson, G.D. (Eds., 1973) *The experimental study of Freudian theories*. London: Methuen.

Eysenck, M.W. (1979) Depth, elaboration and distinctiveness. In L.S. Cermak & F.I.M. Craik (Eds.), *Levels of processing in human memory*. Hillsdale, New Jersey: Lawrence Erlbaum Associates Inc.

Eysenck, M.W. (1984) *A Handbook of cognitive psychology*. London: Lawrence Erlbaum Associates Ltd.

Eysenck, M.W. (1986) Working memory. In G. Cohen, M.W. Eysenck & M.A. Le Voi, *Memory: A cognitive approach*. Milton Keynes: Open University Press.

Eysenck, M.W. & Eysenck, M.C. (1980) Effects of processing depth, distinctiveness and word frequency on retention. *British Journal of Psychology*, 71, 263–74.

Eysenck, M.W. & Keane, M.J. (1990) *Cognitive psychology*. Hove, East Sussex: Lawrence Erlbaum Associates Ltd.

Fairbairn, G. (1987) Responsibility, respect for persons and psychological change. In S. Fairbairn & G. Fairbairn (Eds.), *Psychology, ethics and change*. London: RKP.

Fairbairn, G. & Fairbairn, S. (1987) Introduction: Psychology, ethics and change. In S. Fairbairn & G. Fairbairn (Eds.), *Psychology, ethics and change*. London: RKP.

Fantz, R.L. (1961) The origin of form perception. *Scientific American*, 204 (5), 66–72.

Faraday, A. (1973) *Dream power*. London: Pan Books.

Faris, J.C. (1972) *Nuba personal art*. London: Temple Smith.

Fazio, R.H. & Zanna, M.D. (1981) Direct experience and attitude-behaviour consistency. In L. Berkowitz (Ed.), *Advances in Experimental Social Psychology, Vol. 14*. New York: Academic Press.

Fazio, R.H., Zanna, M.P. & Cooper, J. (1977) Dissonance and self-perception: An integrative view of each theory's major domain of application. *Journal of Experimental and Social Psychology*, 13, 464–79.

Feighner, J.P., Robins, E., Guze, S.B., Woodruff, R.A., Winokur, G. & Munz, R. (1972) Diagnostic criteria for use in psychiatric research. *Archives of General Psychiatry*, 26, 57–63.

Felipe, N.J. & Sommer, R. (1966) Invasion of personal space. *Social Problems*, 14, 206–14.

Ferster, C.B. & Skinner, B.F. (1957) *Schedules of reinforcement*. New York: Appleton-Century-Crofts.

Feshbach, S. (1964) The function of aggression and the regulation of aggressive drive. *Psychological Review*, 71, 257–72.

Festinger, L. (1957) *A theory of cognitive dissonance*. New York: Harper & Row.

Festinger, L. & Carlsmith, J.M. (1959) Cognitive consequences of forced compliance. *Journal of Abnormal and Social Psychology*, 58, 203–10.

Festinger, L., Schachter, S. & Back, K. (1950) *Social pressures in informal groups: A study of human factors in housing*. Stanford, California: Stanford University Press.

Fiedler, F.E. (1967) *A theory of leadership effectiveness*. New York: McGraw Hill.

Fiedler, F.E. (1968) Personality and situational determinants of leadership effectiveness. In D. Cartwright & A. Zander (Eds.), *Group dynamics*. New York: Harper & Row.

Fiedler, F.E. (1971) Validation and extension of the contingency model of leadership effectiveness: A review of empirical findings. *Psychological Bulletin*, 76, 128–48.

Fiedler, F.E. (1972) Personality motivational systems and the behaviour of high and low LPC. *Human Relations*, 25, 391–2.

Fishbein, H.D. (1984) *The psychology of infancy and childhood-evolutionary and cross-cultural perspectives*. Hillsdale, New Jersey: Lawrence Erlbaum Associates Inc.

Fisher, S. (1978) Dirt-anality and attitudes towards negros. A test of Kubie's hypothesis. *Journal of Nervous and Mental Disease*, 166, 280–91.

Fisher, S. & Greenberg, R.P. (1977) *The scientific credibility of Freud's theories and therapy*. New York: Basic Books.

Flanagan, O.J. (1984) *The science of the mind*. London: MIT Press.

Flavell, J.H. (1977) *Cognitive development*. Englewood Cliffs, New Jersey: Prentice-Hall.

Fodor, J.A. (1983) *The modularity of mind*. Cambridge, Massachusetts: MIT Press.

Fodor, J.A. & Pylyshyn, Z.W. (1981) How direct is visual perception? Some reflections on Gibson's "ecological approach". *Cognition*, 9, 139–96.

Fogelman, K. (1976) *Britain's sixteen-year-olds*. London: National Childrens' Bureau.

Fonagy, P. (1981) Research on psychoanalytic concepts. In F. Fransella, (Ed.), *Personality—theory, measurement and research*. London: Methuen.

Fonagy, P. & Higgitt, A. (1984) *Personality, theory and clinical practice*. London: Methuen.

Fontana, D. (1982) Intelligence. In D. Fontana (Ed.), *Psychology for teachers*. London: British Psychological Society/Macmillan Press.

Fransella, F. (1972) *Personal change and reconstruction: Research on a treatment of stuttering*. London: Academic Press.

Fransella, F. (1975) *Need to change?* London: Methuen.

Fransella, F. (1981) Personal construct psychology and repertory grid technique. In F. Fransella (Ed.), *Personality—theory, measurement and research*. London: Methuen.

Fransella, F. (1984) Personal construct therapy. In W. Dryden (Ed.), *Individual therapy in Britain*. London: Harper & Row.

Freedman, J.L. (1963) Attidudinal effects of inadequate justification. *Journal of Personality*, 31, 371–385.

Friedman, M. & Rosenman, R.H. (1974) *Type A behaviour and your heart*. New York: Knopf.

Freud, A. (1936) *The ego and the mechanisms of defence*. London: Chatto & Windus.

Freud, A. & Dann, S. (1951) An experiment in group upbringing. *Psychoanalytic Study of the Child*, 6, 127–68.

Freud, S. (1976) *The interpretation of dreams*. Pelican Freud Library (4) Harmondsworth, Middlesex: Penguin. (Original work published 1900).

Freud, S. (1976) *The psychopathology of everyday life*. Pelican Freud Library (5) Harmondsworth, Middlesex: Penguin. (Original work published 1901).

Freud, S. (1977a) *Three essays on the theory of sexuality*. Pelican Freud Library (7) Harmondsworth, Middlesex: Penguin. (Original work published 1905).

Freud, S. (1977b) *Analysis of a phobia in a five-year-old boy*. Pelican Freud Library (8) Harmondsworth, Middlesex: Penguin. (Original work published 1909).

Freud, S. (1984) *Beyond the pleasure principle*. Pelican Freud Library (11) Harmondsworth, Middlesex: Penguin. (Original work published 1922).

Freud, S. (1984) *The ego and the id*. Pelican Freud Library (11) Harmondsworth, Middlesex: Penguin. (Original work published 1923.)

Frisby, J.P. (1986) The computational approach to vision. In I. Roth & J.P. Frisby (Eds.), *Perception and representation*. Milton Keynes: Open University Press.

Fromm, E. (1941) *Escape from freedom*. New York: Farrar & Rhinehart.

Fromm, E. (1962) *The art of loving*. London: Unwin Books.

Fromm, E. (1970) *The crisis of psychoanalysis—Essays on Freud, Marx and social psychology*. Harmondsworth, Middlesex: Penguin.

Fromm, E. (1977) *The anatomy of human destructiveness*. Harmondsworth, Middlesex: Penguin.

Frueh, T. & McGhee, P.E. (1975) Traditional sex-role development and amount of time spent watching television. *Developmental Psychology*, 11, 109.

Furth, H.G. (1966) *Thinking without language*. New York: Free Press.

Gagné, R.M. (1974) *Essentials of learning for instruction*. New York: Dryden Press.

Gagné, R.M. (1977) *The conditions of learning*. New York: Holt, Rinehart & Winston.

Gahagan, J. (1975) *Interpersonal and group behaviour*. London: Methuen.

Gahagan, J. (1984) *Social interaction and its management*. London: Methuen.

Galin, D. (1974) Implication for psychiatry of left and right cerebral specialization. *Archives of General Psychiatry*, 31, 572–83.

Gallup, G.G. (1977) Self-recognition in primates. *American Psychologist*, 32, 329–38

Garcia, J. & Koelling, R.A. (1966) Relation of cue to consequence in avoidance learning. *Psychonomic Science*, 4, 123–4.

Garcia, J., Ervin, F.R. & Koelling, R. (1966) Learning with prolonged delay of reinforcement. *Psychonomic Science*, 5 (3), 121–2.

Gardner, B.T. & Gardner, R.A. (1971) Two-way communication with an infant chimpanzee. In A. Schrier & F. Stollitz (Eds.), *Behaviour of non-human primates, Vol. 4*. New York: Academic Press.

Gardner, B.T. & Gardner, R.A. (1975) Evidence for sentence constituents in the early utterances of child and chimp. *Journal of Experimental Psychology: General*, 104, 244–67.

Gardner, B.T. & Gardner, R.A. (1983) Two comparative psychologists look at language acquisition. In K. Nelson (Ed.), *Childrens' language, Vol. 2*. New York: Gardner Press.

Gardner, H. (1983) *Frames of mind: The theory of multiple intelligence*. New York: Basic Books.

Gardner, H. (1985) *The mind's new science*. New York: Basic Books.

Gardner, H. (1987) Epilogue: Cognitive science after 1984. In Gardner, H. (1985), *The mind's new science*. New York: Basic Books.

Gardner, R.A. & Gardner, B.T. (1969) Teaching sign language to a chimpanzee. *Science*, 165 (3894), 664–72.

Gardner, R.A. & Gardner, B.T. (1978) Comparative psychology and language acquisition. *Psychology: The state of the art*. Annals of the New York Academy of Sciences, 309, 37–76.

Garner, W.R. & Clement, D.E. (1963) Goodness of pattern and pattern redundancy. *Journal of Verbal Learning and Verbal Behaviour*, 2, 446–52.

Garnham, A. (1988) *Artificial intelligence: An introduction*. London: RKP.

Garnham, A. (1991) *The mind in action*. London: Routledge.

Gauker, C. (1990) How to learn a language like a chimpanzee. *Philosophical Psychology*, 3 (1), 31–53.

Gazzaniga, M.S. (1985) *The social brain: Discovering the networks of the mind*. New York: Basic Books.

Geen, R.G. (1990) *Human aggression*. Milton Keynes: Open University Press.

Gelder, M., Gath, D. & Mayon, R. (1989) *Oxford textbook of psychiatry* (2nd ed.). Oxford: Oxford University Press.

Gerard, H.B., Wilhelmy, R.A. & Connolly, E.S. (1968) Conformity and group size. *Journal of Personality and Social Psychology*, 8, 79–82.

Gerbner, G. (1972) Violence in television drama: Trends and symbolic functions. In G.A Comstock & E.A. Rubinstein (Eds.), *Television and social behaviour, Vol. 1, Media content and control*. Washington, DC: US Government Printing Office.

Gerbner, G. & Gross, L. (1976) Living with television: The violence profile. *Journal of Communication*, 26, 173–99.

Gergen, K.J. & Gergen, M.M. (1981) *Social psychology*. New York: Harcourt Brace Jovanovich.

Gergen, K.J., Gergen, M.M. & Barton, W. (1973) Deviance in the dark. *Psychology Today*, 7, 129–30.

Gibson, E.J. & Walk, P.D. (1960) The visual cliff. *Scientific American*, 202, 64–71.

Gibson, J.J. (1950) *The perception of the visual world*. Boston: Houghton Mifflin.

Gibson, J.J. (1966) *The senses considered as perceptual systems*. Boston: Houghton Mifflin.

Gibson, J.J. (1979) *The ecological approach to visual perception*. Boston: Houghton Mifflin.

Gillham, W.E.C. (1975) Intelligence: The persistent myth. *New Behaviour*, June 26, 433–5.

Gillham, W.E.C. (1978) Measurement constructs and psychological structure: Psychometrics. In A. Burton & J. Radford (Eds.), *Thinking in perspective*. London: Methuen.

Gilligan, C. (1977) In a different voice: Womens' conceptions of self and morality. *Harvard Educational Review*, 47, 481–517.

Gilligan, C. (1982) *In a different voice: Psychological theory and womens' development*. Cambridge, Massachusetts: Harvard University Press.

Gilling, D. & Brightwell, R. (1982) *The human brain*. London: Orbis Publishing.

Ginsburg, H.P. (1981) Piaget and education: The contributions and limits of genetic epistemology. In K. Richardson & S. Sheldon (Eds.), *Cognitive development to adolescence*. Hove, E. Sussex/Milton Keynes: Lawrence Erlbaum/Open University.

Glanzer, M. & Cunitz, A.R. (1966) Two storage mechanisms in free recall. *Journal of Verbal Learning and Verbal Behaviour*, 5, 351–60.

Goffman, E. (1968) *Asylums—essays on the social situation of mental patients and other inmates*. Harmondsworth, Middlesex: Penguin.

Goffman, E. (1968) *Stigma—notes on the management of spoiled identity*. Harmondsworth, Middlesex: Penguin.

Goffman, E. (1971) *The presentation of self in everyday life*. Harmondsworth, Middlesex: Penguin.

Goldfarb, W. (1943a) The effects of early institutional care on adolescent personality. *Journal of Experimental Education*, 12, 106–29.

Goldfarb, W. (1943b) Infant rearing and problem behaviour. *American Journal of Orthopsychiatry*, 13, 249–65.

Goldfarb, W. (1945) Effects of psychological deprivation in infancy and subsequent stimulation. *American Journal of Psychiatry*, 102, 18–33.

Goldman-Eisler, F. (1948) Breast-feeding and character formation. *Journal of Personality*, 17, 83–103.

Goldman-Eisler, F. (1951) The problem of 'orality' and its origin in early childhood. *Journal of Mental Science*, 97, 765–82.

Goldwyn, E. (1979) The fight to be male. *Listener*, May 24, 709–12.

Golombok, S., Spencer, A. & Rutter, M. (1983) Children in lesbian and single-parent households: Psychosexual and psychiatric appraisal. *Journal of Child Psychology and Psychiatry*, 24, 551–72.

Gombrich, E.H. (1960) *Art and illusion*. London: Phaidon.

Gordon, I.E. (1989) *Theories of visual perception*. Chichester: John Wiley & Sons.

Gottesman, I.I. & Shields, J. (1976) A critical review of recent adoption, twin and family studies of schizophrenia: Behavioural genetics perspectives. *Schizophrenia Bulletin*, 2, 360–98.

Gould, R.L. (1978) *Transformations: Growth and change in adult life.* New York: Simon & Schuster.

Gould, R.L. (1980) Transformational tasks in adulthood. In S.I. Greenspan & G.H. Pollock (Eds.), *The course of life: Psychoanalytic contributions toward understanding personality development, Vol. 3: Adulthood and the ageing process.* Washington DC: National Institution for Mental Health.

Gould, S.J. (1981) *The mismeasure of man.* Harmondsworth, Middlesex: Penguin.

Graham, H. (1986) *The human face of psychology.* Milton Keynes: Open University Press.

Grasha, A.F. (1983) *Practical applications of psychology* (2nd ed.). Boston: Little, Brown & Co.

Gray, J. & Wedderburn, A. (1960) Grouping strategies with simultaneous stimuli. *Quarterly Journal of Experimental Psychology*, 12, 180–4.

Gray, J.A. (1971) *The psychology of fear and stress.* London: Weidenfeld & Nicolson.

Gray, J.A. (1975) *Elements of a two-process theory of learning.* London: Academic Press.

Gray, J.A. (1987) The ethics and politics of animal experimentation. In H. Beloff & A.M. Colman (Eds.), *Psychology Survey, No. 6.* Leicester: British Psychological Society.

Gray, J.A. (1991) On the morality of speciesism. *The Psychologist*, 4 (5), 196–8.

Green, R. (1978) Sexual identity of 37 children raised by homosexual or transsexual parents. *American Journal of Psychiatry*, 135, 692–7.

Green, S. (1980) Physiological studies I and II. In J. Radford & E. Govier (Eds.), *A textbook of psychology.* London: Sheldon Press.

Greene, J. (1987) *Memory, thinking and language.* London: Methuen.

Greene, J. (1990) Perception. In I. Roth (Ed.), *Introduction to psychology, Vol. 2.* Milton Keynes/Hove: Open University/Lawrence Erlbaum Associates Ltd.

Greene, J. & Hicks, C. (1986) *Basic cognitive processes.* Milton Keynes: Open University Press.

Greer, A., Morris, T. & Pettingale, K.W. (1979) Psychological response to breast cancer: Effect on outcome. *Lancet*, 13, 785–7.

Gregor, A.J. & McPherson, D. (1965) A study of susceptibility to geometric illusions among cultural outgroups of Australian aborigines. *Psychologia, Africana*, 11, 490–9.

Gregory, R.L. (1966) *Eye and brain.* London: Weidenfeld & Nicolson.

Gregory, R.L. (1970) *The intelligent eye.* London: Weidenfeld & Nicolson.

Gregory, R.L. (1972) Visual illusions. In B.M. Foss (Ed.), *New horizons in psychology*, 1. Harmondsworth, Middlesex: Penguin.

Gregory, R.L. (1980) Perceptions as hypotheses. *Philosophical Transactions of the Royal Society of London, Series B*, 290, 181–97.

Gregory, R.L. (1981) *Mind in science.* Harmondsworth, Middlesex: Penguin.

Gregory, R.L. (1983) Visual illusions. In J. Miller (Ed.), *States of mind.* London: BBC Publications.

Gregory, R.L. (1987) In defence of artificial intelligence—a reply to John Searle. In C. Blakemore & S. Greenfield (Eds.), *Mindwaves.* Oxford: Blackwell.

Gregory, R.L. & Wallace, J. (1963) *Recovery from early blindness.* Cambridge: Heffer.

Griffit, W. & Veitch, R. (1974) Preacquaintance attitude similarity and attraction revisited: Ten days in a fallout shelter. *Sociometry*, 37, 163–73.

Gross, A.E. & Crofton, C. (1977) What is good is beautiful. *Sociometry*, 40, 85–90.

Gross, R.D. (1990) *Key studies in psychology.* Sevenoaks: Hodder & Stoughton.

Guilford, J.P. (1959) Three faces of intellect. *American Psychologist*, 14, 469–79.

Guiton, P. (1958) The effect of isolation on the following response of brown leghorn chicks. *Proceeding of the Royal Physical Society, Edinburgh*, 27, 9–14.

Guiton, P. (1966) Early experience and sexual object choice in the brown leghorn. *Animal Behaviour*, 14, 534–8.

Gunter, B. (1986) *Television and sex-role stereotyping.* London: IBA and John Libbey.

Gunter, B. & McAleer, J.L. (1990) *Children and television—the one-eyed monster?* London: Routledge.

Guntrip, H. (1968) *Schizoid phenomena: Object relations and the self.* London: Hogarth.

Guthrie, E.R. (1938) *Psychology of human conflict.* New York: Harper.

Hall, C.S. (1966) *The meaning of dreams.* New York: McGraw-Hill.

Hall, C.S. & Nordby, V.J. (1973) *A primer of Jungian psychology.* New York: Mentor.

Hall, E.T. (1959) *The silent language.* New York: Doubleday.

Hall, G.S. (1904) *Adolescence.* New York: Appleton & Co.

Halloran, J.D. & Croll, P. (1973) Television programmes in Great Britain. In G.A. Comstock & E.A. Rubinstein (Eds.), *Television and social behaviour, Vol. 1., Medial content and control.* Washington DC: US Government Printing Office.

Hampson, P.J. (1989) Aspects of attention and cognitive science. *Irish Journal of Psychology*, 10, 261–75.

Harari, H. & McDavid, J.W. (1973) Teachers' expectations and name stereotypes. *Journal of Educational Psychology*, 65, 222–5.

Hardy, G.R. & Legge, D. (1968) Cross-modal induction of changes in sensory thresholds. *Quarterly Journal of Experimental Psychology*, 20, 20–9.

Hargreaves, D., Molloy, C. & Pratt, A. (1982) Social factors in conservation. *British Journal of Psychology*, 73, 231–4.

Harlow, H.F. (1949) Formation of learning sets. *Psychological Review*, 56, 51–65.

Harlow, H.F. (1959) Love in infant monkeys. *Scientific American*, 200 (6), 68–74.

Harlow, H.F. & Harlow, M.K. (1962) Social deprivation in monkeys. *Scientific American*, 207 (5), 136.

Harlow, H.F., Harlow, M.K. & Meyer, D.R. (1950) Learning motivated by a manipulation drive. *Journal of Experimental Psychology*, 40, 228–34.

Harlow, H.F., Harlow, M.K. & Suomi, S.J. (1971) From thought to therapy: Lessons from a primate laboratory. *American Scientist*, 59, 74–83.

Harlow, H.F. & Zimmerman, R.R. (1959) Affectional responses in the infant monkey. *Science*, 130, 421–32.

Harré, R., Clarke, D. & De Carlo, N. (1985) *Motives and mechanisms.* London: Methuen.

Hartshorne, H. & May, M. (1930) *Studies in the nature of character.* New York: Macmillan.

Hass, R.G. & Linder, D.E. (1972) Counterargument availability and the effects of message structure on persuasion. *Journal of Personality and Social Psychology*, 23, 319–33.

Hass, R.G. & Mann, R. (1976) Anticipatory belief change: Persuasion or impression management? *Journal of Personality and Social Psychology*, 34, 105–11.

Hatfield, E., Traupmann, J. & Walster, G.W. (1978) Equity and extramarital sexuality. *Archives of Sexual Behaviour*, 7, 127–42.

Hatfield, E., Walster, G.W. & Traupmann, J. (1978) Equity and premarital sex. *Journal of Personality and Social Psychology*, 37, 82–92.

Havighurst, R.J., Neugarten, B.L. & Tobin, S.S. (1968) Disengagement and patterns of ageing. In B.L. Neugarten (Ed.), *Middle age and ageing.* Chicago: University of Chicago Press.

Hawkins, L.H. & Armstrong-Esther, C.A. (1978) Circadian rhythms and night shift working in nurses. *Nursing Times, May 4*, 49–52.

Hayslip, B. & Panek, P.E. (1989) *Adult development and ageing.* New York: Harper & Row.

Heather, N. (1976) *Radical perspectives in psychology.* London:

Methuen.

Hebb, D.O. (1949) *The organization of behaviour*. New York: Wiley.

Hediger, H. (1951) *Wild animals in captivity*. London: Butterworth.

Heider, E. (1972) Universals in colour naming and memory. *Journal of Experimental Psychology*, *93*, 10–20.

Heider, F. (1958) *The psychology of interpersonal relations*. New York: John Wiley & Sons.

Heider, F. & Simmel, M. (1944) An experimental study of apparent behaviour. *American Journal of Psychology*, *57*, 243–59.

Heim, A. (1970) *Intelligence and personality—their assessment and relationship*. Harmondsworth, Middlesex: Penguin.

Held, R. (1965) Plasticity in sensory-motor systems. *Scientific American*, *213* (5), 84–94.

Held, R. & Hein, A. (1963) Movement-produced stimulation in the development of visually guided behaviour. *Journal of Comparative and Physiological Psychology*, *56*, 607–13.

Hendrick, C. & Constanini, A. (1970) Effects of varying trait inconsistency and response requirements on the primacy effect on impression formation. *Journal of Personality and Social Psychology*, *15*, 158–64.

Heron, W. (1957) The pathology of boredom. *Scientific American*, *196*, 52–69.

Hershenson, M., Munsinger, H. & Kessen, W. (1965) Preference for shapes of intermediate variability in the newborn human. *Science*, *147*, 630–1.

Hess, E.H. (1956) Space perception in the chick. *Scientific American*, July, 71–80.

Hess, E.H. (1958) Imprinting in animals. *Scientific American*, March, 71–80.

Hess, R.D. & Shipman, V. (1965) Early experience and the socialization of cognitive modes in children. *Child Development*, *36*, 860–86.

Heston, L.J. (1966) Psychiatric disorders in foster home reared children of schizophrenic mothers. *British Journal of Psychiatry*, *112*, 819–25.

Hetherington, E.M., Cox, M. & Cox, R. (1978) The aftermath of divorce. In M.H. Stevens & M. Mathews (Eds.), *Mother/child, father/child relationships*. Washington DC: National Association for the Education of Young Children.

Hewstone, M. & Brown, R.J. (1986) Contact is not enough: An intergroup perspective on the contact hypothesis. In M. Hewstone & R. Brown (Eds.), *Contact and conflict in intergroup encounters*. Oxford: Basil Blackwell.

Hilgard, E.R. (1974) Towards a neo-dissociationist theory: Multiple cognitive controls in human functioning. *Perspectives in Biology and Medicine*, *17*, 301–16.

Hilgard, E.R. (1975) Hypnosis. *Annual Review of Psychology*, *26*, 19–44.

Hilgard, E.R. (1977) Neodissociation theory of multiple cognitive control systems. In G.E. Schwartz & D. Shapiro (Eds.), *Consciousness and self-regulation*, *Vol. 1*. New York: Plenum Press.

Hilgard, E.R. (1978) Hypnosis and consciousness. *Human Nature*, January, 42–9.

Hilgard, E.R. (1981) Hypnosis gives rise to fantasy and is not a truth serum. *Skeptical enquirer*, *5*, 25.

Hilgard, E.R., Atkinson, R.L. & Atkinson, R.C. (1979) *Introduction to Psychology* (7th ed.). New York: Harcourt Brace Jovanovich.

Hilgard, J.R. (1970) *Personality and hypnosis*. Chicago: University of Chicago Press.

Hinde, R.A. (1959) Unitary drives. *Animal Behaviour*, *7*, 130–41.

Hinde, R.A. (1974) *Biological bases of human social behaviour*. New York: McGraw Hill.

Hinde, R.A. (1982) *Ethology*. London: Fontana.

Hinde, R.A. & Spencer-Booth, Y. (1970) Individual differences in the responses of rhesus monkeys to a period of separation from their mothers. *Journal of Child Psychology and Psychiatry*, *11*, 159–76.

Hinton, J. (1975) *Dying*. Harmondsworth, Middlesex: Penguin.

Hobson, J.A. & McCarley, R.W. (1977) The brain as a dream state generator: An activation–synthesis hypothesis of the dream process. *American Journal of Psychiatry*, *134*, 121.

Hochberg, J. (1978) Art and perception. In E.C. Carterette & H. Friedman (Eds.), *Handbook of perception*. *Vol. 10*. London: Academic Press.

Hocket, C.D. (1960) The origins of speech. *Scientific American*, *203*, 88–96.

Hodges, B. (1974) Effect of volume on relative weighting in 'impression' formation. *Journal of Personality and Social Psychology*, *30*, 378–81.

Hodges, J. & Tizard, B. (1989) I.Q. and behavioural adjustment of ex-institutional adolescents. *Journal of Child Psychology and Psychiatry*, *30* (1), 53–75.

Hodges, J. & Tizard, B. (1989) Social and family relationships of ex-institutional adolescents. *Journal of Child Psychology and Psychiatry*, *30* (1), 77–97.

Hoffman, L.W. (1977) Fear of success in 1965 and 1974: A follow-up study. *Journal of Consulting and Clinical Psychology*, *45*, 310–12.

Hoffman, M.L. (1970) Conscience, personality and socialization techniques. *Human Development*, *13*, 90–126.

Hofling, K.C., Brotzman, E., Dalrymple, S., Graves, N. & Pierce, C.M. (1966) An experimental study in the nurse-physician relationship. *Journal of Nervous and Mental Disorders*, *143*, 171–80.

Hohman, G.W. (1966) Some effects of spinal cord lesions on experienced emotional feelings. *Psychophysiology*, *3*, 143–56.

Hollander, E.P. & Willis, R.H. (1964) Conformity, independence and anticonformity as determiners of perceived influence and attraction. In E.P. Hollander (Ed.), *Leaders, groups and influence*. New York: Oxford University Press.

Holmes, T.H. & Masuda, M. (1974) Life change and illness susceptibility. In B.S. Dohrenwend and B.P. Dohrenwend (Eds.), *Stressful life events: Their nature and effects*. New York: Wiley.

Holmes, T.H. & Rahe, R.H. (1967) The social readjustment rating scale. *Journal of Psycho-somatic Research*, *11*, 213–18.

Homans, G.C. (1961) *Social behaviour: Its elementary forms*. New York: Harcourt Brace Jovanovich.

Homans, G.C. (1974) *Social behaviour: Its elementary forms* (2nd ed.). New York: Harcourt Brace Jovanovich.

Honzik, M.P., Macfarlane, J.W. & Allen, L. (1948) The stability of mental test performance between two and eighteen years. *Journal of Experimental Education*, *17*, 309–24.

Hopson, B. & Scally, M. (1980) Change and development in adult life: Some implications for helpers. *British Journal of Guidance and Counselling*, *8* (2), 175–87.

Horn, J.L. & Cattell, R.B. (1967) Age differences in fluid and crystallized intelligence. *Acta Psychologica*, *26*, 107–29.

Horn, J.L. & Cattell, R.B. (1982) Whimsy and misunderstanding of Gf–Gc theory: A comment on Guilford. *Psychology Bulletin*, *91*, 623–33.

Horn, J.M., Loehlin, J.L. & Willerman, L. (1979) Intellectual resemblance among adoptive and biological relatives: The Texas adoption project. *Behaviour Genetics*, *9*, 177–207.

Horne, J. (1988) *Why we sleep: The functions of sleep in humans and other mammals*. Oxford: Oxford University Press.

Horner, M.S. (1970) The motive to avoid success and changing aspirations of college women. In *Women on campus 1970: A symposium*. Ann Arbor, Michigan: Center for Continuing Education of Women.

Horner, M.S. (1972) Toward an understanding of achievement-related conflicts in women. *Journal of Social Issues*, *28*, 157–76.

Horney, K. (1924) On the genesis of the castration complex in women. *International Journal of Psychoanalysis*, *V*, 50–65.

Hovland, C.I., Campbell, E. & Brock, B.T. (1957) The effects of 'commitment' on opinion change following communication. In C.I. Hovland (Ed.), *The order of presentation in persuasion*. New Haven, Connecticut: Yale University Press.

Hovland, C.I. & Janis, I.L. (1959) *Personality and persuasibility*. New Haven, Connecticut: Yale University Press.

Hovland, C.I., Lumsdaine, A.A. & Sheffield, F.D. (1949) *Experiments in mass communication*. Princeton, New Jersey: Princeton University Press.

Hovland, C.I. & Weiss, W. (1951) The influence of source credibility on communication effectiveness. *Public Opinion Quarterly*, 15, 635–50.

Howard, J.W. & Rothbart, M. (1980) Social categorization and memory for ingroup and outgroup behaviour. *Journal of Personality and Social Psychology*, 38, 301–10.

Howe, M.J.A. (1980) *The psychology of human learning*. London: Harper & Rowe.

Howe, M.J.A. (1989) The strange achievements of idiots savants. In A.M. Colman & J.G. Beaumont (Eds.), *Psychology Survey, No. 7*. Leicester: British Psychological Society.

Howes, D. & Solomon, R.L. (1950) A note on McGinnies' emotionality and perceptual defence. *Psychological Review*, 57, 229–34.

Howie, D. (1952) Perceptual defence. *Psychological Review*, 59, 308–15.

Howlin, P.A. (1981) The effectiveness of operant language training with autistic children. *Journal of Autism and Developmental Disorders*, 11, 89–106.

Hrdy, S.B. (1977) *The Langurs of Abu*. Cambridge, Massachusetts: Harvard University Press.

Hubel, D.H. (1979) The brain. *Scientific American, September*, 38–47.

Hubel, D.H. & Wiesel, T.N. (1959) Receptive fields of single neurons in the cat's striate cortex. *Journal of Physiology*, 148, 579–91.

Hubel, D.H. (1962) Receptive fields, binocular interaction and functional architecture in the cat's visual cortex. *Journal of Physiology*, 160, 106–54.

Hubel, D.H. (1968) Receptive fields and functional architecture of monkey striate cortex. *Journal of Physiology*, 195, 215–43.

Hubel, D.H. (1977) Functional architecture of macaque monkey visual cortex. *Proceedings of the Royal Society of London, Series B*, 198, 1–59.

Hudson, W. (1960) Pictorial depth perception in sub-cultural groups in Africa. *Journal of Social Psychology*, 52, 183–208.

Hudson, W. (1962) Pictorial perception and educational adaptation in Africa. *Psychologica Africana*, 9, 226–39.

Hull, C.L. (1943) *Principles of behaviour*. New York: Appleton, Century Crofts.

Humphreys, G.W. & Reddoch, M.J. (1987) *To see but not to see—a case study of visual agnosia*. London: Lawrence Erlbaum Associates Ltd.

Hunt, J.McV. (1961) *Intelligence and experience*. New York: Ronald Press.

Hunt, J.McV. (1969) Has compensatory education failed? Has it been attempted? *Harvard Educational Review*, 39, 278–300.

Hunter, I. (1957) *Memory*. Harmondsworth, Middlesex: Penguin.

Hutt, C. (1972) *Males and females*. Harmondsworth, Middlesex: Penguin.

Hyde, T.S. & Jenkins, J.J. (1973) Recall for words as a function of semantic, graphic and syntactic orienting tasks. *Journal of Verbal Learning and Behaviour*, 12, 471–80.

Illman, J. (1977) ECT: Therapy or trauma? *Nursing Times, August 11*, 1226–7.

Immelman, K. & Suomi, S.J. (1981) Sensitive phases in development. In K. Immelman, G. Barlow, M. Main & L. Petrinovich (Eds.), *Issues in behavioural development. The Bielefelt Interdisciplinary Conference*. New York: Cambridge University Press.

Imperato-McGinley, J., Guerro, L., Gautier, T. & Peterson, R.E. (1974) Steroid 5-reductase deficiency in man: An inherited form of male pseudohermaphroditism. *Science*, 186, 1213–16.

Insko, C.A., Arkoff, A. & Insko, V.M. (1965) Effects of high and low fear-arousing communications upon opinion change towards smoking. *Journal of Experimental Social Psychology*, 1, 256–66.

Insko, C.A., Drenan, S., Solomon, M.R., Smith, R. & Wade, T.J. (1983) Conformity as a function of the consistency of positive self-evaluation with being liked and being right. *Journal of Experimental Social Psychology*, 19, 341–58.

Ittleson, W.H. (1952) *The Ames demonstrations in perception*. Princeton, New Jersey: Princeton University Press.

Iversen, L.L. (1979) The chemistry of the brain. *Scientific American*, 241, 134–49.

Izard, C. (1977) *Human emotions*. New York: Plenum Press.

Jacobs, M. (1984) Psychodynamic therapy: The Freudian approach. In W. Dryden (Ed.), *Individual therapy in Britain*. London: Harper & Row.

Jacoby, L.L. & Craik, F.I.M. (1979) Effects of elaboration of processing at encoding and retrieval: Trace distinctiveness and recovery of initial context. In C.S. Cermak & F.I.M. Craik (Eds.), *Levels of processing in human memory*. Hillsdale, New Jersey: Lawrence Erlbaum Associates Inc.

Jahoda, G. (1966) Geometric illusions and environment: A study in Ghana. *British Journal of Psychology*, 57, 193–9.

Jahoda, M. (1958) *Current concepts of positive mental health*. New York: Basic Books.

Jahoda, M. (1979) The impact of unemployment in the 1930s and the 1970s. *Bulletin of the British Psychological Society*, 32, 309–14.

James, W. (1884) What is an emotion? *Mind*, 9, 188–205.

James, W. (1890) *Principles of psychology*. New York: Holt.

Janis, I.L. & Feshbach, S. (1953) Effects of fear-arousing communication. *Journal of Abnormal and Social Psychology*, 48, 78–92.

Janis, I.L. & Field, P.B. (1959) Sex differences and personality factors related to persuasability. In C.I. Hovland & I.L. Janis (Eds.), *Personality and persuasability*. New Haven, Connecticut: Yale University Press.

Janis, I.L. & Mann, L. (1965) Effectiveness of emotional role-playing in modifying smoking habits and attitudes. *Journal of Experimental Personality Research*, 1, 84–90.

Janis, I.L. & Terwillinger, R.T. (1962) An experimental study of psychological resistance to fear-arousing communication. *Journal of Abnormal and Social Psychology*, 65, 403–10.

Janov, A. (1973) *The primal scream*. London: Abacus.

Jenkins, J.G. & Dallenbach, K.M. (1924) Oblivescence during sleep and waking. *American Journal of Psychology*, 35, 605–12.

Jenness, A. (1932) The role of discussion in changing opinion regarding matter of fact. *Journal of Abnormal and Social Psychology*, 27, 279–96.

Jensen, A.R. (1969) How much can we boost IQ and scholastic achievement? *Harvard Educational Review*, 39, 1–123.

Jensen, A.R. (1980) *Bias in mental testing*. London: Methuen.

Jersild, A.T. (1963) *The psychology of adolescence* (2nd ed.). New York: Macmillan.

Johansson, G. (1975) Visual motion perception. *Scientific American*, 232, 76–88.

Johnson, J.H. & Scileppi, I.D. (1969) Effects of ego involvement conditions on attitude change in high and low credibility communications. *Journal of Personality and Social Psychology*, 13, 31–6.

Johnson-Laird, P.N., Herrman, D.J. & Chaffin, R. (1984) Only connections: A critique of semantic networks. *Psychological Bulletin*, 96 (2), 292–315.

Johnston, W.A. & Heinz, S.P. (1978) Flexibility and capacity demands of attention. *Journal of Experimental Psychology: General*, 107, 420–35.

Johnston, W.A. & Wilson, J. (1980) Perceptual processing of non-targets in an attention task. *Memory and Cognition*, 8, 372–7.

Jolly, H. (1969) Play is work—the role of play for sick and healthy children. *Lancet*, 2, 487–8.

Jones, E.E. & Davis, K.E. (1965) From acts to dispositions: The attribution process in person perception. In L. Berkowitz (Ed.), *Advances in experimental social psychology, Vol. 2*. New York: Academic Press.

Jones, E.E., Caputo, C., Legant, P. & Marecek, J. (1973) Behaviour as seen by the actor and as seen by the observer. *Journal of Personality and Social Psychology*, 27 (2), 154–64.

Jones, E.E. & Nisbett, R.E. (1971) *The actor and the observer:*

Divergent perceptions of the causes of behaviour. Morristown, New Jersey: General Learning Press.

Jones E.E., Rock, L., Shaver, K.G., Goethals, G.R. & Wand, L.M. (1968) Patterns of performance and ability attribution: An unexpected primacy effect. *Journal of Personality and Social Psychology*, *10*, 317–40.

Jones, M.C. (1924a) A laboratory study of fear: The case of Peter. *Pedagogical Seminary*, *31*, 308–15.

Jones, M.C. (1924b) The elimination of childrens' fears. *Journal of Experimental Psychology*, *7*, 382–90.

Jones, M.C. & Bayley, N. (1950) Physical maturity among boys related to behaviour. *Journal of Educational Psychology*, *41*, 129–48.

Jones, M.C. & Mussen, P.H. (1958) Self-conceptions, motivations and interpersonal attitudes of early and late maturing girls. *Child Development*, *29*, 491–501.

Jost, A. (1970a) Hormonal factors in the development of the male genital system. In E. Rosenberg & C.A. Paulsen (Eds.), *The human testis*. New York: Plenum Press.

Jost, A. (1970b) Hormonal factors in sexual differentiation. *Philosophical Transactions of the Royal Society of London*, *B259*, 119–30.

Jourard, S.M. (1966) An exploratory study of body accessibility. *British Journal of Social and Clinical Psychology*, *5*, 221–31.

Jourard, S.M. (1971) *Self-disclosure: An experimental analysis of the transparent self*. New York: Wiley Interscience.

Jouvet, M. (1967) Mechanisms of the states of sleep: A neuropharmacological approach. *Research Publications of the Association for the Research in Nervous and Mental Diseases*, *45*, 86–126.

Joynson, R.B. (1972) The return of mind. *Bulletin of the British Psychological Society*, *25*, 1–10.

Joynson, R.D. (1974) *Psychology and common sense*. London: RKP.

Juel-Nielson, N. (1965) Individual and environment: A psychiatric and psychological investigation of monozygous twins raised apart. *Acta Psychiatrica et Neurologica Scandinavia*, (Suppl. 183).

Jung, C.G. (1963) *Memories, dreams, reflections*. London: Collins/RKP.

Jung, C.G. (Ed.). (1964) *Man and his symbols*. London: Aldus-Jupiter Books.

Kadushin, A. (1970) *Adopting older children*. New York: Columbia University Press.

Kagan, J., Kearsley, R.B. & Zelago, P.R. (1980) *Infancy—its place in human development*. Cambridge, Massachusetts: Harvard University Press.

Kahneman, D. (1973) *Attention and effort*. Englewood Cliffs, New Jersey: Prentice Hall.

Kahneman, D. & Henik, A. (1979) Perceptual organization and attention. In M. Kubovy & J R Pomerants (Eds.), *Perceptual organization*. Hillsdale, New Jersey: Lawrence Erlbaum Associates Inc.

Kalish, R.A. (1975) *Late adulthood: Perspectives on human development*. Monterey, California: Brooks-Cole.

Kalish, R.A. (1979) The new ageism and the failure models: A polemic. *Gerontologist*, *19*, 398 402.

Kamin, L.J. (1977) *The science and politics of IQ*. Harmondsworth, Middlesex: Penguin.

Karlins, M., Coffman, T.L. & Walters, G. (1969) On the fading of social stereotypes: Studies in three generations of college students. *Journal of Personality and Social Psychology*, *13*, 1–16.

Karniol, R. (1978) Childrens' use of intention cues in evaluating behaviour. *Psychological Bulletin*, *85*, 76–85.

Karr, R.G. (1978) Homosexual labelling and the male role. *Journal of Social Issues*, *34*, 73–83.

Kastenbaum, R. (1979) *Growing old—years of fulfilment*. London: Harper & Row.

Katz, D. (1960) The functional approach to the study of attitudes. *Public Opinion Quarterly*, *74*, 163 204.

Katz, D. & Braly, K. (1933) Racial stereotypes of one hundred college students. *Journal of Abnormal and Social Psychology*, *28*, 280–90.

Katz, E. (1957) The two-step flow of conversion. *Public Opinion Quarterly*, *21*, 61–78.

Kazdin, A.E. & Wilcoxin, L.A. (1976) Systematic desensitization and nonspecific treatment effects: A methodological evaluation. *Psychological Bulletin*, *83*, 729–58.

Keasey, C.B. (1978) Childrens' developing awareness and usage of intentionality and motives. In C.B. Keasey (Ed.), *Nebraska Symposium on Motivation, Vol. 25*. Lincoln: University of Nebraska Press.

Kelley, H.H. (1950) The warm–cold variable in first impressions of people. *Journal of Personality*, *18*, 431–9.

Kelley, H.H. (1967) Attribution theory in social psychology. In D. Levine (Ed.), *Nebraska Symposium on Motivation, Vol. 15*. Lincoln: Nebraska University Press.

Kelley, H.H. (1973) The processes of causal attribution. *American Psychologist*, *28*, 107–28.

Kelley, G.A. (1955) *A theory of personality—the psychology of personal constructs*. New York: Norton.

Kellogg, W.N. & Kellogg, L.A. (1933) *The ape and the child*. New York: McGraw Hill.

Kelman, H.C. (1958) Compliance, identification and internalization: Three processes of attitude change. *Journal of Conflict Resolution*, *2*, 51–60.

Kelman, H.C. & Hovland, C.I. (1953) Reinstatement of the communication in delayed measurement of opinion change. *Journal of Abnormal and Social Psychology*, *48*, 327–35.

Kelvin, P. (1981) Work as a source of identity: The implications of unemployment. *British Journal of Guidance and Counselling*, *9* (1), 2 11.

Kelvin, P. & Jarrett, J. (1985) *The social psychological effects of unemployment*. Cambridge: Cambridge University Press.

Kendell, R.E. (1983) The principles of classification in relation to mental disease. In M. Shepherd & O.L. Zangwill (Eds.), *Handbook of psychiatry: 1, general psychopathology*. Cambridge: Cambridge University Press.

Kennell, J.H., Voos, D.K. & Klaus, M.H. (1979) Parent–infant bonding. In J.D. Osofsky, (Ed.), *Handbook of infant development*. New York: Wiley.

Kerckhoff, A.C. (1974) The social context of interpersonal attraction. In T.L. Huston (Ed.), *Foundations of interpersonal attraction*. New York: Academic Press.

Kerckhoff, A.C. & Davis, K.E. (1962) Value consensus and need complementarity in mate selection. *American Sociological Review*, *27*, 295–303.

Kerr, S. (1977) Substitutes for leadership: Some implications for organizational design. *Organization and Administrative Sciences*, *8*, 135 46.

Kety, S., Rosenthal, D., Wender, P.H., Schulsinger, F. & Jacobson, B. (1975) Mental illness in the biological and adoptive families of adoptive individuals who have become schizophrenic. In R.R. Fieve, D. Rosenthal & H. Bull (Eds.), *Genetic research in psychiatry*. Baltimore: Johns Hopkins University Press.

Kilham, W. & Mann, L. (1974) Level of destructive obedience as a function of transmitter and executant roles in the Milgram obedience paradigm. *Journal of Personality and Social Psychology*, *29*, 696–702.

Kimball, R.K. & Hollander, E.P. (1974) Independence in the presence of an experienced but deviant group member. *Journal of Social Psychology*, *93*, 281 92.

Kiminyo, D.M. (1977) A cross-cultural study of the development of conservation of mass, weight and volume among Kamba children. In P.R. Dasen (Ed.), *Piagetian psychology*. New York: Gardner Press.

Kinchla, R.A. & Wolf, J.M. (1979) The order of visual processing: "Top-down", "bottom-up", or "middle-out". *Perception and Psychophysics*, *25*, 225 31.

Kintsch, W. & Buschke, H. (1969) Homphones and synonyms in short-term memory. *Journal of Experimental Psychology*, *80*, 403–7.

Kirby, R. & Radford, J. (1976) *Individual differences*. London: Methuen.

Klaus, H.M. & Kennell, J.H. (1976) *Maternal infant bonding*. St Louis: Mosby.

Klaus, R.A. & Gray, S.W. (1968) The early training project for disadvantaged children: A report after five years. *Monographs of the Society for Research in Child Development 33* (4), (Serial No. 120).

Kleiner, K.A. (1987) Amplitude and phase spectra as indices of infants' pattern preferences. *Infant Behaviour and Development, 10*, 49–59.

Kleinmuntz, B. (1980) *Essentials of abnormal psychology* (2nd ed.). London: Harper & Row.

Kleitman, N. (1927) Studies on the physiology of sleep; V; Some experiments on puppies. *American Journal of Physiology, 84*, 386–95.

Kline, P. (1972) *Fact and fantasy in Freudian theory*. London: Methuen.

Kline, P. (1981) The work of Eysenck and Cattell. In F. Fransella (Ed.), *Personality—theory, measurement and research*. London: Methuen.

Kline, P. (1983) *Personality—measurement and theory*. London: Hutchinson.

Kline, P. (1988) *Psychology exposed*. London: Routledge.

Kline, P. (1989) Objective tests of Freud's theories. In A.M. Colman & J.G. Beaumont (Eds.), *Psychology Survey, No. 7*. Leicester: British Psychological Society.

Klüver, H. & Bucy, P.C. (1937) "Psychic blindness" and other symptoms following bilateral temporal lobectomy in rhesus monkeys. *American Journal of Physiology, 119*, 352–3.

Koestler, A. (1970a) *The ghost in the machine*. London: Pan Books.

Koestler, A. (1970b) *The act of creation*. London: Pan Books.

Kohlberg, L. (1966) A cognitive–developmental analysis of childrens' sex-role concepts and attitudes. In E.E. Maccoby (Ed.), *The development of sex differences*. Stanford, California: Stanford University Press.

Kohlberg, L. (1969) Stage and sequence: The cognitive developmental approach to socialization. In D.A. Goslin (Ed.), *Handbook of socialization theory and research*. Chicago: Rand McNally.

Kohlberg, L. (1975) The cognitive-developmental approach to moral education. *Phi Delta Kappa, June*, 670–7.

Kohlberg, L. (1976) Moral stages and moralization. In T. Likona (Ed.), *Moral development and behaviour*. New York: Holt, Rinehart & Winston.

Kohlberg, L. (1978) Revisions in the theory and practice of moral development. *Directions for Child Development, 2*, 83–8.

Kohlberg, L. (1981) *Essays on moral development, Vol. 1*. New York: Harper & Row.

Kohler, I. (1962) Experiments with goggles. *Scientific American, 206*, 67–72.

Kohler, I. (1964) The formation and transformation of the visual world. *Psychological Issues, 3*, 28–46/116–33.

Köhler, W. (1925) *The mentality of apes*. New York: Harcourt Brace Jovanovich.

Köhler, W. (1947) *Gestalt psychology*. New York: Liveright.

Koffka, K. (1935) *Principles of Gestalt psychology*. New York: Harcourt Brace.

Kolers, P.A. (1972) *Aspects of motion perception*. New York: Pergamon Press.

Koluchova, J. (1972) Severe deprivation in twins: a case study. *Journal of Child Psychology and Psychiatry, 13*, 107–14.

Koluchova, J. (1976) The further development of twins after severe and prolonged deprivation: A second report. *Journal of Child Psychology and Psychiatry, 17*, 181–8.

Konishi, M. (1965) The role of auditory feedback in the control of vocalization in the white-crowned sparrow. *Zeitschrift der Tierpsychologie, 22*, 770–83.

Kraepelin, E. (1913) *Psychiatry* (8th ed.). Leipzig: Thieme.

Kraus, A.S. & Lilienfeld, A.M. (1959) Some epidemiological aspects of the high mortality rate in the young widowed group. *Journal of Chronic Diseases, 10*, 207–17.

Krebs, D. & Adinolfi, A. (1975) Physical attractiveness, social relations and personality style. *Journal of Personality and Social Psychology, 31*, 245–53.

Kretschmer, E. (1936) *Physique and character* (2nd ed.) (W.J.H. Sprott & K. Paul Trench, trans). New York: Trubner.

Kruglanski, A.W. (1977) The place of naive contents in a theory of attribution: Reflections on Calder and Zuckerman's critiques of the endogenous–exogenous partition. *Personality and Social Psychology Bulletin, 3*, 592–605.

Kruglanski, A.W. (1979) Causal explanation, teleological expansion: On radical particularism in attribution theory. *Journal of Personality and Social Psychology, 37*, 1447–57.

Kübler-Ross, E. (1969) *On death and dying*. London: Tavistock/Routledge.

Kuhn, D., Nash, S.C. & Brucker, J.A. (1978) Sex role concepts of two- and three-year-olds. *Child Development, 49*, 445–51.

Kuhn, H.H. (1960) Self attitudes by age, sex and professional training. *Sociology Quarterly, 1*, 39–55.

Kuhn, T.S. (1962) *The structure of scientific revolutions*. Chicago: University of Chicago Press.

Kulick, J.A. & Brown, R. (1979) Frustration, attribution of blame and aggression. *Journal of Experimental and Social Psychology, 15*, 183–94.

Kurtines, W. & Greif, E.B. (1974) The development of moral thought: Review and evaluation of Kohlberg's approach. *Psychological Bulletin, 81* (8), 453–70.

Labouvie-Vief, G. (1979) *Does intelligence decline with age?* Bethesda, Maryland: National Institute of Health.

Labov, W. (1970) The logic of non-standard English. In F. Williams (Ed.), *Language and poverty*. Chicago: Markham.

Lahey, B.B. (1983) *Psychology: An introduction*. Dubugue, Iowa: William C. Brown Co.

Laing, R.D. (1965) *The divided self*. Harmondsworth, Middlesex: Penguin.

Laing, R.D. (1967) *The politics of experience and the bird of paradise*. Harmondsworth, Middlesex: Penguin.

Laing, R.D. (1971) *Knots*. Harmondsworth, Middlesex: Penguin.

Laird, J.D. (1974) Self-attribution of emotion: The effects of facial expression on the quality of emotional experience. *Journal of Personality and Social Psychology, 29*, 475–86.

Lamb, M.E. (1977) Father–infant and mother–infant interaction in the first year of life. *Child Development, 48*, 167–81.

Land, E.H. (1964) The retinex. *American Scientist, 52*, 247–64.

Land, E.H. (1977) The retinex theory of colour vision. *Scientific American, 237* (6), 108–28.

La Piere, R.T. (1934) Attitudes versus action. *Social Forces, 13*, 230–7.

Larsen, K.S. (1974) Conformity in the Asch experiment. *Journal of Social Psychology, 94*, 303–4.

Larsen, K.S. (1982) Cultural conditions and conformity: The Asch effect. *Bulletin of the British Psychological Society, 35*, 347.

Larsen, K.S., Triplett, J.S., Brant, W.D. & Langenberg, D. (1979) Collaborator status, subject characteristics and conformity in the Asch paradigm. *Journal of Social Psychology, 108*, 259–63.

Lashley, K. (1929) *Brain mechanisms and intelligence: A quantitative study of injuries to the brain*. Chicago, Illinois: University of Chicago Press.

Laswell, H.D. (1948) The structures and function of communication in society. In L. Bryson (Ed.), *Communication of ideas*. New York: Harper.

Latané, B. & Darley, J.M. (1968) Group inhibitions of bystander intervention in emergencies. *Journal of Personality and Social Psychology, 10*, 215–21.

Latané, B. & Darley, J.M. (1970) *The unresponsive bystander: Why does he not help?* New York: Appleton-Century-Croft.

Latané, B. & Rodin, J. (1969) A lady in distress: Inhibiting effects of friends and strangers on bystander intervention. *Journal of Experimental Social Psychology, 5*, 189–202.

Latané, B. & Wolf, S. (1981) The social impact of majorities and minorities. *Psychological Review*, 88, 438–53.

Lazarsfeld, P.F., Berelson, B. & Gaudet, H. (1948) *The peoples' choice: How the voter makes up his mind in a presidential campaign*. New York: Columbia University Press.

Lazarus, A.A. (1977) *Behaviour therapy and beyond*. New York: McGraw Hill.

Lazarus, R.S. (1982) Thoughts on the relations between emotion and cognition. *American Psychologist*, 37, 1019–24.

Lazarus, R.S. & McCleary, R.A. (1951) Automatic discrimination without awareness: A study of subception. *Psychological Review*, 58, 113–22.

Lea, S.E.G. (1984) *Instinct, environment and behaviour*. London: Methuen.

Leahy, A.M. (1935) Nature–nurture and intelligence. *Genetic Psychology Monograph*, 17, 235–308.

Leavitt, J.J. (1951) Some effects of certain communication patterns on group performance. *Journal of Abnormal and Social Psychology*, 46, 38–50.

Lee, D.N. & Lishman, J.R. (1975) Visual proprioceptive control of stance. *Journal of Human Movement Studies*, 1, 87–95.

Lee, L. (1984) Sequences in separation: A framework for investigating endings of the personal (romantic) relationship. *Journal of Social and Personal Relationships*, 1, 49–74.

LeFrancois, G.R. (1983) *Psychology*. Belmont, California: Wadsworth Publishing Co.

Legge, D. (1975) *An introduction to psychological science*. London: Methuen.

Lemyre, L. & Smith, P.M. (1985) Intergroup discrimination and self-esteem in the minimal group paradigm. *Journal of Personality and Social Psychology*, 62, 99–105.

Lenneberg, E.H. (1960) Review of speech and brain mechanisms by W. Penfield and L. Roberts. In R.C. Oldfield & J.C. Marshall (Eds.), *Language*. Harmondsworth, Middlesex: Penguin.

Lenneberg, E.H. (1967) *Biological foundations of language*. New York: Wiley.

Lenneberg, E.H. & Roberts, J.M. (1956) *The language of experience, Memoir 13*. Indiana: University of Indiania, Publications in Anthropology & Linguistics.

Lepper, M.R. & Greene, D. (1978) Overjustification research and beyond: Towards a means–end analysis of intrinsic and extrinsic motivation. In M.R. Lepper & D. Greene (Eds.), *The hidden costs of reward*. Hillsdale, New Jersey: Lawrence Erlbaum Associates Inc.

Levinger, G. & Clark, J. (1961) Emotional factors in the forgetting of word associations. *Journal of Abnormal and Social Psychology*, 62, 99–105.

Levinson, D.J., Darrow, D.N., Klein, E.B., Levinson, M.H. & McKee, B. (1978) *The seasons of a man's life*. New York: A.A. Knopf.

Levy-Agresti, J. & Sperry, R.W. (1968) Differential perceptual capacities in major and minor hemispheres. *Proceedings of the National Academy of Sciences*, 61, 1151.

Lewin, K., Lippitt, R. & White, R. (1939) Patterns of aggressive behaviour in experimentally created 'social climates'. *Journal of Social Psychology*, 10, 271–99.

Lewin, R. (1991) Look who's talking now. *New Scientist*, 130 (1766), 48–52.

Lewis, M. & Brooks-Gunn, J. (1979) *Social cognition and the acquisition of self*. New York: Plenum.

Light, P. (1986) Context, conservation and conversation. In M. Richards & P. Light (Eds.), *Children of social worlds*. Cambridge: Polity Press.

Light, P., Buckingham, N. & Robbins, A.H. (1979) The conservation task as an interactional setting. *British Journal of Educational Psychology*, 49, 304–10.

Light, P. & Gilmour, A (1983) Conservation or conversation? Contextual facilitation of inappropriate conservation judgements. *Journal of Experimental Child Psychology*, 36, 356–63.

Likert, R. (1932) A technique for the measurement of attitudes.

Archives of Psychology, 22, 140.

Linder, D.E., Cooper, J. & Jones, E.E. (1967) Decision freedom as a determinant of the role of incentive magnitude in attitude change. *Journal of Personality and Social Psychology*, 6, 245–54.

Lindsay, W.R. (1982) The effects of labelling: Blind and non-blind ratings of social skills in schizophrenic and non-schizophrenic control subjects. *American Journal of Psychiatry*, 139, 216–19.

Linville, P.W. & Jones, E.E. (1980) Polarized appraisals of outgroup members. *Journal of Personality and Social Psychology*, 38, 689–703.

Lipsitt, L.P. (1977) The study of sensory and learning processes of the newborn. *Clinics in Perinatology*, 4, 163–86.

Lippman, W. (1922) *Public opinion*. New York: Harcourt.

Lloyd, P., Mayes, A., Manstead, A.S.R., Mendell, P.R. & Wagner, H.L. (1984) *Introduction to psychology—an integrated approach*. London: Fontana.

Locke, S.E. (1982) Stress, adaptation and immunity: Studies in humans. *General Hospital Psychiatry*, 4, 49–58.

Locksley, A., Ortiz, V. & Hepburn, C. (1980) Social categorization and discriminatory behaviour. Extinguishing the minimal intergroup discrimination effect. *Journal of Personality and Social Psychology*, 39, 773–83.

Loftus, E.F. (1979) Reactions to blatantly contradictory information. *Memory and Cognition*, 7, 368–74.

Loftus, E.F. (1984) Expert testimony on the eyewitness. In G.L. Wells & E.F. Loftus (Eds.), *Eyewitness testimony: Psychological perspectives*. Cambridge: Cambridge University Press.

Loftus, E.F., Freedman, J.L. & Loftus, G.R. (1970) Retrieval of words from sub-ordinate and superordinate categories in semantic hierarchies. *Psychonomic Science*, 21, 235–6.

Loftus, E.F., Miller, D.G. & Burns, H.J. (1978) Semantic integration of verbal information into a visual memory. *Journal of Experimental Psychology*, 4 (1), 19–31.

Loftus, E.F. & Palmer, J.C. (1974) Reconstruction of automobile destruction: An example of the interaction between language and memory. *Journal of Verbal Learning and Verbal Behaviour*, 13, 585–9.

Loftus, E.F. & Zanni, G. (1975) Eyewitness testimony: The influence of the wording of a question. *Bulletin of the Psychonomic Society*, 5, 86–8.

Logan, G.D. (1988) Toward an instance theory of automisation. *Psychological Review*, 95, 492–527.

Lorenz, K.Z. (1935) The companion in the bird's world. *Auk*, 54, 245–73.

Lorenz, K.Z. (1966) *On aggression*. London: Methuen.

Lovaas, O.I., Freitas, L., Nelson, K. & Whalen, C. (1967) The establishment of imitation and its use for the development of complex behaviour in schizophrenic children. *Behaviour Research and Therapy*, 5, 171–81.

Luchins, A.S. (1942) Mechanisation in problem solving. The effect of Einstellung. *Psychological Monographs*, 54 (Whole No. 248).

Luchins, A.S. (1957) Primacy–recency in impression formation. In C. Hovland (Ed.), *The order of presentation in persuasion*. New Haven, Connecticut: Yale University Press.

Luchins, A.S. & Luchins, E.H. (1959) *Rigidity of behaviour*. Eugene, Oregon: University of Oregon Press.

Luria, A.R. (1968) *The mind of a mnemonist*. New York: Basic Books.

Luria, A.R. (1975) *The man with a shattered world*. Harmondsworth, Middlesex: Penguin.

Luria, A.R. (1987) Reductionism. In R. Gregory (Ed.), *The Oxford companion to the mind*. Oxford: Oxford University Press.

Luria, A.R. & Yudovich, F.I. (1971) *Speech and the development of mental processes in the child*. Harmondsworth, Middlesex: Penguin.

Lyons, J. (1970) *Chomsky*. London: Fontana.

Maccoby, E.E. (1980) *Social development—psychological growth and the parent child relationship*. New York: Harcourt Brace Jovanovich.

Maccoby, E.E. & Jacklin, C.N. (1974) *The psychology of sex differences*. Stanford, California: Stanford University Press.

Mackay, D. (1975) *Clinical psychology—theory and therapy*. London: Methuen.

Mackay, D. (1984) Behavioural psychotherapy. In W. Dryden (Ed.), *Individual therapy in Britain*. London: Harper & Row.

Mackinnon, D. (1938) Violations of prohibitions. In H.A. Murray (Ed.), *Explorations in personality*. New York: Oxford University Press.

Mackintosh, N. (1984) In search of a new theory of conditioning. In G. Ferry (Ed.), *The understanding of animals*. Oxford: Blackwell and New Scientist.

MacNamara, J. (1982) *Names for things*. Cambridge, Massachusetts: Bradford MIT Press.

Maddison, D. & Viola, A. (1968) The health of widows in the year following bereavement. *Journal of Psychosomatic Research*, 12, 297.

Mahoney, M.J. (1974) *Cognition and behaviour modification*. Cambridge, Massachusetts: Ballinger.

Maier, N.R.F. (1931) Reasoning in humans II: The solution of a problem and its appearance in consciousness. *Journal of Comparative Psychology*, 12, 181–94.

Maier, S.F. & Seligman, M.E.P. (1976) Learned helplessness: Theory and evidence. *Journal of Experimental Psychology: General*, 105, 3–46.

Malinowski, B. (1929) *The sexual life of savages*. New York: Harcourt, Brace and World.

Mandler, J.M. & Johnson, N.S. (1977) Remembrance of things parsed: Story structure and recall. *Cognitive Psychology*, 9, 111–51.

Mann, L. (1969) *Social psychology*. New York: Wiley.

Mapstone, E. (1991) Special issue on animal experimentation. *The Psychologist*, 4 (5), 195.

Marañon, G. (1924) Contribution a l'etude de l'action emotive de l'adrenaline. *Revue Française Endocrinol.*, 2, 301–25.

Marcia, J.E. (1966) Development and validation of ego identity status. *Journal of Personality and Social Psychology*, 3, 551–8.

Marcia, J.E. (1967) Ego identity status: Relationship to change in self-esteem, general maladjustment and authoritarianism. *Journal of Personality*, 35, 118–33.

Marcia, J.E. (1968) The case history of a construct: Ego identity status. In E. Vinacke (Ed.), *Readings in general psychology*. New York: Van Nostrand–Reinhold.

Marcus, D.E. & Overton, W.F. (1978) The development of cognitive gender constancy and sex role preferences. *Child Development*, 49, 434–44.

Marks, I.M., Gelder, M. & Bancroft, J. (1970) Sexual deviants two years after electric aversion. *British Journal of Psychiatry*, 117, 173–85.

Marr, D. (1982) *Vision*. San Francisco: W.H. Freeman.

Marris, P. (1958) *Widows and their families*. London, RKP.

Marshall, G.D. & Zimbardo, P.G. (1979) Affective consequences of inadequately explained physiological arousal. *Journal of Personality and Social Psychology*, 37, 970–88.

Maslach. C. (1979) Negative emotional biasing of unexplained arousal. *Journal of Personality and Social Psychology*, 37, 953–69.

Maslow, A. (1954) *Motivation and personality*. New York: Harper & Row.

Maslow, A. (1968) *Towards a psychology of being* (2nd ed.). New York: Van Nostrand–Reinhold.

Maslow, A. (1970) *Motivation and personality* (2nd ed.). New York: Harper & Row.

Maslow, C., Yoselson, K. & London, M. (1971) Persuasiveness of confidence expressed via language and body language. *British Journal of Social and Clinical Psychology*, 10, 234–40.

Mason, M.K. (1942) Learning to speak after six and one half years of silence. *Journal of Speech and Hearing Disorders*, 7, 295–304.

Maunsell, J.H.R. & Newsome, W.T. (1987) Visual processing in monkey extrastriate cortex. *Annual Review of Neuroscience*, 10, 363–401.

Maykovich, M.K. (1975) Correlates of racial prejudice. *Journal of Personality and Social Psychology*, 32, 1014–20.

McArthur, L.A. (1972) The how and why of why: Some determinants and consequences of causal attribution. *Journal of Personality and Social Psychology*, 22, 171–93.

McCall, R.B. (1975) *Intelligence and heredity*. Homewood, Illinois: Learning Systems Co.

McCall, R.B., Applebaum, M.I. & Hogarty, P.S. (1973) Developmental changes in mental test performance. *Monographs of the Society for Research in Child Development* 38, (3, Whole No. 150).

McCann, J.J. (1987) Retinex theory and colour constancy. In R. Gregory (Ed.), *Oxford companion to the mind*. Oxford: Oxford University Press.

McCarley, R.M. (1983) REM dreams, REM sleep and their isomorphism. In M.H. Chase & E.D. Weitzman (Eds.), *Sleep disorders: Basic and clinical research, Vol. 8* (published as book). New York: Spectrum.

McClelland, D.C., Atkinson, J., Clark, R. & Lowell, E. (1953) *The achievement motive*. New York: Appleton-Century-Croft.

McGarrigle, J. & Donaldson, M. (1974) Conservation accidents. *Cognition*, 3, 341–50.

McGeoch, J.A. (1942) *The psychology of learning*. New York: Spectrum.

McGinn, C. (1987) Could a machine be conscious? In C. Blakemore & S. Greenfield (Eds.), *Mindwaves*. Oxford: Blackwell.

McGinnies, E. (1949) Emotionality and perceptual defence. *Psychological Review*, 56, 244–51.

McGlynn, F.D., Mealiea, W.L. & Landau, D.L. (1981) The current status of systematic desensitization. *Clinical Psychology Review*, 1, 149–79.

McGuire, W.J. (1957) Order of presentation as a factor in "conditioning" persuasiveness. In C.I. Hovland (Ed.), *The order of presentation in persuasion*. New Haven: Yale University Press.

McGuire, W.J. & Papegeorgis, D. (1961) Effectiveness of forewarning in developing resistance to persuasion. *Public Opinion Quarterly*, 26, 24–34.

McGurk, H. (1975) *Growing and changing*. London: Methuen.

McNally, R.J. & Reiss, S. (1982) The preparedness theory of phobias and human safety-signal conditioning. *Behaviour Research and Therapy*, 20, 153–9.

McNeill, D. (1966) The creation of language. In R.C. Oldfield & J.C. Marshall (Eds.), *Language*. Harmondsworth, Middlesex: Penguin.

McNeill, D. (1970) *The acquisition of language*. New York: Harper & Row.

Mead, G.H. (1925) The genesis of the self and social control. *International Journal of Ethics*, 35, 251–73.

Mead, G.H. (1934) *Mind, self and society*. Chicago: University of Chicago Press.

Mead, M. (1928) *Coming of age in Samoa*. Harmondsworth, Middlesex: Penguin.

Mead, M. (1930) *Growing up in New Guinea*. Harmondsworth, Middlesex: Penguin.

Mead, M. (1935) *Sex and temperament in three primitive societies*. New York: Dell.

Mead, M. (1949) *Male and female: A study of the sexes in a changing world*. New York: Dell.

Meadows, S (1986) *Understanding child development*. London: Hutchinson.

Meadows, S. (1988) Piaget's contribution to understanding cognitive development: An assessment for the late 1980's. In K. Richardson & S. Sheldon (Eds.), *Cognitive development to adolescence*. Milton Keynes/Hove: Open University/Lawrence Erlbaum Associates Ltd.

Medawar, P.B. (1963) *The art of the soluble*. Harmondsworth, Middlesex: Penguin.

Meddis, R. (1975) On the function of sleep. *Animal Behaviour*, 23, 676–91.

Meddis, R. (1977) *The sleep instinct*. London: RKP.

Medvedev, Z.A. (1975) Aging and longevity: New approaches and new perspectives. *The Gerontologist*, 15, 196–201.

Megargee, E.I. (1966) Uncontrolled and overcontrolled personality types in extreme antisocial aggression. *Psychological Monographs: General and Applied* (Whole No. 611).

Meichenbaum, D. (1977) *Cognitive behaviour modification: An integrative approach*. New York: Plenum.

Melhuish, E.C. (1982) Visual attention to mothers' and strangers' faces and facial contrast in 1 month olds. *Developmental Psychology*, 18, 299–331.

Milarsky, J.R., Kessler, R.C., Stipp, H. & Rubens, W.S. (1982) *Television and aggression: A panel study*. New York: Academic Press.

Milgram, S. (1963) Behavioural study of obedience. *Journal of Abnormal and Social Psychology*, 67, 391–8.

Milgram, S. (1974) *Obedience to authority*. New York: Harper & Row.

Millar, S. (1968) *The psychology of play*. Harmondsworth, Middlesex: Penguin.

Miller, E. & Morley, S. (1986) *Investigating abnormal behaviour*. London: Lawrence Erlbaum Associates Ltd.

Miller, G.A. (1956) The magical number seven, plus or minus two: Some limits on our capacity for processing information. *Psychological Review*, 63, 81–97.

Miller, G.A. (1962) *Psychology—the science of mental life*. Harmondsworth, Middlesex: Penguin.

Miller, G.A. (1968) *The psychology of communication—seven essays*. Harmondsworth, Middlesex: Penguin.

Miller, G.A. & McNeill, D. (1969) Psycholinguistics. In G. Lindzey & E. Aronson (Eds.), *The handbook of social psychology*, Vol. 3. Reading, Massachusetts: Adison-Wesley.

Miller, N. & Campbell, D. (1959) Recency and primacy in persuasion as a function of the timing of speeches and measurements. *Journal of Abnormal and Social Psychology*, 59, 1–9.

Miller, N.E. (1941) The frustration–aggression hypothesis. *Psychology Reviews*, 48, 337–42.

Miller, N.E. (1978) Biofeedback and visceral learning. *Annual Review of Psychology*, 29, 373–404.

Miller, N.E. & Dicara, L.V. (1967) Instrumental learning of heart-rate changes in curarised rats: Shaping and specificity to discriminative stimulus. *Journal of Comparative and Physiological Psychology*, 63, 12–19.

Milner, B. (1971) Interhemispheric differences in the localization of psychological processes in man. *British Medical Bulletin*, 27, 272–7.

Minard, R.D. (1952) Race relations in the Pocohontas coalfield. *Journal of Social Issues*, 8, 29–44.

Minsky, M. (1975) A framework for representing knowledge. In P.H. Winston (Ed.), *The psychology of computer vision*. New York: McGraw Hill.

Mischel, W. (1968) *Personality and assessment*. New York: Wiley.

Mischel, W. (1969) Continuities and change in personality. *American Psychologist*, 24, 1012–18.

Mischel, W. (1973) Toward a cognitive social learning reconceptualization of personality. *Psychological Review*, 80, 252–83.

Mischel, W. & Mischel, H.N. (1976) A cognitive social learning approach to morality and self-regulation. In T. Lickona (Ed.), *Moral development and behaviour: Theory, research and social issues*. New York: Holt, Rinehart & Winston.

Mitchell, J. (1974) *Psychoanalysis and feminism*. Harmondsworth, Middlesex: Penguin.

Mitchel, R. (1982) *Phobias*. Harmondsworth, Middlesex: Penguin.

Moltz, H. & Stettner, L.J. (1961) The influences of patterned-light deprivation on the critical period for imprinting. *Journal of Comparative and Physiological Psychology*, 54, 279–83.

Monahan, F. (1941) *Women in crime*. New York: Ives Washburn.

Money, J. (1971) Sexually dimorphous behaviour, normal and abnormal. In N. Kretchner & D.N. Walcher (Eds.), *Environmental influences on genetic expression*. Washington DC: US Government Printing Office.

Money, J. (1974) Prenatal hormones and postnatal socialization in gender identity differentiation. In J.K. Cole & R. Dienstbier (Eds.), *Nebraska Symposium on Motivation*. Lincoln: University of Nebraska Press.

Money, J. & Ehrhardt, A.A. (1972) *Man and woman, boy and girl*. Baltimore: Johns Hopkins University Press.

Moore, C. & Frye, D. (1986) The effect of the experimenter's intention on the child's understanding of conservation. *Cognition*, 22, 283–98.

Moray, N. (1959) Attention in dichotic listening: Affective cues and the influence of instructions. *Quarterly Journal of Experimental Psychology*, 11, 56–60.

Moreno, J.L. (1953) *Who shall survive?* (2nd ed.). New York: Beacon.

Morgan, M. (1982) Television and adolescents' sex role stereotypes: A longitudinal study. *Journal of Personality and Social Psychology*, 43, 947–55.

Morgan, P. (1974) Against clinging: Monkeys and mothers. *New Society*, August 29, 537–40.

Morris, C.D., Bransford, J.D. & Franks, J.J. (1977) Levels of processing versus transfer appropriate processing. *Journal of Verbal Learning and Verbal Behaviour*, 16, 519–33.

Morris, D. (1967) *The naked ape*. London: Jonathan Cape.

Morris, D. (1969) *The human zoo*. London: Jonathan Cape.

Morris, P.E. (1978) Models of long-term memory. In M.M. Gruneberg & P.E. Morris (Eds.), *Aspects of memory*. London: Methuen.

Moruzzi, G. & Magoun, H.W. (1949) Brain stem reticular formation and activation of the EEG. *Electroencephalography and Clinical Neurophysiology*, 1, 455–73.

Moser, K.A., Fox, A.J. & Jones, D.R. (1984) Unemployment and mortality in the OPCS longitudinal study. *Lancet*, 2, 1324–9.

Moskovitz, S. (1983) *Love despite hate—child survivors of the Holocaust and their adult lives*. New York: Schocken.

Mowrer, O.H. (1950) *Learning theory and personality dynamics*. New York: Ronald Press.

Moyer, K.E. (1976) *The psychobiology of aggression*. New York: Harper & Row.

Mundy-Castle, A.C. & Nelson, G.K. (1962) A neuropsychological study of the Kuysma forest workers. *Psychologia Africana*, 9, 240–72.

Murdock, B.B. (1962) The serial position effect of free recall. *Journal of Experimental Psychology*, 64, 482–8.

Murray, E.J. & Foote, F. (1979) The origins of fear of snakes. *Behaviour Research and Therapy*, 17, 489–93.

Murray, H.A. (Ed.) (1938) *Explorations in personality*. New York: Oxford University Press.

Murstein, B.I. (1972) Physical attractiveness and marital choice. *Journal of Personality and Social Psychology*, 22 (1), 8–12.

Murstein, B.I. (1978) *Exploring intimate lifestyles*. New York: Springer.

Murstein, B.I. & MacDonald, M.G. (1983) The relation of "exchange orientation" and "commitment" scales to marriage adjustment. *International Journal of Psychology*, 18, 297–311.

Murstein, B.I., MacDonald, M.G. & Cerreto, M. (1977) A theory of the effect of exchange-orientation on marriage and friendship. *Journal of Marriage and the Family*, 39, 543–8.

Mussen, P.H. & Jones, M. (1957) Self-conceptions, motivations and interpersonal attitudes of late and early maturing boys. *Child Development*, 28, 243–56.

Navon, D. (1977) Forest before trees: The precedence of global features in visual perception. *Cognitive Psychology*, 9, 353–83.

Neisser, U. (1967) *Cognitive psychology*. New York: Appleton-Century-Crofts.

Neisser, U. (1976) *Cognition and reality*. San Francisco: W.H. Freeman.

Neisser, U. (1979) The concept of intelligence. In R.J. Sternberg & D.K. Detterman (Eds.), *Human intelligence: Perspectives on its theory and measurement*. New Jersey: Norwood.

Nelson, K. (1973) Structure and strategy in learning to talk. *Monographs of the Society for Research in Child Development*, 38, 149.

Nelson, T.O. & Vining, S.K. (1978) Effect of semantic versus structural processing on long-term retention. *Journal of Experimental Psychology: Human learning and memory*, 4, 198–209.

Nesselroade, J.R., Schaie, K.W. & Batter, P.B. (1972) Ontogenetic and generational components of structural and quantitative change in adult behaviour. *Journal of Gerontology*, 27, 222–8.

Neugarten, B.L. (1965) Personality and patterns of ageing. *Gawein*, 13, 249–56.

Neugarten, B.L. & Havighurst, R.J. (1969) Disengagement reconsidered in a cross national context. In R.J. Havighurst (Ed.), *Adjustment to retirement*. Assess, Netherlands: Van Gorcum.

Neugarten, B.L., Moore, J.W. & Lowe, J.C. (1965) Age norms, age constraints and adult socialization. *American Journal of Sociology*, 70, 710–17.

Newcomb, T.M. (1947) Autistic hostility and social reality. *Human Relations*, 1, 69–86.

Newcomb, T.M. (1961) *The aquaintanceship process*. New York: Holt, Rinehart & Winston.

Newell, A. (1973) Production systems: Models of control structures. In W.G. Chase (Ed.), *Visual information processing*. New York: Academic Press.

Newell, A., Shaw, J.C. & Simon, H.A. (1958) Elements of a theory of human problem solving. *Psychological Review*, 65, 151–66.

Newell, A. & Simon, H.A. (1972) *Human problem solving*. Englewood Cliffs, New Jersey: Prentice-Hall.

Newman, H.H., Freeman, F.N. & Holzinger, K.J. (1937) *Twins: A study of heredity and environment*. Chicago, Illinois: University of Chicago Press.

Nicholson, J. (1977) *Habits*. London: Macmillan.

Nisbet, R.E. & Borgida, E. (1975) Attribution and the psychology of prediction. *Journal of Personality and Social Psychology*, 32, 923–43.

Nisbet, R.E., Caputo, C., Legant, P. & Maracek, J. (1973) Behaviour as seen by the actor and as seen by the observer. *Journal of Personality and Social Psychology*, 27, 154–65.

Nisbet, R.E. & Ross, L. (1980) *Human inference: Strategies and shortcomings of social judgement*. Englewood Cliffs, New Jersey: Prentice-Hall.

Nisbet, R.E. & Wilson, T. (1972) Telling more than we can know: Verbal reports on mental processes. *Psychology Review*, 84, 231–59.

Nord, W.R. (1969) Social exchange theory: An integrative approach to social conformity. *Psychological Bulletin*, 71, 173–208.

Norman, D.A. (1969) Memory while shadowing. *Quarterly Journal of Experimental Psychology*, 21, 85–93.

Norman, D.A. (1976) *Memory and attention* (2nd ed.). Chichester: Wiley.

Norman, D.A. & Bobrow, D.G. (1975) On data-limited and resource-limited processing. *Cognitive Psychology*, 7, 44–64.

Norman, D.A. & Shallice, T. (1980) *Attention to action: Willed and automatic control of behaviour (CHIP Report 99)*. San Diego, California: University of California.

Novak, M.A. (1979) Social recovery of monkeys isolated for the first year of life 2: Long-term assessment. *Developmental Psychology*, 15, 50–61.

Nyiti, R.M. (1976) The development of conservation in the Meru children of Tanzania. *Child Development*, 47, 1622–9.

Nyiti, R.M. (1982) The validity of "cultural differences explanations" for cross-cultural variation in the rate of Piagetian cognitive development. In D.A. Wagner and H.W. Stevenson (Eds.), *Cultural perspectives in child development*. San Francisco: W.H. Freeman.

Oakes, P.J. & Turner, J.C. (1980) Social categorization and intergroup behaviour: Does minimal intergroup discrimination make social identity more positive? *European Journal of Psychology*, 10, 295–301.

Oatley, K. (1981) The self with others: The person and the interpersonal context in the approaches of C.R. Rogers and R.D. Laing. In Fransella, F. (Ed.), *Personality—theory, measurement and research*. London: Methuen.

Oatley, K. (1984) *Selves in relation: An introduction to psychotherapy and groups*. London: Methuen.

O'Connor, N. & Hermelin, B. (1988) Low intelligence and special abilities. *Journal of Child Psychology and Psychiatry*, 29 (4), 391–6.

Offer, D. & Offer, J.B. (1975) *From teenage to young manhood: A psychological study*. New York: Basic Books.

O'Grady, M. (1977) Effects of subliminal pictorial stimulation on skin resistance. *Perceptual and Motor Skills*, 44, 1051–6.

Olds, J. (1956) Pleasure centres in the brain. *Scientific American*, October, 105–6.

Olds, J. (1958) Self-stimulation of the brain. *Science*, 127, 315–23.

Olds, J. (1962) Hypothalmic substrates of reward. *Physiological Review*, 42, 554–604.

Olds, J. & Milner, P. (1954) Positive reinforcement produced by electrical stimulation of septal area and other regions of the rat brain. *Journal of Comparative and Physiological Psychology*, 47, 419–27.

Oliner, S.P. & Oliner, P.M. (1988) *The altruistic personality: Rescuers of Jews in Nazi Europe*. New York: Free Press.

Olson, R.K. & Attneave, F. (1970) What variables produce similarity grouping? *American Journal of Psychology*, 83, 1–21.

Ora, J.P. (1965) *Characteristics of the volunteer for psychological investigation*. Office of Naval Research, Contract 2149 (03), Technical Report 27.

Orne, M.T. (1962) On the social psychology of the psychological experiment—with particular reference to demand characteristics and their implications. *American Psychologist*, 17 (11), 776–83.

Orne, M.T. (1970) Hypnosis: Motivation and the ecological validity of the psychological experiment. In W.J. Arnold and M.M. Page (Eds.), *Nebraska Symposium on Motivation*. Lincoln, Nebraska: University of Nebraska Press.

Ornstein, R. (1986) *The psychology of consciousness* (2nd ed. revised). Harmondsworth, Middlesex: Penguin.

Orvis, B.R. Cunningham, J.D. & Kelley, H.H. (1975) A closer examination of causal inference: The roles of consensus, distinctiveness and consistency information. *Journal of Personality and Social Psychology*, 32, 605–16.

Osgood, C.E., Suci, G.J. & Tannenbaum, P.H. (1957) *The measurement of meaning*. Urbana, Illinois: University of Illinois Press.

Osgood, C.E. & Tannenbaum, P.H. (1955) The principle of congruity in the prediction of attitude change. *Psychological Review*, 62, 42–55.

Oswald, I. (1966) *Sleep*. Harmondsworth, Middlesex: Penguin.

Oswald, I. (1969) Human brain protein, drugs and dreams. *Nature*, 223, 893–7.

Oswald, I. (1974) *Sleep* (2nd ed.). Harmondsworth, Middlesex: Penguin.

Oswald, I. (1980) Sleep as a restorative process: Human clues. *Process in Brain Research*, 53, 279–88.

Packer, O., Hartmann, E.E. & Teller, D.Y. (1985) Infant colour vision: The effect of test field size on Rayleigh discriminations. *Vision Research*, 24, 1247–60.

Paivio, A. (1969) Mental imagery in associative learning and memory. *Psychological Review*, 76, 241–63.

Paivio, A. (1971) *Imagery and verbal processes*. New York: Holt, Rinehart & Winston.

Palermo, D.S. (1971) Is a scientific revolution taking place in psychology? *Psychological Review*, 76, 241–63.

Palmore, E. (1977) Facts on aging. *The Gerontologist*, 17, 315–20.

Papalia, D.E. (1972) The status of several conservation abilities across the lifespan. *Human Development*, 15, 229–43.

Papez, J.W. (1937) A proposed mechanism of emotion. *Archives of Neurology and Psychiatry*, 38, 725–43.

Parke, R.D. (1969) Effectiveness of punishment as an interaction of intensity, timing agent nurturance and cognitive structuring. *Child Development*, 40, 213–36.

Parke, R.D. (1972) Some effects of punishment on childrens' behaviour. In W.W. Harting (Ed.), *The young child, Vol. 2*. Washington DC: National Association for the Education of Young Children.

Parke, R.D. (1974) Rules, roles and resistance to deviation: Recent advances in punishment, discipline and self control. In A.D. Pick (Ed.), *Minnesota Symposium on Child Psychology*, Vol. 8. Minneapolis, Minnesota: University of Minnesota Press.

Parke, R.D. (1977) Some effects of punishment on childrens' behaviour—revisited. In E.M. Hetherington & R.D. Parke (Eds.), *Contemporary readings in child psychology*. New York: McGraw Hill.

Parke, R.D. (1978) Perspectives on father–infant interaction. In J.D. Osofsky (Ed.), *Handbook of infancy*. New York: John Wiley & Sons.

Parke, R.D. (1981) *Fathering*. London: Fontana.

Parke, R.D., Berkowitz, L., Leyens, J.P., West, S.G. & Sebastian, R.J. (1977) Some effects of violent and non-violent movies on the behaviour of juvenile delinquents. In L. Berkowitz (Ed.), *Advances in experimental psychology, Vol. 10*. New York: Academic Press.

Parkes, C.M. (1962) *Reactions to bereavement*. Unpublished Masters Thesis, London University.

Parkes, C.M. (1964) Recent bereavement as a cause of mental illness. *British Journal of Psychiatry*, 110, 198–204.

Parkes, C.M. (1965) Bereavement and mental illness. *British Journal of Medical Psychology*, 38, 1.

Parkes, C.M. (1970) The first year of bereavement: A longitudinal study of the reaction of London widows to the death of their husbands. *Psychiatry*, 33, 444–67.

Parkes, C.M. (1975) *Bereavement—studies of grief in adult life*. Harmondsworth, Middlesex: Penguin.

Parkes, C.M., Benjamin, B. & Fitzgerald, R.G. (1969) Broken heart: A statistical study of increased mortality among widowers. *British Medical Journal*, 1, 740–3.

Parkes, C.M. & Weiss, R.S. (1983) *Recovery from bereavement*. New York: Basic Books.

Parkin, A.J. (1987) *Memory and amnesia: An introduction*. Oxford: Blackwell.

Parkin, A.J., Lewinson, J. & Folkard, S. (1982) The influence of emotion on immediate and delayed retention: Levinger and Clark reconsidered. *British Journal of Psychology*, 73, 389–93.

Parkinson, B. (1987) Emotion—cognitive approaches. In H. Beloff and A.M. Colman (Eds.), *Psychology survey, No. 6*. Leicester: British Psychological Society.

Pastor, D.L. (1981) The quality of mother–infant attachment and its relationship to toddlers' initial sociability with peers. *Developmental Psychology*, 17, 326–35.

Patterson, F.G. (1978) The gestures of a gorilla: Language acquisition in another pongid. *Brain and Language*, 5, 72–97.

Patterson, F.G. (1980) Innovative uses of language by a gorilla: A case study. In K. Nelson (Ed.), *Childrens' language, Vol. 2*. New York: Gardner Press.

Patterson, F.G. & Linden, E. (1981) *The education of Koko*. New York: Holt, Rinehart & Winston.

Pavlov, I.P. (1927) *Conditioned reflexes*. London: Oxford University Press.

Peck, D. & Whitlow, D. (1975) *Approaches to personality theory*. London: Methuen.

Penfield, W. (1958) The role of the temporal cortex in recall of past experiences and interpretation of the present. In W. Penfield (Ed.), *Neurological bases of behaviour*. Boston: Little Brown.

Perls, F.S. (1969) *Gestalt therapy verbatim*. New York: Bantam.

Perry, D.G. & Bussey, K. (1979) The social learning theory of sex differences: Imitation is alive and well. *Journal of Personality and Social Psychology*, 37 (10), 1699–712.

Perry, D.G. & Parke, R.D. (1975) Punishment and alternative

response training as determinants of response inhibition in children. *Genetic Psychology Monographs*, 91, 257–79.

Pervin, L.A. & Lewis, M. (1978) *Perspective in interactional psychology*. New York: Plenum Press.

Peters, R.S. (1974) Moral development: A plea for pluralism. In R.S. Peters (Ed.), *Psychology and ethical development*. London: Allen & Unwin.

Peterson, L.R. & Peterson, M.J. (1959) Short term retention of individual items. *Journal of Experimental Psychology*, 58, 193–8.

Pettito, L.A. & Seidenberg, M.S. (1979) On the evidence from linguistic abilities in signing apes. *Brain and Language*, 8, 162–83.

Pettigrew, T.F. (1959) Regional difference in anti-negro prejudice. *Journal of Abnormal and Social Psychology*, 59, 28–56.

Pettigrew, T.F. (1971) *Racially separate or together?* New York: McGraw Hill.

Phillips, J.L. (1969) *The origins of intellect: Piaget's theory*. San Francisco: W.H. Freeman.

Piaget, J. (1932) *The moral judgement of the child*. London: RKP.

Piaget, J. (1950) *The psychology of intelligence*. London: RKP.

Piaget, J. (1951) *Play, dreams and imitation in children*. London: RKP.

Piaget, J. (1952) *The child's conception of numbers*. London: RKP.

Piaget, J. (1963) *The origins of intelligence in children*. New York: Norton.

Piaget, J. (1970) Piaget's theory. In P.H. Mussen (Ed.), *Manual of child psychology*. London: Wiley.

Piaget, J. (1972) Intellectual evolution from adolescence to adulthood. *Human Development*, 15, 1–21.

Piaget, J. (1973) *The child's conception of the world*. London: Paladin.

Piaget, J. & Inhelder, B. (1956) *The child's conception of space*. London: RKP.

Piaget, J. & Inhelder, B. (1969) *The psychology of the child*. London: RKP.

Piliavin, I.M., Piliavin, J.A. & Rodin, S. (1975) Costs, diffusion and the stigmatised victim. *Journal of Personality and Social Psychology*, 32, 429–38.

Piliavin, I.M., Rodin, J. & Piliavin, J.A. (1969) Good samaritanism: An underground phenomenon? *Journal of Personality and Social Psychology*, 13, 289–99.

Piliavin, J.A., Dovidio, J.F., Gaertner, S.L. & Clark, R.D. (1981) *Emergency intervention*. New York: Academic Press.

Piliavin, J.A. & Piliavin, I.M. (1972) Effects of blood on reactions to a victim. *Journal of Personality and Social Psychology*, 23, 353–62.

Piliavin, J.A., Piliavin, I.M., Loewenton, E.P., McCauley, C. & Hammond, P. (1969) On observers' reproductions of dissonance effects: The right answers for the wrong reasons? *Journal of Personality and Social Psychology*, 13, 98–106.

Platt, S. (1986) Recent trends in parasuicide ("attempted suicide") and unemployment among men in Edinburgh. In S. Allen (Ed.), *The experience of unemployment*. Basingstoke: Macmillan Education.

Plunkett, K. (1981) Psycholinguistics. In B. Gilliam (Ed.), *Psychology for today* (2nd ed.). Sevenoaks: Hodder & Stoughton.

Plutchik, R. (1986) *Emotion: A psychoevolutionary synthesis*. New York: Harper & Row.

Plutchik, R. & Ax, A.F. (1967) A critique of determinants of emotional state by Schachter and Singer (1962). *Psychophysiology*, 4, 79–82.

Polanyi, M. (1958) *Personal knowledge*. London: RKP.

Pomerantz, J. (1981) Perceptual organization in information processing. In M. Kubovy & J. Pomerantz (Eds.), *Perceptual organization* Hillsdale, New Jersey: Lawrence Erlbaum Associates Inc.

Pomerantz, J. & Garner, W.R. (1973) Stimulus configuration in selective attention tasks. *Perception and Psychophysics*, 14, 565–9.

Pomerantz, J. & Schwaitzberg, S.D. (1975) Grouping by proximity: Selective attention measures. *Perception and Psychophysics*, 18, 355–61.

Popper, K. (1945) *The open society and its enemies*. London: RKP.

Popper, K. (1950) Indeterminism in quantum physics and in classical physics. *British Journal of Philosophy and Science*, 1, 117–33/173–

95.

Popper, K. (1959) *The logic of scientific discovery*. London: Hutchinson.

Popper, K. (1968) *Conjecture and refutations: The growth of scientific knowledge*. New York: Harper & Row.

Popper, K. (1972) *Objective knowledge: An evolutionary approach*. Oxford: Oxford University Press.

Porteous, M.A. (1985) Developmental aspects of adolescent and problem disclosure in England and Ireland. *Journal of Child Psychology and Psychiatry*, 26, 465–78.

Poskocil, A. (1977) Encounters between blacks and white liberals: The collision of stereotypes. *Social Forces*, 55, 715–27.

Postman, L., Bruner, J.S. & McGinnies, E. (1948) Personal values as selective factors in perception. *Journal of Abnormal and Social Psychology*, 43, 142–54.

Postman, L., Bronson, W.C. & Gropper, G.L. (1953) Is there a mechanism of perceptual defence? *Journal of Abnormal and Social Psychology*, 48, 215.

Premack, D. (1971) Language in chimpanzee? *Science*, 172, 808–22.

Premack, D. (1976) *Intelligence in ape and man*. Hillsdale, New Jersey: Lawrence Erlbaum Associates Inc.

Price, R.A. & Vandenberg, S.G. (1979) Matching for physical attractiveness in married couples. *Personality and Social Psychology Bulletin*, 5, 398–400.

Price-Williams, D. (1966) Cross-cultural studies. In B.M. Foss (Ed.), *New horizons in psychology, 1*. Harmondsworth, Middlesex: Penguin.

Pringle, M.L. & Kelmer M. (1986) *The needs of children* (3rd ed.). London: Hutchinson.

Quattrone, G.A. (1982) Overattribution and unit formation: When behaviour engulfs the person. *Journal of Personality and Social Psychology*, 42, 593–607.

Rachman, S. (1967) The conditioning theory of fear-acquisition: A critical examination. *Behaviour Research and Therapy*, 15, 375–87.

Rachman, S. (1978) *Fear and courage*. San Francisco: W.H. Freeman.

Rachman, S. (1984) Agoraphobia—a safety-signal perspective. *Behaviour Research and Therapy*, 22, 59–70.

Rachman, S. & Wilson, G. (1980) *The effects of psychological therapy*. Oxford: Pergamon.

Rahe, R.H. (1974) The pathway between subjects' recent life changes and their near-future illness reports: Representative results and methodological issues. In B.S. Dohrenwend and B.P. Dohrenwend (Eds.), *Stressful life events*. New York: Wiley.

Rahe, R.H. (1981) Developments in life change measurement: Subjective life change unit scaling. In B.S. Dohrenwend and B.P. Dohrenwend (Eds.), *Stressful life events and their contexts*. New York: Wiley.

Rahe, R.H. & Arthur, R.J. (1977) Life change patterns surrounding illness experience. In A. Monat & R.S. Lazarus (Eds.), *Stress and coping*. New York: Columbia University Press.

Ramsey, A.O. & Hess, E.H. (1954) A laboratory approach to the study of imprinting. *Wilson Bulletin*, 66, 196–206.

Raphael, B. (1984) *The anatomy of bereavement*. London: Hutchinson.

Rawlins, R. (1979) Forty years of rhesus research. *New Scientist*, 82 (1150), 105–10.

Rebok, G.W. (1987) *Life-span cognitive development*. New York: Holt, Rinehart & Winston.

Rees, W.D. (1971) The hallucinations of widowhood. *British Medical Journal*, 4, 37–41.

Rees, W.D. & Lutkins, S.G. (1967) Mortality of bereavement. *British Medical Journal*, 4, 13.

Reich, B. & Adcock, C. (1976) *Values, attitudes and behaviour change*. London: Methuen.

Reichard, S., Livson, F. & Peterson, P.G. (1982) *Ageing and personality*. New York: Wiley.

Rescorla, R.A. (1967) Pavlovian conditioning and its proper control procedures. *Psychological Review*, 74, 71–80.

Rescorla, R.A. (1968) Probability of shock in the presence and absence of CS in fear conditioning. *Journal of Comparative and Physiological Psychology*, 66, 1–5.

Rest, J.R. (1983) Mortality. In J.H. Flavell & E.M. Markman (Eds.), *Handbook of child psychology, Vol. 3*. New York: Wiley.

Rest, J., Turiel, E. & Kohlberg, L. (1969) Level of moral development as a determinant of preference and comprehension of moral judgement made by others. *Journal of Personality*, 37, 225–52.

Restle, F. (1957) Discrimination of cues in mazes: A resolution of the "place versus response" question. *Psychological Review*, 64, 217–28.

Restle, F. (1974) Critique of pure memory. In R. Solso (Ed.), *Theories in cognitive psychology: The Loyola symposium*. New York: Wiley.

Rheingold, H.L. (1961) The effect of environmental stimulation upon social and exploratory behaviour in the human infant. In B.M. Foss (Ed.), *Determinants of infant behaviour, Vol. 1*. London: Methuen.

Rheingold, H.L. (1969) The effect of a strange environment on the behaviour of infants. In B.M. Foss (Ed.), *Determinants of infant behaviour, Vol. 4*. London: Methuen.

Rheingold, H.L. & Cook, K.V. (1975) The content of boys' and girls' rooms as an index of parents' behaviour. *Child Development*, 46, 459–63.

Rheingold, H.L. & Eckerman, C.O. (1973) Fear of a stranger—a critical examination. In H.W. Reese (Ed.), *Advances in child development and behaviour, Vol. 8*. New York: Academic Press.

Rice, R.W. (1978) Construct validity of the esteem for least preferred coworker (LPC) scale. *Psychological Bulletin*, 85, 1199–237.

Rice, R.W., Bender, L.R. & Vitters, A.G. (1980) Leader sex, follower attitudes toward women and leadership effectiveness: A laboratory experiment. *Organizational Behaviour and Human Performance*, 25, 46–78.

Richards, M. (1987) Parents and kids: The new thinking. *New Society*, March 27, 12–15.

Richardson, K. (1991) *Understanding intelligence*. Milton Keynes: Open University Press.

Riegel, K.F. (1973) Dialetic operations: The final period of cognitive development. *Human Development*, 16, 346–70.

Riesen, A.H. (1947) The development of visual perception in man and chimpanzee. *Science*, 106, 107–8.

Riesen, A.H. (1965) Effects of early deprivation of photic stimulation. In S. Oster & R. Cook (Eds.), *The biosocial basis of mental retardation*. Baltimore: Johns Hopkins University Press.

Riley, V. (1981) Neuroendocrine influences on immunity and neoplasia. *Science*, 211, 1100–9.

Rips, L.J., Shoben, E.H. & Smith, E.E. (1973) Semantic distance and the verification of semantic relations. *Journal of Verbal Learning and Verbal Behaviour*, 12, 1–20.

Rivers, W.H.R. (1901) Vision. In A.C. Haddon (Ed.), *Reports of the Cambridge Anthropological Expedition to the Torres Straits, Vol. 2, part 1*. Cambridge: Cambridge University Press.

Robinson, J.O. (1972) *The psychology of visual illusions*. London: Hutchinson.

Rogers. C.R. (1951) *Client-centred therapy—its current practices, implications and theory*. Boston: Houghton Mifflin.

Rogers, C.R. (1959) A theory of therapy, personality and interpersonal relationships, as developed in the client-centred framework. In S. Koch (Ed.), *Psychology: A study of a science, Vol. 3*. New York: McGraw Hill.

Rogers, C.R. (1961) *On becoming a person*. Boston: Houghton Mifflin.

Rogers, C.R. (1970) *Encounter groups*. New York: Harper & Row.

Rokeach, M. (1960) *The open and closed mind*. New York: Basic Books.

Rokeach, M. (1968) *Beliefs, attitudes and values*. San Francisco: Jossey-Bass.

Rosch, E. (1973) Natural categories. *Cognitive Psychology*, 4, 328–50.

Rose, S. (1976) *The conscious brain*. Harmondsworth, Middlesex: Penguin.

Rose, S., Lewontin, R.C. & Kamin, L.J. (1984) *Not in our genes*. Harmondsworth, Middlesex: Penguin.

Rose, S.A. & Blank, M. (1974) The potency of context in childrens' cognition: An illustration through conservation. *Child Development*, 45, 499–502.

Rosenberg, M. (1965) *Society and the adolescent self-image*. Princeton, New Jersey: Princeton University Press.

Rosenblatt, F. (1959) Two theorems of statistical separability in the perceptron. In *Mechanisation of thought processes: Proceedings of a symposium held at the National Physical Laboratory, November 1958, Vol. 1*. London: HMSO.

Rosenhan, D.L. (1973) On being sane in insane places. *Science, 179*, 250–8.

Rosenman, R.H., Brand, R.J., Jenkins, C.D., Friedman, M., Strauss, R. & Wurm, M. (1975) Coronary heart disease in the Western Collaborative Group Study. *Journal of the American Medical Association*, 233, 872–7.

Rosenthal, D., Wender, P.H., Kety, S.S. & Welner, J. (1971) The adopted-away offspring of schizophrenics. *American Journal of Psychiatry, 128*, 307–11.

Rosenthal, N.E., Sack, D.A., Gillin, J.C., Lewy, A.J., Goodwin, F.K., Davenport, Y., Mudler, P.S., Newsome, D.A. & Weher, T.A. (1984) Seasonal affective disorder. *Archives of General Psychiatry, 41*, 72–80.

Rosenthal, R. (1966) *Experimenter effects in behavioural research*. New York: Appleton-Century-Crofts.

Rosenthal, R. & Jacobson, L. (1968) *Pygmalion in the classroom*. New York: Holt, Rinehart & Winston

Rosenthal, R. & Rosnow, R.L. (1966) Volunteer subjects and the results of opinion change studies. *Psychological Reports, 19*, 1183.

Rosenwald, G.C. (1972) Effectiveness of defences against anal impulse arousal. *Journal of Consulting and Clinical Psychology, 39*, 292–8.

Rosenzweig, M.R. & Leiman, A.L. (1989) *Physiological psychology* (2nd ed.). New York: Random House.

Roth, I. (1986) An introduction to object perception. In I. Roth and J.P. Frisby (Eds.), *Perception and representation*. Milton Keynes: Open University Press.

Rothbart, M., Evans, M. & Fulero, S. (1979) Recall for confirming events: Memory processes and the maintenance of social stereotyping. *Journal of Experimental Social Psychology, 15*, 343–55.

Rotter, J.B. (1966) Generalized expectancies for internal versus external control of reinforcement. *Psychological Monographs, 30* (1), 1–26.

Rotter, J.P., Seerman, M. & Liverant, S. (1962) Internal versus external locus of control of reinforcement: A major variable in behaviour theory. In N.F. Washburne (Ed.), *Decisions, values and groups*. New York: Pergamon Press.

Rubin, J.Z., Proveyzano, F.J. & Luria, Z. (1974) The eye of the beholder: Parents' views on sex of newborns. *American Journal of Orthopsychiatry, 44*, 512–19.

Rubin, K.H. (1973) Decentration skills in institutionalized and non-institutionalized elderly. *Proceedings of the 81st Annual Convention of American Psychology Association, 8*, 759–60.

Rubin, Z. (1973) *Liking and loving*. New York: Holt Rinehart & Winston.

Rubin, Z. & McNeil, E.B. (1983) *The psychology of being human* (3rd ed.). London: Harper & Row.

Rubinstein, J.L. & Howes, C. (1979) Caregiving and infant behaviour in day care and in homes. *Developmental Psychology, 15*, 1–24.

Ruble, D.N., Balaban, T. & Cooper, J. (1981) Gender constancy and the effects of sex-typed televised toy commercials. *Child Development, 52*, 667–73.

Rubovitz, P.C. & Maehr, M.L. (1973) Pygmalion in black and white. *Journal of Personality and Social Psychology, 25*, 210–18.

Ruch, J.C. (1984) *Psychology—the personal science*. Belmont, California: Wadsworth Publishing Company.

Rumbaugh, D.M., Gill, T.V. & Glaserfeld, E.C. (1973) Reading and sentence completion by a chimpanzee. *Science, 182*, 731–3.

Rumelhart, D.E. (1975) Notes on a schema for stories. In D.G. Bobrow & A. Collins (Eds.), *Representation and understanding: Studies in cognitive science*. New York: Academic Press.

Rumelhart, D.E., Hinton, G.E. & McClelland, J.L. (1986) A general framework for parallel distributed processing. In D. Rumelhart, J.L. McClelland & the PDP Research Group (Eds.), *Parallel distributed processing: Vol. 1. Foundations*. Cambridge, Massachusetts: MIT Press.

Rumelhart, D.E. & Norman, D.A. (1983) Representation in memory. In R.C. Atkinson, R.J. Herrstein, B. Lindzey & R.D. Luce (Eds.), *Handbook of experimental psychology*. Chichester: Wiley.

Rumelhart, D.E. & Norman, D.A. (1985) Representation of knowledge. In M.M. Aitkenhead & J.M. Slack (Eds.), *Issues in cognitive modelling*. London: Lawrence Erlbaum Associates Ltd.

Rushton, J.P. (1980) *Altruism, socialization and society*. Englewood Cliffs, New Jersey: Prentice Hall.

Rushton, W.A.H. (1987) Colour vision: Eye mechanism. In R. Gregory (Ed.), *The Oxford companion to the mind*. Oxford: Oxford University Press.

Rutter, M. (1976) Sex differences in childrens' responses to family stress. In E.J. Anthony and C.M. Konpernick (Eds.), *The child in his family*. New York: Wiley.

Rutter, M. (1979a) Maternal deprivation, 1972–1978: New findings, new concepts, new approaches. *Child Development, 50*, 283–305.

Rutter, M. (1979b) Separation experiences: A new look at an old topic. *Journal of Paediatrics, 95*, 147–54.

Rutter, M. (1981) *Maternal deprivation reassessed* (2nd ed.). Harmondsworth, Middlesex: Penguin.

Rutter, M. (1989) Pathways from childhood to adult life. *Journal of Child Psychology and Psychiatry, 30*, (1), 23–51.

Rutter, M., Graham, P., Chadwick, D.F.D. & Yule, W. (1976) Adolescent turmoil: Fact or fiction. *Journal of Child Psychology and Psychiatry, 17*, 35–56.

Ryan, J. (1972) IQ—the illusion of objectivity. In K. Richardson & D. Spears (Eds.), *Race, culture and intelligence*. Harmondsworth, Middlesex: Penguin.

Ryle, A. (1975) Psychotherapy research: The role of the repertory grid. *New Behaviour, August 28*, 326–8.

Ryle, G. (1949) *The concept of mind*. London: Hutchinson.

Sachs, J. & Truswell, L. (1976) Comprehension of two-word instructions by children in the one-word stage. *Journal of Child Language, 5*, 17–24.

Saegert, S.C., Swap, W. & Zajonc, R.B. (1973) Exposure context and interpersonal attraction. *Journal of Personality and Social Psychology, 25*, 234–42.

Salamé, P. & Baddeley, A.D. (1982) Disruption of short-term memory by unattended speech: Implications for the structure of working memory. *Journal of Verbal Learning and Verbal Behaviour, 21*, 150–64.

Salapatek, P. (1975) Pattern perception in early infancy. In L.B. Cohen and P. Salapatek (Eds.), *Infant perception: From sensation to cognition, Vol. 1. Basic visual processes*. London: Academic Press.

Samuel, J. & Bryant, P. (1984) Asking only one question in the conservation experiment. *Journal of Child Psychology and Psychiatry, 25* (2), 315–18.

Sapir, E. (1929) The status of linguistics as a science. *Language, 5*, 207–14.

Sarbin, T.R. & Mancuso, J.C. (1980) *Schizophrenia: Medical diagnosis or moral verdict?* New York: Pergamon.

Savage-Rumbaugh, E.S. (1990) Language as a cause–effect communication system. *Philosophical Psychology, 3* (1), 55–76.

Savage-Rumbaugh, E.S., Rumbaugh, D.M. & Boysen, S.L. (1978) Symbolic communication between two chimpanzees (*Pan troglodytes*). *Science, 201*, 641–4.

Savage-Rumbaugh, E.S., Rumbaugh, D.M. & Boysen, S.L. (1980) Do apes use language? *American Scientist, 68*, 49–61.

Savin, H.B. (1973) Professors and psychological researchers: Conflicting values in conflicting roles. *Cognition*, 2 (1), 147–9.

Scarr, S. & Weinberg, R.A. (1977) Intellectual similarities within families of both adopted and biological children. *Intelligence*, 1, 170–91.

Scarr, S. & Weinberg, R.A. (1983) The Minnesota adoption studies—genetic difference and malleability. *Child Development*, 54, 260–7.

Scarr-Salapatek, S. (1971) Social class and IQ. *Science*, 174, 28–36.

Scarr-Salapatek, S. (1976) An evolutionary perspective on infant intelligence—species patterns and individual variations. In M. Lewis (Ed.), *Origins of intelligence*. New York: Plenum.

Schachter, S. (1964) The interaction of cognitive and physiological determinants of emotional state. In L. Berkowitz (Ed.), *Advances in experimental social psychology*, Vol. 1. New York: Academic Press.

Schachter, S. & Singer, J.E. (1962) Cognitive, social and physiological determinants of emotional state. *Psychological Review*, 69, 379–99.

Schachter, S. & Wheeler, L. (1962) Epinephrine, chlorpromazine and amusement. *Journal of Abnormal and Social Psychology*, 65, 121–8.

Schaffer, H.R. (1971) *The growth of sociability*. Harmondsworth, Middlesex: Penguin.

Schaffer, K.R. (1977) *Mothering*. London: Fontana/Open Books.

Schaffer, H.R. & Emerson, P.E. (1964) The development of social attachments in infancy. *Monographs of the Society for Research in Child Development*, 29 (Whole No. 3).

Schaie, K.W. & Hertzog, C. (1983) Fourteen year cohort-sequential analysis of adult intellectual development. *Developmental Psychology*, 19, 531–43.

Schaie, K.W. & Labouvie-Vief, G. (1974) Generational versus autogenetic components of change in adult cognitive behaviour: A fourteen year cross-sequential study. *Developmental Psychology*, 101, 305–20.

Schaie, K.W. & Strother, C.R. (1968) The effect of time and cohort differences upon age changes in cognitive behaviour. *Multivariate Behaviour Research*, 3, 259–94.

Schank, R.C. (1975) *Conceptual information processing*. Amsterdam: North-Holland.

Schank, R.C. (1982) *Dynamic memory*. New York: Cambridge University Press.

Schank, R.C. & Abelson, R.P. (1977) *Scripts, plans, goals and understanding*. Hillsdale, New Jersey: Lawrence Erlbaum Associates Inc.

Scheerer, M. (1963) Problem solving. *Scientific American*, 208 (4), 118–28.

Schiff, M., Duyne, M., Dumaret, A., Stewart, J., Tomkiewicz, S. & Fenigold, J. (1978) Intellectual status of working-class children adopted early into upper-middle class families. *Science*, 200, 1503–4.

Schneider, K. (1959) Primary and secondary symptoms in schizophrenia. In S.R. Hirsch & M. Shepherd (Eds.), (1974) *Themes and variations in European psychiatry*. New York: John Wright.

Schneirla, T.C. (1965) Aspects of stimulation and organization in approach/withdrawal processes underlying vertebrate behaviour development. In D.S. Lehrman, R.A. Hinde & E. Shaw (Eds.), *Advances in the study of behaviour. Vol. 1*. New York: Academic Press.

Schreiber, F.R. (1973) *Sybil*. Harmondsworth, Middlesex: Penguin.

Schulman, A. (1974) Memory for words recently classified. *Memory and Cognition*, 2, 47–52.

Schuster, R.H. (1978) Ethological theories of aggression. In I.L. Kutash, S.B. Kutash & L.B. Schlesinger (Eds.), *Violence: Perspectives on murder and aggression*. San Francisco: Jossey-Bass.

Schwartz, S. & Johnson, J.H. (1981) *Psychopathology of childhood*. New York: Pergamon Press.

Science as Ideology Group of the British Society for Social Responsibility in Science (1976) The new synthesis is an old story. *New Scientist, May 13*.

Scodel, A. (1957) Heterosexual somatic preference and fantasy dependence. *Journal of Consulting Psychology*, 21, 371–4.

Searle, J.R. (1980) Minds, brains and programs. *The Behaviour and Brain Sciences*, 3, 417–57.

Searle, J.R. (1987) Minds and brains without programs. In C. Blakemore and S. Greenfield (Eds.), *Mindwaves*. Oxford: Blackwell.

Sears, R.R., Maccoby, E. & Levin, H. (1957) *Patterns of child rearing*. Evanston, Illinois: Row, Petersen and Co.

Sears, R.R., Rau, L. & Alpert, R. (1965) *Identification in child rearing*. Stanford, California: Stanford University Press.

Secord, P.F. & Backman, C.W. (1964) *Social psychology*. New York: McGraw Hill.

Segall, M.H., Campbell, D.T. & Herskovitz, M.J. (1963) Cultural differences in the perception of geometrical illusions. *Science*, 139, 769–71.

Seidenberg, M.S. & Petitto, L.A. (1987) Communication, symbolic communications and language: Comment on Savage-Rumbaugh, McDonald, Sevcik, Hopkins and Rupert (1986). *Journal of Experimental Psychology: General*, 116, 279–87.

Selfridge, O.G. (1959) Pandemonium: A paradigm for learning. In *The mechanisation of thought processes*. London: HMSO.

Selfridge, O.G. & Neisser, U. (1960) Pattern recognition by machine. *Scientific American*, 203, 60–8.

Seligman, M.E.P. (1970) On the generality of the laws of learning. *Psychological Review*, 77, 406–18.

Seligman, M.E.P. (1971) Phobias and preparedness. *Behaviour Therapy*, 2, 307–20.

Seligman, M.E.P. (1972) *Biological boundaries of learning*. New York: Appleton-Century-Crofts.

Seligman, M.E.P. (1975) *Helplessness: On depression, development and death*. San Francisco: W.H. Freeman.

Seligman, M.E.P., Maier, S.F. & Solomon, R,L. (1971) Unpredictable and uncontrollable aversive events. In F.R. Brush (Ed.), *Aversive conditioning and learning*. New York: Academic Press.

Seligman, M.E.P. & Yellen, A. (1987) What is a dream? *Behavioural Research and Therapy*, 25, 1–24.

Selye, H. (1956) *The stress of life*. New York: McGraw-Hill.

Senatore, V., Matson, J.L & Kazdin, A.E. (1982) A comparison of behavioural methods to teach social skills to mentally retarded adults. *Behaviour Therapy*, 13, 313–24.

Serpell, R.S. (1976) *Culture's influence on behaviour*. London: Methuen.

Shackleton, V.J. & Fletcher, C.A. (1984) *Individual differences—theories and applications*. London: Methuen.

Schaffer, D.R. (1985) *Developmental psychology—theory, research and applications*. Monterey, California: Brooks Cole Publisher.

Schaffer, L.H. (1975) Multiple attention in continuous verbal tasks. In P.M.A. Rabbit and S. Dormi (Eds.), *Attention and performance, Vol. 5*. London: Academic Press.

Shah, S.A. & Roth, L.H. (1974) Biological and psychophysiological factors in criminality. In D. Glasen (Ed.), *Handbook of criminology*. Chicago: Rand McNally.

Shallice, T. (1982) Specific impairments of planning. *Philosophical Transactions of the Royal Society of London*, 13298, 199–209.

Shatz, M. & Gelman, R. (1973) The development of communication skills: Modification in the speech of young children as a function of the listener. *Monographs of the Society for Research in Child Development*, 38, No. 152.

Shaver, J.P. & Strong, W. (1976) *Facing value decisions: Rationale-building for teachers*. Belmont, California: Wadsworth.

Shavitt, S. (1990) The role of attitude objects in attitude functions. *Journal of Experimental Social Psychology*, 26, 124–8.

Sheehy, G. (1976) *Passages—predictable crises of adult life*. New York: Bantam Books.

Sherif, M. (1935) A study of sane factors in perception. *Archives of Psychology*, 27 (Whole No. 187).

Sherif, M. (1936) *The psychology of social norms*. New York: Harper & Row.

Sherif, M. (1966) *Group conflict and co-operation: Their social psychology*. London: RKP.

Sherif, M., Harvey, O.J., White, B.J., Hood, W.R. & Sherif, C.W. (1961) *Intergroup conflict and co-operation: The robber's cave experiment*. Norman, Oklahoma: University of Oklahoma Press.

Sherif, M. & Hovland, C.I. (1961) *Social judgement: Assimilation and contrast in communication and attitude change*. New Haven, Connecticut: Yale University Press.

Sherif, M. & Sherif, C. (1969) *Social psychology*. New York: Harper & Row.

Sherrington, C.S. (1900) Experiments on the value of vascular and visceral factors for the genesis of emotion. *Proceedings of the Royal Society*, 66, 390–403.

Shields, J. (1962) *Monozygotic twins brought up apart and brought up together*. London: Oxford University Press.

Shields, J. (1976) Heredity and environment. In H.J. Eysenck & G.D. Wilson (Eds.), *Textbook of human psychology*. Lancaster: MTP.

Shields, J. (1978) Genetics. In J.K. Wing (Ed.), *Schizophrenia—towards a new synthesis*. London: Academic Press.

Shiffrin, R.M. & Schneider, W. (1977) Controlled and automatic human information processing: 11—perceptual learning, automatic attending and a general theory. *Psychological Review*, 84, 127–90.

Shotland, R.L. & Straw, M.K. (1976) Bystander response to an assault: When a man attacks a woman. *Journal of Personality and Social Psychology*, 34, 990–9.

Shotter, J. (1975) *Images of man in psychological research*. London: Methuen.

Shuey, A. (1966) *The testing of negro intelligence*. New York: Social Science Press.

Siann, G. (1985) *Accounting for aggression—perspectives on aggression and violence*. London: Allen & Unwin.

Sigall, H. (1970) The effects of competence and consensual validation of a communicator's liking for the audience. *Journal of Personality and Social Psychology*, 16, 251–8.

Sigall, H. & Landy, D. (1973) Radiating beauty: Effects of having a physically attractive partner on person perception. *Journal of Personality and Social Psychology*, 28, 218–24.

Sigall, H. & Ostrove, N. (1975) Beautiful but dangerous: Effects of offender attractiveness and nature of crime on juridic judgement. *Journal of Personality and Social Psychology*, 31, 410–14.

Simon, H.A. (1979) Information-processing theory of human problem solving. In W. Estes (Ed.), *Handbook of learning and cognitive processes, Vol. 5*. Hillsdale, New Jersey: Lawrence Erlbaum Associates Inc.

Sinclair-de-Zwart, H. (1969) Developmental psycholinguistics. In D. Elkind and J. Flavell (Eds.), *Studies in cognitive development*. New York: Oxford University Press.

Sistruuk, F. & McDavid, J.W. (1971) Sex variable in conforming behaviour. *Journal of Personality and Social Psychology*, 2, 200–7.

Skeels, H.M. (1966) Adult status of children with contrasting early life experiences. *Monographs of the Society for Research in Child Development*, 31 (Whole No. 3).

Skeels, H.M. & Dye, H.B. (1939) A study of the effects of differential stimulation on mentally retarded children. *Proceedings of the American Association of Mental Deficiency*, 44, 114–36.

Skinner, B.F. (1948) *Walden two*. New York: Macmillan.

Skinner, B.F. (1950) Are theories of learning necessary? *Psychological Review*, 57, 193–216.

Skinner, B.F. (1953) *Science and human behaviour*. New York: Macmillan.

Skinner, B.F. (1957) *Verbal behaviour*. New York: Appleton-Century-Crofts.

Skinner, B.F. (1971) *Beyond freedom and dignity*. New York: Knopf.

Skodak, M. & Skeels, H. (1949) A final follow-up study of 100 adopted children. *Journal of Genetic Psychology*, 75, 85–125.

Skuse, D. (1984) Extreme deprivation in early childhood—I. Diverse outcome for three siblings from an extraordinary family. *Journal of Child Psychology and Psychiatry*, 25 (4), 523–41.

Skuse, D. (1984) Extreme deprivation in early childhood—II. Theoretical issues and a comparative review. *Journal of Child Psychology and Psychiatry*, 25 (4), 543–72.

Slaby, R.G. & Frey, K.S. (1975) Development of gender constancy and selective attention to same-sex models. *Child Development*, 46, 849–56.

Slater, A. (1979) Visual memory and perception in early infancy. In A. Slater and G. Bremner (Eds.), *Infant development*. Hove, East Sussex: Lawrence Erlbaum Associates Ltd.

Slater, E. & Roth, M. (1977) *Clinical psychiatry* (3rd ed.). London, Ballière Tindall and Cassell.

Sluckin, W. (1965) *Imprinting and early experiences*. London: Methuen.

Slobin, D.I. (1975) On the nature of talk to children. In E.H. Lenneberg and E. Lenneberg (Eds.), *Foundation of language development, Vol. 1*. New York: Academic Press.

Smail, D. (1987) Psychotherapy and 'change': Some ethical considerations. In S. Fairbairn and G. Fairbairn (Eds.), *Psychology, ethics and change*. London: RKP.

Smith, H.B., Bruner, J.S. & White, R.W. (1956) *Opinions and personality*. New York: John Wiley.

Smith, M.L. & Glass, G.V. (1977) Meta-analysis of psychotherapeutic outcome studies. *American Psychologist*, 32, 752–60.

Smith, M.L., Glass, G.V. & Miller, B.L. (1980) *The benefits of psychotherapy*. Baltimore, Maryland: Johns Hopkins University Press.

Smith, P.K. (1990) Ethology, sociobiology and developmental psychology: In memory of Niko Tinbergen and Konrad Lorenz. *British Journal of Developmental Psychology*, 8 (2), 187–96.

Smith, P.K. & Cowie, H. (1988) *Understanding children's development*. Oxford: Basil Blackwell.

Smith, R.E., Sarason, I.G. & Sarason, B.R. (1986) *Psychology—the frontiers of behaviour* (3rd ed.). New York: Harper & Row.

Smith, V.L. & Ellsworth, P.C. (1987) The social psychology of eyewitness accuracy: Misleading questions and communicator expertise. *Journal of Applied Psychology*, 72, 294–300.

Snow, C.E. (1977) Mother's speech research: From input to interaction. In C.E. Snow & C.A. Ferguson (Eds.), *Talking to children: Language input and acquisition*. New York: Cambridge University Press.

Snyder, F.W. & Pronko, N.H. (1952) *Vision with spatial inversion*. Wichita, Kansas: University of Wichita Press.

Sobesky, W. (1983) The effects of situational factors on moral judgements. *Child Development*, 54, 575–84.

Solomon, R.L. & Howes, D.W. (1951) Word frequency, personal values and visual duration thresholds. *Psychological Review*, 58, 256.

Solso, R.L. (1979) *Cognitive psychology*. New York: Harcourt Brace Jovanovich.

Sorrentino, R.M. & Boutillier, R.G. (1975) The effect of quantity and quality of verbal interaction on ratings of leadership ability. *Journal of Experimental and Social Psychology*, 11, 403–11.

Sorrentino, R.M. & Field, N. (1986) Emergent leadership over time: The functional value of positive motivation. *Journal of Personality and Social Psychology*, 50, 1091–9.

Spearman, C. (1904) General intelligence, objectively determined and measured. *American Journal of Psychology*, 15, 201–93.

Spearman, C. (1967) The doctrine of two factors. In S. Wiseman (Ed.), *Intelligence and ability*. Harmondsworth, Middlesex: Penguin. (Original work published 1927.)

Speisman, J.C., Lazarus, R.S., Mordkoff, A.M. & Davidson, L.A. (1964) The experimental reduction of stress based on ego defence theory. *Journal of Abnormal and Social Psychology*, 68, 397–8.

Spelke, E., Zelazo, P., Kagan, J. & Kotelchuck, M. (1973) Father interaction and separation protest. *Developmental Psychology*, 9, 83–90.

Spelke, E.S., Hirst, W.C. & Neisser, U. (1976) Skills of divided attention. *Cognition*, 4, 215–30.

Spence, J.T. & Helmreich, R.L. (1978) *Masculinity and femininity:*

Their psychological dimensions, correlates and antecedents. Austin, Texas: University of Texas Press.

Spence, J.T., Helmreich, R.L. & Stapp, J. (1975) Ratings of self and peers on sex role attributes and their relation to self-esteem and concepts of masculinity and femininity. *Journal of Personality and Social Psychology*, 32, 29–39.

Sperling, G. (1960) The information available in brief visual presentation. *Psychological Monographs*, 74 (Whole No. 498).

Sperling, G. (1963) A mode for visual memory tasks. *Human Factors*, 5, 19–31.

Sperling, G. & Speelman, R.G. (1970) Acoustic similarity and auditory short-term memory: Experiments and a model. In D.A. Norman (Ed.), *Models of human memory*. New York: Academic Press.

Sperry, R.W. (1943) The effect of 180 degree rotation in the retinal field of visuo-motor co-ordination. *Journal of Experimental Zoology*, 92, 263–79.

Sperry, R.W. (1964) The great cerebral commissure. *Scientific American*, 210 (1), 42–52.

Sperry, R.W. (1968) Hemisphere deconnection and unity in conscious awareness. *American Psychologist*, 23, 723–33.

Sperry, R.W. & Gazzaniga, M.S. (1967) Language following surgical disconnection of the hemispheres. In F. Darley (Ed.), *Brain mechanisms underlying speech and language*. New York: Grune and Stratton.

Spitz, R.A. (1945) Hospitalism: An inquiry into the genesis of psychiatric conditions in early childhood. *Psychoanalytic Study of the Child*, 1, 53–74.

Spitz, R.A. (1946) Hospitalism: A follow-up report on investigation described in Vol. 1, 1945. *Psychoanalytic Study of the Child*, 2, 113–17.

Spitz, R.A. & Wolf, K.M. (1946) Anaclitic depression. *Psychoanalytic Study of the Child*, 2, 313–42.

Spitzer, R.L. (1976) More on pseudoscience in science and the case for psychiatric diagnosis. *Archives of General Psychiatry*, 33, 459–70.

Spitzer, R.L., Endicott, J. & Robins, E. (1978) Research diagnostic criteria: Rationale and reliability. *Archives of General Psychiatry*, 35, 773–82.

Sroufe, L.A. & Waters, E. (1977) Attachment as an organizational construct. *Child Development*, 48, 1184–99.

Staats, A.W. & Staats, C.K. (1963) *Complex human behaviour*. New York: Holt Rinehart & Winston.

Stampfl, T. & Levis, D. (1967) Essentials of implosive therapy. *Journal of Abnormal Psychology*, 72, 496–503.

Stayton, D.J. & Ainsworth, M.D.S. (1973) Individual differences in infant response to brief, everyday separations as related to other infant and maternal behaviours. *Developmental Psychology*, 9, 226–35.

Stayton, D.J., Ainsworth, M.D.S. & Main, M.B. (1973) Development of separation behaviour in the first year of life: Protest, following and greeting. *Developmental Psychology*, 9, 213–25.

Stein, B.S., Morris, C.D. & Bransford, J.D. (1978) Constraints on effective elaboration. *Journal of Verbal Learning and Verbal Behaviour*, 17, 707–14.

Steiner, J.E. (1977) Facial expressions of the neonate infant indicating the hedonics of food-related chemical stimuli. In J.M. Weiffenbach (Ed.), *Taste and Development*. Bethesda, Maryland: DHEW.

Steiner, J.E. (1979) Human facial expressions in response to taste and smell stimulation. In H. Reese & L. Lipsitt (Eds.), *Advances in Child Development and Behaviour, Vol. 13*. New York: Academic Press.

Stephan, W.G. (1978) School desegregation: An evaluation of predictions made in Brown vs. the Board of Education. *Psychological Bulletin*, 85, 217–38.

Stephenson, G.M. (1988) Applied social psychology. In M. Hewstone, W Stroebe, J.P. Codol & G.M. Stephenson (Eds.), *Introduction to social psychology*. Oxford: Basil Blackwell.

Sternberg, R.J. (1985) *Beyond IQ: A triarchic theory of human intelligence*. Cambridge: Cambridge University Press.

Sternberg, R.J. (1987) Intelligence. In R. Gregory (Ed.), *The Oxford companion to the mind*. Oxford: Oxford University Press.

Sternberg, R.J. (1988) *The triarchic mind: A new theory of human intelligence*. New York: Viking.

Sternberg, R.J. (1990) *Metaphors of mind*. Cambridge: Cambridge University Press.

Sternglanz, S.H. & Serbin, L.A. (1974) Sex role stereotyping in childrens' television programs. *Developmental Psychology*, 10, 710–15.

Stewart, V.M. (1973) Tests of the 'carpentered world' hypothesis by race and environment in America and Zambia. *International Journal of Psychology*, 8, 83–94.

Stogdill, R.M. (1974) *Handbook of leadership*. New York: Free Press.

Stones, E. (1971) *Educational psychology*. London: Methuen.

Storr, A. (1966) The concept of cure. In C. Rycroft (Ed.), *Psychoanalysis observed*. London: Constable.

Storr, A. (1966) *Human aggression*. Harmondsworth, Middlesex: Penguin.

Storr, A. (1987) Why psychoanalysis is not a science. In C. Blakemore and S. Greenfield (Eds.), *Mindwaves*. Oxford: Blackwell.

Stouffer, S.A., Suchman, E.A., DeVinney, L.C., Starr, S.A. & Williams, R.M. (1949) *The American soldier: Adjustment during army life, Vol. 1*. Princeton, New Jersey: Princeton University Press.

Stratton, G.M. (1896) Some preliminary experiments on vision. *Psychological Review*, 3, 611–17.

Stroebe, W., Insko, C.A., Thompson, V.D. & Layton, B.D. (1971) Effects of physical attractiveness, attitude similarity, and sex on various aspects of interpersonal attraction. *Journal of Personality and Social Psychology*, 18, 79–91.

Stroop, J.R. (1935) Interference in serial verbal reactions. *Journal of Experimental Psychology*, 18, 643–61.

Sudnow, D. (1967) Dead on arrival. *Transaction, November*.

Sugarman, L. (1986) *Life span development*. London: Methuen.

Sullivan, L. (1976) Selective attention and secondary message analysis: A reconsideration of Broadbent's filter model of selective attention. *Quarterly Journal of Experimental Psychology*, 28, 167–78.

Suomi, S.J. (1982) Biological foundations and developmental psychobiology. In C.B. Kopp and J.B. Krakow (Eds.), *Child development in a social context*. Reading, Massachusetts: Addison-Wesley.

Suomi, S.J. & Harlow, H.F. (1972) Depressive behaviour in young monkeys subjected to vertical chamber confinement. *Journal of Comparative and Physiological Psychology*. 80, 11–18.

Sutherland, S.N. (1976) *Breakdown*. London: Weidenfeld & Nicolson.

Szasz, T. (1960) The myth of mental illness. *American Psychologist*, 15, 113–18.

Szasz, T. (1972) *The myth of mental illness*. London: Paladin.

Szasz, T. (1973) *The manufacture of madness*. London: Paladin.

Szasz, T. (1974) *Ideology and insanity*. Harmondsworth, Middlesex: Penguin.

Tagiuri, R. (1969) Person perception. In G. Lindzey and E. Aronson, (Eds.), *Handbook of psychology, Vol. 2*. Reading, Massachusetts: Addison-Wesley.

Tajfel, H. (1981) *Human group and social categories*. Cambridge: Cambridge University Press.

Tajfel, H., Billig, M.G. & Bundy, R.P. (1971) Social categorization and integroup behaviour. *European Journal of Social Psychology*, 1 (2), 149–78.

Tajfel, H. & Turner, J. (1979) An integrative theory of intergroup conflict. In G.W. Austin and S. Worchel, (Eds.), *The social psychology of intergroup relations*. Monterey, California: Brooks Cole.

Tedeschi, J.T. & Rosenfield, P. (1981) Impression management theory and the forced compliance situation. In J.T. Tedeschi (Ed.), *Impression management theory and social psychological research*. New York: Academic Press.

Tedeschi, J.T., Schlenker, B.R. & Bonoma, T.V. (1971) Cognitive dissonance: Private ratiocination or public spectacle? *American Psychologist*, 26, 685–95.

Teichman, J. (1988) *Philosophy and the mind*. Oxford: Blackwell.

Teitelbaum, P. (1967) Motivation and control of food intake. In C.F. Code (Ed.), *Handbook of physiology: Alimentary canal, Vol. 1*. Washington, DC: American Physiological Society.

Teitelbaum, P. (1971) The encephalization of hunger. In E. Stellar and J.M. Sprague (Eds.), *Progress in physiological psychology, Vol. 4*. London: Academic Press.

Terman, L.M. (1921) In symposium: Intelligence and its measurement. *Journal of Educational Psychology*, 12, 127–33.

Terman, L.M. (1954) The discovery and encouragement of exceptional talent. *American Psychologist*, 9, 221–38.

Terman, L.M. & Merrill, M.A. (1937) *Measuring intelligence*. London: Harrap.

Terman, L.M. & Oden, M.H. (1959) *The gifted group of mid-life*. Stanford, California: Stanford University Press.

Terrace, H.S. (1979) *Nim*. New York: Knopf.

Terrace, H.S. (1987) Thoughts without words. In C. Blakemore & S. Greenfield (Eds.), *Mindwaves*. Oxford: Basil Blackwell.

Thibaut, J.W. & Kelley, H.H. (1959) *The social psychology of groups*. New York: Wiley.

Thigpen, C.H. & Cleckley, H. (1954) A case of multiple personality. *Journal of Abnormal and Social Psychology*, 49, 135–51.

Thigpen, C.H. & Cleckley, H. (1957) *The three faces of Eve*. New York: McGraw Hill.

Thomas, K. (1990) Psychodynamics: The Freudian approach. In I. Roth (Ed.), *Introduction to psychology, Vol. 1*. Hove, E. Sussex/Milton Keynes: Open University/Lawrence Erlbaum Associates Ltd.

Thomas, R.M. (1985) *Comparing theories of child development* (2nd ed.). Belmont, California: Wadsworth Publishing Company.

Thorndike, E.L. (1898) Animal intelligence: An experimental study of the associative processes in animals. *Psychological Review, Monograph Supplement*, 2 (Whole No. 8).

Thorne, B. (1984) Person-centred therapy. In W. Dryden (Ed.), *Individual therapy in Britain*. London: Harper & Row.

Thorpe, W.H. (1963) *Learning and instinct in animals* (2nd ed.). London: Methuen.

Thorpe, W.H. (1979) *The origins and rise of ethology*. London: Heinemann.

Thurstone, L.L. (1938) Primary mental abilities. *Psychometric Monographs, No. 1*.

Thurstone, L.L. & Chave, E.J. (1929) *Primary mental attitudes*. Chicago: University of Chicago Press.

Tillman, W.S. & Carver, C.S. (1980) Actors' and observers' attributions for success and failure: A comparative test of predictions from Kelley's cube, self-serving bias and positivity bias formulations. *Journal of Experimental Social Psychology*, 16, 18–32.

Tinbergen, N. (1951) *The study of instinct*. Oxford: Clarendon Press.

Tinbergen, N. & Perdeck, A.C. (1950) On the stimulus situation releasing the begging response in the newly-hatched herring-gull chick. *Behaviour*, 3, 1–39.

Tizard, B. (1977) *Adoption: A second chance*. London: Open Books.

Tizard, B. (1986) *The care of young children*. London: Institute of Education.

Tizard, B. & Hodges, J. (1978) The effect of early institutional rearing on the development of eight-year old children. *Journal of Child Psychology and Psychiatry*, 19, 99–118.

Tizard, B., Joseph, A., Cooperman, O. & Tizard, J. (1972) Environmental effects on language development: A study of young children in long-stay residential nurseries. *Child Development*, 43, 337–58.

Tizard, B. & Rees, J. (1975) A comparison of the effects of adoption, restoration to the natural mother and continued institutionalization on the cognitive development of four-year old children. *Child Development*, 45, 92–9.

Tizard, J. & Tizard, B. (1971) Social development of 2-year-old children in residential nurseries. In H.R. Schaffer (Ed.), *The origins of human social relations*. London: Academic Press.

Tolman, E.C. (1948) Cognitive maps in rats and men. *Psychological Review*, 55, 189–208.

Tolman, E.C. & Honzik, C.H. (1930) Introduction and removal of reward and maze learning in rats. *University of California Publications in Psychology*, 4, 257–75.

Tomikawa, S.A. & Dodd, D.H. (1980) Early word meanings: Perceptually or functionally based. *Child Development*, 51, 1103–9.

Torrance, S. (1986) Breaking out of the Chinese room. In M. Yazdani, (Ed.), *Artificial intelligence: Principles and applications*. London: Chapman & Hall.

Traupmann, J., Hatfield, E. & Wexer, P. (1983) Equity and sexual satisfaction in dating couples. *British Journal of Social Psychology*, 22, 33–40.

Treisman, A.M. (1960) Contextual cues in selective listening. *Quarterly Journal of Experimental Psychology*, 12, 242–8.

Treisman, A.M. (1964) Verbal cues, language and meaning in selective attention. *American Journal of Psychology*, 77, 206–19.

Treisman, A.M. & Geffen, G. (1967) Selective attention: Perception or response? *Quarterly Journal of Experimental Psychology*, 19, 1–18.

Treisman, A.M. & Gelade, G. (1980) A feature integration theory of selection. *Cognitive Psychology*, 12, 97–136.

Treisman, A.M. & Riley, J.G.A. (1969) Is selective attention selective perception or selective response: A further test. *Journal of Experimental Psychology*, 79, 27–34.

Triplett, N. (1898) The dynamogenic factors in pacemaking and competition. *American Journal of Psychology*, 9, 507–33.

Triseliotis, J. (1980) Growing up in foster care and after. In J. Triseliotis (Ed.), *New developments in foster care and adoption*. London: RKP.

Trivers, R.L. (1971) The evolution of reciprocal altruism. *Quarterly Review of Biology*, 46, 35–57.

Trivers, R.L. & Hare, H. (1976) Haplodiploidy and the evolution of social insects. *Science*, 191, 249–63.

Troscianko, T. (1987) Colour vision: Brain mechanisms. In R. Gregory (Ed.), *The Oxford companion to the mind*. Oxford: Oxford University Press.

Trower, P. (1987) On the ethical bases of 'scientific' behaviour therapy. In S. Fairbairn & G. Fairbairn (Eds.), *Psychology, ethics and change*. London: RKP.

Truax, C. & Mitchell, K. (1971) Research on certain therapist interpersonal skills in relation to process and outcome. In A.E. Bergin & S.L. Garfield (Eds.), *Handbook of psychotherapy and behaviour change: An empirical analysis*. New York: Wiley.

Tulving, E. (1962) Subjective organization in free recall of unrelated words. *Psychological Review*, 69, 344–54.

Tulving, E. (1972) Episodic and semantic memory. In E. Tulving & W. Donaldson (Eds.), *Organization of memory*. London: Academic Press.

Tulving, E. (1985) How many memory systems are there? *American Psychologist*, 40, 385–98.

Tulving, E. (1979) Relation between encoding specificity and levels of processing. In L.S. Cermak & F.I.M. Craik (Eds.), *Levels of processing in human memory*. Hillsdale, New Jersey: Lawrence Erlbaum Associates Inc.

Tulving, E. & Pearlstone, Z. (1966) Availability versus accessibility of information in memory for words. *Journal of Verbal Learning and Verbal Behaviour*, 5, 381–91.

Tulving, E. & Psotka, J. (1971) Retroactive inhibition in free recall: Inaccessibility of information available in the memory store. *Journal of Experimental Psychology*, 87, 1–8.

Turiel, E. (1966) An experimental test of the sequentiality of developmental stages in the child's moral judgements. *Journal of Personality and Social Psychology*, 3, 611–18.

Turiel, E. (1978) Distinct conceptual and developmental domains: Social convention and morality. In C.B. Keasey (Ed.), *Nebraska Symposium on Motivation, Vol. 25*. Lincoln, Nebraska: Nebraska

University Press.

Turing, A.M. (1950) Computing machinery and intelligence. *Mind*, *59*, 433–60.

Turnbull, C.M. (1961) *The forest people*. New York: Simon & Schuster.

Turner, E.A. & Wright, J. (1965) Effects of severity of threat and perceived availability on the attractiveness of objects. *Journal of Personality and Social Psychology*, *2*, 128–32.

Turner, J.C. (1982) Towards a cognitive redefinition of the social group. In H. Tajfel (Ed.), *Social identity and intergroup relations*. Cambridge: Cambridge University Press.

Turner, J.C. (1985) Social categorizations and the self-concept: A social cognitive theory of group behaviour. In E.J. Lawler (Ed.), *Advances in group processes: Theory and research*, Vol. 2. Greenwich, Connecticut: JAI Press.

Turner, J.C. (1991) *Social influence*. Milton Keynes: Open University Press.

Turner, J.S. & Helms, D.B. (1989) *Contemporary adulthood* (4th ed.). Fort Worth, Florida: Holt, Rinehart & Winston.

Tyerman, A. & Spencer, C. (1983) A critical test of the Sherifs' robbers' cave experiment: Intergroup competition and co-operation between groups of well-acquainted individuals. *Small Group Behaviour*, *14* (4), 515–31.

Ullmann, L.P. & Krasner, L.A. (1975) *A psychological approach to abnormal behaviour*. Englewood Cliffs, New Jersey: Prentice Hall.

Underwood, B.J. (1948) Retroactive and proactive inhibition after 5 and 48 hours. *Journal of Experimental Psychology*, *38*, 29–38.

Underwood, B.J. (1957) Interference and forgetting. *Psychological Review*, *64*, 49–60.

Unger, R.K. (1979) *Female and male*. London: Harper & Row.

Vagg, P.R. & Hammond, S.B. (1976) The number and kind of invariant personality Q factors: A partial replication of Eysenck and Eysenck. *British Journal of Social and Clinical Psychology*, *15*, 121–30.

Valentine, E.R. (1982) *Conceptual issues in psychology*. London: Allen & Unwin.

Valins, S. (1966) Cognitive effects of false heart-rate feedback. *Journal of Personality and Social Psychology*, *4*, 400–8.

Van Avermaet, E. (1988) Social influence in small groups. In M. Hewstone, W. Stroebe, J.P. Codol & G.M. Stephenson (Eds.), *Introduction to social psychology*. Oxford: Basil Blackwell.

van Essen, D.C. (1985) Functional organization of primate visual cortex. In A. Peters & E.G. Jones (Eds.), *Cerebral cortex. Vol. 2—Visual cortex*. New York: Plenum Press.

Vaughn, B.E., Gove, F.L. & Egeland, B.R. (1980) The relationship between out-of-home care and the quality of infant–mother attachment in an economically disadvantaged population. *Child Development*, *51*, 1203–14.

Vernon, P.E. (1950) The hierarchy of ability. In S. Wiseman (Ed.), *Intelligence and ability*. Harmondsworth, Middlesex: Penguin.

Vernon, P.E. (1979) *Intelligence: Heredity and environment*. San Francisco: W.H. Freeman.

von Bekesy, G. (1960) *Experiments in hearing*. New York: McGraw-Hill.

Von Senden, M. (1960) *Space and sight: The perception of space and shape in the congenitally blind before and after operations* (P. Heath, trans.). London: Methuen. (Original work published 1932.)

Von Wright, J.M., Anderson, K. & Stenman, U. (1975) Generalization of conditioned GSRs in dichotic listening. In P.M.A. Rabbit & S. Dornic (Eds.), *Attention and performance, Vol. 1*. London: Academic Press.

Vygotsky, L.S. (1962) *Thought and language*. Cambridge, Massachusetts: MIT Press. (Original work published 1934.)

Vygotsky, L.S. (1978) *Mind in society*. Cambridge, Massachusetts: Harvard University Press.

Walker, S. (1984) *Learning theory and behaviour modification*. London: Methuen.

Walster, E. (1966) The assignment of responsibility for an accident. *Journal of Personality and Social Psychology*, *5*, 508–16.

Walster, E. (1970) The effect of self-esteem on liking for dates of various social desirabilities. *Journal of Experimental and Social Psychology*, *6*, 248–53.

Walster, E., Aronson, E. & Abrahams, D. (1966) On increasing the persuasiveness of a low prestige communicator. *Journal of Experimental and Social Psychology*, *2*, 325–42.

Walster, E., Aronson, E., Abrahams, D. & Rottman, L. (1966) Importance of physical attractiveness in dating behaviour. *Journal of Personality and Social Psychology*, *4*, 508–16.

Walster, E.H., Walster, G.W. & Berscheid, E. (1978) *Equity theory and research*. Boston, Massachusetts: Allyn and Bacon.

Walster, E. & Festinger, L. (1962) The effectiveness of 'overheard' persuasive communication. *Journal of Abnormal and Social Psychology*, *65*, 395–402.

Warr, P.B. (1984) Work and unemployment. In P.J.D. Drenth (Ed.), *Handbook of work and organisational psychology*. Chichester: Wiley.

Warr, P.B. (1987) *Work, unemployment and mental health*. Oxford: Clarendon Press.

Warren, N. (1971) Is a scientific revolution taking place in psychology? *Scientific Studies*, *1*, 407–13.

Warren, S. & Jahoda, M. (Eds.). (1973) *Attitudes* (2nd ed.). Harmondsworth, Middlesex: Penguin.

Waters, E. (1978) The reliability and stability of individual differences in infant–mother attachments. *Child Development*, *49*, 483–94.

Waters, E., Wippman, J & Sroufe, L.A. (1979) Attachment, positive affect and competence in the peer group: Two studies in construct validation. *Child Development*, *50*, 821–9.

Watson, J.B. (1913) Psychology as the behaviourist views it. *Psychological Review*, *20*, 158–77.

Watson, J.B. (1919) *Psychology from the standpoint of a behaviourist*. Philadelphia: J.B. Lippincott.

Watson, J.B. (1924) *Behaviourism*. New York: J.B. Lippincott.

Watson, J.B. & Rayner, R. (1920) Conditioned emotional reactions. *Journal of Experimental Psychology*, *3*, 1–14.

Watson, O.N. & Graves, T.D. (1966) Quantitative research in proxemic behaviour. *American Anthropologist*, *68*, 971–85.

Waugh, N.C. & Norman, D. (1965) Primary memory. *Psychological Review*, *72*, 89–104.

Weatherley, D. (1961) Anti-semitism and expression of fantasy aggression. *Journal of Abnormal and Social Psychology*, *62*, 454–7.

Weatherley, D. (1964) Self-perceived rate of physical maturation and personality in late adolescence. *Child Development*, *35*, 1197–210.

Wechsler, D. (1944) *The measurement of adult intelligence* (3rd ed.). Baltimore: Williams & Wilkins.

Wechsler, D. (1958) *The measurement and appraisal of adult intelligence* (4th ed.). Baltimore: Williams & Wilkins.

Wechsler, D. (1974) *Wechsler Intelligence Scale for Children*. New York: Psychological Corporation.

Weiskrantz, L. (1956) Behavioural changes associated with ablation of the amygdaloid complex in monkeys. *Journal of Comparative and Physiological Psychology*, *49*, 381–91.

Weiskrantz, L. (1986) *Blindsight: A case study and implications*. Oxford: Oxford University Press.

Weitzenhoffer, A.M. & Hilgard, E.R. (1959) *Stanford hypnotic susceptibility scale, forms A and B*. Palo Alto, California: Consulting Psychologists' Press.

Wells, G.L. & Harvey, J.H. (1977) Do people use consensus information in making causal attributions? *Journal of Personality and Social Psychology*, *35*, 279–93.

Wender, P., Rosenthal, D., Kety, S.S., Schulsinger, F. & Welner, J. (1974) Cross-fostering: A research strategy for clarifying the role of genetic and experimental factors in the aetiology of schizophrenia. *Archives of General Psychiatry*, *30*, 121–8.

Wessler, R.L. (1986) Conceptualizing cognitions in the cognitive-behavioural therapies. In W. Dryden & W. Golden (Eds.), *Cognitive–behavioural approaches to psychotherapy*. London: Harper & Row.

Westley, W.A. & Elkin, F. (1957) The protective environment and adolescent socialization. *Social Forces*, *35*, 243–9.

Wetherall, M. (1982) Cross-cultural studies of minimal groups: Implications for the social identity theory of intergroup relations. In H. Tajfel (Ed.), *Social identity and intergroup relations*. London: Cambridge University Press.

Whitbourne, S.K. & Weinstock, C.S. (1979) *Adult development: The differentiation of experience*. New York: Holt, Rinehart & Winston.

White, D. (1975) The growth of conscience. *New Society*, December 4th, 538–40.

White, R.W. (1959) Motivation reconsidered: The concept of competence. *Psychological Review*, *66*, 297–333.

Whorf, B.L. (1941) The relation of habitual thought and behaviour to language. In L. Spier (Ed.), *Language, culture and personality*. Provo: University of Utah Press.

Wickelgren, W.A. (1965) Acoustic similarity and retroactive interference in short term memory. *Journal of Verbal Learning and Verbal Behaviour*, *4*, 53–61.

Wickelgren, W.A. (1973) The long and the short of memory. *Psychological Bulletin*, *80*, 425–38.

Wickelgren, W.A. (1974) Single trace fragility theory of memory dynamics. *Memory and Cognition*, *2*, 775–80.

Wickens, C.D. (1984) Processing resources in attention. In R. Parasuraman & D.R. Davies, (Eds.), *Varieties of attention*. London: Academic Press.

Wickens, D.D. (1972) Characteristics of word encoding. In A. Melton & E. Martin (Eds.), *Coding processes in human memory*. Washington, DC: Winston.

Wilder, D.A. (1977) Perceptions of groups, size of opposition and influence. *Journal of Experimental Social Psychology*, *13*, 253–68.

Wilding, J.M. (1982) *Perception—from sense to object*. London: Hutchinson.

Wilkinson, F.R. & Cargill, D.W. (1955) Repression elicited by story material based on the Oedipus complex. *Journal of Social Psychology*, *42*, 209–14.

Williams, J.B.W. & Spitzer, R.L. (1982) Idiopathic pain disorder: A critique of pain-prone disorder and a proposal for a revision of the DSM III Category psychogenic pain disorder. *Journal of Nervous and Mental Disorders*, *170*, 415–19.

Williams, T.M. (Ed.). (1986) *The impact of television: A national experiment in three communities*. New York: Academic Press.

Willis, R.H. (1963) Two dimensions of conformity–nonconformity. *Sociometry*, *26*, 499–513.

Wilson, E.O. (1975) *Sociobiology—the new synthesis*. Cambridge, Massachusetts: Harvard University Press.

Wilson, E.O. (1976) Sociobiology—a new basis for human nature. *New Scientist*, May 13.

Wilson, E.O. (1978) *On human nature*. Cambridge, Massachusetts: Harvard University Press.

Winch, R.F. (1955) The theory of complementary needs in mate selection: A test of one kind of complementariness. *American Sociological Review*, *20*, 52–6.

Winch, R.F. (1958) *Mate selections: A study of complementary needs*. New York: Harper.

Wing, J.K., Cooper, J.E. & Sartorius, N. (1974) *Measurement and classification of psychiatric symptoms*. Cambridge: Cambridge University Press.

Wingfield, A. & Byrnes, D. (1972) Decay of information in short-term memory. *Science*, *176*, 690–2.

Winnicott, D.W. (1958) *Through paediatrics to psycho-analysis*. London: Hogarth Press.

Wishner, J. (1960) Reanalysis of "Impressions of Personality". *Psychological Review*, *67*, 96–112.

Wittgenstein, L. (1953) *Philosophical investigations*. Oxford: Blackwell,

Wober, J.M., Reardon, G. & Fazal, S. (1987) *Personality, character aspirations and patterns of viewing among children*. London: IBA Research Papers.

Wohlwill, J.F. (1965) Texture of the stimulus field and age as variables in the perception of relative distance. *Journal of Experimental Child Psychology*, *2*, 163–77.

Wolf, S. & Wolff, H.G. (1947) *Human gastric function*. New York: Oxford University Press.

Wolf, T.M. (1973) Effects of live-modeled sex-inappropriate play behaviour in a naturalistic setting. *Developmental Psychology*, *9*, 120–3.

Wollheim, R. (1971) *Freud*. London: Fontana.

Wolpe, J. (1958) *Psychotherapy by reciprocal inhibition*. Stanford, California: Stanford University Press.

Wolpe, J. & Rachman, S. (1960) Psychoanalytic evidence: A critique based on Freud's case of little Hans. *Journal of Nervous and Mental Disease*, *131*, 135–45.

Word, C.O., Zanna, M.P. & Cooper, J. (1974) The non-verbal mediation of self-fulfilling prophecies in interracial interaction. *Journal of Experimental Social Psychology*, *10*, 109–20.

World Health Organization (1973) *Report of the International Pilot Study of Schizophrenia, Vol. 1*. Geneva: WHO.

World Health Organization (1978) *Mental Disorders: Glossary and guide to the classification in accordance with the ninth revision of the international classification of diseases*. Geneva: WHO.

World Health Organization (1987) *ICD-10, 1986 Draft of Chapter V. Mental, behavioural and developmental disorders*. Geneva: WHO.

Worthington, A.G. (1964) Differential rates of dark adaptation to 'taboo' and 'neutral' stimuli. *Canadian Journal of Psychology*, *18*, 257–68.

Worthington, A.G. (1969) Paired comparison scaling of brightness judgements: A method for the measurement of perceptual defence. *British Journal of Psychology*, *60* (3), 363–8.

Wortman, C.B. & Brehm, J.W. (1975) Responses to uncontrollable outcomes: An integration of reactance theory and the learned helplessness model. In L. Berkowitz (Ed.), *Advances in experimental social psychology, Vol. 8*. New York: Academic Press.

Wright, D. (1971) *The psychology of moral behaviour*. Harmondsworth, Middlesex: Penguin.

Wynne-Edwards, V.C. (1962) *Animal dispersion in relation to social behaviour*. Edinburgh: Oliver & Boyd.

Yarrow, L.J. (1961) Maternal deprivation: Towards an empirical and conceptual re-evaluation. *Psychological Bulletin*, *58*, 459–90.

Yates, A.J. (1970) *Behaviour therapy*. New York: Wiley.

Yuille, J.C. & Cutshall, J.L. (1986) A case study of eyewitness memory of a crime. *Journal of Applied Psychology*, *71*, 291–301.

Zaidel, E. (1978) Auditory language comprehension in the right hemisphere following cerebral commissurotomy and hemispherectomy. In A. Caramassa & E. Zuriff (Eds.), *Acquisition and language breakdown: Parallels and divergences*. Baltimore, Maryland: Johns Hopkins University Press.

Zajonc, R.B. (1968) Attitudinal effects of mere exposure. *Journal of Personality and Social Psychology*, Monograph Supplement 9, Part 2, 1–27.

Zajonc R.B. (1980) Feeling and thinking: Preferences need no inferences. *American Psychologist*, *35*, 151–75.

Zajonc, R.B. (1984) On the primacy of affect. *American Psychologist*, *39*, 117–23.

Zajonc, R.B., Marcus, H.M. & Wilson, W.R. (1974) Exposure effects and associative learning. *Journal of Experimental Social Psychology*, *10*, 248–63.

Zajonc, R.B., Shaver, P., Tavris, C. & Van Kreveld, D. (1972) Exposure, satiation and stimulus discriminability. *Journal of Personality and Social Psychology*, *21*, 270–80.

Zajonc. R.B., Swap, W.C., Harrison, A. & Roberts, P. (1971) Limiting conditions of the exposure effect: Satiation and relativity. *Journal of Personality and Social Psychology*, *18*, 384–91.

Zanna, M.P. & Cooper, J. (1974) Dissonance and the pill: An attribution approach to studying the arousal propensities of dissonance. *Journal of Personality and Social Psychology*, *29*, 703–9.

Zebrowitz, L.A. (1990) *Social perception*. Milton Keynes: Open University Press.

Zeki, S.M. (1978) Uniformity and diversity of structure and function in rhesus monkey prestriate visual cortex. *Journal of Physiology*, *277*, 273–90.

Zillman, D. (1978) Attribution and misattribution of excitatory reactions. In J.H. Harvey, W. Ickes & R.F. Kidd (Eds.), *New directions in attribution research, Vol. 2*. New York: Lawrence Erlbaum Associates Inc.

Zimbardo, P.G. (1969) The human choice: Individuation, reason and order versus deindividuation, impulse and chaos. In W.J. Arnold and D. Levine (Eds.), *Nebraska Symposium on Motivation*. Lincoln: University of Nebraska Press.

Zimbardo, P.G. (1973) On the ethics of intervention in human psychological research with special reference to the "Stanford Prison Experiment". *Cognition*, *2* (2), 243–55.

Zimbardo, P.G., Banks, W.C., Craig H, & Jaffe, D. (1973) A Pirandellian prison: The mind is a formidable jailor. *New York Times Magazine*, April 8th, 38–60.

Zubin, J. (1967) Classification of the behaviour disorders. *Annual Review of Psychology*, *18*, 312–35.

Zubin, J. & Spring, B. (1977) Vulnerability—a new view of schizophrenia. *Journal of Abnormal Psychology*, *86*, 103–26.

Zuckerman, M. (1978) Actions and occurrences in Kelley's cube. *Journal of Personality and Social Psychology*, *36*, 647–56.

INDEX

abnormality (*see also* clinical psychology
    and psychopathology), 11)
  deviation from norm, 930
  maladaptiveness, 932
  mental illness, 932
  personal distress, 932
  statistical criterion, 929
Aborigines, 446
Abrams, D. et al, 571, 573–4
accommodation and assimilation, 739–40
acetylcholine (ACh), 78, 80
action therapies, 988–90
activation-synthesis model (of dreaming),
    119
activity theory (re-engagement), 730
actor observer effect, 179
adaptation, 739–40
Adler, A.
  and Freud, 591
  leadership, 561
  theories of, 907, 926–8, 931
adolescence
  and anorexia nervosa, 623–4
  and formal operational thinking, 754–5
  and self-concept, 621–4
  and self-identity, 629–34
  and work, 633–4
  theories of, 634–44
adoption studies, 666–9
  and intelligence, 869–71
Adorno, T.W. et al, 541–42, 570
adrenal glands, 102
adrenocorticotrophic hormone (ACTH)
    78, 101–2
  and stress, 106
adrenogenital syndrome, 677, 678–9, 685
adulthood, 10, 700–12
  theories of, 702–9
affectionless psychopathy, 664
affective (mood) disorders, 952–3
affective primacy, 151
ageing, 10, 715–37
  'ages of me', 717–18
  and cognitive changes, 726–7
  and IQ, 723–6
  and memory, 727
  physical aspects of, 719–22
  and social change, 728–32
  and theories of, 636–44, 728–32
ageism (*see also* prejudice), 716–17

aggression, 443–62
  and deindividuation, 460–2
  and television, 454–9
  definitions of, 443–4
  ethological approach to, 444–7
  learning theory approach to, 451–3
  neurophysiological approach to, 447–9
  psychoanalytical approach to, 449–51
  social learning theory approach to, 453–
    60
aggressive cue theory, 456
agoraphobia, 942, 974
Ainsworth, M. et al, 648, 649, 655
Algol, 391
Allport, D.A., 105, 252, 254
Allport, F.H., 555
Allport, G.W., 20, 28, 30
  attitudes and prejudice, 515, 539, 548,
    549, 550
  perception, 252, 254
  stereotyping, 483, 485
  Trait Theory, 880, *882*, 883
Allport, G.W. and Pettigrew, T.F., 274
altruism, 440, 431–444
American Association for the
    Advancement of Science (AAAS), 55
American Psychiatric Association, 52, 60,
    931
American Sign Language (Ameslan or
    ASL), 790–4
Ames distorted room, *236*, 237
amnesia, 944
  and ECT, 966
amnesic syndrome, 321
amphetamines, 80, 950
amygdala and aggression, 448
anaclitic depression, 657
anaclitic identification, 598, 803, 804
anal personality, 605, 606
anal stage, 803
androgyny, 695–9
anima/animus, 924
animal subjects, 9, 34–5, 61–5, 83
  ethics of, 61
  psychology of, 403
  reasons for, 63–5
animism, 474, 746
anorexia nervosa, 623–4
anterior hypothalamus, 90
anterograde amnesia, 321–3

anti-depressants, 80, 964
antidiuretic hormone (ADH), 101
  and thirst, 133
anti-psychiatry, 951–2, 990–1
anti-semitism, (*see* prejudice)
anxiety, 897
anxiety neurosis, 941–2
aphagia, 130
aphasia, 83
appeasement rituals (in aggression), 445–6
approach–approach conflicts in humans,
    154
approach–avoidance conflict, in animals,
    415
  in humans, 154
Arapesh, 692, 693
ARAS, *see* Reticular Activity System
    (RAS)
Arbours Association, 990
archetypes, 923–4
Argyle, M., 613, 622, 710, 711, 714, 715
Aronfeed, J., 811
Aronson, E., 59, 60–1, 505, 530, 551, 561,
    581
Aronson, E. and Linder, D., 505
Aronson, E. and Mills, J., 534, 536
Aronson, E. and Osherow, N., 540
arousal and personality, 137–40
arousal: cost-reward model, 440, 443
artificial intelligence, (*see also* Computers)
  adversary and non-adversary problems,
    377, 380–1
  algorithms, 378–9
  connectionist model, 395–9
  definition of, 388–9
  expert systems, 385–8
  General Problem Solver (GPS), 378
  heuristics, 378–81
  logic theorist, *378–9*
  means end analysis (MEA), 380
  parallel distributed processing, 395–9
  scope of, 388
  strong/weak distinction, 392–4
Asch, S.E., 467–9, 470–1, 563–8, 575
Asanti tribe, 619
assimilation, 739–40
association cortex, 89
ataxia, 92
Atchley/Atchley and Robinson, 713–14
Atkinson, R.C., 5, 142

Atkinson, R.C. and Shiffrin, R.M., 310, 312, 313, 316–17, 319, 321
Atkinson, R.L., 222, 484, 485, 832
Atkinson, R.L. et al, 5, 434–5, 822
attachment, 645–73
  and bonds, 647
  and detachment, 648
  and social competence, 650
  as a secondary drive, 135
  behaviour, 647
  concepts of, 665
  effects of day care on, 660–1
  influences on, 654–6
  stability of, 648–50
  stages of, 645–6
  study of, 648, *649*
  theories of, 650–6, 602–3
  varieties of, 647
  with fathers, 653–4
attention, 296–301
  definitions of, 296–7
  divided attention
    studies of, 302–8
    dual task, 302
  methods of study, 297
  selective attention,
    attenuator model (of Treisman), 299, *300*
    filter model (of Broadbent), 297–9, *298*
    pertinence model, *300*, 301
attitudes,
  and behaviour, 516–17
  beliefs and values, 514–16
  components of, 514
  definitions of, *515*
  functions of, 527–8
  measurement of, 517–19
  persuasive communication, *519*–32
  schemas, 540
  theories of attitude change, 532–9
attribution process, 472–82
  and attitude change, 536–8
audience effect, 555
auditory hallucinations (in schizophrenia), 946
auditory system, 219–22
  nerve, 220
  pathways, 220
  sensory processing, 220
  sounds,
    frequency, 219
    intensity, 219
    pitch, 220
    timbre, 221
  structure, *219*
authoritarian personality, 541–3
  and conformity, 569
autistic hostility, 552
autistic speech, 373
autokinetic effect (*see also* visual illusions), 230, 562–3
automatic versus controlled processing, 304–5

autonomic nervous system (ANS), 90, 99–*100, 101, 102*
automony versus shame and doubt, 628–9
availability versus accessibility (in memory), 309, 334–5, 338
average evoked potentials (AEPs), 84, 108–9
aversion therapy, 976
avoidance learning, 135

babbling, 774–5
Baddeley, A.D., 256, 308, 320, 322, 323, 330, 332, 341, 343, 349, 359
Baddeley, A.D. and Hitch, G., 308, 332
Bandura, A., 109–2, 814, 816–17, 818, 982–3, 993
Bandura, A. et al, 190, 256, 308, 320, 322, 323, 330, 332, 343, 349, 452, 456
Bannister, D., 984
Bannister, D. and Agnew, J. 611, 616
Bannister, D. and Fransella, R., 539, 989–90
Bannister, D., and Mair, M.J.M., 900
Barnes, M., 990
Baron, R.A. and Byrne, D., 444, 521, 529, 531, 539–40, 541, 552, 553
Barrett, M., 778, 779, 780, 781
Bartlett, F.C., 252, 352–4
basal age, 855
basal ganglia, 91
basic trust versus mistrust, 628, 645
Batista family, case of, 677, 682, *683*
Baumrind, D., 53, 54
Bayankole, tribe, 272
Bayley, N., 871
Bayley Scales of Infant Development, 871–2
Beck, A.T., 982
Bee, H.L. and Mitchell, S.K., 702, 709, 719, 780, 872
begging response (of herring/laughing-gull chick), 409–10, 411
behaviour modification, 178, 188, 972, 977–80
behaviour therapy, 13, 972, 974–7
behavioural (functional) analysis, 972
behavioural technology, 972
behaviourism, 4, 21, 26, *166*
  and reductionism, 41–4, *42, 43*
  philosophical and methodological, 21–2, 27
Bem, D.J., 144, 515, 536–7
Bem, D.J., and Allen, A., 813, 885
Bem, S., 695–7, 698, 699
Bem Sex Role Inventory (BSRI), 696–8, *696*
Benedict, R., 637–8
bereavement, 732
Bereiter, C. and Engelmann, S., 370
Berke, J., 874
Berkeley, 21, 47
Berko, J., *782*
Berkowitz, L., 453

Berlyne, D.E., 137
Berne, E., 998
Bernstein, B., 360, 368–70
Berscheid, E., 495
Berscheid, E. and Walster, E., 483, 492, 493
beta-endorphins, 132
Bettelheim, B., 920
biased sampling, 34
Berkeley, 21, 47
Bierhoff and Klein, 438, 439
Binet, A., 738, 840, 861
binocular disparity, 278
biofeedback, 125
biosocial theory, 648–6
bisexual, 675
BITCH test (of intelligence), 371
Blackwell, Mr, case of, *677, 684*
Blakemore, C., 109, 110, 115, 120, 121
Blakemore, C., and Cooper, G.F., 268
Blank, M. and Solomon, F., 874
Blau, P.M., 493
Bleuler, E., 945
Blos, P., 637
Bobo doll (*see also* observational learning and SLT), 816, *817*
Boden, M., 375, 384, 387–8, 389, 391, 392, 393
Bodmer, W.F., 869
body-buffer zone, 502–3
Bogardus Social Distance Scale, 518
Bolles, R.C., 137
Bornstein, M.H., 44, 283, *284*, 291, 295, 366
bottom-up versus top-down approach (in perception), 233, 418
Bower, G.H., 264, 314, 349
Bower, G.H. and Springston, F., 320–1
Bower, G.H. et al, 349
Bower, T.G.R., 290–1, *292*–4, 742
Bower, T.G.R. and Wishart, J.G., 742
Bower, T.G.R. et al, 290–4, 744
Bowlby, J., 9, 425
  maternal deprivation hypothesis, 656, 664–5, 667
  monotropy theory, 652, 653
  mothering, definition of, 645
brain
  major functions of, 93–5, *96, 97*, 98–9
  major structures of, 86–93
  methods of studying, 83–5
  development of, 85–6
brain-damaged patients and memory, 321–4
Braine, M.D.S., 784
Brehm, J.W., 140, 533
Brehm, J.W. and Cohen, A.R., 535
British Ability Scale (BAS), 853
Broadbent, D.E., 19, 37–8, 41, 297, *298*, 301, 312
Broadcasters Audience Research Board (BARB), 689
Broca, P., 83, 93

Broca's area (of brain), 83, 89, 93
Brody, E.B. and Brody, N., 845
Bromley, D.B., 714, 715, 728, 729, 730
Brown, H., 544, 556, 557, 560, 563, 568, 571, 575
Brown, J.A.C., 920, 924–5, 928
Brown, R., 158, 159, 162, 164, 485, 486, 494, 497, 542, 543, 547, 549, 551, 552, 575, 769, 780, 781, 782, 783, 802
Brown, R.W. and Lenneberg, E.H., 363
Brown-Peterson technique, 318
Bruce, V., and Green, P.R., 202
Bruner, J.S., 196, 360, 762–5
Bruner, J.S., and Goodman, C.C., 256–7
Bruner, J.S. and Kenney, H., 763
Bruner, J.S. and Postman L., 254
Bruner, J.S. et al, 253, 753, 764
Burks, B.S., 869
Burns, R.B. and Dobson, C.B., 124
Burt, C., 738, 866, 868–9
Buss, A.H., 444
bystander intervention, 423–43

Campbell, D.T., 487, 545
Campos, J.J., et al, 290
Cannon, W.B., 129, 145–7
Cannon-Bard theory of emotion, 145–7
capacity
    of STM, 312
    of LTM, 314
cardinal traits, 882
Carmichael, L., Hogan, P., and Walter, A., 364
Carroll, D.W. 771–3, 800
catatonic schizophrenia, 947
catecholamines, 160
Cattell, R.B., 38, 847–8, 880, 886–7, 894–8
Cattell, R.B., and Kline, P., 887
cause and effect, definition of, 35, 36
Cayo Santiago, 64
central fissure (Fissure of Rolando), 87
central traits, 882
central versus peripheral traits, 466–9
centration, 745, 750
cerebellum 87
cerebral cortex, 87–91
cerebral hemispheres (cerebrum), 87
chain response (or reflex) theory of learning, 187
Chapanis, N.P. and Chapanis, A., 536
chartered psychologists, 7, 14
Chernobyl, 162
Cherry, E.C., 297
Cheyenne Indians, 637
child abuse, 604, 647–8
    and attachment, 647–8
'Childhood survivors of the Holocaust', case of, 669–670
children as witnesses, 357
'Chinese Room' parable, 393, 394–5
Chomsky, N., 772–3, 785–9, 789–90
chromosome abnormalities, 677
chunking (in memory), 313

circadian rhythms and stress, 154–5
Clare, A., 945, 950, 958, 967
Clarke-Stewart, A., 653
classical conditioning, 4, 167, 168
class-inclusion tasks, 747–8
clinical psychology, 7, 13, 929
cocktail party situation (in attention), 298–300
coding
    in LTM, 314
    in STM, 313
cognitive appraisal theory (of emotion), 151–2
cognitive behaviour therapy (CBT), 980–3
cognitive consistency, theories of, 140–1, 532
cognitive control, 162
cognitive development, stages of (see also Piaget), 740–62
cognitive dissonance theory, 154, 514, 532–9
cognitive labelling, theory (of emotion), 147–8, 149–51
cognitive learning, 8
cognitive (or mental) maps, 186–8
cognitive processes, 8–9
cognitive psychology, 5, 8 9
cognitive science, 9, 15
cohort effect, 725
Coleman, J.C., 638–44
Coleman, J.C. and Hendry, L., 639–40, 641–2, 643–4, 834, 639, 640
collective unconscious, 922–5
Collins, A.M. and Loftus, E.F., 344
Collins, A.M. and Quillan, M., 342–3
colour blindness/vision, 215
colour constancy, 217
common traits, 882
comparative psychology, 9
compatibility, 297–8
competence and self-concept, 505–6
complexes, 922
computational theory of mind (CTM), 391–3
computers, 389–92
    analogue, 390, 391
    digital, 390, 391
    hardware, 391, 399
    parallel distributed processing (PDP), 395, 400
    programming languages, 390, 391
    programs, 349, 385–8
    scope of, 388–91
    software, 391, 399
computer analogy, 5, 10, 19
Computerized Axial Tomography (CATscan), 84
Comte, A., 22
conceptually-driven versus data-driven processing, 261
concrete operational stage, 741, 753–4
concrete representation (in dreams), 908–9
concurrent validity, 860

condensation, 908
conditional positive regard, 906
conditioning, 4, 8, 166–88
    and attachment, 135
    and morality, 810–14
    applications, 188–9
    preparedness for, 183
conditions of worth, 907
connectionist model (parallel distributed processing), 395–400
    and human brain, 398
    connectionist machine, 397
    Gardner on, 398
    Garnham on, 396, 399, 406
    Gordon on, 395, 398, 399
    hidden units, 397
    input, 397
    output, 397
    pandemonium, 397
    perception, 397
    Sternberg on, 400
    Turing test (Imitation Game), 396
confabulation, 815
conformity, 561–75
    definitions of, 561–2
    influences on, 572
    varieties of, 569–70
Conrad, R., 319, 321, 343
conscience, 803, 804–12
consciousness and awareness, 103–26
    and attention, 105–6
    and EEG, 107–9
    arousal and alertness, 104–5
    functions of, 107
    Freud's levels of, 103–4
    Jung's levels of, 921–5
conservation, 750–3
consolidation process, 116, 324, 339
construct validity, 861
constructive alternativism, 898–9
contentives versus functors, 780
context (cue)-dependent memory, 316
contiguity, 181
contingency model (of leader effectiveness), 558–9
contralateral control, 87–8
convergent versus divergent thinking, 846
Cook, M., 466
Cooley, C.H., 610, 611
Coolican, H., 33, 55, 59, 60
Coopersmith, S., 616
coping mechanisms, 161–3
corpus callosum, 83, 87
    and split-brain patients, 96–9
corpus striatum, 79
correspondent inference theory, 474–6
Corteen, R.S. and Dunn, D., 299
Corteen, R.S. and Wood, B., 299
cortical periods, 78
co-variation model, 476–8
covert behaviour, 976–7
Craik, F. and Lockhart, R., 319, 322, 326
Craik, F. and Tulving, E., 327–8

Craik, F. and Watkins, M., 319
criterion analysis, 890
critical and sensitive periods
  and imprinting, 421–3, 424
  and attachment, 652, 666
  and gender identity, 685
  and language development, 788
Cromer, R.F., 765
cross-longitudinal ('cohort-sequential')
  design, 725
cross-sectional studies, 690, 725
Crutchfield, R., 561, 568–70, 575
cue-dependent forgetting, 335
cultural anthropology, 637–8
cultural relativism and gender, 692–4
culture-free/fair IQ test, 862–3
Cumberbatch, G., 445, 454
Cumming, E. and Henry, W.F., 728
Cummins, M.S. and Suomi, S.J., 672
'cupboard-love' theory of attachment,
  650–1
curare, 80
cure, concept of, 971
curiosity drive, 136
Czech twins, case of, 670–1

D-state (see sleep)
Danziger, K., 807, 818
Darley, J.M., 433, 443, 481
Darwin, C., 9, 11, 128, 403, 406, 426
Dawkins, M.S., 61, 62, 63
Dawkins, R., 417, 428
decalage, 754, 757
decrement model versus personal growth
  (of ageing), 715–16, 717
Deese, J., 36
defence mechanisms, 911
deferred imitation, 744
defining the situation (in bystander
  intervention), 436
de-individuation (and aggression), 460–2
Dement, W. and Kleitman, N., 112
denial, 163, 911
dependent variable, definition, 36
depressive disorder, 953
Deregowski, J., 276, 277
Descartes, R., 45
descriptive versus generalizing science,
  883
Deutsch, J.A. and Deutsch, D., 297, 300–1
Deutsch, M. and Collins, M.E., 550
developmental psychology, 10–11
developmental retardation, 657, 665–6
deviation-from-the-norm criterion (of
  abnormality), 930
deviation IQ, 857
Dicara, L.V. and Miller, N.E., 125
dichotic listening, 297–9
diffusion of responsibility (in bystander
  intervention), 436–7
Dion, K.K., 508
Dion, K.K. and Berscheid, E., 508

directive versus non-directive therapies,
  963
discriminative stimulus, 181
discriminatory power (of a test), 858–9,
  885
displacement,
  and aggression, 450, 452
  and conflict in animals, 415–16
  and dreams, 908
  and neurosis, 968
  and prejudice, 549
  as ego defence mechanism, 416, 911
  in authoritarian personality, 542
  theory of forgetting, 334–9
dissociative hysterical neurosis, 943–44
dissolving personal relations, 512–13
distress and separation, 657–63
diurnal rhythms, 105
divided attention (see also attention), 302–
  8
  audio-typing, 302
  automatic processing, 304–5
  automaticity, 306
  central allocation policy, 307
  central processor, 306
  controlled processing, 304
  dual task, 302
  Kahneman's model, 307
  practise, 303, 305–6
  resource allocation, 306
  Stroop effect, 304
Dixon, N.F., 256
dizygotic twins (DZs), 864–9, 948–50
'Doctrine of Specifity' (Character
  Education Inquiry), 809
dogmatism scale, 543
Dollard, J. and Miller, N.E., 135, 651
Dollard, J. et al, 450, 451
dominance hierarchy, 418–19
Donaldson, M., 747–8, 749, 752, 753
Donaldson, M. and McGarrigle, J., 747–8,
  751–2
Donaldson, M. and Wales, R.J., 753
dopamine, 79, 90, 81, 950, 953
dorsal hypothalamus, 90
dorsal root (of spinal cord), 93
dorsomedial hypothalamus, 90
double-aspect theory, 292
double-blind technique, 40
Dove Counterbalance General
  Intelligence Test ('Chitling test'), 877
Down's Syndrome children
  and language, 787
  in institutions, 666
dreaming
  and sleep, 113–14
  dream interpretation, 908–9
  dream series, 925
  Freud's theory of, 118, 120, 908, 910
  Jung's theory of, 925
  physiological theories of, 113–14
Dreyfus, H.L., 128, 129
drive-reduction theory, 133–5, 651

drives, 33–5
drug therapy, 964–5
drugs-effects on neurotransmitters, 79–81,
  80–2
DSM 111-R (Diagnostic and Statistical
  Manual of Mental Disorder), 937–41,
  957
dualism, 45
Duck, S., 490, 494, 508, 509, 510, 511, 512,
  513
Dworetzsky, J.P., 423, 753, 794
dynamic memory theory
  MOPs, 349
  TOPs, 349
dysthymic versus hysterical disorders, 893

ear (see also auditory system), 219, 220
eating and the hypothalamus, 130–1
Ebbinghaus, H., 310–12
ECT (electro-convulsive therapy), 965–7
educational psychology, 7, 12
EEG (electroencephalogram)
  and biofeedback, 125
  and consciousness, 104–5, 107–9
  and hypnosis, 122–3
  and intelligence, 863
  and major tranquillizers, 81
  and study of the brain, 84
egg-rolling in greylag goose, 409
  and herring gull, 410
ego, 592, 908, 910, 920
  and conflict, 908
  defence mechanisms, 162, 636–7, 910–12
  ideal, 803, 804
  identity, 625, 635
  integrity versus despair, 732
egocentric speech, 373
egocentrism, 748–50
  and adolescence, 631
  and morality, 825–6
Eibl-Eibesfeldt, L., 404, 410–11, 445
Eight Ages of Man, 624, 627, 635
Ekman, P. and Friesen, W.V., 143
Electra complex, 687
electrical self-stimulation of brain (ESB),
  134–5
electro-chemical impulses, 74
  and action potential, 77
  and resting potential, 77
  and saltatory conduction, 77
electrooculogram (EOG) and sleep, 111
Eliot, C., 853
Elkind, D., 701, 761
Ellis, A., 981
EMG (electromyogram) and sleep, 111
emotion, 142–53
  classification of, 143
  components of, 143
  theories of, 143–52
empathic understanding, 986
empirical methods, 23, 24
empiricism, 21–2
Empson, J., 112–13, 115, 116–19, 121–2

encephalins, 78
encoding specificity principle (ESP), 340
encounter groups, 987
endocrine system, 78, 91
  and hypothalamus, 99, 100–2
endorphins, 78, 81
emancipation and displacement activity,
  416
engineering model of stress, 152–3
engulfment, 951
epigenetic principle, 625
ephiphenomenalism, 46
equal-status contact, 549–50
equilibration, 739–40
equilibrium model of intimacy, 500–3
equity theory, definition of, 493–4
ergonomics (human engineering), 14
ergs, 898
Erhard Seminars Training (EST), 989–4
Erikson, E.H., 10, 136, 509, 624–44, 708,
  903, 907
  and Freud, 624–5
  'Eight Ages of Man', 10, *626*
  epigenetic principle, 625
  id, 625
  'lifespan approach', *730*, 731
  play, theory of, *627*
  psycho-social stages, theory of, 628–33
Erlenmeyer-Kimling, L., Jarvik, L.F. and
  Jensen A.R., 876–7
erogenous/erotogenic zones, 595
Eros (Life Instincts), 450
escape and avoidance learning, 179–80
Eskimos, 362, 446
Esterson, A., 990
Ethical Rule Theory versus Ethical Act
  Theory, 833–5
ethics of psychological research, 51–69
  American Psychological Association
    (APA), 52, 60
  British Psychological Society (BPS)
    'Principles 1990', 34, *52*, 53, 54, 56,
    57, 59, 60
    and guidelines, 61, 65, 66
    confidentiality, 59
    consent, 53–5, 59–60
    data, access to, 60
    debriefing, 57–9
    deception, 55–6
    obedience experiment, the, 53, 574,
      575–9, 581, 585
    of animal experiments, 61–5
    of psychological research, 34, 35
ethnocentrism, 541, 547
ethogram, 405
ethology (see also imprinting), 9
  and aggression, 444–6
  and attachment, 651–2
  and evolutionary theory, 103
  and motivation, 128
  and psychology, 405
  and sociobiology, 404–6
  concept of instinct, 407–8

FAPs (fixed action patterns), 408–21
  IRMs (innate releasing mechanisms),
    412–16
eusocial insects, 418
Evans, P., 411, 413, 414
evolution, theory of, 26, 406–7
  and FAPs, 416
  and sexual (diploid) reproduction, 406
  (see also ethology and Darwin, C.)
exchange theory, 438, 489, 492–8
executive monkey experiments, 63, 158
existence constancy, 293
existential psychiatry, 951–2
existential therapy, 951–2
exocrine glands, 102
experimental methodology, 32–40
experimental neurosis, 169
experimenter bias, 867–8, 40
expiatory punishment, 824
exposure (in systematic desensitization),
  975
external (reality) conflict (of ego), 593
exvia (-invia), 897
eye (see also visual system), 207, 211
eye movements, 286
eye-witness testimony (EWT), 352–9
Eysenck, H.J., 140, 543, 544, 600, 860,
  877, 880, 887–94, 972, 991, *992*
Eysenck, H.J. and Eysenck, S.B.G., 884,
  889, 890, 897
Eysenck, M.W., 256, 259, 261, 301
Eysenck, M.W. and Keane, M.J., 230, 232,
  233, 234, 238, 245, 246, 254, 302,
  303, 304, 305, 306, 308, 312, 341–2,
  375, 376
Eysenck Personality Inventory (EPI), *889*,
  892, 893, 894
Eysenck Personality Questionnaire
  (EPQ), 890, 893

face (content) validity, 860
facedness, 287, *288*, 289
factor analysis, 886
  see also psychometric approach (to
    personality and intelligence)
  and intelligence, 841–7
  first and second order, 886–7
Fairbairn, G. and Fairbairn, S., 65, 66, 67,
  68
falsifiability criterion, (refutability of
  theory), 28
family interaction model (of
  schizophrenia), 952–64
family (and marital) therapy, 964
Fantz, R.L., 285–7
F (Fascism) scale, 542
fear
  of castration, 803–4
  of failure, 142
  of success, 142
feature detection theories (of pattern
  recognition), 260–1
feature constancy, 293

Ferster, C.B. and Skinner, B.F., 176
Festinger, L., 514, 532–9, 563, 571
Festinger, L. and Carlsmith, J.M., 534–5
Fiedler, F.E., 558–9
fight or flight syndrome (see Autonomic
  Nervous System [ANS])
figural unity versus identity, 264
figural coherence, 284
filter model (of attention), 297–9
Fisher, S. and Greenberg, R.P., 604–5,
  606, 915
Fiske, S.T., 708
Fiske, S.T. and Taylor, S.E., 478, 479,
  488–9, 514, 533, 540
fixation,
  and personality types, 604
fixed action patterns (FAPs), 403, 408–9,
  414–15
fixed role enactment, sketch, therapy,
  984–5
Flanagan, O.J., 47, 48
Flavell, J.H., 750, 757, 760
flooding, 975
fluid versus crystallized intelligence, 723–
  4, 848, 896
focal theory (of adolescence), 643, 644
focal versus peripheral attention, 106
Fonagy, P., 915, 916, 917
Fonagy, P. and Higgit, A. 957, 971, 974,
  980
forebrain, 87–91
forensic/legal psychologists, 13
forgetting, 334, *335–41*
formal operational stage, 741, 754–5
fostering and adoption studies, 869–71
'Four Whys' of Tinbergen, 403, 405
Fox, R.M. and Azrin, N.H., 978
Fransella, F., 611–12, 935, 983, 984
free association, 970–1
free will versus determinism, 49–50
Freud, A., 636–7, 660
Freud, A. and Dann, S., 669–70, 671
Freud, S., 5, 103–4, 106, 120, 127, 136,
  340, 589–606, 802, 803–9, 814, 820,
  880, 907, 908–14, 931, 968–71, 974
  analytic method, 590–1
  and Erikson, 624–5
  and gender role differences, 687–8
  attachment, 650–1, 653
  case of Little Hans, 600–1
  child abuse (seduction theory), 603–4
  instinct theory (psychosexual
    development), 594, *595*
    (0 to 1 year) oral stage, 596
    (1 to 3 years) anal stage, 596–7
    (3 to 6 years) phallic stage, 597
    (6 to puberty) latency stage, 598–9
  drive (psychic energy) 594
  electra complex, 597–8
  libido, 594
  oedipus complex, 597, 599–600, 603 4
  moral conflict, 592, *593*
  personality, structure of, 591

Freud, S. – *cont.*
  ego, 592
  id, 591–2
  psychic apparatus, *593*, 594
  super-ego, 593
  personality types, 604, *605*, 606
  play, theory of, *599*
  'primary' and 'secondary process'
    thinking, 592
  psychoanalytic theory, 589–94
  and adolescence, 636–7
Fromm, E., 450, 460–1, 493, 508, *601*, 928
frontal lobe, 87–9
frustration-aggression hypothesis, 451–3,
  549
functional invariants, 739
functional lateralization (of cerebrum), 92,
  95–6
fundamental attribution error, 479, 883
Furth, H.G., 366, 765

Gagne, R.M., 194–5, 196
Gahagan, J., 465–6, 472, 482, 555
'gain–loss' theory, 505
gamma-amino-butyric acid (GABA), 79,
  81
Garcia, J., 181
Garcia, J. and Koelling, R.A., 181
Gardner, H., 395–6, 398, 400, 851–2
Gardner, R.A. and Gardner, B.T., 514,
  790, 792, 796
Garnham, A., 31, 41, 44, 398, 400
Gebner, G. and Gross, L., 454
Geen, R.G., 79, 81, 449
Gelder, M. et al, 965
gender (*see also* sex and gender)
  constancy, 689, 695
  identity, 674–5, 685, 694–5, 804, 815
  media, effects of, 689–91
  stability, 695
gene-environment interaction, 425, 871
General Adaptation Syndrome (GAS),
  153, 160–1
General Problem Solver (GPS), 378–9
general symbolic function, 744
generalized imitation (*see also*
    identification), 818
generation gap, 640–2
Generalized Delta Rule (GDR)
    (backwards error propagation), 398–
    9
generativity versus stagnation, 701
genes and (apparent) altruism (biological
    altruism), 426–7
genetic epistemology, 738
genetic theory, of intelligence, 864
  of schizophrenia, 948–50
genetic transmission, 8
genital stage, 803
Gergen, K.J. and Gergen, M.M., 460, 462,
  561
Gergen, K.J. et al, 462
geriatrics, 719

gerontology, 717
Gesell developmental test, 878
Gestalt psychology, 4, 8, *241*
  and forgetting, 339
  and insight, 375–6
  and language, 785
  and learning, 192–4
  and perception, 239–46
  and problem solving, 375–6
  and restructuring, 376
  therapy, 988–9
Gibson, E.J. and Walk, P.D., 289–90
Gibson, J.J., 223, 233–9
Gillham, W.E.C., 863
Glanzer, M. and Cunitz, A.R., 317–18
Glanzer, M. and Meinzer, A., 319
glucocorticoid hormones and stress, 160
Glueck, S, and Glueck, E., 806
Goffman, E., 488, 936
Goldfarb, W., 663, 656–7, 667
gonadotrophic hormones, 101
Gordon, I.E., 232, 233, 234–5, 240, 242–3,
  246, 247–8, 251–2, 395, 398
Gottesman, I.I. et al, 950
Gould, R.L., 701, 702, 706–8
Graham, H., 951, 985, 986, 987, 988, 989,
  990
Gray, J.A., 63, 64, 65, 179
Gray, J. and Wedderburn, A., 298
Green, S., 129, 130, 132, 134, 447
Greene, J., 224, 226, 375, 379, 380, 381,
  384
Greene, J. and Hicks, C.J., 296
Gregory, R.L., 223, 224–32, 394, 395, 899
Gregory, R.L., and Wallace, J., 265
Grid Test of Thought Disorder, 899
grief, 732, *734*
  normal and abnormal, 735
  pathological, 736
grief work, 733
Gross, R.D., 64, 276, 668, 669
Gua, 790
Guilford, J.P., 843, 845, 884
Guiton, P., 423
Gunter, B. and McAleer, J.L., 454, 456,
  457, 458, 459, 460, 689, 690

habituation, 92, 105
Hall, C.S. and Lindzey, G., 883
Hall, C.S. and Nordby, V.J., 923, 927
Hall, E.J., *501–3*
Hall, G.S., 636
hallucinations, *139*
  and drugs, 81
hardware and software, 391, 399
Hardy, G.R. and Legge, D., 256
Harlow, H.F., 136, 195–6, 405, 664
Harlow, H.F. and Zimmerman, R.R., *651*,
  652
Hartshorne, H. and May, M., 809
Hass, R.G. and Mann, R., 529
hassles scale, 159
Havighurst, R.J., 730

hearing defects,
  conductive, 222
  sensory neural, 222
Heather, N., 20, 106, 858, 861, 892, 934,
  951, 958
Hebb, D.O., 137, 864, 875
hebephrenic schizophrenia, 946–7
Hediger, H., 415
hedonism, 128
Heider, F., 473, 474, 476, 532
Heim, A., 840, 841, 857, 861, 887, 893
Held, R., 272
Held, R. and Hein, A., 268–9
heredity–environment issue, 8, 864–75,
  875–8
heritability estimate for intelligence, 868–9
hermaphroditism, 677–9
Heron, W., 138–9
Herrnstein, R.J., 877
Hershenson, M., 287
hertz units, 219
Hess, E.H., 422
Hess, R.D. and Shipman, V., 370
heteronomous versus autonomous
    morality, 825, 831, 826
heuristic function of theories, 28
hierarchical model of intelligence, 843
hierarchical nature of personality, 887
hierarchical network model (of semantic
    memory), 342–3
hierarchy of needs, 902–3
high availability factor (in attitude
    change), 524
High School Personality Questionnaire,
  895
Hilgard, E.R., 107, 122–4
hindbrain, 92
Hinde, R.A., 403, 405, 408, 410, 412, 414,
  415, 416, 423, 427, 429, 447
Hinde, R.A. and Spencer-Booth, Y., 648
hippocampus (and memory), 91, 322
Hitch, G.J., 312
Hochberg's minimum principle, 240
Hodges, and Tizard, B., 668
Hoffman, L.W., 142, 661
Hoffman, M.L., 804, 806, 808
Holmes, T.H. and Rahe, R.H., 156–8
holophrase, 779
Homans, G.C., 492
homeostasis, definition of, 720
homeostatic drive theory, 129–35
homosexuality, 675, 687–8, 931
honey-bee 'waggle dance', 418
Hopi Indians, 362, 364–5
hormones (*see also* endocrine system), 6,
  78
Horn, J.L. and Cattell, R.B., 848
Horn, J.L. et al, 870
Horner, M.S., 142
Horney, K., 804
hospitalism, 657
Hovland, C.I., 514
Hovland, C.I., and Janis, I.L., 519

Hovland, C.I. et al, 526, 527
Hovland, C.I. and Weiss, W., 520
Howe, M.J.A., 165, 180, 196
Hubel, D.H. and Wiesel, T.N., 84
Hull, C.L. 128, 129, 135–6, 166
human virtues, 626, 635
humanistic psychology, 11
    and idealism, 46
    and personality, 881, 901–7
    and therapy, 985–7
hunger, 129–32
Hunt, J. McVicker, 874
Huntington's chorea and GABA, 79, 81
Hutt, C., 136
hydraulic model
    and territoriality, 421
    criticisms of, 414–15
    of aggression, 447
    of instinct, 412–13
hyperphagia, 130
hypnogogic period, 111
hypnosis
    and Freud, 590
    and hidden observer, 124
    and pain, 123–4
    definitions of, 122–4
    uses of, 123–4
hypnotics, 82
hypothalamus
    and aggression, 90, 447–8
    and stress, 160
hypothesis, definition of, 19
hypothetical construct, definition of, 16
hysterical conversion neurosis, 910, 944

id, 591–2, 625, 898, 913, 920
idealism, 46
identification
    anaclitic, 598
    and aggression, 600
    and conformity, 570
    and defence, 912
    with the aggressor, 598, 803, 804
identity crisis, 632, 639 40
identity theory, 46, 47
idiographic approach, 880–1, 898
idiography (idiodynamics), 882
idiots savants, 852
imagery, in memory, 315–16, 352
imitation, 814–18
    and identification, 818–19
    and language development, 780, 783, 784
    and moral development, 814–21
    with expansion, 780
    with reduction, 780
imitative aggression, 816–18, 817
imitative self (dis-)approval (see also
        observational learning and Social
        Learning Theory), 820
immanent justice, 825
Immelmann, K. and Suomi, S.J., 425
Imperato-McGinley, J. et al, 683
implicit personality theory (stereotyping)

(see also interpersonal perception),
        482–6
implosion, 951
implosive therapy, 975
impression management, 487–9
imprinting, 404, 421
incidental learning and memory, 319
inclusive fitness, 428
independent variable, 36
individual differences, 11
individual psychology, 926–8
individual traits, 882
individuation, 922
induced movement (see also visual
        illusions), 231
induction (inductive method), 23, 24, 25
industrial (or occupational) psychology, 7,
        13–14
industry versus inferiority, 629
infantile sexuality (see psychosexual
        stages)
inferiority, 926–7
informational conformity, 571, 572
informational control, 162
ingratiational conformity, 571, 572
Inhelder, B. and Piaget, J., 755
initiative versus guilt, 629
innate releasing mechanisms (IRMs), 412–
        13
innoculation (and attitude change), 528–9
insight learning, 8, 192–4
intelligence (see also artificial intelligence),
        11, 839–78
    A, B and C, 875
    alternative models, 847–52
    and ageing, 722–6
    and IQ, 856–8
    components of, 848
    definitions of, 723, 839–41, 840
    factor analytic, 841–7
    fluid and crystallized, 848
    hierarchical model (Burt and Vernon),
        843
    information-processing approach, 848
    IQ correlations, 724–6, 738, 853, 854,
        864, 872
    multiple, 851
    primary mental abilities, 844
    qualitative approach, 839–40, 849
    quotient (IQ), 724–6, 738, 853, 854, 864,
        872
    structure of, 845, 846
    tests, 371
    zone of proximal development, 850
intention movements and conflict, 415–16
interference (theory of forgetting), 336,
        337–8
inter-group conflict (and prejudice), 545–6
interiorized schemas, 744
internal consistency (see also reliability),
        859
internalization (and conformity), 572
International Classification of Diseases

(ICD-10), 937, 957
interpersonal attraction, 492–513
interpersonal perception, 463–91
    accuracy of, 471
    definitions of, 465–6
    inference model, 473–86
    intuitive model, 466–73
interpretation (in psychoanalysis), 970
interviews, 519
intimacy versus isolation, 701
introjection and self-concept, 613
introspection, 3, 4
introversion-extroversion, 140, 888–9, 891
    and arousal, 890
    and conditionability, 891–2
    and Jung, 992
intuitive stage, 747–8
isolation (as ego defence), 163, 913
isomorphism, 46
Ituri pygmies, 446
Iversen, L.L., 950, 953

Jahoda, G., 275, 550, 619
Jahoda, M., 930
James, W., 4, 128, 146, 264, 280, 310, 335,
        610
James-Lange theory of emotion, 143, 144,
        145
Janis, I.L. and Feshbach, S., 523–4, 525
Janis, I.L. and Mann, L., 530
Janis, I.L. and Terwillinger, R.T., 524
Janov, A., 988–9
Jekyll and Hyde, 944
Jenkins, J.J., 313
Jensen, A.R., 869, 876–8
Jersild, A.J., 621
jet-lag and stress, 155, 156
jigsaw classroom, 551
Jolly, H., 660
Jones, E. et al, 475
Jones, E.E. and Charms, R., 481
Jones, E.E. and Davis, K.E., 474–6
Jones, E.E. and Nisbett, R.E., 479
Jones, M.C. and Bayley, N., 622
Jones, M.C., 71
Jost, A., 681
Jourard, S.M., 489, 490
Joynson, R.B., 19
Juel-Nielsen, N., 866–7
Jung, C.G., 104, 590, 888, 907, 921–4,
        925–6

Kadushin, A., 669
Kagan, J., 873
Kagan, J. et al, 660
Kahneman, D., 301
Kahneman, D. and Henik, A., 304
Kahneman's model of attention, 307
Kulahari Bushmen, 185, 446
Kamin, L.J., 865, 867, 868
Kanzi, 797–801
Karlin, M. et al, 484
Karnes, M.B. et al, 874

Katz, D., 527–8, 539
Katz, D. and Braly, K., 484, 485
Kelley, H.H., 467, 476–8
Kellogg, W.N. and Kellogg, L., 790, 797
Kelly, G., 880, 898–901
Kennell, J.H. et al, 646
kibbutzim, 654–5
kin selection, 431, 428
Kirby, R. and Radford, J., 883
kitten carousel, 268–9
Kitty Genovese, case of, 433–5, 437
Klaus, R.A. and Gray, S.W., 874
Klaus, H.M. and Kennell, J.H., 646
Kleinmuntz, B., 976
Kline, P., 38, 39, 44, 858, 860, 861, 883,
    884, 887, 892, 897, 915–18
Kline, P. and Storey, R., 604
Klinefelter's syndrome, 873
Kluver, H. and Bucy, P.C., 968
Kluver-Bucy syndrome, 448
knee-jerk reflex, 93
Koestler, A., 193, 194
Kohlberg, L., 239, 240, 681, 694–5, 808,
    826, 827–35
Kohler, I., 272
Köhler, W., 193, 194
Koko, 792, 793–4, 795, 796
Korsakoff's syndrome, 324
Kraepelin, E., 936, 945
Kuder-Richardson method, 860
Kuhn, T.S., 26, 27
Kurtines, W. and Grief, E.B., 834

Labov, W., on black English, 370–1
lactogenic hormone, 101
Laing, R.D., 464–5, 948, 951–2, 964, 990
Laing, R.D. and Esterson, A., 952
Lamb, M.E., 654, 687
Lana, 792, 793, 795, 796
Language
    acquisition device (LAD), 785–9
    and cognitive development, 763–5
    and gender differences, 680
    as human species-specific behaviour,
        768, 789, 790
    competence versus performance, 784
    creativity of, 784
    criteria of, 789–90, 791
    deep versus surface structure, 785–6
    definition of, 768–9
    grammar, 769–71, 770, 783–4
    linguistic universals, 786, 787
    morphology, 770, 771
    phonology, 769–70
    semantics, 770, 771
    stages of development, 773–83
    syntax, 770, 771
    teaching language to primates, 789–800
    theories of acquisition, 783–8
    transformational grammar, 786, 787, 789
language and thought, 364
    Bitch Test, 371
    codes restricted and elaborated, 368

linguistic determinism, 361
linguistic relativity hypothesis, 361, 362,
    363
    modularity of mind, 374
    peripheralism, 366
    Piaget on, 372, 373
    race and class differences, 185–6
    universal linguistic structures, 365
    Vygotsky's theory, 372
    Wittgenstein on, 361
Larsen, K.S., 568
Lashley, K., 83, 95
Latané, B. and Darley, J.M., 433, 435–6,
    439
Latané, B. and Rodin, J., 436
Latané, B. et al, 437
latency stage, 803
latent learning, 186
lateral fissure (fissure of Sylvius), 87–8
lateral geniculate body (LGB), 90, 212
lateral hypothalamus
    and eating, 130, 132
    and thirst, 132
law of
    effect, 172–3
    equipotentiality, 95
    mass action, 95
    parsimony, 30
    pragnanz, 240
    Weber-Fechner, 204
Lazarfeld, P.F. et al, 521
Lazarus, R.S. and McCleary, R.A., 256
L-data, 894, 897
Lea, S.E.G., 404, 405, 406, 407, 408, 414,
    415, 416, 418, 422, 424
leadership, 554, 555–61
    and communication networks, 559–60
    and power, 559–60, 561
    effectiveness, 558–9
    situational approach, 557–8
    styles of, 555–7, 556
    trait approach, 556–7
learned helplessness, 140, 158, 185
learning, 4–5, 8
    definitions of, 164–5
    sets, 195–7
    versus performance, 165, 186
learning theory and attachment, 650, 651
least preferred co-worker (LPC) scores
    (see also leadership), 559
Leeper's ambiguous lady, 242
Lefrancois, G.R., 126, 130
Legge, D., 6, 20
Leibnitz, G.W., 40
Lenneberg, E.H., 777–8, 784–5, 787, 789
Lepper, M.R., 813
leucotomy, 967–8
level of emotional appeal (in attitude
    change), 523–5
levels (depths) of processing (in memory),
    326–7
Levinson, D.J. et al, 702–6
Lewin, K., Lippit R. and White, R., 556–7

Lewis, M. and Brooks-Gunn, J., 618–19,
    621
libido, 594
Lie Scale, 517, 889–90, 896
life changes and stress, 156–9
Life Events Scale, 157
lifespan approach (in developmental
    psychology), 10, 636, 700
lifespan versus life expectancy, 718–19,
    722
Likert Scale, 518
liking and loving, 508–9
limbic system and aggression, 91, 447–9
limbic leucotomy, 967–8
linguistic relativity hypothesis, 361–5
Lippman, W., 482
lithium carbonate, 964
Little Albert, case of, 170
Little Hans, case of, 600–3, 919, 968
Little Peter, case of, 171
Lloyd, P. et al, 38, 78, 104, 106, 146, 444,
    951
localization of brain function, 89, 93–6
Locke, J., 21
Loftus, E.F., 354–6
logical positivists, 22, 28
long term memory, 314
longitudinal fissure (or sulcus), of cortex,
    37
longitudinal studies, 725
Lorenz, K., 403–5, 413–16, 421–5, 445,
    446, 447, 450, 459, 651–2
Lorenz, K. and Tinbergen, N., 9, 408–9,
    413
locus coeruleus and sleep, 110
locus of control, 140
locus of control scale, 140, 158
love versus object-oriented child rearing,
    807
Luchins, A.S., 469–71
Luria, A.R., 352
Luria, A.R. and Yudovich, F.I., 367
Lyons, J., 786

McCelland, D.C. 142
McCelland, D.C. et al, 142
Maccoby, E.E., 142, 617, 620, 647, 648,
    680, 681, 695, 802
Maccoby, E.E. and Jacklin, C.N., 679–81,
    688
McDougall, W., 128, 747
McGarrigle, J. and Donaldson, M., 751–2
McGarrigle, J. et al, 747
McGeoch, J.A. and McDonald, W.T., 337
McGinnies, E., 254–5
McGuire, W.J., 520, 523, 524, 525, 526,
    530
McGurk, H., 864, 870
Mackay, D., 931, 958, 972, 984
Mackinnon, D., 805, 806, 807
Mackintosh, N.J., 184
McNeill, D., 785, 789
magic number seven, 312–13

Magnetic Resonance Imaging (MRI), 84
Maier, S.F. and Seligman, M.E.P., 185
maintenance versus elaborative rehearsal, 173
Malinowski, B., 599, 693
Mandler, G., 346–7
manic depression, 953
manifest and latent content (of dreams), 908
manipulative drive, 136
Mann, L., 561
Marcia, J.E., 630–1
Marks, I.M., 972, 975, 983
Marr, D., 260, 375
Marr's computational theory of vision, 248–52
   image, 249
   model, 30, 249
   sketch, primal, 249
   sketch, 2 1/2D, 249
Maslow, A., 11, 17, 18, 127, 444, 901–5, 924, 930
Maslow's hierarchy of needs, 902
matching hypothesis, 494–7
materialism (physicalism), 22
maternal deprivation hypothesis, 656–8
matriline, 419
Maudsley Medical Questionnaire (MMQ), 889
Maudsley Personality Inventory (MPI), 889
Mead, G.H., 610–11, 612
Mead, M., 447, 625, 637–8, 653, 692–4
Meadows, S., 398, 400, 643, 757, 758, 761, 833, 834, 835
mean length of utterance (MLU), 782
media-effects on gender role stereotypes (see also Social Learning Theory), 689–91
medial geniculate body (of thalamus), 90
meditation, 124–5
medulla oblongata, 93
Medvedev, Z.A., 719, 721
Me'en tribe, 276
Meichenbaum, D., 980
memory, 341
   aids (see mnemonics)
   amnesia, 321–4
   and learning, 309–10
   articulatory loop, 308
   central executive, 332–3
   Clive Weaving, case of, 321, 323
   declarative, 325
   eye-witness testimony, 352–9
   H.M., case of, 321–2
   imagery, 352
   long term (LTM), 314
   mnemonics, 327, 352
   multistore model, 310, 316–21
   primary acoustic store, 332–3
   primary versus secondary, 311
   procedural, 325
   reconstructive schemas, 345–6, 350

schemas, 345–6, 350
semantic, 342–4
sensory memory, 310–12
short-term (STM), 308, 312–13
storage, 310, 311
three processes of, 309
working, 308, 332
visuospatial scratchpad, 308
(see also forgetting)
Mental Health Act (of 1983), 954
mental illness (see psychopathology)
mental maps (see also cognitive maps), 8
Mi Lai Massacre, 586
microelectrodes and brain, 83
mid-life crisis, 708–9
Miles, T.R., 841
Milgram, S., 53–5, 570, 575–83
Miller, G.A., 21, 127, 312–13, 320
Miller, G.A. and Selfridge, J.A., 320
Miller, N.E., 126, 135, 179
Miller, N.E. and Dicara, L.V., 125
Minard, R.S., 544, 550
MIND, 966
mind, 3–5
mind–body problem, 8, 44–8
mind of a mnemonist, 352–3
minor and major tranquillizers, 964–5
Mischel, W., 820–1, 884–5
Mitchell, R., 942
mnemonics, 327, 352–3
model (definition of), 19
models (and modelling) (see also observational learning), 982–3
modelling therapy, 982
Mohave Indians, 694
Mondrian experiment (Lands), 218
monoamine oxidase (MAO), 80, 964–5
monoamine transmitters, 79, 80
Money, J. and Ehrhardt, A.A., 685, 695
monism, 46
monotropy, 652
monozygotic twins (MZs), 864–9
moral conflict, 593
moral development, 802–35
   cognitive developmental approach, 820–35
   Freud's psychoanalytical theory, 803–9
   Kohlberg's theory, 828–31
   Learning Theory approach, 810–14
   Social Learning Theory approach, 814–19
moral realism versus relativism, 825
Moray, N., 296, 298, 299
Moreno, J., 519, 989–90
morphemes, 769–70
Moruzzi, G. and Magoun, H.W., 105, 110
Moscovici, S. and Faucheux, C., 575
Moss, H.A., 684
motion parallax, 278
motivated forgetting, 341
motivation, 127–42
   and adaptation, 137
   and philosophy, 128–9

and play, 136–7
cognitive motives, 140–2
competence motives, 135–6
definitions, 127
drive reduction theory, 129–33
homeostatic drive theory, 133–5
need for control, 140
theoretical perspectives, 127–8
motor cortex, 87
mourning, 732
Mowrer, O.H., 179, 975
Moyer, K.E., 444, 448
Müller-Lyer illusion (see visual system illusions)
multiple personality, 944
Mundugumor, 692
Murdock, B.B., 317
Murray, H.A., 127, 128, 141
Murray Islanders, 273
Mussen P.H. and Jones M., 622

National Children's Bureau (1976 study), 638, 640, 641
Nativists, 21
'Naughty Teddy', 751–2
Navaho Indians, 363
negative practice, 976–7
Neisser, U., 239, 260, 301, 307, 312, 785
Nelson, K., 779, 784
neo-behaviourists, 30
neogenesis (Spearman's 'g'), 696, 842
nervous system
   absolute refractory period, 77
   all-or-none rule, 77
   characteristics, 73–82
   cranial and spinal nerves, 77
   neuromodulators, 78
   neuropeptides, 78, 79
   neurotransmitters, 73, 78, 79, 80, 81, 82
   pre/post-synaptic membrane, 75
   relative refractory period, 77
   sensory (afferent), motor (efferent) and inter-neurons, 74
   structure of neurons, 73–4
   sub-divisions, 73, 74, 75
   summation, 77
   synapses (excitatory and inhibitory), 76, 77
   synaptic cleft (gap), 75
   threshold of response, 77
Nesselroade, J.R. et al, 724
neural theory (of dreaming), 119–20
neurosis and ego defences, 968
neurosis and psychosis, 940
neurosis, varieties of,
   anxiety, 941
   dissociative (hysterical), 943–4
   obsessive-compulsive, 942–3
   phobias, 942
   psychosomatic disorders, 940
   somatoform conversion, 944
neurotic paradox, 968
neurotic symptoms, 910

neuroticism, 888–94
New Guinea tribes, 692
Newell, A. Shaw and Simon, H.A., 378
Nim Chimpsky, 792, 794, 795, 796
Nisbett, R. and Ross, L., 482
nomothetic approach, 880–2, 883
non-standard English, 370–1
non-verbal behaviour
    and attraction (*see* interpersonal
        attraction)
    and persuasive communication, 522–3
norepinephrine (noradrenaline), 79, 80,
    134
    and stress, 160, 953
normal distribution and IQ, 856–7
Norman, D.A., 297, 299, *300*
Norman, D.A. and Shallice, T., 305
normative conformity, 570
Novak, M.A., 671
Novak, M.A., and Harlow, H.F., 671
Nuclear Magnetic Resonance Imaging,
    (NMR), 84

Oatley, K., 963, 981
obedience, 575–85
object permanence, 741–4
objective (external) versus internal
    responsibility, 823
objectivity (in experiments), *38*
observational learning (*see also* Social
    Learning Theory), 8, 189–91
obsessive-compulsive personality, 954
occipital lobe, 87–8
occupational (industrial) psychology, 7,
    13–14
ocular dominance columns, 267
Oedipus complex, 636, 687, 803–4, 909,
    992
Offer, D. and Offer, J.B., 77, 638–9, 640
Offer self-image questionnaire, 639
Olds, J., 734
Olds, J. and Milner, P., 134
one versus two-sided arguments, 525–6
ontogeny, 11, 403
ontological insecurity, 951
open and closed mind, 543
operant (instrumental) conditioning, 4,
    171–2, 188, 783, 790, 792, 794
Operational Headstart, 874–5
operational definitions
    of intelligence, 839–41
opiates, 82
opinion leaders, 521
opponent colour theory, 216
optimal–level ('arousal') theories, 137
optoids, 78
oral personality, 604–6
oral stage, 803
orbital leucotomy, 967
order of presentation (of persuasive
    message), 526–7
organic versus functional psychosis, 934
organization (in memory), 342–6

organizational psychology, 14
orienting reflex, 92
Orne, M.T., 123
Ornstein, R.E., 82, 96–7, 125, 201, 206
orthogonal versus oblique factor analysis,
    886–7
Osgood, C.E., 143
Osgood, C.E. and Tannenbaum, P.H.,
    532
osmoreceptors, 133
Oswald, I., 116
oxytocin, 101

Pandemonium, 261, 397
Parke, R.D., 653–4, 811, 812
Parkes, C.M., 733, 735–6
Parkes, C.M. and Weiss, R.S., 732–3, 736
pair bond, 417
paired associate learning, 337
Paivio, A., 352
Papez Circuit and aggression, 448
paradox of reward, 813–14
parallel distribution processing (PDP)
    (Connectionist Model), 395–40
paranoia, 896
paranoid personality, 854
paranoid schizophrenia, 947
parapraxes (Freudian slips), 914
parasympathetic branch (of ANS), 99
Parkinson's disease, 949, 950
    and dopamine, 79
    and L-Dopa, 80
passivity experiences (in schizophrenia),
    946
pathogenic ideas, 910
pattern recognition
    and context, 261
    and memory, 317
    theories of, 258–61
Pavlov, I., 166, 167, 168, 169, 170, 184,
    190
peak experiences, 904, 987
Peck, D. and Whitlow, D., 893, 901
pecking order, 419
Penfield, W., 83, 917
penis envy, 598
peptides, 79, 132
perception, 5, 9
    accentuation/sensitization, 254–7
    adaptation (readjustments) studies, 263,
        269–72
    and human cateract patients, 263, 264–6
    animal experiments, 266–9
    as inference, 224
    assessment of Gestalt principles, 242–6
    common illusions, *227*
    constancies, 225–6, 265–6
    cross-cultural studies of, 273–9
    defence, 202, 254–6
    depth cues, *257–8*
    directive perception, 233
    evaluation of theories, 235
    factors influencing set, 252–6

human infants, 262, 279–95
    interactionism, 262, 264
    Marr's computational theory of vision,
        233, 246–52
    Müller-Lyer illusion, *229*
    nativism versus empiricism, 224, 262,
        264, 291
    nature–nurture debate, 262–95
    of movment, 231–2
    perceptual constancy, 225
    Piaget on, 225
    principles of, 223–4, 233, *240*, *241*, *244*
    schema/set, 252–*3*
    theories of, 223–*4*
        Gestalt, *239–42*
        Gibson, 233–9
        Gregory, 224–3, *238*
    visual illusions, 226–*30*, 231
peripheral nervous system (PNS), 99, 744
peripheralism, 366
Perls, F., 988
Perry, D.G. and Parke, R.D., 814
persona, 923–4
Personal Construct Theory (PCT), 898–
    901, 983–4
personal growth model (of ageing), 716
person/process approach, 12
personal space, 500–3
personal unconscious, 922
personal versus positional modelling, 818
personality
    and psychology, 879–81
    and self-concept, 879
    and stereotypes, 879
    biological basis, 890–1
    definition of, 11, 879
    Freudian model, 591–3
    theories of, 421–2, *880*–1, 901–7, 907–28
    trait and type approaches, 11, 886–98
    traits versus situation, 883–5
personality disorders, 953–4
pertinence model (of attention), 300–1
Peterson, L.R., and Peterson, M.J., 318,
    335
petrification (depersonalization), 951
phallic stage, 803–4
phasic alertness, 105
phenylketonuria (PKU), 871, 873
pheromones, 417
phi phenomenon (*see also* visual illusions),
    231
Philadelphia Association, 990
philosophy: influence on psychology, 21–
    5
phobias, 942, 973
phonemes, 769–70, 775
phonemic contraction, 774
phonemic expansion, 774
phylogeny, 11, 404
physical versus psychological treatments,
    961
Piaget, J., 9, 63, 136, 152, 153, 360, 372–3,
    374, 474, 726, 738–62, 762–5, 766,

821–7, 831, 839, 848–9
adaptation, (accommodation and assimilation), 738–40
conservation, 750–3
disequilibrium, 740
egocentrism, 741, *748–50*
General Symbolic Function, 744
object permanence, *742–3*
play, theory of, 755–7
schemas, *739*
stages of development, 740–62
(0–2 years) sensorimotor, 741–4
(2–7 years) pre-operational, 745–53
(7–11 years) concrete-operational, 753–4
(11–15 years) formal-operational, 754–5
syncretic thought, 745
Piliavin, I.M. et al, 437, 439–40, 441
Piliavin, J.A. and Piliavin, I.M., 439
pineal body, 101
and sleep, 110
pituitary gland, anterior and posterior, 102
major hormones and effects, 101
pivotal (and categorical rules), 781
placebos, 78
plasticity of brain, 95
play
and motivation, 136
Erikson's theory of, *627*
Freud's theory of, *599*
mastery (practice), 756
Piaget's theory of, 755–7
play with rules, 757
representational (make-believe), 744
symbolic (make-believe), 756
pleasure principle, 591
polygyny, 418
pons, 92
Popper, K.R., 23, 25, 28, 37, 883, 918
Positron Emission Tomography (PET), 84
positive self-regard (conditional and unconditional), 906–7
positivism, 22
posterior hypothalamus, 90
Postman, L. et al, 265
precocial birds, 421
pre-conscious, 106
predictive validity, 861
prejudice (*see also* ageism), 539–52
components of, 539
definitions of, 539
demonstrations of, 540–1
origins of, 541–9
reduction of, 549–53
Premack, D., 792, 793, 796
pre-operational stage, 740, 745–53
preparedness (in conditioning), 183, 973
Pre-School Personality Quiz (PSPQ), 894
pressupraoptic hypothalamus, 90
primacy-recency effect
and interpersonal perception, 469–71

and memory, 317
and persuasive communication, 526–7
primal therapy, 988–9
primary delusions, 946
Primary Mental Abilities, (PMA) test, 723–4, 725, 844–5
primates (language), 789–801
primordial images, 923
principles of multiple control (brain), 93–6
prison-simulation experiment, 52, 462, 583–5
privation versus deprivation, 657
effects of privation, 663–73
proactive inhibition, 337–8
problem solving, 375–84
adversary, 377, 383–4
AI (artificial intelligence), 378
algorithms, 379
expert versus novice, 384–5
expert systems, 384–8
Garnham, A., 377, 378, 379, 381, 383–4, 385–6, 388–9, 393, 396–7, 398, 399
GPS (General Problem Solver), 378
heuristics, 379
Logical Theorist, *378–9*
Means End Analysis (MEA), *380–1*
Missionaries problem, *381*
non-adversary, 377, 380–3
programs
CADUCEUS, 386–7
ELIZA, 393
GUESSING, 389
MYCIN, 386–7
state-space theory, 381–2, 383
Towers of Hanoi, *380*
programmed learning, 188
projection, 163, 542, 968
prostaglandins, 78
prototype theories (of pattern recognition), 259–60
proxemics, 501
proximity (*see* interpersonal attraction)
psychedelic model (of schizophrenia), 952
psychic determinism, 913–14
psychic energy, 591
psychoanalysis, 961, 968–71
psychoanalytic theory, 5, 880, 881, 907
and adolescence, 636–7
empirical studies of, 915–17
evaluation of, 917–21
psychodrama, 989–90
psychodynamic theories, 907–28
psychogenic versus viscerogenic needs, 141
psychohistory, 635
psycho-hydraulic model (*see* hydraulic model)
psychoimmunology, 162
psycholinguistics, 760–9, 770, 771–3
psychological reactance, 140
psychology,
as value-free, 66, 68
definitions of, 3–6

history of, 3–5
major approaches, *7, 17–18*
scope of, 5–6, *7*
sub-divisions of, *7, 15*
psychometric approach
to intelligence, 841–7
to personality, 880, 881, 886–98
psychopathic (sociopathic) personality, 953–4
psychopathology, 914, 929–59
classification of mental disorders, 937–58
concept of abnormality, 929–32
description of mental disorders, *937–55*
effectiveness of treatments and therapies, 991–4
problems with classification, 955–9
treatments and therapies, 961–94
psychosis, 945–52
organic and functional, 934
psychotics, 896, 916
punishment, 174, 180, 805, 806–8, 811, 812–13, 820
purkinje cells, 92
pyramidal system, 91

Q-data, 894, 895, 896–8
Q-sort, 881

race and IQ, 876–8
Rachman, S., 972–4
Rachman, S. and Wilson, G., 974
Radford, J., 847
radicalism, 896
radioactive labelling, 84
Raphael, B., 709–10, 712
raphe nuclei and sleep, 110
rapid eye-movement sleep (REM), 80
rational emotive therapy (RET), 981
Rationalists, 21, 128
rationalization, 163, 911
Raven's Progessive Matrices, 863
reaction formation, 163, 911, 917–18
reaction range, 871
reactive versus process schizophrenia, 950
reality principle, 592
recall, 315
recapitulation theory, 636
receptive fields, 212
reciprocal inhibition, 974
reciprocal liking, 504–5
recognition memory, 314
reconstructive memory, 315
and eyewitness testimony, 352–8
redintegration, 315
reductionism, 22, 42
reflexivity criterion (of a theory), 29
refutability criterion (of a theory), 28
regression, 163, 912
rehearsal (in STM), 313
Reich, B. and Adcock, C., 521, 545, 528
reification, 847

reinforcement
  and drive-reduction theory, 133
  and language acquisition, 783–95
  definitions of, 173–6
  external versus internal, 820
  positive and negative, 134, 173–4
  primary and secondary, 176
  schedules of, 176–7
re-learning, 315
reliability
  of a test, 859–60, 886
  of classification of mental disorder, 956–57
  of 16 PF, 897
remembering (forms of), 314–15
Repertory Grid (Rep Grid), 881, 899
Repertory Grid Test, 881–2, 899
repeated and serial reproduction (in memory), 353
replicability (experiments), 31–3
repression, 163, 968
Rescorla, R.A., 184
residual rules, 936
resistance-to-temptation (versus guilt), 810
resistance (in psychoanalysis), 971
Rest, J., 831
Restle, F., 188, 351
respondent (versus operant) conditioning, 166
response set (in attitude scales), 517
restricted versus elaborated codes, 368–9
reticular activating system (RAS), 80, 81, 91, 105
  and personality, 890
  and sleep, 110–11
retinex theory, 217–18
retrieval (see remembering)
retroactive inhibition, 337–8
retrograde amnesia, 323–4
reversibility, 750, 753
rewards: extrinsic versus intrinsic, 813–14
Rheingold, H.L., 289
Richardson, K., 32, 739, 853
Riesen, A.H., 266–7
ritualization
  and displacement activity, 416
  in aggression, 416, 445
Robber's cave experiment, 546, 551–2
Robertson, J. and Robertson, J., 647
Rogers, C.R., 880, 901, 905–7
Rokeach, M., 515, 543
Role Construct Repertory Test (Rep Test), 899
Rose, S., 41, 43, 95, 119–20
Rose, S.A. and Blank, M., 751
Rosenhan, D.L., 955–6, 959
rotating trapezoid illusion, 273–4
Rotter, J.B., 140, 158
Rubin vase, 240
Rubin, Z., 493, 504, 508
Rubin, Z., and McNeil, E.B., 104, 105, 122, 140, 143, 492, 504, 506, 509

Ruch, J.C., 104, 107, 123
Rutter, M., 646, 648, 652, 663, 665, 672, 687
Ryan, J., 857, 858, 859, 861, 862
Ryle, A., 985, 994
Ryle, G., 841

safety signal hypothesis, 974
Salapatek, P., 286
Samuel, J. and Bryant, P., 751
Sapir, E., 360, 361–3
Sarah, 792, 794, 796
Savage-Rumbaugh, E.S., 797, 798, 799, 800, 801
Savage-Rumbaugh, E.S. et al, 792, 796, 771
scales of measurement (and IQ), 858
scapegoating, 549
Scarr-Salapatek, S., 870
Scarr, S., and Weinberg, R.A., 871, 878
Schachter, S., 147–51
Schachter, S. and Singer, J.E., 148
Schaffer, H.R., 645, 651
Schaffer, H.R. and Emerson, P.E., 651, 652, 653, 654, 656
Schaie, K.W., 725
Schaie, K.W. and Labouvie-Vief, G., 725
Schaie, K.W. and Strother, C.R., 725
schema, 739, 740
schemas (attitude), 540
schemas (memory), 345–6, 350
Schiff, M. et al, 871
schizoid personality, 954
schizophrenia, 896, 899, 925–52, 984
  and dopamine, 79
  and hallucinogenic drugs, 81
  and L-Dopa, 80
  and major tranquillizers, 81
  DSM III-R, 937–41
  first rank symptoms, 945–6
  theories of, 948–52
  varieties of, 945–8
Schneider, K., 945–6
school phobia (refusal), 661
Scodel, A., 917
Sears, R.R. et al, 807, 812, 819
Segall, M.H. et al, 273
secondary gain, 974
sedatives (depressants), 82
self-actualization, 902–5, 924
self-characterization, 984
self-concept, 10, 487, 607
  archetype, 924
  awareness (consciousness), 607–20
  categorical, 620–1
  definition, 619
  development of, 617–20
  disclosure, 489–90
  esteem inventory, 612, 613
  esteem (self regard), 609
  factors influencing development, 612–17
  ideal self (ego ideal), 609
  image (ego identity), 608–9

in adolescence, 621–4
  monitoring, 491
  psychological self, 620
  recognition, 617–18, 618–9
  theories of, 610–24
self-efficacy, 983
self-fulfilling prophecy, 487, 619
self-instructional training (SIT), 981–2
self-perception theory, 144, 536–7
self-serving attributional bias, 480
Selfridge, O.G., 261
Seligman, M., 181, 183, 973
Selye, H., 153, 160–1
semantic differential, 518
semantic memory, 342–50
  and episodic, 324
  causally related events, 347
  frame, 345
  network model, 343
  SAM, 349
  schema, 345–6, 350
  scripts, 345, 349
  'War of the Ghosts', 346–7
senile dementia, 945
sensation and perception, 201
sensitive periods (see critical periods)
sensorimotor stage, 740, 741–4
sensory deprivation, 137–8
sensory deprivation cubicle, 138
sensory overload, 137
sensory systems
  classifications, 203
  characteristics, 203–5
  thresholds, 204
separation
  and anxiety, 661
  and IQ, 664, 665, 667
  'continuity and discontinuity' view (debate), 666–9, 669–71, 672–3
  deprivation, effects of, short term, 658–61
  deprivation, long term, 661–3
  privation, effects of, 663–73
  maternal deprivation hypothesis (Bowlby), 656–8
sequential functioning versus parallel processing, 398
serial position curve, 317
serial probe technique, 336
seriation, 746
serotonin, 79, 80, 953
  and sleep, 110
sex and gender
  biological categories, 675
  chromosomes, 675, 682
  external genitalia, 676
  gender identity, 674
  gender role, 674
  gender role behaviour, 675
  gender role identity, 675, 681
  gender role stereotypes, 675
  gender (sex) differences, 675, 679–81
  gonads, 675, 682

hormones, 675–6
internal accessory organs, 676
sex typing, 675, 691–2
sexual identity, 674–5
sexual orientation, 675
theories of, 681–5
Shackleton, V.J. and Fletcher, C.A., 881, 890, 894, 899
shadowing (*see also* dichotic listening), 297
Shaffer, D.R., 846
Shallice, T., 305
shape discrimination, 287
shaping, 178, 189
Sheehy, G., 708
Sherif, M., 545, 562–3, 574, 575
Sherif, M. et al, 545, 546, 551
Shields, J., 866–7
short term memory, 312–13
Shuey, A., 877
shuttlebox, 179, 185
Siann, G., 446, 447, 448, 449
sign-learning (place-learning) theory, 187–8
sign stimulus (*see also* releasers), 409–10
signal detection theory, 204
simple schizophrenia, 946
simultaneous conditioning, 168
Sinclair-de-Zwart, H., 765
single channel models (of attention), 297–301
single (and double) blind technique, 40
Sioux Indians, 635
Situationalism, 880, 884
Skeels, H., 664, 665, 873
Skeels, H. and Dye, H.B., 663–4, 665, 873
Skinner, B.F., 8, 19, 128, 134, 166, 167, 171, 172, 173–9, 185, 186, 188, 190, 191, 192, 198, 770, 783, 784, 785, 814, 817, 820
Skinner box, *174*, 181
Skodak, M. and Skeels, H., 869, 870
Slaby, R.G. and Frey, K.S., 695
Slater, E. and Roth, M., 695
sleep
and circadian rhythm, 109–10
and dreaming, 113–14
and drugs, 115
and stress, 154–6
and ultradian rhythm 111–13
as a drive, 115
deprivation of, 114–15
function of, 114–18
physiology of, 110–*11*
NREM, 111–15
REM, 110, 111–18
REM rebound, 114
stages of, 111–*13*
theories of, 115–18
sleeper effect, 520
Slobin, D.I., 784
Slukin, W., 423–4
Smith, M.L., and Glass, G.V., 991

Smith, P.K. and Cowie, H., 759–60
Smith, R.E. et al, 932
Snyder, F.W. and Pronko, N.H., 271
social cognition, 9
social desirability, 517
social disengagement theory, 728–9
social drift versus social causation hypothesis (of schizophrenia), 950
social exchange theory, 731
social facilitation, 554–5
social identity theory, (SIT), 548
social influence, 554
social learning theory (SLT), 8, 30, 189–91, 814–21
social phenomenology, 952
social psychiatry, 990–1
social psychology, 10
Social Readjustment Rating Scale (SRRS), 156–7, 159–9, 161
social roles, 472–3, 475–6
and self concept, 608, 616–7
conflict, 472–3
definitions, 472
social skills training, 978
sociobiology, 427–30
sociometry, 519
Solso, R.L., 300, 301
somatosensory (body sense) cortex, 87
somatotropin (growth hormone), 101
somnambulism, 113, 944
Spearman, C., 842–3
spectrum electromagnetic radiation, *203*
Sperling, G., 311
Sperry, R.W., 83, 96–9, 268
Spitz, R.A., 657
Spitz, R.A. et al, 657, 663
Spitzer, R.L., 956, 957
spinal cord, 93, *94*
reflexes, 93
split brain patients, 83, 96–9, 917
spontaneous visual preference technique, 280
stage one (and two) grammar, 780–3
standard deviation and IQ, 857
standardization of a test, 858–9
Stanford-Binet test, 853, 854–6, 859, 860
state-dependent memory, 315
statistical criterion of abnormality, 929
Stayton, D.J. and Ainsworth, M.D.S., 648
stereotyping, 482–6, 486–7
Sternberg, R.J., 399–400, 759, 761, 766, 848–51, 863
stickleback
courtship dance, 414
threat behaviour, 410
stigmatizing labels, 935
stimulants, 82
stimulus control, 180–1
stimulus-response (S-R) theories, 4, 134, 810–14
stimulus satiation, 976–7
Storm and Stress, 636
Storr, A., 450, 971

Strange Situation, the, 648, *649*, 650
Stratton, G.M., *270*
stress
and personality, 159, 161
causes, 153–60
coping with, 161–3
definitions of models, 152–3
response to, 160–1
strobosscopic motion (*see also* visual illusions), 230
structuralism, 3, 4, 26
structure of intellect model, 845
Suomi, S.J., 90, 424, 425
Suomi, S.J. and Harlow, H.F., 671
sublimation, 163, 912
Sugarman, L., 702, 707
superego, 593, 803, 804, 808, 809, 896, 898, 916
superior colliculus, 213
superstitious behaviour, 178
supraoptic hypothalamus, 90
surface versus source traits, 886
survival versus growth needs, 135
Susannah Fienues, case of, *271*
Swiss mountain scene, 748
Sybil, case of, *944*
symbols, in dreams and neurotic symptoms, 908–9
sympathetic branch (of ANS), 99–100
symptom substitution, 993
synaesthesia, 353
syncretic thought, 745
synpraxic speech, 367
syntactic rules, 784
systematic desensitization (SD), 974–5
Szasz, T., 931, 933–6, 951

T-data, 894–6
Tagiuri, R., 482
Tajfel, H. et al, 546–7
taste aversion studies, 181, 973
Tchambuli, 693
telegraphic speech, 780
television
and aggression, 454–9
Broadcasters Audience Research Board (BARB), 689
and catharsis, 459–60
Cumberbatch (study), 445, 456
and pro-social behaviour, 460
template matching hypothesis, 259
temporal lobe, 87–8
Terman, L.M., 853
terminal versus instrumental values, 515
Terrace, H.S., 792, 794, 796, 797, 800
territoral imperative, 446
territoriality, 406, 420–1, 444
test-retest reliability, 859–60
testosterone, 675
testosterone insensitivity (Testicular Feminizing Syndrome), 677–8
tests, criteria of, 856–62, 886
thalamus, 90

Thanatos (Death Instinct), 450
thematic apperception test (TAT), *141*, 613
theoretical approaches, 16
theory: definitions of, 19, 28–31
therapeutic communities, 990
Thibaut, J.W. and Kelley, H.H., 493
Thigpen, C.H. and Cleckley, H.M., 944
thirst, 132–3
Thomas, R.M., 913, 919
Thorndike, E.L., 166, *172–3*
Thorndike puzzlebox, *172*
Thorpe, W.H., 403, 411
thought disturbances (in schizophrenia), 946
thought stopping, 982
Three Faces of Eve, 944
Three Mile Island, 162
Thurstone, L.L., 844–5, 849
Thurstone scale, 518
thymus, 101
thyrotrophic hormone (TTH), 101
Tinbergen, N., 403, 404, 405, 407, 414
Tinbergen, N. and Perdeck, A.C., 408, 409–10
Tizard, B., 66, 668–9, 671
Tizard, B. and Hodges, J., 666, 667
Tizard, B. and Rees, J., 647, 667
Tizard, B. et al, 784
Tizard, B. and Tizard, J., 666, 667
token economy programmes, 979–80
tolerance (of opiates), 82
Tolman, E.C., 8, *186–7*, 191
Tolman Maze, *187*
tonic alertness, 104–5
total institutions, 936
tough-minded/tender-minded, 543–4
trace conditioning, 168
trace decay, 335–6, 338
trait approach versus situationalism, 884–5
trait theories (of personality), 882–98
tranquillizers, 81
transactional analysis, 988
transactional model of stress, 153
Transactionalists, 236–7, 262
transductive reasoning, 745–6
transfer of learning (or training), 196–7
transference (and counter-transference), 969–70
transitivity tasks, 754
transsexuals, 675
treatments and therapies, 961–94
Treisman, A., 297, 299–*300*, 312
trial-and-error learning, 172–3
trichromatic theory, 216
Trivers, R.L., 428
Triplett, N., 554
Triseliotis, J., 669
Trobriand Islanders, 599, 693
truth value criterion (of a theory), 29
Tulving, E., 324, 325, 327, 328, 332, 338, 339, 340
Turiel, E., 834

Turing Test, 393–4, 396
Turnbull, C.M., 275
Turner, J.C., 488, 554, 556, 558, 560, 563, 568, 571, 573, 574, 580
Turner's syndrome, 873
Turner, J.C. and Helms, D.B., 700, 713, 714, 729, 731
twin studies
    and intelligence, 864–9
    and schizophrenia, 948–50
two-component tasks (in memory), 317–19
two-factor model of intelligence, 842–3
two-factor (two-process) theory of avoidance learning, 179, 973
two-step flow hypothesis (of attitude change), 521
two-word stage (of language development), 780, *781*
Tyerman, A. and Spencer, C., 546
Type A/Type B personality, 159–60
type and trait approach (to personality), 886–97

ultradian rhythms, 105
unconditional positive regard, 986
Underwood, B.J., 337
unemployment, effects of, 709–12
unilateral versus mutual respect, 826
universal linguistic structures, 365–6
uplift scale, 159

Valentine, E.R., 46
validity,
    of EPI, 893
    of IQ tests, 860–2
    of 16PF, 897
    of psychiatric classification, 958
value-free (of psychology), 66–8
value-match (and exchange theory), 495
value-neutral (of therapists), 68–9
vassopressin, 78, 101
ventral root (of spinal cord), 93
ventrobasal complex (of thalamus), 90
ventromedial nucleus (of hypothalamus) (VMH), 90, 130, 132
verbal and performance scales (on WAIS–R), 725
verification principle, 28
Vernon, M.D., 252, 255
Vernon, P.E., 843, 845, 863, 869, 875, 887
Viki, 790
Vilcabamba, 721–2
'Villa 21', 990
visual cliff, 289–*90*
visual cortex, 87
visual system, 206–11, *212*, 218
    colour vision/blindness, 215–28
    illusions, 27, *226–31*
    pathways, 211–15
    rods and cones, 209–11
    saccades (in babies), 284

visuo-spatial ability and sex differences, 680
Von Frisch, K., 418
Von Senden, M., 264, 266
Vygotsky, L.S., 361, 372, 373, 762, 982

Walker, S., 134, 176, 179, 181, 972, 979
Walster, E., 481
Walster, E. and Festinger, L., 522
'War of the Ghosts', 346–7
Warren, N. and Jahoda, M., 515
Warrington, E.K. and Weiskrantz, L., 322
Washoe, 790, 792–3, 794, 796
Watson, J.B., *4*, 9, 21, 36, 47, 104, 166, 170, 171, 172, 190, 360, 366
Watson, J.B. and Rayner, R., 170
Waugh, N.C. and Norman, D., 310, 336
Weatherley, D., 549, 622
Weber-Fechner law, 206
Wechsler, D., 724, 840, 853
Wechsler Adult Intelligence Scale (WAIS-R), 724–5, *855–6*
Wechsler Intelligence Scale for Children (WISC-R), 853
Wechsler Pre-School Primary Scale of Intelligence (WPPSI-R), 853
Weiskrantz, L., 184, 266
Wernicke, C., 83
Wernicke's area, 89, 93, 95
Whorf, B.L., 360, 361–3, 365, 374
Wickelgren, W.A., 320, 321
Wilding, J.M., 296, 297, 301
will-to-power, 926
Wilson, E.O., 426, 427–8, 429–30
Winnicott, D.W., 969
Wishner, J., 467, 468
Wittgenstein, L., 361
'wolf' children, 787
Wollheim, R., 910
womb envy, 804
Wolpe, J., 972, 974, 975, 982
Woodworth, R., 129
work and identity, 633–4
working memory (*see* memory)
World Health Organization (WHO) classification of diseases, 937
Wright, D., 826–7
Wundt, W., *3*, 21, 22, 46, 104, 143, 312

Yates, A., 972, 975
Yerkish, 793
Yerkes Primate Centre, 797
Yurok Indians, 635

Zajonc, R.B., 499–50, 555
Zebrowitz, L.A., 468, 471, 499, 480, 482, 483
Zimbardo, P.G., 54, 58, 461–2
Zimbardo, P.G., et al, 462, 583–5, 585–6
zone of proximal development, 767
Zulus, 273
Zuni Indians, 362, 363